White Collar Crime

White Collar Crime

Cases, Materials, and Problems

FOURTH EDITION

J. Kelly Strader
IRWIN R. BUCHALTER PROFESSOR OF LAW
SOUTHWESTERN LAW SCHOOL

John P. Anderson
J. WILL YOUNG PROFESSOR OF LAW
MISSISSIPPI COLLEGE SCHOOL OF LAW

Mihailis E. Diamantis
PROFESSOR OF LAW
UNIVERSITY OF IOWA COLLEGE OF LAW

Sandra D. Jordan
ADJUNCT PROFESSOR OF LAW
NORTH CAROLINA CENTRAL UNIVERSITY SCHOOL OF LAW

CAROLINA ACADEMIC PRESS
Durham, North Carolina

ISBN   978-1-5310-1604-3
eISBN   978-1-5310-1605-0
LCCN   2021935678

Carolina Academic Press
700 Kent Street
Durham, NC 27701
Telephone (919) 489-7486
www.cap-press.com

Printed in the United States of America

J.K.S.
To Eleanor and Sam

J.P.A
To Jaime, Peyton, Brendan, and Cosette

M.E.D.
To Bill L. and John H. Thank you for your early support,
continued mentorship, and growing friendship.

S.D.J.
To Nedra, B.J., Jordan, and Janelle, and in loving memory of
Byron and Catherine

Summary of Contents

Contents

Preface

Our background and goals

With this book, we hope to put to good use our experience practicing in the area of white collar crime and teaching and writing about the subject. Professor Strader practiced white collar criminal defense with the New York City law firm of Morvillo, Abramowitz, Grand, Iason, and Anello, P.C. He writes principally in the area of criminal law, including topics on white collar criminalization. Professor Anderson practiced in the areas of white collar criminal defense and securities enforcement in Washington, D.C., at Wilmer Hale LLP and Eversheds Sutherland LLP. Currently he teaches White Collar Crime and related courses at Mississippi College School of Law. He has written a number of articles on financial crimes and a book on insider trading. Professor Diamantis started his legal career practicing white collar defense in New York at Debevoise & Plimpton LLP. As a faculty member at the University of Iowa College of Law, he now writes broadly about corporate crime. Professor Jordan served for nearly 10 years as an Assistant United States Attorney for the Western District of Pennsylvania, eventually heading the White Collar Crimes Unit of the United States Attorney's Office. Professor Jordan began her academic career at the University of Pittsburgh School of Law, where she was Professor of Law and served as Associate Dean. She is currently Adjunct Professor of Law at North Carolina Central University School of Law.

Based upon our academic and practice experiences, we have endeavored to write a problem-based casebook that provides a topical, informative, and thought-provoking perspective on this rapidly evolving area of the law. We also believe that the study of white collar criminal law and practice raises unique issues of criminal law and justice policy, and serves as an excellent vehicle for deepening our understanding of criminal justice issues in general. For the fourth edition, we have continued to focus on practice problems while also deepening the policy and theoretical discussion. We have substantially increased the number of practice problems, and hope that they prove both fun and useful for students and teachers alike.

We are very grateful to our contributor, Katrice Bridges Copeland, Professor of Law, Penn State Law, for authoring Chapter Six, Health Care Fraud and Abuse. Professor Copeland practiced law at Sidley Austin LLP in Washington, D.C., focusing on white collar criminal defense and constitutional litigation. As part of her white collar crime practice, she represented pharmaceutical companies in health care fraud and abuse prosecutions.

Coverage

This casebook focuses on the substance and procedure of federal white collar and corporate crime. The book is intended for use in two-, three-, or four-unit courses in White Collar Crime, Federal Criminal Law, Corporate Crime, and related subjects. The book is organized as follows:

- Chapters 1 and 2 (Introduction and Corporate and Individual Liability) introduce themes and concepts discussed throughout the text.

- Chapters 3–14 cover the substantive law of white collar and corporate crime. Chapters 3 and 4 address at length the crimes of conspiracy, mail and wire fraud, and related crimes, the building blocks of many white collar crime prosecutions. Chapters 5–14 address specific types of fraud (securities fraud, health care fraud, and tax fraud), political corruption (bribery, gratuities, and extortion), the cover-up crimes (false statements, perjury, and obstruction of justice), financial crimes (tax crimes and money laundering), and the RICO statute.

- Chapters 15–17 (Internal Investigations, Compliance Programs, and Deferred and Non-Prosecution Agreements; Grand Juries; and Self-Incrimination), cover the principal practical and procedural issues that arise in white collar investigations and prosecutions.

- Chapters 18–20 address the consequences of white collar offenses: civil fines, criminal penalties, and forfeitures.

Selection of materials

Throughout the text, our goal has been to provide leading and illustrative cases in each area, focusing where possible on United States Supreme Court opinions. This goal is challenging, given the lightning speed at which this area of the law evolves. The rapid evolution of federal sentencing law is only the most recent example of how quickly the law in this area changes. We have done our best to provide both foundational cases and the most recent significant cases.

In the introductory materials to each of the substantive crime chapters, we have included an overview of the law and the statutory elements. Because our goal is to teach principally through the study of the cases, we have tried to edit them judiciously.* We include a number of concurring and dissenting opinions, both because these opinions help elucidate the issues and because in close cases today's dissent may be tomorrow's majority. Following the cases, we also include notes on important issues those cases raise on matters of law, policy, and theory. We have tried to keep the notes concise, where possible, and hope that they will serve as starting points for rich class discussions.

---

* We indicate lengthy omissions with centered asterisks, and short omissions with ellipses. We generally have not indicated the omission of citations and footnotes. With respect to footnotes, we have retained the cases' original note numbers. The footnotes that we have written are indicated by letters rather than numbers.

Finally, we intersperse practice problems throughout the casebook. The problems focus on substantive law, procedural issues, and ethical dilemmas that arise in white collar practice. The text is designed to be used flexibly and thus lends itself both to comprehensive study of the black letter law and to a problem-based approach.

A special request

Any book of this length will contain errors. If you find any errors, or have any comments or suggestions, kindly let us know. Please contact Kelly Strader, kstrader @swlaw.edu, John P. Anderson, jpanders@mc.edu, or Mihailis E. Diamantis, mihailis-diamantis@uiowa.edu.

Acknowledgments

J.K.S.

I would like to thank my many colleagues who gave generously of their time to read various of the book's chapters; my mentors at Morvillo, Abramowitz, Grand, Iason, and Anello; my research assistants, especially John Lucas C. Frye and Sydney N. Woods, for their help, including researching and drafting notes and practice problems. Also thanks to the many adopters who made extremely helpful comments and suggestions for the fourth edition of the book. Finally, thanks to my co-authors, with whom collaboration has been a joy.

J.P.A

I thank all the research assistants who have contributed their time to this project over the years, especially Charise Samuel and Gabrielle Wells. Charise and Gabrielle worked a number of late nights to help get this project across the finish line, and I am very grateful for their hard work and dedication. I am also grateful to my coauthors. Their excellent comments and suggestions dramatically improved my contributions to this book. It is a real treat to work with such knowledgeable professionals, and wonderful friends.

M.E.D.

I am exceedingly grateful to my research assistant, Rebekah Cochran, for her diligence, attention to detail, and genuine curiosity about white collar crime. Her assistance on this textbook came during a year filled with many other stresses. Thanks for your excellent work.

S.D.J.

This project is the end result of many months of effort, thought and revision. Several of my colleagues generously offered their suggestions, support and vast legal experience as they read through some of the earlier drafts of the chapters. Thanks to my current and former colleagues who had a role in this publication. Robert B. Harper, Browne C. Lewis, and Robert J. Bondi spent time reviewing drafts, making suggestions or offering valuable insight into the substance of our topics. Thanks also to Nate O'Neil, Sonya Murphy, Andrea Patterson, LaTonia Bills, and Shernika Smith who offered their research assistance on this project.

White Collar Crime

Chapter 1

Overview of White Collar Crime

A. Introductory Notes

It is hard to overstate the impact that white collar crime has on the United States. According to recent estimates from the Federal Bureau of Investigation, the annual economic loss attributable to white collar crime is at least 20 times greater than the economic loss attributable to every other sort of crime combined: $300 billion/year (minimum) versus $15 billion/year. *See* Rodner Huff et al., The 2010 National Public Survey on White Collar Crime 12 (2010), http://www.fraudaid.com /library/2010 national public survey on white collar crime.pdf; Kathrin E. McCollister, Michael T. French & Hai Fang, The Cost of Crime to Society: New Crime-Specific Estimates for Policy and Program Evaluation (Apr. 1, 2010). In an effort to curb its effects, governmental and private parties dedicate massive resources to detection, prevention, and sanction. Corporations collectively spend as much on internal compliance as the entire nation spends on municipal policing. *See* William S. Laufer, *A Very Special Regulatory Milestone*, 20 J. Bus. L. 392, 399 (2017).

We will see throughout this text how white collar crime bends and occasionally breaks the usual logic of criminal justice. *See* Mihailis E. Diamantis, *White-Collar Showdown*, 102 Iowa L. Rev. Online 320 (2017). Ordinarily, criminal conduct that causes more harm should be punished more harshly, whether for reasons of retribution or deterrence. Despite the outsized effects of white collar misconduct, many commentators question whether it really should count as crime at all. Individual white collar defendants who are convicted routinely receive more lenient sentences than street criminals, the effects of whose wrongs are often much smaller and much more contained. *See* Mark W. Bennett et al., *Judging Federal White-Collar Fraud Sentencing: An Empirical Study Revealing the Need for Further Reform*, 102 Iowa L. Rev. 939, 980–88 (2017). As to the largest corporate criminal defendants, criminal justice mechanisms often ensure an extrajudicial resolution that limits the reputational impact of authorities' suspicions.

Over the past several decades, white collar crime has captured the attention of law makers, law enforcement, and the general public. This development has largely been due to a number of high-profile investigations and prosecutions, including:

- *Corporate fraud*, leading to the bankruptcy of major corporations and the destabilization of the U.S. financial system.

- *Insider trading conspiracies*, leading to charges against both hedge fund managers and individual defendants.
- *Political corruption investigations and prosecutions* of members of the United States Congress, high-ranking members of the executive branch of the U.S. government, state governors, and many others.
- *Individual crimes* committed by high-profile defendants.

All these events have produced substantial debate about the nature of white collar crime and methods for combating that crime.

There is little doubt that white collar crime causes enormous harm. For example, when corporations use fraudulent accounting practices to overstate their earnings, overexpand, and then collapse, both investors and employees suffer. When public officials commit bribery and other crimes, the public loses its trust in government. Criminal justice policy therefore must effectively address white collar crime.

This chapter highlights some of the principal issues of law and policy that arise in white collar investigations and prosecutions. Although white collar crimes exist under both state and federal law, most of the significant white collar prosecutions occur at the federal level, and it is upon federal law that this text focuses. Before turning to themes in federal white collar crime, the section below sets the parameters for the study of white collar crime.

B. The Definition of "White Collar Crime"[a]

As seen below, there are many definitions of "white collar crime." This text defines the term in a way that comports with the practices of prosecutors and defenders of those charged with such crime.

1. The Development of the Term "White Collar Crime"

Criminologist and sociologist Edwin Sutherland coined the term "white collar crime" in 1939 to distinguish it from "common" or "street" crime. Sutherland wrote that "[w]hite collar crime may be defined approximately as a crime committed by a person of respectability and high social status in the course of his occupation," and as crime committed by organizations such as corporations. EDWIN H. SUTHERLAND, WHITE COLLAR CRIME: THE UNCUT VERSION 7 (1983).

In seeking to explore the determinants of crime, Sutherland used the study of "white collar crime" to question the assumption that a person's social status or class determines that person's propensity to commit crime. Sutherland's thesis was that,

---

a. This section is adapted from J. Kelly Strader, *The Judicial Politics of White Collar Crime*, 50 HASTINGS L.J. 1199 (1999). Copyright © 1999 J. Kelly Strader.

contrary to popular belief, crime is not primarily caused by social circumstances, nor is it primarily perpetrated by those of low socioeconomic status.

Although historically important, Sutherland's definition is not particularly helpful for studying white collar crime today. It is difficult to draw a principled distinction, for example, between tax fraud committed by a corporate executive and tax fraud committed by a "blue collar" worker.

Nor does a status-based definition comport with white collar cases. For example, the crime of "insider trading" occurs when a person buys or sells stock based upon stolen secret information; "insider trading" is a classic white collar crime. Yet, the United States Supreme Court first addressed insider trading in *United States v. Chiarella*, 445 U.S. 222 (1980), where the defendant was not a corporate executive but a "markup man" for a printing company. In fact, many "white collar" defendants, particularly in cases involving crimes such as bank embezzlement and government benefits fraud, do not look much different from defendants in common crime cases. As Samuel Buell has noted, "[m]any white collar offenses, maybe even most of them, are committed by pedestrian hucksters, scam artists, cheaters, and liars." Samuel W. Buell, *Is the White Collar Offender Privileged?*, 63 DUKE L J. 823, 830–31 (2014). Sutherland's sociologically oriented definition thus fails to provide a workable framework for a substantive legal discussion of the *types* of crimes that lawyers and academics speak of as "white collar offenses." Indeed, in this sense, the term "white collar" crime is a misnomer.

Perhaps the most useful definition of "white collar crime" comes from the way the term is used by those who practice in the field. In common usage, "white collar crime" is best identified by what it does not include. As used in this text, "white collar crime" does *not* include:

1. *Crimes that necessarily involve the use or threat of physical force, either against the victim or the victim's property.*

Whether a crime is "white collar" may sometimes depend upon the criminal means used, rather than upon the crime's statutory definition. For example, under the Hobbs Act, 18 U.S.C. § 1951, the crime of extortion may sometimes be "white collar" (for example, when the defendant threatens the victim with economic harm), and sometimes not (for example, when the defendant threatens the victim with the use of physical force).

2. *Offenses directly related to the possession, sale, or distribution of controlled substances.*

Many narcotics offenses do not involve the use of force. They are excluded from "white collar crime," however, because (a) there is a common perception that the "drug culture" often has a violent context, and (b) criminal investigations and prosecutions of these offenses are typically handled by specialized agencies, such as the United States Drug Enforcement Agency. On the other hand, the money laundering and tax offenses that focus on the illegal proceeds of drug crimes are categorized as a "white collar crime." *See, e.g.*, Chapters 12 (Tax Crimes) and 13 (Money Laundering), *infra*.

3. *Crime directly related to organized crime activities.*

Organized crime can be non-violent and, on the surface, conducted by "legitimate" businesses. It is excluded from "white collar crime," however, because (a) it often has a violent context, and (b) it is investigated and prosecuted by specialized law enforcement departments.

4. *Crime directly related to certain national policy-driven areas such as immigration and civil rights.*

Once again, these areas are considered specialized areas by law enforcement. Each raises particular policy-driven issues specific to its context.

5. *Common theft crimes and "vice" crimes.*

Ordinary theft crimes and "vice" crimes are generally considered common street crimes and not "white collar" offenses. This generalization does not apply to one type of theft crime — fraud — which is criminalized in a wide variety of white collar contexts. *See, e.g.,* Chapters 4 (Mail and Wire Fraud) and 5 (Securities Fraud), *infra.*

After excluding (1) crimes of violence, (2) narcotics offenses, (3) organized crime cases, (4) national policy crimes, and (5) common theft crimes and vice crimes, what remains is a broad, common-sense definition of white collar crime. One commentator defined white collar crimes as "non-violent illegal activities that principally use deceit, deception, concealment, fraud, or misrepresentation to obtain money, property, or some other advantage, or to conceal or cover up other wrongdoing." Randall Eliason, *The Definition of White Collar Crime*, Sidebars: Reflections on White Collar Crime and Federal Criminal Law (Nov. 26, 2014), https://sidebarsblog .com/the-definition-of-white-collar-crime/. Such crimes can lead either to economic harm (for example: mail and wire fraud, securities fraud, and financial crimes) or to harm to the government's ability to function effectively and without conflicts of interest (for example: bribery, extortion, perjury, false statements, obstruction of justice, and currency transaction violations).

White collar offenses thus encompass a wide range of crimes, from simple cases of individual fraud and political corruption to wide-spread financial fraud, bribery, and extortion schemes. This definition removes the pure socioeconomic focus of "white collar crime," but comports with the views of criminal law practitioners and the general public concerning the distinction between white collar and non-white collar crime.

Despite the difficulties in offering a positive definition of white collar crime, it does have some typical features. White collar crimes tend to involve deception to take advantage of victims rather than physical, coercive force. Unlike many street crimes, which may be spur-of-the-moment responses to emotional cues, white collar crime typically requires more planning and is committed for monetary gain. Finally, the people involved in white collar crime tend to be different from those involved in common crime. Perpetrators, while not always professional criminals, are often professionals who have access to the information, resources, power, and/or trust they need to carry out their crime. Victims are often organizations (like the federal government) and institutions (like the stock market) rather than identifiable individuals. These features largely comport with the Department of Justice's definition of white collar crime: "[I]llegal acts that use deceit and concealment ... to obtain money, property, or service; to avoid the payment or loss of money; or to secure a business or personal advantage. White collar criminals occupy positions of responsibility and trust in government, industry, the professions, and civic organizations." U.S. Att'y Gen. Office, *Annual Report of the Attorney General of the United States* (1983).

As you read through these materials, consider whether and why it might be helpful to distinguish white collar crime from other types of crime. Are there any costs to this sort of white collar exceptionalism?

2. White Collar Legal Practice

Although the term "white collar crime" is misnomer because it encompasses crimes committed by defendants who do not fit within the socioeconomic understanding of "white collar," there is still a legal practice divide between well-to-do corporate defendants and other defendants, sometimes called "blue collar" offenders. In this sense, Sutherland's socioeconomic definition of "white collar crime" retains some legitimacy.

One study of major law firms observed that there is "a developing norm that corporate officers and employees ought to be represented in white collar criminal cases not just by accomplished defense counsel, but by a certain type of counsel — those at the nation's leading corporate law firms, most of whom are former federal prosecutors." Charles D. Weisselberg & Su Li, *Big Law's Sixth Amendment: The Rise of Corporate White-Collar Practices in Large U.S. Law Firms*, 53 Ariz. L. Rev. 1221, 1224 (2011). This reality is economically based. "As a practical matter, given the high hourly rates these large firm partners command, very few individual defendants can afford to retain them if their fees are not advanced by their corporate employers." *Id.* at 1249.

There are several other practice features of white collar defense that bear note. White collar defense attorneys typically get involved at a much earlier stage in the criminal justice process, often before the potential defendant has received any formal communication from the government. Their objective at that stage is to find out what might be of interest to prosecutors and to control the flow of information. If authorities decide to pursue their concerns, the defense attorneys want to take a proactive stance in negotiations. When representing corporations, a defense attorney's role will typically be to investigate what happened, to produce any documents the government requests, and to present an account of what happened. All of this is with the goal of persuading prosecutors not to proceed, whether that means declining charges or entering into some form of deferred prosecution agreement. Since much of a white collar defense attorney's work takes place outside of the courtroom — in the grey space where prosecutorial discretion plays a larger role than statute or judicial opinion — there is a special premium placed on defense attorneys who have significant experience working with prosecutors. Many of the top defense attorneys are former Department of Justice prosecutors.

There are important demographic trends to bear in mind when considering white collar crime, and they are often different from familiar trends in other areas of criminal law. For example, while women represent only 13% of federal offenders generally, they represent one-third of economic crime offenders. *See* UNITED STATES SENTENCING COMMISSION, WHAT DOES FEDERAL ECONOMIC CRIME REALLY LOOK LIKE? 12 (2019), https://www.ussc.gov/sites/default/files/pdf/research-and-publications/research-publications/2019/20190130_Econ-Crime.pdf.   Turning to race, white defendants are overrepresented among the highest-value white collar offenders. *See* Tracy Sohoni & Melissa Rorie, *The Whiteness of White-Collar Crime in the United States: Examining the Role of Race in a Culture of Elite White-Collar Offending*, THEORETICAL CRIMINOLOGY (Aug. 2, 2019). Breaking race down by specific types of crime reveals more nuance. "For example, White offenders accounted for a substantial majority of securities and investment fraud (79.9%), computer related fraud (70.5%), and government procurement fraud (62.3%), while Black offenders accounted for the largest proportion of tax fraud (55.0%), identity theft (49.4%), and credit card fraud (45.0%)." *See* UNITED STATES SENTENCING COMMISSION, *supra*, at 2. When reviewing the materials in this text, readers may wish to consider the sorts of factors that may have produced these demographic disparities. For example, have socio-economic circumstances and/or the exercise of prosecutorial discretion likely played a role? What other factors might be at play?

Another issue that arises in white collar crime practice is the diversity (or lack thereof) among prominent white collar counsel. As the study cited above showed,

> [V]irtually all of the leading firms have lawyers in [white collar] practices. Some work primarily as white collar lawyers. Others have different dominant specialties — such as securities or antitrust, where criminal and civil issues often intertwine, or where there may be parallel proceedings — but these attorneys nevertheless still have substantial ongoing white collar practices. The majority are former prosecutors. They are overwhelmingly male. And they tend to be concentrated in select legal markets.

Weisselberg & Li, *supra*, at 1249.[b] What do these observations tell us about the fairness of our judicial system? About the nature of white collar legal practice in the context

---

b. The authors state that they were unable to identify the race and ethnicity of the lawyers included in their study. *Id.* at 1250. With respect to the representation of women, they found:
> Women are dramatically underrepresented in the partnership ranks of major U.S. law firms. [A]mong the 1626 white-collar partners in our data set, only 247 (15%) are women. The gender difference between the white-collar and non-white-collar partners is statistically significant. Interestingly, we note that in both our initial pool of white-collar lawyers and the weighted sample of non-white-collar litigators, women comprise 43% of associates who are recent law school graduates. Inasmuch as women appear to enter these practice areas as new associates at the same rate, it is especially discouraging that women

of large law firms? Interestingly, women led the way in establishing the study of white collar and corporate crime in the nation's law schools during a time when the subject was considered a minor subset of criminal law. *See* Peter J. Henning, *Women Lead the Way in White-Collar Law*, N.Y. Times Dealbook, Apr. 2, 2013, http://dealbook .nytimes.com/2013/04/02/women-lead-the-way-in-white-collar-law/?_r=0.

3. The Overlap between White Collar and Common Crime

By defining "white collar crime" according to the type of criminal activity—or, more accurately, by excluding types of criminal activities from the term "white collar crime"—the focus shifts from the characteristics of the defendant to the characteristics of the crime. Often, this distinction works relatively easily; securities fraud and tax fraud, for example, are "paper" crimes that are "white collar" by nature.

Some crimes, however, and some issues in white collar cases do not observe these neat categories. For example, some of the most important Supreme Court cases interpreting federal conspiracy statutes have arisen in the white collar crime context, and a conspiracy count is often included in a white collar indictment. Governing legal principles in these cases, however, apply to any federal conspiracy case, whether the case involves white collar or common crime. As noted above, the crime of extortion includes some offenses that are "white collar" offenses and others that are not. Also, the "cover-up" offenses of perjury, false statements, and obstruction of justice fall within the definition of "white collar" offenses used here, and often arise in white collar cases. However, when such charges arise in cases of violent crime, they lose their "white collar" association. Finally, the broad-ranging criminal provisions of the federal racketeering ("RICO") and money laundering statutes are most often used outside the white collar context, but of course can also apply in the white collar context. Again, though, governing legal principles remain the same in the white collar and non-white collar contexts.

4. Corporate Crime and White Collar Crime

While white collar enforcement declined during the Trump administration, *see* Patricia Hurtado et al., *Trump Oversees All-Time Low in White-Collar Enforcement*, Bloomberg (Aug. 10, 2020), https://www.bloomberg.com/news/articles/2020-08 -10/trump-oversees-all-time-low-in-white-collar-crime-enforcement, expectations are that the Biden administration will take more of an aggressive stand, *see* Patricia Hurtado & Christopher Yasiejko, *White-Collar Crime Probes Likely to Intensify Under Biden*, Press Herald (Nov. 11, 2020), https://www.pressherald.com/2020/11 /11/white-collar-crime-probes-likely-to-intensify-under-bidens-doj/.

---

are even more poorly represented among the white-collar partners than among the non-white-collar litigation partners.

Id. at 1256–57 (citations omitted).

"Corporate crime" refers to crime committed by business entities rather than just the individuals within those entities. Technically, corporations can commit any type of crime. In 2020, Pacific Gas and Electric pled guilty to 84 counts of manslaughter after its wires caused massive wildfires. More typically, though, corporations will find themselves charged for white collar violations. Corporate employees usually commit crime for economic reasons, whether to benefit the corporation or the employee himself. The next chapter discusses the legal doctrines for attributing criminal conduct to corporations.

5. "Civil" versus "Criminal" Cases

It is important to note that some civil cases are properly included within the category of "white collar" cases. This is so because the rules established in civil cases arising under such statutes as the securities laws and false claims also govern in criminal cases premised on the same misconduct. Thus, a number of the chapters in this textbook include civil cases — initiated either by the government or by private parties — that establish principles applicable in criminal cases as well.

6. "Substantive" versus "Procedural" White Collar Cases

This text focuses both on the substance of white collar crime and on the procedure of white collar investigations and prosecutions. The vast majority of criminal procedure issues that arise in white collar cases mirror issues that arise in common crime cases. Some procedural issues, however, merit special attention in the white collar context. For example, the production of documents to the government by entities such as corporations raises unique issues under the Fifth Amendment's Self-Incrimination Clause. In addition, because white collar investigations typically are conducted by grand juries, issues relating to grand jury proceedings should be included within the category of "white collar" criminal law.

C. Recurring Issues in White Collar Investigations and Prosecutions

Apart from its timeliness, the study of white collar crime presents an opportunity to study criminal law and procedure within a particular context. Studying the processes of enacting white collar crimes and prosecuting those crimes allows us to address critical criminal justice issues, such as the criminalization of economic regulations, the constitutional impact of "over-criminalization," and the balance between federal and state/local law enforcement.

Further, white collar investigations raise interesting and important strategic and ethical issues for prosecutors and defense counsel. Issues relating to the representation of witnesses before grand juries, pre-indictment negotiations between prosecutors and defense counsel, parallel civil and criminal proceedings, and other issues often arise in white collar matters. These issues are discussed in cases and notes throughout this text and are also addressed in many of the practice problems contained in the chapters that follow.

1. Criminalization

The fundamental question in criminal law is determining when it is appropriate to deem conduct "criminal." When should society subject a defendant to the full force of criminal penalties rather than to civil and/or administrative remedies? This issue is particularly acute when the matters at hand involve the regulation of economic activities. Some have argued that it is often not appropriate to criminalize complex economic and business activities, for two reasons. First, such activities are morally ambiguous and may not deserve the full condemnation of the criminal law. White collar crimes tend to be malum prohibitum violations (illegal because law proscribes them) rather than malum in se (illegal because inherently immoral). There is a clear difference in character between, say, failing to report cash transactions over $10,000, and crimes like theft and arson that are familiar from the general part of criminal law. Second, criminal statutes designed to cover such matters are often flawed, in large part because economic crimes are difficult to define. There is often a very indistinct line between sharp business dealing and criminal fraud. As you read the materials in this text, consider whether these criticisms are justified.[c]

a. Distinguishing Civil and Criminal Liability

With respect to the increased criminalization of certain areas of the law, including economic regulations, consider the following excerpt written by Professor John Coffee in 1991:

> [T]he dominant development in substantive federal criminal law over the last decade has been the disappearance of any clearly definable line between civil and criminal law. [T]his blurring of the border between tort and crime predictably will result in injustice, and ultimately will weaken the efficacy of

---

c. For the views of one of the earliest and most influential critics of overcriminalization, *see* Sanford Kadish, *Some Observations on the Use of Criminal Sanctions to Enforce Economic Regulations*, 30 U. Chi. L. Rev. 423 (1963). Many others have explored this topic. *See, e.g.*, J. Kelly Strader, *White Collar Crime and Punishment — Reflections on Michael, Martha, and Milberg Weiss*, 15 Geo. Mason L. Rev. 45 (2007) (arguing that "gray area" financial fraud cases should be pursued using civil and administrative remedies unless there is overwhelming evidence of actual harm); Sara Sun Beale, *The Many Faces of Overcriminalization: From Morals and Mattress Tags to Overfederalization*, 54 Am. U. L. Rev. 747, 748 (2005) (arguing that "a good deal of so-called regulatory or 'white collar crime' should fall outside the ambit of the criminal law, to be dealt with by other bodies of specialized civil law"); Erik Luna, *The Overcriminalization Phenomenon*, 54 Am. U. L. Rev. 703, 743–44 (2005) (concluding that the expansion of federal criminal law is "contrary to the principles of limited government and narrow congressional powers, looking instead like the usurpation of a de facto police power by federal lawmakers").

the criminal law as an instrument of social control. [T]o define the proper sphere of the criminal law, one must explain how its purposes and methods differ from those of tort law. Although it is easy to identify distinguishing characteristics of the criminal law — *e.g.*, the greater role of intent in the criminal law, the relative unimportance of actual harm to the victim, the special character of incarceration as a sanction, and the criminal law's greater reliance on public enforcement — none of these is ultimately decisive.

Rather, the factor that most distinguishes the criminal law is its operation as a system of moral education and socialization. The criminal law is obeyed not simply because there is a legal threat underlying it, but because the public perceives its norms to be legitimate and deserving of compliance. Far more than tort law, the criminal law is a system for public communication of values. As a result, the criminal law often and necessarily displays a deliberate disdain for the utility of the criminalized conduct to the defendant.

Thus, while tort law seeks to balance private benefits and public costs, criminal law does not (or does so only by way of special affirmative defenses), possibly because balancing would undercut the moral rhetoric of the criminal law. Characteristically, tort law prices, while criminal law prohibits.

John C. Coffee, Jr., *Does "Unlawful" Mean "Criminal"?: Reflections on the Disappearing Tort/Crime Distinction in American Law*, 71 B.U. L. Rev. 193, 193–94 (1991).

According to Professor Coffee, what are the principal purposes of the criminal law? As we study white collar crime in different contexts, it will be helpful to ask whether the particular criminal statute — or particular criminal prosecution — serves those goals. When reading any particular case in this text, consider whether the conduct at issue merits criminal sanctions and, if so, what purposes criminal sanctions serve.

b. The Effects of Over-Criminalization

The difficulty in clearly drawing the boundaries between white collar crime and legitimate business transactions is a theme that runs throughout the materials in this text. For example, in the securities business, it is often the job of brokers and analysts to gain as much information as they can about the companies in which they are trading stock. But when a broker trades on "inside information," a term that has proven notoriously difficult to define (*see* Chapter 5, *infra*), the trading may constitute securities fraud. And when analyzing the criminal application of an antitrust statute, the Supreme Court in *United States v. United States Gypsum Co.*, 438 U.S. 422, 441 (1978), noted that the statute does not always distinguish criminal conduct from the "gray zone of socially acceptable and economically justifiable business conduct."

The difficulty in separating criminal from non-criminal acts is not limited to the business context. For example, as discussed in more detail in the chapters below, Congress and the Supreme Court have had difficulty distinguishing legitimate political campaign fundraising from the crimes of bribery, extortion "under color of official right," and honest services fraud. *See, e.g., McCormick v. United States*, 500 U.S. 257, 272 (1991) (expressing concern that an overly broad reading of the federal extortion statute could lead to criminalization of routine political fundraising activities). Consider the following observations concerning the conviction of former Virginia governor Robert McDonnell on political corruption charges:

> It would be both wise (to avoid prison) and good policy for officials to discourage large donations, avoid decisions that benefit big donors and generally disengage from contributors. But until that happens, we are stuck with a system in which lots of public officials could be convicted of a felony but few are prosecuted.
>
> That's not healthy for a democracy. It gives prosecutors vast discretion to choose targets, undermines the credibility of prosecutions that do occur and, ultimately, says something very unsettling about our government. Something has to give. We either need to strengthen our campaign finance laws or, if that's impossible, acknowledge that our public corruption laws are merely aspirational. A political system where any given federal, state or local official is just a wink, nod and a motivated prosecutor away from federal prosecution is untenable.

Jeffrey Bellin, *What the McDonnell Verdict Says About U.S. Politics*, Wash. Post (Sept. 5, 2014), http://www.washingtonpost.com/opinions/the-mcdonnell-verdict -shows-how-easily-prosecutors-may-criminalize-politics/2014/09/05/3128202a-3519 -11e4-9e92-0899b306bbea_story.html. Are these criticisms justified? At least in part because of some of these concerns, the United States Supreme Court overturned McDonnell's conviction. *See* Chapter 7, Bribery, *infra.*

Ambiguous and overlapping statutes put more power into the hands of prosecutors. Prosecutors confronting a single act of misconduct have more options in deciding how and what to charge. Among the consequences of ever-broader criminal statutes is an increased emphasis on plea bargaining. Plea bargaining reduces the role of courts and allows prosecutors to push broader understandings of what statutes actually proscribe. One study of plea bargaining in the federal system led to the following conclusions:

> Today, almost ninety-seven percent of criminal convictions in the federal system are resolved through a plea of guilty. As the number, breadth, and sentencing severity of federal criminal statutes continue to increase through overcriminalization, prosecutors gain increased ability to create overwhelming incentives for defendants to waive their constitutional right to a trial by jury and plead guilty. The symbiotic relationship between overcriminalization and plea bargaining has led us to our current state and created an environment in which we have jeopardized the accuracy of our criminal justice system in favor of speed and convenience.
>
> We found that more than half of the innocent participants in our study falsely admitted guilt in return for a perceived benefit. As overcriminalization

continues to create incentives that make plea bargaining so prevalent and powerful, one must ask what constitutional price is being paid when Congress creates yet another law or increases yet another statutory maximum where, despite the intent of Congress in passing them, these reforms appear ineffective at actually achieving their primary goal of deterrence.

Lucian E. Dervan, *White Collar Overcriminalization: Deterrence, Plea Bargaining, and the Loss of Innocence*, 101 Ky. L.J. 723, 751 (2013). As you cover the materials in this book, consider the possible impact of overcriminalization on the criminal justice system.

2. Due Process

The difficulty in defining white collar crimes also raises issues relating to the fairness of the criminal justice system. As Professor John Coffee has written, "the federal law of 'white collar' crime now seems to be judge-made to an unprecedented degree, with courts deciding on a case-by-case, retrospective basis whether conduct falls within often vaguely defined legislative prohibitions." Coffee, *supra*, at 198. Such statutes run the risk of reaching conduct that Congress did not intend to criminalize, failing to provide fair notice to potential defendants, and failing to provide sufficient guidance to prosecutors.

3. Prosecutorial Discretion

White collar investigations and prosecutions raise complex issues of prosecutorial discretion. Prosecutors have the discretion to decide: (a) whether the facts merit criminal charges, (b) whether to seek criminal penalties when civil and/or administrative proceedings have been or may be brought, (c) what criminal statutes to use in bringing a case, (d) what theories to charge when using those statutes, (e) whom to charge in the case, and/or (f) whether to offer a resolution that avoids trial (*e.g.*, a plea deal or a deferred prosecution agreement).

This broad discretion provides prosecutors with substantial powers in the white collar crime arena. As Professor Ellen Podgor has noted:

> Prosecutors have an array of crimes for proceeding against those engaged in white collar criminality. In many instances the involved activity fits the elements of more than one offense. Conduct will be mail fraud, tax fraud, a false statement, perjury, and also be violations of the Travel Act and RICO. A prosecutor, who in some instances may be a relatively inexperienced attorney, will be deciding which of these offenses will be used from the arsenal of possible charges to proceed against the defendant.

Ellen S. Podgor, *Corporate and White Collar Crime: Simplifying the Ambiguous*, 31 Am. Crim. L. Rev. 391, 400 (1994).

Apart from deciding which offenses to charge, a prosecutor may have the discretion to apply a white collar statute in a novel way. Precisely because many white collar criminal statutes are so broad-reaching, these statutes call upon prosecutors to exercise discretion when applying the statutes to new situations and to particular defendants. In addition, prosecutors identify the amount of loss or the number and identity of victims, factors that may contribute heavily to a defendant's sentence. These decisions thus give prosecutors tremendous leverage relating to plea bargaining, restitution, and sentencing.

Courts have traditionally declined to supervise the exercise of prosecutorial discretion, absent some egregious showing such as racial bias. Does reliance on the exercise of sound prosecutorial discretion solve or exacerbate the problem of vagueness in white collar criminalization?

4. A Double Standard?

Consider the common perception that high-level white collar criminal defendants receive special treatment in the criminal justice system. According to commentators, such treatment derives from, among other bases, the greater resources available to corporations and their agents and employees, the government's failure to prosecute such defendants (particularly those who may be considered "too big to jail"), lenient treatment that these defendants receive in the form of deferred- and nonprosecution agreements, and cognitive biases among criminal justice functionaries.

First, as noted above, top-tier white collar counsel charge such high rates that only corporations and the very wealthy generally can afford to retain such counsel. *See* Weisselberg & Li, *supra*, at 1249. This creates at least the appearance of a two-tier system that favors the wealthy.

Second, the government has been widely criticized for failing to prosecute the wealthy and powerful, such as those responsible for major financial crises. The *New York Times*, for example, blamed a lack of "creative thinking on the part of federal prosecutors about the web of federal statutes that could be brought to bear on potential [financial fraud] cases" following the 2008 recession. Editorial, *No Crime, No Punishment*, N.Y. Times (Aug. 26, 2012) at SR10. The *Times* continued:

> The result is a public perception that the big banks and their leaders will never have to answer fully for the [financial] crisis. The shameless pursuit of Wall Street campaign donations by both political parties strengthens this perception, and further undermines confidence in the rule of law.... After all these years, what is still needed are cases with convictions and settlements severe enough to deter future bad behavior. If institutions operating at the heart of the economy really cannot be held to account, the solution should be to break them up, not give them and their leaders a pass.

Id.

Third, the increasing use of deferred and non-prosecution agreements — which allow potential defendants to avoid criminal prosecution — in the corporate context has been the subject of substantial criticism. According to one commentator, such agreements "limit the punitive and deterrent value of the government's law enforcement efforts and extinguish the societal condemnation that should accompany criminal prosecution." David M. Uhlmann, *Deferred Prosecution and Non-Prosecution Agreements and the Erosion of Corporate Criminal Liability*, 72 Md. L. Rev. 1295, 1301 (2013). (This issue is explored in detail in Chapter 15, Internal Investigations, Compliance Programs, and Deferred and Non-Prosecution Agreements, *infra*.)

A fourth explanation, and one endorsed by the U.S. Sentencing Commission when it reformed white collar sentencing guidelines, is cognitive bias:

> Before the reforms, sentences for white-collar criminals were too light, especially when compared to street-crime sentences. One leading explanation was that judges are much more likely to overlap demographically with the sorts of upper-echelon folks who end up committing white-collar crimes. Beneath their robes and powdered wigs, judges are just humans subject to human foibles; like us all, they are more likely to empathize (even if unconsciously) with one of their own. The Sentencing Commission could not cure this suspected cognitive bias, but they could counteract it by raising the sentencing ranges for white-collar crimes.

Diamantis, *supra*, at 323.

Are the foregoing observations valid? For a different perspective, consider the following observations:

> [S]tudy of the routine operation of criminal-justice institutions belies the claim that the American system unjustly shields individual corporate offenders, that is, persons who commit financial crimes in business firms. Privilege cannot be found in sentencing law and practice, which nowadays treat the corporate offender with genuine harshness. Nor in substantive law, which turns out to be more problematic for the financial criminal than for many other offenders. Nor in the laws of evidence and procedure, which do not produce an identifiable advantage in case outcomes for the white collar defendant. Nor in contemporary enforcement regimes, which — though they direct fewer conventional policing resources to the corporate sector — have structural features that heighten the exposure of business actors to criminal sanctions. Clear privilege can be found in access to well-funded counsel. But there, the advantage is not as decisive as generally believed.

Buell, *supra*, at 829.

The perception that white collar defendants — particularly large corporations, their agents and employees, and the politically well-connected — receive favorable treatment is a theme that will recur throughout this text. As you read the materials, consider whether this perception is accurate.

5. Enforcement Barriers

White collar crime often occurs behind closed doors, causing harm of which the victim may not even be aware. Successful fraud is self-concealing. Apart from the difficulty of detection, these crimes are also often highly complex and require substantial resources and expertise to investigate and prosecute. The government continually struggles to make white collar criminal law enforcement more efficient and effective. Important questions arise as to whether the more effective way to achieve these goals is to enact more laws and/or to devote more resources to the effort to fight white collar crime. A third strategy that is gaining traction in recent years is to recruit corporations in the enforcement effort. Through the threat of sanction, authorities hope to induce corporations to implement better prevention and detection mechanisms and to self-report misconduct when they uncover it.

6. Federalism

a. Over-Federalization?

Under our constitutional system, criminal law enforcement is primarily left to the states; historically only about five percent of all criminal cases are brought at the federal level. *See Report of the ABA Task Force on the Federalization of Criminal Law* 4 (1998). In recent decades, however, Congress has enacted an ever-broader array of criminal statutes. The Chairman of the United States House of Representatives Judiciary Committee Over-Criminalization Task Force made the following observation:

> Over the past few decades, the federal criminal code has expanded dramatically, creating an ever-increasing labyrinth of federal statutes and regulations, many of which impose criminal penalties without requiring that criminal intent be shown to establish guilt. We need to make sure our laws and regulations protect freedom, work as efficiently and fairly as possible, and do not duplicate state efforts. This Task Force is taking a detailed look at our criminal code, seeking input from recognized experts in the field, and intends to examine many issues this year.

House Judiciary Committee Reauthorizes Bipartisan Over-Criminalization Task Force (Feb. 5, 2014), https://republicans-judiciary.house.gov/press-release/house -judiciary-committee-reauthorizes-bipartisan-over-criminalization-task-force/. The subcommittee chairman noted that "[t]he criminal code is muddled and outdated." *Id.* Consider the following:

> The United States Code currently contains some 4,500 federal crimes. Recent studies estimate that approximately 60 new federal crimes are enacted each year, and over the past three decades, Congress has averaged

500 new crimes per decade. In addition to the statutory criminal offenses, there are thousands of federal regulations that, if violated, can also result in criminal liability. Some of these new statutes have been accompanied by hundreds of thousands of implementing regulations — studies put the number at more than 300,000 — many of which, if violated, can also result in criminal liability.

Id.

Federal white collar criminalization is a significant part of a broader trend to federalize criminal law. Apart from the increased burdens on the federal judicial system, what are the implications of this development for our federal system of government? One commentator observed:

> The original role of federal criminal law was auxiliary to that of the states. Federal law addressed matters of substantial federal concern that were beyond the reach of the states. The evolution of a national police power paralleled the rise of economic regulation. Increased economic regulation inspired a Congress enamored with commerce-based jurisdiction to add more and more crimes to the books. Thus, as economic regulation ascended, criminal law flourished as well. But somewhere along the line, federal criminal law lost its compass. Congress, disregarding the auxiliary nature of federal law enforcement, placed federal criminal law on an evolutionary collision course with state criminal law. Thus, instead of complementing state criminal law, federal law began competing with it.
>
> Federal duplication of state criminal law unduly burdens the federal justice system, which is ill-equipped to supplant local law enforcement. The federal government's assumption of a major responsibility for maintaining local law and order is not only harmful to the federal justice system. It is also harmful to the states. When the government preempts local prosecutions in areas of overlapping jurisdiction, it interferes with a state's ability to exercise discretion in a way that is responsive to local concerns. Excessive use of federal jurisdiction diminishes the prestige of local law enforcement authorities and thus may interfere with their development of responsibility for and capacity to handle complex matters or detract from the distinctive role states play as "laboratories of change."

Kathleen F. Brickey, *Criminal Mischief: The Federalization of American Criminal Law*, 46 HASTINGS L.J. 1135, 1172–74 (1995); *see also* Adam H. Kurland, *First Principles of American Federalism and the Nature of Federal Criminal Jurisdiction*, 45 EMORY L.J. 1 (1996); Sara Sun Beale, *Too Many and Yet Too Few: New Principles to Define the Proper Limits for Federal Criminal Jurisdiction*, 46 HASTINGS L.J. 979 (1995). For a different view on the federalization of the criminal law, however, see Susan R. Klein & Ingrid B. Grobey, *Debunking Claims of Over-Federalization of Criminal Law*, 62 EMORY L.J. 1 (2012) (challenging common assumptions concerning over-federalization).

What has caused this trend toward "over-federalization"? Some features of white collar crime necessitate a federal response. Prosecutors need ample resources and firm negotiating leverage to handle the complexity of white collar crimes and the high-powered attorneys available to white collar defendants. Since many white collar crimes extend across multiple jurisdictions, federal authorities are uniquely situated to subpoena witnesses, compel production of documents, and, where necessary, seize evidence. Federal prosecutors are also less likely to be subject to local political constraints that might protect influential individuals and businesses.

But structural necessity is not the only driver of the federalization of white collar criminal law. In 1998, the American Bar Association's Criminal Justice Section issued a report prepared by the bipartisan Task Force of the Federalization of Criminal Law. That report stated:

> The Task Force was told explicitly by more than one source that many of these new federal laws are passed not because federal prosecution of these crimes is necessary but because federal crime legislation in general is thought to be politically popular. Put another way, it is not considered politically wise to vote against crime legislation, even if it is misguided, unnecessary, and even harmful.

> The Task Force believes that the Congressional appetite for new crimes regardless of their merit is not only misguided and ineffectual, but has serious adverse consequences, some of which have already occurred and some of which can be confidently predicted.

Report of the ABA Task Force, supra, at 1–2. Throughout this text, you will encounter opportunities to study the increased role of the federal government in the criminal law in matters ranging from routine fraud prosecutions to state and local political corruption cases.

b. Jurisdiction

There must be a jurisdictional basis for any federal criminal prosecution. In most white collar cases, jurisdiction exists under the Commerce Clause of the United States Constitution. U.S. Const. art. I, § 8, cl. 3. That clause provides that Congress may "regulate Commerce with Foreign Nations, and among the several states, and with the Indian Tribes." After years of reading the Commerce Clause broadly, the Supreme Court employed a more restrictive reading in *United States v. Lopez*, 514 U.S. 549, 554–55 (1995). In that case, the Court voided a non-white collar federal statute because the proscribed activity (relating to the possession of firearms on school grounds) did not meet the requirement of "substantially affect[ing] interstate commerce." It is rare, however, for a white collar statute to be voided on jurisdictional grounds. Note also that some white collar statutes rely on other constitutional grants of federal authority, like the postal power (mail fraud) and the taxing power (tax fraud), for their jurisdictional basis.

D. White Collar Crime and General Criminal Law

The study of white collar crime provides a valuable opportunity to gain a more in-depth understanding of how substantive criminal law operates. In common crime cases, the primary issue is often one of identity — have the police caught the right person? In white collar cases, on the other hand, the issues are usually far more complex. First, because of the vagueness of many white collar statutes, the primary issue is often whether the defendant's admitted conduct even constitutes a crime. Second, the defendant's culpable mental state, or mens rea, is more frequently the principal issue in white collar cases than in non-white collar cases. For example, in a business fraud case, the government must prove that the defendant had the purpose to defraud, as opposed to an intent merely to engage in an aggressive but legal business practice. The fact of the misrepresentation is often easy to prove, but misrepresentation only becomes fraud if the defendant *knew* it would mislead.

1. Mens Rea

The required proof of mens rea is a key issue in most white collar cases. Initially, in many contexts, the required level of mens rea may not be clear from the criminal statute at issue. Further, defining precisely what a particular level of mens rea really means is often a difficult task.

Even where a mental state element is clear from the statute, determining which elements of the offense it applies to presents another challenge. *See* Darryl K. Brown, *Federal Mens Rea Interpretation and the Limits of Culpability's Relevance*, 75 L. & Contemp. Probs. 109 (2012). For example, if a statute forbids knowingly submitting a false statement to a federal agency, does violation require only knowledge that the statement is false, or also knowledge that it is being made to a federal agency? In *Flores-Figueroa v. United States*, 556 U.S. 646 (2009), the Supreme Court announced an interpretive principle under which the stated mens rea in a criminal statute applies to all subsequent elements. It remains to be seen, however, whether lower courts will adhere to this principle, particularly with respect to strict liability offenses. *See* Leonid Traps, *"Knowingly" Ignorant: Mens Rea Distribution in Federal Criminal Law after* Flores-Figueroa, 112 Colum. L. Rev. 628 (2012). The subsections below explore mens rea concepts and definitions that arise in cases throughout this text.

a. Strict Liability

Recall that the vast majority of crimes require proof of both the criminal act and the criminal mental state. But what if a criminal statute fails on its face to require proof of mens rea? Should such a requirement be read into the statute? In *United States v. United States Gypsum Co.*, 438 U.S. 422 (1978), the Supreme Court examined whether intent is an element of a criminal antitrust charge under the Sherman Act, 15 U.S.C. §1. That statute proscribes certain anticompetitive business practices, such as price-fixing, and can be enforced in both civil and criminal proceedings. The trial judge had instructed the jury that "the law presumes that a person intends the necessary and natural consequences of his acts. Therefore, if the effect of the exchanges of pricing information was to raise, fix, maintain, and stabilize prices, then the parties to them are presumed, as a matter of law, to have intended that result." *United States Gypsum*, 438 U.S. at 430. The defendant was convicted and, on appeal, challenged this jury instruction.

The Supreme Court reversed, noting that "the instructions . . . given by the trial judge provided that . . . the [defendant's] *purpose* was essentially irrelevant if the jury found that the *effect* of [defendant's conduct] was to raise, fix, maintain, or stabilize prices." *Id.* at 429–30 (emphasis added). The instructions thus imposed strict liability if the actus reus of the crime was present. The Court concluded "a defendant's state of mind or intent is an element of a criminal antitrust offense which must be established by evidence and inferences drawn therefrom and cannot be taken from the trier of fact through reliance on a legal presumption of wrongful intent from proof of an effect on prices. . . . [I]ntent generally remains an indispensable element of a criminal offense. This is as true in a sophisticated criminal antitrust case as in one involving any other criminal offense." *Id.* at 435–37. Absent clear congressional intent to impose strict liability, the Court held, criminal intent must be proven in any criminal case.

The Court in *United States Gypsum* decided that a criminal violation of the Sherman Act is not a "strict liability" offense. As seen in the next chapter, however, the Court has approved of strict liability criminal offenses in other contexts.

b. Types of Mens Rea

Once it had decided that proof of mens rea is required in a criminal prosecution under the Sherman Act, the Court in *United States Gypsum* turned to the task of defining the required level of mens rea. Relying upon the Model Penal Code ("MPC"), the Court identified four possible levels: purpose,[d] knowledge,[e] recklessness,[f]

---

d. Model Penal Code § 2.02(a) provides:
   A person acts purposely . . . when . . . it is his conscious object to engage in the [proscribed] conduct or to cause [the proscribed] result. . . .
e. Model Penal Code § 2.02(b) provides:
   A person acts knowingly . . . when (i) if the element involves the nature of his conduct, he is aware that his conduct is of that nature; and (ii) if the element involves a result of his conduct, he is aware that it is practically certain that his conduct will cause such a result.
f. Model Penal Code § 2.02(c) provides:
   A person acts recklessly . . . when he consciously disregards a substantial and unjustifiable risk that the material element exists or will result from his conduct. The risk must be of such a nature and degree that, considering the nature and purpose of the actor's conduct and the circumstances known to him, its disregard involves a gross deviation from the standard of conduct that a law-abiding person would observe in the actor's situation.

and negligence.[g] (Be sure to take a moment to read the definitions reproduced in the footnotes.) The Court stated that, "[i]n dealing with the kinds of business decisions upon which the antitrust laws focus, the concepts of recklessness and negligence have no place." *Id.* at 444. The Court then stated that:

> Our question instead is whether a criminal violation of the antitrust laws requires ... a demonstration that the disputed conduct was undertaken with the 'conscious object' [i.e., purpose] of producing such effects, or whether it is sufficient that the conduct is shown to have been undertaken with knowledge that the proscribed effects would most likely follow. While the difference between these formulations is a narrow one, we conclude that action undertaken with knowledge of its probable consequences ... can be a sufficient predicate for a finding of criminal liability under the antitrust laws. *Id.*

According to the Court, at least when anticompetitive effects are shown, knowledge is the required mens rea; the Court declined to require proof that the defendants acted with "purpose." As a practical matter, what is the difference? As we will see in the chapters below, Congress has adopted statutes that indeed impose criminal liability based upon reckless and negligent conduct. Can you determine why the Court found these standards inappropriate to a charge of price-fixing?

In addition to actual knowledge, under both federal law and the MPC, "knowledge" also encompasses "constructive knowledge," also termed "willful blindness." This concept is explored more fully in Chapter 3, Conspiracy, *infra*. For present purposes, it is worth noting that "constructive knowledge" is often difficult to distinguish from recklessness, but at least theoretically the two concepts are distinct.

c. "Specific" versus "General" Intent

The MPC and the *United States Gypsum* opinion both reject the old common law distinction between specific and general intent — terms with varying definitions that have produced more confusion than clarity. As a general matter, if the term "specific intent" appears in a case, it is probably used to mean "purpose" as employed by the MPC. The MPC provides that a defendant acted "purposefully" when the defendant acted with the "conscious object to engage in [the proscribed] conduct ... or to cause such a result." Model Penal Code § 2.02(2)(a)(i).

---

g. Model Penal Code § 2.02(d) provides:
   A person acts negligently ... when he should be aware of a substantial and unjustifiable risk that the material element exists or will result from his conduct. The risk must be of such a nature and degree that the actor's failure to perceive it, considering the nature and purpose of his conduct and the circumstances known to him, involves a gross deviation from the standard of care that a reasonable person would observe in the actor's situation.

d. "Willfulness"

Some white collar statutes require proof that the defendant acted "willfully." The interpretation of this term varies according to the context. Consider the following opinion, which interprets the element of willfulness in the context of criminal copyright infringement: "[T]he term 'willfully' is ambiguous. To infringe willfully could simply mean to intentionally commit the act that constitutes infringement. Alternatively, it could mean that the defendant must act with a 'bad purpose' or 'evil motive' in the sense that there was an 'intentional violation of a known legal duty.'" *United States v. Liu*, 731 F.3d 982, 989–90 (9th Cir. 2013) (citations omitted). In the realm of tax fraud, the Supreme Court stated in *Cheek v. United States*, 498 U.S. 192, 201 (1991), that "[w]illfulness . . . requires the government to prove that the law imposed a duty on the defendant, that the defendant knew of this duty, and that he voluntarily and intentionally violated that duty." This unusually high burden of proof defies the usual maxim that "ignorance of the law is no excuse." The Court concluded that the extraordinary complexity of the federal tax code justifies this high level of proof. The Court reached a similar result when interpreting the currency transaction reporting statutes. *See Ratzlaf v. United States*, 510 U.S. 135 (1994).[h]

In other contexts, however, "willfulness" may be defined differently. Instead of knowledge that the act violates a specific law, it may mean only that the defendant knew that the act was generally unlawful. *See Bryan v. United States*, 524 U.S. 184 (1998). In other circumstances, "willfulness" may mean "purpose," "knowledge," or even "recklessness." *See, e.g., United States v. Tarallo*, 380 F.3d 1174, 1180 (9th Cir. 2004) ("[W]e hold that a defendant may commit securities fraud 'willfully' even if the defendant did not know at the time of the acts that the conduct violated the law. We further hold that a defendant may commit securities fraud 'willfully' by intentionally acting with reckless disregard for the truth of material misleading statements."). Care should be taken to identify precisely how courts have interpreted the term "willfulness" under the particular statute.

2. Statutory Interpretation

As is apparent from the preceding sections, statutory interpretation plays a more significant role in white collar crimes than in most other areas of the criminal law. Because the statutes are so often at once broad and vague, courts continually struggle to construe these statutes,. One scholar summarized the process thus:

> A court's first step is to read the statute's text for a plain or ordinary meaning, which can be the best guide to legislative intent. This may require resorting to dictionary definitions and — often in mens rea analysis — inferences

---

h. As discussed in Chapter 13 *infra*, Congress later amended the applicable statute to overturn the *Ratzlaf* result.

of typical grammar or syntax usage, sometimes drawing from writing style manuals as guides on common usage — and therefore — textual meaning. If the text's meaning is unambiguous, the question is settled. If not, courts resort to other strategies, including canons of construction, and other evidence of statutory purpose and legislative intent. They may also seek guidance from a predecessor statute or from the title of the statute. Furthermore, under the doctrine of in pari materia, the construction of related statutes or those employing similar language can guide courts. The priority and influence of these secondary tools vary according to the interpreter's methodology.

All these strategies are means of determining the legislature's intent for the statute. Yet it is easy to see how these different interpretive methods can and do lead to different results.

Brown, *supra*, at 112. Issues that turn on principles of statutory interpretation arise throughout this text.

3. The Rule of Lenity

The defendants in *United States Gypsum* were prosecuted under a statute that, on its face, did not require that the government prove any level of mens rea in order to obtain a criminal conviction. In interpreting Section 1 of the Sherman Act to require proof of a culpable mental state, the Court relied upon the rule of "lenity." The Supreme Court has defined lenity as "the familiar rule that, 'where there is ambiguity in a criminal statute, doubts are to be resolved in favor of the defendant.'" *Adamo Wrecking Co. v. United States*, 434 U.S. 275, 285 (1978), quoting *United States v. Bass*, 404 U.S. 336, 348 (1971). As you read the materials in this text, consider whether lenity provides a meaningful safeguard when construing ambiguous statutes.

E. The "Harm" from White Collar Crime

Does white collar criminal activity cause the sort of harm that might even warrant criminalization? As one scholar has written with respect to white collar crimes, "the harms they cause are often diffuse; and the victims they affect are frequently hard to identify." Stuart P. Green, *Moral Ambiguity in White Collar Criminal Law*, 18 Notre Dame J.L. Ethics & Pub. Pol'y 501, 501 (2004). The indeterminacy of harm is an issue that does not often arise in connection with common crime, where the injury to person or property is usually readily apparent.

Enforcement of some white collar crimes arguably causes more harm than it prevents. In *United States Gypsum*, for example, the Supreme Court suggested that an overly broad reading of the Sherman Act might result in "overdeterrence" that would prevent businesspeople from engaging in beneficial activities. The uncertainty over the "harm" caused by many types of white collar crime underscores the problematic nature of white collar criminalization. One commentator, for example, argued that prosecutors' emphasis on white collar crime is not justified by the harm that such crime causes:

> White-collar criminal prosecutions were a small feature of law enforcement, state and federal, before about 1970. They are still a small feature of local prosecutors' dockets, but they play a large role indeed in many U.S. Attorneys' offices. This large growth in white-collar prosecutions, like the explosion in drug enforcement, has taken place in Republican and Democratic administrations alike, and now appears to be a permanent feature of federal criminal practice.
>
> What explains it? The phenomenon was partly prompted by Edwin Sutherland's skillful propagandizing: Sutherland spent years making exaggerated claims about the high cost of the frauds of the wealthy. . . . But it is hard to credit the popularity of white-collar criminal enforcement to the perceived cost of white-collar crimes. The best study of those crimes and the criminals who commit them concluded that many are fairly small-time frauds that cost their victims a few thousand dollars or less. More importantly, frauds do not impose the biggest costs that more traditional street crime imposes: fear of violence, and the attendant inability to travel about one's neighborhood in peace. Plus, white-collar cases are more costly to investigate and prosecute than street crime, partly because of the nature of the evidence the government must gather, and partly because white-collar defendants are so often represented by counsel even while the investigation is going forward. Sutherland's fulminations notwithstanding, street crime is and always has been more socially costly and more easily punished than its white-collar counterpart.

William J. Stuntz, *Race, Class, and Drugs*, 98 COLUM. L. REV. 1795, 1839–40 (1998).

Problems

1-1. Do you agree that, because street crime involves the fear of violence, it "is and always has been more socially costly" than white collar crime? What are the social costs of white collar crime?

1-2. If you were a prosecutor with limited resources, whom would you pursue — a person who repeatedly and intentionally murdered a number of victims, or a corporate executive whose workplace practices had caused a similar number of employees to be killed?

1-3. Would you pursue a burglar who had stolen thousands of dollars' worth of property from hundreds of homes, or a savings and loan executive who had defrauded a similar number of victims out of an equivalent sum of money? Why?

Chapter 2

Corporate and Individual Liability

A. Introductory Notes

Any study of white collar crime must incorporate a comprehensive understanding of the scope of individual and corporate liability for criminal activity. Legal entities, such as corporations, may be held criminally liable even if the individuals who acted on behalf of the entity are not charged with or convicted of any crime, and vice versa. Further, individuals acting on behalf of entities may be liable even if those individuals were acting solely to benefit the corporation.

The scope of corporate liability has evolved over many decades and runs the gamut from administrative and civil sanctions to criminal liability. Because of the unique nature of artificial entities, such as corporations, corporate liability is subject to considerable public policy debate. Corporations lack the most fundamental aspects of criminal liability: bodies of their own with which to commit criminal acts and minds of their own with which to harbor criminal intent. To locate criminal intent and the guilty acts, courts look to the employees of the corporation. However, locating a culpable employee is not always a straightforward task. Over the years, courts have also struggled with the concept of convicting and sentencing abstract entities such as corporations, partly because punishing a corporation in reality may harm innocent shareholders by depriving them of their property.

Criminal prosecution of corporations has become much more frequent in recent years, reflecting a government shift in priorities and resources. Most recently the impact of financial crimes has devastated many sectors of the national and worldwide economies. Highly publicized scandals focused public attention on corporate wrongdoing. From the financial meltdown of 2008 and continuing to the present, the financial crisis continues to affect all aspects of our society. The ensuing public outcry often leads legislatures and prosecutors to respond swiftly to such scandals. For example, public outrage at the corporate accounting scandals of the early 21st century resulted in the hasty passage of the Sarbanes-Oxley Act of 2002. This law exposes corporations, employees, and officers to expanded criminal sanctions and has resulted in closer scrutiny of individual wrongdoers within corporate entities. In 2010, Congress passed the Dodd-Frank Wall Street Reform and Consumer Protection Act. This law heightened financial regulation and extended criminal liability to additional types of financial instruments. Task forces focusing on corporate wrongdoing exist on the federal, state, and local levels, all with the goal of holding entities accountable through the imposition of sanctions including civil fines, criminal sanctions, and debarment (suspension from doing business with the government).

Corporate criminal liability is an essential part of the government's toolkit for addressing corporate misconduct. As Samuel Buell has pointed out, *criminal liability seems to be a greater motivation for corporations than civil liability. See* Samuel W. Buell, *The Blaming Function of Entity Criminal Liability*, 81 IND. L.J. 473 (2006). Entity-level liability (as opposed to just holding individuals within corporations responsible) is important because culpability for corporate crime often lies with the organization itself. In other words, the ultimate source of misbehavior may be the corporate system or corporate culture. These are larger than any individual and also largely beyond the capacity of any single individual to influence. *See* Mihailis E. Diamantis, *Successor Identity*, 36 YALE J. ON REG. 1 (2019). Even when there are responsible individuals, prosecutors can face significant hurdles proving beyond a reasonable doubt who committed the crime. The corporate structure can obscure the truth of what happened, and individuals within the organization all have an incentive to point blame in a different direction.

Even if corporate criminal liability is a valuable tool, the criminal justice system still needs to have some account of what it wants to accomplish once it finds a corporation guilty. How do you punish a corporation and what should punishment accomplish? The dominant mode of corporate punishment is the fine, largely because the other prevalent mode of criminal punishment — time in prison — is unavailable. But what should courts try to accomplish with fines? Here is one commentator's perspective:

> Criminal law has been punishing corporations for over a century without a defensible theory of corporate punishment. The main alternatives are retribution and deterrence. . . .
>
> Retributivists want corporations to suffer their just deserts. The trouble is corporations don't experience suffering. The best retributivists can offer is the imposition of harms on criminal corporations, typically in the form of a monetary fine. But fines flow directly through the corporate fiction to harm shareholders, who, more often than not, will be innocent of their corporation's misconduct. Shareholders, as natural people, do suffer. So . . . the bulk of the suffering corporate punishment can inflict goes to those who do not deserve it.
>
> Deterrence theorists want to alter corporate incentives so that criminal conduct becomes unappealingly costly. Just as corporations can't suffer, they also don't really have their own incentives. The individuals who act on behalf of corporations have incentives, and one way to deter corporate misconduct would be to target those. But corporate punishment cannot be the way to do it. Whatever benefits an employee may gain from misconduct will more often than not outweigh the fractional share they experience of

any corporate-level sanction. Deterrence theory and corporate fines cannot overcome the basic economic problem of agency costs.

Mihailis E. Diamantis, *The Law's Missing Account of Corporate Character*, GEO. J.L. & PUB. POL'Y 865, 879–80 (2019).

These difficulties have necessitated some creative thinking about how and why to punish corporations. One leading account takes a process-oriented approach, according to which the goal of holding corporations criminally liable is to induce corporations to implement their own internal monitoring systems so that they can detect, address, and report individual misconduct to authorities. *See* Jennifer Arlen & Reinier Kraakman, *Controlling Corporate Misconduct: An Analysis of Corporate Liability Regimes*, 72 N.Y.U. L. REV. 687 (1997). Another account challenges the received wisdom that incapacitation is inapplicable to corporations by conceiving of modes of restricting corporate convicts' behavior without imprisoning them. *See* W. Robert Thomas, *Incapacitating Criminal Corporations*, 72 VAND. L. REV. 905 (2019). A third approach would forgo corporate fines altogether and punish corporations by forcibly rehabilitating them. *See* Mihailis E. Diamantis, *Clockwork Corporations: A Character Theory of Corporate Punishment*, 103 IOWA L. REV. 507 (2018). For a more detailed overview of corporate punishment, see Mihailis E. Diamantis & William S. Laufer, *Prosecution and Punishment of Corporate Criminality*, 15 ANN. REV. L. & SOC. SCI. 453 (2019).

A Note on Prosecutorial Discretion

The goal of bringing to justice those who violate the law and must take into account numerous competing factors. Any decision to indict an individual or a corporation involves tremendous prosecutorial discretion. As prosecutors view the facts of any case, they must first determine whether criminal conduct has occurred. Often this is the easiest issue to resolve. Determining who committed the crime is the next question. As you will see in this chapter, individuals within a corporation must instantiate the physical acts and mental states. Then those acts and mental states must be attributed to the corporation. The potential fallout from a conviction is always in the back of the minds of prosecutors.

With any corporate criminal investigation, the consequences of an indictment or conviction are paramount. A corporation can have thousands of employees, any of whom might commit crime on the company's behalf. The misconduct of a few employees can have devastating consequences for the many. Innocent shareholders, employees, creditors, and clients can be harmed by such misconduct. For these reasons and others, the government has increased the use of deferred prosecution agreements, which allows companies to admit their misconduct but not suffer the effect of a criminal conviction against the institution. (*See* Chapter 15, Internal Investigations, Compliance Programs, and Deferred and Non-Prosecution Agreements, *infra*.)

Of paramount importance are the Department of Justice's Principles of Federal Prosecution of Business Organizations (U.S. Dep't of Just., Just. Manual § 9-28.000 (2020)). Originally formulated in 1999, they have been through several revisions since. The "Principles" list several factors that frontline prosecutors should consider in deciding whether to charge a corporation. Factors include those familiar from the general part of criminal law (e.g., the sufficiency of the evidence) and some particular to the corporate context (e.g., size of the corporation, the adequacy of the corporation's compliance programs, involvement of senior officials in the crime, and the potential for collateral effects of conviction). Although considered by prosecutors, the Principles are not binding and create no legal rights for corporate suspects. Courts have no jurisdiction to review how prosecutors balance the numerous factors in any individual case. This means that the informal norms that the Principles establish are often as important to the practice of corporate criminal defense as the actual criminal statutes.

Prosecutors have a vast amount of discretion to decide whether to charge corporations (and what crimes to charge) or to offer them some form of noncriminal resolution. This discretion has drawn a lot of critical attention. Some scholars observe that similarly situated corporations can receive very different resolutions because the DOJ's guidelines on prosecuting corporations are imprecise and nonbinding. *See* Jennifer Arlen, *Prosecuting Beyond the Rule of Law: Corporate Mandates Imposed Through Deferred Prosecution Agreements*, 8 J. Legal Analysis 191 (2016). This leaves individual prosecutors to make their own decisions in the cases they prosecute, and often considerations of political economy will prevail. One scholar points to what he calls the "corporate compliance game" — a surprising alignment of interests between corporations and prosecutors — because both want to *seem* as though they are tough on crime while also avoiding a lengthy investigation and trial. William S. Laufer, *The Missing Account of Progressive Corporate Criminal Law*, 14 N.Y.U. J.L. & Bus. 71, 112–13 (2018).

As prosecutors consider the potential consequences of criminal prosecution against corporations, U.S. Attorney General Eric H. Holder (testifying before a Senate Judiciary Committee on March 6, 2013), recognized that

> "[T]he size of some of these institutions becomes so large that it does become difficult for us to prosecute them." Indeed, prosecutorial discretion is paramount in any given criminal investigation, but "there is the nagging feeling that prosecutors are trying to have it both ways in deciding whether to file charges against [corporations] by taking steps to ensure they do not cause too much collateral damage. In the end, the issue is whether the misconduct is serious enough to warrant criminal prosecution, and if so, then perhaps the government should let the chips fall where they may."

Peter J. Henning, *Seeking Guilty Pleas from Corporations While Limiting the Fallout*, N.Y. Times (May 5, 2014, 1:20 PM) http://dealbook.nytimes.com/2014/05/05/seeking -guilty-pleas-from-corporations-while-limiting-the-fallout.

As you read through the materials in this chapter, think about the question of whether a corporation should ever be immune from indictment because it is "too big to fail."

B. Corporate Criminal Liability

This chapter will review the basic principles of corporate criminal liability and some of the considerations that might persuade a prosecutor to charge a corporation and/or various individuals within the corporate structure. Corporations can be held liable for acts of employees under two different legal approaches: respondeat superior and the Model Penal Code ("MPC"), depending on the jurisdiction. This section discusses each of these approaches.

1. Respondeat Superior

In the federal court system, the civil doctrine of respondeat superior applies to corporate criminal investigations. The requirements are often incorporated into the statutory language, but courts also use a three-pronged test to determine whether an agent's acts and thoughts can be imputed to the corporation. The essence of the respondeat superior doctrine imposes liability on corporations for acts committed by corporate agents acting: (1) on behalf of the corporation, (2) with intent to benefit the corporation, and (3) within the scope of the agent's authority. As will be seen, determining the presence of these criteria is often a difficult task.

A frequent issue that arises in corporate investigations is whether the agent was acting within the scope of the agent's employment regardless of the agent's position within the corporation. Proof of this fact is necessary for a corporation to be convicted under the respondeat superior theory of criminal liability. The next case demonstrates the breadth of respondeat superior liability and discusses the sufficiency of the evidence on the "scope of employment" and "intent to benefit."

United States v. Automated Medical Laboratories, Inc.
770 F.2d 399 (4th Cir. 1985)

SNEEDEN, CIRCUIT JUDGE:

The defendant, Automated Medical Laboratories, Inc. ("AML"), appeals its conviction of one count of conspiracy, in violation of 18 U.S.C. § 371, and three counts of making and using false documents in a matter within the jurisdiction of a federal agency, in violation of 18 U.S.C. § 1001. AML was convicted of these four counts following a jury trial in March 1984 in the United States District Court for the Eastern District of Virginia. AML was fined $250.00 for each count, for a total fine of $1000.00. AML argues that its convictions should be reversed because several instances of prosecutorial misconduct denied it a fundamentally fair trial and because the evidence adduced at trial was insufficient to sustain its convictions. We disagree with these contentions and consequently affirm AML's conviction on all counts.

On December 12, 1983, a grand jury indicted AML, along with one of its wholly-owned subsidiaries, Richmond Plasma Corporation ("RPC"), and three individuals, Hugo Partucci, Noberto Queris, and Pedro Ramos, for engaging in a conspiracy that included falsification of logbooks and records required to be maintained in connection with the commercial enterprise of producing blood plasma. The indictment alleged that the falsification of logbooks and records was engaged in to conceal from the Food and Drug Administration ("FDA") various violations of federal regulations governing the plasmapheresis process and facilities. The remainder of the eight-count indictment alleged specific violations of the false statements statute, 18 U.S.C. § 1001, with regard to particular logbooks or records at the RPC facility. AML was named as a defendant in six of the seven substantive counts plus the conspiracy count. RPC was found guilty on all counts.

The three individuals indicted — Partucci, Queris, and Ramos — were all involved, at various times, in the management or oversight of RPC. Queris was the manager of RPC from 1979 to 1980. In 1980, Ramos succeeded Queris as manager of RPC. Hugo Partucci was a regional manager and "Responsible Head" for several of AML's plasmapheresis facilities between 1972 and 1979. Queris pleaded guilty to one substantive count prior to trial. Ramos was found guilty of one substantive count. Partucci was not present at trial, having apparently left for his native country, Argentina, about six months before the indictment was returned.

AML, a Florida corporation with its main office in Miami, owns and operates several medically-related businesses, such as kidney dialysis centers, facilities for the manufacture and sale of the cancer drug Interferon, and plasmapheresis facilities. AML's primary line of business, however, is the collection and sale of plasma through its eight commercial plasmapheresis centers. Each center, including RPC, is separately incorporated and wholly-owned by AML.

AML had experienced difficulties with RPC dating back to 1977. The FDA closed RPC twice, once in 1977 and again in late 1978, because of problems with overbleeding of donors (removing more blood from a given donor than is allowed by federal regulations) and incomplete recordkeeping. Following the first closing, the manager and responsible head for RPC were changed. Partucci became responsible head for RPC and was charged with assuring compliance with FDA regulations. Partucci, although technically employed by the Orlando Plasma Center, another AML subsidiary, operated as a regional manager for AML and was responsible for assuring compliance with FDA regulations. Partucci was responsible for assuring compliance at RPC and at least two other plasma centers.

At some point, apparently in 1978, Partucci and Edgar Nugent, an Executive Vice President at AML, established a special office for the specific purpose of assuring compliance with federal regulations at AML plasma centers. The compliance office, headed by Partucci, operated from the Orlando Center. By late 1978, the compliance office included Partucci, Claudia Hayes, and Mary Jo Lawton. Another AML employee, Robert Curry, sometimes accompanied them on inspection trips. The members of the compliance "team" conducted periodic inspections at various AML centers to discover and correct any deficiencies in compliance with FDA regulations. Contrary to AML's later characterizations of their responsibilities, the members of the compliance team clearly drew their authority from AML, not from the Orlando Center where their office was located. Thus, they functioned as agents of AML.

The compliance team often conducted inspections in advance of FDA inspections. Some of the deficiencies, particularly at RPC, were severe enough, however, that the compliance team members began to instruct plasma center employees to falsify and fabricate records to conceal these deficiencies—a practice apparently engaged in on the basis of Partucci's instructions. During the time that RPC was closed in late 1978 and early 1979, the compliance team, sometimes with Queris and Curry, visited RPC to prepare for the FDA inspection prior to its reopening. Faced with numerous problems, the compliance team, Queris, and Curry instructed RPC employees to falsify various records or falsified the records themselves.

Partucci left AML in December of 1979; but, even after his departure, the practice of falsifying records continued. Several RPC employees testified at trial that they were instructed by the compliance team, Queris, or Curry to falsify various records . . . .

After Partucci's departure, members of the compliance team began to report to Mili Lamas, a vice-president at AML. Sometime in March or April of 1980, Queris informed Lamas of the entire history of unlawful practices at RPC. In mid-March 1980, Lois Keith, an AML employee, travelled from the Miami office to the RPC offices, where she discovered a whole blood weight log that had been falsified. Keith telephoned Lamas to inform Lamas of her discovery. Several days later, Lamas met with Keith, Lawton, and Hayes to discuss the falsification of the weight log. Lamas informed them that AML's attorney would notify the FDA of the problem. Unbeknownst to Lamas, however, or anyone else at AML or RPC, several RPC employees had gone to the FDA in mid-March 1980 to report the long-standing and pervasive falsification practices at RPC.

The FDA began an inspection of RPC in March of 1980. By the end of that March, an initial FDA inspection report had been prepared. The investigation was concluded by June of 1980 and a final report prepared by October 1980. From that point until March 1982, various levels of the FDA reviewed what had been recommended. In March of 1982, the FDA referred the matter to the Department of Justice recommending criminal prosecution. The Department of Justice referred it to the U.S. Attorney's office in Richmond in mid-March 1982. An indictment was returned by the grand jury on December 12, 1983. An eight-day jury trial was held in March 1984 resulting in the conviction of AML on four of seven counts. . . .

AML's final argument is that there is insufficient evidence to support its conviction, and thus the district court should have granted AML's motion for a judgment of acquittal. AML asserts that there is no evidence that any officer or director at AML knowingly and willfully participated in or authorized the unlawful practices at RPC, essentially arguing that the Government failed to prove that AML had the requisite intent to violate 18 U.S.C. §1001. AML further maintains that the Government failed to prove the "element" that its agents' criminal acts were undertaken primarily to benefit AML.

In *United States v. Basic Construction Co.*, 711 F.2d 570 (4th Cir. 1983), this Court rejected the argument that the Government had to prove "that the corporation, presumably as represented by its upper level officers and managers, had an intent separate from that of its lower level employees to violate the antitrust laws." *Basic Construction* involved a criminal prosecution under section 1 of the Sherman Act, for bid rigging in state road paving contracts. The conviction of Basic Construction Company, affirmed by the Court, was based on evidence showing that the bid rigging activities were perpetrated by two relatively minor officials and were done without the knowledge of high level corporate officers. Basic introduced evidence indicating that it had a longstanding, well known, and strictly enforced policy against bid rigging. The Court, citing with approval several cases from other circuits, summarized the rule on corporate criminal liability as follows:

> These cases hold that a corporation may be held criminally responsible for antitrust violations committed by its employees if they were acting within the scope of their authority, or apparent authority, and for the benefit of the corporation even if . . . such acts were against corporate policy or express instructions.

Thus, AML may be held criminally liable for the unlawful practices at RPC if its agents were acting within the scope of their employment, which includes a determination of whether the agents were acting for the benefit of the corporation.

The term "scope of employment" has been broadly defined to include acts on the corporation's behalf in performance of the agent's general line of work. *United States v. Hilton Hotels Corporation*, 467 F.2d 1000, 1004 (9th Cir. 1972). To be acting within the scope of his employment, an agent must be "performing acts of the kind which he is authorized to perform, and those acts must be motivated — at least in part — by an intent to benefit the corporation." It is clear that the agents of AML — Partucci, Lawton, Hayes, and Curry — were acting within the scope of their employment. AML had specifically assigned to these individuals the responsibility for assuring compliance by its plasmapheresis centers with FDA regulations. In instructing other employees regarding compliance with applicable regulations, Partucci and the others were acting within the scope of their authority or certainly within their apparent authority. The fact that many of their actions were unlawful and contrary to corporate policy does not absolve AML of legal responsibility for their acts. . . .

The basic purpose of requiring that an agent have acted with the intent to benefit the corporation, however, is to insulate the corporation from criminal liability for actions of its agents which be *inimical* to the interests of the corporation or which may have been undertaken solely to advance the interests of that agent or of a party other than the corporation. It would seem entirely possible, therefore, for an agent to have acted for his own benefit while also acting for the benefit of the corporation.

In light of the foregoing principles, we believe that the jury could reasonably have concluded from the evidence presented at trial that Partucci and other agents of AML acted, at least in part, with the intent of benefiting AML by their unlawful acts. AML attempts to make much of the testimony regarding Partucci's ambitious nature and his desire to ascend the corporate ladder at AML, arguing that he instigated the unlawful practices at RPC to benefit himself, not AML. We are not persuaded by this argument. Partucci was clearly acting in part to benefit AML since his advancement within the corporation depended on AML's well-being and its lack of difficulties with the FDA. At any rate, regardless of Partucci's motivation, the other members of the compliance team appear to have been acting for the benefit of AML.

When viewed in light of the proper principles governing corporate criminal liability, the evidence presented at trial is more than sufficient to sustain AML's conviction on all counts. It is well-established that a jury verdict must be affirmed if there is sufficient evidence, viewed in the light most favorable to the Government, from which a rational jury could have found guilt beyond reasonable doubt. Numerous Government witnesses testified regarding the unlawful actions of and instructions given by Partucci, Lawton, Hayes, and Curry—all agents of AML. Based on our review of the record, we find that there was sufficient evidence to support the jury's verdict. The conviction of AML is AFFIRMED.

Notes and Questions

1. *Civil versus criminal law.* Is it appropriate to apply a civil law tort concept, respondeat superior, to a criminal case? How difficult is it for a corporation to avoid criminal liability under this standard? After reflecting on the different purposes of civil and criminal liability, is respondeat superior better suited to one or the other?

2. *Scope of employment.* Courts and commentators have argued about what evidence can be shown to establish that an employee is acting within the scope of employment. Suppose an employee does not have the express authority to bind the corporation. Will that establish that the employee was not acting within the scope of employment?

3. *The ultra vires doctrine.* Before respondeat superior had the full breadth of application that it enjoys today, there were some strict limits to what an employee could do on behalf of a corporation. Among these was the ultra vires doctrine, which stated that corporations could never do anything not authorized by their corporate

charters. This meant that a corporation could not be liable for so-called "ultra-vires acts" of its employees because, being beyond the powers conferred by its corporate charter, the corporation literally could not do them. Employees who acted ultra vires ("beyond the powers") only acted (and incurred liability) in their personal capacities. Were the ultra vires doctrine in place today, would it be a significant limitation on corporate criminal law?

4. *Debate over corporate criminal liability.* Among commentators, corporate criminal liability has always been controversial. Many see criminal law as overbroad, inefficient, or otherwise inapt when applied to organizations rather than individual human beings. Federal courts have rejected these grounds and have imposed corporate liability based on three main arguments: liability is necessary to ensure that corporations adequately supervise their agents and employees; corporate liability encourages corporations to develop general policies to deter wrongdoing; and corporate liability appropriately places responsibility on the entity that benefits from the wrongdoing rather than solely upon the individual wrongdoer. Additionally, corporations themselves are often the more significant locus of wrongdoing when compared to individual employees. Defective corporate culture, perverse incentive systems, and inadequate employee training can all foster criminal behavior in employees who would not otherwise be disposed to it.

5. *European view of corporate criminal liability.* In contrast to the United States, European countries do not have a long history of recognizing corporate criminal liability. This is based in part on Europe's past belief that legal entities could not be blamed for the actions of their employees. *See* Sarah Sun Beale & Adam G. Safwat, *What Developments in Western Europe Tell us About American Critiques of Corporate Criminal Liability*, 8 Buff. Crim. L. Rev. 89 (2004). However, with the increasing economic influence of corporations in Western Europe in the 1970's, many European nations began to utilize approaches that mirror the American respondeat superior doctrine for establishing corporate criminal liability. *See id.* at 107–08. Over the years, both the European Union and the Council of Europe put forth proposals recommending that member states adopt corporate criminal liability to combat corruption, environmental pollution, and many other facets of criminal law, with many countries ratifying these proposals. *See id.* at 136. Despite widespread support, Germany most notably refuses to adopt corporate criminal liability statutes, instead choosing to adopt administrative sanctions in the hope that such sanctions will have the same deterrent effects as corporate criminal liability. *Id.* at 137–38. Is this a realistic assumption? Why or why not?

6. *Is it fair?* For decades, academics and practitioners alike have debated the issue of corporate criminal liability. The widespread criticism of the scope of criminal liability for corporations is summarized by the observation of District Judge Gerald E. Lynch:

> If a corporation is criminally liable for the unauthorized acts of mid-level managers, the corporation will often not have a viable defense, despite

legitimate questions about the justice of punishing it. . . . Such defendants are increasingly relegated to making their most significant moral and factual arguments to prosecutors, as a matter of "policy" or "prosecutorial discretion," rather than making them to judges, as a matter of law, or to juries, as a matter of factual guilt or innocence.

Gerald E. Lynch, *The Role of Criminal Law in Policing Corporate Misconduct*, 60 LAW & CONTEMP. PROBS. 23, 59 (1997).

Is it fair to hold a large corporation liable for the wrongful actions of a low-level employee? What if the corporation, after finding out about the violation, fires the employee? Should this limit liability? What if, rather than firing the employee, the corporation simply reports the violation itself?

7. *Modern doctrine revisited.* The modern doctrine of corporate criminal liability states that a corporation is liable for the actions of its agents whenever such agents act within the scope of their employment and, at least in part, to benefit the corporation. Should it matter where the employee fits within the corporate hierarchy? Should it matter whether the corporation had policies in place to deter wrongdoing?

8. *Size matters.* Should the size of the corporation be taken into account by prosecutors in deciding whether to indict? Consider the 2012 case of HSBC, a British multinational financial services and banking company, where prosecutors decided not to indict the firm for money laundering but instead settled the case due to concerns that criminal charges could jeopardize one of the world's largest banks and potentially destabilize the world economy. *See* Ben Protess & Jessica Silver-Greenburg, *HSBC to Pay $1.92 Billion to Settle Charges of Money Laundering*, N.Y. TIMES (Dec. 10, 2012, 4:10 PM), http://dealbook.nytimes.com/2012/12/10/hsbc-said -to-near-1-9-billion-settlement-over-money-laundering. HSBC was required to pay $1.92 billion, a record penalty at the time. Is this fair? Should larger corporations be permitted to simply write a check due to their influence and importance in the world economy?

9. *A $1000 fine?* Note that AML only faced a criminal fine of $1000. Why would the corporation litigate such a small fine? They likely spent orders of magnitude more to defend the case.

———

In the next case, the employee was acting in violation of corporate compliance policies. Should a corporation be liable because of the acts of an employee who violated explicit corporate policy?

United States v. Hilton Hotels Corp.

467 F.2d 1000 (9th Cir. 1972)

BROWNING, CIRCUIT JUDGE:

This is an appeal from a conviction under an indictment charging a violation of section 1 of the Sherman Act, 15 U.S.C. § 1.

Operators of hotels, restaurants, hotel and restaurant supply companies, and other businesses in Portland, Oregon, organized an association to attract conventions to their city. To finance the association, members were asked to make contributions in predetermined amounts. Companies selling supplies to hotels were asked to contribute an amount equal to one per cent of their sales to hotel members. To aid collections, hotel members, including appellant, agreed to give preferential treatment to suppliers who paid their assessments, and to curtail purchases from those who did not.

The jury was instructed that such an agreement by the hotel members, if proven, would be a per se violation of the Sherman Act. Appellant argues that this was error.

Appellant's president testified that it would be contrary to the policy of the corporation for the manager of one of its hotels to condition purchases upon payment of a contribution to a local association by the supplier. The manager of appellant's Portland hotel and his assistant testified that it was the hotel's policy to purchase supplies solely on the basis of price, quality, and service. They also testified that on two occasions they told the hotel's purchasing agent that he was to take no part in the boycott. The purchasing agent confirmed the receipt of these instructions, but admitted that, despite them, he had threatened a supplier with loss of the hotel's business unless the supplier paid the association assessment. He testified that he violated his instructions because of anger and personal pique toward the individual representing the supplier.

Based upon this testimony, appellant requested certain instructions bearing upon the criminal liability of a corporation for the unauthorized acts of its agents. These requests were rejected by the trial court. The court instructed the jury that a corporation is liable for the acts and statements of its agents "within the scope of their employment," defined to mean "in the corporation's behalf in performance of the agent's general line of work," including "not only that which has been authorized by the corporation, but also that which outsiders could reasonably assume the agent would have authority to do." The court added: "A corporation is responsible for acts and statements of its agents, done or made within the scope of their employment, even though their conduct may be contrary to their actual instructions or contrary to the corporation's stated policies." Appellant objects only to the court's concluding statement.

Congress may constitutionally impose criminal liability upon a business entity for acts or omissions of its agents within the scope of their employment. *United States v. A & P Trucking Co.*, 358 U.S. 121, 125–26 (1958); *New York Central & Hudson R.R. Co.*

v. United States, 212 U.S. 481 (1909); *cf. United States v. Illinois Central R.R. Co.*, 303 U.S. 239 (1938). Such liability may attach without proof that the conduct was within the agent's actual authority, and even though it may have been contrary to express instructions. . . .

The intention to impose such liability is sometimes express, *New York Central & Hudson R.R. Co. v. United States, supra*, 212 U.S. 481, but it may also be implied. The text of the Sherman Act does not expressly resolve the issue. For the reasons that follow, however, we think the construction of the Act that best achieves its purpose is that a corporation is liable for acts of its agents within the scope of their authority even when done against company orders. . . .

Legal commentators have argued forcefully that it is inappropriate and ineffective to impose criminal liability upon a corporation, as distinguished from the human agents who actually perform the unlawful acts . . . . But it is the legislative judgment that controls, and "the great mass of legislation calling for corporate criminal liability suggests a widespread belief on the part of legislators that such liability is necessary to effectuate regulatory policy." ALI Model Penal Code, Comment on § 2.07. Moreover, the strenuous efforts of corporate defendants to avoid conviction, particularly under the Sherman Act, strongly suggests that Congress is justified in its judgment that exposure of the corporate entity to potential conviction may provide a substantial spur to corporate action to prevent violations by employees. . . .

Complex business structures, characterized by decentralization and delegation of authority, commonly adopted by corporations for business purposes, make it difficult to identify the particular corporate agents responsible for Sherman Act violations. At the same time, it is generally true that high management officials, for whose conduct the corporate directors and stockholders are the most clearly responsible, are likely to have participated in the policy decisions underlying Sherman Act violations, or at least to have become aware of them.

Violations of the Sherman Act are a likely consequence of the pressure to maximize profits that is commonly imposed by corporate owners upon managing agents and, in turn, upon lesser employees. In the face of that pressure, generalized directions to obey the Sherman Act, with the probable effect of foregoing profits, are the least likely to be taken seriously. And if a violation of the Sherman Act occurs, the corporation, and not the individual agents, will have realized the profits from the illegal activity.

In sum, identification of the particular agents responsible for a Sherman Act violation is especially difficult, and their conviction and punishment is peculiarly ineffective as a deterrent. At the same time, conviction and punishment of the business entity itself is likely to be both appropriate and effective.

For these reasons we conclude that as a general rule a corporation is liable under the Sherman Act for the acts of its agents in the scope of their employment, even though contrary to general corporate policy and express instructions to the agent. . . . Affirmed.

Notes and Questions

1. *Relevance of corporate profit.* The Ninth Circuit upheld the conviction of Hilton Hotels partly because it is often difficult to identify the particular agent who engaged in the activity. Do you agree with this rationale as a basis for holding a large, complex organization criminally liable based on the acts of a few individuals? What incentives does such a rule give, and to whom, with respect to detecting and reporting (or concealing) misconduct?

2. *Motivated by intent to benefit the corporation.* Several courts have offered their perspective of what respondeat superior requires regarding an employee's intent to benefit the corporation. In one famous case, an employee diverted corporate funds to assist a personal friend. The friend was a politician who had very little chance of ever being asked to help the corporation. In upholding campaign finance convictions against the corporation, the court noted it did not matter that the employee's intent to benefit the corporation might have been (1) hypothetical, (2) a subsidiary intent among other intents, or (3) actually harmful to the company. *See* United States v. Sun-Diamond Growers of California, 138 F.3d 961 (D.C. Cir. 1998), *aff'd on other grounds,* 526 U.S. 398 (1999). Do you agree with this holding?

3. *The* New York Central *case.* The seminal case applying the tort doctrine of respondeat superior to criminal actions against corporations was *New York Central & Hudson River Railroad v. United States,* 212 U.S. 481 (1909). In *New York Central,* a railroad company and its employee were both convicted of violating the Elkins Act, regulating the rates common carriers could charge. The Elkins Act explicitly provided for corporate liability premised on respondeat superior. The Supreme Court rejected the two primary arguments on appeal: that the conviction should be reversed because it would punish the innocent shareholders, who were not defendants in the suit; and that the conviction was improper because there was no evidence that the actions leading to the offense were authorized by the board of directors.

In upholding application of respondeat superior in the criminal context, the Court stated that "to give [corporations] immunity from all punishment because of the old and exploded doctrine that a corporation cannot commit a crime would virtually take away the only means of effectually controlling the subject matter [of the Elkins Act] and correcting the abuses . . . ." *Id.* at 495–96. Through a process of federal common lawmaking, respondeat superior gained traction beyond the Elkins Act to become the general federal doctrine for establishing corporate criminal liability.

At the time of the *New York Central* decision, punishing a corporation just meant imposing monetary fines against it. Today, criminal conviction might also mean debarment or loss of licenses necessary for conducting business, both of which could amount to a corporate death penalty. Arthur Andersen, formerly one of the largest accounting firms, dissolved after being indicted for obstruction of justice connected to the Enron investigation. (*See Arthur Andersen LLP v. United States,* 544 U.S. 696 (2005), discussed in Chapter 11, Obstruction of Justice, *infra* at § 11.E.)

Arthur Andersen's experience reinvigorated critics who questioned the legal theory that holds a corporation liable for the acts of individual employees. Consider the following criticisms:

a. Civil, not criminal, sanctions should be the primary approach to corporate misbehavior. First, criminal prosecution causes significant collateral damage to innocent individuals. Second, a corporation is not deterred by the primary criminal sanctions of going to jail or feeling shame.

b. The judicial rationale for indicting corporations is outdated. Originally, the Court in *New York Central* applied criminal sanctions to corporations because of the lack of alternatives. Today, the significant expansion of civil and regulatory sanctions makes this rationale moot.

c. Federal prosecutors held too much power over Arthur Andersen because the criminal conviction automatically debarred it from practicing before the SEC. This sort of ultimate power is tantamount to controlling the life and death of the entity.

d. The federal standard of respondeat superior is too broad and dangerous. In its current state, the doctrine allows for conviction of the corporation regardless of whether the employee was a low-level employee or a high-level officer, and regardless of whether the behavior was condoned or prohibited by management.

Elizabeth K. Ainslie, *Indicting Corporations Revisited: Lessons of the Arthur Andersen Prosecution*, 43 AM. CRIM. L. REV. 107 (2006). Are these criticisms justified? Why or why not?

4. *Ripple effects:* The prosecution of a large corporation may not only affect the corporation's viability but may also affect the national and world economies. On the other hand, the premise that a corporation is "too large" to prosecute is counterintuitive and furthers the perception that white collar crime is treated more leniently than traditional crime. Allowing a corporation to shield its activities from criminal scrutiny may only confirm the perception that corporations, the larger they are, enjoy insulation from criminal liability. *See* Josh Gerstein, *Holder: No Banks 'Too Big To Jail*,' POLITICO (May 5, 2014, 9:57 AM), http://www.politico.com/blogs/under -the-radar/2014/05/holder-no-banks-too-big-to-jail-187961.html.

5. *Deferred prosecution agreements.* Since the Enron scandal, the proliferation of deferred prosecution agreements has increased. Deferred prosecution agreements are

> [A] form of probation which enables a corporation to avoid pleading guilty to a crime or even being indicted. Under such an agreement, the company commits to performing certain agreed-upon measures and refraining from criminal conduct for the duration of the agreement's term, at the end of which if the company has complied with all the terms, the government drops all charges.

Andrew Weissman & David Newman, *Rethinking Criminal Corporate Liability*, 82 IND. L.J. 411, 413 (2007). Thus, should a corporation fail to abide by the terms of the agreement, criminal charges may be instituted against the corporation. *Id.* But how do deferred prosecution agreements comport with the belief that imposing criminal liability on corporations will serve as a deterrent to future wrongful actions? *See* Chapter 18, Civil Actions, Civil Penalties, and Parallel Proceedings, *infra*.

6. *Corporate compliance programs.* Should a corporation be held criminally liable where the corporate policies specifically prohibit the behavior? This question is important because corporate compliance programs may affect charging and sentencing decisions. Corporations have instituted compliance programs in an effort to insulate the corporation from criminal scrutiny. If a compliance program cannot be a shield for a criminal investigation, then does this dissuade corporations from instituting and following such programs? To what extent should corporate compliance programs be relevant at the time of sentencing? *See* Chapter 15, Internal Investigations, Compliance Programs, and Deferred and Non-Prosecution Agreements, *infra*.

7. *Additional requirements?* With the potential to destroy a corporation, legal scholars have proposed additional elements to the doctrine of respondeat superior. One proposal would require the government to prove that the corporation failed to take reasonable steps to prevent the employee's conduct. *See* Peter J. Henning, *Corporate Criminal Liability and the Potential for Rehabilitation*, 46 AM. CRIM. L. REV. 1417, 1418 (2009). Some scholars have proposed offering corporations a "compliance defense." Under it, corporations charged with a crime could get a full defense if they could prove that they had an otherwise effective compliance program in place at the time of the crime. *See* Ellen S. Podgor, *A New Corporate World Mandates a "Good Faith" Affirmative Defense*, 44 AM. CRIM. L. REV. 1537, 1537 (2007). What other elements would you consider adding to respondeat superior?

8. *Successor companies.* Many corporations find it strategic and beneficial to merge with other entities for a variety of business reasons. When and under what circumstances should successor companies be held liable for acts of predecessor companies? What if, instead of a merger, a corporation that committed a crime spins off the division in which the crime occurred into a different corporation? Which of the two should face liability? Consider what incentives any rule you settle on would give to corporations who discover (before authorities do) that they committed crime in the past. *See* Mihailis E. Diamantis, *Successor Identity*, 36 YALE J. ON REG. 1, 18 (2019).

Problem

2-1. Suppose that Bank A merges with Bank B, and that together they become one bank under the charter of Bank A. Bank B surrendered its charter after the merger. The new bank entity is called Bank AB. Three years prior to the merger, Bank B committed numerous violations of the Bank Secrecy Act (Chapter 13, Money Laundering and Related Financial Crimes, *infra*) by failing to report substantial cash transactions in violation of federal law. After the merger, Bank AB was indicted for violations of federal law that were committed by Bank B prior to the merger with Bank A.

> *a. Would the government prevail when charging Bank AB through the doctrine of respondeat superior? Should it matter how long has passed since the*

merger? What arguments would you make as a federal prosecutor that Bank AB is liable for the conduct that Bank B committed three years earlier?

b. What arguments would you make as defense counsel for Bank AB?

2. Model Penal Code

Many states have adopted an alternative approach to corporate criminal liability based on the Model Penal Code ("MPC") formulation. Section 2.07(1)(c) of the MPC provides that a corporation may be convicted of a crime where: "[T]he commission of the offense was authorized, requested, commanded, performed, or recklessly tolerated by the board of directors or by a high managerial agent acting on behalf of the corporation within the scope of the agent's office or employment."

Courts and scholars call the MPC and related approaches "control group" tests for corporate liability. The intuition behind them is that elites in the corporate hierarchy (as the corporate "brains") are more likely to embody the corporation than are lower-level employees (the corporate "hands") who have less discretion to make business decisions. Further, MPC § 2.07(5) provides a version of the due diligence defense discussed above: "[I]t shall be a defense if the defendant proves by a preponderance of evidence that the high managerial agent having supervisory responsibility over the subject matter of the offense employed due diligence to prevent its commission."

In jurisdictions where clear standards for corporate liability have not been established, courts have considered the respective merits of respondeat superior and MPC § 2.07(1). As you read the next case, consider the key differences between the MPC approach and the respondeat superior approach to corporate criminal accountability.

Commonwealth v. Beneficial Finance Co.

275 N.E.2d 33 (Mass. 1971)

SPIEGEL, JUSTICE.

We have before us appeals emanating from two separate series of indictments and two separate jury trials of various individual and corporate defendants. . . .

These cases have become generally known as the "small loans" cases. In each case the defendants were charged with various offences under numerous indictments returned in 1964 by a special grand jury. The offences charged were offering or paying, or soliciting or receiving, bribes, or conspiring to do so. These indictments were presented to the special grand jury as a result of an investigation developed by the Massachusetts Crime Commission (Commission). The Commission was specifically created by the Legislature "to investigate and study as a basis for legislative action the existence and extent of organized crime within the Commonwealth and corrupt practices in government at state and local levels."

* * *

[The court then detailed the extensive trial and pre-trial history in these protracted proceedings. The agents of the various companies skirted the law and charged illegal interest rates by bribing public officials. The court instructed the jury that it should apply the common law standard of *respondeat superior*. The defendants argued that the court erred and should have directed the jury to use the MPC formulation, requiring that the jury find that a high level corporate agent had authorized or recklessly tolerated the bribery scheme.]

Having concluded that the evidence was sufficient to establish that the [individual] defendants . . . were part of a conspiracy . . . to bribe [public officials], we turn to the question of whether there was sufficient evidence to support a finding that [the corporations employing the individual defendants] were parties to the conspiracy. Each of the corporate defendants raised this issue by means of a motion for a directed verdict. In view of the fact that this issue is discussed extensively in the briefs of the respective corporate defendants as well as in the Commonwealth's brief, and because the legal principles involved permeate these cases, in this part of the opinion we discuss at length the applicable legal standards concerning the extent to which a corporation may be held criminally responsible for the acts of its directors, officers and agents. We then summarize the evidence admitted against the respective corporations and apply the appropriate legal standard to the evidence.

The defendants and the Commonwealth have proposed differing standards upon which the criminal responsibility of a corporation should be predicated. The defendants argue that a corporation should not be held criminally liable for the conduct of its servants or agents unless such conduct was performed, authorized, ratified, adopted or tolerated by the corporations' directors, officers or other "high managerial agents" who are sufficiently high in the corporate hierarchy to warrant the assumption that their acts in some substantial sense reflect corporate policy. This standard is that adopted by the American Law Institute Model Penal Code, approved in May, 1962. Section 2:07 of the Code provides that, except in the case of regulatory offences and offences consisting of the omission of a duty imposed on corporations by law, a corporation may be convicted of a crime if "the commission of the offence was authorized, requested, commanded, performed or recklessly tolerated by the board of directors or by a high managerial agent acting in behalf of the corporation within the scope of his office or employment." The section proceeds to define "high managerial agent" as "an officer of a corporation . . . or any other agent . . . having duties of such responsibility that his conduct may fairly be assumed to represent the policy of the corporation."

The Commonwealth, on the other hand, argues that the standard applied by the judge in his instructions to the jury was correct. These instructions, which prescribe a somewhat more flexible standard than that delineated in the Model Penal Code, state in part, as follows:

[T]he Commonwealth must prove beyond a reasonable doubt that there existed between the guilty individual or individuals and the corporation which is being charged with the conduct of the individuals, such a relationship that the acts and the intent of the individuals were the acts and intent of the corporation. . . .

It does not mean that the Commonwealth must prove that the individual who acted criminally was a member of the corporation's board of directors, or that he was a high officer in the corporation, or that he held any office at all. If the Commonwealth did prove that an individual for whose act it seeks to hold a corporation criminally liable was an officer of the corporation, the jury should consider that. But more important than that, it should consider what the authority of that person was as such officer in relation to the corporation. The mere fact that he has a title is not enough to make the corporation liable for his criminal conduct. The Commonwealth must prove that the individual for whose conduct it seeks to charge the corporation criminally was placed in a position by the corporation where he had enough power, duty, responsibility and authority to act for and in behalf of the corporation to handle the particular business or operation or project of the corporation in which he was engaged at the time that he committed the criminal act, with power of decision as to what he would or would not do while acting for the corporation, and that he was acting for and in behalf of the corporation in the accomplishment of that particular business or operation or project, and that he committed a criminal act while so acting. . . .

You will note from what I said that it is not necessary that the Commonwealth prove that an individual had any particular office or any office at all or that he had any particular title or any title at all. It isn't the title that counts. It isn't the name of the office that counts, but it's the position in which the corporation placed that person with relation to its business, with regard to the powers and duties and responsibilities and authority which it gave to him which counts. If it placed him in a position with such power, duty, authority, and responsibility that it can be found by you that, when he acted in the corporation's business, the corporation was acting, then you may find the corporation equally guilty of the criminal acts which he commits and of the intent which he holds, if you first find that the individual was guilty of the crime.

Now, this test doesn't depend upon the power, duty, the responsibility, or the authority which the individual has with reference to the entire corporation business. The test should be applied to his position with relation to the particular operation or project in which he is serving the corporation.

The difference between the judge's instructions to the jury and the Model Penal Code lies largely in the latter's reference to a "high managerial agent" and in the

Code requirement that to impose corporate criminal liability, it at least must appear that its directors or high managerial agent "authorized . . . or recklessly tolerated" the allegedly criminal acts. The judge's instructions focus on the authority of the corporate agent in relation to the particular corporate business in which the agent was engaged. The Code seems to require that there be authorization or reckless inaction by a corporate representative having some relation to framing corporate policy, or one "having duties of such responsibility that his conduct may fairly be assumed to represent the policy of the corporation." Close examination of the judge's instructions reveals that they preserve the underlying corporate policy rationale of the Code by allowing the jury to infer "corporate policy" from the position in which the corporation placed the agent in commissioning him to handle the particular corporate affairs in which he was engaged at the time of the criminal act. We need not deal with the Model Penal Code in greater detail. Although we give it careful consideration as a scholarly proposal, it has not been enacted in Massachusetts and does not purport to be a restatement of existing law. . . . The judge correctly charged the jury on the basis of decided cases, [rather] than on the basis of a proposed model code.

It may also be observed that the judge's standard is somewhat similar to the traditional common law rule of *respondeat superior*. However, in applying this rule to a criminal case, the judge added certain requirements not generally associated with that common law doctrine. He further qualified the rule of *respondeat superior* by requiring that the conduct for which the corporation is being held accountable be performed on behalf of the corporation. . . .

[T]he judge's instructions, as a whole and in context, required a greater quantum of proof in the practical application of this standard than is required in a civil case. In focusing on the "kinship" between the authority of an individual and the act he committed, the judge emphasized that the jury must be satisfied "beyond a reasonable doubt" that the act of the individual "constituted" the act of the corporation. Juxtaposition of the traditional criminal law requirement of ascertaining guilt beyond a reasonable doubt (as opposed to the civil law standard of the preponderance of the evidence), with the rule of *respondeat superior*, fully justifies application of the standard enunciated by the judge to a criminal prosecution against a corporation for a crime requiring specific intent.

The foregoing is especially true in view of the particular circumstances of this case. In order to commit the crimes charged in these indictments, the defendant corporations either had to offer to pay money to a public official or conspire to do so. The disbursal of funds is an act peculiarly within the ambit of corporate activity. These corporations by the very nature of their business are constantly dealing with the expenditure and collection of moneys. It could hardly be expected that any of the individual defendants would conspire to pay, or would pay, the substantial amount of money here involved, namely $25,000, out of his own pocket. The jury would be warranted in finding that the disbursal of such an amount of money would come from the corporate treasury. A reasonable inference could therefore be drawn that the payment of such money by the corporations was done as a matter of corporate policy and as a reflection of corporate intent, thus comporting with the underlying rationale of the Model Penal Code, and probably with its specific requirements.

Moreover, we do not think that the Model Penal Code standard really purports to deal with the evidentiary problems which are inherent in establishing the quantum of proof necessary to show that the directors or officers of a corporation authorize, ratify, tolerate, or participate in the criminal acts of an agent when such acts are apparently performed on behalf of the corporation. Evidence of such authorization or ratification is too easily susceptible of concealment. As is so trenchantly stated by the judge: "Criminal acts are not usually made the subject of votes of authorization or ratification by corporate Boards of Directors; and the lack of such votes does not prevent the act from being the act of the corporation."

It is obvious that criminal conspiratorial acts are not performed within the glare of publicity, nor would we expect a board of directors to meet officially and record on the corporate records a delegation of authority to initiate, conduct or conclude proceedings for the purpose of bribing a public official. Of necessity, the proof of authority to so act must rest on all the circumstances and conduct in a given situation and the reasonable inferences to be drawn therefrom.

Additional factors of importance are the size and complexity of many large modern corporations which necessitate the delegation of more authority to lesser corporate agents and employees. As the judge pointed out: "There are not enough seats on the Board of Directors, nor enough offices in a corporation, to permit the corporation engaged in widespread operations to give such a title or office to every person in whom it places the power, authority, and responsibility for decision and action." This latter consideration lends credence to the view that the title or position of an individual in a corporation should not be conclusively determinative in ascribing criminal responsibility. In a large corporation, with many numerous and distinct departments, a high ranking corporate officer or agent may have no authority or involvement in a particular sphere of corporate activity, whereas a lower ranking corporate executive might have much broader power in dealing with a matter peculiarly within the scope of his authority. Employees who are in the lower echelon of the corporate hierarchy often exercise more responsibility in the everyday operations of the corporation than the directors or officers. Assuredly, the title or office that the person holds may be considered, but it should not be the decisive criterion upon which to predicate corporate responsibility. . . .

To permit corporations to conceal the nefarious acts of their underlings by using the shield of corporate armor to deflect corporate responsibility, and to separate the subordinate from the executive, would be to permit "endocratic" corporations to inflict widespread public harm without hope of redress. It would merely serve to ignore the scramble and realities of the market place. This we decline to do. We believe that stringent standards must be adopted to discourage any attempt by "endocratic" corporations' executives to place the sole responsibility for criminal acts on the shoulders of their subordinates. . . .

* * *

Considering everything we have said above, we are of [the] opinion that the quantum of proof necessary to sustain the conviction of a corporation for the acts of its agents is sufficiently met if it is shown that the corporation has placed the agent in a position where he has enough authority and responsibility to act for and in behalf of the corporation in handling the particular corporate business, operation or project in which he was engaged at the time he committed the criminal act. The judge properly instructed the jury to this effect and correctly stated that this standard does not depend upon the responsibility or authority which the agent has with respect to the entire corporate business, but only to his position with relation to the particular business in which he was serving the corporation. . . .

All judgments affirmed.

Notes and Questions

1. *Lenient rule.* The *Beneficial* court rejected the MPC's requirement of high managerial approval. The court reasoned that the MPC standard was too lenient because "[e]vidence of such authorization or ratification is too easily susceptible of concealment." The court also found that requiring high managerial approval would simply allow large organizations to avoid liability by delegating decision making to lower-level employees and hiding behind various levels of management. Do you agree with this position?

2. *Respondeat superior.* Other courts and commentators view the respondeat superior rule as more relaxed than the MPC rule. The respondeat superior theory includes those corporate agents who are high level, such as managers, supervisors, and executives, but also entry level agents, such as line employees. Is a rule that allows a subordinate employee to bind the corporation fundamentally fair? What is the basis for this extension of criminal liability? What if the actor is an independent contractor?

Consider the application of *Beneficial* to the following case. In *Commonwealth v. Angelo Todesca Corp.*, 842 N.E.2d 930 (Mass. 2006), the employee, a driver for the defendant trucking company, struck and killed a police officer while backing up without a functioning back-up alarm. The jury found the company guilty of vehicular homicide as a result of the incident. The appeals court reversed the conviction, but the Massachusetts Supreme Judicial Court reinstated the conviction based on *Beneficial*. The court found that a corporation could be held criminally liable even if the conduct were not "'performed, authorized, ratified, adopted or tolerated by' corporate officials or managers." *Id.* at 937. All that was required was

> (1) that an individual committed a criminal offense; (2) that at the time of committing the offense, the individual "was engaged in some particular corporate business or project"; and (3) that the individual had been vested by

the corporation with the authority to act for it, and on its behalf, in carrying out that particular corporate business or project when the offense occurred.

Id. (quoting *Commonwealth v. Angelo Todesca Corp.*, 818 N.E.2d 608, 613 (Mass. App. Ct. 2004)). Is this outcome fair and appropriate?

3. *High managerial agents.* In contrast to the respondeat superior approach to corporate criminal liability used in the federal system, many states have adopted language that limits liability to those criminal acts committed by, or approved by, "high managerial agents." Model Penal Code § 2.07(1)(c). High managerial agents are defined as "officer[s] of a corporation or an unincorporated association, or, in the case of a partnership, a partner, or any other agent of a corporation or association having duties of such responsibility that his conduct may fairly be assumed to represent the policy of the corporation or association." *Id.* § 2.07(4)(c). The MPC imposes criminal liability on a corporation in two types of situations: (a) where the employee behavior was authorized or recklessly tolerated by the board of directors or by a high managerial agent acting on behalf of the corporation within the scope of his or her office or employment; or (b) where such liability is imposed by statute. Thus, the MPC section sets forth a more restrictive test for corporate liability than does respondeat superior. Which approach to combating corporate fraud is preferable? Why?

Problem

2-2. The Gado Corporation is engaged in providing the local school district with a variety of supplies during the school year. Sarah Steady is an account manager at Gado. Sarah handles all of the orders for the corporation. Sarah wants to impress her boss and negotiates a deal with a competing vendor to coordinate the bidding process so that each of them is the low bidder on certain contracts. That way, both of them will see an increase in the level of their business. Assume that this activity is a violation of federal competition law.

Evaluate the corporation's criminal liability under both the MPC and respondeat superior in the following scenarios:

a. Sarah is a low-level employee and acted on her own without any direction from corporate executives. The corporation has a policy that forbids the sort of anti-competitive behavior in which Sara engaged, and trains all its employees in that policy through regular training sessions.

b. The Gado Corporation did not benefit from Sarah's conduct. The evidence is that Gado was awarded as many contracts as it would have received without Sarah's conduct. She engaged in this wrongdoing to benefit only herself by impressing her boss and improving her chances for promotion.

c. Sarah only intended to benefit herself, but Gado benefited from Sarah's conduct because it was awarded more business than it would have received otherwise.

C. Corporate Mens Rea

1. Criminal Intent

As in every criminal case, the prosecution must prove all elements of the crime — actus reus and mens rea — even when the defendant is a corporation. The same doctrines discussed above for attributing corporate acts also apply to establishing corporate mental states. As you read the case, consider the scope of corporate criminal liability under both the doctrine of respondeat superior and the Model Penal Code.

State v. Chapman Dodge Center

428 So. 2d 413 (La. 1983)

FRED C. SEXTON, JR., JUSTICE AD HOC.

Chapman Dodge Center, Inc., a Baton Rouge Dodge dealership, closed its doors because of financial difficulty on September 12, 1980. Shortly thereafter the district attorney's office began receiving complaints from Dodge customers that they had not received their permanent license plates for their cars because the dealership had neither registered the cars purchased, nor paid the sales tax due. The usual practice was for the customer to pay the amount due for sales tax to the car dealer who, in turn, would register the car with the state and tender the tax. After a car is registered and the tax paid, the state issues a permanent license plate. In the meantime, the dealership is authorized to give the customer a temporary plate that is valid for 35 days. Dodge customers were being stopped for expired temporary license plates since they had not received their permanent tags.

Chapman Dodge had been in financial trouble for about a year prior to its closing. Aside from the general economic situation, Chapman's difficulties were due in great part to Chapman's financial relationship to the financially troubled Chrysler Corporation. According to the trial record, at the time Chapman closed, Chrysler Corporation owed between $250,000 and $400,000 to Chapman Dodge. In addition, Chrysler Credit Corporation, a subsidiary of Chrysler Motors, had $140,000 of Chapman's money "on reserve" for potential losses on loans Chrysler Credit made to Chapman customers.

After Chapman Dodge closed its doors, Chrysler Credit Corporation took possession of Chapman Dodge. On the premises, employees of Chrysler Credit Corporation found between 180 and 190 registration forms for purchased cars which had not been filed with the state and for which no sales tax had been paid. Since Chrysler Credit Corporation owned the mortgages on 159 of these cars, it paid the sales taxes due on them (approximately $68,000) in order to register the cars and the chattel mortgages with the state.

The defendant, John Swindle, personally paid the sales taxes (about $11,000) on the remaining cars which had not been financed by Chrysler Credit Corporation.

The defendant did so after he was notified by the district attorney's office that the taxes were due. The defendant's attorney in Mississippi, however, testified that he advised the defendant that Chrysler Credit Corporation should be responsible for all taxes due since it had possession of all of Chapman Dodge's assets, and was therefore responsible for discharging Chapman's tax liability.

The original bill of information charged 159 counts of theft, but was later amended to 20 counts with a reservation to prosecute the remaining 139 at a later time. Defendant John Swindle testified that he was the sole owner of Barony Corporation, a holding company for several food service corporations. Barony Corporation owned a subsidiary called Center Management which was formed to hold automobile dealerships when Swindle expanded his operations to include that business. Chapman Dodge was one of four dealerships owned by Center Management. Center Management, after acquiring the necessary funding, then purchased Chapman Dodge. Subsequently Chapman Dodge endorsed the notes Center Management had signed in obtaining financing. Each month a check was sent by Chapman Dodge to Center Management to cover the payment due by Center Management on the notes.

The evidence showed that the defendant, a resident of Jackson, Mississippi, was seldom at the dealership more than twice a month. It was Donald Barrett that was in charge of the daily operations of Chapman Dodge as general manager. All department managers were responsible to Barrett, who in turn answered to Swindle. According to the testimony of James Duvall, Chapman Dodge's accountant, he and Barrett made the decisions as to which bills were to be paid.

Swindle testified that when the dealership was showing continued financial trouble, he discussed this matter with James Duvall. Since the dealership was behind in paying withholding taxes, as well as sales taxes, he ordered Duvall to pay all of the taxes owed, particularly the federal withholdings. When the dealership was closed, Swindle asked Barrett if all the taxes had been paid. The record shows that in the presence of Johnilyn Smith, an administrative assistant to Swindle, and Frank Peel, a business associate of Swindle, Barrett stated that *all* taxes had been paid. Barrett testified that he did not say *all* the taxes had been paid, only that the *federal* taxes had been paid. On cross-examination however Barrett stated that he "may" have said that all the taxes were paid.

The defendant received no indication that the sales taxes were not paid until a week or ten days after closing the dealership when the district attorney contacted Chapman Dodge's lawyer. Duvall testified that he was instructed by Donald Barrett to retain the sales tax money. Donald Barrett however testified that he had told James Duvall in June of 1980 to pay only those obligations necessary to keep the dealership open; but that he never told Duvall to retain the contracts and sales taxes on the purchased vehicles.

Donald Barrett was originally indicted on the theft charges along with John Swindle and Chapman Dodge. Both he and James Duvall were granted "use" immunity in order to compel their testimony against Chapman Dodge and John Swindle. Duvall was granted immunity at the preliminary examination. Barrett was granted immunity when his counsel invoked his privilege against compulsory self-incrimination when he was called to testify at the trial. Barrett stated on cross-examination that the district attorney's office had told him three weeks earlier that he would not be prosecuted if he testified for the state.

John Swindle was charged with the crime of theft. The jury, however, apparently found that the elements of theft had not been proven by the state and returned a verdict of the lesser included offense of unauthorized use of a movable.

In the instant case, the state has failed to prove *any* intent on the part of Swindle, fraudulent or otherwise. . . .

The question of the criminal liability of the corporate defendant in this cause is a more difficult proposition involving fundamental issues of the nature of criminal responsibility. These issues have not been generally considered with respect to corporations in this jurisdiction. Certainly our law contemplates corporate criminal defendants. Louisiana law delineates a number of acts the commission or omission of which creates corporate criminal responsibility.

The problem of what criminal liability a corporation should bear for the unauthorized acts of its officers and managers is indeed a grave and troubling one. Recent allegations of corporate responsibility for large train derailments and massive pollution of water sources underscore the importance of this troubling topic. Certainly there is civil responsibility under such circumstances. The question is whether a corporation should be criminally responsible in the absence of a specific statute which defines and describes the corporate act, prohibits that act, and establishes a specific punishment therefor.

Criminal liability in our system of justice has always been founded upon the simultaneous existence of two distinct elements namely: (1) *actus reus*, and (2) *mens rea*. The existence of only one of these elements does not make one criminally liable. Both must be present to invoke the sanctions society has placed on what is termed "criminal conduct." Certainly one cannot be held criminally liable for simply thinking of a criminal act without the act occurring. A somewhat more difficult, but logically consistent idea, is that an act, committed without the required criminal intent or *mens rea*, is not criminally punishable. We do not criminally punish those that do not know what they are doing — such as the insane. Neither do we punish those who, while aware of what they are doing, have no control over their actions — the victims of threats or coercion. We do not impose criminal liability on those who act without criminal intent for the simple reason that such an imposition would not achieve the main goal of our criminal law: deterrence.

Given these basic ruminations on the topic of criminal intent, we should now consider the nature of a corporation. Our Civil Code in Article 427 defines a corporation as:

. . . an intellectual body, created by law, composed of individuals united under a common name, the members of which succeed each other, so that the body continues always the same, notwithstanding the change of the individuals which compose it, and which, for certain purposes, *is considered as a natural person.* (emphasis added.)

The corporation as a fictitious person is capable of entering into contracts, owning property and making and receiving donations. In short, it is capable of doing virtually anything that a natural person is capable of doing.

A corporation by the very nature of its operation is dependent upon people to carry out its business. Some of these people may rightfully be regarded as the "mind" of the corporation. This group, known as the board of directors, is responsible for the direction that the corporation takes in its business activity. Plans for the corporation, developed by the board of directors, are transmitted to the officers of the corporation and through them to the employees. This latter group may be regarded as the "hands" of the corporation. But here our analogy to the human form must end. For unlike ordinary human hands, corporate "hands" have minds of their own and are capable of self direction.

When a corporation is accused of committing a crime which requires intent, it must be determined who within the corporate structure had the intent to commit the crime. If the crime was the product of a board of directors' resolution authorizing its employees to commit specific criminal acts, then intent on the part of the corporation is manifest. However, a more difficult question arises if the crime is actually committed by an employee of the corporation not authorized to perform such an act. Holding a corporation criminally responsible for the acts of an employee may be inconsistent with basic notions of criminal intent, since such a posture would render a corporate entity responsible for actions which it theoretically had no intent to commit.

Common law jurisdictions hold corporations criminally liable for the acts of low-ranking employees. In such jurisdictions, corporate criminal liability is based on an extension of the tort doctrine of vicarious liability. The theme of vicarious criminal liability, however, is varied. Some jurisdictions impose criminal liability where there has been an act or an authorization to act by a managerial officer, some where there has been an act committed within the scope of the actor's employment, and still others where there has been an act done which benefits the corporation. These varied applications notwithstanding, common law jurisdictions have found corporations liable for forms of homicide, theft, extortion — in short, virtually every crime other than rape and carnal knowledge.

Although this merger of tort and criminal law doctrine has found wide acceptance, it has also generated significant theoretical problems. Admittedly, tort law and criminal law are cousins, causing concern as to whether their relationship is within the prohibited degree such that a union of the two might produce unwanted offspring. It should be remembered that the main function of the law of torts is compensation and to a much lesser degree, deterrence.

Tort law attempts to distribute the loss of a harmful occurrence. Causation is the important ingredient therein. Holding a corporation vicariously liable for the torts of its employees dovetails with the idea of compensating the victim. The corporation is in a more likely position to compensate.

On the other hand, as mentioned earlier, the primary function of criminal law is to deter future criminal liability. To impose such liability on another party who had no part in the act and, as in the case of most corporate crimes, no intent to commit such an act, seems at first glance to be contrary to the purpose of our criminal legal system. . . .

The instant defendant is a closely held holding corporation which is accused of a basic "Ten Commandment Crime" — theft — and convicted of a lesser included offense. Thus the finder of fact in effect determined that the defendant corporation kept the money in question with fraudulent intent, but with the intent to eventually return the funds. The evidence further indicates that "retention" of the funds was not specifically authorized by the board of directors or by the president or any other officer of the corporation. The record does not indicate, moreover, that any of these entities had any real knowledge of that action. Of course the corporation, its board of directors, its parent corporations and its president are for all practical purposes the same entity — the individual defendant Swindle. Furthermore, as discussed earlier, the evidence preponderates that it was a party other than Swindle who determined to "retain the funds."

Thus, the facts of this case can be narrowed to a fine point. In so doing, however, broad questions of a complex nature are visited upon us. While recognizing the potential disservice to the jurisprudence we are nevertheless unable, within the confines of this appeal, to resolve these extremely complex issues. We simply determine that under the circumstances of this case, criminal intent has not been adequately established. We determine that under the circumstances of this case, there was insufficient intent shown in the trial court analysis [for any rational trier of fact to find criminal intent], and therefore this corporate defendant may not be found criminally responsible. We hold that since this record reveals no evidence of complicity by the officers or the board of directors, explicit or tacit, that the actions of these managers and/or employees were insufficient to cause this corporate entity to be guilty of the offense of an unauthorized use of a movable.

We thus reverse as to both defendants and order their discharge.

Notes and Questions

1. *High managerial agent status not always predictable.* The Louisiana Supreme Court used a narrow interpretation of the MPC's concept "high managerial agent" in finding that the general manager did not satisfy that definition. Even though he engaged in ongoing fraud, the manager's intent could not be imputed to the corporation, which

was owned solely by a person who did not live in Louisiana and who had no knowledge of the general manager's activities. In your view, based on the evidence in the case, did Swindle qualify as a "high managerial agent?" Did Barrett? Why or why not?

2. *Employee immunity.* In order to prosecute Chapman Dodge and Swindle, the government offered immunity from prosecution to two of the company's employees. Immunity deals are an especially powerful tool for prosecutors in the corporate context. Under respondeat superior, corporate crime and employee crime are two sides of the same coin. A corporation confesses to crime by providing evidence of employee crime and, when an employee confesses to crime, that employee effectively provides a roadmap to proving the corporation committed crime too. Using immunity, prosecutors can play corporations and their employees against each other. Is one type of immunity more concerning than the other?

3. *Deterrence.* The *Chapman* court asserted that "the main goal of our criminal law [is] deterrence." *Chapman*, 428 So. 2d at 417. Do you agree? Would focusing on a different function of criminal law dictate a different result?

4. *Piercing the corporate veil.* The *Chapman* court opined: "Of course the corporation, its board of directors, its parent corporations and its president are for all practical purposes the same entity — the individual defendant Swindle." *Chapman*, 428 So. 2d at 419. A fundamental tenet of corporate law is that a corporation is distinct from its owners. Equally fundamental are the formal distinctions between parent corporations and subsidiaries and between corporations and those who run them. This is how corporations help limit liability; the successful party can only claim assets held by the corporation, and not those held by its shareholders. Under certain circumstances, such as when a corporation is effectively functioning as the alter ego of its owner, courts recognize that there is no real distinction between a corporation and those who own or run it. In such cases, plaintiffs may "pierce the corporate veil," and assert claims against the assets of the individual owners. *See* Irwin & Leighton, Inc. v. W.M. Anderson Co., 532 A.2d 983 (Del. Ch. 1987). Is the *Chapman* court discussing something similar here?

5. *Splitting mens rea from actus reus.* What if the employee who satisfies the actus reus element is different from the employee who satisfies the mens rea element? For example, suppose a pharmaceutical company is releasing a report to its shareholders about a new drug. The CEO publishes the report thinking all the positive news about the drug is true, but scientists at the pharmaceutical company know the news is fake. Should the corporation still be liable, or liable only under certain circumstances? What sorts of incentives would this give to corporations and motivated prosecutors?

2. Collective Knowledge

As the preceding materials show, applying the concept of mens rea to artificial entities such as corporations raises complex issues. This is particularly true in the context of a large national or multinational corporation. Even in a jurisdiction that applies respondeat superior, courts often look for some sort of corporate acquiescence to, or conscious avoidance of knowledge of, wrongdoing by corporate employees or agents. Still, prosecutors have to be able to identify one employee who instantiates the full criminal mens rea. But what happens if a corporation parcels out responsibility among several employees in such a way that none can know enough to satisfy the mens rea requirement? Under a strict application of respondeat superior, the corporation could not be convicted. It would not even necessarily matter whether the corporation purposely distributed responsibility to avoid liability, or just did so through happenstance.

One controversial doctrine, known as "collective knowledge," addresses this circumstance exactly, at least for crimes that require culpable knowledge. The doctrine aggregates all of the knowledge of all individual corporate agents and then attributes this aggregate knowledge to the organization. The first case to discuss this doctrine in corporate criminal law was the First Circuit decision in *United States v. Bank of New England, N.A.*, 821 F.2d 844 (1st Cir. 1987). In that decision, the court held that the corporation was criminally liable based upon the "collective knowledge" of all the employees within the corporation. The Bank of New England failed to file Currency Transaction Reports ("CTRs") triggered by 31 separate cash withdrawals made by a customer over the course of a year. The government charged the Bank with violations of 31 U.S.C. § 5322, which attached when a financial institution "willfully" fails to file the required reports. The court acknowledged the difficulty of establishing willfulness "since it is a state of mind; it is usually established by drawing reasonable inferences from the available facts." *Id.* The court determined that in the context of the statute, "willfulness" required proof of knowledge (1) of what facts would trigger a reporting requirement and (2) that those facts had materialized.

The evidence established that individual employees each possessed one component of the required knowledge, but none possessed both. Compliance personnel knew about the reporting requirements, but not about the withdrawals. Tellers knew about the withdrawals, but not the reporting requirements. Indeed, the individual employees had each been acquitted of criminal charges. When it came to assessing the Bank's liability, however, the court aggregated the individual knowledge and held that the Bank knew it all. The court considered modern-day corporate structure in developing its rationale:

> A collective knowledge instruction is entirely appropriate in the context of corporate criminal liability. The acts of a corporation are, after all, simply the acts of all of its employees operating within the scope of their employment. The law on corporate criminal liability reflects this. Similarly, the knowledge obtained by corporate employees acting within the scope of their employment is imputed to the corporation. Corporations compartmentalize knowledge, subdividing the elements of specific duties and operations into smaller components. The aggregate of those components constitutes the corporation's knowledge of a particular operation. It is

irrelevant whether employees administering one component of an operation know the specific activities of employees administering another aspect
of the operation: "[A] corporation cannot plead innocence by asserting that
the information obtained by several employees was not acquired by any
one individual who then would have comprehended its full import. Rather
the corporation is considered to have acquired the collective knowledge of
its employees and is held responsible for their failure to act accordingly."
United States v. T.I.M.E.-D.C., Inc., 381 F. Supp. at 738. Since the Bank had
the compartmentalized structure common to all large corporations, the
court's collective knowledge instruction was not only proper but necessary.

821 F.2d 844, 856 (1st Cir. 1987).

Since the *Bank of New England* case, most commentators have rejected this doctrine as overly broad and inconsistent with principles of criminal accountability.
On the other hand, in the absence of a collective knowledge doctrine a corporation could "avoid liability by simply dividing up duties to ensure that the fraudulent [activity was] only [committed] by uninformed employees." *United States v.
Philip Morris USA, Inc.,* 449 F. Supp. 2d 1, 897 (D.D.C. 2006), *aff'd in part, vacated in
part,* 566 F.3d 1095 (D.C. Cir. 2009). These considerations have failed to sway many
judges; very few jurisdictions have followed the First Circuit's lead in permitting
collective knowledge.

Notes and Questions

1. *Knowledge.* The collective knowledge doctrine applies, as its name would suggest, only to knowledge. It is hard to see how it could extend to other mental states,
like intent, since there is no obvious way to aggregate the intentions of individuals, which, unlike knowledge, might conflict. Knowledge, though, is an extremely
important mens rea in white collar criminal law, and, in one form or another, is an
element of most white-collar violations. As *Bank of New England* intimates, knowledge — and the law's mechanisms for attributing it to corporations — plays a crucial
role in structuring corporate incentives to implement compliance programs. In the
words of one scholar:

> Corporations worried about criminal liability have a Janus-faced stake in
> knowledge. From one perspective, knowledge can be power and security.
> Regular audits of employee performance can help corporations streamline
> operations, increase efficiencies, and boost profitability. Audits also gener-
> ate information critical for designing and implementing programs to pre-
> vent employees — and hence their corporate employers — from committing
> crime and incurring criminal liabilities. From another perspective, knowl-
> edge can be a great vulnerability. The line between criminal and innocent
> conduct frequently turns on what defendants knew. Monitoring employees
> can sometimes make corporations worse off. The same internal corporate
> compliance and audit programs that gather information crucial to helping

corporations prevent crime can also produce knowledge that converts otherwise permissible corporate conduct into crime.

Mihailis E. Diamantis, *Functional Corporate Knowledge*, 61 Wm. & Mary L. Rev. 319, 325–26 (2019). Does the collective knowledge doctrine make it more or less likely that corporations will invest in the right level of compliance?

2. *Willful blindness.* The collective knowledge theory of mens rea is analogous in many ways to the willful blindness theory used in both drug and white collar criminal prosecutions. Proof of "willful blindness," also known as "constructive knowledge" or "conscious avoidance," has recently been defined by the United States Supreme Court: "(1) the defendant must subjectively believe that there is a high probability that a fact exists and (2) the defendant must take deliberate actions to avoid learning of that fact." *Global-Tech Appliances, Inc. v. SEB S.A.*, 131 S. Ct. 2060, 2070 (2011). *Global-Tech* is discussed in Chapter 3, Conspiracy, *infra*. Willful blindness has also been called the "ostrich" approach—burying one's head in the sand to avoid knowledge. Should this type of criminal liability, a hybrid between knowledge and recklessness, be applied to the corporate and white collar criminal arenas? To what extent can willful blindness address the concerns that motivated the *Bank of New England* court?

D. Individual Liability within the Corporate Setting

While individuals within a corporation can subject their employer to criminal liability, they are, of course, also individually accountable for their conduct. This section discusses two special doctrines that help prosecutors bring cases in white collar settings.

1. Responsible Corporate Officer Doctrine

Statistically speaking, most criminal conduct within corporations occurs in the middle and lower echelons of the corporate hierarchy. *See* Mihailis E. Diamantis, *Corporate Criminal Minds*, 91 Notre Dame L. Rev. 2049, 2068–69 (2016) Gregory Gilchrist, *Individual Accountability for Corporate Crime*, 34 Ga. St. U.L. Rev. 365 (2018). This is the case even *though those higher up* are in a better position both to appreciate the criminal significance of that conduct and to effectuate corporation-wide change. The responsible corporate officer doctrine is a partial legal fix in some arenas, like pharmaceuticals and food production. It holds corporate officers responsible for the criminal acts of their subordinates. It functions like respondeat superior in reverse, attributing acts of the corporation to individual officers. Importantly, the doctrine only allows attribution of acts to corporate officers; to be convicted, the officer must still independently satisfy applicable mens rea (if any).

The foundational case for the corporate officer doctrine is *United States v. Dotterweich*, 320 U.S. 277, 284 (1943), which held under the doctrine that an "offense is committed . . . by all who do have such a responsible share in the furtherance of the transaction which the statute outlaws." More than three decades later, the Court again addressed the responsible corporate officer doctrine in *United States v. Park*, which remains one of the few major Supreme Court cases that elaborate on the doctrine. As you read this case, consider what, if anything, Park could have done to avoid criminal liability under the facts.

United States v. Park
421 U.S. 658 (1975)

Mr. CHIEF JUSTICE BURGER delivered the opinion of the Court.

We granted certiorari to consider whether the jury instructions in the prosecution of a corporate officer under § 301(k) of the Federal Food, Drug, and Cosmetic Act, 21 U.S.C. § 331(k), were appropriate under *United States v. Dotterweich*, 320 U.S. 277 (1943).

Acme Markets, Inc., is a national retail food chain with approximately 36,000 employees, 874 retail outlets, 12 general warehouses, and four special warehouses. Its headquarters, including the office of the president, respondent Park, who is chief executive officer of the corporation, are located in Philadelphia, Pa. In a five-count information filed in the United States District Court for the District of Maryland, the Government charged Acme and respondent with violations of the Federal Food, Drug and Cosmetic Act. Each count of the information alleged that the defendants had received food that had been shipped in interstate commerce and that, while the food was being held for sale in Acme's Baltimore warehouse following shipment in interstate commerce, they caused it to be held in a building accessible to rodents and to be exposed to contamination by rodents. These acts were alleged to have resulted in the food's being adulterated within the meaning of 21 U.S.C. §§ 342(a) (3) and (4), in violation of 21 U.S.C. § 331(k).

Acme pleaded guilty to each count of the information. Respondent pleaded not guilty. The evidence at trial demonstrated that in April 1970 the Food and Drug Administration (FDA) advised respondent by letter of insanitary conditions in Acme's Philadelphia warehouse. In 1971 the FDA found that similar conditions existed in the firm's Baltimore warehouse. An FDA consumer safety officer testified concerning evidence of rodent infestation and other insanitary conditions discovered during a 12-day inspection of the Baltimore warehouse in November and December 1971. He also related that a second inspection of the warehouse had been conducted in March 1972. On that occasion the inspectors found that there had been improvement in the sanitary conditions, but that "there was still evidence of rodent activity in the building and in the warehouses and we found some rodent-contaminated lots of food items."

The Government also presented testimony by the Chief of Compliance of the FDA's Baltimore office, who informed respondent by letter of the conditions at the Baltimore warehouse after the first inspection. There was testimony by Acme's Baltimore division vice president, who had responded to the letter on behalf of Acme and respondent and who described the steps taken to remedy the insanitary conditions discovered by both inspections. The Government's final witness, Acme's vice president for legal affairs and assistant secretary, identified respondent as the president and chief executive officer of the company and read a bylaw prescribing the duties of the chief executive officer. He testified that respondent functioned by delegating "normal operating duties," including sanitation, but that he retained "certain things, which are the big, broad, principles of the operation of the company," and had "the responsibility of seeing that they all work together."

At the close of the Government's case in chief, respondent moved for a judgment of acquittal on the ground that "the evidence in chief has shown that Mr. Park is not personally concerned in this Food and Drug violation." The trial judge denied the motion, stating that *United States v. Dotterweich*, 320 U.S. 277 (1943), was controlling.

Respondent was the only defense witness. He testified that, although all of Acme's employees were in a sense under his general direction, the company had an "organizational structure for responsibilities for certain functions" according to which different phases of its operation were "assigned to individuals who, in turn, have staff and departments under them." He identified those individuals responsible for sanitation, and related that upon receipt of the January 1972 FDA letter, he had conferred with the vice president for legal affairs, who informed him that the Baltimore division vice president "was investigating the situation immediately and would be taking corrective action and would be preparing a summary of the corrective action to reply to the letter." Respondent stated that he did not "believe there was anything [he] could have done more constructively than what [he] found was being done."

On cross-examination, respondent conceded that providing sanitary conditions for food offered for sale to the public was something that he was "responsible for in the entire operation of the company," and he stated that it was one of many phases of the company that he assigned to "dependable subordinates." Respondent was asked about and, over the objections of his counsel, admitted receiving, the April 1970 letter addressed to him from the FDA regarding insanitary conditions at Acme's Philadelphia warehouse.[1] He acknowledged that, with the exception of the division vice

---

1. The April 1970 letter informed respondent of the following "objectionable conditions" in Acme's Philadelphia warehouse:
    1. Potential rodent entry ways were noted via ill fitting doors and door in disrepair at Southwest corner of warehouse; at dock at old salvage room and at receiving and shipping doors which were observed to be open most of the time.
    2. Rodent nesting, rodent excreta pellets, rodent stained bale bagging and rodent gnawed holes were noted among bales of flour stored in warehouse.

president, the same individuals had responsibility for sanitation in both Baltimore and Philadelphia. Finally, in response to questions concerning the Philadelphia and Baltimore incidents, respondent admitted that the Baltimore problem indicated the system for handling sanitation "wasn't working perfectly" and that as Acme's chief executive officer he was responsible for "any result which occurs in our company."

At the close of the evidence, respondent's renewed motion for a judgment of acquittal was denied. The relevant portion of the trial judge's instructions to the jury challenged by respondent is set out in the margin.[2] Respondent's counsel objected to the instructions on the ground that they failed fairly to reflect our decision in *United States v. Dotterweich, supra*, and to define "responsible relationship." The trial judge overruled the objection. The jury found respondent guilty on all counts of the information, and he was subsequently sentenced to pay a fine of $50 on each count.

The Court of Appeals reversed the conviction and remanded for a new trial. That court viewed the Government as arguing "that the conviction may be predicated solely upon a showing that . . . [respondent] was the President of the offending corporation," and it stated that as "a general proposition, some act of commission or omission is an essential element of every crime." It reasoned that, although our decision in *United States v. Dotterweich, supra*, 320 U.S. at 281, had construed the statutory provisions under which respondent was tried to dispense with the traditional element of "awareness of some wrongdoing," the Court had not construed them as dispensing with the element of "wrongful action." The Court of Appeals concluded that the trial judge's instructions "might well have left the jury with the erroneous impression that Park could be found guilty in the absence of 'wrongful action' on his part," and that proof of this element was required by due process. It held, with one dissent, that the instructions did not "correctly state the law of the case," and directed that on retrial the jury be instructed as to "wrongful action," which might be "gross negligence and inattention in discharging . . . corporate duties and obligations or any of a host of other acts of commission or omission which would 'cause' the contamination of food." . . .

We granted certiorari because of an apparent conflict among the Courts of Appeals with respect to the standard of liability of corporate officers under the

---

3. Potential rodent harborage was noted in discarded paper, rope, sawdust and other debris piled in corner of shipping and receiving dock near bakery and warehouse doors. Rodent excreta pellets were observed among bags of sawdust (or wood shavings).

2. "In order to find the Defendant guilty on any count of the Information, you must find beyond a reasonable doubt on each count. . . .

"[T]hat John R. Park held a position of authority in the operation of the business of Acme Markets, Incorporated. . . .

"The individual is or could be liable under the statute, even if he did not consciously do wrong. However, the fact that the Defendant is president and is a chief executive officer of the Acme Markets does not require a finding of guilt. Though, he need not have personally participated in the situation, he must have had a responsible relationship to the issue. The issue is, in this case, whether the Defendant, John R. Park, by virtue of his position in the company, had a position of authority and responsibility in the situation out of which these charges arose."

Federal Food, Drug, and Cosmetic Act as construed in *United States v. Dotterweich*, *supra*, and because of the importance of the question to the Government's enforcement program. We reverse.

The question presented by the Government's petition for certiorari in *United States v. Dotterweich*, *supra*, and the focus of this Court's opinion, was whether "the manager of a corporation, as well as the corporation itself, may be prosecuted under the Federal Food, Drug, and Cosmetic Act of 1938 for the introduction of misbranded and adulterated articles into interstate commerce." In *Dotterweich*, a jury had disagreed as to the corporation, a jobber purchasing drugs from manufacturers and shipping them in interstate commerce under its own label, but had convicted *Dotterweich*, the corporation's president and general manager. The Court of Appeals reversed the conviction on the ground that only the drug dealer, whether corporation or individual, was subject to the criminal provisions of the Act, and that where the dealer was a corporation, an individual connected therewith might be held personally only if he was operating the corporation "as his 'alter ego.'"

In reversing the judgment of the Court of Appeals and reinstating Dotterweich's conviction, this Court looked to the purposes of the Act and noted that they "touch phases of the lives and health of the people which, in the circumstances of modern industrialism, are largely beyond self-protection." It observed that the Act is of "a now familiar type" which "dispenses with the conventional requirement for criminal conduct — awareness of some wrongdoing. In the interest of the larger good it puts the burden of acting at hazard upon a person otherwise innocent but standing in responsible relation to a public danger."

Central to the Court's conclusion that individuals other than proprietors are subject to the criminal provisions of the Act was the reality that "the only way in which a corporation can act is through the individuals who act on its behalf." The Court also noted that corporate officers had been subject to criminal liability under the Federal Food and Drugs Act of 1906, and it observed that a contrary result under the 1938 legislation would be incompatible with the expressed intent of Congress to "enlarge and stiffen the penal net" and to discourage a view of the Act's criminal penalties as a "license fee for the conduct of an illegitimate business."

At the same time, however, the Court was aware of the concern which was the motivating factor in the Court of Appeals' decision that literal enforcement "might operate too harshly by sweeping within its condemnation any person however remotely entangled in the proscribed shipment." A limiting principle, in the form of "settled doctrines of criminal law" defining those who "are responsible for the commission of a misdemeanor," was available. In this context, the Court concluded, those doctrines dictated that the offense was committed "by all who . . . have . . . a responsible share in the furtherance of the transaction which the statute outlaws."

The Court recognized that, because the Act dispenses with the need to prove "consciousness of wrongdoing," it may result in hardship even as applied to those who share "responsibility in the business process resulting in" a violation. It regarded as "too treacherous" an attempt "to define or even to indicate by way of illustration the class of employees which stands in such a responsible relation." The question of responsibility, the Court said, depends "on the evidence produced at the trial and its submission — assuming the evidence warrants it — to the jury under appropriate guidance." The Court added: "In such matters the good sense of prosecutors, the wise guidance of trial judges, and the ultimate judgment of juries must be trusted."

The rule that corporate employees who have "a responsible share in the furtherance of the transaction which the statute outlaws" are subject to the criminal provisions of the Act was not formulated in a vacuum. Cases under the Federal Food and Drugs Act of 1906 reflected the view both that knowledge or intent were not required to be proved in prosecutions under its criminal provisions, and that responsible corporate agents could be subjected to the liability thereby imposed. Moreover, the principle had been recognized that a corporate agent, through whose act, default, or omission the corporation committed a crime, was himself guilty individually of that crime. The principle had been applied whether or not the crime required "consciousness of wrongdoing," and it had been applied not only to those corporate agents who themselves committed the criminal act, but also to those who by virtue of their managerial positions or other similar relation to the actor could be deemed responsible for its commission.

In the latter class of cases, the liability of managerial officers did not depend on their knowledge of, or personal participation in, the act made criminal by the statute. Rather, where the statute under which they were prosecuted dispensed with "consciousness of wrongdoing," an omission or failure to act was deemed a sufficient basis for a responsible corporate agent's liability. It was enough in such cases that, by virtue of the relationship he bore to the corporation, the agent had the power to prevent the act complained of.

The rationale of the interpretation given the Act in *Dotterweich*, as holding criminally accountable the persons whose failure to exercise the authority and supervisory responsibility reposed in them by the business organization resulted in the violation complained of, has been confirmed in our subsequent cases. Thus, the Court has reaffirmed the proposition that "the public interest in the purity of its food is so great as to warrant the imposition of the highest standard of care on distributors." In order to make "distributors of food the strictest censors of their merchandise," the Act punishes "neglect where the law requires care, or inaction where it imposes a duty." "The accused, if he does not will the violation, usually is in a position to prevent it with no more care than society might reasonably expect and no more exertion than it might reasonably exact from one who assumed his responsibilities." Similarly, in cases decided after *Dotterweich*, the Courts of Appeals have recognized that those corporate agents vested with the responsibility, and power commensurate with that responsibility, to devise whatever measures are necessary to ensure compliance with the Act bear a "responsible relationship" to, or have a "responsible share" in, violations.

Thus *Dotterweich* and the cases which have followed reveal that in providing sanctions which reach and touch the individuals who execute the corporate mission — and this is by no means necessarily confined to a single corporate agent or employee — the Act imposes not only a positive duty to seek out and remedy violations when they occur but also, and primarily, a duty to implement measures that will insure that violations will not occur. The requirements of foresight and vigilance imposed on responsible corporate agents are beyond question demanding, and perhaps onerous, but they are no more stringent than the public has a right to expect of those who voluntarily assume positions of authority in business enterprises whose services and products affect the health and well-being of the public that supports them.

The Act does not, as we observed in *Dotterweich*, make criminal liability turn on "awareness of some wrongdoing" or "conscious fraud." The duty imposed by Congress on responsible corporate agents is, we emphasize, one that requires the highest standard of foresight and vigilance, but the Act, in its criminal aspect, does not require that which is objectively impossible. The theory upon which responsible corporate agents are held criminally accountable for "causing" violations of the Act permits a claim that a defendant was "powerless" to prevent or correct the violation to "be raised defensively at a trial on the merits." *United States v. Wiesenfield Warehouse Co.*, 376 U.S. 86, 91 (1964). If such a claim is made, the defendant has the burden of coming forward with evidence, but this does not alter the Government's ultimate burden of proving beyond a reasonable doubt the defendant's guilt, including his power, in light of the duty imposed by the Act, to prevent or correct the prohibited condition. Congress has seen fit to enforce the accountability of responsible corporate agents dealing with products which may affect the health of consumers by penal sanctions cast in rigorous terms, and the obligation of the courts is to give them effect so long as they do not violate the Constitution.

We cannot agree with the Court of Appeals that it was incumbent upon the District Court to instruct the jury that the Government had the burden of establishing "wrongful action" in the sense in which the Court of Appeals used that phrase. The concept of a "responsible relationship" to, or a "responsible share" in, a violation of the Act indeed imports some measure of blameworthiness; but it is equally clear that the Government establishes a prima facie case when it introduces evidence sufficient to warrant a finding by the trier of the facts that the defendant had, by reason of his position in the corporation, responsibility and authority either to prevent in the first instance, or promptly to correct, the violation complained of, and that he failed to do so. The failure thus to fulfill the duty imposed by the interaction of the corporate agent's authority and the statute furnishes a sufficient causal link. The considerations which prompted the imposition of this duty, and the scope of the duty, provide the measure of culpability.

Turning to the jury charge in this case, it is of course arguable that isolated parts can be read as intimating that a finding of guilt could be predicated solely on respondent's corporate position. But this is not the way we review jury instructions, because "a single instruction to a jury may not be judged in artificial isolation, but must be viewed in the context of the overall charge."

Reading the entire charge satisfies us that the jury's attention was adequately focused on the issue of respondent's authority with respect to the conditions that formed the basis of the alleged violations. Viewed as a whole, the charge did not permit the jury to find guilt solely on the basis of respondent's position in the corporation; rather, it fairly advised the jury that to find guilt it must find respondent "had a responsible relation to the situation," and "by virtue of his position . . . had . . . authority and responsibility" to deal with the situation. The situation referred to could only be "food . . . held in unsanitary conditions in a warehouse with the result that it consisted, in part, of filth or . . . may have been contaminated with filth."

Moreover, in reviewing jury instructions, our task is also to view the charge itself as part of the whole trial. "Often isolated statements taken from the charge, seemingly prejudicial on their face, are not so when considered in the context of the entire record of the trial." The record in this case reveals that the jury could not have failed to be aware that the main issue for determination was not respondent's position in the corporate hierarchy, but rather his accountability, because of the responsibility and authority of his position, for the conditions which gave rise to the charges against him.

We conclude that, viewed as a whole and in the context of the trial, the charge was not misleading and contained an adequate statement of the law to guide the jury's determination.

Reversed.

Mr. Justice Stewart, with whom Mr. Justice Marshall and Mr. Justice Powell join, dissenting.

Although agreeing with much of what is said in the Court's opinion, I dissent from the opinion and judgment, because the jury instructions in this case were not consistent with the law as the Court today expounds it.

As I understand the Court's opinion, it holds that in order to sustain a conviction under § 301(k) of the Federal Food, Drug, and Cosmetic Act the prosecution must at least show that by reason of an individual's corporate position and responsibilities, he had a duty to use care to maintain the physical integrity of the corporation's food products. A jury may then draw the inference that when the good is found to be in such condition as to violate the statute's prohibitions, that condition was "caused" by a breach of the standard of care imposed upon the responsible official. This is the language of negligence, and I agree with it.

To affirm this conviction, however, the Court must approve the instructions given to the members of the jury who were entrusted with determining whether the respondent was innocent or guilty. Those instructions did not conform to the standards that the Court itself sets out today.

As the Court today recognized, the *Dotterweich* case did not deal with what kind of conduct must be proved to support a finding of criminal guilt under the Act.

Dotterweich was concerned, rather, with the statutory definition of "person" — with what kind of corporate employees were even "subject to the criminal provisions of the Act." The Court held that those employees with "a responsible relation" to the violative transaction or condition were subject to the Act's criminal provisions, but all that the Court had to say with respect to the kind of conduct that can constitute criminal guilt was that the Act "dispenses with the conventional requirement for criminal conduct — awareness of some wrongdoing."

The *Dotterweich* case stands for two propositions, and I accept them both. First, "any person" within the meaning of 21 U.S.C. § 333 may include any corporate officer or employee "standing in responsible relation" to a condition or transaction forbidden by the Act. Second, a person may be convicted of a criminal offense under the Act even in the absence of "the conventional requirement for criminal conduct — awareness of some wrongdoing."

But before a person can be convicted of a criminal violation of this Act, a jury must find — and must be clearly instructed that it must find — evidence beyond a reasonable doubt that he engaged in wrongful conduct amounting at least to common-law negligence. There were no such instructions, and clearly, therefore, no such finding in this case.

For these reasons, I cannot join the Court in affirming Park's criminal conviction.

Notes and Questions

1. *Mens rea and actus reus.* What level of mens rea (guilty mind) did Park possess? What actus reus (guilty act) did he commit? Given the proof adduced on these essential elements of criminal liability, why did the Court affirm Park's criminal conviction?

2. *Justifying the responsible corporate officer doctrine. Dotterweich* identified what may be the most powerful justification for the responsible corporate officer doctrine — corporate officers are often what economists would call the "least cost avoiders" of certain types of harm.

> Balancing relative hardships, Congress has preferred to place it upon those who have at least the opportunity of informing themselves of the existence of conditions imposed for the protection of consumers before sharing in illicit commerce, rather than to throw the hazard on the innocent public who are wholly helpless.

Dotterweich, 320 U.S. at 285 (1943). What are other possible justifications?

3. Dotterweich *and strict liability.* The Court in *Park* relied heavily on its opinion in *United States v. Dotterweich*, 320 U.S. 277 (1943). In that case, the defendant was the president and general manager of a pharmaceutical company that shipped adulterated and misbranded products in interstate commerce. He was convicted of violating the Food, Drug, and Cosmetic Act. The Court upheld the conviction based on proof that Dotterweich had a "responsible share in the furtherance of the transaction."

Dotterweich, 320 U.S. at 284. *Dotterweich* involved a strict liability offense where the public welfare was threatened. Is the responsible corporate officer doctrine appropriate for strict liability offenses?

4. *The "no intent" defense.* In many of the recent corporate scandals, chief executives have claimed that they are not liable for corporate wrongdoing because they did not intend to commit a crime. These executives have claimed that they simply relied on the assurances of managers and on the advice of attorneys and accountants. To support this claim, the executives have often minimized their own roles in their corporations. How much evidence should be required to prosecute a corporate executive? How can prosecutors go about obtaining this evidence?

5. *Responsible corporate officers.* What arguments can executives advance that they were not "responsible corporate officers" for purposes of criminal liability?

Problems

2-3. David acquired a wastewater treatment facility. The facility treated water for various municipalities. During his association with the facility, David changed the name several times, eventually calling it Crystal Clear Processing Corp. ("CCP"). David moved CCP's operations to a new location and controlled the finances. His name did not appear on the corporate records and he did not have a formal association with CCP in its daily operations. David had an office at CCP, where he maintained the books and records but did not otherwise exercise managerial authority. CCP employed 50 people.

In an effort to secure a contract from the City of Water's Edge, CCP's general manager Klark acquired a special carbon filtration system. Although this system was to be used as a final step in water treatment, and was not intended to be used on untreated water, CCP used it as the sole treatment process. The salesperson who sold the filtration system told Klark and David that the system would not function properly unless it was preceded by a more comprehensive filtration system. David inspected the carbon filtration system on at least one occasion, and did not install an additional filtration system.

CCP began to "treat" the water in the Water's Edge community. CCP began to discharge untreated water into the municipality's sewage facility. Based on this conduct, CCP was criminally charged with violating federal law that required the pretreatment of water under the Clean Water Act. Each count alleged that David committed the violations as the responsible corporate officer. The provision of the Clean Water Act under which David was charged applies to "any person who negligently violates the pretreatment requirements." The law defines a person as an "individual, corporation, partnership, association," and extends liability to "any responsible corporate officer."

> *a. David comes to you seeking legal advice to defend against the charges. David tells you that he was never formally designated as a corporate officer of CCP and that he never exercised sufficient control over the operations to*

come under the law's parameters. What additional information do you need to know in order to defend him?

b. You are the prosecutor in this case. Do you have sufficient information to establish that David had the required mens rea? Do you need any additional information to proceed with prosecution?

c. Is Klark, CCP's general manager, criminally liable for the conduct in the processing of the water for Water's Edge? What theories would apply to Klark?

2-4. Harvey was the manager of Harvey's Cars, a car dealership located in Oklahoma. The dealership was a subsidiary of General Autos, located in Texas. Harvey sold cars under a licensing agreement with General Autos. Harvey ran the dealership's day-to-day operations. He had authority to hire and fire employees and to sign and process all payroll checks. General Autos was running its spring sale campaign and offered customers the option of receiving rebate checks when they purchased certain current-model cars. The rebate campaign applied to all of General Autos' dealerships. The rebate checks were issued from the corporate offices of General Autos once the sale was completed and were sent to each of the participating dealerships for them to forward to the qualifying customer. This procedure was designed to allow for the dealership to have additional contact with the customer in order to provide additional goods and services.

Harvey's Cars was in financial trouble because it was not meeting its quarterly goals. Harvey began to not advise certain customers that their car purchases would qualify for the national rebate being offered by General Autos. In addition, he falsely told certain customers that their particular cars were not covered by the rebate or that the program had expired at the end of the previous month. Because the rebates applied to all of these purchases, when Harvey processed the paperwork, he included the rebate request in the submission to General Autos and forwarded it with all of the other documentation. Harvey then deposited the rebates into an account held by Harvey's Cars. The government seeks to charge General Autos with fraud based upon Harvey's acts.

a. Assume the role of the prosecution or defense in this case. Assume that the jurisdiction has not yet determined whether to follow the respondeat superior or the MPC approach to corporate criminal liability. Argue for the adoption of the approach that best supports your case.

b. Argue for and against General Autos' liability under each approach.

2. The Public Welfare Doctrine

While the responsible corporate officer doctrine helps prosecutors when it comes to establishing actus reus, the public welfare doctrine is about mens rea. As mentioned in the previous chapter, federal criminal laws are often ambiguous in regard to mens rea. The public welfare doctrine is an interpretive rule according to which, when no mens rea is specified in a statute or the mens rea is ambiguous, courts will generally require a mens rea of recklessness or negligence (rather than purpose or knowledge) when dangerous devices or obnoxious waste are involved. In the words of the Supreme Court,

> [A]s long as a defendant knows that he is dealing with a dangerous device of a character that places him "in responsible relation to a public danger," he should be alerted to the probability of strict regulation, and we have assumed that in such cases Congress intended to place the burden on the defendant to "ascertain at his peril whether [his conduct] comes within the inhibition of the statute."

Staples v. United States, 511 U.S. 600, 607 (1994) (internal citations omitted). The public welfare doctrine eases the burden on prosecutors when bringing cases where public safety is at stake. This is generally thought to be an efficient result because the party who is in control of the dangerous device or obnoxious waste is typically in a better position to prevent its potentially harmful effects than are the potential victims.

However, application of the public welfare doctrine is not automatic when dangerous materials or obnoxious wastes are involved. Courts will often also refer to factors such as:

1. How severe the potential penalty is.

2. How dangerous the regulated conduct is.

3. How probable public harm resulting from the conduct is.

4. How obvious it is that the defendant's conduct is likely to be subject to regulation.

5. Whether applying the doctrine would risk criminalizing innocent conduct.

How do you expect the factors would bear on the likelihood of a court applying the public welfare doctrine? As you read the following case, consider which way each of the factors leans.

United States v. International Minerals & Chemical Corp.

402 U.S. 558 (1971)

MR. JUSTICE DOUGLAS delivered the opinion of the Court.

The information charged that appellee shipped sulfuric acid and hydrofluosilicic acid in interstate commerce and 'did knowingly fail to show on the shipping papers the required classification of said property, to wit, Corrosive Liquid, in violation of 49 C.F.R. 173.427.'

Title 18 U.S.C. s 834(a) gives the Interstate Commerce Commission power to 'formulate regulations for the safe transportation' of 'corrosive liquids' and 18 U.S.C. s 834(f) states that whoever 'knowingly violates any such regulation' shall be fined or imprisoned.

Pursuant to the power granted by s 834(a) the regulatory agency promulgated the regulation already cited which reads in part:

'Each shipper offering for transportation any hazardous material subject to the regulations in this chapter, shall describe that article on the shipping paper by the shipping name prescribed in s 172.5 of this chapter and by the classification prescribed in s 172.4 of this chapter, and may add a further description not inconsistent therewith. Abbreviations must not be used.' 49 CFR s 173.427. . . .

The sole and narrow question is whether 'knowledge' of the regulation is also required. It is in that narrow zone that the issue of 'mens rea' is raised; and appellee bears down hard on the provision in 18 U.S.C. s 834(f) that whoever 'knowingly violates any such regulation' shall be fined, etc. . . .

There is no issue in the present case of the propriety of the delegation of the power to establish regulations and of the validity of the regulation at issue. We therefore see no reason why the word 'regulations' should not be construed as a shorthand designation for specific acts or omissions which violate the Act. The Act, so viewed, does not signal an exception to the rule that ignorance of the law is no excuse and is wholly consistent with the legislative history. . . .

In *St. Johnsbury Trucking Co. v. United States*, 220 F.2d 393, 397, Chief Judge Magruder had concluded that knowledge of the regulations was necessary. But whether the House Committee was referring to *Boyce Motor Lines* or the opinion of Chief Judge Magruder is not clear since both views of the section were before Congress. It is clear that strict liability was not intended. The Senate Committee felt it would be too stringent and thus rejected the position of the Interstate Commerce Commission. But despite protestations of avoiding strict liability the Senate version was very likely to result in strict liability because knowledge of the facts would have been unnecessary and anyone involved in the business of shipping dangerous materials would very likely know of the regulations involved. Thus in rejecting the Senate version the House was rejecting strict liability. But it is too much to conclude that in rejecting strict liability the House was also carving out an exception to the general rule that ignorance of the law is no excuse.

The principle that ignorance of the law is no defense applies whether the law be a statute or a duly promulgated and published regulation. In the context of these proposed 1960 amendments we decline to attribute to Congress the inaccurate view that that Act requires proof of knowledge of the law, as well as the facts, and that it intended to endorse that interpretation by retaining the word 'knowingly.' We conclude that the meager legislative history of the 1960 amendments makes unwarranted the conclusion that Congress abandoned the general rule and required knowledge of both the facts and the pertinent law before a criminal conviction could be sustained under this Act.

So far as possession, say, of sulfuric acid is concerned the requirement of 'mens rea' has been made a requirement of the Act as evidenced by the use of the word 'knowingly.' A person thinking in good faith that he was shipping distilled water when in fact he was shipping some dangerous acid would not be covered. As stated in *Morissette v. United States*, 342 U.S. 246, 250 (1952):

'The contention that an injury can amount to a crime only when inflicted by intention is no provincial or transient notion. It is as universal and persistent in mature systems of law as belief in freedom of the human will and a consequent ability and duty of the normal individual to choose between good and evil.'

There is leeway for the exercise of congressional discretion in applying the reach of 'mens rea.' *United States v. Balint*, 258 U.S. 250 (1922). *United States v. Murdock*, 290 U.S. 389 (1933), closely confined the word 'willfully' in the income tax law to include a purpose to bring about the forbidden result:

'He whose conduct is defined as criminal is one who 'willfully' fails to pay the tax, to make a return, to keep the required records, or to supply the needed information. Congress did not intend that a person, by reason of a bona fide misunderstanding as to his liability for the tax, as to his duty to make a return, or as to the adequacy of the records he maintained, should become a criminal by his mere failure to measure up to the prescribed standard of conduct. And the requirement that the omission in these instances must be willful, to be criminal, is persuasive that the same element is essential to the offense of failing to supply information.' Id., at 396.

In *Balint* the Court was dealing with drugs, in *Freed* with hand grenades, in this case with sulfuric and other dangerous acids. Pencils, dental floss, paper clips may also be regulated. But they may be the type of products which might raise substantial due process questions if Congress did not require, as in *Murdock*, 'mens rea' as to each ingredient of the offense. But where, as here and as in *Balint* and *Freed*, dangerous or deleterious devices or products or obnoxious waste materials are involved, the probability of regulation is so great that anyone who is aware that he is in possession of them or dealing with them must be presumed to be aware of the regulation.

Reversed.

Mr. Justice Stewart, with whom Mr. Justice Harlan and Mr. Justice Brennan join, dissenting.

This case stirs large questions — questions that go to the moral foundations of the criminal law. Whether postulated as a problem of 'mens rea,' of 'willfulness,' of 'criminal responsibility,' or of 'scienter,' the infliction of criminal punishment upon the unaware has long troubled the fair administration of justice. But there is no occasion here for involvement with this root problem of criminal jurisprudence, for it is evident to me that Congress made punishable only knowing violations of the regulation in question. That is what the law quite clearly says, what the federal courts have held, and what the legislative history confirms.

The statutory language is hardly complex. Section 834(a) of Title 18, U.S.C., gives the regulatory agency power to 'formulate regulations for the safe transportation' of, among other things, 'corrosive liquids.' Section 834(f) provides that '(w)hoever knowingly violates any such regulation shall be fined not more than $1,000 or imprisoned not more than one year, or both.' In dismissing the information in this case because it did not charge the appellee shipper with knowing violation of the applicable labeling regulation, District Judge Porter did no more than give effect to the ordinary meaning of the English language. . . .

The Court today thus grants to the Executive Branch what Congress explicitly refused to grant in 1960. It effectively deletes the word 'knowingly' from the law. I cannot join the Court in this exercise, requiring as it does such a total disregard of plain statutory language, established judicial precedent, and explicit legislative history. . . .

I respectfully dissent from the opinion and judgment of the Court.

Notes and Questions

1. *Strict liability.* In statutory interpretation, courts apply a presumption against strict liability crimes. Even if a statute specifies no mens rea, courts will generally read the statute to require intent, unless the statute explicitly makes a contrary congressional purpose clear. Does the public welfare doctrine violate that interpretive presumption? If the public welfare doctrine applies, could it convert a statute into a strict liability statute? Would the result in *International Minerals* be any different if the defendant thought the shipping container was loaded with marshmallows rather than dangerous chemicals?

2. *Innocent conduct.* One of the factors courts consider in applying the public welfare doctrine is whether a lower mens rea would end up criminalizing innocent conduct. What should "innocent" mean here? Non-dangerous? Morally unobjectionable? Not obviously subject to regulation? Commonplace?

Problem

2-5. Splat is a major manufacturer of oil-based paint and a supplier to local hardware stores. As part of its go-green campaign this quarter, Splat advertised free recycling of empty paint canisters. Unfortunately, customers started returning all sorts of paint — not just Splat brand — and distributors soon became overwhelmed by the number of cans they were receiving from local stores. John, a low-level manager of a Splat distribution center, directed his workers to toss the non-Splat brand products in the dumpster, but continue to properly dispose of the donated Splat containers.

> *a. Splat is charged with "improper disposal of a Class IV carcinogen." The statute provides a detailed definition of "Class IV" carcinogen, but states no mens rea element. What mens rea, if any, might the court read into the statute?*

> *b. Would your answer change if all paint containers were affixed, as required by statute, with disposal instructions printed on the packaging?*

> *c. Under your answers to the previous two questions, is Splat likely to be convicted?*

Chapter 3

Conspiracy

A. Introductory Notes

1. The Importance of a Conspiracy Charge

Conspiracy is an inchoate offense that is frequently charged in federal and state criminal cases. In the simplest terms, a conspiracy exists whenever two or more people agree to commit a criminal offense. Some modern statutes, such as the general federal conspiracy statute (18 U.S.C. § 371), also require that the government prove an "overt act" in furtherance of the conspiracy. Because white collar crimes often involve multiple actors, a conspiracy charge is common in white collar cases. For example, a corporate officer who gives a stockbroker secret corporate information that the broker uses to trade stock may well be guilty conspiring with the broker to commit insider trading.

The crime of conspiracy is the principal avenue for punishing uncompleted white collar criminal conduct.[a] Under federal law, conspiracy does not merge with the crimes that are the objects of the conspiracy. Thus, if the criminal objectives are achieved, the co-conspirators generally may be punished both for the crime of conspiracy and for the object crimes.

As noted by Justice Jackson in his oft-cited concurring opinion in *Krulewitch v. United States*, 336 U.S. 440, 446 (1949), conspiracy is a controversial crime. The boundaries of the crime are notoriously unclear; as Justice Jackson wrote, conspiracy is "so vague that it almost defies definition." *Id.* Thus, prosecutors have tremendous discretion in deciding when to bring a conspiracy charge. In addition, as discussed in the cases below, a conspiracy charge provides the prosecutor with substantial strategic and tactical advantages.

---

a. There is no general provision that criminalizes all attempts to commit federal crimes, but there are statutes that criminalize attempts to commit specific federal crimes. *See, e.g.,* 18 U.S.C. § 1349 (Chapter 63 — Mail Fraud and Other Fraud Offenses); 21 U.S.C.A. § 846 (narcotics offenses). In addition, some specific federal criminal statutes impose inchoate liability under the terms of the statutes themselves. For example, the federal obstruction of justice statute criminalizes "endeavors" to obstruct justice. *See* 18 U.S.C. § 1503, discussed in Chapter 11, Extortion, *infra*. And the criminal tax evasion statute applies to "[a]ny person who willfully attempts in any manner to evade or defeat any tax." 26 U.S.C. § 7201, discussed in Chapter 12, Tax Fraud, *infra*. In fact, many white collar crimes may be considered to be inchoate offenses. Fraud offenses, for example, require a scheme to defraud, but do not require that the scheme succeed in order for the defendant to be liable. *See, e.g.,* Chapter 4, Mail Fraud, Wire Fraud, and Related Offenses, *infra*.

2. Advantages of a Conspiracy Charge

Including a conspiracy charge in a white collar case places the prosecution at an advantage, and the defense at a disadvantage, in several important ways. Most importantly, a conspiracy charge enables the government to bring together at a single trial all defendants who were allegedly part of the conspiracy, including minor participants against whom the evidence may not be strong.

As to venue, the government may bring the conspiracy case in any district where the agreement was entered into or where any co-conspirator committed any act in furtherance of the conspiracy. It may advantage the government to bring the case in a venue that is convenient for the government and/or inconvenient for the defense.

A conspiracy charge also gives the government important evidentiary advantages. First, a conspiracy charge typically expands the scope of relevant evidence. Thus, evidence as to any co-conspirators' acts in furtherance of the conspiracy may be admissible. Second, as discussed in § E, 2 below, co-conspirator statements made during and in furtherance of a conspiracy are admissible under the "co-conspirators exception" to the hearsay rule.

A defendant charged with conspiracy also faces possible expanded liability. As noted above, the defendant can be found guilty both of the conspiracy and of the conspiracy's object crimes. And, as discussed in § F below, the defendant may also be vicariously liable for substantive offenses committed by other co-conspirators.

Finally, including a conspiracy charge may also extend the statute of limitations, which does not begin to run until the conspiratorial goals are achieved or abandoned. Even if the limitations period for some or all of the conspiracy's object crimes has expired, all co-conspirators may be liable for the *crime of conspiracy* so long as any co-conspirator committed an overt act within five years of the indictment. This delayed running of the statute of limitations may benefit the government substantially in cases where co-conspirators continue to commit overt acts even after the conspiracy's goals have been largely accomplished.

3. Federal Conspiracy Statutes

Federal law contains both a general conspiracy provision and more specific conspiracy provisions. The general conspiracy law is set forth at § 371 of the criminal code, 18 U.S.C. § 371. Federal law also contains distinct provisions that criminalize conspiring to commit certain types of offenses, such as narcotics, antitrust, and racketeering offenses (*see, e.g.,* 21 U.S.C. § 846; 15 U.S.C. §§ 1, 2; 18 U.S.C. § 1962(d)). Furthermore, the Sarbanes-Oxley Act, passed in response to financial scandals of the early twenty-first century, includes a conspiracy statute specifically applicable to a number of white collar crimes, including mail and wire fraud and certain financial crimes. (18 U.S.C. § 1349). Most federal conspiracy charges arise under § 371, and it is upon that statute that this chapter focuses.

4. The Elements of Conspiracy

a. Section 371

Section 371 provides: "If two or more persons conspire either to commit any offense against the United States, or to defraud the United States, or any agency thereof in any manner or for any purpose, and one or more of such persons do any act to effect the object of the conspiracy, each shall be fined under this title or imprisoned not more than five years, or both." Under this statute, the government must show that:

(1) An agreement existed to

    (a) commit an offense against the United States, *and/or*

    (b) defraud the United States;

(2) Two or more persons were parties to that agreement (the "plurality" requirement);

(3) The defendant intended

    (a) to enter into the agreement, *and*

    (b) that the object offense or fraud come to pass; *and*

(4) A co-conspirator committed an "overt act" in furtherance of the offense.

The precise level of intent, or mens rea, required for conspiracy is the subject of § B below.

b. The "Plurality" Requirement

Because so many white collar cases arise in the corporate context, complex issues may arise as to whether the plurality requirement has been satisfied. For example, two or more corporations, or a corporation and its subsidiary, are capable of conspiring with one another. Thus, a conspiracy may exist solely between or among artificial entities. Also, a corporation may be vicariously liable under respondeat superior for a conspiracy entered into by its agents. Finally, special rules apply to antitrust law, which focuses on unlawful business combinations. The United States Supreme Court held that, under Section 1 of the Sherman Act, 15 U.S.C. § 1, a conspiracy cannot be composed solely of a corporation and its wholly owned subsidiary, or solely of a corporation and agents who are acting on behalf of the corporation. *Copperweld Corp. v. Independence Tube Corp.*, 467 U.S. 752, 769 (1984) ("The officers of a single firm are not separate economic actors pursuing separate economic interests, so . . . officers or employees of the same firm do not provide the plurality of actors imperative for a § 1 conspiracy."). For an analysis of this rule, see J.S. Nelson, *The Intracorporate Conspiracy Trap*, 36 CARDOZA L. REV. 969 (2015).

c. The Overt Act Requirement

Under the common law, the actus reus of conspiracy was the agreement itself. Many modern conspiracy statutes follow the same approach.[b] Some statutes, including § 371, also require that the government prove an "overt act" in furtherance of the conspiracy. This requirement serves to corroborate the conspiratorial intent that is at the heart of the crime.

The overt act requirement is not hard to meet. Any act by a coconspirator that occurs during the conspiracy and in furtherance of the conspiracy will qualify. This could include, for example, sending an email, introducing participants in the conspiracy, or traveling to a location for purposes of furthering the conspiracy. Significantly, the overt act need not meet the test required for the actus reus of attempt at common law; the overt act need not constitute a "substantial step" toward nor be "dangerously proximate" to the criminal objective, as attempt liability would require. Thus, a conspiracy prosecution rarely fails for lack of an overt act.

Coconspirators are considered to be agents of each other. An overt act by one coconspirator will therefore meet the proof requirement for all coconspirators who are members of the conspiracy, even if they join later. *See Salinas v. United States*, 522 U.S. 52 (1997).

5. Sentencing

The maximum sentence under § 371 is five years. As with all federal crimes, however, the actual sentence will depend on the application of the federal sentencing guidelines to the facts of the case. *See* Chapter 19, Sentencing, *infra*. In conspiracy cases, the sentences are tied to those for the substantive offenses, and thus will vary considerably from case to case.

B. Mens Rea

The crime of conspiracy is often considered difficult to prove. Because it is primarily a mental crime, the existence of a conspiracy is usually demonstrated by circumstantial evidence. With respect to proving the necessary intent, or mens rea, the United States Supreme Court has stated that "in a conspiracy, two different types of intent are generally required — the basic intent to agree, which is necessary to establish the existence of the conspiracy, and the more traditional intent to effectuate the object of the conspiracy." *United States v. United States Gypsum Co.*, 438 U.S. 422, 444 n.20 (1978). In order to enter into a criminal conspiracy, a defendant thus must have some knowledge of its wrongful objective. With respect to the knowledge

---

b. *See, e.g.*, 18 U.S.C. § 1962(d) (RICO conspiracy), discussed in the Chapter 14, RICO, *infra*.

requirement, as is true in other areas of white collar crime, courts hold that proof of "willful blindness," also known as "constructive knowledge" or "conscious avoidance," will suffice.

The next case applies the willful blindness standard to a conspiracy to trade securities on inside information. Very generally, and as explained more fully in Chapter 5, Securities Fraud, *infra*, the crime of insider trading may occur when a "tipper" (Svoboda in the case below), acting in breach of a fiduciary duty, provides material, nonpublic information to a "tippee" (Robles in the case) who trades on the information with knowledge that it is material, nonpublic information obtained by breach of duty. (The law also has particular restrictions applicable to trading with respect to tender offers, where the offering company offers to buy all of a "target" company's stock at a specified price over the then-current market price for the stock.)

As you read the decision, consider why courts allow the government to satisfy the knowledge element even in the absence of proof of actual knowledge. Also consider whether this approach is fair to defendants.

United States v. Svoboda

347 F.3d 471 (2d Cir. 2003)

SCULLIN, Chief District Judge.

[A]fter a thirteen-day jury trial, Robles was convicted of one count of conspiracy to commit securities and tender offer fraud pursuant to 18 U.S.C. §371 and thirteen individual securities and tender offer fraud counts. On appeal, Robles principally contends that the district court erred in giving a conscious avoidance instruction with respect to the conspiracy charge. . . .

At trial, the Government sought to prove that Robles and his long-time friend Richard Svoboda[4] engaged in a conspiracy to commit securities and tender offer fraud for profit between approximately November 1994 and December 1997. During that period, Svoboda was employed in Dallas, Texas, as a "credit policy officer" at Nations Bank, a financial institution engaged, *inter alia,* in commercial lending. As a credit policy officer, Svoboda was charged with structuring and approving loans to corporate clients. In the course of his duties at Nations Bank, Svoboda was privy to confidential information about Nations Bank's clients, such as earnings information and merger and acquisition plans. Svoboda testified that he obtained confidential information about certain securities and tender offers through his position at Nations Bank; that he passed the information to Robles, who, in turn, used the insider information to make trades; and that he and Robles shared the profits realized from their illicit trading. Svoboda further testified that he and Robles discussed and agreed upon the details of the above-described scheme and that Robles was

---

4. Svoboda was originally indicted along with Robles but later entered into a plea agreement with the Government in which he agreed, *inter alia,* to testify against Robles at trial.

fully aware that he was trading on the basis of unlawfully obtained insider information. Robles, however, took the stand in his own defense and denied knowledge of the unlawful source of Svoboda's information.

At the close of evidence, the Government requested a conscious avoidance instruction; i.e., an instruction to the effect that the Government could satisfy its obligation to prove Robles' knowledge of the unlawful source of the information by proving that he deliberately avoided acquiring that knowledge. Over Robles' objection, the district court granted the Government's request and included a conscious avoidance instruction in the jury charge.[5]

The instant case requires us to determine whether and under what circumstances the doctrine of conscious avoidance may be employed in a conspiracy prosecution. Robles' principal contention on appeal is that the conscious avoidance doctrine cannot be employed in the course of establishing a conspiratorial agreement between two persons. We disagree.

Robles was convicted of conspiracy to engage in insider trading under 18 U.S.C. § 371 . . . . A conspiracy conviction under § 371 requires proof of three essential elements: (1) an agreement among two or more persons, the object of which is an offense against the United States; (2) the defendant's knowing and willful joinder in that conspiracy; and (3) commission of an overt act in furtherance of the conspiracy by at least one of the alleged co-conspirators. . . .[6]

"The gist of conspiracy is, of course, agreement." *United States v. Beech-Nut Nutrition Corp.,* 871 F.2d 1181, 1191 (2d Cir. 1989). "A conspiracy need not be shown by proof of an explicit agreement but can be established by showing that the parties have a tacit understanding to carry out the prohibited conduct." *United States v. Samaria,* 239 F.3d 228, 234 (2d Cir.2001). In either case, "the evidence must be

---

5. While objecting to the giving of a conscious avoidance charge, Robles requested that the district court utilize Judge Sand's model instruction rather than the Government's proposed instruction. The district court granted Robles' request and instructed the jury as follows:

> In determining whether the defendant acted knowingly, you may consider whether the defendant deliberately closed his eyes to what would otherwise have been obvious to him. If you find, beyond a reasonable doubt, that the defendant acted with a conscious purpose to avoid learning the truth, that he was trading on the basis of insider information, then this element may be satisfied.
>
> However, guilty knowledge may not be established by demonstrating that the defendant was merely negligent, foolish or mistaken. If you find that the defendant was aware of a high probability that he was trading on the basis of insider information, and that the defendant acted with a deliberate disregard of the facts, you may find that the defendant acted knowingly. However, if you find that the defendant actually believed that he was not receiving insider information, he may not be convicted.

6. We note that this formulation of the elements of conspiracy under § 371 is somewhat redundant when applied to a scheme involving only two persons. . . . [T]o find that an agreement existed amongst the alleged conspirators, the finder of fact must necessarily find some knowledge of the aims of the agreement and the intent to bring them about.

sufficient to permit the jury to infer that the defendant and other alleged coconspirators entered into a joint enterprise with consciousness of its general nature and extent." *United States v. Beech-Nut Nutrition Corp.,* 871 F.2d 1181, 1191 (2d Cir. 1989).

Conspiracies are secretive by their very nature, and it is thus well-settled that the elements of a conspiracy may be proved by circumstantial evidence. . . .

In certain conspiracy prosecutions, the Government often seeks to prove that a particular defendant joined a preexisting conspiracy. In other cases, the question is whether a conspiracy existed at all and, if so, whether a particular defendant was a party to the alleged conspiratorial agreement. Of course, the nature of the evidence used to establish the existence of a conspiratorial agreement may vary slightly, depending on the circumstances of the case. In the case of a preexisting conspiracy, the critical evidentiary question is often whether the defendant joined in the charged conspiracy (1) with some knowledge of the conspiracy's unlawful aims and (2) with the intent of helping the scheme succeed. In other cases, the evidentiary question is frequently whether there is proof that the defendant (1) had knowledge of the unlawful aims of the charged scheme and (2) evinced, by his actions, an intention to further or promote its unlawful aims. In either case, the fundamental legal question is the same: whether the evidence establishes beyond a reasonable doubt that a particular defendant entered into an agreement with others with knowledge of the criminal purpose of the scheme and with the specific intent to aid in the accomplishment of those unlawful ends.

"The conscious avoidance doctrine provides that a defendant's knowledge of a fact required to prove the defendant's guilt may be found when the jury is persuaded that the defendant consciously avoided learning that fact while aware of a high probability of its existence." *Samaria,* 239 F.3d at 239. "In such circumstances, a conscious avoidance instruction to the jury permits a finding of knowledge even where there is no evidence that the defendant possessed actual knowledge." *Id.*

Relying on dictum in one of our opinions, *United States v. Reyes,* 302 F.3d 48, 54 (2d Cir.2002), Robles contends that "the doctrine of conscious avoidance cannot be used at all in the context of a two-person conspiracy." We disagree. The *Reyes* decision does not mean what Robles reads into it. Even if it did, it would not support his argument.

In *Reyes,* we upheld the defendant's conviction by the jury, overturning the district court's grant of a directed verdict. The defendant was in the business of selling auto parts. The jury found him guilty of engaging in the transportation and sale of stolen airbags and conspiracy to do the same. There was evidence that the defendant, when being interviewed by an FBI agent, said he was aware that the bags were stolen, making "an analogy to . . . when you see a friend using drugs, you see what's happening, but you turn the other way." *Id.* at 52. In analyzing the sufficiency of the evidence to support the conviction, we found that the evidence was sufficient to prove that the defendant knew the airbags were stolen, or in any event "thought the airbags were stolen, but deliberately avoided confirming that fact." *Id.* at 56. We further found that evidence supported the defendant's intentional participation in the conspiracy.

Prior to analyzing the evidence, our opinion discoursed on the nature of the conscious avoidance doctrine and observed, "[We] do not permit the doctrine to be used to prove intent to participate in a conspiracy." *Id.* at 54. This observation played no role in the decision.

Robles relies on this sentence for his argument. His argument is essentially that conspiracy by definition requires the participation of two or more conspirators, both of whom must intend to participate. If intent to participate may not be proved by reliance on conscious avoidance, then in a case of only two conspirators where the prosecution must rely on the doctrine of conscious avoidance to prove intent to participate on the part of one, the necessary proof of intent to participate by at least two conspirators will be lacking.

This argument fails for three reasons. First, the statement in *Reyes* on which Robles relies was pure dictum. As noted, it played no role whatever in the decision, which was to *uphold* the defendant's conviction upon the jury's guilty verdict. . . .

Second, the district court's instruction [in this case] did not conflict with the *Reyes* dictum. The court instructed the jury only to the effect that, "[i]n determining whether the defendant acted *knowingly,* you may consider whether the defendant deliberately closed his eyes to what would otherwise have been obvious to him." In giving the instruction, the court made no reference to the defendant's "intent to participate."

Finally, we doubt that the dictum in *Reyes* intended what the defendant reads into it. The broad assertion that conscious avoidance may not be used to prove "intent to participate" has a capacity to cause confusion, and Robles' argument draws on that confusion. Properly understood, "intent to participate" is a shorthand phrase used to encompass both aspects of the joinder element of conspiracy, i.e., a defendant's knowledge or awareness of the illegal nature of the charged activity and his intent to advance the illegal objective.[8]

Thus, when *Reyes* states that conscious avoidance cannot prove intent to participate, we do not understand it to mean that conscious avoidance cannot be used to prove any aspect of intent to participate; it simply means that just as actual

---

8. It is to ensure that jurors do not mistakenly conflate the knowledge and intent aspects of the mens rea necessary to prove a defendant's joinder in a conspiracy that trial judges routinely charge:

> Mere knowledge [of a criminal conspiracy] . . . without participation, in the unlawful plan is not sufficient. Moreover, the fact that . . . a defendant, without knowledge, merely happen[s to act] to further the purposes or objectives of the conspiracy, does not make the defendant a member. . . . What is necessary is that the defendant must have participated with knowledge of at least some of the purposes or objectives of the conspiracy and with the intention of aiding in the accomplishment of those unlawful ends.

1 L. Sand et al., MODERN FEDERAL JURY INSTRUCTIONS 18-6.

knowledge of the illegal purpose of a conspiracy is insufficient to prove a defendant's joinder in a conspiracy, so conscious avoidance of such knowledge is also insufficient. There must be further proof that the defendant joined in the illegal agreement with the intent of helping it succeed in its criminal purpose.

In sum, we can see no reason why the factfinder may not rely on conscious avoidance to satisfy at least the knowledge component of intent to participate in a conspiracy. . . . [9] The defendant's conscious avoidance of knowledge of the unlawful aims of the conspiracy thus may be invoked as the equivalent of knowledge of those unlawful aims. In the context of a two-person conspiracy, intent to participate may be shown by a finding that the defendant either knew, or consciously avoided knowing, the unlawful aims of the charged scheme and intended to advance those unlawful ends.

Having found no doctrinal obstacle to employing a conscious avoidance instruction in the context of a two-person conspiracy, we now turn to the question of whether the facts in the instant case support such an instruction. . . .

A conscious avoidance instruction "may only be given if (1) the defendant asserts the lack of some specific aspect of knowledge required for conviction, . . . and (2) the appropriate factual predicate for the charge exists, i.e., 'the evidence is such that a rational juror may reach [the] conclusion beyond a reasonable doubt . . . that [the defendant] was aware of a high probability [of the fact in dispute] and consciously avoided confirming that fact[.]'" *Unites States v. Ferrarini*, 219 F.3d 145, 154 (2d Cir. 2000) (internal citations omitted). The second prong of this test thus has two components — there must be evidence that the defendant (1) was aware of a high probability of the disputed fact and (2) deliberately avoided confirming that fact. . . .

Here, the first prerequisite is easily met, as Robles denied knowledge of the unlawful source of Svoboda's investment advice. The second prerequisite is also easily met. First, the source of Svoboda's information was suspicious — Robles knew that Svoboda was a credit officer at Nations Bank and would thus be privy to confidential financial information. Second, the timing of Robles' trades was suspicious — for example, some of Robles' trades occurred as little as a day before a tender offer announcement. Third, the success of the trades was suspicious — Robles realized large returns, up to 400%, on trades based on Svoboda's advice. These facts suggest a high probability that Svoboda's tips were based on inside information and that any lack of actual knowledge on Robles' part was due to a conscious effort to avoid confirming an otherwise obvious fact. We therefore find that there was a sufficient factual predicate in the instant case to warrant a conscious avoidance instruction.

---

9. Significantly, Robles *does not* challenge the sufficiency of the evidence supporting his conspiracy conviction. Accordingly, we assume, for purposes of this appeal, that the evidence was, in fact, sufficient to establish beyond a reasonable doubt (1) Robles' knowledge that he was trading on inside information and (2) his active participation in the charged scheme. We have no difficulty concluding that this evidence provides a proper evidentiary foundation, as a matter of law, to infer the existence of an agreement to violate federal securities laws.

Finally, Robles argues that, even if the conscious avoidance instruction was theoretically proper, its content impermissibly diluted the *mens rea* requirement for the conspiracy charge, i.e., specific intent to engage in the proscribed conduct, and thus allowed the jury to convict on a negligence theory. . . .

[Robles's] argument is unavailing. To begin, the conscious avoidance instruction itself made clear that "guilty knowledge may not be established by demonstrating that the defendant was merely negligent, foolish or mistaken." Moreover, the jury charge, taken as a whole, repeatedly and emphatically instructed the jury that it had to find that Robles intentionally engaged in the charged scheme. [The court instructed the jury that "the government must prove beyond a reasonable doubt that Mr. Robles knowingly, *willfully*, and unlawfully entered into the conspiracy. . . . Willfully means to act with knowledge that one's conduct is unlawful *and with the intent* to do something that the law forbids. . . .") (emphasis added). Accordingly, although the conspiracy charge made reference to knowledge of the illegal scheme, it also "clearly and conjunctively" required a finding of intent to participate. We therefore perceive no error in the substance of the charge.

For the foregoing reasons, the judgment of the district court is hereby AFFIRMED.

Notes and Questions

1. *Appellate practice.* Many of the cases in this text raise issues of appellate practice in addition to substantive legal issues. In this case, what precisely are the defendant's arguments? Did he raise issues of law? Of fact? What is the standard of appellate review for these issues?

2. *Two levels of mens rea.* As noted above, the government must prove two levels of mens rea in a conspiracy case: (1) the intent to agree and (2) the intent that the object offense(s) be committed. As the Court in *Svoboda* stated, the evidence must "establish beyond a reasonable doubt that a particular defendant entered into an agreement with others [1] with knowledge of the criminal purpose of the scheme and [2] with the specific intent to aid in the accomplishment of those unlawful ends." At least on the second level of mens rea, then, conspiracy is generally considered to be a "specific intent" crime. Why is this high level of mens rea required in conspiracy cases?

3. *Conscious avoidance and the* Global-Tech *decision.* What is the conscious avoidance doctrine, often termed "willful blindness"? What is the basis for the defendant's argument that it should not have been applied in the above case? Of course, the conscious avoidance doctrine is not limited to conspiracy cases, but generally applies when proof of knowledge is an element of a crime. Why do courts allow proof of "knowledge" based upon evidence that concededly may not show actual knowledge?

The United States Supreme Court defined willful blindness as follows:

[T]he Courts of Appeals . . . all appear to agree on two basic requirements [for willful blindness]: (1) the defendant must subjectively believe that there

is a high probability that a fact exists and (2) the defendant must take deliberate actions to avoid learning of that fact. We think these requirements
give willful blindness an appropriately limited scope that surpasses recklessness and negligence. Under this formulation, a willfully blind defendant
is one who takes deliberate actions to avoid confirming a high probability of
wrongdoing and who can almost be said to have actually known the critical
facts.

Global-Tech Appliances, Inc. v. SEB S.A., 563 U.S. 754, 769 (2011).

By requiring proof that the defendant undertook "deliberate actions" to avoid
learning the truth, the Supreme Court in *Global-Tech* seemed to adopt a stricter
willful blindness standard than had existed in many circuits. *See* Jeremy Adler &
Dane C. Ball, *Improving 'Willful Blindness' Jury Instructions in Criminal Cases After
High Court's Decision in* Global-Tech, 6 WHITE COLLAR CRIME REP. (BNA) 762
(2011). Nonetheless, lower courts generally seem to assume that *Global-Tech* did not
alter existing law. *See, e.g., United States v. Hale*, 857 F.3d 158, 173 (4th Cir. 2017);
United States v. Thomson, 634 Fed. Appx. 100 (4th Cir. 2016); *United States v. Gof-
fer*, 721 F.3d 113, 127–28 (2d Cir. 2013); *United States v. Jinwright*, 683; F.3d 471, 480
(4th Cir. 2012), *cert. denied*, 568 U.S. 1093 (2013).

Although *Global-Tech* was a civil case, the Court used criminal law mens rea concepts throughout its decision. The case thus has important implications for federal
criminal cases. *See* 563 at 2072 (Kennedy, J., dissenting) ("[t]he Court appears to
endorse the willful blindness doctrine here for all federal criminal cases involving
knowledge."). Courts have recognized that the *Global-Tech* decision has important
implications for criminal cases. *See, e.g., United States v. Sharp*, 879 F.3d 327, 333–34
(8th Cir. 2018); *United States. v. Parker*, 872 F.3d 1, 13–14 (1st Cir. 2017).

As the Court acknowledged in *Global-Tech*, the willful blindness concept rests on
the assumption that a defendant who acted with willful blindness is as culpable as
one who acted with actual knowledge. *See* 563 U.S. at 769. Many disagree with this
assumption. *See id.* at 772 (Kennedy, J., dissenting) ("Willful blindness is not knowledge; and judges should not broaden a legislative proscription by analogy."). Which
is the correct view? Why?

4. *Conscious avoidance compared to recklessness*. The Court in Global-Tech stated
that its requirements for willful blindness "give willful blindness an appropriately
limited scope that surpasses recklessness and negligence." 563 U.S. at 769. What is
the distinction between willful blindness and recklessness? Is there a danger that
juries applying a willful blindness standard will convict a defendant based on conduct that was merely reckless? For a critique of the willful blindness standard, see
Geraldine Szott Moohr, *Playing with the Rules: An Effort to Strengthen the Mens Rea
Standards of Federal Criminal Laws*, 7 J.L. ECON. & POL'Y 685, 696 (2011).

5. *Mens rea and jurisdiction*. Must the government prove mens rea as to the jurisdictional element of a conspiracy case? Assume, for example, that the defendants conspire to harm a person who, unbeknownst to them, is an undercover federal agent.

Are the defendants guilty of conspiring to commit the crime of assaulting a federal officer? Would the purposes of conspiracy law be served in such a case? *See United States v. Feola*, 420 U.S. 671 (1975).

6. *Inconsistent verdicts.* In a conspiracy case, the government must show that two or more persons agreed to enter into a conspiracy. Suppose that, in a two-person conspiracy, the jury acquits one of the alleged coconspirators but convicts the other. May the conviction stand? Most federal circuit courts answer in the affirmative. *See, e.g., United States v. Ching Tang Lo*, 447 F.3d 1212, 1226 (9th Cir. 2006) ("It is well established that a person may be convicted of conspiring with a co-defendant even when the jury acquits that co-defendant of conspiracy"). *See also United States v. Powell*, 469 U.S. 57 (1984) (affirming conviction of defendant who was acquitted of narcotics charges but convicted of using a telephone to commit those charges). *Cf. United States v. Moran-Toala*, 762 F.3d 334 (2d Cir. 2013) (holding that it is error for the trial court to instruct the jury during deliberations that it may issue inconsistent verdicts because such an instruction encourages improper jury nullification). Can you explain these results? Note that some states do not follow the *Powell* rule (allowing for inconsistent verdicts) as a matter of state law. *See, e.g., State v. Halstead*, 791 N.W.2d 805 (Iowa 2010); *Price v. State*, 959 A.2d 28 (Del. 2008).

7. *Co-conspirator as victim.* May an alleged coconspirator be considered part of a conspiracy even when that alleged coconspirator was an intended victim of the conspiracy? As discussed more fully in Chapter 8, Extortion, *infra*, at least in the context of violation of the federal extortion statute, known as the Hobbs Act (18 U.S.C. § 1951), the Supreme Court has held in the affirmative. In *Ocasio v. United States*, 136 S. Ct. 1423 (2016), the defendant was convicted of participating in an extortion scheme in which he was the intended victim. In upholding the conviction, the Court reasoned:

> Under longstanding principles of conspiracy law, a defendant may be convicted of conspiring to violate the Hobbs Act based on proof that [that defendant] entered into a conspiracy that had as its objective the [extorting] of property from another conspirator. . . .
>
> These basic principles of conspiracy law resolve this case. In order to establish the existence of a conspiracy to violate the Hobbs Act, the government has no obligation to demonstrate that each conspirator agreed personally to commit — or was even capable of committing — the substantive offense of Hobbs Act extortion. It is sufficient to prove that the conspirators agreed that the underlying crime *be committed* by a member of the conspiracy who was capable of committing it. In other words, each conspirator must have specifically intended that *some conspirator* commit each element of the substantive offense.

Id. at 1432 (emphasis in original). Is this an appropriate outcome? Why or why not? For a critique of this case, see Michael F. Dearington, Ocasio v. United States: *The Supreme Court's Sudden Expansion of Conspiracy Liability (And Why Bribe-Taking Foreign Officials Should Take Note)*, 74 WASH. & LEE L. REV. ONLINE 204 (2017).

Problems

3-1. In a bank fraud trial, the government has alleged that defendant, Sara, and her coconspirators conspired to defraud National Bank ("NB") when applying for mortgages on Sara's home and other properties. The misrepresentations in the loan application included false employment and income information, and property appraisal values that had no basis in fact. Most of the mortgaged properties did not even exist. Based on the fraudulent loan applications, NB issued loans that totaled more than $1 million to Sara, her son, and her son's girlfriend.

At trial, Sara denied knowledge of the fraudulent nature of the scheme. Sara testified that she never read the papers she submitted to obtain a mortgage for her home, explaining that she "signed the papers as they told me." Those papers were prepared by Sara's son and his girlfriend and contained false information about Sara's income, marital status, and previous employment. Four months earlier, she learned that her son had made misstatements on a bank loan application. Sara testified that she trusted her son when she signed the documents and had no reason to believe the documents she signed contained false information. She also said that she had no reason to view large cash gifts from her son as anything other than signs of their gratitude for all she had done for him.

Assume that the trial has now concluded, and that the government has requested an instruction telling the jury that the government can meet the knowledge element of conspiracy by proving that Sara was willfully blind as to the fraudulent nature of the loan scheme. Should the court give the instruction? Why or why not? Assuming that the court does give the instruction, what should it say?

3-2. In order to avoid a state probation violation hearing, Larry designed a plan to fake his death with the assistance of his girlfriend. Larry's scheme was to rent a boat to go fishing with his unsuspecting brother and, while his brother was preoccupied with fishing, to jump off the boat, swim to shore, meet his girlfriend, and flee the state. Larry expected that, when his brother discovered his absence, his brother would make a distress call; that the U.S. Coast Guard would respond and conduct an unsuccessful search; and that Larry would be declared dead after a period of time.

It all happened as planned, except that Larry was not declared dead. He was arrested, indicted, and convicted of conspiring with his girlfriend to cause a false distress call to be communicated to the U.S. Coast Guard, in violation of 18 U.S.C. § 371, and the substantive offense of causing a false distress call to be sent to the U.S. Coast Guard, in violation of 14 U.S.C. § 521(c).

On appeal, Larry argues that the government failed to prove a conspiracy because his girlfriend did not share in the object of the conspiracy to commit a *federal* offense. He contends that, because she was not aware that the false distress call would go to the U.S. Coast Guard, she did not share his conspiratorial intent and that the plurality requirement was therefore not met.

How should the court rule? Why?

3-3. Defendant was convicted along with various coconspirators for running a massive insider trading network involving hundreds of publicly traded companies. At trial, the government argued that wiretap evidence demonstrated that Defendant consciously avoided learning the source of a tip, which Defendant used when trading on stock in furtherance of the conspiracy. During a taped conversation among Defendant and two other coconspirators, one of Defendant's coconspirators told the third coconspirator that the third coconspirator was "better off not knowing where the tips were coming from," and that "if the government ever asks, you don't have any idea." Defendant stated in the conversation that Defendant had "heard from [a fourth coconspirator] that the tip came from a janitor" working at one of the publicly traded companies the stock of which was traded in furtherance of the alleged conspiracy.

At trial, Defendant denied knowledge of the tip's source. At the government's request, the trial judge instructed the jury that it could find that Defendant had knowledge of the source of the tip if Defendant consciously avoided learning the identity of the source. The judge rejected Defendant's request that the jury instruction provide that "the mental state of recklessness is insufficient for a finding of conscious avoidance." The jury convicted Defendant of conspiracy to commit insider trading.

On appeal, Defendant argues that: (1) the trial judge should not have given the conscious avoidance instruction, (2) the failure to include defendant's requested language was error, and (3) in any event the evidence was insufficient for the jury to have found conscious avoidance. (For purposes of this problem only, please assume that if the tip actually had come from a janitor then Defendant could not have been convicted of insider trading.)

How should the court rule on appeal? Why?

3-4. Defendants, lawyers for Waste Corp., were indicted for allegedly conspiring with company employees under the Racketeer Influenced and Corrupt Organizations (RICO) Act stemming from allegations that the employees, assisted by Defendants, engaged in a scheme to steal company assets through a number of unethical and illegal business practices, and thus committed securities fraud among several other federal crimes. The government's case hinged on Defendants' admissions that Waste Corp. had engaged in "inappropriate billing practices" when billing company clients, that Defendants failed to see to it that the company rectified these practices, and that Defendants failed to review a huge document-drop of some 60 gigabytes of electronically stored information that the employees delivered to Defendants and that would have revealed the employees' illegal scheme.

At trial, the government argued that Defendants consciously avoided learning of the illegal nature of the scheme. Customarily, corporate lawyers such as Defendants review business clients' billing practices to ensure regulatory compliance and root out unlawful activity. Defendants testified that they intentionally declined to review the company's billing practices because Waste Corp. did not wish to pay for a proper review of company billing. No direct evidence exists that Waste Corp.'s lawyers knew anything about securities fraud or any other crimes committed against Waste Corp. shareholders. After receiving a conscious avoidance instruction, the jury convicted Defendants.

Defendants appeal. How should the court rule? Be specific.

C. The "Offense Clause" and the "Defraud Clause"

Section 371 makes it a crime for "two or more persons to conspire either to commit any offense against the United States, or to defraud the United States, or any agency thereof in any manner or for any purpose." The following case deals with the scope of the "offense clause," and the relationship between the "offense clause" and the "defraud clause."

United States v. Arch Trading Co.
987 F.2d 1087 (4th Cir. 1993)

NIEMEYER, CIRCUIT JUDGE:

On August 2, 1990, Iraq invaded Kuwait. On that same day President Bush invoked the emergency powers provided to him by Congress and issued executive orders prohibiting United States persons from, among other things, traveling to Iraq and dealing with the government of Iraq and its agents. In the present appeal, Arch Trading Company, Inc., a Virginia corporation, challenges its convictions for various crimes arising from violations of these prohibitions. The company was convicted of conspiring to commit an offense against the United States, in violation of 18 U.S.C. § 371.

Arch Trading contends principally that the indictment charging it with conspiracy to *commit an offense* under § 371 was defective because in the circumstances the company could only have been charged with conspiracy *to defraud*. . . .

In November 1988 Arch Trading entered into a $1.9 million contract with Agricultural Supplies Company, a "quasi-governmental body owned by the government of Iraq" (Agricultural of Iraq), to ship to Iraq and install there laboratory equipment, including a "virology fermenter" and a "bacteriology machine," purportedly for veterinary use. . . .

From April 1990 through July 1990 Arch Trading acquired the equipment and related chemicals and arranged for their delivery to Iraq. By early August 1990, five of a planned six shipments had arrived in Iraq, but none had been installed. The sixth shipment, which was never actually delivered, was en route. On August 2,

1990, when Iraq invaded Kuwait, President Bush, issued Executive Order No. 12722 prohibiting United States persons from, among other things, exporting goods, technology, or services to Iraq; performing any contract in support of an industrial, commercial or governmental project in Iraq; and engaging in any transaction related to travel to Iraq by United States persons. At Arch Trading's request, that same day the Treasury Department's [Office of Foreign Assets Control ("OFAC")] faxed a copy of the Executive Order to Arch Trading's offices. A week later the President issued a slightly more detailed order.

Notwithstanding the prohibitions of the first executive order, two executives of Arch Trading immediately attempted to enter Iraq via Cyprus to install the laboratory equipment that had already been delivered. When that effort failed, Arch Trading retained a Jordanian firm, Biomedical Technologies, Inc., to perform the installation. One of the Arch Trading executives who had earlier attempted to enter Iraq later joined Biomedical employees in Baghdad to help coordinate the installation, which was accomplished between October 24 and November 2, 1990. The travel expenses of both the Arch Trading executive and the Biomedical Technologies employees were reimbursed by Arch Trading, on authority of its president, Kamal Sadder, and upon completion of the installation, Biomedical Technologies was paid a bonus. . . .

Arch Trading's dealings with Iraq ultimately came to the attention of the United States Customs Service during an investigation into a shipment unrelated to this case. In late July 1990, customs agents discovered a personal computer at Dulles International Airport in Washington, D.C., that Arch Trading was shipping to Baghdad, Iraq, without proper documentation. During the course of the investigation the government questioned Arch Trading executives and subsequently executed a search warrant which led to the indictment and conviction in this case. This appeal followed.

Arch Trading contends that it was improperly charged under 18 U.S.C. § 371. That section criminalizes conspiracies of two sorts: conspiracies *to commit an offense* against the United States and conspiracies *to defraud* the United States. Arch Trading was charged with, and convicted of, conspiring to commit an "offense" against the United States government. It asserts, however, it could only have been charged, if at all, with having conspired to "defraud" the United States, because violations of executive orders and regulations do not constitute an "offense." Arch Trading argues that the conspiracy count must therefore be dismissed, relying on *United States v. Minarik*, 875 F.2d 1186, 1193–94 (6th Cir.1989).

We reject this argument because we do not agree that violation of an executive order cannot constitute an offense as that term is used in 18 U.S.C. § 371. While it may be that executive orders cannot alone establish crimes, when such orders are duly authorized by an act of Congress and Congress specifies a criminal sanction for their violation, the consequence is different. In this case the International Emergency Economic Powers Act (IEEPA), 50 U.S.C. § 1701, *et seq.*, authorized the President to issue executive orders proscribing conduct, and 50 U.S.C. § 1705(b) makes criminal the disobedience of an order issued under the Act.[2] There is no question that violation of a federal criminal statute may properly be charged under the "offense" clause. We therefore hold that when Congress provides criminal sanctions for violations of executive orders that it empowers the President to issue, such violation constitutes an "offense" for the purposes of 18 U.S.C. § 371.

While Arch Trading's conduct could arguably have been charged also as a conspiracy "to defraud," the two prongs of § 371 are not mutually exclusive. Because of the broad interpretation which has been given the "defraud" clause, § 371's two clauses overlap considerably. The wide breadth of the "defraud" clause has long been established:

> To conspire to defraud the United States means to cheat the government out of property or money, but it also means to interfere with or obstruct one of its lawful functions by deceit, craft or trickery, or at least by means that are dishonest. It is not necessary that the government shall be subjected to property or pecuniary loss by the fraud, but only that its legitimate official actions and purpose shall be defeated by misrepresentation, chicane, or the overreaching of those charged with carrying out the governmental intention.

Hammerschmidt v. United States, 265 U.S. 182, 188 (1924).

Because of this overlap, given conduct may be proscribed by both of the section's clauses. In such a situation, the fact that a particular course of conduct is chargeable under one clause does not render it immune from prosecution under the other. When both prongs of § 371 apply to the conduct with which a particular defendant is charged, the government enjoys considerable latitude in deciding how to proceed. *See United States v. Jones*, 976 F.2d 176, 183 (4th Cir.1992) ("[F]aced with two equally applicable penal statutes, there is nothing wrong with the government's decision [absent an improper purpose] to prosecute under one and not the other"). Convictions under the "defraud" clause for conspiracies *to commit particular offenses* are commonly upheld. Conversely, convictions under the "offense" clause for conspiracy to engage in conduct which would defraud the United States are also proper. Many courts have even found it permissible to list both prongs of § 371 in a single indictment count rather than specifying whether the alleged conspiracy was one to defraud or one to commit an offense.

The case upon which Arch Trading primarily relies, *United States v. Minarik*, is in no way inconsistent with our conclusions. In *Minarik*, the Sixth Circuit found that

---

2. 50 U.S.C. § 1705(b) provides:

Whoever willfully violates any license, order, or regulation issued under this chapter shall, upon conviction, be fined not more than $50,000, or, if a natural person, may be imprisoned for not more than ten years, or both; and any officer, director, or agent of any corporation who knowingly participates in such violation may be punished by a like fine, imprisonment, or both.

(*This language has since been amended. — Eds.*)

the prosecution had "used the defraud clause in a way that created great confusion about the conduct claimed to be illegal." *Minarik*, 875 F.2d at 1196. In light of the prejudice to the defendant that resulted from the confusion in that case, the Sixth Circuit reversed the defendant's conviction. *Id.* at 1186, 1193–96. As that court has since stressed, however, *Minarik* did not hold that the two clauses of § 371 are mutually exclusive, but only that in the case then before the court confusion prejudicial to the defendant had arisen from the government's choice of proceeding under the "defraud" clause. In cases such as the present one, however, where the defense will not be unfairly burdened by invocation of either clause, the prosecution may frame the indictment at its discretion.

In short, the evidence in this case against Arch Trading would have supported conviction under either the "offense" or the "defraud" clause, and absent an improper motive, which is not alleged here, the government's choice of invoking the offense clause was an appropriate exercise of discretion.

Affirmed.

Notes and Questions

1. *The "defraud" clause.* According to the court in *Arch Trading*, what is the scope of the defraud clause? When would a conspiracy to defraud not also be a conspiracy to commit an offense against the United States? In other words, does the defraud clause add anything to the statute? If so, what?

2. *The required connection to the United States government.* The defraud clause only applies when there is a sufficiently close connection between the criminal objective and the United States government. In *Tanner v. United States*, 483 U.S. 107 (1987), for example, the defendants defrauded a private corporation that received aid from the federal government. The Supreme Court held that, because the aid did not remain subject to government supervision, the federal aid did not provide a sufficient tie to the federal government to form the basis for a defraud clause conviction. In essence, the facts were not sufficient to show an intent to defraud the United States. *Id.* at 128–132.

3. *Punishment.* A conspiracy to commit an offense is punished as a felony where the object crime was a felony, and as a misdemeanor where the object crime was a misdemeanor. Conspiracies to defraud the United States, however, are punished as felonies. Why should this be so?

Problem

3-5. Defendant was a partner in a produce distribution business, Wholesale Foods Company, Inc. (Wholesale). Wholesale bought produce from the growers and sold it, almost exclusively, to Retail Foods Co. (Retail). Almost 90 percent of Retail's purchases were from Wholesale. Over the last five years, there was a sharp rise in the price of organic produce. At the same time, the overall prices of non-organic produce remained relatively constant.

Because of the price increase, Defendant decided last year to begin distributing organic produce, even though Defendant had no experience with the regulations governing such produce. In a scheme to turn a quick profit, Defendant agreed with Nick Barracuda, a produce grower, for Barracuda to deliver to Defendant non-organic produce fraudulently labeled as organic. Barracuda also had no previous experience with regulations governing organic produce. Defendant then sold this mislabeled produce to Retail. The difference between the actual value of non-organic produce sold and the price charged was $4.2 million.

Federal laws and regulations require accuracy in labeling organic produce sold in interstate commerce. The United States Department of Agriculture has the function of enforcing these standards, which Retail violated because of Defendant's and Barracuda's misrepresentations. Intentional violations of the regulations may be subject to criminal sanctions.

Defendant and Barracuda were charged with one count of violating 18 U.S.C. § 371. The indictment alleged, in the alternative, that the defendants conspired to defraud the United States and conspired to commit an offense against the United States. Barracuda agreed to plead guilty and to testify against Defendant. By means of a general verdict, the jury convicted Defendant.

Defendant appeals the conviction on the grounds that the evidence was insufficient to support either theory. How should the court rule? Why?

3-6. Defendant was indicted under § 371 for allegedly conspiring to defraud the United States Department of Transportation's Disadvantaged Business Enterprise Program ("DBE Program"). The DBE Program is structured to increase the participation of DBEs in federally funded highway construction projects, setting a goal of 10 percent participation. The State Department of Transportation ("DOT") and the State Turnpike Commission ("STC") receive federal funds for federally funded highway projects and, as a result, are required to establish goals and objectives in administering the DBE Program. State and local authorities are also delegated the responsibility to administer the program by, among other things, certifying entities as DBEs; tracking the usage of DBEs on federally funded highway projects through the award of credits to general contractors on specific projects; and reporting compliance with the participation goals to the federal authorities.

The indictment alleges that Defendant and Century Steel Contractors ("CSC") used MMCC, Inc., a DBE qualified entity, as a "front" to obtain 13 federally funded highway construction subcontracts requiring DBE status, and that CSC (which is not a DBE) performed the work on the jobs while it was represented to the state agencies and the general contractors that MMCC would be performing the work. The government contends that MMCC did not perform a "commercially useful function" on the jobs as the DBE regulations require and that CSC personnel did the actual work, taking great efforts to conceal from general contractors and state entities that CSC and its personnel were doing the work.

Defendant has moved to dismiss, arguing that the allegations do not allege a scheme to defraud the United States. How should the court rule? Why?

Notes on § 371 and the Double Jeopardy Clause

As the United States Supreme Court has stated, "the Double Jeopardy Clause of the Fifth Amendment provides that no person may be 'twice put in jeopardy' 'for the same offence.' [A]t its core, the Clause means that those acquitted or convicted of a particular 'offence' cannot be tried a second time for the same 'offence.'" *Gamble v. United States*, 139 S. Ct. 1960, 1963–64 (2019). Prosecutions under § 371 raise two distinct issues under the Double Jeopardy Clause.

1. *Does § 371 create one offense with alternative theories, or two separate offenses?*

A question not raised in *Arch Trading* is whether the offense and defraud clauses of § 371 create a single offense with two possible underlying theories, or whether those two clauses create two different offenses. If the latter is true, then defendants could be separately punished under each clause for the same conspiracy and this would not violate the Double Jeopardy Clause.

This issue arose in *United States v. Rigas*, 605 F.3d 194 (3d Cir. 2010) (*en banc*). John Rigas was the founder of Adelphia Communications Corporation, and his son Timothy was a board member and Chief Financial Officer. Until its collapse in 2002, Adelphia was the sixth-largest cable television provider in the United States. The Rigas family effectively controlled the company. According to the government, the defendants engaged in sham transactions to support Adelphia's stock price and also looted the company of its assets. When the company's true financial condition became known, the company collapsed.

These facts gave rise to two separate prosecutions. First, in 2002, the Rigases were indicted and convicted under § 371's offense clause in the Southern District of New York. The indictment in that case alleged a wide-ranging conspiracy to loot Adelphia and to hide both the looting and Adelphia's weak financial condition from the public and the United States Securities and Exchange Commission. Second, in 2005, the Rigases were indicted in the Middle District of Pennsylvania for conspiracy to defraud the United States in violation of 18 U.S.C. § 371 by evading the taxes due on their gains from the fraudulent scheme.

Seeking to dismiss the second prosecution, the defendants argued that § 371 creates a single offense that can be violated in alternative ways. According to the defendants, the government had charged the same crime in successive prosecutions and the second prosecution therefore violated the Double Jeopardy Clause. The government asserted that § 371 creates two separate crimes and that the Pennsylvania prosecution therefore did not constitute double jeopardy.

The court agreed with the defendants. The Court found that the plain and literal meaning of the words "either . . . or" indicates that, when Congress enacted § 371, it intended to create a single criminal offense that may be committed in two alternative ways.

Having decided this threshold question, the court then turned to establishing the proper test for determining the factual question whether the two prosecutions charged the same conspiracy. The court held that the appropriate test required examination of the totality of the circumstances. Under this test, a court must examine whether the successive indictments concern the same underlying transactions, relate to the same time and place, and involve the same core group of participants.

The court found that both indictments alleged a common goal, and individual overt acts in both indictments were interdependent. Accordingly, the court found that the Rigases had established a strong inference that there was a single agreement. On remand, the government would have the burden of proving by a preponderance of the evidence that the Rigases entered into two separate agreements. Not surprisingly, on remand the district court dismissed the indictment. *United States v. Rigas*, No. 4:05-cr-402 (M.D. Pa. Jan. 26, 2012) (order dismissing superseding indictment).

Is this the correct result? Should the defendants have been charged, tried, and punished twice for their acts? Why or why not?

2. *May a defendant be punished under both § 371 and another federal conspiracy statute?*

A separate issue is whether it would violate the Double Jeopardy Clause to punish a defendant under both § 371 and one of the specific federal criminal conspiracy statutes. As discussed more fully in Chapter 9, False Statements, *infra*, in *Blockburger v. United States*, 284 U.S. 299, 304 (1932), the Supreme Court set forth the applicable test for determining whether two statutes create the same crime. Under that test, a defendant may not be punished under two separate statutes for the same act if: (1) the two crimes have the same elements or (2) Congress did not intend that a defendant be punished twice for those crimes. Applying that test, charges under § 371 and another federal conspiracy statute for the same act generally will not constitute double jeopardy.

The Eleventh Circuit considered this issue in *United States v. Gonzales*, 834 F.3d 1206, 2019–20 (11th Cir. 2016). In that case, the court held that punishment both for conspiracy to defraud under § 371 and for conspiracy to commit health care fraud under 18 U.S.C. §§ 1347, 1349 does not constitute double jeopardy because each crime requires proof of an element that the other does not:

> Section 371 requires as elements proof of an overt act and proof that the intended victim was the United States or one of its agencies. In contrast, the language of § 1349 does not require the commission of an overt act. Nor, does it require that the United States or one of its agencies be the intended victim of the fraud. Indeed, conspiring to commit health care fraud under §§ 1347 and 1349 can encompass targeting either a public or a private plan that provides medical benefits. Likewise, § 1349 requires that the conspiracy must relate to one of a specific subset of statutes found in Chapter 63 of Title 18. But § 371 explicitly applies to conspiracies to commit any offense against the United States or to defraud the United States. Thus, a conviction under

§ 371 would not require proof that the conspiracy was for the purpose of committing one of the offenses required by § 1349. Section 371 simply lacks that element.

Is it appropriate to punish a defendant under two separate conspiracy statutes for the same acts? As a matter of constitutional law? As a matter of prosecutorial discretion?

Problems

3-7. Last July 28, Albert arranged to purchase a BMW automobile from West German Motor Imports for approximately $70,000. The sales contract provided that Albert would pay a down payment of $27,000 toward the purchase price on or before the date of delivery, and that the remainder of the purchase price would be financed. The salesman was co-defendant Richard. Albert left with Richard a personal check for $500 toward the down payment.

Albert's car became available on September 12. Albert made cash remittals to Motor Imports of $5,000 on September 30, $2,500 on October 4, and $1,500 on October 5, for a total of $9,000 within that week. A single cash payment of more than $10,000 would have triggered Motor Imports' obligation to file an IRS Form 8300 for cash payments of over $10,000. The employee manual given to all Motor Imports employees discusses this reporting requirement. There is no direct evidence that Richard read the employee manual or that Albert knew of the reporting requirement.

On October 5, Albert paid cash for a $9,500 money order from the State Avenue Branch of Metropolitan Bank payable to Motor Imports and delivered the money order to Motor Imports that day. Albert obtained the money order from Theresa, the head bank teller at the branch and a close personal friend of Albert's. On October 7, Albert purchased with cash another $8,000 money order payable to Motor Imports from the State Avenue Branch and delivered the money order to Motor Imports that day. On October 9, Albert took delivery of his new car. Money orders are considered "cash" for purposes of this case.

Federal law provides that it is illegal for an individual to "structure," that is, to conduct one or more cash transactions at one or more financial institutions, for purposes of evading the financial institution's reporting requirements. Structuring includes reducing a sum of cash exceeding $10,000 into smaller sums and is subject to both civil and criminal penalties. *See* Chapter 13, Money Laundering and Related Financial Crimes, *infra*.

Albert and Richard were charged in Count I with violating 18 U.S.C. § 371 by conspiring to defraud the United States and in Count II with violating 18 U.S.C. § 371 by conspiring to commit an offense against the United States. Richard and Albert declined to testify at trial. They were convicted of both counts.

The defendants appeal the conspiracy convictions on the grounds that there was insufficient evidence to prove mens rea and that the two separate convictions violate the Double Jeopardy Clause. How should the court rule? Why?

3-8. Defendant was a truck driver for a shipping company and was indicted in the United States District Court in Oregon on one count of conspiracy to transport stolen goods in interstate commerce in violation of 18 U.S.C. § 371 and two counts of transporting stolen goods in interstate commerce in violation of 18 U.S.C. § 2314. After a jury trial, Defendant was acquitted on all counts. One month later, Defendant was indicted in the United States District Court in Idaho on one count of conspiracy to steal from an interstate shipment of goods in violation of 18 U.S.C. § 371, one count of theft from an interstate shipment of goods in violation of 18 U.S.C. § 659, and one count of receipt and concealment of stolen goods in violation of 18 U.S.C. § 2315. Defendant entered a plea of not guilty and filed a motion to dismiss the indictment on double jeopardy grounds. The trial court denied the motion, and Defendant appealed.

Both indictments allege that Defendant and others conspired to and did steal merchandise from trucks in Oregon. Each indictment alleges that Defendant coordinated the thefts. The Oregon indictment alleged that Defendant and coconspirators A and B participated in a conspiracy extending from September 28, Year 00 to October 1, Year 00. The Idaho indictment alleged that Defendant and coconspirators A and C participated in a conspiracy beginning on or about August 13, Year 00 and ending on December 3, Year 00. The Idaho indictment alleged that those charged, along with unindicted coconspirators, conspired to transport, and did transport, a stolen trailer load of goods from Oregon to Idaho.

How should the appeals court rule? Why? Please be precise.

D. Scope of the Conspiracy

Under federal joinder rules, one defendant may be tried with another defendant only when the evidence shows that both defendants participated in "the same act or transaction or in the same series of acts or transactions." Fed. R. Crim. P. 8(b). Because the scope of a conspiracy is not always clear, defendants often argue that they were not part of the conspiracy charged by the government and thus cannot be jointly tried with the other defendants. In effect, the argument is that, instead of one grand conspiracy, there were two or more conspiracies constituting different crimes. Thus, the defendants argue, they should be tried at a separate trial for the smaller conspiracy rather than at a single trial for the grand conspiracy. As discussed in the notes below, a defendant in a conspiracy trial faces substantial risks from simply being associated at trial with other, perhaps more culpable, defendants.

The following is the leading United States Supreme Court case on the issue of when the government has sufficiently pleaded and proven a single, overarching conspiracy. Note that, to prevail, the defendant must prove both that the government failed to prove a single conspiracy and that the error was prejudicial.

Kotteakos v. United States

328 U.S. 750 (1946)

MR. JUSTICE RUTLEDGE delivered the opinion of the Court.

The only question is whether petitioners have suffered substantial prejudice from being convicted of a single general conspiracy by evidence which the government admits proved not one conspiracy but some eight or more different ones of the same sort executed through a common key figure, Simon Brown. Petitioners were convicted under the general conspiracy section of the Criminal Code of conspiring to violate the provisions of the National Housing Act. . . .

The indictment named thirty-two defendants, including the petitioners.[1] The gist of the conspiracy, as alleged, was that the defendants had sought to induce various financial institutions to grant credit, with the intent that the loans or advances would then be offered to the Federal Housing Administration for insurance upon applications containing false and fraudulent information.

Of the thirty-two persons named in the indictment nineteen were brought to trial[3] and the names of thirteen were submitted to the jury.[4] Two were acquitted; the jury disagreed as to four; and the remaining seven, including petitioners, were found guilty.

Simon Brown, who pleaded guilty, was the common and key figure in all of the transactions proven. He was president of the Brownie Lumber Company. Having had experience in obtaining loans under the National Housing Act, he undertook to act as broker in placing for others loans for modernization and renovation, charging a five per cent commission for his services. Brown knew, when he obtained the loans, that the proceeds were not to be used for the purposes stated in the applications.

In May, 1939, petitioner Lekacos told Brown that he wished to secure a loan in order to finance opening a law office, to say the least a hardly auspicious professional launching. Brown made out the application, as directed by Lekacos, to state that the purpose of the loan was to modernize a house belonging to the estate of Lekacos' father. Lekacos obtained the money. Later in the same year Lekacos secured another loan through Brown, the application being in the names of his brother and sister-in-law. Lekacos also received part of the proceeds of a loan for which one Gerakeris, a defendant who pleaded guilty, had applied.

In June, 1939, Lekacos sent Brown an application for a loan signed by petitioner Kotteakos. It contained false statements. Brown placed the loan, and Kotteakos

---

1. Four other persons were alleged to be conspirators but were not made defendants.

3. As to four, a severance was granted. The indictment was nol-prossed as to one, and eight others pleaded guilty.

4. One pleaded guilty during trial. The indictment was nol-prossed as to another, and a severance was ordered for a third. Verdicts of acquittal were directed as to three others.

thereafter sent Brown applications on behalf of other persons. Two were made out in the names of fictitious persons. The proceeds were received by Kotteakos and petitioner Regenbogen, his partner in the cigarette and pinball machine business. Regenbogen, together with Kotteakos, had indorsed one of the applications. Kotteakos also sent to Brown an application for a loan in Regenbogen's name. This was for modernization of property not owned by Regenbogen. The latter, however, repaid the money in about three months after he received it.

The evidence against the other defendants whose cases were submitted to the jury was similar in character. They too had transacted business with Brown relating to National Housing Act loans. But no connection was shown between them and petitioners, other than that Brown had been the instrument in each instance for obtaining the loans. In many cases the other defendants did not have any relationship with one another, other than Brown's connection with each transaction. As the Circuit Court of Appeals said, there were "at least eight, and perhaps more, separate and independent groups, none of which had any connection with any other, though all dealt independently with Brown as their agent." As the government puts it, the pattern was "that of separate spokes meeting at a common center," though we may add without the rim of the wheel to enclose the spokes.

The proof therefore admittedly made out a case, not of a single conspiracy, but of several, notwithstanding only one was charged in the indictment. The Court of Appeals aptly drew analogy in the comment, "Thieves who dispose of their loot to a single receiver — a single 'fence' — do not by that fact alone become confederates: they may, but it takes more than knowledge that he is a 'fence' to make them such." It stated that the trial judge "was plainly wrong in supposing that upon the evidence there could be a single conspiracy; and in the view he took of the law, he should have dismissed the indictment." Nevertheless the appellate court held the error not prejudicial, saying among other things that "especially since guilt was so manifest, it was 'proper' to join the conspiracies," and "to reverse the conviction would be a miscarriage of justice." This is indeed the government's entire position. It does not now contend that there was no variance in proof from the single conspiracy charged in the indictment. Admitting that separate and distinct conspiracies were shown, it urges that the variance was not prejudicial to the petitioners.

If, when all is said and done, the conviction is sure that the error did not influence the jury, or had but very slight effect, the verdict and the judgment should stand, except perhaps where the departure is from a constitutional norm or a specific command of Congress. But if one cannot say, with fair assurance, after pondering all that happened without stripping the erroneous action from the whole, that the judgment was not substantially swayed by the error, it is impossible to conclude that substantial rights were not affected. The inquiry cannot be merely whether there was enough to support the result, apart from the phase affected by the error. It is rather, even so, whether the error itself had substantial influence. If so, or if one is left in grave doubt, the conviction cannot stand.

The government's theory seems to be, in ultimate logical reach, that the error presented by the variance is insubstantial and harmless, if the evidence offered specifically and properly to convict each defendant would be sufficient to sustain his conviction, if submitted in a separate trial. For reasons we have stated and in view of the authorities cited, this is not and cannot be the test. But in apparent support of its view the government argues that there was no prejudice here because the results show that the jury exercised discrimination as among the defendants whose cases were submitted to it. As it points out, the jury acquitted some, disagreed as to others, and found still others guilty. From this it concludes that the jury was not confused and, apparently, reached the same result as would have been reached or would be likely, if the convicted defendants had been or now should be tried separately.

One difficulty with this is that the trial court itself was confused in the charge which it gave to guide the jury in deliberation. The court instructed:

> The indictment charges but one conspiracy, and to convict each of the defendants of a conspiracy, the government would have to prove, and you would have to find, that each of the defendants was a member of that conspiracy. You cannot divide it up. It is one conspiracy, and the question is whether or not each of the defendants or which of the defendants, are members of that conspiracy.

On its face, as the Court of Appeals said, this portion of the charge was plainly wrong in application to the proof made; and the error pervaded the entire charge, not merely the portion quoted. The jury could not possibly have found, upon the evidence, that there was only one conspiracy. The trial court was of the view that one conspiracy was made out by showing that each defendant was linked to Brown in one or more transactions, and that it was possible on the evidence for the jury to conclude that all were in a common adventure because of this fact and the similarity of purpose presented in the various applications for loans.

This view, specifically embodied throughout the instructions, obviously confuses the common purpose of a single enterprise with the several, though similar, purposes of numerous separate adventures of like character. It may be that, notwithstanding the misdirection, the jury actually understood correctly the purport of the evidence, as the government now concedes it to have been; and came to the conclusion that the petitioners were guilty only of the separate conspiracies in which the proof shows they respectively participated. But, in the face of the misdirection and in the circumstances of this case, we cannot assume that the lay triers of fact were so well informed upon the law or that they disregarded the permission expressly given to ignore that vital difference.

As we have said, the error permeated the entire charge, indeed the entire trial. Not only did it permit the jury to find each defendant guilty of conspiring with thirty-five other potential co-conspirators, or any less number as the proof might turn out for acquittal of some, when none of the evidence would support such a conviction, as the proof did turn out in fact. It had other effects. One was to prevent the court from giving a precautionary instruction such as would be appropriate, perhaps, required, in cases where related but separate conspiracies are tried together, namely, that the jury should take care to consider the evidence relating to each conspiracy separately from that relating to each other conspiracy charged. The court here was careful to caution the jury to consider each defendant's case separately, in determining his participation in "the scheme" charged. But this obviously does not, and could not, go to keeping distinct conspiracies distinct, in view of the court's conception of the case.

Moreover, the effect of the court's misconception extended also to the proof of overt acts. Carrying forward his premise that the jury could find one conspiracy on the evidence, the trial judge further charged that, if the jury found a conspiracy, "then the acts or the statements of any of those whom you so find to be conspirators between the two dates that I have mentioned, may be considered by you in evidence as against all of the defendants whom you so find to be members of the conspiracy." The instructions in this phase also declared: "It is not necessary, as a matter of law, that an overt act be charged against each defendant. It is sufficient if the conspiracy be established and the defendant be found to be a member of the conspiracy — it is sufficient to allege overt acts on the part of any others who may have been members of the conspiracy, if those acts were done in furtherance of, and for the purpose of accomplishing the conspiracy."

On those instructions it was competent not only for the jury to find that all of the defendants were parties to a single common plan, design and scheme, where none was shown by the proof, but also for them to impute to each defendant the acts and statements of the others without reference to whether they related to one of the schemes proven or another, and to find an overt act affecting all in conduct which admittedly could only have affected some. We do not understand how it can be concluded, in the face of the instruction, that the jury considered and was influenced by nothing else.

Numbers are vitally important in trial, especially in criminal matters. Guilt with us remains individual and personal, even as respects conspiracies. It is not a matter of mass application. There are times when of necessity, because of the nature and scope of the particular federation, large numbers of persons taking part must be tried together or perhaps not at all, at any rate as respects some. When many conspire, they invite mass trial by their conduct. Even so, the proceedings are exceptional to our tradition and call for use of every safeguard to individualize each defendant in his relation to the mass. Wholly different is it with those who join together with only a few, though many others may be doing the same and though some of them may line up with more than one group.

Criminal they may be, but it is not the criminality of mass conspiracy. They do not invite mass trial by their conduct. Nor does our system tolerate it. That way lies the drift toward totalitarian institutions. True, this may be inconvenient for prosecution. But our government is not one of mere convenience or efficiency. It too has a stake, with every citizen, in his being afforded our historic individual protections, including those surrounding criminal trials. About them we dare not become careless or complacent when that fashion has become rampant over the earth.

Here toleration went too far. We do not think that either Congress intended to authorize the government to string together, for common trial, eight or more separate and distinct crimes, conspiracies related in kind though they might be, when the only nexus among them lies in the fact that one man participated in all. Leeway there must be for [cases] where proof may not accord with exact specifications in indictments. Otherwise criminal conspirators never could be brought to halt. But if the practice here followed were to stand, we see nothing to prevent its extension to a dozen, a score, or more conspiracies and at the same time to scores of men involved, if at all, only separately in them. The dangers for transference of guilt from one to another across the line separating conspiracies, subconsciously or otherwise, are so great that no one really can say prejudice to substantial right has not taken place. The line must be drawn somewhere.

Accordingly the judgments are reversed and the causes are remanded for further proceedings in conformity with this opinion.

Reversed.

Mr. Justice Douglas, with whom Mr. Justice Reed agrees, dissenting.

It is clear that there was error in the charge. An examination of the record in *Berger v. United States*, 295 U.S. 78 (1935), shows that the same erroneous instructions were in fact given in that case. But I do not think the error "substantially injured" the defendants in this case any more than it did in the *Berger* case.

Whether injury results from the joinder of several conspiracies depends on the special circumstances of each case. Situations can easily be imagined where confusion on the part of the jury is likely by reason of the sheer number of conspirators and the complexities of the facts which spell out the series of conspiracies. The evidence relating to one defendant may be used to convict another.

Those possibilities seem to be non-existent here. Nothing in the testimony of the other defendants even remotely implicated petitioners in the other frauds. Nothing in the evidence connected petitioners with the other defendants, except Brown, in the slightest way. On the record no implication of guilt by reason of a mass trial can be found. The dangers which petitioners conjure up are abstract ones.

Moreover, the true picture of the case is not thirty-two defendants engaging in eight or more different conspiracies which were lumped together as one. The jury convicted only four persons in addition to petitioners. The other defendants and the evidence concerning them were in effect eliminated from the case. We have then a case of two closely related conspiracies involving petitioners and two additional conspiracies in which petitioners played no part — but all of the same character and revolving around the same central figure, Brown. And the strong and irresistible inference that the jury was not confused is bolstered by their failure to convict six of the thirteen defendants on trial before them.

Notes and Questions

1. *Advantages of a "mass" trial.* Why would the government choose to bring a case like *Kotteakos* rather than bringing a number of separate trials? Would it not be simpler and more straightforward to bring separate trials? If you were the prosecutor in the case, how would you structure such a case? Why?

2. *Reversible error.* Even if the defendant shows that the case was improperly charged and tried as a single conspiracy, is a reversal necessarily required? What was the basis for the government's argument that the conviction should have been affirmed in *Kotteakos*? Why did the Court reject the argument? Although the Court in *Kotteakos* reversed the conviction, most defendants fail to obtain a reversal even if the appeals court finds that multiple conspiracies were improperly charged as a single conspiracy. If you were the trial judge in a similar case, what would your incentives be when confronted with such arguments?

3. *Mandatory versus discretionary severance.* Rule 8(b) provides that defendants may be joined if the government sufficiently alleges that they participated in "the same act or transaction or in the same series of acts or transactions." If a defendant has been misjoined, then the trial judge *must* sever that defendant's trial under Rule 8(b).

Even if joinder is proper under Rule 8(b), a trial judge has the *discretion* to grant the defendant a separate trial under Fed. R. Crim. P. 14, in the interest of fairness. A judge might grant such an order, for example, as to a minor defendant, where there is substantial evidence that is only admissible against the principal defendants. Defendants in conspiracy trials frequently bring Rule 14 motions, but such motions rarely succeed. Why do you think this is so?

4. *Wheels and chains.* What if an alleged co-conspirator knows of the existence of other participants, but does not know their identities? Is that sufficient to render the alleged co-conspirator part of a single conspiracy with the other participants? In *Blumenthal v. United States*, 332 U.S. 539 (1947), defendants were charged with conspiracy to sell whiskey at illegal prices. The alleged conspiracy was composed of the owner of the whiskey, two distributors, and two salespeople. The salespeople argued that they did not know each other or the owner, and could not have conspired with each other or the owner. The Court rejected the argument, finding it sufficient that the salespeople knew that they were selling portions of one large lot of whiskey and thus that others were involved. The *Blumenthal*-type conspiracy is often charged in narcotics cases and has come to be known as a "chain" or "ladder" conspiracy.

In a "chain" conspiracy case — as compared with a *Kotteakos*-type "wheel" conspiracy case — the government seeks to show that each participant in the conspiracy constituted a "link." The various links can be charged as part of a single conspiracy so long as each link was aware of the other links' existence. In both types of conspiracies, the government must prove that each co-conspirator knew that the other conspirators existed but need not prove that each co-conspirator knew the identities of the other co-conspirators. "Wheel" and "chain" analysis is often used in white collar cases. In many cases, large conspiracies may be too complex to fit neatly within either category and there can be significant overlap between these two theories.

5. *The "Varsity Blues" case.* In *United States v. Sidoo et al.*, Crim. No. 19-10080-NMG, 2020 WL 2308807 (W.D. Mass. May 8, 2020), often referred to as the "College Admissions Prosecutions" or "Varsity Blues" case, venue was a central issue that defendants raised in their pretrial motions. In that case, parents of college applicants were charged in connection with multiple schemes across the country to bribe various college administrators and others to rig the college admissions process. The government used the residence of David Sidoo, one of several defendants in the case, to establish venue in the District of Massachusetts by alleging a single conspiracy. *See* Mem. of Law in Supp. of Defs. Mot. to Dismiss for Lack of Venue at 2, Crim. No. 19-10080-NMG, 2020 WL 1698009 (D. Mass. April 1, 2020). Many of Sidoo's alleged coconspirators lived far away from the District of Massachusetts, in locales such as Los Angeles and Chicago, presenting tactical and practical hardships for Sidoo's alleged coconspirators. Does the broad application of venue provisions in conspiracy cases lead to the potential for abuse? If so, what is the solution?

Problem

3-9. Attorney worked for a large New York law firm. After a couple of years with the firm, Attorney decided to leave the practice of law and to become a securities broker. To that end and while still at the firm, Attorney began to observe "new matter" memos, confidential documents that were circulated among attorneys at the law firm announcing new business. In this way, Attorney was able to determine when companies were involved in transactions that had the strong potential to affect stock prices. Attorney discussed this information with acquaintances in the securities industry in order to curry their favor.

In violation of federal securities laws, Attorney personally gave confidential "new matter" information to Broker, a principal at a major securities firm. Broker used this information to trade on stocks, at a substantial profit. Attorney also gave the information to Attorney's friend, Trader, who worked at a different securities firm. Trader gave the information to Trader's boss, Supervisor. Supervisor also traded in the stock of the companies discussed, again making a substantial profit. Supervisor and Attorney were casual acquaintances, but the two never discussed the "new matter" information.

Attorney, Trader, Broker, and Supervisor were indicted for conspiracy to commit insider trading in violation of the federal securities laws. Attorney and Trader agreed to plead guilty, and to testify against Broker and Supervisor.

At trial, Attorney admitted giving the stolen, secret information directly to Broker and to Trader, but denied ever speaking directly with Supervisor. Trader admitted getting the information and passing along both the substance of the tips and the source (Attorney) to Supervisor, though Supervisor denied hearing the source of the information.

There is no evidence that Broker and Supervisor ever discussed the information from Attorney. Attorney did testify that Attorney was visiting Broker at Broker's office one day, and that Supervisor happened to be there paying a social visit to Broker. According to Attorney, Supervisor said to Attorney, "What are you doing here? Shouldn't you be at the law firm?"

At the end of the government's case, Broker and Supervisor moved to dismiss the conspiracy count on the ground that it charges multiple conspiracies in a single count. How should the court rule? Why?

3-10. Defendant has been indicted for conspiring to commit multiple federal crimes. Defendant was head commodities trader at the New York office of Southern New York Commodities, Regional ("SNYCR"). Defendant had the authorization to trade in bulk and individually on the behalf of SNYCR's clients. Defendant was guaranteed a commission for each successful profitable sale completed. The government alleges that Defendant, with the agreement and urging of his friend and business associate, Associate, concocted a scheme to maximize their personal profits. Prosecutors allege that Defendant agreed to funnel the most profitable contracts to Associate's account, and in turn Associate would pay Defendant both a commission and half of all profits earned through their scheme, defrauding SNYCR's high-paying clientele by reducing the amount of profits to which they were entitled and siphoning those profits to Defendant and Associate.

The government then alleges that, at some point, another employee at SNYCR, Trader, noticed Defendant's improved lifestyle and became curious. Trader approached Defendant, who described the scheme to Trader. Trader then asked to be part of Defendant's and Associate's scheme. Defendant agreed to enter into a scheme with Trader, without Associate's knowledge. Eventually, Defendant's and Associate's scheme and Defendant's and Trader's scheme developed into larger schemes at SNYCR, with a few persons participating in each scheme. Defendant was the only person involved in both schemes. Based on these facts, Defendant has been charged with participating in a single conspiracy under § 371, in violation of federal wire fraud, mail fraud, and money laundering statutes.

Defendant has moved to dismiss the conspiracy count, or to sever the case into two separate trials. How should the court rule? Why?

E. Duration and Withdrawal

Because the crime of conspiracy essentially rests on a meeting of the minds, it can only begin when the agreement is formed and, if the statute requires, when an overt act is committed. Determining when a conspiracy ends, however, is more complicated. The first case below deals with the issue of when a conspiracy terminates.

1. Defining the Termination Point

United States v. Jimenez Recio

537 U.S. 270 (2003)

JUSTICE BREYER delivered the opinion of the Court.

We here consider the validity of a Ninth Circuit rule that a conspiracy ends automatically when the object of the conspiracy becomes impossible to achieve — when, for example, the government frustrates a drug conspiracy's objective by seizing the drugs that its members have agreed to distribute. In our view, conspiracy law does not contain any such "automatic termination" rule.

In *United States v. Cruz*, 127 F.3d 791, 795 (9th Cir 1997), the Ninth Circuit, following the language of an earlier case, *United States v. Castro*, 972 F.2d 1107, 1112 (9th Cir. 1992), wrote that a conspiracy terminates when "'there is affirmative evidence of abandonment, withdrawal, disavowal *or defeat of the object of the conspiracy*'" (emphasis added). It considered the conviction of an individual who, the government had charged, joined a conspiracy (to distribute drugs) after the government had seized the drugs in question. The Circuit found that the government's seizure of the drugs guaranteed the "defeat" of the conspiracy's objective, namely, drug distribution. The Circuit held that the conspiracy had terminated with that "defeat," *i.e.*, when the government seized the drugs. Hence the individual, who had joined the conspiracy after that point, could not be convicted as a conspiracy member.

In this case the lower courts applied the *Cruz* rule to similar facts: On November 18, 1997, police stopped a truck in Nevada. They found, and seized, a large stash of illegal drugs. With the help of the truck's two drivers, they set up a sting. The government took the truck to the drivers' destination, a mall in Idaho. The drivers paged a contact and described the truck's location. The contact said that he would call someone to get the truck. And three hours later, the two defendants, Francisco Jimenez Recio and Adrian Lopez-Meza, appeared in a car. Jimenez Recio drove away in the truck; Lopez-Meza drove the car away in a similar direction. Police stopped both vehicles and arrested both men.

A federal grand jury indicted Jimenez Recio, Lopez-Meza, and the two original truck drivers, charging them with having conspired, together and with others, to possess and to distribute unlawful drugs. . . . [A jury convicted the defendants.]

Jimenez Recio and Lopez-Meza appealed [their convictions]. They pointed out that, given *Cruz*, the jury had to find that they had joined the conspiracy before the Nevada stop, and they claimed that the evidence was insufficient at both trials to warrant any such jury finding. The Ninth Circuit panel . . . agreed. The government sought certiorari. It noted that the Ninth Circuit's holding in this case was premised upon the legal rule enunciated in *Cruz*. And it asked us to decide the rule's validity, *i.e.*, to decide whether "a conspiracy ends as a matter of law when the government frustrates its objective." We agreed to consider that question.

In *Cruz*, the Ninth Circuit held that a conspiracy continues "'until there is affirmative evidence of abandonment, withdrawal, disavowal or defeat of the object of the conspiracy.'" 127 F.3d at 795 (quoting *Castro*, 972 F.2d at 1112). The critical portion of this statement is the last segment, that a conspiracy ends once there has been "defeat of [its] object." The Circuit's holdings make clear that the phrase means that the conspiracy ends through "defeat" when the government intervenes, making the conspiracy's goals impossible to achieve, even if the conspirators do not know that the government has intervened and are totally unaware that the conspiracy is bound to fail. In our view, this statement of the law is incorrect. A conspiracy does not automatically terminate simply because the government, unbeknownst to some of the conspirators, has "defeat[ed]" the conspiracy's "object."

Two basic considerations convince us that this is the proper view of the law. First, the Ninth Circuit's rule is inconsistent with our own understanding of basic conspiracy law. The Court has repeatedly said that the essence of a conspiracy is "an agreement to commit an unlawful act." *Iannelli v. United States*, 420 U.S. 770, 777 (1975). That agreement is "a distinct evil," which "may exist and be punished whether or not the substantive crime ensues." *Salinas v. United States*, 522 U.S. 52, 65 (1997). The conspiracy poses a "threat to the public" over and above the threat of the commission of the relevant substantive crime — both because the "[c]ombination in crime makes more likely the commission of [other] crimes" and because it "decreases the probability that the individuals involved will depart from their path of criminality." *Callanan v. United States*, 364 U.S. 587, 593–594 (1961). Where police have frustrated a conspiracy's specific objective but conspirators (unaware of that fact) have neither abandoned the conspiracy nor withdrawn, these special conspiracy-related dangers remain. *Cf.* 2 W. LaFave & A. Scott, Substantive Criminal Law § 6.5, p. 85 (1986) ("[i]mpossibility" does not terminate conspiracy because "criminal combinations are dangerous apart from the danger of attaining the particular objective"). So too remains the essence of the conspiracy — the agreement to commit the crime. That being so, the government's defeat of the conspiracy's objective will not necessarily and automatically terminate the conspiracy.

Second, the view we endorse today is the view of almost all courts and commentators but for the Ninth Circuit. No other Federal Court of Appeals has adopted the Ninth Circuit's rule. Three have explicitly rejected it. . . .

The *Cruz* majority argued that the more traditional termination rule threatened "endless" potential liability. To illustrate the point, the majority posited a sting in which police instructed an arrested conspirator to go through the "telephone directory . . . [and] call all of his acquaintances" to come and help him, with the government obtaining convictions of those who did so. The problem with this example, however, is that, even though it is not necessarily an example of entrapment itself, it draws its persuasive force from the fact that it bears certain resemblances to entrapment. The law independently forbids convictions that rest upon entrapment. And the example fails to explain why a different branch of the law, conspiracy law, should be modified to forbid entrapment-like behavior that falls outside the bounds of current entrapment law. At the same time, the *Cruz* rule would reach well beyond arguable police misbehavior, potentially threatening the use of properly run law enforcement sting operations. . . .

We conclude that the Ninth Circuit's conspiracy-termination law holding set forth in *Cruz* is erroneous in the manner discussed. We reverse the present judgment insofar as it relies upon that holding.

Notes and Questions

1. *Why have the crime of conspiracy?* According to the Court in *Jimenez Recio*, what particular danger does the crime of conspiracy address? Does prosecution of the defendants in this case fulfill those aims? Why? According to the Court, what would the problem be for law enforcement if the Ninth Circuit's approach had prevailed? Are the Court's concerns valid? Why?

2. *Duration of a conspiracy.* A conspiracy begins upon the agreement and, where required, the commission of an overt act in furtherance of the conspiracy. According to the Court, when exactly does a conspiracy end? Is that also when the dangers of a conspiracy end?

3. *Statute of limitations.* A conspiracy charge can extend the limitations period for bringing the charge in some cases. The five-year limitations period for conspiracy does not begin to run until the commission of the last overt act, even if the criminal objectives have all been achieved and even if charges for object offenses would be time-barred. Thus, all co-conspirators may be charged with the crime of conspiracy if at least one co-conspirator committed an overt act within five years of the indictment. In addition, overt acts that occur beyond the five year limitation period can extend the conspiracy charge well beyond five years into the future.

What flexibility does a prosecutor have in alleging the *starting point* of a conspiracy? Would it be appropriate for a prosecutor, in order to extend the limitations period, to allege that the conspiracy began even after the agreement was formed and an overt act that was committed? Similarly, how much discretion should a prosecutor have in picking the last overt act or acts? What constitutes an overt act that would prevent the limitations period from beginning to run? *See United States v. Grimm*, 738 F.3d 498, 503 (2d Cir. 2013) ("generally, overt acts have ended when the conspiracy has completed its influence on an otherwise legitimate course of common dealing that remains ongoing for a prolonged time, without measures of concealment, adjustment or any other corrupt intervention by any conspirator."). In *Grimm*, the court found that interest payments on bonds that were issued in a big-rigging scheme did not constitute overt acts for statute of limitations purposes.

2. The Implications of Termination

Determining when a conspiracy ends may have important implications for the defendant. For example, the end of a conspiracy will trigger the running of the statute of limitations. In addition, a conspiracy charge provides important evidentiary advantages to the prosecution, including an expanded application of relevancy and the admissibility of coconspirators' statements.[f] Those advantages will not apply to evidence of acts that occurred after the conspiracy ends. The next case deals with the admissibility of a coconspirator's statement. Pay particular attention to Justice Jackson's concurring opinion, which contains perhaps the most often-cited critique of modern conspiracy law.

Krulewitch v. United States

336 U.S. 440 (1949)

Mr. Justice Black delivered the opinion of the Court.

A federal district court indictment charged in three counts that petitioner and a woman defendant had (1) induced and persuaded another woman to go on October 20, 1941, from New York City to Miami, Florida, for the purpose of prostitution, in violation of 18 U.S.C. § 399 [now § 2422]; (2) transported or caused her to be transported from New York to Miami for that purpose, in violation of 18 U.S.C. § 398 [now § 2421]; and (3) conspired to commit those offenses in violation of 18 U.S.C. § 88 [now § 371]. Tried alone, the petitioner was convicted on all three counts of the indictment. The Court of Appeals affirmed. We granted certiorari limiting our review to consideration of alleged error in admission of certain hearsay testimony against petitioner over his timely and repeated objections.

The challenged testimony was elicited by the government from its complaining witness, the person whom petitioner and the woman defendant allegedly induced to go from New York to Florida for the purpose of prostitution. The testimony narrated the following purported conversation between the complaining witness and petitioner's alleged coconspirator, the woman defendant.

> "She asked me, she says, 'You didn't talk yet?' And I says, 'No.' And she says, 'Well, don't,' she says, 'until we get you a lawyer.' And then she says, 'Be very careful what you say.' And I can't put it in exact words. But she said, 'It would be better for us two girls to take the blame than Kay [the defendant] because he couldn't stand it, he couldn't stand to take it.'"

The time of the alleged conversation was more than a month and a half after October 20, 1941, the date the complaining witness had gone to Miami. Whatever

---

f. A "coconspirator statement" would normally be considered hearsay and would be inadmissible. "Hearsay" includes a statement that is: (a) made out of court by one person (the "declarant"), (b) repeated in court by another person (the witness), and (c) offered for its truth. Such statements are generally inadmissible because they are unreliable and because the declarant is not available for cross-examination. Rule 801(d)(2)(E) of the Federal Rules of Evidence, however, provides that such a statement may be admissible under the "co-conspirators' exception" if the party offering the statement shows that it was "made by the coconspirator of a party during the course of and in furtherance of the conspiracy." This exception exists both because coconspirators are considered agents who adopt each other's statements, and because prosecutors need leeway in proving what is essentially a mental crime.

original conspiracy may have existed between petitioner and his alleged coconspirator to cause the complaining witness to go to Florida in October, 1941, no longer existed when the reported conversation took place in December, 1941. For on this latter date the trip to Florida had not only been made — the complaining witness had left Florida, had returned to New York, and had resumed her residence there. Furthermore, at the time the conversation took place, the complaining witness, the alleged coconspirator, and the petitioner had been arrested. They apparently were charged in a United States District Court of Florida with the offense of which petitioner was here convicted.

It is beyond doubt that the central aim of the alleged conspiracy — transportation of the complaining witness to Florida for prostitution — had either never existed or had long since ended in success or failure when and if the alleged coconspirator made the statement attributed to her. The statement plainly implied that petitioner was guilty of the crime for which he was on trial. It was made in petitioner's absence and the government made no effort whatever to show that it was made with his authority. The testimony thus stands as an unsworn, out-of-court declaration of petitioner's guilt. This hearsay declaration, attributed to a coconspirator, was not made pursuant to and in furtherance of objectives of the conspiracy charged in the indictment, because if made, it was after those objectives either had failed or had been achieved. Under these circumstances, the hearsay declaration attributed to the alleged coconspirator was not admissible on the theory that it was made in furtherance of the alleged criminal transportation undertaking.

Although the government recognizes that the chief objective of the conspiracy — transportation for prostitution purposes — had ended in success or failure before the reported conversation took place, it nevertheless argues for admissibility of the hearsay declaration as one in furtherance of a continuing subsidiary objective of the conspiracy. Its argument runs this way. Conspirators about to commit crimes always expressly or implicitly agree to collaborate with each other to conceal facts in order to prevent detection, conviction and punishment. Thus the argument is that even after the central criminal objectives of a conspiracy have succeeded or failed, an implicit subsidiary phase of the conspiracy always survives, the phase which has concealment as its sole objective. . . .

We cannot accept the government's contention. There are many logical and practical reasons that could be advanced against a special evidentiary rule that permits out-of-court statements of one conspirator to be used against another. But however cogent these reasons, it is firmly established that where made in furtherance of the objectives of a going conspiracy, such statements are admissible as exceptions to the hearsay rule. This prerequisite to admissibility, that hearsay statements by some conspirators to be admissible against others must be made in furtherance of the conspiracy charged, has been scrupulously observed by federal courts. The government now asks us to expand this narrow exception to the hearsay rule and hold admissible a declaration, not made in furtherance of the alleged criminal transportation conspiracy charged, but made in furtherance of an alleged implied but uncharged conspiracy aimed at preventing detection and punishment. . . . The rule contended for by the government could have far-reaching results. For under this rule plausible arguments could generally be made in conspiracy cases that most out-of-court statements offered in evidence tended to shield coconspirators. We are not persuaded to adopt the government's implicit conspiracy theory which in all criminal conspiracy cases would create automatically a further breach of the general rule against the admission of hearsay evidence.

It is contended that the statement attributed to the alleged coconspirator was merely cumulative evidence, that without the statement the case against petitioner was so strong that we should hold the error harmless. In *Kotteakos v. United States*, 328 U.S. 750 (1946), we said that error should not be held harmless under the harmless error statute if upon consideration of the record the court is left in grave doubt as to whether the error had substantial influence in bringing about a verdict. We have such doubt here. The Florida District Court grand jury failed to indict. After indictment in New York petitioner was tried four times with the following results: mistrial; conviction; mistrial; conviction with recommendation for leniency. The revolting type of charges made against this petitioner by the complaining witness makes it difficult to believe that a jury convinced of a strong case against him would have recommended leniency. There was corroborative evidence of the complaining witness on certain phases of the case. But as to all vital phases, those involving the sordid criminal features, the jury was compelled to choose between believing the petitioner or the complaining witness. The record persuades us that the jury's task was difficult at best. We cannot say that the erroneous admission of the hearsay declaration may not have been the weight that tipped the scales against petitioner.

Reversed.

Mr. Justice Jackson, concurring in the judgment and opinion of the Court.

This case illustrates a present drift in the federal law of conspiracy which warrants some further comment because it is characteristic of the long evolution of that elastic, sprawling and pervasive offense. Its history exemplifies the "tendency of a principle to expand itself to the limit of its logic." The unavailing protest of courts against the growing habit to indict for conspiracy in lieu of prosecuting for the substantive offense itself, or in addition thereto, suggests that loose practice as to this offense constitutes a serious threat to fairness in our administration of justice.

The modern crime of conspiracy is so vague that it almost defies definition.[3] Despite certain elementary and essential elements, it also, chameleon-like, takes on a special coloration from each of the many independent offenses on which it may

---

3. Albert J. Harno, *Intent in Criminal Conspiracy*, 89 U. Pa. L. Rev. 624: "In the long category of crimes there is none, not excepting criminal attempt, more difficult to confine within the boundaries of definitive statement than conspiracy." An English author — Wright, The Law of Criminal Conspiracies, p. 11 — gives up with the remark: "But no intelligible definition of 'conspiracy' has yet been established."

be overlaid. It is always "predominantly mental in composition" because it consists primarily of a meeting of minds and an intent.

It is not intended to question that the basic conspiracy principle has some place in modern criminal law, because to unite, back of a criminal purpose, the strength, opportunities and resources of many is obviously more dangerous and more difficult to police than the efforts of a lone wrongdoer. However, even when appropriately invoked, the looseness and pliability of the doctrine present inherent dangers which should be in the background of judicial thought wherever it is sought to extend the doctrine to meet the exigencies of a particular case.

A recent tendency has appeared in this Court to expand this elastic offense and to facilitate its proof. In *Pinkerton v. United States*, 328 U.S. 640, it sustained a conviction of a substantive crime where there was no proof of participation in or knowledge of it, upon the novel and dubious theory that conspiracy is equivalent in law to aiding and abetting.

Of course, it is for prosecutors rather than courts to determine when to use a scatter-gun to bring down the defendant, but there are procedural advantages from using it which add to the danger of unguarded extension of the concept.

An accused, under the Sixth Amendment, has the right to trial "by an impartial jury of the State and district wherein the crime shall have been committed." The leverage of a conspiracy charge lifts this limitation from the prosecution and reduces its protection to a phantom, for the crime is considered so vagrant as to have been committed in any district where any one of the conspirators did any one of the acts, however innocent, intended to accomplish its object. The government may, and often does, compel one to defend at a great distance from any place he ever did any act because some accused confederate did some trivial and by itself innocent act in the chosen district. Circumstances may even enable the prosecution to fix the place of trial in Washington, D. C., where a defendant may lawfully be put to trial before a jury partly or even wholly made up of employees of the government that accuses him.

When the trial starts, the accused feels the full impact of the conspiracy strategy. Strictly, the prosecution should first establish prima facie the conspiracy and identify the conspirators, after which evidence of acts and declarations of each in the course of its execution are admissible against all. But the order of proof of so sprawling a charge is difficult for a judge to control. As a practical matter, the accused often is confronted with a hodgepodge of acts and statements by others which he may never have authorized or intended or even known about, but which help to persuade the jury of existence of the conspiracy itself. In other words, a conspiracy often is proved by evidence that is admissible only upon assumption that conspiracy existed. The naive assumption that prejudicial effects can be overcome by instructions to the jury all practicing lawyers know to be unmitigated fiction. . . .

The trial of a conspiracy charge doubtless imposes a heavy burden on the prosecution, but it is an especially difficult situation for the defendant. The hazard from loose application of rules of evidence is aggravated where the government institutes mass trials. Moreover, in federal practice there is no rule preventing conviction on uncorroborated testimony of accomplices, as there are in many jurisdictions, and the most comfort a defendant can expect is that the court can be induced to follow the "better practice" and caution the jury against "too much reliance upon the testimony of accomplices." *Caminetti v. United States*, 242 U.S. 470, 495 (1917).

A co-defendant in a conspiracy trial occupies an uneasy seat. There generally will be evidence of wrongdoing by somebody. It is difficult for the individual to make his own case stand on its own merits in the minds of jurors who are ready to believe that birds of a feather are flocked together. If he is silent, he is taken to admit it and if, as often happens, co-defendants can be prodded into accusing or contradicting each other, they convict each other. There are many practical difficulties in defending against a charge of conspiracy which I will not enumerate.

Against this inadequately sketched background, I think the decision of this case in the court below introduced an ominous expansion of the accepted law of conspiracy. The prosecution was allowed to incriminate the defendant by means of the prostitute's recital of a conversation with defendant's alleged co-conspirator, who was not on trial. The conversation was said to have taken place after the substantive offense was accomplished, after the defendant, the co-conspirator and the witness had all been arrested, and after the witness and the other two had a falling out. The Court of Appeals sustained its admission upon grounds stated as follows: "We think that implicit in a conspiracy to violate the law is an agreement among the conspirators to conceal the violation after as well as before the illegal plan is consummated."

I do not see the slightest warrant for judicially introducing a doctrine of implied crimes or constructive conspiracies. . . .

There is, of course, strong temptation to relax rigid standards when it seems the only way to sustain convictions of evildoers. But statutes authorize prosecution for substantive crimes for most evil-doing without the dangers to the liberty of the individual and the integrity of the judicial process that are inherent in conspiracy charges. We should disapprove the doctrine of implied or constructive crime in its entirety and in every manifestation. And I think there should be no straining to uphold any conspiracy conviction where prosecution for the substantive offense is adequate and the purpose served by adding the conspiracy charge seems chiefly to get procedural advantages to ease the way to conviction.

Although a reversal after four trials is, of course, regrettable, I cannot overlook the error as a harmless one. But I should concur in reversal even if less sure that prejudice resulted, for it is better that the crime go unwhipped of justice than that this theory of implied continuance of conspiracy find lodgment in our law, either by affirmance or by tolerance. Few instruments of injustice can equal that of implied or presumed or constructive crimes. The most odious of all oppressions are those which mask as justice.

Notes and Questions

1. *The hearsay rule.* What did Justice Jackson mean when he said that "a conspiracy often is proved by evidence that is admissible only upon assumption that conspiracy existed"? Note that the government may adduce co-conspirator statements even before the conspiracy has been proven beyond a reasonable doubt at trial, so long as it has established that (a) a conspiracy existed by a preponderance of the evidence and (b) the defendant and declarant were members of the conspiracy when the statement was made. And under *Bourjaily v. United States*, 483 U.S. 171 (1987), the trial court may use a coconspirator's statement to decide whether the government has made such a showing. Most courts required, however, that the government adduce further proof—in addition to the coconspirator's statement—of the existence of the conspiracy. *See, e.g., United States v. Silverman*, 861 F.2d 571 (9th Cir. 1988). In response to *Bourjaily*, Congress amended Federal Rule of Evidence 801(d)(2)(E) to require that "the statement must be considered but does not itself establish . . . the existence of the conspiracy or participation in it."

2. *The advantages of a conspiracy charge.* In his concurring opinion, Justice Jackson identified several ways in which a conspiracy charge advantages the government: (a) coconspirator liability under the *Pinkerton* doctrine (discussed more fully below); (b) flexible venue rules; (c) the admissibility of co-conspirator statements; and (d) the tactical advantages flowing from the joining of multiple defendants at a single trial. Another advantage, discussed in the *Kotteakos* case, is the broadened scope of relevant evidence in a conspiracy case. Can you specify exactly how these factors may assist the government in a conspiracy case? Are these advantages unfair to defendants? Why or why not?

3. *Reliance on uncharged theories.* In *Krulewitch*, the Court rejected the government's assertion that the out-of-court statement was made during and in furtherance of a conspiracy to cover up the original crime. The Court stated that "[t]he government now asks us to expand [the] narrow [co-conspirator's] exception to the hearsay rule and hold admissible a declaration, *not made in furtherance of the alleged criminal transportation conspiracy charged*, but made in furtherance of *an alleged implied but uncharged conspiracy* aimed at preventing detection and punishment." The government in *Krulewitch* neither charged a cover-up conspiracy nor attempted to prove such a conspiracy at trial. The Court was unwilling to affirm the conviction based upon this alternate conspiracy theory, implicitly applying the general Due Process Clause principle that a criminal defendant is entitled to be informed of the charges against the defendant in order to prepare a defense at trial and the Fifth Amendment right to a grand jury indictment.

4. *Is conspiracy necessary?* As seen by Justice Jackson's opinion, conspiracy is a controversial crime that has been deemed by some to be unnecessary. *See* Phillip E. Johnson, *The Unnecessary Crime of Conspiracy*, 61 Cal. L. Rev. 1137 (1973). Nonetheless, the crime remains deeply rooted in both federal law and in state penal codes. Why is this so? Does the Court's opinion in *Krulewitch* provide the answer?

3. Withdrawal

A defendant who has joined a conspiracy may nonetheless withdraw from the conspiracy after it has commenced. To withdraw from a conspiracy, a conspirator must do more than merely cease participation. The conspirator must commit affirmative acts inconsistent with the object of the conspiracy and communicate the withdrawal in a manner reasonably designed to reach the co-conspirators. *United States v. United States Gypsum Co.*, 438 U.S. 422, 464–465 (1978). The defendant need not notify law enforcement or otherwise attempt to prevent the crime from occurring. If the defendant continued to benefit from the conspiracy even after attempting to withdraw, however, the withdrawal will not be effective.

Withdrawal may: (1) trigger the running of the statute of limitations period as to the defendant who withdrew, (2) limit the admissibility of coconspirator statements as to that defendant, and (3) limit that defendant's vicarious liability for the acts of coconspirators. With respect to withdrawal, a conspirator's membership in the ongoing scheme continues until the defendant withdraws.

Note on Smith v. United States

When a defendant argues that the defendant withdrew from a conspiracy, should the defendant or the government bear the burden of proving the elements of withdrawal? In *Smith v. United States*, 568 U.S. 106 (2013), the Court addressed this issue, resolving a circuit split. Five circuits had held that the burden of producing evidence of withdrawal and of proving withdrawal rests on the defendant. Five other circuits held that, once the defendant meets the burden of producing the evidence of withdrawal from the conspiracy prior to the limitations, the government has the burden of disproving withdrawal beyond a reasonable doubt. The latter courts raised two concerns with placing the burden on the defendant. First, this approach requires that the defendant disprove an element of the offense in violation of the Due Process Clause. Second, placing the burden on the defendant may compel the defendant either to take the witness stand, implicating the Fifth Amendment right against compelled testimony, or forgo the defense of withdrawal altogether.

Smith was convicted of crimes, including narcotics and RICO conspiracy, connected to his role in an organization that distributed narcotics for about a decade. Before trial, Smith argued that the conspiracy counts were barred by the applicable five-year statute of limitations, 18 U.S.C. § 3282, because he had spent the last six years of the charged conspiracies in prison for a felony conviction and therefore had withdrawn from the conspiracy outside the limitations period.

In its analysis, the Court noted that withdrawal terminates the defendant's liability for post-withdrawal acts of his coconspirators, but that the defendant remains guilty of conspiracy. Placing the burden on the defense therefore does not violate the Due Process Clause because a defense of withdrawal does not negate an element of the crime of conspiracy. Instead, it assumes that the crime has occurred and starts the clock on the statute of limitations period for the prosecution. The Court held that a defense of withdrawal is an affirmative defense that places the burden of proof on the defendant. The Court also held that placing the burden on the prosecution to disprove withdrawal would be unfair to the government because witnesses would invoke the Fifth Amendment right against self-incrimination and decline to provide the necessary evidence.

Problem

3-11. Seller owned a used car lot that sold automobiles and offered financing to its customers who could not afford to make large down payments. Seller conducted the financing part of the business through a relationship with Lender.

On July 9, Year 00, Lender removed $900,000 in cash from Lender's parents' safety deposit box and put the cash in a suitcase. Lender put the suitcase in the trunk of a car that was parked at the used car lot and went to dinner. Seller and Seller's domestic partner, Partner, witnessed this event. While Lender was at dinner, Seller and Partner removed the suitcase from the car. Seller denied having taken the money in public confrontations with Lender.

On August 19, Year 00, a month after the theft, Seller signed a purchase and sale agreement to buy a property, 89 Ivanhoe Road, for $120,000. Seller made a $12,000 down payment by check; that check was returned for insufficient funds, and Seller replaced it with $12,000 cash. Seller paid the $108,000 balance of the purchase price with 13 cashier's checks, which had been obtained in several stages, over a span of three days. Seller's brother, two friends, and one of the used car lot's employee assisted Seller and Partner. Seller provided the cash to these four people. Then each person deposited the cash into a personal bank account to purchase one or more cashier's checks. The checks were made out to Seller or to Partner. Assume that this activity constituted the crime of money laundering under federal law.

Partner took title to the property in the name of "AU Trust." That trust, created on the day of the closing, August 29, Year 00, bears Partner's and Seller's initials. Also on the day of the closing, Partner granted a sham mortgage on the property to "Bostonians Trust," which then did not even exist. The property was then rented out for $1,000 per month. Assume that the creation of the sham mortgage and receipt of rental income also constituted money laundering.

The 89 Ivanhoe Road property was sold on January 5, Year 02, for $200,000. On January 6, the real estate attorney wrote separate checks to Seller and Partner for $40,000 each, and less than a week later, purchased bank checks made out to Seller and Partner for $60,000 each. Bank records indicate that these checks were deposited into the accounts of the used car lot and Partner, respectively, in January Year 02. Assume that the deposits constituted money laundering.

In July Year 03, Seller eventually filed Seller's Year 00 federal income tax return, reporting a total income of $14,165. The Year 00 return was false in that it did not disclose any portion of the $900,000 stolen from Lender, nor did it disclose any portion of the rental income from 89 Ivanhoe Road for the partial Year 00. Partner's tax returns for Year 00, filed in August Year 01, also neglected to report any portion of the stolen money or the rental income. Seller did not file a return for Year 01. Partner filed a false return for Year 01 in October Year 02, again failing to report rental income. Neither Seller nor Partner filed a tax return for Year 02, the year in which each earned a substantial capital gain from the sale of the property.

In February Year 07, the government seeks to charge Seller and Partner with, among other charges, conspiracy to commit money laundering.

Defendants move to dismiss the conspiracy charge, arguing that the conspiracy was completed by January Year 02, when the defendants sold the 89 Ivanhoe Road property that the government alleged had been purchased with the stolen money. How should the court rule? Why?

3-12. In Year 00, Underwood and Ross, each individual owners of import-export companies, entered into an agreement and began exporting finishing machinery to the Republic of Pacifica, in violation of United States regulations establishing trade sanctions against the Republic. The two developed an intricate business plan where Underwood's company would procure the machines and Ross's company would handle the process of smuggling the machinery into the country. In Year 01, Underwood began to suspect that Ross was not honoring an agreement to split the profits equally with Underwood . After Underwood requested receipts from one of Ross's low-level employees, Underwood discovered that Ross had indeed been keeping a large portion of the Republic of Pacifica's payments. Incensed, Underwood immediately called Ross and the two had a heated argument. Underwood and Ross never spoke again, with Ross finding a new supplier and Underwood advising other exporters on how to evade United States sanctions against the Republic of Pacifica. Both thus continued their unlawful activities with new business partners, some of whom worked with both Underwood and Ross. Six years after the two stopped speaking, Underwood and Ross were indicted under § 371 on one count of conspiracy to defraud the United States.

The defendants have moved to dismiss the indictment on the grounds that the conspiracy ended in year 01 and that the statute of limitations for conspiracy had therefore expired. Underwood alternatively argues that his falling-out with Ross constituted withdrawal from the conspiracy. How should the court rule here? Why?

3-13. Defendant has been convicted of conspiracy to commit bribery, in violation of numerous federal laws, on behalf of Allstrong Power Co. The proof at trial showed that Defendant worked for Allstrong for less than three years, from October Year 00 to August Year 03, when he resigned from his position at the company and severed all ties to Allstrong, the alleged conspiracy, and his alleged coconspirators. The indictment against Defendant was returned on July 1, Year 12, almost nine years later. The most recent overt act in furtherance of the conspiracy in which Defendant is alleged to have engaged occurred on March 3, Year 03, five months before his resignation from Allstrong, and each of the substantive counts in the indictment charged other defendants with specific bribes of which Defendant had no knowledge or personal involvement, and that substantially post-date Defendant's employment with Allstrong. The bribes allegedly occurred between November Year 04 and October Year 08.

The government alleged that between Year 01 and Year 03, acting on behalf of Allstrong Power, Defendant helped negotiate contracts with two consultants to funnel bribes to Central Republic officials so that Allstrong Power would win a contract to build a power station in Capital City. The terms of the contracts that Defendant helped negotiate allegedly made clear that once Allstrong won the Capital City project in July Year 03, Allstrong's obligation to funnel bribes through consultants was triggered and would occur over several years. The government further alleged that when Defendant resigned from Allstrong on August 1 Year 04, his role—and that of most, if not all, of his co-conspirators—was principally fulfilled already, and the subsequent bribe payments—from November Year 04 through October Year 08—were triggered automatically at various points during the project.

At trial, the defense argued that because Defendant's personal involvement in the conduct at issue ceased long before the inception of the five-year statute of limitations period, the charges against him are time-barred. Defendant argued that the resignation from Allstrong and severing of ties with the alleged co-conspirators operated as an effective withdrawal from the alleged conspiracy on August 1, Year 03, absolved Defendant from culpability for any subsequent acts of his alleged coconspirators, and triggered the five-year statute of limitations period, which thus expired on August 1, Year 08 (four years before Defendant was first indicted).

Prepare and present closing arguments to the jury on Defendant's withdrawal defense. (2) How is the jury likely to decide on this issue? Why?

F. Vicarious Liability

The crime of conspiracy under federal law provides a form of vicarious liability that is somewhat different from traditional aiding and abetting liability. In general terms, an accessory can be liable for the crime committed by the principal when the accessory has (1) aided, abetted, or encouraged the principal's commission of the crime, and (2) acted with the intention to aid and abet and with the intention that the object crime be committed. In reading this case, be sure to identify the ways in which "*Pinkerton*" liability is different from aiding and abetting liability.

Pinkerton v. United States

328 U.S. 640 (1946)

Mr. Justice Douglas delivered the opinion of the Court.

Walter and Daniel Pinkerton are brothers who live a short distance from each other on Daniel's farm. They were indicted for violations of the Internal Revenue Code. The indictment contained ten substantive counts and one conspiracy count. The jury found Walter guilty on nine of the substantive counts and on the conspiracy count. It found Daniel guilty on six of the substantive counts and on the conspiracy count. Walter was fined $500 and sentenced generally on the substantive counts to imprisonment for thirty months. On the conspiracy count he was given a two year sentence to run concurrently with the other sentence. Daniel was fined $1,000 and sentenced generally on the substantive counts to imprisonment for thirty months. On the conspiracy count he was fined $500 and given a two year sentence to run concurrently with the other sentence. The judgments of conviction were affirmed by the Circuit Court of Appeals.

It is contended that there was insufficient evidence to implicate Daniel in the conspiracy. But we think there was enough evidence for submission of the issue to the jury. . . .

There is, however, no evidence to show that Daniel participated directly in the commission of the substantive offenses on which his conviction has been sustained, although there was evidence to show that these substantive offenses were in fact committed by Walter in furtherance of the unlawful agreement or conspiracy existing between the brothers. The question was submitted to the jury on the theory that each petitioner could be found guilty of the substantive offenses, if it was found at the time those offenses were committed petitioners were parties to an unlawful conspiracy and the substantive offenses charged were in fact committed in furtherance of it.[6]

Daniel relies on *United States v. Sall*, 116 F.2d 745 (3d Cir. 1940). That case held that participation in the conspiracy was not itself enough to sustain a conviction for the substantive offense even though it was committed in furtherance of the conspiracy. The court held that, in addition to evidence that the offense was in fact committed in furtherance of the conspiracy, evidence of direct participation in the commission of the substantive offense or other evidence from which participation might fairly be inferred was necessary.

We take a different view. We have here a continuous conspiracy. There is here no evidence of the affirmative action on the part of Daniel which is necessary to establish his withdrawal from it. *Hyde v. United States*, 225 U.S. 347 (1912). As stated in that case, "having joined in an unlawful scheme, having constituted agents for

---

6. Daniel was not indicted as an aider or abettor, nor was his case submitted to the jury on that theory.

its performance, scheme and agency to be continuous until full fruition be secured, until he does some act to disavow or defeat the purpose he is in no situation to claim the delay of the law. As the offense has not been terminated or accomplished, he is still offending. And we think, consciously offending, offending as certainly, as we have said, as at the first moment of his confederation, and consciously through every moment of its existence." *Id.* at 369. And so long as the partnership in crime continues, the partners act for each other in carrying it forward. It is settled that "an overt act of one partner may be the act of all without any new agreement specifically directed to that act." *United States v. Kissel*, 218 U.S. 601, 608 (1910). Motive or intent may be proved by the acts or declarations of some of the conspirators in furtherance of the common objective. The governing principle is the same when the substantive offense is committed by one of the conspirators in furtherance of the unlawful project. The criminal intent to do the act is established by the formation of the conspiracy. Each conspirator instigated the commission of the crime. The unlawful agreement contemplated precisely what was done. It was formed for the purpose. The act done was in execution of the enterprise. The rule which holds responsible one who counsels, procures, or commands another to commit a crime is founded on the same principle. That principle is recognized in the law of conspiracy when the overt act of one partner in crime is attributable to all. An overt act is an essential ingredient of the crime of conspiracy. . . . If that can be supplied by the act of one conspirator, we fail to see why the same or other acts in furtherance of the conspiracy are likewise not attributable to the others for the purpose of holding them responsible for the substantive offense.

A different case would arise if the substantive offense committed by one of the conspirators was not in fact done in furtherance of the conspiracy, did not fall within the scope of the unlawful project, or was merely a part of the ramifications of the plan which could not be reasonably foreseen as a necessary or natural consequence of the unlawful agreement. But as we read this record, that is not this case.

Affirmed.

MR. JUSTICE RUTLEDGE, dissenting in part.

The judgment concerning Daniel Pinkerton should be reversed. In my opinion it is without precedent here and is a dangerous precedent to establish.

Daniel and Walter, who were brothers living near each other, were charged in several counts with substantive offenses, and then a conspiracy count was added naming those offenses as overt acts. The proof showed that Walter alone committed the substantive crimes. There was none to establish that Daniel participated in them, aided and abetted Walter in committing them, or knew that he had done so. Daniel in fact was in the penitentiary, under sentence for other crimes, when some of Walter's crimes were done.

There was evidence, however, to show that over several years Daniel and Walter had confederated to commit similar crimes concerned with unlawful possession, transportation, and dealing in whiskey, in fraud of the federal revenues. On this evidence both were convicted of conspiracy. Walter also was convicted on the substantive counts on the proof of his committing the crimes charged. Then, on that evidence without more than the proof of Daniel's criminal agreement with Walter and the latter's overt acts, which were also the substantive offenses charged, the court told the jury they could find Daniel guilty of those substantive offenses. They did so.

I think this ruling violates both the letter and the spirit of what Congress did when it separately defined the three classes of crime, namely, (1) completed substantive offenses; (2) aiding, abetting or counseling another to commit them; and (3) conspiracy to commit them. Not only does this ignore the distinctions Congress has prescribed shall be observed. It either convicts one [person] for another's crime or punishes the [person] convicted twice for the same offense.

The gist of conspiracy is the agreement; that of aiding, abetting or counseling is in consciously advising or assisting another to commit particular offenses, and thus becoming a party to them; that of substantive crime, going a step beyond mere aiding, abetting, counseling to completion of the offense.

These general differences are well understood. But when conspiracy has ripened into completed crime, or has advanced to the stage of aiding and abetting, it becomes easy to disregard their differences and loosely to treat one as identical with the other, that is, for every purpose except the most vital one of imposing sentence. And thus the substance, if not the technical effect, of double jeopardy or multiple punishment may be accomplished. Thus also may one be convicted of an offense not charged or proved against him, on evidence showing he committed another. . . .

Daniel has been held guilty of the substantive crimes committed only by Walter on proof that he did no more than conspire with him to commit offenses of the same general character. There was no evidence that he counseled, advised or had knowledge of those particular acts or offenses. There was, therefore, none that he aided, abetted or took part in them. There was only evidence sufficient to show that he had agreed with Walter at some past time to engage in such transactions generally. As to Daniel this was only evidence of conspiracy, not of substantive crime.

The Court's theory seems to be that Daniel and Walter became general partners in crime by virtue of their agreement and because of that agreement without more on his part Daniel became criminally responsible as a principal for everything Walter did thereafter in the nature of a criminal offense of the general sort the agreement contemplated, so long as there was not clear evidence that Daniel had withdrawn from or revoked the agreement. Whether or not his commitment to the penitentiary had that effect, the result is a vicarious criminal responsibility as broad as, or broader than, the vicarious civil liability of a partner for acts done by a co-partner in the course of the firm's business.

Such analogies from private commercial law and the law of torts are dangerous, in my judgment, for transfer to the criminal field. Guilt there with us remains personal, not vicarious, for the more serious offenses. It should be kept so. The effect of

Daniel's conviction in this case, to repeat, is either to attribute to him Walter's guilt or to punish him twice for the same offense, namely, agreeing with Walter to engage in crime. Without the agreement Daniel was guilty of no crime on this record. With it and no more, so far as his own conduct is concerned, he was guilty of two. [Daniel's conviction for Walter's substantive crimes should be reversed.]

Notes and Questions

1. *Vicarious liability.* The federal aiding and abetting statute, now codified at 18 U.S.C. § 2, provides that "[w]hoever commits an offense against the United States or aids, abets, counsels, commands, induces or procures its commission, is punishable as a principal." As the majority stated in note 6, Daniel was not charged on this theory. Review the dissent's comments concerning aiding and abetting. Could Daniel Pinkerton have been liable as an aider and abettor? Why or why not?

2. *Conspiracy and substantive offenses.* As noted above, under federal law the crime of conspiracy does not merge with the substantive offenses. Thus, it is critical to distinguish between liability for (a) the crime of conspiracy itself and (b) liability for substantive offenses. Was the principal issue in this case Daniel Pinkerton's liability for the crime of conspiracy? Why or why not?

3. *Is foreseeability an element of* Pinkerton *liability?* The Court in *Pinkerton* stated that a coconspirator could not be liable for a substantive offense committed by another coconspirator if that offense "[1] was not in fact done in furtherance of the conspiracy, [2] did not fall within the scope of the unlawful project, or [3] was merely a part of the ramifications of the plan which could not be reasonably foreseen as a necessary or natural consequence of the unlawful agreement."

Does this language require that all three of the listed elements be met? In particular, is reasonable foreseeability an element of *Pinkerton* liability that the government must prove beyond a reasonable doubt? *Compare, e.g., United States v. Baker*, 923 F.3d 390, 406 (9th Cir. 2019) ("The substantial evidence of Baker's involvement establishes that the fraudulent acts were reasonably foreseeable by him and done in furtherance of the conspiracy") *with United States v. Aramony*, 88 F.3d 1369, 1379–81 (4th Cir. 1996) (relying on circuit precedent to hold that it is not error to fail to instruct the jury that foreseeability is an element of *Pinkerton* liability).

4. *The merits of the* Pinkerton *rule.* The *Pinkerton* rule applies in federal courts and in at least 12 states. *See* Andrew Ingram, *Pinkerton* Short-Circuits the Model Penal Code, 64 VILL. L. REV. 71, 78 (2019). Justice Rutledge strongly objected to the outcome in *Pinkerton*. The Model Penal Code and a number of states have rejected *Pinkerton* liability. Is *Pinkerton* liability fair and appropriate? Consider the following commentary:

> The belief that criminal liability should not exceed culpability was a basic premise of the drafters of the Model Penal Code. This commitment was baked into the text through the Code's provisions on mens rea: the section of the Code dealing with mens rea is titled 'General Requirements of

Culpability.' It makes committing a crime 'purposely' the most culpable mens rea and committing a crime 'negligently' the least. Consistent with this view of culpability, the drafters of the Code rejected the *Pinkerton* theory of vicarious liability for all crimes committed in furtherance of the conspiracy that were reasonably foreseeable to the conspirator . . . .

The Code's pattern of careful attention to the mental states of offenders and its modulation of punishment thereby is in keeping with the drafter's goal 'to differentiate on reasonable grounds between serious and minor offenses.' The same spirit animates the rejection of the *Pinkerton* doctrine by the Code's drafters, who feared that the 'law would lose all sense of just proportion' if the rule in *Pinkerton* were embraced. They were aware that conspiracy law had been applied to large conspiracies, formed of a leadership group and scattered lieutenants. Courts call these hub-and-spoke conspiracies because the lieutenants, the spokes, may have no knowledge of the other spokes or their activities. The Code's drafters did not want each 'spoke' subject to criminal liability for 'thousands of additional offenses of which [the spoke] was completely unaware and which he did not influence at all.'

Id. at 72, 76–77. *See also* Bruce A. Antkowiak, *The* Pinkerton *Problem*, 115 PENN. ST. L. REV. 3. 607, 639 (2011) (arguing that the *Pinkerton* doctrine undermines basic criminal law principles assessing criminal law liability according to an individual defendant's mens rea). Others have generally criticized the Supreme Court's role in expanding criminal liability under federal conspiracy laws. *See* Paul Marcus, *The Crime of Conspiracy Thrives in the Decisions of the United States Supreme Court,* 64 U. KAN. L. REV. 373 (2015).

Returning to the facts of *Pinkerton*, exactly what was Daniel's role in the crimes that Walter committed? Under *Pinkerton*, Daniel could be convicted of a specific intent crime under the tax code based on a finding that he could have "reasonably foreseen [Walter's crimes] as a necessary or natural consequence of the unlawful agreement"—essentially a negligence standard. Here, Daniel's liability does not seem to correspond to the mens rea required for proof of tax crimes. *See* Chapter 12, Tax Crimes, *infra*.

In this light, is *Pinkerton* liability fair to defendants? Did the case unnecessarily expand the scope of federal criminal liability? Is aiding and abetting liability sufficient to serve the punishment goals of deterrence and retribution that underlie the imposition of derivative liability? Using *Pinkerton* as a case study for this inquiry, should Daniel have been punished for Walter's tax crimes? Why or why not?

Problems

3-14. Associate worked for a personal injury law firm, and conducted a federal jury trial in January Year 00. Concerned that the trial had gone poorly, Associate spoke with Partner at the law firm about paying a juror $10,000. Partner approved, and

Investigator made the payment on January 30, Year 00. This payment constituted an illegal bribe. In addition, without Associate's knowledge, Partner approved a separate $20,000 bribe to another juror in the same case the following week.

In July, Year 00, Partner asked Investigator to pay $5,000 to bribe a witness in a trial that Partner would be conducting the following October. Investigator paid the bribe on October 1, Year 00. In September, Year 00, Associate left the law firm to take another job. Other than social engagements with friends at the law firm, Associate had no further dealings with the law firm after that time.

On September 15, Year 05, Associate, Partner, and Investigator were each indicted on four charges: for conspiracy under § 371 to obstruct justice (18 U.S.C. § 1503) based upon (1) the $10,000 payment, (2) the $20,000 payment, and (3) the $5,000 payment, and three counts of obstruction. Investigator and Partner pleaded guilty and agreed to cooperate with the government. At Associate's trial, the government introduced the July, Year 00, conversation between Partner and Investigator. Associate was convicted of all charges.

Associate has appealed the four convictions, focusing on Associate's alleged withdrawal from the conspiracy. Assuming that the substance of the obstruction charges was proven beyond a reasonable doubt, should the defendant prevail as to any or all of the charges? Why or why not?

3-15. Defendants Accountant and Trader were charged under § 371 with conspiring to commit securities fraud in violation of Section 10(b) of the Securities Exchange Act of 1934, 15 U.S.C. § 78j. The indictment alleged an insider trading scheme under which Accountant gave Trader confidential information belonging to Accountant's employer ("Firm") during years 01 and 02. The information related to various of Firm's clients' business dealings. Trader used the information to trade in the clients' stock, netting substantial profits that Trader then shared with Accountant.

For tax years 01 and 02, Accountant did not file tax returns pursuant to valid extensions, but Trader filed tax returns for both years that falsely stated the source of the insider trading income. In addition to the insider trading charge, the government charged Trader with two counts of tax evasion under 26 U.S.C. § 7201 and also charged Accountant with two counts under that same statute under a *Pinkerton* theory. At trial, the government offered no evidence that Accountant participated in or knew of Trader's alleged tax evasion.

Over the defendants' objection, at the close of trial the judge instructed the jury as follows:

> In this case, a person may be guilty of a crime on one or more of three different bases. First, a person is guilty if the person himself or herself committed the crime, that is actually perpetrated the crime. Second, a person is guilty as a co-conspirator if the person was a member of the conspiracy when the crime was committed, and if it was committed (a) in furtherance of, *or* (b) as a foreseeable consequence of the conspiracy. Third, a person is

guilty of a crime committed by someone else if the person aids and abets the commission of the crime.

If any one or more of these three bases is shown by the evidence beyond a reasonable doubt, that is that the person was the actual perpetrator of the crime, that the person was responsible as a co-conspirator, or that the person was an aider or abetter, the person may be found guilty of the crime charged.

Defendants were convicted of all charges by means of a general verdict that did not specify the theory or theories upon which the jury relied. *You are advising Accountant in preparation for a possible appeal. What viable arguments do you have on appeal? How will the court likely rule? Why?*

Chapter 4

Mail Fraud, Wire Fraud, and Related Crimes

A. Introductory Notes

1. Breadth of the Mail and Wire Fraud Statutes

The mail and wire fraud statutes, 18 U.S.C. §§ 1341, 1343, have long been among federal prosecutors' favorite tools for fighting white collar crime. The mail fraud statute was first enacted in 1872, and has been amended many times; the current version is based upon amendments enacted in 1948. One former prosecutor (now federal judge) went so far as to describe the mail and wire fraud statutes as the prosecutor's "Stradivarius, [their] Colt 45, [their] Louisville Slugger . . . and [their] true love." Jed S. Rakoff, *The Federal Mail Fraud Statute (Part I)*, 18 Duq. L. Rev. 771, 771 (1980). The statutes' popularity with prosecutors is no doubt explained by the relative ease with which they can be "invoked to impose criminal penalties upon a staggeringly broad swath of behavior." *Sorich v. United States*, 129 S. Ct. 1308, 1309 (2009) (Scalia, J., dissenting from denial of certiorari). On their face, the statutes are indeed straightforward. Subject to qualifications discussed below, the statutes require the government to prove that the defendant engaged in a scheme to defraud, and that the scheme involved the use of the United States mails, a private courier operating in interstate commerce, or interstate wires.

Because of their breadth and simplicity, the mail and wire fraud statutes may be used in a wide range of circumstances:

- To prosecute traditional financial fraud schemes, ranging from complex interstate schemes to ordinary intrastate fraud cases;

- To prosecute private employees who have breached their fiduciary duties to their employers;

- To prosecute public officials who have abused their positions of public trust;

- To prosecute cases that are primarily focused on other substantive crimes; for example, mail and wire fraud may be the basis for charges arising out of the same acts that form the basis for securities fraud (*see* Chapter 5, *infra*); and

- As predicate crimes that form the basis for charges under the federal racketeering (RICO) and money laundering statutes discussed later in this text (*see* Chapters 13 and 14, *infra*).

The very flexibility of the mail and wire fraud statutes raises important law-enforcement policy issues. Because the statutes reach ordinary fraud cases that would normally be prosecuted at the state level, they pose significant questions concerning the role of federal law enforcement. Also, the statutes broadly criminalize breaches of fiduciary duties and have triggered debate over the role of the criminal law in regulating everyday economic activity. *See* John C. Coffee Jr., *Hush!: The Criminal Status of Confidential Information after* McNally *and* Carpenter *and the Enduring Problem of Overcriminalization*, 26 Am. Crim. L. Rev. 121 (1988). Finally, the statutes raise vagueness concerns under the Due Process Clause, including issues of notice and abuse of prosecutorial discretion. These themes recur throughout the materials in this chapter.

2. The Statutory Elements

The language of the mail and wire fraud statutes does not provide much guidance to courts. Therefore, the statutes have been subject to substantial judicial interpretation. Under the mail and wire fraud statutes and the cases interpreting those statutes, in a mail or wire fraud case, the government must prove that:

(1) The defendant engaged in a scheme to defraud;

(2) The defendant acted with the specific intent to defraud;

(3) The scheme resulted, or would result upon completion, in the loss of money, property, and/or honest services; and

(4) The United States mail, a private courier operating in interstate commerce, or interstate or international wires (a) were used in furtherance of the scheme to defraud, and (b) the defendant used, or caused the use, of the mail, courier, or wires.

The substantive elements of the mail fraud statute and the wire fraud statute are the same, and judicial interpretations of each statute apply to the other. Mail/wire fraud is an inchoate crime. Thus, the crime is complete if the above elements are met, regardless of whether the scheme comes to fruition.

Each instance of the use of the mail or wire gives rise to a separate count under the statutes. A single fraudulent scheme that uses multiple mailings could, for example, lead to a huge number of criminal charges. The Sarbanes-Oxley Act of 2002 increased the penalty for each count from five to 20 years' imprisonment. The Federal Sentencing Guidelines do place some limits on consecutive sentences for convictions of multiple counts.[a] Nevertheless, a mail or wire fraud conviction for schemes resulting in significant actual or intended loss will likely give rise to a substantial sentence.

---

a. *See* Chapter 19, Sentencing, *infra*.

3. Jurisdiction

There are two possible bases for federal jurisdiction under the mail fraud statute. First, any use of the federal mails — regardless of where the package or letter goes — provides jurisdiction pursuant to the federal government's postal power under the United States Constitution. Second, the use of "any private or commercial interstate carrier" qualifies under the statute. Under the Commerce Clause, *interstate* use of a private courier will plainly provide federal jurisdiction. In addition, *intrastate* use of a private courier will suffice under the Commerce Clause when, as is generally the case, the courier's business affects interstate commerce. *See, e.g., United States v. Photogrammetric Data Servs., Inc.*, 259 F.3d 229, 247 (4th Cir. 2001). Under the plain language of the wire fraud statute, wires used in *interstate* or foreign commerce provide federal jurisdiction under the Commerce Clause.

Complex issues have arisen in determining what constitutes the interstate use of wires in the context of web postings and Internet access. These issues arise under the wire fraud statute and other statutes requiring interstate transmissions. For example, in *United States v. Wright*, 625 F.3d 583, 588 (9th Cir. 2010), the defendant was convicted of interstate transportation of child pornography in violation of 18 U.S.C. § 2252A. On appeal, the defendant argued that there was insufficient evidence that the transmission crossed state lines. At trial, an expert testified that the images could not have crossed state lines because they were transferred using a direct client-to-client connection. The court held "the defendant's mere connection to the Internet does not satisfy the jurisdictional requirement where there is undisputed evidence that the files in question never crossed state lines." *Id.* at 595. For a case addressing a number of related issues, see *United States v. Kieffer*, 681 F.3d 1143 (10th Cir. 2012).

Must a defendant be aware of the facts giving rise to federal jurisdiction? For example, if the defendant sends an email that is routed interstate, must the defendant be aware of that fact to be charged with wire fraud? The general rule under federal law is that the government need not prove that the defendant possessed any particular mens rea in connection with a purely jurisdictional element of a crime. *See, e.g., United States v. Feola*, 420 U.S. 671, 684 (1975) (holding the government is not required to show that the defendant had knowledge of a fact — in this case, that the intended victim was a federal officer — that provides the basis for federal jurisdiction). Courts have applied this principle to the wire fraud statute, holding that jurisdiction is present even if the defendant did not know, and could not reasonably have known, that the wire transmission would travel interstate. *See, e.g., United States v. Lindemann*, 85 F.3d 1232, 1241–42 (7th Cir. 1996).

B. Scheme and Intent to Defraud

The mail and wire fraud statutes punish one who has used the mail or wires in "any scheme or artifice *to defraud*, or for obtaining money or property by means of *false or fraudulent* pretenses, representations, or promises." The statutes, however, do not define the fraudulent schemes that fall within their ambit. In the cases in this section, the courts attempt to define the "fraud" that is at the heart of these statutes.

Many white collar crimes require prosecutors and courts to draw the line between merely aggressive business practices and those practices that are properly deemed criminal. The following case addresses this issue in the mail and wire fraud context. In this case, the defendants clearly made false representations, and did so for the purpose of obtaining money from the alleged victims. Is that all that the statute requires?

United States v. Regent Office Supply Co.
421 F.2d 1174 (2d Cir. 1970)

MOORE, CIRCUIT JUDGE.

* * *

The appellants are in the business of selling stationery supplies through salesmen (called "agents") who solicit orders for their merchandise by telephone. [Defendants] stipulated in writing that their agents "secured sales" by making false representations to potential customers that:

(a) the agent had been referred to the customer by a friend of the customer.

(b) the agent had been referred to customer firms by officers of such firms.

(c) the agent was a doctor, or other professional person, who had stationery to be disposed of.

(d) stationery of friends of the agent had to be disposed of because of a death and that the customer would help to relieve this difficult situation by purchasing it.

* * *

The government's case consisted entirely of the defendants' stipulation. . . . For [their] defense, the accused corporations called the president of Regent, Harold Hartwig, who testified that the firms sell well-known, nationally advertised brands of stationery and some paper to large users among which are corporations; that many of these customers provide a large volume of reorder business; that the Regent-Oxford enterprise has over 20,000 customers; that sales are made exclusively through their customers' purchasing agents; that the false representations listed in the stipulation were made as a preliminary part of the salesmen's solicitation; that price and quality of the merchandise are always discussed honestly; that the price offered has been lower than the purchasing agent is or was paying at the time of the solicitation; that the goods could be returned if found to be unsatisfactory; and that when a complaint is made an additional discount is offered to induce the customer to keep the goods.

Cross-examination elicited that visits to the Regent-Oxford offices had been made by the Better Business Bureau and by a Post Office Inspector; that the "lies" were to "get by" secretaries on the telephone and to get "the purchasing agent to listen to our agent;" and that for business reasons various fictitious names were used both for their companies in different localities and for individuals. . . .

* * *

The important substantive question on this appeal is: Does solicitation of a purchase by means of false representations not directed to the quality, adequacy or price of goods to be sold, or otherwise to the nature of the bargain, constitute a "scheme to defraud" or "obtaining money by false pretenses" within the prohibition of 18 U.S.C. § 1341? We hold that, as here presented, it does not and the convictions should be reversed. We do not, however, condone the deceitfulness such business practices represent. On the contrary, we find these "white lies" repugnant to "standards of business morality." Nevertheless, the facts as stipulated in the case before us do not, in our view, constitute a scheme to defraud or to obtain money by false pretenses punishable under § 1341. But this is not to say that we could not, on different facts or more specific proof, arrive at a different conclusion.

The case presented by the Regent-Oxford operation is unique (as the government, in effect, concedes) among prosecutions for violation of § 1341. The most nearly analogous cases sustaining convictions for mail fraud have involved sales tactics and representations which have tended to mislead the purchaser, or prospective purchaser, as to the quality or effectiveness of the thing being sold, or to mislead him with regard to the advantages of the bargain which should accrue to him. Thus claims or statements in advertising may go beyond mere puffing and enter the realm of fraud where the product must inherently fail to do what is claimed for it. *United States v. Andreadis*, 366 F.2d 423 (2d Cir. 1966) (claim that "Regimen Tablets" could reduce weight without dieting contradicted scientific evidence); *United States v. New South Farm and Home Company*, 241 U.S. 64 (1916) (false representations regarding climate, ability to grow crops, and expected future improvements in promotion of land sales); *Wilson v. United States*, 190 F. 427 (2d Cir. 1911) (sale of intrinsically worthless stock). And promotion of an inherently useful item may also be fraud when the scheme of promotion is based on claims of additional benefits to accrue to the customer, if the benefits as represented are not realistically attainable by the customer. *United States v. Armantrout*, 411 F.2d 60, 64 (2d Cir. 1969) (carpet sold at inflated price on customer's expectation that defendant's "chain referral" scheme would return purchase price and produce profit for him); *United States v. Baren*, 305 F.2d 527 (2d Cir. 1962) (promotion of knitting machines on representation that women customers could easily make complicated knitted garments for profitable resale, after it became known that average prospects could not so operate them). . . .

The government does not contend that the Regent-Oxford agents made any false representations regarding the quality or price of their nationally advertised merchandise. Nor is there any suggestion of material benefits which the customer might expect from the transaction beyond the inherent utility of the goods purchased and the discount price at which they were offered. Thus the present case cannot fall within either of the classes of commercial fraud cases we have previously considered. We must, therefore, examine the government's theory that fraud may exist in a commercial transaction even when the customer gets exactly what he expected and at the price he expected to pay. . . .

It is generally stated that there are two elements to the offense of mail fraud: use of the mails and a scheme to defraud. Since only a "scheme to defraud" and not actual fraud is required for conviction, we have said that "it is not essential that the Government allege or prove that purchasers were in fact defrauded." *United States v. Andreadis*, 366 F.2d 423, 431 (2d Cir. 1966). But this does not mean that the government can escape the burden of showing that some actual harm or injury was *contemplated* by the schemer. Of course proof that someone was actually victimized by the fraud is good evidence of the schemer's intent. . . .

* * *

[W]e have found no case in which an intent to deceive has been equated with an "intent to defraud" where the deceit did not go to the nature of the bargain itself. Where the false representations are directed to the quality, adequacy or price of the goods themselves, the fraudulent intent is apparent because the victim is made to bargain without facts obviously essential in deciding whether to enter the bargain. In closer cases, where the representations do not mislead as to the quality, adequacy or inherent worth of the goods themselves, fraud in the bargaining may be inferable from facts indicating a discrepancy between benefits reasonably anticipated because of the misleading representations and the actual benefits which the defendant delivered, or intended to deliver. In either instance, the intent of the schemer is to injure another to his own advantage by withholding or misrepresenting material facts. Although proof that the injury was accomplished is not required to convict under 1341, we believe the statute does require evidence from which it may be inferred that some actual injury to the victim, however slight, is a reasonably probable result of the deceitful representations if they are successful.

The Regent-Oxford agents did not attempt to deceive their prospective customers with respect to the bargain they were offering; rather, they gave a false reason for being able to offer the bargain. There was no substitution of merchandise contrary to the customer's understanding of the offer, and no "quid pro quo of equal value" exchanged for the customer's money which did not meet his reasonable expectations. No customer testified that he felt he had been cheated. The government asks us to infer some injury from the mere fact of the falseness of the representations and their connection with a commercial transaction. On the evidence before us, we conclude that the defendants intended to deceive their customers but they did not intend to defraud them, because the falsity of their representations was not shown to be capable of affecting the customer's understanding of the bargain nor of influencing his assessment of the value of the bargain to him, and thus no injury was shown to flow from the deception. . . .

[T]he convictions are reversed.

Notes and Questions

1. *Fraudulent intent.* Courts have consistently held that mail and wire fraud require proof of specific intent to defraud. *See, e.g., United States v. Gelb*, 700 F.2d 875, 879 (2d Cir. 1983). As the *Regent Office Supply* opinion makes clear, the "intent to defraud" is an essential part of the "scheme to defraud" that is at the core of a mail or wire fraud charge. In its opinion, the Second Circuit characterized the defendants' conduct as "repugnant" and found that the defendants undoubtedly intended to deceive their customers. Given these conclusions, why did the court find that there was no scheme to defraud? The court provided a number of examples where a scheme to defraud *was* proven. Are you convinced that those cases are substantially different from the *Regent Office Supply* case? Why or why not?

2. *When is a breach of contract fraud?* In *United States ex rel. O'Donnell v. Country-wide Home Loans, Inc.*, 822 F.3d 650 (2d Cir. 2016), the Second Circuit addressed the issue of when an intentional breach of contract can also constitute a scheme to defraud. In that case, loan officers at a bank were alleged to have intentionally sold inferior quality loans to government-sponsored entities in breach of the express terms of their contract with those entities. The court held that even a willful breach of contract does not constitute a scheme to defraud unless the contract was entered into with a contemporaneous intent not to perform. Only if a contractual promise is made with "no intent ever to perform it can the promise itself constitute a fraudulent misrepresentation." *Id.* at 662. Since there was no evidence the bank had entered into the agreement with the contemporaneous fraudulent intent not to perform according to its terms, the post-formation breach (even if intentional) did not constitute a scheme to defraud. The court noted that a contrary rule would be in tension with the principle of "efficient breach" in contract law. The doctrine of efficient breach holds that intentional breaches of contract should be tolerated — and perhaps even encouraged — where the nonbreaching party can be made whole with money damages and the breaching party is thereby left free to pursue a more economically advantageous opportunity.

3. *Literally true and misleading statements.* Can a defendant who has not made a false statement be convicted of mail or wire fraud? For example, assume that an enterprising salesperson marketed plots of land, stating in mailings to prospective customers that a lake would be available for recreational use only five miles from the property. The statement was literally true. The driving distance to the lake, however, was 15 to 40 miles on roads not suitable for passenger vehicles. Have property purchasers been defrauded under the mail fraud statute? *See Lustiger v. United States*, 386 F.2d 132 (9th Cir. 1967). Though not an "outright lie," a misleading statement can be described as "true as far as it goes but creat[ing] a false impression by omitting information necessary to correct the false impression." *O'Donnell* 822 F.3d at 655.

As we will see in Chapter 10, Perjury, *infra*, a literally true but misleading statement will *not* support a perjury charge under federal law. Should the result be different in a fraud case? Why or why not?

4. *Materiality.* In *Neder v. United States*, 527 U.S. 1 (1999), the Supreme Court held that a scheme to defraud under the mail and wire fraud statutes must include a *material* deception. Neder was convicted of mail and wire fraud based upon fraudulent bank loan applications. On appeal, the Court unanimously held that the trial judge erred in failing to require that the jury find that the defendant's misstatements were material to the transactions. Although the statutory language does not contain such a requirement, the Court reasoned that Congress incorporated the common law definition of "defraud" in the statutes. That definition includes a "misrepresentation or concealment of *material* fact." *Id.* at 22.

Although the Court did not define "material" in its opinion, the Court did cite the definition provided by the Restatement (Second) of Torts § 538. The Restatement provides that a matter is material when:

> (a) a reasonable [person] would attach importance to its existence or nonexistence in determining his choice of action in the transaction in question; or

> (b) the maker of the representation knows or has reason to know that its recipient regards or is likely to regard the matter as important in determining his choice of action, although a reasonable [person] would not so regard it.

Id. at 22 n.5.

5. *Lack of candor about negotiation position?* In *United States v. Weimert*, 819 F.3d 351 (7th Cir. 2016), the Seventh Circuit considered the question of whether a party's misrepresentations concerning his or her negotiating position in a transaction constitutes fraud. The court explained, "[n]ot all conduct that strikes a court as sharp dealing or unethical conduct is a 'scheme or artifice to defraud.'" *Id.* at 357. And, specifically, the court held that "Congress could not have meant to criminalize deceptive misstatements or omissions about a buyer's or seller's negotiating positions." *Id.* at 357. For, "[t]o state the obvious, [one party] will often try to mislead the other party about the prices and terms they are willing to accept. Such deceptions are not criminal." *Id.* Since Weimert's misrepresentations related only to his negotiation position, and not to the underlying subject matter of the agreement itself, they were not material and therefore there was no scheme to defraud.

6. *What about especially gullible victims?* Insofar as federal mail and wire fraud is an inchoate crime (requiring proof of only a "scheme to defraud," and not a completed fraud), prosecutors are not required to show the victim actually relied on a would-be fraudster's misrepresentations, or that the victim incurred actual damages (as common law fraud requires). *See, e.g., O'Donnell*, 822 F.3d at 657. Nevertheless, focusing on the false or misleading statement itself, does a defendant commit mail or wire fraud by making misleading statements that would not fool a reasonable person? In *United States v. Brown*, 79 F.3d 1550 (11th Cir. 1996), the court said no. The court found that the misstatements in the case—relating to the market and rental values of houses that the defendants were selling—would not have fooled

a reasonable customer because a reasonable home buyer would conduct independent research into the home's market value. In a later en banc decision, however, the Eleventh Circuit overturned its decision in *Brown*. *United States v. Svete*, 556 F.3d 1157, 1166 (11th Cir. 2009) (en banc). The court agreed with the other circuits that had considered the issue, and held that mail fraud and wire fraud occur even if the misrepresentations would not fool a reasonable person. Is this the correct result? Even without the reasonable person rule, was there sufficient evidence of intent to defraud in *Brown* under the *Regent Office Supply* standard? Why or why not?

Problems

4-1. James Goodall was the president of Direct Mail, Inc., a direct mail marketing company. Goodall created a "mailgram" that was mailed to more than one million people. The mailgram stated:

CONGRATULATIONS! YOU ARE DEFINITELY TO RECEIVE ONE OR MORE OF THE GIFTS LISTED BELOW:

GIFT(S): (1) $5,000 CASH; (2) $2,500.00 CASH; (3) $1,000.00 DISCOUNT SHOPPING SPREE.

SEE REVERSE SIDE FOR DETAILS.

On the reverse, the mailgram stated:

Odds of receiving each gift: for $5,000, 1 in 300,000; for $2,500, 5 in 300,000; and for the discount shopping spree coupons, 1 in 1.

Below these odds, the mailgram indicated that the coupons could be used only toward the purchase of merchandise out of a catalog. The mailgram stated that the offer would expire 48 hours from receipt and told the recipients to call immediately "to see which gift(s) you will receive." It listed a "900" telephone number and indicated that a call would cost $3.98 plus 97 cents per minute, with a minimum three minute charge.

Of the one million mailgrams sent, 25,000 people called in response, and 22,000 discount shopping spree coupons were mailed out. Recipients of the coupons could use them to purchase one of 14 items contained in the catalog, items ranging from autographed basketballs and photographs to game-worn boxer shorts. After applying the coupons to the total prices, the price of these items still exceeded Direct Mail's cost in obtaining the items. A defense expert testified that the mark-ups were nonetheless, "very fair, even on the low side."

The government charged Goodall with mail fraud based on the theory that the mailgrams induced recipients to call the "900" number and to incur telephone charges in the belief that the callers would thereby receive money and things of value. In fact, the callers merely received an opportunity to purchase one of 14 items, the stated value of which was far in excess of their wholesale cost to Direct Mail.

Goodall was convicted and appeals, claiming, inter alia, that there was insufficient evidence of a scheme to defraud. What arguments should Goodall make on appeal? What are the government's best responses? How should the court rule? Why?

4-2. For the last three years, Defendant, a correctional officer employed by the State Department of Corrections, was a board member of the Correction Officer's Benevolent Association ("COBA"). As part of his union contract with COBA, Defendant was entitled to death benefits with Life Insurance Company of America ("LICA") in the event of the death of his lawful spouse. In May of last year, Defendant filed for divorce from his estranged wife, Mary. The divorce was granted on July 23 of this year. Mary died on July 29.

On August 23, Defendant submitted via United States mail a claim to LICA for a $15,000 death benefit for Mary's death, listing his relationship to the deceased as "husband." On or about November 17, Defendant received by mail a $15,000 check on the policy from LICA. Shortly thereafter, other COBA board members learned about Defendant's divorce. At an emergency COBA Board meeting on November 20, the President of COBA, confronted Defendant. On or around November 25, Defendant returned to LICA the $15,000 he had received on the policy and resigned from the COBA board.

Defendant has been indicted for mail fraud for devising a scheme to defraud an insurance company of life insurance benefits to which he was not entitled and in which the United States Postal Service was used.

The government's evidence included: (1) a copy of the divorce judgment signed by the county clerk on July 23 and filed with the County Clerk's Office on August 7; (2) testimony that notices of divorce decrees are mailed to both parties within one week of the date that the divorce is finalized; and (3) a log entry at the County Clerk's Office showing that the notice was mailed to Defendant at his COBA office. The Defendant declined to testify at the trial.

Defendant was convicted of mail fraud and appeals. How should the court rule? Why?

4-3. Andrea is an electronics wholesaler, and Bill owns an electronics store. Andrea and Bill execute a contract, in which Andrea agrees to periodically provide smart TVs to Bill over a five-year term. Andrea represents that each delivery of smart TVs will meet certain minimum specifications detailed in the contract. For the first two years, Andrea sent Bill smart TVs by mail that met or exceeded the specifications of their agreement. In the third year, however, Andrea began having trouble with her usual suppliers and she could not obtain sufficient volume to satisfy the needs of her retail buyers. Consequently, she began buying smart TVs from low-quality manufacturers in order to meet her contractual obligations. Andrea mailed a number of these law-quality TVs to Bill, despite the fact that she *knew* when she sent them that they did not meet the required specifications per her contract with Bill. Andrea said nothing to Bill about these TVs' substandard quality.

When customers began complaining about the poor quality, Bill took a close look at the specifications and discovered what Andrea had done. When Bill learned that Andrea sent the TVs with full knowledge that they were subpar, he was so upset that he alerted the U.S. Attorney's office and complained that Andrea had committed mail fraud.

Did Andrea's willful but silent noncompliance with the terms of her contract with Bill constitute a scheme to defraud?

4-4. Suppose Albert is representing Bob in the sale of Bob's truck to Chuck. Bob instructed Albert that his rock-bottom sale price for the truck is $15,000, and that he would be very pleased with any sale price above $17,000. When Albert and Chuck meet to discuss the potential sale, Chuck begins negotiations by offering $17,500 for the truck. Albert laughs the offer off and states, "Bob gave me express instructions that I am not permitted to accept any offer less than $18,500 — that's his rock-bottom price." Chuck refuses to buy the truck for $18,500 and negotiations break off. The next day, without having discussed the matter with Bob, Albert sends Chuck a letter stating, "I have just talked the truck sale over with Bob. Though he was really firm on his floor price of $18,500, I have talked him into coming down to a new rock-bottom price of $18,000 — but he says that that is it. He will not go lower." Chuck receives the letter and decides to buy the truck for $18,000. A few weeks later, Chuck runs into Bob and discovers that Bob never said any of those things, and that Albert had lied to him about his discussions with Bob.

Did Albert's misrepresentations to Chuck constitute a scheme to defraud?

C. Deprivation of Money, Property, or Honest Services

As seen in the materials below, when proving the existence of a scheme to defraud, the government must show that the defendant intended to deprive a victim of money, property, or "honest services." This section traces the evolution of this requirement and the difficulties that courts have had in defining the terms "property" and "honest services."

1. The *McNally* Decision

In *McNally v. United States*, the United States Supreme Court found that mail or wire fraud could be based upon an intended loss of money or property, but not on a deprivation of honest services. In so holding, the Court overturned every court of appeals decision on this issue. Why did the Court take this unusual step?

McNally v. United States

483 U.S. 350 (1987)

JUSTICE WHITE delivered the opinion of the Court.

This action involves the prosecution of petitioner Gray, a former public official of the Commonwealth of Kentucky, and petitioner McNally, a private individual, for alleged violation of the federal mail fraud statute, 18 U.S.C. § 1341. The prosecution's principal theory of the case, which was accepted by the courts below, was that petitioners' participation in a self-dealing patronage scheme defrauded the citizens and government of Kentucky of certain "intangible rights," such as the right to have the Commonwealth's affairs conducted honestly. We must consider whether the jury charge permitted a conviction for conduct not within the scope of the mail fraud statute.

We accept for the sake of argument the government's view of the evidence, as follows. Petitioners and a third individual, Howard P. "Sonny" Hunt, were politically active in the Democratic Party in the Commonwealth of Kentucky during the 1970's. After Democrat Julian Carroll was elected Governor of Kentucky in 1974, Hunt was made chairman of the state Democratic Party and given *de facto* control over selecting the insurance agencies from which the Commonwealth would purchase its policies. In 1975, the Wombwell Insurance Company of Lexington, Kentucky (Wombwell), which since 1971 had acted as the Commonwealth's agent for securing a workmen's compensation policy, agreed with Hunt that in exchange for a continued agency relationship it would share any resulting commissions in excess of $50,000 a year with other insurance agencies specified by him. The commissions in question were paid to Wombwell by the large insurance companies from which it secured coverage for the Commonwealth.

From 1975 to 1979, Wombwell funneled $851,000 in commissions to 21 separate insurance agencies designated by Hunt. Among the recipients of these payments was Seton Investments, Inc. (Seton), a company controlled by Hunt and petitioner Gray and nominally owned and operated by petitioner McNally.

Gray served as Secretary of Public Protection and Regulation from 1976 to 1978 and also as Secretary of the Governor's Cabinet from 1977 to 1979. Prior to his 1976 appointment, he and Hunt established Seton for the sole purpose of sharing in the commissions distributed by Wombwell. Wombwell paid some $200,000 to Seton between 1975 and 1979, and the money was used to benefit Gray and Hunt. Pursuant to Hunt's direction, Wombwell also made excess commission payments to the Snodgrass Insurance Agency, which in turn gave the money to McNally.

On account of the foregoing activities, Hunt was charged with and pleaded guilty to mail and tax fraud and was sentenced to three years' imprisonment. Petitioners were charged with one count of conspiracy and seven counts of mail fraud, six of which were dismissed before trial. The remaining mail fraud count was based on the mailing of a commission check to Wombwell by the insurance company from which it had secured coverage for the State. This count alleged that petitioners had devised a scheme (1) to defraud the citizens and government of Kentucky of their right to have the Commonwealth's affairs conducted honestly, and (2) to obtain, directly and indirectly, money and other things of value by means of false pretenses and the concealment of material facts. The conspiracy count alleged that petitioners had (1) conspired to violate the mail fraud statute through the scheme just described and (2) conspired to defraud the United States by obstructing the collection of federal taxes.

* * *

The jury convicted petitioners on both the mail fraud and conspiracy counts, and the Court of Appeals affirmed the convictions. In affirming the substantive mail fraud conviction, the court relied on a line of decisions from the Courts of Appeals holding that the mail fraud statute proscribes schemes to defraud citizens of their intangible rights to honest and impartial government. Under these cases, a public official owes a fiduciary duty to the public, and misuse of his office for private gain is a fraud.

We granted certiorari and now reverse.

The mail fraud statute clearly protects property rights, but does not refer to the intangible right of the citizenry to good government. As first enacted in 1872, as part of a recodification of the postal laws, the statute contained a general proscription against using the mails to initiate correspondence in furtherance of "any scheme or artifice to defraud." The sponsor of the recodification stated, in apparent reference to the antifraud provision, that measures were needed "to prevent the frauds which are mostly gotten up in the large cities . . . by thieves, forgers, and rapscallions generally, for the purpose of deceiving and fleecing the innocent people in the country." Insofar as the sparse legislative history reveals anything, it indicates that the original impetus behind the mail fraud statute was to protect the people from schemes to deprive them of their money or property.

Durland v. United States, 161 U.S. 306 (1896), the first case in which this Court construed the meaning of the phrase "any scheme or artifice to defraud," held that the phrase is to be interpreted broadly insofar as property rights are concerned, but did not indicate that the statute had a more extensive reach. The Court rejected the argument that "the statute reaches only such cases as, at common law, would come within the definition of 'false pretenses,' in order to make out which there must be a misrepresentation as to some existing fact and not a mere promise as to the future." *Id.* at 312. Instead, it construed the statute to "include everything designed to defraud by representations as to the past or present, or suggestions and promises as to the future." *Id.* at 313. Accordingly, the defendant's use of the mails to sell bonds which he did not intend to honor was within the statute. The Court explained that "it was with the purpose of protecting the public against all such intentional efforts to despoil, and to prevent the post office from being used to carry them into effect, that this statute was passed." *Id.* at 314.

Congress codified the holding of *Durland* in 1909, and in doing so gave further indication that the statute's purpose is protecting property rights. The amendment added the words "or for obtaining money or property by means of false or fraudulent pretenses, representations, or promises" after the original phrase "any scheme or artifice to defraud." The new language is based on the statement in *Durland* that the statute reaches "everything designed to defraud by representations as to the past or present, or suggestions and promises as to the future." 161 U.S. at 313. However, instead of the phrase "everything designed to defraud" Congress used the words "[any scheme or artifice] for obtaining money or property."

After 1909, therefore, the mail fraud statute criminalized schemes or artifices "to defraud" or "for obtaining money or property by means of false or fraudulent pretenses, representation, or promises." Because the two phrases identifying the proscribed schemes appear in the disjunctive, it is arguable that they are to be construed independently and that the money-or-property requirement of the latter phrase does not limit schemes to defraud to those aimed at causing deprivation of money or property. This is the approach that has been taken by each of the Courts of Appeals that has addressed the issue: schemes to defraud include those designed to deprive individuals, the people, or the government of intangible rights, such as the right to have public officials perform their duties honestly.

As the Court long ago stated, however, the words "to defraud" commonly refer "to wronging one in his property rights by dishonest methods or schemes," and "usually signify the deprivation of something of value by trick, deceit, chicane or overreaching." *Hammerschmidt v. United States*, 265 U.S. 182, 188 (1924). The codification of the holding in *Durland* in 1909 does not indicate that Congress was departing from this common understanding. As we see it, adding the second phrase simply made it unmistakable that the statute reached false promises and misrepresentations as to the future as well as other frauds involving money or property.

We believe that Congress' intent in passing the mail fraud statute was to prevent the use of the mails in furtherance of such schemes. The Court has often stated that when there are two rational readings of a criminal statute, one harsher than the other, we are to choose the harsher only when Congress has spoken in clear and definite language. As the Court said in a mail fraud case years ago: "There are no constructive offenses; and before one can be punished, it must be shown that his case is plainly within the statute." *Fasulo v. United States*, 272 U.S. 620, 629 (1926). Rather than construe the statute in a manner that leaves its outer boundaries ambiguous and involves the Federal Government in setting standards of disclosure and good government for local and state officials, we read §1341 as limited in scope to the protection of property rights. If Congress desires to go further, it must speak more clearly than it has.

For purposes of this action, we assume that Hunt, as well as Gray, was a state officer. The issue is thus whether a state officer violates the mail fraud statute if he chooses an insurance agent to provide insurance for the State but specifies that the agent must share its commissions with other named insurance agencies, in one of which the officer has an ownership interest and hence profits when his agency receives part of the commissions. We note that as the action comes to us, there was no charge and the jury was not required to find that the Commonwealth itself was defrauded of any money or property. It was not charged that in the absence of the alleged scheme the Commonwealth would have paid a lower premium or secured better insurance. Hunt and Gray received part of the commissions but those commissions were not the Commonwealth's money. Nor was the jury charged that to convict it must find that the Commonwealth was deprived of control over how its money was spent. Indeed, the premium for insurance would have been paid to some agency, and what Hunt and Gray did was to assert control that the Commonwealth might not otherwise have made over the commissions paid by the insurance company to its agent.[9] Although the government now relies in part on the assertion that petitioners obtained property by means of false representations to Wombwell, there was nothing in the jury charge that required such a finding. We hold, therefore, that the jury instruction on the substantive mail fraud count permitted a conviction for conduct not within the reach of § 1341.

The government concedes that if petitioners' substantive mail fraud convictions are reversed their conspiracy convictions should also be reversed.

The judgment of the Court of Appeals is reversed, and the case is remanded for proceedings consistent with this opinion.

It is so ordered.

JUSTICE STEVENS, with whom JUSTICE O'CONNOR joins as to Parts I, II, and III, dissenting.

Congress has broadly prohibited the use of the United States mails to carry out "any scheme or artifice to defraud." 18 U.S.C. § 1341. . . .

---

9. JUSTICE STEVENS would affirm the convictions even though it was not charged that requiring the Wombwell agency to share commissions violated state law. We should assume that it did not. For the same reason we should assume that it was not illegal under state law for Hunt and Gray to own one of the agencies sharing in the commissions and hence to profit from the arrangement, whether or not they disclosed it to others in the state government. It is worth observing as well that it was not alleged that the mail fraud statute would have been violated, had Hunt and Gray reported to state officials the fact of their financial gain. The violation asserted is the failure to disclose their financial interest, even if state law did not require it, to other persons in the state government whose actions could have been affected by the disclosure. It was in this way that the indictment charged that the people of Kentucky had been deprived of their right to have the Commonwealth's affairs conducted honestly. It may well be that Congress could criminalize using the mails to further a state officer's efforts to profit from governmental decisions he is empowered to make or over which he has some supervisory authority, even if there is no state law proscribing his profiteering or even if state law expressly authorized it. But if state law expressly permitted or did not forbid a state officer such as Gray to have an ownership interest in an insurance agency handling the State's insurance, it would take a much clearer indication than the mail fraud statute evidences to convince us that having and concealing such an interest defrauds the State and is forbidden under federal law.

In the public sector, judges, state governors, chairmen of state political parties, state cabinet officers, city aldermen, Congressmen and many other state and federal officials have been convicted of defrauding citizens of their right to the honest services of their governmental officials. In most of these cases, the officials have secretly made governmental decisions with the objective of benefitting themselves or promoting their own interests, instead of fulfilling their legal commitment to provide the citizens of the state or local government with their loyal service and honest government. Similarly, many elected officials and their campaign workers have been convicted of mail fraud when they have used the mails to falsify votes, thus defrauding the citizenry of its right to an honest election. In the private sector, purchasing agents, brokers, union leaders, and others with clear fiduciary duties to their employers or unions have been found guilty of defrauding their employers or unions by accepting kickbacks or selling confidential information. In other cases, defendants have been found guilty of using the mails to defraud individuals of their rights to privacy and other non-monetary rights. All of these cases have something in common — they involved what the Court now refers to as "intangible rights." They also share something else in common. The many federal courts that have confronted the question whether these sorts of schemes constitute a "scheme or artifice to defraud" have uniformly and consistently read the statute in the same, sensible way. They have realized that nothing in the words "any scheme or artifice to defraud," or in the purpose of the statute, justifies limiting its application to schemes intended to deprive victims of money or property.

The mail fraud statute sets forth three separate prohibitions. It prohibits the use of the United States mails for the purpose of executing "[1] *any* scheme or artifice to defraud, [2] *or* for obtaining money or property by means of false or fraudulent pretenses, representations, or promises, [3] *or* to sell, dispose of, loan, exchange, alter, give away, distribute, supply, or furnish or procure for unlawful use any counterfeit or spurious coin, obligation, security, or other article, or anything represented to be or intimated or held out to be such counterfeit or spurious article." 18 U.S.C. § 1341 (emphasis and brackets added).

As the language makes clear, each of these restrictions is independent. One can violate the second clause — obtaining money or property by false pretenses — even though one does not violate the third clause — counterfeiting. Similarly, one can violate the first clause — devising a scheme or artifice to defraud — without violating the counterfeiting provision. Until today it was also obvious that one could violate the first clause by devising a scheme or artifice to defraud, even though one did not violate the second clause by seeking to obtain money or property from his victim through false pretenses. Every court to consider the matter had so held. . . .

In considering the scope of the mail fraud statute it is essential to remember Congress' purpose in enacting it. Congress sought to protect the integrity of the United States mails by not allowing them to be used as "instruments of crime." *United States v. Brewer*, 528 F.2d 492, 498 (4th Cir. 1975). Once this purpose is considered, it becomes clear that the construction the Court adopts today is senseless. Can it be that Congress sought to purge the mails of schemes to defraud citizens of money but was willing to tolerate schemes to defraud citizens of their right to an honest government, or to unbiased public officials? Is it at all rational to assume that Congress wanted to ensure that the mails not be used for petty crimes, but did not prohibit election fraud accomplished through mailing fictitious ballots?

* * *

Examination of the way the term "defraud" has long been defined, and was defined at the time of the statute's enactment, makes it clear that Congress' use of the term showed no intent to limit the statute to property loss. Similarly, the law dictionaries of the era broadly defined the type of interests subject to deprivation by fraudulent action. One leading dictionary stated that "to defraud is to withhold from another that which is justly due to him, or to deprive him of a right by deception or artifice." Another dictionary defined "defraud" as "to cheat; to deceive; to deprive of a right by an act of fraud to withhold from another what is justly due him, or to deprive him of a right, by deception or artifice."

It is, in fact, apparent that the common law criminalized frauds beyond those involving "tangible rights".

* * *

To support its crabbed construction of the Act, the Court makes a straightforward but unpersuasive argument. Since there is no explicit, unambiguous evidence that Congress actually contemplated "intangible rights" when it enacted the mail fraud statute in 1872, the Court explains, any ambiguity in the meaning of the criminal statute should be resolved in favor of lenity. The doctrine of lenity is, of course, sound, for the citizen is entitled to fair notice of what sort of conduct may give rise to punishment. But the Court's reliance on that doctrine in this case is misplaced. . . .

Especially in light of the statutory purpose, I believe that § 1341 unambiguously prohibits all schemes to defraud that use the United States mails — whether or not they involve money or property.

* * *

Perhaps the most distressing aspect of the Court's action today is its casual — almost summary — rejection of the accumulated wisdom of the many distinguished federal judges who have thoughtfully considered and correctly answered the question these cases present. The quality of this Court's work is most suspect when it stands alone, or virtually so, against a tide of well-considered opinions issued by state or federal courts. In these cases I am convinced that those judges correctly understood the intent of the Congress that enacted this statute. Even if I were not so persuaded, I could not join a rejection of such a longstanding, consistent interpretation of a federal statute.

In the long run, it is not clear how grave the ramifications of today's decision will be. Congress can, of course, negate it by amending the statute. The possibilities that the decision's impact will be mitigated do not moderate my conviction that the Court has made a serious mistake. Nor do they erase my lingering questions about why a Court that has not been particularly receptive to the rights of criminal defendants in recent years has acted so dramatically to protect the elite class of powerful individuals who will benefit from this decision.

I respectfully dissent.

Notes and Questions

1. *A surprise decision.* As Justice Stevens noted in his dissent, the majority opinion rejected "the accumulated wisdom of the many distinguished federal judges who have thoughtfully considered and correctly answered the question these cases present." What concerns led the majority to reach its conclusion? What is the essential disagreement between the majority and the dissent? In any event, as discussed in § C, 3 below, Congress wasted little time in effectively overruling the principal holding of *McNally* by enacting 18 U.S.C. § 1346, which reinstated the deprivation of "the intangible right of honest services" as a viable mail or wire fraud theory.

2. *The rule of lenity.* The *McNally* majority relied in part upon the rule of lenity in reaching its conclusion. Perhaps because of the vagueness of many white collar statutes, defendants in white collar cases often argue that the statutory language is ambiguous and should be read in their favor. Sometimes the Court accepts the argument, sometimes not. What precisely was the statutory language at issue in *McNally*? Why did the members of the majority find the language ambiguous? Were they correct?

3. *The* Durland *decision.* The Court in *McNally* discussed its earlier decision in *Durland v. United States*, 161 U.S. 306 (1896). That case was the United States Supreme Court's most important early decision interpreting a predecessor to the modern mail and wire fraud statutes. In *Durland*, the Court found that the mail fraud statute reached more broadly than the then-existing version of the common law crime of false pretenses. The Court thus found that the statute covered false promises of future actions. The Court's approach foretold subsequent, expansive readings of the mail and wire fraud statutes.

4. *Why are white collar cases different?* As seen throughout this text, Supreme Court justices who are usually perceived to be "conservative" in criminal cases often decide for the defendant in white collar cases, while "liberal" justices often decide for the government. *See* J. Kelly Strader, *The Judicial Politics of White Collar Crime*, 50 Hastings L. Rev. 1 (1999). In his dissent, Justice Stevens emphasized "lingering questions about why a Court that has not been particularly receptive to the rights of criminal defendants in recent years has acted so dramatically to protect the elite class of powerful individuals who will benefit from this decision." Do you agree that the *McNally* decision is class-based?

2. Intangible Property Rights

In the next case, the Court applied *McNally* to what it termed "intangible" property rights. What exactly were the rights at issue in this case? How were they different from the "intangible" rights at issue in *McNally*?

Carpenter v. United States
484 U.S. 19 (1987)

JUSTICE WHITE delivered the opinion of the Court.

Petitioners Kenneth Felis and R. Foster Winans were convicted of violating section 10(b) of the Securities Exchange Act of 1934 and Rule 10b-5. They were also found guilty of violating the federal mail and wire fraud statutes, 18 U.S.C. §§ 1341, 1343, and were convicted for conspiracy under 18 U.S.C. § 371. Petitioner David Carpenter, Winans' roommate, was convicted for aiding and abetting. With a minor exception, the Court of Appeals for the Second Circuit affirmed; we granted certiorari.

In 1981, Winans became a reporter for the *Wall Street Journal* (the Journal) and in the summer of 1982 became one of the two writers of a daily column, "Heard on the Street." That column discussed selected stocks or groups of stocks, giving positive and negative information about those stocks and taking "a point of view with respect to investment in the stocks that it reviews." Winans regularly interviewed corporate executives to put together interesting perspectives on the stocks that would be highlighted in upcoming columns, but, at least for the columns at issue here, none contained corporate inside information or any "hold for release" information. Because of the "Heard" column's perceived quality and integrity, it had the potential of affecting the price of the stocks which it examined. The District Court concluded on the basis of testimony presented at trial that the "Heard" column "does have an impact on the market, difficult though it may be to quantify in any particular case."

The official policy and practice at the Journal was that prior to publication, the contents of the column were the Journal's confidential information. Despite the rule, with which Winans was familiar, he entered into a scheme in October 1983 with Peter Brant and petitioner Felis, both connected with the Kidder Peabody brokerage firm in New York City, to give them advance information as to the timing and contents of the "Heard" column. This permitted Brant and Felis and another conspirator, David Clark, a client of Brant, to buy or sell based on the probable impact of the column on the market. Profits were to be shared. The conspirators agreed that the scheme would not affect the journalistic purity of the "Heard" column, and the District Court did not find that the contents of any of the articles were altered to further the profit potential of petitioners' stock-trading scheme. Over a four-month period, the brokers made prepublication trades on the basis of information given them by Winans about the contents of some 27 "Heard" columns. The net profits from these trades were about $690,000.

In November 1983, correlations between the "Heard" articles and trading in the Clark and Felis accounts were noted at Kidder Peabody and inquiries began. Brant and Felis denied knowing anyone at the Journal and took steps to conceal the trades. Later, the Securities and Exchange Commission ("SEC") began an investigation. Questions were met by denials both by the brokers at Kidder Peabody and by Winans at the Journal. As the investigation progressed, the conspirators quarreled, and on March 29, 1984, Winans and Carpenter went to the SEC and revealed the entire scheme. This indictment and a bench trial followed. Brant, who had pleaded guilty under a plea agreement, was a witness for the government. . . .

The Court is evenly divided with respect to the convictions under the securities laws and for that reason affirms the judgment below on those counts. For the reasons that follow, we also affirm the judgment with respect to the mail and wire fraud convictions.[b]

Petitioners assert that their activities were not a scheme to defraud the Journal within the meaning of the mail and wire fraud statutes; and that in any event, they did not obtain any "money or property" from the Journal, which is a necessary element of the crime under our decision last Term in *McNally v. United States*, 483 U.S. 350 (1987). We are unpersuaded by either submission and address the latter first.

We held in *McNally* that the mail fraud statute does not reach "schemes to defraud citizens of their intangible rights to honest and impartial government," and that the statute is "limited in scope to the protection of property rights." Petitioners argue that the Journal's interest in prepublication confidentiality for the "Heard" columns is no more than an intangible consideration outside the reach of §1341; nor does that law, it is urged, protect against mere injury to reputation. This is not a case like *McNally*, however. The Journal, as Winans' employer, was defrauded of much more than its contractual right to his honest and faithful service, an interest too ethereal in itself to fall within the protection of the mail fraud statute, which "had its origin in the desire to protect individual property rights." *McNally*, 483 U.S. at 359 n.8. Here, the object of the scheme was to take the Journal's confidential business information — the publication schedule and contents of the "Heard" column — and its intangible nature does not make it any less "property" protected by the mail and wire fraud statutes. *McNally* did not limit the scope of §1341 to tangible as distinguished from intangible property rights. . . .

Confidential business information has long been recognized as property. "Confidential information acquired or compiled by a corporation in the course and conduct of its business is a species of property to which the corporation has the exclusive right and benefit, and which a court of equity will protect through the injunctive process or other appropriate remedy." 3 W. Fletcher, Cyclopedia of Law of Private Corporations §857.1 at 260 (1986). The Journal had a property right in

---

b. The Supreme Court affirmed the misappropriation theory of insider trading in United States v. O'Hagan, 521 U.S. 642 (1997). *See* Chapter 5, Securities Fraud, *infra*.

keeping confidential and making exclusive use, prior to publication, of the schedule and contents of the "Heard" column. As the Court has observed before:

> [N]ews matter, however little susceptible of ownership or dominion in the absolute sense, is stock in trade, to be gathered at the cost of enterprise, organization, skill, labor, and money, and to be distributed and sold to those who will pay money for it, as for any other merchandise.

International News Service v. Associated Press, 248 U.S. 215, 236 (1918).

Petitioners' arguments that they did not interfere with the Journal's use of the information, or did not publicize it and deprive the Journal of the first public use of it, miss the point. The confidential information was generated from the business, and the business had a right to decide how to use it prior to disclosing it to the public. Petitioners cannot successfully contend that a scheme to defraud requires a monetary loss, such as giving the information to a competitor; it is sufficient that the Journal has been deprived of its right to exclusive use of the information, for exclusivity is an important aspect of confidential business information and most private property for that matter.

We cannot accept petitioners' further argument that Winans' conduct in revealing prepublication information was no more than a violation of workplace rules and did not amount to fraudulent activity that is proscribed by the mail fraud statute. Sections 1341 and 1343 reach any scheme to deprive another of money or property by means of false or fraudulent pretenses, representations, or promises. . . .

The District Court found that Winans' undertaking at the Journal was not to reveal prepublication information about his column, a promise that became a sham when in violation of his duty he passed along to his co-conspirators confidential information belonging to the Journal, pursuant to an ongoing scheme to share profits from trading in anticipation of the "Heard" column's impact on the stock market. As the New York courts have recognized: "It is well established, as a general proposition, that a person who acquires special knowledge or information by virtue of a confidential or fiduciary relationship with another is not free to exploit that knowledge or information for his own personal benefit but must account to his principal for any profits derived therefrom." *Diamond v. Oreamuno*, 24 N.Y.2d 494, 497 (1969); *see also* Restatement (Second) of Agency §§ 388, Comment *c*, 396(c) (1958).

We have little trouble in holding that the conspiracy here to trade on the Journal's confidential information is not outside the reach of the mail and wire fraud statutes, provided the other elements of the offenses are satisfied. The Journal's business information that it intended to be kept confidential was its property; the declaration to that effect in the employee manual merely removed any doubts on that score and made the finding of specific intent to defraud that much easier. Winans continued in the employ of the Journal, appropriating its confidential business information for his own use, all the while pretending to perform his duty of safeguarding it. In fact, he told his editors twice about leaks of confidential information not related to the stock-trading scheme, demonstrating both his knowledge that the Journal viewed information concerning the "Heard" column as confidential and his deceit as he played the role of a loyal employee. Furthermore, the District Court's conclusion that each of the petitioners acted with the required specific intent to defraud is strongly supported by the evidence.

Lastly, we reject the submission that using the wires and the mail to print and send the Journal to its customers did not satisfy the requirement that those mediums be used to execute the scheme at issue. The courts below were quite right in observing that circulation of the "Heard" column was not only anticipated but an essential part of the scheme. Had the column not been made available to Journal customers, there would have been no effect on stock prices and no likelihood of profiting from the information leaked by Winans.

The judgment below is *affirmed*.

Notes and Questions

1. *Intangible property rights.* What exactly was the property right at stake in *Carpenter*? How was the *Journal* harmed in *Carpenter*, if at all? Why did the Court reach a different result than the one it reached in *McNally*? Does *Carpenter* limit *McNally*'s significance?

2. *Criticisms of Carpenter.* Scholars have criticized the *Carpenter* decision's expansive reading of the mail and wire fraud statutes. As Professor Coffee has written,

> [I]nsider trading revelations have produced a Supreme Court decision, *Carpenter v. United States*, that exhibits all the characteristics of an overbroad, moralistic legislative response. In *Carpenter*, the Court held unanimously that an employee who leaks to third parties confidential business information belonging to his employer embezzles property in violation of the federal mail and wire fraud statutes, even though the employer suffers no apparent economic injury as a result. At bottom, *Carpenter* rests on an analogy that broadly characterizes the unauthorized communication of trade secrets as equivalent to the crime of embezzlement.

> [T]his view of "confidential information" as a form of property covered by the laws against larceny is (a) historically unsound, (b) inconsistent with most statutory law dealing with the subject of trade secrets, and (c) capable of trivializing the Court's decision only months earlier in *McNally v. United States*, which clearly sought to cut back on the amoebalike growth of the mail and wire fraud statutes. More important than all these considerations, however, is the fact that *Carpenter*'s logic has the potential to alter significantly the relationship between employers and employees across the landscape of American business life.

> More than any other theory that the Court could have chosen to address the evil of insider trading, *Carpenter*'s doctrinal invention — the idea that divulging confidential information of one's employer amounts to

embezzlement — has the ability to chill employee mobility and increase the social control that employers have over employees.

John C. Coffee, Jr., *Hush!: The Criminal Status of Confidential Information after McNally and Carpenter and the Enduring Problem of Overcriminalization*, 26 Am. Crim. L. Rev. 121, 122–23 (1988). Are Professor Coffee's criticisms sound? Why or why not?

More recently, Professor Ellen Podgor raised the concern that Winans and Carpenter being an openly gay couple may have adversely impacted their defense. *See* Ellen Podgor, Carpenter v. United States: *Did Being Gay Matter?*, 15 Tenn. J.L. & Pol'y 116 (2020). Professor Podgor's excellent discussion addresses important concerns of prosecutorial and jury bias that extend well beyond the facts of *Carpenter*.

3. *The "right-to-control" theory.* Is the right to control how property is used a "property" interest for purposes of the mail and wire fraud statutes? In *United States v. Catalfo*, 64 F.3d 1070, 1076–1077 (7th Cir. 1995), *cert. denied*, 517 U.S. 1192 (1996), for example, the defendant engaged in a scheme to prevent the victim, a commodities firm, from controlling its *risk* of loss. The court found that this satisfied the property requirement. *See also United States v. Gray*, 405 F.3d 227, 234 (4th Cir. 2005) (finding an insurance company's right to control to whom the benefits of an insurance policy would be paid amounted to a property interest). Under this "right-to-control theory," the scheme to defraud need not seek to impose an actual economic loss on the victim; it need only deprive the victim of information necessary to exercise discretion in how its property is to be used or disposed of.

There has been varied treatment among the circuits concerning the scope of the "right-to-control" theory. Some courts have limited application of the theory to only those cases where the misrepresentation goes to an essential element of the bargain (e.g., merely being a "but for" cause of assent is not enough) and exposes the victim to either some tangible economic risk or liability for a violation of the law. For example, in *United States v. Davis*, 2017 WL 3328240 (S.D.N.Y. Aug. 3, 2017), a builder won a contract for a post-9-11 World Trade Center project by misrepresenting that it was a minority-owned and woman-owned business enterprise ("MWBE"). It was a goal of the New York Port Authority to grant a certain percentage of its contracts to MWBEs. Despite its false representation, the contractor completed the work on budget and without deficiency. The district court set aside the jury's verdict against the builder for wire fraud, concluding that the facts did not support a scheme to defraud under the right-to-control theory. According to the court, the builder's false representations regarding their minority status did not go to an "essential element" of the bargain (even if it may have been a "but-for" cause of the Port Authority's assent to the bargain) because MWBE status was only an "aspiration" of the Port Authority; it was not a crucial condition or legal requirement. *Id.* at *8, *16. Moreover, the Port Authority suffered no actual (or risk of) economic harm because of the deception. The heart of the bargain was for the construction of a 104-floor building at a contracted-for price, and the builder's deception neither impacted that contractual promise nor placed it at risk. *Id.* at *15.

Though the Supreme Court's recent opinion in *Kelly v. United States, infra*, does not expressly address the right-to-control theory, as you read through the case, consider its potential implications for the theory's application.

Note and Questions on Cleveland v. United States

Following *McNally* and *Carpenter*, courts struggled to define the term "property," particularly in cases where the government alleged that the "property" at issue was a license or permit. In *Cleveland v. United States*, 531 U.S. 12 (2000), the Supreme Court addressed the question whether a state license is "property" for purposes of the mail and wire fraud statutes. In that case, Cleveland and others misrepresented the true ownership of their business to the state in applications for licenses to operate video poker machines. Based on these false applications, the defendants were convicted of mail fraud — and of RICO, money laundering, and conspiracy, all predicated on the mail fraud. On appeal, the defendants argued that their mail fraud convictions should be overturned because the government did not have a property interest in the unissued licenses. The Court agreed, holding that the state's principal interest in the unissued licenses was *regulatory*, not as property. The Court rejected the government's claims that the state had a property interest in the unissued licenses because they: (1) generated significant revenue for the state and (2) gave the state a right of control over gambling practices in the state. Concerning the first claim, the Court held that although the state had a substantial economic stake in the video poker industry, it "receives the lion's share of its expected revenue not while the licenses remain in its own hands, but only after they have been issued to licensees." *Id*. at 22. Regarding the second claim, "far from composing an interest that has long been recognized as property," the state's "intangible rights of allocation, exclusion, and control [through the issue of licenses] amount to no more and no less than Louisiana's sovereign power to regulate." *Id*. at 23. In addition, the Court rejected the government's broad understanding of property rights per the rule of lenity, emphasizing that this "interpretive guide is especially appropriate in construing §1341 because, as this case demonstrates, mail fraud is a predicate offense under RICO, 18 U.S.C. §1961(1), and the money laundering statute, §1956 (c)(7)(A)." Finally, the Court rejected the government's broad conception of "property" under the mail and wire fraud statutes because such a reading "invites us to approve a sweeping expansion of federal criminal jurisdiction in the absence of a clear statement by Congress." *Id*. at 24.

1. *Varying interpretations of the mail and wire fraud statutes.* In *Carpenter*, the Court broadly interpreted the concept of "property" under the statutes. In *Cleveland*, the Court reverted to a narrow construction of the statutes. Can you explain the varying outcomes?

2. *Federalism.* In *Cleveland*, the Court stated, "We resist the government's reading of §1341 . . . because it invites us to approve a sweeping expansion of federal criminal jurisdiction in the absence of a clear statement by Congress." Does this observation also apply to the government's reading of the statute in *Carpenter*? Why or why not?

3. *The right to collect taxes as a property interest.* By a five-to-four vote, the Supreme Court, in *Pasquantino v. United States*, 544 U.S. 349 (2005), held that Canada's right to collect taxes on imported liquor constitutes "property" under the wire fraud statute. The defendants had smuggled liquor from the United States into Canada, depriving Canada of importation and sales taxes on the liquor. The Court found that Canada's right to collect these taxes is a "straightforward 'economic' interest" that is distinguishable from the alleged property interest at issue in *Cleveland. Pasquantino*, 544 U.S. at 357. The case also extended the mail and wire fraud statutes to cases where the alleged victim was a foreign government. In her dissent, Justice Ginsburg concluded that "the Court has ascribed an exorbitant scope to the wire fraud statute." *Id.* at 373 (Ginsburg, J., dissenting). Is she correct? Why or why not?

In the following case, the Supreme Court continued to fill out the concept of "property" under the mail and wire fraud statutes. In addition, the Court took up the important question of whether deceptive conduct that just happens to result in the loss of money or property is enough to incur liability, or whether, instead, the victim's loss of money or property must be the *aim* or *object* of the deceptive scheme.

Kelly v. United States

140 S. Ct. 1565 (2020)

JUSTICE KAGAN delivered the opinion of the Court.

For four days in September 2013, traffic ground to a halt in Fort Lee, New Jersey. The cause was an unannounced realignment of 12 toll lanes leading to the George Washington Bridge, an entryway into Manhattan administered by the Port Authority of New York and New Jersey. For decades, three of those access lanes had been reserved during morning rush hour for commuters coming from the streets of Fort Lee. But on these four days — with predictable consequences — only a single lane was set aside. The public officials who ordered that change claimed they were reducing the number of dedicated lanes to conduct a traffic study. In fact, they did so for a political reason — to punish the mayor of Fort Lee for refusing to support the New Jersey Governor's reelection bid.

Exposure of their behavior led to the criminal convictions we review here. The Government charged the responsible officials under the federal statutes prohibiting wire fraud and fraud on a federally funded program or entity. Both those laws target fraudulent schemes for obtaining property. The jury convicted the defendants, and the lower courts upheld the verdicts.

The question presented is whether the defendants committed property fraud. The evidence the jury heard no doubt shows wrongdoing — deception, corruption, abuse of power. But the federal fraud statutes at issue do not criminalize all such conduct. Under settled precedent, the officials could violate those laws only if an object of their dishonesty was to obtain the Port Authority's money or property. The Government contends it was, because the officials sought both to "commandeer" the Bridge's access lanes and to divert the wage labor of the Port Authority employees used in that effort. We disagree. The realignment of the toll lanes was an exercise of regulatory power — something this Court has already held fails to meet the statutes' property requirement. And the employees' labor was just the incidental cost of that regulation, rather than itself an object of the officials' scheme. We therefore reverse the convictions.

The setting of this case is the George Washington Bridge. Running between Fort Lee and Manhattan, it is the busiest motor-vehicle bridge in the world. Twelve lanes with tollbooths feed onto the Bridge's upper level from the Fort Lee side. Decades ago, the then-Governor of New Jersey committed to a set allocation of those lanes for the morning commute. And (save for the four days soon described) his plan has lasted to this day. Under the arrangement, nine of the lanes carry traffic coming from nearby highways. The three remaining lanes, designated by a long line of traffic cones laid down each morning, serve only cars coming from Fort Lee.

The case's cast of characters are public officials who worked at or with the Port Authority and had political ties to New Jersey's then-Governor Chris Christie. The Port Authority is a bi-state agency that manages bridges, tunnels, airports, and other transportation facilities in New York and New Jersey. At the time relevant here, William Baroni was its Deputy Executive Director, an appointee of Governor Christie and the highest ranking New Jersey official in the agency. Together with the Executive Director (a New York appointee), he oversaw "all aspects of the Port Authority's business," including operation of the George Washington Bridge. David Wildstein (who became the Government's star witness) functioned as Baroni's chief of staff. And Bridget Anne Kelly was a Deputy Chief of Staff to Governor Christie with special responsibility for managing his relations with local officials. She often worked hand-in-hand with Baroni and Wildstein to deploy the Port Authority's resources in ways that would encourage mayors and other local figures to support the Governor.

The fateful lane change arose out of one mayor's resistance to such blandishments. In 2013, Governor Christie was up for reelection, and he wanted to notch a large, bipartisan victory as he ramped up for a presidential campaign. On his behalf, Kelly avidly courted Democratic mayors for their endorsements — among them, Mark Sokolich of Fort Lee. As a result, that town received some valuable benefits from the Port Authority, including an expensive shuttle-bus service. But that summer, Mayor Sokolich informed Kelly's office that he would not back the Governor's campaign. A frustrated Kelly reached out to Wildstein for ideas on how to respond. He suggested that getting rid of the dedicated Fort Lee lanes on the Bridge's toll plaza would cause rush-hour traffic to back up onto local streets, leading to gridlock there. Kelly agreed to the idea in an admirably concise e-mail: "Time for some traffic problems in Fort Lee." In a later phone conversation, Kelly confirmed to Wildstein that she wanted to "creat[e] a traffic jam that would punish" Mayor Sokolich and "send him a message." And after Wildstein relayed those communications, Baroni gave the needed sign-off.

To complete the scheme, Wildstein then devised "a cover story"—that the lane change was part of a traffic study, intended to assess whether to retain the dedicated Fort Lee lanes in the future. Wildstein, Baroni, and Kelly all agreed to use that "public policy" justification when speaking with the media, local officials, and the Port Authority's own employees. And to give their story credibility, Wildstein in fact told the Port Authority's engineers to collect "some numbers on how[ ] far back the traffic was delayed." That inquiry bore little resemblance to the Port Authority's usual traffic studies. According to one engineer's trial testimony, the Port Authority never closes lanes to study traffic patterns, because "computer-generated model[ing]" can itself predict the effect of such actions. And the information that the Port Authority's engineers collected on this singular occasion was mostly "not useful" and "discarded." Nor did Wildstein or Baroni show any interest in the data. They never asked to review what the engineers had found; indeed, they learned of the results only weeks later, after a journalist filed a public-records request. So although the engineers spent valuable time assessing the lane change, their work was to no practical effect.

Baroni, Wildstein, and Kelly also agreed to incur another cost—for extra toll collectors—in pursuit of their object. Wildstein's initial thought was to eliminate all three dedicated lanes by not laying down any traffic cones, thus turning the whole toll plaza into a free-for-all. But the Port Authority's chief engineer told him that without the cones "there would be a substantial risk of sideswipe crashes" involving cars coming into the area from different directions. So Wildstein went back to Baroni and Kelly and got their approval to keep one lane reserved for Fort Lee traffic. That solution, though, raised another complication. Ordinarily, if a toll collector on a Fort Lee lane has to take a break, he closes his booth, and drivers use one of the other two lanes. Under the one-lane plan, of course, that would be impossible. So the Bridge manager told Wildstein that to make the scheme work, "an extra toll collector" would always have to be "on call" to relieve the regular collector when he went on break. Once again, Wildstein took the news to Baroni and Kelly. Baroni thought it was "funny," remarking that "only at the Port Authority would [you] have to pay a toll collector to just sit there and wait." Still, he and Kelly gave the okay.

The plan was now ready, and on September 9 it went into effect. Without advance notice and on the (traffic-heavy) first day of school, Port Authority employees placed traffic cones two lanes further to the right than usual, restricting cars from Fort Lee to a single lane. Almost immediately, the town's streets came to a standstill. According to the Fort Lee Chief of Police, the traffic rivaled that of 9/11, when the George Washington Bridge had shut down. School buses stood in place for hours. An ambulance struggled to reach the victim of a heart attack; police had trouble responding to a report of a missing child. Mayor Sokolich tried to reach Baroni, leaving a message that the call was about an "urgent matter of public safety." Yet Baroni failed to return that call or any other: He had agreed with Wildstein and Kelly that they should all maintain "radio silence." A text from the Mayor to Baroni about the locked-in school buses—also unanswered—went around the horn to

Wildstein and Kelly. The last replied: "Is it wrong that I am smiling?" The three merrily kept the lane realignment in place for another three days. It ended only when the Port Authority's Executive Director found out what had happened and reversed what he called their "abusive decision."

The fallout from the scheme was swift and severe. Baroni, Kelly, and Wildstein all lost their jobs. More to the point here, they all ran afoul of federal prosecutors. Wildstein pleaded guilty to conspiracy charges and agreed to cooperate with the Government. Baroni and Kelly went to trial on charges of wire fraud, fraud on a federally funded program or entity (the Port Authority), and conspiracy to commit each of those crimes. The jury found both of them guilty on all counts. The Court of Appeals for the Third Circuit affirmed, rejecting Baroni's and Kelly's claim that the evidence was insufficient to support their convictions. We granted certiorari.

The Government in this case needed to prove *property* fraud. The federal wire fraud statute makes it a crime to effect (with use of the wires) "any scheme or artifice to defraud, or for obtaining money or property by means of false or fraudulent pretenses, representations, or promises." 18 U.S.C. §1343. Construing that disjunctive language as a unitary whole, this Court has held that "the money-or-property requirement of the latter phrase" also limits the former. *McNally v. United States*, 483 U.S. 350, 358 (1987). The wire fraud statute thus prohibits only deceptive "schemes to deprive [the victim of] money or property." *Id.*, at 356. Similarly, the federal-program fraud statute bars "obtain[ing] by fraud" the "property" (including money) of a federally funded program or entity like the Port Authority. §666(a)(1)(A). So under either provision, the Government had to show not only that Baroni and Kelly engaged in deception, but that an "object of the[ir] fraud [was] 'property.'" *Cleveland v. United States*, 531 U.S. 12, 26 (2000).

That requirement, this Court has made clear, prevents these statutes from criminalizing all acts of dishonesty by state and local officials. Some decades ago, courts of appeals often construed the federal fraud laws to "proscribe[ ] schemes to defraud citizens of their intangible rights to honest and impartial government." *McNally*, 483 U.S. at 355. This Court declined to go along. The fraud statutes, we held in *McNally*, were "limited in scope to the protection of property rights." They did not authorize federal prosecutors to "set[ ] standards of disclosure and good government for local and state officials." Congress responded to that decision by enacting a law barring fraudulent schemes "to deprive another of the intangible right of honest services" — regardless of whether the scheme sought to divest the victim of any property. §1346. But the vagueness of that language led this Court to adopt "a limiting construction," confining the statute to schemes involving bribes or kickbacks. *Skilling v. United States*, 561 U.S. 358, 405, 410 (2010). We specifically rejected a proposal to construe the statute as encompassing "undisclosed self-dealing by a public official," even when he hid financial interests. *Id.*, at 409.[c] The upshot is that federal fraud law leaves

---

c. Honest services fraud and the Court's *Skilling* opinion are addressed later in this chapter at §C, 3, *infra*.

much public corruption to the States (or their electorates) to rectify. Save for bribes or kickbacks (not at issue here), a state or local official's fraudulent schemes violate that law only when, again, they are "for obtaining money or property."

The Government acknowledges this much, but thinks Baroni's and Kelly's convictions remain valid. According to the Government's theory of the case, Baroni and Kelly "used a lie about a fictional traffic study" to achieve their goal of reallocating the Bridge's toll lanes. The Government accepts that the lie itself— *i.e.,* that the lane change was part of a traffic study, rather than political payback—could not get the prosecution all the way home. As the Government recognizes, the deceit must also have had the "object" of obtaining the Port Authority's money or property. The scheme met that requirement, the Government argues, in two ways. First, the Government claims that Baroni and Kelly sought to "commandeer[ ]" part of the Bridge itself—to "take control" of its "physical lanes." Second, the Government asserts that the two defendants aimed to deprive the Port Authority of the costs of compensating the traffic engineers and back-up toll collectors who performed work relating to the lane realignment. On either theory, the Government insists, Baroni's and Kelly's scheme targeted "a 'species of valuable right [or] interest' that constitutes 'property' under the fraud statutes."

We cannot agree. As we explain below, the Government could not have proved— on either of its theories, though for different reasons—that Baroni's and Kelly's scheme was "directed at the [Port Authority's] property." Baroni and Kelly indeed "plotted to reduce [Fort Lee's] lanes." But that realignment was a quintessential exercise of regulatory power. And this Court has already held that a scheme to alter such a regulatory choice is not one to appropriate the government's property. See *Cleveland*, 531 U.S. at 23. By contrast, a scheme to usurp a public employee's paid time is one to take the government's property. But Baroni's and Kelly's plan never had that as an object. The use of Port Authority employees was incidental to—the mere cost of implementing—the sought-after regulation of the Bridge's toll lanes.

Start with this Court's decision in *Cleveland*, which reversed another set of federal fraud convictions based on the distinction between property and regulatory power. The defendant there had engaged in a deceptive scheme to influence, to his own benefit, Louisiana's issuance of gaming licenses. The Government argued that his fraud aimed to deprive the State of property by altering its licensing decisions. This Court rejected the claim. The State's "intangible rights of allocation, exclusion, and control"—its prerogatives over who should get a benefit and who should not—do "not create a property interest." *Id.* Rather, the Court stated, those rights "amount to no more and no less than" the State's "sovereign power to regulate." Or said another way: The defendant's fraud "implicate[d] the Government's role as sovereign" wielding "traditional police powers"—not its role "as property holder." *Id.* at 23–24. And so his conduct, however deceitful, was not property fraud.

The same is true of the lane realignment. Through that action, Baroni and Kelly changed the traffic flow onto the George Washington Bridge's tollbooth plaza. Contrary to the Government's view, the two defendants did not "commandeer" the Bridge's access lanes (supposing that word bears its normal meaning). They (of course) did not walk away with the lanes; nor did they take the lanes from the Government by converting them to a non-public use. Rather, Baroni and Kelly regulated use of the lanes, as officials responsible for roadways so often do — allocating lanes as between different groups of drivers. To borrow *Cleveland*'s words, Baroni and Kelly exercised the regulatory rights of "allocation, exclusion, and control" — deciding that drivers from Fort Lee should get two fewer lanes while drivers from nearby highways should get two more. They did so, according to all the Government's evidence, for bad reasons; and they did so by resorting to lies. But still, *what* they did was alter a regulatory decision about the toll plaza's use — in effect, about which drivers had a "license" to use which lanes. And under *Cleveland*, that run-of-the-mine exercise of regulatory power cannot count as the taking of property.

A government's right to its employees' time and labor, by contrast, can undergird a property fraud prosecution. Suppose that a mayor uses deception to get "on-the-clock city workers" to renovate his daughter's new home. *United States v. Pabey,* 664 F.3d 1084, 1089 (CA7 2011). Or imagine that a city parks commissioner induces his employees into doing gardening work for political contributors. See *United States v. Delano*, 55 F.3d 720, 723 (CA2 1995). As both defendants agree, the cost of those employees' services would qualify as an economic loss to a city, sufficient to meet the federal fraud statutes' property requirement. No less than if the official took cash out of the city's bank account would he have deprived the city of a "valuable entitlement." *Pasquantino v. United States,,* 544 U.S. 349, 357 (2005).

But that property must play more than some bit part in a scheme: It must be an "object of the fraud." *Id.,* at 355. Or put differently, a property fraud conviction cannot stand when the loss to the victim is only an incidental byproduct of the scheme. In the home-and-garden examples cited above, that constraint raised no problem: The entire point of the fraudsters' plans was to obtain the employees' services. But now consider the difficulty if the prosecution in *Cleveland* had raised a similar employee-labor argument. As the Government noted at oral argument here, the fraud on Louisiana's licensing system doubtless imposed costs calculable in employee time: If nothing else, some state worker had to process each of the fraudster's falsified applications. But still, the Government acknowledged, those costs were "[i]ncidental." The object of the scheme was never to get the employees' labor: It was to get gaming licenses. So the labor costs could not sustain the conviction for property fraud.

This case is no different. The time and labor of Port Authority employees were just the implementation costs of the defendants' scheme to reallocate the Bridge's access lanes. Or said another way, the labor costs were an incidental (even if foreseen) byproduct of Baroni's and Kelly's regulatory object. Neither defendant sought to obtain the services that the employees provided. The back-up toll collectors — whom Baroni joked would just "sit there and wait" — did nothing he or Kelly thought useful. Indeed, those workers came onto the scene only because the Port

Authority's chief engineer managed to restore one of Fort Lee's lanes to reduce the risk of traffic accidents. In the defendants' original plan, which scrapped all reserved lanes, there was no reason for extra toll collectors. And similarly, Baroni and Kelly did not hope to obtain the data that the traffic engineers spent their time collecting. By the Government's own account, the traffic study the defendants used for a cover story was a "sham," and they never asked to see its results. Maybe, as the Government contends, all of this work was "needed" to realize the final plan — "to accomplish what [Baroni and Kelly] were trying to do with the [B]ridge." Even if so, it would make no difference. Every regulatory decision . . . requires the use of some employee labor. But that does not mean every scheme to alter a regulation has that labor as its object. Baroni's and Kelly's plan aimed to impede access from Fort Lee to the George Washington Bridge. The cost of the employee hours spent on implementing that plan was its incidental byproduct.

To rule otherwise would undercut this Court's oft-repeated instruction: Federal prosecutors may not use property fraud statutes to "set[ ] standards of disclosure and good government for local and state officials." *McNally*, 483 U.S. at 360. Much of governance involves (as it did here) regulatory choice. If U.S. Attorneys could prosecute as property fraud every lie a state or local official tells in making such a decision, the result would be — as *Cleveland* recognized — "a sweeping expansion of federal criminal jurisdiction." 531 U.S. at 24. And if those prosecutors could end-run *Cleveland* just by pointing to the regulation's incidental costs, the same ballooning of federal power would follow. In effect, the Federal Government could use the criminal law to enforce (its view of) integrity in broad swaths of state and local policymaking. The property fraud statutes do not countenance that outcome. They do not "proscribe[ ] schemes to defraud citizens of their intangible rights to honest and impartial government." *McNally*, 483 U.S. at 355. They bar only schemes for obtaining property.

As Kelly's own lawyer acknowledged, this case involves an "abuse of power." For no reason other than political payback, Baroni and Kelly used deception to reduce Fort Lee's access lanes to the George Washington Bridge — and thereby jeopardized the safety of the town's residents. But not every corrupt act by state or local officials is a federal crime. Because the scheme here did not aim to obtain money or property, Baroni and Kelly could not have violated the federal-program fraud or wire fraud laws. We therefore reverse the judgment of the Court of Appeals and remand the case for further proceedings consistent with this opinion.

It is so ordered.

Notes and Questions

1. *Loss of money or property must be an aim or object of deception.* The *Kelly* Court makes it clear that mail and wire fraud liability requires more than the loss of money or property as a mere "incidental by-product" of a deception (even if that loss is foreseen). According to the Court, the victim's loss of money or property must "play more than some bit part in a scheme: it must be an 'object of the fraud.'" But was this

the correct result? After all, the victim's loss is the same regardless of whether the perpetrator sought that loss as an aim or object of the deception.

2. *Exercise of regulatory power is not property.* Both *Cleveland* and *Kelly* explain that a deceptive scheme to alter a state's exercise of regulatory power (of "allocation, exclusion, and control") does not deprive the state of a property interest. The *Kelly* Court was, however, prepared to find that the deceptive misuse of regulatory authority to divert state-employee time and labor for personal use would deprive the state of a property interest for purposes of the mail and wire fraud statutes, so long as the prosecution can show that usurping such property was an aim or object of the deception. What are some examples?

3. *Mail and wire fraud statutes do not criminalize bad government.* The Court's decision in *Kelly* offers another confirmation of *McNally's* "oft-repeated instruction" that "Federal prosecutors may not use property fraud statutes to 'set[] standards of disclosure and good government for local and state officials.'" *McNally*, 483 U.S., at 360. The *Kelly* Court offers some of the same federalism-based arguments made in *Cleveland* in support of this instruction. What are they?

Problems

4-5. Terry Howard was the Comptroller of the State Bridge Commission (the "Commission"). The Commission operates and maintains bridges within the state. Among these bridges are seven toll bridges that generate more than $10 million in revenue annually. Mike Moose was the state's executive auditor and was Howard's close personal friend. Ten people are members of the Commission.

The Commission invested toll bridge revenues in short-term certificates of deposit at banks selected through competitive bidding. As the Commission's Comptroller, Howard was responsible for this process. Howard would notify interested banks that the Commission had money it wished to deposit and would advise banks that they could submit confidential bids to him in writing or by telephone by a certain deadline. Commission guidelines required that, after the bidding deadline passed, the funds be deposited with the bank that had offered the highest interest rate on the certificates of deposit.

On 10 occasions, Howard disclosed bidding information to Moose, who in turn disclosed the information to a representative of Acme Bank. Acme Bank was thus able to outbid the other banks by offering a slightly higher rate of interest and, as a result, received deposits of $40,000,000 in Commission funds. Howard and Moose were both investors in Acme bank.

The government indicted Howard and Moose on the theory that they engaged in a scheme to defraud banks who submitted failed bids in the bidding process. According to the government, the victim banks were deprived of their intangible property interest in the chance to compete in a fair bidding process.

The defendants have moved to dismiss the indictment because the competing banks were not deprived of a cognizable property interest. How should the court rule? Why?

4-6. The defendants have been charged with defrauding the United States government by arranging sales of privately owned, U.S.-made weapons to Iran. United States law prohibits such sales. As part of the scheme, the defendants allegedly used the mail to deceive the United States into believing that the true destination of the arms was Israel, not Iran. The United States government has a right to veto the sale of U.S.-made weapons from one government to another, and thus would have had the right to veto a sale of the weapons by Israel to Iran. The weapons actually were sold directly to Iran. The government's theory is that the right to veto sales of U.S.-made or licensed weapons by one foreign government to another is a property right for wire and mail fraud purposes.

Defendants have moved to dismiss the indictment. Should they succeed? Why or why not?

4-7. The defendant lives in a city that operates under a charter providing that its citizens elect a mayor for a four-year term. Last January, the defendant was the incumbent mayor and a candidate for re-election.

Candidates for public office in the state must abide by the provisions of the state's Campaign Finance Disclosure Act ("CFDA"). The CFDA requires any candidate for elective office to disclose contributions, loans, or loan guarantees in excess of $2,000 from any individual. Candidates must also file campaign finance disclosure reports with the state Board of Ethics (the "Board" or "Board of Ethics"). The reports are to detail all campaign contributions, loans, loan guarantors, and expenditures.

According to the indictment, the defendant obtained but did not disclose several loans from September to November of last year. On September 23, the defendant obtained a $50,000 bank loan for the purpose of financing his reelection campaign. The defendant had insufficient income and assets to qualify for the loan, and a local businessperson with sufficient assets served as cosigner. One week later, on October 7, the defendant obtained another $50,000 loan with the same businessperson as cosigner. The cosigner also assigned a $50,000 certificate of deposit as collateral.

On October 22, the defendant obtained two new loans to pay off the loans that had been guaranteed by the businessperson. The indictment charges that the new loans were secured by a pledge of $99,000 in cash, supplied by one of the defendant's wealthy supporters who had a financial interest in the transfer of a permit for operation of a city landfill to Waste Management, Inc. ("Waste Management"). The transfer, allegedly supported by the defendant, was a major election issue. The defendant obtained another $50,000 loan on November 3, allegedly secured by a pledge of $55,000 in cash supplied by the same wealthy supporter. The indictment asserts that the defendant knew that his failure to disclose all four loans violated the CFDA.

The defendant was reelected as mayor on November 20. During the course of the campaign, the defendant had contracted with a political consultant to help with the re-election bid, and by the time of the election, the defendant owed the consultant over $57,000. On November 22, a Waste Management lobbyist allegedly gave the defendant approximately $44,000 in cash for the defendant's political consultant to hold as collateral until the defendant paid the consultant the money he owed. Defendant failed to disclose these amounts.

The defendant not only failed to report the amount and source of cash and loans, but he also allegedly misled the Board of Ethics during its investigation of his activities. Specifically, the indictment alleges that the defendant falsely represented that he had the creditworthiness to obtain the original loans on September 23 and October 7 without a cosigner and that the replacement loans were obtained on the basis of independent creditworthiness. And despite requests from the Board for information on the use of collateral to secure the replacement loans, the defendant allegedly failed to disclose that the collateral was borrowed cash. The indictment also asserts that the defendant used the mail to submit a false campaign finance disclosure report and two letters concerning the ethics investigation to the Board of Ethics, as well as to receive the financial benefits of office.

The defendant filed a motion to dismiss the mail fraud charges, and the trial court granted the motion. The government appeals, contending that the defendant's indictment sufficiently charged the offense of mail fraud because the salary and employment benefits of elected office constitute "money or property" under the mail fraud statute. The government also reasons that fraudulent job procurement can constitute mail fraud in the election context just as it can in the typical hiring context.

How should the court rule? Why?

4-8. Abigail is the Mayor of Wonder City. Abigail and Charlotte have had a long history of playing practical jokes on one another ever since their sorority days in college. Abigail was looking for an opportunity to really get Charlotte and she finally had an idea. She emailed Charlotte and invited her to a surprise party for their mutual friend, Barbara. The address Abigail gave Charlotte was for an empty lot 45 minutes outside of town. Charlotte went out and bought a present for Barbara and a new dress for herself. She didn't have a lot of money, but she wasn't going to disappoint Barbara! On the day of the party, Charlotte punched the address into her car's GPS. When she arrived at the empty lot an hour later, she found a note from Abigail nailed to the tree in the empty lot: "GOT YOU AGAIN!" Charlotte was not amused this time. Abigail's deception had cost her the price of a present, a new dress, and 10 gallons of gas—and she couldn't afford any of it. Charlotte mentioned the incident to her friend, Joe, who happens to be a U.S. Attorney. Abigail is a politically unpopular mayor, and the federal prosecutor sees that he could make a name for himself by charging her.

You are the U.S. Attorney's new intern. He asks you to research the issue and tell him whether you think these facts support a wire fraud charge against Abigail. What's your answer?

4-9. Charles is the head coach of a Division 1 college football program. He was approached by Bill, a professional sports agent, with a "business" proposal. If Charles would encourage his players to sign with Bill while they are still in college, then Bill will pay Charles money for each player he signs from the team. Per NCAA rules, if a college football player signs with a professional agent, he is no longer eligible to play at the collegiate level. Any college that permits ineligible players to participate is subject to significant NCAA fines and penalties. Charles was aware of these NCAA rules, and he understood that doing what Bill suggested would expose the college (his employer) to significant fines and penalties. After giving it some thought, Charles called Bill on the phone and agreed to encourage his players to sign with Bill — and many did. Charles received $200,000 from Bill as a result of his participation. During the course of his agreement with Bill, Charles signed and mailed multiple employment contracts with his college in which he agreed to run an NCAA-compliant program; he also mailed multiple false certifications to the college asserting that his players were eligible to play when he knew some of them were not.

Charles never informed the college of his agreement with Bill, but he won three conference championships for the college and his team's success likely generated many millions of dollars of revenue for the college. Charles's agreement with Bill eventually came to light and he was charged with money and property mail and wire fraud. The government alleges that Charles's misrepresentations deprived the college of the right to control the use of its assets, including, but not limited to, the decision of how to allocate a limited number of coaching staff positions, and exposed the college to tangible economic harm in the form of NCAA fines and penalties.

Charles moves to dismiss the indictment on grounds that he never intended to deprive the college of any money or property. Indeed, the only money Charles ever received pursuant to his side deal was from Bill. Moreover, Charles argues that he ultimately provided the college with everything it hoped for from its employment contract with Charles — an extremely successful college football program.

How should the court rule? Why?

3. Honest Services

Recall that *McNally* held that, in a mail or wire fraud prosecution, the government must prove an intended deprivation of money or property. The Court therefore reversed a conviction where the alleged loss was of "honest services." Congress, however, responded to *McNally*, and reinstated the deprivation of "honest services" as a viable mail or wire fraud theory. Specifically, Congress adopted the following provision, enacted at 18 U.S.C. § 1346, "Definition of 'scheme or artifice to defraud,'" as part of the Drug-Abuse Act of 1988:

> For the purpose of this chapter, the term "scheme or artifice to defraud" includes a scheme or artifice to deprive another of the intangible right of honest services.

As is apparent from the text of § 1346, the statute does not define the term "honest services." As one appellate court noted, "[t]he central problem is that the concept of 'honest services' is vague and undefined by the statute." *United States v. Urciuoli*, 513 F.3d 290, 294 (1st Cir. 2008). The circuit courts adopted widely divergent approaches to this issue, in the contexts of both public sector and private sector defendants.

In the next case, the United States Supreme Court attempted to resolve the issues surrounding the honest services statute in the context of a high profile white collar prosecution. As you read the case, consider whether the Court succeeded in its attempt to provide clarity to the statute. Also consider whether the criticisms that Justice Scalia articulated in his concurrence are valid.

Skilling v. United States
561 U.S. 358 (2010)

JUSTICE GINSBURG delivered the opinion of the Court.

In 2001, Enron Corporation, then the seventh highest-revenue-grossing company in America, crashed into bankruptcy. We consider in this opinion [whether] the jury improperly convict[ed] Skilling of conspiracy to commit "honest-services" wire fraud, 18 U.S.C. §§ 371, 1343, 1346. . . .

Founded in 1985, Enron Corporation grew from its headquarters in Houston, Texas, into one of the world's leading energy companies. Skilling launched his career there in 1990 when Kenneth Lay, the company's founder, hired him to head an Enron subsidiary. Skilling steadily rose through the corporation's ranks, serving as president and chief operating officer, and then, beginning in February 2001, as chief executive officer. Six months later, on August 14, 2001, Skilling resigned from Enron. . . .

Less than four months after Skilling's departure, Enron spiraled into bankruptcy. The company's stock, which had traded at $90 per share in August 2000, plummeted to pennies per share in late 2001. Attempting to comprehend what caused the corporation's collapse, the U.S. Department of Justice formed an Enron Task Force, comprising prosecutors and FBI agents from around the Nation. The government's investigation uncovered an elaborate conspiracy to prop up Enron's short-run stock prices by overstating the company's financial well-being. In the years following Enron's bankruptcy, the government prosecuted dozens of Enron employees who participated in the scheme. In time, the government worked its way up the corporation's chain of command: On July 7, 2004, a grand jury indicted Skilling, Lay, and Richard Causey, Enron's former chief accounting officer.

These three defendants, the indictment alleged,

> engaged in a wide-ranging scheme to deceive the investing public, including Enron's shareholders, . . . about the true performance of Enron's businesses by: (a) manipulating Enron's publicly reported financial results; and (b) making public statements and representations about Enron's financial performance and results that were false and misleading.

Skilling and his co-conspirators, the indictment continued, "enriched themselves as a result of the scheme through salary, bonuses, grants of stock and stock options, other profits, and prestige."

Count 1 of the indictment charged Skilling with conspiracy to commit securities and wire fraud; in particular, it alleged that Skilling had sought to "depriv[e] Enron and its shareholders of the intangible right of [his] honest services." The indictment further charged Skilling with more than 25 substantive counts of securities fraud, wire fraud, making false representations to Enron's auditors, and insider trading.

* * *

Following a 4-month trial and nearly five days of deliberation, the jury found Skilling guilty of 19 counts, including the honest-services-fraud conspiracy charge, and not guilty of 9 insider-trading counts. The District Court sentenced Skilling to 292 months' imprisonment, 3 years' supervised release, and $45 million in restitution.

On appeal, Skilling raised a host of challenges to his convictions. . . . The Court of Appeals . . . rejected Skilling's claim that his conduct did not indicate any conspiracy to commit honest-services fraud. "[T]he jury was entitled to convict Skilling," the court stated, "on these elements": "(1) a material breach of a fiduciary duty . . . (2) that results in a detriment to the employer," including one occasioned by an employee's decision to "withhold material information, i.e., information that he had reason to believe would lead a reasonable employer to change its conduct." The Fifth Circuit did not address Skilling's argument that the honest-services statute, if not interpreted to exclude his actions, should be invalidated as unconstitutionally vague.

Arguing that the Fifth Circuit erred in its consideration of these claims, Skilling sought relief from this Court. We granted certiorari, and now affirm in part, vacate in part, and remand for further proceedings. We consider first Skilling's allegation of juror prejudice, and next, his honest-services argument. [The Court rejected Skilling's argument that his convictions should be reversed because of jury prejudice due to pre-trial publicity.]

* * *

We next consider whether Skilling's conspiracy conviction was premised on an improper theory of honest-services wire fraud. The honest-services statute, §1346, Skilling maintains, is unconstitutionally vague. Alternatively, he contends that his conduct does not fall within the statute's compass.

To place Skilling's constitutional challenge in context, we first review the origin and subsequent application of the honest-services doctrine.

Enacted in 1872, the original mail-fraud provision, the predecessor of the modern-day mail- and wire-fraud laws, proscribed, without further elaboration, use of the mails to advance "any scheme or artifice to defraud." *See McNally v. United States*, 483 U.S. 350, 356 (1987). In 1909, Congress amended the statute to prohibit, as it does today, "any scheme or artifice to defraud, *or for obtaining money or property by means of false or fraudulent pretenses, representations, or promises."* § 1341 (emphasis added). Emphasizing Congress' disjunctive phrasing, the Courts of Appeals, one after the other, interpreted the term "scheme or artifice to defraud" to include deprivations not only of money or property, but also of intangible rights. . . .

Over time, "[a]n increasing number of courts" recognized that "a recreant employee" — public or private — "c[ould] be prosecuted under [the mail-fraud statute] if he breache[d] his allegiance to his employer by accepting bribes or kickbacks in the course of his employment," *United States v. McNeive*, 536 F.2d 1245, 1249 (C.A.8 1976); by 1982, all Courts of Appeals had embraced the honest-services theory of fraud. . . .

In 1987, this Court, in *McNally v. United States*, stopped the development of the intangible-rights doctrine in its tracks. *McNally* involved a state officer who, in selecting Kentucky's insurance agent, arranged to procure a share of the agent's commissions via kickbacks paid to companies the official partially controlled. 483 U.S. at 360. The prosecutor did not charge that, "in the absence of the alleged scheme[,] the Commonwealth would have paid a lower premium or secured better insurance." *Id.* Instead, the prosecutor maintained that the kickback scheme "defraud[ed] the citizens and government of Kentucky of their right to have the Commonwealth's affairs conducted honestly." *Id.* at 353.

We held that the scheme did not qualify as mail fraud. "Rather than constru[ing] the statute in a manner that leaves its outer boundaries ambiguous and involves the Federal government in setting standards of disclosure and good government for local and state officials," we read the statute "as limited in scope to the protection of property rights." *Id.* at 360. "If Congress desires to go further," we stated, "it must speak more clearly." *Id.*

Congress responded swiftly. The following year, it enacted a new statute "specifically to cover one of the 'intangible rights' that lower courts had protected . . . prior to *McNally*: 'the intangible right of honest services.'" *Cleveland v. United States*, 531 U.S. 12, 19–20 (2000). In full, the honest-services statute stated:

> For the purposes of th[e] chapter [of the United States Code that prohibits, *inter alia*, mail fraud, § 1341, and wire fraud, § 1343], the term 'scheme or artifice to defraud' includes a scheme or artifice to deprive another of the intangible right of honest services. § 1346.

Congress, Skilling charges, reacted quickly but not clearly: He asserts that § 1346 is unconstitutionally vague. To satisfy due process, "a penal statute [must] define the criminal offense [1] with sufficient definiteness that ordinary people can understand what conduct is prohibited and [2] in a manner that does not encourage arbitrary and discriminatory enforcement." *Kolender v. Lawson*, 461 U.S. 352, 357 (1983). The void-for-vagueness doctrine embraces these requirements.

According to Skilling, § 1346 meets neither of the two due process essentials. First, the phrase "the intangible right of honest services," he contends, does not adequately define what behavior it bars. Second, he alleges, §1346's "standardless sweep allows policemen, prosecutors, and juries to pursue their personal predilections," thereby "facilitat[ing] opportunistic and arbitrary prosecutions."

In urging invalidation of §1346, Skilling swims against our case law's current, which requires us, if we can, to construe, not condemn, Congress' enactments. Alert to §1346's potential breadth, the Courts of Appeals have divided on how best to interpret the statute.[36] Uniformly, however, they have declined to throw out the statute as irremediably vague.

We agree that §1346 should be construed rather than invalidated. First, we look to the doctrine developed in pre-*McNally* cases in an endeavor to ascertain the meaning of the phrase "the intangible right of honest services." Second, to preserve what Congress certainly intended the statute to cover, we pare that body of precedent down to its core: In the main, the pre-*McNally* cases involved fraudulent schemes to deprive another of honest services through bribes or kickbacks supplied by a third party who had not been deceived. Confined to these paramount applications, §1346 presents no vagueness problem.

There is no doubt that Congress intended §1346 to refer to and incorporate the honest-services doctrine recognized in Court of Appeals' decisions before *McNally* derailed the intangible-rights theory of fraud. Congress enacted §1346 on the heels of *McNally* and drafted the statute using that decision's terminology. As the Second Circuit observed in its leading analysis of §1346:

> The definite article "the" suggests that "intangible right of honest services" had a specific meaning to Congress when it enacted the statute-Congress was recriminalizing mail- and wire-fraud schemes to deprive others of *that* "intangible right of honest services," which had been protected before *McNally*, not *all* intangible rights of honest services whatever they might be thought to be.

United States v. Rybicki, 354 F.3d 124, 137–138 (2003) (en banc).

Satisfied that Congress, by enacting §1346, "meant to reinstate the body of pre-*McNally* honest-services law," we have surveyed that case law. In parsing the Courts of Appeals decisions, we acknowledge that Skilling's vagueness challenge has force, for honest-services decisions preceding *McNally* were not models of clarity or consistency. While the honest-services cases preceding *McNally* dominantly and consistently applied the fraud statute to bribery and kickback schemes—schemes that

---

36. Courts have disagreed about whether §1346 prosecutions must be based on a violation of state law, compare, *e.g., United States v. Brumley*, 116 F.3d 728, 734–735 (C.A.5 1997) (en banc), with, *e.g., United States v. Weyhrauch*, 548 F.3d 1237, 1245–1246 (C.A.9 2008), vacated and remanded; whether a defendant must contemplate that the victim suffer economic harm, compare, *e.g., United States v. Sun-Diamond Growers of Cal.*, 138 F.3d 961, 973 (C.A.D.C. 1998), with, *e.g., United States v. Black*, 530 F.3d 596, 600–602 (C.A.7 2008), vacated and remanded; and whether the defendant must act in pursuit of private gain, compare, *e.g., United States v. Bloom*, 149 F.3d 649, 655 (C.A.7 1998), with, *e.g., United States v. Panarella*, 277 F.3d 678, 692 (C.A.3 2002).

were the basis of most honest-services prosecutions — there was considerable disarray over the statute's application to conduct outside that core category. In light of this disarray, Skilling urges us, as he urged the Fifth Circuit, to invalidate the statute *in toto*.

It has long been our practice, however, before striking a federal statute as impermissibly vague, to consider whether the prescription is amenable to a limiting construction. We have accordingly instructed "the federal courts . . . to avoid constitutional difficulties by [adopting a limiting interpretation] if such a construction is fairly possible." *Boos*, 485 U.S. at 331.

Arguing against any limiting construction, Skilling contends that it is impossible to identify a salvageable honest-services core; "the pre-*McNally* caselaw," he asserts, "is a hodgepodge of oft-conflicting holdings" that are "hopelessly unclear." . . .

Although some applications of the pre-*McNally* honest-services doctrine occasioned disagreement among the Courts of Appeals, these cases do not cloud the doctrine's solid core: The "vast majority" of the honest-services cases involved offenders who, in violation of a fiduciary duty, participated in bribery or kickback schemes. Indeed, the *McNally* case itself, which spurred Congress to enact § 1346, presented a paradigmatic kickback fact pattern. Congress' reversal of *McNally* and reinstatement of the honest-services doctrine, we conclude, can and should be salvaged by confining its scope to the core pre-*McNally* applications. . . .

[T]he honest-services doctrine had its genesis in prosecutions involving bribery allegations. Both before *McNally* and after § 1346's enactment, Courts of Appeals described schemes involving bribes or kickbacks as "core . . . honest services fraud precedents." *United States v. Czubinski*, 106 F.3d 1069, 1077 (1st Cir. 1997).

In view of this history, there is no doubt that Congress intended § 1346 to reach *at least* bribes and kickbacks. Reading the statute to proscribe a wider range of offensive conduct, we acknowledge, would raise the due process concerns underlying the vagueness doctrine.[42] To preserve the statute without transgressing constitutional limitations, we now hold that § 1346 criminalizes *only* the bribe-and-kickback core of the pre-*McNally* case law.

The government urges us to go further by locating within § 1346's compass another category of proscribed conduct: "undisclosed self-dealing by a public official or private employee — *i.e.*, the taking of official action by the employee that furthers his own undisclosed financial interests while purporting to act in the interests of those to whom he owes a fiduciary duty." "[T]he theory of liability in *McNally* itself was nondisclosure of a conflicting financial interest," the government observes, and "Congress clearly intended to revive th[at] nondisclosure theory." Moreover,

---

42. Apprised that a broader reading of § 1346 could render the statute impermissibly vague, Congress, we believe, would have drawn the honest-services line, as we do now, at bribery and kickback schemes.

"[a]lthough not as numerous as the bribery and kickback cases," the government asserts, "the pre-*McNally* cases involving undisclosed self-dealing were abundant."

Neither of these contentions withstands close inspection. *McNally*, as we have already observed, involved a classic kickback scheme: A public official, in exchange for routing Kentucky's insurance business through a middleman company, arranged for that company to share its commissions with entities in which the official held an interest. This was no mere failure to disclose a conflict of interest; rather, the official conspired with a third party so that both would profit from wealth generated by public contracts. Reading § 1346 to proscribe bribes and kickbacks — and nothing more — satisfies Congress' undoubted aim to reverse *McNally* on its facts.

Nor are we persuaded that the pre-*McNally* conflict-of-interest cases constitute core applications of the honest-services doctrine. Although the Courts of Appeals upheld honest-services convictions for "some schemes of non-disclosure and concealment of material information," *Mandel*, 591 F.2d at 1361, they reached no consensus on which schemes qualified. In light of the relative infrequency of conflict-of-interest prosecutions in comparison to bribery and kickback charges, and the intercircuit inconsistencies they produced, we conclude that a reasonable limiting construction of § 1346 must exclude this amorphous category of cases.

Further dispelling doubt on this point is the familiar principle that "ambiguity concerning the ambit of criminal statutes should be resolved in favor of lenity." *Cleveland*, 531 U.S. at 25. "This interpretive guide is especially appropriate in construing [§ 1346] because . . . mail [and wire] fraud [are] predicate offense[s] under [the Racketeer Influenced and Corrupt Organizations Act], 18 U.S.C. § 1961(1), and the money laundering statute, § 1956(c)(7)(A)." *Cleveland*, 531 U.S. at 25. Holding that honest-services fraud does not encompass conduct more wide-ranging than the paradigmatic cases of bribes and kickbacks, we resist the government's less constrained construction absent Congress' clear instruction otherwise.

In sum, our construction of § 1346 "establish[es] a uniform national standard, define[s] honest services with clarity, reach[es] only seriously culpable conduct, and accomplish[es] Congress's goal of 'overruling' *McNally*." "If Congress desires to go further," we reiterate, "it must speak more clearly than it has." *McNally*, 483 U.S. at 360.[44]

---

44. If Congress were to take up the enterprise of criminalizing "undisclosed self-dealing by a public official or private employee," it would have to employ standards of sufficient definiteness and specificity to overcome due process concerns. The Government proposes a standard that prohibits the "taking of official action by the employee that furthers his own undisclosed financial interests while purporting to act in the interests of those to whom he owes a fiduciary duty," so long as the employee acts with a specific intent to deceive and the undisclosed conduct could influence the victim to change its behavior. That formulation, however, leaves many questions unanswered. How direct or significant does the conflicting financial interest have to be? To what extent does the official action have to further that interest in order to amount to fraud? To whom should the disclosure be made and what information should it convey? These questions and others call for particular care in attempting to formulate an adequate criminal prohibition in this context.

Interpreted to encompass only bribery and kickback schemes, §1346 is not unconstitutionally vague. Recall that the void-for-vagueness doctrine addresses concerns about (1) fair notice and (2) arbitrary and discriminatory prosecutions. See *Kolender*, 461 U.S. at 357. A prohibition on fraudulently depriving another of one's honest services by accepting bribes or kickbacks does not present a problem on either score.

As to fair notice, "whatever the school of thought concerning the scope and meaning of §1346, it has always been 'as plain as a pikestaff that' bribes and kickbacks constitute honest-services fraud," *Williams v. United States*, 341 U.S. 97, 101 (1951), and the statute's *mens rea* requirement further blunts any notice concern. Today's decision clarifies that no other misconduct falls within §1346's province.

As to arbitrary prosecutions, we perceive no significant risk that the honest-services statute, as we interpret it today, will be stretched out of shape. Its prohibition on bribes and kickbacks draws content not only from the pre-*McNally* case law, but also from federal statutes proscribing-and defining-similar crimes. *See, e.g.,* 18 U.S.C. §§201(b), 666(a)(2); 41 U.S.C. §52(2) [which now appears at 41 U.S.C. §8701(2)] ("The term 'kickback' means any money, fee, commission, credit, gift, gratuity, thing of value, or compensation of any kind which is provided, directly or indirectly, to [enumerated persons] for the purpose of improperly obtaining or rewarding favorable treatment in connection with [enumerated circumstances].").[45] A criminal defendant who participated in a bribery or kickback scheme, in short, cannot tenably complain about prosecution under §1346 on vagueness grounds.

It remains to determine whether Skilling's conduct violated §1346. Skilling's honest-services prosecution, the government concedes, was not "prototypical." The government charged Skilling with conspiring to defraud Enron's shareholders by misrepresenting the company's fiscal health, thereby artificially inflating its stock price. It was the government's theory at trial that Skilling "profited from the fraudulent scheme . . . through the receipt of salary and bonuses, . . . and through the sale of approximately $200 million in Enron stock, which netted him $89 million."

The government did not, at any time, allege that Skilling solicited or accepted side payments from a third party in exchange for making these misrepresentations. It is therefore clear that, as we read §1346, Skilling did not commit honest-services fraud.

Because the indictment alleged three objects of the conspiracy—honest-services wire fraud, money-or-property wire fraud, and securities fraud—Skilling's conviction is flawed. This determination, however, does not necessarily require reversal

---

45. Overlap with other federal statutes does not render §1346 superfluous. The principal federal bribery statute, §201, for example, generally applies only to federal public officials, so §1346's application to state and local corruption and to private-sector fraud reaches misconduct that might otherwise go unpunished.

of the conspiracy conviction. The parties vigorously dispute whether the error was harmless. We leave this dispute for resolution on remand.

Whether potential reversal on the conspiracy count touches any of Skilling's other convictions is also an open question. All of his convictions, Skilling contends, hinged on the conspiracy count and, like dominoes, must fall if it falls. The District Court, deciding Skilling's motion for bail pending appeal, found this argument dubious, but the Fifth Circuit had no occasion to rule on it. That court may do so on remand.

For the foregoing reasons, we affirm the Fifth Circuit's ruling on Skilling's fair-trial argument, vacate its ruling on his conspiracy conviction, and remand the case for proceedings consistent with this opinion.

It is so ordered.

Justice Scalia, with whom Justice Thomas joins [along with Justice Kennedy on the sections of the opinion here], concurring.

I . . . agree that the decision upholding Skilling's conviction for so-called "honest-services fraud" must be reversed, but for a different reason. In my view, the specification in 18 U.S.C. §1346 that "scheme or artifice to defraud" in the mail-fraud and wire-fraud statutes, §§1341 and 1343, includes "a scheme or artifice to deprive another of the intangible right of honest services," is vague, and therefore violates the Due Process Clause of the Fifth Amendment. The Court strikes a pose of judicial humility in proclaiming that our task is "not to destroy the Act . . . but to construe it." But in transforming the prohibition of "honest-services fraud" into a prohibition of "bribery and kick-backs" it is wielding a power we long ago abjured: the power to define new federal crimes.

A criminal statute must clearly define the conduct it proscribes. A statute that is unconstitutionally vague cannot be saved by a more precise indictment, nor by judicial construction that writes in specific criteria that its text does not contain. Our cases have described vague statutes as failing "to provide a person of ordinary intelligence fair notice of what is prohibited, or [as being] so standardless that [they] authoriz[e] or encourag[e] seriously discriminatory enforcement." *United States v. Williams*, 553 U.S. 285, 304 (2008). Here, Skilling argues that §1346 fails to provide fair notice and encourages arbitrary enforcement because it provides no definition of the right of honest services whose deprivation it prohibits. In my view Skilling is correct.

The Court maintains that "the intangible right of honest services "means the right not to have one's fiduciaries accept "bribes or kickbacks." Its first step in reaching that conclusion is the assertion that the phrase refers to "the doctrine developed" in cases decided by lower federal courts prior to our decision in *McNally v. United States*, 483 U.S. 350 (1987). I do not contest that. I agree that Congress used the novel phrase to adopt the lower-court case law that had been disapproved by *McNally*-what the Court calls "the pre-*McNally* honest-services doctrine." The problem is that that doctrine provides no "ascertainable standard of guilt," *United States v. L. Cohen Grocery Co.*, 255 U.S. 81, 89 (1921), and certainly is not limited to "bribes or kickbacks."

Investigation into the meaning of "the pre-*McNally* honest-services doctrine" might logically begin with *McNally* itself, which rejected it. That case repudiated the many Court of Appeals holdings that had expanded the meaning of "fraud" in the mail-fraud and wire-fraud statutes beyond deceptive schemes to obtain property. If the repudiated cases stood for a prohibition of "bribery and kickbacks," one would have expected those words to appear in the opinion's description of the cases. In fact, they do not. *Not at all.* Nor did *McNally* even provide a consistent definition of the pre-existing theory of fraud it rejected. It referred variously to a right of citizens "to have the [State]'s affairs conducted honestly," to "honest and impartial government," to "good government," and "to have public officials perform their duties honestly." It described prior case law as holding that "a public official owes a fiduciary duty to the public, and misuse of his office for private gain is a fraud."

But the pre-*McNally* Court of Appeals opinions were not limited to fraud by public officials. Some courts had held that those fiduciaries subject to the "honest services" obligation included private individuals who merely participated in public decisions, and even private employees who had no role in public decisions. Moreover, "to say that a man is a fiduciary only begins [the] analysis; it gives direction to further inquiry. . . . What obligations does he owe as a fiduciary?" *SEC v. Chenery Corp.*, 318 U.S. 80, 85–86 (1943). None of the "honest services" cases, neither those pertaining to public officials nor those pertaining to private employees, defined the nature and content of the fiduciary duty central to the "fraud" offense.

There was not even universal agreement concerning the *source* of the fiduciary obligation-whether it must be positive state or federal law, or merely general principles, such as the "obligations of loyalty and fidelity" that inhere in the "employment relationship," *Lemire, supra,* at 1336. The decision *McNally* reversed had grounded the duty in general (not jurisdiction-specific) trust law. Another pre-*McNally* case referred to the general law of agency, which imposes duties quite different from those of a trustee.

This indeterminacy does not disappear if one assumes that the pre-*McNally* cases developed a federal, common-law fiduciary duty; the duty remained hopelessly undefined. Some courts described it in astoundingly broad language. . . .

The indefiniteness of the fiduciary duty is not all. Many courts held that some *je-ne-sais-quoi* beyond a mere breach of fiduciary duty was needed to establish honest-services fraud. There was, unsurprisingly, some dispute about that, at least in the context of acts by persons owing duties to the public. And even among those courts that did require something additional where a public official was involved, there was disagreement as to what the addition should be.

Similar disagreements occurred with respect to private employees. Courts disputed whether the defendant must use his fiduciary position for his own gain. . . .

In short, the first step in the Court's analysis — holding that "the intangible right of honest services" refers to "the honest-services doctrine recognized in Court of Appeals' decisions before *McNally*" — is a step out of the frying pan into the fire. The pre-*McNally* cases provide no clear indication of what constitutes a denial of the right of honest services. The possibilities range from any action that is contrary to public policy or otherwise immoral, to only the disloyalty of a public official or employee to his principal, to only the secret use of a perpetrator's position of trust in order to harm whomever he is beholden to. The duty probably did not have to be rooted in state law, but maybe it did. It might have been more demanding in the case of public officials, but perhaps not. At the time § 1346 was enacted there was no settled criterion for choosing among these options, for conclusively settling what was in and what was out. . . .

Arriving at [the Court's] conclusion requires not interpretation but invention. The Court replaces a vague criminal standard that Congress adopted with a more narrow one (included within the vague one) that can pass constitutional muster. I know of no precedent for such "paring down," and it seems to me clearly beyond judicial power. . . .

I would therefore reverse Skilling's conviction under § 1346 on the ground that it fails to define the conduct it prohibits. The fate of the statute in future prosecutions-obvious from my reasoning in the case-would be a matter for *stare decisis*.

* * *

Justice Alito, concurring in part and concurring in the judgment. [Omitted.] Justice Sotomayor, with whom Justice Stevens and Justice Breyer join, concurring in part and dissenting in part. [Omitted.] [All four Justices fully joined the honest services holding.]

Notes and Questions

1. *Public official "honest services" cases.* As Justice Stevens noted in his *McNally* dissent, "In the public sector, judges, state governors, chairmen of state political parties, state cabinet officers, city aldermen, Congressmen and many other state and federal officials have been convicted of defrauding citizens of their right to the honest services of their governmental officials." Are the mail and wire fraud statutes properly used as political corruption statutes? What does the *Skilling* majority say on this issue? For a critique, *see* Randall D. Eliason, *Surgery with a Meat Axe: Using Honest Services Fraud to Prosecute Federal Corruption*, 99 Crim. L. & Criminology 929, 933, 956–57 (2009).

2. *Private sector "honest services" cases.* Prosecutors have also used the honest services statutes in the private sector context, as the *Skilling* case shows. Are the mail and wire fraud statutes necessary to police private sector fraud, or do other statutes suffice?

3. *Undisclosed self-dealing.* What was the government's proposed interpretation of the statute concerning undisclosed self-dealing? Should the Court have adopted the government's approach? Why or why not?

4. *Legislative history.* The legislative history behind § 1346 provides scant guidance in defining "honest services." One opinion summarized the history as follows:

> The specific text of what has become 18 U.S.C. § 1346 was inserted in the Omnibus Drug Bill for the first time on the very day that the Omnibus Drug Bill was finally passed by both the House and the Senate. The text of what is now § 1346 was never included in any bill as filed in either the House of Representatives or the Senate. As a result, the text of § 1346 was never referred to any committee of either the House or the Senate, was never the subject of any committee report from either the House or the Senate, and was never the subject of any floor debate reported in the Congressional Record.

Brumley, 116 F.3d at 742 (Jolly, J. dissenting). Does this history provide any basis for the *Skilling* majority's reading of the statute? If not, what was the source of the majority's interpretation of the statute?

5. *Vagueness.* What is the purpose of the vagueness doctrine? Did the Court in *Skilling* hold that, without the Court's gloss on the honest services statute, the statute would be unconstitutionally vague? How did Justice Scalia respond to the Court's reasoning on the vagueness issue? Who has the more persuasive argument? Why? How far should a court go to fill in the blanks of an ambiguous statute? Is Justice Scalia correct to say that Court exceeded its proper role in this case by "wielding a power we long ago abjured: the power to define new federal crimes"? Why or why not?

6. *Remand and sentencing.* On remand from the Supreme Court's decision, one issue before the court of appeals was whether Skilling's conspiracy conviction could be sustained when one of the objects of the conspiracy — honest services fraud — was invalid. The court found that there was overwhelming evidence that Skilling and his co-conspirators had schemed to commit securities fraud by manipulating Enron's reported earnings and concealing Enron's losses from the investing public with the intent to affect Enron's stock price. The court therefore found that the district court's error in presenting the honest-services theory to the jury was harmless error beyond a reasonable doubt and sustained Skilling's conspiracy conviction. *See United States v. Skilling*, 638 F.3d 480, 481 (5th Cir. 2011).

Skilling was sentenced to 24 years in prison. Based upon an agreement with the government after the Fifth Circuit determined that his original sentence was miscalculated, *see id.*, the sentence was later reduced to 14 years. In exchange, Skilling gave up about $42 million to be distributed to victims of the Enron fraud scheme and agreed not to pursue any further appeals. *See* Peter Lattman, *Ex-Enron Chief's Sentence Is Cut by 10 Years, to 14*, N.Y. TIMES DEALBOOK (June 21, 2013).

7. *The congressional response to* Skilling. Legislation has been proposed that would effectively reverse *Skilling*. That legislation, however, appears to suffer from many of the vagueness problems that the Court addressed in *Skilling*. *See* J. Kelly Strader, Skilling *Reconsidered: The Legislative-Judicial Dynamic, Honest Services Fraud, and*

the Ill-Conceived "Clean Up Government Act," 39 FORDHAM URB. L.J. 309 (2011). Should Congress overturn *Skilling*? Why or why not? If so, what should the new law provide?

8. *The* Carpenter *case.* Reconsider the *Carpenter* decision. In that case, the government did not assert a deprivation of honest services theory because the case was post-*McNally* and pre-§1346. Would the honest services theory have succeeded on the *Carpenter* facts under *Skilling*'s interpretation of §1346? Why or why not?

9. *Open questions after* Skilling. As Justice Scalia noted in his concurring opinion, the *Skilling* majority did not resolve a number of questions that have plagued lower courts over the proper scope of the honest services statute.

a. *Personal gain?* Some pre-*Skilling* courts limited honest services fraud cases to instances where the defendant was misusing a public position for personal gain. *See United States v. Thompson*, 484 F.3d 877, 883–84 (7th Cir. 2007) (reversing conviction of state official who arranged to have a state contract awarded to a politically favored travel agency). Is that requirement met where the defendant schemed to benefit a third party? *See United States v. Sorich*, 523 F.3d 702, 710–11 (7th Cir. 2008) (finding defendants who were city employees who violated city hiring rules so that political allies would get city jobs satisfied the private gain requirement).

b. *State law violation?* As one court stated:

> The relationship between state law and the federal honest services statute is unsettled. The Fifth Circuit has held that §1346 extends only to conduct that independently violates state law. Other circuits have denied that state law plays any necessary role. It is plain that §§1341 and 1346 enact a federal crime — but beyond that, broad generalizations may be unsafe.

United States v. Urciuoli, 513 F.3d 290, 298 (1st Cir. 2008). Does *Skilling* clarify the role that state law should play in defining bribes and kickbacks?

c. *Bribes and kickbacks.* Are you persuaded by the Court's reasoning when concluding that the mail and wire fraud statutes should be limited to bribes and kickbacks? Why or why not? How do we ascertain the proper definitions of those terms in the absence of any statutory guidance in §1346 itself?

d. *Defining "kickbacks."* In *Skilling*, the Court looks to 41 U.S.C. §52(2) for the definition of a "kickback" as "any money, fee, commission, credit, gift, gratuity, thing of value, or compensation of any kind which is provided, directly or indirectly, to [enumerated persons] for the purpose of improperly obtaining or rewarding favorable treatment in connection with [enumerated circumstances]." 561 U.S. at 412–13. In *United States v. DeMizio*, 741 F.3d 373, 381 (2d Cir. 2014), the court explained that a kickback scheme "typically involves an employee steering business of his employer to a third party in exchange for a share of the third party's profits on that business." In that case, the scheme benefited the defendant's father and brother, who did minimal work for payments they received from the defendant's employer. The defendant argued that there was no kickback scheme because "kickbacks" do not include:

(a) payments made to third parties and (b) payments in exchange for some minimal amount of work. The court rejected the arguments and affirmed the conviction.

e. *Defining bribery and "official acts."* Courts look to federal statutes such as 18 U.S.C. § 201 to define "bribery" for purposes of honest services fraud. This statute makes it a crime for a public official to "directly or indirectly," corruptly demand, seek, receive, accept, or agree to receive or accept, "anything of value . . . in return for . . . being influenced in the performance of any official act." 18 U.S.C. § 201(b) (2). The definition requires that there be a *quid pro quo*, but it need not be explicit in most cases. *United States v. Ring*, 706 F.3d 460 (D.C. Cir. 2013). If, however, the benefit conferred is a campaign contribution (as opposed to gifts or other benefits), courts may require proof of an explicit *quid pro quo* to prevent the prosecution of conduct that implicates First Amendment rights and that "has long been thought to be well within the law [and] in a very real sense unavoidable" in politics. *United States v. Menendez*, 2018 WL 526746 (D. NJ. 2018) (*quoting McCormick v. United States*, 500 U.S. 257, 272 (1991)). *See* Elkan Abramowitz & Jonathan Sack, *'Menendez' Decision Clarifies Issues in Public Corruption Cases*, New York Law Journal (March 21, 2018). As discussed in Chapter 7, Bribery and Gratuities, *infra*, § 201(c) also proscribes illegal gratuities (giving or offering to give something of value as compensation for an official act). *Skilling* does not explicitly reference illegal "gratuities" as grounds for honest services fraud. Given its close relation to bribery, however, courts continue to struggle with the question of whether an illegal gratuity should also provide a basis for honest services fraud.

The federal bribery statute defines an "official act" as "any decision or action on any question, matter, cause, suit, proceeding or controversy, which may at any time be pending, or which may by law be brought before any public official, in such official's official capacity. . . ." *Id*. at § 201(a)(3). The federal courts, however, struggled to settle on the range of conduct constituting an official act under this statutory definition. The Supreme Court therefore took up the question of what constitutes an "official act" for purposes of honest services fraud liability in *McDonnell v. United States*, 136 S.Ct. 2355 (2016). Applying familiar principles of statutory interpretation, the Court adopted a "bounded" interpretation of what constitutes an official act as:

> a decision or action on a "question, matter, cause, suit, proceeding or controversy." The "question, matter, cause, suit, proceeding or controversy" must involve a formal exercise of government power that is similar in nature to a lawsuit before a court, a determination before an agency, or a hearing before a committee. It must also be something specific and focused that is "pending" or "may by law be brought" before a public official. To qualify as an "official act," the public official must make a decision or take an action on that "question, matter, cause, suit, proceeding or controversy," or agree to do so. . . . Setting up a meeting, talking to another official, or organizing an event (or agreeing to do so) — without more — does not fit that definition of "official act."

Id. at 2371–72. *See* Chapter 7, Bribery and Gratuities, *infra*, for a complete treatment of *McDonnell.*

f. *Breaches of fiduciary duties.* The *Skilling* Court suggested that honest services fraud only reaches bribery or kickback schemes that violate a fiduciary duty. *See, e.g.,* 561 U.S. at 407 (noting that the "vast majority of [pre-*McNally*] honest-services cases involved offenders who, in violation of a fiduciary duty, participated in bribery or kickback schemes"). But some controversy has persisted over the strictness of the fiduciary duty requirement (e.g., is it always required in private and public sector cases?), and over the nature of the fiduciary relationship contemplated (e.g., must it be a formal common law fiduciary relationship, or could an informal relationship of trust and confidence satisfy the requirement?). The Ninth Circuit addressed these issues in *United States v. Milovanovic*, 678 F.3d 713 (9th Cir. 2012) (en banc).

In *Milovanovic*, defendants Milovanovic and Lamb were charged with conspiracy to commit honest services fraud by soliciting bribes to help unqualified, nonresident applicants obtain Washington State commercial driver's licenses through false applications. Lamb was an independent contractor hired directly by the state to conduct commercial driving tests on the state's behalf. Milovanovic was also an independent contractor, but he was hired by a private translation company that was, in turn, hired as an independent contractor of the State of Washington to help conduct written commercial driving exams. Milovanovic recruited Bosnian speakers to pay $2500 for his aid in cheating on the written commercial driving exam and for Lamb's aid in cheating on the driving exam. The district court dismissed the charges, holding (*inter alia*) that honest services fraud requires the "existence of a formal fiduciary duty" to the victim (here, the state), and that independent contractors such as Milovanovic and Lamb had no such fiduciary duties to the State of Washington. The Ninth Circuit reversed. The court held that, under *Skilling*, honest services fraud does require the government to prove a breach of fiduciary duty. But, the court explained, the fiduciary duty contemplated by § 1346 need not be formal (e.g., public official/state, employer/employee); it could instead be an informal, loose relationship of trust or confidence, including any "trusting relationship in which one party acts for the benefit of another and induces the trusting party to relax the care and vigilance which it would ordinarily exercise." *Id.* at 724.

In this case, the court explained that there is no question but that Lamb and Milovanovic would have owed the requisite fiduciary duty if they had been actual employees of the state. But, according to the court, they could also owe such a fiduciary duty as independent contractors on these facts because the "State entrusted Milovanovic and Lamb to honestly and truthfully administer the written skills tests and to interpret and certify the result. The defendants well knew that the State relied on their fidelity in administering and translating the tests in order to grant [commercial driver's licenses] to applicants." *Id.* at 724. Milovanovic argued that his relationship (as an independent contractor of an independent contractor of the State) was too attenuated for him to be regarded as a fiduciary of the State under any test. The court, however, dismissed this argument, holding that even if the fact finder were to conclude that Milovanovic was not a fiduciary himself, his role in assisting Lamb (who had a direct contractual relationship to the state) could nevertheless expose him to aider and abettor liability.

g. *Foreseeable economic harm versus materiality.* Does the government need to show that a scheme to commit honest services fraud involved a foreseeable economic harm to the victim (as with money or property fraud), or is it enough that the deception was material to the victim (even if there is no foreseeable economic harm)? In *United States v. Rybicki*, 354 F.3d 124 (2d Cir. 2003), the Second Circuit (en banc) discussed these competing tests in the context of a private sector honest services case. The panel decision in that case adopted a test requiring that "it must have been 'reasonably foreseeable that the scheme could cause some economic or pecuniary harm to the victim that [was] more than *de minimis.*'" 287 F.3d at 266. The en banc court rejected that approach in favor of a materiality test:

> [T]he misrepresentation or omission at issue for an "honest services" fraud conviction must be "material," such that the misinformation or omission would naturally tend to lead or is capable of leading a reasonable employer to change its conduct. . . .

> The reasonably foreseeable harm test of the *Rybicki* panel opinion is limited to "economic or pecuniary harm." In this respect "materiality" may be a somewhat broader test: It may capture some cases of non-economic, yet serious, harm in the private sphere.

Rybicki, 354 F.3d at 146. What is the essential difference between the two tests? Is there a danger of vagueness from the materiality approach? The court in *Rybicki* adopted the materiality test in private sector cases. In a portion of its decision not referenced above, the Ninth Circuit later adopted the materiality test for public sector honest-services cases in *Milovanovic* (but it left the decision on whether this test would also apply in private sector cases for another day). *See* 678 F.3d at 727. Should the approach be the same for both categories of honest-services cases?

10. *Participants in a scheme to defraud.* Both *Skilling* and *Milovanovic* rely heavily on *United States v. Rybicki*, 354 F.3d 124, 137–138 (2003) (en banc). In *Rybicki*, the government's theory was that insurance adjusters failed to disclose to their employers that the adjusters were receiving kickbacks. In a case based on an omission, the government must show that the person engaging in the deception had a duty to disclose the omitted information. Because the adjusters had fiduciary duties to their employers, the adjusters had a duty to reveal the scheme. Their omission to do so was fraudulent. The individual defendants in the case, however, were two attorneys who themselves had no duties to the insurance companies; the attorneys thus had no duty to reveal the kickback scheme. On these facts, why were the attorneys guilty of defrauding the companies?

The answer is that a defendant in a mail or wire fraud case need not be the person making the misrepresentation or engaging in the omission. Nor does the defendant need to have a personal duty to the victim in an omission case. All that the statutes require is proof that the defendant *participated in a scheme* to deprive the victim of money, property, or honest services. Because the defendants aided and abetted a scheme to deprive the insurance companies of the honest services of their employees (the insurance adjusters), the attorneys engaged in a scheme to defraud the companies.

11. *Reframing the theory.* Will *Skilling* and its honest-services progeny substantially hamper prosecutors? In many cases, could the government simply reframe the issue and argue a deprivation of intangible property rights—such as the right to control—rather than honest services? *See* Brette M. Tannenbaum, Note, *Reframing the Right: Using Theories of Intangible Property to Target Honest Services Fraud After Skilling,* 112 Colum. L. Rev. 359 (2012). What impact might cases like *Kelly* and *Davis* have on this strategy?

Problems

4-10. Defendants Bob Urchin and Frank Dresser served respectively as CEO and Senior Vice President of City Medical Center ("CMC"). CMC's subsidiaries included a local hospital, a local nursing home, and an assisted living facility called "The Village." The two executives were friends of state senator Joan Carona. State legislators worked part-time in the state legislature, and typically held outside jobs. Carona was having financial difficulties, and approached Urchin about obtaining employment with CMC. Ultimately, Carona signed and sent by U.S. mails a contract that purported to employ her as a part-time consultant to The Village at a salary of $1,000 per week.

Thereafter, Carona did engage in some minimal work on behalf of The Village, including referring several prospective residents to The Village. In addition, Carona engaged in three kinds of activities while employed by The Village:

1. Carona communicated with Urchin and Dresser about various pieces of legislation; defendants allegedly asked Carona to try to "kill" certain bills and otherwise to promote CMC's interests with respect to pending legislative matters.

2. Carona lobbied a number of municipal officials (mayors and fire chiefs) in order to increase the number of patients brought to the CMC hospital by ambulance service ("rescue runs"). Specifically, Carona correctly told the officials that state law required that patients be taken to the hospital of the patients' choosing. State law permitted this kind of lobbying activity.

3. Carona facilitated meetings at her government office between Urchin and representatives of two major insurance companies, pressing the companies to pay outstanding reimbursements owed to CMC. Carona told the companies that if they did not make the reimbursements they would be treated unfavorably during the legislative process.

Carona did not publicly disclose in any of these instances that she was acting on behalf of CMC or its hospital.

Urchin and Dresser were indicted on counts of conspiracy to commit "honest services" mail fraud and various counts of such mail fraud; 18 U.S.C. §§ 371, 1341, 1346. In substance, the government asserted that the defendants had devised a scheme to offer Carona a disguised bribe in the form of a sham or largely sham job at The Village; in exchange, the government asserted, Carona advanced CMC's financial interests by exploiting her public office in the three ways described above. Carona entered into a plea agreement and cooperated with the government.

At the trial, the judge instructed the jury that any of the three types of Carona's activities could be covered by the honest services statutes. The judge instructed the jury:

> The honest services that an elected official owes to citizens is not limited to the official's formal votes on legislation. It includes the official's behind-the-scenes activities and influence in the legislation, and it also includes other actions that the official takes in an official capacity, not what he does as a private individual but what he does under the cloak of his office.

During the trial, the government strongly relied on all three types of activities.

Both defendants were convicted by means of a general verdict, and appeal. How should the court rule? Why?

4-11. Davis was a member of the City of Metropolis City Council, having been elected last year to a four-year term. Davis's friend, Terry Thompson, owned a construction company, Terry's Construction, which specialized in city building construction projects. Davis owns a five percent interest in Terry's Construction.

Last March 1, the City Council began considering a major construction project to provide new office space for city agencies. The Council decided to acquire land with the assistance of a real-estate broker, and to hire a contractor to construct a new building on the site once it was purchased. The Council agreed to meet on March 18 to continue the discussions.

On March 12, Davis met with Thompson, and another acquaintance, real-estate broker Pat Parsons, over coffee at Davis's home. Parsons specialized in purchases of land for commercial and municipal building projects. During the meeting, Davis said to Parsons, "We have this big city project coming up. I sure would like for you to be our broker. Would you like a shot?" Parsons responded, "Of course." Davis then said, "Well, I can assure you that you will be considered, with a substantial brokerage fee. You know, it's a competitive business. But the only way I can assure that you will be considered would be for me to have a, you know, stake in the venture." Parsons said, "How does a half percent sound of my share sound?" Davis nodded in response.

Davis next told Parsons that the City Council had already reached a confidential decision that it would only hire an agent who agreed to accept a real-estate commission of lower than the standard six percent of the purchase price. Davis also told Thompson and Parsons that, in required forms to be sent to the city, Davis would have to reveal Davis's interest in Terry's Construction but that Davis hoped to keep the arrangement with Parsons secret.

On March 18, prior to the continuation of City Council discussions of the construction project, Davis completed a conflict-of-interest form. The form quoted Metropolis City Ordinance § 100.10, which provides:

> No city officer, employee, or agent shall acquire any interest, direct or indirect, in any city construction project or in any property included or planned to be included in such a project, nor shall such person have any interest, direct or indirect, in any contract or proposed contract for materials or services to be furnished or used in connection with any project. If any such person owns or controls an interest, direct or indirect, in any property included or planned to be included in any such project, the member or employee shall immediately disclose the same in writing to the city. Nor shall any officer, employee, or agent of the city disclose confidential information relating to such projects.

Violation of § 100.10 subjects the violator to a civil fine of up to $10,000.

In response to a question on the form asking for disclosure of all potential conflicts, Davis revealed his ownership interest in Terry's construction, but not his arrangement with Parsons. Davis then sent the form from the City Council office to the City's Attorney's office via Federal Express.

Davis refrained from participating in all City Council debates relating to the construction project. Davis also refrained from voting on all matters relating to the project. The City Council subsequently retained both Parsons and Terry's Construction for the project. The Council chose Parsons because Parsons' proposal to the Council indicated Parsons' willingness to accept less than the usual six percent real estate commission.

On July 1, the city purchased the property at a fair market value of $25 million. That day, Parsons gave Davis $125,000 in cash, Davis's share of Parsons' commission.

Davis has been convicted of honest services mail fraud based upon the foregoing. What viable arguments does Davis have on appeal? What is the likely outcome? Why?

4-12. In order to communicate their clients' policy goals more effectively, lobbyists often seek to cultivate personal relationships with public officials. This involves not only making campaign contributions, but sometimes also hosting events or providing gifts of value such as drinks, meals, and tickets to sporting events and concerts. Appellant, after stints working for a member of the U.S. House of Representatives and a U.S. Senate committee, joined Jerry Abramson's lobbying team 10 years ago. The Abramson group maintained a successful and wide-ranging lobbying practice in Washington, D.C. Playing a role some characterized as the team's "chief operating officer," Appellant managed some of Abramson's most important clients and maintained close relationships with several public officials. Appellant and the other Abramson lobbyists relied heavily on campaign contributions to maintain relationships with elected officials and promote their clients' political interests. But it was Appellant's other lobbying tactics that got him in trouble. These tactics chiefly included treating congressional and executive branch officials to dinners, drinks, travel, concerts, and sporting events. Appellant referred to officials with whom he had the closest ties and with whom his lobbying efforts were most successful as his "champions." As regular beneficiaries of Appellant's largesse, these "champions" often took actions that were favorable to Appellant's clients.

Five years ago, a targeted federal investigation of a kickback scheme mastermined by Abramson and another of his associates, Scanlon, spawned the broader investigation that ultimately ensnared Appellant. Discovering that meals, tickets, and travel Appellant provided to public officials were impermissibly linked to official acts that benefitted Appellant and his clients, the government indicted Appellant on six counts of aiding and abetting honest-services fraud, one count of paying an illegal gratuity, and one count of conspiracy to pay illegal gratuities and commit honest-services fraud. After his first trial resulted in a hung jury, the district court postponed retrial to await the Supreme Court's decision in *Skilling*. Then, following a two-week trial, a jury convicted Appellant on three of the six honest-services counts, the illegal gratuity count, and the conspiracy count. Appellant was sentenced to 20 months' incarceration, but the district court, observing that his case "presented challenging and novel questions of law," stayed that sentence pending appeal.

Appellant now challenges the honest services convictions. He argues that Skilling *only encompasses bribery and not gratuities. How should the court rule? Why?*

4-13. Savage made both a name and a fortune as a plaintiffs' attorney in asbestos and tobacco litigation. Along the way, he became entangled in many fee-sharing disputes with co-counsel, one of which resulted in a lawsuit filed by Roberts Williams ("the *Williams* Case"). Robert Cruz sat on the state Circuit Court, where he was assigned the *Williams* Case and his path crossed with Savage. Savage wanted a sure thing in the *Williams* Case, having recently lost a similar fee fight. As the presiding judge, Cruz could put his finger on the scales. Cruz coveted a federal judgeship more than anything else; as the brother-in-law of a United States Senator, Savage could influence the person who sent judicial candidates to the President. Early last year, Savage retained Ed Peters, a close friend and mentor of Cruz's, as a secret go-between who conveyed an offer: If Cruz would help Savage win the *Williams* Case, Savage would recommend Cruz to the Senator for a district court judgeship. Savage and Cruz mailed a total of three letters in furtherance of this scheme.

Cruz kept his end of the bargain: When Savage badly needed a trial continuance, Cruz entered, verbatim, a scheduling order prepared by one of Savage's attorneys, despite having disclaimed input from either party. Cruz also reviewed yet-to-be-filed motions for Savage, advising how he would rule and which arguments needed work.

Early last year, three judicial vacancies opened up on federal district courts in the state. In March, after being passed over for nomination to one of those seats, Cruz relayed to Savage his dissatisfaction and concern that "he was doing his part of the bargain and that Savage was not going to fulfill his part of the deal." Immediately thereafter, Savage had the Senator call Cruz. Although the record suggests that the Senator did not say that Cruz was being considered, Cruz nonetheless came away with the impression that he was in the running for a seat.

Mollified that Savage was keeping his end of the bargain, Cruz continued secretly to tilt the scales in the *Williams* Case. These machinations came to light when members of Savage's legal team began cooperating with the government's investigation of an unrelated judicial bribery scheme. A grand jury returned an indictment, charging Savage and Cruz with three counts of honest-services mail fraud, in violation of 18 U.S.C. §§ 1341 and 1346. Cruz agreed to plead guilty and to cooperate with the government.

Savage has filed a motion to dismiss the charges on the ground that he did not owe a fiduciary duty that would support such a charge. How should the court rule? Why?

4-14. William is the former majority leader of the state legislature of a large state. His influence as a legislator was immense. William typically ran for reelection on a "pro-business" platform, and he regularly set up meetings (by phone and email) between local business leaders and state agencies that may be in a position to facilitate or fund those businesses' projects and research. Occasionally, the businesses he helped would hire William's son, Bill, for odd jobs. Bill was paid more than $300,000 for these "jobs," but he didn't seem to do any real work to earn the money. Based on these facts, prosecutors charged William with honest-services wire fraud. During the trial, prosecutors introduced a great deal of evidence of William setting up meetings between the businesses who hired Bill and a number of state agencies. Prosecutors also introduced evidence that a number of these meetings resulted in state funding and other favorable treatment for these businesses. At the conclusion of the trial, the judge included the following as part of the jury instructions:

> I have used the term "official act" in connection with the bribery element of the honest services wire fraud charges against the defendant. The term "official act" includes any act taken under color of official authority. These decisions or actions do not need to be specially described in any law, rule, or job description, but may also include acts customarily performed by a public official with a particular position. In addition, official action can include actions taken in furtherance of longer-term goals, and an official action is no less official because it is one in a series of steps to exercise influence or achieve an end.

William was convicted of honest-services wire fraud and now appeals his conviction by challenging (among other things) the above jury instruction as erroneous in light of the Supreme Court's decision in McDonnell. *How should the court of appeals rule?*

D. The Use of the Mails and Wires

1. The "In Furtherance" Requirement

In a number of mail and wire fraud cases, the Supreme Court has stated that the government must show that the use of the mail or wires was "in furtherance" of the fraudulent scheme. Defining this element has not proven easy, as the cases that follow show.

Schmuck v. United States

489 U.S. 705 (1989)

Justice Blackmun delivered the opinion of the Court.

In August 1983, petitioner Wayne T. Schmuck, a used-car distributor, was indicted in the United States District Court for the Western District of Wisconsin on 12 counts of mail fraud, in violation of 18 U.S.C. §§ 1341 and 1342.

The alleged fraud was a common and straightforward one. Schmuck purchased used cars, rolled back their odometers, and then sold the automobiles to Wisconsin retail dealers for prices artificially inflated because of the low-mileage readings. These unwitting car dealers, relying on the altered odometer figures, then resold the cars to customers, who in turn paid prices reflecting Schmuck's fraud. To complete the resale of each automobile, the dealer who purchased it from Schmuck would submit a title-application form to the Wisconsin Department of Transportation on behalf of his retail customer. The receipt of a Wisconsin title was a prerequisite for completing the resale; without it, the dealer could not transfer title to the customer and the customer could not obtain Wisconsin tags. The submission of the title application form supplied the mailing element of each of the alleged mail frauds.

Before trial, Schmuck moved to dismiss the indictment on the ground that the mailings at issue—the submissions of the title-application forms by the automobile dealers—were not in furtherance of the fraudulent scheme and, thus, did not satisfy the mailing element of the crime of mail fraud. The District Court denied the motion. After trial, the jury returned guilty verdicts on all 12 counts.

* * *

"The federal mail fraud statute does not purport to reach all frauds, but only those limited instances in which the use of the mails is a part of the execution of the fraud, leaving all other cases to be dealt with by appropriate state law." *Kann v. United States*, 323 U.S. 88, 95 (1944). To be part of the execution of the fraud, however, the use of the mails need not be an essential element of the scheme. *Pereira v. United States*, 347 U.S. 1, 8 (1954). It is sufficient for the mailing to be "incident to an essential part of the scheme," *id.*, or "a step in [the] plot," *Badders v. United States*, 240 U.S. 391, 394 (1916).

Schmuck, relying principally on this Court's decisions in *Kann, supra, Parr v. United States*, 363 U.S. 370 (1960), and *United States v. Maze*, 414 U.S. 395 (1974), argues that mail fraud can be predicated only on a mailing that affirmatively assists the perpetrator in carrying out his fraudulent scheme. The mailing element of the offense, he contends, cannot be satisfied by a mailing, such as those at issue here, that is routine and innocent in and of itself, and that, far from furthering the execution of the fraud, occurs after the fraud has come to fruition, is merely tangentially related to the fraud, and is counterproductive in that it creates a "paper trail" from which the fraud may be discovered. We disagree both with this characterization of the mailings in the present case and with this description of the applicable law.

We begin by considering the scope of Schmuck's fraudulent scheme. Schmuck was charged with devising and executing a scheme to defraud Wisconsin retail automobile customers who based their decisions to purchase certain automobiles at least in part on the low-mileage readings provided by the tampered odometers. This was a fairly large-scale operation. Evidence at trial indicated that Schmuck had employed a man known only as "Fred" to turn back the odometers on about 150 different cars. Schmuck then marketed these cars to a number of dealers, several of whom he dealt with on a consistent basis over a period of about 15 years. Indeed, of the 12 automobiles that are the subject of the counts of the indictment, five were sold to "P and A Sales," and 4 to "Southside Auto." Thus, Schmuck's was not a "one-shot" operation in which he sold a single car to an isolated dealer. His was an ongoing fraudulent venture. A rational jury could have concluded that the success of Schmuck's venture depended upon his continued harmonious relations with, and good reputation among, retail dealers, which in turn required the smooth flow of cars from the dealers to their Wisconsin customers.

Under these circumstances, we believe that a rational jury could have found that the title-registration mailings were part of the execution of the fraudulent scheme, a scheme which did not reach fruition until the retail dealers resold the cars and effected transfers of title. Schmuck's scheme would have come to an abrupt halt if the dealers either had lost faith in Schmuck or had not been able to resell the cars obtained from him. These resales and Schmuck's relationships with the retail dealers naturally depended on the successful passage of title among the various parties. Thus, although the registration-form mailings may not have contributed directly to the duping of either the retail dealers or the customers, they were necessary to the passage of title, which in turn was essential to the perpetuation of Schmuck's scheme. As noted earlier, a mailing that is "incident to an essential part of the scheme," *Pereira*, 347 U.S. at 8, satisfies the mailing element of the mail fraud offense. The mailings here fit this description.

Once the full flavor of Schmuck's scheme is appreciated, the critical distinctions between this case and the three cases in which this Court has delimited the reach of the mail fraud statute — *Kann, Parr*, and *Maze* — are readily apparent. The defendants in *Kann* were corporate officers and directors accused of setting up a dummy corporation through which to divert profits into their own pockets. As part of this fraudulent scheme, the defendants caused the corporation to issue two checks payable to them. The defendants cashed these checks at local banks, which then mailed the checks to the drawee banks for collection. This Court held that the mailing of the cashed checks to the drawee banks could not supply the mailing element of the mail fraud charges. The defendants' fraudulent scheme had reached fruition. "It was immaterial to them, or to any consummation of the scheme, how the bank which paid or credited the check would collect from the drawee bank." 323 U.S. at 94.

In *Parr*, several defendants were charged, *inter alia*, with having fraudulently obtained gasoline and a variety of other products and services through the unauthorized use of a credit card issued to the school district which employed them. The mailing element of the mail fraud charges in *Parr* was purportedly satisfied when the oil company which issued the credit card mailed invoices to the school district for payment, and when the district mailed payment in the form of a check. Relying on *Kann*, this Court held that these mailings were not in execution of the scheme as required by the statute because it was immaterial to the defendants how the oil company went about collecting its payment. 363 U.S. at 393.

Later, in *Maze*, the defendant allegedly stole his roommate's credit card, headed south on a winter jaunt, and obtained food and lodging at motels along the route by placing the charges on the stolen card. The mailing element of the mail fraud charge was supplied by the fact that the defendant knew that each motel proprietor would mail an invoice to the bank that had issued the credit card, which in turn would mail a bill to the card owner for payment. The Court found that these mailings could not support mail fraud charges because the defendant's scheme had reached fruition when he checked out of each motel. The success of his scheme in no way depended on the mailings; they merely determined which of his victims would ultimately bear the loss. 414 U.S. at 402.

The title-registration mailings at issue here served a function different from the mailings in *Kann*, *Parr*, and *Maze*. The intrabank mailings in *Kann* and the credit card invoice mailings in *Parr* and *Maze* involved little more than post-fraud accounting among the potential victims of the various schemes, and the long-term success of the fraud did not turn on which of the potential victims bore the ultimate loss. Here, in contrast, a jury rationally could have found that Schmuck by no means was indifferent to the fact of who bore the loss. The mailing of the title-registration forms was an essential step in the successful passage of title to the retail purchasers. Moreover, a failure of this passage of title would have jeopardized Schmuck's relationship of trust and goodwill with the retail dealers upon whose unwitting cooperation his scheme depended. Schmuck's reliance on our prior cases limiting the reach of the mail fraud statute is simply misplaced.

To the extent that Schmuck would draw from these previous cases a general rule that routine mailings that are innocent in themselves cannot supply the mailing element of the mail fraud offense, he misapprehends this Court's precedents. In *Parr* the Court specifically acknowledged that "innocent" mailings—ones that contain no false information—may supply the mailing element. 363 U.S. at 390. In other cases, the Court has found the elements of mail fraud to be satisfied where the mailings have been routine. *See, e.g., Carpenter v. United States*, 484 U.S. 19, 28 (1987) (mailing newspapers).

We also reject Schmuck's contention that mailings that someday may contribute to the uncovering of a fraudulent scheme cannot supply the mailing element of the mail fraud offense. The relevant question at all times is whether the mailing is part of the execution of the scheme as conceived by the perpetrator at the time, regardless of whether the mailing later, through hindsight, may prove to have been counterproductive and return to haunt the perpetrator of the fraud. The mail fraud statute includes no guarantee that the use of the mails for the purpose of executing a fraudulent scheme will be risk free. Those who use the mails to defraud proceed at their peril.

For these reasons, we agree with the Court of Appeals that the mailings in this case satisfy the mailing element of the mail fraud offenses.

* * *

We conclude that Schmuck's conviction was consistent with the statutory definition of mail fraud. The judgment of the Court of Appeals, accordingly, is affirmed.

It is so ordered.

JUSTICE SCALIA, with whom JUSTICE BRENNAN, JUSTICE MARSHALL, and JUSTICE O'CONNOR join, dissenting.

* * *

The purpose of the mail fraud statute is "to prevent the post office from being used to carry [fraudulent schemes] into effect." *Durland v. United States*, 161 U.S. 306, 314 (1896); *Parr v. United States*, 363 U.S. 370, 389 (1960). The law does not establish a general federal remedy against fraudulent conduct, with use of the mails as the jurisdictional hook, but reaches only "those limited instances in which the use of the mails is *a part of the execution of the fraud*, leaving all other cases to be dealt with by appropriate state law." *Kann v. United States*, 323 U.S. 88, 95 (1944) (emphasis added). In other words, it is mail fraud, not mail and fraud, that incurs liability. This federal statute is not violated by a fraudulent scheme in which, at some point, a mailing happens to occur — nor even by one in which a mailing predictably and necessarily occurs. The mailing must be in furtherance of the fraud.

In *Kann v. United States*, we concluded that even though defendants who cashed checks obtained as part of a fraudulent scheme knew that the bank cashing the checks would send them by mail to a drawee bank for collection, they did not thereby violate the mail fraud statute, because upon their receipt of the cash "[t]he scheme had reached fruition," and the mailing was "immaterial to any consummation of the scheme." *Id.* at 94. We held to the same effect in *United States v. Maze*, 414 U.S. 395, 400–402 (1974), declining to find that credit card fraud was converted into mail fraud by the certainty that, after the wrongdoer had fraudulently received his goods and services from the merchants, they would forward the credit charges by mail for payment. These cases are squarely on point here. For though the government chose to charge a defrauding of retail customers (to whom the innocent dealers resold the cars), it is obvious that, regardless of who the ultimate victim of the fraud may have been, the fraud was complete with respect to each car when petitioner pocketed the dealer's money. As far as each particular transaction was concerned, it was as inconsequential to him whether the dealer resold the car as it was inconsequential to the defendant in *Maze* whether the defrauded merchant ever forwarded the charges to the credit card company.

Nor can the force of our cases be avoided by combining all of the individual transactions into a single scheme, and saying, as the Court does, that if the dealers' mailings obtaining title for each retail purchaser had not occurred then the dealers would have stopped trusting petitioner for future transactions. (That conclusion seems to me a non sequitur, but I accept it for the sake of argument.) This establishes, at most, that the scheme could not technically have been consummated if the mechanical step of the mailings to obtain conveyance of title had not occurred. But we have held that the indispensability of such mechanical mailings, not strictly in furtherance of the fraud, is not enough to invoke the statute. For example, when officials of a school district embezzled tax funds over the course of several years, we held that no mail fraud had occurred even though the success of the scheme plainly depended on the officials' causing tax bills to be sent by mail (and thus tax payments to be received) every year. *Parr v. United States*, 363 U.S. at 388–392. Similarly, when those officials caused the school district to pay by mail credit card bills — a step plainly necessary to enable their continued fraudulent use of the credit card — we concluded that no mail fraud had occurred.

I find it impossible to escape these precedents in the present case. Assuming the Court to be correct in concluding that failure to pass title to the cars would have threatened the success of the scheme, the same could have been said of failure to collect taxes or to pay the credit card bills in *Parr*. And I think it particularly significant that in *Kann* the government proposed a theory *identical* to that which the Court today uses. Since the scheme was ongoing, the government urged, the fact that the mailing of the two checks had occurred after the defendants had pocketed the fraudulently obtained cash made no difference. The Court rejected this argument, concluding that "the subsequent banking transactions between the banks concerned were merely incidental and collateral to the scheme and not a part of it." I think the mailing of the title application forms equivalently incidental here. . . .

Notes and Questions

1. *The "in furtherance" rule.* After reading *Schmuck*, what "rule" can you divine from the case? In particular, if you were advising a client, could you distinguish between the outcomes in *Kann, Parr,* and *Maze*, on the one hand, and *Schmuck* on the other? The four-member dissent in *Schmuck* argued that *Kann, Parr,* and *Maze* in fact cannot be distinguished from *Schmuck*. Is the dissent right?

2. *A federal case?* As noted elsewhere in this text, the vast majority of criminal cases, including fraud cases, are brought at the state and local level. Can you think of possible reasons why *Schmuck* was prosecuted at the federal level?

3. *Identity of the deceived party.* Suppose that an insurance company officer schemes to steal money from the company. As part of the scheme, the officer mails forms to the state insurance commissioner that contain material false statements. Has the officer committed mail fraud? *See Corcoran v. American Plan Corp,* 886 F.2d 16 (2d Cir. 1989).

Courts have split as to whether there must be a "convergence" between the party the defendant intended to deceive and the party the defendant intended to be the victim of the fraud. *Compare, e.g., United States v. Christopher,* 142 F.3d 46, 54 (1st Cir. 1998) (finding the *McNally* holding does not contain a convergence requirement) and *United States v. Greenberg,* 835 F.3d 295 (2^d Cir. 2016) (joining the First, Fifth, Seventh, and Eighth Circuits in holding that mail and wire fraud "does not require convergence between the parties intended to be deceived and those whose property is sought in a fraudulent scheme"), *with United States v. Lew,* 875 F.2d 219, 221–222 (9th Cir. 1989) (holding that *McNally* implicitly requires that "the intent must be to obtain money or property from the one who is deceived").

In a civil RICO case based on mail fraud predicate acts, however, the United States Supreme Court seemed to assume — without explicitly holding — that convergence is not required. In *Bridge v. Phoenix Bond & Indemnity Co.,* 533 U.S. 639, 648 (2008), the defendants made false statements in mailings to local governments in a bid-rigging scheme. The victims in the scheme were other bidders who were deprived of the right to compete fairly in the bidding process and of the financial benefits of potentially successful bids. The Court found that this amounted to mail fraud.

In this light, the correct question may not be whether the deceived party (the government in *Phoenix Bond*) was the victim (the other bidders in *Phoenix Bond*). Instead of focusing on "convergence," it may be better to focus on the "in furtherance" requirement. Take a material, false statement made to a third party who is not the intended victim of the scheme and who therefore would not be deprived of money, property, or honest services if the scheme succeeded. A statement to the third party would not be "in furtherance" of the scheme to defraud unless it is directly related to the intended injury to the scheme's victim. Thus, in *Phoenix Bond*, the statements to the local government led directly to the intended injury to the victims and satisfied the requirement from *Schmuck, Parr,* and *Maze* that the use of the mails or wires be sufficiently tied to the scheme to be considered "in furtherance" of the scheme.

4. *The "lulling" rule.* Can a use of the mails or wires be "in furtherance" of a fraudulent scheme where such use occurs *after* the scheme has reached fruition and the deceived party has already been deprived of the money, property, or honest services? The Supreme Court has answered in the affirmative in situations in which the use of the mail or wires was designed to "lull" the victim into a false sense of security. For

example, in *United States v. Sampson*, 371 U.S. 75 (1962), the defendants offered services to potential customers that the defendants never intended to provide. After the customers paid for the services, the defendants mailed the customers letters assuring them that the defendants indeed would perform the promised services. Similarly, in *United States v. Lane*, 474 U.S. 438 (1986), the defendant defrauded an insurance company; after he received the payment for the fraudulent claim, he sent the company documentation supporting the claim. The Supreme Court affirmed both convictions. As the Court stated in *Lane*, "Mailings occurring after receipt of the goods obtained by fraud are within the statute if they 'were designed to lull the victims into a false sense of security, postpone their ultimate complaint to the authorities, and therefore, make the apprehension of the defendants less likely than if no mailings had taken place.'" *Id.* at 451–452, *quoting United States v. Maze*, 414 U.S. at 403.

5. *The required mailings exception.* Under *Schmuck*, most mailings necessary to the continuation of an ongoing scheme will qualify under the mail fraud statute. Most circuits, however, recognize a required mailings exception to this rule. *See United States v. Lake*, 472 F.3d 1247, 1256 (10th Cir. 2007) (noting that "[m]ost other circuits to address the issue have interpreted *Parr* to hold that 'mailings of documents which are required by law to be mailed, and which are not themselves false and fraudulent, cannot be regarded as mailed for the purpose of executing a fraudulent scheme'"). Why have the courts created this exception?

Problem

4-15. The defendant, an engineer, was involved in designing airport plans in the defendant's state. Before an airport project could proceed in the state, the plans had to receive formal written approval from interested state agencies confirmed by an official stamped seal from each agency. The defendant placed a state Office of Health and Environmental Control ("OHEC") seal onto a set of construction plans without OHEC approval. The defendant mailed the plans to officials in the county where the airport project was located. The county officials then approved the plan and construction commenced. Approximately three months after the project was completed, a county official contacted the defendant, told the defendant that the plans had been misplaced, and asked the defendant to send another copy of the plans to place in the county's files. While in another state, the defendant scanned and emailed a copy of the plans containing the OHEC seal to the county official.

Among other charges, a grand jury has charged the defendant with mail fraud based upon the mailing and wire fraud based upon the email. The defendant has moved to dismiss the charges. How should the court rule? Why?

2. The Causation Requirement

Under the terms of the mail and wire fraud statutes, a defendant must either use, or "cause[]" the use of, the mails, a private courier, or the wires. In some cases, even when a mailing may arguably have been "in furtherance" of the fraud, the defendant may not have "caused" the mailing. The meaning of the causation requirement is explored in the next case.

United States v. Walters

997 F.2d 1219 (7th Cir. 1993)

EASTERBROOK, CIRCUIT JUDGE.

Norby Walters, who represents entertainers, tried to move into the sports business. He signed 58 college football players to contracts while they were still playing. Walters offered cars and money to those who would agree to use him as their representative in dealing with professional teams. Sports agents receive a percentage of the players' income, so Walters would profit only to the extent he could negotiate contracts for his clients. The athletes' pro prospects depended on successful completion of their collegiate careers. To the National Collegiate Athletic Association (NCAA), however, a student who signs a contract with an agent is a professional, ineligible to play on collegiate teams. To avoid jeopardizing his clients' careers, Walters dated the contracts after the end of their eligibility and locked them in a safe. He promised to lie to the universities in response to any inquiries. Walters inquired of sports lawyers at Shea & Gould whether this plan of operation would be lawful. The firm rendered an opinion that it would violate the NCAA's rules but not any statute.

Having recruited players willing to fool their universities and the NCAA, Walters discovered that they were equally willing to play false with him. Only 2 of the 58 players fulfilled their end of the bargain; the other 56 kept the cars and money, then signed with other agents. They relied on the fact that the contracts were locked away and dated in the future, and that Walters' business depended on continued secrecy, so he could not very well sue to enforce their promises. When the 56 would neither accept him as their representative nor return the payments, Walters resorted to threats. One player, Maurice Douglass, was told that his legs would be broken before the pro draft unless he repaid Walters' firm. A 75-page indictment charged Walters and his partner Lloyd Bloom with conspiracy, RICO violations (the predicate felony was extortion), and mail fraud. The fraud: causing the universities to pay scholarship funds to athletes who had become ineligible as a result of the agency contracts. The mail: each university required its athletes to verify their eligibility to play, then sent copies by mail to conferences such as the Big Ten.

After a month-long trial and a week of deliberations, the jury convicted Walters and Bloom. We reversed, holding that the district judge had erred in declining to instruct the jury that reliance on Shea & Gould's advice could prevent the formation of intent to defraud the universities. Any dispute about the adequacy of Walters' disclosure to his lawyers and the bona fides of his reliance was for the jury, we concluded. On remand, Walters asked the district court to dismiss the indictment, arguing that the evidence presented at trial is insufficient to support the convictions. After the judge denied this motion, Walters agreed to enter a conditional *Alford* plea: he would plead guilty to mail fraud, conceding that the record of the first trial supplies a factual basis for a conviction while reserving his right to contest the sufficiency of that evidence.

"Whoever, having devised any scheme or artifice to defraud, or for obtaining money or property by means of false or fraudulent pretenses, representations, or promises places in any post office or authorized depository for mail matter, any matter or thing whatever to be sent or delivered by the Postal Service or knowingly causes [such matter or thing] to be delivered by mail" commits the crime of mail fraud. 18 U.S.C. § 1341. Norby Walters did not mail anything or cause anyone else to do so (the universities were going to collect and mail the forms no matter what Walters did), but the Supreme Court has expanded the statute beyond its literal terms, holding that a mailing by a third party suffices if it is "incident to an essential part of the scheme," *Pereira v. United States*, 347 U.S. 1, 8 (1954). While stating that such mailings can turn ordinary fraud into mail fraud, the Court has cautioned that the statute "does not purport to reach all frauds, but only those limited instances in which the use of the mails is a part of the execution of the fraud." *Kann v. United States*, 323 U.S. 88, 95 (1944). Everything thus turns on matters of degree. Did the schemers foresee that the mails would be used? Did the mailing advance the success of the scheme? Which parts of a scheme are "essential"? Such questions lack obviously right answers, so it is no surprise that each side to this case can cite several of our decisions in support.

"The relevant question is whether the mailing is part of the execution of the scheme as conceived by the perpetrator at the time." *Schmuck v. United States*, 489 U.S. 705, 715 (1989). Did the evidence establish that Walters conceived a scheme in which mailings played a role? We think not — indeed, that no reasonable juror could give an affirmative answer to this question. For all Walters cared, the forms could sit forever in cartons. Movement to someplace else was irrelevant. In *Schmuck*, where the fraud was selling cars with rolled-back odometers, the mailing was essential to obtain a new and apparently "clean" certificate of title; no certificates of title, no marketable cars, no hope for success. Even so, the Court divided five to four on the question whether the mailing was sufficiently integral to the scheme. A college's mailing to its conference has less to do with the plot's success than the mailings that transferred title in *Schmuck*.

To this the United States responds that the mailings were essential because, if a college had neglected to send the athletes' forms to the conference, the NCAA would have barred that college's team from competing. Lack of competition would spoil the athletes' pro prospects. Thus the use of the mails was integral to the profits Walters hoped to reap, even though Walters would have been delighted had the colleges neither asked any questions of the athletes nor put the answers in the mail. Let us take this as sufficient under *Schmuck* (although we have our doubts). The question remains whether Walters caused the universities to use the mails. A person "knowingly causes" the use of the mails when he "acts with the knowledge that the use of the mails will follow in the ordinary course of business, or where such use can reasonably be foreseen." *United States v. Kuzniar*, 881 F.2d 466, 472 (7th Cir. 1989), *quoting Pereira*, 347 U.S. at 8–9. The paradigm is insurance fraud. Perkins tells his auto insurer that his car has been stolen, when in fact it has been sold. The local employee mails the claim to the home office, which mails a check to Perkins. Such mailings in the ordinary course of business are foreseeable. Similarly, a judge who takes a bribe derived from the litigant's bail money causes the use of the mails when the ordinary course is to refund the bond by mail. The prosecutor contends that the same approach covers Walters.

No evidence demonstrates that Walters *actually* knew that the colleges would mail the athletes' forms. The record is barely sufficient to establish that Walters knew of the forms' existence; it is silent about Walters' knowledge of the forms' disposition. So the prosecutor is reduced to the argument that mailings could "reasonably be foreseen." Yet why should this be so? Universities frequently collect information that is stashed in file drawers. Perhaps the NCAA just wants answers available for inspection in the event a question arises, or the university wants the information for its own purposes (to show that it did not know about any improprieties that later come to light). What was it about these forms that should have led a reasonable person to foresee their mailing? Recall that Walters was trying to break into the sports business. Counsel specializing in sports law told him that his plan would not violate any statute. These lawyers were unaware of the forms (or, if they knew about the forms, were unaware that they would be mailed). The prosecutor contends that Walters neglected to tell his lawyers about the eligibility forms, spoiling their opinion; yet why would Walters have to brief an expert in sports law if mailings were foreseeable even to a novice?

In the end, the prosecutor insists that the large size and interstate nature of the NCAA demonstrate that something would be dropped into the mails. To put this only slightly differently, the prosecutor submits that all frauds involving big organizations necessarily are mail frauds, because big organizations habitually mail things. No evidence put before the jury supports such a claim, and it is hardly appropriate for judicial notice in a criminal case. Moreover, adopting this perspective would contradict the assurance of *Kann*, 323 U.S. at 95, and many later cases that most frauds are covered by state law rather than §1341. That statute has been expanded considerably by judicial interpretation, but it does not make a federal crime of every deceit. The prosecutor must prove that the use of the mails was foreseeable, rather than calling on judicial intuition to repair a rickety case.

[Having concluded the causation element of mail fraud was not satisfied, the court went on to conclude that Walter's scheme was also not mail fraud because it did not have as its aim or object any loss of money or property on the part of the university (the purported victim). In a portion of the decision that was later embraced by the Supreme Court in *Kelly* (*see supra* at C; 2 and Problem 4-7), the court held that "[l]osses that occur as byproducts of a deceitful scheme do not satisfy the statutory requirement" for mail or wire fraud.]

Anticipating that we might come to this conclusion, the prosecutor contends that Walters is nonetheless guilty as an aider and abettor. If Walters did not defraud the universities, the argument goes, then the athletes did. Walters put them up to it and so is guilty under 18 U.S.C. § 2, the argument concludes. But the indictment charged a scheme by Walters to defraud; it did not depict Walters as an aide de camp in the students' scheme. The jury received a boilerplate § 2 instruction; this theory was not argued to the jury, or for that matter to the district court either before or after the remand. Independent problems dog this recasting of the scheme — not least the difficulty of believing that the students hatched a plot to employ fraud to receive scholarships that the universities had awarded them long before Walters arrived on the scene, and the lack of evidence that the students knew about or could foresee any mailings. Walters is by all accounts a nasty and untrustworthy fellow, but the prosecutor did not prove that his efforts to circumvent the NCAA's rules amounted to mail fraud.

Reversed.

Notes and Questions

1. *The "causation" and "in furtherance" requirements.* Did the *Walters* court find that the mailings were not in furtherance of the scheme? Did it find that Walters had not caused the mailings? What is the difference between the two requirements?

2. *The* Pereira *case.* In *Pereira v. United States*, 347 U.S. 1 (1954), the defendant engaged in a scheme to defraud a wealthy widow by deceiving her as to his financial and professional status and then marrying her. The defendant received funds from the victim, including funds represented by a check written on a California bank account that the victim endorsed to Pereira. Pereira deposited the check in a Texas bank, which mailed the check to California for collection. Did Pereira "cause" the mailing? The Court held in the affirmative, stating that "[w]here one does an act with knowledge that the use of the mails will follow in the ordinary course of business, or where such use can reasonably be foreseen, even though not actually intended, then he 'causes' the mails to be used." Was this the correct result? Is it consistent with *Walters*? Why or why not?

3. *The* Schmuck *decision revisited.* The Supreme Court found that the mailings in *Schmuck* were sufficient, in large part because the mailings were part of an ongoing scheme that would collapse if the mailings never occurred. Cannot the same be said for *Walters*? Then why the different outcome? In light of *Schmuck*, was *Walters* correctly decided?

4. *Reliance on counsel.* The court in *Walters* noted that it had reversed the defendants' original conviction, "holding that the district judge had erred in declining to instruct the jury that reliance on [a law firm's] advice could prevent the formation of intent to defraud the universities." A successful good faith advice of counsel defense typically requires the following:

> 1. Before taking action, he in good faith sought the advice of an attorney whom he considered competent to advise him on the matter; and

> 2. He consulted this attorney for the purpose of securing advice on the lawfulness of his possible future conduct; and

3. He made a full and accurate report to his attorney of all material facts that he knew; and

4. He then acted strictly in accordance with the advice of this attorney.

United States v. Scully, 877 F.3d 464, 478 (2d Cir. 2017) (quoting the Seventh Circuit Pattern Criminal Jury Instructions, § 6.12 (2012 ed.)). The jury may consider the reasonableness of the attorney's advice when determining the defendant's good faith. *Id.* Recall the maxim that "ignorance of the law is no excuse." In that light, why is reliance on counsel a defense to a mail fraud charge?

Problems

4-16. The government has indicted Defendant for mail and wire fraud based upon the following evidence. Defendant was the Chief Executive Officer of Energy Corp., based in New York City. During the last four years, Defendant conspired with Energy Corp's accountant, Dern, to inflate Energy Corp's earnings and stock prices artificially. Many investors bought stock in the company, which is now worthless. Approximately 1,000 investors have lost a total of tens of millions of dollars. Many of these investors received copies of Energy Corp's annual reports in the mail and relied on the reports when making their investment decisions. The annual reports contained the inflated earnings statements, along with a proviso that said, "These statements are preliminary and subject to change upon final review by our auditors."

Last July, Dern and Defendant had lunch. During the lunch, they discussed ways to hide the ongoing fraud. Dern made notes on a legal pad during this lunch. In August, Defendant learned that Energy Corp. was being investigated by the Securities and Exchange Commission for alleged securities fraud. From the Energy Corp. offices, Defendant called Dern, who was on vacation in Vermont, and asked Dern to throw away the notes. Dern complied. Dern is now cooperating with the government.

The government has charged Defendant with mail fraud based upon the mailings of the annual reports, and with wire fraud based upon the phone call. Defendant has moved to dismiss the charges. What is the likely outcome? Why?

4-17. Defendant is an immigration attorney who was retained by a number of clients. The clients paid Defendant to obtain labor certification that would allow them to work legally in the country. Defendant performed the services for which Defendant was retained. During the course of representing the clients, Defendant mailed documents to the federal government that made false, material misrepresentations concerning the clients' eligibility for labor certification.

Defendant has been indicted for mail fraud based upon the foregoing facts and has filed a motion to dismiss. Should the motion be granted? Why or why not?

4-18. Wilson, a Colorado real estate broker, was indicted on several counts of mail fraud, wire fraud, and witness tampering. The indictment alleged that Wilson organized a scheme to obtain mortgage loans for low-income, unsophisticated homebuyers through a Federal Housing Administration ("FHA") program sponsored by the United States Department of Housing and Urban Development ("HUD"). In furtherance of this scheme, Wilson helped borrowers obtain subsidized loans through the FHA's Single Family Home Mortgage program even though they were ineligible, provided lenders with false information about the buyers, and paid the buyers' down payments in violation of HUD rules.

The charged mailings in the mail fraud counts were recorded deeds of trust sent from the Denver County Clerk and Recorder to the lenders involved in the various home sales which comprised Wilson's scheme. Each lender required its closing agent to have a deed of trust executed at the closing and required the deed of trust to be promptly recorded and sent to the lender. The lenders needed these original recorded deeds of trust to facilitate the smooth securitization and marketing of the mortgages in the secondary market.

Representatives from several lenders, as well as the Government National Mortgage Association ("Ginnie Mae"), testified as to the importance of these recorded deeds of trusts in marketing FHA loans in the secondary mortgage market. A manager at Old Kent Mortgage testified that federally insured loans were particularly attractive to lenders because they could easily be sold to Ginnie Mae to generate funds for future loans. The manager also testified that lenders needed the original recorded deeds of trust to meet Ginnie Mae's certification requirements and that lenders such as Old Kent tried to avoid any deviation from this practice.

Wilson was convicted of eight counts of mail fraud. Wilson appealed, arguing that there was insufficient evidence to support his mail fraud convictions because the mailings were not "part of the execution of the scheme as conceived by the perpetrator at the time." How should the court hold? Why?

4-19. Dudley was a police officer employed by the Alton Police Department ("APD"). During the time period relevant to this case, Dudley was the evidence custodian for the APD; in this capacity, he was responsible for collecting and processing evidence at the scenes of major crimes committed within the APD's jurisdiction. He was also in charge of receiving, maintaining, and preserving the evidence that was stored in the APD's evidence vault.

The APD's evidence vault was subject to strict security measures. Only five members of the APD, including Mr. Dudley, had access cards allowing entry to the vestibule area outside the evidence vault. The cash locker inside the vault required another key for access; only two copies existed. One was assigned to Mr. Dudley and the other was stored in the secured administration wing.

In June two years ago, the Olin Community Credit Union in Alton was robbed (the "OCU robbery"). In October that year, a local branch of the U.S. Bank was robbed (the "US Bank robbery"). The APD investigated the robberies; it ultimately was able to recover $4,200 in proceeds from the June robbery and $21,000 from the October robbery. Dudley participated in both investigations and personally deposited the money into the APD evidence vault. On Friday, April 7 last year,

FBI Special Agent Vasquez contacted Dudley's supervisor to request that evidence from the OCU robbery be turned over to the FBI for use in the federal prosecution in that case. That same day, Dudley's supervisor sent him an email to inform him that the FBI wished to retrieve that evidence the following week. On Sunday, April 9 — one of Mr. Dudley's days off — surveillance cameras recorded Mr. Dudley inside the evidence vault removing the box containing evidence from the OCU robbery.

On the following Monday, April 10, Special Agent Vasquez called Dudley to arrange to pick up the evidence. Mr. Dudley told Vasquez that he would provide a container in which to carry the evidence. He also asked her to delay the evidence pickup until the following day. Vasquez agreed. When Vasquez arrived the next day, Dudley gave her an inventory list to check off while he handled the evidence packages. While Vasquez was looking at the list, the surveillance camera captured Dudley placing one of the packages under another; as a result, Vasquez never examined the contents of the concealed package, from which Dudley had removed several thousand dollars.

The government charged Dudley with wire fraud based on the email message sent by Dudley's supervisor to Dudley on April 7. The government submits that, although Mr. Dudley did not send that message himself, he nevertheless "caused" it to be sent because he "acted with knowledge that the use of a wire was reasonably foreseeable." Dudley has moved to dismiss the charge. How will the court likely rule? Why?

E. Related Crimes

In addition to the mail and wire fraud statutes, the federal criminal code contains many provisions directed to specific types of fraud. The next two chapters of this text, for example, focus on securities fraud and health care fraud, respectively. Among other important fraud statutes are the computer and bank fraud statutes. This section provides a brief overview of these laws.

1. Computer Fraud

a. Scope of Computer Crimes

Computer-related crimes present tremendous challenges for law enforcement, the public, and defense counsel. Today's technological explosion provides unlimited ways for criminals to prey upon businesses and individuals via computers and the Internet. The scope of criminal activity that falls within the broad range of "computer crimes" is restricted only by the creative criminal mind. Computers can be used as tools to facilitate a wide range of criminal activity. Thus, computer crimes frequently overlap with other crimes, such as wire fraud, theft offenses, espionage, and privacy crimes. Computers have also been used in stalking cases, child pornography cases, and lottery fraud schemes, as well as many other types of fraud.

There is no universal definition of computer crime or cybercrime. It is impractical to formulate a comprehensive definition because most elements of modern life revolve around some use of computer systems. The United States Department of Justice ("DOJ") defines computer crimes as including "any violations of criminal law that involve a knowledge of computer technology for their perpetration, investigation, or prosecution." Nat'l Inst. of Justice, U.S. Dept. of Justice, Computer Crime: Criminal Justice Resource Manual 2 (1989).

One way to approach the study of computer crimes is to categorize the criminal activity depending on whether the computer is the (1) object, (2) subject, or (3) instrument of the criminal activity. An example of the first category occurs when computer hardware or software is stolen. Cases in this category involve the computer as a typical storage device, equivalent to a filing cabinet. The focus is on the computer itself because of what it contains. Crimes in the second category occur when the computer is the subject of the crimes. In today's technological environment, the computer is particularly vulnerable to infrastructure attacks including viruses and worms designed to create widespread disruption or even destruction. This type of criminal activity focuses on the integrity or confidentiality of the computer information. Crimes in the third category — where the computer is used as an instrument or tool of crime — involve more traditional crimes that are committed with the assistance of computers. Examples of such crimes include child pornography and identity theft. Within these three general types of offenses, most cybercrime centers on the unauthorized access to computer systems and the transmission of information stored on a computer for illegal purposes.

There has been a rapid emergence of legislation designed to address the vulnerability of this spawning technology. As much of our country's security system is computerized, recent terrorist activities have been promulgated on the Internet in an effort to disarm United States security measures or to disrupt fundamental services. The USA PATRIOT Act of 2001 has intersected with the computer crime legislation to enhance punishment and widen the scope of the government's powers.[d]

Computer crimes are exceedingly difficult to investigate and prosecute partly because there is no single law enforcement organization that polices the use of computers and the Internet. Computer technology evolves at lightning speed. Ever increasing technical training thus is required to investigate these types of offenses. Juveniles, who typically have more up-to-date computer savvy than even law enforcement personnel, often commit technologically-based offenses with ease. The perpetrators of computer crimes have been called "hackers" and "crackers."[e]

---

d. The Uniting and Strengthening America by Providing Appropriate Tools Required to Intercept and Obstruct Terrorist Act of 2001 (USA PATRIOT Act), Pub. L. No 107-56, 115 Stat. 272 (as amended by the Cyber Security Enhancement Act of 2002, Pub. L. No 107-298, § 225, 116 Stat. 2135, 2156).

e. "Hackers" have been defined as individuals who "access [computer] systems, without any authorization, for their own interest and not for economic profit, and traditionally lack the criminal

The damage to computer systems caused by sabotage is often calculated in the billions of dollars. Nearly 80% of the losses come from three types of computer crime: virus attacks, unauthorized access, and information theft. Viruses and worms in particular are both fast moving and extremely destructive to businesses, governments, and individuals.[f] In addition, companies face data security attacks on a massive scale.

b. Computer Crimes Statutes

The computer crimes statutory scheme was initially entitled the "Counterfeit Access Device and Computer Fraud and Abuse Act" when it was passed in 1984. Some courts still refer to 18 U.S.C. § 1030 as the Computer Fraud and Abuse Act. The original act was narrowly tailored to protect only computers containing classified governmental defense and foreign relations information, financial institution and consumer reporting agency files, and access to computers operated for the government. Congress continued to expand the scope of the law through the 1980s and 1990s. The USA PATRIOT Act of 2001, Pub. L. No. 107-56, § 814, 115 (2001), amended sections of the computer crime laws, significantly extending the scope of the law to reach protected computers outside of the borders of the United States. Another key effort directed at computer-related offenses was the Cyber Security Enhancement Act of 2002, enacted as part of the Homeland Security Act of 2002, Cyber Security Enhancement Act of 2001, Pub. L. No. 107-296, 116 Stat. 2135, 2156 (2002).[g]

Prior versions of the law covered crimes involving computers located in more than one state. The 1996 National Information Infrastructure Protection Plan amended § 1030 and extended the definition of "protected computer" to include any computer attached to the Internet, in order to protect computers against attack from within their home state. The government has continued to update the existing statutes related to traditional crimes, such as wire fraud, to address computer abuse. In addition, the United States Sentencing Guidelines provide for the enhancement of criminal punishment if the offense was committed with the use of a computer.

---

intent to damage systems." Cybercrime: The Investigation, Prosecution and Defense of a Computer-Related Crime 125 (Ralph D. Clifford, ed. 2001). "Crackers" are "hackers with criminal intent." *Id.*

f. "A virus is a program that copies itself into other programs and becomes active when a program is run (*e.g.*, clicked on); from there, a virus infects other files." Mark G. Milone, *Hactivism: Securing the National Infrastructure*, 20 Computer & Internet L. 2 n.18 (2003). "A worm is a self-replicating virus that does not alter files but resides in active memory and duplicates itself. Worms use parts of an operating system that are automatic and usually invisible to the user. It is common for worms to be noticed only when their uncontrolled replication consumes system resources, slowing or halting other tasks." *Id.* at 2 n.20.

g. A 2010 Department of Justice manual entitled *"Prosecuting Computer Crimes"* explores statutes, including the Computer Fraud and Abuse Act and the Wiretap Act, that may be used in computer crime prosecutions. *See* https://www.justice.gov/sites/default/files/criminal-ccips/legacy/2015/01/14/ccmanual.pdf.

The computer crimes statute, 18 U.S.C. §1030, *et seq.*, contains seven different violations, each with its own specific elements and requisite mental states. As you review the statutory scheme, keep in mind that the elements of proof will differ depending on what subsection the government uses, and what relevant conduct is alleged. As is clear from the statute, its coverage extends far beyond traditional fraud schemes:

- *Electronic espionage.* Section 1030(a)(1) criminalizes acts by one who "[A] having knowingly accessed a computer without authorization or exceeding authorized access" and having thereby "[B] obtained information that has been determined by the United States Government . . . [to] require protection against unauthorized disclosure for reasons of national defense or foreign relations . . . [C] with reason to believe that such information so obtained could be used to the injury of the United States, or to the advantage of any foreign nation [D] willfully communicates, delivers, transmits, or causes to be communicated, delivered, or transmitted, or attempts to communicate, deliver, transmit or cause to be communicated, delivered, or transmitted the same to any person not entitled to receive it, or willfully retains the same and fails to deliver it to the officer or employee of the United States entitled to receive it."

- *Theft of information.* Section 1030(a)(2) criminalizes one who "intentionally accesses a computer without authorization or exceeds authorized access, and thereby obtains (A) information contained in a financial record of a financial institution, or of a card issuer . . . , or contained in a file of a consumer reporting agency on a consumer . . . ; (B) information from any department or agency of the United States; or (C) information from any protected computer."

- *Accessing government computers.* Section 1030(a)(3) criminalizes the acts of one who "intentionally, without authorization to access any nonpublic computer of a department or agency of the United States, accesses such a computer of that department or agency that is exclusively for the use of the Government of the United States or, in the case of a computer not exclusively for such use, is used by or for the Government of the United States and such conduct affects that use by or for the Government of the United States."

- *Fraud.* Section 1030(a)(4) criminalizes the acts of one who "knowingly and with intent to defraud, accesses a protected computer without authorization, or exceeds authorized access, and by means of such conduct furthers the intended fraud and obtains anything of value, unless the object of the fraud and the thing obtained consists only of the use of the computer and the value of such use is not more than $5,000 in any one-year period."

- *Hacking.* Section 1030(a)(5) criminalizes the acts of one who "(A) knowingly causes the transmission of a program, information, code, or command, and as a result of such conduct, intentionally causes damage without authorization, to a protected computer; (B) intentionally accesses a protected computer without authorization, and as a result of such conduct, recklessly causes damage; or

(C) intentionally accesses a protected computer without authorization, and as a result of such conduct, causes damage and loss."

- *Trafficking of passwords.* Section 1030(a)(6) criminalizes the acts of one who "knowingly and with intent to defraud traffics . . . in any password or similar information through which a computer may be accessed without authorization, if (A) such trafficking affects interstate or foreign commerce; or (B) such computer is used by or for the Government of the United States."

- *Extortion.* § 1030(a)(7) criminalizes the acts of one who "with intent to extort from any person any money or other thing of value, transmits in interstate or foreign commerce any communication containing any (A) threat to cause damage to a protected computer; (B) threat to obtain information from a protected computer without authorization or in excess of authorization or to impair the confidentiality of information obtained from a protected computer without authorization or by exceeding authorized access; or (C) demand or request for money or other thing of value in relation to damage to a protected computer, where such damage was caused to facilitate the extortion."

Several of these subsections grade the offense depending on the level of harm and the mens rea. The government also utilizes a number of other laws to prosecute computer-related crimes, including mail and wire fraud, copyright infringement, espionage, interstate transportation of stolen property, and conspiracy.

c. Proving the Elements of Computer Crimes

The following case was one of the first to test the application of § 1030(a)(4), which is the fraud section of the computer crimes statute. The case turns on what constitutes a "thing of value" for purposes of computer fraud. As you read the case, consider why the government failed to meet its burden of proof.

United States v. Czubinski

106 F.3d 1069 (1st Cir. 1997)

TORRUELLA, CHIEF JUDGE.

[Czubinski worked for the Internal Revenue Service. His primary duties were answering taxpayers' questions about their returns. Czubinski was authorized to use his Boston computer to retrieve information from the IRS computer database in West Virginia. Acting outside the scope of official responsibilities, and in violation of IRS policy, Czubinski retrieved information about various individuals. These individuals included two persons involved in a political campaign — a District Attorney who had prosecuted Czubinski's father in an unrelated case and a Boston Housing Authority Police Officer who was involved in an organization with Czubinski's brother. The government alleged that Czubinski intended to use this information to build dossiers on people involved in the white supremacist movement and for other personal reasons. The government charged Czubinski with computer fraud and with wire fraud. At trial, the government did not prove that Czubinski actually used the information in any way, or that he disclosed the information to any third parties.]

Czubinski was convicted on all four of the computer fraud counts on which he was indicted; these counts arise out of unauthorized searches that also formed the basis of four of the ten wire fraud counts in the indictment. Specifically, he was convicted of violating 18 U.S.C. § 1030(a)(4), a provision enacted in the Computer Fraud and Abuse Act of 1986. Section 1030(a)(4) applies to:

> whoever . . . knowingly and with intent to defraud, accesses a Federal interest computer without authorization, or exceeds authorized access, and by means of such conduct furthers the intended fraud <u>and obtains anything of value</u>, unless the object of the fraud and the thing obtained consists only of the use of the computer.

We have never before addressed § 1030(a)(4). Czubinski unquestionably exceeded authorized access to a Federal interest computer.[14] On appeal he argues that he did not obtain "anything of value." We agree, finding that his searches of taxpayer return information did not satisfy the statutory requirement that he obtain "anything of value." The value of information is relative to one's needs and objectives; here, the government had to show that the information was valuable to Czubinski in light of a fraudulent scheme. The government failed, however, to prove that Czubinski intended anything more than to satisfy idle curiosity.

The plain language of § 1030(a)(4) emphasizes that more than mere unauthorized use is required: the "thing obtained" may not merely be the unauthorized use. It is the showing of some additional end — to which the unauthorized access is a means — that is lacking here. The evidence did not show that Czubinski's end was anything more than to satisfy his curiosity by viewing information about friends, acquaintances, and political rivals. No evidence suggests that he printed out, recorded, or used the information he browsed. No rational jury could conclude beyond a reasonable doubt that Czubinski intended to use or disclose that information, and merely viewing information cannot be deemed the same as obtaining something of value for the purposes of this statute.

The legislative history further supports our reading of the term "anything of value." "In the game of statutory interpretation, statutory language is the ultimate trump card," and the remarks of sponsors of legislation are authoritative only to the extent that they are compatible with the plain language of § 1030(a)(4). *Rhode Island v. Narragansett Indian Tribe*, 19 F.3d 685, 699 (1st Cir. 1994). Here, a Senate co-sponsor's comments suggest that Congress intended § 1030(a)(4) to punish attempts to steal valuable data, and did not wish to punish mere unauthorized access:

---

14. "[T]he term 'exceeds authorized access' means to access a computer with authorization and to use such access to obtain or alter information in the computer that the accessor is not entitled so to obtain or alter." 18 U.S.C. § 1030(e)(6).

> The acts of fraud we are addressing in proposed § 1030(a)(4) are essentially thefts in which someone uses a federal interest computer to wrongly obtain something of value from another.... Proposed § 1030(a)(4) is intended to reflect the distinction between the theft of information, a felony, and mere unauthorized access, a misdemeanor.

132 Cong. Rec. 7129, 99th Cong., 2d Sess. (1986). The Senate Committee Report further underscores the fact that this section should apply to those who steal information through unauthorized access as part of an illegal scheme:

> The Committee remains convinced that there must be a clear distinction between computer theft, punishable as a felony [under § 1030(a)(4)], and computer trespass, punishable in the first instance as a misdemeanor [under a different provision]. The element in the new paragraph (a)(4), requiring a showing of an intent to defraud, is meant to preserve that distinction, as is the requirement that the property wrongfully obtained via computer furthers the intended fraud.

[W]e find that Czubinski has not obtained valuable information in furtherance of a fraudulent scheme for the purposes of § 1030(a)(4).

Notes and Questions

1. *Proving the "thing of value."* The district court denied a motion to dismiss the computer fraud counts in the indictment, finding that the indictment sufficiently alleged that the confidential taxpayer information was itself a "thing of value" to Czubinski, given his ends. The indictment, of course, alleged specific uses for the information that were not proven at trial, such as creating dossiers on KKK members. In light of the evidence admitted at trial, the circuit court said that because "there was no recording, disclosure or further use of the confidential information — we find that Czubinski did not obtain 'anything of value' through his unauthorized searches." 106 F.3d at 1078 n.15. Was this a case of failure of proof by the government? Should the determination of "value" be made from the perspective of the victim or the defendant? Does it matter? The defendant was also charged with wire fraud based upon the theory that he deprived the IRS of its intangible property right to confidential taxpayer information. The court found that this did not qualify as an intangible property interest and reversed the conviction. (The court also found the evidence insufficient for a conviction under a deprivation of honest services theory based on reasoning similar to that in the Supreme Court's later *Skilling* decision.)

2. *Quantifying value.* Given that the government spends considerable sums of money in order to protect confidential government information, is such information inherently valuable? If so, how should this value be quantified?

3. *Choosing a theory.* At the time Czubinski was prosecuted, § 1030(a)(4) punished one who "knowingly and with intent to defraud, accesse[d] a Federal interest computer without authorization, or exceed[ed] authorized access, and by means of such conduct further[ed] the intended fraud and obtain[ed] anything of value, unless the

object of the fraud and the thing obtained consist[ed] only of the use of the computer." The current version of that statute states that the "thing of value" may be the computer time alone if that time is valued as more than $5,000 within one year. Could *Cuzbinski* be successfully charged under § 1030(a)(4) today? Also, the Taxpayer Browsing Protection Act, codified at 26 U.S.C. § 7213A, makes it misdemeanor for a federal employee to gain unauthorized access to tax return information. In addition, under the current version of § 1030(a)(2), Czubinski arguably could be convicted for the misdemeanor of gaining access to the information in excess of his authorization.

4. *The* Van Buren *case and defining "authorized access."* One of the trickier interpretive issues raised by § 1030 is determining when a computer user "exceeds authorized access." The statute defines the term "exceeds authorized access" as meaning "to access a computer with authorization and to use such access to obtain or alter information in the computer that the accesser is not entitled so to obtain or alter." 18 U.S.C. § 1030(e)(6). The circuits have split between narrow and broad interpretations of this language. The Second, Fourth, Sixth, and Ninth Circuits have interpreted "exceeds authorized access" more narrowly to apply only to those computer users who access information they are prohibited from accessing. *See, e.g., United States v. Valle*, 807 F.3d 508, 526–27 (2d Cir. 2015) (finding a police officer's authorized accessing of an official database for a personal purpose did not "exceed authorized access" under § 1030). The First, Fifth, Seventh, and Eleventh Circuits, by contrast, have adopted an expansive interpretation such that a person exceeds authorized access if that person uses authorized access to a computer for an improper or unauthorized purpose. *See, e.g., United States v. Van Buren*, 940 F.3d 1192 (11th Cir. 2019) (finding a police officer "exceeded authorized access" when the officer used authorized access to a police database to acquire information for a purpose that violated department policy), *cert. granted*, 140 S. Ct. 2667 (2020); *see also* Elkan Abramowitz & Jonathan S. Sack, *The Supreme Court Will Interpret Another White-Collar Criminal Statute*, 264 N.Y.L.J. (Nov. 10, 2020), https://www.law.com/newyorklawjournal /2020/11/09/in-current-term-the-supreme-court-will-interpret-another-white-collar -criminal-statute/.

As this text went to press, the Supreme Court had granted certiorari in *Van Buren* to settle this circuit split. *Van Buren* offers the Supreme Court its first opportunity to interpret the Computer Fraud and Abuse Act. There are significant policy considerations in favor of both the narrow and broad interpretations of "exceeds authorized access." As one commentator notes:

> Van Buren points, for example, to a student who views material on amazon .com during a law-school class, flagrantly violating computer-use restrictions imposed by the professor. The government has no obvious answer for why that is beyond the scope of the statute under its reading, except for the implicit suggestion that prosecutors rarely would bring cases of this sort.

Ronald Mann, *Case Preview: Justices to Consider Breadth of Federal Computer Fraud Statute*, SCOTUSBLOG (Nov. 29, 2020), https://www.scotusblog.com/2020/11 /case-preview-justices-to-consider-breadth-of-federal-computer-fraud-statute/. On the other hand, "it seems clear that the government has a legitimate need for prosecution in many cases that the narrow reading of ["exceeding authorized access"] would not reach." *Id.*

2. Bank Fraud

Federal law criminalizes a wide range of banking related crimes. The Bank Secrecy Act, for example, contains criminal penalties for failure to file required currency transaction reports, among other crimes. *See* Chapter 13, Money Laundering and Related Financial Crimes, *infra.* For an overview of the various crimes related to banking activities, *see* Helen Gredd & Gabriella Geanuleas, *Banking Crimes, in* White Collar Crime: Business and Regulatory Offenses §§ 2.01–08 (Otto Obermaier et al., eds., 2015). This section focuses on the bank fraud statute, a crime that is closely analogous to the mail and wire fraud statutes.

a. Statutory Overview

Passed in 1984, the bank fraud statute was modeled on the mail fraud statute. As explained below, Congress enacted the bank fraud statute in order to fill in gaps left by the mail and wire fraud statutes. The bank fraud statute is just one of many fraud statutes in the United States Code applicable to particular types of fraud.

The statute provides:

Whoever knowingly executes, or attempts to execute, a scheme or artifice —

(1) to defraud a financial institution; or

(2) to obtain any of the moneys, funds, credits, assets, securities, or other property owned by, or under the custody or control of, a financial institution, by means of false or fraudulent pretenses, representations, or promises; shall be fined not more than $1,000,000 or imprisoned not more than 30 years, or both.

18 U.S.C. § 1344.

The term "financial institution" is broadly defined in 18 U.S.C. § 20 to encompass a wide range of institutions, including federally insured banks, credit unions, branches and agencies of foreign banks, mortgage lending businesses, and other institutions.

b. Defining the Elements

In the next case, the United States Supreme Court addressed an issue concerning the scope of the bank fraud statute's second prong. The opinion provides an important application of basic principles of statutory interpretation. As you read the case, note the interplay between interpretations of the bank fraud statute and the mail fraud statute. The case also raises important issues of federalism that are a recurring theme throughout this text.

Loughrin v. United States

134 S. Ct. 2384 (2014)

JUSTICE KAGAN delivered the opinion of the Court.

A provision of the federal bank fraud statute, 18 U.S.C. §1344(2), makes criminal a knowing scheme to obtain property owned by, or in the custody of, a bank "by means of false or fraudulent pretenses, representations, or promises." The question presented is whether the government must prove that a defendant charged with violating that provision intended to defraud a bank. We hold that the government need not make that showing.

Petitioner Kevin Loughrin executed a scheme to convert altered or forged checks into cash. Pretending to be a Mormon missionary going door-to-door in a neighborhood in Salt Lake City, he rifled through residential mailboxes and stole any checks he found. Sometimes, he washed, bleached, ironed, and dried the checks to remove the existing writing, and then filled them out as he wanted; other times, he did nothing more than cross out the name of the original payee and add another. And when he was lucky enough to stumble upon a blank check, he completed it and forged the accountholder's signature. Over several months, Loughrin made out six of these checks to the retailer Target, for amounts of up to $250. His *modus operandi* was to go to a local store and, posing as the accountholder, present an altered check to a cashier to purchase merchandise. After the cashier accepted the check (which, remarkably enough, happened time after time), Loughrin would leave the store, then turn around and walk back inside to return the goods for cash.

Each of the six checks that Loughrin presented to Target was drawn on an account at a federally insured bank, including Bank of America and Wells Fargo. Employees in Target's back office identified three of the checks as fraudulent, and so declined to submit them for payment. Target deposited the other three checks. The bank refused payment on one, after the accountholder notified the bank that she had seen a man steal her mail. Target appears to have received payment for the other two checks, though the record does not conclusively establish that fact.

The Federal government eventually caught up with Loughrin and charged him with six counts of committing bank fraud — one for each of the altered checks presented to Target. . . .

Ruling (for a reason not material here) that Circuit precedent precluded convicting Loughrin under the statute's first clause, §1344(1), the District Court allowed the case to go to the jury on the statute's second, §1344(2).

The court instructed the jury that it could convict Loughrin under that clause if, in offering the fraudulent checks to Target, he had "knowingly executed or attempted to execute a scheme or artifice to obtain money or property from the [banks on which the checks were drawn] by means of false or fraudulent pretenses, representations, or promises." Loughrin asked as well for another instruction: The jury, he argued, must also find that he acted with "intent to defraud a financial institution." The court, however, declined to give that charge, and the jury convicted Loughrin on all six counts. . . .

We granted certiorari to resolve a Circuit split on whether § 1344(2) requires the government to show that a defendant intended to defraud a federally insured bank or other financial institution. We now affirm the Tenth Circuit's decision.

We begin with common ground. All parties agree, as do we and the Courts of Appeals, that § 1344(2) requires that a defendant "knowingly execute[ ], or attempt[ ] to execute, a scheme or artifice" with at least two elements. First, the clause requires that the defendant intend "to obtain any of the moneys . . . or other property owned by, or under the custody or control of, a financial institution." (We refer to that element, more briefly, as intent "to obtain bank property.") And second, the clause requires that the envisioned result — *i.e.*, the obtaining of bank property — occur "by means of false or fraudulent pretenses, representations, or promises." . . .

The single question presented is whether the government must prove yet another element: that the defendant intended to defraud a bank. As Loughrin describes it, that element would compel the government to show not just that a defendant intended to obtain bank property (as the jury here found), but also that he specifically intended to deceive a bank. And that difference, Loughrin claims, would have mattered in this case, because his intent to deceive ran only to Target, and not to any of the banks on which his altered checks were drawn.

But the text of § 1344(2) precludes Loughrin's argument. That clause focuses, first, on the scheme's goal (obtaining bank property) and, second, on the scheme's means (a false representation). We will later address how the "means" component of § 1344(2) imposes certain inherent limits on its reach. But nothing in the clause additionally demands that a defendant have a specific intent to deceive a bank. And indeed, imposing that requirement would prevent § 1344(2) from applying to a host of cases falling within its clear terms. In particular, the clause covers property "owned by" the bank but in someone else's custody and control (say, a home that the bank entrusted to a real estate company after foreclosure); thus, a person violates § 1344(2)'s plain text by deceiving a non-bank custodian into giving up bank property that it holds. Yet under Loughrin's view, the clause would not apply to such a case except in the (presumably rare) circumstance in which the fraudster's intent to deceive extended beyond the custodian to the bank itself. His proposed inquiry would thus function as an extra-textual limit on the clause's compass.

And Loughrin's construction of § 1344(2) becomes yet more untenable in light of the rest of the bank fraud statute. That is because the *first* clause of § 1344, as all agree, includes the requirement that a defendant intend to "defraud a financial institution"; indeed, that is § 1344(1)'s whole sum and substance. To read the next clause, following the word "or," as somehow repeating that requirement, even while using different words, is to disregard what "or" customarily means. As we have recognized, that term's "ordinary use is almost always disjunctive, that is, the words it connects are to be given separate meanings." Yet Loughrin would have us construe the two entirely distinct statutory phrases that the word "or" joins as containing an identical element. And in doing so, his interpretation would make §1344's second clause a mere subset of its first: If, that is, §1344(2) implicitly required intent to defraud a bank, it would apply only to conduct already falling within §1344(1). Loughrin's construction thus effectively reads "or" to mean "including"—a definition foreign to any dictionary we know of. . . .

Loughrin makes two principal arguments to avoid the import of the statute's plain text. First, he relies on this Court's construction of comparable language in the federal mail fraud statute to assert that Congress intended §1344(2) merely to explicate the scope of §1344(1)'s prohibition on scheming to defraud a bank, rather than to cover any additional conduct. And second, he contends that unless we read the second clause in that duplicative way, its coverage would extend to a vast range of fraudulent schemes, thus intruding on the historic criminal jurisdiction of the States. Neither argument is without force, but in the end, neither carries the day.

"[D]espite appearances," Loughrin avers, §1344(2) has no independent meaning: It merely specifies part of what §1344(1) already encompasses. To support that concededly counterintuitive argument, Loughrin invokes our decision in *McNally v. United States*, 483 U.S. 350 (1987), interpreting similar language in the mail fraud statute, 18 U.S.C. §1341. That law, which served as a model for §1344, prohibits using the mail to further "any scheme or artifice to defraud, or for obtaining money or property by means of false or fraudulent pretenses, representations, or promises." Loughrin rightly explains that, despite the word "or," *McNally* understood that provision as setting forth just one offense—using the mails to advance a scheme to defraud. The provision's back half, we held, merely codified a prior judicial decision applying the front half: In other words, the back clarified that the front included certain conduct, rather than doing independent work. According to Loughrin, we should read the bank fraud statute in the same way.

But the two statutes, as an initial matter, have notable textual differences. The mail fraud law contains two phrases strung together in a single, unbroken sentence. By contrast, §1344's two clauses have separate numbers, line breaks before, between, and after them, and equivalent indentation—thus placing the clauses visually on an equal footing and indicating that they have separate meanings. The legislative structure thus reinforces the usual (even if not *McNally*'s) understanding of the word "or" as meaning . . . well, "or"—rather than, as Loughrin would have it, "including." . . .

According to *McNally*, Congress added the mail fraud statute's second, money-or-property clause merely to affirm a decision of ours interpreting the ban on schemes "to defraud": The second clause, *McNally* reasoned, thus worked no substantive change in the law. *See* 483 U.S. at 356–359 (discussing Congress's codification of *Durland v. United States*, 161 U.S. 306 (1896)). By contrast, Congress passed the bank fraud statute to *disapprove* prior judicial rulings and thereby expand federal criminal law's scope—and indeed, partly to cover cases like Loughrin's. One of the decisions prompting enactment of the bank fraud law, *United States v. Maze*, 414 U.S. 395 (1974), involved a defendant who used a stolen credit card to obtain food and lodging. (Substitute a check for a credit card and Maze becomes Loughrin.) The government brought charges of mail fraud, relying on post-purchase mailings between the merchants and issuing bank to satisfy the statute's mailing element. But the Court held those mailings insufficiently integral to the fraudulent scheme to support the conviction. Hence, *Maze* created a "serious gap[ ] . . . in Federal jurisdiction over frauds against banks." S. Rep. No. 98-225, p. 377 (1983). Congress passed § 1344 to fill that gap, enabling the federal government to prosecute fraudsters like Maze and Loughrin. We will not deprive that enactment of its full effect because *McNally* relied on different history to adopt a counter-textual reading of a similar provision.

Loughrin also appeals to principles of federalism to support his proffered construction. Unless we read § 1344(2) as requiring intent to defraud a bank, Loughrin contends, the provision will extend to every fraud, no matter how prosaic, happening to involve payment with a check — even when that check is perfectly valid. Consider, for example, a garden-variety con: A fraudster sells something to a customer, misrepresenting its value. There are countless variations, but let's say the fraudster passes off a cheap knock-off as a Louis Vuitton handbag. The victim pays for the bag with a good check, which the criminal cashes. Voila!, Loughrin says, bank fraud has just happened — unless we adopt his narrowing construction. After all, the criminal has intended to "obtain . . . property . . . under the custody or control of" the bank (the money in the victim's checking account), and has made "false or fraudulent . . . representations" (the lies to the victim about the handbag).[5] But if the bank fraud statute were to encompass all such schemes, Loughrin continues, it would interfere with matters "squarely within the traditional criminal jurisdiction of the state courts." We should avoid such a "sweeping expansion of federal criminal" law, he concludes, by reading § 1344(2), just like § 1344(1), as requiring intent to defraud a bank. Reply Brief (quoting *Cleveland v. United States*, 531 U.S. 12, 24 (2000)).

We agree with this much of what Loughrin argues: Unless the text requires us to do so, we should not construe § 1344(2) as a plenary ban on fraud, contingent only on use of a check (rather than cash). As we have often (and recently) repeated, "we will not be quick to assume that Congress has meant to effect a significant change in the sensitive relation between federal and state criminal jurisdiction." *Bond v. United States*, 134 S. Ct. 2077, 2089 (2014). Just such a rebalancing of criminal jurisdiction

---

5. One might think the federal government would never use the bank fraud statute to prosecute such ordinary frauds just because they happen to involve payment by check rather than cash. But in fact, the government has brought a number of cases alleging violations of § 1344(2) on that theory (so far, it appears, unsuccessfully). *See, e.g., United States v. Thomas*, 315 F.3d 190, 197 (3d Cir. 2002) (a home health care worker got a valid check from a patient to buy groceries, but then cashed the check and pocketed the money); *United States v. Rodriguez*, 140 F.3d 163 (C.A.2 1998) (an employee filed fake invoices with her employer, causing the company to issue valid checks to her friend for services never rendered).

would follow from interpreting §1344(2) to cover every pedestrian swindle happening to involve payment by check, but in no other way affecting financial institutions. Indeed, even the government expresses some mild discomfort with "federalizing frauds that are only tangentially related to the banking system."

But in claiming that we must therefore recognize an invisible element, Loughrin fails to take account of a significant *textual* limitation on §1344(2)'s reach. Under that clause, it is not enough that a fraudster scheme to obtain money from a bank and that he make a false statement. The provision as well includes a relational component: The criminal must acquire (or attempt to acquire) bank property "by means of" the misrepresentation. That phrase typically indicates that the given result (the "end") is achieved, at least in part, *through* the specified action, instrument, or method (the "means"), such that the connection between the two is something more than oblique, indirect, and incidental. In other words, not every but-for cause will do. If, to pick an example out of a hat, Jane traded in her car for money to take a bike trip cross-country, no one would say she "crossed the Rockies by means of a car," even though her sale of the car somehow figured in the trip she took. The relation between those things would be (as the government puts it) too "tangential[ ]" to make use of the phrase at all appropriate.

Section 1344(2)'s "by means of" language is satisfied when, as here, the defendant's false statement is the mechanism naturally inducing a bank (or custodian of bank property) to part with money in its control. That occurs, most clearly, when a defendant makes a misrepresentation to the bank itself — say, when he attempts to cash, at the teller's window, a forged or altered check. In that event, the defendant seeks to obtain bank property by means of presenting the forgery directly to a bank employee. But no less is the counterfeit check the "means" of obtaining bank funds when a defendant like Loughrin offers it as payment to a third party like Target. After all, a merchant accepts a check only to pass it along to a bank for payment; and upon receipt from the merchant, that check triggers the disbursement of bank funds just as if presented by the fraudster himself. So in either case, the forged or altered check — *i.e.*, the false statement — serves in the ordinary course as the means (or to use other words, the mechanism or instrumentality) of obtaining bank property. To be sure, a merchant might detect the fraud (as Target sometimes did) and decline to submit the forged or altered check to the bank. But that is to say only that the defendant's scheme to obtain bank property by means of a false statement may not succeed. And we have long made clear that such failure is irrelevant in a bank fraud case, because §1344 punishes not "completed frauds," but instead fraudulent "scheme [s]." *Neder*, 527 U.S. at 25. . . .

For the reasons stated, we affirm the judgment of the Tenth Circuit.

JUSTICE SCALIA, with whom JUSTICE THOMAS joins, concurring in part and concurring in the judgment. (Omitted.)

JUSTICE ALITO, concurring in part and concurring in the judgment. (Omitted.)

Notes and Question

1. *Plain language.* What was the appellant's argument concerning the statutory language? How did he attempt to use *McNally* to bolster his argument? Why did the Court reject this argument?

2. *Federalism.* The appellant argued that his interpretation of the statute was necessary in order to avoid the sort of federal encroachment onto state criminal law that the Court took into account in its decision in *Cleveland.* Is the Court's response persuasive? Why or why not?

3. *The "means" test.* The Court responded to the federalism concerns by noting that the "'means' component of §1344(2) imposes certain inherent limits on its reach." What exactly did the Court mean by this? In his concurring opinion, Justice Scalia rejected the "means" test, stating that "I do not know where the Court's crabbed definition of 'means' comes from." He continued, "I certainly agree that this statute must be interpreted, if possible, in a manner that will not make every fraud effected by receipt of a check a federal offense. But deciding this case does not require us to identify that manner, and I would leave that for another case." Is the "means component" an effective limitation on the reach of the statute? And is this limitation inherent in the statutory language, or is it an additional court-created statutory element?

Chapter 5

Securities Fraud

A. Introductory Notes

1. The Quintessential White Collar Crime?

Securities fraud encompasses a wide range of crimes. For example, if a company makes material misstatements or omissions about the company in public documents, then the company and its agents may be liable for defrauding investors in that company. Such fraud has been alleged in a number of high-profile corporate scandals in recent decades.[a] In addition, securities fraud encompasses fraud committed by individual investors. The latter type of securities fraud includes what is perhaps the quintessential white collar crime — insider trading. The government has pursued a number of high-profile insider trading investigations and prosecutions of public figures.[b] Consequently, as a former director of enforcement at the Securities and Exchange Commission noted, "insider trading has a unique hold on the American popular imagination," and is worthy of special attention. Linda Chatman Thomsen, *Remarks Before the Australian Securities and Investments Commission 2008 Summer School: U.S. Experience of Insider Trading Enforcement* (February 19, 2008), https://www.sec.gov/news/speech/2008/spch021908lct.htm.

This chapter provides an overview of the principal securities fraud statutes, while focusing primarily upon insider trading. Securities fraud is just one specific type of fraud covered in the federal criminal code.[c] It will be important during the course of this chapter to observe the interplay between specific securities fraud statutes on

---

a. For example, securities fraud was the principal allegation in the criminal cases arising out of the massive collapses of both Enron and WorldCom. *See* John R. Emshwiller, *Executives on Trial; Enron Ex-Official Pleads Not Guilty to Fraud, Agrees to Aid Probe*, WALL ST. J., Aug. 2, 2004, at C3; Ken Belson, *Ex-Chief of WorldCom Is Found Guilty in $11 Billion Fraud*, WALL ST. J., Mar. 16, 2005, at A1. More recently, Theranos founder, Elizabeth Holmes, was charged with massive securities fraud for making false and misleading statements to investors concerning her company's technology and financial performance. *See* Joel Rosenblatt, *The Spectacular Rise and Fall of Elizabeth Holmes and Theranos*, BLOOMBERG (December 3, 2020), https://www.bloomberg.com/news/storythreads/2020-12-03/the-spectacular-rise-and-fall-of-elizabeth-holmes-and-theranos.

b. As commentators have noted, "insider trading prosecutions have drawn more public attention to the securities markets than virtually any other event since the passage of the federal securities laws." Charles A. Stillman et al., *Securities Fraud*, *in* WHITE COLLAR CRIME: BUSINESS AND REGULATORY OFFENSES § 12.03 (Law Journal Press, Otto G. Obermaier et al., eds., 2015).

c. *See, e.g.*, 18 U.S.C. §§ 1341 and 1343 (Chapter 4, Mail and Wire Fraud, *supra*), and 18 U.S.C. § 1347 (Chapter 6, Health Care Fraud and Abuse, *infra*).

the one hand, and the more generally applicable crimes covered in the previous two chapters (conspiracy and mail and wire fraud) on the other. In addition, charges may also arise in specific fraud cases under the "cover-up" statutes involving false statements, perjury, and obstruction of justice covered later in this text. Readers may ask themselves, as they review the securities fraud materials below, why the defendants in these cases are so often charged with attempting to cover up their acts.[d]

The interplay among these various criminal laws also raises important questions that appear throughout this book concerning enforcement obstacles, prosecutorial discretion, and statutory vagueness. In particular, the relationships among these crimes provide some sense of the choices prosecutors must make in deciding whether and how to charge a criminal case. This is particularly true in the securities fraud context because, as noted below, the government in many cases will be able to choose among pursuing administrative and/or civil remedies in addition to, or instead of, criminal sanctions.

2. Civil and Criminal Enforcement

Securities fraud may be alleged in a number of different contexts. First, the government, through the Securities and Exchange Commission (the "SEC" or the "Commission"), may initiate an administrative proceeding or civil lawsuit alleging a violation of the federal securities laws. Second, private parties may bring causes of action and seek damages for alleged violations of those laws. Third, the United States Department of Justice may bring a criminal case in addition to, or instead of, any civil action brought by the SEC and/or a private party. Note that the legal issues decided in civil cases may also apply to criminal cases; many of the cases discussed in this chapter were civil cases brought by the SEC or by private parties. Because securities fraud is subject to parallel civil and criminal actions, the wise counsel will be mindful of the particulars and consequences of liability in each context. While this chapter focuses on criminal liability for securities fraud, § C below highlights some important aspects of civil enforcement and issues that may arise in parallel proceedings. (*See also* Chapter 18, *infra*, for issues that arise in parallel criminal and civil enforcement generally.)

3. The Federal Securities Regulation Scheme[e]

Congress enacted the two principal securities laws in the aftermath of the stock market crash of 1929. The Securities Act of 1933 (the "Securities Act" or the "1933 Act"), 15 U.S.C. §§77a–77aa, generally regulates a company's original *registration*

---

d. *See, e.g.*, United States v. Stewart, 323 F. Supp. 2d 606 (S.D.N.Y. 2004); United States v. Arthur Andersen, 374 F.3d 281 (5th Cir. 2004), *rev'd*, 544 U.S. 696 (2005).

e. The states have their own securities laws and regulations, which are referred to as "blue sky laws." Most of the important securities cases are brought at the federal level, although states have been increasingly active in enforcing their own securities statutes.

and *issuance* of securities, known as the "primary" or "new-issue" securities market. This statute, and the regulations adopted pursuant to the statute, govern the disclosure of information to potential purchasers of those securities. The Securities Exchange Act of 1934 (the "Exchange Act" or the "1934 Act"), 15 U.S.C. §§ 78a–78ll, on the other hand, generally governs what is known as the "secondary" or "trading" market. Thus, this statute and the regulations adopted under the statute apply to *trading* in the securities markets.

The civil and criminal fraud provisions of these statutes only apply when there has been a purchase or sale of a "security." The definition of the term "security" is a technical one that is a mixed question of law and fact. *See United States v. McKye*, 734 F.3d 1104 (10th Cir. 2013). For present purposes, the most important securities include stocks (equity interests that give a stockholder an ownership interest in the issuing company) and bonds (debt instruments that essentially are loans that the bond holder makes to the company).

Section 24 of the 1933 Act, 15 U.S.C. § 77x, and Section 32(a) of the 1934 Act, 15 U.S.C. § 78ff, make it a crime to commit a "willful" violation of the statutes or of the rules and regulations adopted under the statutes. Most criminal securities fraud cases are brought for willful violations of the statutes' "catch-all" anti-fraud provisions, set forth at Section 17(a) of the 1933 Act, 15 U.S.C. § 77q(a), Section 10b of the 1934 Act, 15 U.S.C. § 78j, and Rule 10(b)(5) thereunder, 17 C.F.R. § 240.10b-5.[f] Although sentences vary widely under the discretionary federal sentencing guidelines, the statutory maximum for securities fraud under Section 10b is 20 years for each count and fines of up to $5 million for individuals and $25 million for organizations. 15 U.S.C. §§ 77x, 78j(b), 77ff. In white collar cases, the sentences recommended by the guidelines are often driven up dramatically by the amount of loss. *See* U.S.S.G. § 2B1.1; Chapter 19, Sentencing, *infra*.

In addition, the corporate accounting scandals of the early 21st century led to the passage of the Sarbanes-Oxley Act of 2002.[g] This broad-ranging legislation imposed new corporate compliance and corporate audit procedures on publicly traded companies and created new crimes relating to securities fraud. The latter is codified at 18 U.S.C. § 1348.[h] Some commentators have questioned whether the new crimes truly differ from the existing securities fraud statutes, or whether they will make

---

f. The 1933 and 1934 Acts grant the SEC the power to issue regulations under the securities statutes. Rule 10b-5 is one such regulation and renders it unlawful "[t]o make any untrue statement of a material fact or to omit to state a material fact necessary in order to make the statements made ... not misleading ... in connection with the purchase or sale of a security."

g. Pub. L. No. 107-204, 116 Stat. 745 (2002). The Act touches on many areas of securities regulation, and has been aptly termed "a securities regulation smorgasbord." Harold S. Bloomenthal, *Sarbanes-Oxley Act in Perspective*, SEC-SOAP § 1:10 (2007).

h. This new securities fraud statute (set forth in the statutory supplement) was intended to "supplement the patchwork of existing technical securities law violations with a more general and less technical provision, with elements and intent requirements comparable to current bank fraud and health care fraud statutes." 148 Cong. Rec. S7418-01, S7418 (2002) (statement of Sen. Leahy).

prosecutions for securities fraud any easier.[i] To date, case law involving prosecutions under §1348 is limited, but some courts have indeed found it to be broader in scope.[j]

4. Elements of Securities Fraud

Most of the cases discussed in this chapter were brought under Section 10b of the 1934 Act and Rule 10b-5 thereunder. To obtain a conviction under these provisions, the government must prove that:

(1) the defendant

    (a) engaged in a fraudulent scheme, or

    (b) made a material misstatement, or

    (c) omitted material information to one to whom the defendant owed a duty;

(2) the scheme, misstatement, or omission occurred in connection with the purchase or sale of a security; and

(3) the defendant acted willfully.

With this general introduction to securities fraud in place, we turn now to the principal focus of this chapter — insider trading.

B. Insider Trading

The "insider" trader provides a classic image of the white collar criminal — the wealthy corporate officer who steals a company's secret information and profits at the expense of the average investor. But the reality, of course, is more complex. Initially, it is important to note that the term "insider" trading is a misnomer. The crime actually applies to a broad range of people who trade on nonpublic information, including, but not limited to, corporate "insiders."

There are two different, albeit overlapping, definitions of insider trading. First, under the "traditional" or "classical" theory, a corporate employee or agent — the "insider" — takes information from the corporation and uses the information to trade in the corporation's stock in violation of a duty to its shareholders. This theory

---

i. *See, e.g.*, Phillip Lambert, *Worlds are Colliding: A Critique of the Need for the Additional Criminal Securities Fraud Section in Sarbanes-Oxley*, 53 Case W. Res. L. Rev. 839, 851 (Spring 2003) ("[T]he language contained in section 807 of Sarbanes-Oxley . . . covers virtually identical transactions and conduct as the language in the Securities Act and Exchange Act.").

j. For example, the Second Circuit recently held in *United States v. Blaszczak*, 947 F.3d 19, 26 (2d Cir. 2019), that the personal benefit test (which is so crucial to tipper-tippee insider trading liability under the Title 15 securities fraud statutes, *see infra* § B, 4), does not apply to insider trading charges brought under §1348. As noted below, the future of the *Blaszczak* court's holding was uncertain at the time this text went to press.

applies to two distinct categories of defendants: (a) officers and employees of that corporation ("insiders"); and (b) outside lawyers, accountants, and others who work for that corporation on a temporary basis ("quasi-" or "temporary-" insiders). Second, the broader "misappropriation" theory applies to anyone who steals confidential information in violation of a fiduciary duty to the information's source and then uses the information to buy or sell securities. This theory would apply, for example, to a reporter who stole confidential, pre-publication information from the financial magazine that employs him and then traded on that information.

This section highlights the historical development of insider trading law. Though Section 10b of the Exchange Act (see § A, *supra*) provides the principal statutory authority for our current federal insider trading enforcement regime, you may have noticed that the statute neither defines nor even references insider trading. The insider trading laws have therefore effectively developed through administrative decisions and federal common law.[k] The Supreme Court did not rule on the validity of insider trading as a form of Section 10b securities fraud until *United States v. Chiarella*, the first case in this section. *Chiarella* was brought under the classical theory. While the *Chiarella* Court recognized the validity of the classical theory, it reversed the defendant's conviction because an essential element of that theory was not met. Almost 20 years later, in the second case in this section, *United States v. O'Hagan*, the Supreme Court approved of the misappropriation theory of insider trading. This theory dramatically expands the potential scope of insider trading liability, far beyond corporate insiders, and has been the subject of substantial criticism because of its broad and somewhat uncertain scope. The third case is *Dirks v. Securities and Exchange Commission*, which examines the liability of "tippers" and "tippees," that is, people who give and receive confidential information used in connection with securities trading. The *Dirks* rule sets forth the specific requirements for tipper-tippee liability.

Finally, while insider trading is one of the more headline-grabbing of white collar crimes, it is also one of the more controversial. Its lack of statutory definition, and the ambiguity in its common law elements, have led to persistent due process and notice challenges from defendants charged with insider trading. Moreover, some jurists and economists have argued that insider trading should not be illegal at all, claiming that it harms no one and is actually good for securities markets. This section will address these and other controversies alongside its treatment of the law's development.

1. The Elements of Insider Trading

Violations of laws prohibiting insider trading essentially constitute a subset of the general category of securities fraud. For this reason, it is helpful to identify the specific elements of a criminal insider trading case. Based upon the applicable statutes,

---

k. The SEC brought its first insider trading enforcement action pursuant to Rule 10b-5 in *Cady, Roberts & Co.*, 40 S.E.C. 907 (1961).

regulations, and Supreme Court decisions, in a case brought against the principal[1] under Section 10b and Rule 10b-5, the government must prove that:

1. The defendant knowingly possessed material, nonpublic information;

2. The defendant bought or sold securities on the basis of that information;

3. The defendant —

   (a) Was an insider of the company the securities of which were traded;

   (b) Was a temporary insider of the company the securities of which were traded; and/or

   (c) Was a misappropriator of the material, nonpublic information from a person or entity to whom the defendant owed a fiduciary duty; and

4. The defendant acted willfully.

As we shall see, the law of insider trading is notoriously complex, largely because of the overlap between the classical and misappropriation theories and vagueness in many of the elements just identified. To successfully navigate these complexities in each case in this section, you will find it helpful to track the answers to the following questions: (a) To whom does the defendant owe a duty? (b) What theory — "classical" and/or "misappropriation" — provides the basis for that duty? And (c) what company's stock was traded?

2. The Classical Theory

In the case that follows, a printing company employee uncovered secret information during his employment and traded on that information. A majority of the Supreme Court determined that the classical insider trading theory did not apply to the defendant. Why did the Court reach this conclusion?

Chiarella v. United States

445 U.S. 222 (1980)

Mr. JUSTICE POWELL delivered the opinion of the Court.

Petitioner is a printer by trade. In 1975 and 1976, he worked as a "markup man" in the New York composing room of Pandick Press, a financial printer. Among documents that petitioner handled were five announcements of corporate takeover bids. When these documents were delivered to the printer, the identities of the acquiring and target corporations were concealed by blank spaces or false names. The true names were sent to the printer on the night of the final printing.

The petitioner, however, was able to deduce the names of the target companies before the final printing from other information contained in the documents. Without disclosing his knowledge, petitioner purchased stock in the target companies and

---

1. Accessory liability is discussed in connection with the *Dirks* decision, *infra*.

sold the shares immediately after the takeover attempts were made public. By this method, petitioner realized a gain of slightly more than $30,000 in the course of 14 months. Subsequently, the Securities and Exchange Commission (Commission or SEC) began an investigation of his trading activities. In May 1977, petitioner entered into a consent decree with the Commission in which he agreed to return his profits to the sellers of the shares. On the same day, he was discharged by Pandick Press.

In January 1978, petitioner was indicted on 17 counts of violating Section 10(b) of the Securities Exchange Act of 1934 (1934 Act) and SEC Rule 10b-5. After petitioner unsuccessfully moved to dismiss the indictment, he was brought to trial and convicted on all counts.

The Court of Appeals for the Second Circuit affirmed petitioner's conviction. 588 F.2d 1358 (1978). We granted certiorari, and we now reverse.

Section 10(b) of the 1934 Act, 15 U.S.C. § 78j, prohibits the use "in connection with the purchase or sale of any security . . . [of] any manipulative or deceptive device or contrivance in contravention of such rules and regulations as the Commission may prescribe." Pursuant to this section, the SEC promulgated Rule 10b-5 which provides in pertinent part:

> It shall be unlawful for any person, directly or indirectly, by the use of any means or instrumentality of interstate commerce, or of the mails or of any facility of any national securities exchange,
>
> (a) To employ any device, scheme, or artifice to defraud, [or] . . .
>
> (c) To engage in any act, practice, or course of business which operates or would operate as a fraud or deceit upon any person, in connection with the purchase or sale of any security.

17 CFR § 240.10b-5 (1979).

This case concerns the legal effect of the petitioner's silence. The District Court's charge permitted the jury to convict the petitioner if it found that he willfully failed to inform sellers of target company securities that he knew of a forthcoming takeover bid that would make their shares more valuable. In order to decide whether silence in such circumstances violates Section 10(b), it is necessary to review the language and legislative history of that statute as well as its interpretation by the Commission and the federal courts.

Although the starting point of our inquiry is the language of the statute, Section 10(b) does not state whether silence may constitute a manipulative or deceptive device. Section 10(b) was designed as a catch-all clause to prevent fraudulent practices. But neither the legislative history nor the statute itself affords specific guidance for the resolution of this case. When Rule 10b-5 was promulgated in 1942, the SEC did not discuss the possibility that failure to provide information might run afoul of Section 10(b).

The SEC took an important step in the development of Section 10(b) when it held that a broker-dealer and his firm violated that section by selling securities on the basis of undisclosed information obtained from a director of the issuer corporation who was also a registered representative of the brokerage firm. In *Cady, Roberts & Co.*, 40 S.E.C. 907 (1961), the Commission decided that a corporate insider must abstain from trading in the shares of his corporation unless he has first disclosed all material inside information known to him. The obligation to disclose or abstain derives from

> [a]n affirmative duty to disclose material information[, which] has been traditionally imposed on corporate "insiders," particular officers, directors, or controlling stockholders. We, and the courts have consistently held that insiders must disclose material facts which are known to them by virtue of their position but which are not known to persons with whom they deal and which, if known, would affect their investment judgment.

Id. at 911.

The Commission emphasized that the duty arose from (i) the existence of a relationship affording access to inside information intended to be available only for a corporate purpose, and (ii) the unfairness of allowing a corporate insider to take advantage of that information by trading without disclosure. *Id.* at 912, and n.15.[8]

That the relationship between a corporate insider and the stockholders of his corporation gives rise to a disclosure obligation is not a novel twist of the law. At common law, misrepresentation made for the purpose of inducing reliance upon the false statement is fraudulent. But one who fails to disclose material information prior to the consummation of a transaction commits fraud only when he is under a duty to do so. And the duty to disclose arises when one party has information "that the other [party] is entitled to know because of a fiduciary or other similar relation of trust and confidence between them." In its *Cady, Roberts* decision, the Commission recognized a relationship of trust and confidence between the shareholders of a corporation and those insiders who have obtained confidential information by reason of their position with that corporation. This relationship gives rise to a duty to disclose because of the "necessity of preventing a corporate insider from . . . [taking] unfair advantage of the uninformed minority stockholders." *Speed v. Transamerica Corp.*, 99 F. Supp. 808, 829.

The federal courts have found violations of Section 10(b) where corporate insiders used undisclosed information for their own benefit. The cases also have emphasized, in accordance with the common-law rule, that "[t]he party charged with failing to disclose market information must be under a duty to disclose it." *Frigitemp Corp. v. Financial Dynamics Fund, Inc.*, 524 F.2d 275, 282 (2d Cir. 1975). Accordingly, a

---

8. The transaction in *Cady, Roberts* involved sale of stock to persons who previously may not have been shareholders in the corporation. 40 S.E.C., at 913 and n.21. The Commission embraced the reasoning of Judge Learned Hand that "the director or officer assumed a fiduciary relation to the buyer by the very sale; for it would be a sorry distinction to allow him to use the advantage of his position to induce the buyer into the position of a beneficiary although he was forbidden to do so once the buyer had become one." *Id.* at 914, n.23.

purchaser of stock who has no duty to a prospective seller because he is neither an insider nor a fiduciary has been held to have no obligation to reveal material facts. . . .

Thus, administrative and judicial interpretations have established that silence in connection with the purchase or sale of securities may operate as a fraud actionable under Section 10(b) despite the absence of statutory language or legislative history specifically addressing the legality of nondisclosure. But such liability is premised upon a duty to disclose arising from a relationship of trust and confidence between parties to a transaction. Application of a duty to disclose prior to trading guarantees that corporate insiders, who have an obligation to place the shareholder's welfare before their own, will not benefit personally through fraudulent use of material, nonpublic information.

In this case, the petitioner was convicted of violating Section 10(b) although he was not a corporate insider and he received no confidential information from the target company. Moreover, the "market information" upon which he relied did not concern the earning power or operations of the target company, but only the plans of the acquiring company. Petitioner's use of that information was not a fraud under Section 10(b) unless he was subject to an affirmative duty to disclose it before trading. In this case, the jury instructions failed to specify any such duty. In effect, the trial court instructed the jury that petitioner owed a duty to everyone; to all sellers, indeed, to the market as a whole. The jury simply was told to decide whether petitioner used material, nonpublic information at a time when "he knew other people trading in the securities market did not have access to the same information."

The Court of Appeals affirmed the conviction by holding that "[a]nyone — corporate insider or not — who regularly receives material nonpublic information may not use that information to trade in securities without incurring an affirmative duty to disclose." 588 F.2d at 1365 (emphasis in original). Although the court said that its test would include only persons who regularly receive material, nonpublic information, its rationale for that limitation is unrelated to the existence of a duty to disclose. The Court of Appeals, like the trial court, failed to identify a relationship between petitioner and the sellers that could give rise to a duty. Its decision thus rested solely upon its belief that the federal securities laws have "created a system providing equal access to information necessary for reasoned and intelligent investment decisions." Id. at 1362. The use by anyone of material information not generally available is fraudulent, this theory suggests, because such information gives certain buyers or sellers an unfair advantage over less informed buyers and sellers.

This reasoning suffers from two defects. First, not every instance of financial unfairness constitutes fraudulent activity under Section 10(b). Second, the element required to make silence fraudulent — a duty to disclose — is absent in this case. No duty could arise from petitioner's relationship with the sellers of the target company's securities, for petitioner had no prior dealings with them. He was not their agent, he was not a fiduciary, he was not a person in whom the sellers had placed their trust and confidence. He was, in fact, a complete stranger who dealt with the sellers only through impersonal market transactions.

We cannot affirm petitioner's conviction without recognizing a general duty between all participants in market transactions to forgo actions based on material, nonpublic information. Formulation of such a broad duty, which departs radically from the established doctrine that duty arises from a specific relationship between two parties, should not be undertaken absent some explicit evidence of congressional intent.

As we have seen, no such evidence emerges from the language or legislative history of Section 10(b). Moreover, neither the Congress nor the Commission ever has adopted a parity-of-information rule. . . .

We see no basis for applying such a new and different theory of liability in this case. . . . Section 10(b) is aptly described as a catchall provision, but what it catches must be fraud. When an allegation of fraud is based upon nondisclosure, there can be no fraud absent a duty to speak. We hold that a duty to disclose under Section 10(b) does not arise from the mere possession of nonpublic market information. The contrary result is without support in the legislative history of Section 10(b) and would be inconsistent with the careful plan that Congress has enacted for regulation of the securities markets.[20]

[T]he United States offers an alternative theory to support petitioner's conviction. It argues that petitioner breached a duty to the acquiring corporation when he acted upon information that he obtained by virtue of his position as an employee of a printer employed by the corporation. The breach of this duty is said to support a conviction under Section 10(b) for fraud perpetrated upon both the acquiring corporation and the sellers.

We need not decide whether this theory has merit for it was not submitted to the jury. . . .

The jury instructions demonstrate that petitioner was convicted merely because of his failure to disclose material, nonpublic information to sellers from whom he bought the stock of target corporations. The jury was not instructed on the nature or elements of a duty owed by petitioner to anyone other than the sellers. Because we cannot affirm a criminal conviction on the basis of a theory not presented to the jury, we will not speculate upon whether such a duty exists, whether it has been breached, or whether such a breach constitutes a violation of Section 10(b).

The judgment of the Court of Appeals is *reversed*.

Mr. Chief Justice Burger, dissenting.

---

20. It is worth noting that this is apparently the first case in which criminal liability has been imposed upon a purchaser for Section 10(b) nondisclosure. Petitioner was sentenced to a year in prison, suspended except for one month, and a 5-year term of probation.

I believe that the jury instructions in this case properly charged a violation of Section 10(b) and Rule 10b-5, and I would affirm the conviction.

As a general rule, neither party to an arm's-length business transaction has an obligation to disclose information to the other unless the parties stand in some confidential or fiduciary relation. This rule permits a businessman to capitalize on his experience and skill in securing and evaluating relevant information; it provides incentive for hard work, careful analysis, and astute forecasting. But the policies that underlie the rule also should limit its scope. In particular, the rule should give way when an informational advantage is obtained, not by superior experience, foresight, or industry, but by some unlawful means. . . . I would read Section 10(b) and Rule 10b-5 to encompass and build on this principle: to mean that a person who has misappropriated nonpublic information has an absolute duty to disclose that information or to refrain from trading.

The language of Section 10(b) and of Rule 10b-5 plainly supports such a reading. By their terms, these provisions reach *any* person engaged in *any* fraudulent scheme. This broad language negates the suggestion that congressional concern was limited to trading by "corporate insiders" or to deceptive practices related to "corporate information." Just as surely Congress cannot have intended one standard of fair dealing for "white collar" insiders and another for the "blue collar" level. . . .

The history of the statute and of the Rule also supports this reading. The antifraud provisions were designed in large measure "to assure that dealing in securities is fair and without undue preferences or advantages among investors." H.R. Conf. Rep. No. 94-229, p. 91 (1975), U.S. Code Cong. & Admin. News 1975, p. 323. An investor who purchases securities on the basis of misappropriated nonpublic information possesses just such an "undue" trading advantage; his conduct quite clearly serves no useful function except his own enrichment at the expense of others.

This interpretation of Section 10(b) and Rule 10b-5 is in no sense novel. It follows naturally from legal principles enunciated by the Securities and Exchange Commission in its seminal *Cady, Roberts* decision. 40 S.E.C. 907 (1961). There, the Commission relied upon two factors to impose a duty to disclose on corporate insiders: (1) ". . . access . . . to information intended to be available only for a corporate purpose *and not for the personal benefit of anyone*" (emphasis added); and (2) the unfairness inherent in trading on such information when it is inaccessible to those with whom one is dealing. Both of these factors are present whenever a party gains an informational advantage by unlawful means. . . .

* * *

In sum, the evidence shows beyond all doubt that Chiarella, working literally in the shadows of the warning signs in the printshop misappropriated — stole to put it bluntly — valuable nonpublic information entrusted to him in the utmost confidence. He then exploited his ill-gotten informational advantage by purchasing securities in the market. In my view, such conduct plainly violates Section 10(b) and Rule 10b-5. Accordingly, I would affirm the judgment of the Court of Appeals.

Mr. Justice Blackmun, with whom Mr. Justice Marshall joins, dissenting.

Although I agree with much of what is said in Part I of the dissenting opinion of THE CHIEF JUSTICE, *ante,* I write separately because, in my view, it is unnecessary to rest petitioner's conviction on a "misappropriation" theory. . . . I also would find petitioner's conduct fraudulent within the meaning of Section § 10(b) of the Securities Exchange Act of 1934, 15 U.S.C. § 78j(b), and the Securities and Exchange Commission's Rule 10b-5, 17 CFR § 240.10b-5, even if he had obtained the blessing of his employer's principals before embarking on his profiteering scheme. Indeed, I think petitioner's brand of manipulative trading, with or without such approval, lies close to the heart of what the securities laws are intended to prohibit.

The Court continues to pursue a course, charted in certain recent decisions, designed to transform Section 10(b) from an intentionally elastic "catchall" provision to one that catches relatively little of the misbehavior that all too often makes investment in securities a needlessly risky business for the uninitiated investor. Such confinement in this case is now achieved by imposition of a requirement of a "special relationship" akin to fiduciary duty before the statute gives rise to a duty to disclose or to abstain from trading upon material, nonpublic information. The Court admits that this conclusion finds no mandate in the language of the statute or its legislative history. Yet the Court fails even to attempt a justification of its ruling in terms of the purposes of the securities laws, or to square that ruling with the long-standing but now much abused principle that the federal securities laws are to be construed flexibly rather than with narrow technicality.

I, of course, agree with the Court that a relationship of trust can establish a duty to disclose under § 10(b) and Rule 10b-5. But I do not agree that a failure to disclose violates the Rule only when the responsibilities of a relationship of that kind have been breached. As applied to this case, the Court's approach unduly minimizes the importance of petitioner's *access* to confidential information that the honest investor no matter how diligently he tried, could not legally obtain. In doing so, it further advances an interpretation of Section 10(b) and Rule 10b-5 that stops short of their full implications. Although the Court draws support for its position from certain precedent, I find its decision neither fully consistent with developments in the common law of fraud, nor fully in step with administrative and judicial application of Rule 10b-5 to "insider" trading.

* * *

Whatever the outer limits of the Rule, petitioner Chiarella's case fits neatly near the center of its analytical framework. He occupied a relationship to the takeover companies giving him intimate access to concededly material information that was sedulously guarded from public access. Petitioner, moreover, knew that the information was unavailable to those with whom he dealt. And he took full, virtually riskless advantage of this artificial information gap by selling the stocks shortly after each takeover bid was announced. This misuse of confidential information was clearly placed before the jury. Petitioner's conviction, therefore, should be upheld, and I dissent from the Court's upsetting that conviction.

Notes and Questions

1. *Theories of "insider trading."* Why, precisely, did the majority reverse the conviction? Is it not clear that Chiarella did something wrong? In their dissents, what theories did Chief Justice Burger and Justice Blackmun cite in support of their arguments that the conviction should have been affirmed? In each case, how did the majority respond?

2. *"Inside" information.* There are many different types of "inside" information. Most insider trading cases, including *Chiarella*, arise in the context of "extraordinary corporate transactions." Such transactions include mergers, tender offers, and proxy contests.[m] In these situations, rapid fluctuations in stock prices make it possible to make (or lose) a lot of money very quickly. In other cases, such as the case relating to Sam Waksal, Martha Stewart, and ImClone stock — where the stock was sold shortly before an unfavorable United States Food and Drug Administration ruling was announced[n] — the defendants allegedly traded based upon secret, un-released information that would likely affect the stock price. Other kinds of nonpublic information include financial projections, earnings statements, and similar information that reflect the company's strengths and weaknesses. Some insider trading schemes involve large-scale arrangements to trade on various forms of information, such as the cases arising out of the investigations of hedge fund giant SAC Capital Investors LP and Raj Rajaratnam, the head of the Galleon Group hedge fund. *See* Patricia Hurtado et al., *SAC Record $1.8 Billion Plea Caps Seven-Year Insider Trading Probe*, 9 WHITE COLLAR CRIME REP. (BNA) No. 242 (April 14, 2014); *United States v. Rajaratnam*, 719 F.3d 139 (2d Cir. 2013).

3. *Materiality.* As the Court noted in *Chiarella*, for insider trading to be illegal, the information traded upon must be "material." *See, e.g., Chiarella*, 445 U.S. at 230. In *Basic Inc. v. Levinson*, 485 U.S. 224 (1988), the Supreme Court held that information is "material" for purposes of § 10(b) securities fraud liability if "there is a substantial likelihood that a reasonable shareholder would consider it important" in making an investment decision. *Id.* at 231 (quoting *TSC Industries, Inc. v. Northway, Inc.*, 426 U.S. 438, 449 (1976)). In addition, "there must be a substantial likelihood that the disclosure of the omitted fact would have been viewed by the reasonable investor as

---

m. In a tender offer, the offering company offers to buy all of a "target" company's stock at a specified price over the then-current market price for the stock. In a proxy contest, the shareholders vote, by giving their votes to "proxies," on corporate decisions such as the election of a board of directors or a merger.

n. Waksal pleaded guilty to insider trading and was sentenced to more than seven years in prison. Kara Scannell, *Waksal's Sentence in Trading Case Tops Seven Years*, WALL ST. J., June 11, 2003, at A2. Stewart was not criminally charged with insider trading, but was named in an SEC civil suit based on that theory. Kara Scannell & Laurie P. Cohen, *Homemaking Maven Pleads Not Guilty to Criminal Counts; SEC Files Civil Insider Charges*, WALL ST. J., June 5, 2003, at C1.

having significantly altered the 'total mix' of information made available." *Id.* at 232. This definition of materiality leaves a number of questions unanswered. For example, who is a "reasonable shareholder"? *See, e.g.,* Joan MacLeod Heminway, *Materiality Guidance in the Context of Insider Trading: A Call for Action*, 52 Am. U.L. Rev. 1131, 1152 (2003); *see also* Donald C. Langevoort, *Commentary: Stakeholder Values, Disclosure, and Materiality*, 48 Cath. U.L. Rev. 93, 98 (1988) (noting that "investors are not homogeneous").

Another difficulty in determining whether information is material for purposes of insider trading liability arises in the context of "soft information." Information is "soft" if it "inherently involves some subjective analysis or extrapolation, such as projections, estimates, opinions, motives, or intentions." Bruce A. Hiler, *The SEC and the Courts' Approach to Disclosure of Earnings Projections, Asset Appraisals, and Other Soft Information: Old Problems, Changing Views*, 46 Md. L. Rev. 1114, 1116 (1987). The *Basic* Court held that the materiality of soft information should be determined by the application of a probability-magnitude test: If, by multiplying the magnitude of the substance of the soft information (e.g., a merger negotiation with an uncertain outcome) by the probability of its becoming hard (e.g., the likelihood the merger will be finalized), the factfinder determines the reasonable investor would deem the information important and as significantly altering the total mix of information, then it is material. *See Basic*, 485 U.S. at 238. Unfortunately, as Professor Stephen Bainbridge has noted, the Supreme Court has not offered guidance on "how high a probability or how large a magnitude is necessary for information to be deemed material." Stephen Bainbridge, Insider Trading: Law and Policy 67 (2014).

4. *What is the harm?* In *Cady, Roberts & Co.*, 40 S.E.C. 907 (1961), the SEC stated that it is unfair for an insider to profit from secret information belonging to the company and its shareholders. And as the United States Supreme Court stated in *United States v. O'Hagan*, 521 U.S. 642, 658 (1997), "an animating purpose of the Exchange Act [is] to insure honest securities markets and thereby promote investor confidence." Is this the correct view? Consider the following:

> Insider trading is a relatively "new" crime, and is emblematic of the broadening scope of white collar criminalization. A debate has raged over whether insider trading is harmful or, in fact, beneficial. The courts and the SEC adhere to the view that insider trading harms both individual traders and the market in general. Under this view, the person who trades with someone who possesses the inside information is damaged because that person is operating at an informational disadvantage. Further, the market itself is harmed by the perception of an uneven playing field; average investors will shy away if they believe they are handicapped vis-a-vis insiders.

> Many commentators argue, however, that insider trading is neither unfair nor harmful to the market. As to harm to individual investors, as one commentator has noted, "it is difficult to conceptualize how public investors

are any worse off simply because the person with whom they trade did not disclose her intent to trade to the source of her information." As to harm to the market, many argue that trading based upon nonpublic information causes stock prices to change based upon that information. The market price will adjust to the new (nonpublic) information. Those who trade after the market has absorbed the effect of the insider trading will thus benefit from the insider trading because the stock price will more accurately reflect the stock's value. One recent survey of the literature thus found that "most commentators conclude that insider trading prohibitions are probably not worth the heavy regulatory cost and that the underlying efficiencies, rather than more amorphous 'fairness' concepts, should rule the day."

J. Kelly Strader, *White Collar Crime and Punishment — Reflections on Michael, Martha, and Milberg Weiss*, 15 Geo. Mason L. Rev. 45, 69–70 (2007). In addition to the arguments just referenced, economists and other scholars have offered a number of other reasons for and against the criminalization of insider trading.

Additional arguments *in favor* of the criminalization of insider trading:

a. *Adverse selection*. Economists have argued that insider trading results in the problem of *adverse selection*. That is, if insider trading is prevalent, "because of order imbalances and the difficulty of sustaining a liquid market only with matching [orders], a liquidity provider [or market maker]° has to transact with his own inventory and thus bears the risk of consistently buying 'high' from and selling 'low' to insiders." Stanislov Dolgopolov, *Insider Trading and the Bid-Ask Spread: A Critical Evaluation of Adverse Selection in Market Making*, 33 Cap. U.L. Rev. 104–05 (2004). Persistent losses to insiders forces market makers to increase their bid-ask spreads to offset these persistent losses. In short, the concern is that insider trading forces market makers to impose a tax on all traders to offset losses imposed by insiders.

b. *Moral hazard*. Some also argue that insider trading creates a moral hazard for firm employees. For example, because insiders can profit from trading when their firm's stock goes down in price (e.g., by shorting their firm's shares), they may have a perverse incentive to create bad news for the firm. *See, e.g.*, Saul Levmore, *Securities and Secrets: Insider Trading and the Law of Contracts*, 68 Va. L. Rev. 117, 149 (1982). Insiders may also have an incentive to delay public disclosures that would otherwise be made in order to gain time to free up capital for trading, or to tip others. *See* Roy A. Schotland, *Unsafe at Any Price: A Reply to Manne, Insider Trading and the Stock Market*, 53 Va. L. Rev. 1425, 1448–49 (1967).

c. *Harms firm by denying right of exclusive use*. Finally, whenever insiders or others trade on a firm's material nonpublic information against the express wishes of the firm, there will almost always be some loss to the firm — otherwise the firm's instructions not to trade would never have be issued in the first place. *See,*

---

o. Market makers are securities dealers that provide market liquidity by standing ready to step in and transact where buy and sell orders for a security fail to achieve equilibrium.

e.g., John P. Anderson, *What's the Harm in Issuer-Licensed Insider Trading?*, 69 U. MIAMI L. REV. 795, 799 (2015).

Additional arguments *against* the criminalization of insider trading:

d. *Market smoothing.* Insider trading can function as a "market smoother" and reduce volatility. If insiders trade prior to disclosure, prices will move more gradually—avoiding the rapid price fluctuations (and windfall gains and losses) that result from the immediate digestion of information upon the release of information to the general public. *See, e.g.*, Stephen Bainbridge, *Insider Trading*, ENCYC. L. & ECON. § 5650 (2000).

e. *Real-time information to management.* Some economists have suggested that price movements resulting from insider trading can raise "red flags" of a fraud or some other issue to upper management in real time without having to wait "for the bureaucratic pipeline to deliver a memorandum." *See* JONATHAN R. MACEY, INSIDER TRADING: ECONOMICS, POLITICS, AND POLICY 10 (1991).

f. *Efficient form of executive compensation.* Insider trading may also serve as an efficient means of executive compensation. Allowing employees to trade on good news they generate for the company may offer savings to shareholders in terms of reduced executive salaries, while incentivizing and rewarding entrepreneurship within the firm. *See, e.g.*, Ian Ayers & Steven Choi, *Internalizing Outsider Trading*, 101 MICH. L. REV. 313, 338 (2002); Henry G. Manne, *Insider Trading and the Law Professors*, 23 VAND. L. REV. 533 (1970). Indeed, there is evidence that firms adjust salary based on the stringency of their insider trading policies. *See, e.g.*, M. Todd Henderson, *Insider Trading and CEO Pay*, 64 VAND. L. REV. 505, 509–10 (2011).

Which view do you believe is correct? Why? Can you think of other considerations (ethical or economic) for or against the criminalization of insider trading?

5. *Should issuer-licensed insider trading be permissible?* Some scholars have argued that insider trading should be (and perhaps already is) legally permitted when the firm that owns the information expressly licenses such trading. For example, Professor John P. Anderson has argued that issuer-licensed insider trading should be permitted if the following conditions are satisfied:

- *The insider submits a written plan to the issuer of the shares that details the proposed trade(s).*

- *The issuing firm authorizes the trading plan.*

- *The firm has previously disclosed to the investing public that it will permit its employees (or others) to trade on the firm's material nonpublic information through these plans when it is in the interest of the firm to do so.*

- *The firm discloses ex post all trading profits resulting from the execution of these plans.*

See JOHN P. ANDERSON, INSIDER TRADING: LAW, ETHICS, AND REFORM 243–244 (2018). Professor Anderson argues that issuer-licensed insider trading is not deceptive and would have few, if any, of the drawbacks outlined in the preceding note (*see* Note 3.a., b., and c. above), while allowing firms and markets to enjoy all the potential benefits of insider trading in the preceding note (*see* Note 3.d., e., and f. above). Based on your understanding of *Chiarella*, do you think issuer-licensed insider trading is legal under the current regime? Do you think issuer-licensed insider trading *should* be legal? Can you foresee any moral or economic problems that might arise from issuer-licensed insider trading? If legal, do you think firms would take advantage of issuer-licensed insider trading? Why or why not?

3. The Misappropriation Theory

In *Chiarella*, the Supreme Court declined to consider whether an insider trading conviction could be based upon the "misappropriation" theory. Seven years later, in *Carpenter v. United States*, 484 U.S. 19 (1987), the Court divided four-to-four on this issue. Finally, in the case that follows, a split court resolved the question. As you read the decision, consider whether the majority made a persuasive case for the rule it adopted.

United States v. O'Hagan

521 U.S. 642 (1997)

JUSTICE GINSBURG delivered the opinion of the Court.

* * *

Respondent James Herman O'Hagan was a partner in the law firm of Dorsey & Whitney in Minneapolis, Minnesota. In July 1988, Grand Metropolitan PLC (Grand Met), a company based in London, England, retained Dorsey & Whitney as local counsel to represent Grand Met regarding a potential tender offer for the common stock of the Pillsbury Company, headquartered in Minneapolis. Both Grand Met and Dorsey & Whitney took precautions to protect the confidentiality of Grand Met's tender offer plans. O'Hagan did no work on the Grand Met representation. Dorsey & Whitney withdrew from representing Grand Met on September 9, 1988. Less than a month later, on October 4, 1988, Grand Met publicly announced its tender offer for Pillsbury stock.

On August 18, 1988, while Dorsey & Whitney was still representing Grand Met, O'Hagan began purchasing call options for Pillsbury stock. Each option gave him the right to purchase 100 shares of Pillsbury stock by a specified date in September 1988. Later in August and in September, O'Hagan made additional purchases of Pillsbury call options. By the end of September, he owned 2,500 unexpired Pillsbury options, apparently more than any other individual investor. O'Hagan also purchased, in September 1988, some 5,000 shares of Pillsbury common stock, at a price just under $39 per share. When Grand Met announced its tender offer in October, the price of Pillsbury stock rose to nearly $60 per share. O'Hagan then sold his Pillsbury call options and common stock, making a profit of more than $4.3 million.

The Securities and Exchange Commission (SEC or Commission) initiated an investigation into O'Hagan's transactions, culminating in a 57-count indictment. The indictment alleged that O'Hagan defrauded his law firm and its client, Grand Met, by using for his own trading purposes material, nonpublic information regarding Grand Met's planned tender offer. According to the indictment, O'Hagan used the profits he gained through this trading to conceal his previous embezzlement and conversion of unrelated client trust funds. O'Hagan was charged with 20 counts of mail fraud, in violation of 18 U.S.C. §1341; 17 counts of securities fraud, in violation of Section 10(b) of the Securities Exchange Act of 1934 (Exchange Act), 15 U.S.C. §78j(b), and SEC Rule 10b-5, 17 CFR §240.10b-5 (1996); 17 counts of fraudulent trading in connection with a tender offer, in violation of §14(e) of the Exchange Act, 15 U.S.C. §78n(e), and SEC Rule 14e-3(a), 17 CFR §240.14e-3(a) (1996); and 3 counts of violating federal money laundering statutes, 18 U.S.C. §§1956(a)(1)(B)(I), 1957. A jury convicted O'Hagan on all 57 counts, and he was sentenced to a 41-month term of imprisonment.

A divided panel of the Court of Appeals for the Eighth Circuit reversed all of O'Hagan's convictions. Liability under Section 10(b) and Rule 10b-5, the Eighth Circuit held, may not be grounded on the "misappropriation theory" of securities fraud on which the prosecution relied.... The Eighth Circuit further concluded that O'Hagan's mail fraud and money laundering convictions rested on violations of the securities laws, and therefore could not stand once the securities fraud convictions were reversed....

We address first the Court of Appeals' reversal of O'Hagan's convictions under Section 10(b) and Rule 10b-5. Following the Fourth Circuit's lead, the Eighth Circuit rejected the misappropriation theory as a basis for Section 10(b) liability. We hold, in accord with several other Courts of Appeals, that criminal liability under Section 10(b) may be predicated on the misappropriation theory.

The statute proscribes (1) using any deceptive device (2) in connection with the purchase or sale of securities, in contravention of rules prescribed by the Commission. The provision, as written, does not confine its coverage to deception of a purchaser or seller of securities; rather, the statute reaches any deceptive device used "in connection with the purchase or sale of any security." ...

→   Under the "traditional" or "classical theory" of insider trading liability, Section 10(b) and Rule 10b-5 are violated when a corporate insider trades in the securities of his corporation on the basis of material, nonpublic information. Trading on such information qualifies as a "deceptive device" under Section 10(b), we have affirmed, because "a relationship of trust and confidence [exists] between the shareholders of a corporation and those insiders who have obtained confidential information by reason of their position with that corporation." *Chiarella v. United States*, 445 U.S. 222, 228 (1980). That relationship, we recognized, "gives rise to a duty to disclose [or to abstain from trading] because of the 'necessity of preventing a corporate insider from ... tak[ing] unfair advantage of ... uninformed ... stockholders.'" *Id.* at 228–229 (citation omitted). The classical theory applies not only to officers, directors, and other permanent insiders of a corporation, but also to attorneys, accountants, consultants, and others who temporarily become fiduciaries of a corporation.

The "misappropriation theory" holds that a person commits fraud "in connection with" a securities transaction, and thereby violates Section 10(b) and Rule 10b-5, when he misappropriates confidential information for securities trading purposes, in breach of a duty owed to the source of the information. Under this theory, a fiduciary's undisclosed, self-serving use of a principal's information to purchase or sell securities, in breach of a duty of loyalty and confidentiality, defrauds the principal of the exclusive use of that information. In lieu of premising liability on a fiduciary relationship between company insider and purchaser or seller of the company's stock, the misappropriation theory premises liability on a fiduciary-turned-trader's deception of those who entrusted him with access to confidential information.

The two theories are complementary, each addressing efforts to capitalize on nonpublic information through the purchase or sale of securities. The classical theory targets a corporate insider's breach of duty to shareholders with whom the insider transacts; the misappropriation theory outlaws trading on the basis of nonpublic information by a corporate "outsider" in breach of a duty owed not to a trading party, but to the source of the information. The misappropriation theory is thus designed to "protec[t] the integrity of the securities markets against abuses by 'outsiders' to a corporation who have access to confidential information that will affect th[e] corporation's security price when revealed, but who owe no fiduciary or other duty to that corporation's shareholders." *Id.*

In this case, the indictment alleged that O'Hagan, in breach of a duty of trust and confidence he owed to his law firm, Dorsey & Whitney, and to its client, Grand Met, traded on the basis of nonpublic information regarding Grand Met's planned tender offer for Pillsbury common stock. This conduct, the government charged, constituted a fraudulent device in connection with the purchase and sale of securities.[5]

We agree with the government that misappropriation, as just defined, satisfies Section 10(b)'s requirement that chargeable conduct involve a "deceptive device or contrivance" used "in connection with" the purchase or sale of securities. We observe, first, that misappropriators, as the government describes them, deal in deception. A fiduciary who "[pretends] loyalty to the principal while secretly converting the principal's information for personal gain," Brief for United States 17, "dupes" or defrauds the principal.

---

5. The government could not have prosecuted O'Hagan under the classical theory, for O'Hagan was not an "insider" of Pillsbury, the corporation in whose stock he traded. Although an "outsider" with respect to Pillsbury, O'Hagan had an intimate association with, and was found to have traded on confidential information from, Dorsey & Whitney, counsel to tender offeror Grand Met. Under the misappropriation theory, O'Hagan's securities trading does not escape Exchange Act sanction, as it would under Justice THOMAS' dissenting view, simply because he was associated with, and gained nonpublic information from, the bidder, rather than the target.

We addressed fraud of the same species in *Carpenter v. United States*, 484 U.S. 19 (1987), which involved the mail fraud statute's proscription of "any scheme or artifice to defraud," 18 U.S.C. § 1341. Affirming convictions under that statute, we said in *Carpenter* that an employee's undertaking not to reveal his employer's confidential information "became a sham" when the employee provided the information to his co-conspirators in a scheme to obtain trading profits. 484 U.S. at 27. A company's confidential information, we recognized in *Carpenter*, qualifies as property to which the company has a right of exclusive use. The undisclosed misappropriation of such information, in violation of a fiduciary duty, the Court said in *Carpenter*, constitutes fraud akin to embezzlement — "'the fraudulent appropriation to one's own use of the money or goods entrusted to one's care by another.'" *Id.* at 27. *Carpenter*'s discussion of the fraudulent misuse of confidential information, the government notes, "is a particularly apt source of guidance here, because [the mail fraud statute] (like Section 10(b)) has long been held to require deception, not merely the breach of a fiduciary duty." Brief for United States 18 n.9.

Deception through nondisclosure is central to the theory of liability for which the government seeks recognition. As counsel for the government stated in explanation of the theory at oral argument: "To satisfy the common law rule that a trustee may not use the property that [has] been entrusted [to] him, there would have to be consent. To satisfy the requirement of the Securities Act that there be no deception, there would only have to be disclosure." Tr. of Oral Arg. 12.[6]

The misappropriation theory advanced by the government is consistent with *Santa Fe Industries, Inc. v. Green*, 430 U.S. 462 (1977), a decision underscoring that Section 10(b) is not an all-purpose breach of fiduciary duty ban; rather, it trains on conduct involving manipulation or deception. In contrast to the government's allegations in this case, in *Santa Fe Industries*, all pertinent facts were disclosed by the persons charged with violating Section 10(b) and Rule 10b-5, therefore, there was no deception through nondisclosure to which liability under those provisions could attach. Similarly, full disclosure forecloses liability under the misappropriation theory: Because the deception essential to the misappropriation theory involves feigning fidelity to the source of information, if the fiduciary discloses to the source that he plans to trade on the nonpublic information, there is no "deceptive device" and thus no Section 10(b) violation — although the fiduciary-turned-trader may remain liable under state law for breach of a duty of loyalty.[7]

---

6. Under the misappropriation theory urged in this case, the disclosure obligation runs to the source of the information, here, Dorsey & Whitney and Grand Met. Chief Justice Burger, dissenting in *Chiarella*, advanced a broader reading of § 10(b) and Rule 10b-5; the disclosure obligation, as he envisioned it, ran to those with whom the misappropriator trades. The government does not propose that we adopt a misappropriation theory of that breadth.

7. Where, however, a person trading on the basis of material, nonpublic information owes a duty of loyalty and confidentiality to two entities or persons — for example, a law firm and its client — but makes disclosure to only one, the trader may still be liable under the misappropriation theory.

We turn next to the Section 10(b) requirement that the misappropriator's deceptive use of information be "in connection with the purchase or sale of [a] security." This element is satisfied because the fiduciary's fraud is consummated, not when the fiduciary gains the confidential information, but when, without disclosure to his principal, he uses the information to purchase or sell securities. The securities transaction and the breach of duty thus coincide. This is so even though the person or entity defrauded is not the other party to the trade, but is, instead, the source of the nonpublic information. A misappropriator who trades on the basis of material, nonpublic information, in short, gains his advantageous market position through deception; he deceives the source of the information and simultaneously harms members of the investing public.

The misappropriation theory targets information of a sort that misappropriators ordinarily capitalize upon to gain no-risk profits through the purchase or sale of securities. Should a misappropriator put such information to other use, the statute's prohibition would not be implicated. The theory does not catch all conceivable forms of fraud involving confidential information; rather, it catches fraudulent means of capitalizing on such information through securities transactions.

The Government notes another limitation on the forms of fraud § 10(b) reaches: "The misappropriation theory would not . . . apply to a case in which a person defrauded a bank into giving him a loan or embezzled cash from another, and then used the proceeds of the misdeed to purchase securities." In such a case, the Government states, "the proceeds would have value to the malefactor apart from their use in a securities transaction, and the fraud would be complete as soon as the money was obtained." In other words, money can buy, if not anything, then at least many things; its misappropriation may thus be viewed as sufficiently detached from a subsequent securities transaction that § 10(b)'s "in connection with" requirement would not be met.

JUSTICE THOMAS' charge that the misappropriation theory is incoherent because information, like funds, can be put to multiple uses misses the point. The Exchange Act was enacted in part "to insure the maintenance of fair and honest markets,"15 U.S.C. § 78b, and there is no question that fraudulent uses of confidential information fall within § 10(b)'s prohibition if the fraud is "in connection with" a securities transaction. It is hardly remarkable that a rule suitably applied to the fraudulent uses of certain kinds of information would be stretched beyond reason were it applied to the fraudulent use of money. . . .

The misappropriation theory comports with Section 10(b)'s language, which requires deception "in connection with the purchase or sale of any security," not deception of an identifiable purchaser or seller. The theory is also well tuned to an animating purpose of the Exchange Act: to insure honest securities markets and thereby promote investor confidence. Although informational disparity is inevitable in the securities markets, investors likely would hesitate to venture their capital in a market where trading based on misappropriated nonpublic information is unchecked by law. An investor's informational disadvantage vis-à-vis a misappropriator with material, nonpublic information stems from contrivance, not luck; it is a disadvantage that cannot be overcome with research or skill.

[C]onsidering the inhibiting impact on market participation of trading on misappropriated information, and the congressional purposes underlying Section 10(b), it makes scant sense to hold a lawyer like O'Hagan a Section 10(b) violator if he works for a law firm representing the target of a tender offer, but not if he works for a law firm representing the bidder. The text of the statute requires no such result. The misappropriation at issue here was properly made the subject of a Section 10(b) charge because it meets the statutory requirement that there be "deceptive" conduct "in connection with" securities transactions.

In sum, the misappropriation theory, as we have examined and explained it in this opinion, is both consistent with the statute and with our precedent. Vital to our decision that criminal liability may be sustained under the misappropriation theory, we emphasize, are two sturdy safeguards Congress has provided regarding scienter. To establish a criminal violation of Rule 10b-5, the government must prove that a person "willfully" violated the provision.[12] Furthermore, a defendant may not be imprisoned for violating Rule 10b-5 if he proves that he had no knowledge of the Rule. O'Hagan's charge that the misappropriation theory is too indefinite to permit the imposition of criminal liability, thus fails not only because the theory is limited to those who breach a recognized duty. In addition, the statute's "requirement of the presence of culpable intent as a necessary element of the offense does much to destroy any force in the argument that application of the [statute]" in circumstances such as O'Hagan's is unjust. *Boyce Motor Lines, Inc. v. United States*, 342 U.S. 337, 342 (1952).

The Eighth Circuit erred in holding that the misappropriation theory is inconsistent with Section 10(b). The Court of Appeals may address on remand O'Hagan's other challenges to his convictions under § 10(b) and Rule 10b-5. . . .

JUSTICE SCALIA, concurring in part and dissenting in part. (Omitted.)

JUSTICE THOMAS, with whom THE CHIEF JUSTICE joins, concurring in the judgment in part and dissenting in part.

Today the majority upholds respondent's convictions for violating Section 10(b) of the Securities Exchange Act of 1934, and Rule 10b-5 promulgated thereunder, based upon the Securities and Exchange Commission's "misappropriation theory." Central to the majority's holding is the need to interpret Section 10(b)'s requirement that a deceptive device be "use[d] or employ[ed], in connection with the purchase or sale of any security." 15 U.S.C. § 78j(b). Because the Commission's misappropriation

---

12. In relevant part, Section 32 of the Exchange Act, as set forth in 15 U.S.C. § 78ff(a), provides: "Any person who willfully violates any provision of this chapter . . . shall upon conviction be fined not more than $1,000,000 [now $5,000,000], or imprisoned not more than 10 years [now 20 years], or both . . . ; but no person shall be subject to imprisonment under this section for the violation of any rule or regulation if he proves that he had no knowledge of such rule or regulation."

theory fails to provide a coherent and consistent interpretation of this essential requirement for liability under Section 10(b), I dissent.

I do not take issue with the majority's determination that the undisclosed misappropriation of confidential information by a fiduciary can constitute a "deceptive device" within the meaning of Section 10(b). Nondisclosure where there is a preexisting duty to disclose satisfies our definitions of fraud and deceit for purposes of the securities laws.

Unlike the majority, however, I cannot accept the Commission's interpretation of when a deceptive device is "use[d] ... in connection with" a securities transaction. . . .

[The misappropriation theory should not] cover cases, such as this one, involving fraud on the source of information where the source has no connection with the other participant in a securities transaction. It seems obvious that the undisclosed misappropriation of confidential information is not necessarily consummated by a securities transaction. In this case, for example, upon learning of Grand Met's confidential takeover plans, O'Hagan could have done any number of things with the information: He could have sold it to a newspaper for publication; he could have given or sold the information to Pillsbury itself; or he could even have kept the information and used it solely for his personal amusement, perhaps in a fantasy stock trading game.

Any of these activities would have deprived Grand Met of its right to "exclusive use" of the information and, if undisclosed, would constitute "embezzlement" of Grand Met's informational property. Under *any* theory of liability, however, these activities would not violate § 10(b) and, according to the Commission's monetary embezzlement analogy, these possibilities are sufficient to preclude a violation under the misappropriation theory even where the informational property *was* used for securities trading. That O'Hagan actually did use the information to purchase securities is thus no more significant here than it is in the case of embezzling money used to purchase securities. In both cases the embezzler *could have* done something else with the property, and hence the Commission's necessary "connection" under the securities laws would not be met. If the relevant test under the "in connection with" language is whether the fraudulent act is *necessarily* tied to a securities transaction, then the misappropriation of confidential information used to trade no more violates § 10(b) than does the misappropriation of funds used to trade. As the Commission concedes that the latter is not covered under its theory, I am at a loss to see how the same theory can coherently be applied to the former.

In upholding respondent's convictions under the new and improved misappropriation theory, the majority also points to various policy considerations underlying the securities laws, such as maintaining fair and honest markets, promoting investor confidence, and protecting the integrity of the securities markets. But the repeated reliance on such broad-sweeping legislative purposes reaches too far and is misleading in the context of the misappropriation theory. It reaches too far in that, regardless of the overarching purpose of the securities laws, it is not illegal to run afoul of the "purpose" of a statute, only its letter. . . .

[A]s we have repeatedly held, use of nonpublic information to trade is not itself a violation of Section 10(b). Rather, it is the use of fraud "in connection with" a securities transaction that is forbidden. Where the relevant element of fraud has no impact on the integrity of the subsequent transactions as distinct from the nonfraudulent element of using nonpublic information, one can reasonably question whether the fraud was used in connection with a securities transaction. And one can likewise question whether removing that aspect of fraud, though perhaps laudable, has anything to do with the confidence or integrity of the market.

The absence of a coherent and consistent misappropriation theory and, by necessary implication, a coherent and consistent application of the statutory "use or employ, in connection with" language, is particularly problematic in the context of this case. The government claims a remarkable breadth to the delegation of authority in Section 10(b), arguing that "the very aim of this section was to pick up unforeseen, cunning, deceptive devices that people might cleverly use in the securities markets." Tr. of Oral Arg. 7. As the Court aptly queried, "[t]hat's rather unusual, for a criminal statute to be that open-ended, isn't it?" *Id.* Unusual indeed. Putting aside the dubious validity of an open-ended delegation to an independent agency to go forth and create regulations criminalizing "fraud," in this case we do not even have a formal regulation embodying the agency's misappropriation theory. . . .[p]

Notes and Questions

1. *The misappropriation theory.* Neither Section 10b nor Rule 10b-5 sets forth a "misappropriation" theory. Why did the majority affirm the use of that theory? Is the decision consistent with *Chiarella*? What is the dissent's complaint? Is the dissent correct?

What sorts of duties will support a misappropriation case? For example, assume that a patient discusses material nonpublic information during a session with a psychiatrist and that the psychiatrist and the psychiatrist's broker then trade on the information. Does that suffice? *See, e.g., United States v. Willis*, 737 F. Supp. 269 (S.D.N.Y. 1990); *SEC v. Willis*, 825 F. Supp. 617 (S.D.N.Y. 1993) (upholding misappropriation theory based upon the psychiatrist's breach of duty to his patient).

2. *The "in connection with" requirement.* What is the dissent's argument concerning whether O'Hagan's deception was "in connection with" his securities trading? The majority concludes that one who embezzles an employer's money to use in trading securities has not committed insider trading, while one who steals an employer's

---

p. The SEC subsequently adopted Rule 10b5-2, which attempts to define the fiduciary duties that may give rise to liability under the misappropriation theory. This Rule is discussed after the notes and questions following *O'Hagan*.

confidential information for such use *has* committed insider trading. Does this distinction make sense? Why or why not?

3. *The* Carpenter *case*. In *Carpenter* (presented in Chapter 4, Mail and Wire Fraud, *supra*), a *Wall Street Journal* reporter traded on information from a column he wrote for the journal. Under newspaper policy, the information was confidential and was not to be disclosed prior to publication. The column often affected stock prices, and the reporter and his cohorts traded in advance of publication and made handsome profits. Note that the *Wall Street Journal* reporter had no duty to any of the participants in the transactions involved in the trading in *Carpenter*. In contrast, O'Hagan did have a duty to his firm's former client, which was the offering party in the Pillsbury transaction. What was the potential harm from O'Hagan's actions? From the *Wall Street Journal* reporter's actions? Was the former more serious than the latter? Why or why not?

4. *The market confidence theory of harm*. The *O'Hagan* Court claimed that "investors likely would hesitate to venture their capital in a market where [insider trading] is unchecked by law." 521 U.S. at 658. The suggestion that a general awareness of rampant insider trading would undermine confidence in our markets and make it more difficult for firms to raise capital is one of the more frequently cited justifications for the regulation of insider trading. There appear to be three claims implicit in the market confidence justification for the criminalization of insider trading: (1) A significant portion of the investing public believes that insider trading is unfair and widespread; (2) this perception leads those who share it to reduce or end their market participation; and (3) aggressive enforcement of insider trading restrictions is therefore necessary to prevent the harm to capital markets that would result from (2). A recent empirical study sought to test the market confidence theory against actual public attitudes. *See* John P. Anderson, Jeremy Kidd & George Mocsary, *Public Perceptions of Insider Trading*, 51 Seton Hall L. Rev. 1035 (2021). For example, the survey participants were asked, "If you knew insider trading was common in the stock market, would you be more likely to invest, less likely, or would it make no difference?" Overall, 43.3% said they would be less likely to trade, 40.6% said such knowledge would make no difference to their trading, and 14.9% said knowledge of insider trading would make them more likely to trade. *Id*. at 1082. How would you respond to this question? Do you think the survey results confirm the market confidence theory? Why or why not?

5. *Tender offer rules*.

a. *Rule 14e-3(a)*. Insider trading can be prosecuted under laws other than Section 10b and Rule 10b-5. Section 14 of the Exchange Act and Rule 14e-3(a) thereunder, for example, prohibit trading while in possession of material nonpublic information relating to a tender offer. A tender offer is a takeover bid that involves a public offer to current shareholders of the target company to purchase some or all of their shares within a specified period. Because the tender offer price typically involves a significant premium over the current trading price of the target shares, trading on the basis of advance knowledge of the offer can generate massive profits. Rule 14e-3(a), 17 C.F.R. 240.14e-3(a), provides:

> If any person has taken a substantial step or steps to commence, or has commenced, a tender offer (the "offering person"), it shall constitute a fraudulent, deceptive or manipulative act or practice within the meaning of section 14(e) of the [Exchange] Act for any other person who is in possession of material information relating to such tender offer which information he knows or has reason to know is nonpublic and which he knows or has reason to know has been acquired directly or indirectly from:
>
> (1) The offering person,
>
> (2) The issuer of the securities sought or to be sought by such tender offer, or
>
> (3) Any officer, director, partner or employee or any other person acting on behalf of the offering person or such issuer, to purchase or sell or cause to be purchased or sold any of such securities . . . , unless within a reasonable time prior to any purchase or sale such information and its source are publicly disclosed by press release or otherwise.

O'Hagan was also convicted under this provision. On appeal, he argued that the SEC exceeded its rulemaking authority when it adopted Rule 14e-3(a). Because that Rule imposes liability even where the defendant has not obtained the information in breach of a fiduciary duty, O'Hagan argued, the Rule violates the *Chiarella* holding. The Court rejected O'Hagan's argument. The Court noted that O'Hagan had indeed breached a fiduciary duty and stated that the SEC, "to the extent relevant to this case, did not exceed its authority."

b. *Warehousing.* By the language quoted above, the Court implied that Rule 14e-3(a) might *not* be valid where there has been no breach of duty. What if, for example, the owner of the information specifically approved of the trading? In *O'Hagan*, the Court stated that "[w]e leave for another day, when the issue requires decision, the legitimacy of Rule 14e-3(a) as applied to 'warehousing,' which the government describes as 'the practice by which bidders leak advance information of a tender offer to allies and encourage them to purchase the target company's stock before the bid is announced.'" Should such trading be forbidden? Why or why not?

c. *Mens rea for Rule 14e-3.* There is also some uncertainty as to the mens rea requirement under Section 14 and Rule 14e-3(a). What if a defendant obtained material, nonpublic information relating to a tender offer, but (a) did not breach a duty in obtaining the information and (b) did not *know* the information involved a tender offer? Could that defendant be liable under those provisions? Courts have not resolved this question. In one case, the court did hold that a defendant who traded on material, nonpublic information, but who did not breach a duty in obtaining the information and did not know that the information involved a tender offer, was not guilty under Section 14. *United States v. Cassese*, 290 F. Supp. 2d 443 (S.D.N.Y. 2003), *aff'd*, 428 F.3d 92 (2d Cir. 2005).

Note on United States v. Chestman *and Rule 10b5-2*

The Court in *O'Hagan* did not define the sorts of fiduciary duties that may give rise to a misappropriation case. In a pre-*O'Hagan* case, *United States v. Chestman*, 947 F.2d 551 (2d Cir. 1991) (en banc), the Second Circuit attempted to draw the boundaries of fiduciary duties among family members. In that case, Ira Waldbaum gave inside information concerning the sale of his company to his sister so that she could make the financial arrangements attendant to the sale. In turn, the sister gave the information to her daughter, who gave it to her husband. The husband, Keith Loeb, and Chestman, the husband's stockbroker, then traded on the information. Each of these persons knew that the information was material and nonpublic information relating to a tender offer.

Loeb pleaded guilty and testified against Chestman, who was convicted under Section 10b. The Second Circuit reversed. As will be seen below in the discussion of tippee liability, for Chestman to be guilty under Section 10b, the government was required to show that Loeb breached a fiduciary duty when giving Chestman the information. The Second Circuit found that there was no such breach because the husband owed no duty to the company, to his wife, or to his wife's family to keep the information secret. The husband was not employed by the company, and had no history of maintaining the business confidences of his wife or his wife's family. (Because no such breach of duty is required under Section 14, however, the court affirmed the husband's conviction for illegal trading in connection with a tender offer.)

In the wake of *Chestman* and *O'Hagan*, the SEC, in 2000, adopted Rule 10b5-2. Entitled "Duties of trust or confidence in misappropriation insider trading cases," the rule attempts to define the fiduciary duties that may give rise to misappropriation liability:

> For purposes of this section, a "duty of trust or confidence" exists in the following circumstances, among others:
>
> (1) Whenever a person *agrees* to maintain information in confidence;
>
> (2) Whenever the person communicating the material nonpublic information and the person to whom it is communicated have a *history, pattern, or practice of sharing confidences*, such that the *recipient of the information knows or reasonably should know* that the person communicating the material nonpublic information expects that the recipient will maintain its confidentiality; or
>
> (3) Whenever a person receives or obtains material nonpublic information from his or her *spouse, parent, child, or sibling*; provided, however, that the person receiving or obtaining the information may demonstrate that no duty of trust or confidence existed with respect to the information, by

establishing that he or she *neither knew nor reasonably should have known* that the person who was the source of the information expected that the person would keep the information confidential, because of the parties' history, pattern, or practice of sharing and maintaining confidences, and because there was no agreement or understanding to maintain the confidentiality of the information.

17 C.F.R. § 240.10b5-2(b) (emphasis added).

Does this section provide clarity to the misappropriation theory? Does it overturn the result in *Chestman*?

1. *Trust and/or confidence?* Recall that in *Chiarella* and *O'Hagan*, the Court held that Section 10b insider trading liability presupposes a breach of a fiduciary or similar duty of "trust and confidence." *See, e.g., O'Hagan*, 521 U.S. at 652–53. SEC Rule 10b5-2, however, defines misappropriation liability in terms of a duty of "trust *or* confidence." Is the shift from the conjunctive to the disjunctive significant for the scope of liability? If so, is the expanded scope under the administrative rule authorized by the statute?

2. *The* Cuban *case and question of confidentiality agreements.* In June 2004 the CEO of Mamma.com called Mark Cuban (owner of the Dallas Mavericks and regular on the show *Shark Tank*) and left a message for Cuban to call him back. When Cuban called back, the CEO said "I've got confidential information;" Cuban responded, "Okay, uh huh, go ahead." At this point the CEO told Cuban (who was a major shareholder at Mamma.com—but not an insider at the company) that the company would likely issue new shares to raise capital. This was bad news for Cuban because his existing shares would be diluted in value with the issuance of the new shares. Shortly after this call (but before the public announcement of this material information), Cuban sold all his 600,000 shares in the company. By selling when he did, Cuban avoided losses of approximately $750,000. *See SEC v. Cuban*, 620 F.3d 551, 556 (5th Cir. 2010). The SEC brought an insider trading enforcement action against Cuban. The case raised the important question of whether a mere contractual or other commitment to confidence (without more) is enough to trigger insider trading liability. We have seen that the Supreme Court has consistently held that insider trading liability under Section 10b presupposes the breach of a fiduciary or similar duty of loyalty to either the shareholders (which Cuban, who was not an insider at the company, did not have) or the source of the information (which Cuban also did not appear to have, since he was only a shareholder of Mamma.com—and therefore owed no duty of loyalty to the CEO or the company). But we have also seen that SEC Rule 10b5-2(b)(1) defines the relevant duty of "trust or confidence" to include "whenever a person agrees to maintain information in confidence." At a minimum, Cuban was aware that the CEO wished him to keep the information in confidence.

The district court held that, without an express or implied commitment not to trade (duty of trust or loyalty), a mere commitment to keep information in confidence does not give rise to insider trading liability. *SEC v. Cuban*, 643 F. Supp. 2d

713, 725 (2009). On appeal, however, the Fifth Circuit refused to affirm the district court's ruling on the question of whether an express or implied commitment not to trade was required, explaining its decision to punt on the issue as follows:

> Given the paucity of jurisprudence on the question of what constitutes a relationship of "trust and confidence" and the inherently fact-bound nature of determining whether such a duty exists, we decline to first determine or place our thumb on the scale in the district court's determination of its presence or to now draw the contours of any liability that it might bring, including the force of Rule 10b5-2(b)(1).

Cuban, 643 F.3d at 558. The case was remanded and Cuban ultimately won the case on the merits before a jury. *See* Jana Pruet, *Billionaire Mark Cuban Cleared of Insider Trading; Blasts U.S. Government*, REUTERS (Oct. 16, 2013, 3:34 PM), https://www.reuters.com/article/us-usasec-cuban-verdict-idUSBRE99F0ZM20131016. The issue of whether a mere agreement to keep information in confidence (without an express or implicit agreement not to trade) is enough to incur insider trading liability under the misappropriation theory, however, remains unresolved. How do you think this issue should be resolved? Do you think Cuban did something wrong here? Do you think the CEO may have had some improper motive in sharing the information with Cuban?

Problems

5-1. Keith Joon was Chief Executive Officer ("CEO") of Goose Foods, Inc. He had also been a member, for 10 years, of the National Leaders Organization ("NLO"), a national organization of company executives under 50 years old. The NLO is organized into regional chapters, and further divided into small forums. Joon was a member of the Northern California Forum.

The "Forum Principles" of the Northern California Forum stated that: "We operate in an atmosphere of absolute confidentiality. Nothing discussed in forum will be discussed with outsiders. Confidentiality, in all ways and for always." Members were also required to comply with a written "Confidentiality Commitment" as a condition of membership. That agreement provided: "I understand that to achieve the level of trust necessary to ensure the interchange we all seek in the Forum, all information shared by the membership must be held in absolute confidence." Joon knew of the Confidentiality Commitment, but did not sign an agreement to that effect or otherwise promise to adhere to the commitment. During his time as a member of NLO, Joon occasionally discussed confidential business information with other members. At no time during those conversations did Joon or the other members promise to maintain each others' confidences.

The CEO of Data, Inc. was also a member of the Northern California Forum. Data is a publicly traded corporation that manufactures computer storage devices. On March 1, the Northern California Forum members departed in a private plane for their annual retreat. Prior to departure, the CEO of Data informed the Forum

Moderator that he could not attend because Data was involved in merger discussions with another company — Quantum Corporation. He authorized the Forum Moderator to tell the other members why he would be absent but asked the Moderator to emphasize the confidential nature of the information. The Forum Moderator relayed the information to Joon and other members of the Northern California Forum.

Based on this confidential information, between March 1 and March 4 last year, Joon purchased 187,300 shares of Data stock for between $2.00 and $4.12 per share. On May 11, Data publicly announced that it had agreed to be acquired by Quantum. Data's share price jumped to $7.56. Joon, thereby, realized a profit of $832,627 on an investment of $583,360.

The government is investigating whether Joon violated the federal securities laws. Does the government have a viable case against Joon? If so, what theory or theories should the government use? What are the likely defenses?

5-2. Alexandra Gogol owned an Internet-based stock brokerage firm. Last October 17, Gogol hacked into the computer network of Thomas Financial Advisers, Inc., and gained access to ONC Health's soon-to-be-released negative earnings announcement for the third quarter. There had been no media or analyst reports anticipating negative earnings for ONC Health, which was a client of Thomas Financial. Approximately 35 minutes after hacking into Thomas Financial's computer network, and two hours before the earnings announcement was to be made public, Gogol sold $300,000 worth of ONC Health stock that she owned. This purchase represented 90% of all sales of ONC stock that day. When the stock market opened at 9:30 the next morning, ONC Health stock immediately dropped 50% on news of the negative earnings.

The SEC has alleged that Gogol, by "hacking and trading," has violated Section 10(b) and Rule 10b-5. Gogol has moved to dismiss the charge. How should the court rule? Why?

5-3. Samantha Jones, a letter carrier, was serving on a federal grand jury investigating accounting fraud at ABC Pharmaceuticals. Jones was aware that matters occurring before a grand jury are confidential under federal law and that only witnesses appearing before a grand jury may reveal their testimony. The Assistant United States Attorney in charge of the investigation, in accordance with the law concerning grand jury secrecy, publicly revealed that the grand jury was investigating ABC for accounting fraud but did not reveal any information relating to the investigation. ABC's stock price fell sharply after the announcement. Jones later learned during a grand jury session that the government had decided not to seek an indictment. Before prosecutors publicly announced their decision not to seek an indictment, Jones bought stock in ABC. After the announcement, ABC's stock price rose sharply. Jones then sold her stock, netting a $100,000 profit.

Has Jones committed securities fraud? Why or why not?

4. Tipper/Tippee Liability

The cases above show that a corporate insider, temporary insider, or misappropriator may be liable for insider trading. However, what about a "tippee," that is, one who is not an insider, a quasi-insider, or a misappropriator but who has been "tipped" with secret information? The United States Supreme Court first addressed this issue in the case that follows. As you read the case, be sure to identify precisely what the government must prove in a case against a tippee, particularly with respect to mens rea.

Dirks v. Securities and Exchange Commission

463 U.S. 646 (1983)

JUSTICE POWELL delivered the opinion of the Court.

Petitioner Raymond Dirks received material nonpublic information from "insiders" of a corporation with which he had no connection. He disclosed this information to investors who relied on it in trading in the shares of the corporation. The question is whether Dirks violated the antifraud provisions of the federal securities laws by this disclosure.

In 1973, Dirks was an officer of a New York broker-dealer firm who specialized in providing investment analysis of insurance company securities to institutional investors. On March 6, Dirks received information from Ronald Secrist, a former officer of Equity Funding of America. Secrist alleged that the assets of Equity Funding, a diversified corporation primarily engaged in selling life insurance and mutual funds, were vastly overstated as the result of fraudulent corporate practices. Secrist also stated that various regulatory agencies had failed to act on similar charges made by Equity Funding employees. He urged Dirks to verify the fraud and disclose it publicly.

Dirks decided to investigate the allegations. He visited Equity Funding's headquarters in Los Angeles and interviewed several officers and employees of the corporation. The senior management denied any wrongdoing, but certain corporation employees corroborated the charges of fraud. Neither Dirks nor his firm owned or traded any Equity Funding stock, but throughout his investigation he openly discussed the information he had obtained with a number of clients and investors. Some of these persons sold their holdings of Equity Funding securities, including five investment advisers who liquidated holdings of more than $16 million.

While Dirks was in Los Angeles, he was in touch regularly with William Blundell, *The Wall Street Journal*'s Los Angeles bureau chief. Dirks urged Blundell to write a story on the fraud allegations. Blundell did not believe, however, that such a massive fraud could go undetected and declined to write the story. He feared that publishing such damaging hearsay might be libelous.

During the two-week period in which Dirks pursued his investigation and spread word of Secrist's charges, the price of Equity Funding stock fell from $26 per share to less than $15 per share. This led the New York Stock Exchange to halt trading on March 27. Shortly thereafter California insurance authorities impounded Equity Funding's records and uncovered evidence of the fraud. Only then did the Securities and Exchange Commission (SEC) file a complaint against Equity Funding and only then, on April 2, did *The Wall Street Journal* publish a front-page story based largely on information assembled by Dirks. Equity Funding immediately went into receivership.

The SEC began an investigation into Dirks' role in the exposure of the fraud. After a hearing by an administrative law judge, the SEC found that Dirks had aided and abetted violations of Section 17(a) of the Securities Act of 1933, Section 10(b) of the Securities Exchange Act of 1934, and SEC Rule 10b-5 by repeating the allegations of fraud to members of the investment community who later sold their Equity Funding stock. The SEC concluded: "Where 'tippees' — regardless of their motivation or occupation — come into possession of material 'information that they know is confidential and know or should know came from a corporate insider,' they must either publicly disclose that information or refrain from trading." 21 S.E.C. Docket 1401, 1407 (1981) (quoting *Chiarella v. United States*, 445 U.S. 222, 230 n. 12 (1980)). Recognizing, however, that Dirks "played an important role in bringing [Equity Funding's] massive fraud to light," 21 S.E.C. Docket at 1412, the SEC only censured him.

Dirks sought review in the Court of Appeals for the District of Columbia Circuit. The court entered judgment against Dirks "for the reasons stated by the Commission in its opinion." . . . In view of the importance to the SEC and to the securities industry of the question presented by this case, we granted a writ of certiorari. We now reverse.

In the seminal case of *In re Cady, Roberts & Co.*, 40 S.E.C. 907 (1961), the SEC recognized that the common law in some jurisdictions imposes on "corporate 'insiders,' particularly officers, directors, or controlling stockholders" an "affirmative duty of disclosure . . . when dealing in securities." *Id.* at 911, and n.13.[10] The SEC found that not only did breach of this common-law duty also establish the elements of a Rule 10b-5 violation,[12] but that individuals other than corporate insiders could

---

10. The duty that insiders owe to the corporation's shareholders not to trade on inside information differs from the common-law duty that officers and directors also have to the corporation itself not to mismanage corporate assets, of which confidential information is one. In holding that breaches of this duty to shareholders violated the Securities Exchange Act, the *Cady, Roberts* Commission recognized, and we agree, that "[a] significant purpose of the Exchange Act was to eliminate the idea that use of inside information for personal advantage was a normal emolument of corporate office."

12. The SEC views the disclosure duty as requiring more than disclosure to purchasers or sellers: "Proper and adequate disclosure of significant corporate developments can only be effected by a public release through the appropriate public media, designed to achieve a broad dissemination to the investing public generally and without favoring any special person or group." *In re* Faberge, Inc., 45 S.E.C. 249, 256 (1973).

be obligated either to disclose material nonpublic information before trading or to abstain from trading altogether. In *Chiarella*, we held that "a duty to disclose under Section 10(b) does not arise from the mere possession of nonpublic market information." 445 U.S. at 235. Such a duty arises rather from the existence of a fiduciary relationship.

Not "all breaches of fiduciary duty in connection with a securities transaction," however, come within the ambit of Rule 10b-5. *Santa Fe Industries, Inc. Green*, 430 U.S. 462, 472 (1977). There must also be "manipulation or deception." *Id.* at 473. In an inside-trading case this fraud derives from the "inherent unfairness involved where one takes advantage" of "information intended to be available only for a corporate purpose and not for the personal benefit of anyone." *In re Merrill Lynch, Pierce, Fenner & Smith, Inc.*, 43 S.E.C. 933, 936 (1968). Thus, an insider will be liable under Rule 10b-5 for inside trading only where he fails to disclose material nonpublic information before trading on it and thus makes "secret profits." *Cady, Roberts*, 40 S.E.C. at 916 n.31.

We were explicit in *Chiarella* in saying that there can be no duty to disclose where the person who has traded on inside information "was not [the corporation's] agent, . . . was not a fiduciary, [or] was not a person in whom the sellers [of the securities] had placed their trust and confidence." 445 U.S. at 232. Not to require such a fiduciary relationship, we recognized, would "depar[t] radically from the established doctrine that duty arises from a specific relationship between two parties" and would amount to "recognizing a general duty between all participants in market transactions to forgo actions based on material, nonpublic information." *Id.* at 232, 233. This requirement of a specific relationship between the shareholders and the individual trading on inside information has created analytical difficulties for the SEC and courts in policing tippees who trade on inside information. Unlike insiders who have independent fiduciary duties to both the corporation and its shareholders, the typical tippee has no such relationships.[14] In view of this absence, it has been unclear how a tippee acquires the *Cady, Roberts* duty to refrain from trading on inside information.

The SEC's position, as stated in its opinion in this case, is that a tippee "inherits" the *Cady, Roberts* obligation to shareholders whenever he receives inside information from an insider. . . .

---

14. Under certain circumstances, such as where corporate information is revealed legitimately to an underwriter, accountant, lawyer, or consultant working for the corporation, these outsiders may become fiduciaries of the shareholders. The basis for recognizing this fiduciary duty is not simply that such persons acquired nonpublic corporate information, but rather that they have entered into a special confidential relationship in the conduct of the business of the enterprise and are given access to information solely for corporate purposes. When such a person breaches his fiduciary relationship, he may be treated more properly as a tipper than a tippee. For such a duty to be imposed, however, the corporation must expect the outsider to keep the disclosed nonpublic information confidential, and the relationship at least must imply such a duty.

This view differs little from the view that we rejected as inconsistent with congressional intent in *Chiarella*. Here, the SEC maintains that anyone who knowingly receives nonpublic material information from an insider has a fiduciary duty to disclose before trading.

In effect, the SEC's theory of tippee liability in both cases appears rooted in the idea that the antifraud provisions require equal information among all traders. This conflicts with the principle set forth in *Chiarella* that only some persons, under some circumstances, will be barred from trading while in possession of material nonpublic information. . . . We reaffirm today that "[a] duty [to disclose] arises from the relationship between parties . . . and not merely from one's ability to acquire information because of his position in the market." 445 U.S. at 231–32, n.14.

Imposing a duty to disclose or abstain solely because a person knowingly receives material nonpublic information from an insider and trades on it could have an inhibiting influence on the role of market analysts, which the SEC itself recognizes is necessary to the preservation of a healthy market. It is commonplace for analysts to "ferret out and analyze information," 21 S.E.C. at 1406, and this often is done by meeting with and questioning corporate officers and others who are insiders. And information that the analysts obtain normally may be the basis for judgments as to the market worth of a corporation's securities. The analyst's judgment in this respect is made available in market letters or otherwise to clients of the firm. It is the nature of this type of information, and indeed of the markets themselves, that such information cannot be made simultaneously available to all of the corporation's stockholders or the public generally.

The conclusion that recipients of inside information do not invariably acquire a duty to disclose or abstain does not mean that such tippees always are free to trade on the information. The need for a ban on some tippee trading is clear. Not only are insiders forbidden by their fiduciary relationship from personally using undisclosed corporate information to their advantage, but they may not give such information to an outsider for the same improper purpose of exploiting the information for their personal gain. Thus, the tippee's duty to disclose or abstain is derivative from that of the insider's duty. As we noted in *Chiarella*, "[t]he tippee's obligation has been viewed as arising from his role as a participant after the fact in the insider's breach of a fiduciary duty." 445 U.S. at 230 n.12.

Thus, some tippees must assume an insider's duty to the shareholders not because they receive inside information, but rather because it has been made available to them *improperly*.[19] And for Rule 10b-5 purposes, the insider's disclosure is improper only where it would violate his *Cady, Roberts* duty. Thus, a tippee assumes a fiduciary duty to the shareholders of a corporation not to trade on material nonpublic

---

19. The SEC itself has recognized that tippee liability properly is imposed only in circumstances where the tippee knows, or has reason to know, that the insider has disclosed improperly inside corporate information.

information only when the insider has breached his fiduciary duty to the shareholders by disclosing the information to the tippee and the tippee knows or should know that there has been a breach. . . . Tipping thus properly is viewed only as a means of indirectly violating the *Cady, Roberts* disclose-or-abstain rule.

In determining whether a tippee is under an obligation to disclose or abstain, it thus is necessary to determine whether the insider's "tip" constituted a breach of the insider's fiduciary duty. All disclosures of confidential corporate information are not inconsistent with the duty insiders owe to shareholders. In contrast to the extraordinary facts of this case, the more typical situation in which there will be a question whether disclosure violates the insider's *Cady, Roberts* duty is when insiders disclose information to analysts. In some situations, the insider will act consistently with his fiduciary duty to shareholders, and yet release of the information may affect the market. For example, it may not be clear — either to the corporate insider or to the recipient analyst — whether the information will be viewed as material nonpublic information. Corporate officials may mistakenly think the information already has been disclosed or that it is not material enough to affect the market. Whether disclosure is a breach of duty therefore depends in large part on the purpose of the disclosure. This standard was identified by the SEC itself in *Cady, Roberts:* a purpose of the securities laws was to eliminate "use of inside information for personal advantage." Thus, the test is whether the insider personally will benefit, directly or indirectly, from his disclosure. Absent some personal gain, there has been no breach of duty to stockholders. And absent a breach by the insider, there is no derivative breach. . . .

The SEC argues that, if inside-trading liability does not exist when the information is transmitted for a proper purpose but is used for trading, it would be a rare situation when the parties could not fabricate some ostensibly legitimate business justification for transmitting the information. We think the SEC is unduly concerned. In determining whether the insider's purpose in making a particular disclosure is fraudulent, the SEC and the courts are not required to read the parties' minds. . . . But to determine whether the disclosure itself "deceive[s], manipulate[s], or defraud[s]" shareholders, *Aaron v. SEC,* 446 U.S. 680, 686 (1980), the initial inquiry is whether there has been a breach of duty by the insider. This requires courts to focus on objective criteria, *i.e.,* whether the insider receives a direct or indirect personal benefit from the disclosure, such as a pecuniary gain or a reputational benefit that will translate into future earnings. There are objective facts and circumstances that often justify such an inference. For example, there may be a relationship between the insider and the recipient that suggests a *quid pro quo* from the latter, or an intention to benefit the particular recipient. The elements of fiduciary duty and exploitation of nonpublic information also exist when an insider makes a gift of confidential information to a trading relative or friend. The tip and trade resemble trading by the insider himself followed by a gift of the profits to the recipient.

Determining whether an insider personally benefits from a particular disclosure, a question of fact, will not always be easy for courts. But it is essential, we think, to have a guiding principle for those whose daily activities must be limited and instructed by the SEC's inside-trading rules, and we believe that there must be a breach of the insider's fiduciary duty before the tippee inherits the duty to disclose or abstain. In contrast, the rule adopted by the SEC in this case would have no limiting principle.

Under the inside-trading and tipping rules set forth above, we find that there was no actionable violation by Dirks. It is undisputed that Dirks himself was a stranger to Equity Funding, with no pre-existing fiduciary duty to its shareholders. He took no action, directly or indirectly, that induced the shareholders or officers of Equity Funding to repose trust or confidence in him. There was no expectation by Dirks' sources that he would keep their information in confidence. Nor did Dirks misappropriate or illegally obtain the information about Equity Funding. Unless the insiders breached their *Cady, Roberts* duty to shareholders in disclosing the non-public information to Dirks, he breached no duty when he passed it on to investors as well as to *The Wall Street Journal*.

It is clear that neither Secrist nor the other Equity Funding employees violated their *Cady, Roberts* duty to the corporation's shareholders by providing information to Dirks. The tippers received no monetary or personal benefit for revealing Equity Funding's secrets, nor was their purpose to make a gift of valuable information to Dirks. As the facts of this case clearly indicate, the tippers were motivated by a desire to expose the fraud. In the absence of a breach of duty to shareholders by the insiders, there was no derivative breach by Dirks. Dirks therefore could not have been "a participant after the fact in [an] insider's breach of a fiduciary duty." *Chiarella*, 445 U.S. at 230 n.12.

We conclude that Dirks, in the circumstances of this case, had no duty to abstain from use of the inside information that he obtained. The judgment of the Court of Appeals therefore is

Reversed.

JUSTICE BLACKMUN, with whom JUSTICE BRENNAN and JUSTICE MARSHALL join, dissenting.

The Court today takes still another step to limit the protections provided investors by Section 10(b) of the Securities Exchange Act of 1934. The device employed in this case engrafts a special motivational requirement on the fiduciary duty doctrine. This innovation excuses a knowing and intentional violation of an insider's duty to shareholders if the insider does not act from a motive of personal gain. Even on the extraordinary facts of this case, such an innovation is not justified.

* * *

No one questions that Secrist himself could not trade on his inside information to the disadvantage of uninformed shareholders and purchasers of Equity Funding securities. Unlike the printer in *Chiarella*, Secrist stood in a fiduciary relationship with these shareholders. . . .

The Court also acknowledges that Secrist could not do by proxy what he was prohibited from doing personally. But this is precisely what Secrist did. Secrist used Dirks to disseminate information to Dirks' clients, who in turn dumped stock on unknowing purchasers. Secrist thus intended Dirks to injure the purchasers of Equity Funding securities to whom Secrist had a duty to disclose. Accepting the Court's view of tippee liability, it appears that Dirks' knowledge of this breach makes him liable as a participant in the breach after the fact. . . .

The fact that the insider himself does not benefit from the breach does not eradicate the shareholder's injury. It makes no difference to the shareholder whether the corporate insider gained or intended to gain personally from the transaction; the shareholder still has lost because of the insider's misuse of nonpublic information. The duty is addressed not to the insider's motives, but to his actions and their consequences on the shareholder. Personal gain is not an element of the breach of this duty. . . .

The improper purpose requirement not only has no basis in law, but it rests implicitly on a policy that I cannot accept. The Court justifies Secrist's and Dirks' action because the general benefit derived from the violation of Secrist's duty to shareholders outweighed the harm caused to those shareholders — in other words, because the end justified the means. Under this view, the benefit conferred on society by Secrist's and Dirks' activities may be paid for with the losses caused to shareholders trading with Dirks' clients.

Although Secrist's general motive to expose the Equity Funding fraud was laudable, the means he chose were not. Moreover, even assuming that Dirks played a substantial role in exposing the fraud, he and his clients should not profit from the information they obtained from Secrist. . . .

In my view, Secrist violated his duty to Equity Funding shareholders by transmitting material nonpublic information to Dirks with the intention that Dirks would cause his clients to trade on that information. Dirks, therefore, was under a duty to make the information publicly available or to refrain from actions that he knew would lead to trading. Because Dirks caused his clients to trade, he violated Section 10(b) and Rule 10b-5. Any other result is a disservice to this country's attempt to provide fair and efficient capital markets. I dissent.

Notes and Questions

1. *The* Dirks *rule.* What precisely must the government prove in order to gain a conviction of a "tippee"? What element was missing in the case against Dirks?

2. *The role of market analysts.* The Court was apparently concerned about imposing broad liability on "tippees." What exactly was the Court's concern? According to the dissent, what are the negative consequences of *not* imposing liability on tippees like Dirks? Who has the better of the argument? Why?

According to the dissent, what actions should Dirks have taken? Was it appropriate for Dirks to investigate Equity Funding's finances on behalf of his clients? If so, once Dirks had the information, what would have been the effect on Dirks' clients if Dirks had publicly disclosed the information before revealing it to his clients? How would his clients have likely reacted? Also, how would Dirks have made the disclosure? Why did *The Wall Street Journal* decline to make the information public? Finally, what was the effect of Dirks' disclosure on the market's valuation of Equity Funding's stock? Did the disclosure provide a market benefit? Why or why not?

3. *The mens rea requirement.* As noted above, § 32(a) of the Exchange Act makes it a crime to commit a "willful" violation of the statute or rules and regulations adopted thereunder, and the Supreme Court has confirmed that criminal insider trading liability requires proof that the defendant "willfully violated [Rule 10b-5]." *O'Hagan*, 521 U.S. at 665. The Court has also noted, however, that the word "willful" "is a word of many meanings." *Ratzlaf v. United States*, 510 U.S. 135, 141 (1994). For criminal securities fraud in violation of Rule 10b-5, "willfully" has been interpreted to mean "intentionally undertaking an act that one knows to be wrongful." *United States v. Tarallo*, 380 F.3d 1174, 1188 (9th Cir. 2004). In this context, "willfully" does "not require that the actor know specifically that the conduct was unlawful." *Id.* You may have noticed, however, that the *Dirks* Court said that if a tippee knows or "should know" of the breach of fiduciary duty by the tipper, then the tippee can be held liable. This language, which sounds like a negligence or recklessness standard, has produced a great deal of confusion in criminal tipper-tippee cases. Professor Kelly Strader has noted that, given "the common understanding of securities fraud as an intentional crime, the only rational explanation of the [*Dirks*] Court's use of the ['should know'] language was that it was being sloppy." J. Kelly Strader, *(Re) Conceptualizing Insider Trading: United States v. Newman and the Intent to Defraud*, 80 BROOK. L. REV. 1419, 1473 (2015). Nevertheless, courts have regularly cited the "or should have known" language from *Dirks* in articulating the relevant mens rea for tippees in criminal insider trading cases. *See, e.g., United States v. Newman*, 773 F.3d 438, 455 (2d Cir. 2014). The result has been that courts have applied a number of different mens rea tests for tippee liability, ranging from knowledge to recklessness. *See id.* If you were a trader on Wall Street who received a "hot tip" from an anonymous source concerning a company's future earnings, how would legal uncertainty concerning the relevant mens rea for tippee liability affect your trading?

4. *Remote tippees.* What if A tips B, who then tips C. Can C be liable? So long as the *Dirks* elements are met for both A and B as tippers, and for C as the tippee, then C can be liable. *See, e.g., Salman v. United States*, 137 S. Ct. 420 (2016) (affirming conviction of a remote tippee).

5. *Tipper-tippee liability in misappropriation cases?* The *Dirks* case arose under the classical theory of insider trading — Secrist was an insider of Equity Funding. Since the relevant fiduciary duties are different under the classical theory (duty to the shareholder-counterparty) and the misappropriation theory (duty to the source of the information), some have questioned whether tipper-tippee liability applies in both contexts — and, if so, whether the elements are the same (e.g., does the personal benefit test apply in misappropriation cases?). *See, e.g.,* Donald C. Langevoort,

"Fine Distinctions" in the Contemporary Law of Insider Trading, 2013 COLUM. BUS. L. REV. 429, 452 (2013); *see also* J. Kelly Strader, *White Collar Crime and Punishment—Reflections on Michael, Martha, and Milberg Weiss*, 15 GEO. MASON L. REV. 45 (2007). As we shall see below, both questions appear to have been answered (albeit implicitly) in *Salman v. United States*, 137 S. Ct. 420 (2016). In *Salman*, the Supreme Court affirmed the criminal conviction of a tippee under the misappropriation theory. *Id.* at 429. In the same case, the government conceded that the *Dirks* "personal-benefit analysis applies in both classical and misappropriation cases." *Id.* at n. 2 (this footnote is not included in the edited version of the case below). The Court therefore noted that it "need not resolve the question." *Id.*

6. *What constitutes a personal benefit?* Recall that the *Dirks* Court adopted the personal benefit test for when a tipper has breached the relevant fiduciary or similar duty of trust and confidence as a means of imposing some form of "limiting principle" on insider trading liability in the tipper/tippee context. *Dirks* at 664. The Court explained that such a limiting principle was important in order to offer market analysts (whose job it is to gather market information from insiders and other sources) some clear guidance on when their efforts to "ferret out and analyze" information have crossed the line. *Id.*, 658–59. The SEC expressed concern at the time that, under the personal benefit test, "it would be a rare situation when the parties could not fabricate some" justification that does not involve self-dealing on the part of the tipper. *Id.* at 663. In response, the Court offered "objective facts and circumstances" that could be relied upon as proof of a personal benefit, such as when "the insider receives a direct or indirect personal benefit from the disclosure, such as a pecuniary gain or a reputational benefit that will translate into future earnings. . . ." Other objective evidence of a personal benefit could arise "when an insider makes a gift of confidential information to a trading relative or friend. The tip and trade resemble trading by the insider himself followed by a gift of the profits to the recipient." *Id.* at 664.

In most tipper/tippee cases, the personal benefit test is not difficult to satisfy because there is a payment to the tipper, a sharing of profits, or some clear reputational benefit. But recently a great deal of controversy has centered around when a mere "gift" of information satisfies the personal benefit test, particularly in the context of remote tippees. For example, who counts as a "friend" or "relative" under *Dirks*? Also, how much does a remote tippee need to know about the original tipper's motives to satisfy the test for liability? The Second Circuit took up these questions in *United States v. Newman*, 773 F.3d 438 (2d Cir. 2014). In that case, the court held that a factfinder may not infer a tipper personally benefited from gifting material nonpublic information to a trading relative or friend absent evidence "of a meaningfully close personal relationship" between the tipper and tippee "that generates an exchange that is objective, consequential, and represents at least a potential gain of a pecuniary or similar valuable nature." *Id.* at 452. This test was far more demanding of prosecutors than their preferred test that a personal benefit could be inferred from any gift of confidential information for a noncorporate purpose. The *Newman* court tied its "meaningfully close personal relationship" requirement to the *Dirks* Court's expectation that the personal benefit test would provide a clear limiting principle. According to the *Newman* court, if the government were allowed to meet its burden by proving the "mere fact of friendship, particularly of a casual or social nature," then the government would be "allowed to meet its burden by proving that two individuals were alumni of the same school or attended the same church." This, according to the court, would render "the personal benefit requirement . . . a nullity." *Id.* In addition to this more circumscribed articulation of the personal benefit test, the *Newman* court also held that tippee liability requires the government to prove that the tippee knew of the tipper's personal benefit at the time of trading. *Id.* at 447.

The Second Circuit's *Newman* decision spurred a number of persons who had recently been convicted of insider trading to request rehearings and caused prosecutors to complain that the court's narrow interpretation of the personal benefit test would "limit the ability to prosecute people who trade on leaked information." Matthew Goldstein & Ben Protess, *U.S. Attorney Preet Bharara Challenges Insider Trading Ruling*, N.Y. Times (Jan. 23, 2015).

In our next case, a remote tippee, Bassam Salman, appealed his conviction for insider trading on information he received from his brother-in-law. He claimed that his conviction should be overturned in light of the personal benefit test articulated in *Newman*. The Ninth Circuit affirmed the conviction and partially challenged the holding in *Newman*. The Supreme Court granted certiorari to resolve the apparent circuit split.

Salman v. United States

137 S. Ct. 420 (2016)

Justice Alito delivered the opinion of the Court.

Section 10(b) of the Securities Exchange Act of 1934 and the Securities and Exchange Commission's Rule 10b-5 prohibit undisclosed trading on inside corporate information by individuals who are under a duty of trust and confidence that prohibits them from secretly using such information for their personal advantage. Individuals under this duty may face criminal and civil liability for trading on inside information (unless they make appropriate disclosures ahead of time).

These persons also may not tip inside information to others for trading. The tippee acquires the tipper's duty to disclose or abstain from trading if the tippee knows the information was disclosed in breach of the tipper's duty, and the tippee may commit securities fraud by trading in disregard of that knowledge. In *Dirks v. Securities and Exchange Commission*, 463 U.S. 646 (1983), this Court explained that a tippee's liability for trading on inside information hinges on whether the tipper breached a fiduciary duty by disclosing the information. A tipper breaches such a fiduciary duty, we held, when the tipper discloses the inside information for a personal benefit. And, we went on to say, a jury can infer a personal benefit — and thus a breach of the tipper's duty — where the tipper receives something of value in exchange for the tip or "makes a gift of confidential information to a trading relative or friend." *Id.*, at 664.

Petitioner Bassam Salman challenges his convictions for conspiracy and insider trading. Salman received lucrative trading tips from an extended family member, who had received the information from Salman's brother-in-law. Salman then traded on the information. He argues that he cannot be held liable as a tippee because the tipper (his brother-in-law) did not personally receive money or property in exchange for the tips and thus did not personally benefit from them. The Court of Appeals disagreed, holding that *Dirks* allowed the jury to infer that the tipper here breached a duty because he made a "'gift of confidential information to a trading relative.'" Because the Court of Appeals properly applied *Dirks,* we affirm the judgment below.

Maher Kara was an investment banker in Citigroup's healthcare investment banking group. He dealt with highly confidential information about mergers and acquisitions involving Citigroup's clients. Maher enjoyed a close relationship with his older brother, Mounir Kara (known as Michael). After Maher started at Citigroup, he began discussing aspects of his job with Michael. At first he relied on Michael's chemistry background to help him grasp scientific concepts relevant to his new job. Then, while their father was battling cancer, the brothers discussed companies that dealt with innovative cancer treatment and pain management techniques. Michael began to trade on the information Maher shared with him. At first, Maher was unaware of his brother's trading activity, but eventually he began to suspect that it was taking place.

Ultimately, Maher began to assist Michael's trading by sharing inside information with his brother about pending mergers and acquisitions. Maher sometimes used code words to communicate corporate information to his brother. Other times, he shared inside information about deals he was not working on in order to avoid detection. Without his younger brother's knowledge, Michael fed the information to others — including Salman, Michael's friend and Maher's brother-in-law. By the time the authorities caught on, Salman had made over $1.5 million in profits that he split with another relative who executed trades via a brokerage account on Salman's behalf.

Salman was indicted on one count of conspiracy to commit securities fraud, and four counts of securities fraud. . . .

The evidence at trial established that Maher and Michael enjoyed a "very close relationship." Maher "love[d] [his] brother very much," Michael was like "a second father to Maher," and Michael was the best man at Maher's wedding to Salman's sister. Maher testified that he shared inside information with his brother to benefit him and with the expectation that his brother would trade on it. . . . .

Michael testified that he became friends with Salman when Maher was courting Salman's sister and later began sharing Maher's tips with Salman. As he explained at trial, "any time a major deal came in, [Salman] was the first on my phone list." . . .

After a jury trial . . . , Salman was convicted on all counts. He was sentenced to 36 months of imprisonment, three years of supervised release, and over $730,000 in restitution. After his motion for a new trial was denied, Salman appealed to the Ninth Circuit. While his appeal was pending, the Second Circuit issued its opinion in *United States v. Newman*, 773 F.3d 438 (2014). There, the Second Circuit reversed the convictions of two portfolio managers who traded on inside information. The *Newman* defendants were "several steps removed from the corporate insiders" and the court found that "there was no evidence that either was aware of the source of the inside information." The court acknowledged that *Dirks* and Second Circuit case law allow a factfinder to infer a personal benefit to the tipper from a gift of confidential information to a trading relative or friend. But the court concluded that, "[t]o the extent" *Dirks* permits "such an inference," the inference "is impermissible in the absence of proof of a meaningfully close personal relationship that generates an exchange that is objective, consequential, and represents at least a potential gain of a pecuniary or similarly valuable nature."[1]

Pointing to *Newman,* Salman argued that his conviction should be reversed. While the evidence established that Maher made a gift of trading information to Michael and that Salman knew it, there was no evidence that Maher received anything of "a pecuniary or similarly valuable nature" in exchange — or that Salman knew of any such benefit. The Ninth Circuit disagreed and affirmed Salman's conviction. The court reasoned that the case was governed by *Dirks* 's holding that a tipper benefits personally by making a gift of confidential information to a trading relative or friend. . . . To the extent *Newman* went further and required additional gain to the tipper in cases involving gifts of confidential information to family and friends, the Ninth Circuit "decline[d] to follow it." We granted certiorari to resolve the tension between the Second Circuit's *Newman* decision and the Ninth Circuit's decision in this case.

In this case, Salman contends that an insider's "gift of confidential information to a trading relative or friend," is not enough to establish securities fraud. Instead, Salman argues, a tipper does not personally benefit unless the tipper's goal in disclosing inside information is to obtain money, property, or something of tangible value. He claims that our insider-trading precedents, and the cases those precedents cite, involve situations in which the insider exploited confidential information for the insider's own "tangible monetary profit. . . ." More broadly, Salman urges that defining a gift as a personal benefit renders the insider-trading offense indeterminate and overbroad: indeterminate, because liability may turn on facts such as the closeness of the relationship between tipper and tippee and the tipper's purpose for disclosure; and overbroad, because the Government may avoid having to prove a

---

1. The Second Circuit also reversed the *Newman* defendants' convictions because the Government introduced no evidence that the defendants knew the information they traded on came from insiders or that the insiders received a personal benefit in exchange for the tips. This case does not implicate those issues.

concrete personal benefit by simply arguing that the tipper meant to give a gift to the tippee. . . . Finally, Salman contends that gift situations create especially troubling problems for remote tippees — that is, tippees who receive inside information from another tippee, rather than the tipper — who may have no knowledge of the relationship between the original tipper and tippee and thus may not know why the tipper made the disclosure.

The Government disagrees and argues that a gift of confidential information to anyone, not just a "trading relative or friend," is enough to prove securities fraud. Under the Government's view, a tipper personally benefits whenever the tipper discloses confidential trading information for a noncorporate purpose. Accordingly, a gift to a friend, a family member, or anyone else would support the inference that the tipper exploited the trading value of inside information for personal purposes and thus personally benefited from the disclosure. . . .

We adhere to *Dirks,* which easily resolves the narrow issue presented here. In *Dirks,* we explained that a tippee is exposed to liability for trading on inside information only if the tippee participates in a breach of the tipper's fiduciary duty. Whether the tipper breached that duty depends "in large part on the purpose of the disclosure" to the tippee. "[T]he test," we explained, "is whether the insider personally will benefit, directly or indirectly, from his disclosure." Thus, the disclosure of confidential information without personal benefit is not enough. In determining whether a tipper derived a personal benefit, we instructed courts to "focus on objective criteria, *i.e.,* whether the insider receives a direct or indirect personal benefit from the disclosure, such as a pecuniary gain or a reputational benefit that will translate into future earnings." This personal benefit can "often" be inferred "from objective facts and circumstances," we explained, such as "a relationship between the insider and the recipient that suggests a *quid pro quo* from the latter, or an intention to benefit the particular recipient." In particular, we held that "[t]he elements of fiduciary duty and exploitation of nonpublic information also exist *when an insider makes a gift of confidential information to a trading relative or friend.*" In such cases, "[t]he tip and trade resemble trading by the insider followed by a gift of the profits to the recipient." We then applied this gift-giving principle to resolve *Dirks* itself, finding it dispositive that the tippers "received no monetary or personal benefit" from their tips to Dirks, "*nor was their purpose to make a gift of valuable information to Dirks.*" *Dirks,* at 667 (emphasis added).

Our discussion of gift giving resolves this case. Maher, the tipper, provided inside information to a close relative, his brother Michael. *Dirks* makes clear that a tipper breaches a fiduciary duty by making a gift of confidential information to "a trading relative," and that rule is sufficient to resolve the case at hand. As Salman's counsel acknowledged at oral argument, Maher would have breached his duty had he personally traded on the information here himself then given the proceeds as a gift to his brother. It is obvious that Maher would personally benefit in that situation. But Maher effectively achieved the same result by disclosing the information to Michael, and allowing him to trade on it. . . . In such situations, the tipper benefits personally because giving a gift of trading information is the same thing as trading by the tipper followed by a gift of the proceeds. Here, by disclosing confidential information as a gift to his brother with the expectation that he would trade on it, Maher breached his duty of trust and confidence to Citigroup and its clients—a duty Salman acquired, and breached himself, by trading on the information with full knowledge that it had been improperly disclosed.

To the extent the Second Circuit held that the tipper must also receive something of a "pecuniary or similarly valuable nature" in exchange for a gift to family or friends, we agree with the Ninth Circuit that this requirement is inconsistent with *Dirks*.

* * *

Salman's conduct is in the heartland of *Dirks's* rule concerning gifts. It remains the case that "[d]etermining whether an insider personally benefits from a particular disclosure, a question of fact, will not always be easy for courts." But there is no need for us to address those difficult cases today, because this case involves "precisely the 'gift of confidential information to a trading relative' that *Dirks* envisioned."

Salman's jury was properly instructed that a personal benefit includes "the benefit one would obtain from simply making a gift of confidential information to a trading relative." As the Court of Appeals noted, "the Government presented direct evidence that the disclosure was intended as a gift of market-sensitive information." And . . . this evidence is sufficient to sustain his conviction under our reading of *Dirks*. Accordingly, the Ninth Circuit's judgment is affirmed.

Notes and Questions

1. *Did* Salman *add anything to* Dirks? The Supreme Court waited almost 20 years after *O'Hagan* to take an insider trading case. Did the Court really offer any significant guidance beyond simply reaffirming its prior holdings in *Dirks*?

2. *What (if anything) remains of* Newman *today?* In affirming Salman's conviction, the Supreme Court expressly overruled *Newman* to the extent that it required that a "tipper must receive something of a 'pecuniary or similar valuable nature' in exchange for a gift to family or friends." *Salman*, 137 S. Ct. at 428. The *Salman* Court did, however, appear to leave the remainder of *Newman's* other core limiting principles untouched (e.g., that the tippee must have knowledge of the tipper's personal benefit and the liability for a gift of information to a trading relative or friend requires proof of a "meaningfully close personal relationship" between tipper and tippee). Indeed, the Court explained that "[i]t remains the case that '[d]etermining whether an insider personally benefits from a particular disclosure, a question of fact, will not always be easy for courts.' But there is no need for us to address those difficult cases today, because this involves 'precisely the "gift of confidential information to a trading relative" that *Dirks* envisioned.'" *Id.* at 429. The implication is that there are some gifts that would *not* result in a personal benefit to the tipper.

Yet despite the fact that the *Salman* Court appeared to have left *Newman*'s "meaningfully close personal relationship" requirement intact, just one year later the Second Circuit itself effectively overruled *Newman* on this point in *U.S. v. Martoma*, 894 F.3d 64 (2d Cir. 2017) (Amended: June 25, 2018). In *Martoma*, the court held that a tipper receives a personal benefit whenever the tipper "intended to benefit the tippee" with the disclosure of material nonpublic information. *Id.* 76. Since arguably *any* gift intends to benefit the recipient, there appears to be nothing left of the *Newman* "meaningfully close personal relationship" test — at least in the Second Circuit. But if the personal benefit test under *Martoma* can be read so broadly, is it consistent with *Dirks*? Recall the facts of *Dirks*; do you think Dirks would have been liable under the *Martoma* test?

3. *The Blaszczak case and § 1348.* With so much controversy and uncertainty surrounding the personal benefit test for tipper-tippee liability pursuant to Section 10b insider trading liability, prosecutors have recently looked to other statutory bases for obtaining convictions. As part of the Sarbanes-Oxley Act of 2002, Congress enacted 18 U.S.C. § 1348, Securities and Commodities Fraud. This general anti-fraud provision provides that: → not willfully

> Whoever knowingly executes, or attempts to execute, a scheme or artifice . . . [t]o defraud any person in connection with . . . any security . . . or [t]o obtain, by means of false or fraudulent pretenses, representations, or promises, any money or property in connection with the purchase or sale of any . . . security . . . shall be fined under this title, or imprisoned not more than 25 years, or both.

While the language of § 1348 is similar to Section 10b, very few insider trading cases have been brought under it. This may, however, be changing in the wake of a recent Second Circuit decision holding that the controversial personal-benefit test does not apply to tipper-tippee actions brought under § 1348. In *United States v. Blaszczak*, 947 F.3d 19 (2d Cir. 2019), the court held that § 1348 and Section 10b were adopted for different purposes. According to the court, "Congress enacted [Section 10b's] fraud provisions . . . with the limited 'purpose of eliminate[ing] [the] use of inside information for personal advantage,'" and the personal benefit test is consistent with this purpose. *Id.* at 35. By contrast, § 1348 was adopted "to overcome the 'technical legal requirements' of [Section 10b]," so the personal-benefit test should not be read into the latter's elements. *Id.* at 36–37. The *Blaszczak* decision raised a number of important questions. *See, e.g.,* Karen E. Woody, *The New Insider Trading*, 52 ARIZ. ST. L. J. 594 (2020). For example, going forward, why would prosecutors ever bring a tipper-tippee case under Section 10b if they can simply bypass the personal-benefit element by bringing it under § 1348? Commentators have also noted the problem that the test for criminal insider trading liability under § 1348 (with a maximum penalty of 25 years imprisonment) is *easier* to satisfy under the *Blaszczak* rule than the test for civil liability (which must be brought under Section 10b because the SEC has no enforcement authority under § 1348).

Highlighting these and other concerns, the *Blaszczak* defendants petitioned the Supreme Court for writ of certiorari in September 2020. In an unusual move, the government responded by asking the Court to grant the petitioners' writs, vacate the Second Circuit's decision, and remand the case for consideration in light of the Court's recent wire-fraud decision, *Kelly v. United States*, 140 S. Ct. 1565 (2020). In *Kelly*, the Court held that "a scheme to alter . . . regulatory choice is not one to take the government's property." *Id.* at 1572. (*Kelly* is presented in Chapter 4, Mail and Wire Fraud, *supra*.) Since the defendants in *Blaszczak* tipped and traded on confidential government information concerning proposed medical treatment reimbursement regulations, the government conceded that the Second Circuit should revisit the question of whether such regulatory information is "property" for purposes of a §1438 prosecution after *Kelly*. (The request to vacate was pending at the time this text went to press.) The government only proposed a remand on the limited issue of what constitutes "property," *not* on the question of whether the personal benefit test applies to insider trading prosecutions under §1348. Nevertheless, if the Court vacates *Blaszczak*, then the Second Circuit's controversial personal benefit holding will no longer be law unless it is embraced on remand or in some other case. *See* Robert J. Anello & Richard F. Albert, *Days Seem Numbered for Circuit's Controversial Insider Trading Decision*, 264 N.Y.L. J. (Dec. 10, 2020), https://www.law.com/newyorklawjournal/2020/12/09/days-seem-numbered-for-circuits-controversial-insider-trading-decision/.

Note on Rule 10b5-1

In an insider trading case, the government must show that the defendant acted "*on the basis of*" material nonpublic information. But what does this mean? For example, assume that before Dirks spoke with Secrist, Dirks had done independent research into the value of Equity Funding securities and had decided to recommend that his clients sell the stock. If Dirks had then recommended the sale to his clients after speaking with Secrist, would the trading have been "on the basis" of the secret information? In other words, is the element met when a person who possesses inside information has another, independent reason for trading?

The circuit courts split on this issue. In *United States v. Teicher*, 987 F.2d 112 (2d Cir. 1993), for example, the defendants appealed their insider trading convictions, arguing that the trial court erred by charging the jury that the defendants could be convicted if they traded while merely in *knowing possession* of the inside information. The Second Circuit found that the instruction was not erroneous. The court reasoned that requiring proof that the defendants actually used the information would place too great an evidentiary burden on the government. The Ninth and Eleventh Circuits held to the contrary, reasoning that proof that the defendant knowingly *used* the information is an essential element of the crime. *See United States v. Smith*, 155 F.3d 1051, 1067 (9th Cir. 1998); *SEC v. Adler*, 137 F.3d 1325, 1334–36 (11th Cir. 1998).

In 2000, the SEC issued Rule 10b5-1, which rejects the "use" standard and adopts the "knowing possession" standard. The rule provides that, in the insider trading context, a person has traded "on the basis" of inside information when the person was "aware" of the information when making the purchase or sale. The rule provides an affirmative defense where the person making the purchase or sale demonstrates that, before becoming aware of the information, the person had: (a) entered into a binding contract to purchase or sell the security, (b) instructed another person to purchase or sell the security for the instructing person's account, or (c) adopted a written trading plan for trading securities (a 10b5-1(c) trading plan). The rule further requires that the contract, instruction, or trading plan meet specific conditions before the defense will be allowed.

Although adopted to mitigate the potentially harsh consequences of the "awareness" test and to allow corporate insiders (who are only rarely without knowledge of at least some material nonpublic information) to diversify their portfolios, the 10b5-1(c) trading plan affirmative defense has been a source of controversy in its own right. A number of recent studies have shown that insiders are using these trading plans strategically (e.g., by selectively terminating established plans based on material nonpublic information). Since the termination of a planned, future order is not itself the purchase or sale of security, it is not clear that such strategic use of trading plans is illegal. *See, e.g.,* John P. Anderson, *Anticipating a Sea Change for Insider Trading Law: From Trading Plan Crisis to Rational Reform*, 2015 UTAH L. REV. 339 (2015). Nevertheless, Congress may soon act to close this potential loophole. For example, the Promoting Transparent Standards for Corporate Insiders Act passed the House of Representatives with bipartisan support in 2019. H.R. 624, 116th Cong. (1st Sess. 2019). This act would force the SEC to revisit Rule 10b5-1(c) trading plans and propose reforms. For a discussion of some challenges to trading-plan reform, *see* John P. Anderson, *Undoing a Deal with the Devil: Some Challenges for Congress's Proposed Reform of Insider Trading Plans*, 13 VA. L. & BUS. REV. 303 (2019).

Even with 10b5-1(c) trading plans available as an affirmative defense, is the "awareness" rule fair? For example, in the hypothetical above, assume that Dirks had done his research and made his decision to disclose the information to his clients before he learned of the inside information but that he could not meet the affirmative defense requirements of Rule 10b5-1. Also assume that Secrist breached a duty in giving Dirks the information. Would insider trading liability be appropriate in such circumstances? Why or why not? Would such a result improperly remove the "willfulness" element? For an argument that it would, see Carol B. Swanson, *Insider Trading Madness: Rule 10b5-1 and the Death of Scienter*, 52 U. KAN. L. REV. 147 (2003).

Problems

5-4. A grand jury has investigated Deana for securities fraud and has found the following facts. Deana is a self-employed businessperson who bought an independent sidewalk newsstand in New York City last January 3. She sells a wide variety of news and financial magazines, including "Business News." Business News magazine imposes a strict confidentiality policy on all employees who work for and are paid by the magazine. The policy forbids the employees to use nonpublic information contained in the magazine. Business News employees are required to sign a copy of this policy when first hired.

In addition, on March 1 every year, a copy of the confidentiality policy is sent by U.S. mail to all sellers of the magazine. A magazine representative testified that a copy of the policy was sent last year to Deana's business address, but there is no direct proof that Deana received, read, or knew of the policy.

In its confidentiality policy and notice sent to sellers, the magazine states that material, nonpublic information must be kept secret until the magazine appears on the newsstands. In particular, the magazine knows that its "Wall Street Week" column tends to affect the amount of trading and the prices of the stocks discussed in the column. The magazine arrives at stores each Wednesday before 5:00 p.m. Attached to each magazine are instructions that the magazine is not to be placed on shelves before 5:00 p.m. the following day. Individual subscribers generally receive the magazine in the mail on Fridays.

The evening of Wednesday, June 6, Deana attended a movie. Deana's brother Miles, a stockbroker in New York City, accompanied her to the movie. Miles and Deana regularly discuss the stock market. Waiting for the movie to begin, Deana told her brother that she had read the latest issue of Business News magazine and told him that the magazine would appear on newsstands late the next day. Deana also said that this issue's Wall Street Week column repeated a rumor, said to be based on inside sources, that Stealth Corp. was planning to announce a tender offer for the stock of X-Ray Corp. within two weeks. Deana also said that she thought the information was "probably hush-hush" and that Miles should not repeat or use the information in any way.

Miles responded that the story sounded "interesting" and, based on his knowledge of the market, was "probably true." Miles had been following X-Ray stock for a number of months and the previous week, he had sent his broker an e-mail instructing the broker to buy 1,000 shares no later than June 8.

That night, Miles went home and logged on to a financial website where he researched the financial conditions of the two companies involved in the rumored merger. At 9:00 a.m. the next day, he called his broker and instructed the broker to execute the purchase immediately.

The following Wednesday, June 13, Stealth Corp. announced its tender offer bid for X-Ray Corp. Miles later sold his stock at a large profit.

The government is preparing to indict Deana and Miles for insider trading. What theory or theories will the government likely use? What defenses are Deana and Miles likely to raise?

5-5. Albert Penn has owned and operated a barbershop for the past 45 years. Penn enjoys investing in the stock market and often asks his clients about the corporations for which they work. Max Davis, a district manager at Wooster Foods, a wholesale food distribution company, has been getting his haircut by Penn for the past 15 years. During the barber appointments, Penn and Davis discussed family and personal matters, but they were not close personal friends and did not socialize with each other.

Penn knew that Davis worked for Wooster Foods in some capacity and had asked Davis on several occasions if Wooster Foods was going to be sold. On one of those occasions, Davis recommended that Penn buy stock in Wooster Foods because it was a good company and would probably be acquired at some point.

Two weeks later, Davis told Penn, during a barber appointment, of a rumor that there were one or two buyers interested in Wooster, that he was confident a deal was going to happen, and that it was very likely Wooster's stock price would double as a result. In fact, Davis knew of negotiations between Wooster and Best Foods and had been actively participating in preparations for the sale of Wooster to Best Foods. Davis also knew that Wooster had a policy prohibiting insider trading, that he was prohibited from trading in Wooster stock based on his knowledge of material, non-public information, and that he was also prohibited from tipping any others about the information.

Based on his conversation with Davis, Penn began buying Wooster stock. He first bought $14,000 worth of common stock, then another $18,000 in common stock. Penn sold all his Wooster stock on the day Wooster's sale to Best Foods was announced to the public. Penn's total profit from the sales was over $32,000.

Is Davis guilty of securities fraud? Is Penn guilty of securities fraud? Why or why not?

5-6. Strommer was an executive at General Capital. Alliance hired General Capital to assist in arranging financing for Alliance's potential acquisition of SunBurst, Inc. General Capital assigned Strommer the task of performing due diligence on the acquisition, including analysis of SunBurst's financial performance. Strommer called Blunt to discuss the potential deal. Blunt was a college friend of Strommer's who worked as a securities analyst at Winstrom Capital. Strommer stated that the conversation was part of Strommer's due diligence work and that he called Blunt because he knew that Winstrom owned a large amount of SunBurst stock. Shortly after the phone call, Blunt spoke with Oliver, Winstrom's Chief Executive Officer. Two weeks later, Winstrom bought a substantial additional amount of SunBurst stock. After Alliance's bid to acquire SunBurst was announced, Winstrom sold the stock that it bought after Blunt's conversation with Oliver, netting a profit of more than $2 million.

Shortly after the deal was finalized, General Capital learned of the above facts. After an internal investigation conducted by counsel, General Capital concluded that Strommer had not breached a duty to General Capital by disclosing the information concerning the deal to Blunt.

The government seeks to charge Strommer, Blunt, and Oliver under Section 10b and Rule 10b-5, alleging that Strommer violated duties as a tipper under both the traditional and misappropriation theories. The defendants have moved to dismiss the charge. How should the court rule? Why?

5-7. Dom Dornan was the Chairman and President of Horizons Corporation, a company located in Newark, New Jersey. Horizons engaged in the business of providing temporary staffing of computer and information technology personnel. The common stock of Horizons was registered with the United States Securities and Exchange Commission and publicly traded on the New York Stock Exchange. As Chairman and President of Horizons, Dornan participated in negotiating mergers and acquisitions involving Horizons and other companies, including other publicly traded companies.

Dornan socialized from time to time with other executives in the same field. One of Dornan's social acquaintances was Kris Karman, Chief Executive Officer of Compuware Corporation. Compuware was also engaged in the business of providing temporary staffing of computer and information technology personnel. Dornan and Karman were casual acquaintances, having met at business conferences four different times over the last 10 years. During conference meetings, they discussed their businesses, mentioning at times financial projections and other business information that was only available to those persons within their respective businesses. Neither Karman nor Dornan ever revealed this information for an improper purpose, and neither ever explicitly said that the information they discussed should not be repeated.

Last April 12, Dornan met with Karman at Karman's office. Karman told Dornan that Compuware was interested in acquiring Horizons through a merger by means of a friendly tender offer. Dornan responded positively, and the two engaged in an initial negotiation of the terms of the acquisition. After the meeting, negotiations regarding the proposed acquisition continued. On May 4, Compuware sent Horizons a letter of intent setting forth the proposed terms of Compuware's acquisition of Horizons through a tender offer.

In April and May, while the negotiations between Compuware and Horizons were ongoing, representatives of Compuware met with executives from Millennium Corp. to discuss a potential merger of those two companies. On May 26, Compuware advised Millennium Corp. that it was interested in acquiring all of the shares of Millennium Corp. through a tender offer of $25 per share, a price substantially above the then-prevailing market price of Millennium Corp. On June 2, Millennium Corp. privately advised Compuware that it would accept its $25 offer.

On June 21, Karman telephoned Dornan and advised Dornan that Compuware would not acquire Horizons, and told Dornan that "we have had initiated very preliminary merger negotiations with Millennium Corp. instead. We don't have a clear idea whether this deal will materialize, but I didn't want to leave you in the lurch." At the time of this conversation, as Dornan knew, Compuware had not yet publicly announced its discussions with Millennium Corp.

The following day, Dornan placed two orders to purchase a total of 15,000 shares of Millennium Corp. Shortly thereafter, Dornan's orders were executed at prices of approximately $13.25 per share. Dornan did not disclose to the sellers of the shares the information Dornan had gotten from Compuware's Chief Executive Officer concerning Millennium Corp.

On June 23, the Board of Directors of Millennium Corp. and Compuware voted to approve Compuware's acquisition of Millennium Corp. by tender offer for $24 per share. On June 24, prior to the opening of trading on the New York Stock Exchange, Compuware and Millennium Corp. issued a press release publicly announcing that Compuware would acquire Millennium Corp. at approximately $24 per share. When trading began, the price of Millennium Corp.'s stock opened at approximately $23.50 per share, representing an increase of approximately $11.25 per share from the previous day's closing price.

On June 24, following the public announcements of the tender offer for Millennium Corp., Dornan sold the 15,000 shares of Millennium Corp. stock that Dornan had purchased on June 22. The securities were sold at an average price of $23.31, yielding profits for Dornan of approximately $150,937.50.

Is Dornan guilty of insider trading? Why or why not?

5-8. Marcia is the CEO of Machine-Corp. In December, Marcia looks ahead to June 25 of the next year when a $100,000 balloon payment will come due on her home mortgage and she decides she would like to sell some of her Machine-Corp shares to make the payment. Marcia does not want to sell the shares in December because of the tax consequences. She is, however, also concerned that if she waits until June to sell the shares she will be aware of material nonpublic information at the time of the sale (Machine-Corp always announces its earnings in late June) and will therefore be exposed to insider trading liability. She talks to Machine-Corp's general counsel and he advises her to set up a 10b5-1(c) trading plan in December (when she is not aware of material nonpublic information) that will execute the sale of her 10,000 shares in June. She follows this advice and sets up a trading plan to sell 10,000 Machine-Corp shares on June 20. On June 10, the CFO informs Marcia that Machine-Corp's new product line far exceeded expectations and the company is going to beat earnings estimates by 50%. Marcia realizes that Machine-Corp's stock will skyrocket when the company discloses this information to the market on June 30. Marcia calls up her broker and tells her to cancel the trading plan she entered into in December. The 10,000 shares Marcia did not sell under her December trading plan end up increasing $50,000 in value after the company's earnings are released on June 30.

Is Marcia liable for Section 10b insider trading?

C. Parallel Civil Proceedings

As noted above (at § A, 2), and as evidenced by a number of cases included in this chapter, some federal securities fraud statutes, such as Exchange Act Section 10b, can form the basis of civil enforcement actions brought by the SEC. The courts have also consistently recognized Section 10b as providing a private right of action against violators. With this in mind, the wise white collar criminal defense counsel should be mindful of some of the particulars and consequences of a possible parallel civil proceeding for securities fraud.

The remedies available to the SEC in a civil enforcement action for securities fraud are varied and can be quite severe. The SEC has authority to pursue injunctive relief, disgorgement, and monetary sanctions for violations of the securities laws.

For example, Exchange Act § 21(d) gives the SEC authority to pursue a temporary or permanent injunction against any person to prevent them from continuing or prospective violations of Section 10b. *See* 15 U.S.C. § 78u(d)(1). As Professor Stephen Bainbridge notes, the courts have made it "quite easy" for the SEC to win such injunctions: "The SEC must make a 'proper showing,' but that merely requires the SEC to demonstrate that a violation of the securities laws occurred and there is a reasonable likelihood of future violations." Stephen M. Bainbridge, Insider Trading: Law and Policy 141 (2014). The Commission may also ask the court to prohibit those who violate Section 10b "from acting as an officer or director of any issuer that has a class of securities registered pursuant to [sections of this title] if the person's conduct demonstrates unfitness to serve as an officer or director of any such issuer." 15 U.S.C. § 78u(d)(2). In addition, Exchange Act Section 21(d)(5) provides that "the Commission may seek, and any Federal court may grant, any equitable relief that may be appropriate or necessary for the benefit of investors." 15 U.S.C. § 78u(d)(5). The SEC may pursue the equitable relief of disgorgement of any profits obtained from securities fraud via the courts under this provision, or through its own administrative proceedings pursuant to Exchange Act Section 21B. 15 U.S.C. § 78u-2(e).

In addition to such injunctive and other equitable relief, the SEC may seek money penalties for securities fraud in civil actions before the federal courts. 15 U.S.C. § 78u(d)(3). The Commission also has its own power to impose fines through administrative proceedings. 15 U.S.C. § 78u-2. The penalties in both fora are structured pursuant to a three-tiered scheme. Under this scheme, available penalties per violation may increase from $5,000 to $100,000 for a natural person (or the gross amount of the violator's gain — whichever is greater). The penalties increase depending on whether the violation involved "fraud, deceit, manipulation, or deliberate or reckless disregard of a regulatory requirement," and depending on whether the violation "directly or indirectly resulted in substantial losses or created a significant risk of substantial losses to other persons." 15 U.S.C. § 78u(d)(3)(B); 15 U.S.C. § 78u-2(b).

Congress has imposed special statutory civil penalties available to the SEC in the context of insider trading. The Insider Trading Sanctions Act of 1984 (ITSA) strengthened the SEC's hand by permitting it to seek treble damages (three times any profits gained or losses avoided) in its civil enforcement actions. 15 U.S.C. §78u-1(a)(2). The SEC may seek ITSA damages in addition to disgorgement, potentially exposing the insider trader to a penalty of four times the profits earned or losses avoided from any given trade. *See*, e.g., Bainbridge, *supra*, at 146. The Insider Trading and Securities Fraud Enforcement Act of 1988 (ITSFEA) later extended the penalty of treble damages to controlling persons. 15 U.S.C. §78u-1(a)(3). ITSFEA does, however, limit the penalty of treble damages to only those controlling persons who (A) "knew or recklessly disregarded the fact that [their] controlled person was likely to engage in the act or acts [of insider trading] and failed to take appropriate steps to prevent such act or acts before they occurred," or (B) failed to establish and maintain effective insider trading compliance programs. 15 U.S.C. §78u-1(b).

In addition to the risk of parallel proceedings brought by the SEC, counsel must be mindful of the possibility of private party litigation for Section 10b securities fraud. Though Section 10b does not expressly authorize a private party to bring an action under its provisions, the courts have recognized an implied right of action. *See, e.g., Herman & MacLean v. Huddleston*, 459 U.S. 375, 380 (1983) (noting that the implied right of private action under Section 10b is "beyond peradventure"). In addition, Congress granted an express private right of action to parties who trade contemporaneously with insider traders in Exchange Act Section 20A. 15 U.S.C. §78t-1.

Finally, beyond the obvious financial and career risks of civil actions for securities fraud, such proceedings also implicate important evidentiary and self-incrimination issues under the Fifth Amendment for any parallel criminal action. Chapter 18, Civil Actions, Civil Penalties, and Parallel Proceedings, *infra*, addresses these (and related) issues in detail.

Chapter 6

Health Care Fraud and Abuse

Katrice Bridges Copeland[*]

A. Introductory Notes

The Federal Bureau of Investigation (FBI) estimates that health care fraud costs taxpayers tens of billions of dollars a year. FBI, Health Care Fraud, http://www.fbi .gov/about-us/investigate/white_collar/health-care-fraud (explaining that "[r]ooting out health care fraud is central to the well-being of both our citizens and the overall economy"). Not surprisingly, the federal government has made cracking down on health care fraud one of its top enforcement priorities. The federal government has used both criminal and civil laws to pursue health care entities and individuals for fraud. Thus, it is critical for attorneys who specialize in white collar crime to understand the various health care fraud laws and their enforcement mechanisms.

Federal health care programs,[a] such as Medicare[b] and Medicaid,[c] are ripe for fraud and abuse because they largely operate based on a fee-for-service reimbursement model. Under the fee-for-service model, health care providers receive payments based on each service provided, such as an office visit, medical procedure, or test. Thus, health care providers are incentivized to provide more services than are necessary to adequately treat patients because the government pays the providers based on the quantity, not the quality, of medical services provided. In recent years, however, there has been a movement toward value-based reimbursement which focuses more on the quality rather than the quantity of treatment. The incentives toward overutilization are lessened in a value-based reimbursement model. Value-based reimbursement may, however, pose different fraud risks such as incentives to manipulate or falsify data used to verify performance and outcomes.

---

[*] Professor of Law, Penn State Law, University Park, PA.

a. A federal health care program is defined as any plan or program that provides health benefits, whether directly, through insurance, or otherwise, and that is funded directly, in whole or in part, by the U.S. Government or a state health care program (except for the Federal Employees Health Benefits Program) (section 1128B(f) of the Social Security Act (the Act)). Among the most significant federal health care programs are Medicare, Medicaid, TRICARE, and the veterans' programs.

b. Medicare is a federally funded insurance program for individuals who are 65 or older, have certain disabilities, or have end-stage renal disease. 42 U.S.C. §§ 1395–1395h.

c. Medicaid is a joint federal-state insurance program for certain categories of low-income individuals. 42 U.S.C. §§ 1395–1395h.

The Office of Inspector General (OIG) of the Department of Health and Human Services (HHS) is responsible for eliminating fraud and abuse in HHS programs, such as Medicare and Medicaid. The OIG works in partnership with the FBI, Department of Justice (DOJ), and state agencies to investigate health care fraud and abuse. FBI, Financial Crimes Report 2010–2011, https://www.fbi.gov/stats-services/ publications/financial-crimes-report-2010-2011. The DOJ Criminal Division's Fraud Section has a Health Care Fraud ("HCF") Unit that focuses exclusively on prosecuting health care fraud-related cases. DOJ, Health Care Fraud Unit, https://www .justice.gov/criminal-fraud/health-care-fraud-unit. The HCF Unit employs a Strike Force model of interagency teams that pursue the worst offenders engaged in fraudulent activities. DOJ, Strike Force Operations, https://www.justice.gov/criminal -fraud/strike-force-operations. The teams focus on health care fraud "hot spots" where there are high levels of billing fraud as well as emerging fraudulent schemes that move around the country. *Id.*

In the past, the government relied heavily on whistleblowers in False Claims Act cases to alert it to health care fraud and abuse by entities or individuals. Now, in addition to whistleblowers, the government relies upon data mining. FBI, Financial Crimes Report 2010–2011, https://www.fbi.gov/stats-services/publications/financial-crimes-report-2010-2011. Data mining is an examination of the billing records of health care companies to determine if the company is billing for certain items, procedures, or services at an abnormally high rate. *Id.* If the rate of billing is abnormal, then an investigation will ensue to determine why that may be happening. *Id.* The HCF Unit has an internal data analytics team that examines billing abnormalities.

In addition to investigating fraud and abuse, the OIG issues advisory opinions about the application of OIG's fraud and abuse authorities to specific factual situations. 42 U.S.C. § 1320a-7d(b); 42 C.F.R. § 1008. The opinions are only legally binding on the requestor, but are often used by practitioners to counsel their clients on the requirements of the health care fraud and abuse laws. In addition to the power to investigate and issue advisory opinions, the OIG has the authority to impose administrative sanctions on individuals and entities.

B. The Federal Anti-Kickback Statute

The Anti-Kickback Statute ("AKS"), 42 U.S.C. § 1320a-7b, is the centerpiece of criminal health care fraud enforcement. The Anti-Kickback Statute is designed to remove economic incentives from medical referrals of items or services that are reimbursable by a federal health care program. It provides criminal penalties for individuals or entities that knowingly and willfully solicit or receive remuneration for the purpose of inducing the referral of federal health care program-related business. A violation of the AKS is a felony that is punishable by up to 10 years' imprisonment and fines of up to $100,000. In addition, criminal conviction under the AKS leads to mandatory exclusion from participation in federal health care programs. A violation may also result in the imposition of civil monetary penalties.

A common example of a prohibited action would be a doctor sending a Medicare patient to a particular laboratory for blood work in exchange for a referral fee. The concern is that the doctor's medical judgment would be compromised by the referral fee to the detriment of the patient. There is also a concern that, due to the referral fee, the doctor will send the patient for unnecessary treatment that will increase the government's health care costs.

By preventing health care providers from paying remuneration to other providers, the statute aims to contain federal health care costs and protect patients. The problem, however, is that the broad language of the AKS also criminalizes many potentially beneficial compensation arrangements and business practices.

1. The Elements of the Anti-Kickback Statute

The government must show that the defendant:

(1) knowingly and willfully;

(2) offered or paid, solicited or received any remuneration;

(3) to induce or in return for

(4) the referral of program-related business.

a. The Mens Rea Requirement

Because the Anti-Kickback Statute is incredibly broad, there is a danger that innocuous conduct could be criminalized under the statute. The original statute did not contain a mens rea requirement, but Congress added a knowing and willful mens rea requirement in 1980. Omnibus Reconciliation Act of 1980, Pub. L. No. 96-499, 94 Stat. 2599 (1980). After the enactment of the knowing and willful mens rea requirement, the circuits were split over whether it required proof of specific intent to violate the statute or simply proof that the individual knew the conduct was unlawful. *Compare Hansleter Network v. Shalala*, 51 F.3d 1390 (9th Cir. 1995) (requiring specific intent to violate the law), *with United States v. Stark*, 157 F.3d 833 (11th Cir. 1998) (refusing to follow *Hansleter* and require a specific intent to violate the law).

The Patient Protection and Affordable Care Act (PPACA) resolved the issue. The PPACA amendment to the AKS provides that "a person need not have actual knowledge of [the AKS] or specific intent to commit a violation of [the AKS]." 42 U.S.C. § 1320a-7b(h) (2018). Ultimately, this amendment makes it easier to obtain a conviction under the AKS because there is no need to prove that the defendant had knowledge of the AKS and specifically intended to violate its requirements.

b. The Any Remuneration Requirement

The AKS prohibits the solicitation, offer, payment or receipt of any remuneration (including any kickback, bribe, or rebate) directly or indirectly, in cash or in kind in exchange for referrals. The phrase "any remuneration" refers to anything of value. Thus, almost any benefit by and between medical providers can be considered remuneration and serve as the basis for an AKS violation if it is provided for the purpose of inducing referrals.

c. The Inducement Requirement

To violate the AKS, the defendant must offer or receive remuneration for the purpose of inducing a referral. An important question arises, however, when remuneration has both the purpose of inducing a referral and some other legitimate purpose. The following case is the most influential decision on that issue.

United States v. Greber

760 F.2d 68 (3d Cir. 1985)

WEIS, CIRCUIT JUDGE.

In this appeal, defendant argues that payments made to a physician for professional services in connection with tests performed by a laboratory cannot be the basis of Medicare fraud. We do not agree and hold that if one purpose of the payment was to induce future referrals, the Medicare statute has been violated. *** We find the district court's rulings consistent with our determinations and accordingly will affirm.

After a jury trial, defendant was convicted on 20 of 23 counts in an indictment charging violations of the mail fraud, Medicare fraud, and false statement statutes. Post-trial motions were denied, and defendant has appealed.

Defendant is an osteopathic physician who is board certified in cardiology. In addition to hospital staff and teaching positions, he was the president of Cardio-Med, Inc., an organization which he formed. The company provides physicians with diagnostic services, one of which uses a Holter-monitor. This device, worn for approximately 24 hours, records the patient's cardiac activity on a tape. A computer operated by a cardiac technician scans the tape, and the data is later correlated with an activity diary the patient maintains while wearing the monitor.

Cardio-Med billed Medicare for the monitor service and, when payment was received, forwarded a portion to the referring physician. The government charged that the referral fee was 40 percent of the Medicare payment, not to exceed $65 per patient.

Based on Cardio-Med's billing practices, counts 18–23 of the indictment charged defendant with having tendered remuneration or kickbacks to the referring physicians in violation of 42 U.S.C. §1395nn(b)(2)(B) (1982).[d]

---

d. The Anti-Kickback Statute, 42 U.S.C. §1320a-7b, was previously codified at 42 U.S.C. §1395nn(b)(2).

* * *

The proof as to the Medicare fraud counts (18–23) was that defendant had paid a Dr. Avallone and other physicians "interpretation fees" for the doctors' initial consultation services, as well as for explaining the test results to the patients. There was evidence that physicians received "interpretation fees" even though defendant had actually evaluated the monitoring data. Moreover, the fixed percentage paid to the referring physician was more than Medicare allowed for such services.

The government also introduced testimony defendant had given in an earlier civil proceeding. In that case, he had testified that ". . . if the doctor didn't get his consulting fee, he wouldn't be using our service. So the doctor got a consulting fee." In addition, defendant told physicians at a hospital that the Board of Censors of the Philadelphia County Medical Society had said the referral fee was legitimate if the physician shared the responsibility for the report. Actually, the Society had stated that there should be separate bills because "for the monitor company to offer payment to the physicians . . . is not considered to be the method of choice." . . .

The Department of Health and Human Services had promulgated a rule providing that it would pay for Holter-monitoring only if it was in operation for eight hours or more. Defendant routinely certified that the temporal condition had been met, although in fact it had not.

On appeal, defendant raises several alleged trial errors. He presses more strongly, however, his contentions that the evidence was insufficient to support the guilty verdict on the Medicare fraud counts, and that the charge to the jury on that issue was not correct. . . .

I. Medicare Fraud

The Medicare fraud statute was amended by P.L. 95-142, 91 Stat. 1183 (1977). Congress, concerned with the growing problem of fraud and abuse in the system, wished to strengthen the penalties to enhance the deterrent effect of the statute. To achieve this purpose, the crime was upgraded from a misdemeanor to a felony.

Another aim of the amendments was to address the complaints of the United States Attorneys who were responsible for prosecuting fraud cases. They informed Congress that the language of the predecessor statute was "unclear and needed clarification." H. Rep. No. 393, PART II, 95 Cong., 1st Sess. 53, reprinted in 1977 U.S .CODE CONG. & AD.NEWS 3039, 3055.

A particular concern was the practice of giving "kickbacks" to encourage the referral of work. Testimony before the Congressional committee was that "physicians often determine which laboratories would do the test work for their Medicaid patients by the amount of the kickbacks and rebates offered by the laboratory. . . . Kickbacks take a number of forms including cash, long-term credit arrangements, gifts, supplies and equipment, and the furnishing of business machines." *Id*. at 3048–3049.

To remedy the deficiencies in the statute and achieve more certainty, the present version of 42 U.S.C. § 1395nn(b)(2) was enacted. It provides:

"whoever knowingly and willfully offers or pays any remuneration (including any kickback, bribe or rebate) directly or indirectly, overtly or covertly in cash or in kind to induce such person-

(B) to purchase, lease, order, or arrange for or recommend purchasing . . . or ordering any . . . service or item for which payment may be made . . . under this title, shall be guilty of a felony."

The district judge instructed the jury that the government was required to prove that Cardio-Med paid to Dr. Avallone some part of the amount received from Medicare; that defendant caused Cardio-Med to make the payment; and did so knowingly and willfully as well as with the intent to induce Dr. Avallone to use Cardio-Med's services for patients covered by Medicare. The judge further charged that even if the physician interpreting the test did so as a consultant to Cardio-Med, that fact was immaterial if a purpose of the fee was to induce the ordering of services from Cardio-Med.

Defendant contends that the charge was erroneous. He insists that absent a showing that the only purpose behind the fee was to improperly induce future services, compensating a physician for services actually rendered could not be a violation of the statute.

The government argues that Congress intended to combat financial incentives to physicians for ordering particular services patients did not require.

The language and purpose of the statute support the government's view. Even if the physician performs some service for the money received, the potential for unnecessary drain on the Medicare system remains. The statute is aimed at the inducement factor.

The text refers to "any remuneration." That includes not only sums for which no actual service was performed but also those amounts for which some professional time was expended. "Remunerates" is defined as "to pay an equivalent for service." Webster Third New International Dictionary (1966). By including such items as kickbacks and bribes, the statute expands "remuneration" to cover situations where no service is performed. That a particular payment was a remuneration (which implies that a service was rendered) rather than a kickback, does not foreclose the possibility that a violation nevertheless could exist.

In *United States v. Hancock*, 604 F.2d 999 (7th Cir.1979), the court applied the term "kickback" found in the predecessor statute to payments made to chiropractors by laboratories which performed blood tests. The chiropractors contended that the amounts they received were legitimate handling fees for their services in obtaining, packaging, and delivering the specimens to the laboratories and then interpreting the results. The court rejected that contention and noted, "The potential for increased costs to the Medicare-Medicaid system and misapplication of federal funds is plain, where payments for the exercise of such judgments are added to the legitimate cost of the transaction . . . [T]hese are among the evils Congress sought to prevent by enacting the kickback statutes. . . ." *Id.* at 1001.

Hancock strongly supports the government's position here, because the statute in that case did not contain the word "remuneration." The court nevertheless held that "kickback" sufficiently described the defendants' criminal activity. By adding "remuneration" to the statute in the 1977 amendment, Congress sought to make it clear that even if the transaction was not considered to be a "kickback" for which no service had been rendered, payment nevertheless violated the Act.

We are aware that in *United States v. Porter*, 591 F.2d 1048 (5th Cir.1979), the Court of Appeals for the Fifth Circuit took a more narrow view of "kickback" than did the court in *Hancock*. *Porter's* interpretation of the predecessor statute which did not include "remuneration" is neither binding nor persuasive. We agree with the Court of Appeals for the Sixth Circuit, which adopted the interpretation of "kickback" used in *Hancock* and rejected that of the *Porter* case. *United States v. Tapert*, 625 F.2d 111 (6th Cir.1980). *See also United States v. Duz-Mor Diagnostic Laboratory, Inc.*, 650 F.2d 223, 227 (9th Cir.1981).

We conclude that the more expansive reading is consistent with the impetus for the 1977 amendments and therefore hold that the district court correctly instructed the jury. If the payments were intended to induce the physician to use Cardio-Med's services, the statute was violated, even if the payments were also intended to compensate for professional services.

A review of the record also convinces us that there was sufficient evidence to sustain the jury's verdict.

* * *

Notes and Questions

1. *The implications of* Greber. What are the implications of *Greber's* holding that if "one purpose" of a payment is to induce referrals the payment violates the AKS? What will happen in other cases where the financial arrangement has more than one purpose? What are the potential criticisms of *Greber's* holding?

2. *Payments for professional services.* Greber demonstrates that an agreement does not have to expressly provide for payments for referrals to violate the AKS. Courts will look beyond the stated intention of the parties to determine whether the contract is actually for patient referrals. Courts will also look at the value of the services provided and whether providers are being over compensated for their services.

3. *The influence of* Greber's *"one purpose" test.* Courts have overwhelmingly embraced the *Greber* court's "one purpose" test. *See United States v. McClatchey*, 217 F.3d 823 (10th Cir. 2000) (adopting the *Greber* "one purpose" test and rejecting the "primary purpose" test advanced by the defense); *United States v. Kats*, 871 F.2d 105 (9th Cir. 1989) (adopting the *Greber* "one purpose" test); *United States v. Bay State Ambulance and Hospital Rental, Inc.*, 874 F.2d 20 (1st Cir. 1989) (citing the *Greber* "one-purpose" test with approval).

4. *The federal government's health care costs.* In making its determination, should the court have considered whether the remuneration actually increased the

government's health care costs? Or would considering the increase in costs unduly complicate the court's inquiry?

5. *Carving out federal health care patients.* Would the scheme in *Greber* have run afoul of the AKS if the "interpretation fees" were only paid to referring physicians for non-federally insured patients? The OIG has been skeptical of attempts to carve out federal health care patients from arrangements that provide remuneration in return for referrals when the referral source is referring both federal and non-federal health care patients. In the OIG's view, the remuneration is for the referral of both the federal and non-federal health care patients. In OIG Advisory Opinion 11-08, the OIG stated:

> The Existing Arrangement covers services provided to non-Federally insured patients only. Thus, as a threshold matter, we must address whether the "carve out" of Federal business is dispositive of the question of whether the Existing Arrangement implicates the anti-kickback statute. It is not. The OIG has a long-standing concern about arrangements pursuant to which parties "carve out" Federal health care program beneficiaries or business generated by Federal health care programs from otherwise questionable financial arrangements. Such arrangements implicate and may violate the anti-kickback statute by disguising remuneration for Federal business through the payment of amounts purportedly related to non-Federal business. OIG Advisory Opinion 11-08 (Jun. 14, 2011).

d. The Referral Requirement

One key question with respect to the referral requirement is who must be the recipient of the remuneration for the referral. Is it "any person" as stated in the statute or is there some limitation on who must be the recipient of the remuneration in order to violate the statute? Some courts have analyzed the amount of influence that the individual making the referral must have over the health care decision before liability can attach. *See, e.g. United States v. Miles*, 360 F.3d 472 (5th Cir. 2004); *United States v. Polin*, 194 F.3d 863 (7th Cir. 1999). The following case, however, forcefully argues against any such limitation on liability.

United States v. Shoemaker
746 F.3d 614 (5th Cir. 2014)

Garza, Circuit Judge.

* * *

This case concerns a bribe and kickback scheme involving Tri-Lakes Medical Center ("TLMC"), a community hospital in Panola County, Mississippi. In 2004, when the County owned 60% of TLMC, the County's Board of Supervisors appointed David Chandler ("Chandler") to serve as the Chairman of TLMC's Board of Trustees. Chandler had been the County Administrator for almost twenty years, and he was appointed to oversee the sale of the hospital on behalf of the Board of Supervisors. As Chairman, Chandler scheduled and set the agenda for hospital board meetings, contacted department heads for reports, and regularly dealt with Shoemaker, then TLMC's Chief Operating Officer ("COO").

Garner owned and operated a nurse staffing business known as Guardian Angel Nursing and, later, as On-Call Staffing, which provided temporary nurses to area hospitals. In early 2005, TLMC entered into a contract with Guardian Angel Nursing after Chandler had arranged two meetings between company representatives and Shoemaker. Soon thereafter, Chandler requested that Garner pay him $5 for every nursing hour his company billed at TLMC. According to Chandler, the $5 per hour was in return for Chandler's ensuring that TLMC used Garner's company for contract nurses and paid Garner's bills in a timely manner. About once a month, Garner would push Chandler to increase hours for his nurse staffing business at TLMC, and Chandler would lobby Shoemaker accordingly. A few months after this arrangement commenced, Chandler signed a board authorization giving Shoemaker a $50,000 raise. Upon Garner's request, Chandler created invoices that did not directly correlate to billed hours but rather looked as if they were for consulting or tax services; the memo "Accounting Fees" or "Accounting Services" appeared on checks from Garner.

In total, Garner paid Chandler $268,000 as a result of the agreement, and TLMC paid Garner's company approximately $2.3 million for nursing services. Shoemaker's executive assistant testified that Chandler, on behalf of Garner's company, regularly delivered invoices to and picked up checks directly from Shoemaker's office, while other vendors had no such billing practices. Moreover, Garner's nursing company was typically the first vendor paid by TLMC. Over the course of one year, when TLMC engaged a total of seven nursing companies, Garner's company received 40% of the hospital's business.

Meanwhile, in mid-2005, Robert Corkern ("Corkern") contracted to purchase TLMC. However, in order to secure financing, he needed a nonprofit entity that would qualify for a loan backed by the United States Department of Agriculture ("USDA"). Shoemaker offered Corkern the use of a non-profit under his control called Kaizen, and Corkern transferred to Kaizen his right to purchase TLMC. Subsequently, Kaizen's name was changed to Physicians and Surgeons Hospital Group ("PSHG"). In the fall of 2005, Chandler signed on behalf of TLMC a contract providing PSHG with rights to purchase the hospital from Panola County and the City of Batesville. Thereafter, PSHG purchased TLMC for approximately $27 million. Once the sale was finalized, Chandler left the Board, and Shoemaker was promoted from COO to Chief Executive Officer ("CEO").

Soon thereafter, Shoemaker began claiming that Garner and Corkern owed him money. Just prior to the sale of the hospital, Chandler had arranged a meeting between Shoemaker and Garner at the Como Steakhouse. During the meeting, Garner excused Chandler from the table, whereupon Garner and Shoemaker conversed privately for approximately thirty minutes. After the sale of the hospital, Shoemaker demanded $25,000 from Chandler, claiming that Garner had "promised" that sum in return for Shoemaker's maintaining the flow of nursing hours and payments to

Garner's business. Chandler recounted this conversation to Garner, who initially did not respond. Chandler then proposed that he would begin paying Shoemaker $2,000 per month, and Garner replied that he did not care what Chandler did as long as the money came out of Chandler's $5-per-hour fee. Chandler testified that he ultimately paid Shoemaker a total of $12,000 over six months.

* * *

Garner and Shoemaker were subsequently charged in twelve counts of the Superseding Indictment. Both Garner and Shoemaker were charged with two counts of conspiracy in violation of 18 U.S.C. § 371: Count One charged conspiracy to violate 18 U.S.C. § 666 by bribing Chandler and Shoemaker, and Count Four charged conspiracy to violate 42 U.S.C. § 1320a-7b, based on the same facts alleged in Count One. . . .

After a nine-day trial, the jury found both Garner and Shoemaker guilty on all counts. Both defendants filed motions for judgment of acquittal on all counts or, in the alternative, a new trial. The district court then granted judgments of acquittal and, in the alternative, new trials to Garner as to Counts One, Two, Four, and Five, and to Shoemaker on Counts One and Four. . . .

The Government now appeals all judgments of acquittal and grants of new trials. Shoemaker appeals from his remaining convictions.

Regarding the first conspiracy in Count Four, the district court reasoned that in order for the convictions under 42 U.S.C. § 1320a-7b(b)(2) to stand, the Government had to present evidence establishing that Chandler was a "relevant decisionmaker." The district court concluded that because "[i]t is undisputed that Chandler had no decision-making authority in regard to the actual procurement of nursing staff," he could not be a "relevant decisionmaker."

Enacted as part of the Medicare-Medicaid Anti-Fraud and Abuse Amendments, 42 U.S.C. § 1320a-7b(b)(2) criminalizes the payment of remuneration under two related circumstances:

> (2) whoever knowingly and willfully offers or pays any remuneration (including any kickback, bribe, or rebate) directly or indirectly, overtly or covertly, in cash or in kind to any person to induce such person —
>
> (A) to refer an individual to a person for the furnishing or arranging for the furnishing of any item or service for which payment may be made in whole or in part under a Federal health care program, or
>
> (B) to purchase, lease, order, or arrange for or recommend purchasing, leasing, or ordering any good, facility, service, or item for which payment may be made in whole or in part under a Federal health care program, shall be guilty of a felony and upon conviction thereof, shall be fined not more than $25,000 or imprisoned for not more than five years, or both.

42 U.S.C. § 1320a-7b(b)(2)(A), (B). Thus, the statute prohibits payments to "any person," so long as the payment is made with the requisite intent: The payer must

"knowingly and willfully" offer or make a payment to induce the recipient either "to refer an individual to a person" for the provision of a covered healthcare good or service under subsection (A), or "to purchase, lease, order, or arrange for or recommend" procuring a covered healthcare good or service under subsection (B).

Here, applying the statute and viewing the evidence in the light most favorable to the jury's verdict, we hold that sufficient evidence supported Garner's and Shoemaker's convictions for conspiring to pay Chandler with the intent "to induce [Chandler to] arrange for or recommend" procuring nursing services from Garner. 42 U.S.C. §1320a-7b(b)(2)(B). The Government introduced evidence that Chandler requested that Garner pay him $5 per hour for every nursing hour billed and collected at TLMC—payments that, according to Chandler, were in return for his ensuring that TLMC used Garner's company for contract nurses. About once a month, Garner would push Chandler to increase his company's nursing hours at TLMC, and Chandler would lobby Shoemaker accordingly. Moreover, Chandler testified that he ultimately paid Shoemaker a total of $12,000 over six months in order to maintain influence over Shoemaker. In short, the evidence sufficiently established that a conspiracy existed to violate 42 U.S.C. §1320a-7b(b)(2)(B) by paying Chandler— a recipient who was "any person"—to induce him to recommend that Shoemaker direct business to Garner's company.

The district court, however, read *United States v. Miles*, 360 F.3d 472 (5th Cir.2004), to limit drastically the meaning of "any person," such that liability cannot attach unless the "person" who receives remuneration is a "relevant decisionmaker" with formal authority to effect the desired referral or recommendation. The Government, Shoemaker, and Garner all agree that the district court's reading of *Miles* is correct; the Government submits only that Chandler was in fact a "relevant decisionmaker" by virtue of his role in TLMC's senior administration. But as explained below, *Miles* imposed no such limitation on the meaning of "any person" and is wholly inapplicable to this case.

In *Miles*, we considered whether sufficient evidence supported convictions under §1320a-7b(b)(2)(A) for alleged healthcare kickbacks paid in return for advertising services. *Id.* at 480. The *Miles* defendants were owners of APRO, a home healthcare company. Premier, a public relations firm, distributed promotional materials about APRO to local doctors' offices. After a physician decided to use APRO's services for a patient, the physician would contact Premier, which then furnished APRO with billing information. *Id.* at 479. For every patient who used APRO's services because of Premier's advertising, the defendants paid Premier $300. *Id.* We prefaced our analysis by explaining that "[t]he only issue in dispute is whether Premier's activities constituted referrals within the meaning of the statute," as the statute only criminalizes payments with the intent to induce such referrals. *Miles*, 360 F.3d at 480. We reasoned that "[t]here was no evidence that Premier had any authority to act on behalf of a physician in selecting the particular home health care provider." *Id.* at 480. We explained that "[t]he payments from APRO to Premier were not made to the relevant decisionmaker as an inducement or kickback for sending patients to APRO." *Id.* Accordingly, we concluded that "APRO's payments to Premier were not illegal kickbacks" prohibited by 42 U.S.C. §1320a7b(b)(2)(A), and vacated the relevant convictions.

Thus, *Miles* drew a distinction not between types of payees — "relevant decision-makers" and others — but between a payer's intent to induce "referrals," which is illegal, and the intent to compensate advertisers, which is permissible. Moreover, the factual and procedural context of that case constrained our holding. *Miles* accordingly stands for a narrow legal proposition: Where advertising facilitates an independent decision to purchase a healthcare good or service, and where there is no evidence that the advertiser "unduly influence[s]" or "act[s] on behalf of" the purchaser, the mere fact that the good or service provider compensates the advertiser following each purchase is insufficient to support the provider's conviction for making a payment "to refer an individual to a person" under 42 U.S.C. §1320a-7b(b)(2)(A). *Miles*, 360 F.3d at 480.

Miles is inapplicable to the facts before us. Here, advertising services are not at issue. Moreover, sufficient evidence established that the payments to Chandler aimed to induce him to "recommend" Garner's company. 42 U.S.C. §1320a7b(b)(2)(B). That is, in paying Chandler, Garner was not asking for a brochure bearing his company's name to be distributed to TLMC staff; rather, enough evidence showed that he wanted Chandler to exploit his personal access to TLMC executives, including Shoemaker, and to ensure that TLMC favored Garner's company when it chose nursing services. This conduct is an archetypal example of the undue influence prohibited by the statute.

Contrary to the district court's opinion and the parties' submissions, we did not hold in *Miles* that a payee with "relevant decisionmaker" status is an independent, substantive requirement of the statute. Such a novel move would be tantamount to re-writing the statutory text, which, as noted above, criminalizes payments to "any person[s]," so long as they are made with the requisite intent. *See United States v. Polin*, 194 F.3d 863, 866 (7th Cir.1999) ("The different subsections [(A) and (B)] do not distinguish between physicians and lay-persons."). Rather, we merely used the term "relevant decisionmaker" as shorthand — to characterize remuneration recipients who were paid with the culpable intent to induce "referrals." *Miles*, 360 F.3d at 480. Premier, as a public relations firm that did not unduly influence doctors through its advertising services, could not have been paid with the requisite corrupt intent to induce such "referrals"; therefore, it was not a "relevant decisionmaker." *Id.* In short, this label merely represents the statute's requirement that remuneration must be paid with certain illegal ends in mind.

The consequences of the district court's reading of the statute and *Miles* would be untenable. By its logic, if a bribe-giver wanted to avoid liability, he could simply identify the individual with direct operational authority over the desired decision, and bribe a manager who is at least one level removed in the chain of command, since the manager would have no direct, formal, day-to-day authority over the targeted decision. Alternatively, he could also avoid liability by paying a third party external to the organization to, in turn, bribe the decisionmaker within the organization. Such a view of the law ignores the statutory text, which limits liability not by narrowing the field of "any person," but by defining culpable intent. Indeed, intent was the focus of our inquiry in *Miles*—specifically the question of whether the evidence could establish intent to induce "referrals." *Id.* at 480. The focus on intent, not titles or formal authority, also accords with Congress's concerns in enacting the statute—to broaden liability to reach operatives who leverage fluid, informal power and influence. *Cf. Polin*, 194 F.3d at 866 (concluding that reading § 1320a-7b(b)(2) to criminalize only payments to physicians who select pacemaker monitoring service providers, and not payments to a pacemaker salesperson who influences physicians' choices, is "clearly a perversion of the Act").

For the foregoing reasons, we VACATE the district court's grants of Garner's and Shoemaker's motions for judgment of acquittal and new trial, AFFIRM Shoemaker's other convictions, and REMAND for reinstatement of the jury verdict and for sentencing.

Notes and Questions

1. *Relevant decisionmaker.* In this case, both the government and defendant agreed that the payee had to be a "relevant decisionmaker" in order for liability to attach. Does the court's rejection of the "relevant decisionmaker" standard make sense? Are you convinced by the court's explanation that the "relevant decisionmaker" inquiry is really a question about intent? Should intent to induce a referral be the only consideration?

2. *Any person.* Do you agree that "any person" can be the payee? The court makes an important point about being able to avoid liability under the "relevant decisionmaker" test by paying someone external to the organization who can influence the decisionmaker. Even if the court does not use the "relevant decisionmaker" test, should there be some other limitation on who could be the payee? Should it be relevant whether the payee actually has the ability to influence the referral decision?

Problem

6-1. Richard Anthony owns a commercial building in a major metropolitan area where he has a medical laboratory that performs routine medical tests. The medical laboratory is one of the largest and most respected laboratories in the city. The medical laboratory does not occupy the entire building. Richard is considering renting space in the building. He puts an ad in the local medical journal advertising the space for $15 per square foot per year. The space ranges from 1,000 to 2,000 square feet. Dr. Charlene Fisher is a primary care physician who has a family medical practice. She regularly treats Medicare and Medicaid patients. She sees the ad in the local medical journal and is excited because other buildings in the area rent space for $20 to $25 per square foot per year. She calls Richard Anthony about the space. During the conversation, Richard mentions that the laboratory is located in the building and Dr. Fisher tells him that she has used the laboratory on many occasions over the years. After Dr. Fisher visits the space, she signs a lease to rent 1500 square feet at $15 per square foot per year. After she signs the lease, Dr. Fisher refers 80% of her Medicare and Medicaid patients who need routine medical tests to Richard Anthony's medical laboratory because it is convenient for her patients to obtain their tests in the same building as her office.

The government launches an investigation into Dr. Fisher's referrals to Richard Anthony's medical laboratory. Assume that you represent Dr. Fisher.

What arguments might you assert if the government pursues charges against Dr. Fisher under 42 U.S.C. § 1320a-7b? What is the government's likelihood of success at trial on AKS charges? Why? Would the government have a stronger or weaker case against Richard Anthony?

2. Statutory Exceptions and Safe Harbors

The AKS contains a number of statutory exceptions and safe harbor provisions. In 1987, Congress required HHS to create regulatory safe harbors to designate commercial arrangements as legal that would otherwise violate the plain language of AKS. Medicare and Medicaid Patient & Program Protection Act of 1987, Pub. L. No. 100-93, 101 Stat. 682 (1987). Congress explained that "the breadth of [AKS] ... created uncertainty among health care providers as to which commercial arrangements are legitimate, and which are prohibited." S. Rep. 109, 100th Congress, 1st Sess. 27 (1987). The government will not prosecute a provider for a transaction that satisfies all of the elements of a safe harbor provision "even though unlawful intent may be present." 62 Fed. Reg. 7350, 7351 (Feb. 19, 1997).

The fact that a transaction does not satisfy all of the elements of a safe harbor provision, however, does not automatically mean that the transaction is illegal. Instead, the legality of the transaction must be decided on a case-by-case basis. The OIG will seek to determine whether the arrangement is abusive and warrants prosecution. An arrangement may be considered abusive if it increases costs to the federal health care programs, but the OIG has not specified generic criteria to be used in assessing every business arrangement. 56 Fed. Reg. 35952, 35956 (Jul. 19, 1991). Some of the safe harbors correspond to exceptions within the statute.

As explained in the Introductory Notes to this chapter, health care providers have been moving away from fee-for-service reimbursement and toward value-based reimbursement. HHS has been analyzing the issue to determine whether regulatory reforms are necessary to assist in the transition. On November 20, 2020, HHS issued a final rule, "Revisions to Safe Harbors under the Anti-Kickback Statute, and Civil Monetary Penalties Rules Regarding Beneficiary Inducements" [the "Final Rule"], that will go into effect on January 19, 2021. 85 Fed. Reg. 77684 (Dec. 2, 2020). The Final Rule is designed to improve coordination of patient care among providers and across care settings. Care coordination often involves arrangements between providers that refer Medicare and Medicaid patients to one another as well as an exchange of remuneration making them likely to run afoul of the AKS. In this context, the remuneration could be staff sharing, such as care coordinators, or technology, such as data analytics tools used to achieve performance outcomes. The new safe harbors will protect financial arrangements among parties participating in value-based arrangements and care coordination activities. It will also enhance the protection for transfers of information technology, data, and cybersecurity tools. The safe harbors vary by the types of remuneration protected, level of financial risk assumed by the parties, and types of safeguards included as safe harbor conditions. The new safe harbors will be critical in allowing health care providers to coordinate care and improve health outcomes without running afoul of the AKS. It is too soon to know, however, whether the safe harbor conditions will be strong enough to protect against fraud.

a. The Employment Exception and Safe Harbor

One of the more important statutory exceptions is for payments to employees. Without an exception or safe harbor, employers and employees may be in violation of the AKS if the employee assists in the solicitation of program-related business. The claim would be that the payment to the employee is to induce referrals of program-related business. Even if the employee performs other services as part of the employment, it would violate the AKS because of *Greber's* "one purpose" test. The employment exception applies to "any amount paid by an employer to an employee (who has a bona fide employment relationship with such employer) for employment in the provision of covered items or services." 42 U.S.C. § 1320a-7b(b)(3)(B). Importantly, independent contractors fall outside of the statutory exception for employees. The safe harbor provision similarly states that "remuneration does not include any amount paid by an employer to an employee, who has a bona fide employment relationship with the employer, for employment in the furnishing of an item or service for which payment may be made in whole or in part under Medicare, Medicaid or other federal health care programs." 42 C.F.R. § 1001.952(i).

The safe harbor relies on the Internal Revenue Code's definition of an employee in 26 U.S.C. § 3121(d)(2). Under that definition, an employee is "any individual who, under the usual common law rules applicable in determining the employer-employee relationship, has the status of an employee." 26 U.S.C. § 3121(d)(2). The Supreme Court has held that when a federal statute refers to the common law definition of employee, the statute incorporates the "general common law of agency." *Nationwide Mut. Ins. Co. v. Darden*, 503 U.S. 318, 323 (1992). The status of the worker as an "employee" is based on "the hiring party's right to control the manner and means" of the work performed, which is determined by the following factors:

> the skill required; the source of the instrumentalities and tools; the location of the work; the duration of the relationship between the parties; whether the hiring party has the right to assign additional projects to the hired party; the extent of the hired party's discretion over when and how long to work; the method of payment; the hired party's role in hiring and paying assistants; whether the work is part of the regular business of the hiring

party; whether the hiring party is in business; the provision of employee benefits; and the tax treatment of the hired party.

Id. at 323–24 (internal quotation marks omitted).

* * *

Despite the fact that the employment exception and safe harbor is of critical importance for health care providers, there have been very few reported cases that address the exception or safe harbor. In addition, the OIG is not permitted to provide advisory opinions on the question of whether an individual is a bona fide employee within the requirements of section 3121(d)(2) of the Internal Revenue Code. The following case is one of the only cases to address the question of whether someone is a bona fide employee for purposes of the AKS exception and safe harbor.

United States v. Borrasi

639 F.3d 774 (7th Cir. 2011)

KANNE, CIRCUIT JUDGE.

Roland Borrasi, a medical doctor, was convicted of Medicare fraud after he accepted a salary from a hospital in exchange for continually referring patients to the facility, a violation of 42 U.S.C. §1320a-7b. In this appeal, Borrasi attacks both his conviction and his sentence. We find that the district court did not err by admitting minutes from hospital committee meetings to prove attendance records while excluding discussion of reports to which the minutes refer, as the latter constituted inadmissible hearsay. Because the Medicare fraud statute criminalizes payments when induction of referrals is among the purposes for the payments, we also find that the district court did not err in instructing the jury. Accordingly, we affirm his conviction....

Dr. Borrasi owned Integrated Health Centers, S.C. ("Integrated"), a corporate group of healthcare providers in Romeoville, Illinois. He worked primarily at nursing homes and hospitals. Through this work, he became acquainted with Chief Executive Officer Wendy Mamoon, Director of Operations Mahmood Baig, and other officers and directors of Rock Creek Center, L.P., a licensed inpatient psychiatric hospital in Lemont, Illinois. Reimbursements from the Medicare federal health care program constituted the vast majority of payments received by Rock Creek.

At some time between 1999 and 2002, Borrasi, Mamoon, Baig, and others conspired to pay bribes to Borrasi and other individuals at Integrated in exchange for an increasing stream of Medicare patient referrals. Doctors Zafer Jawich, Bruce Roper, and Abhin Singla, as well as psychologist Agnes Jonas, were among those employed at Integrated at that time. Over that period, a sum of $647,204 in potential bribes was paid to Borrasi and Integrated physicians by Rock Creek. In 2001 alone, Borrasi referred approximately 484 Medicare patients to Rock Creek.

In order to conceal these bribes, Borrasi and other Integrated employees were placed on the Rock Creek payroll, given false titles and faux job descriptions, and asked to submit false time sheets. Borrasi, for example, was named "Service Medical Director" and was allegedly required to be available at all times; Baig later testified that Borrasi was not expected to perform any of the duties listed in his job description. According to minutes of Rock Creek's various committee meetings, Borrasi and some Integrated physicians occasionally attended meetings and submitted reports of their work. But they attended only a very small percentage of the actual meetings, and multiple witnesses testified to rarely seeing them in the Rock Creek facility for meetings or other duties. Jonas, Jawich, and Roper each testified that the Integrated physicians did not perform their assigned administrative duties, their reports and time sheets notwithstanding. Baig testified that he, Borrasi, and Mamoon did not expect the Integrated physicians to perform any actual administrative duties.

In addition, Rock Creek paid the salary for Integrated's secretary, as well as lease payments for one of Integrated's offices. This arrangement purportedly gave Rock Creek an outpatient clinic at Borrasi's building and certainly supplemented Borrasi's rent. Further, Baig was paid both to oversee the admission and stays of Integrated's referrals to Rock Creek and also to ensure the referred patients were returned to nursing homes and facilities that Borrasi could access and control. These methods enabled Rock Creek and Borrasi to maximize their Medicare reimbursement claims.

In December 2006, a grand jury returned an indictment against Borrasi, Mamoon, and Baig, charging them with one count of conspiracy to defraud the United States government, in violation of 18 U.S.C. § 371, and six counts each of Medicare-related bribery, in violation of 42 U.S.C. § 1320a-7b et seq. Baig pled guilty to all seven counts, but Mamoon and Borrasi proceeded to trial. The three-week trial included testimony from Integrated and Rock Creek employees; documentary evidence comprising time sheets, attendance records from meeting minutes, and Medicare reimbursement claims; and recordings of Borrasi's conversations with Integrated physicians recorded by Singla, including one in which Borrasi admitted to referring patients in exchange for "free money" from Rock Creek. The jury returned verdicts of guilty on each count against Borrasi and Mamoon.

A. Challenges to Conviction

At the conclusion of his trial, Borrasi moved for a new trial or, in the alternative, a judgment of acquittal, alleging twelve separate grounds for relief that included alleged evidentiary, procedural, and instructional errors. On appeal, he wisely limits his attack on his conviction to two allegations of error. . . . His first allegation of error involves an evidentiary ruling, and the second focuses on the government's commentary during closing arguments regarding the statute he was charged with violating. We find neither argument persuasive.

* * *

2. Interpretation of 42 U.S.C. § 1320a-7b

Borrasi's second challenge to his conviction turns on the interpretation of the criminal statute he was charged with violating and conspiring to violate. Because medical services for the patients Borrasi referred to Rock Creek were paid for by Medicare, his referrals and conduct were subject to certain statutory restrictions. Borrasi was charged, for example, with violating one statute designed to help combat health care fraud:

> [W]hoever knowingly and willfully solicits or receives any remuneration (including any kickback, bribe, or rebate) . . . in return for referring an individual to a person for the furnishing or arranging for the furnishing of any item or service for which payment may be made in whole or in part under a Federal health care program . . . shall be guilty of a felony and upon conviction thereof, shall be fined not more than $25,000 or imprisoned for not more than five years, or both.

42 U.S.C. §1320a-7b(b)(1). The government theorized that Borrasi and the other Integrated physicians received payments—in the guise of salaries—from Rock Creek for their referrals of Medicare patients.

Borrasi points out, however, that the statute exempts some behavior from its coverage. It does not criminalize "any amount paid by an employer to an employee (who has a bona fide employment relationship with such employer) for employment in the provision of covered items or services." 42 U.S.C. §1320a-7b(b)(3). Seizing this language, Borrasi argues that the prosecution prejudicially misstated the law in its closing argument by suggesting that it did not matter if any portion of Rock Creek's payments to him or other Integrated physicians was pursuant to legitimate employment relationships because the statute was violated if any portion of the payments was for patient referrals. He contends that the government's argument to the jury nullified his theory of defense and that the district court did not cure the misconduct by striking the argument and by giving an adequate curative instruction.

Because Borrasi's challenge to the district court's jury instructions necessarily implicates a question of law — the scope of §1320a-7b(b)(3)'s exemption — we review the district court's instructions de novo. . . .

Borrasi urges us to adopt a "primary motivation" doctrine, under which the trier of fact would determine the defendants' intent in any given case and find them not guilty if the primary motivation behind the remuneration was to compensate for bona fide services provided. Under the primary motivation doctrine, the district court's instructions in this case would have been both inaccurate as to the law and inadequate to cure any prejudice from the government's statements during its closing arguments. He contends that such a construction is necessary both to avoid the possibility of conviction based on innocent or de minimis conduct and also to give effect to the rule of lenity in the face of statutory ambiguity.

Persuasive authority weighs heavily against Borrasi's proposal. He relies on *United States v. Bay State Ambulance and Hosp. Rental Serv., Inc.*, 874 F.2d 20 (1st Cir.1989), where the First Circuit affirmed the appellants' convictions after "the district court instructed that the defendants could only be found guilty if the payments were made primarily as [referral] inducements." *Id.* at 30. But contrary to his allegation, there does not appear to be a circuit split regarding the appropriate interpretation of §1320a-7b(b). The First Circuit did not decide in Bay State "whether the government must show that such payments were made primarily or solely with a corrupt intent." *Id.* Rather, it held that the district court's instruction at least "comport[ed] with congressional intent." *Id.* Each circuit to actually reach the issue has rejected the primary motivation theory Borrasi advocates. *See United States v. Greber*, 760 F.2d 68, 71 (3d Cir.1985) ("The text refers to 'any remuneration.' That includes not only sums for which no actual service was performed but also those amounts for which some professional time was expended."); *United States v. Davis*, 132 F.3d 1092, 1094 (5th Cir.1998) (holding that §1320a-7b(b)(2) is violated whenever the benefits extended were partially to induce patient referrals); *United States v. Kats*, 871 F.2d 105, 108 (9th Cir.1989) ("[T]he Medicare fraud statute is violated if 'one purpose of the payment was to induce future referrals.'" (quoting *Greber*, 760 F.2d at 69)); *United States v. McClatchey*, 217 F.3d 823, 835 (10th Cir.2000) ("[A] person who offers or pays remuneration to another person violates the Act so long as one purpose of the offer or payment is to induce Medicare or Medicaid patient referrals.").

We find the reasoning of the Third, Fifth, Ninth, and Tenth Circuits convincing, and we decline Borrasi's invitation to create a circuit split. Nothing in the Medicare fraud statute implies that only the primary motivation of remuneration is to be considered in assessing Borrasi's conduct. We join our sister circuits in holding that if part of the payment compensated past referrals or induced future referrals, that portion of the payment violates 42 U.S.C. §1320a-7b(b)(1).

The district court's instructions comported with this common-sense holding. The instruction tracked the language of §1320a-7b(b)(1), combining it with a definition of remuneration. To convict Borrasi, the instruction required the jury to find — beyond a reasonable doubt — that some amount was paid not pursuant to a bona fide employment relationship. The trial court did not err in instructing the jury, and the government's comments during its closing arguments did not entitle Borrasi to a curative instruction. Because at least part of the payments to Borrasi was "intended to induce" him to refer patients to Rock Creek, "the statute was violated, even if the payments were also intended to compensate for professional services." *Greber*, 760 F.2d at 72.

* * *

The district court erred in neither its evidentiary rulings nor its jury instructions, so we AFFIRM the district court's judgment of conviction. . . .

Notes and Questions

1. *Bona fide employment relationship and the Greber "one purpose" test.* Did the court conclude that there was no bona fide employment relationship between Borrasi and Rock Creek? If so, what is the basis for that conclusion? Does the court confuse the

analysis by citing *Greber*? If the court is concluding that there wasn't a bona fide employment relationship (which would be well supported due to the sham arrangements), then the statutory exception is irrelevant to the analysis and the court should examine the intent of the parties. But the court never expressly came to that conclusion before invoking *Greber*. As a result, it allows for a much broader interpretation of the holding. One could interpret *Borrasi* as holding that if one purpose of the employment agreement is to induce referrals then it is in violation of the AKS, notwithstanding a bona fide employment relationship. That seems to be contrary to the purpose of the exception and safe harbor and would call into question many employment arrangements. It is probably true that compensation cannot be paid to employees *solely* for referrals because the exception and safe harbor both refer to remuneration being paid for employment in furnishing or providing covered items or services. That is different, however, from saying that a bona fide employment relationship runs afoul of the AKS because one purpose of the compensation is to induce referrals.

2. *Contract Performance.* Most of the AKS exceptions and safe harbor provisions require written agreements. The problem in *Borrasi* was that the contract was not performed but payment was made on the contract. From a compliance perspective, it is very important to make sure that the performance of contracts are tracked and appropriately documented. If contracts are not performed, the mere creation of an employment relationship through the contract will not bring one within the protection of the bona fide employment relationship exception or safe harbor.

Problem

6-2. South Shore Hospital is a for-profit hospital that participates in various federal health care programs. South Shore Hospital acquires the cardiology practice of Drs. Lincoln and Pratt. The price that South Shore Hospital pays to acquire the practice is similar to prices paid by other hospitals for comparable practices in the area. As a result of the acquisition, Drs. Lincoln and Pratt sign employment contracts with South Shore Hospital. The employment contracts require Drs. Lincoln and Pratt to refer their patients to South Shore Hospital or an affiliated hospital whenever their patients require hospital services. In addition, the employment contract requires that Drs. Lincoln and Pratt give up their surgical privileges at hospitals other than South Shore or its affiliates. Under the contract, Drs. Lincoln and Pratt are not provided an annual salary. Instead, the doctors are compensated based on a percentage of receipts for their professional services. In some cases the percentage differs, depending on whether the doctors provide the services in the hospital or the doctor's office. Regardless of where the work is performed, however, the overall compensation depends on the value of work performed by the individual doctors. South Shore Hospital also pays for malpractice insurance and continuing medical education for Drs. Lincoln and Pratt.

Has there been a violation of the AKS by South Shore Hospital and Drs. Lincoln and Pratt? Why or why not?

b. The Personal Services and Management Contract Safe Harbor

The OIG heavily scrutinizes consulting contracts between physicians and pharmaceutical and medical device manufacturers. In 1994, the OIG issued a special fraud alert on pharmaceutical marketing practices involving physicians. The OIG warned that:

> Physicians, suppliers and, increasingly, patients are being offered valuable, non-medical benefits in exchange for selecting specific prescription drug brands. Traditionally, physicians and pharmacists have been trusted to provide treatments and recommend products in the best interest of the patient. In an era of aggressive drug marketing, however, patients may now be using prescription drug items, unaware that their physician or pharmacist is being compensated for promoting the selection of a specific product.

OIG Special Fraud Alert: Prescription Drug Marketing Schemes (Issued Aug. 1994), republished at 59 Fed. Reg. 65372, 65376 (Dec. 19, 1994). The OIG explained that payments to physicians would be improper under the AKS if the payments were tied to the volume of business generated for the payer and if the compensation is more than nominal in value and exceeds the fair market value for services rendered to the payer, or is unrelated to any service at all other than referral of patients. *Id.*

If a physician consulting agreement is to be legal under the AKS, it must fall into one of the safe harbors. The most likely safe harbor is the provision for personal services and management contracts. The personal services and management contract safe harbor applies to agreements between medical practitioners and providers to perform services for each other. The payments in these agreements may be structured such that the payment is a fixed amount or hourly rate; the parties each perform services and share the profits; or the party may perform a service acting as an agent for a company. Fraud and Abuse OIG Anti-Kickback Provisions, 54 Fed. Reg. 3088-01 (Jan. 23, 1989). The agent might perform administrative services such as billing and collection or management services for the company. *Id.* Although these arrangements may involve referrals between the parties, the arrangements are not per se illegal. "However, if the nature of the agreement is such that payments are intended to induce referrals, or there is an implicit or explicit arrangement where the amount of the payment varies with the volume of referral, the anti-kickback law would apply." *Id.*

To satisfy the safe harbor, the agreement must meet six requirements that are designed to limit the opportunity to provide remuneration in exchange for referrals:

(1) the agreement is in writing and signed by the parties;

(2) the agreement specifies and covers all of the services provided;

(3) the term of the agreement is at least one year;

(4) the methodology for determining the compensation is set in advance, is consistent with fair market value, and is not determined in a manner that takes into account the volume or value of any referrals;

(5) the services under the contract do not involve the counseling or promotion of a business arrangement or other activity that violates any State or federal law; and

(6) the aggregate services contracted for do not exceed those which are reasonably necessary to accomplish the commercially reasonable business purpose of the services.

Although the personal services and management contract safe harbor is of critical importance to pharmaceutical and medical device manufacturers, the courts have not had the opportunity to interpret the safe harbor. Many cases involving improper marketing practices by pharmaceutical manufacturers are settled before going to trial. The OIG has also not had many opportunities to examine the safe harbor in the context of arrangements between pharmaceutical or medical device manufacturers and physicians.

In the Final Rule that addresses the transition from fee-for-service to value-based reimbursement, HHS added a new provision to the personal services and management contracts safe harbor that would protect certain outcome-based payments. An outcome-based payment is either a reward for successfully achieving an outcome measure or a reduction in payment for the failure to achieve an outcome measure. Importantly, the outcome-based payments provision does not apply to pharmaceutical or medical device manufacturers.

Problems

6-3. Big Pharma has a drug that is used for the treatment of multiple sclerosis. The drug has steep competition from a drug produced by Top Pharma. Big Pharma purchases subscriber data for its drug and Top Pharma's drug. Big Pharma enters into contracts with the top 100 physicians who prescribe Top Pharma's drug and the top 50 physicians who prescribe Big Pharma's drug to train them on the benefits of Big Pharma's multiple sclerosis drug so that they can speak at continuing medical education seminars and presentations paid for by Big Pharma. Under the one-year contracts, each doctor receives fixed compensation for speaking at seminars and presentations over the course of one year. The speaking engagements are clearly set forth in the contract. Big Pharma pays the doctors who are top prescribers of Top Pharma's drug 50% more than they pay the top prescribers of Big Pharma's drug. Big Pharma flies the 150 physicians and their spouses to St. Thomas, USVI for the week long training at a five-star resort hotel. The training is three hours per day.

Assume that the doctors do not fulfill their speaking duties under the contract but Big Pharma pays them anyway. Will the contract fall into the safe harbor for personal services contracts? Would your analysis change if the doctors fulfill their speaking duties under the contract?

6-4. Sleep Incorporated is an entity owned by non-physicians that provides sleep disorder diagnostic testing and related services in both freestanding and hospital-owned facilities. City Hospital enters into a one-year contract with Sleep Incorporated to operate a sleep testing facility within City Hospital. Under the contract, City Hospital provides the space for the sleep testing facility and Sleep Incorporated provides the necessary staff, equipment, technology, and supplies to run the hospital sleep testing facility. In addition, Sleep Incorporated provides marketing services for the sleep testing facility in City Hospital. Specifically, Sleep Incorporated provides a marketing manager who visits offices of physician referral sources to educate the physicians and their staffs about City Hospital's sleep testing services and the test ordering process. The marketing manager addresses patient satisfaction issues or referring physician concerns. Physicians refer patients to City Hospital's sleep testing facility. Sleep Incorporated schedules the sleep studies and its technicians perform the studies, evaluate the data, and transmit the results to the interpreting physician. Pursuant to the Agreement, Sleep Incorporated charges the Hospital a per-test fee that covers all items and services furnished in connection with the sleep test, including marketing services. The per-test fee is comparable to fees charged by other providers of sleep tests. After the testing is complete, City Hospital bills insurance companies, federal health care programs, and patients for the sleep studies under its own name. The government has launched an investigation into whether the arrangement between Sleep Incorporated and City Hospital violates 42 U.S.C. §1320a-7b.

Would this arrangement be protected by the personal services and management contract safe harbor? Why or why not? If it is not protected by the safe harbor, what arguments would you make in favor or against finding a violation of the AKS?

6-5. Assume the same factual situation as above except that instead of a per-test fee, City Hospital pays Sleep Incorporated three separate fees: (1) a fixed annual rent for the equipment; (2) a fixed annual fee for marketing services; and (3) a fixed annual fee for supplies and other services.

Does this change your analysis concerning the personal services and management contract safe harbor? Why or why not?

3. The Use of the AKS as a Basis for False Claims Act Cases

As explained in Chapter 18, Civil Actions, Civil Penalties, and Parallel Proceedings, *infra*, the False Claims Act ("FCA"), 18 U.S.C. §§3729–3731, incentivizes whistleblowers to bring claims against individuals or entities that have defrauded the federal government. The FCA imposes liability on anyone who knowingly presents or causes to be presented, a false or fraudulent claim for payment or approval to the federal government. Unlike the FCA, there is no private right of action under the AKS. *U.S. ex rel. Barrett v. Columbia/HCA Healthcare Corp.*, 251 F.Supp.2d 28 (D.D.C. 2003). Thus, in order for an individual to bring a suit alleging a violation of the AKS, she must do so through use of the FCA.

Courts were split on whether or not claims submitted in violation of the AKS were "false" for purposes of the FCA even if all of the items and services on the claim were necessary and provided as claimed. The Patient Protection and Affordable Care Act (PPACA) added a new section to the AKS to resolve the issue. It states that "a claim that includes items or services resulting from a violation of [the AKS] constitutes a false or fraudulent claim" for purposes of the FCA. 42 U.S.C. §1320-7b(g). Therefore, it is now clearly established that a violation of the AKS is actionable under the FCA.

C. Administrative Sanctions: Civil Monetary Penalties, Corporate Integrity Agreements, and Exclusion

In addition to criminal penalties, Congress has also created many civil remedies for violations of the health care fraud and abuse statutes. The government may decide to pursue civil remedies in addition to or instead of criminal charges.

1. Civil Money Penalties — 42 U.S.C. §1320a-7a

The OIG has broad authority to seek administrative remedies to combat fraud and abuse in Medicare and Medicaid. The OIG may impose civil money penalties under the Civil Monetary Penalties Law ("CMPL"), 42 U.S.C. §1320a-7a, to address incidences of health care fraud. For example, the OIG may seek civil money penalties against any person who: (1) presents or causes to be presented claims to a federal health care program that the person knows or should know is for an item or service that was not provided as claimed or is false or fraudulent; or (2) violates the Anti-Kickback Statute. In a case of false or fraudulent claims, the OIG may seek a penalty of up to $20,000 for each item or service improperly claimed, and an assessment of up to three times the amount improperly claimed. 42 U.S.C. §1320a-7a(a). In a kickback case, the OIG may seek a penalty of up to $100,000 for each improper act and damages of up to three times the amount of remuneration at issue (regardless of whether some of the remuneration was for a lawful purpose). 42 U.S.C. §1320a-7a(a).

To bring a civil money penalties case, the OIG issues a demand letter describing the sanction sought. The subject of the action has the right to request a hearing before an administrative law judge ("ALJ") within HHS. In such a hearing, the OIG and the respondent have the right to present evidence and make arguments to the ALJ. Most of the CMPL's provisions have a "know or should know" intent requirement. The CMPL explains that the "term 'should know' means that a person, with respect to information — (A) acts in deliberate ignorance of the truth or falsity of the information; or (B) acts in reckless disregard of the information, and no proof of specific intent to defraud is required." 42 U.S.C. 1320a-7a(i)(7). The ALJ issues a written decision which may be appealed administratively and to federal court.

2. Exclusion

The Social Security Act grants the Secretary of the Department of Health and Human Services the power to exclude individuals and entities from participation in federal health care programs. The Secretary has delegated the exclusion authority to the OIG. The exclusion authority protects the federal health care programs and its beneficiaries from "untrustworthy healthcare providers, i.e. individuals and entities whose behavior has demonstrated that they pose a risk to program beneficiaries or to the integrity of these programs." 67 Fed. Reg. 11,928 (Mar. 18, 2002).

Further, the exclusion authority is not limited to direct providers, such as hospitals or physicians, that receive payment directly from the federal health care programs. Indirect providers, such as pharmaceutical manufacturers, can also be excluded. If the OIG excludes a pharmaceutical company, no hospital or physician can submit a claim for payment for any of the pharmaceutical company's drugs. 42 C.F.R. § 1001.2001. In turn, any Medicare or Medicaid patient who uses that pharmaceutical company's drugs would have to pay for the drugs out of pocket or obtain a prescription for a similar drug from a non-excluded pharmaceutical company.

The exclusion is mandatory in some cases and within the OIG's discretion in other cases. Exclusion is mandatory if the individual or entity is convicted of "program-related" crimes. 42 U.S.C. § 1320a-7(a)(1). The AKS is considered a "program-related" crime that would require mandatory exclusion upon conviction. Exclusion is also mandatory upon a felony conviction "relating to health care fraud." 42 U.S.C. § 1320a-7(a)(1). The mandatory exclusion period for a first-time conviction is a minimum of five years unless the exclusion would pose a hardship on federal health care beneficiaries. 42 U.S.C. § 1320a-7(c)(3)(B). If the AKS violation is found in an administrative proceeding, however, the exclusion is permissive rather than mandatory. 42 U.S.C. § 1320a-7(b)(7). Exclusion is also permissive if the individual or entity is convicted of a misdemeanor offense "relating to" fraud in connection with the delivery of a health care item or service or the unlawful distribution of a controlled substance. 42 U.S.C. § 1320a-7(b)(1). Under this provision, the permissive exclusion period is for three years unless there are mitigating or aggravating circumstances that lead to a shorter or longer period of exclusion. 42 U.S.C. § 1320a-7(c)(3)(D).

At the end of the exclusion period, the excluded individual or entity must request reinstatement to federal health care programs. To be reinstated, the OIG must determine that the individual or entity has not continued to engage in the actions that subjected it to exclusion and that those activities will not recur. The OIG's reinstatement decision is not subject to administrative or judicial review. 42 C.F.R. § 1001.3004(c).

3. Corporate Integrity Agreements

For some entities, such as pharmaceutical manufacturers, exclusion would harm not only the excluded entity, but also federal health care participants. To minimize the harm, the government will pursue a global resolution of the criminal and civil claims against the entity. The DOJ will enter into a settlement to resolve FCA violations and may also require the entity to plead guilty to charges that would not result in a mandatory exclusion. Contemporaneously, OIG will enter into a Corporate Integrity Agreement (CIA) in lieu of excluding the entity from participation in federal health care programs. CIAs are administrative settlements negotiated with OIG to settle alleged violations of federal health care program requirements. Typically, the CIA requires the entity to pay a large fine and enact compliance measures to ensure that violations will not recur. In return, the OIG agrees not to exclude the entity. CIAs typically include the following: (1) a statement that the entity has a compliance program in place; (2) the scope of the agreement, including the responsibility of individuals; (3) corporate integrity obligations, such as the creation of a compliance committee and selection of a compliance officer; (4) training requirements; (5) a toll-free hotline system to allow individuals to anonymously disclose misconduct; (6) reporting requirements for allegations of misconduct; (7) periodic or annual reports to OIG; and (8) the terms under which a breach of the agreement will be found. Ralph F. Hall, *Corporate Integrity Agreements*, in Punishing Corporate Crime: Legal Penalties for Criminal and Regulatory Violations 97, 99–108 (James T. O'Reilly et al., eds. 2009).

Many CIAs also require the entity to hire an independent review organization ("IRO") (typically an accounting firm, law firm, or a consultant) to assess and evaluate the entity's systems and procedures. *Id.* at 106–07. As part of the entity's annual report, CIAs require that the IRO conduct a random review of the entity's paid claims either quarterly or annually. Office of Inspector General, Corporate Integrity Agreement FAQ, https://oig.hhs.gov/faqs/corporate-integrity-agreements-faq .asp. Many CIAs also require the IRO to review the entity's paid claims to ensure that they were correctly coded, submitted, and reimbursed. *Id.* More recent CIAs add on an additional requirement that the IRO determine whether the items or services furnished were medically necessary and appropriately documented. *Id.* Entities must certify compliance with the CIA and all federal health care requirements in their annual report. More recent CIAs require high-level executives to certify compliance, which may subject the executives to personal liability in the event of noncompliance. Hall, *Corporate* Integrity Agreements, *supra*, at 104.

Notes and Questions

1. *The pharmaceutical company enforcement problem.* Most of the major pharmaceutical companies have entered into CIAs for violations related to their marketing practices. The government enters into CIAs with pharmaceutical companies to protect patients from the adverse effects of exclusion. For pharmaceutical manufacturers, the benefits of the CIA far outweigh the potential costs because Medicare and Medicaid bring in billions of dollars of revenue which far surpasses the cost of fines and compliance. *See* Katrice Bridges Copeland, *Enforcing Integrity*, 87 Ind. L.J. 1033, 1053–55 (2012). At the same time, however, the illegal marketing practices bring in revenue that substantially exceeds the costs of CIA fines and compliance. The end

result has been a lack of deterrence. Pharmaceutical companies have continued to engage in illegal marketing practices and the government has not excluded them, even in the face of an existing CIA, because of the harm to patients. Some pharmaceutical companies, like Pfizer, have entered into multiple CIAs. Pfizer's most recent settlement was for $2.3 billion. *Id.* at 1034. What can the government do to curb the illegal marketing practices of pharmaceutical companies? Should they exclude the companies despite the harm to patients? Should Congress create a new exclusion remedy that limits the exclusion to the drugs from the illegal marketing scheme? Should the government have the ability to take away a pharmaceutical company's patent for an illegally marketed drug? Should the government exclude executives for illegal marketing?

2. *The exclusion of responsible corporate officers.* The government has decided to direct some of its enforcement efforts toward responsible corporate officers of pharmaceutical companies. One prominent example involves high-level officers who were charged with misdemeanor violations of the Food, Drug, and Cosmetic Act ("FDCA") as responsible corporate officers after Purdue Pharma entered into a CIA for marketing violations. *See* Chapter 2, Corporate and Individual Liability, *supra,* for a discussion of the responsible corporate officer doctrine. A key question that arose after their guilty pleas was whether it was possible for the OIG to exclude the executives from participation in federal health care programs when they had no knowledge of the misconduct of their subordinates and there was no showing of intent because their crimes were strict liability. In *Friedman v. Sebelius*, the D.C. Circuit upheld the OIG's ability to exclude the executives. 686 F.3d 813 (D.C. Cir. 2012).

Does this send a strong message to executives that they need to monitor their employees more carefully? Is it fair to exclude executives when the company is spared from exclusion by entering into a CIA? If executives should be excluded, what is the appropriate length of exclusion? The baseline period of exclusion in this type of case is three years, but the OIG's exclusion of the Purdue Pharma executives was 12 years. The D.C. Circuit found the length of exclusion to be arbitrary and capricious because the OIG could not justify it based on prior exclusions under the applicable statute. *Id.* at 828. Should the OIG have to show knowledge of the underlying misconduct or other extraordinary factors to lengthen the exclusion period?

Chapter 7

Bribery and Gratuities

A. Introductory Notes

The federal bribery and gratuity statutes, along with the federal extortion statute discussed in the next chapter, provide powerful tools in the effort to combat governmental corruption. Federal law broadly criminalizes both giving bribes and gratuities to federal public officials and receiving such bribes and gratuities. As seen in the cases below, the bribery and gratuity statutes have been interpreted to apply to a wide range of public officials and official acts. In addition, the Foreign Corrupt Practices Act (FCPA) criminalizes bribery of foreign officials.

The expanded federal power raises issues relating to matters traditionally reserved to state and local law enforcement. In addition, this power has given rise to questions as to whether some political bribery prosecutions have been politically motivated. Further, the expanded scope of the federal bribery statutes raises issues of fair notice to potential defendants.

Section 201 of the federal criminal code contains the principal federal bribery and gratuity statute. 18 U.S.C. § 201. Also, § 666 of the federal criminal code criminalizes giving and receiving bribes in connection with federal programs. 18 U.S.C. § 666. Finally, the FCPA, 15 U.S.C. §§ 78dd-1, 78dd-2, 78dd-3, 78m, 78ff, applies to bribery of foreign officials. This chapter covers these three statutes in detail.

B. Section 201

1. Section 201 — Statutory Elements

Section 201 sets forth the distinct crimes of bribery and gratuities, and defines the terms used in those offenses. Under § 201(b), in a case alleging that the defendant *gave, or offered to give, or promised* a bribe, the government must prove that:

(1) The defendant gave, offered to give, or promised something of value;

(2) The recipient or offeree was a federal public official;

(3) The defendant acted with corrupt intent; and

(4) The defendant's scheme was designed to:

    (a) influence the public official in an official act,

    (b) influence the public official to commit a fraud on the United States, or

(c) induce the public official to act in violation of a lawful duty.

In a case alleging that the defendant *demanded, sought, received, accepted, or agreed to receive or accept*, a bribe, the government must prove that:

(1) The defendant demanded, sought, received, accepted, or agreed to receive or accept something of value;

(2) The defendant was a federal public official;

(3) The defendant acted with corrupt intent; and

(4) The scheme was designed to:

  (a) influence the defendant in an official act,

  (b) influence the defendant to commit a fraud on the United States, or

  (c) induce the defendant to act in violation of a lawful duty.

The statute provides that the defendant may be punished by a fine, by imprisonment of not more than 15 years, or both.

In a gratuities prosecution under § 201(c) for *giving, offering, or promising to give* an illegal gratuity, the government must prove that:

(1) The defendant gave or offered to give something of value;

(2) The recipient or offeree was a federal public official; and

(3) The defendant intended that the thing of value be given as compensation for an official act already performed or to be performed otherwise than as provided by law for the proper discharge of the recipient's official duty.

In a case alleging that the defendant *demanded, sought, received, accepted, or agreed to receive or accept* an illegal gratuity, the government must show that:

(1) The defendant received or agreed to receive something of value;

(2) The defendant was a federal public official; and

(3) The defendant received or agreed to receive the thing of value as compensation for an official act already performed or to be performed otherwise than as provided by law for the proper discharge of the defendant's official duty.

The statute provides that the defendant may be punished by a fine, by imprisonment of not more than two years, or both.

2. Defining Bribery and Gratuities

Prior to the United States Supreme Court's decision in the next case, lower courts had long disagreed about the intent that the government must show in order to obtain a conviction for the illegal receipt of a gratuity. In resolving that dispute, the Court endeavored clearly to delineate the difficult distinction between the crimes of bribery and gratuity. As you read this case, consider whether the Court succeeded in that effort.

United States v. Sun-Diamond Growers of California

526 U.S. 398 (1999)

JUSTICE SCALIA delivered the opinion of the Court.

Talmudic sages believed that judges who accepted bribes would be punished by eventually losing all knowledge of the divine law. The Federal Government, dealing with many public officials who are not judges, and with at least some judges for whom this sanction holds no terror, has constructed a framework of human laws and regulations defining various sorts of impermissible gifts, and punishing those who give or receive them with administrative sanctions, fines, and incarceration. One element of that framework is 18 U.S.C. § 201(c)(1)(A), the "illegal gratuity statute," which prohibits giving "anything of value" to a present, past, or future public official "for or because of any official act performed or to be performed by such public official." In this case, we consider whether conviction under the illegal gratuity statute requires any showing beyond the fact that a gratuity was given because of the recipient's official position.

Respondent is a trade association that engaged in marketing and lobbying activities on behalf of its member cooperatives, which were owned by approximately 5,000 individual growers of raisins, figs, walnuts, prunes, and hazelnuts. Petitioner United States is represented by Independent Counsel Donald Smaltz, who, as a consequence of his investigation of former Secretary of Agriculture Michael Espy, charged respondent with, *inter alia*, making illegal gifts to Espy in violation of § 201(c)(1)(A). . . .

Count One of the indictment charged Sun-Diamond with giving Espy approximately $5,900 in illegal gratuities: tickets to the 1993 U.S. Open Tennis Tournament (worth $2,295), luggage ($2,427), meals ($665), and a framed print and crystal bowl ($524). The indictment alluded to two matters in which respondent had an interest in favorable treatment from the Secretary at the time it bestowed the gratuities. First, respondent's member cooperatives participated in the Market Promotion Plan (MPP), a grant program administered by the Department of Agriculture to promote the sale of U.S. farm commodities in foreign countries. The cooperatives belonged to trade organizations, such as the California Prune Board and the Raisin Administrative Committee, which submitted overseas marketing plans for their respective commodities. If their plans were approved by the Secretary of Agriculture, the trade organizations received funds to be used in defraying the foreign marketing expenses of their constituents. Each of respondent's member cooperatives was the largest member of its respective trade organization, and each received significant MPP funding. Respondent was understandably concerned, then, when Congress in 1993 instructed the Secretary to promulgate regulations giving small-sized entities preference in obtaining MPP funds. If the Secretary did not deem respondent's member cooperatives to be small-sized entities, there was a good chance they would no longer receive MPP grants. Thus, respondent had an interest in persuading the Secretary to adopt a regulatory definition of "small-sized entity" that would include its member cooperatives.

Second, respondent had an interest in the Federal Government's regulation of methyl bromide, a low-cost pesticide used by many individual growers in respondent's member cooperatives. In 1992, the Environmental Protection Agency announced plans to promulgate a rule to phase out the use of methyl bromide in the United States. The indictment alleged that respondent sought the Department of Agriculture's assistance in persuading the EPA to abandon its proposed rule altogether, or at least to mitigate its impact. In the latter event, respondent wanted the Department to fund research efforts to develop reliable alternatives to methyl bromide.

Although describing these two matters before the Secretary in which respondent had an interest, the indictment did not allege a specific connection between either of them — or between any other action of the Secretary — and the gratuities conferred. The District Court denied respondent's motion to dismiss Count One because of this omission. 941 F. Supp. 1262 (D.D.C. 1996). The court stated:

> [T]o sustain a charge under the gratuity statute, it is not necessary for the indictment to allege a direct nexus between the value conferred to Secretary Espy by Sun-Diamond and an official act performed or to be performed by Secretary Espy. It is sufficient for the indictment to allege that Sun-Diamond provided things of value to Secretary Espy because of his position.

Id. at 1265.

At trial, the District Court instructed the jury along these same lines. It read § 201(c)(1)(A) to the jury twice, but then placed an expansive gloss on that statutory language, saying, among other things, that "[i]t is sufficient if Sun-Diamond provided Espy with unauthorized compensation simply because he held public office," and that "[t]he government need not prove that the alleged gratuity was linked to a specific or identifiable official act or any act at all." The jury convicted respondent on, *inter alia*, Count One (the only subject of this appeal), and the District Court sentenced respondent on this count to pay a fine of $400,000. . . . [The Court of Appeals reversed, and the Supreme Court granted certiorari.]

Initially, it will be helpful to place § 201(c)(1)(A) within the context of the statutory scheme. Subsection (a) of § 201 sets forth definitions applicable to the section — including a definition of "official act," § 201(a)(3). Subsections (b) and (c) then set forth, respectively, two separate crimes — or two pairs of crimes, if one counts the giving and receiving of unlawful gifts as separate crimes — with two different sets of elements and authorized punishments. The first crime, described in § 201(b)(1) as to the giver, and § 201(b)(2) as to the recipient, is bribery, which requires a showing that something of value was corruptly given, offered, or promised to a public official (as to the giver) or corruptly demanded, sought, received, accepted, or agreed to be received or accepted by a public official (as to the recipient) with intent, *inter alia*, "to influence any official act" (giver) or in return for "being influenced in the performance of any official act" (recipient). The second crime, defined in § 201(c)(1)(A) as to the giver, and in § 201(c)(1)(B) as to the recipient, is illegal gratuity, which requires a showing that something of value was given, offered, or promised to a public official (as to the giver), or demanded, sought, received, accepted, or agreed to be received or accepted by a public official (as to the recipient), "for or because of any official act performed or to be performed by such public official."

➔ The distinguishing feature of each crime is its intent element. Bribery requires intent "to influence" an official act or "to be influenced" in an official act, while illegal gratuity requires only that the gratuity be given or accepted "for or because of" an official act. In other words, for bribery there must be a *quid pro quo* — a specific intent to give or receive something of value *in exchange* for an official act. An illegal gratuity, on the other hand, may constitute merely a reward for some future act that the public official will take (and may already have determined to take), or for a past act that he has already taken. The punishments prescribed for the two offenses reflect their relative seriousness: Bribery may be punished by up to 15 years' imprisonment, a fine of $250,000 ($500,000 for organizations) or triple the value of the bribe, whichever is greater, and disqualification from holding government office. Violation of the illegal gratuity statute, on the other hand, may be punished by up to two years' imprisonment and a fine of $250,000 ($500,000 for organizations).

The District Court's instructions in this case, in differentiating between a bribe and an illegal gratuity, correctly noted that only a bribe requires proof of a *quid pro quo*. The point in controversy here is that the instructions went on to suggest that § 201(c)(1)(A), unlike the bribery statute, did not require any connection between respondent's intent and a specific official act. It would be satisfied, according to the instructions, merely by a showing that respondent gave Secretary Espy a gratuity because of his official position — perhaps, for example, to build a reservoir of goodwill that might ultimately affect one or more of a multitude of unspecified acts, now and in the future. The United States, represented by the Independent Counsel, and the Solicitor General as *amicus curiae*, contend that this instruction was correct. The Independent Counsel asserts that "section 201(c)(1)(A) reaches any effort to buy favor or generalized goodwill from an official who either has been, is, or may at some unknown, unspecified later time, be *in a position to act* favorably to the giver's interests." The Solicitor General contends that § 201(c)(1)(A) requires only a showing that a "gift was motivated, at least in part, by the recipient's *capacity to exercise governmental power or influence* in the donor's favor" without necessarily showing that it was connected to a particular official act.

In our view, this interpretation does not fit comfortably with the statutory text, which prohibits only gratuities given or received "for or because of *any official act* performed or to be performed" (emphasis added). It seems to us that this means "for or because of some particular official act of whatever identity" — just as the question "Do you like any composer?" normally means "Do you like some particular composer?" It is linguistically possible, of course, for the phrase to mean "for or because of official acts in general, without specification as to which one" — just as the question "Do you like any composer?" could mean "Do you like all composers, no matter what their names or music?" But the former seems to us the more natural meaning, especially given the complex structure of the provision before us here. Why go through the trouble of requiring that the gift be made "for or because of any official act performed or to be performed by such public official," and then defining "official act" (in § 201(a)(3)) to mean "any decision or action on any question, matter, cause, suit, proceeding or controversy, which may at any time be pending, or which may by law be brought before any public official, in such official's official capacity," when, if the Government's interpretation were correct, it would have sufficed to say "for or because of such official's ability to favor the donor in executing the functions of his office"? The insistence upon an "official act," carefully defined, seems pregnant with the requirement that some particular official act be identified and proved.

Besides thinking that this is the more natural meaning of § 201(c)(1)(A), we are inclined to believe it correct because of the peculiar results that the Government's alternative reading would produce. It would criminalize, for example, token gifts to the President based on his official position and not linked to any identifiable act — such as the replica jerseys given by championship sports teams each year during ceremonial White House visits. Similarly, it would criminalize a high school principal's gift of a school baseball cap to the Secretary of Education, by reason of his office, on the occasion of the latter's visit to the school. That these examples are not fanciful is demonstrated by the fact that counsel for the United States maintained at oral argument that a group of farmers would violate § 201(c)(1)(A) by providing a complimentary lunch for the Secretary of Agriculture in conjunction with his speech to the farmers concerning various matters of USDA policy — so long as the Secretary had before him, or had in prospect, matters affecting the farmers. Of course the Secretary of Agriculture *always* has before him or in prospect matters that affect farmers, just as the President always has before him or in prospect matters that affect college and professional sports, and the Secretary of Education matters that affect high schools.

It might be said in reply to this that the more narrow interpretation of the statute can also produce some peculiar results. In fact, in the above-given examples, the gifts could easily be regarded as having been conferred, not only because of the official's position as President or Secretary, but also (and perhaps principally) "for or because of" the official acts of receiving the sports teams at the White House, visiting the high school, and speaking to the farmers about USDA policy, respectively. The answer to this objection is that those actions — while they are assuredly "official acts" in some sense — are not "official acts" within the meaning of the statute, which, as we have noted, defines "official act" to mean "any decision or action on any question, matter, cause, suit, proceeding or controversy, which may at any time be pending, or which may by law be brought before any public official, in such official's official capacity, or in such official's place of trust or profit." 18 U.S.C. § 201(a)(3). Thus, when the violation is linked to a particular "official act," it is possible to eliminate the absurdities *through the definition of that term.* When, however, no particular "official act" need be identified, and the giving of gifts by reason of the recipient's mere tenure in office constitutes a violation, nothing but the Government's discretion prevents the foregoing examples from being prosecuted.

The Government insists that its interpretation is the only one that gives effect to all of the statutory language. Specifically, it claims that the "official position" construction is the only way to give effect to § 201(c)(1)(A)'s forward-looking prohibition on gratuities to persons who have been selected to be public officials but have not yet taken office. Because, it contends, such individuals would not know of specific matters that would come before them, the only way to give this provision effect is to interpret "official act" to mean "official position." But we have no trouble envisioning the application of § 201(c)(1)(A) to a selectee for federal office under the more narrow interpretation. If, for instance, a large computer company that has planned to merge with another large computer company makes a gift to a person who has been chosen to be Assistant Attorney General for the Antitrust Division of the Department of Justice and who has publicly indicated his approval of the merger, it would be quite possible for a jury to find that the gift was made "for or because of" the person's anticipated decision, once he is in office, not to challenge the merger. The uncertainty of future action seems to us, in principle, no more an impediment to prosecution of a selectee with respect to some future official act than it is to prosecution of an officeholder with respect to some future official act.

Our refusal to read § 201(c)(1)(A) as a prohibition of gifts given by reason of the donee's office is supported by the fact that when Congress has wanted to adopt such a broadly prophylactic criminal prohibition upon gift giving, it has done so in a more precise and more administrable fashion. For example, another provision of Chapter 11 of Title 18, the chapter entitled "Bribery, Graft, and Conflicts of Interest," criminalizes the giving or receiving of any "supplementation" of an Executive official's salary, without regard to the purpose of the payment. Other provisions of the same chapter make it a crime for a bank employee to give a bank examiner, and for a bank examiner to receive from a bank employee, "any loan or gratuity," again without regard to the purpose for which it is given. A provision of the Labor Management Relations Act makes it a felony for an employer to give to a union representative, and for a union representative to receive from an employer, anything of value. With clearly framed and easily administrable provisions such as these on the books imposing gift-giving and gift-receiving prohibitions specifically based upon the holding of office, it seems to us most implausible that Congress intended the language of the gratuity statute — "for or because of any official act performed or to be performed" — to pertain to the office rather than (as the language more naturally suggests) to *particular* official acts.

More important for present purposes, however, this regulation, and the numerous other regulations and statutes littering this field, demonstrate that this is an area where precisely targeted prohibitions are commonplace, and where more general prohibitions have been qualified by numerous exceptions. Given that reality, a statute in this field that can linguistically be interpreted to be either a meat axe or a scalpel should reasonably be taken to be the latter. Absent a text that clearly requires it, we ought not expand this one piece of the regulatory puzzle so dramatically as to make many other pieces misfits. As discussed earlier, not only does the text here not require that result; its more natural reading forbids it.

We hold that, in order to establish a violation of 18 U.S.C. § 201(c)(1)(A), the Government must prove a link between a thing of value conferred upon a public official and a specific "official act" for or because of which it was given. Our decision today casts doubt upon the lower courts' resolution of respondent's challenge to the sufficiency of the indictment on Count One—an issue on which certiorari was neither sought nor granted. We leave it to the District Court to determine whether that issue should be reopened on remand.

It is so ordered.

Notes and Questions

1. *The difference between bribery and gratuity.* In *Sun-Diamond*, the government argued that the gratuities statute "requires only a showing that a 'gift was motivated, at least in part, by the recipient's *capacity to exercise governmental power or influence* in the donor's favor' without necessarily showing that it was connected to a particular official act." Under this reading, the crime of offering or receiving a gratuity would be much broader than the crime of offering or receiving a bribe. The Court, however, rejected the government's approach and offered its own distinction between the crimes of bribery and gratuity. Is the distinction as clear as the Court indicates? If a client asked you for an explanation of the law, how would you explain the difference between the two crimes?

2. *Double jeopardy.* Could a defendant be charged, convicted, and punished under both the bribery and gratuity statutes? Some courts have concluded that gratuity is a lesser-included offense of bribery. *See, e.g., United States v. Alfisi*, 308 F.3d 144, 152 (2d Cir. 2002); *United States v. Young*, 87 F. Supp. 3d 805, 809 (W.D. Va. 2015). Thus, if the government were to charge both bribery and gratuity, the jury would determine whether the defendant had committed a crime and, if so, whether it amounted to bribery or gratuity. How would the jury make this distinction?

3. *Corrupt intent.* Bribery under § 201(b)(1) requires proof that the defendant acted "corruptly." As the Court in *Sun-Diamond* made clear, proof of corrupt intent for the crime of bribery rests on the party's understanding that the payment was offered for a *quid pro quo*. In that light, has bribery been committed in the following circumstances?

a. *The public official—unbeknownst to the bribing party—has already performed the official act at the time the bribe is offered or received. See United States v. Arroyo*, 581 F.2d 649, 652 (7th Cir. 1978) (holding that an official can act corruptly without intending to be influenced; the official need only "solicit or receive the money on the representation that the money is for the purpose of influencing [the official's] performance of some official act.").

b. *The bribed party either does not have the power to perform the official act or has no intention of doing so. See United States v. Peleti*, 576 F.3d 377, 383 (7th Cir. 2009) (holding that "[w]hether [the public official] actually intended to be influenced is irrelevant, so long as [that official] conveyed to [the bribing party] that the money would influence [the official].").

How far does the definition of "corrupt intent" extend? If one is threatened with harm, and makes a payoff to a federal official to avoid the harm, has one acted corruptly? This issue arose in *Alfisi*, 308 F.3d 144. Alfisi was employed by a produce wholesaler and made payments to a federal food inspector in exchange for favorable treatment by the inspector. At trial, the defendant argued that the inspector had extorted him and that the defendant made the payments so that the inspector would perform the inspector's duties in a lawful manner. On appeal, the defendant asserted that the jury should have been required to find an intent to induce a *quid pro quo* beyond performance of the public official's lawful duties. The majority rejected the argument and affirmed the conviction. The dissent argued that the bribery statute should not apply in such circumstances. Which result seems correct to you? Why?

4. *The harm.* The harm from offering or receiving a bribe seems clear enough; the act calls into question the integrity of the official's performance of public duties. But where is the harm from offering or receiving a gratuity? Under the statutory scheme, gratuities are punished much less severely than bribery — two years as opposed to 15 years in prison. Is offering or receiving a gratuity something that properly rises to the level of a criminal offense? Why or why not?

3. Public Official

Section 201(a) defines the term "public official" to include members of Congress and officers, employees, and other persons "acting for or on behalf of the United States, or any department, agency or branch of government thereof . . . in any official function." The statute, however, does not provide any guidance for determining when one is "acting for or on behalf of the United States." That task fell to the Supreme Court in the case that follows.

Dixson v. United States

465 U.S. 482 (1984)

JUSTICE MARSHALL delivered the opinion of the Court.

These consolidated cases present the question whether officers of a private, nonprofit corporation administering and expending federal community development block grants are "public officials" for purposes of the federal bribery statute. 18 U.S.C. § 201(a).

In 1979, the City of Peoria received two federal block grants from the Department of Housing and Urban Development (HUD). The first was a $400,000 Community Development Block Grant; the second a $636,000 Metro Reallocation Grant. Both grants were funded through the Housing and Community Development Act of 1974. Under that Act, the Secretary of HUD is authorized to dispense federal block grants to state and local governments and nonprofit community organizations for urban renewal programs such as the rehabilitation of residential structures, code enforcement in deteriorating areas, and the construction of public works projects.

The City of Peoria subsequently designated United Neighborhoods, Inc. (UNI), a community-based, social-service organization, to be the City's subgrantee in charge of the administration of the federal block grant funds.[1] UNI in turn hired petitioner Dixson to serve as the corporation's Executive Director and petitioner Hinton as its Housing Rehabilitation Coordinator. Petitioner Dixson was responsible for the general supervision of UNI's programs, including fiscal control and execution of contracts. Petitioner Hinton's duties included contracting with persons applying for housing rehabilitation assistance, and contracting with demolition firms.

A federal grand jury named petitioners in an 11-count indictment filed on March 12, 1981. The indictment charged that petitioners, as "public officials" under 18 U.S.C. § 201(a), had sought a series of bribes in return for "being influenced in their performance of an official act in respect to the awarding of housing rehabilitation contracts" in violation of 18 U.S.C. § 201(c)(1), (2).

According to the Government's evidence at trial, petitioners used their positions to extract $42,604 in kick-backs from contractors seeking to work on UNI's housing rehabilitation projects. One contractor testified how he was approached by petitioner Hinton and persuaded to pay petitioners ten percent of each housing rehabilitation contract that petitioners awarded him. The contractor explained that on ten occasions, he received first draw checks from UNI for 20 percent of the contract price, deposited the check at his bank, and paid half the amount of the check in cash to petitioners. A second contractor testified as to substantially the same arrangement.

Before trial, petitioners moved to dismiss the indictment on the grounds that they were not "public officials" within the meaning of the federal statute. Their motions were denied, and following a jury trial in the United States District Court for the Central District of Illinois, petitioners were convicted as charged. The District Court sentenced each to 7 1/2 years imprisonment, to be followed by three years' probation. Petitioners appealed to the United States Court of Appeals for the Seventh Circuit, which affirmed. Both petitioners filed petitions for writs of certiorari, and we granted the writs. We now affirm.

Petitioners' sole claim is that they were not "public officials" within the meaning of 18 U.S.C. § 201(a) and therefore not subject to prosecution under the federal bribery statute. Since our disposition of this claim turns on the relationship between petitioners and the federal government, we begin our discussion with an analysis of

---

1. Local recipients of Housing and Community Development Act (HCDA) block grants have the option of distributing the funds directly or of subcontracting the administration of the funds to private, nonprofit organizations.

the Housing and Community Development Act (HCDA) block grant program and petitioners' role in administering that program.

Congress passed the HCDA to meet the social, economic, and environmental problems facing cities. 42 U.S.C. § 5301(a). The primary objective of the Act is "the development of viable urban communities." § 5301(c). While the HCDA addressed a national problem, Congress enacted the legislation as a federal block grant statute, under which the day-to-day administration of the federal program, including the actual expenditure of federal funds, is delegated to State and local authorities.

The HCDA creates a "consistent system of Federal aid," § 5301(d), by distributing funds committed by Congress through organizations outside the federal government, while retaining federal control to assure compliance with statutory federal objectives and implementing regulations. Congress itself specified the 17 categories of community projects upon which HCDA grants can be spent. Within the federal constraints, grant recipients design programs addressing local needs. To obtain federal funds, local communities must submit to the Secretary a plan made in accordance with national urban growth policies, and supplement the plan with annual performance reports. The federal government retains the right to audit the records of HCDA programs, and to recover improperly expended funds.

HCDA grantees give assurances to HUD that they, and their subgrantees, will abide by specific financial accountability, equal opportunity, fair labor, environmental, and other requirements. By administering HCDA funds, private nonprofit organizations subject themselves to numerous federal restrictions beyond those imposed directly by HUD. Like other recipients of federal grant funds, HUD grantees and subgrantees are subject to a uniform audit procedure, adopted by the federal government as "an integral element" of "full accountability by those entrusted with responsibility for administering the programs."

UNI voluntarily assumed the status of CDA subgrantee when UNI and the City of Peoria signed five separate grant agreements in March and October 1979, pursuant to which UNI hired petitioners. . . .

Petitioners contend now, as they have throughout this litigation, that, as executives of a private nonprofit corporation unaffiliated with the federal government, they were never "public officials" as Congress defined that term. . . .

Petitioners argue that they can not be considered to have acted "for or on behalf of the United States" because neither they nor their employer UNI ever entered into any agreement with the United States or any subdivision of the federal government. . . .

As is often the case in matters of statutory interpretation, the language of § 201(a) does not decide the dispute. The words can be interpreted to support either petitioners' or the Government's reading. We must turn, therefore, to the legislative history of the federal bribery statute to determine whether these materials clarify which of the proposed readings is consistent with Congress's intent. If the legislative history fails to clarify the statutory language, our rule of lenity would compel us to construe the statute in favor of petitioners, as criminal defendants in these cases.

Congress passed the current federal bribery provision, including § 201(a), in 1962, as part of an effort to reformulate and rationalize all federal criminal statutes dealing with the integrity of government. At the time of the 1962 revisions, general federal bribery statutes had been in existence for more than a century. From the start, Congress drafted its bribery statutes with broad jurisdictional language, and periodically amended the provisions to ensure that the scope of federal criminal liability kept pace with the growth and diversification of the federal government. Prior to 1962, in recognition of Congress's apparent desire for the federal bribery statutes to have wide application, the federal judiciary interpreted the statutes and, indeed, the phrase "person acting for or on behalf of the United States" to have a broad jurisdictional reach.

We find the legislative history of § 201(a) inconsistent with the view that the words "person acting for or on behalf of the United States" were added simply to bring within the jurisdiction of the federal bribery laws those individuals tied to the federal government by direct contractual obligations.

Of particular relevance to the instant case is the House Judiciary Committee's citation of the Second Circuit's decision in United States v. Levine, 129 F.2d 745 (2d Cir. 1942), as an example of how the judiciary had in the past properly construed the federal bribery laws. *See* H.R. Rep. No. 748 at 17. The *Levine* decision involved the application of the 1909 bribery statute to a low-level official in a decentralized federal assistance program. The defendant in *Levine* worked for a locally-administered price stabilization program, the Market Administrator of the New York Metropolitan Milk Marketing Area, and was responsible for receiving milk handlers' market surplus claims, and checking them for accuracy. Levine solicited a bribe from one of the handlers within his jurisdiction in return for his promise to prevent investigations of the claims.

Although hired by a Market Administrator who, in turn, had been appointed by the Secretary of Agriculture, Levine himself was neither employed by the United States nor paid with federal funds. Nevertheless, Levine's duties were critical to the proper administration of the federally assisted New York Milk Marketing Area. Because claims for payment were not rechecked by anyone else, his duties resulted in expenditures from the federal treasury. After reviewing these facts, the Second Circuit concluded that, notwithstanding the absence of a direct contractual bond between the defendant and the United States, Levine's responsible position made him a "public official" for purposes of the federal bribery laws. 129 F.2d at 747. By explicitly endorsing the Second Circuit's analysis in *Levine*, the House Judiciary Committee strongly intimated that the phrase "acting for or on behalf of the United States" covers something more than a direct contractual bond.

Congress's long-standing commitment to a broadly-drafted federal bribery statute, its expressed desire to continue that tradition with the 1962 revisions, its affirmative adoption of the language at issue in this case, and the House Report's endorsement of the Second Circuit's reasoning in *Levine*, combine to persuade us that Congress never intended § 201(a)'s open-ended definition of "public official" to be given the cramped reading proposed by petitioners. We agree with the Government that § 201(a) has been accurately characterized as a "comprehensive statute applicable to all persons performing activities for or on behalf of the United States," whatever the form of delegation of authority. To determine whether any particular individual falls within this category, the proper inquiry is not simply whether the person had signed a contract with the United States or agreed to serve as the Government's agent, but rather whether the person occupies a position of public trust with official federal responsibilities. Persons who hold such positions are public officials within the meaning of § 201 and liable for prosecution under the federal bribery statute.

Given the structure of the Housing and Community Development Act program and petitioners' responsible positions as administrators of the subgrant, we have little difficulty concluding that these persons served as public officials for purposes of § 201(a). As executives of UNI, petitioners had operational responsibility for the administration of the HCDA grant program within the City of Peoria. In allocating the federal resources made available to the City through the HCDA grant program, petitioners were charged with abiding by federal guidelines, which dictated both where and how the federal funds could be distributed. By accepting the responsibility for distributing these federal fiscal resources, petitioners assumed the quintessentially official role of administering a social service program established by the United States Congress.

Lest there be any doubt that Congress intended § 201(a) to cover local officials like petitioners, one need only compare petitioners to the defendant in *Levine*, whose conviction the House Judiciary Committee explicitly endorsed. Both Levine and petitioners worked in decentralized federal assistance programs. Both Levine and petitioners effectively determined who would be the beneficiary of federal dollars, and both solicited bribes to influence their official decisions. Levine held a position of public trust with official federal responsibilities: to collect and investigate the accuracy of data submitted by milk producers in support of their claims for federal subsidies. Petitioners held a position of public trust with official federal responsibilities: allocating federal resources, pursuant to complex statutory and regulatory guidelines, in the form of residential rehabilitation contracts. Indeed, in certain respects, petitioners performed duties that were more clearly "official" and more obviously undertaken "for or on behalf of the United States" than the responsibilities of the defendant in *Levine*. Where Levine was paid through a levy imposed on local businesses participating in the marketing order, petitioners' salaries were completely funded by the HCDA grant. Where Levine simply compiled data that was submitted to the Department of Agriculture for eventual disbursement, petitioners personally bestowed the benefits of the HCDA program to residents of Peoria.

By finding petitioners to be public officials within the meaning of § 201(a), we do not mean to suggest that the mere presence of some federal assistance brings a local organization and its employees within the jurisdiction of the federal bribery statute or even that all employees of local organizations responsible for administering federal grant programs are public officials within the meaning of § 201(a). To be a public official under § 201(a), an individual must possess some degree of official responsibility for carrying out a federal program or policy. Our opinion today is, therefore, fully consistent with Krichman v. United States, 256 U.S. 363 (1921), in which this Court ruled that a baggage porter, although employed by a federally controlled railroad, could not be said to have "acted for or on behalf of the United States" because the porter lacked any duties of an official character. Similarly, individuals who work for block grant recipients and business people who provide recipients with goods and services cannot be said to be public officials under § 201(a) unless they assume some duties of an official nature.

We recognize that the manner in which the HCDA block grant program combines local administration with federal funding initially creates some confusion as to whether local authorities administering HCDA grants should be considered public officials under the federal bribery statute. However, when one examines the structure of the program and sees that the HCDA vests in local administrators like petitioners Hinton and Dixson the power to allocate federal fiscal resources for the purpose of achieving congressionally-established goals, the confusion evaporates and it becomes clear that these local officials hold precisely the sort of positions of national public trust that Congress intended to cover with the "acting for or on behalf of" language in the bribery statute. The federal government has a strong and legitimate interest in prosecuting petitioners for their misuse of government funds. As this Court has said in another, closely related context, grant funds to state and local governments "are as much in need of protection from [fraud] as any other federal money, and the statute does not make the extent of [grant monies'] safeguard dependent upon the bookkeeping devices used for their distribution." United States ex rel. Marcus v. Hess, 317 U.S. 537, 544 (1943) (holding that one who contracts with a local governmental unit to work on federally-funded projects can "cheat the United States" through the state intermediary).

Because we agree with the Seventh Circuit that petitioners were public officials under § 201(a), the judgment of the Court of Appeals is affirmed.

JUSTICE O'CONNOR, with whom JUSTICE BRENNAN, JUSTICE REHNQUIST, and JUSTICE STEVENS join, dissenting.

The rule of lenity demands that "ambiguity concerning the ambit of criminal statutes should be resolved in favor of lenity." Rewis v. United States, 401 U.S. 808, 812 (1971). The Court concludes that congressional intent to include persons like petitioners within the coverage of 18 U.S.C. § 201 is clear enough to make the rule of lenity inapplicable. The statutory language admits of the Court's reading, and the case for that reading would be strong, though perhaps not persuasive, if § 201 were a civil statute. I differ with the Court in that I find the evidence of congressional intent too weak to meet the higher standard for resolving facial ambiguity against a defendant when interpreting a criminal statute. In my view, the evidence of intent offered by the Court's opinion cannot carry the weight the Court places on it, and there is good reason to reject the Court's interpretation of the statute.

The language of § 201 and of its predecessors, as the Court's opinion points out, is intentionally broad. But that fact merely creates the interpretive problem—it does not resolve it. Congress intended to carry forward the pre-1962 bribery statute when it enacted § 201, and it understood the coverage of the bribery law to be broad. Moreover, the purpose of the statute was undoubtedly to proscribe bribery of all those who carry out a federal trust. To say that the statute is broadly aimed at all persons bearing a federal trust, however, is not to resolve the ambiguity over what constitutes a federal trust. Indeed, the statutory language—"acting for or on behalf of the United States"—is merely a formulation of the public trust idea, and the Court concedes that the statutory language can accommodate both petitioners' and respondent's views. The breadth of the language accordingly offers little help in defining the ambiguous coverage of the statute.

The legislative history likewise provides no significant support for the Court's reading of the statute. The critical statutory language has been a part of the federal bribery statute for more than one hundred years. Yet, as the Court's opinion indicates, Congress apparently has never specifically considered the statute's coverage of federal grant recipients. The legislative history is simply silent on the question to be answered in these cases.

Moreover, the *Levine* case itself does not suggest inclusion of such individuals. The individual involved in *Levine* was an employee of a person appointed by the Federal Government to carry out a federally defined regulatory task. As an employee of an agent of the United States, he was obviously acting for the United States. An employee of a grantee or subgrantee of the United States is in a quite different position.

Finally, I think it especially inappropriate to construe an ambiguous criminal statute unfavorably to the defendant when the construction that is adopted leaves the statute as unclear in its coverage as the bare statutory language. The rule of lenity rests on the notion that people are entitled to know in advance whether an act they contemplate taking violates a particular criminal statute, even if the act is obviously condemnable and even if it violates other criminal statutes. The "public trust" standard adopted by the Court provides no more guidance to employees of a grant recipient or its subgrantee than does the statutory language, "acting for or on behalf of the United States." There are hundreds of federal grant programs. Yet it is impossible to tell from the Court's analysis just what sorts of federal regulation make a grant recipient subject to the bribery statute. A criminal statute, after if not before it is judicially construed, should have a discernible meaning. I do not think the Court offers one.

I respectfully dissent.

Notes and Questions

1. *The* Dixson *standard.* The dissent asserted that "it is impossible to tell from the Court's analysis just what sorts of federal regulation make a grant recipient subject

to the bribery statute." Does the Court's test for determining whether a person is a federal public official provide clear notice to potential defendants? Can you devise a clearer rule? Lower courts have found that the *Dixson* definition of "federal public official" encompasses a wide range of potential defendants. *See, e.g., United States v. Hang*, 75 F.3d 1275, 1279–1280 (8th Cir. 1996) (a low-level corporate employee responsible for determining eligibility for federally subsidized housing); *United States v. Strissel*, 920 F.2d 1162, 1165–1166 (4th Cir. 1990) (a city housing authority director); *United States v. Velazquez*, 847 F.2d 140, 142 (4th Cir. 1988) (a state deputy sheriff with authority over federal and state prisoners). *But see United States v. Evans*, 344 F.3d 1131, 1134–1136 (11th Cir. 2003) (holding that an executive director of a nonprofit acting at the direction of the federal government did not qualify as a federal public official because of the tenuous link between that nonprofit and the federal government).

2. *The vote.* The Court in *Dixson* split five-to-four along lines rarely seen in criminal cases. Why did Justice Marshall, typically a strong pro-defendants' rights justice, write an opinion adopting a broad rule of criminal liability in this case? Conversely, why did Justices Rehnquist and O'Connor, generally known as "law and order" justices, favor the defense position? Are there policy issues at work in the case that may have produced these alliances?

3. *The "thing of value."* As noted above, an element in any § 201 case is that the defendant offered to give or receive something "of value." How broadly should this term be interpreted? Suppose that the thing offered is the perception that someone will be awarded a federal judgeship, though this may not actually be within the reach of the donee nor the power of the donor. Is this element met? *See United States v. Scruggs*, 714 F.3d 258, 268 (5th Cir. 2013) (holding in the affirmative, that the offer to influence one's United States Senator brother was enough even though it was not in the donee's immediate power); *United States v. Williams*, 705 F.2d 603, 623–624 (2d Cir. 1983) (holding the same when one promises to use their influence as a United States Senator to steer government contracts to a titanium mining venture in which defendants held an interest). How does this compare to what you learned about honest services fraud in Chapter 4, Mail and Wire Fraud, *supra*? Do these holdings conflict with principles underscored in *Skilling*, or do these holdings cover other areas of conduct akin to behavior that may not be perfectly considered honest services fraud?

Problems

7-1. FLY International, Inc. (FLY) is a large publicly traded company that, among other things, does extensive government engineering contract work with the United States Department of Defense. Ken is the manager of the Runway Repair Branch of FLY.

The Department of Defense awarded Moon Flight, Inc. (Moon) a contract to build a runway edge-marker system for an Air Force runway repair program. Susan is the president of Moon.

Ken was introduced to Susan. He told her that he was the primary contact on the project, and that if any problem arose, she should contact him. Ken also told Susan that he would be the "eyes and ears" of the Air Force during the project. As a result, Susan believed that Ken was the engineer on the project and had the decision-making authority concerning the project.

In reality, Ken did not have final decision-making authority and his decisions could not bind the government. He did, however, advise government decision makers with respect to certain technical issues involved in the edge-marker contract. Ken's salary was not paid by Air Force, but by FLY with funds it received from the government in payment for government services.

A week after Susan met Ken, Ken contacted her and suggested that Moon could cut costs by using a different brand of materials than that specified in Moon's contract. Ken offered to approve the change if Susan would pay him one-half of the cost savings. The contract was in fact modified to allow for a different brand of materials. Instead of paying Ken one-half of the cost savings, however, Susan reported Ken's suggestion to Air Force officials.

Ken has been charged with soliciting a bribe under 18 U.S.C. § 201. Ken has moved to dismiss the charge on the ground that he is not a federal public official. How should the court rule? Why?

7-2. Neder is a case manager for the Internal Revenue Service (IRS). This position requires Neder to supervise a group of revenue agents assigned to audit certain corporate income tax returns filed by Gulf Coast Oil (Gulf). Neder's responsibilities include developing and giving final approval of the audit plan, which is a detailed outline of the specific procedures to be utilized during the course of a particular audit. During the development of an audit plan, Neder had the power to make all final decisions regarding the scope and depth of the areas of corporate taxation that were to be reviewed in the audit. Neder has been supervising the audits of Gulf's tax returns for more than 10 years.

Evidence presented to a federal grand jury demonstrates the following facts. In January of last year, Neder spent four days at a country club with the Manager of Federal Tax Compliance for Gulf. Neder's entire bill was paid for by the Manager. In August and September, Neder and his wife spent four days on vacation with Gulf's Vice-President of Tax Administration. All expenses were paid for by the Vice-President. In December, again Neder spent three days on vacation in the company of both the Manager and Vice-President. Once again, the Gulf employees paid all of Neder's expenses.

You are the Assistant United States Attorney in charge of the investigation of Neder. What charges, if any, would ask the grand jury to bring against Neder under 18 U.S.C. § 201? Why?

7-3. The City of Metropolis created the Metropolitan Housing Authority ("the Authority") to develop and operate public housing units for eligible families. The

Authority received millions of dollars annually from the United States Department of Housing and Urban Development ("HUD") to assist it in providing housing. Among the HUD funds received by the Authority were "Section 8" funds, which were used by the Authority to pay the rent of qualified families who lived outside of Authority owned public housing. The Authority made rent payments for low income families who became clients of the Authority and resided in private housing.

The River Development Corp. ("RDC") is a nonprofit corporation created at the direction of the Authority to provide and develop affordable housing opportunities for low income persons. RDC was created as an instrumentality of the Authority for the purpose of implementing the housing plans and programs of the Authority. RDC is an independent corporation that is not under city control.

RDC owned and operated several residential properties. RDC received Section 8 funds from the Authority for eligible families who resided in RDC properties. In each of the last two calendar years, RDC received more than $350,000 in HUD funds. All of these funds were paid by the Authority to RDC to offset the rent payments of eligible low income residents in RDC properties.

In January of last year, defendant Evers became the Executive Director of RDC. Evers was essentially the general manager of the RDC properties. Beginning in February, Evers awarded three RDC contracts to Construction Corp., Inc.; the first contract was awarded in February, the second in March, and the third in May. Construction Corp. was controlled by Evers' friend, Chadwick. In April, Chadwick had Construction Corp. post a $50,000 letter of credit as collateral to allow Evers to take out a loan. The letter was necessary because of Evers' low credit rating. Evers repaid the loan the following month, and the letter of credit was never used. In June, Chadwick had Construction Corp. pay $125,000 to one of Evers' creditors. Evers repaid the $125,000 two months later, with a market rate of interest.

The government later initiated a grand jury investigation. Chadwick agreed to testify against Evers in exchange for immunity. The government has charged Evers with (1) bribery under § 201(b)(2)(A) for the $50,000 letter of credit, (2) bribery under § 201(b)(2)(A) for the $125,000 payment, (3) gratuities under § 201(c)(1)(B) for the $50,000 letter of credit, and (4) gratuities under § 201(c)(1)(B) for the $125,000 payment. Evers has moved to dismiss all the charges.

Should the court grant the motion as to any or all of the charges? Why or why not?

4. Official Act

Courts have differed over what constitutes an "official act" under Section 201. In the next case, the United States Supreme Court attempted to provide guidance on this issue. Did the Court succeed? What are the competing concerns at stake?

McDonnell v. United States

136 S. Ct. 2355 (2016)

ROBERTS, C.J., delivered the opinion for a unanimous Court.

In 2014, the Federal government indicted former Virginia Governor Robert McDonnell and his wife, Maureen McDonnell, on bribery charges. The charges related to the acceptance by the McDonnells of $175,000 in loans, gifts, and other benefits from Virginia businessman Jonnie Williams, while Governor McDonnell was in office. Williams was the chief executive officer of Star Scientific, a Virginia-based company that had developed a nutritional supplement made from anatabine, a compound found in tobacco. Star Scientific hoped that Virginia's public universities would perform research studies on anatabine, and Williams wanted Governor McDonnell's assistance in obtaining those studies.

To convict the McDonnells of bribery, the government was required to show that Governor McDonnell committed (or agreed to commit) an "official act" in exchange for the loans and gifts. The parties did not agree, however, on what counts as an "official act." The government alleged in the indictment, and maintains on appeal, that Governor McDonnell committed at least five "official acts." Those acts included "arranging meetings" for Williams with other Virginia officials to discuss Star Scientific's product, "hosting" events for Star Scientific at the Governor's Mansion, and "contacting other government officials" concerning studies of anatabine. The government also argued more broadly that these activities constituted "official action" because they related to Virginia business development, a priority of Governor McDonnell's administration. Governor McDonnell contends that merely setting up a meeting, hosting an event, or contacting an official — without more — does not count as an "official act."

* * *

Governor McDonnell was indicted for accepting payments, loans, gifts, and other things of value from Williams and Star Scientific in exchange for "performing official actions on an as-needed basis, as opportunities arose, to legitimize, promote, and obtain research studies for Star Scientific's products." The charges against him comprised one count of conspiracy to commit honest services fraud, three counts of honest services fraud, one count of conspiracy to commit Hobbs Act extortion, six counts of Hobbs Act extortion, and two counts of making a false statement. *See* 18 U.S.C. §§ 1343, 1349 (honest services fraud); § 1951(a) (Hobbs Act extortion); § 1014 (false statement). Mrs. McDonnell was indicted on similar charges, plus obstructing official proceedings, based on her alleged involvement in the scheme. *See* § 1512(c)(2) (obstruction).

The theory underlying both the honest services fraud and Hobbs Act extortion charges was that Governor McDonnell had accepted bribes from Williams. *See Skilling v. United States,* 561 U.S. 358, 404 (2010) (construing honest services fraud to forbid "fraudulent schemes to deprive another of honest services through bribes or kickbacks"); *Evans v. United States,* 504 U.S. 255, 260, 269 (1992) (construing Hobbs Act extortion to include "'taking a bribe'").

The parties agreed that they would define honest services fraud with reference to the federal bribery statute, 18 U.S.C. § 201. That statute makes it a crime for "a public official or person selected to be a public official, directly or indirectly, corruptly" to demand, seek, receive, accept, or agree "to receive or accept anything of value" in return for being "influenced in the performance of any official act." § 201(b)(2). An "official act" is defined as "any decision or action on any question, matter, cause, suit, proceeding or controversy, which may at any time be pending, or which may by law be brought before any public official, in such official's official capacity, or in such official's place of trust or profit." § 201(a)(3).

The parties also agreed that obtaining a "thing of value ... knowing that the thing of value was given in return for official action" was an element of Hobbs Act extortion, and that they would use the definition of "official act" found in the federal bribery statute to define "official action" under the Hobbs Act. 792 F.3d 478, 505 (C.A.4 2015) (internal quotation marks omitted).

As a result of all this, the government was required to prove that Governor McDonnell committed or agreed to commit an "official act" in exchange for the loans and gifts from Williams.

The case proceeded to a jury trial, which lasted five weeks. Pursuant to an immunity agreement, Williams testified that he had given the gifts and loans to the McDonnells to obtain the Governor's "help with the testing" of Anatabloc at Virginia's medical schools. Governor McDonnell acknowledged that he had requested loans and accepted gifts from Williams. He testified, however, that setting up meetings with government officials was something he did "literally thousands of times" as Governor, and that he did not expect his staff "to do anything other than to meet" with Williams.

Several state officials testified that they had discussed Anatabloc with Williams or Governor McDonnell, but had not taken any action to further the research studies. A UVA employee in the university research office, who had never spoken with the Governor about Anatabloc, testified that she wrote a pro/con list concerning research studies on Anatabloc. The first "pro" was the "[p]erception to Governor that UVA would like to work with local companies," and the first "con" was the "[p]olitical pressure from Governor and impact on future UVA requests from the Governor."

Following closing arguments, the District Court instructed the jury that to convict Governor McDonnell it must find that he agreed "to accept a thing of value in exchange for official action." The court described the five alleged "official acts" set forth in the indictment, which involved arranging meetings, hosting events, and contacting other government officials. The court then quoted the statutory definition of "official act," and — as the government had requested — advised the jury that the term encompassed "acts that a public official customarily performs," including acts "in furtherance of longer-term goals" or "in a series of steps to exercise influence or achieve an end."

Governor McDonnell had requested the court to further instruct the jury that the "fact that an activity is a routine activity, or a 'settled practice,' of an officeholder does not alone make it an 'official act,'" and that "merely arranging a meeting, attending an event, hosting a reception, or making a speech are not, standing alone, 'official acts,' even if they are settled practices of the official," because they "are not decisions on matters pending before the government." He also asked the court to explain to the jury that an "official act" must intend to or "in fact influence a specific official decision the government actually makes — such as awarding a contract, hiring a government employee, issuing a license, passing a law, or implementing a regulation." The District Court declined to give Governor McDonnell's proposed instruction to the jury.

The jury convicted Governor McDonnell on the honest services fraud and Hobbs Act extortion charges, but acquitted him on the false statement charges. Mrs. McDonnell was also convicted on most of the charges against her. Although the government requested a sentence of at least ten years for Governor McDonnell, the District Court sentenced him to two years in prison. Mrs. McDonnell received a one-year sentence. . . .

The issue in this case is the proper interpretation of the term "official act." Section 201(a)(3) defines an "official act" as "any decision or action on any question, matter, cause, suit, proceeding or controversy, which may at any time be pending, or which may by law be brought before any public official, in such official's official capacity, or in such official's place of trust or profit."

According to the government, "Congress used intentionally broad language" in § 201(a)(3) to embrace "*any* decision or action, on *any* question or matter, that may at *any time* be pending, or which may by law be brought before *any* public official, in such official's official capacity." The government concludes that the term "official act" therefore encompasses nearly any activity by a public official. In the government's view, "official act" specifically includes arranging a meeting, contacting another public official, or hosting an event — without more — concerning any subject, including a broad policy issue such as Virginia economic development.

Governor McDonnell, in contrast, contends that statutory context compels a more circumscribed reading, limiting "official acts" to those acts that "direct [ ] a particular resolution of a specific governmental decision," or that pressure another official to do so. He also claims that "vague corruption laws" such as § 201 implicate serious constitutional concerns, militating "in favor of a narrow, cautious reading of these criminal statutes.

Taking into account the text of the statute, the precedent of this Court, and the constitutional concerns raised by Governor McDonnell, we reject the government's reading of § 201(a)(3) and adopt a more bounded interpretation of "official act."

Under that interpretation, setting up a meeting, calling another public official, or hosting an event does not, standing alone, qualify as an "official act."

The text of § 201(a)(3) sets forth two requirements for an "official act": First, the government must identify a "question, matter, cause, suit, proceeding or controversy" that "may at any time be pending" or "may by law be brought" before a public official. Second, the government must prove that the public official made a decision or took an action "on" that question, matter, cause, suit, proceeding, or controversy, or agreed to do so. The issue here is whether arranging a meeting, contacting another official, or hosting an event — without more — can be a "question, matter, cause, suit, proceeding or controversy," and if not, whether it can be a decision or action on a "question, matter, cause, suit, proceeding or controversy."

The first inquiry is whether a typical meeting, call, or event is itself a "question, matter, cause, suit, proceeding or controversy." The government argues that nearly any activity by a public official qualifies as a question or matter — from workaday functions, such as the typical call, meeting, or event, to the broadest issues the government confronts, such as fostering economic development. We conclude, however, that the terms "question, matter, cause, suit, proceeding or controversy" do not sweep so broadly.

The last four words in that list — "cause," "suit," "proceeding," and "controversy" — connote a formal exercise of governmental power, such as a lawsuit, hearing, or administrative determination. Although it may be difficult to define the precise reach of those terms, it seems clear that a typical meeting, telephone call, or event arranged by a public official does not qualify as a "cause, suit, proceeding or controversy."

But what about a "question" or "matter"? A "question" could mean any "subject or aspect that is in dispute, open for discussion, or to be inquired into," and a "matter" any "subject" of "interest or relevance." Webster's Third New International Dictionary 1394, 1863 (1961). If those meanings were adopted, a typical meeting, call, or event would qualify as a "question" or "matter." A "question" may also be interpreted more narrowly, however, as "a subject or point of debate or a proposition being or to be voted on in a meeting," such as a question "before the senate." Id. at 1863. Similarly, a "matter" may be limited to "a topic under active and usually serious or practical consideration," such as a matter that "will come before the committee." Id. at 1394.

To choose between those competing definitions, we look to the context in which the words appear. Under the familiar interpretive canon *noscitur a sociis,* "a word is known by the company it keeps." *Jarecki v. G.D. Searle & Co.,* 367 U.S. 303, 307 (1961). . . .

Applying that same approach here, we conclude that a "question" or "matter" must be similar in nature to a "cause, suit, proceeding or controversy." Because a typical meeting, call, or event arranged by a public official is not of the same stripe as a lawsuit before a court, a determination before an agency, or a hearing before a committee, it does not qualify as a "question" or "matter" under § 201(a)(3). . . .

Because a typical meeting, call, or event is not itself a question or matter, the next step is to determine whether arranging a meeting, contacting another official, or hosting an event may qualify as a "decision or action" *on* a different question or matter. That requires us to first establish what counts as a question or matter in this case. . . .

The Fourth Circuit found at least three questions or matters at issue in this case: (1) "whether researchers at any of Virginia's state universities would initiate a study of Anatabloc"; (2) "whether the state-created Tobacco Indemnification and Community Revitalization Commission" would "allocate grant money for the study of anatabine"; and (3) "whether the health insurance plan for state employees in Virginia would include Anatabloc as a covered drug." We agree that those qualify as questions or matters under § 201(a)(3). Each is focused and concrete, and each involves a formal exercise of governmental power that is similar in nature to a lawsuit, administrative determination, or hearing.

The question remains whether — as the government argues — merely setting up a meeting, hosting an event, or calling another official qualifies as a decision or action on any of those three questions or matters. Although the word "decision," and especially the word "action," could be read expansively to support the government's view, our opinion in *United States v. Sun-Diamond Growers of Cal.*, 526 U.S. 398 (1999), rejects that interpretation. . . .

It is apparent from *Sun-Diamond* that hosting an event, meeting with other officials, or speaking with interested parties is not, standing alone, a "decision or action" within the meaning of § 201(a)(3), even if the event, meeting, or speech is related to a pending question or matter. Instead, something more is required: § 201(a)(3) specifies that the public official must make a decision or take an action *on* that question or matter, or agree to do so. . . .

Under this Court's precedents, a public official is not required to actually make a decision or take an action on a "question, matter, cause, suit, proceeding or controversy"; it is enough that the official agree to do so. The agreement need not be explicit, and the public official need not specify the means that he will use to perform his end of the bargain. Nor must the public official in fact intend to perform the "official act," so long as he agrees to do so. A jury could, for example, conclude that an agreement was reached if the evidence shows that the public official received a thing of value knowing that it was given with the expectation that the official would perform an "official act" in return. It is up to the jury, under the facts of the case, to determine whether the public official agreed to perform an "official act" at the time of the alleged *quid pro quo*. The jury may consider a broad range of pertinent evidence, including the nature of the transaction, to answer that question.

Setting up a meeting, hosting an event, or calling an official (or agreeing to do so) merely to talk about a research study or to gather additional information, however, does not qualify as a decision or action on the pending question of whether to initiate the study. Simply expressing support for the research study at a meeting, event, or call — or sending a subordinate to such a meeting, event, or call — similarly does not qualify as a decision or action on the study, as long as the public official does not intend to exert pressure on another official or provide advice, knowing or intending such advice to form the basis for an "official act." Otherwise, if every action somehow related to the research study were an "official act," the requirement that the public official make a decision or take an action on that study, or agree to do so, would be meaningless. . . .

In sum, an "official act" is a decision or action on a "question, matter, cause, suit, proceeding or controversy." The "question, matter, cause, suit, proceeding or controversy" must involve a formal exercise of governmental power that is similar in nature to a lawsuit before a court, a determination before an agency, or a hearing before a committee. It must also be something specific and focused that is "pending" or "may by law be brought" before a public official. To qualify as an "official act," the public official must make a decision or take an action on that "question, matter, cause, suit, proceeding or controversy," or agree to do so. That decision or action may include using his official position to exert pressure on another official to perform an "official act," or to advise another official, knowing or intending that such advice will form the basis for an "official act" by another official. Setting up a meeting, talking to another official, or organizing an event (or agreeing to do so) — without more — does not fit that definition of "official act."

In addition to being inconsistent with both text and precedent, the government's expansive interpretation of "official act" would raise significant constitutional concerns. Section 201 prohibits *quid pro quo* corruption — the exchange of a thing of value for an "official act." In the government's view, nearly anything a public official accepts — from a campaign contribution to lunch — counts as a *quid*; and nearly anything a public official does — from arranging a meeting to inviting a guest to an event — counts as a *quo*.

But conscientious public officials arrange meetings for constituents, contact other officials on their behalf, and include them in events all the time. The basic compact underlying representative government *assumes* that public officials will hear from their constituents and act appropriately on their concerns — whether it is the union official worried about a plant closing or the homeowners who wonder why it took five days to restore power to their neighborhood after a storm. The government's position could cast a pall of potential prosecution over these relationships if the union had given a campaign contribution in the past or the homeowners invited the official to join them on their annual outing to the ballgame. Officials might wonder whether they could respond to even the most commonplace requests for assistance, and citizens with legitimate concerns might shrink from participating in democratic discourse.

This concern is substantial. White House counsel who worked in every administration from that of President Reagan to President Obama warn that the government's "breathtaking expansion of public-corruption law would likely chill federal officials' interactions with the people they serve and thus damage their ability effectively to perform their duties." Six former Virginia attorneys general — four Democrats and two Republicans — also filed an *amicus* brief in this Court echoing those concerns, as did 77 former state attorneys general from States other than Virginia — 41 Democrats, 35 Republicans, and 1 independent.

None of this, of course, is to suggest that the facts of this case typify normal political interaction between public officials and their constituents. Far from it. But the government's legal interpretation is not confined to cases involving extravagant gifts or large sums of money, and we cannot construe a criminal statute on the assumption that the government will "use it responsibly." *United States v. Stevens,* 559 U.S. 460, 480, (2010). . . .

A related concern is that, under the government's interpretation, the term "official act" is not defined "with sufficient definiteness that ordinary people can understand what conduct is prohibited," or "in a manner that does not encourage arbitrary and discriminatory enforcement." *Skilling,* 561 U.S. at 402–403 (internal quotation marks omitted) . . . .

The government's position also raises significant federalism concerns. Here, where a more limited interpretation of "official act" is supported by both text and precedent, we decline to "construe the statute in a manner that leaves its outer boundaries ambiguous and involves the Federal Government in setting standards" of "good government for local and state officials." *McNally v. United States,* 483 U.S. 350, 360, (1987).

Governor McDonnell argues that his convictions must be vacated because the jury was improperly instructed on the meaning of "official act" under §201(a)(3) of the federal bribery statute. According to Governor McDonnell, the District Court "refused to convey any meaningful limits on 'official act,' giving an instruction that allowed the jury to convict [him] for lawful conduct." We agree.

The jury instructions included the statutory definition of "official action," and further defined the term to include "actions that have been clearly established by settled practice as part of a public official's position, even if the action was not taken pursuant to responsibilities explicitly assigned by law." The instructions also stated that "official actions may include acts that a public official customarily performs," including acts "in furtherance of longer-term goals" or "in a series of steps to exercise influence or achieve an end." In light of our interpretation of the term "official acts," those instructions lacked important qualifications, rendering them significantly overinclusive.

First, the instructions did not adequately explain to the jury how to identify the "question, matter, cause, suit, proceeding or controversy." . . . .

The problem with the District Court's instructions is that they provided no assurance that the jury reached its verdict after finding those questions or matters.

To prevent this problem, the District Court should have instructed the jury that it must identify a "question, matter, cause, suit, proceeding or controversy" involving the formal exercise of governmental power.

Second, the instructions did not inform the jury that the "question, matter, cause, suit, proceeding or controversy" must be more specific and focused than a broad policy objective. [T]he District Court should have instructed the jury that the pertinent "question, matter, cause, suit, proceeding or controversy" must be something specific and focused that is "pending" or "may by law be brought before any public official," such as the question whether to initiate the research studies.

Third, the District Court did not instruct the jury that to convict Governor McDonnell, it had to find that he made a decision or took an action — or agreed to do so — *on* the identified "question, matter, cause, suit, proceeding or controversy," as we have construed that requirement. At trial, several of Governor McDonnell's subordinates testified that he asked them to attend a meeting, not that he expected them to do anything other than that. If that testimony reflects what Governor McDonnell agreed to do at the time he accepted the loans and gifts from Williams, then he did not agree to make a decision or take an action on any of the three questions or matters described by the Fourth Circuit.

The jury may have disbelieved that testimony or found other evidence that Governor McDonnell agreed to exert pressure on those officials to initiate the research studies or add Anatabloc to the state health plan, but it is also possible that the jury convicted Governor McDonnell without finding that he agreed to make a decision or take an action on a properly defined "question, matter, cause, suit, proceeding or controversy." To forestall that possibility, the District Court should have instructed the jury that merely arranging a meeting or hosting an event to discuss a matter does not count as a decision or action on that matter.

Because the jury was not correctly instructed on the meaning of "official act," it may have convicted Governor McDonnell for conduct that is not unlawful. For that reason, we cannot conclude that the errors in the jury instructions were "harmless beyond a reasonable doubt." We accordingly vacate Governor McDonnell's convictions. . . .

There is no doubt that this case is distasteful; it may be worse than that. But our concern is not with tawdry tales of [gifts of] Ferraris, Rolexes, and ball gowns. It is instead with the broader legal implications of the government's boundless interpretation of the federal bribery statute. A more limited interpretation of the term "official act" leaves ample room for prosecuting corruption, while comporting with the text of the statute and the precedent of this Court.

Notes and Questions

1. *The "official act."* As noted above, § 201 criminalizes offering to give or agreeing to receive something of value for any of three purposes: (a) to influence a public official in an official act; (b) to influence a public official to commit a fraud on the United

States; or (c) to induce a public official to act in violation of a lawful duty. When the first theory is used, the government must prove the "official act" as an element of the offense. The Court attempted to define this term in *McDonnell*. Is the definition sufficiently clear? Why or why not?

2. *Applying § 201's definition of "official act" to extortion and honest services.* As discussed more fully below, because *McDonnell* did not involve charges brought under § 201, it was not clear that the Court needed to apply the § 201 definition of "official act." Because the defendants were not federal public officials, the government used other anti-corruption statutes — the honest services statute and the extortion statute — to prosecute the alleged bribery in this case. Was the Court required to apply § 201's definition to these statutes? The government conceded this point. Was that an error on the government's part? *See* Randall Eliason, *The Bob McDonnell Case May Have Been Won Months Before Trial*, SIDEBARS: REFLECTIONS ON WHITE COLLAR CRIME AND FEDERAL CRIMINAL LAW (July 14, 2016), https://sidebarsblog.com/the-bob-mcdonnell-case-may-have-been-won-months-before-trial/.

3. *Was* McDonnell *correctly decided?* Because it was a unanimous decision, it may seem that the outcome was obvious and noncontroversial. Not so. It seems clear that McDonnell provided access in exchange for gifts. Should this behavior constitute a crime? *See* Randall Eliason, McDonnell v. United States: *A Cramped Vision of Public Corruption*, GEO. WASH. L. REV. ON THE DOCKET (Oct. Term 2015) (July 2, 2016), https://www.gwlr.org/mcdonnell-v-united-states-a-cramped-vision-of-public-corruption/ (opining that "[t]his unfortunate decision dramatically limits the reach of federal bribery law. It was a win for McDonnell, but a loss for anyone concerned about public corruption and the influence of money in politics.").

4. McDonnell's *reach.* How far does the *McDonnell* holding extend? So far, courts have tended to limit its holding. *See, e.g., United States v. Ng Lap Seng*, 934 F.3d 110 (2d Cir. 2019) (holding that *McDonnell* does not apply to scheme where defendant used his influence to cause United Nations official to influence another UN official); *United States v. Boyland*, 862 F.3d 279 (2d Cir. 2017) (holding that *McDonnell* does not apply to federal program bribery). *See generally* Elkan Abramowitz & Jonathan S. Sack, *Limiting the Reach of the Supreme Court's* McDonnell *Decision*, N.Y.L.J. Vol. 262, No. 65, Oct. 1, 2019 (positing that the "what" and the "when" of the term "official act" will remain important questions in both corruption and bribery prosecutions in the years to come).

5. *Bribery and the Trump impeachment.* On December 18, 2019, the United States House of Representatives impeached President Donald Trump on several grounds. *See* United States House of Representatives, *Articles of Impeachment against Donald John Trump*, Dec. 18, 2019. The allegations in the First Article of Impeachment stemmed from Trump's communications with the president of Ukraine, Volodymyr Zelensky. The Article alleged that President Trump attempted to induce the Ukrainian government to provide information damaging to Trump's political rival in the 2020 election, Joe Biden, in exchange for military aid. Although the allegations seemed to make out a bribery case, the House declined to include a bribery

charge in the Articles of Impeachment and instead accused Trump of broad "abuses of power" based upon allegations of corruption that mirror bribery in substance. *See id.* (alleging that "President Trump engaged in this scheme or course of conduct for corrupt purposes in pursuit of personal political benefit.").

During the Impeachment Proceedings, House Republicans and their expert witness, George Washington Law School Professor Jonathan Turley, argued that there was insufficient evidence to show that Trump acted with the corrupt intent necessary for a bribery charge. Their view was that the President, during his communications with Zelensky, acted out of sincere concern about Ukrainian corruption in connection with the activities of Biden's son, Hunter. *See* Jonathan Turley, Written Statement, *The Impeachment Inquiry Into President Donald J. Trump: The Constitutional Basis For Presidential Impeachment*, Dec. 4, 1019. House Democrats and other commentators disagreed, asserting that Trump corruptly sought something of value (assistance in his reelection) in exchange for an official act (providing military aid to Ukraine). *See* Randall D. Eliason, *Opinion: The Republicans' Expert Is Wrong about Bribery*, Wash. Post, Dec. 5, 2019, https://www.washingtonpost.com/opinions/2019/12/05/republicans-expert-is-wrong-about-bribery/.

Should the House have included bribery as one of the "high crimes and misdemeanors" in the Articles of Impeachment? Was there sufficient evidence that President Trump acted with corrupt intent? *See* Sean Elling, *Did Trump Commit Bribery? I Asked 7 Legal Experts. It's Complicated*, VOX (Dec. 17, 2019, 11:00 a.m.), https://www.vox.com/policy-and-politics/2019/12/17/21024235/impeachment-trump-bribery-democrats.

6. *Defining bribery.* As examined in Chapter 8, Extortion, distinguishing bribery from lawful activity, such as making legitimate contributions, is a daunting task. The Court in *McDonnell* stated that "[t]he government's position could cast a pall" on legitimate interactions between public officials and their constituents. Is this a valid concern? *See* George Brown, McDonnell *and the Criminalization of Politics*, 5 Va. J. Crim. L. 1, 34–36 (2017) (positing that *McDonnell* is a distinct rebuke of expansive statutory interpretation).

Is drawing the distinction between legal and illegal activity in the political realm properly a job for courts or legislatures? In either case, how could we clearly distinguish legitimate activity from bribery? In that context, consider the following:

> Could Virginia or another state prohibit the exchange of luxury items for access? [T]his Article [proposes an] external value theory of bribery according to which an agreement to exchange *X* for *Y* only constitutes bribery if *X* and *Y* are values from different spheres. As a result, an agreement to exchange something of value for a political act only constitutes bribery when the value exchanged for the political act is something external to politics. Unlike the campaign contribution context, in *McDonnell* we have no doubt that the purchase of a Rolex watch or a shopping trip for the Governor's wife are not political acts. Rather, the controversy is on the other

side of the quid pro quo exchange. If access is not an official act, then an agreement to exchange a Rolex for access does not constitute an agreement to exchange one type of value for another. As a result, we have no bribery.

Is the granting of access an official act? [N]othing in the nature of bribery provides an answer to this question. The Court is correct that granting access must be an official act in order for the sale of access to constitute bribery. This is so not only as a matter of statutory interpretation but also because bribery requires a boundary crossing between spheres of value. Moreover, the theory of bribery put forward here tells us that this question is empirical or descriptive in nature rather than normative. It asks whether granting access is an official act in our political culture. Statutory interpretation is a good way to begin to answer this question.

The theory of bribery also gives rise to two normative questions. First, where should such boundaries between spheres of value be drawn, and second, who decides the answer to this first question? In the context of the *McDonnell* case, these questions are: Should access be considered an official act and who should make this determination? Chief Justice Roberts hints at his answers to each of these questions. He suggests that access should not be considered an official act and in so doing, he assumes that it is the Court, rather than the legislature, that determines whether access is or is not an official act. However, each of these assertions is far more controversial than this short unanimous opinion would lead one to believe.

Deborah Hellman, *A Theory of Bribery*, 38 Cardozo L. Rev. 1947, 1992 (2017). What is your view of this approach? Why?

Problems

7-4. The defendant is a Social Security Administration employee who, in exchange for money, helped people fraudulently obtain benefits. The defendant is charged with bribery under § 201. The defendant moves to dismiss on the grounds that the defendant simply helped people prepare false documents when applying for government benefits. Because the defendant did not have the authority to approve or disapprove the applications, he argues, he did not engage in "official acts."

How should the court rule? Why?

7-5. Montgomery worked for the United States Department of Housing and Urban Development ("HUD"), and had labor relations duties. While employed by HUD, Montgomery used the contacts with labor unions that he developed through his duties at HUD and schemed with insurance companies to sell group automobile insurance policies to labor unions. As part of the scheme, Montgomery received free trips and other things of value from the insurance companies. Based on these facts, Montgomery was convicted of receiving illegal gratuities. Montgomery now appeals.

How should the court rule? Why?

7-6. An undercover federal agent paid a federal law enforcement official to search for publicly available information in the federal agency for which the official worked. Based upon these facts, federal prosecutors are considering charging the federal law enforcement official under Section 201.

Has the defendant violated the statute? Why or why not?

7-7. Thomas was a federal inmate at United States Penitentiary-Lee County (USP-Lee). Thomas paid a prison nurse, Susan, to smuggle coveted items such as cell phones and tobacco into the prison. Eventually, investigators discovered their arrangement, and both were arrested. Susan pled guilty and testified against Thomas. Thomas pled not guilty to charges of bribing a government official. At trial, Thomas argued that the bribe was not for an "official act" as defined by statute and that the court erred in instructing that it was immaterial as to whether the government official in question initiated the illicit transactions. Thomas was convicted.

On appeal, is the court likely to uphold Thomas' conviction? Why or why not?

C. Federal Program Bribery — § 666

1. Statutory Elements

Section 666 criminalizes bribery in connection with federal programs. Unlike § 201, § 666 is not limited to cases involving federal public officials, and encompasses bribery involving a wide range of private and governmental entities. Prosecutors have become increasingly aggressive in using § 666, particularly in cases involving state and local corruption.

In a prosecution under § 666(a)(1)(B) against the *bribed party*, the government must prove that:

(1) The defendant solicited or demanded, or accepted or agreed to accept, a thing of value;

(2) The defendant was an agent of a private organization or of a state, local, or tribal government or agency that received more than $10,000 a year in federal benefits;

(3) The defendant solicited or received the thing of value in connection with business or transactions of the entity valued at $5,000 or more; and

(4) The defendant acted corruptly.

In a prosecution under § 666(a)(2) against the *bribing party*, the government must prove that:

(1) The defendant gave, offered, or agreed to give a thing of value;

(2) The offeree was an agent of a private organization or of a state, local, or tribal government or agency that received more than $10,000 a year in federal benefits;

(3) The defendant offered or gave the thing of value in connection with business or transactions of the entity valued at $5,000 or more; and

(4) The defendant acted corruptly.

Section 666 provides that the defendant may be punished by a fine, by imprisonment of not more than 10 years, or both.

2. The Reach of the Statute

In a pair of decisions, the United States Supreme Court has rejected attempts to narrow the reach of § 666. In *Salinas v. United States*, 522 U.S. 52 (1997), the defendant argued that his conviction under § 666 could not stand because the bribes he received did not involve the misuse or misappropriation of federal funds. Salinas was a sheriff's deputy at a county prison that received over $10,000 a year in federal money in exchange for housing federal prisoners.[a] A prisoner paid bribes to Salinas, who in return arranged "contact visits" with the prisoner's girlfriend. The Court affirmed the conviction under § 666, holding that the government is not required to prove that the bribes led to the misappropriation or misuse of federal funds.

In *Salinas*, the Court did not answer the question whether § 666 "requires some other kind of connection between a bribe and the expenditure of federal funds." The circuit courts split on this issue, and the Supreme Court resolved the split in the case that follows.

Sabri v. United States
541 U.S. 600 (2004)

JUSTICE SOUTER delivered the opinion of the Court.

The question is whether 18 U.S.C. § 666(a)(2), proscribing bribery of state, local, and tribal officials of entities that receive at least $10,000 in federal funds, is a valid exercise of congressional authority under Article I of the Constitution. We hold that it is.

Petitioner Basim Omar Sabri is a real estate developer who proposed to build a hotel and retail structure in the city of Minneapolis. Sabri lacked confidence, however, in his ability to adapt to the lawful administration of licensing and zoning laws, and offered three separate bribes to a city councilman, Brian Herron, according to the grand jury indictment that gave rise to this case. At the time the bribes were allegedly offered (between July 2, 2001, and July 17, 2001), Herron served as a member of the Board of Commissioners of the Minneapolis Community Development Agency (MCDA), a public body created by the city council to fund housing and economic development within the city.

---

a. Another aspect of this case is discussed in Chapter 14, RICO, *infra*.

Count 1 of the indictment charged Sabri with offering a $5,000 kickback for obtaining various regulatory approvals, and according to Count 2, Sabri offered Herron a $10,000 bribe to set up and attend a meeting with owners of land near the site Sabri had in mind, at which Herron would threaten to use the city's eminent domain authority to seize their property if they were troublesome to Sabri. Count 3 alleged that Sabri offered Herron a commission of 10% on some $800,000 in community economic development grants that Sabri sought from the city, the MCDA, and other sources. . . .

Before trial, Sabri moved to dismiss the indictment on the ground that § 666(a)(2) is unconstitutional on its face for failure to require proof of a connection between the federal funds and the alleged bribe, as an element of liability. The government responded that "even if an additional nexus between the bribery conduct and the federal funds is required, the evidence in this case will easily meet such a standard" because Sabri's alleged actions related to federal dollars. Although Sabri did not contradict this factual claim, the District Court agreed with him that the law was facially invalid. A divided panel of the Eighth Circuit reversed, holding that there was nothing fatal in the absence of an express requirement to prove some connection between a given bribe and federally pedigreed dollars, and that the statute was constitutional under the Necessary and Proper Clause in serving the objects of the congressional spending power. Judge Bye dissented out of concern about the implications of the law for dual sovereignty. We granted certiorari to resolve a split among the Courts of Appeals over the need to require connection between forbidden conduct and federal funds. We now affirm.

Sabri raises what he calls a facial challenge to § 666(a)(2): the law can never be applied constitutionally because it fails to require proof of any connection between a bribe or kickback and some federal money. It is fatal, as he sees it, that the statute does not make the link an element of the crime, to be charged in the indictment and demonstrated beyond a reasonable doubt. Thus, Sabri claims his attack meets the demanding standard set out in United States v. Salerno, 481 U.S. 739, 745 (1987), since he says no prosecution can satisfy the Constitution under this statute, owing to its failure to require proof that its particular application falls within Congress's jurisdiction to legislate.

We can readily dispose of this position that, to qualify as a valid exercise of Article I power, the statute must require proof of connection with federal money as an element of the offense. We simply do not presume the unconstitutionality of federal criminal statutes lacking explicit provision of a jurisdictional hook, and there is no occasion even to consider the need for such a requirement where there is no reason to suspect that enforcement of a criminal statute would extend beyond a legitimate interest cognizable under Article I, § 8.

Congress has authority under the Spending Clause to appropriate federal monies to promote the general welfare, Art. I, § 8, cl. 1, and it has corresponding authority under the Necessary and Proper Clause, Art. I, § 8, cl. 18, to see to it that taxpayer dollars appropriated under that power are in fact spent for the general welfare, and not frittered away in graft or on projects undermined when funds are siphoned off or corrupt public officers are derelict about demanding value for dollars. Congress does not have to sit by and accept the risk of operations thwarted by local and state improbity. Section 666(a)(2) addresses the problem at the sources of bribes, by rational means, to safeguard the integrity of the state, local, and tribal recipients of federal dollars.

It is true, just as Sabri says, that not every bribe or kickback offered or paid to agents of governments covered by § 666(b) will be traceably skimmed from specific federal payments, or show up in the guise of a *quid pro quo* for some dereliction in spending a federal grant. *Cf.* Salinas v. United States, 522 U.S. 52, 56–57 (1997) (the "expansive, unqualified" language of the statute "does not support the interpretation that federal funds must be affected to violate § 666(a)(1)(B)"). But this possibility portends no enforcement beyond the scope of federal interest, for the reason that corruption does not have to be that limited to affect the federal interest. Money is fungible, bribed officials are untrustworthy stewards of federal funds, and corrupt contractors do not deliver dollar-for-dollar value. Liquidity is not a financial term for nothing; money can be drained off here because a federal grant is pouring in there. And officials are not any the less threatening to the objects behind federal spending just because they may accept general retainers. It is certainly enough that the statutes condition the offense on a threshold amount of federal dollars defining the federal interest, such as that provided here, and on a bribe that goes well beyond liquor and cigars.

For those of us who accept help from legislative history, it is worth noting that the legislative record confirms that § 666(a)(2) is an instance of necessary and proper legislation. The design was generally to "protect the integrity of the vast sums of money distributed through Federal programs from theft, fraud, and undue influence by bribery," *see* S. Rep. No. 98-225, p. 370 (1983), in contrast to prior federal law affording only two limited opportunities to prosecute such threats to the federal interest: 18 U.S.C. § 641, the federal theft statute, and § 201, the federal bribery law. Those laws had proven inadequate to the task. The former went only to outright theft of unadulterated federal funds, and prior to this Court's opinion in Dixson v. United States, 465 U.S. 482 (1984), which came after passage of § 666, the bribery statute had been interpreted by lower courts to bar prosecution of bribes directed at state and local officials. Thus we said that § 666 "was designed to extend federal bribery prohibitions to bribes offered to state and local officials employed by agencies receiving federal funds," Salina, 522 U.S. at 58, thereby filling the regulatory gaps. Congress's decision to enact § 666 only after other legislation had failed to protect federal interests is further indication that it was acting within the ambit of the Necessary and Proper Clause.

Petitioner presses two more particular arguments against the constitutionality of § 666(a)(2), neither of which helps him. First, he says that § 666 is all of a piece with the legislation that a majority of this Court held to exceed Congress's authority under the Commerce Clause in United States v. Lopez, 514 U.S. 549 (1995), and

United States v. Morrison, 529 U.S. 598 (2000). But these precedents do not control here. In *Lopez* and *Morrison*, the Court struck down federal statutes regulating gun possession near schools and gender-motivated violence, respectively, because it found the effects of those activities on interstate commerce insufficiently robust. The Court emphasized the noneconomic nature of the regulated conduct, commenting on the law at issue in *Lopez*, for example, "that by its terms [it] has nothing to do with 'commerce' or any sort of economic enterprise, however broadly one might define those terms." 514 U.S. at 561. The Court rejected the government's contentions that the gun law was valid Commerce Clause legislation because guns near schools ultimately bore on social prosperity and productivity, reasoning that on that logic, Commerce Clause authority would effectively know no limit. *Cf.* Morrison, 529 U.S. at 615–616 (rejecting comparable congressional justification for Violence Against Women Act of 1994). In order to uphold the legislation, the Court concluded, it would be necessary "to pile inference upon inference in a manner that would bid fair to convert congressional authority under the Commerce Clause to a general police power of the sort retained by the States." Lopez, 514 U.S. at 567.

No piling is needed here to show that Congress was within its prerogative to protect spending objects from the menace of local administrators on the take. The power to keep a watchful eye on expenditures and on the reliability of those who use public money is bound up with congressional authority to spend in the first place, and Sabri would be hard pressed to claim, in the words of the *Lopez* Court, that §666(a)(2) "has nothing to do with" the congressional spending power. Id. at 561.

Sabri next argues that §666(a)(2) amounts to an unduly coercive, and impermissibly sweeping, condition on the grant of federal funds as judged under the criterion applied in South Dakota v. Dole, 483 U.S. 203 (1987). This is not so. Section 666(a)(2) is authority to bring federal power to bear directly on individuals who convert public spending into unearned private gain, not a means for bringing federal economic might to bear on a State's own choices of public policy.*

We remand for proceedings consistent with this opinion. The judgment of the Court of Appeals for the Eighth Circuit is Affirmed.

JUSTICE KENNEDY, with whom JUSTICE SCALIA joins, concurring in part. (Omitted.)JUSTICE THOMAS, concurring in the judgment. (Omitted).

Notes and Questions

1. *Scope of §666.* What exactly is the scope of §666? In light of the Court's holding in *Dixson*, does §666 give the government any power that it does not have under §201? If so, what?

---

* In enacting §666, Congress addressed a legitimate federal concern by licensing federal prosecution in an area historically of state concern. In upholding the constitutionality of the law, we mean to express no view as to its soundness as a policy matter.

2. *Federalism.* Many commentators believed that, after Lopez, 514 U.S. 549, the Court would strike down federal criminal statutes that intruded into matters historically reserved to the states. Why did the reasoning in *Lopez* fail to control the outcome in *Sabri*? In a footnote in *Sabri*, the Court stated, "[i]n enacting § 666, Congress addressed a legitimate federal concern by licensing federal prosecution in an area historically of state concern. In upholding the constitutionality of the law, we mean to express no view as to its soundness as a policy matter." Does § 666 rest on sound policy? Why or why not?

3. *The meaning of "benefits."* Section 666 requires that the "organization, government, or agency receive, in any one year period, benefits in excess of $10,000 under a Federal program involving a grant, contract, subsidy, loan, guarantee, insurance, or other form of Federal assistance." In Fischer v. United States, 529 U.S. 667 (2000), the Supreme Court considered whether a health care provider participating in the Medicare program receives "benefits" under § 666. The defendant in that case was convicted of paying bribes to an agent of a local hospital authority. Although the authority received Medicare payments of more than $10,000 a year, the defense asserted that these payments did not constitute "benefits." According to this argument, the only "benefits" were received by the covered patients.

The Court rejected the defendant's argument, concluding that "the payments are made not simply to reimburse for treatment of qualifying patients but to assist the hospital in making available and maintaining a certain level and quality of medical care, all in the interest of both the hospital and the greater community." Id. at 679–680. The Court continued:

> To determine whether an organization participating in a federal assistance program receives "benefits," an examination must be undertaken of the program's structure, operation, and purpose. The inquiry should examine the conditions under which the organization receives the federal payments. The answer could depend, as it does here, on whether the recipient's own operations are one of the reasons for maintaining the program. Health care organizations participating in the Medicare program satisfy this standard.

Id. at 681.

Justices Thomas and Scalia dissented, concluding that "the only persons who receive 'benefits' under Medicare are the individual elderly and disabled Medicare patients, not the medical providers who serve them." Id. at 682 (Thomas, J., dissenting). The dissent characterized the majority's approach to defining "benefits" as "unpersuasive and boundless," and as violating the rule of lenity. Id. at 686, 691.

Which side has the better of the argument? Under the majority's approach, what are the limits of the definition of "benefits"? Take a corner grocery store that receives food stamp payments of more than $10,000 a year. To receive the payments, the store is subject to federal regulations concerning the store's inventory and business integrity. Would these payments qualify as "benefits" under the statute? *See* id. at 691–692.

Courts have continued to apply a broad definition of "benefits" under § 666. For example, in *United States v. Bahel*, 662 F.3d 610, 630 (2d Cir. 2011), the court affirmed the conviction of an employee of the United Nations. The court concluded that, "the payment of the United States' dues to the U.N. is a 'Federal program,' because there is a specific statutory scheme authorizing the assistance, i.e., the U.N. Participation Act. Further, the U.N. Participation Act plainly seeks to promote the United States' foreign policy objectives, and thus is properly considered a 'benefit' subject to the strictures of 18 U.S.C. § 666."

4. *Does § 666 encompass gratuities?* Section 666 requires proof that the defendant acted "corruptly." Some courts have interpreted this language to require proof of a *quid pro quo.* For example, in *United States v. Fernandez,* 722 F.3d 1 (1st Cir. 2013), the First Circuit engaged in a lengthy review of the language, history, and purpose of § 666, and concluded that the statute does not criminalize gratuities. *See also* United States v. Jennings, 160 F.3d 1006, 1015 n.4 (4th Cir. 1998) (opining that gratuities are not prohibited by § 666, but declining to decide the issue).

Other federal circuit courts, however, have held that § 666 does encompass gratuities. In United States v. McNair, 605 F.3d 1152 (11th Cir. 2010), the Eleventh Circuit held that the government is not required to prove a quid pro quo under §§ 666(a)(1)(B) and (a)(2). The court relied upon the plain language of §§ 666(a)(1)(B) and (a)(2), neither of which either mentions a *quid pro quo* or contains such language as "in exchange for" or "in return for" a specific official act. A contrary holding, the court stated, "would permit a person to pay a significant sum to [a covered agent] intending the payment to produce a future, as yet unidentified, favor without violating § 666." *Accord,* United States v. Bonito, 57 F.3d 167, 171 (2d Cir. 1995).

Which is the correct result? Why?

5. *Defining the quid pro quo.* Assuming that a quid pro quo is required under § 666, how should that element be defined? In one high profile case, the government prosecuted former Alabama governor Don Siegelman on various political corruption charges, including federal program bribery. *See* United States v. Siegelman, 640 F.3d 1159, 1169–72 (11th Cir. 2011). In affirming the conviction, the court addressed the definition of quid pro quo under the statute. The court held that the offer or payment must be in exchange for an explicit, but not necessarily express, agreement. The court explained:

> No generalized expectation of some future favorable action will do. The official must agree to take or forego some specific action in order for the doing of it to be criminal under § 666. In the absence of such an agreement on a specific action, even a close-in-time relationship between the donation and the act will not suffice.

In reaching this conclusion, the court relied upon United States Supreme Court precedent in the context of the closely related crime of extortion, Chapter 8, *infra.*

6. *The official act.* In *Sun-Diamond Growers*, the Supreme Court held that the benefit to the public official must be in connection with a specific official act. 526 U.S. 398.

Does the same requirement apply to cases brought under § 666 based on a bribery theory? The court in *United States v. Ganim*, 510 F.3d 134, 134 (2d Cir. 2007), held not. The court reasoned that the language in the gratuities statute—referring to giving benefits to a public official "for or because of *any official act* performed or to be performed,"—compelled the outcome in *Sun-Diamond*. By contrast, the court reasoned, the elements of § 666 bribery are met so long as the official accepted the benefit in exchange for a promise to perform official acts for the giver; the government need not specify the official acts.

In *McDonnell*, the Supreme Court narrowed the definition of an "official act" under § 201. Does that definition apply to § 666? In *United States v. Ng Lap Seng*, 934 F.3d 110, 133–36 (2d Cir. 2019), the Second Circuit held not. The court stated that, based on the "textual differences among various bribery statutes, we conclude that the *McDonnell* 'official act' standard, derived from the *quo* component of bribery as defined by § 201(a)(3), does not necessarily delimit the *quo* components of other bribery statutes, such as § 666." *Id.* at 133–34. *Accord United States v. Porter*, 886 F.3d 562, 565 (6th Cir. 2018).

7. *The meaning of "misapplies."* Section 666(a) criminalizes, among other acts, "intentionally misapply[ing]" property valued at $5,000 or more. In *United States v. Thompson*, 484 F.3d 877 (7th Cir. 2007), a state official arranged to have a state contract awarded to a politically favored travel agency. The defendant was charged under § 666 under the theory that she misapplied the property by steering the contract away from another bidder, who would have been awarded the contract had the defendant not interfered in the process. The benefit to the defendant, according to the government, was the raise she received that reflected, in part, her actions concerning the contract. Although she received the raise through normal civil service means, on appeal she did not argue that the evidence was insufficient to show that the raise was related to the travel contract; the court thus assumed that the connection was established. *Id.* at 879. In a decision written by Judge Easterbrook, the Seventh Circuit reversed the conviction. The court reasoned:

> Section 666 is captioned 'Theft or bribery concerning programs receiving Federal funds,' and the Supreme Court refers to it as an anti-bribery rule. Neither Thompson nor anyone else in state government was accused of taking a bribe or receiving a kickback. A statute's caption does not override its text, but the word "misapplies" is not a defined term. We could read that word broadly, so that it means any disbursement that would not have occurred had all state laws been enforced without any political considerations. Or we could read it narrowly, so that it means a disbursement in exchange for services not rendered (as with ghost workers), or to suppliers that would not have received any contract but for bribes, or for services that were overpriced (to cover the cost of baksheesh), or for shoddy goods at the price prevailing for high-quality goods. All of these conditions were satisfied in [earlier] cases. . . . None is satisfied here.

Faced with a choice between a broad reading that turns all (or a goodly fraction of) state-law errors or political considerations in state procurement into federal crimes, and a narrow reading that limits § 666 to theft, extortion, bribery, and similarly corrupt acts, a court properly uses the statute's caption for guidance. That plus the Rule of Lenity, which insists that ambiguity in criminal legislation be read against the prosecutor, lest the judiciary create, in common-law fashion, offenses that have never received legislative approbation, and about which adequate notice has not been given to those who might be ensnared.

Id. at 881. Do you agree that the government's theory in this case was flawed? Why or why not?

8. *The meaning of "agent."* Although the Court in *Sabri* expanded the reach of § 666, some federal courts of appeal have begun to narrow the statute's application by limiting the definition of "agent." In the case of a bribed party, the government must show that the defendant was an agent of a private organization or of a state, local, or tribal government or agency that received more than $10,000 a year in federal benefits. The statute defines "agent" as a "person authorized to act on behalf of another person or a government and, in the case of an organization or government, [the term "agent"] includes a servant or employee, and a partner, director, officer, manager, and representative."

In *United States v. Langston*, 590 F.3d 1226 (11th Cir. 2009), the court found that an official paid by a state commission with state money was not a state "agent" under § 666 because he was not authorized to act on behalf of the state under applicable state law. *See also United States v. Whitfield*, 590 F.3d 325 (5th Cir. 2009) (holding that, even assuming that the defendant judges were "agents" of the state court administrative agency insofar as they performed functions that involved agency funds, their decisions as presiding judges in two lawsuits were not made "in connection with any business, transaction, or series of transactions" of the agency under § 666). For a decision applying a broad construction of "agent," see *United States v. Keen*, 676 F.3d 981, 989 (11th Cir. 2012) (rejecting a claim that to qualify as an "agent" the defendant "must be authorized to act on behalf of the entity specifically with respect to its funds").

What is the appropriate definition of "agent" under § 666? Why?

9. *Potential for abuse?* As the materials in this chapter show, the federal bribery statutes have been broadly interpreted by both courts and prosecutors. Are there dangers in such interpretations? Do the broad readings open the door for politically motivated prosecutions?

The *Siegelman* case discussed above raised these issues. Many observers, including members of both political parties, questioned whether the case may have been politically motivated. *See* Editorial, *A Case of Politics*, N.Y. Times, June 16, 2008, at A18. Commentators have suggested that "the conversion of traditionally accepted political practices into aggressively interpreted criminal law violations by 'good government' prosecutors flirts with the danger of unfairness, or worse, revenge politics." Robert G. Morvillo & Robert J. Anello, *Criminalization of Political Processes*, N.Y.L.J., Oct. 3, 2006, at 3. Do you agree? Why or why not?

Problem

7-8. Defendant was a manager of Aerospace, Inc. ("Aerospace") and was responsible for acquiring property for Aerospace. Acting in that capacity, defendant retained Broker in connection with the acquisition of property and agreed to pay Broker an above-market rate of commission. In return, Broker paid Defendant $20,000 in kickbacks. During the year in question, Aerospace received more than $1 million under contracts to produce weapons systems for the United States Department of Defense.

A grand jury targeted Defendant and Broker in connection with this arrangement. Broker entered into a cooperation agreement with the government and testified against Defendant. Defendant was convicted of federal program bribery under § 666. Defendant appeals the conviction, arguing that the "benefits" element was not met.

What is the likely outcome? Why?

D. Foreign Corrupt Practices Act[*]

1. Background

In 1977, Congress passed the Foreign Corrupt Practices Act ("FCPA"), which criminalizes commercial bribery under certain circumstances and requires publicly traded companies to submit relevant information to the government. Congress acted, at least in part, as a response to discoveries of extensive corruption concerning payments to foreign officials. A Senate Report declared that: "Corporate bribery is bad business. In our free market system it is basic that the sale of products should take place on the basis of price, quality, and service. Corporate bribery is fundamentally destructive of this basic tenet." S. Rep. No. 95-114, at 4 (1977). A House Report stated that bribing foreign officials and others is also unethical and "counter to the moral expectations and values of the American public." H.R. Rep. No. 950640, at 4–5 (1977).

The FCPA modified the Securities Exchange Act of 1934. *See* 15 U.S.C. §§ 78dd-1, 78dd-2, 78dd-3, 78m, 78ff. Both the Department of Justice and the Securities and Exchange Commission have enforcement authority concerning violations of the FCPA. *See* Miriam F. Weisman, *Corporate Crime & Financial Fraud: Legal and Financial Implications of Corporate Misconduct* 116 (2012); Department of Justice

---

[*] Steven L. Chanenson, Professor of Law, Villanova University School of Law, contributed to an earlier version of this section.

and Securities and Exchange Commission, A Resource Guide to the U.S. Foreign Corrupt Practices Act 4–5 (2012), *available at* http://www.justice.gov/criminal/fraud/fcpa/guide.pdf (hereinafter "FCPA Guide"). In a jointly issued guide, the DOJ and the SEC describe the FCPA this way:

> The FCPA contains both anti-bribery and accounting provisions. The anti-bribery provisions prohibit U.S. persons and businesses (domestic concerns), U.S. and foreign public companies listed on stock exchanges in the United States or which are required to file periodic reports with the Securities and Exchange Commission (issuers), and certain foreign persons and businesses acting while in the territory of the United States (territorial jurisdiction) from making corrupt payments to foreign officials to obtain or retain business. The accounting provisions require issuers to make and keep accurate books and records and to devise and maintain an adequate system of internal accounting controls. The accounting provisions also prohibit individuals and businesses from knowingly falsifying books and records or knowingly circumventing or failing to implement a system of internal controls. * * *
>
> In general, the FCPA prohibits offering to pay, paying, promising to pay, or authorizing the payment of money or anything of value to a foreign official in order to influence any act or decision of the foreign official in his or her official capacity or to secure any other improper advantage in order to obtain or retain business."

FCPA Guide at 2, 10.

In a prosecution under § 78dd-1 against an agent of a publicly traded corporation for payments to a foreign official, the government must prove that:

(1) The defendant used the mails or an instrumentality of interstate commerce in furtherance of a payment, gift, etc. of anything of value;

(2) The payment, gift, etc. was to a foreign official for an enumerated purpose, including securing any improper advantage, in order to assist the corporation in obtaining or retaining business for or with, or directing business to, any person; and

(3) The defendant acted willfully and corruptly.

The statute does exempt what it refers to as a "facilitating or expediting payment" — commonly known as a "grease" payment — as long as the purpose of the payment was "to expedite or to secure the performance of a routine governmental action." Currently, the law provides for affirmative defenses if the payments were lawful under the written law of the foreign country or the payments were "a reasonable and bona fide expenditure." 15 U.S.C. 78dd-1(b).

As noted above, the FCPA also applies to what the statute refers to as "domestic concerns," which includes U.S. citizens, nationals, or residents as well as corporations, partnerships, or sole proprietorships with their principal place of business in the United States or organized under U.S. law. *See* 15 U.S.C. 78dd-2(h).

The FCPA provides that the defendant may be punished by a fine, by imprisonment of not more than five years, or both. The actual sentence will depend upon the application of the federal sentencing guidelines to the case.

2. The Scope of the FCPA

The FCPA covers a broad array of behavior. This "wide net over foreign bribery" is not, of course, unlimited. In the following case, the Fifth Circuit addressed what satisfies the so-called "business nexus element," which is the requirement that the allegedly unlawful payment be "in order to assist . . . in obtaining or retaining business for or with, or directing business to, any person." 15 U.S.C. 78dd-1(s).

United States v. Kay
359 F.3d 738 (5th Cir. 2004)

WEINER, CIRCUIT JUDGE:

Plaintiff-appellant, the United States of America ("government") appeals the district court's grant of the motion of defendants-appellees David Kay and Douglas Murphy ("defendants") to dismiss the Superseding Indictment ("indictment") that charged them with bribery of foreign officials in violation of the Foreign Corrupt Practices Act ("FCPA"). In their dismissal motion, defendants contended that the indictment failed to state an offense against them. The principal dispute in this case is whether, if proved beyond a reasonable doubt, the conduct that the indictment ascribed to defendants in connection with the alleged bribery of Haitian officials to understate customs duties and sales taxes on rice shipped to Haiti to assist American Rice, Inc. in obtaining or retaining business was sufficient to constitute an offense under the FCPA. Underlying this question of sufficiency of the contents of the indictment is the preliminary task of ascertaining the scope of the FCPA, which in turn requires us to construe the statute.

American Rice, Inc. ("ARI") is a Houston-based company that exports rice to foreign countries, including Haiti. Rice Corporation of Haiti ("RCH"), a wholly owned subsidiary of ARI, was incorporated in Haiti to represent ARI's interests and deal with third parties there. As an aspect of Haiti's standard importation procedure, its customs officials assess duties based on the quantity and value of rice imported into the country. Haiti also requires businesses that deliver rice there to remit an advance deposit against Haitian sales taxes, based on the value of that rice, for which deposit a credit is eventually allowed on Haitian sales tax returns when filed.

In 2001, a grand jury charged Kay with violating the FCPA and subsequently returned the indictment, which charges both Kay and Murphy with 12 counts of FCPA violations. . . .

In granting defendants' motion to dismiss the indictment for failure to state an offense, the district court held that, as a matter of law, bribes paid to obtain favorable tax treatment are not payments made to "obtain or retain business" within the intendment of the FCPA, and thus are not within the scope of that statute's proscription of foreign bribery. The government timely filed a notice of appeal. . . .

Because an offense under the FCPA requires that the alleged bribery be committed for the purpose of inducing foreign officials to commit unlawful acts, the results of which will assist in obtaining or retaining business in their country, the questions before us in this appeal are (1) whether bribes to obtain illegal but favorable tax and customs treatment can ever come within the scope of the statute, and (2) if so, whether, in combination, there are minimally sufficient facts alleged in the indictment to inform the defendants regarding the nexus between, on the one hand, Haitian taxes avoided through bribery, and, on the other hand, assistance in getting or keeping some business or business opportunity in Haiti.

None contend that the FCPA criminalizes every payment to a foreign official: It criminalizes only those payments that are intended to (1) influence a foreign official to act or make a decision in his official capacity, or (2) induce such an official to perform or refrain from performing some act in violation of his duty, or (3) secure some wrongful advantage to the payor. And even then, the FCPA criminalizes these kinds of payments only if the result they are intended to produce — their *quid pro quo* — will *assist* (or is intended to assist) the payor in efforts to get or keep some *business* for or with "any person." Thus, the first question of statutory interpretation presented in this appeal is whether payments made to foreign officials to obtain unlawfully reduced customs duties or sales tax liabilities can ever fall within the scope of the FCPA, i.e., whether the illicit payments made to obtain a reduction of revenue liabilities can *ever* constitute the kind of bribery that is proscribed by the FCPA. The district court answered this question in the negative; only if we answer it in the affirmative will we need to analyze the sufficiency of the factual allegations of the indictment as to the one element of the crime contested here.

The principal thrust of the defendants' argument is that the business nexus element, i.e., the "assist . . . in obtaining or retaining business" element, narrowly limits the statute's applicability to those payments that are intended to obtain a foreign official's approval of a bid for a new government contract or the renewal of an existing government contract. In contrast, the government insists that, in addition to payments to officials that lead directly to getting or renewing business contracts, the statute covers payments that indirectly advance ("assist") the payor's goal of obtaining or retaining foreign business with or for some person. The government reasons that paying reduced customs duties and sales taxes on imports, as is purported to have occurred in this case, is the type of "improper advantage" that *always* will assist in obtaining or retaining business in a foreign country, and thus is always covered by the FCPA.

In approaching this issue, the district court concluded that the FCPA's language is ambiguous, and proceeded to review the statute's legislative history. We agree with the court's finding of ambiguity for several reasons. Perhaps our most significant statutory construction problem results from the failure of the language of the FCPA to give a clear indication of the exact scope of the business nexus element; that is, the proximity of the required nexus between, on the one hand, the anticipated results of the foreign official's bargained-for action or inaction, and, on the other hand, the assistance provided by or expected from those results in helping the briber to obtain or retain business. Stated differently, how attenuated can the linkage be between the effects of that which is sought from the foreign official in consideration of a bribe (here, tax minimization) and the briber's goal of finding assistance or obtaining or retaining foreign business with or for some person, and still satisfy the business nexus element of the FCPA?

Second, the parties' diametrically opposed but reasonable contentions demonstrate that the ordinary and natural meaning of the statutory language *is* genuinely debatable and thus ambiguous. For instance, the word "business" can be defined at any point along a continuum from "a volume of trade," to "the purchase and sale of goods in an attempt to make a profit," to "an assignment" or a "project." Thus, dictionary definitions can support both (1) the government's broader interpretation of the business nexus language as encompassing any type of commercial activity, and (2) defendants' argument that "obtain or retain business" connotes a more pedestrian understanding of establishing or renewing a particular commercial arrangement. Similarly, although the word "assist" suggests a somewhat broader statutory scope, it does not connote specificity or define either how proximate or how remote the foreign official's anticipated actions that constitute assistance must or may be to the business obtained or retained. . . .

As the statutory language itself is amenable to more than one reasonable interpretation, it is ambiguous as a matter of law. We turn therefore to legislative history in our effort to ascertain Congress's true intentions.

1. 1977 Legislative History

Congress enacted the FCPA in 1977, in response to recently discovered but widespread bribery of foreign officials by United States business interests. Congress resolved to interdict such bribery, not just because it is morally and economically suspect, but also because it was causing foreign policy problems for the United States. . . .

Congress expressly emphasized that it did not intend to prohibit "so-called grease or facilitating payments," such as "payments for expediting shipments through customs or placing a transatlantic telephone call, securing required permits, or obtaining adequate police protection, transactions which may involve even the proper performance of duties." Instead of making an express textual exception for these types of non-covered payments, the respective committees of the two chambers sought to distinguish permissible grease payments from prohibited bribery by only prohibiting payments that induce an official to act "corruptly," i.e., actions requiring him "to misuse his official position" and his discretionary authority, not those "essentially ministerial" actions that "merely move a particular matter toward an eventual act or decision or which do not involve any discretionary action."

In short, Congress sought to prohibit the type of bribery that (1) prompts officials to misuse their discretionary authority and (2) disrupts market efficiency and United States foreign relations, at the same time recognizing that smaller payments intended to expedite ministerial actions should remain outside of the scope of the statute. . . .

To divine the categories of bribery Congress did and did not intend to prohibit, we must look to the Senate's proposal, because the final statutory language was drawn from it, and from the SEC Report on which the Senate's legislative proposal was based. In distinguishing among the types of illegal payments that United States entities were making at the time, the SEC Report identified four principal categories: (1) payments "made in an effort to procure special and unjustified favors or advantages in the enactment or *administration of the tax* or other *laws*" of a foreign country; (2) payments "made with the intent to assist the company in obtaining or retaining government contracts"; (3) payments "to persuade low-level government officials to perform functions or services which they are obliged to perform as part of their governmental responsibilities, but which they may refuse or delay unless compensated" ("grease"), and (4) political contributions. The SEC thus exhibited concern about a wide range of questionable payments (explicitly including the kind at issue here) that were resulting in millions of dollars being recorded falsely in corporate books and records. . . .

The statute's ultimate language of "obtaining or retaining" mirrors identical language in the SEC Report. But, whereas the SEC Report highlights payments that go toward "obtaining or retaining *government contracts*," the FCPA, incorporating the Senate Report's language, prohibits payments that assist in obtaining or retaining *business*, not just government contracts. Had the Senate and ultimately Congress wanted to carry over the exact, narrower scope of the SEC Report, they would have adopted the same language. We surmise that, in using the word "business" when it easily could have used the phraseology of SEC Report, Congress intended for the statute to apply to bribes beyond the narrow band of payments sufficient only to "obtain or retain government contracts." The Senate's express intention that the statute apply to corrupt payments that *maintain* business opportunities also supports this conclusion.

For purposes of deciding the instant appeal, the question nevertheless remains whether the Senate, and concomitantly Congress, intended this broader statutory scope to encompass the administration of tax, customs, and other laws and regulations affecting the revenue of foreign states. To reach this conclusion, we must ask whether Congress's remaining expressed desire to prohibit bribery aimed at getting assistance in retaining business or maintaining business opportunities was sufficiently broad to include bribes meant to affect the administration of revenue laws. When we do so, we conclude that the legislative intent was so broad.

Congress was obviously distraught not only about high profile bribes to high-ranking foreign officials, but also by the pervasiveness of foreign bribery by United States businesses and businessmen. Congress thus made the decision to clamp down on bribes intended to prompt foreign officials to misuse their discretionary authority for the benefit of a domestic entity's business in that country. This observation is not diminished by Congress's understanding and accepting that relatively small facilitating payments were, at the time, among the accepted costs of doing business in many foreign countries. . . .

In short, the 1977 legislative history, particularly the Senate's proposal and the SEC Report on which it relied, convinces us that Congress meant to prohibit a range of payments wider than only those that directly influence the acquisition or retention of government contracts or similar commercial or industrial arrangements. On the other end of the spectrum, this history also demonstrates that Congress explicitly excluded facilitating payments (the grease exception). In thus limiting the exceptions to the type of bribery covered by the FCPA to this narrow category, Congress's intention to cast an otherwise wide net over foreign bribery suggests that Congress intended for the FCPA to prohibit all other illicit payments that are intended to influence non-trivial official foreign action in an effort to aid in obtaining or retaining business for some person. The congressional target was bribery paid to engender assistance in improving the business opportunities of the payor or his beneficiary, irrespective of whether that assistance be direct or indirect, and irrespective of whether it be related to administering the law, awarding, extending, or renewing a contract, or executing or preserving an agreement. . . .

[Discussions of 1988 and 1998 amendments and legislative history omitted.]

Given the foregoing analysis of the statute's legislative history, we cannot hold as a matter of law that Congress meant to limit the FCPA's applicability to cover only bribes that lead directly to the award or renewal of contracts. Instead, we hold that Congress intended for the FCPA to apply broadly to payments intended to assist the payor, either directly or indirectly, in obtaining or retaining business for some person, and that bribes paid to foreign tax officials to secure illegally reduced customs and tax liability constitute a type of payment that can fall within this broad coverage. In 1977, Congress was motivated to prohibit rampant foreign bribery by domestic business entities, but nevertheless understood the pragmatic need to exclude innocuous grease payments from the scope of its proposals. The FCPA's legislative history instructs that Congress was concerned about both the kind of bribery that leads to discrete contractual arrangements and the kind that more generally helps a domestic payor obtain or retain business for some person in a foreign country; and that Congress was aware that this type includes illicit payments made to officials to obtain favorable but unlawful tax treatment. . . .

Thus, in diametric opposition to the district court, we conclude that bribes paid to foreign officials in consideration for unlawful evasion of customs duties and sales taxes *could* fall within the purview of the FCPA's proscription. We hasten to add, however, that this conduct does not automatically constitute a violation of the FCPA: It still must be shown that the bribery was intended to produce an effect — here, through tax savings — that would "assist in obtaining or retaining business."

We are satisfied that — for purposes of the statutory provisions criminalizing payments designed to induce foreign officials unlawfully to perform their official duties in *administering* the laws and regulations of their country to produce a result intended to assist in obtaining or retaining business in that country — an unjustified reduction in duties and taxes can, under appropriate circumstances, come within the scope of the statute.

As the district court held the indictment insufficient based on its determination that the kind of bribery charged in the indictment does not come within the scope of the FCPA, that court never reached the question whether the indictment was sufficient as to the business nexus element of the crime, for which the charging instrument merely tracked the statute without alleging any discrete facts whatsoever. [W]e hold that the indictment in this case is sufficient as a matter of law. For the foregoing reasons, therefore, the judgment of the district court dismissing the indictment charging defendants with violations of the FCPA is reversed and the case is remanded for further proceedings consistent herewith.

REVERSED and REMANDED.

Notes and Questions

1. *Corruptly?* The FCPA requires a "corrupt" intent. Based in part on legislative history, the government takes the view that this means a measure of wrongfulness regardless of whether the scheme succeeded. *United States v. Ford*, 435 F.3d 204, 211–213 (2d Cir. 2006) (holding that jury instruction describing "intent to influence" was not sufficient to describe "corrupt" intent). Therefore, according to the government, "an executive who authorizes others to pay 'whoever you need to' in a foreign government to obtain a contract has violated the FCPA — even if no bribe is ultimately offered or paid." FCPA Guide at 14.

2. *Willfully?* The FCPA requires that individual defendants act "willfully." This remains a difficult term to interpret when, as here, the statute does not define it. The Supreme Court has stated that, "[a]s a general matter, when used in the criminal context, a 'willful' act is one undertaken with a 'bad purpose.'" *Bryan v. United States*, 524 U.S. 184, 191 (1998); *see also* FCPA Guide at 14. The Court in *Bryan* stated that there are exceptions — most notably tax law crimes — when defendants must know they are violating a specific law. Id. at 194–95. Two courts of appeal, including a decision in the subsequent litigation in *Kay*, have concluded that the FCPA is not one of those exceptions. *See United States v. Kay*, 513 F.3d 432, 450–51 (5th Cir. 2007), *aff'd on reh'g en banc*, 513 F.3d 461 (2008); *Stichting Ter Behartiging Van de Belangen Van Oudaandeelhouders In* Het Kapitaal Van Saybolt Int'l B.V. v. Schreiber, 327 F.3d 173, 181 (2d Cir. 2003). Should the FCPA being treated like tax crimes? Why or why not?

3. *Anything of value?* The FCPA condemns the willful and corrupt offering of "anything of value" under specific circumstances. *See* 15 U.S.C. 78dd-1(a). This reflects Congress's view that "bribes can come in many shapes and sizes." FCPA Guide at 14; *United States v. Liebo*, 923 F.2d 1308, 1311–1312 (8th Cir. 1991) (finding that "anything of value" includes airplane tickets and cash payments to a third party within the sphere of influence of a target official). While cash payments are an obvious form of a bribe, "anything of value" can mean innumerable things, including travel and entertainment expenses or charitable contributions that do not have a proper business purpose. *See* Jacelyn Jager, *Debating "Anything of Value" Under the FCPA*, Compliance Week (Jan. 18, 2017), https://www.complianceweek.com/debating -anything-of-value-under-the-fcpa/2802.article.

4. *Defining a foreign official.* The FCPA defines a "foreign official," in part, as "any officer or employee of a foreign government or a department, agency, or instrumentality thereof." *See* 15 U.S.C. 78dd-1(f)(1)(A). In some situations, such as a direct employee of a foreign governmental agency like the Ministry of Defense, it will be clear that a person is a foreign official. It may be more difficult, however, if the putative foreign official works for state-owned (or partially state-owned) entity like a telecommunications company. Is such an organization an "instrumentality" of a foreign government such that the person is a foreign official under the FCPA? In a case of first impression, the Eleventh Circuit took the following approach:

> An 'instrumentality' under . . . the FCPA is an entity controlled by the government of a foreign country that performs a function the controlling government treats as its own. Certainly, what constitutes control and what constitutes a function the government treats as its own are fact-bound questions. It would be unwise and likely impossible to exhaustively answer them in the abstract.

United States v. Esquenazi, 752 F.3d 912, 925 (11th Cir. 2014) (finding sufficient evidence that the telecommunications company was an instrumentality of a foreign government within the meaning of the FCPA). *See United States v. Duperval*, 777 F.3d 1324, 1333–1334 (11th Cir. 2015) (holding that a telecommunications company 97% owned by the Haitian government was sufficiently an "instrumentality"). How, if at all, should Congress amend the FCPA in light of this judicial approach to potential foreign instrumentalities?

5. *No private right of action.* The lower federal courts have consistently concluded that there is no private right of action under the FCPA. The Second Circuit recently observed as follows:

> The antibribery provisions of the FCPA prohibit certain entities and persons from, inter alia, corruptly making payments to foreign officials for the purpose of influencing official action in order to obtain business. The text of the statute contains no explicit provision for a private right of action, although it does provide for civil and criminal penalties, and permits the Attorney General to seek injunctive relief. Because "[t]he express provision of one

method of enforcing a substantive rule suggests that Congress intended to preclude others," [*Alexander v.*] *Sandoval*, 532 U.S. [275, 290 (2001)], the structure of the statute, by focusing on public enforcement, tends to indicate the absence of a private remedy.

Republic of Iraq v. ABB AG, 768 F.3d 145, 170 (2d Cir. 2014). In light of this reasoning and the fact that Congress chose not to overrule earlier cases reaching the same conclusion when it amended the FCPA in 1998 (and despite some legislative history to the contrary), the Second Circuit held "that there is no private right of action under the antibribery provisions of the FCPA" Id., at 172. Would it be better policy to have a private right of action under the FCPA? Why or why not?

6. *Anti-bribery efforts outside of the United States.* International anti-bribery efforts have grown over the years. For example, the Convention on Combating Bribery of Foreign Officials in International Business Transactions, also known as the Anti-Bribery Convention, requires the parties to criminalize bribing foreign officials. Congress's 1998 amendments to the FCPA, including expanding the FCPA's scope to prohibit payments made to obtain "any improper advantage," were designed to meet the requirements of the Anti-Bribery Convention. *See* FCPA Guide at 3–4.

The United Nations General Assembly subsequently adopted the United Nations Convention Against Corruption ("UNCAC") in 2003, and it came into force in 2005. More than 170 countries are parties to the Convention. *See* United Nations Convention Against Corruption, https://www.unodc.org/unodc/en/treaties/CAC/. The 2010s saw further developments in the international fight against bribery and corruption, with the United Nations and other nongovernmental organizations urging cooperation and transparency, describing corruption as a "sinister enabler" of some of the "worst problems we face." *At this 'Critical Moment' UN Chief Urges Anti-Corruption Conference to Adopt United Front*, UN News (Dec. 16, 2019), https://news.un.org/en/story/2019/12/1053601. *See also* Janine R. Wedel, *Beyond Bribery*, Foreign Policy (Feb. 17, 2015), https://foreignpolicy.com/2015/02/17/beyond-bribery-corruption/ (discussing the implications of "legal" bribery and the "new corruption").

Furthermore, the United Kingdom passed the Bribery Act of 2010, creating a new offense "which can be committed by commercial organisations which fail to prevent persons associated with them from committing bribery on their behalf. It is a full defence for an organisation to prove that despite a particular case of bribery it nevertheless had adequate procedures in place to prevent persons associated with it from bribing." Ministry of Justice, *The Bribery Act 2010: Guidance About Procedures Which Relevant Commercial Organisations Can Put into Place To Prevent Persons Associated with Them from Bribing* 6 (2011), *available at* http://www.justice.gov.uk/downloads/legislation/bribery-act-2010-guidance.pdf.

As for any legislation meant to bring the foreign activities of corporate entities under the scrutiny of its home country, many criticisms arose in the wake of the Bribery Act's passage in 2010. Some commentators stressed that the law would stifle economic growth in the United Kingdom because such payments and hospitalities are commonplace throughout the world, and rendering these practices illegal would bring a halt to business as usual. *See* A. Anwar & G. Deeprose, *The Bribery Act 2010*, SCOTS LAW TIMES, (2010) 23, 125–128.

In 2014, the World Bank issued a report discussing international anti-bribery enforcement and the role of settlements. The report highlights some of the challenges that lie ahead as anti-bribery efforts become more internationalized.

> The main conclusion of the report is that significant monetary sanctions have been imposed with hardly any of the respective assets being returned to the countries whose officials have allegedly been bribed. The report highlights how the overwhelming majority of the jurisdictions harmed by foreign bribery are in the developing world and that the vast majority of the settlements involve state-owned enterprises and public procurement contracts, including projects that range from tens to hundreds of millions of dollars in infrastructure and natural resources sectors.
>
> The reality is that, in the majority of settlements, the countries whose officials were allegedly bribed have not been involved in the settlements and have not found any other means to obtain redress.

Jacinta Oduor et al., *Left Out of the Bargain: Settlements in Foreign Bribery Cases and Implications for Asset Recovery* 2 (2014), *available at* http://star.worldbank.org/star/sites/star/files/9781464800863.pdf.

7. *Growing importance of compliance programs.* As the frequency and sources of international anti-corruption enforcement increases, corporations with even a modest global reach may find themselves in difficult circumstances as discussed above. A key strategy for corporations will revolve around meaningful compliance programs designed to prevent, detect, and respond to violations. *See, e.g.*, Michael K. Loucks & Alexandra M. Gorman, *Is the DOJ FCPA Enforcement Hegemony Dead?* (June 26, 2014), *available at* https://openknowledge.worldbank.org/handle/10986/16271 (noting that "the risk can be well-managed through effective compliance programs and appropriate internal investigative responses in the event that facts regarding foreign bribery surface."). The importance of compliance programs to prosecutorial discretion is further explored in Chapter 15.

8. *Increased enforcement but few reported decisions.* The rise in FCPA actions has been well-documented. *See* Otto G. Obermaier et al., *The Foreign Corrupt Practices Act*, in WHITE COLLAR CRIME: BUSINESS AND REGULATORY OFFENSES § 16.02 (Otto Obermaier et al., eds. 2021) ("Since 2001, FCPA enforcement has seen significant growth with little sign of abatement . . ."); Weisman, *supra*, at 128 ("[S]ince 2005, the [the DOJ] has prosecuted more cases than were prosecuted in the first 28 years of the FCPA's existence combined.").

As enforcement actions have increased, the reach of the statute has also grown. As one commentator noted, "[e]nforcement agencies continue to assert novel and expansive theories of jurisdiction and liability, and the range of defendants brought within the FCPA's purview has only widened." Obermaier, *supra*.

The vast majority of FCPA actions have been resolved through negotiated resolutions, such as deferred-prosecution and non-prosecution agreements (DPAs and NPAs), rather than litigation. (For a discussion of the use of such agreements in general, see Chapter 15, *infra*.) As a result, the government's theories in these cases have gone largely untested. One observer noted:

> As a matter of general jurisprudence, it is troubling when any area of law largely develops outside of the judicial process. The judicial process facilitates the thoughtful presentation of opposing views, mitigating facts and circumstances, and potential defenses in an adversarial proceeding culminating in an impartial decision-maker weighing the facts and applying the law in rendering a decision in a transparent manner.
>
> These fundamental hallmarks are largely missing in FCPA enforcement. Rather, the enforcement agencies, occupying positions of advocate, judge, and rule-maker, induce settlement through the 'carrots' and 'sticks' they possess even though many of the enforcement theories leading to these resolutions are untested and dubious, and in some cases in direct conflict with the FCPA's statutory provisions. The end result is resolution vehicles that do not facilitate the thoughtful presentation of opposing views, mitigating facts and circumstances, potential defenses, or testing of legal theories. Yet, these resolution vehicles largely define the FCPA. When the parameters of any law develop through such an opaque process, public confidence in that law, as well as the rule of law, suffers.

Mike Koehle, *The Façade of FCPA Enforcement*, 41 Geo. J. Int'l L. 907, 994 (2010).

What are the costs and benefits, to the government and private parties, of resolving FCPA actions through negotiated settlements? Do negotiated resolutions such as DPAs and NPAs have the same deterrent effect as prosecutions that result in trials? *See* Weisman, *supra*, at 130 (recounting skepticism over the deterrent effects of such resolutions).

For private parties and entities under investigation, responding to a FCPA investigation may be enormously expensive. *See* Joe Palazzolo, *The Business of Bribery*, Wall. St. J., Oct. 2, 2012, at B1 (describing expenses of nearly half a billion dollars incurred by three corporations during internal investigations into possible FCPA violations). What are the incentives to reach a deal with the government rather than going to trial?

9. *Why criminalize?* Why does the United States criminalize the bribery of foreign officials? One scholar notes that "[t]he legislative history of the FCPA suggests that moralism and self-interest played the most significant roles in shaping the original Act and its 1988 Amendments. Since then, altruism [through promoting the economic development of foreign countries] has played a more prominent role in

shaping the FCPA and other initiatives aimed at foreign bribery." Kevin E. Davis, *Why Does the United States Regulate Foreign Bribery: Moralism, Self-Interest, or Altruism?*, 67 N.Y.U. ANN. SURV. AM. L. 497, 498 (2012). What is the proper rationale for the criminalization of such activities? What is the harm from the bribery of foreign officials? How does that harm affect the interests of the United States?

10. *The "official act."* Does the *McDonnell* definition of "official act" for purposes of § 201 also apply to the FCPA? In *United States v. Ng*, discussed above in the notes following the *Sabri* case, the Second Circuit held that *McDonnell* applies neither to Federal Program Bribery under § 666 nor to the FCPA.

Problems

7-9. Electro, Inc. is a large U.S. engineering company with global operations in more than 50 countries, including a number that have a high risk of corruption, such as Outer Slobovia. Electro's stock is listed on a national U.S. stock exchange. In conducting its business internationally, Electro's officers and employees come into regular contact with foreign officials, including officials in various ministries and state-owned entities. At a trade show, Electro has a booth at which it offers free pens, hats, t-shirts, and other similar promotional items with Electro's logo. Electro also serves free coffee, other beverages, and snacks at the booth. Some of the visitors to the booth are foreign officials.

Is Electro, Inc. violating the FCPA?

7-10. Please incorporate the facts from the previous problem. Now assume that, two years ago, Electro won a long-term contract to supply goods and services to the state-owned Electricity Commission in Outer Slobovia. The Electricity Commission is 100% owned, controlled, and operated by the government of Outer Slobovia, and employees of the Electricity Commission are subject to Outer Slobovia's domestic bribery laws. During the course of the contract, Electro periodically provides training to Electricity Commission employees at its facilities in Michigan. The training is paid for by the Electricity Commission as part of the contract. Senior officials of the Electricity Commission inform Electro that they want to inspect the facilities and ensure that the training is working well. Electro pays for the airfare, hotel, and transportation for the Electricity Commission senior officials to travel to Michigan to inspect Electro's facilities. Because it is a lengthy international flight, Electro agrees to pay for business class airfare, to which its own employees are entitled for lengthy flights. The foreign officials visit Michigan for several days, during which the senior officials perform an appropriate inspection. Electro executives take the officials to a moderately priced dinner, a baseball game, and a play.

a. Do any of these actions violate the FCPA?

b. Would this analysis be different if Electro instead paid for the senior officials to travel first-class with their spouses for an all-expenses-paid, week-long trip to Las Vegas, where Electro has no facilities?

7-11. A U.S. lobbying firm ("the firm") hired a consulting company ("the consultants") that is partially owned by a member of the governing royal family ("the family member") of the country at issue. The firm represented the foreign country's embassy in the United States, and used the services of the consultants to obtain business in the foreign country. The family member, who was paid over $200,000 for the consulting work, did not hold any official government position, and did not purport to act on behalf of the ruling family.

Do any of these acts violate the FCPA? Do you need more facts before you can answer this question?

Chapter 8

Extortion

A. Introductory Notes

1. The Breadth of the Federal Extortion Statute

Extortion is a crime that is closely related to bribery. The Hobbs Act, codified at 18 U.S.C. § 1951, is the principal federal extortion statute and is often used to prosecute political corruption. Congress passed the Hobbs Act in 1946 in an effort to deter and punish robbery and extortion in interstate commerce. Section (a) of the Hobbs Act provides that "[w]hoever in any way obstructs, delays, or affects commerce . . . by robbery or extortion or attempts or conspires so to do" shall be punished under the Act. Section (b) defines extortion as "the obtaining of property from another, with his consent, induced by wrongful use of actual or threatened force, violence, or fear, *or* under color of official right."

Thus, there are two types of extortion under the Hobbs Act — (1) extortion "under color of official right," and (2) extortion by force, violence, or fear. The first theory is used in white collar crime political corruption cases against federal, state, and local officials. In addition, extortion under the second theory — extortion by the use of fear — includes a subset of cases where the defendant has allegedly induced a fear of economic harm in the victim. This theory may fall within the "white collar" rubric, and is discussed in this chapter in cases involving public official defendants and private defendants. As these definitions show, in some respects the federal extortion statute applies more broadly than the federal bribery and gratuities statutes, 18 U.S.C. § 201, or the federal program bribery statute, 18 U.S.C. § 666.

2. Statutory Elements and Definitions

In an extortion case brought in the white collar context, the government must prove that:

(1) The defendant's acts affected interstate commerce;

(2) The defendant obtained, or attempted or conspired to obtain, property of another;

(3) The property was obtained, or would have been obtained, with the other person's consent;

(4) The defendant acted with the required mens rea; and

(5) The property was obtained, or would have been obtained,

    (a) by the wrongful use of fear of economic harm; and/or

    (b) under color of official right.

The mens rea required for an extortion conviction depends upon the theory — use of fear or color of official right — that the government has asserted. *See* §§ 8, C–D, *infra*. Under the terms of the statute, extortion includes the inchoate conduct of conspiring or attempting to commit extortion. It is the consent element of extortion that distinguishes this crime from the crime of robbery, during which the victim's will is overborne by the defendant's immediate use of physical force or violence, or fear of force or violence. Extortion is punished by a fine and imprisonment of not more than 20 years, though of course the sentence in any case will depend on the application of the federal sentencing guidelines to that case.

3. Jurisdiction

As noted above, extortion under color of official right under the Hobbs Act is not limited to extortion by federal public officials or to extortion relating to federal programs. The crime thus relies upon the Interstate Commerce Clause to confer federal jurisdiction. The statute provides that jurisdiction is present where the defendant has obstructed, delayed, or affected commerce "in any way or degree."

In *Taylor v. United States*, 136 S. Ct. 2074 (2016), the United States Supreme Court explained the breadth of federal jurisdiction under the Hobbs Act:

> The Hobbs Act makes it a crime for a person to affect commerce, or to attempt to do so, by robbery. The Act defines "commerce" broadly as interstate commerce "and all other commerce over which the United States has jurisdiction." This case requires us to decide what the government must prove to satisfy the Hobbs Act's commerce element when a defendant commits a robbery that targets a marijuana dealer's drugs or drug proceeds.

> The answer to this question is straightforward and dictated by our precedent. We held in *Gonzales v. Raich,* 545 U.S. 1 (2005), that the Commerce Clause gives Congress authority to regulate the national market for marijuana, including the authority to proscribe the purely intrastate production, possession, and sale of this controlled substance. Because Congress may regulate these intrastate activities based on their aggregate effect on interstate commerce, it follows that Congress may also regulate intrastate drug *theft*. And since the Hobbs Act criminalizes robberies and attempted robberies that affect any commerce "over which the United States has jurisdiction," the prosecution in a Hobbs Act robbery case satisfies the Act's

commerce element if it shows that the defendant robbed or attempted to rob a drug dealer of drugs or drug proceeds. By targeting a drug dealer in this way, a robber necessarily affects or attempts to affect commerce over which the United States has jurisdiction.

In this case, petitioner was convicted on two Hobbs Act counts based on proof that he attempted to rob marijuana dealers of their drugs and drug money. We hold that this evidence was sufficient to satisfy the Act's commerce element.

Id. at 2076–77.

Courts have also broadly applied the Commerce Clause in white collar crime cases. In *United States v. Stillo*, 57 F.3d 553 (7th Cir. 1995), for example, the Seventh Circuit held that the jurisdictional element was satisfied where a judge took money from a lawyer in return for fixing cases. The court found that interstate commerce was affected because the payment would have depleted the lawyer's firm's assets, and the firm purchased supplies in interstate commerce. For similar reasoning outside the white collar context, see *United States v. Jimenez-Torres*, 435 F.3d 3 (1st Cir. 2006), a murder and robbery case. The court found two ways in which the robbery of the victim's home affected interstate commerce: "First, [the victim's] murder led to the closing of the gas station, a business which had been engaged in interstate commerce. Second, the robbery depleted the assets available to the gas station to participate in interstate commerce . . .."). *Id.* at 8. For an example of the rare white collar case where the court found that the jurisdictional element was not satisfied, see *United States v. Perrotta*, 313 F.3d 33, 39–41 (2d Cir. 2002). In that case, the court held that mere evidence that the alleged victim worked at a business involved in interstate commerce was not sufficient to establish federal jurisdiction. Under these cases, however, it is generally not difficult for the government to show jurisdiction in a Hobbs Act prosecution.

B. The Property Requirement

In the following case, the Supreme Court interpreted the property element of extortion. As you read the case, carefully consider the policy implications upon which the majority, concurring, and dissenting opinions focus.

Scheidler v. National Organization for Women

537 U.S. 393 (2003)

CHIEF JUSTICE REHNQUIST delivered the opinion of the Court.

We once again address questions arising from litigation between petitioners, a coalition of antiabortion groups called the Pro-Life Action Network (PLAN), Joseph Scheidler, and other individuals and organizations that oppose legal abortion, and respondents, the National Organization for Women, Inc. (NOW), a national non-profit organization that supports the legal availability of abortion, and two health care centers that perform abortions.[a]

In 1986, respondents sued in the United States District Court for the Northern District of Illinois alleging, *inter alia*, that petitioners violated RICO's §§ 1962(a), (c), and (d). They claimed that petitioners, all of whom were associated with PLAN, the alleged racketeering enterprise, were members of a nationwide conspiracy to "shut down" abortion clinics through a pattern of racketeering activity that included acts of extortion in violation of the Hobbs Act.

After a seven-week trial, a six-member jury concluded that petitioners violated the civil provisions of RICO. By answering a series of special interrogatory questions, the jury found, *inter alia*, that petitioners' alleged "pattern of racketeering activity" included 21 violations of the Hobbs Act, 18 U.S.C. § 1951. . . . The jury awarded $31,455.64 to respondent, the National Women's Health Organization of Delaware, Inc., and $54,471.28 to the National Women's Health Organization of Summit, Inc. These damages were trebled pursuant to § 1964(c). Additionally, the District Court entered a permanent nationwide injunction prohibiting petitioners from obstructing access to the clinics, trespassing on clinic property, damaging clinic property, or using violence or threats of violence against the clinics, their employees, or their patients.

The Court of Appeals for the Seventh Circuit affirmed in relevant part. The Court of Appeals rejected petitioners' contention that the things respondents claimed were "obtained" — the class women's right to seek medical services from the clinics, the clinic doctors' rights to perform their jobs, and the clinics' rights to provide medical services and otherwise conduct their business — were not "property" for purposes of the Hobbs Act. The court explained that it had "repeatedly held that intangible property such as the right to conduct a business can be considered 'property' under the Hobbs Act." Likewise, the Court of Appeals dismissed petitioners' claim that even if "property" was involved, petitioners did not "obtain" that property; they merely forced respondents to part with it. Again relying on Circuit precedent, the court held that "'as a legal matter, an extortionist can violate the Hobbs Act without either seeking or receiving money or anything else. A loss to, or interference with

---

a. An earlier United States Supreme Court decision in this litigation is set forth in Chapter 14, RICO, *infra*. — Eds.

the rights of, the victim is all that is required.'" We granted certiorari, and now reverse.

We first address the question whether petitioners' actions constituted extortion in violation of the Hobbs Act. That Act defines extortion as "the obtaining of property from another, with his consent, induced by wrongful use of actual or threatened force, violence, or fear, or under color of official right." 18 U.S.C. §1951(b)(2). Petitioners allege that the jury's verdict and the Court of Appeals' decision upholding the verdict represent a vast and unwarranted expansion of extortion under the Hobbs Act. They say that the decisions below "rea[d] the requirement of 'obtaining' completely out of the statute" and conflict with the proper understanding of property for purposes of the Hobbs Act.

Respondents, throughout the course of this litigation, have asserted, as the jury instructions at the trial reflected, that petitioners committed extortion under the Hobbs Act by using or threatening to use force, violence, or fear to cause respondents "to give up" property rights, namely, "a woman's right to seek medical services from a clinic, the right of the doctors, nurses or other clinic staff to perform their jobs, and the right of the clinics to provide medical services free from wrongful threats, violence, coercion and fear." Perhaps recognizing the apparent difficulty in reconciling either its position (that "giv[ing] up" these alleged property rights is sufficient) or the Court of Appeals' holding (that "interfer[ing] with such rights" is sufficient) with the requirement that petitioners "obtain[ed] . . . property from" them, respondents have shifted the thrust of their theory. Respondents now assert that petitioners violated the Hobbs Act by "seeking to get control of the use and disposition of respondents' property." They argue that because the right to control the use and disposition of an asset is property, petitioners, who interfered with, and in some instances completely disrupted, the ability of the clinics to function, obtained or attempted to obtain respondents' property.

The United States offers a view similar to that of respondents, asserting that "where the property at issue is a business's *intangible* right to exercise exclusive control over the use of its assets, [a] defendant obtains that property by obtaining control over the use of those assets." Brief for United States as *Amicus Curiae* 22. Although the Government acknowledges that the jury's finding of extortion may have been improperly based on the conclusion that petitioners deprived respondents of a liberty interest, it maintains that under its theory of liability, petitioners committed extortion.

We need not now trace what are the outer boundaries of extortion liability under the Hobbs Act, so that liability might be based on obtaining something as intangible as another's right to exercise exclusive control over the use of a party's business assets. Whatever the outer boundaries may be, the effort to characterize petitioners' actions here as an "obtaining of property from" respondents is well beyond them. Such a result would be an unwarranted expansion of the meaning of that phrase.

Absent contrary direction from Congress, we begin our interpretation of statutory language with the general presumption that a statutory term has its common-law meaning. At common law, extortion was a property offense committed by a public official who took "any money or thing of value" that was not due to him under the pretense that he was entitled to such property by virtue of his office. 4 W. Blackstone, Commentaries on the Laws of England 141 (1765). In 1946, Congress enacted the Hobbs Act, which explicitly "expanded the common-law definition of extortion to include acts by private individuals." *Evans v. United States*, 504 U.S. 255, 261 (1992). While the Hobbs Act expanded the scope of common-law extortion to include private individuals, the statutory language retained the requirement that property must be "obtained."

We have said that the words of the Hobbs Act "do not lend themselves to restrictive interpretation" because they "'manifes[t] . . . a purpose to use all the constitutional power Congress has to punish interference with interstate commerce by extortion, robbery or physical violence.'" *United States v. Culbert*, 435 U.S. 371, 373 (1978). We have also said, construing the Hobbs Act in *United States v. Enmons*, 410 U.S. 396, 411 (1973): "Even if the language and history of the Act were less clear than we have found them to be, the Act could not properly be expanded as the Government suggests — for two related reasons. First, this being a criminal statute, it must be strictly construed, and any ambiguity must be resolved in favor of lenity."

We think that these two seemingly antithetical statements can be reconciled. *Culbert* refused to adopt the view that Congress had not exercised the full extent of its commerce power in prohibiting extortion which "affects commerce or the movement of any article or commodity in commerce." But there is no contention by petitioners here that their acts did not affect interstate commerce. Their argument is that their acts did not amount to the crime of extortion as set forth in the Act, so the rule of lenity referred to in *Enmons* may apply to their case quite consistently with the statement in *Culbert*. "[W]hen there are two rational readings of a criminal statute, one harsher than the other, we are to choose the harsher only when Congress has spoken in clear and definite language." *McNally v. United States*, 483 U.S. 350, 359–360 (1987). . . .

Because we find that petitioners did not obtain or attempt to obtain property from respondents, we conclude that there was no basis upon which to find that they committed extortion under the Hobbs Act. Because all of the predicate acts supporting the jury's finding of a RICO violation must be reversed, the judgment that petitioners violated RICO must also be reversed.

The judgment of the Court of Appeals is accordingly *reversed*.

Justice Ginsburg, with whom Justice Breyer joins, concurring.

I join the Court's opinion, persuaded that the Seventh Circuit's decision accords undue breadth to the Racketeer Influenced and Corrupt Organizations Act (RICO or Act). As Justice Stevens recognizes, "Congress has enacted specific legislation responsive to the concerns that gave rise to these cases." In the Freedom of Access to Clinic Entrances Act of 1994, 18 U.S.C. § 248, Congress crafted a statutory response that homes in on the problem of criminal activity at health care facilities. Thus, the principal effect of a decision against petitioners here would have been on other cases pursued under RICO.

RICO, which empowers both prosecutors and private enforcers, imposes severe criminal penalties and hefty civil liability on those engaged in conduct within the Act's compass. *See, e.g.,* § 1963(a) (up to 20 years' imprisonment and wide-ranging forfeiture for a single criminal violation); § 1964(a) (broad civil injunctive relief); § 1964(c) (treble damages and attorneys' fees for private plaintiffs). The Court is rightly reluctant, as I see it, to extend RICO's domain further by endorsing the expansive definition of "extortion" adopted by the Seventh Circuit.

JUSTICE STEVENS, dissenting.

The term "extortion" as defined in the Hobbs Act refers to "the obtaining of property from another." 18 U.S.C. § 1951(b)(2). The Court's murky opinion seems to hold that this phrase covers nothing more than the acquisition of tangible property. No other federal court has ever construed this statute so narrowly.

For decades federal judges have uniformly given the term "property" an expansive construction that encompasses the intangible right to exercise exclusive control over the lawful use of business assets. The right to serve customers or to solicit new business is thus a protected property right. The use of violence or threats of violence to persuade the owner of a business to surrender control of such an intangible right is an appropriation of control embraced by the term "obtaining." That is the commonsense reading of the statute that other federal judges have consistently and wisely embraced in numerous cases that the Court does not discuss or even cite. Recognizing this settled definition of property, as I believe one must, the conclusion that petitioners obtained this property from respondents is amply supported by the evidence in the record.

Notes and Questions

1. *The* Scheidler *litigation.* As the above opinion notes, the Supreme Court's decision in this case was just one of a number of judicial decisions in litigation that stretched over nearly two decades. Yet the Court in this case concluded that the theory of the plaintiff's case was fundamentally flawed. Do you agree? If so, why did this case consume so much of the federal judiciary's resources?

2. *The dissent.* Justice Stevens' interpretation of the Hobbs Act is fundamentally different from the majority's interpretation. Do you agree with Justice Stevens? Why or why not?

3. *Intangible rights.* Under *Scheidler,* does the extortion statute apply when the defendant attempted to deprive the alleged victim of intangible rights? Suppose that the government shows that the defendant fixed labor union elections and controlled how the elected officials performed their union duties, depriving union members of their statutory right to participate in union governance. In *United States v. Gotti,* 459 F.3d 296, 326 (2d Cir. 2006), the court held that this conduct amounted to extortion. Because the defendant obtained the benefits of which the victims were

deprived, the *Scheidler* requirement was met. According to this reasoning, it did not matter that the right obtained was an intangible right.

Was the Court correct that the rights at issue were intangible "property rights"? Would these rights qualify as property under the mail and wire fraud statutes? Why or why not?

4. *Nontransferable interests.* Consider the following facts. The defendant managed an investment fund, and the state controller's office was considering whether to invest state money in the fund. The defendant sent emails to the official in the controller's office who made investment recommendations. The emails threatened to expose an affair in which the official had purportedly engaged unless the official recommended that the state invest in the fund. The defendant was convicted of extortion under the theory that the emails were designed to obtain property, specified as the official's investment recommendation. Does this amount to a cognizable property interest under § 1951?

In a unanimous ruling, the United States Supreme Court held not. *United States v. Sekhar*, 570 U.S. 729 (2013). Writing for six members of the Court, Justice Scalia reasoned that under *Scheidler* the defendant must attempt to obtain transferrable property belonging to another. The official's right to make a recommendation was not transferable and thus was not a property interest under the Hobbs Act. The Court explained:

> The Hobbs Act punishes 'extortion,' one of the oldest crimes in our legal tradition. The crime originally applied only to extortionate action by public officials, but was later extended by statute to private extortion. As far as is known, no case predating the Hobbs Act — English, federal, or state — ever identified conduct such as that charged here as extortionate. Extortion required the obtaining of items of value, typically cash, from the victim. It did not cover mere coercion to act, or to refrain from acting.
>
> The text of the statute at issue confirms that the alleged property here cannot be extorted. Enacted in 1946, the Hobbs Act defines its crime of 'extortion' as 'the *obtaining of property from another*, with his consent, induced by wrongful use of actual or threatened force, violence, or fear, or under color of official right.' Obtaining property requires 'not only the deprivation but also the acquisition of property.' *Scheidler*, 537 U.S. at 404. That is, it requires that the victim 'part with' his property, and that the extortionist 'gain possession of it. *Id.* at 403 n.8. The property extorted must therefore be *transferable* — that is, capable of passing from one person to another. The alleged property here lacks that defining feature.

570 U.S. at 734. Did *Scheidler* compel this result? Why or why not?

5. *The government as beneficiary.* Does the Hobbs Act apply when the federal government is the intended beneficiary of the extortion? In *Wilkie v. Robbins*, 551 U.S. 537, 586 (2007), the Court held not. In that case, the plaintiff alleged that the government

attempted to extort him to force him to grant the government an easement over his property. The Court found that neither the text of the statute nor the common law of extortion supported this theory. The Court also opined that a contrary holding would subject federal employees to possible extortion charges in a wide range of circumstances.

6. *RICO.* This case provides a preview of the federal racketeering statute, 18 U.S.C. §§ 1961–68, commonly referred to as "RICO." *See* Chapter 14, RICO, *infra.* That statute allows the government to charge wide-ranging criminal activity in a single case, and can lead to severe sanctions, including asset forfeitures. According to Justice Ginsburg's concurring opinion in *Scheidler,* what is the danger of allowing a case like this to go forward under the RICO statute?

Problems

8-1. Last year, Alpine Corporation ("Alpine") and Sunny Energy Corporation ("Sunny") were competing to secure the right to build a power plant at a site in the Port of Stockdale. McFalon and his partners (acting through a partnership agreement) entered into a consulting contract with Sunny under which the partners stood to reap substantial financial rewards if Sunny obtained the right to build at the Port of Stockdale site, and an even greater sum if the plant was actually built. According to the evidence, McFalon and his partners sought to undermine Alpine's chances of prevailing at the Port of Stockdale by mounting political opposition to another pending Alpine project in neighboring Allmeda County.

Alpine was in the process of securing a permit from the state Energy Commission for its Allmeda County project. McFalon warned Alpine representatives that if they did not drop their bid for the Port of Stockdale site, he would use his political influence to create a "public outcry" over the project, thereby complicating the permitting process. After Alpine declined to withdraw its bid, McFalon and his partners conspired to pass a resolution through the Board of Supervisors of neighboring San Juan County raising environmental, health, and safety concerns about Alpine's Allmeda County project. McFalon appeared at the meeting and denounced Alpine's project as a threat to public safety. The resolution passed.

McFall was convicted of extortion by threat of economic harm, and appeals on the ground that the property requirement has not been met. How should the court rule? Why?

8-2. Defendant was the Executive Director of the Poverty Point Reservoir District ("PPRD"), a political subdivision of Missouri whose purpose is to develop the natural resources of the district. Joe Cleaver ("Cleaver") was an independent contractor who performed maintenance services for PPRD and was compensated on an hourly basis. Cleaver's wife, Kathy Cleaver, worked as Defendant's administrative assistant, which involved processing her husband's time sheets and submitting them to PPRD for payment. In response to accusations that Kathy Cleaver was embezzling PPRD funds, she and her husband entered into agreements with the government to testify against Defendant. In particular, the Cleavers would testify that Defendant orchestrated a scheme in which Cleaver was paid nearly $18,000 of PPRD funds for work performed for Defendant personally over the course of five years.

The government alleges that, using his position as Executive Director of PPRD, Defendant coerced Cleaver under color of official right into performing a myriad of jobs at Defendant's home and farm, while paying Cleaver with PPRD funds. According to the government, the labor provided by Clever qualifies as "property" within the meaning of the Hobbs Act. The government obtained a single-count indictment against Defendant charging a violation of the Hobbs Act based on these facts.

Defendant has moved to dismiss the indictment, arguing that the government failed to charge a Hobbs Act violation because Cleaver was not deprived of property within the meaning of the Hobbs Act. Defendant contends that, because Cleaver was fully compensated for his labor, he was not deprived of any property. How should the court rule? Why?

8-3. Defendant, then a member of Congress, along with a former business partner, started a real estate company called Desert Sea Investments. After three years, Defendant's partner bought Defendant's remaining interest in the company, worth approximately $1,000,000. The partner wrote Defendant a $200,000 cashier's check and then gave Defendant a note for $800,000, promising to pay the remaining amount in the future.

Two years later, Orichalcum Metals, a large metal refining company, wished to enter into a land exchange with the federal government. A land exchange is a contract with the federal government that entitles a party to use federal land for profit, at an agreed rate. Orichalcum wished to buy the mineral rights to a tract of land owned by the federal government. Defendant, as congressional representative for the district in which the tract was located, oversaw negotiations with the company, which would only be granted the land exchange by way of a bill passed by Congress. Defendant told Orichalcum that Defendant would assure the bill's passage, but only if Orichalcum would also buy $800,000 in real estate from Defendant's former business partner, who had still failed to pay Defendant. "No Desert Sea purchase, no deal," Defendant told Orichalcum's CEO in an email.

Defendant has been indicted for Hobbs Act extortion. Defendant has moved to dismiss the indictment, citing Wilkie v. Robbins. *Defendant asserts that, because the federal government stood to benefit from the land exchange with Orichalcum Metals, Defendant is absolved from Hobbs Act liability. How will the court likely rule? Why?*

C. The Color of Official Right Theory

In the next two cases, the Supreme Court attempted to delineate the reach of the color of official right theory in the context of campaign contributions. Are the outcomes consistent? Can you divine a clear rule from the cases? As you read the opinions, consider whether the individual Justices' votes help to answer these questions.

McCormick v. United States

500 U.S. 257 (1991)

JUSTICE WHITE delivered the opinion of the Court.

This case requires us to consider whether the Court of Appeals properly affirmed the conviction of petitioner, an elected public official, for extorting property under color of official right in violation of the Hobbs Act, 18 U.S.C. §1951.

Petitioner Robert L. McCormick was a member of the West Virginia House of Delegates in 1984. He represented a district that had long suffered from a shortage of medical doctors. For several years, West Virginia had allowed foreign medical school graduates to practice under temporary permits while studying for the state licensing exams. Under this program, some doctors were allowed to practice under temporary permits for years even though they repeatedly failed the state exams. McCormick was a leading advocate and supporter of this program.

In the early 1980's, following a move in the House of Delegates to end the temporary permit program, several of the temporarily licensed doctors formed an organization to press their interests in Charleston. The organization hired a lobbyist, John Vandergrift, who in 1984 worked for legislation that would extend the expiration date of the temporary permit program. McCormick sponsored the House version of the proposed legislation and a bill was passed extending the program for another year. Shortly thereafter, Vandergrift and McCormick discussed the possibility of introducing legislation during the 1985 session that would grant the doctors a permanent medical license by virtue of their years of experience. McCormick agreed to sponsor such legislation.

During his 1984 reelection campaign, McCormick informed Vandergrift that his campaign was expensive, that he had paid considerable sums out of his own pocket, and that he had not heard anything from the foreign doctors. Vandergrift told McCormick that he would contact the doctors and see what he could do. Vandergrift contacted one of the foreign doctors and later received from the doctors $1,200 in cash. Vandergrift delivered an envelope containing nine $100 bills to McCormick. Later the same day, a second delivery of $2,000 in cash was made to McCormick. During the fall of 1984, McCormick received two more cash payments from the doctors. McCormick did not list any of these payments as campaign contributions[1] nor did he report the money as income on his 1984 federal income tax return. And although the doctors' organization kept detailed books of its expenditures, the cash payments were not listed as campaign contributions. Rather, the

---

1. West Virginia law prohibits cash campaign contributions in excess of $50 per person. W. Va. Code § 3-8-5d (1990).

entries for the payments were accompanied only by initials or other codes signify-
ing that the money was for McCormick.

In the spring of 1985, McCormick sponsored legislation permitting experienced
doctors to be permanently licensed without passing the state licensing exams.
McCormick spoke at length in favor of the bill during floor debate and the bill ultimately was enacted into law. Two weeks after the legislation was enacted, McCormick received another cash payment from the foreign doctors.

Following an investigation, a federal grand jury returned an indictment charging McCormick with five counts of violating the Hobbs Act, by extorting payments
under color of official right, and with one count of filing a false income tax return
in violation of 26 U.S.C. §7206(1), by failing to report as income the cash payments
he received from the foreign doctors. At the close of a 6-day trial, the jury was
instructed that to establish a Hobbs Act violation the Government had to prove that
McCormick induced a cash payment and that he did so knowingly and willfully by
extortion.

The next day the jury informed the court that it "would like to hear the instructions again with particular emphasis on the definition of extortion under the color
of official right and on the law as regards the portion of moneys received that does
not have to be reported as income." The court then reread most of the extortion
instructions to the jury, but reordered some of the paragraphs and made the following significant addition:

> Extortion under color of official right means the obtaining of money by a
> public official when the money obtained was not lawfully due and owing to
> him or to his office. Of course, extortion does not occur where one who is
> a public official receives a legitimate gift or a voluntary political contribu-
> tion even though the political contribution may have been made in cash in
> violation of local law. Voluntary is that which is freely given without expec-
> tation of benefit.

It is also worth noting that with respect to political contributions, the last two
paragraphs of the supplemental instructions on the extortion counts were as follows:

> It would not be illegal, in and of itself, for Mr. McCormick to solicit or
> accept political contributions from foreign doctors who would benefit from
> this legislation.

> In order to find Mr. McCormick guilty of extortion, you must be convinced
> beyond a reasonable doubt that the payment alleged in a given count of the
> indictment was made by or on behalf of the doctors with the expectation
> that such payment would influence Mr. McCormick's official conduct, and
> with knowledge on the part of Mr. McCormick that they were paid to him
> with that expectation by virtue of the office he held.

The jury convicted McCormick of the first Hobbs Act count (charging him with
receiving the initial $900 cash payment) . . . but could not reach verdicts on the

remaining four Hobbs Act counts. The District Court declared a mistrial on those four counts.

The Court of Appeals affirmed.

Because of disagreement in the Courts of Appeals regarding the meaning of the phrase "under color of official right" as it is used in the Hobbs Act, we granted certiorari. We reverse and remand for further proceedings.

McCormick's challenge to the judgment below affirming his conviction is limited to the Court of Appeals' rejection of his claim that the payments made to him by or on behalf of the doctors were campaign contributions, the receipt of which did not violate the Hobbs Act.

We agree with the Court of Appeals that in a case like this it is proper to inquire whether payments made to an elected official are in fact campaign contributions, and we agree that the intention of the parties is a relevant consideration in pursuing this inquiry. But we cannot accept the Court of Appeals' approach to distinguishing between legal and illegal campaign contributions. The Court of Appeals stated that payments to elected officials could violate the Hobbs Act without proof of an explicit quid pro quo by proving that the payments "were never intended to be legitimate campaign contributions."

Serving constituents and supporting legislation that will benefit the district and individuals and groups therein is the everyday business of a legislator. It is also true that campaigns must be run and financed. Money is constantly being solicited on behalf of candidates, who run on platforms and who claim support on the basis of their views and what they intend to do or have done. Whatever ethical considerations and appearances may indicate, to hold that legislators commit the federal crime of extortion when they act for the benefit of constituents or support legislation furthering the interests of some of their constituents, shortly before or after campaign contributions are solicited and received from those beneficiaries, is an unrealistic assessment of what Congress could have meant by making it a crime to obtain property from another, with his consent, "under color of official right." To hold otherwise would open to prosecution not only conduct that has long been thought to be well within the law but also conduct that in a very real sense is unavoidable so long as election campaigns are financed by private contributions or expenditures, as they have been from the beginning of the Nation. It would require statutory language more explicit than the Hobbs Act contains to justify a contrary conclusion.

This is not to say that it is impossible for an elected official to commit extortion in the course of financing an election campaign. Political contributions are of course vulnerable if induced by the use of force, violence, or fear. The receipt of such contributions is also vulnerable under the Act as having been taken under color of official right, but only if the payments are made in return for an explicit promise or undertaking by the official to perform or not to perform an official act. In such situations the official asserts that his official conduct will be controlled by the terms of the promise or undertaking. This is the receipt of money by an elected official under color of official right within the meaning of the Hobbs Act.

This formulation defines the forbidden zone of conduct with sufficient clarity. As the Court of Appeals for the Fifth Circuit observed in *United States v. Dozier*, 672 F.2d 531, 537 (5th Cir. 1982):

> A moment's reflection should enable one to distinguish, at least in the abstract, a legitimate solicitation from the exaction of a fee for a benefit conferred or an injury withheld. Whether described familiarly as a payoff or with the Latinate precision of *quid pro quo*, the prohibited exchange is the same: a public official may not demand payment as inducement for the promise to perform (or not to perform) an official act.

The United States agrees that if the payments to McCormick were campaign contributions, proof of a quid pro quo would be essential for an extortion conviction, and quotes the instruction given on this subject in 9 Department of Justice Manual § 9-85A.306, p. 9-1938.134: "campaign contributions will not be authorized as the subject of a Hobbs Act prosecution unless they can be proven to have been given in return for the performance of or abstaining from an official act; otherwise any campaign contribution might constitute a violation."

We thus disagree with the Court of Appeal's holding in this case that a quid pro quo is not necessary for conviction under the Hobbs Act when an official receives a campaign contribution.[10] By the same token, we hold, as McCormick urges, that the District Court's instruction to the same effect was error.

Accordingly we reverse the judgment of the Court of Appeals and remand for further proceedings consistent with this opinion.

JUSTICE SCALIA, concurring (omitted).

JUSTICE STEVENS, with whom JUSTICE BLACKMUN and JUSTICE O'CONNOR join, dissenting.

As I understand its opinion, the Court would agree that these facts would constitute a violation of the Hobbs Act if the understanding that the money was a personal payment rather than a campaign contribution had been explicit rather than implicit and if the understanding that, in response to the payment, petitioner would endeavor to provide the payers with the specific benefit they sought had also been explicit rather than implicit. In my opinion there is no statutory requirement that illegal agreements, threats, or promises be in writing, or in any particular form. Subtle extortion is just as wrongful — and probably much more common — than the kind of express understanding that the Court's opinion seems to require.

---

10. As noted previously, McCormick's sole contention in this case is that the payments made to him were campaign contributions. Therefore, we do not decide whether a quid pro quo requirement exists in other contexts, such as when an elected official receives gifts, meals, travel expenses, or other items of value.

Nevertheless, to prove a violation of the Hobbs Act, I agree with the Court that it is essential that the payment in question be contingent on a mutual understanding that the motivation for the payment is the payer's desire to avoid a specific threatened harm or to obtain a promised benefit that the defendant has the apparent power to deliver, either through the use of force or the use of public office. In this sense, the crime does require a "*quid pro quo.*" Because the use of the Latin term "*quid pro quo*" tends to confuse the analysis, however, it is important to clarify the sense in which the term was used in the District Court's instructions.

The crime of extortion was complete when petitioner accepted the cash pursuant to an understanding that he would not carry out his earlier threat to withhold official action and instead would go forward with his contingent promise to take favorable action on behalf of the unlicensed physicians. What he did thereafter might have evidentiary significance, but could neither undo a completed crime nor complete an uncommitted offense. When petitioner took the money, he was either guilty or not guilty. For that reason, proof of a subsequent *quid pro quo* — his actual support of the legislation — was not necessary for the Government's case. And conversely, evidence that petitioner would have supported the legislation anyway is not a defense to the already completed crime. The thug who extorts protection money cannot defend on the ground that his threat was only a bluff because he would not have smashed the shopkeeper's windows even if the extortion had been unsuccessful. It was in this sense that the District Court correctly advised the jury that the Government did not have to prove the delivery of a postpayment *quid pro quo.*

Notes and Questions

1. *The Travel Act.* In a concurring opinion, Justice Scalia concluded that the crime that McCormick committed was bribery, not extortion. Justice Scalia also concluded that McCormick, although not a federal official for purposes of the federal bribery statute, could be guilty under the Travel Act, 18 U.S.C. §1952, which criminalizes the use of interstate commerce for bribery.

2. *Bribery v. extortion.* Re-consider the trial judge's instruction to the jury. Under this instruction, is there a distinction between bribery and extortion under color of official right? If a client asked you to distinguish the two crimes, how would you do so?

3. *The policy debate.* What was the primary policy concern of the majority? Of the dissent? Which side has the better of the argument? Why? In this context, reconsider the observations of one commentator, quoted in Chapter 1, *supra,* in connection with the conviction of former Virginia governor Robert McDonnell, *United States v. McDonnell,* 136 S. Ct. 2355 (2016), on political corruption charges:

> It would be both wise (to avoid prison) and good policy for officials to discourage large donations, avoid decisions that benefit big donors and generally disengage from contributors. But until that happens, we are stuck with a system in which lots of public officials could be convicted of a felony but few are prosecuted.

That's not healthy for a democracy. It gives prosecutors vast discretion to choose targets, undermines the credibility of prosecutions that do occur and, ultimately, says something very unsettling about our government. Something has to give. We either need to strengthen our campaign finance laws or, if that's impossible, acknowledge that our public corruption laws are merely aspirational. A political system where any given federal, state or local official is just a wink, nod and a motivated prosecutor away from federal prosecution is untenable.

Jeffrey Bellin, *What the* McDonnell *Verdict Says About U.S. Politics*, WASH. POST, Sept. 5, 2014, http://www.washingtonpost.com/opinions/the-mcdonnell-verdict -shows-how-easily-prosecutors-may-criminalize-politics/2014/09/05/3128202a -3519-11e4-9e92-0899b306bbea_story.html. *Compare* Alan Feuer, *Silver May Start 'Parade of Horribles' Out of McDonnell Case, Critics Say*, N.Y. TIMES, July 13, 2017, https://www.nytimes.com/2017/07/13/nyregion/sheldon-silver-bob-mcdonnell.html (arguing that the United States Supreme Court's reversal of McDonnell's conviction [*see* Chapter 7, Bribery, *supra*] will pave the way for politicians to avoid liability for "reprehensible behavior," including self-dealing).

What is the inherent tension in the criminalization of payments and gifts to public officials? Is the federal extortion statute an appropriate vehicle for distinguishing legitimate from illegitimate donations? Why?

————————

In the next case, the Court addressed the issue whether extortion under color of official right occurs when the public official does not initiate the transaction. In the course of resolving this issue, the Court attempted to reconcile its holding with the *McCormick* decision. Did the Court succeed in that effort? Pay particular attention to Justice Kennedy's concurring opinion in this regard.

Evans v. United States

504 U.S. 255 (1992)

JUSTICE STEVENS **delivered the opinion of the Court.**

We granted certiorari to resolve a conflict in the Circuits over the question whether an affirmative act of inducement by a public official, such as a demand, is an element of the offense of extortion "under color of official right" prohibited by the Hobbs Act, 18 U.S.C. § 1951. We agree with the Court of Appeals for the Eleventh Circuit that it is not, and therefore affirm the judgment of the court below.

Petitioner was an elected member of the Board of Commissioners of DeKalb County, Georgia. During the period between March 1985 and October 1986, as part of an effort by the Federal Bureau of Investigation (FBI) to investigate allegations of public corruption in the Atlanta area, particularly in the area of rezonings of property, an FBI agent posing as a real estate developer talked on the telephone and met with petitioner on a number of occasions. Virtually all, if not all, of those conversations were initiated by the agent and most were recorded on tape or video. In those conversations, the agent sought petitioner's assistance in an effort to rezone a 25-acre tract of land for high-density residential use. On July 25, 1986, the agent handed petitioner cash totaling $7,000 and a check, payable to petitioner's campaign, for $1,000. Petitioner reported the check, but not the cash, on his state campaign-financing disclosure form; he also did not report the $7,000 on his 1986 federal income tax return. Viewing the evidence in the light most favorable to the Government, as we must in light of the verdict, we assume that the jury found that petitioner accepted the cash knowing that it was intended to ensure that he would vote in favor of the rezoning application and that he would try to persuade his fellow commissioners to do likewise. Thus, although petitioner did not initiate the transaction, his acceptance of the bribe constituted an implicit promise to use his official position to serve the interests of the bribe-giver.

In a two-count indictment, petitioner was charged with extortion in violation of 18 U.S.C. § 1951 and with failure to report income in violation of 26 U.S.C. § 7206(1). He was convicted by a jury on both counts. With respect to the extortion count, the trial judge gave the following instruction:

> The defendant contends that the $8,000 he received from agent Cormany was a campaign contribution. The solicitation of campaign contributions from any person is a necessary and permissible form of political activity on the part of persons who seek political office and persons who have been elected to political office. Thus, the acceptance by an elected official of a campaign contribution does not, in itself, constitute a violation of the Hobbs Act even though the donor has business pending before the official.

> However, if a public official demands or accepts money in exchange for [a] specific requested exercise of his or her official power, such a demand or acceptance does constitute a violation of the Hobbs Act regardless of whether the payment is made in the form of a campaign contribution.

In affirming petitioner's conviction, the Court of Appeals noted that the instruction did not require the jury to find that petitioner had demanded or requested the money, or that he had conditioned the performance of any official act upon its receipt. The Court of Appeals held, however, that "passive acceptance of a benefit by a public official *is* sufficient to form the basis of a Hobbs Act violation if the official knows that he is being offered the payment in exchange for a specific requested exercise of his official power. The official need not take any specific action to induce the offering of the benefit." (emphasis in original).

This statement of the law by the Court of Appeals for the Eleventh Circuit is consistent with holdings in eight other Circuits. Two Circuits, however, have held that an affirmative act of inducement by the public official is required to support a conviction of extortion under color of official right. Because the majority view is consistent with the common-law definition of extortion, which we believe Congress intended to adopt, we endorse that position.

It is a familiar "maxim that a statutory term is generally presumed to have its common-law meaning." *Taylor v. United States*, 495 U.S. 575, 592 (1990). As we have explained, "where Congress borrows terms of art in which are accumulated the legal tradition and meaning of centuries of practice, it presumably knows and adopts the cluster of ideas that were attached to each borrowed word in the body of learning from which it was taken and the meaning its use will convey to the judicial mind unless otherwise instructed. In such case, absence of contrary direction may be taken as satisfaction with widely accepted definitions, not as a departure from them." *Morissette v. United States*, 342 U.S. 246, 263 (1952).

At common law, extortion was an offense committed by a public official who took "by colour of his office" money that was not due to him for the performance of his official duties. A demand, or request, by the public official was not an element of the offense. Extortion by the public official was the rough equivalent of what we would now describe as "taking a bribe." It is clear that petitioner committed that offense. The question is whether the federal statute, insofar as it applies to official extortion, has narrowed the common-law definition.

Congress has unquestionably expanded the common-law definition of extortion to include acts by private individuals pursuant to which property is obtained by means of force, fear, or threats. It did so by implication in the Travel Act, 18 U.S.C. §1952, and expressly in the Hobbs Act. The portion of the Hobbs Act that is relevant to our decision today provides: . . . "(2) The term 'extortion' means the obtaining of property from another, with his consent, induced by wrongful use of actual or threatened force, violence, or fear, or under color of official right." 18 U.S.C. §1951.

Although the present statutory text is much broader than the common-law definition of extortion because it encompasses conduct by a private individual as well as conduct by a public official, the portion of the statute that refers to official misconduct continues to mirror the common-law definition. There is nothing in either the statutory text or the legislative history that could fairly be described as a "contrary direction," *Morissette v. United States*, 342 U.S. at 263, from Congress to narrow the scope of the offense.

The two courts that have disagreed with the decision to apply the common-law definition have interpreted the word "induced" as requiring a wrongful use of official power that "begins with the public official, not with the gratuitous actions of another." If we had no common-law history to guide our interpretation of the statutory text, that reading would be plausible. For two reasons, however, we are convinced that it is incorrect.

First, we think the word "induced" is a part of the definition of the offense by the private individual, but not the offense by the public official. In the case of the private individual, the victim's consent must be "induced by wrongful use of actual or threatened force, violence or fear." In the case of the public official, however, there is no such requirement. The statute merely requires of the public official that he obtain "property from another, with his consent, . . . under color of official right." The use of the word "or" before "under color of official right" supports this reading.[15]

Second, even if the statute were parsed so that the word "induced" applied to the public officeholder, we do not believe the word "induced" necessarily indicates that the transaction must be initiated by the recipient of the bribe. Many of the cases applying the majority rule have concluded that the wrongful acceptance of a bribe establishes all the inducement that the statute requires. They conclude that the coercive element is provided by the public office itself. And even the two courts that have adopted an inducement requirement for extortion under color of official right do not require proof that the inducement took the form of a threat or demand.

Petitioner argues that the jury charge with respect to extortion allowed the jury to convict him on the basis of the "passive acceptance of a contribution."[18] He contends that the instruction did not require the jury to find "an element of duress such as a demand," and it did not properly describe the quid pro quo requirement for conviction if the jury found that the payment was a campaign contribution.

We reject petitioner's criticism of the instruction, and conclude that it satisfies the quid pro quo requirement of *McCormick v. United States*, 500 U.S. 257 (1991), because the offense is completed at the time when the public official receives a payment in return for his agreement to perform specific official acts; fulfillment of the quid pro quo is not an element of the offense. We also reject petitioner's contention that an affirmative step is an element of the offense of extortion "under color of official right" and need be included in the instruction. As we explained above, our construction of the statute is informed by the common-law tradition from which the term of art was drawn and understood. We hold today that the Government need only show that a public official has obtained a payment to which he was not entitled, knowing that the payment was made in return for official acts. . . .

The judgment is affirmed.

JUSTICE KENNEDY, concurring in part and concurring in the judgment.

The Court gives a summary of its decision in these words: "We hold today that the Government need only show that a public official has obtained a payment to

---

15. This meaning would, of course, have been completely clear if Congress had inserted the word "either" before its description of the private offense because the word "or" already precedes the description of the public offense. The definition would then read: "The term 'extortion' means the obtaining of property from another, with his consent, either induced by wrongful use of actual or threatened force, violence, or fear, or under color of official right."

18. Petitioner also makes the point that "[t]he evidence at trial against [petitioner] is more conducive to a charge of bribery than one of extortion." Although the evidence in this case may have supported a charge of bribery, it is not a defense to a charge of extortion under color of official right that the defendant could also have been convicted of bribery. Courts addressing extortion by force or fear have occasionally said that extortion and bribery are mutually exclusive, while that may be correct when the victim was intimidated into making a payment (extortion by force or fear), and did not offer it voluntarily (bribery), that does not lead to the conclusion that extortion under color of official right and bribery are mutually exclusive under either common law or the Hobbs Act.

which he was not entitled, knowing that the payment was made in return for official acts." In my view the dissent is correct to conclude that this language requires a *quid pro quo* as an element of the Government's case in a prosecution under 18 U.S.C. § 1951, and the Court's opinion can be interpreted in a way that is consistent with this rule. Although the Court appears to accept the requirement of a *quid pro quo* as an alternative rationale, in my view this element of the offense is essential to a determination of those acts which are criminal and those which are not in a case in which the official does not pretend that he is entitled by law to the property in question. Here the prosecution did establish a *quid pro quo* that embodied the necessary elements of a statutory violation.

With regard to the question whether the word "induced" in the statutory definition of extortion applies to the phrase "under color of official right," 18 U.S.C. § 1951(b)(2), I find myself in substantial agreement with the dissent. Scrutiny of the placement of commas will not, in the final analysis, yield a convincing answer, and we are left with two quite plausible interpretations. Under these circumstances, I agree with the dissent that the rule of lenity requires that we avoid the harsher one. We must take as our starting point the assumption that the portion of the statute at issue here defines extortion as "the obtaining of property from another, with his consent, induced . . . under color of official right."

I agree with the Court, on the other hand, that the word "induced" does not "necessarily indicat[e] that the transaction must be *initiated* by the" public official. Something beyond the mere acceptance of property from another is required, however, or else the word "induced" would be superfluous. That something, I submit, is the *quid pro quo*. The ability of the official to use or refrain from using authority is the "color of official right" which can be invoked in a corrupt way to induce payment of money or to otherwise obtain property. The inducement generates a *quid pro quo*, under color of official right, that the statute prohibits. The term "under color of" is used, as I think both the Court and the dissent agree, to sweep within the statute those corrupt exercises of authority that the law forbids but that nevertheless cause damage because the exercise is by a governmental official.

The requirement of a *quid pro quo* means that without pretense of any entitlement to the payment, a public official violates § 1951 if he intends the payor to believe that absent payment the official is likely to abuse his office and his trust to the detriment and injury of the prospective payor or to give the prospective payor less favorable treatment if the *quid pro quo* is not satisfied. The official and the payor need not state the *quid pro quo* in express terms, for otherwise the law's effect could be frustrated by knowing winks and nods. The inducement from the official is criminal if it is express or if it is implied from his words and actions, so long as he intends it to be so and the payor so interprets it.

The criminal law in the usual course concerns itself with motives and consequences, not formalities. And the trier of fact is quite capable of deciding the intent with which words were spoken or actions taken as well as the reasonable construction given to them by the official and the payor. [F]or a public official to commit extortion under color of official right, his course of dealings must establish a real understanding that failure to make a payment will result in the victimization of the prospective payor or the withholding of more favorable treatment, a victimization or withholding accomplished by taking or refraining from taking official action, all in breach of the official's trust.

Moreover, the mechanism which controls and limits the scope of official right extortion is a familiar one: a state of mind requirement. Hence, even if the *quid pro quo* requirement did not have firm roots in the statutory language, it would constitute no abuse of judicial power for us to find it by implication.

The requirement of a *quid pro quo* in a §1951 prosecution such as the one before us, in which it is alleged that money was given to the public official in the form of a campaign contribution, was established by our decision last Term in *McCormick v. United States*, 500 U.S. 257 (1991). Readers of today's opinion should have little difficulty in understanding that the rationale underlying the Court's holding applies not only in campaign contribution cases, but in all §1951 prosecutions. That is as it should be, for, given a corrupt motive, the *quid pro quo*, as I have said, is the essence of the offense.

Because I agree that the jury instruction in this case complied with the *quid pro quo* requirement, I concur in the judgment of the Court.

Justice Thomas, with whom The Chief Justice and Justice Scalia join, dissenting.

* * *

The "under color of office" element of extortion had a definite and well-established meaning at common law. "At common law it was essential that the money or property be obtained under color of office, *that is, under the pretense that the officer was entitled thereto by virtue of his office.* The money or thing received must have been claimed or accepted in right of office, and the person paying must have yielded to official authority." 3 R. Anderson, Wharton's Criminal Law and Procedure §1393, pp. 790–791 (1957) (emphasis added). Thus, although the Court purports to define official extortion under the Hobbs Act by reference to the common law, its definition bears scant resemblance to the common-law crime Congress presumably codified in 1946.

The Court errs in asserting that common-law extortion is the "rough equivalent of what we would now describe as 'taking a bribe.'" Regardless of whether extortion contains an "inducement" requirement, bribery and extortion are different crimes. An official who solicits or takes a bribe does *not* do so "under color of office;" i.e., under any pretense of official entitlement. "The distinction between bribery and extortion seems to be that the former offense consists in offering a present or receiving one, the latter in demanding a fee or present by color of office." *State v. Pritchard*, 12 S.E. 50, 52 (1890). Where extortion is at issue, the public official is the sole wrongdoer; because he acts "under color of office," the law regards the payor as an innocent victim and not an accomplice. With bribery, in contrast, the payor knows the recipient official is not entitled to the payment; he, as well as the official, may be punished for the offense. Congress is well aware of the distinction between the crimes; it has always treated them separately. By stretching the bounds of extortion to make it encompass bribery, the Court today blurs the traditional distinction between the crimes.

Perhaps because the common-law crime — as the Court defines it — is so expansive, the Court, at the very end of its opinion, appends a qualification: "We hold today that the Government need only show that a public official has obtained a payment to which he was not entitled, *knowing that the payment was made in return for official acts.*" (emphasis added). This *quid pro quo* requirement is simply made up. The Court does not suggest that it has any basis in the common law or the language of the Hobbs Act, and I have found no treatise or dictionary that refers to any such requirement in defining "extortion."

Its only conceivable source, in fact, is our opinion last Term in *McCormick v. United States*, 500 U.S. 257 (1991). Quite sensibly, we insisted in that case that, unless the Government established the existence of a *quid pro quo*, a public official could not be convicted of extortion under the Hobbs Act for accepting a campaign contribution.

Because the common-law history of extortion was neither properly briefed nor argued in *McCormick*, the *quid pro quo* limitation imposed there represented a reasonable first step in the right direction. Now that we squarely consider that history, however, it is apparent that that limitation was in fact overly modest: at common law, McCormick was innocent of extortion *not* because he failed to offer a *quid pro quo* in return for campaign contributions, but because he did not take the contributions under color of official right. Today's extension of *McCormick*'s reasonable (but textually and historically artificial) *quid pro quo* limitation to *all* cases of official extortion is both unexplained and inexplicable — except insofar as it may serve to rescue the Court's definition of extortion from substantial overbreadth.

As serious as the Court's disregard for history is its disregard for well-established principles of statutory construction. The Court chooses not only the harshest interpretation of a criminal statute, but also the interpretation that maximizes federal criminal jurisdiction over state and local officials. I would reject both choices.

Our duty in construing this criminal statute, then, is clear: "The Court has often stated that when there are two rational readings of a criminal statute, one harsher than the other, we are to choose the harsher only when Congress has spoken in clear and definite language." *McNally v. United States*, 483 U.S. 350, 359–360 (1987). Because the Court's expansive interpretation of the statute is not the only plausible one, the rule of lenity compels adoption of the narrower interpretation.

The Court's construction of the Hobbs Act is repugnant not only to the basic tenets of criminal justice reflected in the rule of lenity, but also to basic tenets of federalism. Over the past 20 years, the Hobbs Act has served as the engine for a stunning expansion of federal criminal jurisdiction into a field traditionally policed by state and local laws — acts of public corruption by state and local officials. . . .

I have no doubt that today's opinion is motivated by noble aims. Political corruption at any level of government is a serious evil, and, from a policy perspective, perhaps one well suited for federal law enforcement. But federal judges are not free to devise new crimes to meet the occasion. Chief Justice Marshall's warning is as timely today as ever: "It would be dangerous, indeed, to carry the principle that a case which is within the reason or mischief of a statute, is within its provisions, so far as to punish a crime not enumerated in the statute, because it is of equal atrocity, or of kindred character, with those which are enumerated." *United States v. Wiltberger*, 5 Wheat. 76, 96 (1820).

Our criminal-justice system runs on the premise that prosecutors will respect and courts will enforce the boundaries on criminal conduct set by the legislature. Where, as here, those boundaries are breached, it becomes impossible to tell where prosecutorial discretion ends and prosecutorial abuse, or even discrimination, begins. The potential for abuse, of course, is particularly grave in the inherently political context of public-corruption prosecutions.

Notes and Questions

1. *Defining the quid pro quo post-*Evans.

a. *Does the quid pro quo requirement apply in non-campaign contribution cases?* In *McCormick*, the Court explicitly declined to decide whether the quid pro quo requirement applies in all color of official right extortion cases, or only in campaign contribution cases. 500 U.S. at 274 n.10. The majority in *Evans* did not address the question, although Justice Kennedy in concurrence opined that a quid pro quo must be proven in all color of official right extortion prosecutions. 504 U.S. at 278 (Kennedy, J., concurring).

b. *Explicit vs. implicit?* Assuming that the quid pro quo requirement applies, what is the standard for determining whether the government has met its burden of proof? In *McCormick*, the Court stated that the government must prove that the defendant made "an explicit" promise to engage in an official act in return for the payment. 500 U.S. at 273. In *Evans*, however, the Court stated that the evidence was sufficient because the defendant's "acceptance of the bribe constituted an implicit promise to use his official position to serve the interests of the bribe-giver." 504 U.S. at 257. One commentator has described the *Evans* approach as a "watered-down version of the [*McCormick*] quid pro quo requirement." James Lindgren, *The Theory, History, and Practice of the Bribery-Extortion Distinction*, 141 U. Pa. L. Rev. 1695, 1733 (1993).

2. *Uncertain state of the law post-*Evans. As the previous note shows, in a number of respects, *Evans* is difficult to reconcile with *McCormick*, raising the question whether *Evans* implicitly overturned *McCormick* at least in part. Needless to say, the law as it now stands has produced a fair amount of confusion, and the federal courts

of appeal have understandably reached differing results when applying the cases. As one commentator summed up:

> [I]n *McCormick v. United States*, [the Court held] that campaign donations to a public official would cross the line into illegal bribery or extortion only if made in return for an explicit quid pro quo agreement from an official to perform or not perform a specific act. Only a year later, however, the Supreme Court weighed in on another case of Hobbs Act extortion by a public official in *Evans v. United States*. The Evans court determined that in such a case of extortion, "the government need only show that a public official has obtained a payment to which he was not entitled, knowing that the payment was made in return for official acts." The Court did not indicate, however, whether *Evans* was to be treated as a campaign contribution case, as opposed to a non-campaign case simply dealing with a bribe to a public official, or whether the holding in *Evans* modified *McCormick*'s holding in any sense.
>
> Since *Evans*, three Circuits — the Second, Sixth, and Ninth — have determined that *McCormick* and *Evans* established different standards, with *McCormick* governing campaign contribution cases and *Evans* governing any other instances of public officials receiving bribes. Two other Circuits — the Third and Seventh — have indicated that they will hold *McCormick* to be the sole standard for campaign contribution cases in the future. The Eleventh Circuit stands alone in trying to reconcile *McCormick* and *Evans* in the campaign context. . . .

Ilissa B. Gold, *Explicit, Express, and Everything in Between: The Quid Pro Quo Requirement for Bribery and Hobbs Act Prosecutions in the 2000s*, 36 Wash. U. J.L. & Pol'y 261, 262–63 (2011) (citations omitted). For other discussions of the complexity of the law post-*Evans*, see John S. Gawey, *The Hobbs Leviathan: The Dangerous Breadth of the Hobbs Act and Other Corruption Statutes*, 87 Notre Dame L. Rev. 383 (2011); David Mills, *Corrupting the Harm Requirement in White Collar Crime*, 60 Stan. L. Rev. 1371 (2008); Jeremy N. Gayed, *"Corruptly:" Why Corrupt State of Mind Is an Essential Element for Hobbs Act Extortion Under Color of Official Right*, 78 Notre Dame L. Rev. 1731 (2003).

3. *Role of the courts in interpreting statutes.* The majority and dissent in *Evans* plainly disagree over whether the court should undertake to interpret the Hobbs Act in an expansive way. What considerations underlie this debate? Which side has the better of the argument?

4. *Bribery versus extortion.* After *Evans*, what is the difference between bribery and extortion under color of official right? Does your answer to this question affect your view as to whether *Evans* was correctly decided?

5. *Lenity.* The dissent in *Evans* relies upon the rule of lenity in reaching its conclusion. This rule is cited by majority and dissenting opinions in many of the cases in this text. Can you discern when the rule should, and should not, be applied?

6. *Potential for abuse?* Revisit the concluding note in the previous chapter, raising the question of whether the expansive reading of the federal bribery statutes creates the potential for abuse. Also recall Justice Thomas's dissent in *Evans*, concluding that because of the Court's broad reading of the extortion statute it will "become[] impossible to tell where prosecutorial discretion ends and prosecutorial abuse, or even discrimination, begins. The potential for abuse, of course, is particularly grave in the inherently political context of public corruption prosecutions." Is Justice Thomas correct? If so, what is the solution?

———————

After *Evans*, what is the breadth of the crime of extortion under color of official right? In the next decision, the various opinions show that the answer is far from clear and that *Evans* is perhaps on shaky ground. The case involves the issue whether a conspiracy to extort one of the members of the conspiracy qualifies as a conspiracy to commit extortion. As you consider this question, keep in mind the basic conspiracy principles discussed in Chapter 3. In light of those principles, was this case correctly decided? Why or why not? Does the answer depend upon whether the *Evans* holding is still good law?

United States v. Ocasio

136 S. Ct. 1423 (2016)

Justice ALITO delivered the opinion of the Court.

Petitioner Samuel Ocasio, a former officer in the Baltimore Police Department, participated in a kickback scheme with the owners of a local auto repair shop. When petitioner and other Baltimore officers reported to the scene of an auto accident, they persuaded the owners of damaged cars to have their vehicles towed to the repair shop, and in exchange for this service the officers received payments from the shopowners. Petitioner was convicted of obtaining money from the shopowners under color of official right, in violation of the Hobbs Act, 18 U.S.C. § 1951, and of conspiring to violate the Hobbs Act, in violation of 18 U.S.C. § 371. He now challenges his conspiracy conviction, contending that, as a matter of law, he cannot be convicted of conspiring with the shopowners to obtain money from them under color of official right. We reject this argument because it is contrary to age-old principles of conspiracy law. . . .

Hernan Alexis Moreno Mejia (known as Moreno) and Edwin Javier Mejia (known as Mejia) are brothers who co-owned and operated the Majestic Auto Repair Shop (Majestic). In 2008, Majestic was struggling to attract customers, so Moreno and Mejia made a deal with a Baltimore police officer, Jhonn Corona. In exchange for kickbacks, Officer Corona would refer motorists whose cars were damaged in accidents to Majestic for towing and repairs. Officer Corona then spread the word to other members of the force, and eventually as many as 60 other officers sent damaged cars to Majestic in exchange for payments of $150 to $300 per referral.

Petitioner began to participate in this scheme in 2009. . . .

Because police are often among the first to arrive at the scene of an accident, the Baltimore officers were well positioned to route damaged vehicles to Majestic. As a result, the kickback scheme was highly successful: It substantially increased Majestic's volume of business and profits, and by early 2011 it provided Majestic with at least 90% of its customers.

Moreno, Mejia, petitioner, and nine other Baltimore officers were indicted in 2011. The shopowners and most of the other officers eventually pleaded guilty pursuant to plea deals, but petitioner did not.

[P]etitioner was charged with three counts of violating the Hobbs Act, 18 U.S.C. § 1951, by extorting money from Moreno with his consent and under color of official right. . . . Petitioner and another Baltimore officer, Kelvin Quade Manrich, were also charged with violating the general federal conspiracy statute, 18 U.S.C. § 371. The indictment alleged that petitioner and Manrich conspired with Moreno, Mejia, and other Baltimore officers to bring about the same sort of substantive violations with which petitioner was charged. . . .

The jury found petitioner guilty on both the conspiracy count and the three substantive extortion counts, and the District Court sentenced him to concurrent terms of 18 months in prison on all four counts. On appeal to the Fourth Circuit, petitioner's primary argument was the same one he had pressed before the District Court: that his conspiracy conviction was fatally flawed because the conspirators had not agreed to obtain money from a person who was not a member of the conspiracy. The Fourth Circuit rejected petitioner's argument and affirmed his convictions. 750 F.3d 399 (2014).

Under longstanding principles of conspiracy law, a defendant may be convicted of conspiring to violate the Hobbs Act based on proof that he entered into a conspiracy that had as its objective the obtaining of property from another conspirator with his consent and under color of official right.

In analyzing petitioner's arguments, we begin with the text of the statute under which he was convicted, namely, the general federal conspiracy statute, which makes it a crime to "*conspire* . . . to commit any offense against the United States." 18 U.S.C. § 371 (emphasis added). Section 371's use of the term "conspire" incorporates long-recognized principles of conspiracy law. And under established case law, the fundamental characteristic of a conspiracy is a joint commitment to an "endeavor which, if completed, would satisfy all of the elements of [the underlying substantive] criminal offense." *Salinas v. United States*, 522 U.S. 52, 65 (1997.

Although conspirators must "pursue the same criminal objective," "a conspirator [need] not agree to commit or facilitate each and every part of the substantive offense." *Salinas, supra*, at 63. A defendant must merely reach an agreement with the "specific intent that the underlying crime be *committed*" by some member of the conspiracy. . . .

These basic principles of conspiracy law resolve this case. In order to establish the existence of a conspiracy to violate the Hobbs Act, the government has no obligation to demonstrate that each conspirator agreed personally to commit—or was even capable of committing—the substantive offense of Hobbs Act extortion. It is sufficient to prove that the conspirators agreed that the underlying crime *be committed* by a member of the conspiracy who was capable of committing it. In other words, each conspirator must have specifically intended that *some conspirator* commit each element of the substantive offense.

That is exactly what happened here: Petitioner, Moreno, and Mejia "share[d] a common purpose," namely, that *petitioner* and other police officers would commit every element of the substantive extortion offense. Petitioner and other officers would obtain property "under color of official right," something that Moreno and Mejia were incapable of doing because they were not public officials. And petitioner and other officers would obtain that money from "another," *i.e.,* from Moreno, Mejia, or Majestic. Although Moreno and Mejia were incapable of committing the underlying substantive offense as principals, they could conspire to commit Hobbs Act extortion by agreeing to help petitioner and other officers commit the substantive offense. For these reasons, it is clear that petitioner could be convicted of conspiring to obtain property from the shopowners with their consent and under color of official right.

In an effort to escape this conclusion, petitioner argues that the usual rules do not apply to the type of Hobbs Act conspiracy charged in this case. His basic argument, as ultimately clarified, is as follows. All members of a conspiracy must share the same criminal objective. The objective of the conspiracy charged in this case was to obtain money "from another, with his consent . . . under color of official right." But Moreno and Mejia did not have the objective of obtaining money "from another" because the money in question was their own. Accordingly, they were incapable of being members of the conspiracy charged in this case. And since there is insufficient evidence in the record to show that petitioner conspired with anyone other than Moreno and Mejia, he must be acquitted.

This argument fails for a very simple reason: Contrary to petitioner's claim, he and the shopowners *did* have a common criminal objective. The objective was not that each conspirator, including Moreno and Mejia, would obtain money from "another" but rather that petitioner and other Baltimore officers would do so. Petitioner does not dispute that he was properly convicted for three substantive Hobbs Act violations based on proof that he obtained money "from another." The criminal objective on which petitioner, Moreno, and Mejia agreed was that *petitioner and other Baltimore officers* would commit substantive violations of this nature. Thus, under well-established rules of conspiracy law, petitioner was properly charged with and convicted of conspiring with the shopowners. Nothing in the text of the Hobbs Act even remotely undermines this conclusion, and petitioner's invocation of the rule of lenity and principles of federalism is unavailing.

Petitioner argues that our interpretation makes the Hobbs Act sweep too broadly, creating a national antibribery law and displacing a carefully crafted network of state and federal statutes. He contends that a charge of conspiring to obtain money from a conspirator with his consent and under color of official right is tantamount to a charge of soliciting or accepting a bribe and that allowing such a charge undermines 18 U.S.C. § 666 (a federal bribery statute applicable to state and local officials) and state bribery laws. He also argues that extortion conspiracies of this sort were not known prior to the enactment of the Hobbs Act and that there is no evidence that Congress meant for that Act to plow this new ground.

The subtext of these arguments is that it seems unnatural to prosecute bribery on the basis of a statute prohibiting "extortion," but this Court held in *Evans* that Hobbs Act extortion "under color of official right" includes the "rough equivalent of what we would now describe as 'taking a bribe.'" Petitioner does not ask us to overturn *Evans,* and we have no occasion to do so. Having already held that § 1951 prohibits the "rough equivalent" of bribery, we have no principled basis for precluding the prosecution of conspiracies to commit that same offense.

Petitioner also exaggerates the reach of our decision. It does not, as he claims, dissolve the distinction between extortion and conspiracy to commit extortion. Because every act of extortion under the Hobbs Act requires property to be obtained with "consent," petitioner argues, proof of that consent will always or nearly always establish the existence of a conspiratorial agreement and thus allow the Government to turn virtually every such extortion case into a conspiracy case. But there are plenty of instances in which the "consent" required under the Hobbs Act will not be enough to constitute the sort of agreement needed under the law of conspiracy.

As used in the Hobbs Act, the phrase "with his consent" is designed to distinguish extortion ("obtaining of property from another, *with his consent,*" from robbery ("obtaining of personal property from the person or in the presence of another, *against his will.*" Thus, "consent" simply signifies the taking of property under circumstances falling short of robbery, and such "consent" is quite different from the *mens rea* necessary for a conspiracy.

This conclusion is clear from the language of § 1951 prohibiting the obtaining of property "from another, with his consent, *induced by wrongful use of actual or threatened force, violence, or fear.*" This language applies when, for example, a store owner makes periodic protection payments to gang members out of fear that they will otherwise trash the store. While these payments are obtained with the store owner's grudging consent, the store owner, simply by making the demanded payments, does not enter into a conspiratorial agreement with the gang members conducting the shakedown. Our interpretation thus does not turn virtually every act of extortion into a conspiracy.

Nor does our reading transform every bribe of a public official into a conspiracy to commit extortion. The "consent" required to pay a bribe does not necessarily create a conspiratorial agreement. In cases where the bribe payor is merely complying with an official demand, the payor lacks the *mens rea* necessary for a conspiracy. For example, imagine that a health inspector demands a bribe from a restaurant owner, threatening to close down the restaurant if the owner does not pay. If the owner reluctantly pays the bribe in order to keep the business open, the owner has "consented" to the inspector's demand, but this mere acquiescence in the demand does not form a conspiracy. . . .

A defendant may be convicted of conspiring to violate the Hobbs Act based on proof that he reached an agreement with the owner of the property in question to obtain that property under color of official right. Because petitioner joined such an agreement, his conspiracy conviction must stand.

The judgment of the United States Court of Appeals for the Fourth Circuit is affirmed.

Justice BREYER, concurring.

I agree with the sentiment expressed in the dissenting opinion of Justice THOMAS that *Evans v. United States* may well have been wrongly decided. I think it is an exceptionally difficult question whether "extortion" within the meaning of the Hobbs Act is really "the rough equivalent of . . . taking a bribe," especially when we admittedly decided that question in that case without the benefit of full briefing on extortion's common-law history. . . .

Nonetheless, we must in this case take *Evans* as good law. *See* Tr. of Oral Arg. 20 (Petitioner "take[s] th[e] holding [in *Evans*] as a given"). That being so, I join the majority's opinion in full.

Justice THOMAS, dissenting.

Today the Court holds that an extortionist can conspire to commit extortion with the person whom he is extorting. This holding further exposes the flaw in this Court's understanding of extortion. In my view, the Court started down the wrong path in *Evans v. United States,* which wrongly equated extortion with bribery. In so holding, *Evans* made it seem plausible that an extortionist could conspire with his victim. Rather than embrace that view, I would not extend *Evans'* errors further. . . .

Today the Court again broadens the Hobbs Act's reach to enable federal prosecutors to punish for conspiracy all participants in a public-official bribery scheme. The invasion of state sovereign functions is again substantial. The federal government can now more expansively charge state and local officials. And it can now more easily obtain pleas or convictions from these officials: Because the government can prosecute bribe-payors with sweeping conspiracy charges, it will be easier to induce those payors to plead out and testify against state and local officials. The Court thus further wrenches from States the presumptive control that they should have over their own officials' wrongdoing. . . .

Justice SOTOMAYOR, with whom THE CHIEF JUSTICE joins, dissenting.

If a group of conspirators sets out to extort "another" person, we ordinarily think that they are proposing to extort money or property from a victim outside their group, not one of themselves. Their group is the conspiratorial entity and the victim is "another" person.

But in upholding the conspiracy conviction here, the Court interprets the phrase extorting property "from another" in the Hobbs Act contrary to that natural understanding. It holds that a group of conspirators can agree to obtain property "from another" in violation of the Act even if they agree only to transfer property among themselves.

That is not a natural or logical way to interpret the phrase "from another." ...

Notes and Questions

1. *The nature of extortion under color of official right.* The Court in *Ocasio* was deeply split when applying basic conspiracy principles to the law of extortion. As the majority stated in *Ocasio*, under *Evans* "extortion 'under color of official right' includes the 'rough equivalent of what we would now describe as "taking a bribe."'"... Having already held that § 1951 prohibits the 'rough equivalent' of bribery, we have no principled basis for precluding the prosecution of conspiracies to commit that same offense."

As Justice Thomas's dissent highlights, the split in some respects reflects disagreement on the Court over the nature of extortion under color of official right: Is that crime more akin to classic extortion, with a clear wrongdoer and victim, or to bribery, in which both parties are culpable? As examined in the notes after *Evans*, it is now difficult to distinguish bribery from extortion in many circumstances.

2. *The law of conspiracy applied to extortion.* Justice Sotomayor's dissent, joined by Chief Justice Roberts, focuses on the nature of conspiracy. She asserted that it is illogical for a group of conspirators to conspire to commit a crime against one of the conspirators. In the case, the garage owners were not public officials, but were convicted of conspiring with public officials (the police officers) to extort themselves. Is the dissent correct that this conclusion does not make sense? Why or why not?

3. *Reconsidering* Evans. In his dissent, Justice Thomas explicitly called for overturning *Evans*. Justice Breyer in concurrence questioned whether *Evans* was correctly decided, but ultimately determined that overruling *Evans* was not an issue before the Court. Justice Sotomayor, joined by Chief Justice Roberts, in dissent did not take on *Evans* so directly, though we might ask whether she implicitly did so when questioning whether a victim could legitimately be considered a Hobbs Act co-conspirator.

Is *Evans* on shaky ground? The Court in *Ocasio* was deeply split, five-to-three, with Justice Breyer in concurrence, making clear that he believed that the principal precedent upon which the majority relied (*Evans*) was perhaps wrongly decided—leaving the Court at the time potentially evenly split on *Evans*'s validity.

Do the complexities inherent in extortion under color of official right after *Evans* illustrate the underlying weaknesses in that decision? As Professor Eliason has written, "The linguistic gymnastics required to frame a charge against the bribe payers in what is really a bribery case do highlight the shaky foundation of the *Evans* holding. But as the majority noted, if you accept *Evans*, then basic conspiracy law dictates the result in *Ocasio*." Randall D. Eliason, *The Extortionist Contortionist*, Geo. Wash. L. Rev. On The Docket (May 10, 2016), http://www.gwlr.org/ocasio-v-united-states -the-contortionist-extortionist/.

4. *Unusual alliances.* Once again, we see in a white collar case that justices generally perceived to be "liberal" or "conservative" line up in ways seldom seen in criminal cases outside the white collar context. In this case, Justice Alito's majority opinion was joined by Justices Kennedy, Ginsburg, Breyer, and Kagan. Justices Thomas, Sotomayor, and Chief Justice Roberts dissented. Why the unusual alliances? Might it have to do with the nature of the perceived harm in white collar cases? With issues of federalism?

Problems

8-4. Antonio held various positions at the Department of Licenses and Inspections ("L & I") for the City. L & I's function is to administer and enforce the City's code requirements, including building, electrical, fire, health, housing, business, and zoning regulations. Officials of L & I are empowered to issue zoning and use permits and licenses according to a first-come-first-served policy, conduct inspections, and enforce applicable codes and regulations. In his positions, Antonio had the discretionary authority to approve zoning and use permits and licenses, and to cite and close businesses for violations.

On December 20 last year, L & I closed for zoning violations one of Westside Check Cashing and Pawn Shop ("Westside") stores. The controller of the check cashing business met with Antonio to discuss reopening the business. Antonio explained that Westside had to file a new application for a zoning and/or use registration permit and make other changes. Several days later, Antonio called the controller and told her that he wanted a piece of jewelry to give his wife for their anniversary. The controller selected a diamond pendant appraised at $4,275 and sent it to Antonio's office by courier. The controller decided not to bill Antonio for the pendant because of Antonio's position with L & I. The zoning issue that led to the store closing on December 20 was still pending and the controller was concerned that Antonio would use his position to keep the business closed. Shortly after the exchange of the jewelry, Antonio permitted the store to reopen.

A federal grand jury indicted Antonio for extortion under color of official right under the Hobbs Act. At the trial, the judge instructed the jury that one of the elements of the offense was proof beyond a reasonable doubt of an implicit quid pro quo. Antonio was convicted, and appeals.

What arguments should Antonio assert? How should the government respond? How should the court rule? Why?

8-5. Pat Oaks is a newly elected state senator. During Oaks's campaign, Oaks did not take a position on the troublesome issue of logging in state forest land in Oaks's state. Such logging occurs in Oaks's state under temporary permits. Last year, as the expiration date for the temporary permit program approached, Oaks unsuccessfully opposed legislation granting a temporary permit for an additional year. Thereafter, Oaks discussed the logging issue with the logger's lobbyist.

At one point, Oaks personally advised the loggers' lobbyist, Larry Larsons, that Oaks was "surprised that the loggers had not been more supportive of me." Larsons responded, "We certainly need your support." Over the next two months, Oaks received the first of several cash payments from the loggers. When Oaks's campaign manager thereafter called the lobbyist to ask for more money, the lobbyist assured Oaks that more would be forthcoming. The payments were made directly to Oaks, and Oaks did not inform the staff accountant or campaign finance director of the payments. The money was not reported as income on Oaks's personal income tax returns, and was not reported on Oaks's campaign finance disclosure forms.

During the next legislative session, Oaks sponsored and secured the passage of legislation permitting permanent logging permits to be issued to the loggers. Over the succeeding two months, Oaks received three more cash payments from the loggers. Again, Oaks did not reveal the payments to Oaks's staff, and the money was not reported as personal income for Oaks or on Oaks's campaign finance disclosure forms. All the payments together totaled $127,000.

Oaks is charged with extortion under color of official right under 18 U.S.C. § 1951. The defense position at trial is that the payments were campaign contributions, and that they were not reported as such because Oaks assumed that Oaks's accountant and campaign finance manager would discover the deposits from bank records Oaks provided them. The staffers have substantiated that the bank records revealed the deposits, which they failed to notice. The lobbyist has declined to testify, citing the Fifth Amendment privilege against compelled testimony.

> *a. Prepare proposed jury instructions, outlining the elements of the offense, for the government and for the defense.*

> *b. Prepare closing arguments to the jury for the government and for the defense.*

8-6. Defendant is a customer service representative for the Internal Revenue Service (IRS). For five years, Defendant used knowledge of available IRS tax credits and fraud detection practices to entice claimants to provide their personal information; Defendant would then ensure them that if the claimants provided Defendant with their information, Defendant had the influence to ensure the claimants would receive a cash payment from the IRS. Defendant would then file fraudulent returns and split a portion of those proceeds with the claimants. If the claimants refused to pay the fee from Defendant requested from the claimants, Defendant threatened them with a "red flag" or potential audit on their IRS accounts.

Defendant was indicted on charges of conspiracy, filing false claims with the IRS, and Hobbs Act extortion. Defendant has moved to dismiss the Hobbs Act charge on the ground that no reasonable person would honestly believe that Defendant, a customer service representative at IRS, had any sway or power over whether the claimants would receive cash payments.

How should the court rule? Why? Does the likelihood of bona fide subjective belief of a party to the alleged extortion matter? If so, why?

D. The Use of Fear Theory

In the next case, the government employed both the "use of fear" theory and the "color of official right" theory in a political corruption prosecution. As you read the case, consider which theory better fits the facts. Given that the court found one of the theories sufficient, why did the court feel compelled to reverse the conviction?

United States v. Garcia

907 F.2d 380 (2d Cir. 1990)

George C. Pratt, Circuit Judge:

Defendants Robert and Jane Garcia appeal from judgments of conviction on two counts of extortion (18 U.S.C. § 1951) and one count of conspiracy to commit extortion (18 U.S.C. § 371) entered against them in the United States District Court for the Southern District of New York. For the reasons that follow, we reverse the Garcias' convictions and remand to the district court for further proceedings.

Robert and Jane Garcia were charged with conspiracy, extortion, bribery, and receiving gratuities in connection with Robert Garcia's congressional activities on behalf of the now infamous Wedtech Corporation. The extortion and conspiracy charges were premised on two theories: (1) extortion by wrongful use of fear and (2) extortion under color of official right. At the close of the government's case, the Garcias moved for dismissal of the first theory. The district judge denied this request, concluding — erroneously, as we establish below — that the government had adequately demonstrated that the Garcias intended to exploit Wedtech's fear of economic loss.

The Garcias were acquitted by the jury of the bribery and gratuity charges, but were convicted of the substantive and conspiracy charges of extortion. Following the jury's verdicts, the Garcias moved for a new trial, claiming that the jury's acquittal of them on the bribery and gratuity counts suggested that the guilty verdicts on the extortion counts were based not on the second theory — under color of official right — but instead on the first theory of extortion — wrongful use of fear — and that the evidence could not support that conclusion. Neither the government nor the Garcias had requested that special interrogatories be given to the jury in order to learn the actual basis for their decision. The district judge denied the new trial motion, and the Garcias appeal their convictions.

Since the jury was not given special interrogatories we cannot determine on this record the precise basis for the guilty verdicts. Therefore, for our purposes, we must assume the jury could have found the Garcias guilty of extortion under either theory presented by the government. Consequently, if there was insufficient evidence for one of the theories, then the verdict is ambiguous and a new trial must be granted. By their Rule 29 motion to withhold from the jury the theory of extortion by fear of economic loss, the Garcias preserved their right to argue here that if the evidence was insufficient to support their extortion convictions on that theory, we should reverse and order a new trial on the remaining theory — extortion under color of official right. We turn, then, to the sufficiency of the evidence to prove extortion by fear of economic loss.

Extortion is defined in the Hobbs Act as "the obtaining of property from another, with his consent, induced by wrongful use of actual or threatened force, violence, or fear, or under color of official right." 18 U.S.C. § 1951(b)(2). Over the years, our cases have concluded that the fear required in extortion cases "can be satisfied by putting the victim in fear of economic loss." *United States v. Brecht*, 540 F.2d 45, 52 (2d Cir. 1976).

In *United States v. Capo*, 817 F.2d 947 (2d Cir. 1987), our court, sitting in banc, focused specifically on what factors are necessary to establish fear of economic loss. The present appeal requires us to apply the standards that we developed in *Capo* to a factual setting involving an elected official who sold his influence and power. *Capo* involved a job-selling scheme that took place at a plant of the Eastman Kodak Company. In 1982 Kodak announced that production of its new "disc camera" created the need for approximately 2,300 new employees. In the rush to fill these jobs, standard hiring procedures were ignored. Exploiting this situation, the defendants used their influence with an employment counselor at Kodak to see that individuals who paid them were hired as Kodak employees. This job-selling network formed the basis of an indictment for extortion based on a fear of economic loss, and the jury convicted.

On appeal, a panel of this court affirmed, but after an in banc rehearing we reversed, holding that a fear of economic loss must be viewed from the victim's perspective and that the victim must have reasonably believed "first, that the defendant had the power to harm the victim, and second, that the defendant would exploit that power to the victim's detriment." *Capo*, 817 F.2d at 951. Concluding that the Kodak job-selling scheme was not extortion, we emphasized that the "victims" had paid the defendants in an attempt to obtain influence. The "victims" in *Capo* thus did not act out of fear of the defendants or of what the defendants might do to them; rather, they were willing participants who were seeking to secure the defendants' assistance in order to improve their chances of obtaining a job.

The Garcias claim that their situation is similar to the one in *Capo*. They argue, in effect, that the payments that they received, like the payments in *Capo*, were not made out of fear but as a way of obtaining influence. For this reason, they claim, there was insufficient evidence to convict them of extortion based on a fear of economic loss. While a defendant challenging the sufficiency of the evidence "bears a very heavy burden," *United States v. Chang An-Lo*, 851 F.2d 547, 553 (2d Cir. 1988), we nevertheless agree with the Garcias and conclude that the evidence in this case was insufficient to support an extortion conviction based on a fear of economic loss.

At trial the government relied on two claimed extortionate events: (1) a dinner meeting at a Manhattan restaurant and (2) a $20,000 loan by Wedtech to the Garcias.

A. The Alleged Dinner Extortion.

In 1978 Robert Garcia was elected to the United States Congress as a representative of the South Bronx, where the Wedtech Corporation was located. During his first years in office, Garcia extended normal congressional assistance to Wedtech in connection with a $550,000 loan from the Small Business Administration, $4 million in loans from the Economic Development Administration, and a bid for an army contract.

In April of 1984, Wedtech received a $24 million dollar contract to build pontoons for the navy. A few weeks after Garcia, along with other congressional figures, had attended a press conference announcing the award of this contract, Garcia called Mario Moreno, a Wedtech officer, and told him that it was important that the two of them meet. They agreed to have dinner the next evening at a midtown Manhattan restaurant.

Garcia and his wife, Jane, met Moreno. The congressman complained that Moreno had not kept him properly informed about Wedtech's activities. Moreno first described Wedtech's success and rapid growth in recent months. Then, when Moreno told the Garcias that Wedtech was having difficulties with the navy pontoon contract, Jane Garcia interjected that she and her husband were friendly with a classmate of then Secretary of the Navy John Lehman and that they could arrange a meeting with Lehman to resolve some of the problems with the contract. Robert Garcia boasted of his increasing influence in congress, and then proposed that Wedtech hire Jane Garcia as a public relations consultant.

Moreno told the Garcias that Wedtech, which was dealing primarily with government contracts, had no need for a public relations consultant and even if it did, it would be "crazy" to hire the wife of a congressman for the position. Garcia persisted, commenting that perhaps the payments to his wife could be made in another way. Jane Garcia then suggested that she be paid through an intermediary, Ralph Vallone, Jr., a lawyer in Puerto Rico who was a good friend of the Garcias.

As the dinner came to an end, the Garcias emphasized their influence with top officials at the navy and at the United States Postal Service. They did this knowing that Wedtech was attempting not only to resolve its problems with the navy pontoon contract, but also that the company was attempting to obtain postal contracts. At this point, Moreno told the Garcias that he personally supported their proposal and would seek approval for it from other Wedtech officials.

Fearing that a denial of payments to Jane Garcia would induce Garcia to withhold his support for the postal contracts Wedtech sought, the Wedtech officers approved the payments.

Wedtech began to send monthly checks to Vallone, who then deposited them and sent Jane Garcia's consulting company, Leesonia Enterprises, checks of comparable amounts. During the period that these payments were made, Jane Garcia received $76,000.

In support of its claim that Wedtech made these payments out of economic fear, the government points primarily to Robert Garcia's statement at the beginning of the dinner conversation. Moreno testified that Garcia had said:

> We have been apart for a long period of time. We don't communicate as much as we used to before, several years before, two or three years before. We had to find out from somebody else that the company had gone public, and that other people had benefitted from the company.... Can you explain to me what has happened there at the company in reality in the last year or so?

The government claims that Garcia made this statement knowing that Wedtech's economic life depended on continued political influence. This statement, it argues, was therefore an implicit threat: Garcia was warning Wedtech that unless he and his wife were paid, the company could no longer count on Garcia as a congressional advocate. This could in turn lead to a failure to obtain any more government contracts. But did Moreno perceive this statement as such a threat? There is no evidence that he did; on the contrary, the evidence shows that he did not.

During the dinner, the Garcias mentioned their contacts in the Postal Service, from which Wedtech was attempting to obtain a contract. Moreno stated that during the dinner he was thinking "that the Congressman [Garcia] could be a tremendous ally in . . . trying to get [the] contracts from the Postal Service."

When asked at trial why he approved the payment of money to Jane Garcia, Moreno answered:

> Because I felt that if we were not going to make those payments, the Congressman was not going to do the kind of activity that we would need to have done to convince Postmaster General Bolger to set aside those contracts for Wedtech.

Later, Moreno testified: "I felt that if we were not to satisfy those payments, we were not going to receive any activity beneficial to us regarding those postal contracts."

This is not the mindset of a victim of economic extortion; rather, it is the thinking of a shrewd, unethical businessman who senses and seeks to capitalize on a money-making opportunity.

The central fact is clear: even in the face of Garcia's disgraceful request for money, Wedtech was not risking the loss of anything to which it was legally entitled.

Wedtech would still be permitted to bid on government contracts. But without Garcia's favorable attitude, the company might not be able to count on continued preferential treatment, nor could it secure Garcia's favorable intervention in the future. Garcia, in turn, was in effect offering to sell his congressional power, but he was not using that power as a way to intimidate Wedtech. By paying the Garcias, Wedtech was purchasing an advocate, not buying off a thug.

On redirect examination of Moreno, the prosecutor crystallized the motivating reason behind Moreno's decision to make the payments:

Q. Now, sir, you were asked questions about — by both lawyers about the meeting at Lelo's [the Manhattan restaurant]. Did you consider it legal or illegal to agree to Congressman Garcia's request that you pay his wife through Vallone?

A. Illegal.

Q. Why did you consider it illegal?

A. Because we were the constituents in Congressman Garcia's district. And to my knowledge, he is not supposed to be receiving any payments for any services he may perform for the company with the government. And I always viewed him and his wife as one unit.

Q. When you made that agreement in Lelo's in May of 1984, did you agree to pay the money for services from Jane Garcia or Congressman Robert Garcia?

A. For Congressman Garcia's services.

In short, the dinner meeting did not generate in Moreno or Wedtech any fear of economic loss within the meaning of the federal extortion statute as we have interpreted it in *Capo*.

B. The Alleged $20,000 Loan Extortion.

The Garcias were also convicted of extorting a $20,000 loan from Wedtech. On August 2, 1985, Robert Garcia told Moreno it was urgent that they meet and discuss a matter that was too sensitive to discuss over the phone. Moreno agreed and met Garcia at his Bronx congressional office. When Moreno arrived, Garcia asked to borrow $20,000 immediately, since he was leaving shortly for the Middle East. Moreno, who was $12,000 overdrawn at the bank himself, told Garcia that this loan could probably be arranged, but that he would have to check with other Wedtech officials. After getting the necessary funds from Wedtech's "slush fund," Moreno returned the same day to Garcia's office where Garcia suggested that the check be made payable to his sister, the Reverend Aimee Cortese, who would in turn forward the money to the Garcias. Garcia then directed a congressional aide to prepare documentation showing a loan between Moreno and Cortese. In Garcia's office, Moreno gave a check for $20,000 to Cortese, who deposited it and wrote another check to Jane Garcia for the same amount. Moreno testified that he believed that if he did not lend Garcia the money, Garcia would no longer help Wedtech.

Although the loan was supposed to be repaid in October of 1985, the Garcias did not repay it until March of 1986. Before finally repaying the loan, Robert Garcia asked Moreno to donate the $20,000 to the Reverend Cortese's church. Moreno declined, telling Garcia that he needed the money himself but that perhaps he would make a donation to the church in the future.

Recognizing that it has presented no evidence to demonstrate that even an implicit threat accompanied Robert Garcia's request that Wedtech lend him $20,000, the government argues that the Garcias' original "threat" created a "climate of fear" that colored all their future dealings with the company. While Moreno testified that he had agreed to the loan because without it Garcia "would not continue to do things in the same way that [Moreno] felt he could do," this does not demonstrate the kind of fear that is required by our decision in *Capo*. Had Garcia actually established a climate of fear, as the government contends, Wedtech would not have refused Robert Garcia's request that Wedtech convert its loan into a "donation" to his sister's church. But this is precisely what Wedtech did, and its refusal powerfully illustrates Wedtech's lack of fear.

The government does not have to prove that a climate of fear was created by a direct threat; nevertheless, the government must at least prove the existence of the victim's belief that the defendant had the power to harm it and the victim's fear that the defendant would exploit that power. However, there was no evidence that in making these payments Wedtech acted out of fear. At the time the alleged initial "threat" was made, Moreno viewed Garcia as an "ally." Moreover, the Garcias did not threaten Wedtech with harm, but instead underscored the mutual benefits that would flow from Wedtech's payments: the Garcias would obtain badly needed cash, and Wedtech would receive more government contracts than was likely without Garcia's help.

While the evidence readily proved that Wedtech paid the Garcias in the hope of receiving future favors, it did not establish that the company acted out of fear that without these payments it would lose existing contracts or even opportunities to which it was legally entitled. As in *Capo*, there was an "absence of any evidence of detrimental action for nonpayment. . . ." 817 F.2d at 953. Garcia never even hinted that he was prepared to use his power to harm Wedtech.

Without expressing — however implicitly — such a threat, the Garcias did not create in Moreno or Wedtech any feeling of fear; there is no evidence of any other cause of fear; and without the victim feeling some fear, extortion through fear of economic loss cannot exist. Wedtech paid the Garcias to ensure that it would receive special, preferential treatment; in making the payments, the company was motivated by desire, not fear; by opportunity, not by concern with retribution. As we sought to make clear in *Capo*, that is not the stuff of which extortion is made.

Because there were no special jury interrogatories, we have no way of knowing on which theory of extortion the Garcias were convicted. The district court, over objection, permitted the jury to consider the theory of economic loss, but we have concluded that the evidence presented was insufficient to support that conviction. Accordingly, we must reverse the judgments of conviction and remand to the district court for further proceedings.

Notes and Questions

1. *Inconsistent verdicts?* Consider the specific charges against the defendants, and the outcome at the trial. On its face, the jury's verdict may seem inconsistent. Was it? Can you explain the trial outcome?

2. *The* Garcia *result.* Is it not clear that Congressman Garcia behaved in a blatantly corrupt way? Why did the appeals court reverse his conviction? Are you persuaded that the result was compelled by the holding in *Capo*? Why or why not?

3. *The retrial.* Following the reversal, the government retried the defendants on the color of official right theory, and obtained partial convictions. In instructing the jury, the trial judge declined to require proof of a quid pro quo, holding that such proof is only required in campaign contribution cases. *See United States v. Garcia*, 774 F. Supp. 848, 848–849 (S.D.N.Y. 1991). On appeal, the Second Circuit reversed, holding that *Evans* requires that the jury find a quid pro quo in all color of official right extortion cases. *United States v. Garcia*, 992 F.2d 409, 414–415 (2d Cir. 1993). The government chose not to retry the defendants for a third time. Were the government's resources wisely spent in this case? Why or why not?

4. *The line between ally and enemy.* In *Garcia*, the court concluded that, "[b]y paying the Garcias, Wedtech was purchasing an advocate, not buying off a thug." Because the purported victim viewed the defendants as allies rather than adversaries, the facts did not show extortion by threat of economic harm. But suppose the Congressman had said, "I only allow bills supporting my friends to come before Congress when my friends have helped me out." Would that amount to the use of fear? Take the case where state officials solicit financial benefits from out-of-state banks, and thereafter arrange for those banks to obtain state business that they otherwise would not have obtained. Would this amount to extortion by use of fear? *See United States v. Collins*, 78 F.3d 1021, 1030 (6th Cir. 1996) (holding that, because failure to provide the benefits would have deprived the banks of an opportunity to compete on a fair basis for the state business, facts supported conviction for extortion by use of fear).

5. *Reversible error?* The court above held that providing an invalid theory to the jury requires reversal where the jury returned a general verdict. Note that the United States Supreme Court has since held that an error in submitting an invalid theory to the jury does not require reversal but is subject to harmless error analysis. *See Hedgpeth v. Pulido*, 129 S. Ct. 530 (2008).

Problems

8-7. Dern is a member of the City of Metropolis City Council, having been elected last year to a four-year term. Last March 1, the City Council began considering a major construction project to provide new office space for city agencies. The Council decided to acquire land with the assistance of a real estate broker and to hire a contractor to construct a new building on the site once it was purchased. The Council agreed to meet on March 18 to continue the discussions.

On March 12, Dern met with real estate broker Pat Parsons over coffee at Dern's home. Parsons specialized in purchases of land for commercial and municipal building projects. During the meeting, Dern said to Parsons, "We have this big city project coming up. I sure would like for you to be our broker. Would you like a shot?" Parsons responded, "Of course." Dern then said, "Well, I can assure you that you will be considered, with a substantial brokerage fee. You know, it's a competitive business. But the only way I can assure that you will be considered would be for me to have a, you know, stake in the venture." Parsons said, "How does a half percent sound?" Dern nodded in response. Parsons then said, "I think it would also be a good idea to contribute to your campaign, don't you think?" Dern responded, "I never turn down an offer for a contribution." The next day, Parsons sent a $5,000 check to Dern for Dern's reelection campaign. Dern reported the contribution in accordance with local election regulations.

Dern next told Parsons that the City Council had already reached a confidential decision that it would only hire an agent who agreed to accept a real estate commission of lower than the standard six percent of the purchase price.

The City Council subsequently retained Parsons for the project. The Council chose Parsons because Parsons' proposal to the Council indicated Parsons' willingness to accept less than the usual six percent real estate commission.

On July 1, the city purchased the property at a fair market value of $25 million. That day, Parsons gave Dern $125,000 in cash, Dern's share of Parsons' commission, which Dern reported to election officials.

In a jurisdiction that follows the *Capo* rule, a jury convicted Dern of extortion, 18 U.S.C. §1951, based upon the foregoing. In the indictment and at trial, the government asserted that Dern was guilty under (a) the use of force theory, and (b) the color of official right theory. By means of a general verdict form, the jury convicted Dern.

What viable arguments does Dern have on appeal? What is the likely outcome? Why?

8-8. Defendant Felicia Suarez has had a career as attorney, judge, and politician. After practicing law, she served as a Central City Court Judge. Subsequently, Suarez was elected to the County Board of Commissioners. She served alongside her friends and co-commissioners Larry Kim and Noelle Spam. This elected three-member Board of Commissioners has exclusive authority to transact county business, including entering into contracts on behalf of the County. By law, contracts with the county are awarded through sealed bidding to the lowest responsible and responsive bidder.

The Commissioners, however, decided not to award contracts by following the law, but instead, awarded contracts to their "friends." Among the contracts that the Commissioners controlled was the contract to clean the County Government Complex. The cleaning contract was for about $200,000 annually. After Suarez was elected, she and the other commissioners had a meeting with the owner of Professional Building Maintenance ("PBM"), Harold Mitchell, to inform him that he would have to pay the Commissioners kickback money in order to keep the cleaning contract. The commissioners devised the following plan: PBM would submit invoices to the County for additional work — for example, carpet cleaning, wall washing, and other services not included in the general cleaning contract — and inflate the price for the work. The Commissioners would approve the invoices for the extra work, and PBM would receive a check from the County for the inflated amount. After receiving the check from the County, PBM would give the Commissioners the difference between the actual price of the extra work and the amount paid by the County. Mitchell agreed to plead guilty and cooperate with the government. At defendant's trial, Mitchell testified that he believed PBM would lose the cleaning contract if he did not give kickbacks to the Commissioners.

A few years later, PBM stopped paying kickbacks and lost the cleaning contract. Suarez suggested to Kim that they give the cleaning contract to Global Management Services ("GMS"), owned by her friends Larry Crowel and Randy Norris. Suarez told Kim that Crowel "knows how to play the game" and "could do a better job" for them. Crowel had known Suarez for approximately 20 years and had worked on Suarez's campaign for County Commissioner. Crowel had several conversations with Suarez and Kim about getting the cleaning contract. Kim told Crowel that PBM was paying him $600 to $700 a month. Crowel offered Kim $900 to $1000. In a similar meeting with Commissioner Spam, Crowel offered Spam $1000 to $1100 a month. Shortly thereafter, Suarez, Spam, and Kim had a secret meeting and awarded the cleaning contract to GMS.

For the next two years, GMS made monthly payments to the Commissioners. GMS financed the bribes by inflating the annual contract price. Then, after GMS received its monthly check from the County, Crowel would cash the check for the inflated amount and meet with each Commissioner to give the kickback money.

A federal grand jury returned an indictment against Suarez. Count 1, which related to the payments obtained from PBM and GMS, charged Suarez with conspiracy to affect commerce by extortion through the use of fear of economic harm, in violation of the Hobbs Act, 18 U.S.C. § 1951. Suarez appeals her conviction on Count 1, contending there was insufficient evidence to prove extortion under the Hobbs Act.

How should the court rule? Why?

Chapter 9

False Statements

A. Introductory Notes

The principal federal false statements statute, 18 U.S.C. §1001, criminalizes the making of a wide range of both sworn and unsworn statements to the federal government. A false statements charge typically arises in one of two ways. First, prosecutors may employ this statute to charge those who have lied to cover up other illegal activities. In this context, the charge is a "cover-up" crime akin to the perjury and obstruction of justice statutes discussed in the next two chapters. Second, the government may also use §1001 to prosecute those who have lied in efforts to defraud the government or to disrupt government functions in such matters as federal employment, government benefits, and federal regulations. Here, the statute acts as a fraud statute in much the same way as the mail and wire fraud statutes discussed in Chapter 4. Because of its breadth, §1001 is one of the most frequently charged crimes in white collar investigations.[a]

B. Elements of False Statements Statute

Section 1001 makes it a crime "knowingly and willfully" to engage in one of three types of conduct:

(1) Falsifying, concealing, or covering up a material fact by any trick, scheme, or device;

(2) Making any materially false, fictitious, or fraudulent statement, or representation; or

(3) Making or using any false writing or document knowing it to contain any materially false, fictitious, or fraudulent statement or entry.

The first theory requires proof that the defendant engaged in an affirmative act of nondisclosure or concealment by means of a trick, scheme, or device. As discussed

---

a. For an analysis of the false statements statute, see Stuart P. Green, *False Statements*, *in* Lying, Cheating, and Stealing: A Moral Theory of White Collar Crime 161–70 (2006). In addition to §1001, there are dozens of statutes that criminalize false statements to the government in specific contexts. *See, e.g.*, 18 U.S.C. §1014 (false statements for the purpose of influencing certain financial institutions). Another important and related statute is the False Claims Act, 18 U.S.C. §287, which criminalizes knowing submission of a false or fraudulent claim to the federal government.

in § E below, courts also generally require, when the charge is based on an omission, that the government prove that the defendant had a legal duty to disclose the omitted facts. The second and third theories require proof that the defendant verbally or in writing made a false or fraudulent statement.

Courts generally interpret § 1001 to require proof of the following elements:

(1) The defendant (a) made or used an oral or written statement, or (b) concealed information that the defendant had a legal duty to disclose;

(2) The statement or information was false or fraudulent;

(3) The statement or information was material;

(4) The defendant acted knowingly and willfully; and

(5) The defendant made the statement or concealed the information on any matter within the subject matter jurisdiction of the executive, legislative, or judicial branch of the federal government.

As discussed below, the statute explicitly excludes from its coverage (a) certain statements made by parties or attorneys in court proceedings and (b) certain statements made in connection with Congressional proceedings. The statutory maximum sentence under § 1001 is five years.

C. Jurisdiction

Defendants in false statements cases have frequently argued that the particular statements at issue did not qualify under the statute. The following case is the principal United States Supreme Court case delineating the jurisdictional scope of the statute.

United States v. Rodgers

466 U.S. 475 (1984)

JUSTICE REHNQUIST delivered the opinion of the Court.

Respondent Larry Rodgers was charged in a two-count indictment with making "false, fictitious or fraudulent statements" to the Federal Bureau of Investigation (FBI) and the United States Secret Service, in violation of 18 U.S.C. § 1001. Rodgers allegedly lied in telling the FBI that his wife had been kidnaped and in telling the Secret Service that his wife was involved in a plot to kill the President. Rodgers moved to dismiss the indictment for failure to state an offense on the grounds that the investigation of kidnappings and the protection of the President are not matters "within the jurisdiction" of the respective agencies, as that phrase is used in § 1001. The District Court for the Western District of Missouri granted the motion, and the United States Court of Appeals for the Eighth Circuit affirmed. We now reverse. The statutory language clearly encompasses criminal investigations conducted by the FBI and the Secret Service, and nothing in the legislative history indicates that Congress intended a more restricted reach for the statute.

On June 2, 1982, Larry Rodgers telephoned the Kansas City, Missouri, office of the FBI and reported that his wife had been kidnaped. The FBI spent over 100 agent hours investigating the alleged kidnaping only to determine that Rodgers' wife had left him voluntarily. Two weeks later, Rodgers contacted the Kansas City office of the Secret Service and reported that his "estranged girlfriend" (actually his wife) was involved in a plot to assassinate the President. The Secret Service spent over 150 hours of agent and clerical time investigating this threat and eventually located Rodgers' wife in Arizona. She stated that she left Kansas City to get away from her husband. Rodgers later confessed that he made the false reports to induce the federal agencies to locate his wife.

In granting Rodgers' motion to dismiss the indictment, the District Court considered itself bound by a prior decision of the Eighth Circuit in *Friedman v. United States*, 374 F.2d 363 (8th Cir. 1967). *Friedman* also involved false statements made to the FBI to initiate a criminal investigation. In that case, the Court of Appeals reversed the defendant's conviction under § 1001, holding that the phrase "within the jurisdiction," as used in that provision, referred only to "the power to make final or binding determinations." . . .

Reading the term "jurisdiction" in this restrictive light, the Court of Appeals included within its scope the "power to make monetary awards, grant governmental privileges, or promulgate binding administrative and regulative determinations," while excluding "the mere authority to conduct an investigation in a given area without the power to dispose of the problems or compel action." *Id.* at 367. The court concluded that false statements made to the FBI were not covered by § 1001 because the FBI "had no power to adjudicate rights, establish binding regulations, compel the action or finally dispose of the problem giving rise to the inquiry." *Id.* at 368.

In the present case, the Court of Appeals adhered to its decision in *Friedman* and affirmed the dismissal of the indictment. The court acknowledged that two other Courts of Appeals had expressly rejected the reasoning of *Friedman*. But the Eighth Circuit found its own analysis more persuasive. We granted certiorari to resolve this conflict.

It seems to us that the interpretation of § 1001 adopted by the Court of Appeals for the Eighth Circuit is unduly strained. Section 1001 expressly embraces false statements made "in any matter within the jurisdiction of any department or agency of the United States." A criminal investigation surely falls within the meaning of "any matter," and the FBI and the Secret Service equally surely qualify as "department[s] or agenc[ies] of the United States." The only possible verbal vehicle for narrowing the sweeping language Congress enacted is the word "jurisdiction." But we do not think that that term, as used in this statute, admits of the constricted construction given it by the Court of Appeals.

"Jurisdiction" is not defined in the statute. We therefore "start with the assumption that the legislative purpose is expressed by the ordinary meaning of the words used." *Richards v. United States*, 369 U.S. 1, 9 (1962). The most natural, nontechnical reading of the statutory language is that it covers all matters confided to the authority of an agency or department. Thus, Webster's Third New International Dictionary 1227 (1976) broadly defines "jurisdiction" as, among other things, "the limits or territory within which any particular power may be exercised: sphere of authority." A department or agency has jurisdiction, in this sense, when it has the power to exercise authority in a particular situation. Understood in this way, the phrase "within the jurisdiction" merely differentiates the official, authorized functions of an agency or department from matters peripheral to the business of that body.

There are of course narrower, more technical meanings of the term "jurisdiction." For example, an alternative definition provided by Webster's is the "legal power to interpret and administer the law." But a narrow, technical definition of this sort, limiting the statute's protections to judicial or quasi-judicial activities, clashes strongly with the sweeping, everyday language on either side of the term. It is also far too restricted to embrace some of the myriad governmental activities that we have previously concluded § 1001 was designed to protect.

* * *

There is no doubt that there exists a "statutory basis" for the authority of the FBI and the Secret Service over the investigations sparked by respondent Rodgers' false reports. The FBI is authorized "to detect and prosecute crimes against the United States," including kidnaping. 28 U.S.C. § 533(1). And the Secret Service is authorized "to protect the person of the President." 18 U.S.C. § 3056. It is a perversion of these authorized functions to turn either agency into a Missing Person's Bureau for domestic squabbles. The knowing filing of a false crime report, leading to an investigation and possible prosecution, can also have grave consequences for the individuals accused of crime. There is, therefore, a "valid legislative interest in protecting the integrity of [such] official inquiries," an interest clearly embraced in, and furthered by, the broad language of § 1001.

Limiting the term "jurisdiction" as used in this statute to "the power to make final or binding determinations," as the Court of Appeals thought it should be limited, would exclude from the coverage of the statute most, if not all, of the authorized activities of many "departments" and "agencies" of the federal government, and thereby defeat the purpose of Congress in using the broad inclusive language which it did. If the statute referred only to courts, a narrower construction of the word "jurisdiction" might well be indicated; but referring as it does to "any department or agency" we think that such a narrow construction is simply inconsistent with the rest of the statutory language.

The Court of Appeals supported its failure to give the statute a "literal interpretation" by offering several policy arguments in favor of a more limited construction.

For example, the court noted that §1001 carries a penalty exceeding the penalty for perjury and argued that Congress could not have "considered it more serious for one to informally volunteer an untrue statement to an F.B.I. agent than to relate the same story under oath before a court of law." *Friedman v. United States, supra,* at 366. A similar argument was made and rejected in *United States v. Gilliland,* 312 U.S. 86, 95 (1941). The fact that the maximum possible penalty under §1001 marginally exceeds that for perjury provides no indication of the particular penalties, within the permitted range, that Congress thought appropriate for each of the myriad violations covered by the statute. Section 1001 covers "a variety of offenses and the penalties prescribed were maximum penalties which gave a range for judicial sentences according to the circumstances and gravity of particular violations." *Id.*

Perhaps most influential in the reasoning of the court below was its perception that "the specter of criminal prosecution" would make citizens hesitant to report suspected crimes and thereby thwart "the important social policy that is served by an open line of communication between the general public and law enforcement agencies." *Friedman v. United States, supra,* at 369. But the justification for this concern is debatable. Section 1001 only applies to those who "knowingly and willfully" lie to the government. It seems likely that "individuals acting innocently and in good faith, will not be deterred from voluntarily giving information or making complaints to the F.B.I." *United States v. Adler,* 380 F.2d 917, 922 (2d Cir. 1967).

Even if we were more persuaded than we are by these policy arguments, the result in this case would be unchanged. Resolution of the pros and cons of whether a statute should sweep broadly or narrowly is for Congress. Its decision that the perversion of agency resources and the potential harm to those implicated by false reports of crime justifies punishing those who "knowingly and willfully" make such reports is not so "absurd or glaringly unjust," *Sorrells v. United States,* 287 U.S. 435, 450 (1932), as to lead us to question whether Congress actually intended what the plain language of §1001 so clearly imports.

Finally, respondent urges that the rule of lenity in construing criminal statutes should be applied to §1001, and that because the *Friedman* case has been on the books in the Eighth Circuit for a number of years a contrary decision by this Court should not be applied retroactively to him. The rule of lenity is of course a well-recognized principle of statutory construction, but the critical statutory language of §1001 is not sufficiently ambiguous, in our view, to permit the rule to be controlling here. And any argument by respondent against retroactive application to him of our present decision, even if he could establish reliance upon the earlier *Friedman* decision, would be unavailing since the existence of conflicting cases from other Courts of Appeals made review of that issue by this Court and decision against the position of the respondent reasonably foreseeable.

The judgment of the Court of Appeals is reversed, and the case is remanded for further proceedings consistent with this opinion.

Notes and Questions

1. *The policy debate.* In *Rodgers*, the Supreme Court quickly rejected the Eighth Circuit's interpretation of § 1001's statutory history and language. The Court seemed to take more seriously, however, the lower court's concerns that a broad application of the statute might have negative consequences. What were the Eighth's Circuit's concerns? Why did the Supreme Court fail to find those concerns compelling?

Consider that the federal government can elect to charge a defendant under § 1001 for lying to the government even in situations where the government does not pursue the underlying criminal activity. Many suspects facing criminal investigation may lie to a government agent in informal conversations, even though they have the right to remain silent. The investigator need not advise the suspect of the *Miranda* rights unless and until the suspect is under arrest. Thus, the informal questions and answers can give rise to a separate charge under § 1001. In addition, the government can link these false statements to the underlying criminal charges for additional and separate counts in the indictment. As a policy matter, should the government be encouraged to pursue this type of cover up charge if it chooses to abandon filing charges on the underlying criminal conduct? *See* Erin Murphy, *Manufacturing Crime: Process, Pretext, and Criminal Justice*, 97 Geo. L.J. 1435, 1463–68 (2009).

2. *Statutory coverage.*

a. *Judicial proceedings.* As noted above, Congress explicitly excluded from § 1001's reach all "statements, representations, writings or documents submitted by [a party to a judicial proceeding, or that party's counsel] to a judge or a magistrate in that proceeding." 18 U.S.C. § 1001(b). Courts have applied the exception to a wide range of representations in judicial proceedings, including, for example, a false claim of indigency on a CJA-23 form seeking court-appointed counsel. *See United States v. McNeil*, 362 F.3d 570 (9th Cir. 2004). It has been found to cover even false statements to courts that induce the expenditure of federal resources. *United States v. Bankston*, 820 F.3d 215, 229–31 (6th Cir. 2016). Congress added this judicial proceeding exception in order to prevent the use of § 1001 to "chill advocacy in judicial proceedings." *See United States v. Manning*, 526 F.3d 611, 617 (10th Cir. 2008). Courts have not read the "judicial proceeding" exception literally, however, and have applied the exception to statements made to agents, such as court clerks, acting on a judge's behalf.

In this light, would a false statement made by a defendant to a probation officer preparing a report in advance of the defendant's sentencing fall within § 1001? *Compare Manning*, 526 F.3d at 619–21 (holding that because probation officer did not act as mere conduit to the judge but performed an independent function, defendant's false statements did not fall within the judicial proceeding exception), *with United States v. Horvath*, 492 F.3d 1075 (9th Cir. 2007), *reh'g en banc denied*, 522 F.3d 904 (9th Cir. 2008) (finding a statement made to probation officer concerning a matter that the law required to be included in the presentence report fell within the judicial proceeding exception).

b. *Congressional matters.* Section 1001's application to congressional matters is limited to specified administrative matters, such as personnel and employment practices, and to investigative proceedings. *See* 18 U.S.C. § 1001(c). So, for example, false statements made by a sitting U.S. Senator in his financial disclosure statements to the Secretary of the Senate would be subject to § 1001 liability. *See United States v. Menendez*, 137 F. Supp. 3d 688, 693 (D.N.J. 2015). And false statements made pursuant to or *"in"* a pending congressional investigation or review are also subject to liability, though false statements made only *concurrently* with (but not *in*) such an investigation or review are not subject to liability (even if they concern the same subject matter). *See United States v. Pickett*, 353 F.3d 62, 69 (D.C. Cir. 2004). All false statements made in matters within the jurisdiction of the legislative branch that fall outside of these narrow categories are, however, excluded from the statute's reach. Why should this be so? What policy concerns might have led Congress to adopt this exclusion?

c. *Contractors and subcontractors.* Private parties who enter into contracts and subcontracts with entities other than the federal government are sometimes paid with federal funds and/or are subject to certain federal regulations. When are statements made by such parties within § 1001's reach?

In *United States v. Blankenship*, 382 F.3d 1110 (11th Cir. 2004), a private construction company entered into a contract with the Florida Department of Transportation, which received federal funds and agreed with the United States Department of Transportation to adhere to federal requirements. In order to appear to meet the federal requirements, subcontractors of the construction company made false statements in their contracts with the construction company. Did the statements made in the contracts fall within federal jurisdiction under § 1001? The majority held not, explaining that "if § 1001 were interpreted to prohibit any false statement to any private entity whose funds, in whole or in part, happened to originate with the federal government, the results would be shocking. To start with a simple example, any employee of either [the construction company] or its subcontractors who may have padded his resume to obtain a job on the project would be guilty of a federal offense." *Id.* at 1137–1138. The dissent argued that jurisdiction was present because the state was obliged to follow federal requirements and, if it failed to do so, it would lose the federal funds. Which approach best comports with *Rodgers*? Why?

Compare *Blankenship* with *United States v. Lutz*, 154 F.3d 581, 587–588 (6th Cir. 1998), where the defendant made false statements to a mortgage brokerage company that was authorized by the U.S. government to originate home loans. Although the statements were not submitted to the U.S. government, the court found that they fell within § 1001 because the statements were material to the U.S. government's supervisory powers over the company.

Are these cases distinguishable? Why or why not?

d. *State and local government benefits.* State and local government programs, such as unemployment benefit programs, may be supported by federal funding. Does a recipient who makes a false statement in connection with the receipt of such a benefit fall within § 1001? *Compare United States v. Holmes*, 111 F.3d 463, 466 (6th Cir. 1997) (finding no federal jurisdiction because the state has control over the award of benefits, and the only federal funding is for administration of the state program, not for the actual benefits), *with United States v. Herring*, 916 F.2d 1543, 1547 (11th Cir. 1990) (finding federal administrative funding and control provided sufficient nexus for federal jurisdiction).

Even if the subject of the statement is a federal program, it is important to focus on to whom the statement is made or owed. In *United States v. Ford*, 639 F.3d 718 (6th Cir. 2011), a jury convicted a Tennessee State Senator under § 1001 for, in part, failing to disclose to the Tennessee Senate and the Tennessee Registry of Election Finance his financial interests in certain organizations working with a Tennessee state healthcare group that receives federal funds. The court noted that, "[h]owever, the disclosures that Ford was supposed to make were owed to state entities — the Tennessee Senate and Tennessee Registry of Election Finance. Herein lies the distinction central to Ford's argument. While the facts that he failed to disclose concerned an entity inseparable from federal ties, the entities to which he failed to disclose those facts were anything but federal." *Id.* at 720. The court explained:

> Here, Ford's failures to disclose financial interests were related to functions of the state government of Tennessee — the senate's and election registry's reporting requirements. The senate and election registry likely could have exercised authority in this situation. They could have reprimanded Ford or exacted some equitable remedy, but no federal entity had similar authority in this situation. Furthermore, the United States presented no evidence that the senate or election registry operate on federal funds.

Id. at 721. The court reversed Ford's convictions under § 1001. Is this an appropriate limit on the statute? Why or why not?

Problems

9-1. Nell was indicted on one count of possessing stolen property. She asserted that she did not have sufficient funds to retain an attorney, and requested that the United States District Court appoint counsel to represent her. In support of the request, Nell submitted a signed financial status form. The form required the defendant to list her assets to determine if she qualified for a court-appointed attorney. Nell completed the form, omitting references to real estate and other assets that she held at the time. The government has indicted Nell under § 1001. Nell has filed a motion to dismiss the charge, relying on the judicial proceedings exception to § 1001.

Should the court grant Nell's motion? Why or why not?

9-2. Larry owns a gas station, LJ's Auto. Energy Authority, an agency of the United States government, owns nearby land. Peaberry Coal Company uses the land to mine for coal under a contract between Peaberry and Energy Authority.

Energy Authority's contract with Peaberry requires that Peaberry's subcontractors agree to obey certain federal laws and requires advance approval from Energy Authority for any Peaberry subcontracts exceeding $100,000. The contract further requires that Peaberry submit all documents related to any transactions with subcontractors to Energy Authority upon request. Peaberry advised Larry of these requirements.

LJ's Auto sold tires and equipment to Peaberry for use on the trucks used in the mining project. An investigation uncovered that LJ's Auto overcharged Peaberry by nearly $120,000 over several years. A federal grand jury indicted Larry under 18 U.S.C. §1001 based on the inflated prices and charges written on purchase orders that Larry submitted to Peaberry. A jury convicted Larry of the charges, and he appeals on the grounds that the facts did not support federal jurisdiction.

How should the court rule on Larry's appeal? Why?

9-3. Federal officers arrested Arnold for violating federal immigration laws and placed Arnold in the Gotham Detention Center ("GDC"). Federal law allows the United States Attorney General to contract with local officials to house federal prisoners. The U.S. Marshal and Gotham City Sheriff entered into such an agreement. GDC is completely supervised and operated by the Sheriff's office, and all employees are local officials. The federal government neither has supervision over the day-to-day operations of GDC nor does it have the authority to determine the security level in which the federal prisoners are housed.

Approximately one week after Arnold was arrested, his sister Susan went to the GDC to visit her brother. When the deputy sheriff in charge told her that Arnold could not have visitors, Susan falsely told the deputy sheriff that she was a "medical doctor summoned to render medical treatment to Arnold."

Susan was indicted for making a false statement in violation of 18 U.S.C. §1001. She has now hired you to seek dismissal of the false statement charge, arguing that the alleged false statement was not within federal jurisdiction.

How do you advise her as to the likelihood of success?

9-4. Max Corp was a subcontractor of Arrow Corp, which had a major defense contract to build top-secret spy satellites for the National Security Agency (NSA). James, an employee of Max Corp, was assigned to this satellite project. The work required a top-secret government clearance, which James applied for and received. The project also required that James do his work on an Air Force base. Since James was working remotely, Max Corp asked that he submit his time sheets by email. James soon figured out that, since he was working offsite, it would be hard for Max Corp to verify his hours. He started submitting false timesheets that regularly overstated his hours by 25%. Max Corp submitted these false timesheets to Arrow Corp for payment. Arrow Corp, in turn, invoiced NSA for the hours — and the NSA therefore paid for hours James did not work. Max Corp eventually discovered that the timesheets were false. The company fired James and alerted Arrow Corp, which in turn alerted the NSA. Based on these facts, the government charged James for making multiple false statements on his timesheets in violation of 18 U.S.C. § 1001. James moved to dismiss the charges, arguing that the alleged false statements were not within federal jurisdiction.

How should the court rule?

9-5. Jonathan helped manage a housing development known as The Shoreline. The development bordered a lake in Happytown. Happytown's municipal housing authority, which focuses on providing housing to low-income residents, received a $10 million federal grant from the Department of Housing and Urban Development (HUD) to build new low-income housing in the town. Jonathan pitched a plan to the housing authority whereby The Shoreline would build a new multi-use shopping and apartment complex at the entrance to the community that would include 50 low-income units. The Happytown housing authority approved Jonathan's plan, and set aside $5 million of the federal grant money to pay for the 50 low-income units. As the project progressed, Jonathan submitted pay applications to the housing authority, and the funds were then paid from the federal grant money. HUD developed the pay application form that Jonathan used. Per the terms of the grant, HUD reserved the right to revoke the town's grant money if the project did not meet its timeline and material specifications. A couple months into the project, The Shoreline started having cash-flow problems, and Jonathan submitted false pay applications to the municipal housing authority (for work that had not actually been done) in order to pay some of the company's creditors. The municipal housing authority soon discovered that the pay applications were not corresponding with progress at the site. After a brief investigation, they discovered that the pay orders were false. After the housing authority informed HUD of the problem, the government charged Jonathan with making false statements on the pay applications in violation of 18 U.S.C. § 1001. Jonathan moved to dismiss the charges, claiming that the pay applications were not within the jurisdiction of the executive, legislative, or judicial branch of the federal government.

How should the court rule?

D. The "False Statement"

When proceeding under the theory that the defendant made or used a false statement or writing, courts have broadly interpreted the term "false statement" so as to include, for example, false invoices, false marriage vows to obtain citizenship, and false information given to federal investigators. *See* Jeremy Baker & Rebecca Young, *False Statements and False Claims*, 42 Am. Crim. L. Rev. 427, 432–33 (2005). As the cases in this section illustrate, however, the boundaries of the term "false statement" are not always immediately apparent.

1. The "Exculpatory 'No'" Doctrine and Related Issues

One issue under §1001 that had produced a distinct split among the courts of appeal involved prosecutions based upon statements that merely denied wrongdoing. Some lower courts had held that such statements—termed "exculpatory 'nos'"—could not be the basis for false statements prosecutions. The Supreme Court resolved this issue in the case that follows. Seven members of the Court agreed with the result in the case. In her concurring opinion, however, Justice Ginsburg expressed an unusual degree of concern over the outcome. Consider why she did so as you read her opinion.

Brogan v. United States
522 U.S. 398 (1998)

JUSTICE SCALIA delivered the opinion of the Court.

This case presents the question whether there is an exception to criminal liability under 18 U.S.C. §1001 for a false statement that consists of the mere denial of wrongdoing, the so-called "exculpatory no."

While acting as a union officer during 1987 and 1988, petitioner James Brogan accepted cash payments from JRD Management Corporation, a real estate company whose employees were represented by the union. On October 4, 1993, federal agents from the Department of Labor and the Internal Revenue Service visited petitioner at his home. The agents identified themselves and explained that they were seeking petitioner's cooperation in an investigation of JRD and various individuals. They told petitioner that if he wished to cooperate, he should have an attorney contact the United States Attorney's Office, and that if he could not afford an attorney, one could be appointed for him.

The agents then asked petitioner if he would answer some questions, and he agreed. One question was whether he had received any cash or gifts from JRD when he was a union officer. Petitioner's response was "no." At that point, the agents disclosed that a search of JRD headquarters had produced company records showing the contrary. They also told petitioner that lying to federal agents in the course of an investigation was a crime. Petitioner did not modify his answers, and the interview ended shortly thereafter. . . .

At the time petitioner falsely replied "no" to the government investigators' question, 18 U.S.C. §1001 provided:

> Whoever, in any matter within the jurisdiction of any department or agency of the United States knowingly and willfully falsifies, conceals or covers up by any trick, scheme, or device a material fact, or makes any false, fictitious or fraudulent statements or representations, or makes or uses any false writing or document knowing the same to contain any false, fictitious or fraudulent statement or entry, shall be fined not more than $10,000 or imprisoned not more than five years, or both.

By its terms, 18 U.S.C. § 1001 covers "any" false statement — that is, a false statement "of whatever kind," *United States v. Gonzales*, 520 U.S. 1, 5 (1997). The word "no" in response to a question assuredly makes a "statement," *see, e.g.*, Webster's New International Dictionary 2461 (2d ed.1950) (def. 2: "That which is stated; an embodiment in words of facts or opinions"), and petitioner does not contest that his utterance was false or that it was made "knowingly and willfully." In fact, petitioner concedes that under a "literal reading" of the statute he loses.

Petitioner asks us, however, to depart from the literal text that Congress has enacted, and to approve the doctrine adopted by many Circuits which excludes from the scope of § 1001 the "exculpatory no." The central feature of this doctrine is that a simple denial of guilt does not come within the statute. There is considerable variation among the Circuits concerning, among other things, what degree of elaborated tale-telling carries a statement beyond simple denial. In the present case, however, the Second Circuit agreed with petitioner that his statement would constitute a "true 'exculpatory n[o]' as recognized in other circuits," but aligned itself with the Fifth Circuit in categorically rejecting the doctrine.

Petitioner's argument in support of the "exculpatory no" doctrine proceeds from the major premise that § 1001 criminalizes only those statements to government investigators that "pervert governmental functions;" to the minor premise that simple denials of guilt to government investigators do not pervert governmental functions; to the conclusion that § 1001 does not criminalize simple denials of guilt to government investigators. Both premises seem to us mistaken. As to the minor: We cannot imagine how it could be true that falsely denying guilt in a government investigation does not pervert a governmental function. Certainly the investigation of wrongdoing is a proper governmental function; and since it is the very *purpose* of an investigation to uncover the truth, any falsehood relating to the subject of the investigation perverts that function. It could be argued, perhaps, that a *disbelieved* falsehood does not pervert an investigation. But making the existence of this crime turn upon the credulousness of the federal investigator (or the persuasiveness of the liar) would be exceedingly strange; such a defense to the analogous crime of perjury is certainly unheard of. Moreover, as we shall see, the only support for the "perversion of governmental functions" limitation is a statement of this Court referring to the *possibility* (as opposed to the certainty) of perversion of function — a possibility that exists whenever investigators are told a falsehood relevant to their task.

In any event, we find no basis for the major premise that only those falsehoods that pervert governmental functions are covered by § 1001. . . .

[Petitioner] argues that a literal reading of § 1001 violates the "spirit" of the Fifth Amendment because it places a "cornered suspect" in the "cruel trilemma" of admitting guilt, remaining silent, or falsely denying guilt. This "trilemma" is wholly of the guilty suspect's own making, of course. An innocent person will not find himself in a similar quandary. And even the honest and contrite guilty person will not regard the third prong of the "trilemma" (the blatant lie) as an available option. . . .

Whether or not the predicament of the wrongdoer run to ground tugs at the heartstrings, neither the text nor the spirit of the Fifth Amendment confers a privilege to lie. "[P]roper invocation of the Fifth Amendment privilege against compulsory self-incrimination allows a witness to remain silent, but not to swear falsely." *United States v. Apfelbaum*, 445 U.S. 115, 117 (1980). Petitioner contends that silence is an "illusory" option because a suspect may fear that his silence will be used against him later, or may not even know that silence is an available option. As to the former: It is well established that the fact that a person's silence can be used against him — either as substantive evidence of guilt or to impeach him if he takes the stand — does not exert a form of pressure that exonerates an otherwise unlawful lie. And as for the possibility that the person under investigation may be unaware of his right to remain silent: In the modern age of frequently dramatized "Miranda" warnings, that is implausible. Indeed, we found it implausible (or irrelevant) 30 years ago, unless the suspect was "in custody or otherwise deprived of his freedom of action in any significant way," *Miranda v. Arizona*, 384 U.S. 436, 445 (1966).

Petitioner repeats the argument made by many supporters of the "exculpatory no," that the doctrine is necessary to eliminate the grave risk that § 1001 will become an instrument of prosecutorial abuse. The supposed danger is that overzealous prosecutors will use this provision as a means of "piling on" offenses — sometimes punishing the denial of wrongdoing more severely than the wrongdoing itself. The objectors' principal grievance on this score, however, lies not with the hypothetical prosecutors but with Congress itself, which has decreed the obstruction of a legitimate investigation to be a separate offense, and a serious one. It is not for us to revise that judgment. Petitioner has been unable to demonstrate, moreover, any history of prosecutorial excess, either before or after widespread judicial acceptance of the "exculpatory no." And finally, if there is a problem of supposed "overreaching" it is hard to see how the doctrine of the "exculpatory no" could solve it. It is easy enough for an interrogator to press the liar from the initial simple denial to a more detailed fabrication that would not qualify for the exemption.

* * *

In sum, we find nothing to support the "exculpatory no" doctrine except the many Court of Appeals decisions that have embraced it. Courts may not create their own limitations on legislation, no matter how alluring the policy arguments for doing so, and no matter how widely the blame may be spread. Because the plain language of § 1001 admits of no exception for an "exculpatory no," we affirm the judgment of the Court of Appeals.

Justice Ginsburg, with whom Justice Souter joins, concurring in the judgment.

Because a false denial fits the unqualified language of 18 U.S.C. § 1001, I concur in the affirmance of Brogan's conviction. I write separately, however, to call attention to the extraordinary authority Congress, perhaps unwittingly, has conferred on prosecutors to manufacture crimes. I note, at the same time, how far removed the "exculpatory no" is from the problems Congress initially sought to address when it proscribed falsehoods designed to elicit a benefit from the government or to hinder government operations.

At the time of Brogan's offense, §1001 made it a felony "knowingly and willfully" to make "any false, fictitious or fraudulent statements or representations" in "any matter within the jurisdiction of any department or agency of the United States." That encompassing formulation arms government agents with authority not simply to apprehend lawbreakers, but to generate felonies, crimes of a kind that only a government officer could prompt.

This case is illustrative. Two federal investigators paid an unannounced visit one evening to James Brogan's home. The investigators already possessed records indicating that Brogan, a union officer, had received cash from a company that employed members of the union Brogan served. (The agents gave no advance warning, one later testified, because they wanted to retain the element of surprise.) When the agents asked Brogan whether he had received any money or gifts from the company, Brogan responded "No." The agents asked no further questions. *After* Brogan just said "No," however, the agents told him: (1) the government had in hand the records indicating that his answer was false; and (2) lying to federal agents in the course of an investigation is a crime. Had counsel appeared on the spot, Brogan likely would have received and followed advice to amend his answer, to say immediately: "Strike that; I plead not guilty." But no counsel attended the unannounced interview, and Brogan divulged nothing more. Thus, when the interview ended, a federal offense had been completed — even though, for all we can tell, Brogan's unadorned denial misled no one.

A further illustration. In *United States v. Tabor*, 788 F.2d 714 (11th Cir. 1986), an Internal Revenue Service (IRS) agent discovered that Tabor, a notary public, had violated Florida law by notarizing a deed even though two signatories had not personally appeared before her (one had died five weeks before the document was signed). With this knowledge in hand, and without "warn[ing] Tabor of the possible consequences of her statements," the agent went to her home with a deputy sheriff and questioned her about the transaction. When Tabor, regrettably but humanly, denied wrongdoing, the government prosecuted her under §1001. An IRS agent thus turned a violation of state law into a federal felony by eliciting a lie that misled no one. (The Eleventh Circuit reversed the §1001 conviction, relying on the "exculpatory no" doctrine.)

As these not altogether uncommon episodes show, §1001 may apply to encounters between agents and their targets "under extremely informal circumstances which do not sufficiently alert the person interviewed to the danger that false statements may lead to a felony conviction." *United States v. Ehrlichman*, 379 F. Supp. 291, 292 (D.D.C. 1974). Because the questioning occurs in a noncustodial setting, the suspect is not informed of the right to remain silent. Unlike proceedings in which a false statement can be prosecuted as perjury, there may be no oath, no pause to concentrate the speaker's mind on the importance of his or her answers. As in Brogan's case, the target may not be informed that a false "No" is a criminal offense until *after* he speaks.

At oral argument, the Solicitor General forthrightly observed that § 1001 could even be used to "escalate completely innocent conduct into a felony." More likely to occur, "if an investigator finds it difficult to prove some elements of a crime, she can ask questions about other elements to which she already knows the answers.... If the suspect lies, she can then use the crime she has prompted as leverage or can seek prosecution for the lie as a substitute for the crime she cannot prove." Comment, *False Statements to Federal Agents: Induced Lies and the Exculpatory No*, 57 U. Chi. L. Rev. 1273, 1278 (1990). If the statute of limitations has run on an offense — as it had on four of the five payments Brogan was accused of accepting — the prosecutor can endeavor to revive the case by instructing an investigator to elicit a fresh denial of guilt. Prosecution in these circumstances is not an instance of government "punishing the denial of wrongdoing more severely than the wrongdoing itself;" it is, instead, government generation of a crime when the underlying suspected wrongdoing is or has become nonpunishable.

* * *

Since *Nunley v. United States*, 434 U.S. 962 (1977), the Department of Justice has maintained a policy against bringing § 1001 prosecutions for statements amounting to an "exculpatory no." At the time the charges against Brogan were filed, the United States Attorneys' Manual firmly declared: "Where the statement takes the form of an 'exculpatory no,' 18 U.S.C. § 1001 does not apply regardless who asks the question." United States Attorneys' Manual (Oct. 1, 1988). After the Fifth Circuit abandoned the "exculpatory no" doctrine in *United States v. Rodriguez-Rios*, 14 F.3d 1040 (5th Cir. 1994) (en banc), the manual was amended to read: "It is the Department's policy that it is not appropriate to charge a § 1001 violation where a suspect, during an investigation, merely denies his guilt in response to questioning by the government." United States Attorneys' Manual (Feb. 12, 1996).[6]

These pronouncements indicate, at the least, the dubious propriety of bringing felony prosecutions for bare exculpatory denials informally made to government agents. Although today's decision holds that such prosecutions can be sustained under the broad language of § 1001, the Department of Justice's prosecutorial guide continues to caution restraint in each exercise of this large authority....

The prospect remains that an overzealous prosecutor or investigator — aware that a person has committed some suspicious acts, but unable to make a criminal

---

6. While this case was pending before us, the Department of Justice issued yet another version of the manual, which deleted the words "that it is" and "appropriate" from the sentence just quoted. The new version reads: "It is the Department's policy not to charge a § 1001 violation in situations in which a suspect, during an investigation, merely denies guilt in response to questioning by the government." United States Attorneys' Manual 9-42.160 (Sept. 1997).

case—will create a crime by surprising the suspect, asking about those acts, and receiving a false denial. Congress alone can provide the appropriate instruction.

* * *

JUSTICE STEVENS, with whom JUSTICE BREYER joins, dissenting.

The mere fact that a false denial fits within the unqualified language of 18 U.S.C. § 1001 is not, in my opinion, a sufficient reason for rejecting a well-settled interpretation of that statute. It is not at all unusual for this Court to conclude that the literal text of a criminal statute is broader than the coverage intended by Congress. Although the text of § 1001, read literally, makes it a crime for an undercover narcotics agent to make a false statement to a drug peddler, I am confident that Congress did not intend any such result. It seems equally clear that Congress did not intend to make every "exculpatory no" a felony. . . . Even if that were not clear, I believe the Court should show greater respect for the virtually uniform understanding of the bench and the bar that persisted for decades with the approval of this Court as well as the Department of Justice. . . .

Accordingly, I respectfully dissent.

Notes and Questions

1. *The purpose of § 1001.* The majority rejected the defendant's argument that "only those falsehoods that pervert governmental functions are covered by § 1001." Why? If that is not the purpose of § 1001, what is?

2. *The Fifth Amendment.* What exactly was the defendant's Fifth Amendment argument? Does the Fifth Amendment provide a right to lie to the government? If not, why had lower courts relied upon that amendment in adopting an "exculpatory 'no'" exception for § 1001 prosecutions?

   How does the majority respond to the defendant's argument? Upon what precise assumptions does the majority rely? Do you agree with those assumptions?

3. *Prosecutorial guidelines.* In *Brogan*, the Supreme Court approved the use of "exculpatory 'nos'" as the basis for false statements prosecutions. As Justice Ginsburg noted in her concurring opinion, however, the Department of Justice has adopted various versions of a guideline that disapproves of prosecutions based upon "exculpatory 'nos.'" The current guidelines provide that "[i]t is the Department's policy not to charge a § 1001 violation in situations in which a suspect, during an investigation, merely denies guilt in response to questioning by the government." Justice Manual ¶ 9-42.160. In your opinion, why did the DOJ adopt this guideline? The guideline, of course, is just that; it does not have the force of law. Can you ascertain why the government decided to violate its own guideline in Brogan's case?

4. *Potential for abuse?* Four Justices, two in concurrence and two in dissent, expressed concern that the *Brogan* decision leaves the door open for prosecutorial abuse. What exactly is the possible abuse that concerned those Justices? Why did those concerns appear not to trouble the remaining members of the Court?

5. *The Michael Flynn false statements case.* In a highly politically charged case, Michael Flynn, former campaign and national security advisor to President Donald Trump, pleaded guilty to one count under § 1001. The charge, brought by Special Counsel Robert Mueller's office, was based upon statements that Flynn made to the FBI as part of its investigation into possible Russian interference in the 2016 presidential election. The criminal information stated:

> [On January 17, 2017, Defendant] did willfully and knowingly make materially false, fictitious, and fraudulent statements and representations in a matter within the jurisdiction of the executive branch of the Government of the United States, to wit, the defendant falsely stated and represented to agents of the Federal Bureau of Investigation, in Washington, D.C., that:

> (i) On or about December 29, 2016, FLYNN did not ask the Government of Russia's Ambassador to the United States ("Russian Ambassador") to refrain from escalating the situation in response to sanctions that the United States had imposed against Russia that same day; and FLYNN did not recall the Russian Ambassador subsequently telling him that Russia had chosen to moderate its response to those sanctions as a result of his request; and

> (ii) On or about December 22, 2016, FLYNN did not ask the Russian Ambassador to delay the vote on or defeat a pending United Nations Security Council resolution; and that the Russian Ambassador subsequently never described to FLYNN Russia's response to his request.

Information, *United States v. Flynn*, No. 17CR00232 (D.D.C. Nov. 30, 2017), 2017 WL 5908165. Flynn's statements did not mislead the government, which had audio recordings of Flynn's conversations with the Ambassador.

After Flynn's guilty plea, the U.S. Department of Justice took the highly unusual step of seeking to have Flynn's case dismissed, leading to substantial political controversy. According to the government, Flynn's falsities could not have been material to the investigation, at least in part because Flynn's statements did not have the capacity to mislead the FBI and there was no proof that Flynn had acted as a Russian agent and the statements were therefore "not 'material' to any viable counterintelligence investigation — or any investigation for that matter — initiated by the FBI." Government's Motion to Dismiss, *United States v. Flynn*, No. 17-232 (D.D.C. May 7, 2020), 2020 WL 2213634. The government also suggested that the FBI had interviewed Flynn in order to set him up for a false statements charge. *Id.* President Trump later pardoned Flynn. *See* Charlie Savage, *Trump Pardons Michael Flynn, Ending Case His Justice Dept. Sought to Shut Down*, N.Y. TIMES, Nov. 25, 2020.

Reconsider Justice Ginsburg's concurring opinion in *Brogan.* Justice Ginsburg expressed the concern that § 1001 "arms government agents with authority not simply to apprehend lawbreakers, but to generate felonies, crimes of a kind that only a government officer could prompt." 522 U.S. at 409. Did investigators attempt to manufacture a crime in Flynn's case? If so, how might this conduct be justified? Keeping in mind that Flynn believed (correctly) that the FBI had a recording of his conversations with the Russian Ambassador, if you had been present at the January 2017 interview as Flynn's counsel, how would you have advised him?

6. *Promises concerning future actions.* Can a promise to undertake, or not undertake, a future action be the basis for a false statements charge? Can such a promise be literally false? Courts have upheld such charges. *See, e.g., United States v. Sattar*, 272 F. Supp. 2d 348, 377 (S.D.N.Y. 2003) (holding an attorney's false promise to adhere to government regulations regarding the representation of an alleged terrorist was a false representation of present intent and could therefore qualify as a false statement within the meaning of § 1001). *Accord, United States v. Shah*, 44 F.3d 285, 293 (5th Cir. 1995) ("[A] promise to perform is not only a prediction, but is generally also a representation of present intent. Promises and representations are simply not mutually exclusive categories. The plain terms of the statute can therefore be said to cover representations of present intent.").

2. Implied False Statements

The Court in *Brogan* held that an "exculpatory 'no'" is a "false statement" covered by § 1001. But how do we define the boundaries of a "false statement" under the statute? Suppose, for example, that a person intentionally writes checks on an account with insufficient funds to cover the checks and cashes the checks at a federally insured bank. Under 18 U.S.C. § 1014, it is a crime knowingly to make a false statement for the purpose of influencing a federally insured bank. Is the bad check a "false statement" under this statute because it implies that there are sufficient funds in the account to cover the check? In *Williams v. United States*, 458 U.S. 279 (1982), the Supreme Court — in a decision that also applies to § 1001 — held five-to-four that it is not. The Court stated:

> Although [the defendant] deposited several checks that were not supported by sufficient funds, that course of conduct did not involve the making of a "false statement," for a simple reason: technically speaking, a check is not a factual assertion at all, and therefore cannot be characterized as "true" or "false." Petitioner's bank checks served only to direct the drawee banks to pay the face value to the bearer, while committing petitioner to make good on the obligations if the bank dishonored the drafts. Each check did not, in terms, make any representations as to the state of petitioner's bank balance.

Id. at 284–285. The dissent countered that "[i]t defies common sense and everyday practice to maintain, as the majority does, that a check carries with it no representation as to the drawer's account balance." *Id.* at 291 (White, J., dissenting).

What is the reach of the *Williams* decision? Assume, for example, that a state department of transportation received grants from the federal government to subsidize highway construction. As a condition of receiving the grants, the state was contractually obligated to ensure that a portion of the funds went to businesses owned by women and minorities. Company A qualified for the program and was awarded a construction contract. Company A, however, did not have sufficient equipment to actually perform the contract. Company A therefore arranged with Company B — which did *not* qualify for the program — to do the work. Companies A and B then entered into sham contracts that obligated Company A to do the construction, although both companies intended that Company B do the work. The contracts were then forwarded to the federal government.

Are the companies guilty of making false statements to the government? In *United States v. Blankenship*, 382 F.3d 1110, 1135 (11th Cir. 2004), the Eleventh Circuit relied upon *Williams* in reversing the §1001 conviction on these facts. The court stated: "Like a check, a contract is not a factual assertion, and therefore cannot be characterized as 'true' or 'false.' Just as a check is not 'false' simply because neither the drawer nor the drawee intends that the drawee cash it, a contract is not false simply because neither party intends to enforce it."

The *Williams* and *Blankenship* decisions raise two distinct but related issues. First, can an implied false statement be the basis for a false statement conviction? The *Williams* dissent clearly would have answered this question in the affirmative. Second, if an implied false statement is actionable under §1001, did the check in *Williams* and the contact in *Blankenship* impliedly assert facts — that is, that the drawer had sufficient funds to cover the check in *Williams*, and that Companies A and B in *Blankenship* intended to perform their contractual obligations?

Problem

9-6. Concerned about protecting their elderly father's assets, Ellen and her brother William opened a three-party account at a federally insured bank into which they placed the father's funds. The account provided that Ellen, William, and their father would each be a principal. A check drawn on the account would be negotiable only if it carried the endorsement of each of the three principals. Ellen held her father's power-of-attorney. Over a four-year period before the father's death, Ellen deposited 10 checks from the three-party account into her personal account. Although the checks bore what looked to be signatures of all three account holders, William did not sign the checks or otherwise agree to the transfer of the funds. On each of the checks, Ellen had forged William's signature.

Based on the forged endorsements, Ellen was indicted on 10 counts under 18 U.S.C. §1014, which criminalizes knowingly making any false statement for the purpose of influencing in any way the action of any federally-insured financial institution.

Ellen was convicted and appeals. What arguments should she make on appeal? How should the government respond? How should the court rule? Why?

9-7. John, a chemical engineer, got mixed up with the wrong crowd a few years back and was convicted of felony drug charges for running a crystal meth lab. He had difficulty finding a job after he was released from prison. His biggest problem was that all of his prior work experience was for defense contractors, and they required a security clearance for employees working on engineering projects. John, however, could not obtain a security clearance as a convicted felon. John proposed a plan to one of his former employers. He would enter into a contract with the defense contractor to purportedly work as a janitor at one of the contractor's U.S. Army weapons project sites (a position that did not require a clearance), but he would secretly work on the project as an engineer — not as a janitor. John and the defense contractor drafted and executed a contract reflecting only that John promised work on the project as a janitor. At the time of the contract, neither John nor the defense contractor had any intention that John would do janitorial work; they both knew he would only work as an engineer. The defense contractor paid John according to the terms of his janitor's contract, and the company provided a copy of this contract to the U.S. Army to receive reimbursement from the Army for money it paid John. When a routine Army inspection of the site uncovered that John was working as an engineer without a clearance (and not as a janitor), a government investigation followed. The government charged John and the defense contractor with making a false statement in violation of 18 U.S.C. § 1001 based strictly upon the contract for purported janitorial work that was submitted to the Army. John and the defense contractor move to dismiss the charges, arguing that the contract was not a false statement.

How should the court rule?

E. Concealment

A charge under § 1001 may be based upon the theory that the defendant concealed facts the defendant had a duty to disclose. The following case arose from a high-profile political corruption scandal. In the case, the court addressed whether the defendant had a duty to disclose facts to the government. As you read the decision, consider whether prosecutors exercised their discretion wisely when bringing the § 1001 charges.

United States v. Safavian
528 F.3d 957 (D.C. Cir. 2008)

RANDOLPH, CIRCUIT JUDGE.

A jury convicted David H. Safavian of three counts of concealing material facts and making false statements in violation of 18 U.S.C. § 1001(a)(1). . . . The prosecution arose from investigations into a golfing trip he took with lobbyist Jack Abramoff in August 2002 while Safavian was chief of staff of the General Services Administration. We reverse on all counts.

The evidence, viewed most favorably to the government, showed as follows. Safavian and Abramoff met in 1994 when Safavian joined a law firm in which Abramoff was a partner. Abramoff became a mentor to Safavian there, and the two remained close friends after Safavian left the firm. They continued to play golf and racquetball together and saw each other socially for drinks and dinner. And when Safavian was looking to leave the congressman for whom he was working in 2002, Abramoff arranged for Safavian to interview at his new firm, though he did not receive an offer.

Safavian instead became the General Services Administration's (GSA) deputy chief of staff in May 2002 and was named chief of staff two months later. GSA is responsible for procurement and property management on behalf of federal agencies. Shortly after Safavian arrived at GSA, Abramoff asked him for information about two GSA-controlled properties: the White Oak property in Silver Spring, Maryland, a 600-acre former Naval facility; and the Old Post Office in Washington, D.C.

Abramoff was interested in having a portion of the White Oak property serve as a new location for the religious school his children attended. As to the Old Post Office building, GSA was considering redeveloping it and had been asking private parties about that possibility. Abramoff thought opportunities for one of his clients might develop.

Safavian and Abramoff exchanged e-mails about these properties between May and August 2002. Abramoff sent messages to both Safavian's work and home accounts, sometimes e-mailing his work account only to inform him a message was waiting on his home account. Safavian's assistance ranged from simply obtaining information that GSA had already compiled for distribution to other parties, to more involved support that Safavian could provide as a GSA insider. For example, he supplied Abramoff with internal GSA information, told Abramoff that he had "overruled" a GSA employee who had "reservations," reviewed and edited Abramoff's letters to GSA, and set up a meeting to discuss the White Oak property. Nothing ever came of any of this and both properties remained with GSA through Safavian's tenure.

While these discussions were ongoing, Abramoff invited Safavian to join him on a five-day golfing trip to Scotland in August 2002, to which Abramoff later added a weekend in London. In addition to Abramoff and Safavian, the group included Abramoff's son and colleagues, a congressman and his chief of staff, and the staff director for the House Administration Committee. Abramoff arranged the schedule and accommodations and chartered a plane for the group.

On July 25, 2002, Safavian requested an ethics opinion from GSA's general counsel about whether he could accept the air transportation as a gift. His e-mail stated:

> I am in need of an ethics opinion. I (along with wto [sic] members of Congress and a few Congressional staff) have been invited by a friend and former colleague on a trip to Scotland to play golf for four days. I will be paying for all of my hotels, meals, and greens fees. The issue is airfare.

> The host of the trip is chartering a private jet to take the eight of us from BWI to Scotland [sic] and back. He is paying the cost for the aircraft regardless of whether I go or not. In fact, none of the other guest [sic] will

be paying a proportional share of the aircraft costs. I need to know how to treat this activity.

One other point of relevance: the host is a lawyer and lobbyist, but one that has no business before GSA (he does all of his work on Capitol Hill).

The GSA ethics officer responded in part:

This is in response to your inquiry on whether you can accept a gift of free air transportation from a friend to attend an [sic] golf trip. You stated that a friend and former colleague, Jack Abramhoff [sic], invited you, along with several members of Congress and a few Congressional staff, to Scotland to play golf for four days. You stated that you will be paying for all of your hotel expenses, meals and greens fees. You noted, however, that your friend would be providing the air transportation at no cost to you and the other guests attending the event. You stated that your friend, who is a lawyer and lobbyist with Greenberg and Traurig, is chartering a private jet to take you and the other participants from BWI Scotland and back. You stated that neither Mr. Abramhoff [sic] nor his firm does business with or is seeking to do business with GSA. Based upon the information you have provided, you may accept the gift of free transportation from your friend.

The ethics opinion recited information not provided in Safavian's e-mail request, such as Abramoff's name and firm, so it appears that further communications must have occurred. Notably, the response also suggests that Safavian said Abramoff is not "seeking to do business with GSA." At trial the government presented no evidence that Safavian had ever told this to an ethics officer and the district judge therefore struck the "seeking to do business" language from the indictment.

After receiving the ethics advice, Safavian forwarded a copy to Abramoff, indicating that he would go on the trip. Abramoff sent Safavian an itinerary showing the travel schedule, hotels, golfing times, a dinner and a lunch with the notation "included in package," and several other scheduled meals. Safavian told Abramoff he wanted to pay for his share of the trip. On the evening of the departure date — August 3, 2002 — Safavian gave Abramoff a check for $3,100, the amount Abramoff said would cover the costs.

The chartered plane landed the morning of August 4th at a small airport adjacent to the St. Andrews Links Old Course, where the group's hotel also was located. Most of their five days in Scotland were spent golfing. They played at several different courses and smoked cigars and drank while playing. Some, including Safavian, played golf more than once per day at various courses. At the Old Course, greens fees and caddy tips for one person totaled $400. The group also ate and had drinks together. Meals — some at the hotel, some elsewhere — ranged from $20–$100 a person, and sometimes a round of drinks reached $100. . . .

The group flew from Scotland to London on Thursday the 9th, using the same chartered plane. Upon landing, they were driven to their hotel, the Mandarin

Oriental. . . . On Sunday, Safavian and Abramoff flew back to the United States on the chartered jet.

Both Safavian and another participant testified that they believed the trip was prepaid. Safavian also paid for some costs himself. He withdrew $500 from his bank account before leaving and $150 on the trip's second day. He tipped the caddies once for two people and bought a few rounds of drinks. Safavian also used his credit card to buy some gifts, a few meals, and some other goods.

In March 2003, acting on an anonymous tip, the GSA Office of Inspector General (GSA-OIG) began investigating the trip. GSA agent Gregory Rowe interviewed Safavian twice. Rowe testified that Safavian told him that he "paid for the trip," including airfare, and that Abramoff did not have any business with GSA. Safavian also provided Rowe with a copy of the $3,100 check he had given to Abramoff on the day they had left and a work attendance sheet showing that he took five days of leave. Safavian did not mention the weekend in London or Abramoff's interest in the two GSA properties. Rowe closed the investigation. Rowe did not review the ethics opinion Safavian had received about the trip.

A year later, in March 2004, the Senate Committee on Indian Affairs began investigating Abramoff. The Committee asked Safavian to produce "all records reflecting, referring, or relating to the 2002 Scotland golf trip." Safavian's letter responded in part:

> When the invitation was made, I was the chief of staff to the U.S. General Services Administration ("GSA"). Mr. Abramoff did not have any business before the agency at that time. Prior to departure, I consulted the GSA Office of General Counsel to obtain guidance on the propriety of this trip. Counsel determined that I could accept the value of the trip gratis; it did not meet the definition of a 'gift from a prohibited source' under the applicable regulations, nor was it considered a gift because of my official position. Nevertheless, in the exercise of discretion, I gave Mr. Abramoff a check for the value of the trip prior to departure. In addition, I took leave without pay to travel.

Safavian also provided, among other things, his July 25 request for the ethics opinion, the opinion, and a copy of the $3,100 check.

A grand jury indicted Safavian on October 5, 2005, on three counts of "falsify[ing], conceal[ing] and cover[ing] up by a trick, scheme, and device material facts" in violation of 18 U.S.C. § 1001(a)(1) (Counts 2, 3, and 5) . . . .[b] [Count 3 was] based on Safavian's interviews with GSA inspector Rowe. Count 2 was based on Safavian's request for the ethics opinion. And Count[] . . . 5 related to his letter to the Senate Committee.

---

b. In Counts 1 and 4, the government charged Safavian with obstruction of justice, 18 U.S.C. § 1505, based upon his interview with the GSA inspector and his letter to the Senate Committee. The jury convicted Safavian on Count 1 and acquitted him on Count 4. — Eds.

The trial began May 22, 2006, and included testimony from Rowe, the ethics officer, the investigative counsel for the Committee, and one of Abramoff's colleagues
who went on the Scotland trip, among others. Safavian, testifying in his defense,
discussed the golf trip, his work at GSA, and his interactions with Abramoff. Safavian testified that in his view, Abramoff was "not doing business with GSA" because
Abramoff "is not a contractor, he is not exchanging property or services for money,
he does not have a business relationship with GSA." As to the golf trip, Safavian
claimed that he thought it was a prepaid package and that he was reimbursing
Abramoff fully with the $3,100 check. . . .

On June 20, the jury convicted Safavian [of Counts 2, 3, and 5, the false statements
charges]. Count 2 was based on the exchange with the ethics officer. On a special verdict form, the jury found that Safavian "concealed his assistance to Mr. Abramoff in
GSA-related activities" (Specification A) and "falsely stated to the GSA ethics officer
that Mr. Abramoff did all his work on Capitol Hill" (Specification C). Count 3 was
based on Safavian's statements and omissions during his interviews with GSA-OIG
agent Rowe. The jury found that Safavian "concealed his assistance to Mr. Abramoff
in GSA-related activities" (Specification A). Count 5 was based on Safavian's letter
to the Committee. The jury found that he "falsely stated in a letter to the Committee
that Mr. Abramoff did not have any business with GSA at the time Mr. Safavian was
invited on the trip to Scotland" (Specification C) . . . .

The court sentenced Safavian to concurrent terms of 18 months imprisonment on
each count, followed by two years of supervised release.

We will begin with Safavian's convictions on Counts 2 and 3. Each of these counts,
and Count 5, charged violations of 18 U.S.C. § 1001(a)(1): a person "in any matter
within the jurisdiction of the executive, legislative, or judicial branch of the Government of the United States," commits an offense if he "knowingly and willfully
falsifies, conceals, or covers up by any trick, scheme, or device a material fact." *Id.*
On Count 2, which dealt with Safavian's request for a GSA ethics opinion, the jury
found that he violated § 1001(a)(1) when he "concealed his assistance to [Abramoff]
in official GSA-related activities." On Count 3, which dealt with the GSA Inspector
General's investigation, the jury found that Safavian violated § 1001(a)(1) when he
"concealed his assistance to [Abramoff] in official GSA-related activities," the same
concealment allegation contained in Count 2.

Safavian raises several serious objections to his convictions on the concealment
charges, though we only reach the question whether he had a duty to disclose his
assistance. As to Count 2, he points out that officers and employees of the executive,
judicial, and legislative branches regularly seek advice from their respective ethics committees. They are encouraged to do so. The value of the advice they receive
depends upon the accuracy and fullness of the information they provide. At GSA,
as elsewhere in the federal government, the officer or employee making the inquiry
may or may not follow the advice of the ethics committee. That he did not follow
that advice does not in itself constitute an ethical transgression. The prosecutors in
this case are mistaken when they write that the GSA "ethics opinion . . . permitted

[Safavian] to engage in behavior that would be prohibited if he had disclosed all relevant information." The ethics opinion did no such thing. It was not up to the GSA ethics officers to permit or forbid; their function was to offer advice. It is not apparent how this voluntary system, replicated throughout the government, imposes a duty on those seeking ethical advice to disclose — in the government's words — "all relevant information" upon pain of prosecution for violating § 1001(a)(1).[5] As Safavian argues and as the government agrees, there must be a legal duty to disclose in order for there to be a concealment offense in violation of § 1001(a)(1), yet the government failed to identify a legal disclosure duty except by reference to vague standards of conduct for government employees.

These standards are formulated as fourteen "general principles" that executive branch "employees shall apply . . . in determining whether their conduct is proper." 5 C.F.R. § 2635.101(b). They range from exceedingly vague — "Employees shall put forth honest effort in the performance of their duties," § 2635.101(b)(5) — to somewhat more descriptive — "Employees shall not use public office for private gain." § 2635.101(b)(7). Only one has anything to do with disclosure. *See* § 2635.101(b) (11) ("Employees shall disclose waste, fraud, abuse, and corruption to appropriate authorities."). These strictures are of no more help to the government's argument than the regulation on seeking ethics advice. Their relationship to Safavian's duty under § 1001(a)(1) is tenuous at best. If an employee violates a standard of conduct, he may be subject to disciplinary action. § 2635.106(a). We cannot see how this translates into criminal liability under 18 U.S.C. § 1001(a)(1) whenever someone seeking ethical advice or being interviewed by a GSA investigator omits "relevant information."

Concealment cases in this circuit and others have found a duty to disclose material facts on the basis of specific requirements for disclosure of specific information. There is good reason for demanding such specificity: to comply with Fifth Amendment due process, the defendant must have "fair notice . . . of what conduct is forbidden. . . . [T]his 'fair warning' requirement prohibits application of a criminal statute to a defendant unless it was reasonably clear at the time of the alleged action that defendants' actions were criminal." *United States v. Kanchanalak*, 192 F.3d 1037, 1046 (D.C. Cir. 1999) (*citing United States v. Lanier*, 520 U.S. 259 (1997)). The ethical principles give no indication of the particular facts or information an executive employee must disclose. Nor do they suggest that they have any bearing on conduct during a GSA investigation or a request for an ethics opinion.

The government also invoked, in support of the verdict on the concealment charges in Count 2 and Count 3, "the principle that once one begins speaking when

---

5. Disclosing all relevant circumstances merely offers the employee protection from disciplinary action: "Disciplinary action for violating this part or any supplemental agency regulations will not be taken against an employee who has engaged in conduct in good faith reliance upon the advice of an agency ethics official, provided that the employee, in seeking such advice, has made full disclosure of all relevant circumstances." 5 C.F.R. § 2635.107(b).

seeking government action or in response to questioning, one must disclose all relevant facts." The government cites no regulation, form, or statute to this effect and the defense maintains that no such general principle exists. Attorneys commonly advise their clients to answer questions truthfully but not to volunteer information. Are we to suppose that once the client starts answering a government agent's questions, in a deposition or during an investigation, the client must disregard his attorney's advice or risk prosecution under § 1001(a)(1)? The government essentially asks us to hold that once an individual starts talking, he cannot stop. We do not think § 1001 demands that individuals choose between saying everything and saying nothing. No case stands for that proposition.[7] We therefore conclude that Safavian had no legal duty to disclose and that his concealment convictions cannot stand.

The remaining charges are the alleged false statements Safavian made, as specified in Counts 2 and 5 (§ 1001(a)(1)).[9] Each of the statements was to the effect that Abramoff had no business with GSA at the time of the golf trip. In defense of these charges, Safavian maintained that when he made the statements he intended the meaning common to government contracts professionals — that is, someone who does not have a contract with GSA is not doing business or working with GSA. Safavian contended that his statements were truthful because Abramoff never secured any GSA contract. With respect to the White Oak property, the headmaster of the school never requested a lease and GSA never transferred the property to the school. As to the Old Post Office, GSA issued no proposal during the tenure of the GSA Administrator for whom Safavian worked.

We agree with Safavian that the district court abused its discretion in excluding favorable expert testimony on how government contracting professionals view having business or working with GSA. Safavian's expert would have testified that an individual is not doing business with GSA until a contract is awarded and that getting information from GSA is simply that, getting information. Defense counsel offered this testimony to show that Safavian's definition "isn't made up out of whole cloth." The testimony would have bolstered Safavian's contention that, as a government contracts professional himself, he had this meaning in mind when he communicated with the GSA ethics official, Rowe, and with the Senate Committee.

---

7. The government cites United States v. Moore, 446 F.3d 671 (7th Cir. 2006), and United States v. Cisneros, 26 F. Supp. 2d 24 (D.D.C. 1998), as supporting its position. However, the jury instructions in *Moore* stated, "The duty to disclose a particular fact to the executive branch of the federal government or its agent arises from requirements in federal statutes, regulations, or government forms." 446 F.3d at 680. In *Cisneros*, the questions posed to the defendant by the FBI agent were rooted in a government form that the defendant had filled out. *See* 26 F. Supp. 2d at 32.

9. Safavian argues that his statements should not have been submitted to the jury because they were fundamentally ambiguous and thus the jurors "could only guess what he may have meant." Assuming *arguendo* that the doctrine of fundamental ambiguity applies to false statements such as these, it was well within the province of the jury to determine what Safavian meant. Likewise, we reject Safavian's argument that there was insufficient evidence for the jury to conclude that the statements were false as Safavian intended them.

In excluding this testimony, the district court reasoned that it would not help the jury and would be confusing. The court asserted that the meaning of "business" "is within the common parlance of the jury," and thus "the layman's definition of these terms are the best guide for the jury. There's no need for expert testimony." This ruling usurped the jury's role by deciding that the lay meaning of "business" is what Safavian meant to convey. The court at one point recognized that "[w]hat was in the defendant's mind is at issue in this case." But excluding the expert testimony effectively preempted the jury's conclusion on this issue. . . .

We do not find the exclusion of the expert's testimony harmless. With respect to Counts 2 and 5, which charged violations of § 1001(a)(1), literal truth would have been a complete defense. The jury's duty was to decide which meaning Safavian intended — the contracting meaning or the "lay" meaning — "by considering the term in context, taking into account the setting in which it appeared and the purpose for which it was used." Evidence showed that Safavian had substantial experience in the field of government contracts. The expert's testimony would have supplied crucial context and support for Safavian's proposed meaning. This testimony would have been especially important in light of the fact that two government witnesses, though not appearing as experts, testified regarding their own interpretations of the phrase "doing business." Excluding the expert's testimony thus was not harmless.

[The court thus reversed Safavian's conviction on the omission theory under Counts 2 and 3, and remanded for a new trial on Count 2 based on the alternative theory that Safavian made an affirmative material misstatement when he stated that the $3,100 payment covered the entire cost of the trip. The court also vacated and remanded Count 5 for a new trial.]

Notes and Questions

1. *Duty to disclose.* When does a duty to disclose arise under § 1001? Courts have found such duties in varying circumstances. *See, e.g., United States v. Moore*, 446 F.3d 671 (7th Cir. 2006) (finding a duty to disclose existed when a HUD form contract incorporated a conflict of interest regulation); *United States v. Stewart*, 433 F.3d 273, 318–319 (2d Cir. 2006) (finding a government agency's specific inquiry can trigger a duty to disclose); *United States v. Kingston*, 971 F.2d 481, 489 (10th Cir. 1992) (holding that "a defendant's duty to disclose is established where a government form required a disclosure of concealed information."). *But see United States v. White Eagle*, 721 F.3d 1108 (9th Cir. 2013) (reversing a § 1001 conviction because the government did not show the defendant violated a specific duty to report Credit Program fraud); *United States v. Curran*, 20 F.3d 560, 566 (3d Cir. 1994) (holding no duty to disclose existed where duty to disclose source of campaign contributions to Federal Election Commission was that of campaign treasurers, rather than defendant at whose behest contributions were purportedly made); *United States v. Crop Growers Corp.*, 954 F. Supp. 335, 348 (D.D.C. 1997) (finding that "to the extent that any duty to disclose is predicated on professional standards not codified in any statute or regulation, there can be no criminal liability").

Why did the court in *Safavian* find that no duty was present in his case?

2. *Literal truth.* Most courts agree with the *Safavian* court that a literally true statement, even if misleading, cannot be the basis for a false statement charge under § 1001. *See, e.g., United States v. Castro*, 704 F.3d 125, 139 (3d Cir. 2013) (holding that "to properly convict Castro of violating § 1001, the government must be able to show that he made a statement to government agents that was untrue, and the government cannot satisfy that burden by showing that the defendant intended to deceive, if in fact he told the literal truth"). *Accord United States v. Kosth*, 257 F.3d 712, 719–20 (7th Cir. 2001); *United States v. Hixon*, 987 F.2d 1261, 1265–68 (6th Cir. 1993). The same rule holds under the federal perjury statutes examined in the next chapter. *See* Chapter 10, Perjury and False Declarations, *infra*, § C. How does a jury determine whether a defendant's statement, as the defendant intended the statement's meaning, was literally true? Why did the appeals court find that the trial court had erred on this issue?

3. *Ambiguous answers.* Reconsider footnote 9 in the *Safavian* opinion. Was the statement that "Abramoff had no business with GSA" ambiguous? Why or why not? The court stated that it is up to the jury to decide, in the event of an ambiguous statement, what meaning the defendant intended. This is also the general rule with respect to ambiguous statements made under oath that are the basis of perjury charges. *See* Chapter 10, Perjury and False Declarations, *infra*, § C.

Problem

9-8. Captain Salty was the commanding officer of a naval base. One evening, Salty attended a party at the Officer's Club. Jimbo, a private contractor on the base, and his wife, Sara, also attended the party. Jimbo had too much to drink and started accusing Salty of having an affair with Sara. Some of Salty's friends urged him to leave the party to avoid a physical altercation and he did so. Later that evening, Jimbo showed up at Salty's home and attacked him. He knocked Salty out and left him lying on the floor. When Salty woke up, Jimbo was nowhere to be found. Sara reported Jimbo missing the next day. After days of searching, Jimbo's dead body was found floating in the bay. U.S. Navy's operational reporting instructions require that commanding officers of a base report up the chain of command any critical incidents, including "those likely to garner media attention, natural disasters, death or serious injury of someone within the command, misconduct by senior officers, and others." Pursuant to this regulation, Captain Salty reported to the Admiral in charge of the region that Jimbo had gone missing and that he was later found dead in the bay. Salty did not disclose to the Admiral that Jimbo had accused him of having an affair with his wife at a party and had assaulted him at his home on the evening of the disappearance. When an investigation later brought these events to light, Salty was charged with making false statements by concealment under § 1001(a)(1).

Salty moves to dismiss the false statements by concealment charge. He relies on Safavian *to argue that he had no duty to disclose personal matters that occurred between Jimbo and him prior to Jimbo's disappearance. How should the court rule?*

F. Mens Rea

Section 1001 requires that the government prove that the defendant acted "knowingly and willfully." As seen in the *Safavian* opinion, *supra*, § E, and as discussed more fully in the notes below, the government must show beyond a reasonable doubt that the defendant intended to make a false statement. Thus, Safavian's proffered expert testimony — regarding the commonly understood meaning of his statement that Abramoff did not do "business" with the GSA — was relevant to Safavian's intent when he made the alleged false statement.

Now assume for a moment that Safavian was not speaking to a person whom Safavian knew to be an agent of the United States government. Also assume that Safavian did not know that his statement would be relayed to the federal government. Even if Safavian acted with the intent to deceive the listener, did he act "knowingly and willfully" under the statute?

Section 1001 states that the statute applies to "whoever, in any matter within the jurisdiction of the executive, legislative, or judicial branch of the Government of the United States, *knowingly and willfully* . . . makes any materially false, fictitious, or fraudulent statement or representation . . ." Thus, the question is whether the words "knowingly and willfully" modify not only the acts that follow those words but also the preceding requirement that the acts be "in any matter within the jurisdiction" of the U.S. government.

Note on United States v. Yermian

The Supreme Court addressed this issue in *United States v. Yermian*, 468 U.S. 63 (1984). Yermian was charged with three counts of violating § 1001 based upon material false statements that he made on a security clearance questionnaire that he completed for his employer. The employer was a private defense contracting firm that did business with the United States government. The employer forwarded Yermian's completed questionnaire to the United States Department of Defense.

On appeal from his conviction, Yermian admitted that he had known that his statements were false. He argued that his conviction should nonetheless be reversed because the jury instructions had not required the jury to find that he had "actual knowledge that his false statements would be transmitted to a federal agency." In a five-to-four decision, the Supreme Court affirmed Yermian's conviction. Interpreting the statutory language, the Court noted that "[t]he jurisdictional language appears in a phrase separate from the prohibited conduct modified by the terms 'knowingly and willfully.'" Thus, the terms "knowingly and willfully" naturally relate only to the making of "false, fictitious, or fraudulent statements . . . and not the predicate circumstance that those statements be made in a matter within the jurisdiction of a federal agency." The Court in *Yermian* held that the government need not prove that the defendant had actual knowledge of federal jurisdiction; it did not determine whether the statute requires that the government prove some lower level of mens rea, such as negligence.

Justice Rehnquist dissented in an opinion joined by Justices Brennan, Stevens, and O'Connor. The dissent concluded that both Congressional intent and the statutory language were ambiguous, and that under the doctrine of lenity, the issue should have been resolved in favor of the defendant.

Notes and Questions

1. *The jurisdictional element.*

a. *Statements within federal jurisdiction.* Why were Yermian's false statements within federal jurisdiction? Were they made directly to the United States government? Reconsider the *Blankenship* case, discussed in the notes following *United States v. Rodgers*, § C, *supra.* If the facts in *Yermian* arose today, could the defendant successfully argue that, under the *Blankenship* reasoning, the statements were not made within federal jurisdiction under § 1001? Why or why not?

b. *Mens rea as to jurisdiction.* In *Yermian*, the Court relied upon its earlier holding in *United States v. Feola*, 420 U.S. 671 (1975). In *Feola*, the defendants were convicted of conspiring to assault a federal officer, whom the defendants did not know was an undercover federal officer. The court of appeals reversed the conspiracy conviction, holding that the jury should have been required to find that the defendants *knew* that their intended victim was a federal officer. The Supreme Court reinstated the conviction. The Court found that knowledge of the victim's status is not required for the object crime of assault. The Court reasoned that such a requirement would frustrate the statute's intent to protect both federal officers and federal functions. The Court concluded that "[t]he concept of criminal intent does not extend so far as to require that the actor understand not only the nature of his act but also its consequence for the choice of a judicial forum." Consequently, the Court also found that the crime of conspiring to violate § 111 does not require proof that the defendant knew that the intended victim was a federal officer. Does this make sense from a culpability standpoint?

2. *The rule from* Yermian.

a. *The majority decision.* The Court in *Yermian* did not decide if the government must prove that the defendant acted negligently, that is, that the defendant should have known the statement was within federal jurisdiction. If you were a judge in a case with facts similar to those in *Yermian*, would you require the jury to find that the defendant possessed any particular mental state concerning jurisdiction? If so, what precise instruction would you give? Why?

b. *The lower courts' responses.* Those circuit courts that have considered the issue have held that the government need not prove any mental state with respect to facts giving rise to federal jurisdiction under § 1001. *See, e.g., United States v. Leo*, 941 F.2d 181, 190 (3d Cir. 1991) (agreeing with four other circuits that no mens rea as to jurisdiction is required under § 1001). The United States Supreme Court has yet to resolve the issue as to whether the government must prove that the defendant reasonably should have known that the false statement fell within federal jurisdiction.

c. *Effect of strict liability.* Are there dangers from imposing strict liability on the jurisdictional element? One circuit court judge has noted that "*Yermian* might be read to permit § 1001 to reach any material, knowing false statement that turns out to have a fortuitous federal involvement — for example, a statement that the IRS happens upon in the course of a tax audit, or a casual falsehood made in the unknown presence of a federal officer and somehow pertinent to his mission." *Unites States v. Oakar*, 111 F.3d 146, 161 (D.C. Cir. 1997) (Williams, J., dissenting in part). The court in *Blankenship*, discussed in the notes following *United States v. Rodgers*, § C, *supra*, voiced similar concerns. Are these courts' concerns legitimate? Why or why not?

d. *The rule of lenity.* As so often happens in white collar prosecutions, the defendant in *Yermian* — like the defendant in *Rodgers* — cited the rule of lenity in support of his interpretation of the statute. What precisely is the alleged ambiguity in *Yermian*? Do you agree with the dissent that the statute is indeed ambiguous? Why or why not?

e. *The votes.* The *Yermian* decision is just one of many important Supreme Court white collar cases decided by a bare majority. Why do these cases split the Court so narrowly? Further, once again we see an unusual alignment of justices. Rare indeed were the criminal cases in which the Court was closely divided and Justices Rehnquist (seen as a strong "law and order" Justice) and Brennan (generally viewed as highly supportive of defendants' rights in criminal cases) found themselves on the same side. Can you explain why the dissenters joined forces in this case?

3. *The general mens rea requirement under § 1001.* As noted above, § 1001 requires that the government prove that the defendant acted "knowingly and willfully." Several interpretive issues arise when considering proof of mens rea under § 1001.

a. *Constructive knowledge.* As in other areas of the criminal law, knowledge can be proven by actual or constructive knowledge (also termed "willful blindness"). The United States Supreme Court stated that willful blindness is shown where "(1) the defendant . . . subjectively believe[d] that there [was] a high probability that a fact exist[ed] and (2) the defendant [took] deliberate actions to avoid learning of that fact." *Global-Tech Appliances, Inc. v. SEB S.A.*, 563 U.S. 754, 769 (2011).

b. *Willfulness.* Does willfulness under § 1001 require proof of an intent to violate a known legal duty, as the Supreme Court has required in some areas? *See, e.g., Cheek v. United States*, 498 U.S. 192 (1991) (willfulness in tax fraud statutes requires proof of an intentional violation of a known legal duty). Or is the requirement met when a defendant knows that the statement is false and knows that making a false statement is generally unlawful? Courts have generally held that the latter is sufficient. *See, e.g., United States v. Whab*, 355 F.3d 155, 162 (2d Cir. 2004) (holding it was not plain error for the district court to instruct the jury that "willfully" under § 1001 requires only that the defendant have been aware of the generally unlawful nature of the conduct).

c. *Specific intent.* Many courts also require that the government show an intent to deceive — sometimes described as "specific intent" — under § 1001. *See, e.g., United States v. Brown*, 151 F.3d 476, 484 (6th Cir. 1998). Such intent can be proven by circumstantial evidence, including knowledge of falsity. As a practical matter, does the "specific intent" requirement impose a significant additional burden on the government?

Problem

9-9. Defendants Broom and Meade were employees of a city Public Housing Authority (PHA). The PHA administered a program that provided housing for low-income families with funding from the United States Department of Housing and Urban Development (HUD). The applicable federal statutes, regulations, and policies were designed to ensure that beneficiaries of the program received assistance through an impartial system based on (1) the degree of the family's need, and (2) the time of the family's application. Because the program did not have sufficient funding to assist all who would qualify, the program required an allocation system based on (a) the date of application, (b) the percentage of income currently spent on housing, and (c) the current housing situation. In addition, the program established a procedure for choosing qualified families in a particular order based upon a waiting list.

Broom was a PHA supervisor. Meade was a PHA staff member in charge of processing applications. Because of ongoing problems with the low-income housing program, the PHA provided employees with various training videotapes and with pamphlets and booklets. There is no evidence, however, that Meade ever saw this material or ever discussed the waiting list procedure with representatives of HUD or PHA. Broom did request and receive the relevant regulations, some of which referred to the use of waiting lists. Broom also discussed the waiting lists with an HUD representative.

In order to favor certain applicants, including friends and political allies, the defendants did not require that those applicants be placed on the waiting list. Rather, the defendants submitted applications for those people as soon as the applications were received. On these applications, the defendants stated that the applicants were "eligible" for the federal program. The evidence showed that the applicants met the program criteria listed above. The defendants were convicted of violating § 1001 based upon PHA applications that the agency forwarded to the federal government.

What theory or theories would support the convictions? What arguments do the defendants have on appeal? Are the arguments likely to succeed? Why or why not?

G. Materiality

In many white collar crime contexts, materiality is a potential issue for the finder of fact. For example, as discussed in other chapters in this text, materiality is an element in any securities fraud case and is also an element in perjury cases. In the False Statements Accountability Act of 1996, Congress amended § 1001 to make it clear that the government must prove materiality as an element in a case brought under that section.

In *United States v. Gaudin*, 515 U.S. 506 (1995), the Supreme Court described a material statement under § 1001 as a statement having "'a natural tendency to influence, or [be] capable of influencing, the decision of the decisionmaking body to which it was addressed.'" *Id.* at 510, *quoting Kungys v. United States*, 485 U.S. 759, 770 (1988). The Court in *Gaudin* further stated:

> Deciding whether a statement is "material" requires the determination of at least two subsidiary questions of purely historical fact: (a) "what statement was made?" and (b) "what decision was the agency trying to make?" The ultimate question: (c) "whether the statement was material to the decision," requires applying the legal standard of materiality . . . to these historical facts.

Id. at 512. Court in *Gaudin* also held that materiality is a mixed question of law and fact that must be decided by the trier of fact.

A false statement can be material even if it does not succeed in misleading or influencing the government. *See, e.g., United States v. Clay*, 832 F.3d 1259, 1309 (11th Cir. 2016) (explaining that a "false statement can be material even if the decision maker actually knew or should have known that the statement was false or even if the decision maker did not actually rely on the statement"). As the First Circuit explained in *United States v. Meehanna*, 735 F.3d 32, 55 (1st Cir. 2013):

> the statement need not actually have influenced the governmental function. It is enough that the statement could have provoked governmental action. . . . [W]here a defendant's statements are intended to misdirect government investigators, they may satisfy the materiality requirement of section 1001 even if they stand no chance of accomplishing their objective. This principle makes eminently good sense: it would stand reason on its head to excuse a defendant's deliberate prevarication merely because his interrogators were a step ahead of him.

Finally, it should be noted that while the government must prove materiality to convict for false statements under § 1001, other false statements statutes in the federal criminal code have no materiality element. *See, e.g.*, 18 U.S.C. § 1519 ("Destruction, alteration, or falsification of records in Federal investigations and Bankruptcy"); *United States v. Powell*, 680 F.3d 350 (4th Cir. 2012) (holding that "the government need not prove materiality of the falsification for an offense under 18 U.S.C. § 1519").

Problems

9-10. Reread the facts of the Michael Flynn Russia Investigation, *supra*, Chapter 9, at § D, 1, Note 5. Assume Flynn sought to dismiss the § 1001 false statement charge against him because his false statements were not material to any government investigation.

How should the court rule?

9-11. Defendant was a federal agent ("Agent") who drove a government-issued car. Agent's car was parked illegally and was towed by local parking enforcement officials. Angry that the car had been towed, Agent went to the lot where the car was being kept and removed the car from the tow lot without paying the towing fee, damaging a fence in the process. Agent later paid $500 for the towing fee and damage to the property. Agent received an invoice for $500 from the towing company, and submitted the invoice to the federal government for reimbursement. Embarrassed by the property damage, Agent altered the invoice to remove the reference to the damage. Under applicable federal regulations, Agent would have been entitled to be reimbursed for the $500 regardless of whether the invoice was altered.

Was the altered invoice a material false statement? If so, under what theory?

H. Double Jeopardy and Related Issues

In many white collar contexts, multiple charges or successive prosecutions based upon the same incident may give rise to a challenge under the Fifth Amendment's Double Jeopardy Clause. That Clause provides that a defendant may not be "subject for the same offense to be twice put in jeopardy of life or limb." Because so many federal statutes criminalize false statements and omissions in different contexts, double jeopardy issues are particularly relevant to these cases. The next case is a leading Supreme Court decision dealing with the application of the Double Jeopardy Clause to multiple criminal charges arising out of the same event.

United States v. Woodward

469 U.S. 105 (1985)

PER CURIAM.

On March 1, 1980, respondent Charles Woodward and his wife arrived at Los Angeles International Airport on a flight from Brazil. In passing through Customs, respondent was handed the usual form that included the following question: "Are you or any family member carrying over $5,000 (or the equivalent value in any currency) in monetary instruments such as coin, currency, traveler's checks, money orders, or negotiable instruments in bearer form?"[c] Respondent checked the "no" box.

After questioning respondent for a brief period, customs officials decided to search respondent and his wife. As he was being escorted to a search room, respondent told an official that he and his wife were carrying over $20,000 in cash.

---

c. After *Woodward* was decided, Congress increased the triggering amount to cash in excess of $10,000. Note also that the monetary reporting statutes at issue in this case, 13 U.S.C. §§1058, and 1101, were recently recodified without substantive change at 31 U.S.C. §§5322(a) and 5316. — Eds.

Woodward removed approximately $12,000 from his boot; another $10,000 was found in a makeshift money belt concealed under his wife's clothing.

Woodward was indicted on charges of making a false statement to an agency of the United States, 18 U.S.C. §1001, and willfully failing to report that he was carrying in excess of $5,000 into the United States, 31 U.S.C. §§1058, 1101. The same conduct—answering "no" to the question whether he was carrying more than $5,000 into the country—formed the basis of each count. A jury convicted Woodward on both charges; he received a sentence of six months in prison on the false statement count, and a consecutive three-year term of probation on the currency reporting count. During the proceedings in the district court, the respondent never asserted that Congress did not intend to permit cumulative punishment for conduct violating the false statement and the currency reporting statutes.

The United States Court of Appeals for the Ninth Circuit held that respondent's conduct could not be punished under both 18 U.S.C. §1001 and 31 U.S.C. §§1058, 1101. The court applied the rule of statutory construction contained in *Blockburger v. United States*, 284 U.S. 299, 304 (1932)—"whether each provision requires proof of a fact which the other does not"—and held that the false statement felony was a lesser included offense of the currency reporting misdemeanor. In other words, every violation of the currency reporting statute necessarily entails a violation of the false statement law.[3] The court reasoned that a willful failure to file a required report is a form of concealment prohibited by 18 U.S.C. §1001. Concluding that Congress presumably intended someone in respondent's position to be punished only under the currency reporting misdemeanor, the Court of Appeals reversed respondent's felony conviction for making a false statement.

The Court of Appeals plainly misapplied the *Blockburger* rule for determining whether Congress intended to permit cumulative punishment; proof of a currency reporting violation does *not* necessarily include proof of a false statement offense. Section 1001 proscribes the nondisclosure of a material fact only if the fact is "conceal[ed] . . . by any *trick, scheme, or device*" (emphasis added). A person could, without employing a "trick, scheme, or device," simply and willfully fail to file a currency disclosure report. A traveler who enters the country and passes through Customs prepared to answer questions truthfully, but is never asked whether he is carrying over $5,000 in currency, might nonetheless be subject to conviction under 31 U.S.C. §1058 for willfully transporting money without filing the required currency report. However, because he did not conceal a material fact by means of a "trick, scheme, or device" (and did not make any false statement) his conduct would not fall within 18 U.S.C. §1001.[4]

---

3. The converse is clearly not true; 31 U.S.C. §§1058, 1101, but not 18 U.S.C. §1001, involve the failure to file a currency disclosure report.

4. In Woodward's case, the government did not have to prove the existence of a trick, scheme, or device. Woodward was charged with violating §1001 because he made a false statement on the

There is no evidence in 18 U.S.C. § 1001 and 31 U.S.C. §§ 1058, 1101 that Congress did not intend to allow separate punishment for the two different offenses. Sections 1058 and 1101 were enacted by Congress in 1970 as part of the Currency and Foreign Transactions Reporting Act. Section 203(k) of that Act expressly provided: "For the purposes of § 1001 of title 18, United States Code, the contents of reports required under any provision of this title are statements and representations in matters within the jurisdiction of an agency of the United States." 31 U.S.C. § 1052(k).[6]

It is clear that in passing the currency reporting law, Congress' attention was drawn to 18 U.S.C. § 1001, but at no time did it suggest that the two statutes could not be applied together. We cannot assume, therefore, that Congress was unaware that it had created two different offenses permitting multiple punishment for the same conduct.

Finally, Congress' intent to allow punishment under both 18 U.S.C. § 1001 and 31 U.S.C. §§ 1058, 1101 is shown by the fact that the statutes "are directed to separate evils." The currency reporting statute was enacted to develop records that would "have a high degree of usefulness in criminal, tax, or regulatory investigations." 31 U.S.C. § 1051. The false statement statute, on the other hand, was designed "to protect the authorized functions of governmental departments and agencies from the perversion which might result from the deceptive practices described." *United States v. Gilliland*, 312 U.S. 86, 93 (1941).

All guides to legislative intent reveal that Congress intended respondent's conduct to be punishable under both 18 U.S.C. § 1001, and 31 U.S.C. §§ 1058, 1101. Accordingly, the petition for a writ of certiorari is granted, and that part of the Court of Appeals' judgment reversing respondent's 18 U.S.C. § 1001 conviction is reversed.

Notes and Questions

1. *The* Blockburger *test.* On its face, the *Blockburger* test is easy to apply: a defendant generally may not be punished for multiple crimes for the same act if: (1) (a) the crimes have the same elements, or (b) one of the crimes is a lesser included offense of the other; or (2) Congress did not intend that a defendant be punished for both crimes.

It is not always easy to determine whether one crime is a lesser included offense of another. In simple terms, under federal law, Crime A is a lesser included offense of Crime B when proof of Crime B always requires proof of Crime A. Thus, if Crime A requires proof of elements 1 & 2, and Crime B requires proof of elements 1, 2, & 3, then Crime A is a lesser included offense of Crime B, and the defendant generally

---

customs form. This type of affirmative misrepresentation is proscribed under the statute even if not accompanied by a trick, scheme, or device.

6. When Title 31 was recodified in 1982, this provision was eliminated as "[u]nnecessary" because "§ 1001 applies unless otherwise provided." H.R. Rep. No. 97-651, p. 301 (1982).

cannot be punished for both crimes.[d] For example, as discussed in Chapter 7, Bribery and Gratuities, *supra*, the crime of receiving an illegal gratuity requires proof that a federal public official received something of value as compensation for an official act other than as provided by law. The crime of bribery essentially requires proof of these elements, plus the public official's "corrupt" intent — receiving the payment knowing that it is being given specifically to influence how the public official carries out the official act. For this reason, gratuity is generally considered to be a lesser included offense of bribery. *See* Chapter 7, Bribery and Gratuities, *supra*, § B, 3.

Thus, if a defendant is charged with the separate crimes of receiving a bribe and of receiving a gratuity, the defendant may be convicted of and punished for either crime, but not both. A prosecutor may make a tactical decision to include the lesser offense in the hope of gaining some conviction if the jury rejects the more serious charge, or may decide to omit the lesser charge in an attempt to avoid jury compromise.

What were the elements of the crimes in *Woodward*? Why did the Court conclude that they are separate crimes?

2. *Multiple charges in a single trial.* The issue in *Woodward* involved multiple charges in a single trial. The Court assumed that, even if the crimes have different elements, multiple punishments would not be appropriate if Congress had expressed an intent not to allow multiple punishments. Conversely, the Supreme Court has held that *Blockburger* does not bar multiple punishments for the same act at one trial where the legislature intended to permit such punishment. *See Missouri v. Hunter*, 459 U.S. 359 (1983). Thus, if Congressional intent were clear, then the government could obtain multiple convictions at a single prosecution for the same act for crimes that have the same elements or for crimes where one is a lesser included offense of the other.

3. *Successive prosecutions.* Issues under *Blockburger* arise in many contexts, including both multiple charges at the same trial, and successive prosecutions arising out of the same facts. Successive prosecutions are prohibited by the Double Jeopardy Clause if the charges violate the *Blockburger* test. For an excellent overview of these and other issues relating to the *Blockburger* rule, see Joshua Dressler & Alan C. Michaels, *Understanding Criminal Procedure, Vol. 2: Adjudication* §§ 14.07–08 (4th ed. 2013).

Problems

9-12. Defendant was convicted under 18 U.S.C. § 542, which provides:

> Whoever enters or introduces, or attempts to enter or introduce, into the commerce of the United States any imported merchandise by means of any

---

d. Some states use different tests for determining whether one crime is a lesser included offense of another. For an overview of legal and strategic issues concerning lesser included offenses, see Catherine L. Carpenter, *The All-or-Nothing Doctrine in Criminal Cases: Independent Trial Strategy or Gamesmanship Gone Awry?* 26 AM. J. CRIM. L. 257 (1999).

fraudulent or false invoice, declaration, affidavit, letter, paper, or by means of any false statement, written or verbal, or by means of any false or fraudulent practice or appliance, or makes any false statement in any declaration without reasonable cause to believe the truth of such statement, or procures the making of any such false statement as to any matter material thereto without reasonable cause to believe the truth of such statement, whether or not the United States shall or may be deprived of any lawful duties . . . shall be fined for each offense under this title or imprisoned not more than two years, or both.

Defendant was also convicted under § 1001 for the same statement.

Can defendant be punished under both statutes? Why or why not?

9-13. Defendant has been convicted under both 18 U.S.C. § 1035 and 18 U.S.C. § 1001. Section 1035 provides:

(a) Whoever, in any matter involving a health care benefit program, knowingly and willfully —

(1) falsifies, conceals, or covers up by any trick, scheme, or device a material fact; or

(2) makes any materially false, fictitious, or fraudulent statements or representations, or makes or uses any materially false writing or document knowing the same to contain any materially false, fictitious, or fraudulent statement or entry, in connection with the delivery of or payment for health care benefits, items, or services, shall be fined under this title or imprisoned not more than 5 years, or both.

Assuming that both charges arose out of the same false statement, assess whether defendant can be convicted and punished under both statutes.

Chapter 10

Perjury and False Declarations

A. Introductory Notes

1. The Federal Perjury Statutes

The federal criminal code contains a number of perjury statutes. The most significant of these are the general perjury statute, 18 U.S.C. §1621, which applies to various types of federal proceedings, and the false declarations statute, 18 U.S.C. §1623, which applies only to federal judicial and grand jury proceedings. In addition, there are federal statutes that make it a crime to lie under oath in connection with particular matters. For example, the federal tax code, 26 U.S.C. §7206, criminalizes perjury in connection with the filing of a tax return. Because perjury potentially affects the functioning of the body to which it is directed, it is a serious crime that carries significant penalties. The false statement statute, 18 U.S.C. §1001, is closely akin to the perjury statutes. It outlaws false statements in any matter within the jurisdiction of a federal agency or department, even if not made under oath. *See* Chapter 9, *supra*.

Perjury charges may arise in one of two ways. First, the government may believe that the defendant has lied under oath and may initiate an investigation and bring an indictment focused solely on the alleged perjury. The investigation and subsequent impeachment of former President Bill Clinton regarding his sworn testimony in a civil lawsuit is perhaps the most famous example of a perjury-focused investigation.[a]

Second, the government may bring a perjury charge in addition to or instead of the primary subject of the criminal investigation. For example, assume that the SEC subpoenas the testimony of one suspected of securities fraud and that the witness denies the fraud during an SEC deposition. If the defendant is later charged in a criminal securities fraud case, the government may decide to include in that case a perjury charge in addition to the substantive securities fraud charges. High-profile defendants in perjury cases that resulted from investigations into other types of wrongdoing include baseball players Barry Bonds and Roger Clemens, media personality Martha Stewart, and vice presidential aid Scooter Libby.[b]

---

a. For an insightful analysis of the Clinton matter, see Stuart P. Green, *Perjury, in* Lying, Cheating, and Stealing: A Moral Theory of White Collar Crime 140–47 (2006).

b. Initially, under investigation for the use of illegal performance-enhancing substances, Bonds and Clemens were ultimately charged only with perjury, false statements, and obstruction of justice based upon their testimony before a grand jury and Congress denying such use. *See* Michael S.

2. Overview and Elements of §§ 1621 and 1623

a. Coverage

Initially, it is important to note the differences in the proceedings covered by § 1621 and § 1623. Section 1621 applies to court proceedings, grand jury proceedings, and all other federal proceedings in which an oath is authorized by law. The latter include Congressional and administrative agency proceedings. By way of contrast, § 1623 *only* applies to proceedings "before or ancillary to any court or grand jury." Thus, the two statutes overlap. Perjury committed in a judicial or grand jury proceeding can be charged under either statute. Perjury not committed before a court or grand jury, but rather during an administrative agency or Congressional proceeding, for example, can only be charged under § 1621. In instances where both statutes apply, courts have generally allowed prosecutors discretion in choosing which statute to employ. The maximum statutory prison sentence under both statutes is five years.[c]

b. The Elements

Under § 1621, the government must prove the following elements:

(1) The defendant undertook an oath administered by one authorized by federal law to do so;

(2) The defendant undertook the oath before a competent tribunal, officer, or person;

(3) The oath was administered in a case in which federal law allowed an oath to be administered;

(4) The defendant made a false statement;

(5) The statement was material to the proceedings; and

(6) The defendant acted willfully and with knowledge of the statement's falsity.

Under § 1623, the government must prove the following elements:

(1) The defendant undertook an oath;

Schmidt, *Prosecutors Rework Indictment of Bonds*, N.Y. Times, May 14, 2008, at D4; *see also Roger Clemens Acquitted on All Charges in Perjury Trial*, CBS News (June 18, 2012), https://www.cbsnews.com/news/roger-clemens-acquitted-on-all-charges-in-perjury-trial/. Martha Stewart was under investigation for insider trading, but ultimately was found guilty only of cover-up crimes, including conspiracy to commit perjury. Peter Bacanovic, her broker and co-defendant, was found guilty of perjury. *See United States v. Stewart*, 323 F. Supp. 2d 606 (S.D.N.Y. 2004). Libby was under investigation for violating national security laws in connection with the CIA leak case, but was charged and convicted only of cover-up crimes, including perjury. *United States v. Libby*, 498 F. Supp. 2d 1 (D.D.C. 2007).

c. For an analysis of the principal federal perjury statutes, see Green, *supra* note a, at 133–147; James Nesland, *Perjury and False Declarations, in* White Collar Crime: Business and Regulatory Offenses § 10.01[1]–[3] (Otto Obermaier et al., eds. 2021).

(2) The oath was administered before or ancillary to a court or grand jury proceeding;

(3) The defendant made a false statement or used false information;

(4) The false statement or information was material to the proceeding; and

(5) The defendant knew the statement or information was false.

c. Differences between §§ 1621 and 1623

Congress enacted § 1623, the false declarations statute, as a supplement to § 1621, the general perjury statute. Congress intended that the new statute promote truthfulness in court and grand jury proceedings. Thus, Congress made it easier in several respects for the government to prove a case under § 1623 than under § 1621:

1. *Inconsistent statements.* Section 1623 contains an "inconsistent statements" provision. Under this provision, the government may prove a false declaration by showing that the defendant made "two or more declarations, which are inconsistent to the degree that one of them is necessarily false." Section 1621 contains no such provision.

2. *Two-witness rule.* Section 1623 does away with the "two-witness" rule that courts have applied to cases brought under § 1621. The two-witness rule requires that a perjury charge be proven by one witness *plus* corroborating evidence. That requirement still applies under § 1621.

3. *False information.* Under § 1623, the prosecution may be based not only on a false statement but also on the use of false information.

4. *Mens rea.* Section 1621 requires proof of willfulness and knowledge of falsity, while § 1623 only requires proof of the latter. In practice, however, the willfulness requirement is usually met whenever the government is able to prove knowledge of falsity.

Although § 1623 does provide these advantages to prosecutors, Congress apparently did intend to limit those advantages to prosecutors in one respect. Thus, § 1623 provides a defense for a witness who takes back, or "recants," earlier sworn testimony. Section § 1621 does not provide for this defense. In practice, however, and as discussed more fully in § E below, the recantation defense is seldom successful.

B. Tribunals and Proceedings

Prosecutions under § 1623 may raise the issue whether the alleged falsity occurred "before or ancillary to any court or grand jury." The statute itself does not define or describe ancillary proceedings. That task fell to the United States Supreme Court in the case that follows. In addition, the case illustrates the use of the inconsistent statements provision of § 1623. Finally, the Court discusses an alleged "variance," a due process issue that often arises in white collar cases.

Dunn v. United States

442 U.S. 100 (1979)

Mr. JUSTICE MARSHALL delivered the opinion of the Court.

Title IV of the Organized Crime Control Act of 1970, 18 U.S.C. § 1623, prohibits false declarations made under oath "in any proceeding before or ancillary to any court or grand jury of the United States." This case turns on the scope of the term ancillary proceeding in § 1623, a phrase not defined in that provision or elsewhere in the Criminal Code. More specifically, we must determine whether an interview in a private attorney's office at which a sworn statement is given constitutes a proceeding ancillary to a court or grand jury within the meaning of the statute.

On June 16, 1976, petitioner Robert Dunn testified before a federal grand jury under a grant of immunity pursuant to 18 U.S.C. § 6002. The grand jury was investigating illicit drug activity at the Colorado State Penitentiary where petitioner had been incarcerated. Dunn's testimony implicated a fellow inmate, Phillip Musgrave, in various drug-related offenses. Following petitioner's appearance, the grand jury indicted Musgrave for conspiracy to manufacture and distribute methamphetamine.

Several months later, on September 30, 1976, Dunn arrived without counsel in the office of Musgrave's attorney, Michael Canges. In the presence of Canges and a notary public, petitioner made an oral statement under oath in which he recanted his grand jury testimony implicating Musgrave. Canges subsequently moved to dismiss the indictment against Musgrave, alleging that it was based on perjured testimony. In support of this motion, the attorney submitted a transcript of Dunn's September 30 statement.

The District Court held an evidentiary hearing on Musgrave's motion to dismiss on October 21, 1976. At that hearing, petitioner, who was then represented by counsel, adopted the statement he had given in Canges' office and testified that only a small part of what he had told the grand jury was in fact true. As a result of petitioner's testimony, the government reduced the charges against Musgrave to misdemeanor possession of methamphetamine.

Petitioner was subsequently indicted on five counts of making false declarations in violation of 18 U.S.C. § 1623. The indictment charged that Dunn's testimony before the grand jury was inconsistent with statements made "on September 30, 1976, while under oath as a witness in a proceeding ancillary to *United States v. Musgrave*, . . . to the degree that one of said declarations was false. . . ." In response to petitioner's motion for a bill of particulars, the government indicated that it would rely on the "inconsistent declarations" method of proof authorized by § 1623(c). Under that subsection, the government must establish the materiality and inconsistency of declarations made in proceedings before or ancillary to a court or grand jury, but need not prove which of the declarations is false.

At trial, the government introduced over objection pertinent parts of Dunn's grand jury testimony, his testimony at the October 21 evidentiary hearing, and his sworn statement to Musgrave's attorney. After the government rested its case, petitioner renewed his objections in a motion for acquittal. He contended that the September 30 statement was not made in a proceeding ancillary to a federal court or grand jury as required by § 1623(c). The court denied the motion and submitted the case to the jury. Petitioner was convicted on three of the five counts of the indictment and sentenced to concurrent five-year terms on each count.

The Court of Appeals for the Tenth Circuit affirmed. Although it agreed with petitioner that the interview in Canges' office was not an ancillary proceeding under § 1623, the court determined that the October 21 hearing at which petitioner adopted his September statement was a proceeding ancillary to a grand jury investigation. Acknowledging that the indictment specified the September 30 interview rather than the October 21 hearing as the ancillary proceeding, the Court of Appeals construed this discrepancy as a nonprejudicial variance between the indictment and proof at trial. . . .

We granted certiorari. Because we disagree with the Court of Appeals' ultimate disposition of the ancillary-proceeding issue, we reverse.

A variance arises when the evidence adduced at trial establishes facts different from those alleged in an indictment. In the instant case, since the indictment specified the September 30 interview rather than the October 21 hearing as the ancillary proceeding, the Court of Appeals identified a variance between the pleadings and the government's proof at trial. However, reasoning that petitioner's October 21 testimony was "inextricably related" to his September 30 declaration, the court concluded that petitioner could have anticipated that the prosecution would introduce the October testimony. The court therefore determined that the variance was not fatal to the government's case.

In our view, it is unnecessary to inquire, as did the Court of Appeals, whether petitioner was prejudiced by a variance between what was alleged in the indictment and what was proved at trial. For we discern no such variance. The indictment charged inconsistency between petitioner's statements in the September 30 interview and his grand jury testimony. That was also the theory on which the case was tried and submitted to the jury. But while there was no variance between the indictment and proof at trial, there was a discrepancy between the basis on which the jury rendered its verdict and that on which the Court of Appeals sustained petitioner's conviction. Whereas the jury was instructed to rest its decision on Dunn's September statement, the Tenth Circuit predicated its affirmance on petitioner's October testimony. The government concedes that this ruling was erroneous. We agree.

To uphold a conviction on a charge that was neither alleged in an indictment nor presented to a jury at trial offends the most basic notions of due process. Few constitutional principles are more firmly established than a defendant's right to be heard on the specific charges of which he is accused. There is, to be sure, no glaring distinction between the government's theory at trial and the Tenth Circuit's analysis on appeal. The jury might well have reached the same verdict had the prosecution built its case on petitioner's October 21 testimony adopting his September 30 statement rather than on the September statement itself. But the offense was not so defined, and appellate courts are not free to revise the basis on which a defendant is convicted simply because the same result would likely obtain on retrial. As we recognized in *Cole v. Arkansas*, 333 U.S. 196, 201 (1948) "[i]t is as much a violation of due process to send an accused to prison following conviction of a charge on which he was never tried as it would be to convict him upon a charge that was never made." Thus, unless the September 30 interview constituted an ancillary proceeding, petitioner's conviction cannot stand.

Congress enacted § 1623 as part of the 1970 Organized Crime Control Act to facilitate perjury prosecutions and thereby enhance the reliability of testimony before federal courts and grand juries. Invoking this broad congressional purpose, the government argues for an expansive construction of the term ancillary proceeding. Under the government's analysis, false swearing in an affidavit poses the same threat to the fact-finding process as false testimony in open court. Thus, the government contends that any statements made under oath for submission to a court, whether given in an attorney's office or in a local bar and grill, fall within the ambit of § 1623. In our judgment, the term "proceeding," which carries a somewhat more formal connotation, suggests that Congress had a narrower end in view when enacting § 1623. And the legislative history of the Organized Crime Control Act confirms that conclusion.

Section 1623 was a response to perceived evidentiary problems in demonstrating perjury under the existing federal statute, 18 U.S.C. § 1621. As Congress noted, the strict common-law requirements for establishing falsity which had been engrafted onto the federal perjury statute often made prosecution for false statements exceptionally difficult. By relieving the government of the burden of proving which of two or more inconsistent declarations was false, *see* § 1623(c), Congress sought to afford "greater assurance that testimony obtained in grand jury and court proceedings will aid the cause of truth." S. Rep. No. 91-617, p. 59 (1969). But nothing in the language or legislative history of the statute suggests that Congress contemplated a relaxation of the government's burden of proof with respect to all inconsistent statements given under oath. Had Congress intended such a result, it presumably would have drafted § 1623 to encompass all sworn declarations irrespective of whether they were made in proceedings before or ancillary to a court or grand jury. Particularly since Congress was aware that statements under oath were embraced by the federal perjury statute without regard to where they were given, the choice of less comprehensive language in § 1623 does not appear inadvertent.

That Congress intended § 1623 to sweep less broadly than the perjury statute is also apparent from the origin of the term ancillary proceeding. As initially introduced in Congress, the Organized Crime Control Act contained a version of § 1623 which encompassed only inconsistent statements made in any "trial, hearing, or proceeding before any court or grand jury." When asked to comment on the proposed statute, the Department of Justice noted that the scope of the inconsistent declarations provision was "not as inclusive" as the perjury statute. *See* Hearings on S. 30 *et al.* before the Subcommittee on Criminal Laws and Procedures of the Senate Committee on the Judiciary, 91st Cong., 1st Sess., 372 (1969) (hereinafter S. 30 Hearings). Significantly, the Justice Department did not suggest that the provision be made coextensive with the perjury statute. However, in subsequent Senate Subcommittee hearings, Assistant Attorney General Wilson indicated, without elaboration, that the Department advocated "including [under § 1623] other testimony, preliminary testimony and other statements, in the perjury field." *Id.* at 389.

In response to that general suggestion, Senator McClellan, on behalf of the Subcommittee, sent a letter to the Assistant Attorney General clarifying its purpose:

> You also read Title IV not to cover "pre-trial depositions, affidavits and certifications." This was not our intent in drafting the bill. We had hoped that it would be applicable, for example, to situations such as [the] kind of pre-trial depositions that the enforcement of S. 1861 would present. If we included in the statute the phrase "proceedings before or ancillary to any court or grand jury," do you feel that this intent would be adequately expressed?

Id. at 409.

The government attaches great significance to the qualification, "for example," in Senator McClellan's letter. Because pretrial depositions were mentioned as illustrative, the government interprets the term ancillary proceeding to subsume affidavits and certifications as well. But that is not the inference the Department of Justice originally drew from the Senator's letter. Responding to the proposed modification of § 1623, Assistant Attorney General Wilson did not advert to affidavits or certifications but stated only that

> [i]nclusion of the phrase "proceedings before or ancillary to any court or grand jury" in the false statement provision would in our opinion adequately bring within the coverage of the provision pre-trial depositions such as that contained in S. 1861.

S. 30 Hearings 411.

In our view, the Justice Department's contemporaneous rather than its current interpretation offers the more plausible reading of the Subcommittee's intent. Its attention having been drawn to the issue, had the Subcommittee wished to bring *all* affidavits and certifications within the statutory prohibition, Senator McClellan presumably would have so stated....

Thus, both the language and history of the Act support the Court of Appeals' conclusion that petitioner's September 30 interview "lack[ed] the degree of formality" required by § 1623. 577 F.2d at 123. For the government does not and could not seriously maintain that the interview in Canges' office constituted a deposition. Musgrave's counsel made no attempt to comply with the procedural safeguards for depositions set forth in Fed. Rule Crim. Proc. 15 and 18 U.S.C. § 3503. A court order authorizing the deposition was never obtained. Nor did petitioner receive formal notice of the proceeding or of his right to have counsel present. Indeed, petitioner did not even certify the transcript of the interview as accurate.

To characterize such an interview as an ancillary proceeding would not only take liberties with the language and legislative history of § 1623, it would also contravene this Court's long-established practice of resolving questions concerning the ambit of a criminal statute in favor of lenity. This practice reflects not merely a convenient maxim of statutory construction. Rather, it is rooted in fundamental principles of due process which mandate that no individual be forced to speculate, at peril of indictment, whether his conduct is prohibited. Thus, to ensure that a legislature speaks with special clarity when marking the boundaries of criminal conduct, courts must decline to impose punishment for actions that are not "'plainly and unmistakably'" proscribed. *United States v. Gradwell*, 243 U.S. 476, 485 (1917).

We cannot conclude here that Congress in fact intended or clearly expressed an intent that § 1623 should encompass statements made in contexts less formal than a deposition. Accordingly, we hold that petitioner's September 30 declarations were not given in a proceeding ancillary to a court or grand jury within the meaning of the statute.

The judgment of the Court of Appeals is reversed.

Notes and Questions

1. *Inconsistent declarations.*

a. According to the Court, why did Congress include the § 1623(c) inconsistent declarations provision when it enacted § 1623? Does this provision appear to accomplish Congress' objective? Why or why not?

b. What declarations did the defendant make? Which of those declarations, according to the government's argument before the Court, were inconsistent? Which declarations did the Court of Appeals find to be inconsistent?

2. *Variance.*

a. What was the "variance" issue discussed by the court? Why does it matter to a defendant whether there is such a variance?

b. The Court found that there was no variance. Why?

c. Given that the Court did not find a variance, why did it reverse?

3. *Ancillary proceedings.*

a. In determining that Dunn's statement did not constitute a declaration in a proceeding ancillary to a court or grand jury, the Court relied heavily on § 1623's legislative history. The defense argued that the legislative history of the statute supported its proposed interpretation. Precisely what language in the legislative history supported the defendant's argument? Absent an effective defense argument on this point, would the result likely have been different? Why or why not?

b. The Court in *Dunn* did not establish precise boundaries for determining which proceedings qualify under § 1623. This issue thus continues to arise in prosecutions under that section. For example, in *United States v. Lamplugh*, 17 F. Supp. 2d 354 (M.D. Pa. 1998), the court held that a declaration signed under penalty of perjury in support of a motion in a civil law suit does not qualify under § 1623. Courts have, however, found depositions in civil cases, as well as a variety of proceedings in criminal cases to be "proceedings before or ancillary to any court or grand jury of the United States."[d]

4. *Oath.* No particular formality is required in the administration of a legally sufficient oath to tell the truth. Courts have held "[i]t is sufficient that, in the presence of a person authorized to administer an oath ... the affiant by an unequivocal act consciously takes on himself the obligation of an oath, and the person undertaking the oath understood that what was done is proper for the administration of the oath and all that is necessary to complete the act of swearing." *United States v. Yoshida*, 727 F.2d 822, 823 (9th Cir. 1983); *see also Moore v. United States*, 348 U.S. 966 (1955) (eschewing any requirement of the use of the word "solemnly" in affirming to tell the truth). Section 1623(a) loosens the requirement of an oath for proof of a false declaration by also including within its scope "any declaration, certificate, verification, or statement under penalty of perjury as permitted under [28 U.S.C. § 1746]." Note, however, that § 1623(a)'s more permissive language does not appear among the requirements for § 1623(c)'s inconsistent statement rule, and courts have taken this omission literally — requiring that both statements be made under oath. *See, e.g., United States v. Jaramillo*, 69 F.3d 388, 390 (9th Cir. 1995).

Problem

10-1. Federal agents asked Witness to assist them in an investigation of Target's drug trafficking activities. Witness submitted a written statement. Witness read the statement, made corrections, and reviewed numerous drafts. At the United States Attorney's Office, an Assistant U.S. Attorney told Witness that a lie in the statement would constitute perjury and he would be criminally punished. Witness signed the statement and a notary public acknowledged the signature. Under the signature, the statement provided that Witness affirmed the truth of the statement under "penalty of perjury." In the statement, Witness said:

> I saw a huge stack of money on top of a table in Target's kitchen. It was about two feet high and in the shape of a volcano. It was in stacks of 100 dollar bills, separated by rubber bands. I went to Target's house and he was in the garage. He had a huge cardboard box that was stuffed with newspaper. He

---

d. *See, e.g., United States v. Zhen Zhou Wu*, 716 F.3d 159, 173–74 (5th Cir. 2013) (depositions in civil cases); *United States v. Johnson*, 325 F.3d 205, 209 (4th Cir. 2003) (habeas corpus proceeding); United States v. Greene, 591 F.2d 471 (8th Cir. 1979) (bail hearings); *United States v. Brugnara*, 856 F.3d 1198 (9th Cir. 2017) (supervised release revocation hearings).

was taking out brown packages wrapped in shiny brown tape and marked with a black squiggly line. I realized it was cocaine.

Witness was called as a witness at Target's trial and testified under oath as follows:

Q: "Did you ever see a large amount of money on the table in Target's house?"

A: "No."

Q: "Have you ever seen Target with any cocaine?"

A: "No."

The government has charged Witness with perjury, using the inconsistent statements provision of § 1623.

Witness has moved to dismiss the charge. How should the court rule? Why?

C. Falsity

Under § 1621, the government must show that the defendant *willfully* and *knowingly* committed perjury. Under § 1623, the government must prove that the defendant *knowingly* made a false statement or declaration. Either level of mens rea is likely met if the defendant is shown to have knowingly given false testimony.

Assume that a witness, deliberately intending to produce a false impression, gives a misleading but literally true answer during sworn testimony. Would this suffice for a perjury conviction? The Supreme Court addressed this question in the following § 1621 case. Note that the Court's analysis also applies to § 1623 prosecutions. *See, e.g., United States v. Gorman,* 613 F.3d 711, 716 (7th Cir. 2010).

Bronston v. United States
409 U.S. 352 (1973)

Mr. Chief Justice Burger delivered the opinion of the Court.

We granted the writ in this case to consider a narrow but important question in the application of the federal perjury statute, 18 U.S.C. § 1621: whether a witness may be convicted of perjury for an answer, under oath, that is literally true but not responsive to the question asked and arguably misleading by negative implication.

Petitioner is the sole owner of Samuel Bronston Productions, Inc., a company that between 1958 and 1964, produced motion pictures in various European locations. For these enterprises, Bronston Productions opened bank accounts in a number of foreign countries; in 1962, for example, it had 37 accounts in five countries. As president of Bronston Productions, petitioner supervised transactions involving the foreign bank accounts.

In June 1964, Bronston Productions petitioned for an arrangement with creditors under Chapter XI of the Bankruptcy Act. On June 10, 1966, a referee in bankruptcy held a hearing to determine, for the benefit of creditors, the extent and location of the company's assets. Petitioner's perjury conviction was founded on the answers given by him as a witness at that bankruptcy hearing, and in particular on the following colloquy with a lawyer for a creditor of Bronston Productions:

Q. Do you have any bank accounts in Swiss banks, Mr. Bronston?

A. No, sir.

Q. Have you ever?

A. The company had an account there for about six months, in Zurich.

Q. Have you any nominees who have bank accounts in Swiss banks?

A. No, sir.

Q. Have you ever?

A. No, sir.

It is undisputed that for a period of nearly five years, between October 1959 and June 1964, petitioner had a personal bank account at the International Credit Bank in Geneva, Switzerland, into which he made deposits and upon which he drew checks totaling more than $180,000. It is likewise undisputed that petitioner's answers were literally truthful. (a) Petitioner did not at the time of questioning have a Swiss bank account. (b) Bronston Productions, Inc., did have the account in Zurich described by petitioner. (c) Neither at the time of questioning nor before did petitioner have nominees who had Swiss accounts. The government's prosecution for perjury went forward on the theory that in order to mislead his questioner, petitioner answered the second question with literal truthfulness but unresponsively addressed his answer to the company's assets and not to his own — thereby implying that he had no personal Swiss bank account at the relevant time.

At petitioner's trial, the District Court instructed the jury that the "basic issue" was whether petitioner "spoke his true belief." Perjury, the court stated, "necessarily involves the state of mind of the accused" and "essentially consists of wilfully testifying to the truth of a fact which the defendant does not believe to be true;" petitioner's testimony could not be found "wilfully" false unless at the time his testimony was given petitioner "fully understood the questions put to him but nevertheless gave false answers knowing the same to be false." The court further instructed the jury that if petitioner did not understand the question put to him and for that reason gave an unresponsive answer, he could not be convicted of perjury. Petitioner could, however, be convicted if he gave an answer "not literally false but when considered in the context in which it was given, nevertheless constitute[d] a false statement."[3]

---

3. The District Court gave the following example "as an illustration only:"

[I]f it is material to ascertain how many times a person has entered a store on a given day and that person responds to such a question by saying five times when in fact he knows that he entered the store 50 times that day, that person may be guilty of perjury even though it is technically true that he entered the store five times.

The jury began its deliberations at 11:30 a.m. Several times it requested exhibits or additional instructions from the court, and at one point, at the request of the jury, the District Court repeated its instructions in full. At 6:10 p.m., the jury returned its verdict, finding petitioner guilty on the count of perjury before us today. . . .

In the Court of Appeals, petitioner contended, as he had in post-trial motions before the District Court, that the key question was imprecise and suggestive of various interpretations. In addition, petitioner contended that he could not be convicted of perjury on the basis of testimony that was concededly truthful, however unresponsive. A divided Court of Appeals held that the question was readily susceptible of a responsive reply and that it adequately tested the defendant's belief in the veracity of his answer. The Court of Appeals further held that, "[f]or the purposes of 18 U.S.C. § 1621, an answer containing half of the truth which also constitutes a lie by negative implication, when the answer is intentionally given in place of the responsive answer called for by a proper question, is perjury." In this Court, petitioner renews his attack on the specificity of the question asked him and the legal sufficiency of his answer to support a conviction for perjury. The problem of the ambiguity of the question is not free from doubt, but we need not reach that issue. Even assuming, as we do, that the question asked petitioner specifically focused on petitioner's personal bank accounts, we conclude that the federal perjury statute cannot be construed to sustain a conviction based on petitioner's answer.

The statute, 18 U.S.C. § 1621, substantially identical in its relevant language to its predecessors for nearly a century, is "a federal statute enacted in an effort to keep the course of justice free from the pollution of perjury." *United States v. Williams*, 341 U.S. 58, 68 (1951). We have held that the general federal perjury provision is applicable to federal bankruptcy proceedings. The need for truthful testimony in a bankruptcy proceeding is great, since the proceeding is "a searching inquiry into the condition of the estate of the bankrupt, to assist in discovering and collecting the assets, and to develop facts and circumstances which bear upon the question of discharge." *Travis v. United States*, 123 F.2d 268, 271 (10th Cir. 1941). Here, as elsewhere, the perpetration of perjury "well may affect the dearest concerns of the parties before a tribunal. . . ." *United States v. Norris*, 300 U.S. 564, 574 (1937).

There is, at the outset, a serious literal problem in applying § 1621 to petitioner's answer. The words of the statute confine the offense to the witness who "willfully . . . states . . . any material matter which he does not believe to be true." Beyond question, petitioner's answer to the crucial question was not responsive if we assume,

---

The illustration given by the District Court is hardly comparable to petitioner's answer; the answer "five times" is responsive to the hypothetical question and contains nothing to alert the questioner that he may be sidetracked. Moreover, it is very doubtful that an answer which, in response to a specific quantitative inquiry, baldly understates a numerical fact can be described as even "technically true." Whether an answer is true must be determined with reference to the question it purports to answer, not in isolation. An unresponsive answer is unique in this respect because its unresponsiveness by definition prevents its truthfulness from being tested in the context of the question — unless there is to be speculation as to what the unresponsive answer "implies."

as we do, that the first question was directed at personal bank accounts. There is, indeed, an implication in the answer to the second question that there was never a personal bank account; in casual conversation this interpretation might reasonably be drawn. But we are not dealing with casual conversation and the statute does not make it a criminal act for a witness to willfully state any material matter that *implies* any material matter that he does not believe to be true.[4]

The government urges that the perjury statute be construed broadly to reach petitioner's answer and thereby fulfill its historic purpose of reinforcing our adversary factfinding process. We might go beyond the precise words of the statute if we thought they did not adequately express the intention of Congress, but we perceive no reason why Congress would intend the drastic sanction of a perjury prosecution to cure a testimonial mishap that could readily have been reached with a single additional question by counsel alert — as every examiner ought to be — to the incongruity of petitioner's unresponsive answer. Under the pressures and tensions of interrogation, it is not uncommon for the most earnest witnesses to give answers that are not entirely responsive. Sometimes the witness does not understand the question, or may in an excess of caution or apprehension read too much or too little into it. It should come as no surprise that a participant in a bankruptcy proceeding may have something to conceal and consciously tries to do so, or that a debtor may be embarrassed at his plight and yield information reluctantly. It is the responsibility of the lawyer to probe; testimonial interrogation, and cross-examination in particular, is a probing, prying, pressing form of inquiry. If a witness evades, it is the lawyer's responsibility to recognize the evasion and to bring the witness back to the mark, to flush out the whole truth with the tools of adversary examination.

It is no answer to say that here the jury found that petitioner intended to mislead his examiner. A jury should not be permitted to engage in conjecture whether an unresponsive answer, true and complete on its face, was intended to mislead or divert the examiner; the state of mind of the witness is relevant only to the extent that it bears on whether "he does not believe (his answer) to be true." To hold otherwise would be to inject a new and confusing element into the adversary testimonial system we know. Witnesses would be unsure of the extent of their responsibility for the misunderstandings and inadequacies of examiners, and might well fear having that responsibility tested by a jury under the vague rubric of "intent to mislead" or "perjury by implication." The seminal modern treatment of the history of the offense concludes that one consideration of policy overshadowed all others during the years when perjury first emerged as a common-law offense: "that the measures

---

4. Petitioner's answer is not to be measured by the same standards applicable to criminally fraudulent or extortionate statements. In that context, the law goes "rather far in punishing intentional creation of false impressions by a selection of literally true representations, because the actor himself generally selects and arranges the representations." In contrast, "under our system of adversary questioning and cross-examination the scope of disclosure is largely in the hands of counsel and presiding officer." A.L.I. Model Penal Code § 208.20, Comment (Tent. Draft No. 6, 1957, p. 124).

taken against the offense must not be so severe as to discourage witnesses from appearing or testifying." Study of Perjury, reprinted in Report of New York Law Revision Commission, Legis. Doc. No. 60, p. 249 (1935). . . .

Thus, we must read § 1621 in light of our own and the traditional Anglo-American judgment that a prosecution for perjury is not the sole, or even the primary, safeguard against errant testimony. . . . The cases support petitioner's position that the perjury statute is not to be loosely construed, nor the statute invoked simply because a wily witness succeeds in derailing the questioner — so long as the witness speaks the literal truth. The burden is on the questioner to pin the witness down to the specific object to the questioner's inquiry.

The government does not contend that any misleading or incomplete response must be sent to the jury to determine whether a witness committed perjury because he intended to sidetrack his questioner. As the government recognizes, the effect of so unlimited an interpretation of § 1621 would be broadly unsettling. It is said, rather, that petitioner's testimony falls within a more limited category of intentionally misleading responses with an especially strong tendency to mislead the questioner. Thus the government isolates two factors which are said to require application of the perjury statute in the circumstances of this case; the unresponsiveness of petitioner's answer and the affirmative cast of that answer, with its accompanying negative implication.

This analysis succeeds in confining the government's position, but it does not persuade us that Congress intended to extend the coverage of § 1621 to answers unresponsive on their face but untrue only by "negative implication." Though perhaps a plausible argument can be made that unresponsive answers are especially likely to mislead,[5] any such argument must, we think, be predicated upon the questioner's being aware of the unresponsiveness of the relevant answer. Yet, if the questioner is aware of the unresponsiveness of the answer, with equal force it can be argued that the very unresponsiveness of the answer should alert counsel to press on for the information he desires. It does not matter that the unresponsive answer is stated in the affirmative, thereby implying the negative of the question actually posed; for again, by hypothesis, the examiner's awareness of unresponsiveness should lead him to press another question or reframe his initial question with greater precision. Precise questioning is imperative as a predicate for the offense of perjury.

It may well be that petitioner's answers were not guileless but were shrewdly calculated to evade. Nevertheless, we are constrained to agree that any special problems

---

5. Arguably, the questioner will assume there is some logical justification for the unresponsive answer, since competent witnesses do not usually answer in irrelevancies. Thus the questioner may conclude that the unresponsive answer is given only because it is intended to make a statement — a negative statement — relevant to the question asked. In this case, petitioner's questioner may have assumed that petitioner denied having a personal account in Switzerland; only this unspoken denial would provide a logical nexus between inquiry directed to petitioner's personal account and petitioner's adverting, in response, to the company account in Zurich.

arising from the literally true but unresponsive answer are to be remedied through the "questioner's acuity" and not by a federal perjury prosecution.

Reversed.

Notes and Questions

1. *A prescription for evasion?*

a. The jury in *Bronston* presumably found beyond a reasonable doubt that Bronston intended that his testimony produce a false impression. Would it not serve the purposes of the perjury statute to sustain a conviction in such a circumstance? Does the result in *Bronston* actually encourage witnesses to provide evasive and misleading answers?

The Court was concerned that allowing literally true answers to suffice would result in an overly broad application of the statute. The government responded by proposing a rule limiting convictions based upon literally true answers to the "category of intentionally misleading responses with an especially strong tendency to mislead the questioner." Is this a sufficient response to the Court's concerns? Why or why not?

b. As seen elsewhere in this text, and as the Court acknowledged, a literally true but misleading statement may well be sufficient for a fraud charge. Is perjury so different from fraud as to warrant the result in *Bronston*? Why or why not?

2. *Perjury as a disfavored crime.*

a. Perjury cases are often considered difficult to prove. *See* Robert G. Morvillo & Christopher J. Morvillo, *Untangling the Web: Defending a Perjury Case*, 33 LITIGATION 8 (2007) (noting "[t]he lack of perjury prosecutions is due . . . to the fact that perjury statutes are deliberately (and notoriously) difficult to enforce"). Why should that be so? When enacting § 1623, Congress attempted to overcome this perceived difficulty by: (i) allowing convictions based upon inconsistent declarations and (ii) abolishing the common law "two-witness" rule (discussed in the section below).

b. The Court cited one study for the proposition that "the measures taken against the offense must not be so severe as to discourage witnesses from appearing or testifying." What did the Court mean when it said this? Why did the Court emphasize the risks from perjury charges?

3. *Literal truth and the Clinton case.*

a. *Numerical answers.* Is it always clear when a numerical answer is "literally true"? Revisit footnote 3 in the *Bronston* opinion. If you entered a store 50 times in a day, is it literally true to say that you entered five times that day? Would such an answer obviously be false? In his sworn deposition in the Paula Jones case, the questioner asked then-President Bill Clinton, "[h]as Monica Lewinsky ever given you any gifts?" His answer: "[O]nce or twice. I think she's given me a book or two." In fact, Lewinsky stated, she gave Clinton as many as 38 gifts. Was Clinton's answer literally true? *See* Stuart P. Green, *Perjury*, in Lying, Cheating, and Stealing: A Moral Theory of White Collar Crime 145–146 (2006).

b. *Responsive but misleading answers.* Bronston was asked, "Have you ever [had any Swiss bank accounts]?" The logical reading of the question was that the "you" referred to Bronston personally. Therefore, Bronston's answer, "The Company had an account there for about six months, in Zurich," was nonresponsive. The questioner could easily have realized that the answer was nonresponsive, and could have followed up, "OK, did you *personally* ever have any bank accounts in Swiss banks?"

In the Clinton investigation, Clinton was asked, "[H]ave you ever had sexual relations with Monica Lewinsky, as that term is defined in Deposition Exhibit 1, as modified by the court?" He responded, "I have never had sexual relations with Monica Lewinsky." Exhibit 1 stated that "a person engages in 'sexual relations' when the person knowingly engages or causes contact with the genitalia, anus, groin, breast, inner thigh, or buttocks of any person with an intent to arouse or gratify the sexual desire of any person." Assuming that the contact was limited to Lewinsky performing oral sex on Clinton, was Clinton's answer literally true? *See id.* at 142–44.

4. *Ambiguous questions and qualified answers.* The Court in *Bronston* did not reach the issue whether a perjury conviction can be sustained when the question is ambiguous. Was there an ambiguous question in *Bronston*? If a question is genuinely ambiguous, does the issue of a literally truthful answer arise?

Bronston was charged with perjury based upon an answer that was literally true. Take instead the circumstance in which an answer is subject to two different interpretations, one of which is false. Could such an answer provide the basis for a perjury conviction?

The answers to these questions tend to be very case- and fact-specific. For example, in *United States v. Long*, 534 F.2d 1097 (3d Cir. 1976), the district court dismissed perjury charges, finding that the terms used in the questions — including "bribe," "kickback," and "payoff" — were legal terms that would be ambiguous to a layperson. The court of appeals reversed and reinstated the charges. Finding that the terms used were not technical legal terms, the court concluded that "we may not dismiss a charge of perjury when it is entirely reasonable to expect a defendant to have understood the terms used in the questions." *Id.* at 1101. Therefore, even if a question is confusing or ambiguous, the jury must ultimately determine whether the defendant understood the intended meaning of the question. Nevertheless, courts have held that "when a line of questioning is so vague as to be fundamentally ambiguous, the answers associated with the questions posed may be insufficient as a matter of law to support a perjury conviction." *United States v. Brown*, 843 F.3d 738, 743 (2d Cir. 2016). To be fundamentally ambiguous, the question (or answer) "must lack a meaning about which men of ordinary intellect could agree, nor one which could be used with mutual understanding by a questioner and answerer unless it were defined at the time it were sought and offered as testimony." *United States v. Strohm*, 671 F.3d

1173, 1179 (10th Cir. 2011). However, "to precisely define the point at which a question becomes fundamentally ambiguous [may be] impossible." *Id.* at 1179–80.

Baseball star Barry Bonds testified before a federal grand jury in connection with an investigation into the illegal use of anabolic steroids in major league baseball. He was charged with perjury based upon the following testimony:

Q: And you weren't getting this flax seed oil stuff during that period of time [January 2002]?

A: Not that I can recall. Like I say, I could be wrong. But I'm — I'm going from my recollection it was, like, in the 2002 time and 2003 season.

The trial court granted Bonds' motion to dismiss the perjury count. The court explained:

> Defendant raises several arguments in response to this count, all of which arise from the confusing wording of his answer. He argues that if the government proves that defendant received "flax seed oil stuff" in January 2002, he cannot be convicted on the basis of this statement because at least part of his answer (i.e. that he received the substance "in the 2002 time") was literally true. He also argues that defendant's other qualifiers — "Not that I can recall" and "like I say, I could be wrong" and "I'm going from my recollection" — render the entire passage fundamentally ambiguous.
>
> The government responds that if such qualifiers could create fatal ambiguity, then every defendant could avoid a perjury charge by qualifying all his answers. The problem here, however, is not that defendant may have attempted to mitigate the effect of his "Not that I recall" response by adding qualifiers. The problem is that defendant's answer is so unclear that it is essentially impossible to parse. When a witness in a grand jury investigation gives answers that are "not entirely responsive," or "evades, it is the lawyer's responsibility to recognize the evasion and to bring the witness back to the mark, to flush out the whole truth with the tools of adversary examination." When defendant's interrogator received this meandering, inconclusive and internally inconsistent response, "[t]he burden [was] on the questioner to pin the witness down." The remedy for such evasion, if indeed it was evasion, is "the questioner's acuity, and not [] a federal perjury prosecution." Defendant's motion to dismiss this count is GRANTED.

United States v. Bonds, 580 F. Supp. 2d. 925 (N.D. Cal. 2008), *aff'd*, 608 F.3d 495 (9th Cir. 2010). Usually, courts allow juries to determine whether ambiguous or qualified answers were perjurious. Why did the judge in this particular case dismiss the charge rather than letting the jury decide the question?

5. *Materiality.* As in a false statements prosecution, materiality is an element in a perjury case that must be submitted to the jury. *See United States v. Johnson*, 520 U.S. 461, 464 (1997). The courts of appeal vary in their precise wording of the test for materiality, but it is generally broadly interpreted. For example, some courts state

that, to be material, a statement must be capable of having an effect on the tribunal or proceeding. *See, e.g., United States v. Kantengwa*, 781 F.3d 545, 553–54 (1st Cir. 2015) (holding that a false statement is material for purposes of a perjury prosecution "if it is capable of influencing the tribunal on the issue before it"). And, as with false statements prosecutions, a false statement may be material under §§ 1621 and 1623 even if it does not in fact dupe the tribunal. *Id.* at 555. For a further discussion of the tests for materiality, see Richard H. Underwood, *Perjury! The Charges and the Defenses*, 36 Duq. L. Rev. 715, 727–732 (1998). Although defendants frequently raise the materiality defense, it is rarely successful.

6. *The perjury trap doctrine.* The perjury trap doctrine arises when a witness is called for the sole purpose of eliciting perjurious testimony. In this situation, it is argued that the tribunal has no valid purpose to which a perjurious statement could be considered material. Since the government is usually able to identify a valid reason for the grand jury inquiry, the perjury trap doctrine will not bar prosecution in most cases because the defense must show that that the false answer was illegally procured by the government. *United States v. Burke*, 425 F.3d 400, 408 (7th Cir. 2005) (noting the Seventh Circuit has "not embraced [the perjury trap] doctrine" in the past, "and do[es] not see any reason to adopt it now"); *United States v. Regan*, 103 F.3d 1072, 1079 (2d Cir. 1997) (noting "the existence of a legitimate basis for an investigation and for particular questions answered falsely precludes any application of the perjury trap doctrine"); *United States v. McKenna*, 327 F.3d 830, 837 (9th Cir. 2003) ("Here, the government did not use its investigatory powers to question McKenna before a grand jury. Rather, it merely questioned McKenna in its role as a defendant during the pendency of a civil action in which she was the plaintiff. The perjury trap doctrine is inapplicable to McKenna's case for this reason."). When would the perjury trap doctrine apply, if ever?

Problems

10-2. A robbery takes place at a restaurant on April 1. FBI investigators are convinced that Michael was at the restaurant on the night of the robbery. Michael is also convinced that he was at the restaurant on April 1. In fact, however, Michael was *not* at the restaurant on April 1; he was there on March 31 and he misremembers being there on April 1. The prosecutor calls Michael to testify at trial. The prosecutor asks Michael whether he was at the restaurant on April 1, the evening of the crime. Michael answers, "No — absolutely not." Michael thought he was lying when he said this, but he was accidentally telling the truth.[e]

Has Michael committed § 1621 perjury on these facts?

10-3. In April, a group of individuals, including defendant Zarn, met at Wells' home to discuss raising funds for Smith's gubernatorial campaign. The funds were to be collected at a Memorial Day Party being held at Wells' home. Invitations were sent

---

e. This problem is based upon a fact pattern shared by Prof. Ken Levy.

out, inviting guests to a "Memorial Day Party . . . for an evening of fun on the farm." Sixty guests attended and gubernatorial candidate Smith made a short speech. Zarn collected contributions to Smith's campaign at that event. After he was elected governor, Smith appointed Zarn and other contributors to various government positions, allegedly based upon an agreement made at the time the contributions were given.

Later that summer, Wells held a Labor Day dinner that Zarn also attended. This was a small dinner party, attended only by six people. Governor Smith neither attended nor was invited to that party.

Zarn was subpoenaed to appear before a grand jury investigating bribery in connection with the Smith campaign. Under oath, the prosecutor asked Zarn approximately 60 questions about the Memorial Day Party, but had not questioned Zarn about the Labor Day dinner. Towards the end of his testimony, Zarn stated as follows:

Q: Okay, sir. My question is going to deal with Mr. Wells. Did you attend the Memorial Day Party at issue here?

A: Yes.

Q: How many people were present?

A: About 60 people.

Q: Okay. Sir, was that Labor Day Party a political fundraising activity?

A: *Absolutely not.*

Q: All right, sir. You said it was not a political fundraising activity. Were there any contributions to Governor Smith's campaign made at that party?

A: *I don't know.*

Q: Okay. You did not see any, though?

A: *No.*

Q: And you were not aware of any?

A: *No.*

No questions other than that set forth above referred to the "Labor Day Party." A number of witnesses testified that Zarn attended the Memorial Day Party and actively solicited funds for Smith's campaign during the party. Zarn was later indicted for perjury under § 1621 based upon the italicized answers above.

Assume that Zarn has moved to dismiss the indictment. What are his likely arguments? What are the likely government responses? What is the likely outcome? Why?

10-4. In Mary Mann's criminal case, the defense called Fred Farder as a witness at a pretrial hearing. Cross-examining Farder at the hearing, the prosecutor asked, "Have you talked to Ms. Mann about your testimony here today?" Farder responded, "No." The government charged Farder with perjury under § 1623 based upon this answer.

In order to prove falsity of Farder's answer, the government introduced at Farder's trial a statement that Farder made and signed on the day of his arraignment. The relevant portion of the statement read: "Mary Mann did call me before I got the subpoena to appear at the pretrial hearing. She called me and she was telling me about her arrest. She told me that she could not have sold drugs to a confidential informant because she was at my house the day of the drug sale, but she kept asking me to pinpoint a date. Just before she hung up the phone she told me that I was going to get a subpoena. Mary never told me to lie for her, but she did want me to mention a date she was at my house, but I couldn't remember the date she was there."

Farder was convicted and appeals, arguing that the prosecutor's question was ambiguous. How should the court rule? Why?

10-5. During his Senate confirmation hearings for the position of Attorney General, then-Senator Jeff Sessions was asked about Trump campaign communications with the Russian government. Sessions responded that he "did not have communications with the Russians." He also followed up with written responses answering "no" to a question that asked whether he had "been in contact with anyone connected to any part of the Russian government about the 2016 election, either before or after election day." It turns out, however, that Sessions had met with Russian Ambassador Sergey Kislyak during the Republican National Convention in July 2016 and in his Senate office in September 2016. It also came to light in the Mueller Report that the Russian Ambassador mentioned the presidential campaign to Sessions "on at least one [of these two] occasion[s]." According to the Mueller Report, after these communications surfaced in the media, Sessions later explained to the Senate and the Office of Special Counsel that that "he understood the question as narrowly calling for disclosure of interactions with Russians that involved the exchange of campaign information, as distinguished from more routine contacts with Russian nationals."

Based on these facts, the Office of Special Counsel investigated Sessions for perjury. Should he have been charged? Why or why not?

D. The Two-Witness Rule

In perjury cases, courts have historically required that the government's case rely upon two witnesses or, more accurately, upon one witness plus corroborating evidence. Although Congress removed this burden in prosecutions under § 1623, the government still must satisfy the rule in § 1621 cases.

Courts generally find that the two-witness rule is necessary for two reasons. First, the requirement encourages a witness to testify without the fear of later being charged with perjury simply because the witness has contradicted another witness. Second, the rule prevents prosecutions based solely on a "swearing contest" between two witnesses. Are those purposes served in the following case?

United States v. Chestman

903 F.2d 75 (2d Cir. 1990), *rev'd in part on other grounds,*
947 F.2d 551 (2d Cir. 1991) (en banc)

MINER, CIRCUIT JUDGE:

[The Securities and Exchange Commission ("SEC") investigated whether Chestman, a stock broker, had committed insider trading in the stock of Waldbaum, Inc. The SEC believed that Chestman had obtained the inside information from Keith Loeb. In an SEC deposition, Chestman testified that he did not speak with Loeb prior to purchasing Waldbaum stock at 10:30 a.m. on November 26. Based upon this testimony, Chestman was charged with perjury under § 1621.]

[Loeb, the government's sole witness on the perjury charge, testified that he gave Chestman inside information concerning an impending tender offer for Waldbaum, and that this conversation occurred before 10:30 a.m. on November 26, when Chestman purchased the securities. As additional evidence, the government offered (1) an 8:50 a.m. phone message indicating that Loeb had called Chestman prior to the trading, (2) Chestman's failure to record the trade in his personal blotter notes on the day of the trade, and (3) the timing of the trade. The jury convicted Chestman of perjury under § 1621, and he appealed.]

The undisputed "rule in prosecutions for perjury is that the uncorroborated oath of one witness is not enough to establish the falsity of the testimony of the accused set forth in the indictment...." *Hammer v. United States*, 271 U.S. 620, 626 (1926). The "two-witness" rule requires that the alleged perjurious statement be established either by the testimony of two independent witnesses or by one witness and corroborating evidence that is "inconsistent with the innocence of the [defendant]." *United States v. Weiner*, 479 F.2d 923, 926 (2d Cir. 1973). ...

Loeb's testimony that he spoke to Chestman prior to [Chestman's trade at] 10:30 a.m. would be sufficient, if supported by corroborative evidence, to sustain a perjury conviction. We therefore examine the sufficiency of the corroborative evidence proffered by the government in support of Loeb's testimony.

In assessing the sufficiency of the corroborative evidence, two elements are considered: "(1) that the evidence, if true, substantiates the testimony of a single witness who has sworn to the falsity of the alleged perjurious statement; (2) that the corroborative evidence is trustworthy." *Weiler v. United States*, 323 U.S. 606, 610 (1945). While the independent evidence must be inconsistent with the innocence of the accused, it need only "tend to substantiate that part of the testimony of the principal prosecution witness which is material in showing" the accused's statement is false. *Weiner*, 479 F.2d at 927–28.

The corroborative evidence relied on by the government is wholly insufficient to satisfy the two-witness rule. For instance, the phone message at 8:58 a.m. merely establishes that Loeb attempted to contact Chestman and that Chestman was not in his office. Thus, it is equally supportive of Chestman's contention that he did not speak to Loeb on the morning of November 26. It does not establish that Chestman returned Loeb's call prior to 10:30 a.m. Chestman's position is buttressed further by the testimony of his administrative assistant. She testified that Loeb called between 9 and 10 a.m. and then again in the late morning or early afternoon. She noted that as of the time of the second phone call Loeb had not yet spoken to Chestman. The theory put forth by the government that stockbrokers always return calls by virtue of the nature of their business requires a presumption we do not care to adopt in the context of a perjury charge.

While the government also highlights the fact that Chestman's blotter notes omitted reference to the Loeb trade, we are unconvinced that this provides adequate proof that Chestman spoke to Loeb prior to execution of the trades. These notations were made solely for Chestman's personal use. As an experienced stockbroker, he certainly realized that the Loeb trade could not be concealed because it would be memorialized by the order and subsequent confirmation slip. Under these circumstances, the blotter omissions cannot serve as corroboration.

The government also would have this Court rely on the propitious timing of the trade as sufficient support for Loeb's testimony. Sole reliance on the timing of the trade would nullify the purpose of the two-witness rule. We recognize that the circumstances surrounding an alleged perjurious statement may constitute better corroborative evidence than oral testimony. When a jury relies on circumstantial evidence, however, it must be demonstrated that this evidence has "independent probative value" if "standing alone." *United States v. Freedman*, 445 F.2d 1220, 1226 (2d Cir. 1971). The timing of the trade here does not meet the standard. The fact that Chestman bought Waldbaum stock prior to the announcement of the tender offer is consistent with Chestman's position that he researched the company, assumed it was a takeover target, and invested accordingly. Standing alone, the timing of the trade does not have sufficient independent probative value to support the Loeb testimony at odds with that position.

After careful review, we find the evidence insufficient to sustain the conviction. Accordingly, we reverse Chestman's conviction for perjury.

Notes and Questions

1. *Sufficiency of the evidence.* A defendant bears a heavy burden when arguing that a conviction should be overturned because of insufficient evidence. In such a circumstance, the appellate court must draw all factual inferences in favor of the government. Was the court correct in concluding that the inferences from the corroborative evidence were insufficient, as a matter of law, to sustain Chestman's conviction?

2. *The two-witness rule.* Are there dangers from allowing a perjury conviction based upon a single witness' testimony? What would be the dangers, if any, of allowing Chestman's conviction to stand based solely on Loeb's testimony?

3. *What counts as corroboration?* The two-witness rule was implicated in the criminal case against Martha Stewart's co-defendant, her broker, Peter Bacanovic. (This

case is discussed in Chapter 5, Securities Fraud, *supra*, at §5, C.) Bacanovic was charged with perjury based on testimony he gave before the SEC during its investigation into the trading of ImClone stock. During his testimony, Bacanovic recalled leaving a phone message for Stewart with Stewart's assistant, but denied remembering telling the assistant that the price of ImClone stock was falling. The government alleged that his denial of recollection was a false statement. The government's proof of falsity was (1) the assistant's testimony, and (2) an electronic message that the assistant wrote for Stewart stating that "Peter Bacanovic thinks ImClone is going to start trading downward." On appeal, Bacanovic argued that corroborating evidence consisting solely of a document created by the only witness did not satisfy the two-witness rule. The Second Circuit rejected the argument and affirmed the perjury conviction. *United States v. Stewart*, 433 F.3d 273, 315–17 (2d Cir. 2006). How do you explain this result?

Problems

10-6. Chapman filed for bankruptcy. As part of the bankruptcy proceeding, Chapman gave deposition testimony under oath to determine the extent of the bankruptcy estate's assets. During the deposition, the following exchange took place:

Q: "Did you give Moss $80,000 in currency on October 23 last year?"

A: "I don't recall doing that, no."

Based upon this answer, the government charged Chapman with perjury under § 1621. At Chapman's trial, the government called Moss to testify in the trial. Moss testified as follows:

Q: "Did Chapman give you $80,000 on October 23 last year?"

A: "Yes. Chapman asked me to purchase some real estate to put in Chapman's name. He gave me the money probably about October of last year."

As corroborating evidence, the government introduced Moss's banking records. The records showed that that Moss deposited $80,000 into his bank account on October 23 last year.

At the end of the government's case, Chapman filed a motion to dismiss the perjury charge. How should the court rule? Why?

10-7. In a deposition in a divorce proceeding, Fred Farmer testified concerning the assets that he held with his wife Maria. Fred testified as follows:

Q: "Did you call Ralph on Monday morning, June 19, and tell him that you had a large screen television that you wanted to sell?"

A: "No, sir, I did not. I mean, I might have called him that morning, but I have not called him about any television."

Fred was charged with perjury under § 1621 based upon the above answer. At Fred's trial, Ralph testified as follows:

Q: "Did you have a telephone conversation with Fred on June 19?"

A: "Well, Maria called, then I called back three times that day and each time spoke with Fred."

Q: "What was discussed in those telephone conversations?"

A: "I told Fred that I would buy the TV and give him cash."

The government next called two neighbors of Fred and Maria. They both testified that on June 20, they had helped Fred load a large screen television onto Fred's pickup truck and drove with Fred to Ralph's house, where they unloaded the TV and saw Ralph give Fred a large quantity of cash.

Is the two-witness rule met on these facts? Why or why not?

10-8 Roger Clemens, a legendary Major League Baseball (MLB) pitcher, was invited to testify before a congressional committee about his alleged use of performance-enhancing drugs ("PEDs") during his professional pitching career. The committee possessed the authority to investigate the use and distribution of PEDs and other controlled substances in professional baseball and elsewhere. Clemens appeared before the committee and offered the following testimony, under oath:

(1) "[Strength Coach #1] has never given me growth hormone or steroids."

(2) "And again, this man [Strength Coach #1] has never given me HGH or growth hormone or steroids of any kind . . ."

(3) "Let me be clear. I have never taken steroids or HGH."

The government alleged that Clemens knew these statements were false when he made them and charged him with perjury under §1621. At trial, the government introduced testimony from Strength Coach #1 that he had in fact injected Clemens with the above-referenced PEDs in 1998, 2000, and 2001. The government also introduced into evidence a needle and other materials Strength Coach #1 testified he had used to inject Clemens with the PEDs. These materials had traces of Clemens' DNA and PEDs on them. In addition to this evidence, prosecutors offered the testimony of another MLB pitcher, Andy Pettitte, who testified to overhearing a conversation in which Clemens admitted to using HGH. The government also offered testimony from a convicted drug dealer that he sent HGH to Clemens' home (under Strength Coach #1's name), but he admitted he did not know whether the drugs were used on Clemens himself. Finally, Clemens' wife admitted to receiving an HGH shot from Strength Coach #1.

Clemens' lawyers argued that the physical evidence was "garbage" and claimed that Strength Coach #1 had tampered with it. Moreover, Pettitte admitted on cross-examination that there was a "50-50" chance he misheard Clemens's conversation.

Is the two-witness rule satisfied on these facts? Why or why not?

10-9. A state trooper pulled over Joe's and Jenny's small truck for speeding. When the trooper walked up to the truck, Joe (who weighs 310 pounds) was in the driver's seat and Jenny was in the passenger's seat. The trooper smelled alcohol on Joe's breath and asked that he perform a field sobriety test, which he failed. At trial, Jenny testified that she, not Joe, had been driving the truck. She claimed that they switched seats after they were pulled over because the tags had expired on the truck, and Joe didn't want Jenny to get in trouble. The trooper testified that he had observed Joe driving the truck as it sped past his vehicle and that he did not notice any movement in the truck as he walked up to it. Joe was convicted of driving under the influence, and Jenny was then charged with perjury. At Jenny's perjury trial, the only evidence introduced by the government was: (1) the state trooper's testimony that he saw Joe driving the truck and noticed no movement in the truck after the stop; (2) a video from the trooper's dashboard camera that shows significant movement in the truck when Joe got out of it, but no identifiable movement in the truck before that time; (3) a transcript of Jenny's trial testimony in Joe's trial.

Assume this state's perjury law tracks § 1621. Is the two-witness rule satisfied on these facts? Why or why not?

E. The Recantation Defense

As noted above, perjury prosecutions are easier under § 1623 than under § 1621 because of § 1623's inconsistent declarations provision and because § 1623 abolishes the two-witness rule. On the other hand, § 1623 alone provides a "recantation" defense if the witness takes back, or "recants," the allegedly false testimony. Recantation, however, is rarely a successful defense; as the court notes in the decision that follows, the broad reading of the recantation defense that the court adopts is clearly the minority rule. As you read the case, consider why the majority of courts have read the defense narrowly.

United States v. Smith
35 F.3d 344 (8th Cir. 1994)

BOWMAN, CIRCUIT JUDGE.

Sherry Lynn Smith timely appeals her conviction following her conditional guilty plea to one count of perjury. We vacate and remand for further proceedings.

On May 18, 1993, a grand jury indicted Smith, charging her with three offenses: conspiracy to structure a cash transaction in violation of 18 U.S.C. § 371; structuring a cash transaction with a trade or business in violation of 26 U.S.C. § 6050I(f)(1)(C) and 18 U.S.C. § 2; and perjury in violation of 18 U.S.C. § 1623(a). In exchange for her conditional guilty plea to the perjury charge, the other charges were dismissed.

The perjury charge arose out of Smith's testimony before a grand jury investigating several individuals, including Smith's boyfriend Craig Keltner, and their involvement in a series of crimes including car theft, kidnaping, mail fraud, burglaries, robberies, and money laundering. The grand jury questioned Smith about the source of funds with which Keltner had purchased a Chevrolet Corvette. Keltner first attempted to make the purchase from a dealership with $12,200 in cash. When the dealership informed him that it would have to file a report with the Internal Revenue Service on any cash transaction in excess of $10,000, Keltner arranged to pay with $9,800 in cash and $2,400 in the form of a check from Smith. The dealership held the $12,200 until Keltner returned with Smith's check, then the dealership returned $2,400 in cash to Keltner. Smith deposited $2,400 in cash into her bank account the same day.

Before the grand jury, Smith initially testified that she had invested $3,000 from her savings toward the purchase of the car. She denied that the $2,400 deposited into her bank account after the purchase came from Keltner. After a thirty-eight-minute break in the proceeding, during which Smith reviewed her bank records, she resumed her testimony and recanted her previous statements. Smith admitted that the $2,400 belonged to Keltner and was given to her to deposit as part of the transaction to purchase the Corvette.

Prior to her conditional guilty plea to the perjury charge, Smith moved for dismissal of that charge on the ground that 18 U.S.C. § 1623(d) bars prosecution for perjury on the facts of her case. The District Court disagreed with Smith's interpretation of the statute and denied her motion. Her conditional plea preserved the issue for appellate review, and she now asks this court to address it.

We review questions of statutory interpretation de novo. Our analysis begins with the statutory language. Section 1623(d) states:

> Where, in the same continuous court or grand jury proceeding in which a declaration is made, the person making the declaration admits such declaration to be false, such admission shall bar prosecution under this section if, at the time the admission is made, the declaration has not substantially affected the proceeding, or it has not become manifest that such falsity has been or will be exposed.

18 U.S.C. § 1623(d).

The District Court denied Smith's motion on the ground that § 1623(d) "bars prosecution only if the false statement has not substantially affected the proceeding and if it has not become manifest that the falsity has been or will be exposed." The District Court construed the two conditions as conjunctive, reading "or" to mean "and," and found that Smith did not satisfy the latter condition. Smith contends that the two conditions are disjunctive and thus satisfaction of either bars her prosecution for perjury.

In interpreting § 1623(d), we adhere to the general principle that "when the plain language of a statute is clear in its context, it is controlling." The plain language of the statute indicates that after recantation, a perjury charge is barred if (1) the proceeding has not been substantially affected by the false testimony, or (2) it has not become manifest that the false nature of the testimony has been or will be exposed. Because the wording of § 1623(d) "is plain, simple, and straightforward, the words must be accorded their normal meanings." *United States v. Jones*, 811 F.2d 444, 447

(8th Cir.1987). The ordinary usage of the word "or" is disjunctive, indicating an alternative. Construing the word "or" to mean "and" is conjunctive, and is clearly in contravention of its ordinary usage. Thus, we find the plain language of § 1623(d) controlling and accord the word "or" its ordinary, disjunctive meaning.

According the word "or" its ordinary meaning does not defeat the intent of Congress in enacting the statute and creating the § 1623(d) recantation defense. In *United States v. Del Toro*, the Second Circuit looked to the legislative history and found that the purpose of the statute "was obviously to induce the witness to give truthful testimony by permitting him voluntarily to correct a false statement without incurring the risk of prosecution for doing so." 513 F.2d 656, 665 (2d Cir.1975). "Section 1623(d) balances the need to encourage a witness to correct [false] testimony against the need to prevent perjury at the outset." *United States v. Denison*, 663 F.2d 611, 617 (5th Cir.1981). To meet the congressional goal of encouraging truthful testimony, we need only apply the plain language of the statute in its ordinary usage. Reading the two conditions in the alternative, as the word "or" demands, the statute creates an incentive for witnesses to correct false testimony early in the proceeding. Arguably, construing the word "or" to mean "and" creates a statutory scheme providing a stronger incentive for witnesses to testify truthfully at the outset; however, we defer to Congress's chosen scheme as manifested by its language which balances encouragement of truthful testimony and penalties for perjury.

Additionally, because § 1623(d) is a penal statute, we must apply the rule of lenity. We conclude that to read "or" as "and" in the context of § 1623(d) would "contravene [the Supreme] Court's long-established practice of resolving questions concerning the ambit of a criminal statute in favor of lenity." *Dunn v. United States*, 442 U.S. 100, 112 (1979). Thus, we accord the word "or" its ordinary meaning, reading the statute as setting forth two alternative conditions, satisfaction of either of which will allow a declarant to employ the recantation defense to bar prosecution for perjury.

We recognize that the District Court followed existing authority in construing § 1623(d) against its plain meaning. Each of the other circuits addressing the language of § 1623(d) has construed "or" to mean "and."

Explaining its rationale for this construction, the District of Columbia Circuit stated in *Moore* that "Congress did not countenance in § 1623(d) the flagrant injustice that would result if a witness is permitted to lie to a judicial tribunal and then, upon only learning that he had been discovered, grudgingly to recant in order to bar prosecution." *United States v. Moore*, 613 F.2d 1029, 1043 (D.C. Cir.1979). The court also discussed the legislative history of § 1623(d), noting that it was modeled after the New York recantation defense statute. The New York statute is similar but employs "and" rather than "or," clearly making the two conditions conjunctive. *Id.* at 1042.

While this observation may raise some uncertainty about the language Congress intended to enact, it does not create an ambiguity in an otherwise plainly worded statute nor does it militate against according the enacted language its ordinary meaning. "[I]t is appropriate to assume that the ordinary meaning of [the statutory language] accurately expresses the legislative purpose." *Jones*, 811 F.2d at 447. In this case, where the statute is unambiguous on its face, the language of the statute is conclusive as to legislative intent, and we thus decline to abandon the ordinary disjunctive meaning accorded to "or" in favor of a conjunctive "and," as such a construction would defeat the plain language of the statute and would not foster any clearly articulated legislative intent to the contrary. . . .

In order to employ § 1623(d) to claim protection from prosecution for perjury, a party is not required to recant before it has become manifest that the falsehoods have been or will be exposed; rather, this is but one of two circumstances in which the defense applies. The declarant may also use the defense if she explicitly recants before the false testimony has substantially affected the proceeding.

On remand, Smith may defeat the perjury charge if she can show that she satisfies either of § 1623(d)'s conditions. As to the condition that she recant before her false testimony has substantially affected the proceedings, the District Court did not address the issue at length, but appears to have found that her false statements may not have affected the proceedings. It is not clear to us that the District Court intended to make a definitive finding on this point, and we do not think the court should be precluded from revisiting this issue on remand.

We turn now to the alternative statutory condition, that the declarant recant before it becomes manifest that the falsity of her statement has been or will be exposed, because the District Court relied upon Smith's failure to fulfill this condition in denying her motion to dismiss.

We believe the District Court misapplied the "manifest" test. The court reasoned that because the government had the bank records with which to confront Smith, the falsity of her statements was manifest to the government before she recanted, and the court stopped its analysis at that point. The proper test to apply, however, when determining whether recantation occurred before imminent exposure was manifest, is whether the fact that the statements have been or will be exposed as false is objectively manifest to the declarant. On remand, if the District Court reaches consideration of this condition, it must determine whether it had become objectively manifest to Smith, before she recanted, that the falsity of her statements had been or would be exposed.

For the reasons stated, we hold that the District Court erred in its interpretation of 18 U.S.C. § 1623(d). The judgment of the District Court is vacated and the case is remanded for further consideration of Smith's § 1623(d) recantation defense in a manner consistent with this opinion.

Notes and Questions

1. *The majority rule.* As the court in *Smith* noted, its holding is the minority position; all the other circuits that have considered the issue have interpreted "or" to mean "and." Why precisely did the court in *Moore*, discussed in *Smith*, read "or" to mean "and"? Why did the court in *Smith* reject *Moore*'s reasoning? How do the incentives

differ for a witness under a conjunction and a disjunctive reading? See *United States v. Fornaro*, 894 F.2d 508 (2d Cir. 1990), for an extended discussion of this issue.

2. *When is a proceeding "substantially affected"?* In what circumstances has a proceeding been "substantially affected"? Courts have not established clear standards for this element of the defense. Was it likely that the proceeding had been substantially affected in *Smith*? Why or why not?

3. *When has the falsity become manifest?* Had the falsity become manifest at the time Smith attempted to recant? Why or why not? Do you need additional facts to answer this question?

4. *What constitutes a "recantation"?* Courts have held that, for a change in testimony to constitute a recantation, the defendant must unequivocally retract the earlier testimony. A mere attempt to explain earlier testimony, or to later claim faulty memory, will not constitute recantation. *See, e.g., United States v. Wiggan*, 700 F.3d 1204, 1216 (9th Cir. 2012) ("Recantation requires a defendant to renounce and withdraw the prior statement. And the defendant must unequivocally repudiate his prior testimony to satisfy § 1623(d). It is not enough if the defendant merely attempted to explain his inconsistent statements, but never really admitted to the facts in question"); *United States v. D'Auria*, 672 F.2d 1085, 1085 (2d Cir. 1982) (finding an attempt to recant ineffective where defendant offered to "clarify" his testimony, but did not use the word "recant" and did not admit that his previous testimony was false).

5. *Procedural rules.* Courts agree that, if the defendant fails to raise the recantation defense prior to trial, the defense is waived. Courts are split, however, as to whether the government or the defense has the burden of proof once the issue is raised.

6. *Prosecutorial discretion.* A witness who makes a contemporaneous correction of a false statement may demonstrate the absence of the necessary willful intent to commit perjury. *See, e.g., United States v. McAfee*, 8 F.3d 1010, 1017 (5th Cir. 1993) (noting that "[r]ecantation may have a bearing on whether an accused perjurer intended to commit the crime"). Generally, however, the crime is completed when the false statement is presented to the tribunal. Should an immediate correction lead a prosecutor to exercise discretion and not file a perjury charge? Why or why not?

As noted above, perjury during a court or grand jury proceeding may be prosecuted under either § 1621 or § 1623. Because § 1623 is specifically directed to such proceedings, and because the required proof under that section is less burdensome than under § 1621, prosecutors will generally use § 1623 when the testimony was given before a court or grand jury. But what if the defendant has a recantation defense? May the government then choose to use § 1621, which does not recognize the defense? The issue was raised, but not decided, in *United States v. Kahn*, 472 F.2d 272 (2d Cir. 1973). In that case, the Second Circuit commented, "we find not a little disturbing the prospect of the government employing § 1621 whenever a recantation exists, and § 1623 when one does not, simply to place perjury defendants in the most disadvantageous trial position." *Id.* at 283.

F. Ethical Considerations

Perjury often raises competing ethical concerns. What if a client has committed or is about to commit perjury? The Preamble to the American Bar Association's Model Rules of Professional Conduct affirms the basic principle that it is the "lawyer's obligation zealously to protect and pursue a client's legitimate interests, within the bounds of the law. . . ." Rule 1.6(a) generally provides that "[a] lawyer shall not reveal information relating to the representation of a client unless the client gives informed consent. . . ." This requirement is subject to exceptions, as the following rule demonstrates. How do the attorney's obligations to the client square with the attorney's obligations under Rule 3.3? When a prosecutor advises a witness of the penalties for perjury, should the prosecutor also advise the witness of the possibility of recanting under § 1623(d)?

American Bar Association

Model Rules of Professional Conduct

Rule 3.3. Candor Toward the Tribunal

(a) A lawyer shall not knowingly:

(3) offer evidence that the lawyer knows to be false. If a lawyer, the lawyer's client, or a witness called by the lawyer, has offered material evidence and the lawyer comes to know of its falsity, the lawyer shall take reasonable remedial measures, including, if necessary, disclosure to the tribunal. A lawyer may refuse to offer evidence, other than the testimony of a defendant in a criminal matter, that the lawyer reasonably believes is false.

Comment

[6] If a lawyer knows that the client intends to testify falsely or wants the lawyer to introduce false evidence, the lawyer should seek to persuade the client that the evidence should not be offered. If the persuasion is ineffective and the lawyer continues to represent the client, the lawyer must refuse to offer the false evidence. If only a portion of a witness's testimony will be false, the lawyer may call the witness to testify but may not elicit or otherwise permit the witness to present the testimony that the lawyer knows is false.

[7] The duties stated [above] apply to all lawyers, including defense counsel in criminal cases. In some jurisdictions, however, courts have required counsel to present the accused as a witness or to give a narrative statement if the accused so desires, even if counsel knows that the testimony or statement will be false. The obligation of the advocate under the Rules of Professional Conduct is subordinate to such requirements.

[8] The prohibition against offering false evidence only applies if the lawyer knows that the evidence is false. A lawyer's reasonable belief that evidence is false does not preclude its presentation to the trier of fact. A lawyer's knowledge that

evidence is false, however, can be inferred from the circumstances. Thus, although a lawyer should resolve doubts about the veracity of testimony or other evidence in favor of the client, the lawyer cannot ignore an obvious falsehood.

[9] Although paragraph (a)(3) only prohibits a lawyer from offering evidence the lawyer knows to be false, it permits the lawyer to refuse to offer testimony or other proof that the lawyer reasonably believes is false. Offering such proof may reflect adversely on the lawyer's ability to discriminate in the quality of evidence and thus impair the lawyer's effectiveness as an advocate. Because of the special protections historically provided criminal defendants, however, this Rule does not permit a lawyer to refuse to offer the testimony of such a client where the lawyer reasonably believes but does not know that the testimony will be false. Unless the lawyer knows the testimony will be false, the lawyer must honor the client's decision to testify.

[10] Having offered material evidence in the belief that it was true, a lawyer may subsequently come to know that the evidence is false. Or, a lawyer may be surprised when the lawyer's client, or another witness called by the lawyer, offers testimony the lawyer knows to be false, either during the lawyer's direct examination or in response to cross-examination by the opposing lawyer. In such situations, or if the lawyer knows of the falsity of testimony elicited from the client during a deposition, the lawyer must take reasonable remedial measures. In such situations, the advocate's proper course is to remonstrate with the client confidentially, advise the client of the lawyer's duty of candor to the tribunal and seek the client's cooperation with respect to the withdrawal or correction of the false statements or evidence. If that fails, the advocate must take further remedial action. If withdrawal from the representation is not permitted or will not undo the effect of the false evidence, the advocate must make such disclosure to the tribunal as is reasonably necessary to remedy the situation, even if doing so requires the lawyer to reveal information that otherwise would be protected by Rule 1.6. It is for the tribunal then to determine what should be done — making a statement about the matter to the trier of fact, ordering a mistrial or perhaps nothing.

[15] Normally, a lawyer's compliance with the duty of candor imposed by this Rule does not require that the lawyer withdraw from the representation of a client whose interests will be or have been adversely affected by the lawyer's disclosure. The lawyer may, however, be required . . . to seek permission of the tribunal to withdraw if the lawyer's compliance with this Rule's duty of candor results in such an extreme deterioration of the client-lawyer relationship that the lawyer can no longer competently represent the client. . . . In connection with a request for permission to withdraw that is premised on a client's misconduct, a lawyer may reveal information relating to the representation only to the extent reasonably necessary to comply with this Rule or as otherwise permitted by Rule 1.6.

Justice Manual

Title 9, Section 69.200: Criminal Resource Manual at 1751 (2020)

Recantation was never a defense to perjury in the common law, and is not a complete defense in a Section 1621 prosecution. . . . Recantation in such cases is relevant only as to whether the defendant intended to make a willfully false statement.

Section 1623(d), however, makes recantation a bar to a perjury prosecution in certain cases that meet either three or four requirements. . . . Because recantation is a jurisdictional bar to prosecution, Fed. R. Crim. P. 12(b)(2) requires that it be shown before trial. *United States v. Fornaro*, 894 F.2d 508, 511 (2d Cir. 1990).

PRACTICE TIP: The prosecutor has no duty to advise a witness of the possibility of recanting under Section 1623(d), even if the witness is advised of the penalties for perjury. Nor must the government confront a witness with evidence of the untruthfulness of his statements, or, conversely, delay revealing incriminating evidence so that the witness can consider whether to recant. If, however, the prosecutor specifically allows a witness to "straighten out" testimony, the government may be estopped from challenging a witness's eligibility to recant. Normally, no perjury prosecution should be undertaken after a solicited recantation, even if the defendant was technically ineligible under Section 1623(d).

PRACTICE TIP: If a witness who has completed his or her testimony requests the opportunity to appear before the grand jury to recant testimony, the prosecutor should grant the request, provided it is timely and in keeping with the promotion of truthful testimony. A witness's request for reappearance after the falsity of the previous testimony has become manifest does not preclude prosecution of the prior false declaration and may be denied.

Notes and Questions

1. *Future testimony.* Any criminal defense attorney or prosecutor may well, at some point, face ethical issues involving perjurious testimony. The issue can arise in a number of ways. For example, an attorney may believe that a client or witness plans to commit perjury. The belief may be based upon a suspicion. Or, less often, the attorney may have actual or constructive knowledge that a witness intends to commit perjury. A prosecutor, of course, can simply decline to present the witness. But what if the witness is a criminal defendant who insists on testifying? May the defendant's attorney elicit the testimony during direct examination?

2. *Past testimony.* Another tricky circumstance arises when a witness or criminal defendant commits perjury, and the attorney who offered the testimony later becomes aware that the testimony was perjurious. A prosecutor does not have a duty to the witness as a client. As an officer of the court, must the prosecutor reveal the perjury? Or what about a defense attorney? How does the attorney square the obligation of candor to the court with the obligation to zealously represent the client?

3. *Government witness perjury at trial.* Assume that a government witness commits perjury at a criminal trial and that the defendant is convicted. Must the conviction be overturned when the perjury comes to light? This issue arose in the case against Martha Stewart and her broker Peter Bacanovic, during which a government expert witness committed perjury during trial. *United States v. Stewart*, 323 F. Supp. 2d 606 (S.D.N.Y. 2004). The defendants moved under Fed. R. Crim. P. 33 to vacate the judgment and to hold a new trial. In denying the motion, the court wrote:

> [T]he mere fact that a witness committed perjury is insufficient, standing alone, to warrant relief under Rule 33. "Whether the introduction of perjured testimony requires a new trial initially depends on the extent to which the prosecution was aware of the alleged perjury. To prevent prosecutorial misconduct, a conviction obtained when the prosecution's case includes testimony that was known or should have been known to be perjured must be reversed if there is any reasonable likelihood that the perjured testimony influenced the jury." When the government is unaware of the perjury at the time of trial, "a new trial is warranted only if the testimony was material and the court [is left] with a firm belief that but for the perjured testimony, the defendant would most likely not have been convicted."

Id. at 615 (citations omitted).

Analyzing the facts, the court concluded:

> Defendants have failed to demonstrate that the prosecution knew or should have known of [the] perjury. However, even under the stricter prejudice standard applicable when the government is aware of a witness's perjury, defendants' motions fail. There is no reasonable likelihood that knowledge by the jury that [the witness] lied . . . could have affected the verdict.

Id. at 619.

How likely is it that a defendant will be able to prove that the government knew or should have known of a witness's perjury? How likely is it that a defendant will be able to prove that perjured testimony was prejudicial? As the court noted in *Stewart*, few courts in the circuit in which the case was decided have ever ordered a new trial because of witness perjury. *Id.* at 615. Why is this so?

Problem

10-10. The federal government charged a pharmaceutical company officer, Manny, with knowingly causing 40 barrels of toxic waste to be illegally dumped on August 30 of last year. Manny's trial is now taking place before a jury.

The government believes that David, a truck driver, had hauled the waste. In addition, the government has evidence that, during a telephone conversation on August 29 last year, Manny had instructed David to haul the waste. For tactical reasons, however, the government decided not to call David as a witness in its case-in-chief.

The defense, however, has called David as a witness. Following the direct examination by Manny's attorney, the government cross-examined David. David gave the following testimony during the cross-examination:

Q: Do you know a person by the name of Manny?

A: *No.*

Q: On August 30 last year, how many barrels of waste did you carry?

A: *Somewhere between ten and fifteen.*

At that point, the trial adjourned for the day.

Assume that you are the attorney for David. Prior to testifying, David had told you that a person who identified himself to David to be Manny had telephoned David on August 29. During the conversation, Manny had instructed David to haul the waste the next day. David also tells you that he had never met Manny before the trial and does not believe, in the common meaning of the word, that he "knows" Manny. You have listened to the above testimony.

Should you take any action? If so, what?

10-11. Now assume that David continued the testimony the next day without having discussed the testimony with his attorney. The government played a recording of a telephone conversation between David and Manny. David's testimony continued:

Q: Having had that opportunity to listen to yourself talking to Manny on the telephone, does that refresh your recollection concerning whether you know Manny?

A: I don't know Manny personally.

Q: What do you mean by that?

A: I mean I've never had personal contact with Manny other than the one phone call. I don't know him.

Q: That is your voice on the tape, isn't it, talking to Manny?

A: I do recall that phone call I received, yes.

Q: And that is your voice.

A: Yes.

Q: Yesterday, Mr. David, you were asked, "Do you know a person by the name of Manny?" Your answer was, "No." Was that answer truthful?

A: I do not know the individual in the sense that I've never met him. If you mean do I know who he is, the answer is yes. If I gave another impression yesterday, I'd like to withdraw my testimony of yesterday.

Other witnesses testified that David carried 40 barrels of toxic waste on the date in question. Although Manny was charged with causing the illegal dumping of 40 barrels of waste, the charges and penalties would have been the same for the dumping of 10, 15, or 40 barrels.

Based upon the italicized answers given during his first day of testimony, David is charged with two counts of perjury under §1623. David seeks to dismiss the charges.

What possible argument or arguments could David make? Will David succeed as to any of the arguments? Why or why not?

Chapter 11

Obstruction of Justice

A. Introductory Notes

1. Statutory Scheme

Federal obstruction of justice statutes broadly criminalize efforts to interfere with federal judicial, administrative, and legislative proceedings. Examples of obstructive efforts include destroying or altering physical evidence, procuring false testimony, and threatening witnesses, jurors, and others involved in official proceedings. As with other "cover-up" crimes, an obstruction case may stand on its own, or may arise out of attempts to cover up earlier, illegal activity.

The federal criminal code contains a myriad of obstruction statutes, many of them overlapping. The principal statutes are set forth in §§ 1501–1521. These include § 1503 (obstruction of judicial proceedings), § 1505 (obstruction of administrative and Congressional proceedings), § 1510 (bribery of witnesses), § 1512 (tampering with witnesses and documents), § 1513 (tampering with a witness), § 1519 (destruction, alteration, or falsification of records in federal investigations and bankruptcy), and § 1520 (destruction of corporate audit records). The Sarbanes-Oxley Act of 2002, which Congress enacted in response to the corporate accounting scandals of the early 2000s, expanded § 1512 to include document tampering and added §§ 1519 and 1520 to the federal criminal code. The most wide-ranging provisions are contained in the "omnibus" clauses of §§ 1503 and 1505. These statutes do not overlap; § 1503 applies to federal judicial proceedings, while § 1505 applies only to federal administrative and legislative proceedings. For an overview of the rather complex and disjointed obstruction statutory scheme, see Julie R. O'Sullivan, *The Federal Criminal Code Is a Disgrace: Obstruction Statutes as Case Study*, 96 J. Crim. L. & Criminology 643 (2006).

Most obstruction charges in white collar crime cases are brought under the omnibus clauses of §§ 1503 and 1505 and the subsections of § 1512 that encompass attempts to influence testimony and destroy or alter documents. In addition, the government is increasingly bringing charges under § 1519, sometimes termed an "anti-shredding" statute. It is upon these statutory provisions that this chapter focuses.

2. Statutory Overview and Elements

a. Sections 1503 and 1505

Section 1503(a) encompasses three distinct activities in connection with judicial proceedings. First, the statute criminalizes an endeavor to influence, intimidate, or impede a grand juror or trial juror, or any court officer. The term "court officer" generally applies to judges and other court officials, such as clerks, as well as to attorneys appearing before the court. Second, the statute criminalizes injuring a juror or court officer. Third, the statute criminalizes acting "corruptly" or by threats to influence, obstruct, or impede a judicial proceeding, or to endeavor to influence, obstruct, or impede, a judicial proceeding. The latter is referred to as the catch-all or "omnibus" clause. Section 1505 contains a parallel omnibus provision applicable to legislative and administrative proceedings. The omnibus clauses are extremely broad, and effectively both subsume and expand upon the more specific preceding clauses in §§ 1503 and 1505.

Most obstruction charges under § 1503 and § 1505 are brought under the omnibus clauses of those statutes. Under the omnibus clause of either section, most circuit courts require the government to prove that:

(1) The defendant acted with "corrupt" intent;

(2) The defendant endeavored to interfere with a judicial, administrative, or congressional proceeding;

(3) There was a "nexus" between the endeavor and the proceeding;

(4) The proceeding was actually pending at the time of the endeavor; and

(5) The defendant knew that the proceeding was pending.

In addition, some courts add a materiality element to omnibus clause obstruction charges. *See* Note on Materiality and the Barry Bonds Case following the *Aguilar* case, *infra*. Obstruction under the omnibus clauses is an inchoate offense; the defendant's "endeavor" need not succeed for the crime to be complete. Violations under § 1503 may be punished by imprisonment of not more than 10 years, a fine, or both. Violations under § 1505 may be punished by imprisonment of not more than five years, a fine, or both.

b. Section 1512

Under the portion of § 1512(b) most applicable to white collar cases, and as interpreted by the courts, the government must prove that:

(1) The defendant knowingly acted corruptly;

(2) The defendant persuaded, or attempted to persuade, or misled another person;

(3) The defendant acted with intent to:

(a) influence, delay, or prevent the testimony of any person in an official proceeding (18 U.S.C. §1512(b)(1)); or

(b) cause or induce any person to—

(i) withhold testimony, or withhold a record, document, or other object, from an official proceeding (18 U.S.C. §1512(b)(2)(A)); or

(ii) alter, destroy, mutilate, or conceal an object with intent to impair the object's integrity or availability for use in an official proceeding (18 U.S.C. §1512(b)(2)(B)); and

(4) there was a "nexus" between the obstructive act and the official proceeding.

Under §1512(c), added by the Sarbanes-Oxley Act, the government must show that:

(1) The defendant acted corruptly; *and*

(2) (a)(i) The defendant altered, destroyed, mutilated, or concealed a record, document, or other object, or attempted to do so; and (ii) The defendant acted with the intent to impair the object's integrity or availability for use in an official proceeding; or

(b) The defendant otherwise obstructed, influenced, or impeded any official proceeding, or attempted to do so.

In addition, as discussed in the notes following the *Arthur Andersen* case, §D *infra*, the federal appeals courts have required a "nexus" between the obstructive act and an official proceeding. Violations of §§1512(b) and (c) may be punished by imprisonment of up to 20 years, a fine, or both.

Section 1512(f)(1) provides that "an official proceeding need not be pending or about to be instituted at the time of the offense." As is apparent from the foregoing, §1512(c)(2) contains its own omnibus clause that largely duplicates the omnibus clauses of §§1503 and 1505, though it reaches farther in some cases by not requiring that a proceeding be pending at the time of the obstructive acts. Nonetheless, as discussed in §D below, the government must show that the defendant at least contemplated an official proceeding in order to prove corrupt intent.

c. Sections 1519 and 1520

Two obstruction statutes were enacted as part of the Sarbanes-Oxley Act of 2002, 18 U.S.C. §§1519–20. Section 1519, entitled "Destruction, alteration, or falsification of records in Federal investigations and bankruptcy," is the so-called "anti-shredding" statute. That section applies to "*any matter* within the jurisdiction of any department or agency of the United States or any case filed under title 11, or in relation to or contemplation of any such matter or case." Section 1520, "Destruction of corporate audit records," applies to destruction of records relating to audits of issuers of registered securities. Both of these sections eliminate the pending proceeding element.

The government is increasingly employing §1519 in obstruction cases. Because the statute is fairly new, courts are still interpreting and defining its elements. Under current law, the statute requires proof that:

(1) The defendant knowingly altered, destroyed, mutilated, concealed, covered up, falsified, or made a false entry in any record, document, or tangible object;

(2) with the intent to impede, obstruct, or influence the investigation or proper administration of any matter within the jurisdiction of any department or agency of the United States or any case filed under title 11 [bankruptcy] or in relation to or contemplation of any such matter or case.

Violations of the statute are punishable by imprisonment of not more than 20 years, a statutory fine, or both.

B. The "Endeavor" and "Nexus" Requirements

The omnibus clauses of §§1503 and 1505 criminalize "*endeavor[ing]* to influence, obstruct, or impede" a pending judicial, legislative, or administrative proceeding. The inchoate crime of endeavoring to obstruct justice may give rise to liability in circumstances even broader than those that would qualify for the common law of attempt. In the case that follows, the Supreme Court interpreted the "endeavor" element to require a "nexus" between the alleged obstructive act and the proceeding. Significantly, under the Court's approach, the nexus requirement also implicates the mens rea of the crime.

United States v. Aguilar
515 U.S. 593 (1995)

CHIEF JUSTICE REHNQUIST delivered the opinion of the Court.

A jury convicted United States District Judge Robert Aguilar of one count of endeavoring to obstruct the due administration of justice in violation of §1503. A panel of the Court of Appeals for the Ninth Circuit reversed the conviction under §1503. We granted certiorari to resolve a conflict among the federal circuits over whether §1503 punishes false statements made to potential grand jury witnesses.

Many facts remain disputed by the parties. Both parties appear to agree, however, that a motion for postconviction relief filed by one Michael Rudy Tham represents the starting point from which events bearing on this case unfolded. Tham was an officer of the International Brotherhood of Teamsters, and was convicted of embezzling funds from the local affiliate of that organization. In July 1987, he filed a motion to have his conviction set aside. The motion was assigned to Judge Stanley Weigel. Tham, seeking to enhance the odds that his petition would be granted, asked Edward Solomon and Abraham Chalupowitz, a.k.a. Abe Chapman, to assist him by capitalizing on their respective acquaintances with another judge in the Northern District of California, respondent Aguilar. Respondent knew Chapman as a distant relation by marriage and knew Solomon from law school. Solomon and Chapman met with respondent to discuss Tham's case, as a result of which respondent spoke with Judge Weigel about the matter.

Independent of the embezzlement conviction, the Federal Bureau of Investigation (FBI) identified Tham as a suspect in an investigation of labor racketeering. On April 20, 1987, the FBI applied for authorization to install a wiretap on Tham's business phones. Chapman appeared on the application as a potential interceptee. Chief District Judge Robert Peckham authorized the wiretap. During the course of the racketeering investigation, the FBI learned of the meetings between Chapman and respondent. The FBI informed Chief Judge Peckham, who, concerned with appearances of impropriety, advised respondent in August 1987 that Chapman might be connected with criminal elements because Chapman's name had appeared on a wiretap authorization.

Five months after respondent learned that Chapman had been named in a wiretap authorization, he noticed a man observing his home during a visit by Chapman. He alerted his nephew to this fact and conveyed the message (with an intent that his nephew relay the information to Chapman) that Chapman's phone was being wiretapped. . . .

At this point, respondent's involvement in the two separate Tham matters converged. Two months after the disclosure to his nephew, a grand jury began to investigate an alleged conspiracy to influence the outcome of Tham's habeas case. Two FBI agents questioned respondent. During the interview, respondent lied about his participation in the Tham case and his knowledge of the wiretap. The grand jury returned an indictment; a jury convicted Aguilar of one count of endeavoring to obstruct the due administration of justice, § 1503. The Court of Appeals reversed the conviction for the reason that the conduct was not covered by the statutory language. . . .[a]

Section 1503 is structured as follows: first it proscribes persons from endeavoring to influence, intimidate, or impede grand or petit jurors or court officers in the discharge of their duties; it then prohibits injuring grand or petit jurors in their person or property because of any verdict or indictment rendered by them; it then prohibits injury of any court officer, commissioner, or similar officer on account of the performance of his official duties; finally, the "Omnibus Clause" serves as a catchall, prohibiting persons from endeavoring to influence, obstruct, or impede the due administration of justice. The latter clause, it can be seen, is far more general in scope than the earlier clauses of the statute. Respondent was charged with a violation of the Omnibus Clause, to wit: with "corruptly endeavor[ing] to influence, obstruct, and impede the . . . grand jury investigation."

---

a. The Court of Appeals sitting en banc also reversed the defendant's conviction for unauthorized disclosure of a wiretap. 21 F.3d 1475 (1994). In a portion of the opinion not reproduced here, the Supreme Court reinstated that conviction. — Eds.

The first case from this Court construing the predecessor statute to § 1503 was *Pettibone v. United States*, 148 U.S. 197 (1893). There we held that "a person is not sufficiently charged with obstructing or impeding the due administration of justice in a court unless it appears that he knew or had notice that justice was being administered in such court." Id. at 206. The Court reasoned that a person lacking knowledge of a pending proceeding necessarily lacked the evil intent to obstruct. Recent decisions of Courts of Appeals have likewise tended to place metes and bounds on the very broad language of the catchall provision. The action taken by the accused must be with an intent to influence judicial or grand jury proceedings; it is not enough that there be an intent to influence some ancillary proceeding, such as an investigation independent of the court's or grand jury's authority. Some courts have phrased this showing as a "nexus" requirement — that the act must have a relationship in time, causation, or logic with the judicial proceedings. In other words, the endeavor must have the "'natural and probable effect'" of interfering with the due administration of justice. This is not to say that the defendant's actions need be successful; an "endeavor" suffices. But as in *Pettibone*, if the defendant lacks knowledge that his actions are likely to affect the judicial proceeding, he lacks the requisite intent to obstruct.

Although respondent urges various broader grounds for affirmance, we find it unnecessary to address them because we think the "nexus" requirement developed in the decisions of the Courts of Appeals is a correct construction of § 1503. We have traditionally exercised restraint in assessing the reach of a federal criminal statute, both out of deference to the prerogatives of Congress, and out of concern that "a fair warning should be given to the world in language that the common world will understand, of what the law intends to do if a certain line is passed," *McBoyle v. United States*, 283 U.S. 25, 27 (1931). We do not believe that uttering false statements to an investigating agent — and that seems to be all that was proved here — who might or might not testify before a grand jury is sufficient to make out a violation of the catchall provision of § 1503.

The government did not show here that the agents acted as an arm of the grand jury, or indeed that the grand jury had even summoned the testimony of these particular agents. The government argues that respondent "understood that his false statements would be provided to the grand jury" and that he made the statements with the intent to thwart the grand jury investigation and not just the FBI investigation. The government supports its argument with a citation to the transcript of the recorded conversation between Aguilar and the FBI agent at the point where Aguilar asks whether he is a target of a grand jury investigation. The agent responded to the question by stating:

> [T]here is a Grand Jury meeting. Convening I guess that's the correct word.
> Um some evidence will be heard I'm . . . I'm sure on this issue.

Because respondent knew of the pending proceeding, the government therefore contends that Aguilar's statements are analogous to those made directly to the grand jury itself, in the form of false testimony or false documents.

We think the transcript citation relied upon by the government would not enable a rational trier of fact to conclude that respondent knew that his false statement would be provided to the grand jury, and that the evidence goes no further than showing that respondent testified falsely to an investigating agent. Such conduct, we believe, falls on the other side of the statutory line from that of one who delivers false documents or testimony to the grand jury itself. Conduct of the latter sort all but assures that the grand jury will consider the material in its deliberations. But what use will be made of false testimony given to an investigating agent who has not been subpoenaed or otherwise directed to appear before the grand jury is far more speculative. We think it cannot be said to have the "natural and probable effect" of interfering with the due administration of justice.

Justice Scalia criticizes our treatment of the statutory language for reading the word "endeavor" out of it, inasmuch as it excludes defendants who have an evil purpose but use means that would "only unnaturally and improbably be successful." This criticism is unwarranted. Our reading of the statute gives the term "endeavor" a useful function to fulfill: It makes conduct punishable where the defendant acts with an intent to obstruct justice, and in a manner that is likely to obstruct justice, but is foiled in some way. Were a defendant with the requisite intent to lie to a sub-poenaed witness who is ultimately not called to testify, or who testifies but does not transmit the defendant's version of the story, the defendant has endeavored to obstruct, but has not actually obstructed, justice. Under our approach, a jury could find such defendant guilty.

Justice Scalia's dissent also apparently believes that *any* act, done with the intent to "obstruct . . . the due administration of justice," is sufficient to impose criminal liability. Under the dissent's theory, a man could be found guilty under § 1503 if he knew of a pending investigation and lied to his wife about his whereabouts at the time of the crime, thinking that an FBI agent might decide to interview her and that she might in turn be influenced in her statement to the agent by her husband's false account of his whereabouts. The intent to obstruct justice is indeed present, but the man's culpability is a good deal less clear from the statute than we usually require in order to impose criminal liability.

We affirm the decision of the Court of Appeals with respect to respondent's conviction under § 1503.

Justice Scalia, with whom Justice Kennedy and Justice Thomas join, concurring in part and dissenting in part.

I would reverse the Court of Appeals, and would uphold respondent's conviction, on the count charging violation of 18 U.S.C. § 1503.

The "omnibus clause" of § 1503 . . . makes criminal not just success in corruptly influencing the due administration of justice, but also the "endeavor" to do so. We have given this latter proscription, which respondent was specifically charged with violating, a generous reading: "The word of the section is 'endeavor,' and by using it the section got rid of the technicalities which might be urged as besetting the word 'attempt,' and it describes *any effort or essay* to accomplish the evil purpose that the section was enacted to prevent." *United States v. Russell*, 255 U.S. 138, 143 (1921) (emphasis added) (interpreting substantially identical predecessor statute). Under this reading of the statute, it is even immaterial whether the endeavor to obstruct pending proceedings is possible of accomplishment.

Even read at its broadest, however, § 1503's prohibition of "endeavors" to impede justice is not without limits. To "endeavor" means to strive or work for a certain end. Webster's New International Dictionary 844 (2d ed. 1950); 1 New Shorter Oxford English Dictionary 816 (1993). Thus, § 1503 reaches only *purposeful* efforts to obstruct the due administration of justice, *i.e.*, acts performed with that very object in mind. This limitation was clearly set forth in our first decision construing § 1503's predecessor statute, *Pettibone v. United States*, 148 U.S. 197 (1893), which held an indictment insufficient because it had failed to allege the intent to obstruct justice. That opinion rejected the government's contention that the intent required to violate the statute could be found in "the intent to commit an unlawful act, in the doing of which justice was in fact obstructed"; to justify a conviction, it said, "the specific intent to violate the statute must exist." Id. at 207. *Pettibone* did acknowledge, how-ever — and here is the point that is distorted to produce today's opinion — that the specific intent to obstruct justice could be found where the defendant intentionally committed a wrongful act that had obstruction of justice as its "natural and prob-able consequence." *Id.*

Today's "nexus" requirement sounds like this, but is in reality quite different. Instead of reaffirming that "natural and probable consequence" is one way of estab-lishing intent, it *substitutes* "natural and probable effect" *for* intent, requiring that factor even when intent to obstruct justice is otherwise clear. But while it is quite proper to derive an *intent* requirement from § 1503's use of the word "endeavor," it is quite impossible to derive a *"natural and probable consequence"* requirement. One would be "endeavoring" to obstruct justice if he intentionally set out to do it by means that would only unnaturally and improbably be successful. . . .

The Court apparently adds to its "natural and probable effect" requirement the requirement that the defendant *know* of that natural and probable effect. ("[I]f the defendant lacks knowledge that his actions are likely to affect the judicial proceed-ing, he lacks the requisite intent to obstruct"). Separate proof of such knowledge is not, I think, required for the orthodox use of the "natural and probable effect" rule discussed in *Pettibone*: Where the defendant intentionally commits a wrong-ful act that *in fact* has the "natural and probable consequence" of obstructing jus-tice, "the unintended wrong may derive its character from the wrong that was intended." 148 U.S. at 207. Or, as we would put the point in modern times, the jury is entitled to presume that a person intends the natural and probable consequences of his acts.

I find that a rational juror could readily have concluded beyond a reasonable doubt that respondent had corruptly endeavored to impede the due administration of justice, *i.e.*, that he lied to the FBI agents intending to interfere with a grand jury investigation into his misdeeds.

Recorded conversations established that respondent knew a grand jury had been convened; that he had been told he was a target of its investigation; and that he feared he would be unable to explain his actions if he were subpoenaed to testify. Respondent himself testified that, at least at the conclusion of the interview, it was his "impression" that his statements to the FBI agents would be reported to the grand jury. The evidence further established that respondent made false statements to the FBI agents that minimized his involvement in the matters the grand jury was investigating. Viewing this evidence in the light most favorable to the government, I am simply unable to conclude that no rational trier of fact could have found beyond a reasonable doubt that respondent lied specifically because he thought the agents *might* convey what he said to the grand jury — which suffices to constitute a corrupt endeavor to impede the due administration of justice. In fact, I think it would be hard for a juror to conclude otherwise. . . .

The "nexus" requirement that the Court today engrafts into § 1503 has no basis in the words Congress enacted. I would reverse that part of the Court of Appeals' judgment which set aside respondent's conviction under that statute.

[Opinion of JUSTICE STEVENS, concurring in part and dissenting in part, omitted.]

Notes and Questions

1. *The "endeavor."* The Court in *Aguilar* applied a "nexus" requirement to prosecutions under § 1503's omnibus clause. Courts have also applied that requirement to the omnibus clause of § 1505. *See United States v. Quattrone*, 441 F.3d 153, 174 (2d Cir. 2006). Under both statutes, complex issues arise with respect to whether sufficient evidence of an endeavor has been established.

a. *The role of federal investigators.* The Court held that the government had not proven that the defendant's false statement to the FBI agent would "have the 'natural and probable effect' of interfering with the due administration of justice." Why not? Federal grand juries typically rely upon federal investigators — principally FBI agents — to gather evidence. Such agents often present the evidence they have gathered both at the grand jury and at the defendant's trial. What additional proof would have satisfied the majority?

b. *Subpoenas for documents.* Obstruction charges often arise out of defendants' efforts to destroy, conceal, or hide documents. For example, in *United States v. Lench*, 806 F.2d 1443 (9th Cir. 1986), the defendant was convicted of obstruction for concealing documents responsive to a grand jury subpoena. *See also, United States v. Arthur Andersen, infra.*

c. *False testimony.* Under the *Blockburger* test, discussed in Chapter 9, § H, *supra*, could a defendant be punished for both perjury and obstruction based upon the same false testimony? Most courts have answered in the affirmative where all the elements of obstruction are met. If, however, the government has failed to prove an element of obstruction — such as the defendant's intent to obstruct or the "nexus" between the testimony and the pending proceeding — then perjury alone will not support an obstruction conviction. *See, e.g., United States v. Littleton*, 76 F.3d 614, 619 (4th Cir. 1996) (holding perjury can constitute the actus reus of obstruction, but an obstruction charge cannot rest solely on the allegation of perjury; there must also be proof that the false statement either obstructed or was intended to obstruct justice). Can you imagine a circumstance in which proof of perjury would not also qualify for proof of obstruction?

2. *Obstructive intent.* Even though the FBI agent told Aguilar that a grand jury had been convened, the Court found insufficient proof that Aguilar "made the statements with the intent to thwart the grand jury investigation and not just the FBI investigation." The Court concluded that, to hold otherwise, "a man could be found guilty under § 1503 if he knew of a pending investigation and lied to his wife about his whereabouts at the time of the crime, thinking that an FBI agent might decide to interview her and that she might in turn be influenced in her statement to the agent by her husband's false account of his whereabouts." Is this a correct reading of the dissent's position?

3. *False statement.* Why did the government not simply charge the defendant with making a false statement under § 1001? The *Aguilar* decision was handed down in 1995; it was not until *Brogan v. United States*, 522 U.S. 398 (1998), that the Supreme Court disallowed the "exculpatory 'no'" defense to a § 1001 prosecution.

4. *Applying the "nexus" requirement to other obstruction statutes.* As seen in the materials below, courts have struggled to determine whether *Aguilar*'s nexus requirement also applies to other obstruction of justice statutes, particularly to the various subsections of § 1512 and to § 1519. As you read these materials, consider whether the policy concerns that drove the Court's decision in *Aguilar* also apply to those other statutes.

C. Materiality and the Barry Bonds Case

Barry Bonds is a former major league baseball star who, among other distinctions, holds the record for most career home runs. Bonds testified under immunity before a federal grand jury investigating the use of steroids in major league baseball. During his testimony, Bonds gave the following answers:

> Q: Did Greg [, your trainer,] ever give you anything that required a syringe to inject yourself with?

> A: I've only had one doctor touch me. And that's my only personal doctor. Greg, like I said, we don't get into each other's personal lives. We're friends, but I don't — we don't sit around and talk baseball, because he knows I don't want — don't come to my house talking baseball. If you want to come to my

house and talk about fishing, some other stuff, we'll be good friends. You come around talking about baseball, you go on. I don't talk about his business. You know what I mean?

Q: Right.

A: *That's what keeps our friendship. You know, I am sorry, but that — you know, that — I was a celebrity child, not just in baseball by my own instincts. I became a celebrity child with a famous father. I just don't get into other people's business because of my father's situation, you see.*

United States v. Bonds, 784 F.3d 582 (9th Cir. 2015) (en banc). Bond was convicted of obstruction of justice under § 1503 based upon the answer above; the jury did not reach a verdict on related perjury charges, which were later dismissed.

A Ninth Circuit panel affirmed the obstruction conviction, but the court reversed en banc by a vote of 10-1. In a brief per curiam, opinion the court concluded that the answer upon which the conviction was based did not meet the materiality element that the Ninth Circuit applies to obstruction charges. Three different concurring opinions supported reversal. The five-member lead concurring opinion began with a discussion of the breadth of the omnibus clause:

> As should be apparent, section 1503's coverage is vast. By its literal terms, it applies to all stages of the criminal and civil justice process, not just to conduct in the courtroom but also to trial preparation, discovery and pretrial motions. Indeed, it arguably covers conduct taken in anticipation that a civil or criminal case might be filed, such as tax planning, hiding assets or talking to police. And the text of the omnibus clause, in concert with our definition of corruptly, encompasses any act that a jury might infer was intended to 'influence, obstruct, or impede . . . the due administration of justice.' That's true even if no actual obstruction occurs, because the clause's use of 'endeavors' makes 'success . . . irrelevant.'

> Stretched to its limits, section 1503 poses a significant hazard for everyone involved in our system of justice, because so much of what the adversary process calls for could be construed as obstruction. . . . Witnesses would be particularly vulnerable because, as the Supreme Court has noted, '[u]nder the pressures and tensions of interrogation, it is not uncommon for the most earnest witnesses to give answers that are not entirely responsive.' *Bronston v. United States*, 409 U.S. 352, 358 (1973).

Bonds, 748 F.3d at 584–85.

The lead concurring opinion concluded that the italicized answer above could not form the basis for an obstruction conviction because the answer could not have been material to the grand jury's investigation:

> Because the statute sweeps so broadly, due process calls for prudential limitations on the government's power to prosecute under it. Such a limitation already exists in [Ninth Circuit] case law interpreting § 1503: the requirement

of materiality. [T]he government must prove beyond a reasonable doubt that the charged conduct was capable of influencing a decisionmaking person or entity — for example, by causing it to cease its investigation, pursue different avenues of inquiry or reach a different outcome. . . .

We start with the self-evident proposition that [the statement], standing alone, did not have the capacity to divert the government from its investigation or influence the grand jury's decision whether to indict anyone. . . .

The most one can say about this statement is that it was non-responsive and thereby impeded the investigation to a small degree by wasting the grand jury's time and trying the prosecutors' patience. . . .

This is true even if, as the government now argues, [the statement] is literally false. An irrelevant or wholly non-responsive answer says nothing germane to the subject of the investigation, whether it's true or false. For example, if a witness is asked, 'Do you own a gun?' it makes no difference whether he answers 'The sky is blue' or 'The sky is green.' That the second statement is false makes it no more likely to impede the investigation than the first.

[Bonds' statement] does not, however, stand alone. It was a small portion of a much longer examination, and we must look at the record as a whole to determine whether a rational trier of fact could have found the statement capable of influencing the grand jury's investigation, in light of defendant's entire grand jury testimony. If, for example, a witness engages in a pattern of irrelevant statements, or launches into lengthy disquisitions that are clearly designed to waste time and preclude the questioner from continuing his examination, the jury could find that the witness's behavior was capable of having some sway.

On careful review of the record, we find insufficient evidence to render [the statement] material. . . .

Bonds, 784 F.3d at 585–86.

Because the court found insufficient evidence to support the conviction, Bonds cannot be retried. *Id*. at 582.

Notes and Questions

1. *A jury question?* Do you agree that no rational juror could have found that Bonds' statement could have had the capacity to affect the grand jury proceeding? Is the question closer than the concurring opinion found? A sole dissenting judge argued that "drawing all inferences in favor of the government, a reasonable juror could reasonably conclude that Bonds' evasive testimony diverted the investigation, thereby impeding the administration of justice." Which is the correct view?

2. *Definition of materiality.* Five judges in two separate additional concurring opinions argued that the lead concurring opinion (quoted above) used the wrong test for

materiality. These opinions would have imported *Aguilar*'s nexus definition to define materiality: "[T]he 'natural and probable effect' test articulated in *United States v. Aguilar* constitutes the proper standard for materiality with respect to §1503." The court thus split five-to-five on the appropriate definition of materiality. Which is the appropriate definition? Why?

3. *Is a separate materiality element necessary?* Does a materiality element really add anything to the government's burden in an obstruction case? One observer argues that *Aguilar*'s nexus requirement subsumes a materiality requirement; an alleged obstructive act could not meet the nexus requirement without necessarily being material. *See* Randall Eliason, *Barry Bonds Obstruction Case Splinters the Ninth Circuit*, SIDEBARS REFLECTIONS ON WHITE COLLAR CRIME AND FEDERAL CRIMINAL LAW (April 27, 2015), https://sidebarsblog.com/barry-bonds-obstruction-case-splinters-the-ninth-circuit. Do you agree?

4. *Literal truth.* Does the literal truth defense, applicable to perjury cases, also apply to obstruction cases? The dissent in *Bonds* disagreed with the concurring opinions' reliance on law developed in the perjury context: "It is questionable whether the 'literal truth' underpinnings of *Bronston* apply outside the confines of adversarial proceedings where opposing counsel are expected to continuously hone their questions to require definitive answers, and a judge is present to control uncooperative witnesses. In contrast, the grand jury is a non-adversarial, investigatory proceeding with no judge presiding." Is the view correct?

D. The "Proceeding" Element

The essence of an obstruction case under the omnibus clauses of §§1503 and 1505 is that the defendant endeavored to interfere with a governmental proceeding. Most courts hold that the government must show both that a proceeding was pending at the time of the endeavor and that the defendant knew of the proceeding. It may be difficult to determine, however, exactly when a court case or other "proceeding" begins or when it ends.

Note on United States v. Fulbright

In *United States v. Fulbright*, 105 F.3d 443 (9th Cir. 1997), the Ninth Circuit attempted to define both the "proceeding" element of the omnibus clause and the "court officer" element of the second clause of §1503. Fulbright was a Montana farmer who experienced some financial reverses and filed for bankruptcy. The bankruptcy judge denied relief in early April and then recused himself from the case. Shortly after the recusal, Fulbright mailed a "Notice and Demand for Declaration of Judge's Impartiality" to the judge. The notice charged the judge with "numerous 'crimes,' including sedition, high treason, bank fraud, and armed robbery." *Id.* at 446. Fulbright's case was dismissed on May 10 (after the notice was mailed). On June 2, Fulbright filed a "Citizen's Arrest Warrant for Citizen's Arrest" with the bankruptcy court. The warrant authorized peace officers to arrest the judge. Fulbright was indicted, *inter alia*, for §1503 obstruction of justice based on these facts. The government's theory of obstruction was based on alternative factual bases: Fulbright endeavored to "influence or impede" the judge "in the discharge of his duties" by mailing the notice in April or by filing of the warrant on June 2.

At trial, Fulbright took the stand and "claimed that he had not intended to intimidate or harass [the judge]: 'I was just trying to get a farm foreclosure action hopefully remedied.'" *Id.* Nevertheless, the jury convicted Fulbright on a general verdict.

There were two principal issues before the court on appeal. First, given that the judge had already recused himself, was the judge acting as a "court officer . . . in the discharge of his duty" when the notice was sent or, alternatively, when the warrant was filed? Second, given the case had already been dismissed on March 10, was there an existing "judicial proceeding" at the time the warrant was filed on June 2?

Concerning the first issue, the court held that the judge was acting in the discharge of his duties even after he had recused himself. According to the court, a federal court officer engaged in daily work is always assumed to be in the discharge of federal duties. The court noted that this element has also been interpreted broadly with respect to jurors and witnesses. Since, in this case, the judge was still involved in adjudicating other bankruptcy cases, Fulbright's conduct still risked dissuading him from the zealous execution of his ongoing official duties.

Concerning the second issue, whether a "proceeding" was still pending at the time the warrant was filed, the court explained that this element has been construed "fairly strictly." In the post-trial context, courts have typically found a proceeding to be pending until "disposition is made of any direct appeal taken by the defendant assigning error that could result in a new trial." *Id.* at 450, *quoting United States v. Johnson*, 605 F.2d 729, 731 (4th Cir. 1979). In this case, the court held that the proceeding was over at the expiration of his 10-day appeal period on May 20. Since the proceeding terminated on that date, as a matter of law, the jury could not have convicted Fulbright for the filing of the warrant almost two weeks later on June 2.

Since the jury convicted on a general verdict, it was impossible to determine whether it was based on the mailing of the notice (which occurred while the proceeding was pending — and was therefore valid) or the filing of the warrant (which occurred after — and was therefore invalid). Consequently, the error was not harmless, and the court vacated Fulbright's conviction for §1503 obstruction.

Notes and Questions

1. *The pending proceeding.* The circuits have generally held that the pending proceeding is an element of both §1503 and §1505. Partly because of this requirement, more and more white collar obstruction prosecutions are being brought under §1512 and

§ 1519. As will be seen in the materials below, however, issues relating to "proceedings" do arise under those statutes.

2. *When does a proceeding begin and end?* Determining exactly when a "proceeding" begins and ends is a potentially problematic issue under both § 1503 and § 1505. Why is this question so critical to a prosecution and defense of an obstruction case?

a. *Court proceedings.* With respect to court proceedings, courts generally agree that a proceeding begins when a complaint or indictment initiating the case is filed. Courts also generally hold that a court case is over when the time for appeal has lapsed or been exhausted. *See generally* Andrea Kendall & Kimberly Cuff, *Obstruction of Justice*, 45 Am. Crim. L. Rev. 765, 769–70 (2008).

b. *Grand jury proceedings.* The circuits are split as to whether a grand jury proceeding commences with the gathering of evidence to be presented to a grand jury or whether the proceeding commences only when the grand jury itself initiates the investigation. *See id.* at 770. The fact that a grand jury is sitting in a particular district will not be sufficient. As the court held in *United States v. Davis*, 183 F.3d 231, 241 (3d Cir. 1999), as amended, 197 F.3d 662 (3d Cir. 1999), because in most federal judicial districts a grand jury is sitting at any given time, "the mere existence of a grand jury in a district does not trigger § 1503; the grand jury must have some relationship to the investigation that is obstructed." And as the court noted in *Fulbright*, "'ancillary' proceedings, such as an FBI investigation, independent of a court's or a grand jury's authority, do not satisfy § 1503's 'proceeding' requirement," 105 F.3d at 450 n.4 (quoting *Aguilar*, 515 U.S. at 599).

c. *Congressional and executive agency proceedings.* Courts seem to agree that informal investigations pursuant to statutory authority qualify as proceedings under § 1505. Thus, any authorized investigation, even without the filing of a formal order of investigation, should qualify under the statute. *See, e.g., United States v. Hopper*, 177 F.3d 824, 830–831 (9th Cir. 1999); *United States v. Cisneros*, 26 F. Supp. 2d 24, 39 (D.D.C. 1998).

3. *Discharge of duties.*

a. *Judges.* Fulbright argued that, because the judge had recused himself, the judge was not acting in the discharge of his duties at the time the "notice" and "warrant" were mailed. Given that the court found that the bankruptcy case was over at the time the warrant was sent, why did the court reject Fulbright's argument?

b. *Prosecutors.* In *United States v. Fernandez*, 837 F.2d 1031, 1034 (11th Cir. 1988), a defendant's brother threatened a prosecutor immediately after the defendant's sentencing. The Eleventh Circuit affirmed the brother's conviction under § 1503, finding that the prosecutor was still on the case while the possibility of an appeal or a motion to reduce the sentence of the defendant persisted.

c. *Jurors.* Both prospective jurors and sworn jurors appear to fall within the scope of § 1503. *See United States v. Osborn*, 415 F.2d 1021, 1024 (6th Cir. 1969) (affirming conviction of defendant who attempted to bribe a juror on a jury panel that the defendant expected would hear the case, even though that panel ultimately did not hear the case).

d. *Witnesses.* Courts have held that one is "[i]ndubitably . . . a witness, within the meaning of Section 1503, when [one] knows or is supposed to know material facts, and expectably is to be called to testify to them. Just as clearly, [one] is not a witness when, despite his testimonial potential, there is no present prospect of ever exploiting it . . . [, or] when the proceeding in which [one] has testified is no longer pending." *United States v. Jackson*, 513 F.2d 456, 459 (D.C. Cir. 1975). However, what if the defendant threatens a witness who has testified after all the evidence in the case has been presented but before the closing arguments? The court in *Jackson* affirmed the defendant's § 1503 conviction under such circumstances because the trial was not over, and the trial judge retained "authority to command [the threatened individual's] reappearance as a witness." *Id.* at 460.

4. *Alternative theories and reversible error.* The government charged Fulbright under alternative theories — the April "Notice" and the June "Warrant" — not an uncommon practice in criminal cases. If a jury convicts without using a special verdict form, and one of the alternative theories will not support a conviction, can the conviction rest on the remaining theory or theories? The court in *Fulbright* distinguished charges that are legally deficient from charges that are based upon insufficient evidence. An alternative theory that is legally deficient, the court held, requires reversal, while an alternative theory that is factually deficient does not. Why do you think the *Fulbright* court drew this distinction? Does it make sense? Note that after *Fulbright* was decided the United States Supreme Court held that an error in submitting an invalid theory to the jury does not require reversal but is subject to harmless error analysis. *See Hedgpeth v. Pulido*, 555 U.S. 57 (2008).

Problems

11-1. The United States Department of Justice was investigating insider trading of Clover Industries Inc. ("Clover Industries") stock. The government believed that a number of Clover Industries stockholders traded in Clover Industries stock based upon secret information that Clover Industries was engaged in merger negotiations. In addition, the Securities and Exchange Commission ("SEC") had begun a preliminary investigation of the same matter. Lawyer represented Client, a former Clover Industries investor. An Assistant United States Attorney ("AUSA") called Lawyer to see if Client would submit to an informal interview at the AUSA's office. After consulting with Client, Lawyer informed the AUSA that Client had agreed to be interviewed.

Client and Lawyer subsequently appeared for the interview in the AUSA's office. Also present was another person whom the AUSA introduced as "an SEC staff member." The press had widely reported that the SEC was investigating trading in Clover Industries stock. Although the SEC representative was present for the entire interview, only the AUSA asked questions of Client.

During the meeting, the following exchange took place:

AUSA: As you know, we are investigating trading of Clover Industries stock prior to the announcement of the merger negotiations. Prior to the time you traded in Clover Industries stock, were you aware that the company was engaged in merger talks?

Client: No one told me that specifically.

AUSA: So, when you bought the stock, you did not know that a merger announcement might be forthcoming?

Client: No.

Two weeks later, a federal grand jury was convened to investigate the alleged insider trading, and the SEC launched a formal investigation into the same matter. The grand jury obtained substantial evidence that Client in fact had been aware of the merger negotiations prior to the trade. Based on the above exchange, the grand jury subsequently issued a two-count indictment. Count I alleged that Client had violated 18 U.S.C. §1503 and Count II alleged that Client had violated 18 U.S.C. §1505.

Client has filed a motion to dismiss both counts of the indictment, arguing that Client was not aware of any pending proceeding and that there was no nexus. Will Client succeed? Why or why not?

11-2. Moore was the head of a not-for-profit, tax-exempt organization. Three years ago, Moore deposited $1.5 million of his personal funds into his personal bank account. Moore's attorney advised him to keep his personal assets separate from the organization's assets and to file an individual tax return for the year in question. Moore thereafter hired Accountant to assist in preparing Moore's personal tax return for that year. Moore told Accountant that Accountant should make it appear as though Moore was holding the $1.5 million as a fiduciary for Moore's organization, although Accountant was aware that the funds actually belonged to Moore. Accountant then created and backdated two fraudulent ledgers showing that the money originated from Moore's organization.

The year after Moore filed the individual tax return, a grand jury was convened to investigate whether Moore and Accountant conspired to file a false tax return. The grand jury subpoenaed various documents from Accountant. Among the responsive documents that Accountant produced were the fraudulent ledgers. Accountant did not vouch for the ledgers' accuracy. Accountant also was unaware that production of the documents might have been protected under the Fifth Amendment's Self-Incrimination Clause.

The grand jury has issued an indictment of Accountant for endeavoring to obstruct justice under §1503 based upon Accountant's submission of the fraudulent ledgers. Accountant has filed a motion to dismiss the charges, arguing that there was no pending proceeding at the time the documents were prepared.

How should the court rule on Accountant's motion? Why?

E. Mens Rea

Sections 1512(b) and (c), like the omnibus clauses of §§ 1503 and 1505, require proof that the defendant acted "corruptly." In addition, § 1512(b) and (c) require proof of a second level of mens rea — an intent to engage in further, specified activity, such as witness tampering or document destruction. Section 1512(b) also requires proof that the defendant acted knowingly.

In the next case, the Supreme Court interpreted the mens rea requirement of § 1512(b). (Subsection (c) had not been enacted at the time of the events in the case.) This was a high-profile prosecution that resulted in the first criminal conviction arising from the notorious Enron scandal. The defendant was Arthur Andersen, LLP, then one of the "big five" accounting firms. The facts are unusually complicated. As you read the case, you may find it helpful to (a) diagram the entities and parties involved and (b) develop a time-line of the key events.

Arthur Andersen, LLP v. United States
544 U.S. 696 (2005)

CHIEF JUSTICE REHNQUIST delivered the opinion of the Court.

As Enron Corporation's financial difficulties became public in 2001, petitioner Arthur Andersen LLP, Enron's auditor, instructed its employees to destroy documents pursuant to its document retention policy. A jury found that this action made petitioner guilty of violating 18 U.S.C. §§ 1512(b)(2)(A) and (B). These sections make it a crime to "knowingly us[e] intimidation or physical force, threate[n], or corruptly persuad[e] another person . . . with intent to . . . cause" that person to "withhold" documents from, or "alter" documents for use in, an "official proceeding."[7] The Court of Appeals for the Fifth Circuit affirmed. We hold that the jury instructions failed to convey properly the elements of a "corrup[t] persuas[ion]" conviction under § 1512(b), and therefore reverse.

Enron Corporation, during the 1990's, switched its business from operation of natural gas pipelines to an energy conglomerate, a move that was accompanied by aggressive accounting practices and rapid growth. Petitioner audited Enron's publicly filed financial statements and provided internal audit and consulting services to it. Petitioner's "engagement team" for Enron was headed by David Duncan. Beginning in 2000, Enron's financial performance began to suffer, and, as 2001 wore on, worsened.[8] On August 14, 2001, Jeffrey Skilling, Enron's Chief Executive Officer

---

7. We refer to the 2000 version of the statute, which has since been amended by Congress.

8. During this time, petitioner faced problems of its own. In June 2001, petitioner entered into a settlement agreement with the Securities and Exchange Commission (SEC) related to its audit work of Waste Management, Inc. As part of the settlement, petitioner paid a massive fine. It also was censured and enjoined from committing further violations of the securities laws. In July 2001, the SEC filed an amended complaint alleging improprieties by Sunbeam Corporation, and petitioner's lead partner on the Sunbeam audit was named.

(CEO), unexpectedly resigned. Within days, Sherron Watkins, a senior accountant at Enron, warned Kenneth Lay, Enron's newly reappointed CEO, that Enron could "implode in a wave of accounting scandals." She likewise informed Duncan and Michael Odom, one of petitioner's partners who had supervisory responsibility over Duncan, of the looming problems.

On August 28, an article in the Wall Street Journal suggested improprieties at Enron, and the SEC opened an informal investigation. By early September, petitioner had formed an Enron "crisis-response" team, which included Nancy Temple, an in-house counsel.[9] On October 8, petitioner retained outside counsel to represent it in any litigation that might arise from the Enron matter. The next day, Temple discussed Enron with other in-house counsel. Her notes from that meeting reflect that "some SEC investigation" is "highly probable."

On October 10, Odom spoke at a general training meeting attended by 89 employees, including 10 from the Enron engagement team. Odom urged everyone to comply with the firm's document retention policy.[10] He added: "'[I]f it's destroyed in the course of [the] normal policy and litigation is filed the next day, that's great. . . . [W]e've followed our own policy, and whatever there was that might have been of interest to somebody is gone and irretrievable.'" 374 F.3d 281, 286 (5th Cir. 2004). On October 12, Temple entered the Enron matter into her computer, designating the "Type of Potential Claim" as "Professional Practice — Government/Regulatory Inv[estigation]." App. JA-127. Temple also e-mailed Odom, suggesting that he "'remin[d] the engagement team of our documentation and retention policy.'"

On October 16, Enron announced its third quarter results. That release disclosed a $1.01 billion charge to earnings.[11] The following day, the SEC notified Enron by letter that it had opened an investigation in August and requested certain information and documents. On October 19, Enron forwarded a copy of that letter to petitioner.

---

9. A key accounting problem involved Enron's use of "Raptors," which were special purpose entities used to engage in "off-balance-sheet" activities. Petitioner's engagement team had allowed Enron to "aggregate" the Raptors for accounting purposes so that they reflected a positive return. This was, in the words of petitioner's experts, a "black-and-white" violation of Generally Accepted Accounting Principles.

10. The firm's policy called for a single central engagement file, which "should contain only that information which is relevant to supporting our work." The policy stated that, "in cases of threatened litigation, . . . no related information will be destroyed." It also separately provided that, if petitioner is "advised of litigation or subpoenas regarding a particular engagement, the related information should not be destroyed. See Policy Statement No. 780 — Notification of Litigation." Policy Statement No. 780 set forth "notification" procedures for whenever "professional practice litigation against [petitioner] or any of its personnel has been commenced, has been threatened or is judged likely to occur, or when governmental or professional investigations that may involve [petitioner] or any of its personnel have been commenced or are judged likely."

11. The release characterized the charge to earnings as "non-recurring." Petitioner had expressed doubts about this characterization to Enron, but Enron refused to alter the release. Temple wrote an e-mail to Duncan that "suggested deleting some language that might suggest we have concluded the release is misleading."

On the same day, Temple also sent an e-mail to a member of petitioner's internal team of accounting experts and attached a copy of the document policy. On October 20, the Enron crisis-response team held a conference call, during which Temple instructed everyone to "[m]ake sure to follow the [document] policy." On October 23, Enron CEO Lay declined to answer questions during a call with analysts because of "potential lawsuits, as well as the SEC inquiry." After the call, Duncan met with other Andersen partners on the Enron engagement team and told them that they should ensure team members were complying with the document policy. Another meeting for all team members followed, during which Duncan distributed the policy and told everyone to comply. These, and other smaller meetings, were followed by substantial destruction of paper and electronic documents.

On October 26, one of petitioner's senior partners circulated a New York Times article discussing the SEC's response to Enron. His e-mail commented that "the problems are just beginning and we will be in the cross hairs. The marketplace is going to keep the pressure on this and is going to force the SEC to be tough." On October 30, the SEC opened a formal investigation and sent Enron a letter that requested accounting documents.

Throughout this time period, the document destruction continued, despite reservations by some of petitioner's managers.[12] On November 8, Enron announced that it would issue a comprehensive restatement of its earnings and assets. Also on November 8, the SEC served Enron and petitioner with subpoenas for records. On November 9, Duncan's secretary sent an e-mail that stated: "Per Dave — No more shredding. . . . We have been officially served for our documents." Enron filed for bankruptcy less than a month later. Duncan was fired and later pleaded guilty to witness tampering.

In March 2002, petitioner was indicted in the Southern District of Texas on one count of violating §§ 1512(b)(2)(A) and (B). The indictment alleged that, between October 10 and November 9, 2001, petitioner "did knowingly, intentionally and corruptly persuade . . . other persons, to wit: [petitioner's] employees, with intent to cause" them to withhold documents from, and alter documents for use in, "official proceedings, namely: regulatory and criminal proceedings and investigations." A jury trial followed. When the case went to the jury, that body deliberated for seven days and then declared that it was deadlocked. The District Court delivered an "*Allen* charge" [strongly encouraging the jury to reach a verdict], *Allen v. United States*, 164 U.S. 492 (1896), and, after three more days of deliberation, the

---

12. For example, on October 26, John Riley, another partner with petitioner, saw Duncan shredding documents and told him "this wouldn't be the best time in the world for you guys to be shredding a bunch of stuff." On October 31, David Stulb, a forensics investigator for petitioner, met with Duncan. During the meeting, Duncan picked up a document with the words "smoking gun" written on it and began to destroy it, adding "we don't need this." Stulb cautioned Duncan on the need to maintain documents and later informed Temple that Duncan needed advice on the document retention policy.

jury returned a guilty verdict. The District Court denied petitioner's motion for a judgment of acquittal.

The Court of Appeals for the Fifth Circuit affirmed. It held that the jury instructions properly conveyed the meaning of "corruptly persuades" and "official proceeding"; that the jury need not find any consciousness of wrongdoing; and that there was no reversible error. Because of a split of authority regarding the meaning of §1512(b), we granted certiorari.

Chapter 73 of Title 18 of the United States Code provides criminal sanctions for those who obstruct justice. Sections 1512(b)(2)(A) and (B), part of the witness tampering provisions, provide in relevant part:

> Whoever knowingly uses intimidation or physical force, threatens, or corruptly persuades another person, or attempts to do so, or engages in misleading conduct toward another person, with intent to . . . cause or induce any person to . . . withhold testimony, or withhold a record, document, or other object, from an official proceeding [or] alter, destroy, mutilate, or conceal an object with intent to impair the object's integrity or availability for use in an official proceeding . . . shall be fined under this title or imprisoned not more than ten years, or both.

In this case, our attention is focused on what it means to "knowingly . . . corruptly persuad[e]" another person "with intent to . . . cause" that person to "withhold" documents from, or "alter" documents for use in, an "official proceeding."

"We have traditionally exercised restraint in assessing the reach of a federal criminal statute, both out of deference to the prerogatives of Congress, *Dowling v. United States*, 473 U.S. 207 (1985), and out of concern that 'a fair warning should be given to the world in language that the common world will understand, of what the law intends to do if a certain line is passed,' *McBoyle v. United States*, 283 U.S. 25, 27 (1931)." *United States v. Aguilar*, 515 U.S. 593, 600 (1995).

Such restraint is particularly appropriate here, where the act underlying the conviction — "persua[sion]" — is by itself innocuous. Indeed, "persuad[ing]" a person "with intent to . . . cause" that person to "withhold" testimony or documents from a Government proceeding or Government official is not inherently malign.[13] Consider, for instance, a mother who suggests to her son that he invoke his right against compelled self-incrimination, *see* U.S. Const., Amdt. 5, or a wife who persuades her husband not to disclose marital confidences.

Nor is it necessarily corrupt for an attorney to "persuad[e]" a client "with intent to . . . cause" that client to "withhold" documents from the Government. In *Upjohn Co. v. United States*, 449 U.S. 383 (1981), for example, we held that Upjohn was

---

13. Section 1512(b)(2) addresses testimony, as well as documents. Section 1512(b)(1) also addresses testimony. Section 1512(b)(3) addresses "persuade[rs]" who intend to prevent "the communication to a law enforcement officer or judge of the United States of information" relating to a federal crime.

justified in withholding documents that were covered by the attorney-client privilege from the Internal Revenue Service (IRS). No one would suggest that an attorney who "persuade[d]" Upjohn to take that step acted wrongfully, even though he surely intended that his client keep those documents out of the IRS' hands.

"Document retention policies," which are created in part to keep certain information from getting into the hands of others, including the Government, are common in business. *See generally* Chase, *To Shred or Not to Shred: Document Retention Policies and Federal Obstruction of Justice Statutes*, 8 Ford. J. Corp. & Fin. L. 721 (2003). It is, of course, not wrongful for a manager to instruct his employees to comply with a valid document retention policy under ordinary circumstances.

Acknowledging this point, the parties have largely focused their attention on the word "corruptly" as the key to what may or may not lawfully be done in the situation presented here. Section 1512(b) punishes not just "corruptly persuad[ing]" another, but "*knowingly* . . . corruptly persuad[ing]" another. (Emphasis added.) The Government suggests that "knowingly" does not modify "corruptly persuades," but that is not how the statute most naturally reads. It provides the *mens rea* — "knowingly" — and then a list of acts — "uses intimidation or physical force, threatens, or corruptly persuades." We have recognized with regard to similar statutory language that the *mens rea* at least applies to the acts that immediately follow, if not to other elements down the statutory chain. The Government suggests that it is "questionable whether Congress would employ such an inelegant formulation as 'knowingly . . . corruptly persuades.'" Long experience has not taught us to share the Government's doubts on this score, and we must simply interpret the statute as written.

The parties have not pointed us to another interpretation of "knowingly . . . corruptly" to guide us here. In any event, the natural meaning of these terms provides a clear answer. *See* Black's Law Dictionary 888 (8th ed. 2004) (hereinafter Black's); Webster's Third New International Dictionary 1252–1253 (1993) (hereinafter Webster's 3d); American Heritage Dictionary of the English Language 725 (1981) (hereinafter Am. Hert.). "Corrupt" and "corruptly" are normally associated with wrongful, immoral, depraved, or evil. *See* Black's 371; Webster's 3d 512; Am. Hert. 299–300. Joining these meanings together here makes sense both linguistically and in the statutory scheme. Only persons conscious of wrongdoing can be said to "knowingly . . . corruptly persuad[e]." And limiting criminality to persuaders conscious of their wrongdoing sensibly allows § 1512(b) to reach only those with the level of "culpability . . . we usually require in order to impose criminal liability." *United States v. Aguilar*, 515 U.S. at 602.

The outer limits of this element need not be explored here because the jury instructions at issue simply failed to convey the requisite consciousness of wrongdoing. Indeed, it is striking how little culpability the instructions required. For example, the jury was told that, "even if [petitioner] honestly and sincerely believed that its conduct was lawful, you may find [petitioner] guilty." The instructions also diluted the meaning of "corruptly" so that it covered innocent conduct.

The parties vigorously disputed how the jury would be instructed on "corruptly." The District Court based its instruction on the definition of that term found in the Fifth Circuit Pattern Jury Instruction for §1503. This pattern instruction defined "corruptly" as "'knowingly and dishonestly, with the specific intent to subvert or undermine the integrity' \'" of a proceeding. The Government, however, insisted on excluding "dishonestly" and adding the term "impede" to the phrase "subvert or undermine." The District Court agreed over petitioner's objections, and the jury was told to convict if it found petitioner intended to "subvert, undermine, or impede" governmental factfinding by suggesting to its employees that they enforce the document retention policy.

These changes were significant. No longer was any type of "dishonest[y]" necessary to a finding of guilt, and it was enough for petitioner to have simply "impede[d]" the Government's factfinding ability. As the Government conceded at oral argument, "'impede'" has broader connotations than "'subvert'" or even "'undermine,'" and many of these connotations do not incorporate any "corrupt[ness]" at all. The dictionary defines "impede" as "to interfere with or get in the way of the progress of" or "hold up" or "detract from." Webster's 3d 1132. By definition, anyone who innocently persuades another to withhold information from the Government "get[s] in the way of the progress of" the Government. With regard to such innocent conduct, the "corruptly" instructions did no limiting work whatsoever.

The instructions also were infirm for another reason. They led the jury to believe that it did not have to find *any* nexus between the "persua[sion]" to destroy documents and any particular proceeding. In resisting any type of nexus element, the Government relies heavily on §1512(e)(1), which states that an official proceeding "need not be pending or about to be instituted at the time of the offense." It is, however, one thing to say that a proceeding "need not be pending or about to be instituted at the time of the offense," and quite another to say a proceeding need not even be foreseen. A "knowingly . . . corrup[t] persaude[r]" [sic] cannot be someone who persuades others to shred documents under a document retention policy when he does not have in contemplation any particular official proceeding in which those documents might be material.

We faced a similar situation in Aguilar, supra. Respondent Aguilar lied to a Federal Bureau of Investigation agent in the course of an investigation and was convicted of "'corruptly endeavor[ing] to influence, obstruct, and impede [a] . . . grand jury investigation'" under §1503. 515 U.S. at 599. All the Government had shown was that Aguilar had uttered false statements to an investigating agent "who might or might not testify before a grand jury." Id. at 600. We held that §1503 required something more — specifically, a "nexus" between the obstructive act and the proceeding. Id. at 599–600. "[I]f the defendant lacks knowledge that his actions are likely to affect the judicial proceeding," we explained, "he lacks the requisite intent to obstruct." Id. at 599.

For these reasons, the jury instructions here were flawed in important respects. The judgment of the Court of Appeals is reversed, and the case is remanded for further proceedings consistent with this opinion.

Notes and Questions

1. *Mens rea under § 1512(b).* What was the essential disagreement between the Supreme Court and the lower courts over the proper interpretation of the statute? Which approach is better? Why?

2. *Document retention policies.* Large organizations routinely destroy documents, both as a matter of policy and necessity. Do such policies run the risk of providing the basis for an obstruction charge? Does the Supreme Court's approach provide some protection for such policies? If so, in what circumstances?

3. *Prosecutorial discretion.* Andersen argued strenuously that a criminal charge was not appropriate in its case, particularly because such a charge would likely imperil the organization's existence and cost a large number of jobs. *See* Elkan Abramowitz & Barry A. Bohrer, *White-Collar Crime: Principles of Federal Prosecution of Business Organizations*, N.Y.L.J. Mar. 4, 2003, at 3, col. 1 (noting that "the government's decision to prosecute Arthur Andersen for its role in the Enron debacle amounted to the imposition of the corporate death penalty on that venerable accounting firm").

Was this a case of prosecutorial overkill? One prominent former federal prosecutor thought so. According to a newspaper report, Mary Jo White, former United States Attorney for the Southern District of New York, "called the decision to indict the accounting giant 'very wrongheaded,' and a sacrifice of the best interests of the public in order to 'message send.' White stated, 'To indict a corporation, as a legal matter, is like shooting fish in a barrel.'" David Ziemer, *Seventh Circuit Bar Association Meets in Milwaukee*, Wis. L.J., May 14, 2003. Does the Andersen prosecution require rethinking of the doctrine of corporate liability under respondeat superior?

4. *The proceeding element under § 1512.* In *Arthur Andersen*, the Court held that the trial court erred in instructing the jury "that it did not have to find *any* nexus between the 'persua[sion]' to destroy documents and any particular proceeding." Even though a proceeding need not be "pending" under the statute, the Court held that a defendant must at least contemplate a proceeding: "A 'knowingly . . . corrup[t] persuade[r]' cannot be someone who persuades others to shred documents under a document retention policy when he does not have in contemplation any particular official proceeding in which those documents might be material."

Section 1515(a)(1)(C), which defines the term "proceeding," specifically includes proceedings before federal judges, grand juries, and Congress, and any other "proceeding before a Federal Government agency which is authorized by law." Just how formal does a proceeding need to be to qualify under § 1512? Some courts interpreting § 1512 have found that informal activities do not qualify. *See United States v. Ramos*, 537 F.3d 439, 462–63 (5th Cir. 2008) (finding the "use [of] the preposition 'before' in connection with the term 'Federal Government agency' . . . implies that an 'official proceeding' involves some formal convocation of the agency in which parties are directed to appear, instead of any informal investigation conducted by any member of the agency."). *Accord, United States v. Ermoian*, 752 F.3d 1165 (9th Cir. 2013).

What are the competing policy concerns behind narrow and broad readings of the term "proceeding?" Which approach is better? Why?

5. *The nexus requirement under § 1512(b)*. In *Aguilar*, the Supreme Court required a nexus between the alleged obstructive act and a pending proceeding; the defendant's act must have the "natural and probable" effect of obstructing the proceeding. The Court also held that "if the defendant lacks knowledge that his actions are likely to affect the proceeding, he lacks the requisite intent to obstruct." The *Arthur Andersen* Court applied this requirement to § 1512(b), holding that the obstructive act must be "in contemplation of" a proceeding, but did not describe the type of contemplation required. Courts have also applied the nexus requirement to § 1512(c) (2), which applies to one who "corruptly ... obstructs, influences, or impedes any official proceeding, or attempts to do so." *See United States v. Reich*, 479 F.3d 179 (2d Cir. 2007).

6. *Assertion of privileges*. Would advising someone to assert an evidentiary or constitutional privilege demonstrate an intent to engage in corrupt persuasion? The courts have taken conflicting approaches to this issue.

For example, in *United States v. Doss*, 630 F.3d 1181 (9th Cir. 2011), a husband urged his wife to assert the marital privilege in a criminal investigation targeting the husband. Based on this conduct, the husband was convicted under § 1512(b). The Ninth Circuit reversed. Describing the circuit split, the court stated, "Two of our sister circuits conclude that persuasion with an 'improper purpose' qualifies (such as self-interest in impeding an investigation), while another concludes there must be something more inherently wrongful about the persuasion (such as bribery or encouraging someone to testify falsely)." Id. at 1186. The court held that the latter is the correct interpretation under *Arthur Andersen* and reversed the conviction.

In another case, *United States v. Gotti*, 459 F.3d 296, 342–43 (2d Cir. 2006), the defendant suggested to a co-conspirator that the co-conspirator invoke his Fifth Amendment privilege. The defendant was convicted of corrupt persuasion, and the Second Circuit affirmed. The court held that the defendant had a self-interested motivation in ensuring that the potential witness did not implicate the defendant. The court found that this motivation amounted to an "improper purpose" sufficient to support the conviction.

Are there dangers from allowing a defendant to be convicted based upon advising another person to assert a constitutional or evidentiary privilege? Why or why not?

7. *Obstruction, pending proceedings, and double jeopardy*. Please review the discussion of *United States v. Woodward*, Chapter 9, False Statements, *supra*. In that case,

the Supreme Court held that punishment under both the false statements statute, 18 U.S.C. §1001, and the international currency reporting statutes, 31 U.S.C. §§1508, 1101, based upon the same conduct does not violate the *Blockburger* rule for assessing double jeopardy violations. In *United States v. Peel*, 595 F.3d 763 (7th Cir. 2010), the court considered a similar issue. The defendant was a bankruptcy debtor who had attempted to blackmail a potential creditor into not filing a claim. He was convicted of bankruptcy fraud in violation of 18 U.S.C. §152(6), which criminalizes offering compensation to someone for "forbearing to act" in a bankruptcy case, and for obstruction under 18 U.S.C. §1512(c)(2) based upon the same conduct.

Did this double punishment violate the Double Jeopardy Clause? In an opinion by Judge Posner, the Seventh Circuit held that it did:

> [S]ince a bankruptcy proceeding is an 'official proceeding,' within the meaning of the obstruction of justice statute, the defendant's conviction for having attempted fraudulently to influence the bankruptcy proceeding by blackmailing [the potential creditor] into agreeing to drop her claim convicted him of obstruction of justice as well.

> The test for 'whether there are two offenses or only one, is whether each provision requires proof of a fact which the other does not.' The test was flunked here because convicting Peel of obstruction of justice did not require proof of any fact that didn't have to be proved to convict him of bankruptcy fraud. It was thus a lesser-included offense of bankruptcy fraud and the *Blockburger* test makes clear, and many cases hold, that to punish a person for a lesser-included offense as well as the 'including' offense is double jeopardy unless Congress intended the double punishment. The government does not argue that Congress intended that.

> This is like a case in which a person is tried for both murder and attempted murder. The elements are different, but since conviction for murder automatically convicts the defendant of attempted murder (for there can be no murder without attempting the deed), the defendant cannot be convicted of both crimes.

Peel, 595 F.3d at 767. In light of *Woodward*, was *Peel* correctly decided? If so, then why was the result in *Peel* different from the result in *Woodward*?

Problem

11-3. LeMont was a Central City police officer accused of using unjustified force on Grace, who had insulted LeMont after he arrested Grace for selling illegal narcotics. Grace later filed a complaint with the Central City Police Department, and the Department's Internal Affairs Division ("IAD") initiated an investigation into the incident. As a result of the investigation, LeMont was fired.

A federal grand jury was then convened to investigate whether LeMont had violated federal civil rights laws when inflicting physical abuse on Grace. LeMont approached Delores DeRota, who had witnessed the incident and paid her $7,000 to leave town before the grand jury could subpoena her. The grand jury later indicted LeMont under the corrupt persuasion statute, 18 U.S.C. § 1512(b)(2)(A).

At LeMont's trial, the judge instructed the jury as follows: "In order to find that the defendant intended to corruptly persuade the witness to withhold testimony, you must find that he knowingly persuaded the witness and that he did so with an improper purpose."

LeMont was convicted. On appeal, he argues that the trial judge committed reversible error when instructing the jury.

How should the court rule? Why?

11-4. The defendants were two F.B.I. agents who had engaged in a high-speed pursuit of a suspect. During the chase, the defendants fired their weapons at the suspect, who was wounded but nonetheless managed to escape. The agents filed no reports concerning the shooting, but a witness advised the F.B.I. of the incident. The agents were later charged with and convicted of assault with a deadly weapon and with obstruction of justice, 18 U.S.C. § 1512(c), for failing to follow F.B.I. policy requiring that agents file reports when they fire their guns. The government's theory on the obstruction charge was that the agents, by failing to file the required report, intended to interfere with a likely internal F.B.I. investigation into their conduct and that such an investigation would constitute an "official proceeding."

The defendants appeal their obstruction convictions, arguing that there was no contemplated "official proceeding," as required by the statute. How should the court rule? Why?

11-5. For the last 16 years, Defendant was an executive of the UK-based Murphy Company, Inc. ("Murphy"). For the last five years, Defendant was the Chief Executive Officer of Murphy. During that same period, Murphy and its subsidiaries were engaged in the sale of aluminum products in the United States. Three years ago, the Antitrust Division of the U.S. Department of Justice ("the Division") was conducting a federal grand jury investigation into possible federal antitrust offenses committed by Defendant and others involving aluminum products sold by Murphy. In the course of that investigation, the Division served Murphyite, Industries, Inc. ("Murphyite"), a U.S. subsidiary of Murphy, with a subpoena duces tecum requiring it and its affiliated companies to produce certain business records related to the aluminum products industry.

The government has evidence that, following service of the subpoena, Defendant directed two other Murphy employees to prepare a list of prior meetings with competitors, called a meeting at which he and the competitors discussed the antitrust investigation, agreed with the competitors at a meeting to tell a false story about what had occurred at their prior meetings, and "cross examined" the competitors about the details of the false story.

You are the prosecutor in charge of the investigation and are considering seeking an indictment of Defendant under § 1512. What theory or theories would you use? What are the strengths and weaknesses of each of those theories? Which charge(s) should you bring? Why?

11-6. When Special Counsel Robert Mueller's much-anticipated Report on the Investigation into Russian Interference in the 2016 Presidential Election ("Report") was released in the spring of 2019, there was much discussion and speculation over its language concerning possible obstruction of justice by President Donald Trump. The following are just a few of the instances of possible obstruction of justice by Trump identified in the Report (all quoted text is from the Executive Summary to Volume II of the Report, *available at* https://www.justice.gov/storage/report.pdf):

> *Termination of Comey.*
>
> On May 3, 2017, [FBI Director James] Comey testified in a congressional hearing, but declined to answer questions about whether the President was personally under investigation. Within days, the President decided to terminate Comey. The President insisted that the termination letter, which was written for public release, state that Comey had informed the President that he was not under investigation. The day of the firing, the White House maintained that Comey's termination resulted from independent recommendations from [the DOJ] for mishandling the Hillary Clinton email investigation. But the President had decided to fire Comey before hearing from the Department of Justice. The day after firing Comey, the President told Russian officials that he had "faced great pressure because of Russia," which had been "taken off" by Comey's firing. . . .
>
> *Efforts to Remove the Special Counsel.*
>
> On June 14, 2017, the media reported that the Special Counsel's Office was investigating whether the President had obstructed justice. Press reports called this "a major turning point" in the investigation: while Comey had told the President he was not under investigation, following Comey's firing, the President now was under investigation. The President reacted to this news with a series of tweets criticizing the Department of Justice and the Special Counsel's investigation. On June 17, 2017, the President called [White House Counsel, Don McGahn] at home and directed him to call the Acting Attorney General and say that the Special Counsel had conflicts of interest and must be removed. McGahn did not carry out the direction. . . .
>
> *Trump's Conduct Involving Flynn and Paul Manafort.*
>
> After [Michael] Flynn withdrew from a joint defense agreement with the President and began cooperating with the government, the President's personal counsel left a message for Flynn's attorneys reminding them of the President's warm feelings towards Flynn, which he said "still remains," and asking for a "heads up" if Flynn knew "information that implicates the President." When Flynn's counsel reiterated that Flynn could no longer share information pursuant to a joint defense agreement, the President's

personal counsel said he would make sure that the President knew that Fly-nn's actions reflected "hostility" towards the President. During Manafort's prosecution and when the jury in his criminal trial was deliberating, the President praised Manafort in public, said that Manafort was being treated unfairly, and declined to rule out a pardon. . . ."

The Report concluded that obstruction §§ 1503, 1505, 1512(b)(3), and 1512(c)(2) could all be implicated by the above (and other) facts. Nevertheless, the Office of Special Counsel "did not make a traditional prosecution decision about the facts" due to a number of extenuating circumstances. For example, some of the conduct investigated, such as the termination of the FBI director, "involved facially law-ful acts within his Article II [constitutional] authority." In addition, "unlike cases in which a subject engages in obstruction of justice to cover up a crime, the evi-dence [. . .] obtained did not establish that the President was involved in an under-lying crime related to Russian election interference." The Report explained that, "[a]lthough the obstruction statutes do not require proof of such a crime, the absence of that evidence affects the analysis of the President's intent and requires consideration of other possible motives for his conduct." Finally, "many of the Presi-dent's acts directed at witnesses, including discouragement of cooperation with the government and suggestions of possible future pardons, took place in public view." While "no principle of law excludes public acts from the reach of obstruction laws," the "circumstance is unusual."

With these and other considerations in mind (including some constitutional con-siderations not addressed here), the Office of Special Counsel decided not to reach a conclusion as to whether the President committed obstruction. Nevertheless, the Report explained, "if we had confidence after a thorough investigation of the facts that the President clearly did not commit obstruction of justice, we would so state. . . . Accordingly, while this report does not conclude that the President com-mitted a crime, it also does not exonerate him."

Which of the instances summarized above do you think provides the strongest basis for an obstruction charge? What would be your principal statutory basis for charging obstruction on these facts? What would be the President's best arguments in defense?

The office of Special Counsel noted that it "did not make a traditional prosecution decision" concerning President Trump due to the unusual circumstances surrounding the case. In light of the considerations outlined above, do you think this was the cor-rect decision? Why or why not?

F. Section 1519: The "Anti-Shredding" Statute

Sections 1519 and 1520 were enacted as part of the Sarbanes-Oxley Act of 2002. As discussed in the notes below, § 1520 requires that corporate auditors maintain certain records and provides criminal penalties for failure to do so. Section 1519 is much broader in scope and has been increasingly used to prosecute obstructive acts.

This statute covers not only acts designed to impede pending proceedings but also acts in contemplation of potentially pending proceedings.

The next case deals with a challenge to the breadth of the statute. Although §1519 is commonly known as the "anti-shredding" statute, the case demonstrates that the statute may cover many more activities.

United States v. Kernell

667 F.3d 746 (6th Cir. 2012)

COLE, CIRCUIT JUDGE.

Defendant David Kernell was convicted of obstruction of justice under 18 U.S.C. §1519 for deleting information from his computer that related to his effort to gain access to the email account of then-Alaska governor and Vice Presidential candidate Sarah Palin. Section 1519, passed as part of the Sarbanes-Oxley Act of 2002, prohibits the knowing destruction or alteration of any record "with the intent to impede, obstruct, or influence the investigation . . . of any matter within the jurisdiction of any department or agency of the United States . . . or in relation to or contemplation of any such matter or case. . . ." Kernell argues that §1519 is unconstitutionally vague, and that there is not sufficient evidence to support his conviction. We AFFIRM the conviction and sentence.

During the 2008 Presidential election, David Kernell was a student at the University of Tennessee, Knoxville. In September of 2008, it was reported in the New York Times that Sarah Palin, the then-governor of Alaska and Republican candidate for Vice President, used the email address "gov.palin@yahoo.com" ("the Palin email account") for personal and official business.

In the early morning of September 16, 2008, Kernell attempted to gain access to the Palin email account. To gain access to a Yahoo! email account without knowing the password, a user could type the user ID into the designated space on the Yahoo! home page and click the "help" link. From there, the user could access the "forgotten password" feature. The feature would prompt the user to provide the birthday, country of residence, and zip code of the user of the account. If this information were correctly provided, the user then answers a "secret question," which had been selected when the account was opened. Upon answering the question correctly, the user would be able to create a new password, and then use that password to access the account.

Kernell used this procedure to gain access to the Palin email account. Using information publicly available on the internet, Kernell entered Governor Palin's date of birth, country of residence and zip code. After a couple of unsuccessful attempts, Kernell guessed the correct answer to the secret challenge question: "where did you meet your spouse?" Kernell then changed the password on the Palin email account to "popcorn," and logged on to the account.

Soon after accessing the Palin email account, Kernell logged on to the internet message board "4chan.org". 4chan is known for its culture of anonymous posting, and often contains content that is offensive or socially unacceptable. Kernell began a message thread on the /b/, or "random," board claiming to have "hacked," or surreptitiously accessed, the Palin email account. He supported his claim with screen shots of the Palin email account's Inbox, as well as at least one photograph of members of the Palin family taken from attachments to the emails in the account. At the end of the thread, he disclosed the new password he created for the Palin email account, allowing any user reading the thread to access the account. 4chan site administrators took down the thread soon after the password was shared.

While this first thread was still active, one anonymous 4chan user claimed to have informed the FBI of Kernell's activities. Other users encouraged Kernell to distribute the information before government officials discovered the access. Approximately an hour after Kernell initiated the thread, a 4chan user logged into the Palin email account, changed the password to freeze out other users, and informed a Palin aide that the account had been hacked.

The next day, September 17, 2008, Kernell returned to 4chan and began a new thread that began "Hello, /b/" ("the Hello post"). In this thread, Kernell took credit for hacking the Palin email account, and described in detail how he accomplished the task. Kernell claims that he disclosed the password to the 4chan community because he wanted the information "out there," and claimed to have deleted information from his computer as a result of his fear of being investigated. Kernell also criticized the individual who alerted the Palin staffer to the hack.

Later computer forensic examinations revealed that Kernell had taken numerous actions to remove information from the computer relating to his access to the Palin email account. At some point between the initial post on 4chan and the evening of September 18, Kernell cleared the cache on his Internet Explorer browser, removing the record of websites he had visited during that period. He also uninstalled the Firefox internet browser, which more thoroughly removed the record of his internet access using that browser, and ran the disk defragmentation program on his computer, which reorganizes and cleans up the existing space on a hard drive, and has the effect of removing many of the remnants of information or files that had been deleted. Finally, Kernell deleted a series of images that he had downloaded from the Palin email account.

On the evening of September 18, 2008, the FBI contacted Kernell's father to determine Kernell's whereabouts. The next day, Kernell contacted FBI investigators and attended a brief phone meeting arranged by Kernell's attorney. Kernell called the FBI again on the evening of September 20, but never provided any information to investigators, and later on September 20 the FBI executed a search warrant for Kernell's apartment and seized his computer. The seized computer, despite the deletions, contained numerous items related to accessing the Palin email account, including a draft of the "Hello" post.

A federal grand jury indicted Kernell on four separate offenses. Count One alleged that Kernell committed identity theft in violation of 18 U.S.C. §1028(a)(7). Count Two alleged that Kernell committed wire fraud in relation to improperly obtaining electronic information belonging to Palin in violation of 18 U.S.C. §1343. Count Three alleged Kernell improperly obtained information from a protected computer in violation of 18 U.S.C. §1030(a)(2)(C). Finally, Count Four alleged Kernell obstructed justice stemming from the deletion of information on his computer, in violation of 18 U.S.C. §1519, a component of the Sarbanes-Oxley Act of 2002. . . .

The jury returned an acquittal on Count Two, deadlocked on Count One, found Kernell guilty on the obstruction of justice charge in Count Four and a lesser-included offense under Count Three. Kernell appeals his conviction, seeking only the dismissal of Count Four.

We review the district court's denial of Kernell's challenge to the constitutionality of 18 U.S.C. §1519 de novo. A criminal statute is unconstitutionally vague if it "defines an offense in such a way that ordinary people cannot understand what is prohibited or if it encourages arbitrary or discriminatory enforcement." For challenges to the statute that do not implicate First Amendment concerns, the "defendant bears the burden of establishing that the statute is vague as applied to his particular case, not merely that the statute could be construed as vague in some hypothetical situation."

For appeals from a denial of a judgment of acquittal based on the sufficiency of the evidence, "the standard of review is whether, after viewing the evidence in the light most favorable to the prosecution, any rational trier of fact could have found essential elements of the crime[.]" . . .

Kernell raises two related challenges to the constitutionality of 18 U.S.C. §1519. First, Kernell argues that the structure of the statute creates an ambiguity as to the application of *mens rea* to the various elements of the statute. Second, Kernell argues that the statute's requirement that the defendant act "in contemplation of an investigation" is vague as to the required state of mind.

Section 1519 states:

> Whoever knowingly alters, destroys, mutilates, conceals, covers up, falsifies, or makes a false entry in any record, document, or tangible object with the intent to impede, obstruct, or influence the investigation or proper administration of any matter within the jurisdiction of any department or agency of the United States or any case filed under title 11, or in relation to or contemplation of any such matter or case, shall be fined under this title, imprisoned not more than 20 years, or both.

Kernell argues that the statute prohibits two types of conduct: (1) knowingly destroying documents with the intent to impede an investigation, and (2) knowingly destroying documents in relation to or in contemplation of an investigation.

For this reason, Kernell argues that § 1519 is a general intent statute as it was applied to him, and the lack of specific intent to obstruct for those convicted of destroying documents in contemplation of an investigation renders the statute vague.

Grammatically, Kernell has an argument. The phrase starting "with the intent to impede" requires a direct object, and there is no natural reading of the statute that makes a contemplated investigation that object, particularly given the presence of the word "or" rather than "either" before the phrase "in relation to or in contemplation of." However, the Supreme Court has frequently refused to adopt "the most grammatical reading of the statute" when a lack of intent would risk punishing otherwise innocent conduct. *United States v. X-Citement Video, Inc.*, 513 U.S. 64, 70 (1994). When faced with two readings of the statute, one of which is constitutional and the other which is not, Congress is presumed to have enacted a constitutional statute. Additionally, Congressional statements about § 1519 strongly support the argument that Congress intended a specific intent to apply throughout § 1519. "[T]he intent required is the intent to obstruct, not some level of knowledge." 148 Cong. Rec. S7418, S7419 (daily ed. July 26, 2002) (statement of Senator Leahy).

The Eighth Circuit, in *United States v. Yielding*, 657 F.3d 688, 711 (8th Cir.2011), recently parsed the language § 1519 in a manner we find instructive. *Yielding* identifies three scenarios under which § 1519 would apply: (1) when a defendant acts directly with respect to "the investigation or proper administration of any matter," that is, a pending matter, (2) when a defendant acts "in . . . contemplation of any such matter," and (3) when a defendant acts "in relation to . . . any such matter." Under this reading, "[t]he statute . . . does not allow a defendant to escape liability for shredding documents with intent to obstruct a foreseeable investigation of a matter within the jurisdiction of a federal agency just because the investigation has not yet commenced." *Id.* However, "the statute does not impose liability for 'knowingly . . . destroy[ing] . . . any . . . document . . . in . . . contemplation of any [federal] matter,' *without* an intent to impede, obstruct, or influence a matter." *Id.* (quoting the statute) (alterations and emphasis in the original). By applying this requirement to each of the three scenarios, the construction creates the needed specific intent and avoids Kernell's concern that "the statute would forbid innocent conduct such as routine destruction of documents that a person consciously and in good faith determines are irrelevant to a foreseeable federal matter." *Id.* The district court used *Yielding*'s interpretation of the statute when it instructed the jury. We agree with the district court and *Yielding* in their interpretation of § 1519. . . .

Kernell argues that even under the government's construction, the statute is unconstitutional because of ambiguities regarding whether it contains requirements found in other obstruction-of-justice provisions, such as a nexus between the investigation and the alleged conduct or the requirement for the alleged conduct to be done with "corrupt intentions" or be "inherently malign." *See generally United States v. Aguilar*, 515 U.S. 593 (1995) (nexus requirement); *Arthur Andersen LLP v. United States*, 544 U.S. 696 (2005) ("inherently malign" requirement). Kernell asserts that the fact that some courts have applied requirements from other obstruction of justice statutes to § 1519 while others do not proves that the statute is vague. Even if true, the fact that different courts have interpreted a statute differently does not make the statute vague — if that were true, a circuit split over the interpretation of a criminal statute would by definition render the statute unconstitutional.

It should also be noted that the differences between the courts' approaches to § 1519 are not as great as Kernell implies. To the extent that cases interpreting § 1519 have discussed *Arthur Andersen* and corrupt intent, they have found that § 1519 meets that requirement, or the "intent to obstruct" language subsumes the requirement. Whether or not courts have explicitly discussed *Arthur Andersen,* no decision interpreting § 1519 implies that *Arthur Andersen* imposes an additional requirement beyond that found in the text of § 1519. . . .

Two district courts have applied the nexus requirement to § 1519. We are neither bound by their interpretation, nor do we agree with it. As the government points out, the nexus requirement is derived from the language of other obstruction-of-justice statutes, wording that is not found in § 1519. Congress is not required to use the same structure for all obstruction-of-justice statutes. In addition, the legislative history of § 1519 shows that Congress designed the provision to be more expansive than earlier obstruction of justice statutes by dispensing with some of these collateral requirements. The Senate report that accompanied the Sarbanes-Oxley Act specifically disclaimed a nexus requirement for § 1519. As the Eighth Circuit discussed in *Yielding,* importing requirements from other obstruction of justice cases over to § 1519 is directly contrary to the legislative intent, as well as having no support in the text itself.

Kernell also argues that the "in contemplation of an investigation" element is vague, because it does not specify what a defendant must know or believe about an investigation in order to trigger potential liability under § 1519. Courts considering the question have consistently held that the belief that a federal investigation directed at the defendant's conduct might begin at some point in the future satisfies the "in contemplation" prong. . . .

Moreover, even if this element is potentially vague as it relates to hypothetical defendants, it is not vague as it relates to Kernell. Kernell had a recognition (memorialized in his "Hello" post) that his conduct might result in a Federal investigation:

> "THIS internet was serious business, yes I was behind a proxy, only one, if this sh* * ever got to the FBI I was f* * * * *, I panicked, i still wanted the stuff out there but I didn't know how to rapidsh* * all that stuff, so I posted that pass on /b/, and then promptly deleted everything, and unplugged my internet and just sat there in a comatose state."

(edited from the original). Thus there is no doubt from this post that Kernell "contemplat[ed]" that an investigation would occur when he took his action, since he specifically referenced the possibility of an FBI investigation in his post. As such, to the extent there are any ambiguities in the "contemplation" prong, Kernell may not raise or rely on them.

Section 1519 clearly sets out the elements that the government must prove for a conviction under the statute. All courts looking at the question have rejected the constitutional challenge, and any ambiguities that might exist apply to a hypothetical defendant, not to Kernell and his specific conduct. For this reason, we reject Kernell's challenge to the constitutionality of 18 U.S.C. § 1519. . . .

Notes and Questions

1. *The textual issue.* What argument did the defendant make concerning the appropriate interpretation of the statutory text? How did the court respond? Do you agree with the court's conclusion?

2. *The nexus requirement.* As seen above, courts have applied *Aguilar*'s nexus requirement under § 1503 to §§ 1505, 1512(b), and § 1512(c) as well. Should that requirement also apply to § 1519? *See United States v. Moore*, 708 F.3d 639, 649 (5th Cir. 2013) ("There is no requirement [under § 1519] that a defendant must know that his conduct is impeding or will impede a pending investigation") (citing *United States v. Moyer*, 674 F.3d 192, 208 (3d Cir. 2012)).

3. *Mens rea.* Another issue raised in *Kernell* is whether the mens rea requirement under *Arthur Andersen* should apply to § 1519. The Court in *Aguilar* held that "if the defendant lacks knowledge that his actions are likely to affect the proceeding, he lacks the requisite intent to obstruct." Thus, under the corrupt intent requirement of § 1503 (and § 1505 according to the courts), the defendant must intend to interfere with a pending proceeding. Where there is no pending proceeding, but merely a contemplated proceeding under § 1512(b), *Arthur Andersen* held that "[a] 'knowingly . . . corrup[t] persaude[r]' cannot be someone who persuades others to shred documents under a document retention policy when he does not have *in contemplation* any particular official proceeding in which those documents might be material." According to *Kernell*, does this requirement apply to § 1519? Should it? Why or why not?

4. *The "in contemplation of" element.* Exactly what does the government have to show to prove this element? Is the statute clear in this regard? If not, is the statute vague on its face? As applied to Kernell? What was the evidence with respect to this element in his case?

Problems

11-7. When Andrew, CEO of a small-town bank, learned that the federal government had initiated an investigation into whether he had engaged in anticompetitive conspiracies with other purchasers at local foreclosure auctions in violation of the Sherman Act, he manually deleted emails relating to the relevant auctions from his and his employee Steve's work-computer inboxes. Andrew then ran "scrubbing" software on his and Steve's work computers, as well as the company's email server, in an attempt to preclude any subsequent recovery of the deleted documents. Unbeknownst to Andrew, however, his failure to "double-delete" the emails (i.e., delete the emails from the "deleted items" folder as well as the inbox) left the emails accessible to government agents. The government charged Andrew with §1519 obstruction of justice for these actions. At trial, the government presented undisputed evidence that Andrew had manually deleted the emails from the computers after learning of the subpoena. Andrew moved for acquittal after the government had presented its case, arguing that he could not violate §1519 without having actually destroyed or concealed the emails. In response, the government explained that its obstruction charge was based exclusively on Andrew's having, after learning of the subpoena, manually moved the emails on his and Steve's computers from the inbox to the deleted items folder. According to the government, "All the jury has to do is find that Andrew hit the delete button. That's it. It's that simple."

How should the court rule? Why?

11-8. After arresting Tony, Sheriff Kripke proceeded to punch him twice in the head. Later that evening, Kripke filled out a County Sheriff's Office form, titled "Obstructing an Officer." On the form, which related to his use of force against Tony, Kripke omitted the fact that he struck Tony in the head. Months later, Tony filed a complaint and the federal government began investigating the incident. Fourteen months later, Kripke was charged with deprivation of rights under color of law in violation of 18 U.S.C. §243. He was also charged with §1519 obstruction of justice for omitting the fact that he punched Tony in the head from his County Sheriff's Office form. Kripke moved to dismiss the obstruction charge because: (1) there was no federal investigation or proceeding at the time he filled out the form, and it was not foreseeable that there would be such a proceeding; and (2) his omission did not constitute a falsification or destruction of a document under §1519.

How should the court rule on Kripke's motion to dismiss the obstruction charge? Why?

———————

Does §1519 contribute to what some have termed the "over-criminalization" crisis? Kernell was charged with computer crimes and wire fraud in connection with the hacking. But were Kernell's efforts to remove information from his computer sufficiently serious to merit a separate felony obstruction count? In that regard, consider the case below.

Yates v. United States

574 U.S. 528 (2015)

Justice GINSBURG announced the judgment of the Court and delivered an opinion, in which THE CHIEF JUSTICE, Justice BREYER, and Justice SOTOMAYOR join.

John Yates, a commercial fisherman, caught undersized red grouper in federal waters in the Gulf of Mexico. To prevent federal authorities from confirming that he had harvested undersized fish, Yates ordered a crew member to toss the suspect catch into the sea. For this offense, he was charged with, and convicted of, violating 18 U.S.C. § 1519, which provides:

> Whoever knowingly alters, destroys, mutilates, conceals, covers up, falsifies, or makes a false entry in any record, document, or tangible object with the intent to impede, obstruct, or influence the investigation or proper administration of any matter within the jurisdiction of any department or agency of the United States or any case filed under title 11, or in relation to or contemplation of any such matter or case, shall be fined under this title, imprisoned not more than 20 years, or both.

Yates . . . maintains that fish are not trapped within the term "tangible object," as that term is used in § 1519.

Section 1519 was enacted as part of the Sarbanes-Oxley Act of 2002, 116 Stat. 745, legislation designed to protect investors and restore trust in financial markets following the collapse of Enron Corporation. A fish is no doubt an object that is tangible; fish can be seen, caught, and handled, and a catch, as this case illustrates, is vulnerable to destruction. But it would cut § 1519 loose from its financial-fraud mooring to hold that it encompasses any and all objects, whatever their size or significance, destroyed with obstructive intent. Mindful that in Sarbanes-Oxley, Congress trained its attention on corporate and accounting deception and cover-ups, we conclude that a matching construction of § 1519 is in order: A tangible object captured by § 1519, we hold, must be one used to record or preserve information.

The Sarbanes-Oxley Act, all agree, was prompted by the exposure of Enron's massive accounting fraud and revelations that the company's outside auditor, Arthur Andersen LLP, had systematically destroyed potentially incriminating documents. The government acknowledges that § 1519 was intended to prohibit, in particular, corporate document-shredding to hide evidence of financial wrongdoing. Prior law made it an offense to "intimidat[e], threate[n], or corruptly persuad[e] *another person*" to shred documents. § 1512(b) (emphasis added). Section 1519 cured a conspicuous omission by imposing liability on a person who destroys records himself. The new section also expanded prior law by including within the provision's reach "any matter within the jurisdiction of any department or agency of the United States."

In the government's view, § 1519 extends beyond the principal evil motivating its passage. The words of § 1519, the government argues, support reading the provision as a general ban on the spoliation of evidence, covering all physical items that might be relevant to any matter under federal investigation.

Yates urges a contextual reading of § 1519, tying "tangible object" to the surrounding words, the placement of the provision within the Sarbanes-Oxley Act, and related provisions enacted at the same time, in particular § 1520 and § 1512(c)(1). Section 1519, he maintains, targets not all manner of evidence, but records, documents, and tangible objects used to preserve them, *e.g.,* computers, servers, and other media on which information is stored.

We agree with Yates and reject the government's unrestrained reading. "Tangible object" in § 1519, we conclude, is better read to cover only objects one can use to record or preserve information, not all objects in the physical world.

The ordinary meaning of an "object" that is "tangible," as stated in dictionary definitions, is "a discrete ... thing," Webster's Third New International Dictionary 1555 (2002), that "possess[es] physical form," Black's Law Dictionary 1683 (10th ed. 2014). From this premise, the government concludes that "tangible object," as that term appears in § 1519, covers the waterfront, including fish from the sea.

Whether a statutory term is unambiguous, however, does not turn solely on dictionary definitions of its component words. Ordinarily, a word's usage accords with its dictionary definition. In law as in life, however, the same words, placed in different contexts, sometimes mean different things.

We have several times affirmed that identical language may convey varying content when used in different statutes, sometimes even in different provisions of the same statute. In short, although dictionary definitions of the words "tangible" and "object" bear consideration, they are not dispositive of the meaning of "tangible object" in § 1519. . . .

Familiar interpretive guides aid our construction of the words "tangible object" as they appear in § 1519.

We note first § 1519's caption: "Destruction, alteration, or falsification of records in Federal investigations and bankruptcy." That heading conveys no suggestion that the section prohibits spoliation of any and all physical evidence, however remote from records. Neither does the title of the section of the Sarbanes-Oxley Act in which § 1519 was placed, § 802: "Criminal penalties for altering documents." Furthermore, § 1520, the only other provision passed as part of § 802, is titled "Destruction of corporate audit records" and addresses only that specific subset of records and documents. While these headings are not commanding, they supply cues that Congress did not intend "tangible object" in § 1519 to sweep within its reach physical objects of every kind, including things no one would describe as records, documents, or devices closely associated with them. If Congress indeed meant to make § 1519 an all-encompassing ban on the spoliation of evidence, as the dissent believes Congress did, one would have expected a clearer indication of that intent.

Section 1519's position within Chapter 73 of Title 18 further signals that § 1519 was not intended to serve as a cross-the-board ban on the destruction of physical evidence of every kind. Congress placed § 1519 (and its companion provision § 1520) at the end of the chapter, following immediately after the pre-existing § 1516, § 1517, and § 1518, each of them prohibiting obstructive acts in specific contexts. *See* § 1516 (audits of recipients of federal funds); § 1517 (federal examinations of financial institutions); § 1518 (criminal investigations of federal health care offenses).

But Congress did not direct codification of the Sarbanes-Oxley Act's other additions to Chapter 73 adjacent to these specialized provisions. Instead, Congress directed placement of those additions within or alongside retained provisions that address obstructive acts relating broadly to official proceedings and criminal trials. . . . Congress thus ranked § 1519, not among the broad proscriptions, but together with specialized provisions expressly aimed at corporate fraud and financial audits. This placement accords with the view that Congress' conception of § 1519's coverage was considerably more limited than the government's.

The contemporaneous passage of § 1512(c)(1), which was contained in a section of the Sarbanes-Oxley Act discrete from the section embracing § 1519 and § 1520, is also instructive. Section 1512(c)(1) provides:

(c) Whoever corruptly —

(1) alters, destroys, mutilates, or conceals a record, document, or other object, or attempts to do so, with the intent to impair the object's integrity or availability for use in an official proceeding

. . .

shall be fined under this title or imprisoned not more than 20 years, or both.

The legislative history reveals that § 1512(c)(1) was drafted and proposed after § 1519. The government argues, and Yates does not dispute, that § 1512(c)(1)'s reference to "other object" includes any and every physical object. But if § 1519's reference to "tangible object" already included all physical objects, as the government and the dissent contend, then Congress had no reason to enact § 1512(c)(1): Virtually any act that would violate § 1512(c)(1) no doubt would violate § 1519 as well, for § 1519 applies to "the investigation or proper administration of any matter within the jurisdiction of any department or agency of the United States . . . or in relation to or contemplation of any such matter," not just to "an official proceeding."

The government acknowledges that, under its reading, § 1519 and § 1512(c)(1) "significantly overlap." Nowhere does the government explain what independent function § 1512(c)(1) would serve if the government is right about the sweeping scope of § 1519. We resist a reading of § 1519 that would render superfluous an entire provision passed in proximity as part of the same Act.

The words immediately surrounding "tangible object" in § 1519 — "falsifies, or makes a false entry in any record [or] document" — also cabin the contextual meaning of that term. As explained in *Gustafson v. Alloyd Co.*, 513 U.S. 561, 575 (1995), we rely on the principle of *noscitur a sociis* — a word is known by the company it keeps — to "avoid ascribing to one word a meaning so broad that it is inconsistent with its accompanying words, thus giving unintended breadth to the Acts of Congress." (internal quotation marks omitted).

The *noscitur a sociis* canon operates in a similar manner here. "Tangible object" is the last in a list of terms that begins "any record [or] document." The term is therefore appropriately read to refer, not to any tangible object, but specifically to the subset of tangible objects involving records and documents, *i.e.*, objects used to record or preserve information. . . .

Having used traditional tools of statutory interpretation to examine markers of congressional intent within the Sarbanes-Oxley Act and § 1519 itself, we are persuaded that an aggressive interpretation of "tangible object" must be rejected. It is highly improbable that Congress would have buried a general spoliation statute covering objects of any and every kind in a provision targeting fraud in financial record keeping. . . .

Finally, if our recourse to traditional tools of statutory construction leaves any doubt about the meaning of "tangible object," as that term is used in § 1519, we would invoke the rule that "ambiguity concerning the ambit of criminal statutes should be resolved in favor of lenity." *Cleveland v. United States*, 531 U.S. 12, 25 (2000) (quoting *Rewis v. United States*, 401 U.S. 808, 812 (1971)). That interpretative principle is relevant here, where the government urges a reading of § 1519 that exposes individuals to 20-year prison sentences for tampering with *any* physical object that *might* have evidentiary value in *any* federal investigation into any offense, no matter whether the investigation is pending or merely contemplated, or whether the offense subject to investigation is criminal or civil. In determining the meaning of "tangible object" in § 1519, "it is appropriate, before we choose the harsher alternative, to require that Congress should have spoken in language that is clear and definite." *See Cleveland*, 531 U.S. at 25.

For the reasons stated, we resist reading § 1519 expansively to create a coverall spoliation of evidence statute, advisable as such a measure might be. Leaving that important decision to Congress, we hold that a "tangible object" within § 1519's compass is one used to record or preserve information. The judgment of the U.S. Court of Appeals for the Eleventh Circuit is therefore reversed, and the case is remanded for further proceedings.

JUSTICE KAGAN, with whom JUSTICE SCALIA, JUSTICE KENNEDY, and JUSTICE THOMAS join, dissenting.

A criminal law, 18 U.S.C. § 1519, prohibits tampering with "any record, document, or tangible object" in an attempt to obstruct a federal investigation. This case raises the question whether the term "tangible object" means the same thing in § 1519 as it means in everyday language — any object capable of being touched. The answer should be easy: Yes. The term "tangible object" is broad, but clear. Throughout the U.S. Code and many States' laws, it invariably covers physical objects of all kinds. And in § 1519, context confirms what bare text says: All the words surrounding "tangible object" show that Congress meant the term to have a wide range. That fits with

Congress's evident purpose in enacting § 1519: to punish those who alter or destroy physical evidence — *any* physical evidence — with the intent of thwarting federal law enforcement.

The plurality instead interprets "tangible object" to cover "only objects one can use to record or preserve information." The concurring opinion similarly, if more vaguely, contends that "tangible object" should refer to "something similar to records or documents" — and shouldn't include colonial farmhouses, crocodiles, or fish. (ALITO, J., concurring in judgment). In my view, conventional tools of statutory construction all lead to a more conventional result: A "tangible object" is an object that's tangible. I would apply the statute that Congress enacted and affirm the judgment below.

While the plurality starts its analysis with § 1519's heading, I would begin with § 1519's text. When Congress has not supplied a definition, we generally give a statutory term its ordinary meaning. As the plurality must acknowledge, the ordinary meaning of "tangible object" is "a discrete thing that possesses physical form." A fish is, of course, a discrete thing that possesses physical form. *See generally* Dr. Seuss, *One Fish Two Fish Red Fish Blue Fish* (1960). So the ordinary meaning of the term "tangible object" in § 1519, as no one here disputes, covers fish (including too-small red grouper). . . .

Section 1519 refers to "any" tangible object, thus indicating (in line with *that* word's plain meaning) a tangible object "of whatever kind." Webster's Third New International Dictionary 97 (2002). This Court has time and again recognized that "any" has "an expansive meaning," bringing within a statute's reach *all* types of the item (here, "tangible object") to which the law refers. And the adjacent laundry list of verbs in § 1519 ("alters, destroys, mutilates, conceals, covers up, falsifies, or makes a false entry") further shows that Congress wrote a statute with a wide scope. Those words are supposed to ensure — just as "tangible object" is meant to — that § 1519 covers the whole world of evidence-tampering, in all its prodigious variety. . . .

As Congress recognized in using a broad term, giving immunity to those who destroy non-documentary evidence has no sensible basis in penal policy. A person who hides a murder victim's body is no less culpable than one who burns the victim's diary. A fisherman, like John Yates, who dumps undersized fish to avoid a fine is no less blameworthy than one who shreds his vessel's catch log for the same reason. Congress thus treated both offenders in the same way. It understood, in enacting § 1519, that destroying evidence is destroying evidence, whether or not that evidence takes documentary form. . . .

Finally, when all else fails, the plurality invokes the rule of lenity. But even in its most robust form, that rule only kicks in when, "after all legitimate tools of interpretation have been exhausted, 'a reasonable doubt persists' regarding whether Congress has made the defendant's conduct a federal crime." *Abramski v. United States,* 573 U.S. 169, 193 (2014) (SCALIA, J., dissenting) (quoting *Moskal v. United States,* 498 U.S. 103, 108 (1990)). No such doubt lingers here. The plurality points to the breadth of § 1519 as though breadth were equivalent to ambiguity. It is not. Section 1519 *is* very broad. It is also very clear. Every traditional tool of statutory interpretation points in the same direction, toward "object" meaning object. Lenity offers no proper refuge from that straightforward (even though capacious) construction. . . .

If none of the traditional tools of statutory interpretation can produce today's result, then what accounts for it? The plurality offers a clue when it emphasizes the disproportionate penalties § 1519 imposes if the law is read broadly. That brings to the surface the real issue: overcriminalization and excessive punishment in the U.S. Code.

Now as to this statute, I think the plurality somewhat — though only somewhat — exaggerates the matter. The plurality omits from its description of § 1519 the requirement that a person act "knowingly" and with "the intent to impede, obstruct, or influence" federal law enforcement. And in highlighting § 1519's maximum penalty, the plurality glosses over the absence of any prescribed minimum. (Let's not forget that Yates's sentence was not 20 years, but 30 days.) Congress presumably enacts laws with high maximums and no minimums when it thinks the prohibited conduct may run the gamut from major to minor. That is assuredly true of acts obstructing justice. Most district judges, as Congress knows, will recognize differences between such cases and prosecutions like this one, and will try to make the punishment fit the crime. Still and all, I tend to think, for the reasons the plurality gives, that § 1519 is a bad law — too broad and undifferentiated, with too-high maximum penalties, which give prosecutors too much leverage and sentencers too much discretion. And I'd go further: In those ways, § 1519 is unfortunately not an outlier, but an emblem of a deeper pathology in the federal criminal code.

But whatever the wisdom or folly of § 1519, this Court does not get to rewrite the law. "Resolution of the pros and cons of whether a statute should sweep broadly or narrowly is for Congress." *Rodgers*, 466 U.S. at 484. If judges disagree with Congress's choice, we are perfectly entitled to say so — in lectures, in law review articles, and even in dicta. But we are not entitled to replace the statute Congress enacted with an alternative of our own design.

I respectfully dissent.

[Opinion of Justice Alito, concurring in the judgment, omitted.]

Notes and Questions

1. *Rules of statutory construction.* Ginsburg's opinion and Kagan's dissent in *Yates* each draws heavily on statutory construction rules. Who has the better of the argument? Why?

2. *Overcriminalization.* In her dissent, Justice Kagan characterizes the plurality opinion as essentially policy-driven: "The plurality offers a clue [as to its reasoning] when it emphasizes the disproportionate penalties § 1519 imposes if the law is read broadly. That brings to the surface the real issue: overcriminalization and excessive

punishment in the U.S. Code." Justice Kagan shares these concerns later in her opinion, but still reaches a different result. Why? Who's right?

3. *Prosecutorial discretion.* Is the careful exercise of prosecutorial discretion a solution to a potentially overly-broad criminal statute? In an article for *Politico Magazine*, the defendant argued that "DOJ's criminal indictment against me is an inappropriate and insulting expansion of federal criminal law. The Sarbanes-Oxley Act was never intended to attack unassuming, hardworking Americans for crimes unrelated to the destruction of records or documents." John Yates, *A Fish Story*, Politico (April 24, 2014), *available at* http://www.politico.com/magazine/story/2014/04/a-fish-story -106010.html#ixzz3JkIT2wPL. Does the defendant have a point? Why or why not?

Many argued that the *Yates* prosecution was emblematic of the move towards over-criminalization. As one of the amicus briefs in that case put it:

> The unseemly prosecution in this case . . . is but a symptom of the under-
> lying problem. It is the latest chapter in a long history of the government's
> misuse of vaguely drawn statutes to criminalize behavior far beyond what
> any ordinary person would understand to be prohibited. In the academic
> world, this problem is known as 'overcriminalization.' And the term
> describes two chief evils: first, the quantitative expansion of federal law to
> include countless, and often redundant, criminal provisions; and second,
> the qualitative breadth with which Congress has drafted many of these
> statutes.

See Brief for Eighteen Criminal Law Professors as Amici Curiae in Support of Petitioner, *Yates v. United States*, 2014 WL 3101373 (July 7, 2014).

Is this a fair characterization? If so, what is the solution? Does relying on prosecutorial discretion solve the problem? Why or why not?

G. Legal and Ethical Considerations for Attorneys

All "cover-up" crimes provide potential pitfalls for attorneys, none perhaps more so than the obstruction statutes. *See, e.g., United States v. Cintolo*, 818 F.2d 980 (1st Cir. 1987), discussed below. The wide scope of an "endeavor" to obstruct justice can all too easily sweep an attorney's actions within the obstruction statutes' coverage. Note that 18 U.S.C. §1515(c), adopted in 1986, provides that "[t]his chapter does not prohibit or punish the providing of lawful, bona fide, legal representation services in connection with or anticipation of an official proceeding." A frequently cited concurring opinion in the *Barry Bonds* case, *supra*, states:

> Stretched to its limits, section 1503 poses a significant hazard for everyone
> involved in our system of justice, because so much of what the adversary
> process calls for could be construed as obstruction. Did a tort plaintiff
> file a complaint seeking damages far in excess of what the jury ultimately

awards? That could be viewed as corruptly endeavoring to 'influence . . . the due administration of justice' by seeking to recover more than the claim deserves. So could any of the following behaviors that make up the bread and butter of litigation: filing an answer that denies liability for conduct that is ultimately adjudged wrongful or malicious; unsuccessfully filing (or opposing) a motion to dismiss or for summary judgment; seeking a continuance in order to inflict delay on the opposing party; frivolously taking an appeal or petitioning for certiorari—the list is endless. Witnesses would be particularly vulnerable because, as the Supreme Court has noted, '[u]nder the pressures and tensions of interrogation, it is not uncommon for the most earnest witnesses to give answers that are not entirely responsive.' *Bronston v. United States*, 409 U.S. 352, 358 (1973).

Lawyers face the most pervasive threat under such a regime. Zealous advocacy sometimes calls for pushing back against an adversary's just case and casting a despicable client in a favorable light, yet such conduct could be described as 'endeavor[ing] to . . . impede . . . the due administration of justice.' Even routine advocacy provides ample occasion for stumbling into the heartland of the omnibus clause's sweeping coverage. Oral arguments provide a ready example. One need not spend much time in one of our courtrooms to hear lawyers dancing around questions from the bench rather than giving pithy, direct answers. There is, for instance, the ever popular 'but that is not this case' retort to a hypothetical, which could be construed as an effort to divert the court and thereby 'influence . . . the due administration of justice.'

It is true that any such maneuver would violate section 1503 only if it were done 'corruptly.' But it is equally true that we have given 'corruptly" such a broad construction that it does not meaningfully cabin the kind of conduct that is subject to prosecution. As noted, we have held that a defendant acts "corruptly," as that term is used in section 1503, if he does so 'with the purpose of obstructing justice.' In the examples above, a prosecutor could argue that a complaint was filed corruptly because it was designed to extort a nuisance settlement, or an answer was filed corruptly because its principal purpose was to pressure a needy plaintiff into an unjust settlement, or that the lawyer who parried a judicial hypothetical with 'but that is not this case' was endeavoring to distract the court so it would reach a wrong result. That a jury or a judge might not buy such an argument is neither here nor there; a criminal prosecution, even one that results in an acquittal, is a life-wrenching event. Nor does an acquittal wipe clean the suspicion that a guilty defendant got off on a technicality.

Bonds, 784 F.3d at 584.

Are these concerns justified? For a skeptical view, see Randall Eliason, *Barry Bonds Obstruction Case Splinters the Ninth Circuit*, SIDEBARS: REFLECTIONS ON WHITE COLLAR CRIME AND FEDERAL CRIMINAL LAW (April 27, 2015), https://sidebarsblog

.com/barry-bonds-obstruction-case-splinters-the-ninth-circuit. Keep these poten-tial concerns in mind as you read the materials below.

One particular dilemma arises when the attorney's duties to perform as a zeal-ous advocate on behalf of clients appears to conflict with the government's efforts to obtain facts in a civil or criminal investigation.

Notes and Questions

1. *Role of in-house counsel.* In one high-profile prosecution, the government charged Lauren Stevens, in-house counsel for pharmaceutical company GlaxoSmithKline, with obstruction of justice under §§ 1512(c) and 1519 and with making false state-ments under § 1001. The government alleged that the defendant obstructed an inves-tigation into illegal marketing of one of the company's products by making false statements in response to investigators' requests for information. The alleged false statements were issued after the defendant had extensively consulted with outside counsel concerning the proper responses to the government's inquiry.

At the end of the government's case, the court granted the defendant's motion for a judgment of acquittal, a rare result in a criminal trial. The court found that the defendant had relied upon the advice of counsel when issuing the statements and that a reasonable jury would not be able to find her guilty beyond a reason-able doubt. The judge stated that "the defendant in this case should never have been prosecuted and she should be permitted to resume her career." *See* Alicia Mundy & Brent Kendall, *U.S. Rebuffed in Glaxo Misconduct Case*, WALL ST. J., May 11, 2011, http://online.wsj.com/articles/SB10001424052748703730804576315101670843340. For a detailed analysis of the case, see Virginia S. Gibson & Thomas J. Widor, *Dismissal of the Stevens Case: What Now for In-House Attorneys?*, WHITE COLLAR CRIME REP. (BNA) (June 3, 2011).

This was a hugely controversial prosecution. Should attorneys be prosecuted for actions that they take on behalf of clients? What are the risks of such prosecutions?

2. *Production of documents.* White collar investigations often gain evidence through grand jury subpoenas for the production of documents. A corporate client will likely have to gather and produce the documents largely on its own, under the general supervision of its attorneys. What if the attorney suspects that the client is altering or destroying documents? The attorney has duties to represent the client zealously and to maintain client confidences. If, however, it appears to the government that the attorney has assisted the obstructive efforts in some way, then the prosecutor may well turn the grand jury's attention to the attorney.

3. *Assertion of the Fifth Amendment privilege.* Assume that an attorney instructs a potential witness to assert the Fifth Amendment privilege against compelled self-incrimination and to refuse to testify in an official proceeding. Are there circum-stances under which an attorney would commit obstruction in such a situation? In *United States v. Cintolo*, 818 F.2d 980 (1st Cir. 1987), the defendant was an attorney who advised a potential witness to assert the Fifth Amendment privilege and not

testify before the grand jury, even though the witness had been granted immunity and threatened with contempt for not testifying. The government charged Cintolo with obstruction, alleging that he had acted to protect the target of the investigation, not the interests of the potential witness. The court of appeals affirmed the conviction, finding sufficient evidence of obstructive intent.

4. *Assertion of the attorney-client privilege.* In the tax fraud prosecution of defendants associated with the KPMG accounting firm — a case the government labeled as the largest tax fraud case in U.S. history — the indictment charged that the defendants conspired to commit tax fraud and obstruction of justice. *See United States v. Stein*, 541 F.3d 130 (2d Cir. 2008) (affirming dismissal of the case on Sixth Amendment grounds). (*Stein* is presented in Chapter 15, Internal Investigations, Compliance Programs, and Deferred and Non-Prosecution Agreements, *infra*.) One of the alleged means of the conspiracy was the phony assertion of the attorney-client privilege. According to the government, the assertion was designed to cover up the fraud. Does an obstruction charge based on such an allegation carry the potential for abuse? Consider the following observation with respect to the KPMG case:

> Charging privilege assertions as fraud or obstruction could turn a defense lawyer into a defendant or, at the very least, make the attorney's intent a discoverable issue.... As the privilege belongs to the client, most lawyers are conditioned as an ethical matter to err on the side of protecting the privilege. Defense lawyers may find themselves torn between their duties to their client and the threat of prosecution.

Douglas M. Tween & James D. Bailey, *Over-Assertion of the Attorney-Client Privilege — Can It Be a Crime?*, 13 No. 6, Bus. Crimes Bull. 3 (Feb. 2006). Are these concerns valid? Why or why not?

5. *Testimony.* When an attorney is preparing a witness, where is the line between zealous advocacy and obstruction of justice?

Problem

11-9. You are the attorney for Witness. Witness has been subpoenaed to give grand jury testimony in connection with alleged insider trading by Target. The grand jury believes that Target has tried to hide the profits of the illegal insider trading. Witness has told you that Witness never knowingly assisted Target in hiding the insider trading proceeds and insists on testifying.

The grand jury is aware that Witness and Target are acquainted. The grand jury wants to find out if Witness has information bearing on the investigation. You are now preparing Witness for the grand jury testimony.

Witness advises you that Target is a family friend with whom Witness has discussed business from time to time. Witness also tells you that, as a favor, Witness allowed Target to deposit $20,000 cash into Witness' bank account because Target's bank had gone out of business and Target needed somewhere to put the money. There appears to be no paper record that Witness did this favor for Target.

You believe the grand jury is unaware that Witness allowed Target to deposit money into Witness' bank account. You have concluded that if Target's deposit in Witness' account comes to light, it would lead the government incorrectly to believe that Witness had knowingly participated in Target' efforts to cover up the insider trading scheme.

Assume that Witness is your largest client and that fees from representing Witness are paying your office rent and student loan bills. Witness insists on not revealing the deposit that Target made into Witness' account.

Advise Witness as to how Witness should answer the expected line of grand jury questions concerning dealings with Target:

1. Do you know a person named Target?

2. What is the nature of your relationship with Target?

3. Have you ever discussed any business with Target?

4. Have you had any business dealings with Target?

5. Are you aware of any monetary transactions in which Target has engaged?

Are there any other questions you should raise in order to prepare your client for the grand jury appearance?

Chapter 12

Tax Crimes

A. Introductory Notes

1. Types of Tax Prosecutions

Federal laws relating to tax offenses provide prosecutors with a great deal of flexibility in white collar cases. Proof of tax crimes tends to be fairly straightforward. Thus, in many white collar investigations, it may be easier to bring criminal tax charges rather than other offenses that were originally the focus of the investigation. Also, as in other areas of white collar crime, in tax cases the government has wide latitude in deciding to pursue civil charges in addition to or instead of criminal charges.

Criminal tax charges may arise in two contexts. First, the government may proceed with a pure criminal tax case. Pure tax cases typically arise when routine tax audits and other Internal Revenue Service ("IRS") investigations uncover evidence of tax offenses. Second, tax offenses may be charged in addition to or instead of other substantive offenses. Those engaging in crimes such as money laundering, securities fraud, bribery, and mail and wire fraud often either fail to report their income or mislabel the source of the income on their tax returns. In an investigation originally focused on one of these non-tax offenses, the government may uncover tax crimes and include them in the charges. Or the government may determine that the tax offenses will be easier to prove than the other crimes and thus only bring the tax offenses. This was the approach in the criminal case against notorious racketeer Al Capone, who was convicted of tax crimes rather than murder and other crimes for which he was originally being investigated. Unlike such complex offenses as RICO and money laundering, juries generally have some familiarity with tax laws and may be more likely to convict for tax offenses. Conversely, many tax offenses can also be prosecuted under other general criminal statutes found in Title 18, like conspiracy, false statements, false claims, perjury, and mail fraud.

The federal tax code provides what courts term a "hierarchy" of tax crimes. These range from tax evasion, which is a felony, to failure to file a return or pay, which is a misdemeanor. This chapter focuses on three principal tax offenses—tax evasion (26 U.S.C. § 7201), filing of false returns (26 U.S.C. § 7206), and failing to file a return or pay taxes (26 U.S.C. § 7203). It is critical to distinguish among these different tax crimes and the conduct at which they are directed.

2. Voluntary Compliance and Deterrence

The United States government loses hundreds of billions of dollars annually because of tax evasion. Nonetheless, given the millions of tax returns filed every year, criminal tax cases are relatively rare.[a] Thus, the government has chosen in many instances to bring criminal cases against high-profile defendants in order to encourage voluntary compliance with the tax code and to deter tax crimes.[b]

3. The Process of Tax Investigations

The process of federal criminal tax investigations differs from most other white collar crimes. Most criminal tax cases begin as civil investigations triggered by routine audits. If an audit produces evidence of crime, the matter is referred to the IRS's Criminal Investigation Division for investigation by a "Special Agent."

In addition, criminal tax prosecutions must be reviewed and approved at several points. The Special Agent may refer the matter to the IRS Regional Counsel. If the Regional Counsel determines that the matter should proceed, the Counsel will refer the case to the Tax Division of the United States Department of Justice ("DOJ") in Washington for possible further investigation and prosecution. Unlike most other white collar crimes — RICO being a notable exception — all tax prosecutions must be approved by the DOJ in Washington. Can you imagine why this is so?

Detecting tax violations can prove particularly challenging. The biggest tax cheats tend to be financially sophisticated, have expert accountants, and route financial transactions across the world. While the IRS can force suspects to disclose bank records pursuant to the Banking Secrecy Act, 12 U.S.C.A. § 1951, the Fifth Amendment protects the same defendants from having to disclose potentially self-incriminating information on tax forms. *Youssefzadeh v. Commissioner*, No. 14868-14 L, Order (T.C., Nov. 6, 2015), https://perma.cc/JW9T-PUF6. The challenges of detecting tax evasion are compounded by the fact that the IRS is shrinking; it has 26% fewer agents now than it did in 2012. To fill some of the shortfall in manpower, the IRS is now using data analytics and artificial intelligence to help it spot suspicious activity.

---

a. For an overview of tax crimes, see Kathryn Keneally et al., *Criminal Tax Cases*, *in* White Collar Crime: Business and Regulatory Offenses §§ 13.01 *et seq.* (Otto Obermaier et al., eds., 2021). The Internal Revenue Service publishes a "Data Book" for each tax year, which is available on-line. The Data Book contains statistics on civil penalties and criminal investigations for each tax year. A quick glance for any tax year will show that the number of criminal actions is extremely small compared to the number of civil actions.

b. As one court stated, "selection for prosecution based in part upon the potential deterrent effect on others serves a legitimate interest in promoting more general compliance with the tax laws. Since the government lacks the means to investigate and prosecute every suspected violation of the tax laws, it makes good sense to prosecute those who will receive, or are likely to receive, the attention of the media." *United States v. Catlett*, 584 F.2d 864, 868 (8th Cir. 1978).

4. Statutory Overview

a. Elements of Tax Evasion — § 7201

Tax evasion, 26 U.S.C. § 7201, is the most serious tax violation and carries with it the harshest penalties. The defendant is subject to an evasion count for each year that the defendant evaded the payment of taxes. To establish tax evasion, the government must prove that the defendant:

(1) Underpaid taxes;

(2) Attempted to evade or defeat a tax; and

(3) Acted willfully.

This offense includes both completed acts and the inchoate offense of attempting to evade taxes. With respect to the underpayment, some federal circuit courts require proof that the defendant "substantially" underpaid the taxes due, while others do not. *See Boulware v. United States*, 552 U.S. 421, 424 n.2 (2008) (noting circuit split but not addressing the issue). All circuits require actual underpayment; in other words, a defendant is not guilty of tax evasion if he thought he was underpaying but was mistaken. *Id.* at 433. A defendant convicted of tax evasion can be sentenced to imprisonment of not more than five years along with the costs of the prosecution, a $100,000 fine, and back taxes. For corporations, the penalties include a $500,000 fine.

b. Elements of Filing False Tax Returns — § 7206

Individuals and entities, including the filer and/or preparer of the tax return, may also be investigated for filing a false tax return, 26 U.S.C. § 7206(1). This crime is punished as a felony. To establish this offense, the government must show that:

(1) The defendant signed the tax return or related document;

(2) The defendant signed under penalty of perjury;

(3) The return or related document was false;

(4) The falsity was material; and

(5) The defendant acted willfully.

This provision is sometimes called "tax perjury" because it focuses on the falsification of the documents. Note, though, that § 7206(1) prosecutions are not technically perjury prosecutions, which have other critical features — such as the two-witness rule under 18 U.S.C. § 1621 and no corporate criminal liability — that are inapplicable in the context of § 7206(1). Under § 7206(2), anyone who assists in the filing of a false return is also subject to prosecution. As with all tax offenses, each filing can constitute a separate crime.

Both of these sections subject the offender to a maximum prison term of three years, a maximum fine of $100,000 for individuals and $500,000 for organizations, plus costs of the prosecution. It should be noted that that the consequences of conviction for a tax offense can be significantly greater for alien residents. In addition to the penalties authorized by statute, convicted alien residents are subject to deportation for having committed a crime involving fraud or deceit. *Kawashima v. Holder*, 565 U.S. 478, 484 (2012).

c. Elements of Failure to File — § 7203

To prove a violation of § 7203, the government must show that the defendant:

(1) Failed to (a) file a required return, (b) pay a required tax, (c) keep required records, or (d) supply required information;

(2) Failed to act at the time the law specified; and

(3) Acted willfully.

The fact that a defendant did not possess sufficient funds to pay the tax obligation is no excuse for failing to file. *United States v. Easterday*, 564 F.3d 1004, 1006 (9th Cir. 2009). Frequently, "tax protestors" — those who claim that the federal tax laws are illegal and/or unconstitutional, for example — are charged with failing to file returns. *See* § D, 1, *infra*. Penalties for violations of § 7203, a misdemeanor, are not more than $25,000 and/or imprisonment of not more than one year, or both, together with the costs of prosecution. For organizations, the penalty can be increased to $100,000.

Finally, with respect to sentencing, the actual sentence for any of the tax crimes discussed in this chapter will vary based upon the application of the United States Sentencing Guidelines, discussed in Chapter 19, Sentencing, *infra*.[c]

B. Tax Evasion and Failure to File— §§ 7201 and 7203

The next case illustrates the distinction between the felony of tax evasion (§ 145(b) in the opinion, now codified at 26 U.S.C. § 7201) and the misdemeanor of failing to file a return (§ 145(a) in the opinion, now codified at 26 U.S.C. § 7203). As you read the case, consider why evasion is considered to be a substantially more serious offense than failing to file a return.

---

c. The amount of tax deficiency may have a significant impact on the sentence in an evasion case. *See* Keneally et al., *Criminal Tax Cases*, *supra* note a, at § 13.02[1]. There is some indication that judges are issuing below-Guidelines range sentences fairly often in criminal tax cases. *See* U.S. Sentencing Comm'n, FY 2019 Annual Report and Sourcebook, Table 31 (2019).

Spies v. United States

317 U.S. 492 (1943)

Mr. Justice Jackson delivered the opinion of the Court.

Petitioner has been convicted of attempting to defeat and evade income tax . . . . Petitioner admitted at the opening of the trial that he had sufficient income during the year in question to place him under a statutory duty to file a return and to pay a tax, and that he failed to do either. The evidence during nearly two weeks of trial was directed principally toward establishing the exact amount of the tax and the manner of receiving and handling income and accounting, which the Government contends shows an intent to evade and defeat tax. Petitioner's testimony related to his good character, his physical illness at the time the return became due, and lack of willfulness in his defaults, chiefly because of a psychological disturbance, amounting to something more than worry but something less than insanity.

Section 145(a) makes, among other things, willful failure to pay a tax or make a return by one having petitioner's income at the time or times required by law a misdemeanor. Section 145(b) makes a willful attempt in any manner to evade or defeat any tax such as his a felony. Petitioner was not indicted for either misdemeanor. The indictment contained a single count setting forth the felony charge of willfully attempting to defeat and evade the tax, and recited willful failure to file a return and willful failure to pay the tax as the means to the felonious end.

The petitioner requested an instruction that "You may not find the defendant guilty of a willful attempt to defeat and evade the income tax, if you find only that he had willfully failed to make a return of taxable income and has willfully failed to pay the tax on that income." This was refused, and the Court charged that: "If you find that the defendant had a net income for 1936 upon which some income tax was due, and I believe that is conceded, if you find that the defendant willfully failed to file an income tax return for that year, if you find that the defendant willfully failed to pay the tax due on his income for that year, you may, if you find that the facts and circumstances warrant it, find that the defendant willfully attempted to evade or defeat the tax." The Court refused a request to instruct that an affirmative act was necessary to constitute a willful attempt and charged that: "Attempt means to try to do or accomplish. In order to find an attempt it is not necessary to find affirmative steps to accomplish the prohibited purpose. An attempt may be found on the basis of inactivity or on refraining to act, as well."

It is the Government's contention that a willful failure to file a return together with a willful failure to pay the tax may, without more, constitute an attempt to defeat or evade a tax within §145(b). Petitioner claims that such proof establishes only two misdemeanors under §145(a) and that it takes more than the sum of two such misdemeanors to make the felony under §145(b). The legislative history of the section contains nothing helpful on the question here at issue, and we must find the answer from the section itself and its context in the revenue laws.

The United States has relied for the collection of its income tax largely upon the taxpayer's own disclosures rather than upon a system of withholding the tax from him by those from whom income may be received. This system can function successfully only if those within and near taxable income keep and render true accounts. In many ways taxpayers' neglect or deceit may prejudice the orderly and punctual administration of the system as well as the revenues themselves. Congress has imposed a variety of sanctions for the protection of the system and the revenues. The relation of the offense of which this petitioner has been convicted to other and lesser revenue offenses appears more clearly from its position in this structure of sanctions.

The penalties imposed by Congress to enforce the tax laws embrace both civil and criminal sanctions. The former consist of additions to the tax upon determinations of fact made by an administrative agency and with no burden on the Government to prove its case beyond a reasonable doubt. The latter consist of penal offenses enforced by the criminal process in the familiar manner. Invocation of one does not exclude resort to the other.

The failure in a duty to make a timely return, unless it is shown that such failure is due to reasonable cause and not due to willful neglect, is punishable by an addition to the tax of 5 to 25 per cent thereof, depending on the duration of the default. But a duty may exist even when there is no tax liability to serve as a base for application of a percentage delinquency penalty; the default may relate to matters not identifiable with tax for a particular period; and the offense may be more grievous than a case for civil penalty. Hence the willful failure to make a return, keep records, or supply information when required, is made a misdemeanor, without regard to existence of a tax liability. § 145(a). Punctuality is important to the fiscal system, and these are sanctions to assure punctual as well as faithful performance of these duties.

Sanctions to insure payment of the tax are even more varied to meet the variety of causes of default. . . . Willful failure to pay the tax when due is punishable as a misdemeanor. § 145(a). The climax of this variety of sanctions is the serious and inclusive felony defined to consist of willful attempt in any manner to evade or defeat the tax. § 145(b). The question here is whether there is a distinction between the acts necessary to make out the felony and those which may make out the misdemeanor.

A felony may, and frequently does, include lesser offenses in combination either with each other or with other elements. We think it clear that this felony may include one or several of the other offenses against the revenue laws. But it would be unusual and we would not readily assume that Congress by the felony defined in § 145(b) meant no more than the same derelictions it had just defined in § 145(a) as a misdemeanor. Such an interpretation becomes even more difficult to accept when we consider this felony as the capstone of a system of sanctions which singly or in combination were calculated to induce prompt and forthright fulfillment of every duty under the income tax law and to provide a penalty suitable to every degree of delinquency.

The difference between willful failure to pay a tax when due, which is made a misdemeanor, and willful attempt to defeat and evade one, which is made a felony, is not easy to detect or define. Both must be willful, and willful, as we have said, is a word of many meanings, its construction often being influenced by its context. It may well mean something more as applied to nonpayment of a tax than when applied to failure to make a return. Mere voluntary and purposeful, as distinguished from accidental, omission to make a timely return might meet the test of willfulness. But in view of our traditional aversion to imprisonment for debt, we would not without the clearest manifestation of Congressional intent assume that mere knowing and intentional default in payment of a tax where there had been no willful failure to disclose the liability is intended to constitute a criminal offense of any degree. We would expect willfulness in such a case to include some element of evil motive and want of justification in view of all the financial circumstances of the taxpayer.

Had § 145(a) not included willful failure to pay a tax, it would have defined as misdemeanors generally a failure to observe statutory duties to make timely returns, keep records, or supply information — duties imposed to facilitate administration of the Act even if, because of insufficient net income, there were no duty to pay a tax. It would then be a permissible and perhaps an appropriate construction of § 145(b) that it made felonies of the same willful omissions when there was the added element of duty to pay a tax. The definition of such nonpayment as a misdemeanor we think argues strongly against such an interpretation.

The difference between the two offenses, it seems to us, is found in the affirmative action implied from the term "attempt," as used in the felony subsection. It is not necessary to involve this subject with the complexities of the common-law "attempt." The attempt made criminal by this statute does not consist of conduct that would culminate in a more serious crime but for some impossibility of completion or interruption or frustration. This is an independent crime, complete in its most serious form when the attempt is complete and nothing is added to its criminality by success or consummation, as would be the case, say, of attempted murder. Although the attempt succeed in evading tax, there is no criminal offense of that kind, and the prosecution can be only for the attempt. We think that in employing the terminology of attempt to embrace the gravest of offenses against the revenues Congress intended some willful commission in addition to the willful omissions that make up the list of misdemeanors. Willful but passive neglect of the statutory duty may constitute the lesser offense, but to combine with it a willful and positive attempt to evade tax in any manner or to defeat it by any means lifts the offense to the degree of felony.

Congress did not define or limit the methods by which a willful attempt to defeat and evade might be accomplished and perhaps did not define lest its effort to do so result in some unexpected limitation. Nor would we by definition constrict the scope of the Congressional provision that it may be accomplished "in any manner." By way of illustration, and not by way of limitation, we would think affirmative willful attempt may be inferred from conduct such as keeping a double set of books, making false entries of alterations, or false invoices or documents, destruction of books or records, concealment of assets or covering up sources of income, handling of one's affairs to avoid making the records usual in transactions of the kind, and any conduct, the likely effect of which would be to mislead or to conceal. If the tax-evasion motive plays any part in such conduct the offense may be made out even though the conduct may also serve other purposes such as concealment of other crime.

In this case there are several items of evidence apart from the default in filing the return and paying the tax which the Government claims will support an inference of willful attempt to evade or defeat the tax. These go to establish that petitioner insisted that certain income be paid to him in cash, transferred it to his own bank by armored car, deposited it, not in his own name but in the names of others of his family, and kept inadequate and misleading records. Petitioner claims other motives animated him in these matters. We intimate no opinion. Such inferences are for the jury. If on proper submission the jury found these acts, taken together with willful failure to file a return and willful failure to pay the tax, to constitute a willful attempt to defeat and evade tax, we would consider conviction of a felony sustainable. But we think a defendant is entitled to a charge which will point out the necessity for such an inference of willful attempt to defeat or evade tax from some proof in the case other than that necessary to make out the misdemeanors; and if the evidence fails to afford such an inference, the defendant should be acquitted.

The Government argues against this construction, contending that the milder punishment of a misdemeanor and the benefits of a short statute of limitation should not be extended to violators of the income tax laws such as political grafters, gamblers, racketeers, and gangsters. We doubt that this construction will handicap prosecution for felony of such flagrant violators. Few of them, we think, in their efforts to escape tax stop with mere omission of the duties put upon them by the statute, but if such there be, they are entitled to be convicted only of the offense which they have committed.

Reversed.

Notes and Questions

1. *Distinguishing the crimes.* According to the Court, what is the essential difference between the crimes of tax evasion and failure to file? Why is the former punished more harshly than the latter? What types of evidence, according to the Court, will support an evasion charge?

2. *The trial court's error.* What was the precise error committed by the trial judge? Was there evidence in the record to support an evasion conviction? If so, then why didn't the Court rule that the trial court's error was harmless and allow the conviction to stand?

3. *Proof of deficiency.* As noted above, proof of underpayment is an element in any tax evasion case. Often, such proof will entail enormously complex issues. *See, e.g.,*

Boulware v. United States, 552 U.S. 421 (2008) (addressing the defendant's argument that money he received from a closely held corporation was not taxable income but instead represented returns of capital, up to his basis in his stock, which are not taxable). What problems do such complex issues present for the government? For the defense? For jurors? For an overview on the methods that the government uses to prove underpayment, see *infra* § E.

4. *The tax gap and its causes.* The IRS defines the "gross tax gap" as "the difference between true tax liability for a given period and the amount of tax that is paid on time." *See* https://www.irs.gov/newsroom/irs-releases-new-tax-gap-estimates -compliance-rates-remain-substantially-unchanged-from-prior-study (IR-2019-159, Sept. 26, 2019). The IRS "currently collects more than $3 trillion annually in taxes, penalties, interest and user fees." *Id.* While about 83.6% of taxes are paid voluntarily and on time, recent estimates reveal an average gross tax gap of $441 billion per year and a net tax gap of $381 billion (after late payments and enforcement efforts). Because nonpayment ultimately shifts the tax burden onto those who properly pay, and maintaining high voluntary compliance is intertwined with taxpayer belief in a fair system, "voluntary compliance rate of the U.S. tax system is vitally important for our nation. A one-percentage-point increase in voluntary compliance would bring in about $30 billion in additional tax receipts." *Id.*

Why do so many people underpay their taxes? Professor Stuart Green has suggested a number of possible explanations, including: (1) the difficulty of distinguishing legitimate tax avoidance from illegal evasion, (2) the complexity of the underlying conduct, (3) the inadequacy of enforcement practices, (4) the arbitrariness of enforcement efforts, (5) the difficulty of distinguishing between civil and criminal violations, (6) the sense that "everyone is doing it," (7) the demonization of taxes, and (8) perceived unfairness of the tax code and dissatisfaction with the use of tax revenues. Stuart P. Green, *What Is Wrong with Tax Evasion?*, 9 Hous. Bus. & Tax L.J. 221 (2009). Which explanation is the most compelling, in your opinion? Why? Does your answer depend on the financial sophistication of the taxpayer?

Problems

12-1. During tax Years 01 through 04, appellant operated a private securities investment firm, Central Financial Corporation ("CFC"). Appellant routinely comingled her corporate and personal finances. For example, appellant used funds received from CFC financers to pay for personal expenses as well as gifts. Appellant owed approximately $500,000 in personal income taxes for each of the tax Years 02, 03, and 04, but failed to file a single personal tax return for those years. Appellant was indicted for tax evasion for the Years 02, 03, and 04.

At trial, one of CFC's outside accountants testified that his firm was hired specifically to calculate CFC's income and losses and to prepare and file tax forms for tax Year 02. Upon review of statements from CFC, the accountant discovered that appellant used corporate funds to pay for approximately $2.4 million of personal expenses. When the accountant confronted appellant about this, appellant stated that this was a miscalculation on the part of CFC's bookkeeping department. When the accountant attempted to verify the information with the brokerage firm's bookkeepers, appellant blocked him from doing so. Consequently, the accountant was unable to prepare the required tax forms for Year 02.

The defendant was convicted of tax evasion for all three tax years, and appeals on the grounds of insufficient evidence.

How should the court rule? Why?

12-2. Defendant, the owner and operator of an electrical contracting business, failed to pay payroll taxes for four consecutive quarters. Defendant was assessed a tax penalty. Rather than pay the penalty, defendant submitted an "offer-in-compromise" to the IRS to attempt to settle his liability for a lesser amount. In filing this offer, defendant also submitted the requisite Form 433-A, which contained an accounting of defendant's employment and financial status. On this form, defendant failed to disclose his ownership of one personal residence and two rental properties. He also falsely claimed that he had no personal assets, income, or employment.

Defendant was indicted on one count of tax evasion in violation of § 7201 for making false statements and concealing assets. Defendant moved to dismiss the case on the ground that the government is precluded from charging a violation of evasion where the alleged conduct fits into the lesser offense of a false statement under § 7206.

The government argued that the relationship between § 7201 and other tax offenses is analogous to a Venn diagram. The Venn diagram can best be illustrated using two circles, a larger one representing the prohibited conduct of § 7201 and a smaller one representing the prohibited conduct in § 7206. The two circles intersect where the prohibited conduct would violate both statutes, and the non-intersecting areas represent conduct that would only violate one or the other. Because § 7201 and § 7206 cover different types of conduct, but partially overlap, the government contended that "Congress intended to provide the government with the discretion to prosecute under either statutory provision where the conduct in issues falls within both."

You are the judge; do you grant or deny defendant's motion to dismiss? Why?

12-3. Last November, defendant was driving from the United States to Canada. Upon reaching the Canadian border, a Canadian customs officer inspected defendant's car and discovered two bags in the trunk. The customs officer found that one of the bags contained large sums of cash. When asked how much money was in the bag, defendant said "several thousand dollars." The customs officer sent defendant back to the United States side of the border to talk to U.S. customs officials.

When a U.S. customs agent asked if defendant had anything in the car, he said there was money in the trunk. When asked how much, defendant initially responded $30,000 or $35,000. The agent asked several more times, and each time the amount went up until defendant finally said there was more than $300,000 in the car. The agent had defendant fill out a customs report of international transport of currency in excess of $10,000, and then seized the money because defendant had not filled out the customs report form prior to crossing the Canadian border. The bags contained $359,500 in $10 and $20 bills.

The IRS then served defendant with a termination assessment for $169,973 as income tax due on the money. A termination notice serves to terminate the person's tax year as of a certain date so that any tax liability becomes due immediately, and the IRS files a tax lien to secure payment of the tax debt. The termination assessment does not relieve the taxpayer of the obligation to file a tax return for the year. Upon his lawyer's advice, defendant did not file a tax return for that tax year because of pending litigation concerning defendant's failure to file the required customs report form.

Defendant was convicted of income tax evasion under § 7201 based on the foregoing facts. Defendant now appeals. How should the court rule? Why? Should defendant also be convicted under § 7203?

C. Filing a False Return — § 7206

The next case addresses the crime of "tax perjury." As you read the case, consider the potential scope of those who may be liable for this crime.

United States v. Shortt Accountancy Corp.

785 F.2d 1448 (9th Cir. 1986)

DUNIWAY, CIRCUIT JUDGE:

Shortt Accountancy Corporation appeals from its conviction on seven counts of making and subscribing false tax returns in violation of § 7206(1) of the Internal Revenue Code of 1954. We affirm.

Appellant Shortt Accountancy Corporation (SAC) is a CPA firm that performs accounting services, prepares tax returns and gives tax planning advice to its clients. Ronald Ashida was its chief operating officer and ran its day-to-day activities in 1981–82.

In the fall of 1981, Clifford Wilson contacted SAC for tax planning advice and services. In late December 1981, Ashida told Wilson that he could invest through SAC in a "straddle" position in government securities that would enable Wilson to claim a sizable deduction on his 1981 federal income tax return. A straddle is the simultaneous holding of a contract to purchase and a contract to sell a specific commodity at some time in the future. It is used to minimize risks by offsetting losses and gains. In order to claim the deduction, however, Wilson would have to backdate a promissory note so that the investment would appear to have been made in May, 1981, rather than December. The backdating was necessary, said Ashida, because

Congress had changed the law to disallow deductions to taxpayers who purchased a straddle investment after June 23, 1981. Wilson agreed to consider the investment, but made no decision before the end of the year.

In early January 1982, Wilson told an Assistant U.S. Attorney about Ashida's investment advice. The Attorney put him in touch with the IRS, which proposed that Wilson cooperate with it in building a criminal case against SAC. He agreed upon the condition that the IRS reimburse him for the purchase price of the straddle position and for any fees charged him by SAC. He also understood that if SAC eventually prepared a tax return for him, the IRS would audit it and disallow any improper deductions claimed by SAC on his behalf. In that case, the IRS would assess Wilson for additional taxes owed, but would not require him to pay interest or penalties resulting from the improper deductions.

Wilson ultimately purchased a straddle position from SAC in April 1982. In addition to the purchase price of $3400, SAC charged Wilson interest calculated from May 1, 1981, so that it appeared that the transaction had occurred before the June 1981 cutoff date. No backdated documents were ultimately used in the transaction.

SAC completed preparation of Wilson's 1981 tax return in January 1983. In it, the firm claimed a $23,024 deduction for Wilson relating to his April 1982 straddle investment. Paul Whatley, who supervised the actual preparation of the return and subscribed to its correctness on behalf of SAC, based this figure on information provided to him by Ashida. Whatley did not know, when he signed the return, that the straddle investment was improperly claimed.

After receiving his 1981 return from SAC, Wilson delivered it to an IRS special agent who immediately filed it with the IRS District Director. He forwarded it to a processing center in October 1983 and Wilson has since received the tax refund claimed, plus applicable interest. He has not filed any other 1981 federal income tax return.

In the subsequent investigation of SAC's preparation of Wilson's 1981 return, the grand jury determined that SAC had prepared tax returns for at least six additional clients in which it improperly claimed deductions for straddle investments. In each case, the straddle position at issue was originally owned by other SAC clients who had purchased their interests from SAC before Congress' disallowance of the deduction in June 1981. Although these clients incurred straddle losses in May 1981 that properly could have been claimed on their 1981 tax returns, SAC determined that the original owners were oversheltered for the year and did not need the deductions. As a result, SAC, which was authorized to sell the client's interest in the straddle should it deem it to be in the client's best interest, sold their straddle positions and resulting losses to Wilson and the other new clients. Each sale occurred after the change in the law disallowing straddle deductions and each was structured to appear that it had occurred before the cutoff date.

In June 1984, the grand jury issued a fourteen count indictment charging [SAC] and Ashida with violations of 18 U.S.C. § 371, conspiracy to commit an offense against or to defraud the United States, and 26 U.S.C. §7206(1), false declaration under penalty of perjury, and (2), aiding preparation or presentation of false documents, under the internal revenue laws. The indictment's basis was SAC's alleged sale of interests in straddle positions after Congress disallowed deductions from such investments and its knowing preparation of tax returns claiming improper straddle deductions. . . .

At trial, defendants moved for judgment of acquittal following the opening statement and again at the close of the government's case. They claimed that a preparer of tax returns cannot be charged under §7206(1), which proscribes making and subscribing a false return, because it cannot "make" a return within the meaning of the statute. Defendants also argued that a corporation cannot be guilty of an offense under §7206(1) when the person who actually subscribes the false return believes it to be true and correct. The district court denied the motions. . . .

The jury ultimately convicted SAC on seven counts of willfully making and subscribing as preparer false income tax returns in violation of 26 U.S.C. §7206(1). SAC timely appeals.

SAC claims that its convictions on seven counts of violating §7206(1) should be reversed as a matter of law because a tax return preparer cannot "make" a return within the meaning of the statute. While SAC does not deny its participation in preparing the false returns, it claims that it could only be charged under §7206(2) for *assisting* in the preparation of a false return. It bases its distinction on the fact that the taxpayer alone has the statutory duty to file a federal income tax return.

Nothing in the statute or case law indicates that a charge under §7206(1) for making and subscribing a false return is based on the taxpayer's duty to file or "make" an income tax return. Instead, §§7206(1) and 7206(2) are "closely related companion provisions" that differ in emphasis more than in substance. *United States v. Haynes*, 573 F.2d 236, 240 (5th Cir. 1978). Section 7206(1) is a perjury statute, making any person who knowingly makes and subscribes a false statement on any return criminally liable. Section 7206(2) has a broader sweep, making all forms of willful assistance in preparing a false return an offense. Perjury in connection with the preparation of a federal tax return is chargeable under either section. *Haynes*, 573 F.2d at 240; *see United States v. Miller*, 491 F.2d 638, 649 (5th Cir. 1974). The Fifth Circuit has considered the exact issue of whether a tax preparer can be charged under §7206(1) rather than §7206(2) and held that he could. *Miller*, 491 F.2d at 649; *see Haynes*, 573 F.2d at 240. We are persuaded to do the same.

SAC argues that our decision in *United States v. Miller*, 545 F.2d 1204 (9th Cir. 1976), recognizes the exclusivity of §§7206(1) and (2). We disagree. In *Miller*, we commented *sua sponte* in a footnote that the defendant, who had prepared a false return for his wife, should have been charged under §7206(2) for assisting in the preparation of the return, rather than under §7206(1) for subscribing the return. It is not clear from the opinion whether the defendant actually committed perjury by subscribing his wife's false return or whether he merely prepared it in advance of her subscription. In either case, we went on to hold that the possible error was not fatal because indictment under § 7206(1) contains the elements of the § 7206(2) offense sufficiently to apprise the defendant of what he has to be prepared to meet at trial and is detailed enough to assure against double jeopardy. This holding does not conflict with our conclusion here that a tax return preparer can properly be charged under § 7206(1) for willfully making and subscribing a false return.

SAC also claims that six of its convictions under § 7206(1) should be reversed because Paul Whatley, the corporate agent who actually subscribed six of the seven contested returns on behalf of SAC, did not have the requisite intent of willfully making and subscribing a false return. While it acknowledges that Ashida, who supplied Whatley with all of his information regarding the straddle losses, did have the requisite intent, it contends that his intent is irrelevant to a § 7206(1) charge because he did not physically subscribe the return. SAC concludes that if the government wanted to charge SAC for Ashida's admittedly illegal conduct and intent, it should have drawn up the indictment under § 7206(2) or some other statute, and not under § 7206(1).

SAC's argument is completely meritless. If it were accepted by the courts, any tax return preparer could escape prosecution for perjury by arranging for an innocent employee to complete the proscribed act of subscribing a false return. This interpretation of § 7206(1) defies logic and has no support in the case law. A corporation will be held liable under § 7206(1) when its agent deliberately causes it to make and subscribe to a false income tax return.

AFFIRMED.

Notes and Questions

1. *Choosing the appropriate theory of prosecution.* Section 7206(2) criminalizes the actions of those who assist in the preparation of a false return and is usually directed to tax preparers. Section 7206(1) criminalizes actions of those who make or subscribe the return. Under *Shortt*, must the government charge the tax preparer under § 7206(2) instead of under § 7206(1)? Why or why not?

2. *Mens rea.* In the *Shortt* case, the corporation was convicted of the crime even though the employee who signed the return had no knowledge of the fraudulent scheme. What was the government's evidence of knowledge? Do you agree with the Court's resolution of the charges against the corporation?

3. *Materiality.* In any prosecution under § 7206, the government must prove that the falsity was material. Courts define materiality in different ways, but most define a material falsity as one having the potential to affect the IRS's ability to monitor and assess the tax owed. *See, e.g., United States v. Griffin*, 524 F.3d 71 (1st Cir. 2008).

Prior to the Supreme Court's 1995 decision in *United States v. Gaudin*, 515 U.S. 506 (1995), materiality was generally considered to be a question of law for the judge. In *Gaudin*, however, the Court held that, in a false statements prosecution under § 1001, materiality should be determined by the jury. In 1999, the Supreme Court determined that materiality is likewise a question for the jury in tax perjury cases.

See Neder v. United States, 527 U.S. 1, 8 (1999) (holding that the District Court committed harmless error in a §7206(1) prosecution by determining materiality element itself rather than submitting the issue to the jury).

Can a falsity be material if it did not lead to an underpayment of taxes? In *United States v. DiVarco*, 484 F.2d 670 (7th Cir. 1973), the defendants argued on appeal from their §7206 conviction that their misstatements as to the source of their income were not material because there was no showing that they had underpaid their taxes. The court, in determining materiality, found that "the purpose behind the statute is to prosecute those who intentionally falsify their tax returns regardless of the precise ultimate effect that falsification may have." Does this mean that a false statement may be material even if the statement did not mislead the government and had no potential for affecting the government's assessment of tax liability? Were the false statements material in *Shortt*? Why or why not? Compare the determination of materiality in mail fraud cases, Chapter 4, *supra*.

Problem

12-4. Defendant operated an organization that conducted nationwide seminars on the constitutional history of income taxes. Defendant told attendees that anyone can claim to be a nonresident alien, for federal income tax purposes, to claim no domestic income. Attendees paid $2,500, in cash, to learn how to complete nonresident alien tax returns, or amend previous returns to claim refunds. Defendant was aware that this position was contrary to well-established law. In fact, the IRS rejected many attendees' returns as frivolous, issuing penalties.

Defendant was charged with 69 counts of aiding and abetting in the preparation of false federal tax returns. The indictment stated that defendant helped file tax returns that were "false and fraudulent as to material matters," because the returns indicated the taxpayers were nonresident aliens when defendant knew they were not. In fact, the IRS well knew at the time the returns were filed that the taxpayers did not qualify as nonresident aliens and was not deceived by any of the alleged false tax returns.

Are the misrepresentations material? Why or why not?

D. Mens Rea

1. Defining "Willfulness" in Criminal Tax Cases

In any criminal tax case, the government must prove beyond a reasonable doubt that the defendant acted willfully. Willfulness takes on a distinct meaning when used in the context of criminal tax offenses. The next case is a leading U.S. Supreme Court decision on the meaning of "willfulness" in criminal tax cases. As you read the case, consider whether the majority's approach to defining "willfulness" is justified.

Cheek v. United States

498 U.S. 192 (1991)

Justice White delivered the opinion of the Court.

Title 26, §7201 of the United States Code provides that any person "who willfully attempts in any manner to evade or defeat any tax imposed by this title or the payment thereof" shall be guilty of a felony. Under 26 U.S.C. §7203, "[a]ny person required under this title . . . or by regulations made under authority thereof to make a return . . . who willfully fails to . . . make such return" shall be guilty of a misdemeanor. This case turns on the meaning of the word "willfully" as used in §§7201 and 7203.

Petitioner John L. Cheek has been a pilot for American Airlines since 1973. He filed federal income tax returns through 1979 but thereafter ceased to file returns. He also claimed an increasing number of withholding allowances — eventually claiming 60 allowances by mid-1980 — and for the years 1981 to 1984 indicated on his W-4 forms that he was exempt from federal income taxes. In 1983, petitioner unsuccessfully sought a refund of all tax withheld by his employer in 1982. Petitioner's income during this period at all times far exceeded the minimum necessary to trigger the statutory filing requirement.

As a result of his activities, petitioner was indicted for 10 violations of federal law. He was charged with six counts of willfully failing to file a federal income tax return for the years 1980, 1981, and 1983 through 1986, in violation of §7203. He was further charged with three counts of willfully attempting to evade his income taxes for the years 1980, 1981, and 1983 in violation of 26 U.S.C. §7201. In those years, American Airlines withheld substantially less than the amount of tax petitioner owed because of the numerous allowances and exempt status he claimed on his W-4 forms. The tax offenses with which petitioner was charged are specific intent crimes that require the defendant to have acted willfully.

At trial, the evidence established that between 1982 and 1986, petitioner was involved in at least four civil cases that challenged various aspects of the federal income tax system. In all four of those cases, the plaintiffs were informed by the courts that many of their arguments, including that they were not taxpayers within the meaning of the tax laws, that wages are not income, that the Sixteenth Amendment does not authorize the imposition of an income tax on individuals, and that the Sixteenth Amendment is unenforceable, were frivolous or had been repeatedly rejected by the courts. During this time period, petitioner also attended at least two criminal trials of persons charged with tax offenses. In addition, there was evidence that in 1980 or 1981 an attorney had advised Cheek that the courts had rejected as frivolous the claim that wages are not income.[4]

---

4. The attorney also advised that despite the Fifth Amendment, the filing of a tax return was required and that a person could challenge the constitutionality of the system by suing for a refund

Cheek represented himself at trial and testified in his defense. He admitted that he had not filed personal income tax returns during the years in question. He testified that as early as 1978, he had begun attending seminars sponsored by, and following the advice of, a group that believes, among other things, that the federal tax system is unconstitutional. Some of the speakers at these meetings were lawyers who purported to give professional opinions about the invalidity of the federal income tax laws. Cheek produced a letter from an attorney stating that the Sixteenth Amendment did not authorize a tax on wages and salaries but only on gain or profit. Petitioner's defense was that, based on the indoctrination he received from this group and from his own study, he sincerely believed that the tax laws were being unconstitutionally enforced and that his actions during the 1980–1986 period were lawful. He therefore argued that he had acted without the willfulness required for conviction of the various offenses with which he was charged.

In the course of its instructions, the trial court advised the jury that to prove "willfulness" the Government must prove the voluntary and intentional violation of a known legal duty, a burden that could not be proved by showing mistake, ignorance, or negligence. The court further advised the jury that an objectively reasonable good-faith misunderstanding of the law would negate willfulness, but mere disagreement with the law would not. The court described Cheek's beliefs about the income tax system and instructed the jury that if it found that Cheek "honestly and reasonably believed that he was not required to pay income taxes or to file tax returns," a not guilty verdict should be returned.

After several hours of deliberation, the jury sent a note to the judge that stated in part:

> "'We have a basic disagreement between some of us as to if Mr. Cheek honestly and reasonably believed that he was not required to pay income taxes.
>
> . . . .
>
> "'Page 32 [the relevant jury instruction] discusses good faith misunderstanding and disagreement. Is there any additional clarification you can give us on this point?'"

Id. at 85.

The District Judge responded with a supplemental instruction containing the following statements:

> "[A] person's opinion that the tax laws violate his constitutional rights does not constitute a good faith misunderstanding of the law. Furthermore, a person's disagreement with the government's tax collection systems and policies does not constitute a good faith misunderstanding of the law."

Id. at 86.

---

after the taxes had been withheld, or by putting himself "at risk of criminal prosecution."

At the end of the first day of deliberation, the jury sent out another note saying that it still could not reach a verdict because "[w]e are divided on the issue as to if Mr. Cheek honestly & reasonably believed that he was not required to pay income tax." *Id.* at 87. When the jury resumed its deliberations, the District Judge gave the jury an additional instruction. This instruction stated in part that "[a]n honest but unreasonable belief is not a defense and does not negate willfulness," *id.* at 88, and that "[a]dvice or research resulting in the conclusion that wages of a privately employed person are not income or that the tax laws are unconstitutional is not objectively reasonable and cannot serve as the basis for a good faith misunderstanding of the law defense." *Id.* The court also instructed the jury that "[p]ersistent refusal to acknowledge the law does not constitute a good faith misunderstanding of the law." *Id.* Approximately two hours later, the jury returned a verdict finding petitioner guilty on all counts.[6]

Petitioner appealed his convictions, arguing that the District Court erred by instructing the jury that only an objectively reasonable misunderstanding of the law negates the statutory willfulness requirement. The United States Court of Appeals for the Seventh Circuit rejected that contention and affirmed the convictions. 882 F.2d 1263 (7th Cir. 1989). In prior cases, the Seventh Circuit had made clear that good-faith misunderstanding of the law negates willfulness only if the defendant's beliefs are objectively reasonable; in the Seventh Circuit, even actual ignorance is not a defense unless the defendant's ignorance was itself objectively reasonable. In its opinion in this case, the court noted that several specified beliefs, including the beliefs that the tax laws are unconstitutional and that wages are not income, would not be objectively reasonable. Because the Seventh Circuit's interpretation of "willfully" as used in these statutes conflicts with the decisions of several other Courts of Appeals, . . . we granted certiorari.

The general rule that ignorance of the law or a mistake of law is no defense to criminal prosecution is deeply rooted in the American legal system. Based on the notion that the law is definite and knowable, the common law presumed that every person knew the law. This common-law rule has been applied by the Court in numerous cases construing criminal statutes. . . .

The proliferation of statutes and regulations has sometimes made it difficult for the average citizen to know and comprehend the extent of the duties and obligations imposed by the tax laws. Congress has accordingly softened the impact of the common-law presumption by making specific intent to violate the law an element of certain federal criminal tax offenses. Thus, the Court almost 60 years ago

---

6. A note signed by all 12 jurors also informed the judge that although the jury found petitioner guilty, several jurors wanted to express their personal opinions of the case and that notes from these individual jurors to the court were "a complaint against the narrow & hard expression under the constraints of the law." *Id.* at 90. At least two notes from individual jurors expressed the opinion that petitioner sincerely believed in his cause even though his beliefs might have been unreasonable.

interpreted the statutory term "willfully" as used in the federal criminal tax statutes as carving out an exception to the traditional rule. This special treatment of criminal tax offenses is largely due to the complexity of the tax laws. . . .

[Cheek] . . . challenges the ruling that a good-faith misunderstanding of the law or a good-faith belief that one is not violating the law, if it is to negate willfulness, must be objectively reasonable. We agree that the Court of Appeals and the District Court erred in this respect.

Willfulness, as construed by our prior decisions in criminal tax cases, requires the Government to prove that the law imposed a duty on the defendant, that the defendant knew of this duty, and that he voluntarily and intentionally violated that duty. We deal first with the case where the issue is whether the defendant knew of the duty purportedly imposed by the provision of the statute or regulation he is accused of violating, a case in which there is no claim that the provision at issue is invalid. In such a case, if the Government proves actual knowledge of the pertinent legal duty, the prosecution, without more, has satisfied the knowledge component of the willfulness requirement. But carrying this burden requires negating a defendant's claim of ignorance of the law or a claim that because of a misunderstanding of the law, he had a good-faith belief that he was not violating any of the provisions of the tax laws. This is so because one cannot be aware that the law imposes a duty upon him and yet be ignorant of it, misunderstand the law, or believe that the duty does not exist. In the end, the issue is whether, based on all the evidence, the Government has proved that the defendant was aware of the duty at issue, which cannot be true if the jury credits a good-faith misunderstanding and belief submission, whether or not the claimed belief or misunderstanding is objectively reasonable.

In this case, if Cheek asserted that he truly believed that the Internal Revenue Code did not purport to treat wages as income, and the jury believed him, the Government would not have carried its burden to prove willfulness, however unreasonable a court might deem such a belief. Of course, in deciding whether to credit Cheek's good-faith belief claim, the jury would be free to consider any admissible evidence from any source showing that Cheek was aware of his duty to file a return and to treat wages as income, including evidence showing his awareness of the relevant provisions of the Code or regulations, of court decisions rejecting his interpretation of the tax law, of authoritative rulings of the Internal Revenue Service, or of any contents of the personal income tax return forms and accompanying instructions that made it plain that wages should be returned as income.

We thus disagree with the Court of Appeals' requirement that a claimed good-faith belief must be objectively reasonable if it is to be considered as possibly negating the Government's evidence purporting to show a defendant's awareness of the legal duty at issue. Knowledge and belief are characteristically questions for the factfinder, in this case the jury. Characterizing a particular belief as not objectively reasonable transforms the inquiry into a legal one and would prevent the jury from considering it. It would of course be proper to exclude evidence having no relevance or probative value with respect to willfulness; but it is not contrary to common sense, let alone impossible, for a defendant to be ignorant of his duty based on an irrational belief that he has no duty, and forbidding the jury to consider evidence that might negate willfulness would raise a serious question under the Sixth Amendment's jury trial provision. . . .

It was therefore error to instruct the jury to disregard evidence of Cheek's understanding that, within the meaning of the tax laws, he was not a person required to file a return or to pay income taxes and that wages are not taxable income, as incredible as such misunderstandings of and beliefs about the law might be. Of course, the more unreasonable the asserted beliefs or misunderstandings are, the more likely the jury will consider them to be nothing more than simple disagreement with known legal duties imposed by the tax laws and will find that the Government has carried its burden of proving knowledge.

Cheek asserted in the trial court that he should be acquitted because he believed in good faith that the income tax law is unconstitutional as applied to him and thus could not legally impose any duty upon him of which he should have been aware. Such a submission is unsound, not because Cheek's constitutional arguments are not objectively reasonable or frivolous, which they surely are, but because the *Murdock-Pomponio* [*United States v. Murdock*, 290 U.S. 389 (1933), and *United States v. Pomponio*, 429 U.S. 10 (1976)], line of cases does not support such a position. Those cases construed the willfulness requirement in the criminal provisions of the Internal Revenue Code to require proof of knowledge of the law. This was because in "our complex tax system, uncertainty often arises even among taxpayers who earnestly wish to follow the law," and "[i]t is not the purpose of the law to penalize frank difference of opinion or innocent errors made despite the exercise of reasonable care." *United States v. Bishop*, 412 U.S. 346, 360–361 (1973) . . . .

Claims that some of the provisions of the tax code are unconstitutional are submissions of a different order. They do not arise from innocent mistakes caused by the complexity of the Internal Revenue Code. Rather, they reveal full knowledge of the provisions at issue and a studied conclusion, however wrong, that those provisions are invalid and unenforceable. Thus in this case, Cheek paid his taxes for years, but after attending various seminars and based on his own study, he concluded that the income tax laws could not constitutionally require him to pay a tax.

We do not believe that Congress contemplated that such a taxpayer, without risking criminal prosecution, could ignore the duties imposed upon him by the Internal Revenue Code and refuse to utilize the mechanisms provided by Congress to present his claims of invalidity to the courts and to abide by their decisions. There is no doubt that Cheek, from year to year, was free to pay the tax that the law purported to require, file for a refund and, if denied, present his claims of invalidity, constitutional or otherwise, to the courts. Also, without paying the tax, he could have challenged claims of tax deficiencies in the Tax Court, §6213, with the right to appeal to a higher court if unsuccessful. Cheek took neither course in some years, and, when he did, was unwilling to accept the outcome. As we see it, he is in no position to claim that his good-faith belief about the validity of the Internal Revenue Code negates willfulness or provides a defense to criminal prosecution under §§ 7201 and 7203. Of course, Cheek was free in this very case to present his claims of invalidity and have them adjudicated, but like defendants in criminal cases in other contexts who "willfully" refuse to comply with the duties placed upon them by the law, he must take the risk of being wrong.

We thus hold that, in a case like this, a defendant's views about the validity of the tax statutes are irrelevant to the issue of willfulness, need not be heard by the jury, and if they are, an instruction to disregard them would be proper. For this purpose, it makes no difference whether the claims of invalidity are frivolous or have substance. It was therefore not error in this case for the District Judge to instruct the jury not to consider Cheek's claims that the tax laws were unconstitutional. However, it was error for the court to instruct the jury that petitioner's asserted beliefs that wages are not income and that he was not a taxpayer within the meaning of the Internal Revenue Code should not be considered by the jury in determining whether Cheek had acted willfully.

For the reasons set forth in the opinion above, the judgment of the Court of Appeals is vacated, and the case is remanded for further proceedings consistent with this opinion.

It is so ordered.

JUSTICE SOUTER took no part in the consideration or decision of this case.

JUSTICE SCALIA, concurring in the judgment.

I concur in the judgment of the Court because our cases have consistently held that the failure to pay a tax in the good-faith belief that it is not legally owing is not "willful." I do not join the Court's opinion because I do not agree with the test for willfulness that it directs the Court of Appeals to apply on remand.

As the Court acknowledges, our opinions from the 1930s to the 1970s have interpreted the word "willfully" in the criminal tax statutes as requiring the "bad purpose" or "evil motive" of "intentional[ly] violat[ing] a known legal duty." It seems to me that today's opinion squarely reverses that long-established statutory construction when it says that a good-faith erroneous belief in the unconstitutionality of a tax law is no defense. It is quite impossible to say that a statute which one believes unconstitutional represents a "known legal duty." . . .

JUSTICE BLACKMUN, with whom JUSTICE MARSHALL joins, dissenting.

It seems to me that we are concerned in this case not with "the complexity of the tax laws," but with the income tax law in its most elementary and basic aspect: Is a wage earner a taxpayer and are wages income?

The Court acknowledges that the conclusively established standard for willfulness under the applicable statutes is the "'voluntary, intentional violation of a known legal duty.'" *See United States v. Bishop*, 412 U.S. 346, 360 (1973), and *United States v. Pomponio*, 429 U.S. 10, 12 (1976). That being so, it is incomprehensible to me how, in this day, more than 70 years after the institution of our present federal income tax system with the passage of the Income Tax Act of 1913, any taxpayer of competent mentality can assert as his defense to charges of statutory willfulness the proposition that the wage he receives for his labor is not income, irrespective of a cult that says otherwise and advises the gullible to resist income tax collections. One might note in passing that this particular taxpayer, after all, was a licensed pilot for one of our major commercial airlines; he presumably was a person of at least minimum intellectual competence.

The District Court's instruction that an objectively reasonable and good-faith misunderstanding of the law negates willfulness lends further, rather than less, protection to this defendant, for it added an additional hurdle for the prosecution to overcome. Petitioner should be grateful for this further protection, rather than be opposed to it.

This Court's opinion today, I fear, will encourage taxpayers to cling to frivolous views of the law in the hope of convincing a jury of their sincerity. If that ensues, I suspect we have gone beyond the limits of common sense.

While I may not agree with every word the Court of Appeals has enunciated in its opinion, I would affirm its judgment in this case. I therefore dissent.

Notes and Questions

1. *Intent to violate a known legal duty.* The *Cheek* decision is the principal case on the interpretation of mens rea in tax cases. In this decision, as in *Ratzlaf v. United States*, 510 U.S. 135 (1994), discussed in Chapter 13, Money Laundering, *infra*, the Court imposed proof of specific intent to violate the law as a requirement in cases involving complicated conduct that is not inherently evil, such as certain banking and tax offenses. (Congress subsequently amended the statute at issue in *Ratzlaf*, effectively overturning the decision, but has yet to enact similar legislation in response to the *Cheek* decision.)

The Court in *Cheek* reasoned that the common law notion that every person is presumed to know the law is not applicable in tax offenses because of the complexity and difficulty of the law in this area. Why did the Court find it necessary to establish a higher mens rea requirement in tax cases? Are there any policy justifications for such an imposition? Against? As a practical matter, how often will this requirement substantially assist a defendant?

Some courts continue to express confusion over the precise application of the willfulness requirement in criminal tax cases. This confusion might be attributed to the Court's earlier decisions in which the Court spoke of willfulness as requiring "bad faith," "evil motive," or "evil intent." *See Spies v. United States*, 317 U.S. 492, 498 (1943); *United States v. Bishop*, 412 U.S. 346, 360 (1973); *United States v. Murdock*, 290 U.S. 389, 398 (1933). As the Court stated in *United States v. Pomponio*, 429 U.S. 10, 12 (1976), however, the standard is simply proof of a voluntary, intentional violation of a known legal duty. What, if anything, did *Cheek* add to the *Pomponio* standard?

2. *Mens rea as to constitutionality.* The *Cheek* decision drew a distinction between those who possess a good faith belief that they are not violating the tax laws and those who believe that the tax system itself is invalid. According to Justice Scalia's concurring opinion, is this a valid distinction? Why are people who believe that their conduct does not violate the law less culpable than those who have an honest disagreement with the taxing system itself? How does the holding in *Cheek* comport with the legal maxim "ignorance of the law is no excuse"? Should it matter that tax crimes, as well as many other white collar crimes, are malum prohibitum rather than malum in se? Courts continue to distinguish between a defendant's misinterpretation of the tax laws and a defendant's disagreement with the tax laws, holding that the latter is irrelevant to the issue of willfulness.

3. *An honest but unreasonable belief.* The Court also held that the defendant's belief need not be an objectively reasonable one. This opens the door for even the unreasonable belief to be put forth as a defense to a tax prosecution. Why should an unreasonably held belief be a defense to a criminal tax prosecution?

4. *Tax protestors.* To what extent does the *Cheek* decision assist tax protestors and other defendants in criminal tax cases? As the majority stated, "*the more unreasonable* the asserted beliefs or misunderstandings are, the more likely the jury will consider them to be nothing more than *simple disagreement* with known legal duties imposed by the tax laws and will find that the government has carried its burden of proving knowledge." At his retrial, Cheek was convicted of the charges against him. *See United States v. Cheek*, 3 F.3d 1057 (7th Cir. 1993). Would you have reached the same verdict?

   Cheek was just one of many thousands of tax protestors in the United States. Such protestors have made an array of legal and constitutional arguments in order to avoid paying taxes. One high profile tax protestor case involved actor Wesley Snipes. Based on advice he received from Eddie Ray Kahn, a founder and organizer of two tax protestor organizations, Snipes did not file income tax returns for six consecutive years and sought tax refunds. Snipes, Kahn, and accountant Douglas Rosile were indicted on felony charges of conspiracy to defraud the United States and filing a false, fictitious, or fraudulent claim in violation of 18 U.S.C. § 287. Snipes was also indicted on six counts of failing to file a tax return. At trial, the defense asserted that Snipes was well-intentioned and was misled by Kahn's advice. In a split verdict, Snipes was acquitted of the felony charges but was convicted on three counts of failure to file. Snipes was sentenced to the maximum of three years in prison, and was required to pay back taxes, interest, and penalties of around $15 million. *See* John J. Tigue Jr. & Jeremy H. Temkin, *Tax Litigation Issues: The Wesley Snipes Trial*, 239 N.Y.L.J. 3, col. 1 (May 15, 2008). Both sides asserted that this outcome was a victory. Which side won? Why?

5. *Selective prosecution.* Prior to his trial, Wesley Snipes moved to have the case against him dismissed on selective prosecution grounds. Selective prosecution is not a defense specific to tax crimes, but rather is a general criminal law defense based upon the prosecutor's alleged violation of the Equal Protection Clause due to

racial or other bias. Snipes, who is African American, argued he had been treated differently than Kahn, who is white and was not charged with failure to file despite not filing his own returns for several years. The district court judge rejected this argument. The court stated that prosecuting Snipes on the additional charges served the goal of general deterrence because of the likely attention the media would pay to the case. *See* John J. Tigue Jr. & Jeremy H. Temkin, *Tax Litigation Issues: The Wesley Snipes Trial*, 239 N.Y.L.J. 3 (May 15, 2008). Data seem to show that such selective prosecution can have a significant general deterrent effect. *See* Joshua D. Blank, *In Defense of Individual Tax Privacy*, 61 EMORY L.J. 265, 321 (2011). For a discussion of the selective prosecution defense, see *United States v. Armstrong*, 517 U.S. 456 (1996). Do you believe that Snipes' argument has merit? Is the court's response persuasive? Why or why not?

2. Defenses

There are a number of ways to defend against the government's proof of willfulness. Cheek asserted a good faith defense — that he honestly believed that he was acting within the law. Although the law was clear that wages are "income" under the Internal Revenue Code, Cheek asserted a good faith misunderstanding of the law.

A defendant may make a related argument when an aspect of the tax law is actually unclear. What happens if the defendant claims a good faith interpretation of a complicated, unsettled aspect of tax law, and the government disagrees with that interpretation? That was the issue in the next case, a high-profile prosecution that arose from the Wall Street insider trading scandals of the 1980s. Although the case involved a somewhat technical aspect of securities law, the tax law issue on appeal was a fairly simple one involving the jury instruction. As you read the case, consider (a) the nature of the legal uncertainty in the case, and (b) the essential disagreement between the majority and the dissent on the jury instruction issue.

United States v. Regan
937 F.2d 823 (2d Cir. 1991)

VAN GRAAFEILAND, CIRCUIT JUDGE:

[Regan and the other defendants were affiliated with a stock brokerage firm, Princeton-Newport Partners ("P.N."). Regan was a managing partner of P.N. and was its resident tax expert. The government alleged that the defendants committed tax fraud by arranging for P.N. to engage in "stock parking" transactions that produced phony tax losses. In the alleged stock parking transactions, PN temporarily sold stock to other brokerage firms at a loss. P.N. then deducted the losses on its tax returns. Later, P.N. bought the same stock back from the firms to which it had previously sold the stock.

At trial, Regan asserted that he believed the tax deductions were proper. He said that he based his conclusion on (1) correspondence from P.N.'s accountants, (2) a report of the Tax Section of the Association of the Bar of the City of New York, and (3) Regan's own study of the relevant statute (Internal Revenue Code § 1058) and proposed regulation 1.1058-1.[d]

The government asserted that P.N.'s transactions, evaluated under § 1058, produced phony deductions. These deductions formed the basis for the tax perjury prosecution. Although essentially a tax fraud case, the government also charged the defendants with conspiracy, securities fraud, mail fraud based upon the mailing of the tax returns, and RICO based upon the mail fraud.]

From time to time in the period between 1984 and 1987, P.N. owned substantial quantities of stock that had depreciated in value and whose sale would provide P.N. with opportunities to take tax losses. Regan testified that, prompted by correspondence from his accountants, a report of the Tax Section of the Association of the Bar of the City of New York, and his own study of section 1058 and proposed regulation 1.1058-1, he concluded that P.N. could take those losses by means of sales and repurchase arrangements with other brokerage or investment houses so long as the arrangements between P.N. and the other houses did not satisfy the requirements of section 1058. Regan felt that this very lack of compliance would enable P.N. to take tax losses on the transactions. Based on this belief, P.N. entered into some fifty-nine transactions with other brokerage and investment houses, consisting of sales of stock by P.N. to those houses and agreements to resell to P.N. at fixed prices at later dates.

Appellants, following Regan's lead, believed that these transactions did not satisfy section 1058 requirements in that their terms were not reduced to writing, did not provide for termination upon short notice, and did not contain legally enforceable rights of repurchase. Moreover, the brokerage houses to whom the stock was sold had complete control of the stock in their possession while P.N. had none, thus depriving P.N. of the opportunity to avoid loss or capitalize on gain during that period. Also, the agreed-upon repurchase price might vary substantially from the then-existing market price.

The district court described this as a "sophistical" treatment of section 1058, and rejected it out of hand. Stating that he didn't think he had "to give a contention that was contrary to what [he] regarded] as being the law," he held that appellants' contention concerning section 1058 had no substance and the section had "no applicability to defendants' case." This was prejudicial error. The issue in the case was not whether appellants' construction of section 1058 was correct or even objectively reasonable but whether it was made in good faith. *Cheek v. United States*, 498 U.S. 192 (1991).

---

d. Section 1058 provides that no loss may be taken if the stock transaction agreement (1) provides for the return of securities identical to those transferred; (2) requires that payments be made to the transferor in amounts equal to the interest, dividends, and other distributions paid on the transferred securities; (3) does not reduce the transferor's risk of loss or opportunity for gain on the transferred securities; and (4) meets such other requirements as may be prescribed by Treasury regulations. If these requirements are met, then the stock has been "parked" and no losses from that arrangement may be deducted.

Although appellants were not charged with violating §1058, that section became pivotal in the case because appellants believed that it authorized them to do just what they did, *i.e.*, take tax losses. If this belief was held in good faith, they could not be held criminally liable for proceeding on that basis. Appellants offered substantial evidence of their good faith reliance on their interpretation of §1058, some of which the court received and some of which it rejected. For example, the Tax Section of the Association of the Bar of the City of New York appears to have interpreted §1058 in somewhat the same manner as did Regan. The report of the Committee upon which Regan relied stated in substance that the distinguishing feature between a loan and a sale of securities was whether the risk of loss or opportunity for gain was retained by the person making the transfer. This, of course, was in accord with the generally accepted rule that "for Federal income tax purposes, the owner of property must possess meaningful burdens and benefits of ownership." Appellants also offered the testimony of two acknowledged tax experts to the effect that Regan's interpretation of section 1058 was not unreasonable, but the district court refused to permit these experts to testify.

Whether, as appellants contend, the district court erred in its evidentiary rulings concerning this evidence is a matter we need not decide. The issue of appellants' good faith reliance on §1058 as appellants interpreted it was squarely raised and argued. The district court should have instructed the jury that, if it found the reliance was held in good faith, the defendants could not be held criminally liable for proceeding in accordance with that reliance.

The record is clear that appellants requested a charge specifically directed to their claim of good faith reliance on §1058. . . . In the instant case, where appellants were charged with sixty-four counts covering the waterfront of tax fraud, securities fraud, mail and wire fraud, conspiracy, and RICO, a generalized charge on good faith was insufficient to instruct the jury concerning appellants' specific good faith defense based on §1058. Appellants were entitled to have the trial court clearly instruct the jury, relative to appellants' theory of defense to the tax charges, that the theory if believed justified acquittal on those charges.

One of the most esoteric areas of the law is that of federal taxation. It is replete with "full-grown intricacies," and it is rare that a "simple, direct statement of the law can be made without caveat." 1 Mertens Law of Federal Income Tax §1.01. Justice White, writing for the Court majority in *Cheek*, *supra*, stated that, because of the proliferation of tax statutes and regulations, the common-law presumption that every person knows the law does not apply where violations of federal criminal tax laws are alleged. Instead, proof of guilt in such cases must be predicated upon a "'voluntary, intentional violation of a known legal duty.'"

This rule applies to alleged violations of the "hierarchy of tax offenses set forth in §§7201–7207, inclusive." *United States v. Bishop*, 412 U.S. 346 (1973). It also applies to 18 U.S.C. §371 conspiracies to violate one or more of the hierarchy of tax offenses.

The Government's burden in proving a mail or wire fraud offense, 18 U.S.C. §§1341 and 1343, is even more onerous. These are specific intent crimes. . . . Where, as here, there is little dispute concerning the making and filing of the allegedly fraudulent returns, the existence vel non of culpable intent or lack of good faith is a crucially important issue in the case.

Despite numerous requests by appellants to charge otherwise, the district court persisted in viewing section 1058 objectively, insisting that the court was the sole judge of the law. That, of course, was true. However, the issue for the jury was not how the district court interpreted section 1058; it was how the defendants in good faith interpreted it. "A jury is the ultimate discipline to a silly argument." *United States v. Burton*, 737 F.2d 439, 443 (5th Cir. 1984). The district court's failure to squarely present this issue to the jury was a prejudicial error that tainted all of the tax hierarchy charges.

[The court affirmed the conspiracy and securities fraud convictions, but reversed and remanded the convictions for tax fraud, mail fraud, and RICO.]

MAHONEY, CIRCUIT JUDGE, concurring in part and dissenting in part:

My colleagues conclude:

> The district court should have instructed the jury that, if it found that the reliance [on section 1058 as appellants interpreted it] was held in good faith, the defendants could not be held criminally liable for proceeding in accordance with that reliance.

The district court in fact gave the following instructions with regard to good faith:

> If you find that the defendant acted in good faith in the honest belief that the representations he made were true, that he did not intend to defraud anyone, this constitutes a complete defense to the crime of mail or wire fraud....

The defendants contend the government has failed to prove that they did not act in good faith....

In connection with the false return counts, the court additionally instructed as follows:

> If the defendant signed the tax return in good faith and believed it to be true in all material matters, he has not committed a crime and must be acquitted on these counts, even if the return was incorrect.

> If you find that the tax return was not true as to a material matter, the central question is whether or not the defendant honestly believed that the return was true. The government has the burden of proving that the defendant did not have an honest belief in the truthfulness of the return.

Characterizing these rather extensive instructions as a "generalized charge on good faith," my colleagues find them "insufficient to instruct the jury concerning the appellants' specific good faith defense based on section 1058." In other words, the defendants were prejudiced by an instruction that their good faith defense was premised on Regan's "general knowledge of the tax laws," because defendants more specifically contended that Regan relied on section 1058. I am unpersuaded that a district court is required to present a defendant's contentions with this level of particularity. The fact is that the theory of defense — to wit, bona fide reliance on the tax code — was squarely presented to the jury. It is unlikely that the jurors were misled because the district court failed to remind them of Regan's contention that § 1058 was at the center of his tax analysis. . . .

Notes and Questions

1. *Prejudicial error?* Why did the Court reverse the defendants' tax fraud convictions? Did the trial judge err? Even if so, did the error prejudice the defense? Why or why not? And even if there was error in the jury charge on the tax offenses, why did the error taint the conspiracy, mail fraud, and RICO charges?

2. *Charging tax cases.* As discussed in the introductory materials, criminal tax cases often develop from investigations that originally focused on other sorts of wrongdoing. The *Regan* case, for example, arose out of a 1980s *securities fraud* investigation of major Wall Street figures including Ivan Boesky and Michael Milken. (*See* Introductory Notes to Chapter 5, Securities Fraud, *supra*.) Ultimately, however, the case was charged principally as a tax fraud case, with mail fraud and RICO charges based upon the tax fraud charges. And the racketeering investigation of organized crime figure Al Capone ultimately led to a prosecution for tax law violations. Is it appropriate to charge tax crimes in such circumstances? *See* Harry Litman, *Pretextual Prosecution*, 92 Geo. L.J. 1135 (2004) (evaluating what the author terms the "Al Capone approach" to the exercise of prosecutorial discretion).

3. *Evidence of willfulness.* As in other areas of white collar crime, mens rea in tax cases is often based on circumstantial evidence, often called "badges of fraud." How far can the government go in relying on such evidence? Assume, for example, that the government has charged an attorney with tax evasion and tax perjury based upon the following evidence:

(a) The defendant exhibited a pattern of understating his income on his tax returns over three years;

(b) The defendant had a law degree;

(c) The defendant had substantial professional experience, including the practice of law;

(d) The defendant was able to bill clients and maintain expense records for his private practice; and

(e) The defendant, when asked by an IRS agent to disclose his bank accounts, failed to disclose one of the accounts.

Which of these pieces of evidence, if any, is probative of willfulness? Is this evidence sufficient to show willfulness beyond a reasonable doubt? *See United States v. Rischard*, 471 F.2d 105 (8th Cir. 1973).

4. *Reliance on professional advice.* As in other fraud prosecutions, such as mail fraud and securities fraud, good faith reliance on professional advice is a complete defense to a tax fraud charge. To prove such a defense, the defendant must adduce facts showing that (a) the defendant relied in good faith on a professional, and (b) the defendant made complete disclosure of all the relevant facts. *See United States v. Masat*, 948 F.2d 923 (5th Cir. 1991). If a defendant adduces the facts necessary to show reliance on counsel, is the defendant entitled to a specific jury instruction on this issue or is a general good faith charge sufficient? Under the *Regan* approach, what's the correct answer? *See Bursten v. United States*, 395 F.2d 976 (5th Cir. 1968).

5. *Privilege for tax professionals.* In 1998, the IRS Restructuring and Reform Act, H.R. 2676, 105th Cong. (1998), created a limited privilege for advice provided by tax professionals. As a result, advice from tax professionals may, like advice from an attorney, be protected from discovery in criminal proceedings. Why would Congress create such a tax advice privilege?

6. *Proving willfulness.* What exactly must a defendant know to count as having willfully violated the tax laws? Must the defendant know the precise tax provisions involved, or just generally that the conduct violates tax laws? *United States v. Davis*, 369 F. App'x 456, 458 (4th Cir. 2010) (holding that a conviction for tax evasion does not require that the defendant know the exact amount of tax due, but only that the defendant know that tax is due which is not paid). Many of the tax code's provisions are ambiguous; even where not ambiguous, compliance with the literal text of the tax laws is no guarantee if the economic substance of a transaction departs from it. This "economic substance analysis is flexible," *Long Term Capital Holdings v. United States*, 330 F. Supp. 2d 122, 171 (D. Conn. 2004), and speaking about what a defendant knows with respect to them may not be very helpful. The defendant may know that the conduct comes close to the line between legal and prohibited, but genuinely believe the conduct is on the right side of the line. Or the defendant may think the conduct has crossed the line, but that there is a good faith argument that it has not. In such situations, defendants do not "know" whether they are acting legally or not, but know there is a risk that their conduct violated the law. What level of known risk should qualify as a willful violation if the court decides the defendant's conduct was against the law? What incentives do your answers to these questions give to people who are evaluating their tax obligations? When should the rule of lenity apply? *See United States v. Wanland*, 830 F.3d 947, 954 (9th Cir. 2016) (holding that the tax code is rarely so ambiguous that the rule of lenity comes into play).

Problems

12-5. Horace Kilborne became a United States district judge three years ago, and has presided over five criminal tax cases. Prior to becoming a judge, he had practiced law for over 30 years. His annual salary as a judge was approximately one tenth the income he received during his last years in private practice.

Judge Kilborne was charged with two counts of tax perjury, in violation of §7206, for allegedly underreporting the amount of legal fees he received from his law firm for work he had performed before becoming a judge. At trial, the government introduced duplicates of checks sent to the defendant from attorneys at his prior firm representing fee income the defendant had earned before becoming a judge. The government also introduced bank records showing amounts that the defendant deposited in his personal account after receiving the checks from the law firm. Both sides agreed that he had not deposited all the checks, but had cashed several of them. The evidence showed that the defendant had reported all the deposited checks on his tax returns, but did not report any money from checks that he had cashed.

With respect to the first return, the government contends Kilborne received $141,000 in fee income, but only reported $72,000 as fee income. The government submitted correspondence from Kilborne to his long-time accountant, James White, which understated Kilborne's fee income for that year by $65,000. Kilborne, however, stated that he instructed his secretary to deliver another letter to White which fully disclosed his fee income. The secretary testified she delivered this letter, but White testified that he never received it and had used the figures from Kilborne's initial letter to complete the return.

Kilborne did not use White for the preparation of the second return, but instead hired Joseph Holmes. The government alleged that Kilborne received over $88,000 in fee income during that tax year, but that his tax return showed no fee income. Kilborne stated that he included this fee income as part of a $350,000 sale price of his interest in the law firm. This sale price appeared on Schedule D of his return, where he also claimed a $200,000 capital loss on the sale of his interest in the law firm. He later conceded that his fee income for that year was wrongly categorized as a capital gain. Kilborne stated that he had innocently relied on Holmes to prepare the return correctly, that he was generally ignorant about the details of tax law, and that he had no reason to doubt the return's accuracy. Kilborne perused the return for 10 or 15 minutes before signing it. Holmes did not testify.

At trial, Kilborne sought to assert reliance on professional advice as a defense to each count of filing a false return. The judge declined to instruct the jury on this defense. Kilborne was convicted, and appeals on the basis that the trial judge erred in failing to give the instruction. How is the court likely to rule? Why?

12-6. William Fuller owns and operates a small accounting firm. He is a Certified Public Accountant ("CPA") and has been filing income taxes for clients for the past 10 years. Despite the over 500 filings he has made over the past 10 years for other people, he failed to file his own income tax return for the past three years. He filed his returns for several years prior to this delinquency. William is a college graduate and has routinely completed the yearly continuing education requirements for his accounting license. He is married, has raised three children, and occasionally finds the time to golf. The Department of Justice is seeking to indict William on three counts of willful failure to file under 26 U.S.C. §7203.

Assume that William's attorney seeks a meeting with the prosecutor in an attempt to persuade the government not to indict William. The attorney asserts the following alternative defenses on behalf of William:

a. Good faith misunderstanding of the law. William claims that he believed it was unnecessary for him to file his returns because he didn't have the money necessary to pay his taxes. He claims that he stopped filing returns when his accounting firm became significantly less profitable than it had been in previous years.

b. Chronic depression/sleeping disorder. William's attorney asserts that several medical experts will testify that William has severe depression and a related sleeping disorder. William claims that his failure to file was a result of his medical disorder and not a willful avoidance or omission.

c. Preoccupation with personal and business affairs. William claims that he is so overwhelmed with running his business, especially during tax season, that he is forced to choose between neglecting his clients and neglecting personal business obligations.

d. Habit. William claims that his failure to file was not willful but rather a result of a habit of procrastination established in college.

e. Alcoholism. William claims that his life outside of the office is clouded by severe alcoholism. He manages to fulfill his professional obligations before happy hour, but completely neglects any personal or social obligations.

f. Filing of delinquent returns. William got word from a college friend that the IRS has begun investigating him. In an attempt to avoid prosecution, William filed all of his delinquent tax returns immediately.

g. Intent unrelated to tax consequences. William asserts that during a visit to Las Vegas for a CPA convention, he committed a state crime. He immediately fled back home but stopped filing his tax returns because of a fear that it would alert Las Vegas authorities to his whereabouts.

If you were the prosecutor, would any of these arguments be effective in persuading you not to seek charges against William?

12-7. At the trial of Pat Hayward for tax evasion and for filing false tax returns, the following facts have been proven:

Pat Hayward is a 50-year-old aircraft structural designer with a consulting business. Pat founded the business 15 years ago. Initially, Pat received payments from clients in two ways. First, Pat received set monthly retainer fees to assure that Pat would be available to work for each client. For the last three tax years, Pat received from $500 to $2,000 per month from various clients. Pat received this amount whether or not Pat performed work for the client during a given month. Second, if Pat's hourly billings for a particular client exceeded the retainer fee for a given month, Pat would bill the client for the hours above and beyond the retainer amount. For example, if a client paid Pat a $1,000 monthly retainer fee, and Pat worked 15 hours in a given month at $100 per hour, then Pat would bill the client an additional $500 for that month.

For the first five years, Pat maintained the company books and records and prepared its tax returns. The business began to boom, however, and Pat retained Graphic Accountants ("Graphic") to keep the company books and to prepare both the company's tax returns and Pat's individual returns.

Upon being retained, Graphic set up an accounting system for Pat. Graphic advised Pat to report all consulting fees to Graphic's office, along with all business expenses. In doing so, Pat provided summaries of fees and expenses instead of original invoices. These summaries were prepared from the bank statements of the company's general operating account.

Beginning five years ago, Pat's main client, Boomerang Air, began to pay Pat regular bonuses apart from the retainer fees and hourly consulting fees. Pat deposited these bonuses in the business's petty cash account instead of in the company's general operating account. As a result, these bonuses were not reflected on the summaries Pat provided to the accountants. Pat has no training as a bookkeeper, and Pat states that any error in amounts provided to the accountants was unintentional. Pat also says that the accountants failed to follow professional standards by failing to ask for original information. The government has no direct evidence to contradict these assertions.

Five years ago, Pat joined the Economic Libertarian Party ("ELP"). During ELP meetings, the members discussed whether the federal income taxation system was legal. Pat asserts that labor constitutes property which, when exchanged for fees, produces no net gain subject to taxation as "income." Pat also came to disagree with the philosophy of the IRS concerning the definition of income.

As a result of Pat's new philosophy, beginning three years ago, Pat stopped placing on the summaries given to the accountants any fees that Pat earned above and beyond the regular monthly retainer fees that Pat received from clients.

Pat testified, "I genuinely believed that the ELP's interpretation of the law was the correct one." In support, Pat provided records of regular attendance at ELP meetings and copies of party literature with notes that Pat took during the meetings.

Graphic never requested underlying documentation for the summaries. Even though the documentation was readily available to the Graphic accountants, Graphic did not examine that documentation when conducting its routine audits of Pat's business. Whenever Graphic did request documentation, Pat provided complete and accurate records.

Based upon the company's tax returns, which Pat signed, the government indicted Pat for filing false income tax returns and for tax evasion for the past three tax years. The government relied on Pat's failure to report (1) the bonuses, and (2) the hourly fees Pat earned each month above the regular retainer fees. The understatements of income resulted in tax deficiencies of $33,000, $45,000, and $70,000 for the respective years in question.

In defense, Pat argues that (1) as to the bonuses, although Pat believed them to be taxable because they were not necessarily in return for actual labor, Pat relied on the accounting system set up by Graphic and assumed they would be reported, and (2) as to the hourly fees, Pat held a good faith belief that these monies were not taxable.

Assume that you are on the jury in Pat's case and have heard the foregoing evidence. Also assume that Pat testified, and that you found Pat to be a generally credible witness. You have been instructed according to the decision in *Cheek*.

Evaluate the government's proof on the elements of filing false returns, 26 U.S.C. §7206, and tax evasion, 26 U.S.C. §7201. Would you vote to convict or acquit Pat?

E. Methods of Proof

In a tax evasion case, the government must prove beyond a reasonable doubt that the defendant underpaid taxes. *See Holland v. United States*, 348 U.S. 121, 126 (1954). In many instances, such proof may be hard to adduce. For example, underpayment may be difficult to prove when the defendant kept incomplete or inaccurate records. Courts have thus allowed various "methods of proof" concerning underpayment of taxes. First, the government may employ the "direct" method by showing, for example, that the taxpayer failed to report a specific item of income. Second, the government may use an "indirect" method of proof. The latter category includes proof of (a) net worth, (b) expenditures, and (c) bank deposits. In such cases, the government may show, for example, that a taxpayer's expenditures far exceeded reported income for the tax year. The following case examines the distinction between direct and indirect methods of proving underpayment.

United States v. Black

843 F.2d 1456 (D.C. Cir. 1988)

SILBERMAN, CIRCUIT JUDGE:

This is an appeal from a conviction of income tax evasion. Appellant, Fred Black, complains of insufficiency of the government's evidence . . . .

After a forty day trial, Black was convicted on three counts of tax evasion. The government charged that although Black received $65,827 of taxable income in 1978, $109,251 of taxable income in 1979, and $174,755 of taxable income in 1981, he failed to file a return for any of those years.

The resolution of Black's claims concerning sufficiency of evidence and adequacy of the jury charge turns entirely upon the proper characterization of the actual method used by the government to prove Black's tax evasion. The government contends it employed the "specific items" method of proof, a direct method of demonstrating tax evasion in which the government "produce[s] evidence of the receipt of specific items of reportable income by the defendant that do not appear on his income tax return." Black claims, however, that the government used the "bank deposits/cash expenditures" method. When using that indirect method of proof, the government shows, either through increases in net worth, increases in bank deposits, or the presence of cash expenditures, that the taxpayer's wealth grew during a tax year beyond what could be attributed to the taxpayer's reported income, thereby raising the inference of unreported income.

In any indirect method case, the government must prove that the increased wealth did not come from nontaxable sources. Otherwise the evidence will be insufficient, for

> [t]here is always the possibility that the taxpayer deposited cash that he received from a non-taxable source or from income taxed in a prior year but kept on hand as cash or even from unreported income from a prior year kept on hand in cash. Such events are common human occurrences, and this possibility may of itself create reasonable doubt. Therefore, the government must establish in some fashion the amount of cash the taxpayer had on hand at the start of the period. This is part of the government's duty to negate the possibility that bank deposits or cash expenditures in the year under investigation originated from non-taxable sources.

On the other hand, where the government's case is based on evidence showing *specific items* of unreported income, the safeguards required for indirect methods of proof are not necessary, as the possibility that the defendant may be convicted because non-taxable income is mistakenly presumed to be taxable income, or because cash expenditures are mistakenly assumed to be made from taxable income, is not present.

Black claims that the government relied on a bank deposits/cash expenditures method of proof, but utterly failed to rebut the possibility that his expenditures originated from non-taxable sources, and therefore the evidence was insufficient to sustain a conviction. In particular, Black maintains that the government was obliged to negate the possibility that his bank deposits and cash expenditures were from non-income sources, and to establish his opening net worth for the years in question. In short, Black claims the government tried to convict him of tax evasion "by simply showing that he spent money and did not file a tax return during the tax years in question."

The government's response is that since it introduced evidence of *specific items* of *income* received by Black, it was not required to disprove the likelihood of a cash hoard or a non-taxable source of income. From approximately 1975 to the time of the trial, Black was subject to an IRS lien of approximately three million dollars. During this time, Black created two corporations, Dunbar and Machine-A-Rama, portrayed by the government as dummy corporations which had neither paid employees nor offices. At trial, Black disputed the bogus nature of these entities, claiming the corporations were involved in developing a casino in Atlantic City — a project which never materialized — and he also insisted that any money he took from these corporations was in the form of loans which he felt obligated to repay. Nevertheless, it was uncontroverted that during the period covered by the indictment Black had no personal bank accounts and that many of Black's personal expenses were paid by checks drawn on accounts of these two corporations. Black further conceded that he created Dunbar because he did not want to put property in his own name and because he wished to conceal from the IRS money he was spending.

In the government's view, Black received taxable income each time he wrote a check on the accounts of Dunbar and Machine-A-Rama to cover his personal expenses. Evidence that Black paid for personal expenses with checks drawn on corporate accounts and that Black never truly considered the checks to be loans would be sufficient for conviction, for "[a]ll the law requires is that there be proof sufficient to establish that there has been a receipt of taxable income by the accused and a willful evasion of the tax thereon." *United States v. Nunan*, 236 F.2d 576, 586 (2d Cir. 1956).

Black, by focusing on isolated remarks at trial, argues that the government presented only a cash expenditures case against him. We disagree. If the statements by the prosecutor, the testimony of the government's tax witness, and the trial judge's instructions to the jury, are each considered in light of the evidence actually submitted, it is clear that the government presented direct proof that Black received specific items of taxable income and did not pay tax on that income. . . .

While there were several explicit references to the "personal expenditures method" by the prosecutor, the government's expert witness, and the trial judge in his instructions, at no point in the trial was it suggested to the jury that evidence of personal expenditures, without more, would be sufficient to convict Black of tax evasion. Evidence of personal expenditures was relevant only because the government contended that the very writing of the checks created income to Black. Thus, the danger encountered in a classic "cash expenditure" case — that the defendant could be convicted for spending non-taxable income — is not at all present here. In this case, the use of the phrase "personal expenditures method" was not associated at all with the "cash expenditures method" of proving tax evasion; the phrase was used solely to distinguish Black's business expenditures from his personal expenditures.

Appellant's conviction is therefore *affirmed*.

Notes and Questions

1. *Direct evidence.* Direct evidence is most simply established through the "specific items" method of proof as discussed in *Black*. Often there is direct evidence that the defendant received unreported income, or direct evidence that the defendant claimed an improper deduction. Under this approach, the taxpayer's books and records usually provide the basis for the direct evidence of underpayment.

2. *Indirect methods of proof.* Tax deficiency may also be proven indirectly by circumstantial evidence. In such cases, the government must follow all reasonable leads,

such as gifts and prior savings, that might explain unreported sources of income. Why is it appropriate to use such an "indirect" method of proof in a criminal case with substantial penalties?

a. *The bank deposits method.* In *United States v. Mounkes*, 204 F.3d 1024, 1028 (10th Cir. 2000), the government presented evidence that the defendant's bank deposits exceeded their reported income after adjustments, thus supporting an inference of unreported income. The court stated that, when using the bank deposits method, the government must establish the defendant's "pre-income cash on hand with reasonable certainty, while negating other sources of nontaxable income during the same period." *Id.* The cash on hand figure need not be proven precisely. When using the bank deposits method, the government must prove only a substantial difference between the bank deposits and reported income, and not an exact amount. *See United States v. Boulware*, 384 F.3d 794, 811 (9th Cir. 2004).

b. *The net worth method.* In *Holland v. United States*, 348 U.S. 121 (1954), the Supreme Court approved the use of the "net worth" method of proving a tax deficiency. After showing the total net value of the defendant's assets at the beginning of a tax period, this method requires the government to demonstrate the defendant's total net worth increased over a tax year by an amount substantially greater than the reported income for the year. The government must also investigate all reasonable leads that would tend to establish that any monies were not directly attributable to taxable income. The Supreme Court noted in *Holland* that the net worth method was originally used to corroborate direct proof of unreported income in cases such as *Capone v. United States*, 51 F.2d 609 (7th Cir. 1931), but was increasingly being used as a main tool in ordinary income-bracket investigations. *Holland*, 348 U.S. at 126–27. The Court also pointed out several pitfalls, as well as the need to exercise care and restraint, when using this method. *Id.* at 127–29. The net worth method is perhaps the most challenging indirect method to prove, and investigations using this method are often long and difficult.

c. *The cash expenditures method.* The "cash expenditures" method of proving a deficiency is similar to the net worth method. This method requires the government to prove that the defendant spent more money than was reported to the government during a given tax year.

The court in *Black* stated that any indirect method of proof requires the government "to establish in some fashion the amount of cash the taxpayer had on hand at the start of the period." In *United States v. Khanu*, 675 F. Supp. 2d 55, 65 (D.D.C. 2009), *aff'd*, 662 F.3d 1226 (D.C. Cir. 2011), the court held that "the government is only required to establish the starting cash on hand amount with *reasonable* certainty; it need not exhaustively eliminate every possible nontaxable source of income that defendant may have had prior to the starting date" of the period.

3. *Amount of tax deficiency required.* As noted above, the circuits are split as to whether, in an evasion case, the government must prove a "substantial" deficiency. *See United States v. Daniels*, 387 F.3d 636, 640–41 (7th Cir. 2004) (listing cases).

Should proof of a "substantial" deficiency be an element of tax evasion? Why or why not?

4. *Civil tax collection.* While a precise assessment of tax due is relevant for civil tax collection, it is not critical for a successful criminal prosecution. In a criminal case, the government need only establish that there was an evasion, a false statement, or the failure to file, not the precise amount of taxes due. This question is left for the civil collection action that usually follows the criminal case. Frequently, however, the defendant's records are insufficient to make an accurate determination in a specific items case.

5. *Sentencing in tax cases.* While proving the amount of tax due is not required for conviction in a criminal case, the amount of tax loss caused by the offense is relevant at sentencing. In general, the amount of tax loss caused by the offense affects the base offense level under the U.S. Sentencing Guidelines. *See* John J. Tigue Jr. & Jeremy H. Temkin, *Tax Litigation Issues: Sentencing in Criminal Tax Cases Post-Booker,* 235 N.Y.L.J. 3, col. 1 (May 18, 2006). Sentencing enhancements may apply if the offense involved, among others, "sophisticated means" or if the unreported income came as a result of criminal activity. *Id.*

The Supreme Court's ruling in *United States v. Booker,* 543 U.S. 220, 244 (2005), has had an impact on sentencing in tax cases. Prior to *Booker,* the sentencing guidelines were mandatory. Tax crime sentences tended to be longer than those "for other white-collar offenses involving comparable losses, resulting in a higher rate of incarceration for convicted tax defendants." Tigue & Temkin, *supra,* 235 N.Y.L.J. at 3. In *Booker,* however, the Supreme Court ruled the Guidelines should be advisory and not mandatory. 543 U.S. at 244. *See* Chapter 19, *infra.* Statistics show that, in the years following *Booker,* the tax sentences falling outside the Guidelines have now climbed to more than 60%. Scott A. Schumacher, *Sentencing in Tax Cases after Booker: Striking the Right Balance between Uniformity and Discretion,* 59 VILL. L. REV. 563, 586 (2014) ("[W]hile the overall sentences within the applicable Guidelines range declined [after *Booker*], the tax sentences within the Guidelines declined much more dramatically. The fact that more than 60% of post-*Booker* sentences in tax cases now fall outside the Guidelines range demonstrates that there is substantially more disparity in tax cases post-*Booker.*").

Problems

12-8. Josephine Dickey worked for the Immigration and Naturalization Service ("INS") at a New Mexico port of entry. Her salary as an INS inspector for the tax year in question year was $45,414. Prior to working for the INS, she had had several low paying jobs. Her husband worked as a custodian and earned minimum wage.

Beginning in March for the tax year at issue, Dickey purchased a new truck, a digital camera, a laptop computer, a new car, and furniture. She paid for most of these items in cash. After overhearing a phone call between Dickey and her uncle, her husband asked her if she was doing any "dirty business." She responded, "I just had to close my eyes and I would get $15,000 per car. My uncle was the one arranging the cars that would go across the border." Later, Dickey's husband saw her in possession of large amounts of cash on several occasions.

Dickey had her annual tax return prepared by a professional tax preparer. Dickey told the preparer she had no other income other than her INS salary. Her return showed adjusted gross income of $45,414, taxable income of $34,315, and tax due of $6,013. An IRS investigation, however, found bank deposits of $32,245 and total cash expenditures of $140,264 for the tax year at issue.

You are an Assistant U.S. Attorney in charge of a grand jury investigation into possible criminal tax offenses committed by Dickey. What charges would you likely seek? How would you seek to prove those charges?

12-9. Mr. and Mrs. Moore owned three corporations that were used in a multi-level marketing system selling personal care products — one in the United States, one in Australia, and one in Singapore. The companies in Australia and Singapore sent monthly commission checks directly to the Moores; however, the accounting department in the United States was unaware of this arrangement. The Moores deposited these checks into a trust account in their name to purchase properties for residential and commercial development.

The IRS subsequently began to investigate the corporation located in the United States. Mr. Moore informed the IRS that the properties were purchased with a loan from the Australian company. The Moores, finding no documentation to substantiate the loan, created a backdated loan document. Mr. Moore told the IRS that the Australian company improperly recorded the money as commission and bonus payments, and that they were fixing the problem. When asked to verify this claim, the Australian company responded that all payments were for bonuses and commissions and no loan payments were made. Consequently, the Moores were charged with six counts of tax evasion.

At trial, the government contended that the evidence stated above indicates that the foreign commission checks were not loans to the corporation, but personal income to the Moores. Based on this assumption, the IRS reconstructed the defendants' income and determined that they owed nearly $3 million in unpaid taxes. The government argued that the creation of the false loan document was an affirmative act to evade paying taxes, and the failure to report the commission checks as income established the evasion was willful. The Moores, however, argued that this evidence was insufficient to support a conviction of tax evasion.

Under the specific items method of proof, has the government met its burden to convict defendant of tax evasion?

12-10. Petitioner was self-employed as a licensed stockbroker, investment consultant, and insurance agent. The IRS notified petitioner that his last two tax returns were being examined. Petitioner refused to provide the requested bank statements and records. The IRS issued summonses to petitioner's banks and referred the case to the IRS Criminal Investigation Division.

Due to petitioner's lack of cooperation, lack of adequate bookkeeping, and evidence of acquisition of assets and substantial expenditures, the IRS decided to use the net worth method of proof to establish petitioner's income and the amount of underpayment, if any. The IRS used bank statements to determine the petitioner's opening net worth. From this amount, the IRS was able to determine that petitioner had deficiencies for the two years of $23,904 and $61,292, respectively.

Petitioner contends that the opening net worth was not reasonably accurate because the IRS failed to take into account $500,000 which he maintained as a cash hoard inside a suitcase in an unlocked closet in his residence. The IRS, on the other hand, argued that the opening net worth was reasonably accurate for three reasons. First, petitioner had and regularly used several bank and investment accounts. Second, it is highly "implausible that petitioner, as a stockbroker and investment adviser . . . had accumulated $500,000 in cash, and that he kept that cash in a closet at his house." Third, petitioners failed to introduce evidence that any of the expenditures made in the two years in question were paid for by cash.

Does the presence of an alleged cash hoard affect the viability of the net worth method in determining a taxpayer's taxable income?

Chapter 13

Money Laundering and Related Financial Crimes

A. Introductory Notes

During the 1970s and 1980s, Congress enacted a series of statutes designed to allow the government to track the flow of large sums of cash in the economy — the currency transaction reporting (CTR) statutes — and to criminalize the flow of illegally-generated funds in the economy — the money laundering statutes. The latter are far-reaching, particularly in light of the increased scope of money laundering crimes affected by the USA PATRIOT Act of 2001. Because of their substantial breadth and substantial penalties, including forfeiture, the money laundering statutes have gained wide use in federal criminal cases, including white collar cases.

The CTR and money laundering statutes provide the government with a means both to uncover crimes, such as tax evasion, and to remove the incentive for drug dealers and others to engage in the criminal activity in the first place. The CTR statutes attempt to track the flow of cash, and the money laundering statutes criminalize efforts to hide "dirty" money ("concealment money laundering") or to use dirty money to carry out illegal activity ("promotion money laundering"). In white collar cases, crimes such as bribery, mail and wire fraud, securities fraud, and tax fraud often generate proceeds that need to be hidden or disguised. Considering the frequent profit-driven motives behind white collar misconduct, statutes that target the use of those profits are a wide-reaching and powerful tool for authorities. When considering the materials in this chapter, it is critical to keep in mind the purposes of these financial crimes statutes.

The stakes in money laundering are very high. By some estimates, money laundering accounts for two percent to five percent of global GDP annually, or around $3 trillion to $7 trillion. The Uniting and Strengthening America by Providing Appropriate Tools Required to Intercept and Obstruct Terrorism (USA PATRIOT Act) Act of 2001, Pub. L. No. 107-56, § 302(a)(1), 115 Stat. 272 (2001).

First, this chapter discusses the CTR laws that apply to financial institutions and to trades and businesses. Second, the chapter reviews the "structuring" statutes that criminalize efforts to avoid the CTR requirements. Third, the chapter discusses the money laundering statutes, which are broader than but work in tandem with the CTR laws. Finally, the chapter addresses important issues concerning the attorney-client relationship that arise under these statutes, which require attorneys to disclose information provided by clients in certain circumstances.

B. The Currency Transaction Reporting, Cash Reporting, and Structuring Laws

1. Statutory Overview

The Bank Secrecy Act of 1970 and its companion statute, the Currency and Foreign Transactions Reporting Act, provide the government with mechanisms to track the flow of money both within the United States and to and from the United States. In addition, related provisions of the federal tax code require trades and businesses to report cash transactions to the government.[a] Congress stated that the purpose of the currency transaction reporting laws is to "require certain reports or records where they have a high degree of usefulness in criminal, tax, or regulatory investigations or proceedings, or in the conduct of intelligence or counterintelligence activities, including analysis, to protect against international terrorism." It is important to note that the currency transaction reporting statutes criminalize willful failure to disclose the required information; the government need not prove that the transaction represented any underlying criminal activity.[b]

These statutes make it difficult to move large amounts of cash. This can be an issue for many white collar crimes, like bribery, which involve payments or generate illicit

---

a. The Bank Secrecy Act is codified at 31 U.S.C. § 5311–22. The companion statute, the Currency and Foreign Transactions Reporting Act ("CFTR"), which deals with transactions that cross international borders, is codified at 31 U.S.C. § 5316. Related statutes include 31 U.S.C. § 5314 (record keeping and reporting concerning foreign financial agency transactions); and 31 U.S.C. § 5315 (reports on foreign currency transactions). The CFTR allows the government to monitor large monetary transactions, including exports and imports of currency. The tax code reporting provision is codified at 26 U.S.C. § 6050I. In 2001 Congress passed the USA PATRIOT Act, according to which certain financial institutions are required to implement programs designed to prevent their institutions from being used to facilitate money laundering or the financing of terrorism. For an overview of these laws, see Helen Gredd, *Banking Crimes, in* WHITE COLLAR CRIME: BUSINESS AND REGULATORY OFFENSES § 2.01 (Otto Obermaier et al., eds. 2015).

b. The enforcement of the CTR statutes was given a boost by the decision in *United States v. Bank of New England*, 821 F.2d 844 (1st Cir. 1987), which increased the exposure of financial institutions to felony convictions for failure to file the required CTRs (currency transactions over $10,000 must be reported within 15 days). As discussed in Chapter 2, *supra*, this case was noteworthy for its adoption of the collective knowledge theory of mens rea. The case involved the bank's willful failure to file CTRs "as part of a pattern of illegal activity involving transactions of more than $100,000 in a twelve-month period. . . ." (31 U.S.C. § 5322(b)). No individual within the bank knowingly violated the law, but the court found that the collective knowledge of all of the employees was sufficient to hold the bank accountable for the failure to file the reports.

profits. Money laundering statutes can be a particular impediment to cash-based criminal enterprises like drug dealing. Successful operations will accumulate literal tons of small denomination bills. The logistical challenge of warehousing and physically moving hard currency can prove to be a significant barrier. It is also difficult to engage in large transactions — e.g. purchasing real estate, cars, yachts, etc. — by paying in small denomination bills without raising suspicion. Scaling up a successful cash-based criminal enterprise requires access to banking to make handling, depositing, and spending cash easier. The reporting and structuring statutes are meant to make this access to banks harder to come by.

This section focuses on the principal currency transaction reporting provisions of the Bank Secrecy Act, and on related provisions of the federal tax code. This section also focuses on statutes that criminalize efforts to "structure" transactions so as to avoid the CTR filing requirements. Finally, this section addresses the laws and regulations that require financial institutions "to report any suspicious transaction relevant to a possible violation of law or regulation." These reports are known as "Suspicious Activity Reports," and generally must be filed for transactions of $5,000 or more that the bank suspects involve money laundering or CTR evasion, or that are otherwise unusual for the customer involved.

a. The Currency Transaction and Cash Reporting Laws

. . .

Section 5313(a) of Title 31 sets forth the CTR filing requirement, and provides for criminal penalties when the defendant acted willfully in violating the requirement.[c] To prove a violation of § 5313(a), the government must show that:

(1) A "domestic financial institution" was involved in a transaction;

(2) The transaction involved U.S. currency or specified monetary instruments;[d]

(3) The transaction was for more than $10,000;

(4) The domestic financial institution failed to file the required report; *and*

(5) The defendant acted willfully.

Under § 5312(a)(2) of the Bank Secrecy Act and regulations promulgated thereunder, the term "financial institutions" is broadly defined to include, among other entities, banks, stock brokers, insurance companies, pawn brokers, and car dealers. Courts have also held that individuals who engage in the types of financial matters listed in the statutes and regulations may constitute "financial institutions." Criminal punishment includes a maximum five-year prison term, a $250,000 fine, or both. 31 U.S.C. § 5322(a).

---

c. 31 U.S.C. § 5322.

d. 31 U.S.C. § 5312(a)(3).

In 1984, Congress applied the cash-reporting requirement to all persons "engaged in a trade or business" in an effort to increase reporting and boost tax collection. This requirement is contained in § 6050I of the Internal Revenue Code. 26 U.S.C. § 6050I. Under this provision, all cash transactions of more than $10,000 must be reported to the IRS on Form 8300, which must provide: (a) the name, address, and [tax identification number] of the person from whom the cash was received, (b) the amount of cash received, (c) the date and nature of the transaction, and (d) such other information as the Secretary may prescribe.

To prove that a person *failed to file* a required Form 8300 under Section 6050I, the government must prove all the elements of the crime of failing to file a tax return.[e] To prove *the filing of a false* Form 8300, the government must prove all the elements of the crime of filing a false tax return.[f] These violations are prosecuted as tax crimes, and therefore the government must prove that the defendant both intended to violate the reporting requirements and also that the defendant knew the conduct was illegal.[g] As discussed below, these laws raise important issues concerning the attorney-client relationship.

b. The Structuring Statutes

After passage of the CTR laws and regulations, individuals began to structure their transactions so as to avoid triggering the reporting requirements. This practice came to be known as "smurfing," [h] that is, breaking transactions into amounts below the $10,000 threshold. [i] To address this structuring activity, Congress passed the anti-structuring laws to close this loophole in the statute. 31 U.S.C. § 5324(a). [j] In order for the government to prove a violation of § 5324(a), it must establish that the defendant:

(a) Acted with the purpose of evading the CTR laws and regulations; *and*

---

e. 26 U.S.C. § 7203. This section is discussed in the Tax Crimes Chapter, *supra*, §§ 12, A, 4, c; 12, B.

f. 26 U.S.C. § 7206. This section is discussed in the Tax Crimes Chapter, *supra*, §§ 12, A, 4, b; 12, C.

g. *See* Tax Crimes Chapter, *supra*, § 12, D, 1.

h. The term "smurfing" comes from the children's cartoon show "The Smurfs," which was wildly popular when the structuring statutes were adopted. The smurfs were little blue people who scattered from here to there to perform certain tasks and who were constantly chased by a cat and the big bad guy named Gargamel.

i. In reality the information flowing from the daily processing of millions of CTRs seldom leads to actual criminal prosecutions. Rather, the CTRs themselves provide the necessary underlying information for the investigation and prosecution of any number of crimes involving money.

j. The statute provides: "No person shall for the purpose of evading the reporting requirement of section 5313(a) or 5325 or any regulation prescribed under any such section . . . structure or assist in structuring, or attempt to structure or assist in structuring, any transaction with one or more domestic financial institutions."

(b) One or more of the following:

    (1) Caused or attempted to cause a domestic financial institution to fail to file a CTR;

    (2) Caused or attempted to cause a domestic financial institution to file a CTR that contained a material false statement or omission; *and/or*

    (3) Structured or attempted to structure any transaction with one or more domestic financial institutions.[k]

In addition, § 5324(c)(3) criminalizes structuring in connection with international monetary instrument transactions. All violations of § 5324 are punished criminally. *See* 31 U.S.C. § 5324(d). The penalty includes a prison term of not more than five years, a statutory fine, or both. The statute also specifies an "aggravated" sentence for "[w]hoever violates this section while violating another law of the United States or as part of a pattern of any illegal activity involving more than $100,000 in a 12-month period." 31 U.S.C. § 5324(d)(2). In such cases, the penalty is a prison term of no more than 10 years, twice the statutory fine, or both.

In addition, § 6050I(f) of the Internal Revenue Code prohibits the structuring of transactions to avoid the cash-reporting requirement of 26 U.S.C. § 6050I. As explained in the notes following the next case, an intent to violate the law is an element under § 6050I but not under § 5324. A "willful" *failure to file* a Form 8300 is punished under § 7203 of the Internal Revenue Code; the penalty includes a prison term of not more than one year, or a statutory fine of not more than $25,000 for individuals ($100,000 for entities), or both. A "willful" *submission of a false* Form 8300 is punished under § 7206 of the Internal Revenue Code with a prison term of not more than three years, or a statutory fine of not more than $100,000 for individuals ($500,000 for entities), or both.

2. Mens Rea — The Anti-Structuring Statute (31 U.S.C. § 5324)

The currency transaction reporting statutes criminalize the failure to provide the government with the information required by the applicable statutes and regulations. These statutes do not require that the funds at issue have been derived from criminal activity. As you read the next case, consider the purpose of the CTR laws. Were the defendant's actions in this case sufficiently culpable to warrant a multi-count criminal conviction? Why or why not?

---

k. Section 5324(c) is entitled "International Monetary Instrument Transactions," and contains provisions that parallel the domestic reporting and anti-structuring statutes.

United States v. MacPherson

424 F.3d 183 (2d Cir. 2005)

RAGGI, CIRCUIT JUDGE.

After trial, a jury found William MacPherson guilty of structuring a quarter-million dollars into thirty-two separate cash transactions, each less than $10,000, in violation of 31 U.S.C. § 5324(a)(3). Nevertheless, the United States District Court for the Eastern District of New York (Sterling Johnson, Jr., *Judge*) set aside the verdict and entered a judgment of acquittal, ruling that the trial evidence was insufficient to establish the requisite *mens rea* elements of the charged offense, specifically, MacPherson's knowledge of and intent to avoid federal currency reporting requirements for cash transactions exceeding $10,000. The United States appeals, arguing that the totality of the circumstantial evidence permitted the jury to infer MacPherson's guilty knowledge and intent. We agree and, accordingly, reverse the judgment of acquittal and remand the case to the district court with directions that it reinstate the jury verdict, proceed to sentencing, and enter a judgment of conviction.

I. Background

A. The Structured Cash Deposits

At times relevant to this case, William MacPherson was a New York City police officer who supplemented his salary with rental income from various real estate holdings. In a four-month period between September 26, 2000, and January 16, 2001, MacPherson deposited a total of $258,100 in cash into three Staten Island bank accounts by means of thirty-two transactions, structured so that no single transaction exceeded $10,000. [The Court detailed the chronology of these deposits.] . . .

B. The Background to the Structured Deposits

1. MacPherson's Attempt to Shield Assets from a Civil Judgment

At trial, the government did not contend that the deposited funds derived from any criminal activity. Rather, it suggested that the deposits were made with monies that MacPherson had previously shielded against a possible civil judgment. To support this theory, the government adduced the following evidence.

In December 1997, MacPherson was sued for $2.5 million by an individual who was injured at one of his rental properties. MacPherson was uninsured against a possible damages award. Starting in January 1998 and continuing for some years thereafter while the tort suit was pending against him, MacPherson liquidated or transferred significant assets in an apparent effort to shield them from judgment. For example, between January 1998 and September 2000, MacPherson sold five real properties for just under $1 million, realizing a net profit of approximately $343,000. He also made four large cash withdrawals totaling $220,000 from a Citibank account held jointly with his wife. The first withdrawal, for $80,000, was on January 21, 1998, from a branch located at 577 Bay Street on Staten Island. The other three cash withdrawals were all made on August 31, 1999: $50,000 from the aforementioned Bay Street branch; another $50,000 from a branch at 1492 Hylan Boulevard on Staten Island; and $40,000 from a branch at 1910 Victory Boulevard, also on Staten Island.

In September 2000, MacPherson settled the pending tort suit for $27,000. That same month, he made the first three of the charged structured deposits.[2]

2. The CTR Filings with Respect to MacPherson's 1998–99 Cash Withdrawals

Because MacPherson's large cash withdrawals in 1998 and 1999 each exceeded $10,000, Citibank was required by law to document them to the Internal Revenue Service, which it did by filing a Form 4789 Currency Transaction Report ("CTR"). The January 21, 1998 CTR reported the persons involved in the cash transaction as William J. MacPherson and his wife, Tracy A. MacPherson. The bank verified Mr. MacPherson's identity by reference to his New York State driver's license. Mrs. MacPherson's identity was verified by reference to her Citicard number. Edith Steuerman, a Citibank Manager, testified that she filled out most of the MacPhersons' January 21, 1998 CTR, with a teller filling out other parts. Although Steuerman had no specific recollection of the MacPherson transaction — for example, she could not recall if Mrs. MacPherson was actually present on the occasion — she testified that her uniform practice in preparing CTRs was to have the customer sit down across from her at a desk while she took down identifying data.

Steuerman did not prepare any of the August 31, 1999 CTRs, and no persons involved in their preparation were called to testify. Nevertheless, the CTR filed in connection with the $50,000 cash withdrawal from the Bay Street branch itself indicates that Mr. MacPherson was the sole person involved in that transaction and that his identity was verified on this occasion by reference to his Citicard number. The Hylan Boulevard CTR of the same date indicates that both MacPhersons were involved in that $50,000 cash withdrawal, with their identities verified by reference to their driver's licenses. The Victory Boulevard CTR similarly indicates the involvement of both MacPhersons in that $40,000 withdrawal, with their identities again verified by their driver's licenses.

---

2. MacPherson argues that, with the settlement of the tort case, any interest he may have had in sheltering his cash assets ended, leaving him without any motive to avoid federal reporting requirements. We will not speculate as to what may have prompted MacPherson to engage in the charged structuring. Motive is not an element of the crime, and, thus, the lack of evidence on this point does not, as a matter of law, preclude conviction. We recognize, of course, that evidence of motive, or the lack thereof, is a factor that a jury may weigh in considering whether the totality of the circumstances permits it to infer guilty knowledge and intent beyond a reasonable doubt. For the reasons discussed herein, however, we conclude that the evidence in this case was sufficient, even without proof of motive, to support a jury finding that MacPherson structured the charged cash transactions with the knowledge and intent required to support conviction.

II. Discussion

. . .

B. The Totality of the Circumstantial Evidence Would Permit a Rational Jury to Find the Knowledge and Intent Elements of Structuring Proved Beyond a Reasonable Doubt

1. The Federal Law Prohibiting Structuring

Preliminary to discussing the evidence from which a reasonable jury could have found the requisite knowledge and intent proved in this case, we briefly review the evolution of federal law prohibiting structuring.

In 1970, Congress enacted the Currency and Foreign Transactions Reporting Act ("CFTRA" or "the Act"), also referred to as the "Bank Secrecy Act," which requires, *inter alia*, that domestic financial institutions report to the Internal Revenue Service any cash transactions exceeding $10,000. Underlying this legislation was Congress's recognition of "the importance of reports of large and unusual currency transactions in ferreting out criminal activity." No criminal predicate as to the source of cash in excess of $10,000 was required to prosecute those who failed to comply with the specified reporting requirements.

Prior to 1986, the law did not explicitly prohibit persons from structuring cash transactions so that no one transaction exceeded $10,000 in an effort to avoid CTR filings. Although such structuring was sometimes prosecuted under 18 U.S.C. § 371 as a scheme to defraud the United States, in 1986, Congress decided to address the problem directly by specifically criminalizing structuring in the Money Laundering Control Act § 1354(a). Title 31 U.S.C. § 5324 states, in pertinent part:

> No person shall, for the purpose of evading the reporting requirements of section 5313(a) . . . or any regulation prescribed under any such section . . . (3) structure or assist in structuring, or attempt to structure or assist in structuring, any transaction with one or more domestic financial institutions.

31 U.S.C. § 5324(a). The applicable regulations define "structuring" by reference to both the *actus reus* and *mens rea* elements of § 5324(a):

> [A] person structures a transaction if that person, acting alone, or in conjunction with, or on behalf of, other persons, conducts or attempts to conduct one or more transactions in currency, in any amount, at one or more financial institutions, on one or more days, in any manner, for the purpose of evading the reporting requirements under section 103.22 of this Part. "In any manner" includes, but is not limited to, the breaking down of a single sum of currency exceeding $10,000 into smaller sums, including sums at or below $10,000, or the conduct of a transaction, or series of currency transactions, including transactions at or below $10,000. The transaction or transactions need not exceed the $10,000 reporting threshold at any single financial institution on any single day in order to constitute structuring within the meaning of this definition.

31 C.F.R. § 103.11(gg).

This court construed this willfulness element to require proof that a defendant, with knowledge of the reporting requirement imposed by law, structured a currency transaction "intend[ing] to deprive the government of information to which it is entitled." In *Ratzlaf v. United States*, the Supreme Court took a different view, ruling that structuring was "willful" only if the government further proved "that the defendant acted with knowledge that his conduct was unlawful." 510 U.S. 135, 137 (1994). Within the year, Congress responded by eliminating willfulness as an element necessary to convict a person of structuring in violation of § 5324. The net result, as this court has previously observed, was to conform federal anti-structuring law "to the *Scanio* interpretation." *United States v. Scanio*, 900 F.2d 485, 487 (2d Cir. 1990).

Because the conduct at issue in this case all occurred well after 1994, we look to *Scanio* to identify the three elements that the government was required to prove beyond a reasonable doubt to convict MacPherson of the charged § 5324 offense: (1) the defendant must, in fact, have engaged in acts of structuring; (2) he must have done so with knowledge that the financial institutions involved were legally obligated to report currency transactions in excess of $10,000; and (3) he must have acted with the intent to evade this reporting requirement.

2. The Circumstantial Evidence Supported an Inference of MacPherson's Knowledge of and Intent to Evade Currency Reporting Requirements

As noted in our discussion of the case's procedural history, MacPherson did not argue in the district court, nor does he assert in opposition to the government's appeal, that the trial evidence was insufficient to permit a reasonable jury to find the first element of a § 5324 offense — acts of structuring — proved beyond a reasonable doubt. Indeed, the evidence would not support such an argument. Instead, MacPherson argued, and it appears the district court concluded, that the government's proof failed at the second and third elements: knowledge and intent. Accordingly, we focus our sufficiency discussion on these two aspects of *mens rea*.

a. Inferring Knowledge and Intent from Circumstantial Evidence

The record is devoid of any direct evidence that MacPherson knew of or intended to evade the reporting requirements for cash transactions exceeding $10,000. The law, however, recognizes that the *mens rea* elements of knowledge and intent can often be proved through circumstantial evidence and the reasonable inferences drawn therefrom. Indeed, the law draws no distinction between direct and circumstantial evidence in requiring the government to carry its burden of proof. A verdict of guilty may be based entirely on circumstantial evidence as long as the inferences of culpability drawn from the circumstances are reasonable. The possibility that inferences consistent with innocence as well as with guilt might be drawn from circumstantial evidence is of no matter to sufficiency analysis because "it is the task of the jury, not the court, to choose among competing inferences." . . .

Applying these principles to this case, we conclude that the totality of circumstantial evidence permitted a jury to find beyond a reasonable doubt that MacPherson engaged in the charged structuring with the requisite guilty knowledge and intent. Specifically, the jury could have reasonably inferred from the pattern of MacPherson's structuring, as well as from the record of his earlier cash withdrawals that did generate CTR filings, that MacPherson knew of and, in connection with the charged deposits, intended to evade currency reporting requirements.

b. The Pattern of MacPherson's Cash Transactions Supported a Jury Inference of Knowledge and Intent

1. United States v. Nersesian *Recognizes that Knowledge of and Intent to Evade Reporting Requirements Can Be Inferred from a Pattern of Structured Transactions*

The government submits that the jury could have inferred MacPherson's guilty knowledge and intent from the pattern of his structured transactions. This argument finds support in our decision in *United States v. Nersesian*, 824 F.2d 1294 (2d Cir. 1987). In that case, a defendant and co-conspirators had used $117,000 in cash to purchase more than one hundred $1,000 money orders at numerous banks throughout New York City over a one-month period. In challenging the sufficiency of the evidence supporting his conviction for conspiring to defraud the government by engaging in cash transactions aimed at avoiding currency reporting requirements, the *Nersesian* defendant argued that the pattern of his transactions could not support an inference that he knew of and intended to evade CTR filing requirements. He specifically noted that his money order purchases did not fall "just short of" the $10,000 reporting trigger, no evidence indicated that he had ever been alerted to the CTR filing requirement, and certain evidence in the case was actually inconsistent with such knowledge. This court acknowledged that "the evidence does permit the inference that [the defendant] did not know of the reporting requirements." Nevertheless, given the pattern of transactions, the court could not conclude that the evidence was insufficient to permit "*any* rational trier of fact" to find knowledge and intent: "The jury could have inferred from the fact that [the defendant] chose to carry out his currency exchanges in a series of small transactions over a number of days, rather than in a single transaction or several larger transactions, that he knew of the reporting requirements and was attempting to avoid them."

2. Nersesian's *Reasoning Supports the Jury Verdict in This Case*

Applying *Nersesian*'s reasoning to this case, we conclude that the jury that convicted MacPherson could have reasonably inferred from the fact that the defendant chose to deposit a quarter-million dollars through a series of thirty-two small transactions all under $10,000 that he knew of the reporting requirements applicable to cash transactions over $10,000 and was intent on avoiding them. The trial evidence indicated that the $258,100 at issue did not represent income earned during the four-month period so as to require multiple deposits. Rather, the evidence suggested that the cash was a long-held asset that MacPherson had shielded for some years from a possible tort judgment. Once the tort suit was settled in September 2000, MacPherson apparently concluded that there was no further risk in placing this cash in bank accounts traceable to him. Nevertheless, he deliberately decided not to deposit the money in one lump sum or even through several five-figure transactions. Instead, he employed the more burdensome technique of thirty-two separate transactions, no one of which exceeded $10,000. As the Seventh Circuit observed in a similar context, "it is unlikely, to the point of absurdity, that it was pure coincidence" that a defendant would engage in multiple transactions, all under $10,000, to achieve his purpose. *United States v. Cassano*, 372 F.3d 868, 879 (7th Cir. 2004).

That MacPherson's avoidance of five-figure transactions was calculated rather than coincidental is evidenced by the fact that twenty-three deposits were in amounts of $9,000–$9,200. Indeed, in six out of seven consecutive weeks, MacPherson traveled to three different banks on the same day to make identical deposits of $9,000, thereby providing even stronger circumstantial evidence than existed in *Nersesian* that the defendant knew of and was intent on avoiding the $10,000 trigger for CTR filings. *Cf. United States v. Nersesian*, 824 F.2d at 1314 (rejecting argument that knowledge and intent could not be inferred because monies were not structured in amounts "just short" of the reporting trigger). In sum, MacPherson's willingness to sacrifice efficiency and convenience in depositing a quarter-million dollars through multiple small transactions structured to ensure that no one exceeded $10,000 amply supported a reasonable inference that MacPherson knew of and was intent on avoiding CTR reporting requirements.

3. MacPherson's Arguments for Not Applying Nersesian's Reasoning to This Case Are Unconvincing

In urging affirmance of the district court's judgment of acquittal, MacPherson submits that *Nersesian*'s reasoning is inapplicable to his case because the *Nersesian* defendant was convicted of violating 18 U.S.C. § 371, which did not require the government to prove the elements of structuring under 31 U.S.C. § 5324. We are not convinced. Although the first element of a § 5324 offense—acts of structuring as defined in 31 C.F.R. § 103.11(gg)—may not have been an element of the § 371 charge in *Nersesian*, as we have already noted, the sufficiency of the government's proof as to that § 5324 element is not here at issue. As to the remaining knowledge and intent elements of § 5324, they are, in fact, identical to the *mens rea* elements in *Nersesian*. . . . Precisely because *Nersesian* addressed the same *mens rea* elements as are here at issue, its recognition that knowledge and evasive intent could reasonably be inferred from the pattern of structured transactions is appropriately applied to sufficiency review in this case.

This conclusion is reinforced by the fact that, even when the government's *mens rea* burden in a § 5324 prosecution was heavier, requiring proof of willfulness as defined in *Ratzlaf*, this court ruled that a jury could infer the requisite knowledge of illegality from the pattern of structured transactions.

In a final attempt to avoid application of *Nersesian* to this case, MacPherson argues that, in *Nersesian*, the cash at issue was criminally derived, which is not a contention in his case. Certainly, the criminal origin of structured funds, to the extent it provides a motive for concealment from government authorities, may constitute an additional circumstance from which a jury can infer a defendant's knowledge of and intent to avoid CTR filings. But proof of criminal derivation was not necessary to secure a § 371 conviction in *Nersesian*, and this court did *not* reference this fact in concluding that the pattern of defendant's structured transactions was sufficient to support a jury inference of guilty knowledge and intent. . . . More to the point, whether or not a § 5324 prosecution relates to criminal proceeds, a jury may properly consider the pattern of structuring activities and draw reasonable inferences therefrom as to whether the defendant possessed the requisite *mens rea*.

c. MacPherson's Prior Cash Transactions Prompting CTR Filings Further Supported the Jury Inference of Knowledge

Although the pattern of MacPherson's structured deposits, by itself, provided evidence from which a reasonable jury could have inferred his knowledge of and intent to evade currency reporting requirements, that conclusion was reinforced by circumstantial evidence that MacPherson acquired knowledge of CTR filing requirements in 1998 and 1999 when his four cash withdrawals of sums ranging from $40,000 to $80,000 prompted Citibank to file CTRs. Although no bank employee specifically recalled dealing with MacPherson at the time of these withdrawals, bank manager Edith Steuerman, who filled out part of the CTR relating to the $80,000 withdrawal, testified that it was her practice to prepare the document sitting across the desk from the customer while she obtained necessary identifying information from him. Steuerman's testimony could support a jury inference that MacPherson thereby acquired knowledge of the reporting requirement for cash transactions exceeding $10,000. We conclude that this evidence strongly reinforces the inference that a jury could reasonably draw from MacPherson's careful structuring of his subsequent cash deposits: he was intent on avoiding any further CTR filings with respect to his money movements. . . .

When the circumstances of MacPherson's CTR-triggering withdrawals are reviewed together with the pattern of his charged structured deposits in the light most favorable to the government, we cannot conclude that this evidence was insufficient to permit any rational jury to find that MacPherson knew of and intended to evade currency reporting requirements when he engaged in the charged structuring.

III. Conclusion

To summarize, we conclude that a pattern of structured transactions, such as occurred in this case, may, by itself, permit a rational jury to infer that a defendant had knowledge of and the intent to evade currency reporting requirements. Further supporting a jury inference of knowledge in this case were the circumstances of MacPherson's past cash transactions triggering CTR filings. Because the totality of this circumstantial evidence was sufficient to establish the elements of knowledge and intent required to convict MacPherson of structuring in violation of 31 U.S.C. §5324(a)(3), the jury verdict of guilty should not have been set aside nor a judgment of acquittal entered by the court. Accordingly, we REVERSE the judgment of acquittal and REMAND this case to the district court with directions that it reinstate the jury verdict, proceed to sentencing, and enter a judgment of conviction.

Notes and Questions

1. *Intent and motive.* Why did MacPherson engage in his elaborate pattern of depositing cash in amounts under $10,000? Was there evidence of motive? If not, why did the court find sufficient evidence of knowledge and intent? What *was* MacPherson's likely motive, if any? The court seems to rely on the structuring itself as evidence of knowledge and intent. Is this a legitimate move, given that the court acknowledges that structuring violations have distinct mens rea and actus reus elements?

2. *Evidence of motive.* The Seventh Circuit has held that circumstantial evidence of motive can support an inference of intent to evade the filing requirements. *United States v. Davenport*, 929 F.2d 1169 (7th Cir. 1991). In *Davenport*, a husband and wife were convicted of violating 31 U.S.C. §5324(3). Starting with a cash hoard of $100,000, the defendants made 10 separate cash deposits, totaling $81,500, in multiple branches of two banks over a period of two weeks. While each deposit was less than $10,000, defendants often made multiple deposits in one day, the aggregate of which crossed the $10,000 threshold; the banks reported those amounts to the IRS. In an interview with an IRS agent, the defendants identified the source of the funds as an inheritance from Mr. Davenport's father. Ms. Davenport claimed they received the inheritance as a check, but Mr. Davenport said it was discovered, in the form of cash, in a safe in his father's house. At trial, there was evidence that Mr. Davenport's father left no inheritance because he had spent the last six months living in a car and died in poverty. The court explained that even though motive is not an element of the offense, it was relevant because "[t]he shadier the source, the greater the Davenports' motive to conceal the money from the authorities." In this case, the "fishiness of the inheritance story was circumstantial evidence that the structuring was done with the evasive purpose that the statute requires for liability."

If a prosecutor has evidence that a defendant has lied about the source of money, but has no proof that the money was generated from illegal activity, is it appropriate to bring a structuring charge? Why or why not?

3. *The mens rea requirement and the* Ratzlaf *decision.* As the court in *MacPherson* noted, in 1994, the United States Supreme Court interpreted §5324's "willful violation" requirement to require proof that the defendant "acted with knowledge that the conduct was unlawful." *Ratzlaf v. United States*, 510 U.S. 135, 137 (1994). The Court had previously applied this heightened level of required mens rea—intent to violate the law—to tax crimes in *Cheek v. United States*, 498 U.S. 192 (1991). *See* Chapter 12, Tax Crimes, *supra*, for a discussion of the *Cheek* case. In his *Ratzlaf* dissent, Justice Blackmun strongly objected to the majority's interpretation of the statute, saying it "is at odds with the statutory text, the intent of Congress, and the

fundamental principle that knowledge of illegality is not required for a criminal act." *Id.* at 162. In the aftermath of that case, Congress quickly removed the willfulness requirement from the structuring statute, effectively overturning *Ratzlaf.* Pub. L. No. 103-325, § 411, 108 Stat. 2253 (1994).

4. *Structuring under the Internal Revenue Code.* As discussed in the preceding note, proof of specific intent to violate a known legal duty is an element in the prosecution of tax crimes. This is an exception to the general rule that "ignorance of the law . . . is no defense to criminal prosecution." *Cheek,* 498 U.S. at 199. The Internal Revenue Code prohibits structuring of cash transaction reports by someone engaged in a trade or business. 26 U.S.C. § 6050I. A violation of § 6050I is a tax crime, so, unlike a case brought under § 5324, the government must prove an intent to violate a known legal duty. *See, e.g., United States v. Loe,* 262 F.3d 427 (5th Cir. 2001); *United States v. McLamb,* 985 F.2d 1284 (4th Cir. 1993).

5. *Conspiracy to defraud.* The court noted above that, prior to the enactment of the anti-structuring statute, structuring activities were prosecuted as conspiracies to defraud the United States under 18 U.S.C. § 371. Recall that § 371 contains two distinct offenses — conspiracies to commit offenses against the United States and conspiracies to defraud the United States. *See* Chapter 3, Conspiracy, *supra,* at § 3, C. In what way does structuring represent an effort to "defraud" the United States?

6. *The law enforcement challenge.* Tens of millions of CTRs are filed each year. For example, in 2004–2006, the federal government reported the filing of nearly 37.8 million CTRs pursuant to the Bank Secrecy Act. These CTRs were collected by banks and other financial institutions and forwarded to the government. *See* Report to Congressional Committees, *Bank Secrecy Act: Increased Use of Exemption Provisions Could Reduce Currency Transaction Reporting While Maintaining Usefulness to Law Enforcement Efforts,* United States Government Accountability Office, p. 81 (Feb. 2008). The U.S. Treasury Department directed the Financial Crimes Enforcement Network, commonly called FinCEN, to maintain and control the CTR filings. Given the sheer volume of filings, how can the government identify "structured" transactions?

FinCEN is tasked with the collection and analysis of the millions of CTRs filed yearly. *See* http://www.fincen.gov. The process of sorting through the paperwork is daunting. Surely, tracking the flow of criminally derived money is critically important to the government, but the reporting requirements encompass tens of millions of transactions that are entirely legitimate. FinCEN uses sophisticated computerized technology to cross-reference these filings and to track and trace the domestic and international flow of currency. What are the policy implications of having third parties, such as securities brokers and even attorneys, collect and remit financial information on customers that is ultimately used for law enforcement purposes?

7. *The regulatory scheme.* The currency transaction and structuring statutes are not self-enforcing. The Code of Federal Regulations ("CFR") provides the specific

regulations that govern the implementation of the statutes, including the monetary limits, which are, from time to time, adjusted. In addition, the CFR dictates the ways in which an institution can secure an exemption from the cumbersome reporting requirements. *See* C.F.R. T. 31, Subt. B, Ch. X.

8. *Suspicious activity reports.* Since 1996 the government has been collecting data on suspicious financial activities. A section of the Bank Secrecy Act, 31 U.S.C. § 5318(g), authorizes the U.S. Department of the Treasury to adopt suspicious activity reporting requirements for financial institutions. This information is contained in a Suspicious Activity Report (SAR), which has replaced CTRs as the primary tool of law enforcement for identifying suspicious financial activity. This report has a $5,000 reporting threshold. Many money laundering investigations are initiated with the suspicious activity report or the currency transaction report. *See The SAR Activity Review: Trends, Tips, and Issues*, Bank Secrecy Act Advisory Group, Issue 13, May 2008, *at* www.fincen.gov. This review regularly reports on the types of cases that are prompted by the suspicious activity reports, including international money laundering, terrorism-related investigations, and domestic fraud cases.

9. *Unit of prosecution.* When a defendant structures a $10,000 transaction into several smaller transactions, is this one violation or several? In *United States v. Lang*, 732 F.3d 1246 (11th Cir. 2013), the Eleventh Circuit held that the unit of prosecution is the amount exceeding $10,000 that is structured into smaller transactions. Because the government had charged each of the smaller transactions as separate counts, the court reversed the defendant's conviction on 70 counts of structuring. The two other circuits that have addressed this question agree with this conclusion. *Id.* at 1248 (citing cases). Why have these courts reached this result? Compare the crime of mail fraud, where each mailing constitutes a separate count. [*See* Mail Fraud, Chapter 4, *supra*.]

10. *Are the reporting and anti-structuring statutes too broad?* Is there a danger that the reporting and anti-structuring statutes will ensnare purely innocent conduct? As one commentator noted with respect to banks' obligations to file CTRs and SARs:

> The problem of course is that when you force banks to cast such a wide net, they're going to report a lot of people who have done nothing wrong. And some of those people are going to find themselves in legal trouble. A top bartender who makes, say, $2,000–$2,500 per week in tips might make regular monthly deposits of over $9,000, but less than $10,000. It isn't illegal to deposit $9,500 in your bank account. It's only illegal if you're doing so because you don't want your bank to report the deposit to the government. That's a pretty thin line between an innocuous activity and a felony.

Radley Balko, *The Federal 'Structuring' Laws are Smurfin' Ridiculous*, WASH. POST (March 24, 2014), http://www.washingtonpost.com/news/the-watch/wp/2014/03/24 /the-federal-structuring-laws-are-smurfin-ridiculous/. *See* Michael J. Deblis III, *Money Laundering: Is the Anti-Structuring Statute Netting the Small Fry with the Big Fish?*, 29 CRIM. JUSTICE 19 (Summer 2014) ("as law enforcement continues to pursue more bank transactions as structuring offenses, there is a need to ensure that the statute is not misused in a way that traps unintended victims").

Is the structuring statute too broad? What dangers does the statute create, if any? Are there remedies for this issue?

11. *High-tech money laundering.* How should reporting and anti-structuring statutes adapt to a world where money laundering increasingly occurs using cryptocurrencies like Bitcoin? These currencies are specifically designed to make tracing ownership difficult. Cryptocurrencies are big business, and many U.S. banks are getting in on the game, including some major names like Goldman Sachs. In 2020, the Office of the Comptroller of the Currency took its first action against a bank for failing to put in place sufficient anti-money laundering safeguards respecting its "digital asset customers," including those who hold cryptocurrencies. *In re M.Y. Safra Bank, FSB*, No. 2020-005 (Dep't of the Treasury, Office of the Comptroller of the Currency, Jan. 30, 2020) (consent order), *available at* https://www.occ.gov/static/enforcement -actions/ea2020-005.pdf.

Problems

13-1. A federal grand jury has adduced the following evidence:

Victor Aiden made a living in the used auto parts business, purchasing parts from junkyards and reselling them to auto rebuilders. In running the unincorporated business, Aiden maintained several bank accounts, including an account at Archer Bank.

For a period of two years, Aiden wrote more than 3,000 checks to himself on the Archer account. All of the checks were cashed, mostly at a currency exchange which charged a processing fee. This business practice stemmed (or so Aiden claims) from the nature of the used auto parts business: Aiden's suppliers dealt exclusively in cash, and Aiden wrote checks that he expected to be sufficient to cover each day's purchase of parts. Aiden's customers also paid by cash.

For the two-year period in question, Aiden made 116 cash deposits at Archer Bank. He states that his practice was to collect cash from customers and then deposit the cash at points when he needed to visit the bank or when it was otherwise convenient for him. The deposits in question totaled $240,000, and ranged in amount from $54 to $9,462. The average amount was $2,000. Eight deposits were between $9,000 and $10,000, but none exceeded $10,000.

If you were the Assistant United States Attorney in charge of the investigation, would you ask the grand jury to bring criminal charges? If so, based on what theory or theories? If you were Aiden's defense attorney, what arguments would you make to try to persuade the government not to bring criminal charges?

13-2. For Years 01 through 05, Nancy Humphrey worked as an administrator for a local health care organization. Nancy's only other sources of income were payments from her retired husband's pension and annuity funds. In December Year 02, Nancy withdrew $100,000 cash from her primary savings account, generating a Currency Transaction Report ("CTR") for which Nancy had to provide her driver's license as identification. Between June Year 03 and May Year 04, Nancy made 17 cash deposits into a secondary savings account at the same institution. The deposits, ranging from $5,500 to $9,900, totaled $150,000. Eleven of the deposits were $9,000 or greater. In January Year 05, Nancy withdrew $175,000 from her secondary account, closed that account, and deposited the funds into her primary savings account. Accordingly, the bank filed a CTR for the transaction. No bank employee recalls discussing the CTR filing requirement with Nancy.

Nancy was subsequently interviewed by the Internal Revenue Service (IRS). In the interview, Nancy explained that she kept cash on hand to pay for her husband's medical expenses. Any amount not needed was deposited into her bank account. Records from the health insurance company show the majority of out-of-pocket expenses were paid with checks. Nancy was charged with 17 counts of violating 31 U.S.C. § 5324(a) by structuring her currency transactions into amounts of $10,000 or less to avoid CTR filings.

Nancy filed a motion to dismiss the charges. What arguments should Nancy make in support of the motion? How should the court rule as to each argument? Why?

13-3. Robert Phillips owned and operated a profitable night club, Club Gray. The night club's main sources of revenue came from alcohol sales and entrance fees. Mr. Phillips insisted on handling all the club's finances. The nature of the club necessitated a lot of cash transactions. At any time, the club had $300,000 to $400,000 in cash.

Each morning Phillips compared the cash-on-hand to the revenue logs from the night before. He then deposited the excess cash in the club's bank account directly. However, as a matter of routine and personal preference, Phillips never transported or deposited more than $8,000 at a time. Since he had previously been robbed, he did not feel comfortable carrying more than that amount on his person.

To reduce the frequency of trips to the bank, Phillips installed an ATM at the club. Phillips stocked the ATM with cash from the club. Each night when the ATM was closed out, the bank would refund the club by wire transfer directly into the club's bank account. Bank statements indicated several transmissions of under $10,000 that would total more than $10,000 per day.

The bank suspected structuring activity and sent a letter to Mr. Phillips warning him that his bank account would close. The letter was misaddressed and Mr. Phillips never received it. Mr. Phillips learned his account was closed the next time he went to the bank to make a deposit. The teller could not explain why the account was closed and Mr. Phillips opened an account with another bank.

The government is considering whether to charge Phillips with structuring in violation of 31 U.S.C. § 5324. Assume that you represent Phillips. What argument(s) would you make in attempting to persuade the government not to bring the charge? If you were the prosecutor, would you bring the case? Why or why not?

C. Money Laundering

1. Statutory Overview and Elements

In 1986 Congress enacted the principal money laundering statutes, 18 U.S.C. §§ 1956 and 1957. These statutes criminalize financial and monetary transactions involving proceeds of criminal activity. In that way, the money laundering statutes provide for penalties in addition to the penalties for the underlying offenses alone. As one member of the U.S. Supreme Court wrote in a money laundering case:

> Money laundering provisions serve two chief ends. First, they provide deterrence by preventing drug traffickers and other criminals who amass large quantities of cash from using these funds "to support a luxurious lifestyle" or otherwise to enjoy the fruits of their crimes. Second, they inhibit the growth of criminal enterprises by preventing the use of dirty money to promote the enterprise's growth.

United States v. Santos, 128 S. Ct. 2020, 2038 (2008) (Alito, J., dissenting).

Over time, the money laundering statutes have joined with — and in some cases supplanted — the federal racketeering (RICO) statute as one of the government's principal weapons against large-scale criminal activity.[1] This has occurred because the money laundering statutes reach a broad range of criminal activities, including mail and wire fraud, and can be employed in a wide range of cases. The statutes are potentially in play for any crime committed for profit or that requires money to be carried out. Money laundering is sometimes easier to prove than RICO, and a money laundering case — unlike a RICO case — does not have to be approved by the Department of Justice in Washington. In addition, money laundering can lead to severe penalties, including substantial prison time and forfeitures.[m]

Although initially enacted principally as a means of countering narcotics trafficking activities, the money laundering statutes apply to many kinds of white collar offenses. There are several types of money laundering under the federal criminal code, but the classic form of money laundering is "concealment" money laundering that attempts to make "dirty" money look "clean" or that attempts to hide money

---

l. The RICO statute, 18 U.S.C. §§ 1961–68, is discussed in Chapter 14, *infra*. For an analysis of the money laundering statutes' increasing role in prosecuting large scale criminal activity, *see* Helen Gredd & Karl D. Cooper, *Money Laundering*, *in* White Collar Crime: Business and Regulatory Offenses § 2A.01 (Otto Obermaier et al., eds. 2015).

m. Money laundering offenses may lead to prison terms of up to 20 years. In 2001, however, the United States Sentencing Guidelines were changed so as to tie money laundering sentences to the sentences for the underlying offenses and to avoid overly-harsh money laundering sentences. *See White Collar Crime Institute Focuses on Recent Changes to Sentencing Guidelines*, CRIM. L. REP. 561, 561 (March 27, 2002). For a discussion of the Sentencing Guidelines, see Chapter 19, *infra*.

from the government.[n] For example, money laundering may occur whenever a defendant has attempted to conceal income to avoid paying taxes. And in any fraud or bribery scheme, the defendant may have attempted to conceal the proceeds from the scheme.

Beyond the classic "concealment" sense of money laundering, there are other statutorily defined ways to commit the offense. For example, "promotion" money laundering applies when people use the proceeds of some criminal activity to further criminal activity (either the same or different). "Transportation" money laundering occurs when a person moves money into, out of, or through the United States in order to conceal it or promote unlawful activity. "Transaction" money laundering occurs through attempts to engage financial institutions with criminal proceeds.

a. Section 1956

Section 1956(a)(1) covers domestic money laundering. To establish a violation, the government must show that:

(1) The defendant conducted or attempted to conduct a *financial transaction*;

(2) The defendant knew that the financial transaction involved the proceeds of some type of unlawful activity, which activity constitutes a felony under state, federal, or foreign law;

(3) The funds in fact were proceeds from a *specified unlawful activity*; *and*

(4) Any one or more of the following:

> (a) The defendant engaged in the transaction done with the intent to further a specified unlawful activity ("promotion" money laundering);

> (b) The defendant engaged in the transaction with the intent to commit tax fraud in violation of §7201 (tax evasion) or §7206 (false returns) of the Internal Revenue Code;

> (c) The defendant engaged in the transaction knowing that the transaction is designed in whole or in part to disguise, conceal, or hide the source of the money ("concealment" money laundering); *or*

> (d) The defendant engaged in the transaction knowing that the transaction is designed in whole or in part to avoid the currency transaction reporting laws.

The statute defines "financial transaction" to include a broad range of financial dealings that affect interstate or foreign commerce. The term thus encompasses bank transactions, gifts, and other transfers of money and property.

---

n. One form of concealment is "layering," which occurs by separating the money from its criminal origins in an effort to disguise its source. This is usually done by passing the money through several financial institutions and transferring the money into other negotiable instruments, such as cashier's checks and money orders.

The money laundering offenses—like offenses under the RICO statute—are premised on underlying criminal activity. That underlying offense must be one of several that are "specified" for the money laundering statutes to come into play. Section 1956(c)(7) defines this term to encompass dozens of crimes, including nearly all the RICO predicate crimes. Many prosecutions of money laundering in the white collar and corporate criminal arenas involve mail and wire fraud, financial institution fraud, tax fraud, obstruction of justice, and securities fraud.

Penalties for money laundering include a fine of not more than $500,000 or twice the value of the property involved in the transaction, whichever is greater, or imprisonment for not more than 20 years, or both. In addition, the money laundering statutes contain powerful civil and criminal forfeiture provisions, which are discussed in Chapter 20, Forfeitures, *infra*.

b. Section 1957

Section 1957, known as the monetary transaction money laundering statute, is the companion statute to § 1956. Section 1957 focuses on the use of illegally derived funds within the financial system. Section 1957 is titled "Engaging in Monetary Transactions in Property Derived from Specified Unlawful Activity." Under § 1957, the government must prove that:

(1) The defendant engaged or attempted to engage in a monetary transaction;

(2) The monetary transaction was of a value greater than $10,000;

(3) The transaction was derived from specified unlawful activity;

(4) The transaction took place in the United States or the defendant is a "United States person"; *and*

(5) The defendant knew that the property was criminally derived.

The statute defines the key terms. "Monetary transaction[s]" include "the deposit, withdrawal, transfer, or exchange, in or affecting interstate or foreign commerce, of funds or a monetary instrument by, through, or to a financial institution, including any transaction that would be a financial transaction under § 1956(c)(4)(B) of this title." The "specified unlawful activities" are the same as those in § 1956. The statute defines "criminally derived property" as "any property constituting, or derived from, proceeds obtained from a criminal offense."

c. A Comparison of § 1956 and § 1957

Although the proliferation of drug proceeds was the impetus for the passage of the money laundering provisions, the wide range of "specified unlawful activity" encompasses many of the offenses that we traditionally think of as white collar crimes. Both 18 U.S.C. §§ 1956 and 1957 can often be added to most financial crime indictments. To date, though, prosecutors have brought many more cases under § 1956 than under § 1957. *See* Stefan D. Cassella, *The Forfeiture of Property Involved in Money Laundering Offenses*, 7 Buff. Crim. L. Rev. 583, 612 (2004) (discussing the number of predicate offenses that fall within §1956). Why might this be? Although the statutes have similarities, there are some important differences.

"Financial transaction" (§1956) and "monetary transaction" (§1957) are terms of art that point out a key distinction between these two statutes. Section 1956 is principally concerned with the actual laundering of the money in an effort to hide its true source. There is no monetary threshold for the "financial transactions" that trigger the statute. The transaction could entail the purchase or sale of many items or services, such as artwork, travel, jewelry, precious metals, vehicles, or investments.

With §1957 "monetary transactions," the activity must be "by, through, or to a financial institution," and it must exceed $10,000. Section 1957 could apply to almost any interaction that a criminal has with the financial system, typically with a bank. It prohibits the entry of any dirty money, in excess of $10,000, into the financial channels by deposit, withdrawal, transfer, or exchange.

Sections 1956 and 1957 also differ with respect to the mens rea element. After you read the next section, look at the elements of §1957 again, paying particular attention to mens rea. You will notice that §1957 has a less demanding mens rea requirement. Why would that be? How did Congress use the other elements of §1957 to pare back some of the far-reaching implications of weakening the required mens rea element?

2. Mens Rea — §1956

As seen above, §1956 requires the government to prove two mens rea elements. The first is that the defendant knew the money at issue was derived from a specified criminal activity. Prosecutors can establish this element either by proving defendant's direct knowledge of the criminal activity or by demonstrating the defendant's willful blindness. *See United States v. Campbell*, 977 F.2d 854, 857–859 (4th Cir. 1992) (upholding jury finding that defendant real estate agent "deliberately closed her eyes to what would otherwise have been obvious to her" given suspicious nature of transaction, defendant's awareness of client's extravagant lifestyle, and statement made by defendant that money "might have been drug money"). The second mens rea is a scienter element with respect to the goal of the financial transaction. The statute specifies four different theories that prosecutors may use to satisfy the latter mens rea requirement: that the transaction was undertaken with the (1) intent to promote the illegal activity (the "promotion" theory), (2) intent to commit tax fraud, (3) knowledge of a design to conceal the source of the money (the "concealment" theory), or (4) knowledge of a design to avoid the CTR laws.

a. Concealment Money Laundering

In the decision below, the defendant contested the sufficiency of the proof of mens rea in a concealment case. Be sure to identify the two levels of mens rea required, and the evidence offered as to each level.

United States v. Corchado-Peralta

318 F.3d 255 (1st Cir. 2003)

BOUDIN, CHIEF JUDGE.

Between 1987 and 1996, Ubaldo Rivera Colon ("Colon") smuggled over 150 kilograms of cocaine into Puerto Rico, yielding some $4 million in profits, which he then laundered through a variety of investments and purchases. Colon was indicted on drug, bank fraud, and conspiracy charges and, based on a plea agreement, was sentenced in June 2002 to over 20 years in prison.

Colon's wife, Elena Corchado Peralta ("Corchado"), and two associates, Basilio Rivera Rodriguez ("Rivera") and Oscar Trinidad Rodriguez ("Trinidad") were indicted and tried together on one count of conspiring with Colon to launder money. 18 U.S.C. §§ 1956(a)(1)(B) and (h). Corchado was also indicted on one count of bank fraud. 18 U.S.C. § 1344. During their eight-day trial, Colon provided extensive testimony about his money laundering methods, which included a variety of transactions (purchases, investments, and loans) involving the defendants.

All three defendants were convicted on the charges against them. Corchado received a 27-month sentence, Rivera, 57 months, and Trinidad, 63 months. Corchado appeals. . . . [I]t is helpful to begin by outlining the criminal offense that was the principal charge against all of them.

The money laundering statute, 18 U.S.C. § 1956, among other things makes it criminal for anyone, "knowing that the property involved in a financial transaction represents the proceeds of some form of unlawful activity" to "conduct . . . such a financial transaction which in fact involves the proceeds of specified unlawful activity" —

> (A) (i) with the intent to promote the carrying on of specified unlawful activity; or . . .
>
> (B) knowing that the transaction is designed in whole or in part —
>
> (i) to conceal or disguise the nature, the location, the source, the ownership or the control of the proceeds of specified unlawful activity;
>
> . . .

The three defendants in this case were charged under subsection (B)(i), based on knowledge of "design[ ]", and not under (A)(i), based on an "intent to promote." In each instance, there is no doubt that the defendant did engage in one or more financial transactions involving Colon's drug proceeds. The issue turns, rather, on state of mind elements. Pertinently, as to Corchado, she disputes knowing either that the "property" represented proceeds of drug dealing or that "the transaction" was "designed . . . to conceal or disguise. . . ." The evidence, taken most favorably to the government, showed the following.

Elena Corchado Peralta met Colon sometime in the early 1990s and they were married in 1994. Corchado, then about 25 years old, was a student when they met and later worked part-time in her mother's jewelry store. She has a college degree in business administration and some training in accounting. Colon testified that he held himself out as a successful legitimate businessman throughout their relationship and that his wife knew about neither his drug smuggling nor his own money laundering activities.

Corchado performed many transactions involving Colon's drug proceeds. These transactions fell into two broad categories—expenditures and deposits. On the expenditure side, Colon directed Corchado to write and endorse checks to purchase a cornucopia of expensive cars, boats, real estate, and personal services. Colon maintained that his wife thought that the money was derived from legitimate businesses.

The purchases themselves were extensive and expensive, affording the couple a fancy lifestyle. For example, Corchado purchased a BMW, a Mercedes Benz, and a Porsche for the couple. At another time, she made a single monthly payment to American Express of $18,384 for interior decorating purchases. And on another day, she signed three checks totaling $350,000 that were used to purchase land for one of Colon's businesses. In total, Corchado signed the majority of 253 checks, representing many hundreds of thousands of dollars of purchases.

With respect to deposits, Corchado's main responsibility was to deposit $6,000 checks on a monthly basis into one of Colon's accounts. Colon testified that he had made a $700,000 loan to an associate using his drug profits with the understanding that the associate was to pay him back over the course of many months so as to dissociate Colon from the illegal proceeds. Under the terms of the arrangement, the checks came from legitimate businesses, and Colon testified that his wife was not aware of the circumstances underlying the monthly payments. At trial, the government also presented evidence showing that on one occasion Corchado wired $40,000 to a Florida company at Colon's request.

Tax records signed by Corchado showed that she knew that her husband's reported income from his legitimate businesses was far less than the money she was handling. For example, the joint tax return that Corchado signed for 1995 listed a total amount of claimed income of only $12,390. The government presented evidence showing that the couple's total reported income between 1992 and 1997 was only approximately $150,000. Corchado did not testify at trial.

We begin with the first knowledge requirement—namely, that Corchado was aware, at the time of the transactions she conducted, that the money she was handling, at least much of the time, was derived from drug dealings.[3] Corchado argues, correctly, that there is no direct evidence of her knowledge (say, by an admission by her or testimony from Colon that he told her about his business). Indeed, he testified repeatedly that she was unaware of his drug business; that in response to

---

3. Formally, the charge is "conspiracy," under subsection (h) to violate subsection (a)(1)(B)(i); but the "agreement" requirement is undisputed: many, if not all, of the transactions were performed at Colon's request or with his consent. Thus, the open issue is Corchado's state of mind.

a question from her he had denied doing anything unlawful; that he never allowed her to attend meetings involving his drug business; and that he stopped distributing drugs when they were married.

Needless to say, the jury did not have to accept Colon's exculpatory testimony. It was clearly self-interested since Corchado was his wife and mother of their two children. But here, at least, the jury's disbelief could not count for much in the way of affirmative proof. Rather, whether there was knowledge of drug dealing, or so much awareness that ignorance was willful blindness, turns in this case on the same circumstantial evidence.

What the evidence shows is that Corchado knew that the family expenditures were huge, that reported income was a fraction of what was being spent and that legitimate sources were not so obvious as to banish all thoughts of possible illegal origin — as demonstrated by Colon's testimony that Corchado once raised the issue. Interviewed by an FBI agent, Corchado told him that her husband had been involved in the cattle business and, more recently, in real estate development but that none of the businesses had employees and that Colon had worked mainly out of his house. And, as the government fairly points out, Corchado was herself well educated and involved in the family bookkeeping.

This might seem to some a modest basis for concluding — beyond a reasonable doubt — that Corchado knew that her husband's income was badly tainted. But the issue turns on judgments about relationships within families and about inferences that might be drawn in the community from certain patterns of working and spending. Further, it is enough to know that the proceeds came from "some form, though not necessarily which form," of felony under state or federal law. 18 U.S.C. §1956(c)(1). The jury's judgment on this factual issue cannot be called irrational.

The other knowledge requirement is harder for the government. Here, the statute requires, somewhat confusingly, that Corchado have known that "the transaction" was "designed," at least in part, "to conceal or disguise the nature, the location, the source, the ownership or the control of the proceeds." 18 U.S.C. §1956(a)(1)(B)(i). We will assume that it would be enough if Corchado herself undertook a transaction for her husband, knowing that her husband had such a design to conceal or disguise the proceeds, or if she undertook a transaction on her own having such a design herself. Other variations might exist, but these two seem the foremost possibilities.

It may help to treat separately the purchases on the one hand and the check deposits (and in one case a transfer) on the other. Any purchase of goods or services, whether by cash or by check, has a potential to conceal or disguise proceeds simply because it transforms them from money into objects or dissipates them in the performance of the services. But if this were enough, every expenditure of proceeds known to be tainted would itself be unlawful. Instead, the statute requires that someone — the instigator or spender — must have an intent to disguise or conceal and the spender must share or know of that intent.

Here, the government showed that from their marriage onward Corchado wrote most of the checks used by the couple to purchase expensive items (*e.g.*, several high-priced cars) and pay off credit card bills and that some of these payments were very large (one credit card bill exceeded $18,000). And, for reasons already given, it is assumed that the jury permissibly found that Corchado knew that some of the money she was spending was criminally derived. Finally, the government stresses that she must have known that Colon was bringing in and spending far more than he reported on his income tax returns. Is this enough for the jury to infer a specific intent to conceal or disguise and impute the intent itself, or knowledge of it, to Corchado?

In this case, nothing about the purchases, or their manner, points toward concealment or disguise beyond the fact that virtually *all expenditures* transform cash into something else. Here, the purchased assets were not readily concealable (*e.g.*, diamonds) nor peculiarly concealed (*e.g.*, buried in the garden) nor acquired in someone else's name nor spirited away to a foreign repository (*e.g.*, a Swiss bank deposit box). Indicia of this kind have been stressed in cases upholding money laundering charges and their absence noted in cases coming out the other way.

To hold that a jury may convict on this evidence — that Corchado spent her husband's money knowing that the money was tainted — is to make it unlawful wherever a wife spends any of her husband's money, knowing or believing him to be a criminal. That the purchases here were lavish or numerous hardly distinguishes this case from one in which a thief's wife buys a jar of baby food; if anything, Corchado's more flamboyant purchases were less likely than the baby food to disguise or conceal. Perhaps a hard-nosed Congress might be willing to adopt such a statute, *compare* 18 U.S.C. § 1957 (2000), but it did not do so here.

Less need be said about the deposit and transfer side. So far as we can tell, Corchado mostly did no more than make large regular deposits in an account given to her by her husband; there was no inference of concealment or disguise. As for the single transfer she made to another person at her husband's request, nothing suspicious about the circumstances is cited to us, let alone anything that would suggest knowledge on Corchado's part that the transfer was meant to conceal or disguise proceeds — as opposed to merely paying off a debt, making an investment, or conducting some other transaction incident to a business, lawful or otherwise.

Corchado's bank fraud conviction is *affirmed*; her money laundering conviction is *reversed*; the sentences are *vacated*; and the case is *remanded* for re-sentencing on the bank fraud conviction.

Notes and Questions

1. *The money laundering theory.* What was the money laundering theory in this case? Why did the court find insufficient evidence? What additional facts would likely have sufficed? As one court explained:

> The statute speaks in terms of transactions that are "designed" to conceal the proceeds of unlawful activity. Whenever a drug dealer uses his profits

to acquire any asset — whether a house, a car, a horse, or a television — a jury could reasonably suspect that on some level he is motivated by a desire to convert his cash into a more legitimate form. The requirement that the transaction be "designed" to conceal, however, requires more than a trivial motivation to conceal. [For example:] [S]tatements by a defendant probative of intent to conceal; unusual secrecy surrounding the transaction; structuring the transaction in a way to avoid attention; depositing illegal profits in the bank account of a legitimate business; highly irregular features of the transaction; using third parties to conceal the real owner; a series of unusual financial moves cumulating in the transaction; or expert testimony on practices of criminals.

United States v. Garcia-Emanuel, 14 F.3d 1469, 1474–76 (10th Cir. 1994). For another example of a decision finding insufficient evidence in a concealment case, see *United States v. Richardson*, 658 F.3d 333, 340–42 (3d Cir. 2011) (holding that, although receipts from drug sales, which defendant used to purchase a house, constituted proceeds of specified unlawful activity, there was insufficient evidence that defendant participated in any financial transactions knowing that they were designed to conceal the nature of the drug money).

2. *Section 1957.* The court noted that concealment money laundering under § 1956 is not as far reaching as offenses under § 1957. What was the basis for this conclusion? Could the government have successfully charged the defendant under § 1957 in this case? Why or why not?

3. *Willful blindness.* What amounts to knowledge that the proceeds were "dirty"? As the court stated above, "it is enough to know that the proceeds came from 'some form, though not necessarily which form,' of felony under state or federal law. 18 U.S.C. § 1956(c)(1)." As the court also noted, proof of willful blindness will suffice in proving such knowledge. Was there sufficient proof of willful blindness, also known as "constructive knowledge," in this case? Why or why not?

What facts are necessary to prove willful blindness? In *United States v. Flores*, 454 F.3d 149 (3d Cir. 2006), an attorney who asserted a defense of lack of knowledge as to the illegal source of the client's money was convicted of conspiring with the client to commit money laundering. The court found sufficient proof of willful blindness based upon the defendant's acts of opening bank accounts and conducting financial transactions for the client. The U.S. Department of Justice Manual provides specific examples of conduct that may support a finding of willful blindness in money laundering cases, such as "conducting business under odd circumstances, at irregular hours, or in unusual locations by industry standards." DOJ Manual § 9-105.400 at 9-21128.36.

Can financial institutions satisfy the elements of willful blindness in money laundering prosecutions? Note that the money laundering statutes and the Bank Secrecy Act reporting requirements are intended to ensure that financial institutions do not remain willfully blind about the money laundering activities, but instead investigate and report these transactions to the government. *See United States v. Rodriguez,* 53 F.3d 1439 (7th Cir. 1995).

4. *Concealment from whom?* From whom must the defendant intend to conceal funds in order to be guilty under § 1956? Clearly, trying to conceal funds from authorities is sufficient. What about from other private parties? *See United States v. Chavez,* 951 F.3d 349 (6th Cir. 2020) (holding that conviction did not require finding that defendant wanted to hide money from the whole world, just from private parties who might have asked inconvenient questions).

b. Transportation Money Laundering

Section 1956(a)(1) defines money laundering offenses involving "financial transactions." A companion statute, § 1956(a)(2), the international transportation money laundering statute, criminalizes the transport of a monetary instrument or funds into or out of the United States in specific circumstances. Section 1956(a)(2)(A) is the promotion international money laundering statute, and criminalizes international transport with "the intent to promote the carrying on of specified unlawful activity." Section 1956(a)(2)(B)(i) is the concealment transportation money laundering statute. Concealment transportation money laundering requires knowledge that the proceeds derived from unlawful activity. Section 1956(a)(2)(B)(ii) criminalizes transportation money laundering with the intent to avoid a state or federal reporting requirement, with knowledge that the proceeds derived from unlawful activity.

In *Cuellar v. United States,* 128 S. Ct. 1994, 1997–98 (2008), the Supreme Court evaluated the required proof for transportation money laundering under a concealment theory, § 1956(a)(2)(B)(i). In that case, the defendant was discovered transporting approximately $81,000 in cash proceeds of narcotics trafficking. The cash was hidden in a secret compartment under the floorboard of a Volkswagen Beetle that the defendant was driving in Texas en route to Mexico. The money was bundled in plastic bags and duct tape. Animal hair was spread in the rear of the vehicle, apparently to mask the smell of marijuana that had been transported in the car.

The Court unanimously reversed the money laundering conviction, stating:

> The provision of the money laundering statute under which petitioner was convicted requires proof that the transportation was "designed in whole or in part to conceal or disguise the nature, the location, the source, the ownership, or the control" of the funds. § 1956(a)(2)(B)(i). Although this element does not require proof that the defendant attempted to create the appearance of legitimate wealth, neither can it be satisfied solely by evidence that a defendant concealed the funds during their transport. In this case, the only evidence introduced to prove this element showed that petitioner engaged in extensive efforts to conceal the funds *en route* to Mexico, and thus his conviction cannot stand. We reverse the judgment of the Fifth Circuit.

Id. at 1998. As Justice Alito noted in his concurring opinion, the government did not present any evidence from which the trier of fact could have inferred that petitioner knew that taking the funds to Mexico would have had one of the required effects — that is, to make it more difficult for United States law enforcement officials to determine the nature, location, source, ownership, or control of the funds. *Id.* at 2006 (Alito, J., concurring).

Question

1. Does the holding in *Cuellar* present a significant barrier to concealment prosecutions? What additional facts likely would have satisfied the Court? *Compare United States v. Warshak*, 562 F. Supp. 2d 986, 991–99 (S.D. Ohio 2008) (evidence of convoluted transactions was sufficient to show knowledge of a design to conceal), *aff'd in part, rev'd in part on other grounds*, 631 F.3d 266 (6th Cir. 2011).

Problems

13-4. Nester ran an armored carrier business that transported valuables, such as artwork and jewelry, internationally. On five separate occasions over the past year, Nester placed cash inside containers that held jewelry, artwork, and other valuables. The cash was placed in paper packages that were commingled with the valuables inside the sealed and locked metal shipping containers. The containers were first transferred to Los Angeles International Airport in armored trucks and placed onto planes being loaded with cargo. In each case, the container was moved later that day to a different cargo plane, which then carried the container to a location outside the United States. A total of over $5 million was transported in this manner. As Nester knew, the cash represented the proceeds from sales of illegal narcotics.

Nester has been charged with transportation money laundering in violation of § 1956(a)(2)(B)(i), and moves to dismiss the charges based on Cuellar. *How should the court rule? Why?*

13-5. Defendant and defendant's daughter ran an insurance brokerage firm. Defendant fraudulently obtained a $3,000 check from a client through the use of the mails. Defendant deposited the check into defendant's bank account, which before the deposit had a balance of $200. Two weeks later, defendant wired $3,000 from the bank account into a bank account that the daughter maintained in her own name. Defendant was convicted of concealment money laundering under 18 U.S.C. § 1956(a)(1)(B)(i) based upon the wire transfer.

Defendant appeals. How should the court rule? Why?

13-6. David Smith was arrested and charged with drug violations. The state district court set his bail at $50,000. Smith contacted his mother, Tammy, to request her help in getting him out of jail. Tammy did so using some of the proceeds that David had in a safe in her home and by calling in debts owed to David. David's bail was posted the next day.

Tammy has always kept track of her son's finances. She made bank deposits, allocated spending money to him, and participated in collecting cash from various sources. She knew her son was a drug dealer, but she did not want to know the origin of the money she used to post bail. She simply wanted to get her son out of jail.

The government has charged Tammy Smith with conspiring with her son to commit concealment money laundering when she posted bail. How should the court rule? Why?

c. Promotion Money Laundering

In the next case, the government charged the defendant with promotion money laundering. As you read the decision, consider how the government might have proceeded differently in constructing its theory of the case.

United States v. Brown

186 F.3d 661 (5th Cir. 1999)

Jerry E. Smith, Circuit Judge:

Leonard Graves appeals his money laundering convictions, a number of his fraud convictions, and his sentence. We affirm Graves's fraud convictions, reverse his money laundering convictions, and vacate and remand his sentence.

The fraud and money laundering charges of which Graves was convicted relate to business dealings conducted at Steve Graves Chevrolet-Pontiac-Cadillac, Inc. ("SGC"), an auto dealership in Ruston, Louisiana. Graves was the dealer, president, and 41% owner of SGC, and [co-defendant Gregory] Brown managed its body shop.

The 120-count indictment against Graves alleged six distinct types of fraud, and for each fraud allegation there was a corresponding money laundering charge. Graves was convicted on counts stemming from three of the six types of fraud and was convicted of money laundering the funds derived from these frauds.

The first type of fraud involved SGC's charging car buyers more than the amount authorized by state law for document and license/title fees. SGC charged purchasers $59 in document fees, which is $9 more than Louisiana law permits; automobile dealerships are allowed to charge only $35 for processing paperwork and $15 for a notary fee. For the license and title fees, which varied from vehicle to vehicle, SGC overcharged an average of $50 per automobile listed in the indictment. The eighteen instances of overcharging were charged against Graves as mail frauds, because the Louisiana Department of Motor Vehicles mailed the automobile titles. Graves was also charged with money laundering the proceeds of the excessive fees. The jury found Graves guilty on some of the counts and not guilty on others.

Graves was convicted of fraud based on SGC's financing the purchases of used cars with "cash for gas." In seven instances, SGC advanced to the purchaser all or part of the down payment required by the financing institution—under the guise of giving the buyer some "cash for gas" — and increased the purchase price of the car by a corresponding amount. This conduct constituted fraud, because the lending institution would not have extended credit to the purchaser absent his having some genuine equity interest in the automobile. The counts of which Graves was convicted were charged as mail frauds, because SGC mailed loan documentation to General Motors Acceptance Corporation ("GMAC"), the financing institution. The jury also found Graves guilty of money laundering the funds derived from cash for gas frauds.

The final form of fraud of which Graves was convicted also involved the financing of used cars. For ten cars financed by Union Federal Credit Union, SGC, on behalf of the buyer, forwarded to the credit union 25% of the sale price, which the credit union maintained in a savings account in the purchaser's name until the loan was paid off. The dealership increased the sale price of the vehicle by a corresponding amount. As with "cash for gas," this scheme had the effect of fraudulently inducing advances of credit, for the credit union believed that the 25% down payment represented genuine purchaser equity in the purchased automobiles. These counts were charged as bank frauds, and the jury returned a guilty verdict. It also found Graves guilty of money laundering the proceeds derived from the bank frauds. Graves does not appeal these bank fraud convictions, but he does appeal the corresponding money laundering convictions.

Graves appeals his convictions on fraud counts stemming from excessive document and license/title fees and "cash for gas" frauds. He also appeals all his money laundering convictions and his sentence.

[The Court concluded that there was sufficient evidence to sustain Graves's fraud convictions stemming from the excessive fees and "cash for gas" schemes].

Each money laundering count on which Graves was indicted was charged under 18 U.S.C. §1956(a)(1)(A)(i), which reads, in part:

> (A) Whoever, knowing that the property involved in a financial transaction represents the proceeds of some form of unlawful activity, conducts or attempts to conduct such a financial transaction which in fact involves the proceeds of specified unlawful activity.

> (i) with the intent to promote the carrying on of specified unlawful activity; . . .

To obtain a conviction under §1956(a)(1)(A)(i), the government must prove beyond a reasonable doubt "[t]hat the defendant (1) conducted or attempted to conduct a financial transaction, (2) which the defendant knew involved the proceeds of unlawful activity, (3) with the intent to promote or further unlawful activity." *United States v. Cavalier*, 17 F.3d 90, 92 (5th Cir. 1994). Graves asserts that there was insufficient evidence to establish that the charged money laundering transactions were intended to promote any fraud committed at SGC. We agree.

The transactions the indictment charged as money laundering consisted of expenditures, paid by checks written by SGC, that allegedly promoted the fraud.[4] Graves contends that there was no evidence that the payment of those checks was intended to promote any fraud at SGC; the checks were simply legitimate business expenses of the dealership. Indeed, a review of the checks indicates that they were for "above board" expenses.[5] Graves argues that such expenditures are not the sort of crime-promoting transactions criminalized by § 1956(a)(1)(A)(i), for the promotion element requires some identifiable and affirmative advancement of the specified criminal activity. In support of this claim, he points to a number of cases involving "promotion" money laundering in which the court highlighted how the expenditures explicitly furthered specified unlawful activity. He then contrasts those cases to the case at hand, in which the nexus between the charged expenditures and any fraud activity is non-existent or weak.

Graves also points to *United States v. Jackson*, 935 F.2d 832 (7th Cir. 1991), in which the defendant, who was both a preacher and drug dealer, deposited drug proceeds into his church's checking account. From the church account, he wrote checks to pay for beepers, mobile phones, and rent; he also wrote some checks for cash. The defendant's drug runners used the beepers to communicate with each other, and the court therefore held that the beeper purchases were intended to promote the specified unlawful conduct. The checks for mobile phones, rent, and cash, however, did not promote the criminal activity and thus did not constitute money laundering. The court explained:

---

4. The government, in selecting financial transactions to fulfill the actus reus requirement of the money laundering charges, picked benign business expenditures — purchases of goods and services necessary to maintain SGC's legitimate business operations. It did not have to do so. Courts have held that a promotion money laundering offense may occur when a defendant receives and deposits criminally derived funds, in which case the *deposit* of the funds is the transaction intended to promote the specified unlawful activity. But the government chose not to indict Graves for depositing the proceeds of fraud. Instead, it made a strategic decision to focus on SGC's spending transactions (*i.e.*, the checks the dealership wrote), not on SGC's depositing of funds, perhaps because "receipt and deposit" money laundering prosecutions are disfavored. Such prosecutions have been criticized because the harm of the money laundering transaction (*i.e.*, the deposit) is not significantly greater than that of the underlying offense. Indeed, the Department of Justice issued a Blue Sheet to chapter 9-105.000 of the U.S. Attorney's Manual requiring consultation by a U.S. Attorney's Office with the Department before a receipt and deposit case may be prosecuted. Having chosen to prosecute Graves for spending (not merely depositing) dirty money, the government was required to show that the expenditures were conducted with an "intent to promote" SGC's fraudulent activity.

5. The allegedly laundered funds paid for (1) parts, paints, and materials; (2) the floor plan, cars that had been traded in, floor plan interest, and a charge back; (3) software support and office supplies; (4) conversions; (5) used cars; (6) disposal of waste oil and used oil filters; (7) t-shirts, caps, coffee mugs; (8) yearbook advertisements; (9) a computer system lease; (10) advertising representation; (11) Graves's travel expenses; (12) extended warranties on used automobiles; (13) glass replacement; (14) automobile association membership fees; (15) photocopier supplies; and (16) a health plan.

> The government did not prove that the cellular phones played the same role — or indeed any role — in Davis' drug operations as the beepers. Likewise the rental payments and the checks written to cash; certainly these expenditures maintained Davis' lifestyle, but more than this is needed to establish that they promoted his drug activities.

Id.

Graves argues that the expenditures charged in the money laundering counts of the indictment are analogous to the *Jackson* defendant's expenditures on mobile phones and rent: They were intended to support the dealership's legitimate business activities and evince no intent to promote fraud.

The government insists that the expenditures did promote fraud. Its theory, which the district court accepted, is that the transactions charged in the indictment promoted the ongoing and future criminal activity at SGC, despite the fact that they were expenditures on the basic operations of the car dealership, because the operation of the dealership was one grand scheme to defraud. In other words, any legitimate operating expense that permitted SGC to stay in business and maintain or increase its customer base would also be an expenditure intended to promote fraud, because it would ensure a steady supply of potential victims.

Despite the government's creative argument, we agree with Graves that there is insufficient evidence that the charged expenditures were financial transactions conducted "with the intent to promote the carrying on of specified unlawful activity." The problem with the government's position is that it ignores the *intent* aspect of the promotion element. Section 1956(a)(1)(A)(i) is not satisfied by a showing that a financial transaction involving the proceeds of specified unlawful activity merely promoted the carrying on of unlawful activity. The provision has a specific intent element: The government must show that the "dirty money" transaction was conducted "*with the intent* to promote the carrying on of specified unlawful activity.".....

This does not mean that there must always be direct evidence, such as a statement by the defendant, of an intent to promote specified unlawful activity. In many cases, the intent to promote criminal activity may be inferred from the particular type of transaction. For example, an intent to promote drug trafficking activities could be inferred from the *Jackson* defendant's purchase of beepers, because beepers were not necessary to the defendant's legitimate business operations and played an important role in his drug trafficking scheme.

In the case at hand, had the government produced evidence of, say, payments for postage for mailing fraudulent warranty claims, such payments might have provided evidence of an intent to promote fraud. Mere evidence of legitimate business expenditures that were necessary to support SGC's non-fraudulent operations, however, was not enough to establish an intent to promote fraud at SGC, even though the expenditures may in fact have promoted SGC's fraudulent activities by increasing the number of potential fraud victims.

We have previously stressed the importance of not turning the "money laundering statute into a 'money spending statute.'" Strictly adhering to the specific intent requirement of the promotion element of § 1956(a)(1)(A)(i) helps ensure that the money laundering statute will punish conduct that is really distinct from the underlying specified unlawful activity and will not simply provide overzealous prosecutors with a means of imposing additional criminal liability any time a defendant makes benign expenditures with funds derived from unlawful acts.

In a separate money laundering statute, 18 U.S.C. § 1957(a), Congress did criminalize the mere spending of "criminally derived property that is of a value greater than $10,000" with knowledge of the unlawful source. The fact that Congress established a $10,000 per transaction threshold for convictions for simply spending dirty money further supports our decision to read § 1956(a)(1)(A)(i) to require either direct proof that the charged transaction was intended to promote specified unlawful activity or proof of a type of transaction (such as the *Jackson* defendant's purchase of beepers) that, on its face, indicates an intent to promote such activity.

Absent such proof, § 1956(a)(1)(A)(i) does not permit conviction of a defendant who, like Graves, deposits proceeds of some relatively minor fraudulent transactions into the operating account of an otherwise legitimate business enterprise and then writes checks out of that account for general business purposes. Accordingly, we reverse Graves's money laundering convictions.

Notes and Questions

1. *Deposits and expenditures.* What were the transactions upon which the government based its case? Would a case built on deposits of funds derived from the fraud have succeeded? If so, why did the government decline to bring such a case?

2. *Sections 1956 and 1957.* What is the difference between a promotion case under § 1956 and a case under § 1957? Could the government have used § 1957 to prosecute the defendant in this case? Why or why not?

3. *Choice of theory.* Would the government have been more successful if it accused Graves of a different type of § 1956 money laundering, such as concealment money laundering? Alternatively, what facts, assuming the government could prove them, would have secured Graves' conviction for promotion money laundering?

Problems

13-7. Rick Port was issued a MasterCard by Maryland National Bank ("MNB"). Marla Oaks impersonated Port in notifying MNB that Port's address had changed to a mailbox rented by Oaks in Baltimore, Maryland. MNB later mailed three convenience checks to Oaks' mailbox, one of which later was found at Oaks' residence in a town 30 miles from Baltimore.

One of the checks was used partially to pay off the balance of another credit card owned by Oaks, a Union Bank Visa card. The address for the Visa had also been changed by Oaks, and a requested replacement card had been sent to Oaks' mailbox.

After the credit balance was partially paid by the MNB check, the Visa was used to purchase one computer at each of two different stores in Baltimore. The computers were found in Oaks' residence and were for her personal use.

Based upon the purchase of the two computers. Oaks was convicted of bank fraud and of both concealment and promotion money laundering. Oaks appeals her money laundering convictions. How should the court rule? Why?

13-8. For a period of four years, the defendants Aden and Bowen defrauded banks of millions of dollars through real estate and mortgage transactions involving properties. The scheme consisted of a series of fraudulently executed land "flips:" the defendants bought cheap properties with fake identities and then sold them to each other for artificially high prices, using bank loans to fund the purchases. The defendants fabricated the identities of the buyers, providing the straw buyers with false employment histories, financial records, and addresses. At the defendants' behest, appraisers lied about the properties' values, inflating the listing prices.

The schemers submitted the fraudulent loan applications to banks, which relied on them in making lending decisions. On the issuance of loan checks to the straw buyers, the defendants endorsed the checks with the straw buyers' names, deposited the checks into their personal bank accounts, and then distributed the fraud proceeds by writing checks drawn on their accounts to the various participants in the scheme. The nonexistent buyers failed to make mortgage payments, which eventually led the banks to foreclose.

Aden served as the real-estate broker and orchestrated many facets of the scheme. Aden owned Protech, a company which was listed as the employer of the straw buyers, and signed a variety of loan documents in the straw buyers' names. Bowen, a co-owner and officer of Protech, played various roles, helping to fabricate the straw buyers' financial and employment records and facilitating the purchase and sale of properties.

Bowen and Aden were convicted of bank fraud and of concealment and promotion money laundering based on the deposits of the straw buyers' checks, and appeal the money laundering convictions. How should the court rule? Why?

13-9. A mother and her 17-year-old son went to the Quick Auto Dealership one afternoon to buy a car for the son. After they took a car for a test drive, the mother asked the salesperson if she could pay for the car with cash. He agreed. The son contributed $6,000 that he had saved from "odd jobs," and his mother gave another $5,000 to complete the purchase. The son's "odd jobs" consisted of selling DVDs that he copied on his computer to his friends at the local high school. Surprised by how much money he had saved, the mother asked the son where the money came from. Before he could answer she said, "I don't want to know, let's just get the car." She thought that he was involved in drug activities with his friends.

The total price for the car was $11,000. The mother made an initial cash deposit of $1,500. Two days later, the mother and son returned to get the car and the son brought his $6,000 in cash for the purchase. The mother asked the dealer to title the car in her name "for insurance purposes." The mother added another $3,500 in cash. The son used the car to make timely deliveries of his counterfeit DVDs, and he began to expand his business to the high school in the neighboring county.

> *a. You are the Assistant U.S. Attorney in charge of the investigation, and these facts have been presented to you. Would you ask a grand jury to return criminal charges in this case against the son and/or the mother? If so, based on what theory or theories?*

> *b. You are private counsel and you represent the Quick Auto Dealership. What obligations does the dealership have, if any, in connection with this transaction?*

3. Criminally Derived Property

In a money laundering case, the government must prove that the financial or monetary transaction actually involved criminally derived property. This requirement raises several distinct issues. First, in a case involving "proceeds" of unlawful activity, does that term encompass all receipts from the activity, or only net profits? Second, in an ongoing scheme, at what point in time can property be considered criminally derived? Third, how does a fact-finder identify criminally-derived property when that property has been mixed together — "commingled" — with non-criminally derived property? This section considers each of these issues.

a. "Proceeds" and the Issue of Merger

Federal circuit courts were split over whether the term "proceeds" in the money laundering statutes means gross proceeds or net profits. *Compare, e.g., United States v. Iacaboni*, 363 F.3d 1 (1st Cir. 2004) ("proceeds" means gross income) *with United States v. Scialabba*, 282 F.3d 475 (7th Cir. 2002) ("proceeds" means net profits). Net profits include only surpluses of an enterprise, after deducting the costs of carrying out the enterprise. Gross income includes any revenue from the enterprise, before deducting costs.

In *United States v. Santos*, 128 S. Ct. 2020 (2008), the U.S. Supreme Court attempted to resolve this issue. In *Santos*, the defendant was convicted of money laundering in connection with an illegal lottery scheme. In a fractured decision, the four-member plurality found that the term "proceeds" is ambiguous. Because the rule of lenity applies when interpreting the term, it must be read in favor of the defendant to mean net profits. In addition, the plurality opinion based its conclusion on the "merger" issue that arises under the broader definition of proceeds:

> If 'proceeds' meant 'receipts,' nearly every violation of the illegal-lottery statute would also be a violation of the money-laundering statute, because paying a winning bettor is a transaction involving receipts that the defendant intends to promote the carrying on of the lottery. Since few lotteries, if

any, will not pay their winners, the statute criminalizing illegal lotteries, 18 U.S.C. § 1955, would 'merge' with the money-laundering statute. Congress evidently decided that lottery operators ordinarily deserve up to 5 years of imprisonment, § 1955(a), but as a result of merger they would face an additional 20 years, § 1956(a)(1). Prosecutors, of course, would acquire the discretion to charge the lesser lottery offense, the greater money-laundering offense, or both — which would predictably be used to induce a plea bargain to the lesser charge.

The merger problem is not limited to lottery operators. For a host of predicate crimes, merger would depend on the manner and timing of payment for the expenses associated with the commission of the crime. Few crimes are entirely free of cost, and costs are not always paid in advance. Anyone who pays for the costs of a crime with its proceeds — for example, the felon who uses the stolen money to pay for the rented getaway car — would violate the money-laundering statute. And any wealth-acquiring crime with multiple participants would become money-laundering when the initial recipient of the wealth gives his confederates their shares. . . .

The Government suggests no explanation for why Congress would have wanted a transaction that is a normal part of a crime it had duly considered and appropriately punished elsewhere in the Criminal Code to radically increase the sentence for that crime. Interpreting 'proceeds' to mean 'profits' eliminates the merger problem. Transactions that normally occur during the course of running a lottery are not identifiable uses of profits and thus do not violate the money-laundering statute. More generally, a criminal who enters into a transaction paying the expenses of his illegal activity cannot possibly violate the money-laundering statute, because by definition profits consist of what remains after expenses are paid. Defraying an activity's costs with its receipts simply will not be covered.

Id. at 2026–27.

Concurring in the judgment, Justice Stevens wrote that "the legislative history of § 1956 makes it clear that Congress intended the term 'proceeds' to include gross revenues from the sale of contraband and the operation of organized crime syndicates involving such sales. But that history sheds no light on how to identify the proceeds of many other types of specified unlawful activities. . . ." Thus, according to Justice Stevens, whether "proceeds" means receipts or profits depends upon the legislative history of the specified unlawful activity. *Id.* at 2037 (Stevens, J., concurring in the judgment).

Writing for a four-member dissent, Justice Alito concluded that the term "proceeds" in state and federal money laundering statutes consistently refers to gross receipts. He stated:

Both [goals — preventing criminals from enjoying a luxurious life style and inhibiting the growth of criminal enterprises —] are frustrated if a money laundering statute is limited to profits. Dirty money may be used to support "a luxurious lifestyle" and to grow an illegal enterprise whenever the enterprise possesses large amounts of illegally obtained cash. And illegal enterprises may acquire such cash while engaging in unlawful activity that is unprofitable.

Id. at 2038 (Alito, J., dissenting). The dissent also concluded that the plurality approach would create severe problems of proof both as to "profits" and the defendant's knowledge of such profits. Finally, the dissent noted that "the so-called merger problem is fundamentally a sentencing problem, and the proper remedy is a sentencing remedy. . . ." *Id.* at 2044.

After *Santos* was decided, Congress enacted the Fraud Enforcement and Recovery Act of 2009 (FERA). The Act amended § 1956 by adding a new section: "the term 'proceeds' means any property derived from or obtained or retained, directly or indirectly, through some form of unlawful activity, including the gross receipts of such activity." This language supersedes the decision in *Santos* in support of the dissent's position. *See People v. Gutman*, 959 N.E.2d 621 (Ill. 2011).

Notes and Questions

1. *Difficulties of proof.* The various elements of a money laundering violation present evidentiary challenges for prosecutors.

a. *Profits.* How difficult would be it for the government to prove that the financial transaction involved the proceeds of criminal activity under the plurality's definition of "proceeds"? Is the dissent correct that this proof would pose a formidable barrier in money laundering prosecutions? Why or why not?

b. *Knowledge.* In a money laundering case, the government must prove that the defendant knew the "proceeds" were generated by unlawful activity. Would the plurality approach make this element more difficult to prove? Why or why not?

c. *Which criminal activity?* Note that the government only needs to prove the defendant knew the funds were derived from a specified unlawful activity, not that the defendant knew exactly which sort of unlawful activity. *See United States v. Estrada-Lopez*, 259 F. Supp. 3d 1358 (M.D. Fla. 2017).

2. *The congressional response.* In addition to clarifying that "proceeds" of criminal activity refers to gross income, FERA also includes a provision titled "Sense of the Congress and Report Concerning Required Approval for Merger Cases":

> It is the sense of the Congress that no prosecution of an offense under section 1956 or 1957 of title 18, United States Code, should be undertaken in combination with the prosecution of any other offense, without prior approval of the Attorney General, the Deputy Attorney General, the Assistant Attorney General in charge of the Criminal Division, a Deputy Assistant Attorney General in the Criminal Division, or the relevant United States Attorney, if the conduct to be charged as "specified unlawful activity"

in connection with the offense under section 1956 or 1957 is so closely connected with the conduct to be charged as the other offense that there is no clear delineation between the two offenses.

The bill also requires that the DOJ provide annual reports to Congress for four years reporting whether the DOJ is adhering to the provisions of the Sense of the Congress statement.

Is FERA's amendment to the money laundering statutes an appropriate and effective responses to *Santos*? Does the Sense of the Congress provision adequately address the plurality's "merger" concerns? Why or why not?

Problems

13-10. Carlos was helping Josie with what she described as "a little money flow problem." Josie had a lot of cash that she needed to put into bankable form. Carlos took Josie's cash and purchased an equivalent value (minus a small commission) of Bitcoin in a new digital wallet using his personal virtual currency account. He then gave Josie the digital "key" to the wallet, which effectively transferred control to her.

Carlos knew Josie was a local meth dealer and assumed that is where her money came from. In fact, Josie had recently moved on to dealing cocaine, which provided a higher profit margin. She also ran a side mail fraud hustle to bilk pensioners. The cash she gave to Carlos was a 50/50 split from the two enterprises.

Is Carlos guilty of money laundering? If so, with respect to all the money Josie gave him or just half of it? Which half?

b. Timing

Under § 1956(a)(1), the financial transaction must involve the proceeds of specified unlawful activity. Under § 1957, the government must show that the defendant engaged in a "monetary transaction in criminally derived property." 18 U.S.C. § 1957(a). The term "criminally derived property" is defined as "any property constituting, or derived from, proceeds obtained from a criminal offense." 18 U.S.C. § 1957(f)(2). At what point can funds be considered to be the product of the unlawful activity?

This issue arose in *United States v. Kennedy*, 64 F.3d 1465 (10th Cir. 1995). The defendant used mail and wires to fraudulently obtain funds that he deposited into his bank account as part of a Ponzi scheme. Based on the deposits, he was convicted of promotion money laundering under 18 U.S.C. § 1956(a)(1)(A)(i). On appeal, he argued that the funds were not "proceeds" at the time of the deposits and did not become proceeds until he used them in transactions subsequent to the deposits. The court disagreed, finding that the crimes of mail and wire fraud were complete upon the use of mail and wires, and that the funds therefore were proceeds of the fraud when the defendant received them.

In reaching that conclusion, the court distinguished a case brought under §1957, *United States v. Johnson*, 971 F.2d 562 (10th Cir. 1992). In *Johnson*, the defendant defrauded investors, who wired money to his bank account. The defendant was convicted under §1957 based upon these wire transfers. Reversing the conviction, the court of appeals held that "both the plain language of §1957 and the legislative history behind it suggest that Congress targeted only those transactions occurring after proceeds have been obtained from the underlying unlawful activity." *Id.* at 568. The wiring of the money was itself the wire fraud, which was not complete until the funds were deposited into the defendant's account. Therefore, at the time of the wiring, the funds were not "criminally derived property." *Accord United States v. Piervinanzi*, 23 F.3d 670 (2d Cir. 1994).

Why was the outcome in *Kennedy* different from that in *Johnson*? As the *Kennedy* court explained:

> [T]he only use of the wires alleged in *Johnson* to prove the predicate wire fraud crimes were the very wire transfers that allegedly involved "criminally derived property" under the money laundering statute. In Kennedy's case, in contrast, the government alleged many *prior* mailings to prove the predicate mail fraud crimes, which occurred before the monetary transactions that formed the basis of his money laundering counts. Thus, unlike in *Johnson*, the illegal mailings in this case involved discrete, earlier mailings by Kennedy, rather than the receipt of funds by Kennedy from his victims. It was the subsequent and distinct transfers of funds that were alleged as the separate transactions involving "proceeds of specified unlawful activity" which constituted the alleged money laundering under §1956.

> This factual difference is important because Congress clearly intended the money laundering statutes to punish new conduct that occurs after the completion of certain criminal activity, rather than simply to create an additional punishment for that criminal activity. The "completion" of both wire and mail fraud occurs when any wiring or mailing is used in execution of a scheme; there is no requirement that the scheme actually defraud a victim into investing money for the crime to be complete. Thus, because the money deposits in Kennedy's case occurred after other mailings had already completed the predicate mail fraud crime, those transfers properly could be construed as new transactions involving the proceeds of mail fraud. In contrast, because the specific wire fraud violations alleged in *Johnson* were not complete until the wires were used to transfer the funds, those transfers could not be construed as new transactions to support a money laundering offense. Accordingly, we reject Kennedy's contention that his money laundering convictions must be set aside for failure to allege the "proceeds" element of those crimes.

Is this distinction persuasive? Why or why not?

c. Commingling

Under § 1956, the government must prove that the financial transaction involved the "proceeds" of the specified unlawful activity. Under § 1957, the government must prove that the monetary transaction was "derived" from the unlawful activity. How does the government meet its burden of proof when "clean" money has been mixed or "commingled" with "dirty" money? Under § 1956, courts generally hold that, where clean and dirty money have been commingled, the government need not prove that the financial transaction specifically derived from the dirty money. Courts are split on this issue, however, under § 1957. As you read the next case, consider which approach should be followed on this issue under § 1957.

United States v. Rutgard

116 F.3d 1270 (9th Cir. 1997)

NOONAN, CIRCUIT JUDGE.

Jeffrey Jay Rutgard appeals his conviction of numerous counts of mail fraud on, and false claims to, Medicare, of counts of mail fraud on other insurers, and of transactions in money derived from the frauds. He appeals as well a judgment of forfeiture. . . .

This case . . . has required this court to determine whether proof of particular examples of fraud in billing insurers establishes that the [defendant's medical] practice is, as a whole, a scheme to defraud. It has required us to decide whether 18 U.S.C. § 1957, the statute forbidding certain bank transfers, is violated if the transfers involve commingled criminal and innocent funds. . . .

Dr. Rutgard, the defendant, was born in Chicago, Illinois, in 1951. His father was a physician. He attended the College of Medicine of the University of Illinois. He also enrolled in the university's graduate school where he was a James Scholar. On the basis of his proficiency in these schools he skipped internship and moved directly to a three-year residency in ophthalmology at the Medical School of the University of Iowa. In 1981 he came from this residency to practice in San Diego, California. . . .

In 1982, he secured his own medical practice. . . . His practice flourished. He kept an extraordinary schedule of working 61/2 days per week, 16 hours a day, with trips to medical meetings but without vacations. He also made a great deal of money. From 1988 through May, 1992 he received from Medicare (80% of his practice) over $151/2 million. . . .

[At trial, the government argued that the defendant defrauded Medicare by (a) making false diagnoses, (b) performing unnecessary procedures, and (c) falsely describing the procedures that he performed. The jury found Rutgard guilty of 132 counts of fraud. The Ninth Circuit reversed 23 of the 132 counts of fraud on the grounds of insufficient evidence, and found sufficient evidence to support the remaining counts.]

[The court then turned to the issue whether there was sufficient evidence to show that Rutgard's entire medical practice was a fraud. The government attempted to prove this theory to support its argument that all the monetary transactions at issue were illegally-derived. Because a large part of Rutgard's practice did not involve defrauding insurers, the court rejected the government's argument that the entire medical practice was a fraud. The court then turned its attention to the specific charges under § 1957.]

The Monetary Transactions Count. In May, 1992, [defendant's wife] Linda, at his direction, made two wire transfers to the National Westminster Bank on the Isle of Man, one of $5,629,220.74 on May 5 and one of $1,935,220.48 on May 6. The transfers were made from the Rutgard Family Trust, whose accounts were at the Imperial Trust Company in San Diego.

The government's accounting expert noted $15.8 million paid by Medicare to Rutgard between the beginning of 1988 and April, 1992. He testified that Rutgard deposited $3,754,056 derived from these entities into the family trust account during this period and deposited $1.9 million in municipal bonds so that a total of $5,654,056 entered this account from October 29, 1990, when Rutgard opened the account with a personal check for $560,000, to May, 1992. He testified that the balance of the account came from municipal bonds delivered to the trust account at unspecified times. On appeal the government argues that the jury could take into account the first year, 1987, when insurance fraud began, and come to the conclusion that the entire amount transferred by wire transfers on May 5 and 6 was the proceeds of insurance fraud.

To prove this contention the government advanced the theory that all of Rutgard's practice was a fraud. If the government had succeeded in this proof, it would have properly convicted him of the monetary transaction counts. But we have just determined that the government's proof was deficient. The government, as we have also held, established Rutgard's guilt of particular counts of fraud. The proceeds of that fraud come to over $46,000. Can the convictions under § 1957 be sustained on the theory that at least $20,000 of fruits of fraud were incorporated in the wire transfers of May 6 and 7? To answer that question requires a consideration of the terms and purpose of § 1957 and a close look at the companion statute, § 1956.

These statutes govern monetary transactions in criminally derived property. The standard money laundering statute is 18 U.S.C. § 1956. The other statute, the one under which Rutgard was convicted, is 18 U.S.C. § 1957. In construing § 1956, we referred to § 1957 as "a companion money laundering statute," *United States v. Garcia*, 37 F.3d 1359, 1365 (9th Cir. 1994), without having occasion to mark the differences between the two. We now have occasion to mark those differences.

Section 1956, alone at issue in *Garcia*, bears the title "Laundering of monetary instruments." It punishes by imprisonment of up to 20 years and a fine a defendant who:

knowing that the property involved in a financial transaction represents the proceeds of some form of unlawful activity, conducts or attempts to conduct such a financial transaction which in fact involves the proceeds of specified unlawful activity—

(A) (i) with the intent to promote the carrying on of specified unlawful activity; or

(ii) with intent to engage in conduct constituting a violation of section 7201 or 7206 of the Internal Revenue Code of 1986; or

(B) knowing that the transaction is designed in whole or in part—

(i) to conceal or disguise the nature, the location, the source, the ownership, or the control of the proceeds of specified unlawful activity; or

(ii) to avoid a transaction reporting requirement under State or Federal law.

18 U.S.C. § 1956(a)(1). For present purposes, five elements of § 1956 differentiate it from § 1957, the statute at issue here—its title, its requirement of intent, its broad reference to "the property involved," its satisfaction by a transaction that "in part" accomplishes the design, and its requirement that the intent be to commit another crime or to hide the fruits of a crime already committed.

Section 1957 has a different heading: "Engaging in monetary transactions in property derived from specified unlawful activity." It punishes by up to ten years' imprisonment and a fine anyone who:

knowingly engages or attempts to engage in a monetary transaction in criminally derived property that is of a value greater than $10,000 and is derived from specified unlawful activity.

18 U.S.C. § 1957(a). The description of the crime does not speak to the attempt to cleanse dirty money by putting it in a clean form and so disguising it. This statute applies to the most open, above-board transaction. *See* 18 U.S.C. § 1957(f)(1) (broadly defining "monetary transaction"). The intent to commit a crime or the design of concealing criminal fruits is eliminated. These differences make violation of § 1957 easier to prove. But also eliminated are references to "the property involved" and the satisfaction of the statute by a design that "in part" accomplishes the intended result. These differences indicate that proof of violation of § 1957 may be more difficult.

Section 1957 could apply to any transaction by a criminal with his bank. Two years after its enactment an amendment was necessary to provide that the term "monetary transaction" does not include "any transaction necessary to preserve a person's right to representation as guaranteed by the sixth amendment to the Constitution." Pub. L. 100-690, § 6182, 102 Stat. 4181, 4354 (1988). Without the amendment a drug dealer's check to his lawyer might have constituted a new federal felony.

Section 1957 was enacted as a tool in the war against drugs. It is a powerful tool because it makes any dealing with a bank potentially a trap for the drug dealer or any other defendant who has a hoard of criminal cash derived from the specified crimes. If he makes a "deposit, withdrawal, transfer or exchange" with this cash, he commits the crime; he's forced to commit another felony if he wants to use a bank. This draconian law, so powerful by its elimination of criminal intent, freezes the proceeds of specific crimes out of the banking system. As long as the underlying crime has been completed and the defendant "possesses" the funds at the time of deposit, the proceeds cannot enter the banking system without a new crime being committed. A type of regulatory crime has been created where criminal intent is not an element. *See Morissette v. United States*, 342 U.S. 246, 252–56 (1952). Such a powerful instrument of criminal justice should not be expanded by judicial invention or ingenuity. We "should not enlarge the reach of enacted crimes by constituting them from anything less than the incriminating components contemplated by the words used in the statute." *Id.* at 263.

For these reasons we do not find helpful in interpreting § 1957 the cases applying § 1956, which speaks of design "in whole or in part" and of "a financial transaction involving property." Other circuits, however, have used the § 1956 precedents to eliminate any tracing of funds in a § 1957 case. *See United States v. Moore*, 27 F.3d 969, 976–77 (4th Cir. 1994); *United States v. Johnson*, 971 F.2d 562 (10th Cir. 1992). They have reasoned that otherwise § 1957 could be defeated by a criminal mingling innocently-obtained funds with his ill-gotten moneys.

This reasoning rests on the fungibility of money in a bank. That fungibility, destroying the specific identity of any particular funds, makes the commingling of innocent funds with criminal funds an obvious way to hide the criminal funds. If § 1956 required tracing of specific funds, it could be wholly frustrated by commingling. For that reason, the statute not only proscribes any transaction whose purpose is to hide criminal funds but reaches any funds "involved" in the transaction. Neither the same reasoning nor the same language is present in § 1957, the statute here applied.

The monetary transaction statute cannot be made wholly ineffective by commingling. To prevail, the government need show only a single $10,000 deposit of criminally-derived proceeds. Any innocent money already in the account, or later deposited, cannot wipe out the crime committed by the deposit of criminally-derived proceeds. Commingling with innocent funds can defeat application of the statute to a withdrawal of less than the total funds in the account, but ordinarily that fact presents no problem to the government which, if it has proof of a deposit of $10,000 of criminally-derived funds, can succeed by charging the deposit as the crime; or the government may prevail by showing that all the funds in the account are the proceeds of crime. Commingling will frustrate the statute if criminal deposits have been kept under $10,000. But that is the way the statute is written, to catch only large transfers. Moreover, if the criminal intent was to hide criminal proceeds, as would presumably be the case any time criminally derived cash was deposited with innocently derived funds to hide its identity, § 1956 can kick in and the depositor of amounts under $10,000 will be guilty of a § 1956 crime.

The government did not take its possible course of charging Rutgard with deposits of over $10,000 of fraudulent proceeds. The government had the means of doing so because its accounting expert identified the large deposits Rutgard made. But as Rutgard was neither charged nor convicted of deposits in violation of § 1957, we cannot uphold his convictions on that basis.

Rutgard's convictions may be upheld if he transferred out of the account all the funds that were in it or if there was a rule or presumption that, once criminally-derived funds were deposited, any transfer from the account would be presumed to involve them for the purpose of applying § 1957. Rutgard did not transfer all the funds in the family trust account, however. The government showed that the account held $8.5 million on April 2, 1992 and $13,901 on July 2, 1992, the dates of the quarterly bank statements. But so far as evidence at trial goes, more than $46,000 remained in the account after the May 5 and 6 transfers. These transfers therefore did not necessarily transfer the $46,000 of fraudulent proceeds.

The alternative way of sustaining the convictions depends on a presumption, which the Fourth Circuit created in *Moore*, 27 F.3d at 976–77, but which we decline to create. The statute does not create a presumption that any transfer of cash in an account tainted by the presence of a small amount of fraudulent proceeds must be a transfer of these proceeds. Unlike § 1956, § 1957 does not cover any funds "involved." To create such a presumption in order to sustain a conviction under § 1957 would be to multiply many times the power of that draconian law. It would be an essay in judicial lawmaking, not an application of the statute. As the government did not prove that any fraudulently-derived proceeds left the account on May 5 or May 6, 1992, the monetary transfer counts, Counts 216 and 217, were not proved beyond a reasonable doubt.

Notes and Questions

1. *The circuit split.* The majority of circuits have declined to require the government to prove that financial transactions using commingled funds under § 1957 specifically involved the illegally derived portion of the funds. In *United States v. Johnson*, 971 F.2d 562 (10th Cir. 1992), discussed above, for example, the defendant had commingled dirty and clean money in his bank account. Of the $5.5 million he had deposited into his account, only about half could be traced to the illegal activity. The defendant was charged under § 1957 based upon a $1.8 million withdrawal from the account, all of which was not necessarily from dirty money. The Tenth Circuit affirmed the conviction, holding that to require the government to trace the transaction to dirty money would defeat the purpose of § 1957. *Id.* at 570.

In rejecting the *Johnson* approach, the court in *Rutgard* relied heavily upon the differences between § 1956 and § 1957. Is the court's reasoning persuasive? Was the court's description of § 1957 as "draconian" fair? Why or why not?

2. *The government's theory.* The court in *Rutgard* also stated that the government used the wrong money laundering theory in this case. Would other, viable theories of money laundering have been available to the government in this case?

3. *Section 1956. Rutgard* was prosecuted under § 1957. Could commingling raise challenges for tracing and proof in § 1956 cases? *See United States v. Colon*, 919 F.3d 510 (7th Cir. 2019) (requiring government to show that each deposit at issue in § 1956 case involved some illegal proceeds, but not requiring government to show how much or from which specific illegal transaction the proceeds derived).

4. *Forfeiture.* Issues of commingled funds also arise in forfeiture. As mentioned above, forfeiture is one of the penalties for money laundering. When legitimate and illegitimate funds have been commingled into a single account, what portions of the account should be subject to forfeiture? How does the answer interact with the rules for determining whether transactions using commingled accounts involved the legitimate or illegitimate funds?

Problem

13-11. The following evidence was adduced at Harris's trial for money laundering:

Three years ago, Harris offered to lend $160,000 to his friends Carey and Bourne, to buy a parcel of land. Carey and Bourne accepted Harris's offer and, after executing a mortgage to secure the loan, Harris gave them the loan proceeds in cash. There was testimony that, when later discussing the loan with a friend, Harris stated that the reason he wanted to lend the money was to "get some of his money more legal." Over the next several years, Harris deposited 46 repayment checks from Carey and Bourne into Harris's personal bank account.

When Carey and Bourne asked Harris where he got the money for the loans, Harris told them that he got most of it from an inheritance from his father. But there was evidence that Harris's father had intentionally omitted him from his will and that Harris did not receive anything from his father's estate. There is also evidence that Harris engaged in narcotics trafficking activities in the two months preceding the loan, generating approximately $180,000 in gross receipts that he placed in his personal bank account. Harris paid $50,000 cash for the narcotics. Harris used three dealers, to whom he paid 30% of the sale price in cash, to sell the narcotics. The money that Harris lent out was obtained from Harris's personal bank account. Immediately before Harris made the loan, his account had a balance of approximately $700,000, which consisted of the narcotics trafficking gross proceeds and income that Harris had legitimately earned over the years as a real-estate developer.

Harris was convicted of conspiracy to distribute narcotics and of 46 counts of concealment money laundering under § 1956(a)(1)(B)(i) based upon the deposits of the loan repayment checks.

On appeal, Harris argues that there was insufficient evidence that (a) he acted with knowledge of a design to conceal, and (b) the checks represented "proceeds" of specified unlawful activity. How should the court rule? Why?

D. The USA PATRIOT Act

The USA PATRIOT Act of 2001, Pub. L. No. 107-56, strengthened the government's ability to combat terrorism in several important ways, including the implementation of "more stringent anti-money laundering statutes and regulations." Michael Shapiro, *The USA PATRIOT ACT and Money Laundering*, 123 BANKING L.J. 629, 629 (July/Aug. 2006). Title III of the PATRIOT Act, entitled the International Money Laundering Abatement and Anti-Terrorist Financing Act of 2001, amended the main laws used to combat money laundering: the Bank Secrecy Act ("BSA") of 1970 and the Money Laundering Control Act of 1986 (codified as 18 U.S.C. §1956 and 18 U.S.C. §1957). *Id.* at 630.

Section 1956 was amended in the PATRIOT Act to include foreign corruption offenses, Pub. L. No. 107-56, §315, long-arm jurisdiction over foreign money launderers, §317, and offenses for laundering money through a foreign bank, §318. In addition, the USA PATRIOT Improvement and Reauthorization Act of 2005 ("PATRIOT II"), Pub. L. No. 109-177, added the following to §1956(a)(1): "For purposes of this paragraph, a financial transaction shall be considered to be one involving the proceeds of specified unlawful activity if it is part of a set of parallel or dependent transactions, any one of which involves the proceeds of specified unlawful activity, and all of which are part of a single plan or arrangement." Pub. L. No. 109-177, §405.

The BSA's recordkeeping and reporting requirements, including Currency Transaction Reports (CTRs) and Suspicious Activity Reports (SARs), already put domestic banks at the forefront of anti-money laundering enforcement. Shapiro, 123 BANKING L.J. at 631. The PATRIOT Act expanded those requirements by mandating that each bank, at the minimum, designate a compliance officer, develop internal anti-money laundering controls, provide periodic training, and go through independent audits of their controls. Pub. L. No. 107-56, §352. The PATRIOT Act does allow individual banks some flexibility to adjust their anti-money laundering programs depending on the size, location, and overall nature of the bank's business. §311. However, all banks must have a Customer Identification Program and periodically check their customer lists with the government's lists of known or suspected terrorists, as well as other Treasury Department lists. Shapiro, 123 BANKING L.J. at 633. With increased responsibilities under the PATRIOT Act, banks now shoulder even more of the burden for tracking money laundering activities than in the past:

> With the events of 9/11 the personification of the money launderer changed from drug dealer to terrorist. Despite enormous additional costs necessitated by myriad new laws and regulations, U.S. banks have, for the most part, risen to the additional burdens placed on them. With the new and complex rules comes the need for better and increased compliance, supervision and advice, both internal and external if banks are to navigate successfully the legal and regulatory shoals and shallows created post-9/11.

Id. at 635–636. In addition, the National Commission on Terrorist Attacks (known as the "9/11 Commission") issued a report that focuses on the close connection between international terrorism and money laundering. Specifically, the Commission addressed the use of laundered money to finance international terrorist efforts. For a discussion of the Commission's findings, see Paul Fagyal, Comment, *The Anti-Money Laundering Provisions of the Patriot Act: Should They Be Allowed to Sunset?*, 50 St. Louis U.L.J. 1361 (2006).

E. Attorney-Client Issues

1. Cash Transaction Reporting by Attorneys

Although the criminal defense bar lobbied for an exemption to the currency transaction reporting requirements imposed on trades and businesses, Congress did not exempt attorneys from those requirements. Because attorneys are engaged in a trade or business as that term is contemplated by 26 U.S.C. § 6050I, they must complete a Form 8300 when accepting cash from their clients and prospective clients. Virtually any exchange of money between a client and attorney constitutes a financial transaction and is subject to the reporting requirements if it exceeds $10,000.

For the criminal defense bar, this law has obvious and serious implications. First, the transaction may subject the attorney to money laundering liability if the money is derived from specified unlawful activity. Second, as discussed above, there are criminal penalties for failing to file a Form 8300, for filing a false Form 8300, or for structuring transactions to avoid filing the form. Finally, the reporting requirements have the potential to affect the attorney-client relationship in profound ways. *See generally* 2 Joel M. Androphy, White Collar Crime § 10:26 (2d ed. 2001 & Supp. 2012); Ellen Podgor, *Form 8300: The Demise of Law as a Profession*, Geo. J. Legal Ethics 485 (1992).

2. Attorney-Client Privilege Issues

The general rule is that information relating to client identity and fees is not covered by the attorney-client privilege. That privilege is designed to protect confidential information that a client conveys to the attorney in order to obtain legal advice. In most cases, information about client identity and fees does not relate to legal advice. Courts therefore hold that identity and fee information does not fall within the privilege's purpose.

Courts have identified three specific circumstances, however, in which the attorney-client privilege may protect against the disclosure of client fee and identity information. This may occur where the disclosure would:

1. Implicate the client in the very matter for which the client retained counsel (the "legal advice" exception);

2. Incriminate the client by providing the last piece of evidence needed to convict the client (the "last linkage" exception); or

3. Reveal the nature of a confidential client-attorney communication (the "confidential communication" exception).

The "legal advice" exception is the broadest exception, and the one most favorable to defendants and potential defendants. The last two exceptions apply in relatively few circumstances. Also, these exceptions sometimes overlap and, as seen in the case and notes below, are not always clearly defined.

In the next case, the government and a law firm engaged in what has become an all-too-common battle over the disclosure of client information. The government issued a subpoena to the law firm and claimed that the subpoena really was directed at obtaining information from the law firm about the law firm — a claim the court labeled as a pretext for gaining information about the firm's client. Because the government did not follow the rules for subpoenaing information from the firm's client, this characterization was critical to the outcome of the case on appeal. As you read the case, focus upon the competing policy concerns underlying the ongoing battle between the government and the criminal defense bar.

United States v. Gertner

873 F. Supp. 729 (W.D. Mass. 1995), *aff'd on other grounds,*
65 F.3d 963 (1st Cir. 1995)

Brody, District Judge.

This case presents an issue of first impression in this Circuit, namely, whether the Internal Revenue Service may require an attorney to disclose the identity of a client from whom the attorney received more than $10,000 in cash without violating the client's constitutional rights, the attorney-client privilege, or the attorney's ethical duty to keep client secrets confidential. The Court concludes that, under the special circumstances presented in this case, the information demanded by the IRS is privileged and need not be disclosed.

In 1981, according to Congressional estimates, underreported income in the United States resulted in an estimated $55 billion in lost tax revenues. *United States v. Goldberger & Dubin, P.C.,* 935 F.2d 501, 505 (2d Cir. 1991). Congress also determined that an additional $9 billion in lost tax revenue resulted from unreported income connected with illegal activities. *Id.* In response, Congress enacted 26 U.S.C. § 6050I, which provided the Internal Revenue Service (IRS) with means to identify taxpayers with large cash incomes. Specifically, the legislation requires "any person . . . engaged in a trade or business" to report any cash transaction that exceeds $10,000. 26 U.S.C. § 6050I. The provision also requires the disclosure of information such as: the name, address, and tax identification number of the person from whom the cash was received; and the date and nature of the transaction. *Id.*

The disclosure required by § 6050I is made on a form prepared by the IRS known as "Form 8300." The IRS states, in the directions to Form 8300, that: "Often smugglers and drug dealers use large cash payments to launder money from illegal activities . . . [thus] compliance with the law provides valuable information that can stop those who evade taxes and those who profit from the drug trade and other illegal activities." Samuel J. Rabin, Jr., *A Survey of the Statute and Caselaw Pertaining to 26 U.S.C. § 6050I*, 68 FLA. BAR J. 26 (1994) (quoting Form 8300).

Nancy Gertner and Jody Newman, attorneys at the law firm of Dwyer, Collora & Gertner, represent an unidentified client, referred to in this proceeding as John Doe. Doe was charged in a narcotics case "relating to years prior to 1991 and 1992" and "there are still pending criminal charges against [him]."

From June 1991 to April 1992, Doe paid Gertner and Newman in four cash transactions of $25,000, $17,260, $15,000, and $25,000. Gertner and Newman reported the transactions to the IRS on four separate Forms 8300 dated June 25, 1991; August 5, 1991; November 14, 1991; and April 30, 1992; respectively. Respondents refused, however, to include any identifying information about Doe or the nature of the transaction. Respondents included with the forms, a statement explaining that "the information requested violates the attorney client privilege, conflicts with the broader ethical obligation of an attorney[,] . . . and violates the First, Fifth, and Sixth Amendment rights of attorneys and their clients."

A series of letters between the IRS and Respondents ensued. Respondents informed the IRS, among other things, that there were criminal charges pending against Doe and that Respondents were currently representing him in those proceedings. Nevertheless, the IRS issued summonses demanding that Respondents appear on February 22 and 24, 1993 accompanied by certain records and other information. In part, the IRS sought the complete name, address, business or occupation, social security or taxpayer identification number, passport number, alien registration number and any other identifying data for the client involved in each of the transactions. Neither Respondent appeared as directed by the summonses.

On March 16, 1994, Respondents sought guidance from the Massachusetts Bar Association Committee on Professional Ethics. The Committee responded citing Disciplinary Rule 4-101 which provides that "a lawyer shall not knowingly . . . reveal a confidence or secret of his client" unless the client consents; the disclosure is permitted under the Disciplinary Rules; or the disclosure is "required by law or court order." The opinion concluded:

> Given your client's refusal to consent to disclosure, the Committee believes that, if you have any doubt about the lawfulness of Section 6050(I)'s disclosure obligations as they impinge on your obligations under DR 4-101, you should continue to resist disclosure of the client's identity, and require [the Government] to obtain a court order mandating disclosure.

Id. Both Respondents have continually refused to provide the information requested by the summonses.

The Government filed a Petition to Enforce the IRS Summonses in this Court on March 28, 1994. In support of its Petition, the Government provided the affidavit of Sophia Ameno, an Internal Revenue Agent. Ameno asserted that she was investigating "the compliance by the law firm with Section 6050I of the Code, and its potential liability under Section 6721 through 6723 of the Code." She also alleged that the information sought by the summonses was relevant and not already in the IRS's possession. Finally, she averred that the appropriate administrative procedures had been followed. This Court concluded that the Government, through the Ameno affidavit, made the prima facie showing of good faith required by *United States v. Powell*, 379 U.S. 48, 57–58 (1964). Accordingly, the Court issued an Order directing Respondents to show cause why the summonses should not be enforced.

Subsequently, the Court granted a Motion on the part of the unidentified client, John Doe, to intervene in the proceeding. The matter has now been thoroughly briefed and argued, including *amici curiae* appearances by the Boston Bar Association, the Massachusetts Association of Criminal Defense Lawyers, and the Massachusetts Bar Association. . . .

Respondents and *amici* argue that § 6050I, when applied to attorneys, violates the First, Fifth, and Sixth Amendments of the United States Constitution. They also argue that the disclosures required by § 6050I are protected by the doctrine of attorney-client privilege and that compliance with § 6050I would violate their ethical obligations, pursuant to Massachusetts Disciplinary Rule 4-101, to keep client secrets confidential. Finally, they argue that the summonses are void and unenforceable because the Government failed to provide the procedural protections required for issuing a "John Doe" summons under § 7609 of the Code.

A. Procedure Followed by Government

The Court first addresses Respondents' argument that the Government failed to comply with the procedural requirements of § 7609(f) of the Internal Revenue Code. Section 7609 governs summonses served, not on the taxpayer personally, but rather on third-party recordkeepers, such as banks, accountants, brokers, and attorneys. A summons served on a third-party recordkeeper may or may not "identify the person with respect to whose liability the summons is issued." 26 U.S.C. § 7609(f). A summons that does not identify the taxpayer under investigation is referred to as a "John Doe" summons. Advance notice to the unnamed taxpayer, by the Government, is generally impossible in these situations. In order to protect the interests of the unnamed taxpayer, therefore, Congress requires prior judicial approval for the issuance of John Doe summonses. No such prior judicial approval was either sought or obtained in this case. . . .

The Government argues that it was not required to obtain prior approval because the summonses in this case were not John Doe summonses. Instead, the Government asserts that the summonses in this case identified the taxpayer under investigation — the law firm. Agent Ameno, in her Affidavit, alleged that her investigation was intended "to ascertain the correctness of Forms 8300" filed by Gertner and Newman, and to determine "the liability, if any, of the law firm for penalties imposed by Sections 6721 through 6723 of the Code." Respondents argue, however, that the Government's assertion, that the law firm is the subject of its investigation, is "clearly pretextual." Respondents contend that the omissions on the Forms 8300 they filed are apparent on their face and that the identity of the client is immaterial to the firm's tax liability. The Court agrees with Respondents. The claim by the Government, that it is investigating the law firm is simply not credible. . . . Accordingly, the Court concludes that the Government's contention that it was investigating the law firm is pretextual and that the summonses were, in fact, John Doe summonses. . . .

B. Attorney-Client Privilege

Respondents argue that the disclosures required by § 6050I violate the attorney-client privilege whenever applied to attorneys in general, or, in the alternative, at least when applied to the facts of this case.

The individual asserting the attorney-client privilege has the burden of proving the existence of the privilege. In an action involving questions of federal law, the federal common law of privilege applies.

"It is well recognized in every circuit, . . . that the identity of an attorney's client and the source of payment for legal fees are not normally protected by the attorney-client privilege." *In re Grand Jury Subpoenas (Anderson)*, 906 F.2d 1485, 1488 (10th Cir. 1990). The Court is in agreement with this general rule, and therefore holds that a blanket rule exempting attorneys from complying with § 6050I would be inappropriate.

Despite its rejection of a bright-line test, the Court must nevertheless consider the specific facts presented by this case because it is clear that the identity of a client and the source of legal fees are privileged in certain special circumstances. The *Anderson* court identified the "three major exceptions" to the general rule as "the legal advice exception, the last link exception, and the confidential communication exception." *Anderson*, 906 F.2d at 1488. The Court need consider only the first of these, the legal advice exception.

Several courts, including the First Circuit, have recognized the legal advice exception. Under this exception, a client's identity or fee arrangement may be privileged "where there is a strong probability that disclosure would implicate the client in the very criminal activity for which legal advice was sought." *Anderson*, 906 F.2d at 1488. The legal advice exception is obviously very narrow and strongly fact-driven. The leading case applying this exception is *Baird v. Koerner*, 279 F.2d 623 (9th Cir. 1960). In *Baird*, the Ninth Circuit held that an attorney was not required to disclose the identity of a client when that client consulted him regarding improperly paid taxes and the attorney subsequently forwarded an anonymous check to the IRS on the client's behalf.

The First Circuit also considered this exception in *United States v. Strahl*, 590 F.2d 10 (1st Cir. 1978). In that case, the Government charged *Strahl* with stealing Treasury notes and counterfeiting. At trial, the Government introduced the testimony of Strahl's former attorney, who testified that Strahl gave him a stolen treasury note in partial payment for legal services. The *Strahl* court concluded that the legal advice exception did not apply because "there is no indication, either in the briefs or the record, that appellant Strahl went to [his former attorney] for legal advice concerning his counterfeiting activities." *Id.* at 12.

In this case, John Doe "has been charged in a narcotics case" and "there are still pending criminal charges against [him]." Those charges prompted Doe to seek representation from Respondents. The Court is convinced that there is a "strong probability" that disclosure of a large unexplained cash income could certainly be incriminating evidence in the pending narcotics prosecution. Therefore, given the facts of this case, the information demanded by the Government is privileged under the legal advice exception as articulated by the First Circuit in *Strahl*. The Court emphasizes the narrow scope of this fact-based holding. The decision to find the disclosures required by § 6050I privileged must be made on a case-by-case basis. The Court acknowledges that other courts have declined to hold that the disclosures required by § 6050I are privileged. *See United States v. Goldberger & Dubin, P.C.*, 935 F.2d 501, 505 (2d Cir. 1991); *United States v. Leventhal*, 961 F.2d 936, 940–41 (11th Cir. 1992); and *United States v. Ritchie*, 15 F.3d 592, 602 (6th Cir. 1994). Of these cases, a thorough analysis of this question can be found in the Second Circuit's decision in *United States v. Goldberger & Dubin, P.C.*, 935 F.2d 501, 505 (2d Cir. 1991). That court appears to have at least contemplated that the information required by § 6050I may be privileged under some circumstances. . . . [T]hat court suggested that a "direct linkage" between the disclosure and the incrimination of the client was required. This Court concludes that the disclosures required by the summonses in this case would provide such a "direct linkage." There is a strong probability that the disclosure would not only incriminate John Doe, but incriminate him in the very activity for which he sought legal advice. . . .

Determining that the information is privileged, however, does not end the inquiry. First, "[a] client, for whose benefit the attorney-client privilege exists, should not be permitted to claim the privilege, either directly or through his attorney, for the purpose of concealing his own ongoing or contemplated fraud." *Goldberger*, 935 F.2d at 506 (citations omitted). The Court does not find any evidence of an ongoing or contemplated fraud in this case. The fact that a large cash income may be incriminating on narcotics charges does not make that income an ongoing or contemplated fraud.

Next, a "privilege cannot stand in the face of countervailing law or strong public policy." *Goldberger*, 935 F.2d at 504 (citations omitted). The Second Circuit in *Goldberger* concluded that, even if the information were privileged, the privilege should not be applied because it "collides head on with a federal statute that implicitly precludes its application." *Id.* at 505. The *Goldberger* court reasoned that, because Congress did not exempt attorneys from the phrase "any person . . . engaged in a trade or business" in § 6050I, it intended the provision to override any applicable attorney-client privilege. *Id.* at 506.

This Court disagrees with the conclusion in *Goldberger*. As this Court has concluded above, the summonses in this case are "John Doe" summonses issued to a third-party recordkeeper, the law firm. Congress has specifically stated that, when attorneys are summoned to appear as third-party recordkeepers, they may raise the attorney-client privilege. *See* H.R. Rep. No. 658, 94th Cong., 2d Sess., at 666 (1976) ("where the summons is served on a person who is not the taxpayer (i.e., a third-party summons), the party summoned may challenge the summons for procedural defects . . . on [the] ground[s] of the attorney-client privilege (where applicable) and on other grounds. . . .").

The Court is also not persuaded that the application of the attorney-client privilege in this case would be contrary to public policy. Rather, there are competing public policy concerns, which in this instance, weigh in favor of applying the attorney-client privilege. First, the Court is mindful that this dilemma could have been avoided had Doe paid Respondents in some other manner. Unfortunately, he did not. Second, the Court recognizes that the IRS "has a legitimate interest in large or unusual financial transactions, especially those involving cash." *United States v. Ritchie*, 15 F.3d 592, 601 (6th Cir. 1994). Section 6050I may well be an important tool for the IRS to investigate cash transactions and to uncover tax evasion; and Congress undoubtedly has a legitimate interest in preventing revenue losses resulting from tax evasion. Third, some courts have further suggested that exempting attorneys from § 6050I's reporting requirements would "grant law firms a potential monopoly on money laundering simply because their services are personal and confidential." *Ritchie*, 15 F.3d at 601.

Notwithstanding these policy arguments, the Court is satisfied that the balance of policy concerns weigh in favor of applying the attorney-client privilege in this case. First, it is unlikely that applying the privilege in this case would give lawyers a "potential monopoly on money laundering." *Ritchie*, 15 F.3d at 601. Generally, lawyers would be required to report the identity of clients from whom they receive substantial cash payments. An attorney may only assert the attorney-client privilege when the IRS seeks disclosures regarding a client who is being represented on currently pending criminal charges and the disclosures are likely to incriminate the client in that very proceeding.

Under these circumstances, the attorney-client relationship becomes more than just "personal and confidential." *Ritchie*, 15 F.3d at 601. More than just lost tax revenues or the method of paying one's attorney is at stake. The attorney-client relationship, during a pending criminal prosecution, implicates bedrock constitutional protections such as the right against self-incrimination and the right to be represented by counsel of one's choice. While the Court does not consider the constitutionality of § 6050I, these fundamental precepts must not be ignored when deciding how public policy impacts the application of the attorney-client privilege. Each factual scenario should be considered separately and the policy issues weighed by the Court on a case-by-case basis. Courts could require attorneys refusing to disclose information required by § 6050I to make an in camera showing that their clients are in fact the subject of pending charges which could be substantiated by the § 6050I disclosures. On balance, the Court is satisfied that, given the specific facts of this case, neither the plain language of § 6050I nor public policy weigh against the application of the attorney-client privilege. Accordingly, the Court finds that the disclosures requested by the IRS summonses are privileged. . . .

Notes and Questions

1. *The attorney-client privilege.* As noted above, there are three exceptions to the general rule that client fee and identity information is not protected by the attorney-client privilege. Which of these exceptions did the court adopt in *Gertner*? *Gertner* is the rare case in which the court found the information to be protected; in most cases, courts require that the attorney disclose client identity and fee information. *See, e.g., Lefcourt v. United States,* 125 F.3d 79 (2d Cir. 1997).

2. *The policy debate.* What is the policy tension underlying the decision in *Gertner*? What is the difference between the analysis in *Gertner* and that in *Goldberger,* 935 F.2d at 504–505, as discussed in *Gertner*? How did the policy tension inform the outcomes in those cases? Which decision is more persuasive? Is it fair or appropriate for the government to seek evidence in a criminal case from the defendant's or potential defendant's attorney? Conversely, what dangers might arise if attorneys were exempted from the currency transaction reporting requirement?

3. *The John Doe summons.* The district court found that the summonses were not valid because the government had not followed the required procedures. What was the government's mistake? How did the government attempt to justify its approach? Was its justification plausible? On appeal, the First Circuit thought not, and affirmed the district court's decision on this ground alone; the court therefore did not reach the attorney-client privilege issue. A defendant in this case, Nancy Gertner, went on to become a federal judge for the United States District Court for Massachusetts.

4. *Challenges for defense attorneys.* If you were a criminal defense attorney in the position of the attorneys in these cases, how would you advise a client who wanted to pay you more than $10,000 in cash? If the client offered to make a number of payments in amounts under $10,000, how would you respond? Why?

5. *Lawyers as gatekeepers.* The nature of an attorney's job often means that a lawyer will unwittingly, or in some cases wittingly, become ensnared in CTR or money laundering schemes.

In light of the materials in this chapter, what steps can attorneys take to avoid becoming part of a criminal scheme and subjecting themselves to possible criminal liability?

Problem

13-12. Over a two-year period, attorney Susan received four cash payments totaling over $100,000 from her client John Doe and two cash payments of $20,000 each from her client Jane Doe for legal services rendered. The clients had retained Susan in connection with a pending criminal investigation into tax evasion. Susan had reason to believe that revelation of the payments to the government might provide the government with evidence in that investigation.

Susan reported each of these transactions on IRS Form 8300, but omitted any identifying information regarding the payors or the persons on whose behalf payments were made. In an attachment to each form, Susan stated that disclosure would "violate ethical duties owed said client, and constitutional and/or attorney-client privileges that the reporting attorney is entitled or required to invoke," and that the client had not authorized release of the information. These forms ask the reporting party to check a box if the payment is a "suspicious transaction." The instructions accompanying the form defined a suspicious transaction as "[a] transaction in which it appears that a person is attempting to cause this report not to be filed or a false or incomplete report to be filed; or where there is an indication of possible illegal activity." Susan left the box blank. After filing these forms, Susan was served with an IRS summons requesting the missing information.

The government has brought an enforcement action before the district court. How should the court rule? Why?

Chapter 14

RICO

A. Introductory Notes

1. History and Scope of the RICO Statute

The Racketeer Influenced and Corrupt Organizations ("RICO") statute, 18 U.S.C. §§ 1961–1968, applies to a broad range of white collar and non-white collar criminal cases, and to an even broader range of civil cases. RICO has long been considered a sort of "super-conspiracy" statute because it allows prosecutors to charge disparate participants and crimes, as well as multiple schemes, in a single case. *See* Gerald E. Lynch, *RICO: The Crime of Being a Criminal, Parts III & IV*, 87 COLUM. L. REV. 920, 949–55 (1988). The statute also provides for a broad range of severe criminal and civil sanctions. *See* Part 4, *infra*.

In basic terms, RICO is violated when: (1) a person commits repeated "predicate acts" constituting a "pattern of racketeering activity"; and (2) those acts involve an entity known as a RICO "enterprise" used in a manner the statute specifies. RICO is an unusual statute because it is based upon the commission of crimes—the "predicate acts"—defined elsewhere under federal and state law. Common predicate acts in white collar cases include the federal crimes of mail and wire fraud, securities fraud, obstruction of justice, bribery, extortion, and money laundering, as well as the state law crimes of bribery and extortion. For example, if a city councilperson uses the City Council District Office to engage in a scheme of bribery and honest services fraud over a period of time, then the government might charge the "Office" as the RICO "enterprise," the council member as the "person" who conducted the enterprise, and the instances of bribery and honest services fraud as the predicate acts. *See, e.g., United States v. Huizar*, First Superseding Indictment, CR 20-326(A) (C.D. Ca. Nov. 12, 2020).

As applied in the white collar context, RICO is controversial. Although some have argued that Congress intended the statute primarily to apply to organized crime cases, others assert that a RICO charge is entirely appropriate in a white collar case. *Compare* Gerard E. Lynch, *A Reply to Michael Goldsmith*, 88 COLUM. L. REV. 802, 802 (1988) (arguing that RICO has been used against legitimate businesses in ways Congress never intended), *with* Michael Goldsmith, *RICO and Enterprise Criminality: A Response to Gerard E. Lynch*, 88 COLUM. L. REV. 774, 776 (1988) (arguing that RICO is appropriately applied in a broad range of cases, including cases outside the organized crime context). Despite the controversy, courts have sanctioned the use of RICO in both the white collar crime context and in a broad range of civil cases brought by both private parties and by the government.

RICO is also controversial because it is used in many civil and criminal matters that traditionally would be left to state courts. As Justice Marshall noted in his dissent in *Sedima, S.P.R.L. v. Imrex Co.*, 473 U.S. 479, 501 (1985), the wide-ranging application of RICO has "quite simply revolutionize[d] private litigation" and "validate[d] the federalization of broad areas of state common law of frauds." The latter observation applies equally to criminal RICO cases.

Although the United States Supreme Court has consistently interpreted RICO in a broad manner, federal district courts and courts of appeals are often hostile to private civil RICO suits. As a result, the appeals court decisions enforce technical pleading rules designed to limit civil RICO actions; these rules, however, apply in both criminal and civil cases. Thus, as in other areas such as securities fraud, this chapter includes civil case holdings that also apply in the criminal context.

Partly because of the statute's complex pleading requirements, RICO seems to have come in and out of fashion with prosecutors over the years. For a period, the money laundering statutes seemed to supplant RICO as prosecutors' favored tool for fighting large-scale white collar criminal activity.[a] RICO, however, now has regained its prominent role in complex white collar cases. *See* John R. Mitchell et al., *Beyond the Mob: "Varsity Blues" and DOJ's Expanding Use of RICO to Prosecute White Collar Crime*, 34-FALL CRIM. JUST. 4 (2019). This has occurred for several reasons, including the statute's lengthy prison sentences and forfeiture provisions, as well as its usefulness in combining multiple criminal schemes and acts in a single case. Familiarity with the statute therefore remains essential for white collar criminal practice. In addition, RICO is widely used in complex civil litigation, and for that reason alone the statute merits close examination.

2. Statutory Elements

Section 1962 sets forth the requirements for proving a RICO case. Under this statute, the government must prove that:

(1) A RICO enterprise existed;

---

a. The Travel Act, 18 U.S.C. § 1952, is another statute that provides prosecutors with a tool for fighting large-scale criminal activity. Like RICO, the Travel Act is based on the intent to commit certain predicate acts. The Travel Act criminalizes the use of the mail or any facility in interstate or foreign commerce with the intent to promote such predicate acts. United States v. Welch, 327 F.3d 1081, 1092 (10th Cir. 2003) (explaining that the Travel Act does not make illegal the predicate act of bribery per se, but the "requisite intent to promote such unlawful activity").

(2) The defendant committed two or more predicate acts (the "racketeering activity");[b]

(3) The commission of the predicate acts constituted a "pattern" of racketeering activity;

(4) The defendant:

    (a) invested in or operated an enterprise with money obtained through a pattern of racketeering activity (18 U.S.C. § 1962(a));

    (b) acquired an interest in or maintained control over an enterprise through the pattern of racketeering activity (18 U.S.C. § 1962(b));

    (c) conducted the affairs of an enterprise through the pattern of racketeering activity (18 U.S.C. § 1962(c)); *or*

    (d) conspired to do any of (a)–(c) (18 U.S.C. § 1962(d)); and

(5) The racketeering activity affected interstate commerce, or the enterprise "engaged in . . . interstate or foreign commerce."

As shown above, § 1962 defines three different substantive crimes, as set forth in §§ 1962(a), 1962(b), and 1962(c), and criminalizes conspiring to commit any of those crimes under § 1962(d). Section 1962(c) is by far the most often-used substantive RICO section, and most of the cases discussed below were brought under that section. Congress has mandated that RICO "be liberally construed to effectuate its remedial purposes." Section 904 of Pub. L. 91-452.

3. Jurisdiction

The Supreme Court has broadly interpreted the statutory elements in a number of contexts, including the interstate commerce requirement. In *United States v. Robertson*, 514 U.S. 669 (1995), the Court held that the interstate commerce requirement was met under § 1962(a) where the defendant invested proceeds from narcotics offenses in the enterprise, an Alaskan gold mine. Applying the statutory language, the Court found that the mine produced, distributed, or acquired goods or services in interstate commerce. Under this reasoning, any business that acquires goods or services from or sells goods or services to another state is engaging in interstate commerce.

4. Criminal and Civil Sanctions

Criminal or civil liability under RICO leads to very severe consequences. Initially, a defendant stands to be labeled as a "racketeer," even if — as is often true — the case has nothing to do with organized crime. Further, each count of a RICO

---

b. Note that the government may allege predicate acts that would be barred by the statutes of limitations for those crimes, so long as the last predicate fell within RICO's five year statute of limitations.

conviction may lead to up to 20 years' imprisonment, fines, and forfeiture of the defendant's property.[c] 18 U.S.C. §§ 1963(a)–(b). In a civil case, a private plaintiff is entitled to treble damages and attorneys' fees, 18 U.S.C. § 1964(c), providing a strong incentive for a private plaintiff to assert a RICO claim whenever possible. The government may also bring a civil RICO suit and may obtain broad injunctive relief under the statute. 18 U.S.C. § 1964(b).

B. The Enterprise

1. The Nature of the Enterprise

Under § 1961(4), an "enterprise" includes "any individual, partnership, corporation, association, or other legal entity, and any union or group of individuals associated in fact although not a legal entity." A RICO enterprise thus may be a formal legal entity, such as a corporation, or an "association-in-fact." Considering that RICO was largely designed to ferret crime out of legitimate businesses, does an association that exists solely for criminal purposes qualify as a RICO "enterprise"? The Supreme Court addressed that issue in the case that follows.

United States v. Turkette
452 U.S. 576 (1981)

JUSTICE WHITE delivered the opinion of the Court.

The question in this case is whether the term "enterprise" as used in RICO encompasses both legitimate and illegitimate enterprises or is limited in application to the former. The Court of Appeals for the First Circuit held that Congress did not intend to include within the definition of "enterprise" those organizations which are exclusively criminal. This position is contrary to that adopted by every other Circuit that has addressed the issue. We granted certiorari to resolve this conflict.

Count Nine of a nine-count indictment charged respondent and 12 others with conspiracy to conduct and participate in the affairs of an enterprise engaged in interstate commerce through a pattern of racketeering activities, in violation of 18 U.S.C. § 1962(d). The indictment described the enterprise as "a group of individuals associated in fact for the purpose of illegally trafficking in narcotics and other dangerous drugs, committing arsons, utilizing the United States mails to defraud insurance companies, bribing and attempting to bribe local police officers, and corruptly influencing and attempting to corruptly influence the outcome of state court proceedings. . . ."

---

c. RICO's forfeiture provisions are discussed in Chapter 20, Forfeitures, *infra*. As always, the actual sentence imposed will depend upon the sentencing calculation under the U.S. Sentencing Guidelines. *See* Chapter 19, *infra*.

The other eight counts of the indictment charged the commission of various substantive criminal acts by those engaged in and associated with the criminal enterprise, including possession with intent to distribute and distribution of controlled substances, and several counts of insurance fraud by arson and other means. The common thread to all counts was respondent's alleged leadership of this criminal organization through which he orchestrated and participated in the commission of the various crimes delineated in the RICO count or charged in the eight preceding counts.

After a six-week jury trial, in which the evidence focused upon both the professional nature of this organization and the execution of a number of distinct criminal acts, respondent was convicted on all nine counts. He was sentenced to a term of 20 years on the substantive counts, as well as a two-year special parole term on the drug count. On the RICO conspiracy count he was sentenced to a 20-year concurrent term and fined $20,000.

On appeal, respondent argued that RICO was intended solely to protect legitimate business enterprises from infiltration by racketeers and that RICO does not make criminal the participation in an association which performs only illegal acts and which has not infiltrated or attempted to infiltrate a legitimate enterprise. The Court of Appeals agreed. We reverse.

In determining the scope of a statute, we look first to its language. . . .

Section 1962(c) makes it unlawful "for any person employed by or associated with any enterprise engaged in, or the activities of which affect, interstate or foreign commerce, to conduct or participate, directly or indirectly, in the conduct of such enterprise's affairs through a pattern of racketeering activity or collection of unlawful debt." The term "enterprise" is defined as including "any individual, partnership, corporation, association, or other legal entity, and any union or group of individuals associated in fact although not a legal entity." There is no restriction upon the associations embraced by the definition: an enterprise includes any union or group of individuals associated in fact. On its face, the definition appears to include both legitimate and illegitimate enterprises within its scope; it no more excludes criminal enterprises than it does legitimate ones. Had Congress not intended to reach criminal associations, it could easily have narrowed the sweep of the definition by inserting a single word, "legitimate." But it did nothing to indicate that an enterprise consisting of a group of individuals was not covered by RICO if the purpose of the enterprise was exclusively criminal. . . .

Section 1961(4) describes two categories of associations that come within the purview of the "enterprise" definition. The first encompasses organizations such as corporations and partnerships, and other "legal entities." The second covers "any union or group of individuals associated in fact although not a legal entity." The Court of Appeals assumed that the second category was merely a more general description of the first. Having made that assumption, the court concluded that the more generalized description in the second category should be limited by the specific examples enumerated in the first. But that assumption is untenable. Each category describes a separate type of enterprise to be covered by the statute — those that are recognized as legal entities and those that are not. The latter is not a more general description of the former. The second category itself not containing any specific enumeration that is followed by a general description, *ejusdem generis* has no bearing on the meaning to be attributed to that part of § 1961(4).

A second reason offered by the Court of Appeals in support of its judgment was that giving the definition of "enterprise" its ordinary meaning would create several internal inconsistencies in the Act. With respect to § 1962(c), it was said:

> If "a pattern of racketeering" can itself be an "enterprise" for purposes of section 1962(c), then the two phrases "employed by or associated with any enterprise" and "the conduct of such enterprise's affairs through [a pattern of racketeering activity]" add nothing to the meaning of the section. The words of the statute are coherent and logical only if they are read as applying to legitimate enterprises.

This conclusion is based on a faulty premise. That a wholly criminal enterprise comes within the ambit of the statute does not mean that a "pattern of racketeering activity" is an "enterprise." In order to secure a conviction under RICO, the Government must prove both the existence of an "enterprise" and the connected "pattern of racketeering activity." The enterprise is an entity, for present purposes a group of persons associated together for a common purpose of engaging in a course of conduct. The pattern of racketeering activity is, on the other hand, a series of criminal acts as defined by the statute. The former is proved by evidence of an ongoing organization, formal or informal, and by evidence that the various associates function as a continuing unit. The latter is proved by evidence of the requisite number of acts of racketeering committed by the participants in the enterprise. While the proof used to establish these separate elements may in particular cases coalesce, proof of one does not necessarily establish the other. The "enterprise" is not the "pattern of racketeering activity"; it is an entity separate and apart from the pattern of activity in which it engages. The existence of an enterprise at all times remains a separate element which must be proved by the Government.

Apart from § 1962(c)'s proscription against participating in an enterprise through a pattern of racketeering activities, RICO also proscribes the investment of income derived from racketeering activity in an enterprise engaged in or which affects interstate commerce as well as the acquisition of an interest in or control of any such enterprise through a pattern of racketeering activity. 18 U.S.C. §§ 1962(a) and (b). The Court of Appeals concluded that these provisions of RICO should be interpreted so as to apply only to legitimate enterprises. If these two sections are so limited, the Court of Appeals held that the proscription in § 1962(c), at issue here, must be similarly limited. Again, we do not accept the premise from which the Court of Appeals derived its conclusion. It is obvious that § 1962(a) and (b) address the infiltration by organized crime of legitimate businesses, but we cannot agree that these sections were not also aimed at preventing racketeers from investing or reinvesting in wholly illegal enterprises and from acquiring through a pattern of racketeering activity wholly illegitimate enterprises such as an illegal gambling business or a loan-sharking operation. There is no inconsistency or anomaly in recognizing that § 1962 applies to both legitimate and illegitimate enterprises. Certainly the language of the statute does not warrant the Court of Appeals' conclusion to the contrary. . . .

Finally, it is urged that the interpretation of RICO to include both legitimate and illegitimate enterprises will substantially alter the balance between federal and state enforcement of criminal law. This is particularly true, so the argument goes, since included within the definition of racketeering activity are a significant number of acts made criminal under state law. But even assuming that the more inclusive definition of enterprise will have the effect suggested, the language of the statute and its legislative history indicate that Congress was well aware that it was entering a new domain of federal involvement through the enactment of this measure. Indeed, the very purpose of the Organized Crime Control Act of 1970 was to enable the Federal Government to address a large and seemingly neglected problem. . . .

Contrary to the judgment below, neither the language nor structure of RICO limits its application to legitimate "enterprises." Applying it also to criminal organizations does not render any portion of the statute superfluous nor does it create any structural incongruities within the framework of the Act. The result is neither absurd nor surprising. On the contrary, insulating the wholly criminal enterprise from prosecution under RICO is the more incongruous position.

Section 904(a) of RICO, 84 Stat. 947, directs that "[t]he provisions of this Title shall be liberally construed to effectuate its remedial purposes." With or without this admonition, we could not agree with the Court of Appeals that illegitimate enterprises should be excluded from coverage. We are also quite sure that nothing in the legislative history of RICO requires a contrary conclusion.

[T]he construction of RICO suggested by respondent and the court below is unacceptable. Whole areas of organized criminal activity would be placed beyond the substantive reach of the enactment. For example, associations of persons engaged solely in "loan sharking, the theft and fencing of property, the importation and distribution of narcotics and other dangerous drugs," would be immune from prosecution under RICO so long as the association did not deviate from the criminal path. Yet these are among the very crimes that Congress specifically found to be typical of the crimes committed by persons involved in organized crime, and as a major source of revenue and power for such organizations. In view of the purposes and goals of the Act, as well as the language of the statute, we are unpersuaded that Congress nevertheless confined the reach of the law to only narrow aspects of organized crime, and, in particular, under RICO, *only* the infiltration of legitimate business.

This is not to gainsay that the legislative history forcefully supports the view that the major purpose of Title IX is to address the infiltration of legitimate business by organized crime. The point is made time and again during the debates and in the hearings before the House and Senate. But none of these statements requires the negative inference that Title IX did not reach the activities of enterprises organized and existing for criminal purposes.

On the contrary, these statements are in full accord with the proposition that RICO is equally applicable to a criminal enterprise that has no legitimate dimension or has yet to acquire one. Accepting that the primary purpose of RICO is to cope with the infiltration of legitimate businesses, applying the statute in accordance with its terms, so as to reach criminal enterprises, would seek to deal with the problem at its very source. Supporters of the bill recognized that organized crime uses its primary sources of revenue and power — illegal gambling, loan sharking and illicit drug distribution — as a springboard into the sphere of legitimate enterprise. . . .

As a measure to deal with the infiltration of legitimate businesses by organized crime, RICO was both preventive and remedial. Respondent's view would ignore the preventive function of the statute. If Congress had intended the more circumscribed approach espoused by the Court of Appeals, there would have been some positive sign that the law was not to reach organized criminal activities that give rise to the concerns about infiltration. The language of the statute, however — the most reliable evidence of its intent — reveals that Congress opted for a far broader definition of the word "enterprise," and we are unconvinced by anything in the legislative history that this definition should be given less than its full effect.

The judgment of the Court of Appeals is accordingly reversed.

Notes and Questions

1. *Formal and informal enterprises.* Under RICO, the term "enterprise" includes "any individual, partnership, corporation, association, or other legal entity, and any union or group of individuals associated in fact although not a legal entity." Most issues arise in connection with "association-in-fact" enterprises, which consist of individual persons and/or legal entities, such as corporations. Does this statutory definition provide clear guidance to prosecutors and potential defendants? Why or why not? Does the *Turkette* decision offer guidelines?

2. *Federalism.* The Court noted the concerns about federalism that had influenced the Court of Appeals. What was the Supreme Court's response? Does RICO pose serious issues of federalism? Why or why not?

In the case that follows, the defendants argued that a RICO enterprise must have an economic motive. As you read the case, identify the meaning and purpose of the enterprise requirement.[d]

---

d. A later decision in this litigation is discussed in Chapter 8, Extortion, *supra.*

National Organization for Women v. Scheidler

510 U.S. 249 (1994)

REHNQUIST, C.J., delivered the opinion for a unanimous Court.

We are required once again to interpret the provisions of the Racketeer Influenced and Corrupt Organizations (RICO) chapter of the Organized Crime Control Act of 1970 (OCCA), 18 U.S.C. §§ 1961–1968. Section 1962(c) prohibits any person associated with an enterprise from conducting its affairs through a pattern of racketeering activity. We granted certiorari to determine whether RICO requires proof that either the racketeering enterprise or the predicate acts of racketeering were motivated by an economic purpose. We hold that RICO requires no such economic motive. . . .

Petitioner National Organization For Women, Inc. (NOW), is a national non-profit organization that supports the legal availability of abortion; petitioners Delaware Women's Health Organization, Inc. (DWHO), and Summit Women's Health Organization, Inc. (SWHO), are health care centers that perform abortions and other medical procedures. Respondents are a coalition of antiabortion groups called the Pro-Life Action Network (PLAN), Joseph Scheidler and other individuals and organizations that oppose legal abortion, and a medical laboratory that formerly provided services to the two petitioner health care centers.

Petitioners sued respondents in the United States District Court for the Northern District of Illinois, alleging violations of RICO's §§ 1962(a), (c), and (d). According to respondent Scheidler's congressional testimony, these protesters aim to shut down the clinics and persuade women not to have abortions. Petitioners sought injunctive relief, along with treble damages, costs, and attorneys' fees. . . .

The amended complaint alleged that respondents were members of a nationwide conspiracy to shut down abortion clinics through a pattern of racketeering activity including extortion in violation of the Hobbs Act, 18 U.S.C. § 1951. . . . According to the amended complaint, PLAN constitutes the alleged racketeering "enterprise" for purposes of § 1962(c).

[The District Court] dismissed petitioners' RICO claims under § 1962(a) because the "income" alleged by petitioners consisted of voluntary donations from persons opposed to abortion which "in no way were derived from the pattern of racketeering alleged in the complaint." The District Court then concluded that petitioners failed to state a claim under § 1962(c) since "an economic motive requirement exists to the extent that some profit-generating purpose must be alleged in order to state a RICO claim." Finally, it dismissed petitioners' RICO conspiracy claim under § 1962(d) since petitioners' other RICO claims could not stand.

The Court of Appeals affirmed. . . .

Section 1962(c) makes it unlawful "for any person employed by or associated with any enterprise engaged in, or the activities of which affect, interstate or foreign commerce, to conduct or participate, directly or indirectly, in the conduct of such enterprise's affairs through a pattern of racketeering activity or collection of unlawful debt." Nowhere in either § 1962(c), or in the RICO definitions in § 1961, is there any indication that an economic motive is required.

The phrase "any enterprise engaged in, or the activities of which affect, interstate or foreign commerce" comes the closest of any language in subsection (c) to suggesting a need for an economic motive. . . .

We do not believe that the usage of the term "enterprise" in subsections (a) and (b) leads to the inference that an economic motive is required in subsection (c). The term "enterprise" in subsections (a) and (b) plays a different role in the structure of those subsections than it does in subsection (c). Section 1962(a) provides that it "shall be unlawful for any person who has received any income derived, directly or indirectly, from a pattern of racketeering activity . . . to use or invest, directly or indirectly, any part of such income, or the proceeds of such income, in acquisition of any interest in, or the establishment or operation of, any enterprise which is engaged in, or the activities of which affect, interstate or foreign commerce." Correspondingly, § 1962(b) states that it "shall be unlawful for any person through a pattern of racketeering activity or through collection of an unlawful debt to acquire or maintain, directly or indirectly, any interest in or control of any enterprise which is engaged in, or the activities of which affect, interstate or foreign commerce." The "enterprise" referred to in subsections (a) and (b) is thus something acquired through the use of illegal activities or by money obtained from illegal activities. The enterprise in these subsections is the victim of unlawful activity and may very well be a "profit-seeking" entity that represents a property interest and may be acquired. But the statutory language in subsections (a) and (b) does not mandate that the enterprise be a "profit-seeking" entity; it simply requires that the enterprise be an entity that was acquired through illegal activity or the money generated from illegal activity.

By contrast, the "enterprise" in subsection (c) connotes generally the vehicle through which the unlawful pattern of racketeering activity is committed, rather than the victim of that activity. Subsection (c) makes it unlawful for "any person employed by or associated with any enterprise . . . to conduct or participate . . . in the conduct of such enterprise's affairs through a pattern of racketeering activity. . . ." Consequently, since the enterprise in subsection (c) is not being acquired, it need not have a property interest that can be acquired nor an economic motive for engaging in illegal activity; it need only be an association in fact that engages in a pattern of racketeering activity. Nothing in subsections (a) and (b) directs us to a contrary conclusion. . . .

Respondents . . . overlook the fact that predicate acts, such as the alleged extortion, may not benefit the protestors financially but still may drain money from the economy by harming businesses such as the clinics which are petitioners in this case. . . .

Both parties rely on legislative history to support their positions. We believe the statutory language is unambiguous and find in the parties' submissions respecting legislative history no such "clearly expressed legislative intent to the contrary" that would warrant a different construction.

Respondents finally argue that the result here should be controlled by the rule of lenity in criminal cases. But the rule of lenity applies only when an ambiguity is present. We simply do not think there is an ambiguity here which would suffice to invoke the rule of lenity. . . .

We therefore hold that petitioners may maintain this action if respondents conducted the enterprise through a pattern of racketeering activity. The questions of whether the respondents committed the requisite predicate acts, and whether the commission of these acts fell into a pattern, are not before us.[e] We hold only that RICO contains no economic motive requirement.

The judgment of the Court of Appeals is accordingly reversed.

Notes and Questions

1. *The economic motive requirement.* What led the lower courts to apply an economic motive requirement to the enterprise element? Why did the Supreme Court reject that requirement? Is its reasoning persuasive? Is the result compelled by *Turkette*?

2. *The role of the enterprise.* According to the Court, what role does the enterprise play in a case brought under §1962(a), (b), or (c)? Put another way, can you identify, under each subsection, the reason why Congress required that an enterprise be proven under that specific subsection?

3. *Prosecutorial guidelines.* The United States Department of Justice requires that the Organized Crime and Racketeering Section of the DOJ's Criminal Division approve the initiation of any criminal RICO case or any civil RICO case brought by the government. https://www.justice.gov/jm/jm-9-110000-organized-crime-and -racketeering. The DOJ provides the following guidelines for determining whether to bring a criminal RICO charge:

> Except as hereafter provided, a government attorney should seek approval for a RICO charge only if one or more of the following requirements is present:
>
> 1. RICO is necessary to ensure that the indictment adequately reflects the nature and extent of the criminal conduct involved in a way that prosecution only on the underlying charges would not;

---

e. The Court subsequently held that the predicate acts of extortion were not proven on these facts, and dismissed the case. Scheidler v. National Organization for Women, 537 U.S. 393 (2003). *See* Chapter 8, Extortion, *supra.* — Eds.

2. A RICO prosecution would provide the basis for an appropriate sentence under all the circumstances of the case in a way that prosecution only on the underlying charges would not;

3. A RICO charge could combine related offenses which would otherwise have to be prosecuted separately in different jurisdictions;

4. RICO is necessary for a successful prosecution of the government's case against the defendant or a codefendant;

5. Use of RICO would provide a reasonable expectation of forfeiture which is proportionate to the underlying criminal conduct;

6. The case consists of violations of State law, but local law enforcement officials are unlikely or unable to successfully prosecute the case, in which the federal government has a significant interest;

7. The case consists of violations of State law, but involves prosecution of significant or government individuals, which may pose special problems for the local prosecutor.

The last two requirements reflect the principle that the prosecution of state crimes is primarily the responsibility of state authorities. RICO should be used to prosecute what are essentially violations of state law only if there is a compelling reason to do so.

Id. Why has the DOJ imposed these guidelines? Must courts defer to such guidelines? Why or why not? *See* Ellen S. Podgor, *Department of Justice Guidelines: Balancing "Discretionary Justice,"* 13 Cornell J.L. & Pub. Pol'y 167 (2004).

2. Proving an Association-in-Fact Enterprise

What proof is required to demonstrate an association-in-fact RICO enterprise? This question raises two related issues. First, must the association-in-fact enterprise have an ascertainable structure? Second, must the enterprise's structure be distinct from the structure necessary for the underlying racketeering activity? The Supreme Court addressed these issues in the case that follows.

Boyle v. United States
556 U.S. 938 (2009)

Justice Alito delivered the opinion of the Court.

We are asked in this case to decide whether an association-in-fact enterprise under the Racketeer Influenced and Corrupt Organizations Act (RICO), 18 U.S.C. § 1961 *et seq.*, must have "an ascertainable structure beyond that inherent in the pattern of racketeering activity in which it engages." We hold that such an enterprise must have a "structure" but that an instruction framed in this precise language is not necessary. The District Court properly instructed the jury in this case. We therefore affirm the judgment of the Court of Appeals.

The evidence at petitioner's trial was sufficient to prove the following: Petitioner and others participated in a series of bank thefts in New York, New Jersey, Ohio, and Wisconsin during the 1990's. The participants in these crimes included a core group, along with others who were recruited from time to time. . . .

The group was loosely and informally organized. It does not appear to have had a leader or hierarchy; nor does it appear that the participants ever formulated any long-term master plan or agreement. . . .

In instructing the jury on the meaning of a RICO "enterprise," the District Court relied largely on language in *United States v. Turkette,* 452 U.S. 576 (1981). The court told the jurors that, in order to establish the existence of such an enterprise, the Government had to prove that: "(1) There [was] an ongoing organization with some sort of framework, formal or informal, for carrying out its objectives; and (2) the various members and associates of the association function[ed] as a continuing unit to achieve a common purpose." Over petitioner's objection, the court also told the jury that it could "find an enterprise where an association of individuals, without structural hierarchy, form[ed] solely for the purpose of carrying out a pattern of racketeering acts" and that "[c]ommon sense suggests that the existence of an association-in-fact is oftentimes more readily proven by what it does, rather than by abstract analysis of its structure."

Petitioner requested an instruction that the Government was required to prove that the enterprise "had an ongoing organization, a core membership that functioned as a continuing unit, and an ascertainable structural hierarchy distinct from the charged predicate acts." The District Court refused to give that instruction.

Petitioner was convicted on 11 of the 12 counts against him, including the RICO counts, and was sentenced to 151 months' imprisonment. In a summary order, the Court of Appeals for the Second Circuit affirmed his conviction. . . . [W]e granted certiorari to resolve conflicts among the Courts of Appeals concerning the meaning of a RICO enterprise.

RICO makes it "unlawful for any person employed by or *associated with any enterprise* engaged in, or the activities of which affect, interstate or foreign commerce, to conduct or participate, directly or indirectly, in the conduct of such enterprise's affairs through a pattern of racketeering activity or collection of unlawful debt." 18 U.S.C. § 1962(c) (emphasis added).

The statute does not specifically define the outer boundaries of the "enterprise" concept but states that the term "includes any individual, partnership, corporation, association, or other legal entity, and any union or group of individuals associated in fact although not a legal entity." § 1961(4). This enumeration of included enterprises is obviously broad, encompassing "*any* . . . group of individuals associated in fact." The term "any" ensures that the definition has a wide reach, and the very concept of an association in fact is expansive. In addition, the RICO statute provides that its terms are to be "liberally construed to effectuate its remedial purposes."

In light of these statutory features, we explained in *Turkette* that "an enterprise includes any union or group of individuals associated in fact" and that RICO reaches "a group of persons associated together for a common purpose of engaging in a course of conduct." Such an enterprise, we said, "is proved by evidence of an ongoing organization, formal or informal, and by evidence that the various associates function as a continuing unit."

Notwithstanding these precedents, the dissent asserts that the definition of a RICO enterprise is limited to "business-like entities." We see no basis to impose such an extratextual requirement.

As noted, the specific question on which we granted certiorari is whether an association-in-fact enterprise must have "an ascertainable structure beyond that inherent in the pattern of racketeering activity in which it engages." We will break this question into three parts. First, must an association-in-fact enterprise have a "structure"? Second, must the structure be "ascertainable"? Third, must the "structure" go "beyond that inherent in the pattern of racketeering activity" in which its members engage?

"Structure." We agree with petitioner that an association-in-fact enterprise must have a structure. In the sense relevant here, the term "structure" means "[t]he way in which parts are arranged or put together to form a whole" and "[t]he interrelation or arrangement of parts in a complex entity." American Heritage Dictionary 1718 (4th ed. 2000); see also Random House Dictionary of the English Language 1410 (1967) (defining structure to mean, among other things, "the pattern of relationships, as of status or friendship, existing among the members of a group or society").

From the terms of RICO, it is apparent that an association-in-fact enterprise must have at least three structural features: a purpose, relationships among those associated with the enterprise, and longevity sufficient to permit these associates to pursue the enterprise's purpose. As we succinctly put it in *Turkette*, an association-in-fact enterprise is "a group of persons associated together for a common purpose of engaging in a course of conduct."

That an "enterprise" must have a purpose is apparent from the meaning of the term in ordinary usage, *i.e.*, a "venture," "undertaking," or "project." Webster's Third New International Dictionary 757 (1976). The concept of "associat[ion]" requires both interpersonal relationships and a common interest. . . .

Although an association-in-fact enterprise must have these structural features, it does not follow that a district court must use the term "structure" in its jury instructions. A trial judge has considerable discretion in choosing the language of an instruction so long as the substance of the relevant point is adequately expressed.

"Ascertainable." Whenever a jury is told that it must find the existence of an element beyond a reasonable doubt, that element must be "ascertainable" or else the jury could not find that it was proved. Therefore, telling the members of the jury that

they had to ascertain the existence of an "ascertainable structure" would have been redundant and potentially misleading.

"Beyond that inherent in the pattern of racketeering activity." This phrase may be interpreted in least two different ways, and its correctness depends on the particular sense in which the phrase is used. If the phrase is interpreted to mean that the existence of an enterprise is a separate element that must be proved, it is of course correct. As we explained in *Turkette*, the existence of an enterprise is an element distinct from the pattern of racketeering activity and "proof of one does not necessarily establish the other."[4]

On the other hand, if the phrase is used to mean that the existence of an enterprise may never be inferred from the evidence showing that persons associated with the enterprise engaged in a pattern of racketeering activity, it is incorrect. We recognized in *Turkette* that the evidence used to prove the pattern of racketeering activity and the evidence establishing an enterprise "may in particular cases coalesce."

The crux of petitioner's argument is that a RICO enterprise must have structural features in addition to those that we think can be fairly inferred from the language of the statute. Although petitioner concedes that an association-in-fact enterprise may be an "'informal'" group and that "not 'much'" structure is needed, he contends that such an enterprise must have at least some additional structural attributes, such as a structural "hierarchy," "role differentiation," a "unique *modus operandi*," a "chain of command," "professionalism and sophistication of organization," "diversity and complexity of crimes," "membership dues, rules and regulations," "uncharged or additional crimes aside from predicate acts," an "internal discipline mechanism," "regular meetings regarding enterprise affairs," an "enterprise 'name,'" and "induction or initiation ceremonies and rituals."

We see no basis in the language of RICO for the structural requirements that petitioner asks us to recognize. As we said in *Turkette*, an association-in-fact enterprise is simply a continuing unit that functions with a common purpose. Such a group need not have a hierarchical structure or a "chain of command"; decisions may be made on an ad hoc basis and by any number of methods — by majority vote, consensus, a show of strength, etc. Members of the group need not have fixed roles; different members may perform different roles at different times. The group need not have a name, regular meetings, dues, established rules and regulations, disciplinary procedures, or induction or initiation ceremonies. While the group must function as a continuing unit and remain in existence long enough to pursue a course of conduct, nothing in RICO exempts an enterprise whose associates engage in spurts of activity punctuated by periods of quiescence. Nor is the statute limited to groups

---

4. It is easy to envision situations in which proof that individuals engaged in a pattern of racketeering activity would not establish the existence of an enterprise. For example, suppose that several individuals, independently and without coordination, engaged in a pattern of crimes listed as RICO predicates — for example, bribery or extortion. Proof of these patterns would not be enough to show that the individuals were members of an enterprise.

whose crimes are sophisticated, diverse, complex, or unique; for example, a group that does nothing but engage in extortion through old-fashioned, unsophisticated, and brutal means may fall squarely within the statute's reach.

Because the statutory language is clear, there is no need to reach petitioner's remaining arguments based on statutory purpose, legislative history, or the rule of lenity. . . .

The instructions the District Court judge gave to the jury in this case were correct and adequate. These instructions explicitly told the jurors that they could not convict on the RICO charges unless they found that the Government had proved the existence of an enterprise. The instructions made clear that this was a separate element from the pattern of racketeering activity.

The instructions also adequately told the jury that the enterprise needed to have the structural attributes that may be inferred from the statutory language. As noted, the trial judge told the jury that the Government was required to prove that there was "an ongoing organization with some sort of framework, formal or informal, for carrying out its objectives" and that "the various members and associates of the association function[ed] as a continuing unit to achieve a common purpose."

Finally, the trial judge did not err in instructing the jury that "the existence of an association-in-fact is oftentimes more readily proven by what it does, rather than by abstract analysis of its structure." This instruction properly conveyed the point we made in *Turkette* that proof of a pattern of racketeering activity may be sufficient in a particular case to permit a jury to infer the existence of an association-in-fact enterprise.

We therefore affirm the judgment of the Court of Appeals.

JUSTICE STEVENS, with whom JUSTICE BREYER joins, dissenting.

In my view, Congress intended the term "enterprise" as it is used in the Racketeer Influenced and Corrupt Organizations Act (RICO), 18 U.S.C. § 1961 *et seq.*, to refer only to business-like entities that have an existence apart from the predicate acts committed by their employees or associates. The trial judge in this case committed two significant errors relating to the meaning of that term. First, he instructed the jury that "an association of individuals, without structural hierarchy, form[ed] solely for the purpose of carrying out a pattern of racketeering acts" can constitute an enterprise. And he allowed the jury to find that element satisfied by evidence showing a group of criminals with no existence beyond its intermittent commission of racketeering acts and related offenses. Because the Court's decision affirming petitioner's conviction is inconsistent with the statutory meaning of the term enterprise and serves to expand RICO liability far beyond the bounds Congress intended, I respectfully dissent. . . .

The trial judge also erred in finding the Government's evidence in this case sufficient to support petitioner's RICO convictions. . . . There is no evidence in RICO's text or history that Congress intended it to reach such ad hoc associations of thieves.

Notes and Questions

1. *Proof of the enterprise.* As the Ninth Circuit noted in its en banc opinion in *Odom v. Microsoft Corp.*, 486 F.3d 541, 549 (9th Cir. 2007), over the years the circuit courts split almost evenly on both of the issues that the Court addressed in *Boyle*. Some circuits required proof that the enterprise have an ascertainable structure, and further required proof that the structure be distinct from the structure necessary for the underlying racketeering activity. These circuits reasoned that, without the separate and distinct structure, the enterprise is not distinct from the racketeering activity itself. Other circuits declined to require proof of an ascertainable structure apart from the racketeering activity. The Court attempted to clarify and resolve these issues in *Boyle*. Did it succeed? Why or why not?

2. *Formal versus informal enterprises.* Under RICO, it is generally not difficult to prove that partnerships, corporations, and other formal entities qualify as enterprises. What about organized crime groupings, such as a collection of people who associate solely for the purpose of engaging in criminal activity? Will they typically meet the *Boyle* requirements? Why or why not?

3. *Section 371.* Given *Boyle*'s broad reading of the enterprise element, is RICO conspiracy under 18 U.S.C. §1962(c) a distinct crime from conspiracy under the general conspiracy statute, 18 U.S.C. §371? The *Boyle* dissent argued that the majority decision threatens to make association-in-fact cases under §1962(c) "indistinguishable from conspiracies to commit predicate acts, *see* §371, as the only remaining difference is §1962(c)'s pattern requirement." The majority responded that §1962(c) "demands much more" than the inchoate offense defined in §371 because §1962(c) requires the creation of "a group with a common purpose and course of conduct — and the actual commission of a pattern of predicate offenses." Which argument is more persuasive?

3. The Relationship Between the "Person" and the "Enterprise"

In the next case, the Court turned to the relationship between the enterprise and the "person" who conducts the enterprise under §1962(c). As you read the case, consider whether the outcome comports with the purpose behind §1962(c).

Cedric Kushner Promotions v. King

533 U.S. 158 (2001)

Justice Breyer delivered the opinion of the Court.

The Racketeer Influenced and Corrupt Organizations Act, 18 U.S.C. § 1961 et seq., makes it "unlawful for any person employed by or associated with any enterprise . . . to conduct or participate . . . in the conduct of such enterprise's affairs" through the commission of two or more statutorily defined crimes — which RICO calls "a pattern of racketeering activity." § 1962(c). The language suggests, and lower courts have held, that this provision foresees two separate entities, a "person" and a distinct "enterprise."

This case focuses upon a person who is the president and sole shareholder of a closely held corporation. The plaintiff claims that the president has conducted the corporation's affairs through the forbidden "pattern," though for present purposes it is conceded that, in doing so, he acted within the scope of his authority as the corporation's employee. In these circumstances, are there two entities, a "person" and a separate "enterprise"? Assuming, as we must given the posture of this case, that the allegations in the complaint are true, we conclude that the "person" and "enterprise" here are distinct and that the RICO provision applies.

Petitioner, Cedric Kushner Promotions, Ltd., is a corporation that promotes boxing matches. Petitioner sued Don King, the president and sole shareholder of Don King Productions, a corporation, claiming that King had conducted the boxing-related affairs of Don King Productions in part through a RICO "pattern," i.e., through the alleged commission of at least two instances of fraud and other RICO predicate crimes. The District Court, citing Court of Appeals precedent, dismissed the complaint, and the Court of Appeals affirmed that dismissal. 219 F.3d 115 (2d Cir. 2000) (per curiam). In the appellate court's view, § 1962(c) applies only where a plaintiff shows the existence of two separate entities, a "person" and a distinct "enterprise," the affairs of which that "person" improperly conducts. In this instance, "it is undisputed that King was an employee" of the corporation Don King Productions and also "acting within the scope of his authority." Under the Court of Appeals' analysis, King, in a legal sense, was part of, not separate from, the corporation. There was no "person," distinct from the "enterprise," who improperly conducted the "enterprise's affairs." And thus § 1962(c) did not apply.

Other circuits, applying § 1962(c) in roughly similar circumstances, have reached a contrary conclusion. We granted certiorari to resolve the conflict. We now agree with these circuits and hold that the Second Circuit's interpretation of § 1962(c) is erroneous.

We do not quarrel with the basic principle that to establish liability under § 1962(c) one must allege and prove the existence of two distinct entities: (1) a "person"; and (2) an "enterprise" that is not simply the same "person" referred to by a different name. The statute's language, read as ordinary English, suggests that principle. The

Act says that it applies to "person[s]" who are "employed by or associated with" the "enterprise." In ordinary English one speaks of employing, being employed by, or associating with others, not oneself. In addition, the Act's purposes are consistent with that principle. Whether the Act seeks to prevent a person from victimizing, say, a small business, or to prevent a person from using a corporation for criminal purposes, the person and the victim, or the person and the tool, are different entities, not the same.

The Acting Solicitor General reads § 1962(c) "to require some distinctness between the RICO defendant and the RICO enterprise." And she says that this requirement is "legally sound and workable." We agree with her assessment, particularly in light of the fact that 12 Courts of Appeals have interpreted the statute as embodying some such distinctness requirement without creating discernible mischief in the administration of RICO. . . .

While accepting the "distinctness" principle, we nonetheless disagree with the appellate court's application of that principle to the present circumstances — circumstances in which a corporate employee, "acting within the scope of his authority," allegedly conducts the corporation's affairs in a RICO-forbidden way. The corporate owner/employee, a natural person, is distinct from the corporation itself, a legally different entity with different rights and responsibilities due to its different legal status. And we can find nothing in the statute that requires more "separateness" than that.

Linguistically speaking, an employee who conducts the affairs of a corporation through illegal acts comes within the terms of a statute that forbids any "person" unlawfully to conduct an "enterprise," particularly when the statute explicitly defines "person" to include "any individual . . . capable of holding a legal or beneficial interest in property," and defines "enterprise" to include a "corporation." 18 U.S.C. §§ 1961(3), (4). And, linguistically speaking, the employee and the corporation are different "persons," even where the employee is the corporation's sole owner. After all, incorporation's basic purpose is to create a distinct legal entity, with legal rights, obligations, powers, and privileges different from those of the natural individuals who created it, who own it, or whom it employs. . . .

Further, to apply the RICO statute in present circumstances is consistent with the statute's basic purposes as this Court has defined them. The Court has held that RICO both protects a legitimate "enterprise" from those who would use unlawful acts to victimize it, *United States v. Turkette*, 452 U.S. 576, 591 (1981), and also protects the public from those who would unlawfully use an "enterprise" (whether legitimate or illegitimate) as a "vehicle" through which "unlawful . . . activity is committed," *National Organization for Women*, 510 U.S. at 259. A corporate employee who conducts the corporation's affairs through an unlawful RICO "pattern . . . of activity," § 1962(c), uses that corporation as a "vehicle" whether he is, or is not, its sole owner.

Conversely, the appellate court's critical legal distinction — between employees acting within the scope of corporate authority and those acting outside that authority — is inconsistent with a basic statutory purpose. It would immunize from RICO liability many of those at whom this Court has said RICO directly aims — e.g., high-ranking individuals in an illegitimate criminal enterprise, who, seeking to further the purposes of that enterprise, act within the scope of their authority.· . . .

In reply, King argues that the lower court's rule is consistent with (1) the principle that a corporation acts only through its directors, officers, and agents, (2) the principle that a corporation should not be liable for the criminal acts of its employees where Congress so intends, and (3) the Sherman Act principle limiting liability under 15 U.S.C. §1 by excluding "from unlawful combinations or conspiracies the activities of a single firm," *Copperweld Corp. v. Independence Tube Corp.*, 467 U.S. 752, 769–770, n. 15 (1984). The alternative that we endorse, however, is no less consistent with these principles. It does not deny that a corporation acts through its employees; it says only that the corporation and its employees are not legally identical. It does not assert that ordinary respondeat superior principles make a corporation legally liable under RICO for the criminal acts of its employees; that is a matter of congressional intent not before us. Neither is it inconsistent with antitrust law's intracorporate conspiracy doctrine; that doctrine turns on specific antitrust objectives. Rather, we hold simply that the need for two distinct entities is satisfied; hence, the RICO provision before us applies when a corporate employee unlawfully conducts the affairs of the corporation of which he is the sole owner — whether he conducts those affairs within the scope, or beyond the scope, of corporate authority.

For these reasons, the Court of Appeals' judgment is reversed, and the case is remanded for further proceedings consistent with this opinion.

Notes and Questions

1. *RICO's purposes.* According to the Court, what is the purpose of §1962(c)? Are these purposes served by allowing a sole shareholder to be charged under that section for conducting the affairs of a corporation that has no other owners or officers? Why or why not?

2. *The "person" and the "enterprise."* Under §1962(c), the defendant is the "person" who conducted the enterprise through a pattern of racketeering activity. In *King*, the Supreme Court apparently agreed with lower courts that had held that the person and the enterprise must be distinct under §1962(c). Thus, the *person*, not the enterprise, is the wrongdoer under that subsection. Under this reasoning, the enterprise cannot be named as the defendant in a case brought under §1962(c). *See, e.g., Schofield v. First Commodity Corp. of Boston*, 793 F.2d 28, 29 (1st Cir. 1986).

3. *Sections 1962(a) and (b).* Does *King's* reasoning apply to §§1962(a) and 1962(b)? In other words, could the enterprise be named as the defendant under subsection 1962(a) or (b)? Why or why not? *See Masi v. Ford City Bank and Trust Company*, 779 F.2d 397, 402 (7th Cir. 1985) (finding that the enterprise could be named as a defendant under §1962(a)).

4. *Association-in-fact enterprises.* Could a plaintiff avoid the distinctiveness require-ment under §1962(c) by naming as the defendant an individual or entity that is part of an allegedly larger, association-in-fact enterprise? *See Riverwoods Chappaqua Corp. v. Marine Midland Bank*, 30 F.3d 339, 344 (2d Cir. 1994) (stating that "where employees of a corporation associate together to commit a pattern of predicate acts in the course of their employment and on behalf of the corporation, the employees in association with the corporation do not form an enterprise distinct from the cor-poration"). The Court in *King* distinguished this case without considering its merits. What would be the result in the *Marine Midland Bank* case under the *King* reason-ing? Why? *See generally* Paul Edgar Harold, Note, *Quo Vadis, Association in Fact? The Growing Disparity between How Federal Courts Interpret RICO's Enterprise Pro-vision in Criminal and Civil Cases (With a Little Statutory Background to Explain Why)*, 80 NOTRE DAME L. REV. 781 (2005).

5. *Parents and subsidiaries.* Are parent corporations and their wholly-owned sub-sidiaries distinct entities for purposes of §1962(c)? Although courts have adopted varying approaches to this question, most courts conclude that parents and sub-sidiaries are not distinct entities. For a critical analysis of these decisions, see Com-ment, William B. Ortman, *Parents, Subsidiaries, and RICO Distinctiveness*, 73 U. CHI. L. REV. 377 (2006) (arguing that the courts' conclusion is not supported by the RICO statute and that parents and subsidiaries should be considered distinct enti-ties under §1962(c)).

Problem

14-1. The government has brought a RICO case against defendant Acme Bank. The government alleges that, through acts of extortion and mail fraud, Acme Bank and two of its loan officers, Augusta and Donald, formed an association-in-fact enter-prise (the "Structuring Group") designed to coerce certain of Acme's customers to "restructure" loan agreements in a way that financially advantaged Acme and dis-advantaged its customers. Specifically, the indictment alleges that, through a pat-tern of racketeering activity, Acme conducted and participated in the affairs of the "Structuring Group," in violation of 18 U.S.C. §1962(c).

You are counsel for Acme, and are considering bringing a motion to dismiss the charge. What argument(s) should you assert? How is the court likely to rule? Why?

4. Required Proof for the "Conduct" Element

As the Supreme Court noted in the *King* case, under §1962(c), the person who "conducts" the affairs of the enterprise must be separate from the enterprise. But, in such a case, what does it mean to "conduct" the affairs of the enterprise? The Supreme Court addressed this issue in the case that follows.

Reves v. Ernst & Young

507 U.S. 170 (1993)

JUSTICE BLACKMUN delivered the opinion of the Court.

[The plaintiff alleged that the defendant, accounting firm Arthur Young (later known as Ernst & Young), had conducted and participated in the affairs of the alleged enterprise, a farmer's cooperative known as The Farmer's Cooperative of Arkansas and Oklahoma, Inc. (the "Co-Op"). The accounting firm had performed the annual financial audit for the Co-Op in 1981 and 1982. The accounting firm certified that the Co-Op's records adequately reflected its financial status, and relied upon those records, and a review of past Co-Op transactions, to prepare the audits. In completing these assignments, and without informing the Co-Op's board, the accounting firm utilized questionable measures to verify the Co-Op's solvency.

[The audits failed to disclose the Co-Op's precarious financial condition. The Co-Op later filed for bankruptcy. The bankruptcy trustee, acting on behalf of the Co-Op and certain of its creditors, sued the accounting firm and others. All the defendants except the accounting firm settled. In the complaint, the plaintiffs alleged that the accounting firm had conducted or participated in the conduct of the Co-Op's affairs through a pattern of racketeering activity. The trial court granted summary judgment in favor of the accounting firm on the RICO claim, and the court of appeals affirmed. Both courts applied an "operation or management" test for determining when a person "conducts" an enterprise under § 1962(c). The courts concluded that the accounting firm's conduct did not "rise to the level of participation in the management or operation of the Co-Op." *See Arthur Young & Co. v. Reves*, 937 F.2d 1310, 1324 (8th Cir. 1991).]

The narrow question in this case is the meaning of the phrase "to conduct or participate, directly or indirectly, in the conduct of such enterprise's affairs." The word "conduct" is used twice, and it seems reasonable to give each use a similar construction. As a verb, "conduct" means to lead, run, manage, or direct. Webster's Third New International Dictionary 474 (1976). Petitioners urge us to read "conduct" as "carry on," so that almost any involvement in the affairs of an enterprise would satisfy the "conduct or participate" requirement. But context is important, and in the context of the phrase "to conduct . . . [an] enterprise's affairs," the word indicates some degree of direction.

The dissent agrees that, when "conduct" is used as a verb, "it is plausible to find in it a suggestion of control." The dissent prefers to focus on "conduct" as a noun, as in the phrase "participate, directly or indirectly, in the conduct of [an] enterprise's affairs." But unless one reads "conduct" to include an element of direction when used as a noun in this phrase, the word becomes superfluous. Congress could easily have written "participate, directly or indirectly, in [an] enterprise's affairs," but it chose to repeat the word "conduct." We conclude, therefore, that as both a noun and a verb in this subsection "conduct" requires an element of direction.

The more difficult question is what to make of the word "participate." This Court previously has characterized this word as a "ter[m] . . . of breadth." *Russello v. United States*, 464 U.S. 16, 21–22 (1983). Petitioners argue that Congress used "participate" as a synonym for "aid and abet." That would be a term of breadth indeed, for "aid and abet" "comprehends all assistance rendered by words, acts, encouragement, support, or presence." Black's Law Dictionary 68 (6th ed. 1990). But within the context of § 1962(c), "participate" appears to have a narrower meaning. We may mark the limits of what the term might mean by looking again at what Congress did *not* say. On the one hand, "to participate . . . in the conduct of . . . affairs" must be broader than "to conduct affairs" or the "participate" phrase would be superfluous. On the other hand, as we already have noted, "to participate . . . in the conduct of . . . affairs" must be narrower than "to participate in affairs" or Congress' repetition of the word "conduct" would serve no purpose. It seems that Congress chose a middle ground, consistent with a common understanding of the word "participate" — "to take part in." Webster's Third New International Dictionary 1646 (1976).

Once we understand the word "conduct" to require some degree of direction and the word "participate" to require some part in that direction, the meaning of § 1962(c) comes into focus. In order to "participate, directly or indirectly, in the conduct of such enterprise's affairs," one must have some part in directing those affairs. Of course, the word "participate" makes clear that RICO liability is not limited to those with primary responsibility for the enterprise's affairs, just as the phrase "directly or indirectly" makes clear that RICO liability is not limited to those with a formal position in the enterprise, but *some* part in directing the enterprise's affairs is required. The "operation or management" test expresses this requirement in a formulation that is easy to apply.

This test finds further support in the legislative history of § 1962. . . .

[T]he legislative history confirms what we have already deduced from the language of § 1962(c) — that one is not liable under that provision unless one has participated in the operation or management of the enterprise itself.

RICO's "liberal construction" clause does not require rejection of the "operation or management" test. Congress directed that the "provisions of this title shall be liberally construed to effectuate its remedial purposes." This clause obviously seeks to ensure that Congress' intent is not frustrated by an overly narrow reading of the statute, but it is not an invitation to apply RICO to new purposes that Congress never intended. Nor does the clause help us to determine what purposes Congress had in mind. Those must be gleaned from the statute through the normal means of interpretation. In this case it is clear that Congress did not intend to extend RICO liability under § 1962(c) beyond those who participate in the operation or management of an enterprise through a pattern of racketeering activity.

Petitioners argue that the "operation or management" test is flawed because liability under § 1962(c) is not limited to upper management but may extend to "any person employed by or associated with [the] enterprise." We agree that liability under § 1962(c) is not limited to upper management, but we disagree that the "operation or management" test is inconsistent with this proposition. An enterprise is "operated" not just by upper management but also by lower rung participants in the enterprise who are under the direction of upper management.[9] An enterprise also might be "operated" or "managed" by others "associated with" the enterprise who exert control over it as, for example, by bribery.

The United States also argues that the "operation or management" test is not consistent with § 1962(c) because it limits the liability of "outsiders" who have no official position within the enterprise. The United States correctly points out that RICO's major purpose was to attack the "infiltration of organized crime and racketeering into legitimate organizations," but its argument fails on several counts. First, it ignores the fact that § 1962 has four subsections. Infiltration of legitimate organizations by "outsiders" is clearly addressed in subsections (a) and (b), and the "operation or management" test that applies under subsection (c) in no way limits the application of subsections (a) and (b) to "outsiders." Second, § 1962(c) is limited to persons "employed by or associated with" an enterprise, suggesting a more limited reach than subsections (a) and (b), which do not contain such a restriction. Third, § 1962(c) cannot be interpreted to reach complete "outsiders" because liability depends on showing that the defendants conducted or participated in the conduct of the "*enterprise's* affairs," not just their *own* affairs. Of course, "outsiders" may be liable under § 1962(c) if they are "associated with" an enterprise and participate in the conduct of *its* affairs — that is, participate in the operation or management of the enterprise itself — but it would be consistent with neither the language nor the legislative history of § 1962(c) to interpret it as broadly as petitioners and the United States urge.

In sum, we hold that "to conduct or participate, directly or indirectly, in the conduct of such enterprise's affairs," § 1962(c), one must participate in the operation or management of the enterprise itself.

Both the District Court and the Court of Appeals applied the standard we adopt today to the facts of this case, and both found that respondent was entitled to summary judgment. Neither petitioners nor the United States have argued that these courts misapplied the "operation or management" test. The dissent argues that by creating the Co-Op's financial statements Arthur Young participated in the management of the Co-Op because "'financial statements are management's responsibility.'" Although the professional standards adopted by the accounting profession may be relevant, they do not define what constitutes management of an enterprise for the purposes of § 1962(c).

---

9. At oral argument, there was some discussion about whether low-level employees could be considered to have participated in the conduct of an enterprise's affairs. We need not decide in this case how far § 1962(c) extends down the ladder of operation because it is clear that Arthur Young was not acting under the direction of the Co-Op's officers or board.

In this case, it is undisputed that Arthur Young relied upon existing Co-op records in preparing the 1981 and 1982 audit reports. The AICPA's professional standards state that an auditor may draft financial statements in whole or in part based on information from management's accounting system. It is also undisputed that Arthur Young's audit reports revealed to the Co-op's board that the value of the gasohol plant had been calculated based on the Co-op's investment in the plant. Thus, we only could conclude that Arthur Young participated in the operation or management of the Co-op itself if Arthur Young's failure to tell the Co-op's board that the plant should have been given its fair market value constituted such participation. We think that Arthur Young's failure in this respect is not sufficient to give rise to liability under § 1962(c).

The judgment of the Court of Appeals is affirmed.

JUSTICE SOUTER, with whom JUSTICE WHITE joins, dissenting.

In the word "conduct," the Court today finds a clear congressional mandate to limit RICO liability under 18 U.S.C. § 1962(c) to participants in the "operation or management" of a RICO enterprise. What strikes the Court as clear, however, looks at the very least hazy to me, and I accordingly find the statute's "liberal construction" provision not irrelevant, but dispositive. But even if I were to assume, with the majority, that the word "conduct" clearly imports some degree of direction or control into § 1962(c), I would have to say that the majority misapplies its own "operation or management" test to the facts presented here. I therefore respectfully dissent.

Even if I were to adopt the majority's view of § 1962(c), . . . I still could not join the judgment, which seems to me unsupportable under the very "operation or management" test the Court announces. If Arthur Young had confined itself in this case to the role traditionally performed by an outside auditor, I could agree with the majority that Arthur Young took no part in the management or operation of the Farmer's Cooperative of Arkansas and Oklahoma, Inc. (Co-Op). . . . Most importantly, Reves adduced evidence that Arthur Young took on management responsibilities, and Arthur Young itself conceded below that the alleged activity went beyond traditional auditing. Because I find, then, that even under the majority's "operation or management" test the Court of Appeals erroneously affirmed the summary judgment for Arthur Young, I would (again) reverse. . . .

Notes and Questions

1. *Employees and the "operation or management test."* What are the boundaries of the test the Court adopts? When do mid- or low-level employees of the enterprise meet the test? Note that the Court specifically avoided providing guidance on this issue.

2. *Outside advisors.* When do lawyers, accountants, or others "operate or manage" an enterprise?

In *Reves*, the Supreme Court adopted the "operation or management test." In the next case, the Eighth Circuit Court of Appeals applied the *Reves* test to an interesting set of facts. As you read the case, consider how you would advise a client concerning the circumstances in which an outsider's actions will amount to "conduct[ing]" an enterprise's affairs.

Handeen v. Lemaire

112 F.3d 1339 (8th Cir. 1997)

FLOYD R. GIBSON, CIRCUIT JUDGE.

Paul Handeen appeals the district court's order granting summary judgment in favor of the Orlins & Brainerd Law Firm and its principals (collectively the "Firm") on his claims under the Racketeer Influenced and Corrupt Organizations Act ("RICO"), 18 U.S.C. §§ 1961–1968. Given the procedural posture of this case, we find ourselves constrained to reverse the district court's dismissal of Handeen's RICO cause of action.

The appeal before us traces its genesis to a series of unfortunate events that has already been the subject of extensive litigation in this Court, *see Handeen v. LeMaire (In re LeMaire)*, 898 F.2d 1346, 1347–48 (8th Cir. 1990) (en banc) ("*LeMaire II*") (describing underlying factual foundation), *rev'g* 883 F.2d 1373, 1375–76 (8th Cir. 1989) (containing further elaboration), and we see no present need to retell that sorry tale. Suffice it to say that Gregory Lemaire (individually referred to as "Gregory" or "Lemaire") set out to execute Handeen on July 9, 1978, and he very nearly succeeded.[2] As a result of this intentional deed, Lemaire pleaded guilty to a charge of aggravated

---

2. Lemaire represented himself *pro se* in the instant action, and one of the numerous documents he filed with the district court is a rambling, thirty-one page Answer recounting with chilling detail his version of the events which transpired on that summer day:

> The rifle was a semi-automatic, .22-calibre rifle that I had purchased many years before for the sole purpose of shooting at tin cans with my friends. The rifle was capable of holding 16 bullets. Prior to the shooting, I had loaded bullets into the gun in the front seat of my car; in checking that a bullet was in the chamber, I had ejected one bullet, which landed on the floor on the passenger's side of the front seat. When I began shooting at Mr. Handeen, it was from the car in which I sat, perhaps 150–200 feet away from him. I then left the car and ran toward him, continuing to shoot. At some point in my approach to him, there were no more bullets left in the gun. I ran back to the car, picked up the single remaining bullet from the floor of the car, placed it in the chamber of the rifle, and ran to Mr. Handeen. At the instant that I came to stand directly over Mr. Handeen, there was no thought involved: I clipped-on the safety mechanism of the rifle and placed it on the roof of Mr. Handeen's car, which was directly adjacent to us. From then on, I agitatedly paced back and forth in the street with raised hands, yelling to Mr. Handeen (who repeatedly attempted to rise), "Stay down![ ] Stay down! The ambulance is coming!"...
> I evidently did fire nine shots with the intent to execute Mr. Handeen; I did not fire the tenth shot, which would have done so.

Upon reading Lemaire's submissions to the district court, one comes away with the distinct impression that he considers himself the primary victim in this affair. This is a sentiment we do not share.

assault and spent twenty-seven months in a Minnesota prison. Following his release, Lemaire resumed his graduate studies at the University of Minnesota and in January 1986 received a doctoral degree in, of all things, experimental behavioral pharmacology.

Handeen filed a civil suit against Lemaire and obtained a consent judgment in excess of $50,000. Lemaire used funds received from his father to pay an initial lump sum of $3,000 due under the judgment, but he failed to remit any agreed-upon monthly installments. This prompted Handeen to commence garnishment proceedings to collect the balance due him. Lemaire, who was represented by the Firm, filed a Chapter 13 bankruptcy petition shortly thereafter.

Handeen initiated this suit against the Firm and [Gregory Lemaire and his parents (the "Lemaires")]. The Complaint paints a sordid portrait of an intricate scheme through which Lemaire sought to fraudulently obtain a discharge of Handeen's judgment by manipulating the bankruptcy system.[3] As part of this plot, the Firm and the Lemaires contrived to minimize whatever reduced recovery Handeen might achieve via the bankruptcy process. To this end, the Firm instructed Gregory to inflate the amount of his debts by agreeing to pay his parents rent and by executing a false promissory note payable to the elder Lemaires.[4] Gregory listed his parents as creditors on schedules he filed with the bankruptcy court,[5] and the Firm relied on the parents' claims when preparing proposed repayment plans. Of course, to the extent the bankruptcy court recognized this "indebtedness," it would reduce Handeen's pro rata share of any Chapter 13 distributions. Indeed, the cabal enjoyed success in this venture, for the bankruptcy court in substantial measure approved the parents' petitions against the estate.[6] As such, Gregory's parents received a portion of the sums he paid under the approved plan, and they compounded the fraud by transferring much of this money back to Gregory.

The intrigue, however, does not end there. In 1989, while Handeen was appealing the bankruptcy court's confirmation of the Chapter 13 plan, Gregory found a new job which required him to relocate from Minneapolis to Houston, Texas. This employment significantly enhanced Lemaire's income. Nonetheless, presumably because a person who takes refuge in Chapter 13 must ordinarily devote to the repayment plan

---

3. As we explain below, at the current stage of these proceedings we must accept as true all of the allegations within the Complaint. We pay homage to this requirement during our recitation of the salient facts.

4. Gregory had never before paid his mother and father rent for the privilege of living in their home. Furthermore, the promissory note was dated January 15, 1987, only one day prior to the date Gregory filed for bankruptcy protection.

5. The Complaint also indicates that the Firm advised Gregory not to disclose on his schedules a contingent debt in the amount of $30,000 to $50,000 which he would have been obligated to repay to the United States Public Health Service if he failed to fulfill the terms of a fellowship stipend. This obscuration could have resulted in discrimination among creditors.

6. The Firm also represented Henry and Patricia Lemaire before the bankruptcy court, and it therefore defended their claims against objections lodged by Handeen.

"all of the debtor's projected disposable income," Lemaire did not wish to reveal his increased wages to the bankruptcy trustee. Consequently, Lemaire, his parents, and the Firm formulated an artifice to avoid rousing the trustee's attention. Specifically, the ruse called for Lemaire to mail his father a parcel every month. Within that package would be an envelope addressed to the bankruptcy trustee and containing a check representing Lemaire's monthly payment under the plan. Lemaire's father would, in turn, place the enclosed envelope in the mails, and the trustee would thus receive a letter postmarked from Minneapolis rather than Houston. The object, it is clear, was to fool the trustee into believing that the status quo ante existed, and this exploitation of the postal service remained a monthly ritual until the court dismissed Lemaire's plan in July of 1990.

In his Complaint, Handeen charges that the Firm and the Lemaires, through their duplicitous association with Gregory's bankruptcy estate, violated 18 U.S.C. § 1962(c) by conducting a RICO enterprise (the estate) through a pattern of racketeering activity. Handeen also alleges that the group conspired to violate RICO in violation of 18 U.S.C. § 1962(d).

Handeen now appeals the district court's dismissal of his RICO cause of action. We reverse the court's grant of summary judgment. . . .

Liability under § 1962(c) extends only to those persons associated with or employed by an enterprise who "conduct or participate, directly or indirectly, in the conduct of such enterprise's affairs through a pattern of racketeering activity." 18 U.S.C. § 1962(c). In *Reves v. Ernst & Young*, 507 U.S. 170, 185 (1993), the Supreme Court confirmed that this Circuit has correctly interpreted the "conduct" requirement to authorize recovery only against individuals who "participate in the operation or management of the enterprise itself." The Supreme Court clarified the scope of the operation or management test, observing:

> An enterprise is "operated" not just by upper management but also by lower rung participants in the enterprise who are under the direction of upper management. An enterprise also might be "operated" or "managed" by others "associated with" the enterprise who exert control over it as, for example, by bribery.

> Section 1962(c) cannot be interpreted to reach complete "outsiders" because liability depends on showing that the defendants conducted or participated in the conduct of the "enterprise's affairs," not just their own affairs. Of course, "outsiders" may be liable under § 1962(c) if they are "associated with" an enterprise and participate in the conduct of its affairs — that is, participate in the operation or management of the enterprise itself.

Reves, 507 U.S. at 184–85. Consonant with the dictate of *Reves*, it is not necessary that a RICO defendant have wielded control over the enterprise, but the plaintiff "must prove some part in the direction . . . of the enterprise's affairs." *Darden*, 70 F.3d at 1543.

The Supreme Court's approval and refinement of our operation or management test has had far-reaching implications, particularly in the area of professional liability under RICO. This is not especially surprising, given that *Reves* itself involved an attempt to impute liability to an accounting firm. There, the accounting firm certified that a co-op's records adequately reflected its financial status, and the firm relied upon those existing records, in combination with a review of past co-op transactions, to prepare audits for the organization. *Reves*, 507 U.S. at 173–75. In completing these assignments, and without informing the co-op's board, the firm utilized questionable measures to verify the co-op's solvency. The Supreme Court affirmed our decision finding that the accounting firm's activity did not constitute conduct of a RICO enterprise.

In our view, the *Reves* decision represents a fairly uncomplicated application of the operation or management test. This test, like *Reves* itself, is built upon a recognition that Congress did not mean for §1962(c) to penalize all who are employed by or associated with a RICO enterprise, but only those who, by virtue of their association or employment, play a part in directing the enterprise's affairs. Furnishing a client with ordinary professional assistance, even when the client happens to be a RICO enterprise, will not normally rise to the level of participation sufficient to satisfy the Supreme Court's pronouncements in *Reves*. In acknowledgment of this certainty, a growing number of courts, including our own, have held that an attorney or other professional does not conduct an enterprise's affairs through run-of-the-mill provision of professional services. . . . By the same token, RICO is not a surrogate for professional malpractice actions.

Appreciation for the unremarkable notion that the operation or management test does not reach persons who perform routine services for an enterprise should not, however, be mistaken for an absolute edict that an attorney who associates with an enterprise can never be liable under RICO. An attorney's license is not an invitation to engage in racketeering, and a lawyer no less than anyone else is bound by generally applicable legislative enactments. Neither *Reves* nor RICO itself exempts professionals, as a class, from the law's proscriptions, and the fact that a defendant has the good fortune to possess the title "attorney at law" is, standing alone, completely irrelevant to the analysis dictated by the Supreme Court. It is a good thing, we are sure, that we find it extremely difficult to fathom any scenario in which an attorney might expose himself to RICO liability by offering conventional advice to a client or performing ordinary legal tasks (that is, by acting like an attorney). This result, however, is not compelled by the fact that the person happens to be a lawyer, but for the reason that these actions do not entail the operation or management of an enterprise. Behavior prohibited by §1962(c) will violate RICO regardless of the person to whom it may be attributed, and we will not shrink from finding an attorney liable when he crosses the line between traditional rendition of legal services and active participation in directing the enterprise. The polestar is the activity in question, not the defendant's status.

Bearing these principles in mind, we are confident that Handeen's Complaint could support a verdict against the Firm. At the outset, we think it worthwhile to reflect upon the nature of a Chapter 13 bankruptcy estate. Chapter 13 affords to a debtor with a regular source of income or earnings, and with a relatively small debt load, an opportunity to obtain a discharge of debts after devoting to creditors disposable income received over a period not to exceed five years. Furthermore, the decision to seek Chapter 13 relief is wholly voluntary, and the debtor may, subject to exceptions not presently relevant, dismiss his case at any time. Finally, it is the debtor's exclusive prerogative to file a proposed repayment plan, and he enjoys many of the powers normally reserved to a bankruptcy trustee.

These examples illustrate, in pointed fashion, that the debtor exercises significant control over his Chapter 13 estate. Of current paramountcy is how much of that control the debtor, in this case Lemaire, may have relinquished to others. If the Complaint is to be believed, as it must, the Firm might have been the beneficiary of considerable abdication. In keeping with the contentions in that pleading, Handeen's proof could show that the Firm and the Lemaires joined in a collaborative undertaking with the objective of releasing Gregory from the financial encumbrance visited upon him by Handeen's judgment. To realize that goal, Lemaire sought the assistance of the Firm. The attorneys, in turn, may have suggested that Chapter 13 bankruptcy, which presented a real opportunity for Lemaire to obtain a discharge of the debt arising from infliction of "willful and malicious injury by the debtor to another entity," 11 U.S.C. § 523(a)(6), offered the most propitious opportunity to reach the desired result. While Lemaire, obviously, was the party on whose behalf the Chapter 13 petition was filed, the Complaint could support a showing that the Firm navigated the estate through the bankruptcy system. Under this postulation, the Firm directed Gregory and his parents to enter into a false promissory note and create other sham debts to dilute the estate, the Firm represented the elder Lemaires and defended their fraudulent claims against objections, the Firm prepared Lemaire's filings and schedules containing erroneous information, the Firm formulated and promoted fraudulent repayment plans, and the Firm participated in devising a scheme to conceal Gregory's new job from the bankruptcy trustee. In short, Handeen might prove that Lemaire, who was, after all, ultimately interested solely in ridding himself of the oppressive judgment, controlled his estate in name only and relied upon the Firm, with its legal acuity, to take the lead in making important decisions concerning the operation of the enterprise.

We underscore that we have no basis for speculating whether Handeen will, in the end, be able to substantiate this narrative. We merely include the above hypothetical to show that relief is available "under a[ ] set of facts that could be proved consistent with the allegations." *Hishon*, 467 U.S. at 73. If Handeen's evidence is up to this challenge, we are comfortable that he will have succeeded in proving that the attorneys conducted the bankruptcy estate. In that event, this would not be a case where a lawyer merely extended advice on possible ways to manage an enterprise's affairs. Nor would this be a situation where counsel issued an opinion based on facts provided by a client. Instead, if the Firm truly did associate with the enterprise to the degree encompassed by the Complaint, we would not hesitate to hold that the attorneys "participated in the core activities that constituted the affairs of the [estate]," *Napoli v. United States*, 32 F.3d 31, 36 (2d Cir. 1994), namely, the manipulation of the bankruptcy process to obtain a discharge for Lemaire. In that instance, the Firm would have played some "role in the conception, creation, or execution," *Azrielli*, 21 F.3d at 521, of the illegal scheme, and we could safely say that the lawyers participated in the operation or management of the estate by assuming at least "some part in directing the enterprise's affairs." *Reves*, 507 U.S. at 179. Therefore, we conclude that the Complaint could justify a finding that the Firm participated in the conduct of the alleged RICO enterprise.

For reasons expressed in the preceding pages, we reverse the district court's order to the extent it grants the Firm's motion for summary judgment on Handeen's RICO claims.

Notes and Questions

1. *The* Reves *test.* The issue litigated in *Handeen* recurs often in RICO cases. When applying the operation or management test, the court in *Reves* found that the facts were not sufficient to show that the defendants had "conducted" the affairs of the enterprise. What were the key facts in *Reves* that led to this outcome? Why was the outcome different in *Handeen*?

2. *Civil RICO actions.* How and why did this bankruptcy dispute become a RICO case? Is this an appropriate use of the RICO statute? Why or why not?

Problems

14-2. Jimmy Suarez ran a business, Suarez Importing, that imported counterfeit DVDs. Jimmy arranged for private packages containing the DVDs to be shipped from overseas and off-loaded at his warehouse. Jimmy had numerous associates who worked for him in his business. Sammy Smith arranged for the shipping of the packages. Nick Flint was a forklift operator who removed the packages from the ships, relocated them to Jimmy's warehouse, and unpacked them for shipping. Barbara Richards acted as a security guard at the warehouse. Barbara mostly took directions from and did odd tasks for Jimmy.

After a search warrant was executed at the warehouse, Suarez Importing and the four individuals were charged with and convicted of violating 18 U.S.C. §§ 1962(c) and (d) based on numerous predicate acts of trafficking in goods or services bearing counterfeit marks, 18 U.S.C. § 2320. At trial, the district court gave the jury the following instructions on the RICO charge:

> The government must prove that each of the individual defendants conducted or participated in the affairs of the enterprise, Suarez Importing. The terms "conduct" and "participate in the affairs" of an enterprise include

the performance of acts, functions, or duties that are necessary or helpful to the operation of the enterprise.

A person may participate in the affairs of an enterprise even though he or she had no part in the management or control of the enterprise and no share in any profits. But the participation must be willful and knowing.

All the defendants were convicted on all counts, and appeal, challenging the sufficiency of the evidence and the jury instruction.

How should the court rule? Why?

14-3. Lewis ran M & M Associates ("M & M"), a check-cashing business, out of a small, enclosed area that Lewis rented in the back of Keller's bar. M & M charged its customers a 1% or 1.5% commission on each check cashed. Lewis used some of the commission money to run the business and to buy computers and other office equipment. M & M is a sole proprietorship, and has no employees other than Lewis, although Lewis did retain an accountant who came to M & M once or twice a month to keep the books.

Bookmakers, those who accept and pay off bets on sporting and other events at agreed-upon odds, tended to frequent Keller's and to use M & M as a check-cashing service. Sometimes, M & M cashed bookmaker checks that banks would not accept. For example, some checks were neither made out by nor payable to the bookmakers (or bookmakers' agents) who were cashing them. Lewis neither asked about the names on the checks he cashed nor required that the checks be endorsed. And Lewis never filed a currency transaction report (CTR) notifying the Internal Revenue Service of his many currency transactions involving more than $10,000, thus violating civil and criminal laws. Lewis engaged in dozens of these transactions over a five-year period.

Assume that you are the Assistant United States Attorney in charge of an investigation into Lewis' activities, and that you believe you have sufficient evidence to charge Lewis with multiple counts of money laundering, 18 U.S.C. § 1956(a)(1), and failing to file CTRs, 31 U.S.C. §§ 5313(a) and 5322(b). You are also considering seeking a RICO charge against Lewis.

What RICO theory or theories would be viable? What arguments might the defense assert if you pursued a RICO charge? What is the likelihood of success at trial on the RICO charge? Why?

14-4. Defendant is a corporation that owns and operates more than 385 fitness centers in at least 14 states, as well as overseas. The business has more than three million members and annual revenues of more than $1.1 billion. Defendant sells monthly memberships to its clubs. Within the last four years, Plaintiffs in a class action lawsuit signed a form contract containing the same material form language, which stated that they were entering into a monthly membership.

Defendant requires each new monthly member to pre-pay the first and "Last Month's Dues" at the time of enrollment. A consumer terminating a monthly membership owes no further fees upon cancellation because the "Last Month's Dues" are always pre-paid.

Defendant requires that monthly dues be paid by Electronic Fund Transfers ("EFTs"). EFTs allow Defendant to withdraw money from consumers' accounts without the consumers' active participation in effectuating payments.

Using EFTs, Plaintiffs allege, Defendant wrongly charged additional dues after cancellation of the monthly memberships. In each case, Defendant acknowledged cancellation, but subsequently made at least one unauthorized post-cancellation EFT "tap" against the (former) member's bank account or credit card account.

By tapping consumers' accounts after consumers cancelled their monthly memberships, Plaintiffs allege, Defendant committed wire fraud and bank fraud in a manner amounting to "an ongoing pattern of racketeering activity." Plaintiffs allege that Defendant perpetrated this pattern of wire fraud and bank fraud through its "association-in-fact" with two outside payment processing companies, PayTech and LeSale. Defendant issued instructions to the payment processors on specific "tap" dates. These payment processors relied on Defendant's representation in those wire instructions that Defendant was authorized to collect consumers' money. This RICO enterprise, Plaintiffs allege, is controlled, managed, and directed by Defendant "for the common purpose of making enormous illicit profits for Defendant with the unwitting complicity of [PayTech and LeSale]."

Defendant has moved to dismiss the RICO allegation on the grounds that Plaintiffs have not adequately alleged an enterprise. How should the court rule? Why?

C. The Racketeering Activity

Any RICO case rests upon proof that the defendant committed the required "racketeering activity," consisting of at least two "predicate acts." Section 1961(1)(B) lists the dozens of federal crimes that qualify as "racketeering activity." Section 1961(1)(A) provides a short list of state offenses that also qualify. Under § 1961(1)(A), racketeering activity includes "any act or threat involving murder, kidnaping, gambling, arson, robbery, bribery, extortion, dealing in obscene matter, or dealing in a controlled substance or listed chemical . . . , which is chargeable under State law and punishable by imprisonment for more than one year."

1. State Crimes

In the following case, the defendants argued that the alleged state law predicate act did not qualify under the RICO statute. As you read the case, be sure to identify the state statute that the government used and the reasons for the court's conclusions.

United States v. Genova

333 F.3d 750 (7th Cir. 2003)

Easterbrook, Circuit Judge.

After his election in 1993 as Mayor of Calumet City, Illinois, Jerome Genova appointed Lawrence Gulotta as City Prosecutor and arranged for his law firm, Gulotta & Kawanna, to get the lion's share of the City's legal business. Both a jury (with respect to Genova) and the judge (with respect to Gulotta, who elected a bench trial) concluded that Genova had a financial reason for this decision: Gulotta kicked back to Genova about 30% of all payments his firm received from the City. Genova diverted public resources to private ends in at least one other way: He induced Jerome Stack, the Public Works Commissioner, to make employees available for political duties. Stack gave employees leave (to provide the cover story that they were doing politics on their own) while providing each with a day of "comp time" for every day of political work. For some tasks, such as attending fundraisers, Stack gave the employees overtime credit, which immediately padded their paychecks — and always in an amount enough to cover the cost of tickets that the employees had purchased for themselves and their families.

For these machinations, Genova, Gulotta, and Stack have been convicted of violating the Racketeer Influenced and Corrupt Organizations Act (RICO); they operated the City (an "enterprise") through a pattern of racketeering (the predicate offenses are bribery and mail fraud).

Section 1961(1)(B) enumerates the federal crimes that are "racketeering activity," and § 1961(1)(A) has a shorter but more general list of state offenses:

> [A]ny act or threat involving murder, kidnapping, gambling, arson, robbery, bribery, extortion, dealing in obscene matter, or dealing in a controlled substance or listed chemical (as defined in [21 U.S.C. § 802]), which is chargeable under State law and punishable by imprisonment for more than one year[.]

The indictment charged that Stack's award of comp time for political work was "bribery" under Illinois law, which in 720 ILCS 5/33-1(a) says that a person commits that crime when, with intent to influence the performance of any act related to the employment or function of any public officer, [or] public employee . . . he promises or tenders to that person any property or personal advantage which he is not authorized by law to accept[.]

Stack's RICO conviction is valid only if the use of public money to pay for political assistance violates § 5/33-1(a). . . .

The prosecutor alleged that Genova, too, committed the predicate offense of bribery, but in his case the underlying acts concerned the Statements of Economic Interest that elected officials must make annually. Genova filed statements that did not disclose the money he received from Gulotta & Kawanna; this omission, according to the indictment, violated 720 ILCS 5/33-3, a statute covering several varieties of official misconduct. Relying on *United States v. Garner*, 837 F.2d 1404 (7th Cir. 1987), the district judge instructed the jury that official misconduct in violation of § 5/33-3 is a form of bribery, and the jury then convicted Genova of violating RICO. After trial the judge concluded that this instruction had been mistaken, but that Genova's RICO conviction could stand, because mail fraud (the mailing of these false and misleading forms, as part of a scheme to retain office and continue receiving kickbacks) still supplied the necessary pattern of racketeering activity. Mail fraud, in violation of 18 U.S.C. § 1341, *is* on the list in § 1961(1)(B). The prosecutor defends this decision and also contends that the jury instruction was correct and that all of the jury's findings thus should stand.

Although we understand the temptation to dilate criminal statutes so that corrupt officials get their comeuppance, people are entitled to clear notice of what the criminal law forbids, and courts must take care not to enlarge the scope of illegality. *See, e.g., Scheidler v. National Organization for Women, Inc.*, 537 U.S. 393 (2003) (rejecting an expansive interpretation of extortion designed to bring noxious activity within RICO); *Bailey v. United States*, 516 U.S. 137 (1995) (rejecting an expansive interpretation of "use" in a gun-control statute); *McNally v. United States*, 483 U.S. 350 (1987) (disapproving the creative "intangible rights" theory of mail fraud). Congress responded to *Bailey and McNally* by amending the statutes to provide a basis for the theories the courts had developed. Perhaps RICO should cover political corruption that does not entail bribery or extortion. But such a change should occur through legislation rather than prosecutorial and judicial creativity. [T]his principle leads us to conclude that neither misapplication of public funds nor concealment of illicit income is "bribery."

Let us start with Genova's situation. Gulotta bribed Genova, but Genova did not bribe anyone — certainly not the county bureaucrats who received and put on public view his Statements of Economic Interest. Genova did not pay anyone to perform any official duty. The idea that any violation of 720 ILCS 5/33-3 entails bribery comes from failure to distinguish among its subsections. It provides:

> A public officer or employee commits misconduct when, in his official capacity, he commits any of the following acts:
>
> (a) Intentionally or recklessly fails to perform any mandatory duty as required by law; or
>
> (b) Knowingly performs an act which he knows he is forbidden by law to perform; or
>
> (c) With intent to obtain a personal advantage for himself or another, he performs an act in excess of his lawful authority; or
>
> (d) Solicits or knowingly accepts for the performance of any act a fee or reward which he knows is not authorized by law.
>
> A public officer or employee convicted of violating any provision of this Section forfeits his office or employment. In addition, he commits a Class 3 felony.

Garner dealt with subsection (d), which defines a species of bribery. 837 F.2d at 1417–19. Genova's misconduct, however, was alleged to violate subsection (c). Using § 5/33-3(c) is itself a stretch, for the law requiring officials to file Statements of Economic Interest has its own penalty clause. Someone who files a false or incomplete statement commits a Class A misdemeanor, *see* 5 ILCS 420/4A-107, and no misdemeanor is "racketeering activity" under RICO. We could not find any Illinois decision suggesting that any statute other than § 420/4A-107 applies to a false, incomplete, or misleading Statement of Economic Interest. At all events, § 5/33-3(c) does not read like a definition of bribery and therefore may not be used as a predicate offense under RICO.

Stack's conduct also is hard to see as bribery. . . . The United States concedes that no Illinois decision supports its view that using public funds to pay municipal employees for political labor is bribery under 720 ILCS 5/33-1, and it would deprive Stack of fair warning to put that statute to such a novel use in order to secure his conviction for violating RICO. Stack's RICO conviction cannot stand.

Whether Genova's RICO conviction is tenable depends on the mail fraud convictions (and the predicate acts based on mail fraud). Each count of mail fraud (and each parallel predicate act under the RICO charge) represented one annual Statement of Economic Interest that omitted the money Genova had received the prior year from Gulotta & Kawanna. Genova does not contest the jury's evident conclusion that the statements (and hence the mailings) were false. He does contend that they were not part of a scheme to defraud, but this goes nowhere. Keeping a lid on the kickbacks was essential to permit their continuation. Genova hoodwinked Calumet City out of the money he received as kickbacks; he also defrauded the voters out of their intangible right to his honest services — a theory of culpability resurrected by 18 U.S.C. § 1346, enacted soon after *McNally*. A jury sensibly could conclude that the false mailings were integral to this scheme, so that Genova violated § 1341. *See, e.g., Schmuck v. United States*, 489 U.S. 705 (1989). And because the scheme extended over several years, a jury also sensibly could find a pattern of racketeering. *See H.J., Inc. v. Northwestern Bell Telephone Co.*, 492 U.S. 229 (1989). Because the jury returned special verdicts identifying particular racketeering acts, we know that it determined beyond a reasonable doubt that Genova committed at least two mail frauds, and there is no good reason to think that the verdicts finding mail fraud predicates could have been influenced by the incorrect jury instruction about treating 720 ILCS 5/33-3 as a form of bribery. Both the mail fraud and the RICO convictions therefore are untainted by error.

Bottom line: Genova's and Gulotta's convictions and sentences are affirmed. . . . Stack's RICO conviction is reversed. . . .

Notes and Questions

1. *Defining state law predicate acts.* Why did the court in *Genova* find that the state law violations in that case — 720 ILCS 5/33-1(a) and 720 ILCS 5/33-3(c) — did not

qualify as RICO predicates? Be as specific as you can when answering this question. With respect to Genova's liability, could the prosecutor have alleged another theory of bribery that would have satisfied the court?

With respect to the latter question, consider *United States v. Garner*, 837 F.2d 1404 (7th Cir. 1987), cited by the *Genova* court. The court in *Garner* noted that § 1961(1)(A) describes state crime predicate acts by *substance* rather than by the *title* of the state crime. With respect to the predicate act of state law bribery, the court in *Garner* stated that "Congress intended for 'bribery' to be defined generically when it included bribery as a predicate act. Thus, any statute that proscribes conduct which could be generically defined as bribery can be the basis for a predicate act. . . ." *Id.* at 1418. The state "official misconduct" crime at issue in *Garner* was in effect a gratuity statute; the crime did not require the proof of a quid pro quo that is the essence of bribery under federal law. And "gratuity" is not listed as a state law predicate. However, 18 U.S.C. § 201 sets forth the distinct crimes of bribery and gratuity, both of which are *federal* predicate acts under RICO. Thus, the court in *Garner* concluded, "We see no reason why Congress would have defined bribery more broadly for federal officials than for state officials, particularly when it is remembered that Congress intended for RICO to 'be liberally construed to effectuate its remedial purpose.'" *Id.* Given that bribery and gratuity are distinct crimes under 18 U.S.C. § 201, why did the court in *Garner* conclude that the receipt of an illegal gratuity qualifies as state law "bribery" under § 1961(1)(A)?

2. *Double jeopardy.* The RICO statute presents potentially complicated double jeopardy issues. For example, may the government: (1) prosecute a defendant under RICO based upon the specified predicate acts necessary for a RICO conviction, *and* (2) later prosecute that same defendant for the predicate criminal acts themselves? *See United States v. Luong*, 393 F.3d 913, 917 (9th Cir. 2004) (concluding that "the government was not barred from successively prosecuting [defendants] for violations of RICO and for conspiracy to commit a Hobbs Act robbery when one of the RICO predicate acts was a conspiracy to commit Hobbs Act robberies").

In an analogous circumstance, a plurality of the Supreme Court concluded that, under the facts of the particular case, the defendant could be punished in successive prosecutions for both operating a "continuing criminal enterprise" and for the underlying offenses. *Garrett v. United States*, 471 U.S. 773 (1985).

2. Federal Crimes

As noted above, § 1961(1) includes dozens of federal crimes. Many of these statutes apply in the white collar context. These include bribery, extortion, financial institution fraud, obstruction of justice, money laundering, securities fraud, and — most significantly — mail and wire fraud. But how far can the government go in using the mail and wire fraud statutes to incorporate other offenses that are *not* listed as RICO predicates? For example, perjury is listed neither as a state RICO predicate nor as a federal RICO predicate. But if a defendant used the mail in order to suborn perjury in a fraud scheme, would that act qualify as a RICO predicate under the mail fraud statute? That is the issue in the next case.

United States v. Eisen

974 F.2d 246 (2d Cir. 1992)

JON O. NEWMAN, CIRCUIT JUDGE:

This is an appeal of RICO convictions arising from a law firm's fraudulent conduct of civil litigation as plaintiff's counsel in personal injury cases. . . .

Morris J. Eisen, P.C. ("the Eisen firm") was a large Manhattan law firm that specialized in bringing personal injury suits on behalf of plaintiffs. The defendants, seven of the Eisen firm's attorneys, investigators, and office personnel, were tried jointly on two counts of conducting and conspiring to conduct the affairs of the Eisen firm through a pattern of racketeering activity, in violation of 18 U.S.C. §§ 1962(c), (d). The indictment alleged, as the underlying acts of racketeering, that each of the defendants committed, among other crimes, numerous acts of mail fraud, in violation of 18 U.S.C. § 1341; and bribery of witnesses, in violation of New York Penal Law § 215.00.

Eisen was the founder, sole shareholder, and principal attorney of the Eisen firm. Napoli was associated with the Eisen firm in an "of counsel" capacity, and he was the main trial attorney for the firm. Fishman, a trial attorney, was also "of counsel" to the firm. The Eisen firm regularly used investigators to assist attorneys in the trial preparation of personal injury cases, and defendants Weinstein, Gabe, and Rella were private investigators affiliated with the firm. Morganti was the office administrator of the Eisen firm with responsibility for managing the daily affairs of the firm, including assigning attorneys and investigators to particular cases, monitoring the firm's daily calendar, and managing the financial and personnel operations of the firm.

The evidence at trial established that the defendants conducted the affairs of the Eisen law firm through a pattern of mail fraud and witness bribery by pursuing counterfeit claims and using false witnesses in personal injury trials, and that the Eisen firm earned millions in contingency fees from personal injury suits involving fraud or bribery. The methods by which the frauds were accomplished included pressuring accident witnesses to testify falsely, paying individuals to testify falsely that they had witnessed accidents, paying unfavorable witnesses not to testify, and creating false photographs, documents, and physical evidence of accidents for use before and during trial. The government's proof included the testimony of numerous Eisen firm attorneys and employees as well as Eisen firm clients, defense attorneys, and witnesses involved in the fraudulent personal injury suits. Transcripts, correspondence, and trial exhibits from the fraudulent personal injury suits were also introduced.

The racketeering acts considered by the jury related to the defendants' conduct with regard to 18 fraudulent personal injury lawsuits in which the plaintiff was represented by the Eisen firm. . . . The jury convicted all seven defendants of RICO substantive and conspiracy offenses after three weeks of deliberations.

[W]einstein contends that permitting the mail fraud offenses charged in the Eisen indictment to serve as RICO predicate acts conflicts with the deliberate decision made by Congress in omitting perjury as one of the enumerated RICO predicate offenses within the definition of "racketeering activity." *See* 18 U.S.C. § 1961(1). Contrary to the government's abrupt dismissal of this argument as "baseless," we recognize that there is some tension between the congressional decision to include federal mail fraud as a predicate offense and to exclude perjury, whether in violation of federal or state law. That tension is illustrated by this prosecution in which the fraudulent scheme consists primarily of arranging for state court witnesses to commit perjury.

Though the tension exists, we do not believe it places the indictment in this case beyond the purview of RICO. Congress did not wish to permit instances of federal or state court perjury as such to constitute a pattern of RICO racketeering acts. Apparently, there was an understandable reluctance to use federal criminal law as a back-stop for all state court litigation. Nevertheless, where, as here, a fraudulent scheme falls within the scope of the federal mail fraud statute and the other elements of RICO are established, use of the mail fraud offense as a RICO predicate act cannot be suspended simply because perjury is part of the means for perpetrating the fraud. We do not doubt that where a series of related state court perjuries occurs, it will often be possible to allege and prove both a scheme to defraud within the meaning of the mail fraud statute as well as the elements of a RICO violation. But in such cases, it will not be the fact of the perjuries alone that suffices to bring the matter within the scope of RICO. In any event, we cannot carve out from the coverage of RICO an exception for mail fraud offenses that involve state court perjuries.

The judgments of conviction appealed from are all affirmed.

Notes and Questions

1. *Federalism issues.* Because the mail and wire fraud statutes are included as RICO predicates, and because those statutes are so far-reaching, RICO applies to a huge range of circumstances. Many RICO cases may look like ordinary state criminal or civil cases that have been federalized by RICO. What was the Second Circuit's concern about the government's theory of the case in *Eisen*? Given those concerns, why did the court affirm the conviction?

2. *Mail and wire fraud.* How much latitude does the government have in applying RICO through the mail and wire fraud statutes? For example, tax fraud is not listed as a RICO predicate. But, if a taxpayer submits a fraudulent tax return via mails or wires, may that lead to potential RICO liability? The government employed this

controversial theory in one high-profile case, *United States v. Regan*, 937 F.2d 823 (2d Cir. 1991), *modified*, 946 F.2d 188 (2d Cir. 1991). At least in part because of the controversy over *Regan*, the Department of Justice later issued guidelines restricting the use of tax fraud/mail fraud as a RICO predicate. *See* U.S. Department of Justice, United States Attorneys' Manual, §6-4.210. Does that mean that the government could not again bring a case on this theory? *See* Ellen S. Podgor, *Department of Justice Guidelines: Balancing "Discretionary Justice,"* 13 Cornell J.L. & Pub. Pol'y 167 (2004).

3. *Securities fraud.* Under §1961(1), a defendant generally need not be charged with or convicted of the predicate acts; the statute only requires that the alleged acts be "chargeable," "indictable," or "punishable" under the applicable state or federal statute. There is, however, an exception to this rule in private RICO suits alleging securities fraud as the predicate acts. 18 U.S.C. §1964(c). (This issue is addressed following the *Sedima* case, *infra*.)

Problem

14-5. Defendant Grosser was "Of Counsel" to the law firm of Simon and Garcia, and was one of the four main trial attorneys for the firm. Simon and Garcia were the principals of the firm, which had six other partners and 18 associates. Grosser was the only attorney who acted as "Of Counsel" to the firm. Grosser was tried along with Simon under RICO.

The evidence at trial established that Grosser participated in a pattern of paying off court personnel to fix cases, and that the firm earned millions in contingency fees from these cases. The government's proof included the testimony of numerous firm attorneys, employees, and clients, as well as defense attorneys and witnesses involved in the fraudulent personal injury suits. Transcripts, correspondence, and trial exhibits from the fraudulent personal injury suits were also introduced. Grosser was found guilty under RICO based upon racketeering acts involving four personal injury cases in which he paid substantial sums of money to court clerks to divulge secret jury deliberations. The government's theory was that Grosser conducted the law firm's affairs through a pattern of racketeering activity in violation of §1962(c).

As "Of Counsel" to the firm, Grosser had an office within the firm's offices, for which Grosser paid rent. Grosser assisted the firm on an "as-needed" basis, but was not employed by or a partner in the firm. There was evidence presented to the jury that Grosser handled approximately five percent of the firm's caseload and produced approximately five percent of the firm's income through jury verdicts and settlements. There was no evidence that Grosser participated in firm policy decisions, such as hiring, benefits, or salary decisions. He did not attend firm partnership meetings but did regularly attend the annual firm retreat of all firm lawyers at which general firm policy was discussed.

The indictment alleged that the four pay-offs violated each of the following state statutes, which the government charged as the eight predicate acts in the case:

Penal Code § 100 (Bribery):

A person is guilty of bribery, a felony of the third degree, if he offers, confers, agrees to offer or confer upon another, or solicits, accepts or agrees to accept from another:

(1) any pecuniary benefit as consideration for the decision, opinion, recommendation, vote or other exercise of discretion as a public servant, party official or voter by the recipient;

(2) any benefit as consideration for the decision, vote, recommendation or other exercise of official discretion by the recipient in a judicial, administrative or legislative proceeding; or

(3) any benefit as consideration for a violation of a known legal duty as a public servant or party official.

A violation of this section is punishable by imprisonment up to one year.

Penal Code § 300 (Corrupt Compensation):

Whoever follows the occupation or practice of providing public officers of the State or of any political subdivision thereof with any compensation or thing of value otherwise than as provided for by the law of the state or political subdivision is guilty of the practice of corrupt compensation, a misdemeanor, and upon conviction thereof, shall be sentenced to pay a fine not exceeding one thousand dollars ($1,000), or to undergo imprisonment not exceeding one (1) year, or both.

You are appellate counsel for the defendant. What viable arguments should you assert on appeal? Are you likely to succeed on the argument(s)? Why or why not?

D. The Pattern Requirement

In a RICO case, the government or private plaintiff must allege and prove that the defendant committed or entered into a conspiracy to commit a "pattern of racketeering activity." [f] Under § 1961(5), a RICO pattern "requires at least two acts of racketeering activity, one of which occurred after the effective date of this chapter and the last of which occurred within ten years . . . after the commission of a prior act of racketeering activity." In the next case, the Supreme Court turned its attention to the pattern requirement. As you read the case, pay particular attention to Justice Scalia's concurring opinion. The second case in the section illustrates how lower courts have applied the approach adopted by the Supreme Court for determining the existence of a RICO pattern.

---

f. An individual may also violate § 1962 through "collection of an unlawful debt," as defined by 18 U.S.C. § 1961(6).

H.J. Inc. v. Northwestern Bell Telephone Co.

492 U.S. 229 (1989)

JUSTICE BRENNAN delivered the opinion of the Court.

The Racketeer Influenced and Corrupt Organizations Act (RICO or Act), imposes criminal and civil liability upon those who engage in certain "prohibited activities." Each prohibited activity is defined in 18 U.S.C. § 1962 to include, as one necessary element, proof either of "a pattern of racketeering activity" or of "collection of an unlawful debt." "Racketeering activity" is defined in RICO to mean "any act or threat involving" specified state-law crimes, any "act" indictable under various specified federal statutes, and certain federal "offenses," 18 U.S.C. § 1961(1); but of the term "pattern" the statute says only that it "requires at least two acts of racketeering activity" within a 10-year period, 18 U.S.C. § 1961(5). We are called upon in this civil case to consider what conduct meets RICO's pattern requirement.

Petitioners, customers of respondent Northwestern Bell Telephone Co., filed this putative class action in 1986 in the District Court for the District of Minnesota. Petitioners alleged violations of §§ 1962(a), (b), (c), and (d) by Northwestern Bell and the other respondents — some of the telephone company's officers and employees, various members of the Minnesota Public Utilities Commission (MPUC), and other unnamed individuals and corporations — and sought an injunction and treble damages under RICO's civil liability provisions, §§ 1964(a) and (c).

The MPUC is the state body responsible for determining the rates that Northwestern Bell may charge. Petitioners' five-count complaint alleged that between 1980 and 1986 Northwestern Bell sought to influence members of the MPUC in the performance of their duties — and in fact caused them to approve rates for the company in excess of a fair and reasonable amount — by making cash payments to commissioners, negotiating with them regarding future employment, and paying for parties and meals, for tickets to sporting events and the like, and for airline tickets. Based upon these factual allegations, petitioners alleged in their first count a pendent state-law claim, asserting that Northwestern Bell violated the Minnesota bribery statute, Minn. Stat. § 609.42, as well as state common law prohibiting bribery. They also raised four separate claims under § 1962 of RICO. Count II alleged that, in violation of § 1962(a), Northwestern Bell derived income from a pattern of racketeering activity involving predicate acts of bribery and used this income to engage in its business as an interstate "enterprise." Count III claimed a violation of § 1962(b), in that, through this same pattern of racketeering activity, respondents acquired an interest in or control of the MPUC, which was also an interstate "enterprise." In Count IV, petitioners asserted that respondents participated in the conduct and affairs of the MPUC through this pattern of racketeering activity, contrary to § 1962(c). Finally, Count V alleged that respondents conspired together to violate §§ 1962(a), (b), and (c), thereby contravening § 1962(d).

The District Court granted respondents' Federal Rule of Civil Procedure 12(b)(6) motion, dismissing the complaint for failure to state a claim upon which relief could be granted. The court found that "[e]ach of the fraudulent acts alleged by [petitioners] was committed in furtherance of a single scheme to influence MPUC commissioners to the detriment of Northwestern Bell's ratepayers." It held that dismissal was therefore mandated by the Court of Appeals for the Eighth Circuit's decision in *Superior Oil Co. v. Fulmer*, 785 F.2d 252 (8th Cir. 1986), which the District Court interpreted as adopting an "extremely restrictive" test for a pattern of racketeering activity that required proof of "multiple illegal schemes." The Court of Appeals for the Eighth Circuit affirmed the dismissal of petitioners' complaint, confirming that under Eighth Circuit precedent "[a] single fraudulent effort or scheme is insufficient" to establish a pattern of racketeering activity, and agreeing with the District Court that petitioners' complaint alleged only a single scheme. Most Courts of Appeals have rejected the Eighth Circuit's interpretation of RICO's pattern concept to require an allegation and proof of multiple schemes, and we granted certiorari to resolve this conflict. We now reverse.

In *Sedima, S.P.R.L. v. Imrex Co.*, 473 U.S. 479 (1985), this Court rejected a restrictive interpretation of § 1964(c) that would have made it a condition for maintaining a civil RICO action both that the defendant had already been convicted of a predicate racketeering act or of a RICO violation, and that plaintiff show a special racketeering injury. In doing so, we acknowledged concern in some quarters over civil RICO's use against "legitimate" businesses, as well as "mobsters and organized criminals" — a concern that had frankly led to the Court of Appeals' interpretation of § 1964(c) in *Sedima*. But we suggested that RICO's expansive uses "appear to be primarily the result of the breadth of the predicate offenses, in particular the inclusion of wire, mail, and securities fraud, and the failure of Congress and the courts to develop a meaningful concept of 'pattern'" — both factors that apply to criminal as well as civil applications of the Act. *Id.* at 500. Congress has done nothing in the interim further to illuminate RICO's key requirement of a pattern of racketeering; and as the plethora of different views expressed by the Courts of Appeals since *Sedima* demonstrates, developing a meaningful concept of "pattern" within the existing statutory framework has proved to be no easy task. . . .

We begin, of course, with RICO's text, in which Congress followed a "pattern [of] utilizing terms and concepts of breadth." *Russello v. United States*, 464 U.S. 16, 21 (1983). As we remarked in *Sedima, supra*, 473 U.S. at 496 n.14,[g] the section of the

---

g. Here is the footnote to which the Court refers:

As many commentators have pointed out, the definition of a "pattern of racketeering activity" differs from the other provisions in § 1961 in that it states that a pattern *requires at least two acts of racketeering activity*, § 1961(5) (emphasis added), not that it "means" two such acts. The implication is that while two acts are necessary, they may not be sufficient. Indeed, in common parlance two of anything do not generally form a "pattern." The legislative history supports the view that two isolated acts of racketeering activity do not constitute a pattern. As the Senate Report explained: "The target of [RICO] is thus not sporadic activity. The infiltration of legitimate business normally requires more than one 'racketeering activity' and the threat of continuing activity to be effective. It is this factor

statute headed "definitions," 18 U.S.C. §1961, does not so much define a pattern of racketeering activity as state a minimum necessary condition for the existence of such a pattern. Unlike other provisions in §1961 that tell us what various concepts used in the Act "mean," 18 U.S.C. §1961(5) says of the phrase "pattern of racketeering activity" only that it "requires at least two acts of racketeering activity, one of which occurred after [October 15, 1970,] and the last of which occurred within ten years (excluding any period of imprisonment) after the commission of a prior act of racketeering activity." It thus places an outer limit on the concept of a pattern of racketeering activity that is broad indeed.

Section 1961(5) does indicate that Congress envisioned circumstances in which no more than two predicates would be necessary to establish a pattern of racketeering — otherwise it would have drawn a narrower boundary to RICO liability, requiring proof of a greater number of predicates. But, at the same time, the statement that a pattern "requires at least" two predicates implies "that while two acts are necessary, they may not be sufficient." *Sedima*, 473 U.S. at 496 (Powell, J., dissenting). Section 1961(5) concerns only the minimum *number* of predicates necessary to establish a pattern; and it assumes that there is something to a RICO pattern *beyond* simply the number of predicate acts involved. The legislative history bears out this interpretation, for the principal sponsor of the Senate bill expressly indicated that "proof of two acts of racketeering activity, without more, does not establish a pattern." 116 Cong. Rec. 18940 (1970) (statement of Sen. McClellan). Section 1961(5) does not identify, though, these additional prerequisites for establishing the existence of a RICO pattern.

In addition to §1961(5), there is the key phrase "pattern of racketeering activity" itself, from §1962, and we must "start with the assumption that the legislative purpose is expressed by the ordinary meaning of the words used." *Richards v. United States*, 369 U.S. 1, 9 (1962). In normal usage, the word "pattern" here would be taken to require more than just a multiplicity of racketeering predicates. A "pattern" is an "arrangement or order of things or activity," 11 Oxford English Dictionary 357 (2d ed. 1989), and the mere fact that there are a number of predicates is no guarantee that they fall into any arrangement or order. It is not the number of predicates but

---

of *continuity plus relationship* which combines to produce a pattern." S. Rep. No. 91-617, p. 158 (1969) (emphasis added). Similarly, the sponsor of the Senate bill, after quoting this portion of the Report, pointed out to his colleagues that "[t]he term 'pattern' itself requires the showing of a relationship. . . . So, therefore, proof of two acts of racketeering activity, without more, does not establish a pattern. . . ." 116 Cong. Rec. 18940 (1970) (statement of Sen. McClellan). Significantly, in defining "pattern" in a later provision of the same bill, Congress was more enlightening: "[C]riminal conduct forms a pattern if it embraces criminal acts that have the same or similar purposes, results, participants, victims, or methods of commission, or otherwise are interrelated by distinguishing characteristics and are not isolated events." 18 U.S.C. §3575(e). This language may be useful in interpreting other sections of the Act.

—Eds.

the relationship that they bear to each other or to some external organizing principle that renders them "ordered" or "arranged." The text of RICO conspicuously fails anywhere to identify, however, forms of relationship or external principles to be used in determining whether racketeering activity falls into a pattern for purposes of the Act.

It is reasonable to infer, from this absence of any textual identification of sorts of pattern that would satisfy § 1962's requirement, in combination with the very relaxed limits to the pattern concept fixed in § 1961(5), that Congress intended to take a flexible approach, and envisaged that a pattern might be demonstrated by reference to a range of different ordering principles or relationships between predicates, within the expansive bounds set. For any more specific guidance as to the meaning of "pattern," we must look past the text to RICO's legislative history, as we have done in prior cases construing the Act.

The legislative history, which we discussed in *Sedima*, 473 U.S. at 496 n.14, shows that Congress indeed had a fairly flexible concept of a pattern in mind. A pattern is not formed by "sporadic activity," S. Rep. No. 91-617 at 158 (1969), and a person cannot "be subjected to the sanctions of title IX simply for committing two widely separated and isolated criminal offenses," 116 Cong. Rec. at 18940 (1970) (Sen. McClellan). Instead, "[t]he term 'pattern' itself requires the showing of a relationship" between the predicates, *id.*, and of "'the threat of continuing activity,'" *id.*, quoting S. Rep. No. 91-617, at 158. "It is this factor of *continuity plus relationship* which combines to produce a pattern." *Id.* (emphasis added). RICO's legislative history reveals Congress' intent that to prove a pattern of racketeering activity a plaintiff or prosecutor must show that the racketeering predicates are related, *and* that they amount to or pose a threat of continued criminal activity.

For analytic purposes these two constituents of RICO's pattern requirement must be stated separately, though in practice their proof will often overlap. The element of relatedness is the easier to define, for we may take guidance from a provision elsewhere in the Organized Crime Control Act of 1970 (OCCA), Pub. L. 91-452, 84 Stat. 922, of which RICO formed Title IX. OCCA included as Title X the Dangerous Special Offender Sentencing Act, 18 U.S.C. § 3575 et seq. (now partially repealed). Title X provided for enhanced sentences where, among other things, the defendant had committed a prior felony as part of a pattern of criminal conduct or in furtherance of a conspiracy to engage in a pattern of criminal conduct. As we noted in *Sedima*, Congress defined Title X's pattern requirement solely in terms of the *relationship* of the defendant's criminal acts one to another: "[C]riminal conduct forms a pattern if it embraces criminal acts that have the same or similar purposes, results, participants, victims, or methods of commission, or otherwise are interrelated by distinguishing characteristics and are not isolated events." Section 3575(e). We have no reason to suppose that Congress had in mind for RICO's pattern of racketeering component any more constrained a notion of the relationships between predicates that would suffice.

RICO's legislative history tells us, however, that the relatedness of racketeering activities is not alone enough to satisfy § 1962's pattern element. To establish a RICO pattern it must also be shown that the predicates themselves amount to, or that they otherwise constitute a threat of, *continuing* racketeering activity. As to this continuity requirement, § 3575(e) is of no assistance. It is this aspect of RICO's pattern element that has spawned the "multiple scheme" test adopted by some lower courts, including the Court of Appeals in this case. But although proof that a RICO defendant has been involved in multiple criminal schemes would certainly be highly relevant to the inquiry into the continuity of the defendant's racketeering activity, it is implausible to suppose that Congress thought continuity might be shown *only* by proof of multiple schemes. The Eighth Circuit's test brings a rigidity to the available methods of proving a pattern that simply is not present in the idea of "continuity" itself; and it does so, moreover, by introducing a concept — the "scheme" — that appears nowhere in the language or legislative history of the Act. We adopt a less inflexible approach that seems to us to derive from a commonsense, everyday understanding of RICO's language and Congress' gloss on it. What a plaintiff or prosecutor must prove is continuity of racketeering activity, or its threat, *simpliciter*. This may be done in a variety of ways, thus making it difficult to formulate in the abstract any general test for continuity. We can, however, begin to delineate the requirement.

"Continuity" is both a closed- and open-ended concept, referring either to a closed period of repeated conduct, or to past conduct that by its nature projects into the future with a threat of repetition. It is, in either case, centrally a temporal concept — and particularly so in the RICO context, where *what* must be continuous, RICO's predicate acts or offenses, and the *relationship* these predicates must bear one to another, are distinct requirements. A party alleging a RICO violation may demonstrate continuity over a closed period by proving a series of related predicates extending over a substantial period of time. Predicate acts extending over a few weeks or months and threatening no future criminal conduct do not satisfy this requirement: Congress was concerned in RICO with long-term criminal conduct. Often a RICO action will be brought before continuity can be established in this way. In such cases, liability depends on whether the *threat* of continuity is demonstrated.

Whether the predicates proved establish a threat of continued racketeering activity depends on the specific facts of each case. Without making any claim to cover the field of possibilities — preferring to deal with this issue in the context of concrete factual situations presented for decision — we offer some examples of how this element might be satisfied. A RICO pattern may surely be established if the related predicates themselves involve a distinct threat of long-term racketeering activity, either implicit or explicit. Suppose a hoodlum were to sell "insurance" to a neighborhood's storekeepers to cover them against breakage of their windows, telling his victims he would be reappearing each month to collect the "premium" that would continue their "coverage." Though the number of related predicates involved may be small and they may occur close together in time, the racketeering acts themselves include a specific threat of repetition extending indefinitely into the future, and thus supply the requisite threat of continuity. In other cases, the threat of continuity may be established by showing that the predicate acts or offenses are part of an ongoing entity's regular way of doing business. Thus, the threat of continuity is sufficiently established where the predicates can be attributed to a defendant operating as part of a long-term association that exists for criminal purposes. Such associations include, but extend well beyond, those traditionally grouped under the phrase "organized crime." The continuity requirement is likewise satisfied where it is shown that the predicates are a regular way of conducting defendant's ongoing legitimate business (in the sense that it is not a business that exists for criminal purposes), or of conducting or participating in an ongoing and legitimate RICO "enterprise."

The limits of the relationship and continuity concepts that combine to define a RICO pattern, and the precise methods by which relatedness and continuity or its threat may be proved, cannot be fixed in advance with such clarity that it will always be apparent whether in a particular case a "pattern of racketeering activity" exists. The development of these concepts must await future cases, absent a decision by Congress to revisit RICO to provide clearer guidance as to the Act's intended scope. . . .

Under the analysis we have set forth above, and consistent with the allegations in their complaint, petitioners may be able to prove that the multiple predicates alleged constitute "a pattern of racketeering activity," in that they satisfy the requirements of relationship and continuity. The acts of bribery alleged are said to be related by a common purpose, to influence commissioners in carrying out their duties in order to win approval of unfairly and unreasonably high rates for Northwestern Bell. Furthermore, petitioners claim that the racketeering predicates occurred with some frequency over at least a six-year period, which may be sufficient to satisfy the continuity requirement. Alternatively, a threat of continuity of racketeering activity might be established at trial by showing that the alleged bribes were a regular way of conducting Northwestern Bell's ongoing business, or a regular way of conducting or participating in the conduct of the alleged and ongoing RICO enterprise, the MPUC.

The Court of Appeals thus erred in affirming the District Court's dismissal of petitioners' complaint for failure to plead "a pattern of racketeering activity." The judgment is reversed, and the case is remanded for further proceedings consistent with this opinion.

Justice Scalia, with whom The Chief Justice, Justice O'Connor, and Justice Kennedy join, concurring in the judgment.

. . . Elevating to the level of statutory text a phrase taken from the legislative history, the Court counsels the lower courts: "'continuity plus relationship.'" This seems to me about as helpful to the conduct of their affairs as "life is a fountain." Of the two parts of this talismanic phrase, the relatedness requirement is said to be the "easier to define," *id.*, yet here is the Court's definition, *in toto*: "'[C]riminal conduct forms a pattern if it embraces criminal acts that have the same or similar purposes, results, participants, victims, or methods of commission, or otherwise are interrelated by distinguishing characteristics and are not isolated events.'" . . .

The Court finds "continuity" more difficult to define precisely. "Continuity," it says, "is both a closed- and open-ended concept, referring either to a closed period of repeated conduct, or to past conduct that by its nature projects into the future with a threat of repetition." I have no idea what this concept of a "closed period of repeated conduct" means. Virtually all allegations of racketeering activity, in both civil and criminal suits, will relate to past periods that are "closed" (unless one expects plaintiff or the prosecutor to establish that the defendant not only committed the crimes he did, but is still committing them), and all of them *must* relate to conduct that is "repeated," because of RICO's multiple-act requirement. Since the Court has rejected the concept of separate criminal "schemes" or "episodes" as a criterion of "threatening future criminal conduct," I think it must be saying that at least a few months of racketeering activity (and who knows how much more?) is generally for free, as far as RICO is concerned. The "closed period" concept is a sort of safe harbor for racketeering activity that does not last *too* long, no matter how many different crimes and different schemes are involved, so long as it does not otherwise "establish a threat of continued racketeering activity." A gang of hoodlums that commits one act of extortion on Monday in New York, a second in Chicago on Tuesday, a third in San Francisco on Wednesday, and so on through an entire week, and then finally and completely disbands, cannot be reached under RICO. I am sure that is not what the statute intends, but I cannot imagine what else the Court's murky discussion can possibly mean. . . .

It is, however, unfair to be so critical of the Court's effort, because I would be unable to provide an interpretation of RICO that gives significantly more guidance concerning its application. Today's opinion has added nothing to improve our prior guidance, which has created a kaleidoscope of Circuit positions, except to clarify that RICO may in addition be violated when there is a "threat of continuity." It seems to me this increases rather than removes the vagueness. . . . There is no reason to believe that the Courts of Appeals will be any more unified in the future, than they have in the past, regarding the content of this law.

That situation is bad enough with respect to any statute, but it is intolerable with respect to RICO. For it is not only true, as Justice Marshall commented in *Sedima, S.P.R.L. v. Imrex Co.*, 473 U.S. 479 (1985), that our interpretation of RICO has "quite simply revolutionize[d] private litigation" and "validate[d] the federalization of broad areas of state common law of frauds," *id.* at 501 (dissenting opinion), so that clarity and predictability in RICO's civil applications are particularly important; but it is also true that RICO, since it has criminal applications as well, must, even in its civil applications, possess the degree of certainty required for criminal laws. No constitutional challenge to this law has been raised in the present case, and so that issue is not before us. That the highest Court in the land has been unable to derive from this statute anything more than today's meager guidance bodes ill for the day when that challenge is presented.

However unhelpful its guidance may be, however, I think the Court is correct in saying that nothing in the statute supports the proposition that predicate acts constituting part of a single scheme (or single episode) can never support a cause of action under RICO. Since the Court of Appeals here rested its decision on the contrary proposition, I concur in the judgment of the Court reversing the decision below.

Notes and Questions

1. *Defining a "pattern."* In *H.J. Inc.*, the Supreme Court acknowledged a number of possible approaches to defining a "pattern." One approach would be to require proof of some sort of "organized" criminal activity. Another approach, used by the Court of Appeals in *H.J. Inc.*, requires multiple schemes. Why did the Court reject these approaches? What exactly is required under the Court's holding? Would two predicate acts within 10 years ever be sufficient? Why or why not?

2. *Fair notice.* If you were advising a client, how would you define the term "pattern"? Could you do so in a way that would be comprehensible to a layperson? Was Justice Scalia correct in concluding the vagueness of the term is "intolerable"? Why or why not?

In the next case, the court of appeals applied the test from *H.J. Inc.* As you read the case, consider why the trial court dismissed the case and whether its decision was justified.

Libertad v. Welch

53 F.3d 428 (1st Cir. 1995)

TORRUELLA, CHIEF JUDGE.

A group of individuals and organizations representing women who have sought or will seek family planning services in Puerto Rico ("Appellants") brought this action against certain individuals and organizations ("Appellees") who oppose abortion and coordinate anti-abortion demonstrations at women's health clinics in Puerto Rico. The Appellants appeal from the district court's grant of summary judgment disposing of their claims brought under §§ 1962(c) and (d) of the Racketeer Influenced and Corrupt Organizations Act ("RICO"). In granting summary judgment for Appellees, the district court ruled that Appellants' claims brought under §§ 1962(c) and (d) of RICO failed because Appellants did not show either the existence of an enterprise or a pattern of racketeering activity. . . .

Appellants initiated this action on behalf of women seeking reproductive health services and their health care providers. Among the named plaintiffs are two women using the pseudonyms "Lydia Libertad" and "Emilia Emancipación." Both Libertad and Emancipación are Puerto Rico residents and have sought reproductive health services on the island. Another plaintiff, Rosa Cáceres, is the Clinic Administrator at the Women's Metropolitan Clinic ("WMC") in Río Piedras, Puerto Rico, which provides a range of reproductive health services including abortion. WMC is owned in turn by plaintiff Oficinas Médicas. Plaintiff Mary Rivera is the Clinic Supervisor and Director of Counselling at the Clínica Gineco-Quirúrgica, ("Clínica") which also provides reproductive health services including abortion. Plaintiffs Ana E. González-Dávila ("González") and Dr. Rafael E. Castro-De Jesús ("Castro") are, respectively, the administrator and the medical director of plaintiff Ladies Medical Center ("LMC"), which also provides reproductive health services including abortion. The Grupo Pro Derechos Reproductivos, an abortion rights organization, is also a plaintiff.

Defendant Father Patrick Welch is the head of the anti-abortion rights organization Pro-Life Rescue Team ("PLRT"), also a named defendant. Defendants Donald Treshman and Reverend Ed Martin are, respectively, the National Director and the Executive Director of defendant Rescue America, a nationwide anti-abortion rights group based in Houston. Defendant Norman Weslin is the director of the defendant anti-abortion rights group the Sacrificial Lambs of Christ ("SLC"). Defendant Carlos Sánchez is a member of the anti-abortion rights group Pro-Vida.

We present the facts here in the light most favorable to the Appellants. Some or all of the Appellees staged protest demonstrations, which they refer to as "rescues," at the plaintiff clinics on five occasions: September 26, 1992; September 28, 1992; December 17, 1992; December 24, 1992; and January 8, 1993. During each of the five protests, Appellees blockaded the clinics so that clinic personnel and patients could not enter. Each blockade was carried out in a similar manner. Typically, the protests began before the clinics opened, with Appellees blocking access to the clinics and parking lots by physically obstructing the entrances, linking their arms tightly together and refusing to allow anyone to pass through. Outside, the protesters shouted slogans through megaphones to clinic personnel and patients, told patients that they were "murderers," screamed insults at clinic personnel, and videotaped or photographed people as they attempted to enter and leave the clinics. The protesters also defaced the clinic property by affixing difficult-to-remove stickers depicting fetuses on the walls and entrances, and by scrawling graffiti on the clinic walls. During these blockades, litter was strewn around clinic property and on the properties of surrounding businesses. In addition to effectively shutting down the clinics for all or part of a day, these protests caused extensive and costly property damage to the clinics.

Appellee Welch and some of the minor children who protest with him have on occasion entered the clinics and intimidated or harassed patients and staff. On September 26, 1992, Welch invaded the LMC and pushed plaintiff González from the clinic entrance all the way through the waiting room to the back office, trapping her there for a number of hours. On September 28, 1992, Welch and a young girl entered one of the clinics and remained in the waiting room, despite being told to leave by clinic staff. Patients with appointments would enter and then leave when they recognized Welch in the waiting room. Eventually, the police had to come and remove Welch and the young girl.

The record indicates that of the five protests at issue in this case, the January 8, 1993 protest is the only one at which all of the Appellees, not just Welch and his followers, participated. The tactics employed on January 8 were considerably more aggressive. In addition to the above-mentioned blockade methods, Appellees also blocked clinic access by parking buses in front of clinic entrances and then refusing to move them when instructed to do so by the police. Appellees chain-locked a clinic entrance and then covered the lock with tape to prevent it from being pried open. One clinic supporter received a death threat from a protester. The clinic suffered considerable property damage as well; locks were filled with glue or gum, and gates were broken or otherwise damaged to prevent entry.

On January 8, 1993, Appellants filed the instant action seeking a temporary restraining order, a preliminary injunction, and a permanent injunction enjoining Appellees from using unlawful force, harassment, intimidation, and physical obstruction during their protests in front of Puerto Rico clinics. The district court denied the motion for a temporary restraining order, but held a hearing from February 4–9, 1993 on Appellants' request for a preliminary injunction, during which extensive testimonial and documentary evidence was presented by both parties. [The district court ultimately granted summary judgment to the Appellees.]

Under the terms of the RICO statute, a "pattern of racketeering activity requires at least two acts of racketeering activity." 18 U.S.C. § 1961(5). The definitional section "does not so much define a pattern of racketeering activity as state a minimum necessary condition for the existence of such a pattern." *H.J. Inc. v. Northwestern Bell Telephone Co.*, 492 U.S. 229, 237 (1989). The two predicate acts of racketeering activity must be acts chargeable or indictable under any one or more of certain specified criminal laws. These acts include "extortion" as it is defined in the Hobbs Act, 18 U.S.C. § 1951(b)(2).[13] In addition, a RICO plaintiff must demonstrate that the predicate acts are related, and that they amount to or pose a threat of continued criminal activity. *H.J. Inc.*, 492 U.S. at 237.

We have noted that "the relatedness test is not a cumbersome one for a RICO plaintiff." *Feinstein*, 942 F.2d 34, 44 (1st Cir. 1991). A RICO plaintiff establishes that predicate acts are related by demonstrating that they "have the same or similar purposes, results, participants, victims, or methods of commission, or otherwise are interrelated by distinguishing characteristics and are not isolated events." *H.J. Inc.*,

---

13. As we explained above, this provision defines extortion as "the obtaining of property from another, with his consent, induced by wrongful use of actual or threatened force, violence, or fear." The intangible right to freely conduct one's lawful business constitutes "property" for purposes of this section. [In Scheidler v. National Organization for Women, 537 U.S. 393 (2003), the United States Supreme Court rejected this theory of extortion and reversed a finding of RICO liability. *See* Chapter 8, Extortion, *supra* — eds.]

492 U.S. at 240. A fact-specific allegation of a single common scheme can be used to satisfy the relatedness requirement. As the district court succinctly and correctly noted, there is little doubt in this case that the alleged predicate acts are related. . . .

In order to establish the continuity of the predicate acts, a plaintiff must show either (1) that the acts amount to continued criminal activity, in that the related acts extend over a period of time; or (2) that the predicate acts, though not continuous, pose a threat of continued activity. *H.J. Inc.*, 492 U.S. at 242. Because RICO was intended by Congress to apply only to enduring criminal conduct, predicate acts extending over a few weeks or months do not generally satisfy this requirement. *Feinstein*, 942 F.2d at 45. Under the second, "threat" approach, however, even where the predicate acts occur in a narrow time frame, the requirement can still be satisfied by demonstrating "a realistic prospect of continuity over an open-ended period yet to come." *Id.* This approach "necessitates a showing that 'the acts themselves include a specific threat of repetition extending indefinitely into the future, [or] . . . are part of an ongoing entity's regular way of doing business.'" *Id.* (quoting *H.J. Inc.*, 492 U.S. at 242).

Under the first method of establishing continuity, the district court found, we think correctly, that the five blockades over a three-month period did not constitute a closed-end period of continued criminal conduct. Appellants do not specifically contest this finding here. Rather, they challenge the district court's finding that the record does not reveal "a realistic prospect that the activity challenged in this suit will resume with enduring effects," and that therefore, no continuity was established.

Appellants point out that the predicate acts involved in this case — the blockades, vandalism, and the threatening harassment of clinic personnel and patients — are part of the regular way that the defendants conduct their ongoing activities. The entire purpose of Rescue America, the PLRT, and their leaders, contend the Appellants, is preventing abortions, and they do this by regularly using unlawful as well as lawful tactics. Appellants further argue, and the record shows, that part of the Appellees' strategy is to strike randomly with little or no warning of which clinic they will target, making it inherently difficult or impossible to determine whether and when they will blockade again. There is also evidence that Rescue America has been conducting protests and blockades for several years, and shows no signs of abating or changing its unlawful tactics. Indeed, the March 4, 1994 press release, quoted in relevant part above, strongly indicates that the Appellees plan to continue their activities in Puerto Rico, lawful and unlawful.

Appellees contend that there is nothing about the challenged conduct that by its nature projects into the future with a threat of repetition. The January 8, 1993 blockade, they claim, was a "special gathering," an event unlikely to be repeated. They point out that Treshman left Puerto Rico after the blockade and has "no immediate plans to return." It is not the nature of the conduct itself, however, that suggests a threat of continuing; it is the fact that the Appellees' regular way of conducting their affairs involves the illegal acts conducted at that blockade, and that the Appellees have admitted that they plan to "continue their efforts." Moreover, Treshman's physical presence in Puerto Rico is not necessary for Appellees to plan or threaten future unlawful blockade activities in furtherance of the alleged conspiracy. We therefore find that sufficient evidence in the record raises a genuine issue of material fact as to whether the Appellees' conduct posed a threat of continuing activity, and that the district court thus erred in granting summary judgment against the Appellants on this basis.

Accordingly, we remand the Appellants' RICO claims against Appellees Welch, Treshman, Rescue America, and the PLRT only, for further proceedings to determine whether Appellants can prove the elements of their RICO causes of action. . . .

Notes and Questions

1. *Alleging and proving a "pattern."* With respect to the pattern requirement, what does the government or a private plaintiff need to allege to survive a motion to dismiss? As a practical matter, the burden may be higher on private plaintiffs. As discussed in the introductory notes and shown in the *Libertad* case, federal trial courts are often hostile towards civil RICO actions, which clog the federal dockets with cases that otherwise would be brought in state court.

What if an appeals court determines that some predicate acts were not proven at trial? May a RICO conviction survive nonetheless? *Compare United States v. Regan*, 937 F.2d 823 (2d Cir. 1991) (reversing bulk of predicate acts and reversing RICO convictions), *with United States v. Genova*, 333 F.3d 750 (7th Cir. 2003) (reversing state law predicate act conviction, but affirming RICO conviction based on two counts of mail fraud).

2. *Due process and notice.* As in so many other areas of white collar crime, due process and notice issues abound in RICO cases. The majority in *H.J. Inc.* acknowledged that RICO is a poorly drafted statute, and Justice Scalia in concurrence invited a vagueness challenge. Such challenges are very rarely successful. Is RICO unconstitutionally vague? Is it appropriate for the Court to attempt to clarify the statute, or should that task be left to Congress?

Problems

14-6. Tom Hivers was the elected district attorney for the city of Oakville. He worked closely with fellow deputy district attorney Wilma Katz. While both were working in the prosecutor's office, the federal government had a program providing supplemental funds to state and local prosecutors who did drug enforcement work. Hivers, however, was not eligible for any grant money because of his elected position.

Hivers appointed Katz as his deputy. In several grant applications mailed to the government, Hivers represented that Katz was primarily responsible for the drug enforcement cases. It was Hivers, however, who prosecuted all the drug cases and did all work in connection with the cases. Nevertheless, Katz signed her name on the monthly contractor reports detailing the drug enforcement work. For two years, Katz received monthly checks from the state and deposited the checks into her bank account. She subsequently wrote Hivers checks for the same amounts. Katz funneled approximately $90,000 in federal grant money to Hivers in this way. Katz and Hivers engaged in a similar scheme with money provided through state grants during the same period.

Hivers and Katz were indicted on crimes related to the district attorney's office over the last two years. Count 1 was a substantive RICO count, alleging a pattern of racketeering activity stemming from predicate acts including mail and wire fraud. Both defendants were convicted of two mail fraud counts in connection with the federal grant program and two mail fraud counts relating to the state grant program, and the RICO count based on those predicate acts. One mailing occurred per program in each of the two years in question.

The defendants appeal their RICO conviction, arguing that a pattern was not proven. How should the court rule? Why?

14-7. Joe Knight was the Mayor of Williamstown for three years. After a public outcry that his administration was corrupt, an extensive investigation took place. Two months later, Knight was charged with RICO based on the federal predicate acts of mail fraud (eight counts) and extortion (one count), and on the state law predicate act of bribery. Each of the federal predicate acts was also charged as a substantive count. The extortion and bribery allegations were based upon an incident during which Knight extorted a payment from a city contractor in exchange for granting a city contract to the contractor.

The jury convicted Knight on all counts. On appeal, the court reversed the mail fraud convictions on the grounds of insufficient evidence. Knight now argues that the RICO count must be dismissed for lack of a pattern. In response, the government argues that the federal extortion count and the state bribery predicate act are sufficient.

How should the court of appeals rule? Why?

14-8. The law firm of Simon and Garcia, P.C., is a Philadelphia firm noted for its work on behalf of personal injury plaintiffs. The senior partner, Seth Simon, is known locally as the "King of Torts," and has successfully sued on behalf of thousands of plaintiffs who have recovered millions of dollars from insurance companies, hospitals, and the like. The firm has also made a name for itself by successfully recovering in dozens of law suits brought against the City of Philadelphia.

Simon is something of a hero in the local legal community and among his clients for his ability to gain judgments against or settlements from powerful businesses and corporations on behalf of down-and-out individual plaintiffs. This success has not hurt the firm's or Simon's financial standing, given the firm's typical one-third contingency fee.

In one recent case, Simon brought a suit against the City on behalf of Imma Jones, whose husband, Irving, was killed in an accident on a Philadelphia street. At trial, the main plaintiff's witness was a truck driver named Helen Haley. Haley testified that she had noticed a crack in the pavement a week before the accident, which occurred in January of last year. The crack, everyone agreed, contributed to the accident. The testimony was critical because the plaintiff had to prove that the City was or should have been on notice of the condition in order to recover. The trial was held the following July, and resulted in an award to Jones of $2,000,000.

The next month, Simon tried another suit on behalf of Imma, this time against the driver of the other car. Once again, Haley testified at the trial. She stated that she happened to be driving by at the time of the accident, and noticed that the other driver was speeding just prior to the accident. After the testimony, the case settled for $50,000.

Shortly after the second trial, Haley was arrested and charged with transportation of stolen property. During plea negotiations, Haley admitted that a paralegal with the Simon firm had paid her $5,000 for the first trial and $7,000 for the second trial to testify as she did at both trials. The paralegal told the investigator that Simon had instructed him to make the payment to Haley.

Haley also told investigators that they might want to talk to her friend Keith Carp. Carp, who had his own history of troubles with the police, had worked as a private investigator for the Simon firm. In two of his cases, he admitted to having been instructed by Simon's secretary to pay the court clerk $500 in each of the cases to divulge the progress of jury deliberations. The secretary told the investigators that Simon instructed her to make the payments. When it appeared that the juries were about to find for the defendant in each case, Simon's associate, who was handling the trials, promptly settled the cases for $100,000 and $75,000, respectively. The trials occurred in November and December four years ago.

The government asserts that there were four instances of state law bribery, each punishable by more than a year in prison. The state bribery statute contains a three-year statute of limitations.

> *a. Assume that you are the defense attorney in the case. The prosecutor tells you that the government can prove the above facts at trial. How would you argue that, even assuming the facts, the government should not bring a RICO case? What arguments can you make based upon the law? Based upon the wise exercise of prosecutorial discretion?*

> *b. Now assume that, based upon the foregoing facts, Simon has been convicted under 18 U.S.C. §1962(c) for conducting the enterprise (the law firm) through a pattern of racketeering activity. What are the defendant's likely arguments on appeal? Should he succeed? Why or why not?*

E. RICO Conspiracy

As discussed in Chapter 3, Conspiracy, *supra*, the United States criminal code contains a number of specific conspiracy provisions. One of those is set forth in §1962(d). In the next case, the Supreme Court discussed the elements of RICO conspiracy.[h] The defendant argued that he could not be convicted of RICO conspiracy unless he personally committed or agreed to commit at least two predicate acts. As you read the case, consider how RICO conspiracy compares to the general federal conspiracy statute, 18 U.S.C. § 371, discussed in Chapter 3, *supra*.

Salinas v. United States

522 U.S. 52 (1997)

JUSTICE KENNEDY delivered the opinion of the Court.

This federal prosecution arose from a bribery scheme operated by Brigido Marmolejo, the Sheriff of Hidalgo County, Texas, and petitioner Mario Salinas, one of his principal deputies. In 1984, the United States Marshals Service and Hidalgo County entered into agreements under which the county would take custody of federal prisoners. In exchange, the Federal Government agreed to make a grant to the county for improving its jail and also agreed to pay the county a specific amount per day for each federal prisoner housed. Based on the estimated number of federal prisoners to be maintained, payments to the county were projected to be $915,785 per year. . . .

Homero Beltran-Aguirre was one of the federal prisoners housed in the jail under the arrangement negotiated between the Marshals Service and the county. He was incarcerated there for two intervals, first for 10 months and then for 5 months. During both custody periods, Beltran paid Marmolejo a series of bribes in exchange for so-called "contact visits" in which he remained alone with his wife or, on other occasions, his girlfriend. Beltran paid Marmolejo a fixed rate of six thousand dollars per month and one thousand dollars for each contact visit, which occurred twice a week. Petitioner Salinas was the chief deputy responsible for managing the jail and supervising custody of the prisoners. When Marmolejo was not available, Salinas arranged for the contact visits and on occasion stood watch outside the room where the visits took place. In return for his assistance with the scheme, Salinas received from Beltran a pair of designer watches and a pickup truck.

Salinas and Marmolejo were indicted and tried together, but only Salinas' convictions are before us. Salinas was charged with one count of violating RICO, 18 U.S.C. § 1962(c), one count of conspiracy to violate RICO, § 1962(d), and two counts of bribery in violation of § 666(a)(1)(B). The jury acquitted Salinas on the substantive RICO count but convicted him on the RICO conspiracy count and the bribery counts. A divided panel of the Court of Appeals for the Fifth Circuit affirmed.

Salinas directs his challenge to his conviction for conspiracy to violate RICO. There could be no conspiracy offense, he says, unless he himself committed or agreed to commit the two predicate acts requisite for a substantive RICO offense under § 1962(c). . . .

---

h. Another aspect of the *Salinas* case is discussed in Chapter 7, Bribery & Gratuities, *supra*, at § 7, C, 2.

The Government's theory was that Salinas himself committed a substantive §1962(c) RICO violation by conducting the enterprise's affairs through a pattern of racketeering activity that included acceptance of two or more bribes, felonies punishable in Texas by more than one year in prison. The jury acquitted on the substantive count. Salinas was convicted of conspiracy, however, and he challenges the conviction because the jury was not instructed that he must have committed or agreed to commit two predicate acts himself. His interpretation of the conspiracy statute is wrong.

The RICO conspiracy statute, simple in formulation, provides: "It shall be unlawful for any person to conspire to violate any of the provisions of subsection (a), (b), or (c) of this section." 18 U.S.C. §1962(d). There is no requirement of some overt act or specific act in the statute before us, unlike the general conspiracy provision applicable to federal crimes, which requires that at least one of the conspirators have committed an "act to effect the object of the conspiracy." §371. The RICO conspiracy provision, then, is even more comprehensive than the general conspiracy offense in §371.

In interpreting the provisions of §1962(d), we adhere to a general rule: When Congress uses well-settled terminology of criminal law, its words are presumed to have their ordinary meaning and definition. The relevant statutory phrase in §1962(d) is "to conspire." We presume Congress intended to use the term in its conventional sense, and certain well-established principles follow.

A conspiracy may exist even if a conspirator does not agree to commit or facilitate each and every part of the substantive offense. The partners in the criminal plan must agree to pursue the same criminal objective and may divide up the work, yet each is responsible for the acts of each other. If conspirators have a plan which calls for some conspirators to perpetrate the crime and others to provide support, the supporters are as guilty as the perpetrators. As Justice Holmes observed: "[P]lainly a person may conspire for the commission of a crime by a third person." *United States v. Holte*, 236 U.S. 140, 144 (1915). A person, moreover, may be liable for conspiracy even though he was incapable of committing the substantive offense.

... The RICO conspiracy statute, §1962(d), broadened conspiracy coverage by omitting the requirement of an overt act; it did not, at the same time, work the radical change of requiring the Government to prove each conspirator agreed that he would be the one to commit two predicate acts. ...

A conspirator must intend to further an endeavor which, if completed, would satisfy all of the elements of a substantive criminal offense, but it suffices that he adopt the goal of furthering or facilitating the criminal endeavor. He may do so in any number of ways short of agreeing to undertake all of the acts necessary for the crime's completion. One can be a conspirator by agreeing to facilitate only some of the acts leading to the substantive offense. It is elementary that a conspiracy may exist and be punished whether or not the substantive crime ensues, for the conspiracy is a distinct evil, dangerous to the public, and so punishable in itself. ...

In the case before us, even if Salinas did not accept or agree to accept two bribes, there was ample evidence that he conspired to violate subsection (c). The evidence showed that Marmolejo committed at least two acts of racketeering activity when he accepted numerous bribes and that Salinas knew about and agreed to facilitate the scheme. This is sufficient to support a conviction under §1962(d).

As a final matter, Salinas says his statutory interpretation is required by the rule of lenity. The rule does not apply when a statute is unambiguous or when invoked to engraft an illogical requirement to its text.

The judgment of the Court of Appeals is affirmed.

Notes and Questions

1. *RICO conspiracy and §371*. What was the defendant's contention in *Salinas*? Why did the Court reject the argument? According to the Court, how does §1962(d) compare with the general conspiracy statute, §371?

2. *Double jeopardy and multiple conspiracy statutes*. If you were a prosecutor, and believed that the elements of both the RICO conspiracy provision and another federal conspiracy statute could be proven, which would you employ? Would you have to choose? Would it violate the Double Jeopardy Clause for a defendant to be convicted and punished under both sections for the same act or acts? Why or why not? In *Blockburger v. United States*, 284 U.S. 299, 304 (1932), the Supreme Court held that under the Double Jeopardy Clause a defendant may not be punished under two separate statutes for the same act or acts if: (1) the two crimes have the same elements or (2) Congress did not intend that a defendant be punished twice for those crimes. For a discussion of Double Jeopardy Clause issues arising from charges under multiple federal conspiracy statutes, see Chapter 3, Conspiracy, *supra*.

3. *The rise, fall, and resurgence of RICO in white collar cases*. Prosecutors' use of RICO in complex white collar cases reached an early peak in the 1980s, with the first case brought against a Wall Street investment firm under RICO and other high-profile RICO cases. *See* J. Kelly Strader, *White Collar Crime and Punishment — Reflections on Michael, Martha, and Milberg Weiss,* 15 GEO. MASON L. REV. 45, 58–65 (2007) (describing the RICO case against Drexel Burnham Lambert and related cases against Michael Milken and others). Many began to criticize the use of RICO in such cases, however, and the use of the statute declined as prosecutors increasingly employed the money laundering statutes (see Money Laundering and Related Offenses, Chapter 12, *supra*) in complex white collar cases. *Cf.* Diane Marie Amann, *Spotting Money Launderers: A Better Way to Fight Organized Crime?* 27 SYRACUSE J. INT'L & COM. L.199 (2000).

The tide seems to be turning again, however, with the government employing RICO in a number of high-profile white collar crime cases. These include prosecutions of a major foreign corporation for theft of trade secrets, a pharmaceutical company in connection with an alleged marketing bribery and kickback scheme, and political figures on bribery and related charges.[i]

Is RICO an appropriate tool in white collar cases? By allowing prosecutors to bring multiple crimes and defendants into a single case, is the statute well-suited to complex prosecutions? Or, with its severe sentences, forfeiture provisions, and "racketeering" association, is the statute a blunt instrument used primarily to coerce pleas in difficult-to-prove cases? What do you think?

F. Civil RICO

As seen in the above materials, RICO allows for private parties and for the government to bring civil RICO actions. It is RICO's use in private actions — with the possibility of treble damages and attorneys' fees — that has engendered the most controversy. In the next case, the Supreme Court addressed two substantial restrictions that lower courts had placed upon plaintiffs in RICO cases.

1. Breadth of Civil RICO

Sedima, S.P.R.L. v. Imrex Co.

473 U.S. 479 (1985)

JUSTICE WHITE delivered the opinion of the Court.

The Racketeer Influenced and Corrupt Organizations Act (RICO), 18 U.S.C. §§ 1961–1968, provides a private civil action to recover treble damages for injury "by reason of a violation of" its substantive provisions. 18 U.S.C. § 1964(c). The initial dormancy of this provision and its recent greatly increased utilization[1] are now familiar history. In response to what it perceived to be misuse of civil RICO by private plaintiffs, the court below construed § 1964(c) to permit private actions only against defendants who had been convicted on criminal charges, and only where

---

i. *See* Aila Slisco, *LA Official Indicted on 34 Corruption Charges, Faces 30 Years in Prison*, NEWSWEEK (July 31, 2020) https://www.newsweek.com/la-official-indicted-34-corruption-charges-faces-30-years-prison-1521854; John R. Mitchell et al., *Beyond the Mob: "Varsity Blues" and DOJ's Expanding Use of RICO to Prosecute White Collar Crime*, 34-FALL CRIM. JUST. 4 (2019); Jeanne Whalen, *U.S. Charges China's Huawei with Racketeering and Conspiracy to Steal U.S. Trade Secrets in New Indictment*, WASH. POST (Feb. 13, 2020), https://www.washingtonpost.com/technology/2020/02/13/us-charges-chinas-huawei-with-conspiracy-steal-us-trade-secrets-new-indictment/; Peter J. Henning, *RICO Offers a Powerful Tool to Punish Executives for the Opioid Crisis*, N.Y. TIMES (May 23, 2019) https://www.nytimes.com/2019/05/23/business/dealbook/rico-insys-opioid-executives.html.

1. Of 270 District Court RICO decisions prior to this year, only 3% (nine cases) were decided throughout the 1970s, 2% were decided in 1980, 7% in 1981, 13% in 1982, 33% in 1983, and 43% in 1984. Report of the Ad Hoc Civil RICO Task Force of the ABA Section of Corporation, Banking and Business Law 55 (1985) (hereinafter ABA Report).

there had occurred a "racketeering injury." While we understand the court's concern over the consequences of an unbridled reading of the statute, we reject both of its holdings. . . .

In 1979, petitioner Sedima, a Belgian corporation, entered into a joint venture with respondent Imrex Co. to provide electronic components to a Belgian firm. The buyer was to order parts through Sedima; Imrex was to obtain the parts in this country and ship them to Europe. The agreement called for Sedima and Imrex to split the net proceeds. Imrex filled roughly $8 million in orders placed with it through Sedima. Sedima became convinced, however, that Imrex was presenting inflated bills, cheating Sedima out of a portion of its proceeds by collecting for nonexistent expenses.

In 1982, Sedima filed this action in the Federal District Court for the Eastern District of New York. The complaint set out common-law claims of unjust enrichment, conversion, and breach of contract, fiduciary duty, and a constructive trust. In addition, it asserted RICO claims under §1964(c) against Imrex and two of its officers. Two counts alleged violations of §1962(c), based on predicate acts of mail and wire fraud. A third count alleged a conspiracy to violate §1962(c). Claiming injury of at least $175,000, the amount of the alleged overbilling, Sedima sought treble damages and attorney's fees.

The District Court held that for an injury to be "by reason of a violation of §1962," as required by §1964(c), it must be somehow different in kind from the direct injury resulting from the predicate acts of racketeering activity. While not choosing a precise formulation, the District Court held that a complaint must allege a "RICO-type injury," which was either some sort of distinct "racketeering injury," or a "competitive injury." It found "no allegation here of any injury apart from that which would result directly from the alleged predicate acts of mail fraud and wire fraud," and accordingly dismissed the RICO counts for failure to state a claim.

A divided panel of the Court of Appeals for the Second Circuit affirmed. After a lengthy review of the legislative history, it held that Sedima's complaint was defective in two ways. First, it failed to allege an injury "by reason of a violation of §1962." . . .

The Court of Appeals also found the complaint defective for not alleging that the defendants had already been criminally convicted of the predicate acts of mail and wire fraud, or of a RICO violation. . . .

The decision below was one episode in a recent proliferation of civil RICO litigation within the Second Circuit and in other Courts of Appeals. In light of the variety of approaches taken by the lower courts and the importance of the issues, we grant certiorari. We now reverse.

The language of RICO gives no obvious indication that a civil action can proceed only after a criminal conviction. The word "conviction" does not appear in any relevant portion of the statute. To the contrary, the predicate acts involve conduct that is "chargeable" or "indictable," and "offense[s]" that are "punishable," under various criminal statutes. As defined in the statute, racketeering activity consists not of acts for which the defendant has been convicted, but of acts for which he could be. Thus, a prior conviction-requirement cannot be found in the definition of "racketeering activity." Nor can it be found in §1962, which sets out the statute's substantive provisions. Indeed, if either §1961 or §1962 did contain such a requirement, a prior conviction would also be a prerequisite, nonsensically, for a criminal prosecution, or for a civil action by the Government to enjoin violations that had not yet occurred.

The Court of Appeals purported to discover its prior-conviction requirement in the term "violation" in §1964(c). However, even if that term were read to refer to a criminal conviction, it would require a conviction under RICO, not of the predicate offenses. That aside, the term "violation" does not imply a criminal conviction. It refers only to a failure to adhere to legal requirements. This is its indisputable meaning elsewhere in the statute. Section 1962 renders certain conduct "unlawful"; §1963 and §1964 impose consequences, criminal and civil, for "violations" of §1962. We should not lightly infer that Congress intended the term to have wholly different meanings in neighboring subsections. . . .

The Court of Appeals was of the view that its narrow construction of the statute was essential to avoid intolerable practical consequences. First, without a prior conviction to rely on, the plaintiff would have to prove commission of the predicate acts beyond a reasonable doubt. This would require instructing the jury as to different standards of proof for different aspects of the case. To avoid this awkwardness, the court inferred that the criminality must already be established, so that the civil action could proceed smoothly under the usual preponderance standard.

We are not at all convinced that the predicate acts must be established beyond a reasonable doubt in a proceeding under §1964(c). In a number of settings, conduct that can be punished as criminal only upon proof beyond a reasonable doubt will support civil sanctions under a preponderance standard. There is no indication that Congress sought to depart from this general principle here. That the offending conduct is described by reference to criminal statutes does not mean that its occurrence must be established by criminal standards or that the consequences of a finding of liability in a private civil action are identical to the consequences of a criminal conviction. But we need not decide the standard of proof issue today. For even if the stricter standard is applicable to a portion of the plaintiff's proof, the resulting logistical difficulties, which are accepted in other contexts, would not be so great as to require invention of a requirement that cannot be found in the statute and that Congress, as even the Court of Appeals had to concede, did not envision.

The court below also feared that any other construction would raise severe constitutional questions, as it "would provide civil remedies for offenses criminal in nature, stigmatize defendants with the appellation 'racketeer,' authorize the award of damages which are clearly punitive, including attorney's fees, and constitute a civil remedy aimed in part to avoid the constitutional protections of the criminal law." 741 F.2d at 500 n.49. We do not view the statute as being so close to the constitutional edge. As noted above, the fact that conduct can result in both criminal liability and treble damages does not mean that there is not a bona fide civil action. The familiar provisions for both criminal liability and treble damages under the antitrust laws indicate as much. Nor are attorney's fees "clearly punitive." As for stigma, a civil RICO proceeding leaves no greater stain than do a number of other civil proceedings. Furthermore, requiring conviction of the predicate acts would not protect against an unfair imposition of the "racketeer" label. If there is a problem with thus stigmatizing a garden variety defrauder by means of a civil action, it is not reduced by making certain that the defendant is guilty of *fraud* beyond a reasonable doubt. Finally, to the extent an action under §1964(c) might be considered quasi-criminal, requiring protections normally applicable only to criminal proceedings, the solution is to provide those protections, not to ensure that they were previously afforded by requiring prior convictions.

Finally, we note that a prior-conviction requirement would be inconsistent with Congress' underlying policy concerns. Such a rule would severely handicap potential plaintiffs. A guilty party may escape conviction for any number of reasons — not least among them the possibility that the Government itself may choose to pursue only civil remedies. Private attorney general provisions such as §1964(c) are in part designed to fill prosecutorial gaps. This purpose would be largely defeated, and the need for treble damages as an incentive to litigate unjustified, if private suits could be maintained only against those already brought to justice. . . .

In considering the Court of Appeals' second prerequisite for a private civil RICO action — "injury . . . caused by an activity which RICO was designed to deter" — we are somewhat hampered by the vagueness of that concept. Apart from reliance on the general purposes of RICO and a reference to "mobsters," the court provided scant indication of what the requirement of racketeering injury means. It emphasized Congress' undeniable desire to strike at organized crime, but acknowledged and did not purport to overrule Second Circuit precedent rejecting a requirement of an organized crime nexus. The court also stopped short of adopting a "competitive injury" requirement; while insisting that the plaintiff show "the kind of economic injury which has an effect on competition," it did not require "actual anticompetitive effect." . . .

[W]e perceive no distinct "racketeering injury" requirement. Given that "racketeering activity" consists of no more and no less than commission of a predicate act, §1961(1), we are initially doubtful about a requirement of a "racketeering injury" separate from the harm from the predicate acts. . . . There is no room in the statutory language for an additional, amorphous "racketeering injury" requirement.

A violation of §1962(c), the section on which Sedima relies, requires (1) conduct (2) of an enterprise (3) through a pattern (4) of racketeering activity. The plaintiff must, of course, allege each of these elements to state a claim. Conducting an enterprise that affects interstate commerce is obviously not in itself a violation of §1962, nor is mere commission of the predicate offenses. In addition, the plaintiff only has standing if, and can only recover to the extent that, he has been injured in his business or property by the conduct constituting the violation. . . .

But the statute requires no more than this. Where the plaintiff alleges each element of the violation, the compensable injury necessarily is the harm caused by predicate acts sufficiently related to constitute a pattern, for the essence of the violation is the commission of those acts in connection with the conduct of an enterprise. Those acts are, when committed in the circumstances delineated in § 1962(c), "an activity which RICO was designed to deter." Any recoverable damages occurring by reason of a violation of § 1962(c) will flow from the commission of the predicate acts. . . .

Underlying the Court of Appeals' holding was its distress at the "extraordinary, if not outrageous," uses to which civil RICO has been put. 741 F.2d at 487. Instead of being used against mobsters and organized criminals, it has become a tool for everyday fraud cases brought against "respected and legitimate 'enterprises.'" *Id.* Yet Congress wanted to reach both "legitimate" and "illegitimate" enterprises. The former enjoy neither an inherent incapacity for criminal activity nor immunity from its consequences. The fact that § 1964(c) is used against respected businesses allegedly engaged in a pattern of specifically identified criminal conduct is hardly a sufficient reason for assuming that the provision is being misconstrued. Nor does it reveal the "ambiguity" discovered by the court below. "[T]he fact that RICO has been applied in situations not expressly anticipated by Congress does not demonstrate ambiguity. It demonstrates breadth." *Haroco, Inc. v. American National Bank & Trust Co. of Chicago,* 747 F.2d 384, 398, *aff'd,* 473 U.S. 606 (1984).

It is true that private civil actions under the statute are being brought almost solely against such defendants, rather than against the archetypal, intimidating mobster.[16] Yet this defect — if defect it is — is inherent in the statute as written, and its correction must lie with Congress. It is not for the judiciary to eliminate the private action in situations where Congress has provided it simply because plaintiffs are not taking advantage of it in its more difficult applications.

We nonetheless recognize that, in its private civil version, RICO is evolving into something quite different from the original conception of its enactors. Though sharing the doubts of the Court of Appeals about this increasing divergence, we cannot agree with either its diagnosis or its remedy. The "extraordinary" uses to which civil RICO has been put appear to be primarily the result of the breadth of the predicate offenses, in particular the inclusion of wire, mail, and securities fraud, and the failure of Congress and the courts to develop a meaningful concept of "pattern." We do not believe that the amorphous standing requirement imposed by the

16. The ABA Task Force found that of the 270 known civil RICO cases at the trial court level, 40% involved securities fraud, 37% common-law fraud in a commercial or business setting, and only 9% "allegations of criminal activity of a type generally associated with professional criminals." ABA Report, at 55–56. Another survey of 132 published decisions found that 57 involved securities transactions and 38 commercial and contract disputes, while no other category made it into double figures. American Institute of Certified Public Accountants, *The Authority to Bring Private Treble-Damage Suits Under "RICO" Should be Removed* 13 (Oct. 10, 1984).

Second Circuit effectively responds to these problems, or that it is a form of statutory amendment appropriately undertaken by the courts. . . .

The judgment below is accordingly reversed, and the case is remanded for further proceedings consistent with this opinion.

It is so ordered.

JUSTICE MARSHALL, with whom JUSTICE BRENNAN, JUSTICE BLACKMUN, and JUSTICE POWELL join, dissenting.

The Court today recognizes that "in its private civil version, RICO is evolving into something quite different from the original conception of its enactors." The Court, however, expressly validates this result, imputing it to the manner in which the statute was drafted. I fundamentally disagree both with the Court's reading of the statute and with its conclusion.

The Court's interpretation of the civil RICO statute quite simply revolutionizes private litigation; it validates the federalization of broad areas of state common law of frauds, and it approves the displacement of well-established federal remedial provisions. We do not lightly infer a congressional intent to effect such fundamental changes. To infer such intent here would be untenable, for there is no indication that Congress even considered, much less approved, the scheme that the Court today defines.

The single most significant reason for the expansive use of civil RICO has been the presence in the statute, as predicate acts, of mail and wire fraud violations. Prior to RICO, no federal statute had expressly provided a private damages remedy based upon a violation of the mail or wire fraud statutes, which make it a federal crime to use the mail or wires in furtherance of a scheme to defraud. Moreover, the Courts of Appeals consistently had held that no implied federal private causes of action accrue to victims of these federal violations. The victims normally were restricted to bringing actions in state court under common-law fraud theories.

Under the Court's opinion today, two fraudulent mailings or uses of the wires occurring within 10 years of each other might constitute a "pattern of racketeering activity," leading to civil RICO liability. The effects of making a mere two instances of mail or wire fraud potentially actionable under civil RICO are staggering, because in recent years the Courts of Appeals have tolerated an extraordinary expansion of mail and wire fraud statutes to permit federal prosecution for conduct that some had thought was subject only to state criminal and civil law.

In summary, in both theory and practice, civil RICO has brought profound changes to our legal landscape. Undoubtedly, Congress has the power to federalize a great deal of state common law, and there certainly are no relevant constraints on its ability to displace federal law. Those, however, are not the questions that we face in this case. What we have to decide here, instead, is whether Congress in fact intended to produce these far-reaching results. . . .

Notes and Questions

1. *Breadth of civil RICO.* RICO is a controversial statute, nowhere more so than in its civil application. As the dissent noted, "civil RICO has brought profound changes to our legal landscape." Why is this so? Why did these concerns not sway the majority of the Court? Despite considerable pressure from business lobbyists and others, and subject to a qualification discussed below, Congress has failed to narrow the reach of civil RICO. Why do you think this is so?

2. *Securities fraud as a predicate act in civil RICO cases.* The Supreme Court in *Sedima* declined to require civil RICO plaintiffs to show that the defendants had been convicted of the predicate acts. This remains the law, with one exception. In 1995, Congress added the following language to the civil RICO statute, §1964:

> [N]o person may rely upon any conduct that would have been actionable as fraud in the purchase or sale of securities to establish a violation of §1962. The exception contained in the preceding sentence does not apply to an action against any person that is criminally convicted in connection with the fraud, in which case the statute of limitations shall start to run on the date on which the conviction becomes final.

Pub. L. No. 104-67, 109 Stat. 758 (1995), amending 18 U.S.C. §1964(c). In your opinion, why did Congress add this language?

3. *Burden of proof.* Although the Court did not decide the issue in *Sedima*, lower courts have held that a civil RICO plaintiff must prove the elements by a preponderance of the evidence standard, rather than by the reasonable doubt standard applicable to criminal cases. *See, e.g., United States v. Local 560, International Brotherhood of Teamsters*, 780 F.2d 267, 279 n.12 (3d Cir. 1985).

2. Standing

As in other civil contexts, a private RICO plaintiff must show an injury caused by the defendant's acts. What must a plaintiff allege in order to demonstrate standing in a RICO case? The United States Supreme Court has addressed this issue in a series of cases.

Note on Holmes v. Securities Investor Protection Corp.

In one of the leading RICO standing cases, *Holmes v. Securities Investor Protection Corp.*, 503 U.S. 258 (1992), the Supreme Court addressed the issue of the proof required to demonstrate standing. Plaintiff Securities Investor Protection Corp. (SIPC) is a nonprofit corporation of which most securities brokers and dealers are members. In certain circumstances, SIPC is financially responsible for paying claims that the member broker/dealers' customers have filed against the broker/dealers. SIPC thus operates to insure the customers of member broker/dealers.

SIPC sued the defendants for securities fraud, and under RICO based upon the securities fraud predicate acts. SIPC alleged that the defendants illegally manipulated stock prices, causing those prices to appear to be artificially high. When the stock prices collapsed, the member broker/dealers who had invested in the stocks became insolvent and therefore unable to meet their obligations to their customers. The allegedly injured customers included customers who had not bought or sold the manipulated securities, but who were injured because of the illegal scheme's effect upon the customers' broker/dealers. Because of the harm to the member broker/dealers, SIPC was obliged to pay $13 million in claims to those customers.

The trial court granted the defendants' summary judgment motion. The court held that SIPC did not have standing to seek damages under RICO.

The Supreme Court affirmed on the ground that SIPC had not sufficiently alleged that the defendants proximately caused SIPC's injury. The Court focused on the language of § 1964(c), which provides that "[a]ny person injured in his business or property *by reason of* a violation of § 1962 of this chapter may sue therefor." The Court then rejected a "but for" test for standing, instead imposing a proximate cause requirement. The Court defined this test as requiring "some direct relation between the injury asserted and the injurious conduct alleged." *Id.* at 268. Applying this test to the facts, the Court held that the plaintiff had not alleged proximate causation. The plaintiff's injury resulted entirely from the member broker/dealers' insolvency, not directly from the alleged manipulation of stock by the defendants. Thus, the alleged injury was too attenuated from the securities fraud to sustain a RICO action.

Notes and Questions

1. *The test for standing.* What was the precise injury that the plaintiff asserted in *Holmes*? But for the defendants' actions, would the injury have occurred? If not, why wasn't this injury sufficient under the Court's reasoning?

In 2010, the Court again analyzed civil RICO's causation requirement. In *Hemi Group LLC v. City of New York*, 130 S. Ct. 983 (2010), the plaintiff, New York City, alleged that an out-of-state cigarette vendor failed to file required reports with New York State, resulting in lost city tax revenues. Chief Justice Roberts's four-member plurality opinion applied the *Holmes* proximate cause test, holding that the City's injury was not a sufficiently direct product of the failure to file the reports with the state. Under this reasoning, the fraud was committed against the state rather than the city.

2. *First-party reliance.* In *Bridge v. Phoenix Bond and Indem. Co.*, 553 U.S. 639 (2008), the plaintiffs sued defendants under RICO, alleging that the defendants engaged in a bid-rigging scheme during a local government's auction of certain assets. The defendants mailed false documents to the local government in furtherance of this scheme, thus committing numerous counts of mail fraud. With respect to injury, the complaint alleged that the scheme gave the defendants an unfair advantage in the auction process, depriving plaintiffs of the opportunity to purchase the assets.

The trial court dismissed the complaint on the grounds that the local government, not the plaintiffs, was deceived by the scheme. The plaintiffs therefore lacked standing, the court held, because they had not actually relied upon the defendants' misrepresentations. The court of appeals reinstated the case, and the Supreme Court affirmed. The Court held that first-party reliance is not an element of a RICO case based on mail fraud. The Court further found that the plaintiffs had standing because they had sufficiently alleged that their injuries were proximately caused by defendants' actions.

3. *Overt acts and RICO conspiracy.* May a plaintiff recover in a civil RICO action where the alleged injury resulted from an overt act that was in furtherance of a RICO conspiracy but was not itself a RICO predicate or otherwise unlawful under the statute? In *Beck v. Prupis*, 529 U.S. 494 (2000), the plaintiff claimed that he was fired because he had refused to participate in RICO violations, and that his termination was an overt act giving rise to liability under RICO's conspiracy provision. The Supreme Court held that, because the termination was not itself unlawful under RICO, the plaintiff was not injured by a RICO violation.

Problem

14-9. Plaintiff Metal Supply Corp. has sued Anzara Corp., a business competitor, under RICO. Plaintiff alleges that defendant committed mail and wire fraud when Anzara Corp. submitted state tax returns that fraudulently failed to reveal that it had not charged cash-paying customers state sales tax. The plaintiff alleged that this practice allowed the defendant to lower its prices and increase its market share, thus injuring the plaintiff by taking away business, in violation of § 1962(c).

The jury found for the plaintiff, and the appeals court affirmed. The defendant now appeals to the United States Supreme Court, arguing that the plaintiff lacked standing.

How should the court rule? Why?

Chapter 15

Internal Investigations, Compliance Programs, and Deferred and Non-Prosecution Agreements

A. Introductory Notes

This chapter examines the mechanics of the corporate criminal justice process. Many recent policy developments push in the direction of a public-private partnership between corporations and prosecutors for combating corporate crime. Through a series of incentive structures, the government encourages corporations to police themselves through effective compliance programs, to conduct internal investigations when red flags arise, and to self-report when violations are uncovered. Some of these incentives are discussed later in the context of the Organizational Sentencing Guidelines (Chapter 19, Sentencing, *infra*). As discussed below, compliance, investigation, and self-reporting are also important considerations for prosecutors who are deciding whether and how to charge corporate suspects. Corporations today that are facing Department of Justice scrutiny aim to persuade prosecutors to keep the criminal justice process out of the courtrooms by using some form of pretrial diversion. The corporate bar considers its cases won or lost at this stage.

As you read these materials, consider whether this public-private partnership is good or bad for corporate criminal justice. What benefits does it hold? What risks?

B. Internal Investigations

1. Determining Whether and How to Investigate

Although there is no universally accepted definition of an internal investigation, the phrase is frequently used in its simplest terms to refer to a corporation's efforts to gather information in response to allegations of corporate or employee misconduct. Because of the increased civil and criminal enforcement efforts against corporations and the government's willingness to treat favorably those companies that make efforts to ferret out misconduct, internal investigations have become increasingly frequent. Corporations have begun aggressively investigating claims that, if true, would subject them to criminal and/or civil liability. Although internal investigations have been instituted since the 1970s, their role today takes on renewed significance. Internal investigations often provide a roadmap for government investigators. Thus, such investigations are fraught with risks. A corporation must proceed with caution when designing and managing an internal investigation.

One of the most practical initial considerations is whether to institute an investigation in situations where the government is already pursuing its own inquiry. If the government has opened an inquiry, the corporation should seriously consider the impact of an internal investigation and should determine whether such action will enable it to respond adequately to the government and to defend itself. Only by investigating itself can a corporation develop a mastery of the facts sufficient to persuade prosecutors that criminal charges are unnecessary. In this way, a corporation can argue either that there was no real concern in the first place or, if there were, it was adequately addressed internally.

In circumstances where there is no pending government investigation, the question becomes more acute: if the corporation is aware of wrongdoing and does nothing about it, it bears the risk of adverse government reaction should the conduct become public or result in a full-scale criminal investigation. Corporations must determine whether the underlying activity would potentially subject the company to criminal consequences, civil lawsuits, or other ancillary proceedings. Additionally, continuous internal auditing is crucial to gaining credit for having effective compliance when it comes to charging or sentencing. By detecting misconduct internally, corporations can put an end to it and implement reforms to prevent it from recurring. Each separate offense could potentially form the basis for a new criminal charge. Only after discovering potential crime is a corporation in a position to determine whether it makes sense to get ahead of any potential governmental response by self-reporting and cooperating.

The intricacies of an internal investigation are many, including the hiring of outside counsel versus conducting the investigation with in-house counsel. Outside counsel hold several advantages. Prosecutors are more likely to view findings of outside counsel as more objective. Outside counsel also provide advantages when it comes to preserving attorney-client privilege over materials that result from the investigation. Only communications pursuant to providing or receiving legal advice are protected. Because in-house counsel often provide both business and legal advice, assertions of privilege over their communications are subject to heightened scrutiny.

Public reaction to an internal investigation, including shareholder awareness, can be a two-edged sword. On the one hand, the investigation demonstrates that the corporation is serious about ferreting out misbehavior and it may reduce adverse publicity. Conversely, the action can negatively affect stock prices and the market value of the company.

Depending on the nature of the wrongdoing, the scope of the fact-gathering necessary for a complete investigation can be very wide. Fiscal realities dictate that an appropriately conducted investigation will divert attention away from the day-to-day operations of the company and drain some corporate resources. Despite these risks, most large businesses today regularly conduct voluntary internal investigations.

2. Privilege and Related Issues

Internal investigations can raise complex legal and ethical issues. None of these issues is more vexing than the duties that corporate counsel owes the corporation and, potentially, its agents and employees. Over the course of an investigation, conflicts of interest may arise between a corporation and its employees, as all parties discover what sort of misconduct might have taken place and who participated. Indeed, prosecutors can engineer such conflicts by offering immunity to either an individual or the corporation in exchange for one testifying against the other.

One flashpoint for such conflicts is the attorney-client privilege. Like all privileges, the attorney-client privilege protects some evidence from discovery or use in court. It attaches to any confidential communications made between attorneys and their clients for the purpose of providing or receiving legal advice. The goal of the privilege is to ensure that clients and attorneys can be fully open with each other, not worrying that what they say will later be used against them. The privilege lasts so long as the communications remain confidential. The client, who is the holder of the privilege, may waive it voluntarily, sometimes to the detriment of other parties whom the communications concern. This directly raises the question of whom an attorney conducting an internal investigation represents: the corporation or the employees with whom the attorney interacts.

These issues are explored in the next cases. As you read them, consider the competing interests at stake.

In re Kellogg Brown & Root, Inc.
756 F.3d 754 (D.C. Cir. 2014)

KAVANAUGH, CIRCUIT JUDGE.

More than three decades ago, the Supreme Court held that the attorney-client privilege protects confidential employee communications made during a business's internal investigation led by company lawyers. *See Upjohn Co. v. United States*, 449 U.S. 383 (1981). In this case, the District Court denied the protection of the privilege to a company that had conducted just such an internal investigation. The District Court's decision has generated substantial uncertainty about the scope of the attorney-client privilege in the business setting. We conclude that the District Court's decision is irreconcilable with Upjohn. We therefore grant KBR's petition for a writ of mandamus and vacate the District Court's March 6 document production order.

Harry Barko worked for KBR, a defense contractor. In 2005, he filed a False Claims Act complaint against KBR and KBR-related corporate entities, whom we will collectively refer to as KBR. In essence, Barko alleged that KBR and certain subcontractors defrauded the U.S. Government by inflating costs and accepting kickbacks while administering military contracts in wartime Iraq. During discovery, Barko sought documents related to KBR's prior internal investigation into the alleged fraud. KBR had conducted that internal investigation pursuant to its Code of Business Conduct, which is overseen by the company's Law Department.

KBR argued that the internal investigation had been conducted for the purpose of obtaining legal advice and that the internal investigation documents therefore were protected by the attorney-client privilege. Barko responded that the internal investigation documents were unprivileged business records that he was entitled to discover. *See generally* Fed. R. Civ. P. 26(b)(1).

After reviewing the disputed documents in camera, the District Court determined that the attorney-client privilege protection did not apply because, among other reasons, KBR had not shown that "the communication would not have been made 'but for' the fact that legal advice was sought." *United States ex rel. Barko v. Halliburton Co.*, No. 05-cv-1276, 2014 WL 1016784 (D.D.C. Mar. 6, 2014) (quoting *United States v. ISS Marine Services, Inc.*, 905 F. Supp. 2d 121, 128 (D.D.C. 2012)). KBR's internal investigation, the court concluded, was "undertaken pursuant to regulatory law and corporate policy rather than for the purpose of obtaining legal advice."

KBR vehemently opposed the ruling. The company asked the District Court to certify the privilege question to this Court for interlocutory appeal and to stay its order pending a petition for mandamus in this Court. The District Court denied those requests and ordered KBR to produce the disputed documents to Barko within a matter of days. *See United States ex rel. Barko v. Halliburton Co.*, 4 F. Supp. 3d 162 (D.D.C. 2014) . . . . KBR promptly filed a petition for a writ of mandamus in this Court. A number of business organizations and trade associations also objected to the District Court's decision and filed an amicus brief in support of KBR. We stayed the District Court's document production order and held oral argument on the mandamus petition. . . .

We first consider whether the District Court's privilege ruling was legally erroneous. We conclude that it was.

Federal Rule of Evidence 501 provides that claims of privilege in federal courts are governed by the "common law — as interpreted by United States courts in the light of reason and experience." Fed. R. Evid. 501. The attorney-client privilege is the "oldest of the privileges for confidential communications known to the common law." *Upjohn Co. v. United States*, 449 U.S. 383, 389 (1981). As relevant here, the privilege applies to a confidential communication between attorney and client if that communication was made for the purpose of obtaining or providing legal advice to the client. In *Upjohn*, the Supreme Court held that the attorney-client privilege applies to corporations. The Court explained that the attorney-client privilege for business organizations was essential in light of "the vast and complicated array of regulatory legislation confronting the modern corporation," which required corporations to "constantly go to lawyers to find out how to obey the law . . . particularly since compliance with the law in this area is hardly an instinctive matter." 449 U.S. at 392 (internal quotation marks and citation omitted). The Court stated, moreover, that the attorney-client privilege "exists to protect not only the giving of professional advice to those who can act on it but also the giving of information to the lawyer to enable him to give sound and informed advice." *Id.* at 390. That is so, the Court said, because the "first step in the resolution of any legal problem is ascertaining the factual background and sifting through the facts with an eye to the legally relevant." *Id.* at 390–91. In *Upjohn*, the communications were made by company employees to company attorneys during an attorney-led internal investigation that was undertaken to ensure the company's "compliance with the law." *Id.* at 392; see *id.* at 394. The Court ruled that the privilege applied to the internal investigation and covered the communications between company employees and company attorneys.

KBR's assertion of the privilege in this case is materially indistinguishable from Upjohn's assertion of the privilege in that case. As in *Upjohn*, KBR initiated an internal investigation to gather facts and ensure compliance with the law after being informed of potential misconduct. And as in *Upjohn*, KBR's investigation was conducted under the auspices of KBR's in-house legal department, acting in its legal capacity. The same considerations that led the Court in *Upjohn* to uphold the corporation's privilege claims apply here.

The District Court in this case initially distinguished *Upjohn* on a variety of grounds. But none of those purported distinctions takes this case out from under *Upjohn's* umbrella.

First, the District Court stated that in *Upjohn* the internal investigation began after in-house counsel conferred with outside counsel, whereas here the investigation was conducted in-house without consultation with outside lawyers. But Upjohn does not hold or imply that the involvement of outside counsel is a necessary predicate for the privilege to apply. On the contrary, the general rule, which this Court has adopted, is that a lawyer's status as in-house counsel "does not dilute the privilege." *In re Sealed Case*, 737 F.2d at 99. As the Restatement's commentary points out, "Inside legal counsel to a corporation or similar organization . . . is fully empowered to engage in privileged communications." 1 RESTATEMENT § 72, cmt. c, at 551.

Second, the District Court noted that in *Upjohn* the interviews were conducted by attorneys, whereas here many of the interviews in KBR's investigation were conducted by non-attorneys. But the investigation here was conducted at the direction of the attorneys in KBR's Law Department. And communications made by and to non-attorneys serving as agents of attorneys in internal investigations are routinely protected by the attorney-client privilege. *See* 1 Paul R. Rice, ATTORNEY-CLIENT PRIVILEGE IN THE UNITED STATES § 7:18, at 1230–31 (2013) ("If internal investigations are conducted by agents of the client at the behest of the attorney, they are protected by the attorney-client privilege to the same extent as they would be had thcy been conducted by the attorney who was consulted."). So that fact, too, is not a basis on which to distinguish *Upjohn*.

Third, the District Court pointed out that in *Upjohn* the interviewed employees were expressly informed that the purpose of the interview was to assist the company in obtaining legal advice, whereas here they were not. The District Court further stated that the confidentiality agreements signed by KBR employees did not mention that the purpose of KBR's investigation was to obtain legal advice. Yet nothing in *Upjohn* requires a company to use magic words to its employees in order to gain the benefit of the privilege for an internal investigation. And in any event, here as in Upjohn employees knew that the company's legal department was conducting an investigation of a sensitive nature and that the information they disclosed would be protected. Cf. *Upjohn,* 449 U.S. at 387 (Upjohn's managers were "instructed to treat the investigation as 'highly confidential'"). KBR employees were also told not to discuss their interviews "without the specific advance authorization of KBR General Counsel." . . .

In short, none of those three distinctions of *Upjohn* holds water as a basis for denying KBR's privilege claim.

More broadly and more importantly, the District Court also distinguished *Upjohn* on the ground that KBR's internal investigation was undertaken to comply with Department of Defense regulations that require defense contractors such as KBR to maintain compliance programs and conduct internal investigations into allegations of potential wrongdoing. The District Court therefore concluded that the purpose of KBR's internal investigation was to comply with those regulatory requirements rather than to obtain or provide legal advice. In our view, the District Court's analysis rested on a false dichotomy. So long as obtaining or providing legal advice was one of the significant purposes of the internal investigation, the attorney-client privilege applies, even if there were also other purposes for the investigation and even if the investigation was mandated by regulation rather than simply an exercise of company discretion.

The District Court began its analysis by reciting the "primary purpose" test, which many courts (including this one) have used to resolve privilege disputes when attorney-client communications may have had both legal and business purposes. *See also In re Sealed Case*, 737 F.2d at 98–99. But in a key move, the District Court then said that the primary purpose of a communication is to obtain or provide legal advice only if the communication would not have been made "but for" the fact that legal advice was sought. 2014 U.S. Dist. LEXIS 36490, at *2. In other words, if there was any other purpose behind the communication, the attorney-client privilege apparently does not apply. The District Court went on to conclude that KBR's internal investigation was "undertaken pursuant to regulatory law and corporate policy rather than for the purpose of obtaining legal advice." (citing federal contracting regulations). Therefore, in the District Court's view, "the primary purpose of" the internal investigation "was to comply with federal defense contractor regulations, not to secure legal advice." *United States ex rel. Barko v. Halliburton Co.,* 4 F. Supp.

3d 162 (D.D.C. 2014); *see id.* ("Nothing suggests the reports were prepared to obtain legal advice. Instead, the reports were prepared to try to comply with KBR's obligation to report improper conduct to the Department of Defense.").

The District Court erred because it employed the wrong legal test. The but-for test articulated by the District Court is not appropriate for attorney-client privilege analysis. Under the District Court's approach, the attorney-client privilege apparently would not apply unless the sole purpose of the communication was to obtain or provide legal advice. That is not the law. We are aware of no Supreme Court or court of appeals decision that has adopted a test of this kind in this context. The District Court's novel approach to the attorney- client privilege would eliminate the attorney-client privilege for numerous communications that are made for both legal and business purposes and that heretofore have been covered by the attorney-client privilege. And the District Court's novel approach would eradicate the attorney-client privilege for internal investigations conducted by businesses that are required by law to maintain compliance programs, which is now the case in a significant swath of American industry. In turn, businesses would be less likely to disclose facts to their attorneys and to seek legal advice, which would "limit the valuable efforts of corporate counsel to ensure their client's compliance with the law." *Upjohn*, 449 U.S. at 392. We reject the District Court's but-for test as inconsistent with the principle of Upjohn and longstanding attorney-client privilege law.

Given the evident confusion in some cases, we also think it important to underscore that the primary purpose test, sensibly and properly applied, cannot and does not draw a rigid distinction between a legal purpose on the one hand and a business purpose on the other. After all, trying to find the one primary purpose for a communication motivated by two sometimes overlapping purposes (one legal and one business, for example) can be an inherently impossible task. It is often not useful or even feasible to try to determine whether the purpose was A or B when the purpose was A and B. It is thus not correct for a court to presume that a communication can have only one primary purpose. It is likewise not correct for a court to try to find the one primary purpose in cases where a given communication plainly has multiple purposes. Rather, it is clearer, more precise, and more predictable to articulate the test as follows: Was obtaining or providing legal advice a primary purpose of the communication, meaning one of the significant purposes of the communication? As the Reporter's Note to the Restatement says, "In general, American decisions agree that the privilege applies if one of the significant purposes of a client in communicating with a lawyer is that of obtaining legal assistance." 1 RESTATEMENT §72, Reporter's Note, at 554. We agree with and adopt that formulation—"one of the significant purposes"—as an accurate and appropriate description of the primary purpose test. Sensibly and properly applied, the test boils down to whether obtaining or providing legal advice was one of the significant purposes of the attorney-client communication.

In the context of an organization's internal investigation, if one of the significant purposes of the internal investigation was to obtain or provide legal advice, the privilege will apply. That is true regardless of whether an internal investigation was conducted pursuant to a company compliance program required by statute or regulation, or was otherwise conducted pursuant to company policy. . . .

In this case, there can be no serious dispute that one of the significant purposes of the KBR internal investigation was to obtain or provide legal advice. In denying KBR's privilege claim on the ground that the internal investigation was conducted in order to comply with regulatory requirements and corporate policy and not just to obtain or provide legal advice, the District Court applied the wrong legal test and clearly erred. . . .

In reaching our decision here, we stress, as the Supreme Court did in *Upjohn*, that the attorney-client privilege "only protects disclosure of communications; it does not protect disclosure of the underlying facts by those who communicated with the attorney." *Upjohn Co. v. United States*, 449 U.S. 383, 395 (1981). Barko was able to pursue the facts underlying KBR's investigation. But he was not entitled to KBR's own investigation files. As the *Upjohn* Court stated, quoting Justice Jackson, "Discovery was hardly intended to enable a learned profession to perform its functions . . . on wits borrowed from the adversary." *Id.* at 396 (quoting *Hickman v. Taylor*, 329 U.S. 495, 515 (1947) (Jackson, J., concurring)).

Although the attorney-client privilege covers only communications and not facts, we acknowledge that the privilege carries costs. The privilege means that potentially critical evidence may be withheld from the factfinder. Indeed, as the District Court here noted, that may be the end result in this case. But our legal system tolerates those costs because the privilege "is intended to encourage 'full and frank communication between attorneys and their clients and thereby promote broader public interests in the observance of law and the administration of justice.'" *Swidler & Berlin v. United States*, 524 U.S. 399, 403 (1998) (quoting *Upjohn*, 449 U.S. at 389).

We grant the petition for a writ of mandamus and vacate the District Court's March 6 document production order. To the extent that Barko has timely asserted other arguments for why these documents are not covered by either the attorney-client privilege or the work-product protection, the District Court may consider such arguments.

So ordered.

Notes and Questions

1. *Internal investigation legal advice.* The *Kellogg* decision addressed the difficult intersection between the attorney-client communication strictly for legal advice and the communication that occurs during an internal investigation. This is a very thin line indeed. Do you believe that the court reached the correct decision when weighing these competing interests?

2. *The Fifth Amendment.* During an internal investigation, a corporation may discover a good deal of incriminating information. Ordinarily, the Fifth Amendment would protect this information from discovery by the government, but (as discussed

in Chapter 17, Self-Incrimination, *infra*) the Supreme Court has held that corporations do not benefit from the privilege against self-incrimination. *See Hale v. Henkel*, 201 U.S. 43 (1906). This leaves the attorney-client privilege and the work product doctrine as the sole protections for the fruits of an internal investigation. Do you think corporations considering internal investigations would behave differently if communications with their attorneys were not privileged?

3. *The* Upjohn *holding—who owns the corporate privilege?* The government will often seek to have a corporation waive the attorney-client privilege in order to assemble evidence against corporate agents. Conversely, the very evidence against the corporation often comes from the corporate agents or employees. This evidence from the employees can also be used against them in their individual capacities. *See* note 5, *infra*.

The privilege protects confidential disclosures made by a client to an attorney in order to obtain legal advice, as well as an attorney's advice in response to such disclosures. Because this privilege impedes full and free discovery of the truth, the attorney-client privilege must be strictly construed. In *Upjohn Co. v. United States*, 449 U.S. 383 (1981), the Supreme Court held that communications between corporate counsel and company employees are privileged. The Court also held that the privilege belongs to the corporation and not to the individual employee. As a result, the company controls the privilege and only the company has the authority to waive the privilege. A corporation might waive the privilege as a demonstration of good faith cooperation with government investigators.

In most situations, the attorney cannot serve the professional interests of both the corporation and the employees because of inherent conflicts (or, as mentioned above, because of conflicts that prosecutors might engineer). This can be especially challenging because the attorney-client privilege exists solely for the benefit of the client. *United States v. Yielding*, 657 F.3d 688, 708 (8th Cir. 2011). To whom should the privilege belong when corporate counsel conducts an investigation—the corporation or the employees?

4. *Waiver through disclosure to third parties.* As mentioned, confidentiality is a crucial presumption behind the attorney-client privilege. The privilege is meant to encourage attorney-client communications by protecting those communications from third parties. However, if the communications are disclosed voluntarily to third parties, that suggests such protection was not necessary in the first place. Accordingly, voluntary disclosure of attorney-client communications to third parties will waive the privilege. *See* Fed. R. Evid. 502(a). Furthermore, involuntary disclosure to third parties will also waive the privilege if reasonable measures were not in place to prevent such disclosure. *See* Fed. R. Evid. 502(b). Involuntary disclosure becomes a particular concern in corporate investigations that involve thousands or millions of documents, many of which will be produced to government authorities. Corporations might accidentally hand over privileged materials. In those contexts, courts will evaluate the sufficiency of the procedures the corporation put in place to filter out and redact privileged documents (or privileged parts of documents),

bearing in mind such details as the production timeline and number of documents involved. *Id.*

5. Upjohn *warnings.* To clarify the communications between corporate counsel and the employee witnesses during an internal investigation, corporate counsel will routinely provide employees with an *Upjohn* warning. These clarify the nature of the attorneys' responsibilities to the corporation versus the employee, and the consequences of that for the attorney-client privilege. Because there is often coercive pressure in the interchange between witness and attorney, greater clarification is needed. Former District Judge Frederick Lacey has suggested that the following language be given before the interview:

> I am not your lawyer, I represent the corporation. It is the corporation's interest I have been retained to serve. You are entitled to have your own lawyer. If you cannot afford a lawyer, the corporation may or may not pay his fee. You may wish to consult with him before you confer with me. Among other things, you may wish to claim the privilege against self-incrimination. You may wish not to talk to me at all.

> What you tell me, if it relates to the performance of your duties, and is confidential, will be privileged. The privilege, however, requires explanation. It is not your privilege to claim. It is the corporation's privilege. Thus, not only can I tell, I must tell, others in the corporation what you have told me, if it is necessary to enable me to provide the legal services to the corporation it has retained me to provide.

> Moreover, the corporation can waive its privilege and thus, the president, or I, or someone else, can disclose to the authorities what you tell me if the corporation decides to waive its privilege.

> Also, if I find wrongdoing, I am under certain obligations to report it to the Board of Directors and perhaps the stockholders.

> Finally, the fact that our conversation is privileged does not mean that what you did, or said, is protected from disclosure just because you tell me about it. You may be subpoenaed, for example, and required to tell what you did, or said or observed, even though you told me about it.

> Do you understand?

Dennis J. Block & Nancy E. Barton, *Chapter 2, Implications of the Attorney-Client Privilege and Work-Product Doctrine, in* INTERNAL CORPORATE INVESTIGATIONS 18, 37 (Barry F. McNeil & Brad D. Brian eds., 3d eds. 2007) (remarks by Frederick B. Lacey, former U.S. District Court Judge for the District of New Jersey).

6. *Effect of* Upjohn *warnings.* Individuals can claim a valid Fifth Amendment privilege, but a corporation does not have the right to assert the privilege. The government has the right to obtain certain corporate documents over a Fifth Amendment objection. However, employees are the ones who will ultimately assemble and transfer the information to the government agents. Thus, attorneys who represent the

corporation must gather information from the individual employees of the corporation acting on behalf of the corporation. *See* Chapter 17, Self-Incrimination, *infra*.

While it is true that counsel conducting internal investigations hope to obtain candid information from employees, the risk of disclosure may make employees less likely to reveal potentially incriminating information. This risk is similar to the risk in other criminal investigations where, after a *Miranda* warning is administered, a suspect refuses to continue to speak. Where corporate counsel is examining employees, the *Upjohn* decision does not require withdrawal from simultaneous representation but only discusses the warning to be given. As a best practice, should corporate counsel explain to employees their right to have personal counsel to protect their interests? Should corporate counsel explain clearly that the corporate attorney does not represent the employees' interests if they choose to continue to be interviewed?

Suppose you are an employee in a corporation that is investigating itself. You do not think you have done anything wrong, but you also know that you are no expert on financial crime. Corporate counsel has just provided you with an *Upjohn* warning. Would you speak with an internal investigator after receiving this warning? Would you secure individual counsel? What factors are important in answering this question?

7. *Work-product doctrine.* Closely related to the attorney-client privilege is the work-product doctrine. This doctrine protects the confidentiality of materials prepared by clients and their attorneys in anticipation of litigation, including, as relevant here, materials generated during an internal investigation that include the attorney's opinions and legal theories. The work-product doctrine is designed to facilitate the U.S. adversarial trial system by preventing adversaries from obtaining the benefit of an attorney's labor in anticipation of litigation. As with the attorney-client privilege, issues arise with waiving the work-product protection.

The Supreme Court originally acknowledged the work-product doctrine in *Hickman v. Taylor*, 329 U.S. 495, 510–11 (1947):

> In performing his various duties . . . it is essential that a lawyer work with a certain degree of privacy, free from unnecessary intrusion by opposing parties and their counsel. Proper preparation of a client's case demands that he assemble information, sift what he considers to be the relevant from the irrelevant facts, prepare his legal theories and plan his strategy without undue influence and needless interference. . . . This work is reflected, of course, in interviews, statements, memoranda, correspondence, briefs, mental impressions, personal beliefs, and countless other tangible and intangible ways — aptly . . . termed . . . the "work-product of the lawyer." Were such materials open to opposing counsel on mere demand, much of what is now put down in writing would remain unwritten.

This reasoning is applied both in civil cases, *see* FED. R. CIV. P. 26(b)(3) (discussing disclosure of trial preparation materials), and in criminal cases, *see* FED. R. CRIM.

P. 16(a)(2) (discussing government's nondisclosure); FED. R. CRIM. P. 16(b)(2) (discussing defendant's nondisclosure). In *Upjohn*, the Supreme Court case discussed earlier holding that corporations are protected by the attorney-client privilege, the Court also held that corporations are protected by the work-product protection. *See Upjohn Co. v. United States*, 449 U.S. 383, 395 (1981).

8. *Waivers of the attorney-client privilege.* The Department of Justice previously adopted controversial policies regarding the attorney-client privilege. Under the "Thompson Memorandum," issued by then-Deputy Attorney General Larry Thompson, titled *Principles of Federal Prosecution of Business Organizations*, the DOJ penalized entities that declined to waive the attorney-client privilege during a criminal investigation. Among other things, the Memorandum stated that an entity's decision to waive, or not to waive, the attorney-client privilege may affect the government's decision to prosecute the entity. For an analysis of the Thompson Memorandum, *see* Peter J. Henning, *Overcriminalization: The Politics of Crime*, 54 AM. U. L. REV. 669 (2005).

In August 2008, the DOJ (under pressure from Congress and an unusual alliance between the American Civil Liberties Union and the corporate bar) rescinded its previous policies and published the new Filip memorandum. The Filip memorandum prohibits federal prosecutors from considering the entity's decision not to waive the attorney-client privilege when assessing the degree of an entity's cooperation. *See* "Principles of Federal Prosecution of Business Organizations," Memorandum from Mark R. Filip, Deputy Attorney General, to Heads of Department Components and United States Attorneys (Aug. 28, 2008) at 9-28.760 *available at* http://www.usdoj.gov/opa/documents/corp-charging-guidelines.pdf.

Section 9-28.750 is one of the few provisions in the prosecution manual with any enforcement mechanism. A party that believes a prosecutor is violating the letter or spirit of the DOJ's official ambivalence to privilege waiver can file a complaint with the prosecutor's superiors. U.S. Dep't. of Just. Manual § 9-28.750 (2018). Is this a good policy, or should prosecutors be able to apply pressure to corporations to waive the privilege? Note that when evidence is unavaileble to authorities, the truth becomes harder to discern.

9. *Selective waivers.* Selective waivers would allow corporations to aid government investigation without waiving the privilege as to future civil litigants. This is a recurring issue. To be effective, selective waiver must be backed by a court order. *See* FED. R. EVID. 502(e). What benefits might there be to the public in allowing such waivers? For further discussion of selective waivers and the attorney-client privilege, see Michael H. Dore, *A Matter of Fairness: The Need for a New Look at Selective Waiver in SEC Investigations*, 89 MARQ. L. REV. 761 (2006); Zach Dostart, *Selective Disclosure: The Abrogation of the Attorney-Client Privilege and the Work-Product*, 33 PEPP. L. REV. 723 (2005/2006). In *Diversified Industries, Inc. v. Meredith*, 572 F.2d 598, 611 (8th Cir. 1977), a corporation disclosed results from an internal investigation to the SEC. The court found that the disclosure was a

limited waiver of the attorney-client privilege, and all other materials remained under the protection of the privilege. Many jurisdictions have rejected this doctrine, but some still apply selective waivers.

10. *Scope of waiver.* If privilege is waived as to some materials, the waiver may extend to other materials as well. The scope of waiver used to operate very harshly, so that even inadvertent waiver as to one document would waive privilege as to all others concerning the same subject matter. The Federal Rules of Evidence, as adopted in 1975, only contained Rule 501. Now, where waiver is inadvertent, the waiver does not extend beyond the documents or communications at issue. Fed. R. Evid. 502(b). Where waiver is intentional, it will extend to any other documents or communications that concern the same subject and ought "in fairness" to be considered together. Fed. R. Evid. 502(a). Although the privilege rules are much more protective than they were in 1975, intentional waiver is treated differently because courts are concerned about parties using the attorney-client privilege as "both a shield and a sword." *See United States v. Bilzerian*, 926 F.2d 1285, 1292 (2d Cir. 1991). What do you think the worry is?

11. *The crime-fraud exception.* If a client uses attorney communications or work product to commit a crime, the privileges may not apply. The client must have made or received the communication with the intent to further an unlawful or fraudulent act, and the client must have carried out an unlawful or fraudulent act. *See In re Sealed Case*, 121 F.3d 729 (D.C. Cir. 1997). Note the focus is on the client's intent and action, not the attorney's.

Problems

15-1. You are in-house counsel to a large multistate corporation, ByGone Industries, Inc. ("ByGone"). ByGone has more than 15,000 employees and locations in every state. ByGone is subject to regulatory governance because it produces widgets. You have instituted a wide-ranging and very effective internal compliance program. All employees have been informed of the program and trained on the rules and procedures that pertain to the specifics of the program. In its business, ByGone is required by law to release certain information to state agencies in order to comply with the various state rules and regulations. One state has sent an inquiry to ByGone regarding materials used in assembling widgets because there have been some reports of defects. In complying with this request and turning over the documents, regulations provide that ByGone maintain its attorney-client privilege as to these documents. You discover that the federal government has opened a criminal investigation related to the matters contained in the documents you turned over to the state. You assert the privilege with respect to the released documents.

Will you have to comply with the criminal grand jury subpoena for the documents? (See Chapter 16, The Grand Jury, *infra.)*

15-2. In Problem 15-1 above, does it matter if you were aware of the pending criminal investigation? Suppose the Assistant United States Attorney had not yet divulged the existence of the grand jury investigation. The AUSA was present at the hearings where the testimony and documents were turned over to the state agency.

Would this person's presence make a difference in your conclusion? Why or why not?

15-3. You are attending a meeting with the senior executives of ByGone. The board and executives are discussing the benefits and risks associated with disclosure of the internal investigation to the government. One of the participants remarked, "If the government is going to ask us to waive the privilege all the time then we should conduct a different kind of investigation of misconduct. For example, we might not want to investigate too thoroughly or probe too deeply."

Is it ethical for a corporation to refrain from investigating possible misconduct brought to its attention because it fears that the government might eventually ask for the results of the investigation? Why or why not?

15-4. The principals at the meeting decide not to reveal the details of the internal investigation to the government, even though the government has made the request. The executives begin to discuss this strategy after the meeting and ask your opinion.

What do you tell them?

3. Conflicts between Corporations and Employees during an Investigation

Corporate investigations are rife with possible conflicts between the corporation and its employees. This is particularly true if the corporation or an employee is a candidate for lenient treatment in exchange for cooperation. Prosecutors can and do exploit such conflicts to gain strategic advantages. As the next case illustrates, however, there are limits to just how far prosecutors can go.

United States v. Stein

541 F.3d 130 (2d Cir. 2008)

Opinion for the Court filed by CHIEF JUDGE JACOBS:

The United States appeals from an order of the United States District Court for the Southern District of New York (Kaplan, *J.*), dismissing an indictment against thirteen former partners and employees of the accounting firm KPMG, LLP. Judge Kaplan found that, absent pressure from the government, KPMG would have paid defendants' legal fees and expenses without regard to cost. Based on this and other findings of fact, Judge Kaplan ruled that the government deprived defendants of their right to counsel under the Sixth Amendment by causing KPMG to impose conditions on the advancement of legal fees to defendants, to cap the fees, and ultimately to end payment. *See United States v. Stein,* 435 F.Supp.2d 330, 367–73 (S.D.N.Y.2006) ("*Stein I* ")....

We hold that KPMG's adoption and enforcement of a policy under which it conditioned, capped and ultimately ceased advancing legal fees to defendants followed as a direct consequence of the government's overwhelming influence, and that KPMG's conduct therefore amounted to state action. We further hold that the government thus unjustifiably interfered with defendants' relationship with counsel and their ability to mount a defense, in violation of the Sixth Amendment, and that the government did not cure the violation. Because no other remedy will return defendants to the status quo ante, we affirm the dismissal of the indictment as to all thirteen defendants. . . .

Background

The Thompson Memorandum. In January 2003, then-United States Deputy Attorney General Larry D. Thompson promulgated a policy statement, *Principles of Federal Prosecution of Business Organizations* (the "Thompson Memorandum"), which articulated "principles" to govern the Department's discretion in bringing prosecutions against business organizations. The Thompson Memorandum was closely based on a predecessor document issued in 1999 by then-U.S. Deputy Attorney General Eric Holder, *Federal Prosecution of Corporations.* Along with the familiar factors governing charging decisions, the Thompson Memorandum identifies nine additional considerations, including the company's "timely and voluntary disclosure of wrongdoing and its willingness to cooperate in the investigation of its agents." The Memorandum explains that prosecutors should inquire whether the corporation appears to be protecting its culpable employees and agents [and that] a corporation's promise of support to culpable employees and agents, either *through the advancing of attorneys fees,* through retaining the employees without sanction for their misconduct, or through providing information to the employees about the government's investigation pursuant to a joint defense agreement, may be considered by the prosecutor in weighing the extent and value of a corporation's cooperation. A footnote appended to the highlighted phrase explains that because certain states require companies to advance legal fees for their officers, "a corporation's compliance with governing law should not be considered a failure to cooperate." In December 2006 — after the events in this prosecution had transpired — the Department of Justice replaced the Thompson Memorandum with the McNulty Memorandum, under which prosecutors may consider a company's fee advancement policy only where the circumstances indicate that it is "intended to impede a criminal investigation," and even then only with the approval of the Deputy Attorney General.

Commencement of the Federal Investigation

After Senate subcommittee hearings in 2002 concerning KPMG's possible involvement in creating and marketing fraudulent tax shelters, KPMG retained Robert S. Bennett of the law firm Skadden, Arps, Slate, Meagher & Flom LLP ("Skadden") to formulate a "cooperative approach" for KPMG to use in dealing with federal authorities. . . .

In February 2004, KPMG officials learned that the firm and 20 to 30 of its top partners and employees were subjects of a grand jury investigation of fraudulent tax shelters. On February 18, 2004, KPMG's CEO announced to all partners that the firm was aware of the United States Attorney's Office's ("USAO") investigation and that "[a]ny present or former members of the firm asked to appear will be represented by competent coun[sel] *at the firm's expense.*"

The February 25, 2004 Meeting

In preparation for a meeting with Skadden on February 25, 2004, the prosecutors — including Assistant United States Attorneys ("AUSAs") Shirah Neiman and Justin Weddle — decided to ask whether KPMG would advance legal fees to employees under investigation. Bennett started the meeting by announcing that KPMG had resolved to "clean house," that KPMG "would cooperate fully with the government's investigation," and that its goal was not to protect individual employees but rather to save the firm from being indicted. AUSA Weddle inquired about the firm's plans for advancing fees and about any legal obligation to do so. Later on, AUSA Neiman added that the government would "take into account" the firm's legal obligations to advance fees, but that "the Thompson Memorandum [w]as a point that had to be considered." Bennett then advised that although KPMG was still investigating its legal obligations to advance fees, its "common practice" was to do so. However, Bennett explained, KPMG would not pay legal fees for any partner who refused to cooperate or "took the Fifth," so long as KPMG had the legal authority to do so.

Later in the meeting, AUSA Weddle asked Bennett to ascertain KPMG's legal obligations to advance attorneys' fees. AUSA Neiman added that "misconduct" should not or cannot "be rewarded" under "federal guidelines." One Skadden attorney's notes attributed to AUSA Weddle the prediction that, if KPMG had discretion regarding fees, the government would "look at that under a microscope."

Skadden then reported back to KPMG. In notes of the meeting, a KPMG executive wrote the words "[p]aying legal fees" and "[s]everance" next to "not a sign of cooperation."

Communications Between the Prosecutors and KPMG

On March 2, 2004, Bennett told AUSA Weddle that although KPMG believed it had no legal obligation to advance fees, "it would be a big problem" for the firm not to do so given its partnership structure. But Bennett disclosed KPMG's tentative decision to limit the amount of fees and condition them on employees' cooperation with prosecutors. . . .

On a March 11 conference call with Skadden, AUSA Weddle recommended that KPMG tell employees that they should be "totally open" with the USAO, "even if that [meant admitting] criminal wrongdoing," explaining that this would give him good material for cross-examination. That same day, Skadden wrote to counsel for the KPMG employees who had been identified as subjects of the investigation. The letter set forth KPMG's new fees policy ("Fees Policy"), pursuant to which advancement of fees and expenses would be

[i] capped at $400,000 per employee;

[ii] conditioned on the employee's cooperation with the government; and

[iii] terminated when an employee was indicted.

The government was copied on this correspondence.

On March 12, KPMG sent a memorandum to certain other employees who had not been identified as subjects, urging them to cooperate with the government, advising them that it might be advantageous for them to exercise their right to counsel, and advising that KPMG would cover employees' "reasonable fees." The prosecutors expressed by letter their "disappoint[ment] with [the] tone" of this memorandum and its "one-sided presentation of potential issues," and "demanded that KPMG send out a supplemental memorandum in a form they proposed." The government's alternative language, premised on the "assum[ption] that KPMG truly is committed to fully cooperating with the Government's investigation," advised employees that they could "meet with investigators without the assistance of counsel." KPMG complied, and circulated a memo advising that employees "may deal directly with government representatives without counsel."

At a meeting in late March, Skadden asked the prosecutors to notify Skadden in the event any KPMG employee refused to cooperate. Over the following year, the prosecutors regularly informed Skadden whenever a KPMG employee refused to cooperate fully, such as by refusing to proffer or by proffering incompletely (in the government's view). Skadden, in turn, informed the employees' lawyers that fee advancement would cease unless the employees cooperated. The employees either knuckled under and submitted to interviews, or they were fired and KPMG ceased advancing their fees. . . . As Bennett later assured AUSA Weddle: "Whenever your Office has notified us that individuals have not . . . cooperat[ed], KPMG has promptly and without question encouraged them to cooperate and threatened to cease payment of their attorney fees and . . . to take personnel action, including termination." . . .

[KPMG avoided indictment and received a deferred prosecution agreement. Prosecutors indicted several individual KMPG employees, including appellees in this case. Upon their indictment, KMPG ceased paying their attorney's fees.]

Discussion

. . .

Judge Kaplan found that "KPMG's decision to cut off all payments of legal fees and expenses to anyone who was indicted and to limit and to condition such payments prior to indictment upon cooperation with the government *was the direct consequence* of the pressure applied by the Thompson Memorandum and the USAO." The government protests that KPMG's adoption and enforcement of its Fees Policy was private action, outside the ambit of the Sixth Amendment.

When "[t]he district court's dismissal of [an] indictment raises questions of constitutional interpretation, . . . we review the district court's decision *de novo.*" *United States v. King,* 276 F.3d 109, 111 (2d Cir.2002). Actions of a private entity are attributable to the State if "there is a sufficiently close nexus between the State and the challenged action of the . . . entity so that the action of the latter may be fairly treated as that of the State itself." *Jackson v. Metro. Edison Co.,* 419 U.S. 345, 351, 95 S.Ct. 449, 42 L.Ed.2d 477 (1974). . . ."A nexus of state action exists between a private entity and the state when the state exercises coercive power, is entwined in the management or control of the private actor, or provides the private actor with *significant encouragement,* either overt or covert, or when the private actor operates as a *willful participant in joint activity* with the State or its agents, is controlled by an agency of the State, has been delegated a public function by the state, or is *entwined with governmental policies.*" *Flagg v. Yonkers Sav. & Loan Ass'n,* 396 F.3d 178, 187 (2d Cir.2005) (emphasis added and internal quotation marks omitted). . . .

The prosecutors . . . steered KPMG toward their preferred fee advancement policy and then supervised its application in individual cases. Such "overt" and "significant encouragement" supports the conclusion that KPMG's conduct is properly attributed to the State. . . .

The government responds: . . . [H]ow can KPMG, an *adversary* of the government, also be its partner? . . . An adversarial relationship does not normally bespeak partnership. But KPMG faced ruin by indictment and reasonably believed it must do everything in its power to avoid it. The government's threat of indictment was easily sufficient to convert its adversary into its agent. KPMG was not in a position to consider coolly the risk of indictment, weigh the potential significance of the other enumerated factors in the Thompson Memorandum, and decide for itself how to proceed. We therefore conclude that KPMG's adoption and enforcement of the Fees Policy (both before and upon defendants' indictment) amounted to state action. The government may properly be held "responsible for the specific conduct of which the [criminal defendants] complain[]," *Blum,* 457 U.S. at 1004, 102 S.Ct. 2777(emphasis omitted), *i.e.,* the deprivation of their Sixth Amendment right to counsel, if the violation is established. . . .

The Sixth Amendment protects "an individual's right to choose the lawyer or lawyers he or she desires," *Stein I,* 435 F.Supp.2d at 366 (citing *Wheat v. United States,* 486 U.S. 153, 164, 108 S.Ct. 1692, 100 L.Ed.2d 140 (1988)), and "to use one's own funds to mount the defense that one wishes to present," *id.* (citing *Caplin & Drysdale, Chartered v. United States,* 491 U.S. 617, 624, 109 S.Ct. 2646, 105 L.Ed.2d 528 (1989)). . . . . [Such a] Sixth Amendment violation "is complete irrespective of the quality of the representation they receive." *Id.* at 369. . . .

Although defendants' Sixth Amendment rights attached only upon indictment, the district court properly considered pre-indictment state action that affected defendants post-indictment. When the government acts prior to indictment so as to impair the suspect's relationship with counsel post-indictment, the pre-indictment actions ripen into cognizable Sixth Amendment deprivations upon indictment.12 As Judge Ellis explained in *United States v. Rosen*, 487 F.Supp.2d 721 (E.D.Va.2007), "it is entirely plausible that pernicious effects of the pre-indictment interference continued into the post-indictment period, effectively hobbling defendants' Sixth Amendment rights to retain counsel of choice with funds to which they had a right. . . . [I]f, as alleged, the government coerced [the employer] into halting fee advances on defendants' behalf and the government did so for the purpose of undermining defendants' relationship with counsel once the indictment issued, the government violated defendants' right to expend their own resources towards counsel once the right attached." *Id.* at 734.

Since the government forced KPMG to adopt the constricted Fees Policy — including the provision for terminating fee advancement upon indictment — and then compelled KPMG to enforce it, it was virtually certain that KPMG would terminate defendants' fees upon indictment. We therefore reject the government's argument that its actions (virtually all pre-indictment) are immune from scrutiny under the Sixth Amendment.

We now consider "*what* the [Sixth Amendment] right guarantees." *Rothgery,* 128 S.Ct. at 2592 (Alito, *J.,* concurring).

The Sixth Amendment ensures that "[i]n all criminal prosecutions, the accused shall enjoy the right . . . to have the Assistance of Counsel for his defence." U.S. Const. amend. VI. Thus "the Sixth Amendment guarantees the defendant the right to be represented by an otherwise qualified attorney whom that defendant can afford to hire, or who is willing to represent the defendant even though he is without funds." . . .

The government must "honor" a defendant's Sixth Amendment right to counsel: This means more than simply that the State cannot prevent the accused from obtaining the assistance of counsel. The Sixth Amendment also imposes on the State an affirmative obligation to respect and preserve the accused's choice to seek this assistance. . . . [A]t the very least, the prosecutor and police have an affirmative obligation not to act in a manner that circumvents and thereby dilutes the protection afforded by the right to counsel. . . .

In a nutshell, the Sixth Amendment protects against unjustified governmental interference with the right to defend oneself using whatever assets one has or might reasonably and lawfully obtain. . . .

It is also urged that a company may pretend cooperation while "circling the wagons," that payment of legal fees can advance such a strategy, and that the government has a legitimate interest in being able to assess cooperation using the payment of fees as one factor. Even if that can be a legitimate justification, it would not be in play here: prosecutors testified before the district court that they were never concerned that KPMG was "circling the wagons." Moreover, it is unclear how the circling of wagons is much different from the legitimate melding of a joint defense. . . .

Judge Kaplan found that [some of the] defendants . . . were unable to retain the counsel of their choosing as a result of the termination of fee advancements upon indictment. . . . Therefore, [as to these defendants], the government deprived [them] of their Sixth Amendment right to counsel of choice.

The remaining defendants . . . do not claim they were deprived of their chosen counsel. . . . [T]hese defendants can easily demonstrate interference in their relationships with counsel and impairment of their ability to mount a defense based on Judge Kaplan's non-erroneous findings that the post-indictment termination of fees "caused them to restrict the activities of their counsel," and thus to limit the scope of their pre-trial investigation and preparation. . . . We therefore hold that these defendants were also deprived of their right to counsel under the Sixth Amendment.

For the foregoing reasons, we AFFIRM the judgment of the district court dismissing defendants' indictment.

Note and Question

1. *Prosecutorial ethics.* Like all attorneys, prosecutors are under a professional obligation to represent their client — in this case, the government — zealously. However, their discretion and zeal is tempered by a further obligation to *"do justice." Berger v. United States*, 295 U.S. 78, 88 (1935). Finding the line between zeal and justice can be a delicate balancing act. Did the prosecutors in *Stein* step over the line?

Problem

15-5. You represent a health care agency being investigated by the Department of Justice for possible Medicare and Medicaid fraud. In anticipation of the investigation, the company initiates internal investigations of its records. The DOJ and your client reach a settlement agreement, but in doing so, your client provided the government with some of the documents from the internal investigation. Your client executes a confidentiality agreement in which it reserves the right to assert attorney-client privilege and the work-product doctrine over the documents as to other parties and over other related documents as to all parties. Once the extent and results of the DOJ investigation come to light, private insurance companies and individuals file numerous lawsuits against your client based on the information your client disclosed to the DOJ.

If an opposing party files for a motion to compel production of these documents and others concerning the same subject matter, how would you advise your client of the potential outcomes of such a motion?

4. Common Interests between Corporations and Employees during an Investigation

In complex litigation, individuals and entities who are parties to the litigation often share common interests. A joint defense agreement may create a privilege, also known as the common interest privilege, which protects the free flow of information among such parties. The privilege provides that communications among the parties are protected when the communications are designed to establish a common litigation strategy. As you read the next case, consider what problems the joint defense agreement presents for both the individuals and the corporation.

United States v. LeCroy

348 F. Supp. 2d 375 (E.D. Pa. 2004)

BAYLSON, DISTRICT JUDGE.

Defendants LeCroy and Snell are charged with wire fraud under 18 U.S.C. §§ 1343 and 2, for allegedly soliciting and obtaining from Philadelphia attorney Ronald White (originally a named co-defendant in this case but now deceased) a false $50,000 invoice presented to J.P. Morgan Chase ("JPMC") for legal services purportedly performed by White's law firm.

The issue presented is whether this Court should preclude the government from using certain notes and memoranda it has in its possession, which were taken by JPMC counsel during interviews held with JPMC employees LeCroy and Snell by JPMC counsel, or whether these notes and interviews are protected by either the attorney-client privilege and/or a joint defense agreement entered into by counsel for LeCroy, Snell and JPMC.

I. Procedural History

During the grand jury investigation which preceded the return of the indictment in this case on June 29, 2004, JPMC, as well as Defendants LeCroy and Snell, received grand jury subpoenas. As set forth in further detail below, JPMC's internal counsel questioned LeCroy and Snell about their knowledge of the facts underlying the grand jury subpoena, recognized their need for individual counsel, and JPMC itself retained outside counsel in Philadelphia. LeCroy and Snell were then given recommendations for lawyers and retained their own individual counsel. A Joint Defense Agreement arose, and during the discussions among counsel for JPMC, LeCroy and Snell, JPMC counsel indicated a desire to interview LeCroy and Snell at various times. As the government had requested, JPMC subsequently decided that it would produce, pursuant to its grand jury subpoena, the notes and/or memoranda of the meetings between JPMC counsel and LeCroy and Snell.

Following the return of the indictment, LeCroy and Snell asserted claims of privilege with respect to notes and memoranda of interviews created by counsel for JPMC. The government designated two attorneys who were not connected with the prosecution of the indictment to maintain custody and control of these notes and memoranda, and constructed a "Chinese wall" between the government attorneys who were the prosecutors on the indictment, and the government attorneys designated to represent the government in connection with the claims of privilege by LeCroy and Snell.

II. Factual Background

Defendant Snell was served with a grand jury subpoena at his JPMC office in Atlanta, GA on or about October 17, 2003, and promptly advised Scott Campbell, JPMC's Senior Vice President and Associate General Counsel. Campbell was aware that JPMC itself had received a grand jury subpoena at or about the same time. Campbell had discussions with Snell and his supervisor, LeCroy, on October 20, 2003. At that time, the Court finds Snell and LeCroy were speaking to Campbell in their capacity as JPMC employees. Campbell was acting as JPMC counsel, and there were no discussions about either Snell or LeCroy having individual counsel.

As a result of further discussions with Snell on the following day, October 21, 2003, and with both Snell and LeCroy on October 27, 2003, JPMC recognized the need for both of these individuals to have individual counsel and so advised them of this fact. At this time JPMC itself retained outside counsel, Dodds, a Philadelphia lawyer with experience as both a prosecutor and a defense counsel. Up to and including October 27, 2003, Snell and LeCroy did not seek personal legal advice from Campbell; they had no expectation of getting personal legal advice from Campbell and they did not ask for it. JPMC made recommendations to LeCroy and Snell of certain Philadelphia attorneys to represent them in connection with the grand jury investigation. JPMC agreed to pay the legal fees of Snell and LeCroy.

Snell retained his counsel, Suddath, on or about October 30, 2003. LeCroy retained his counsel, Recker, in the time period of November 10–13, 2003. Both Suddath and Recker are Philadelphia lawyers experienced in grand jury investigations.

The Court finds that JPMC intended to form a Joint Defense Agreement ("JDA") prior to LeCroy and Snell retaining personal counsel. Campbell's handwritten notes for the meeting of October 27, 2003, state "we will work going forward on a joint defense basis." Campbell testified that at the October 27 meeting he informed LeCroy and Snell that he was speaking to them in his capacity as counsel for JPMC and that he was going to "recommend counsel to represent their personal interests." As soon as Suddath and Recker were retained, they confirmed the existence of the JDA with Dodds.

The government does not dispute the existence of a JDA in this case. The JDA was verbal, and although its terms were never specifically articulated, Recker accurately described her understanding of the JDA as follows:

> The joint defense arrangement, primarily the focus is twofold. One, that the lawyers are able to investigate facts and share the results of their investigation with each other, keeping everything under the cloak of privilege. The second important part in the understanding of a joint defense arrangement

is that none of that information that has been shared pursuant to the privilege can be disclosed to a third party without the consult-consent of all the parties involved.

[Counsel for Snell] testified [to a] similar understanding of the JDA. From these facts, the Court concluded that the discussions which took place between JPMC counsel and LeCroy and Snell after October 27, 2003, specifically on October 29, 2003 as to both, and on December 11, 2003 with LeCroy, are protected by the JDA. During these meetings, both LeCroy and Snell had reason to believe that their discussions with either their own counsel or JPMC counsel were protected from disclosure. . . .

The testimony is undisputed that Dodds, on behalf of JPMC, was consistent and insistent that if the government pushed, JPMC would turn over the interview notes taken by JPMC counsel, to the government. Despite this clear warning, LeCroy and Snell went to New York on separate dates in January 2004 and were interviewed by JPMC counsel with their own counsel present.

The March 4, 2004 interviews of Snell and LeCroy were taken without their individual counsel present, and they did not know that the meeting was going to occur.

III. Legal Principles of a Joint Defense Agreement

Although the Third Circuit has not specifically ruled on the applicability of a joint defense agreement in any similar factual situation, it has described a joint defense agreement. . . . "Because the privilege sometimes may apply outside the context of actual litigation, what the parties call a 'joint defense' privilege is more aptly termed the 'common interest' rule." *In re Grand Jury Subpoena, A. Nameless Lawyer,* 274 F.3d 563, 572 (1st Cir. 2001). The burden of demonstrating the existence of a joint defense agreement falls on the person claiming it. A party seeking to assert the joint defense privilege must demonstrate that: 1) the communications were made in the course of a joint defense effort; 2) the statements were made in furtherance of that effort; and 3) the privilege has not been waived. Likewise, the party asserting privilege, both in the context of joint defense agreements and otherwise, bears the burden of proving the applicability of the privilege. In the absence of a JDA, when the party asserting privilege is a corporate officer, the individual corporate officer's assertion of attorney-client privilege cannot prevent the disclosure of corporate communications with corporate counsel when the corporation's privilege has been waived.

Although "privileges should be narrowly construed and expansions cautiously extended," *Weissman,* 195 F.3d at 100, courts have found that an oral joint defense agreement may be valid. *See Nameless Lawyer,* 274 F.3d at 569–70. A person need not be a litigant to be a party to a joint defense agreement.

It is axiomatic that in order for a communication to be privileged that communication must be made in confidence. Even in the context of joint defense agreements, in order for privilege to attach to a communication, the party asserting the privilege bears the burden of demonstrating that "the communication was given in confidence and that the client *reasonably understood it to be so given*." *United States v. Schwimmer*, 892 F.2d 237, 244 (2d Cir. 1989) (emphasis added). Additionally, the burden is on the party asserting a joint defense privilege to demonstrate that the clients reasonably believed that their statements were being made within the context and in furtherance of their joint defense.

IV. Application of Legal Principles to the Facts of this Case

A JDA is not an escape-proof prison. Indeed, public policy mandates that a participant in a JDA must be free to withdraw from it, unilaterally, but the withdrawal or waiver must be prospective only — and the duty of the Court in the present dispute is to determine whether there was such a withdrawal or waiver, and if so, precisely what notes and memoranda the government is entitled to retain and use at trial, and which notes and memoranda are protected by the JDA that was in existence.

A JDA without the right of prospective withdrawal would be void, if only because it would prevent one party to the JDA determining, as JPMC did in this case, that its own interests required it to cooperate with the government, rather than cooperate exclusively with its employees and their counsel. A participant in a JDA may also decide that it wants to "go it alone" and that doing so outweighs the benefits of continuing in the JDA. One party may decide that he, she or it wants to plead guilty to the charges that appear inevitable and that continuance in the JDA would deprive that party of the benefits which would come from negotiating an early plea agreement with the government.

A. Waiver

As to the issue of waiver of the attorney-client privilege, there is no waiver of the individual privilege between LeCroy and his counsel, and Snell and his counsel. The only issue of waiver relates to certain protections of the JDA. The leading case in the Third Circuit on waiver of privilege is *Westinghouse v. Republic of the Philippines*, 951 F.2d 1414, 1423 (3d Cir. 1991), holding that voluntary disclosure to a third party of purportedly privileged communications has long been considered inconsistent with the privilege. It is well settled that when a party voluntarily discloses privileged communications to a third party, the privilege is waived. Similarly, when a party discloses a portion of otherwise privileged material but withholds the remainder, the privilege is waived only as to those communications actually disclosed, unless a partial waiver would be unfair to the party's adversary. Disclosure alone, without intent, may constitute waiver of the attorney-client privilege.

Defendants rely on *In re Grand Jury Subpoenas (89-3 and 89-4)*, 902 F.2d 244, 248 (4th Cir. 1990), for the proposition that the joint defense privilege cannot be waived without the consent of all the parties to the joint defense agreement. That case involved a dispute between a parent company and its wholly owned subsidiary — both of whom had been summoned before a grand jury — regarding the production of records. The Fourth Circuit held that the subsidiary could not unilaterally waive a joint defense privilege, and that the joint defense privilege may attach irrespective of whether an action is criminal or civil, and regardless of whether an action is ongoing or contemplated.

The First Circuit recently made the following observation: "[T]he existence of a joint defense agreement does not increase the number of parties whose consent is needed to waive the attorney-client privilege; it merely prevents disclosure of a communication made in the course of preparing a joint defense by the third party to whom it was made." *Nameless Lawyer*, 274 F.3d at 572–73.

Applying these waiver principles to the present case, the Court finds that LeCroy and Snell waived some protections of the JDA by proceeding with the interviews with JPMC counsel in January 2004 and March 2004. Specifically, they voluntarily and knowingly waived the protection of the JDA to the extent that JPMC would be allowed to turn over the notes of those interviews to the government.

B. Withdrawal

. . .

[I]t is clearly contemplated by the parties to a JDA that one party could withdraw prospectively. Similarly, as the Court has noted above, any prohibition on withdrawal would be decidedly contrary to the public interest. There are some cases where courts have discussed the necessity of one party being able to withdraw from a JDA on a prospective basis.

In *United States v. Stepney*, 246 F. Supp. 2d 1069, 1086 (N.D. Cal. 2003), the court required that each joint defense agreement entered into by the defendants "must explicitly allow withdrawal upon notice to the other defendants." The court in *Stepney* elaborated on the risks inherent in a joint defense arrangement and emphasized that the protections afforded therein are not identical to the protections generally enjoyed under the attorney-client privilege:

> Although a limitation on confidentiality between a defendant and his own attorney would pose a severe threat to the true attorney-client relationship, making each defendant somewhat more guarded about the disclosures he makes to the joint defense effort does not significantly intrude on the function of joint defense agreements. . . . Co-defendants may eliminate inconsistent defenses without the same degree of disclosure that would be required for an attorney to adequately represent her client. *Id.*

C. Modification

As to modification, there can be no dispute that parties to an agreement have the right to modify it. While one party to a contract cannot modify its terms without the assent of the other parties, the fact of agreement as to a modification may be implied from a course of conduct in accordance with its existence.

D. Analysis

. . .

[T]he Court also finds partial withdrawal by JPMC and a partial waiver by LeCroy and Snell. The Court is not obliged to shoehorn its decision into any particular single legal doctrine, but rather, to pragmatically apply the law to the facts and make a decision as to what evidence may be used by the government at the trial.

It is also important to note that although the Court finds that there was a significant modification of the JDA as of January 2004, the JDA nonetheless continued in existence, as modified, throughout the balance of the investigation and indeed continues in existence today, during the pretrial preparation stages.

JPMC had determined for its own good and sufficient reasons — one of which is the fact that it is a highly regulated financial institution, and another may have been that it realized it may have been a victim of a fraudulent scheme — that it would, if the government "pushed," turn over the notes and memoranda of its meetings with LeCroy and Snell. JPMC thought it had the right to do so because LeCroy and Snell had their own counsel, and thus their meetings with JPMC counsel were not covered by their own personal attorney-client privilege. However, the Court finds that JPMC counsel was mistaken in this belief, because having joined the JDA, JPMC was bound by it until and unless it withdrew.

The Court believes that the most important facts on this issue relate to the discussions which Dodds had with Recker and Suddath *prior* to the January meetings in which Dodds explained to them that JPMC was retaining the right to turn over the notes of the interviews. Also significant is the fact that Recker and Suddath clearly made JPMC's intent known to their clients, LeCroy and Snell, respectively. With these facts, there is no dispute that LeCroy and Snell, and their counsel, were thoroughly advised of JPMC's intent and nonetheless decided to proceed with the January 2004 interviews with JPMC counsel. LeCroy and Snell had the option, knowing in advance that these notes may be turned over to the government by JPMC counsel pursuant to the grand jury subpoena, to decline to be interviewed by JPMC counsel. . . . There are risks for every decision in a grand jury investigation, but the right of the grand jury to get the facts, and the right of JPMC, as a recipient of a grand jury subpoena, to decide to cooperate with the grand jury, are paramount. . . .

The grand jury may compel the production of evidence or the testimony of witnesses as it considers appropriate, and its operation generally is unrestrained by the technical procedural and evidentiary rules governing the conduct of criminal trials.

V. Conclusion

The facts of this case demonstrate that although entering into a JDA is often, indeed generally, beneficial to its participants, like skating on thin ice, dangers lurk below the surface. When JPMC insisted on its right of turning over the notes of its interviews with Snell and LeCroy to the government, Snell and LeCroy had the option to reject JPMC's terms and refuse to submit to the interviews. By proceeding the way they did, LeCroy and Snell waived the protections they had under the existing JDA and, by their conduct, agreed to a modification of the JDA. For this Court to refuse the government use of the interview notes which JPMC turned over to the grand jury would amount to judicial suppression of evidence that the recipient of a grand jury subpoena legitimately turned over to the grand jury. . . .

[For these reasons, the Court entered the Order protecting the interview notes while the JDA existed, and refused to protect the interview notes under the modification of the JDA proposed by JPMC and accepted by the conduct of LeCroy and Snell.]

Notes and Questions

1. *Common interests.* A common interest privilege applies where: (1) the communication is made by separate parties in the course of a matter of common interest, (2) the communication is designed to further that effort, and (3) the privilege has not otherwise been waived. *United States v. Bergonzi*, 216 F.R.D. 487, 495 (N.D. Cal. 2003). In conducting an internal investigation, a company is seeking evidence of wrongdoing. If such evidence is discovered, companies sometimes disclose the information to the government in order to forestall a criminal prosecution. In *Bergonzi*, the McKesson Corporation argued that it had a similar interest with the government in the investigation. McKesson was preparing a report on the investigation to submit to the government, and both parties wanted information contained in the internal report. Do you agree that there was a common interest between them? The court said, "The company and the government did not have a true common goal as it could not have been the company's goal to impose liability onto itself, a consideration always maintained by the government." *Id.* at 496. Did the company and the government ever have a similar goal? If so, what was that goal?

With respect to the work-product doctrine, the majority stated in *In re Columbia/ HCA Healthcare*, "The ability to prepare one's case in confidence, which is the chief reason articulated in *Hickman* for the work-product protections, has little to do with talking to the Government." 293 F.3d 289, 306 (6th Cir. 2002). Do you agree?

2. *Confidentiality agreements.* In many cases involving internal investigations, corporations often create confidentiality agreements with the government when disclosing information from internal investigations. However, absent a court order, this confidentiality agreement does not prevent the waiver of the attorney-client privilege as to other parties. What purpose would a confidentiality agreement serve if it still constituted a waiver of the privilege?

3. *Non-waiver agreements.* As seen above, some United States Attorney's offices will enter into "non-waiver" agreements with a corporation under investigation. Questions remain, however, as to the extent to which the courts will recognize such agreements. Given the potential ramifications of disclosure to the government, corporations should consider approaches that lessen the consequences of any waivers. As one commentary stated:

> [A]ttorneys conducting the investigation should do so with the expectation that any documents they generate may ultimately be discovered or even published in newspapers. . . . Any such documents [notes in preparation of memos or reports] should be carefully prepared. . . . [C]orporations can often negotiate with regulators and prosecutors about the particular materials to be disclosed . . . [and] when a corporation does elect to provide privileged materials to the government, it can attempt to frame a non-waiver

agreement in ways that will maximize the chances of the agreement being honored. For example, if a company can negotiate for disclosure to occur after or simultaneously with the company's settlement or other resolution of proceedings with the government, then the company will have a stronger argument that it and the government are not adversaries and that the disclosure is being made to further a common interest in fully investigating the alleged wrongdoing.

Robert C. Myers & Seth C. Farber, Commentary, *Corporate Internal Investigations in the Age of Cooperation: Strategies for Limiting Disclosure of Confidential Information*, 18 WHITE-COLLAR CRIME REP., No. 6, 1 (Jan. 2004) (published in the Westlaw Journal White Collar Crime).

4. *Strategy for counsel.* The *LeCroy* court noted that "[t]here were good and abundant reasons why LeCroy and Snell, with the advice of their counsel, rationally, intelligently and knowingly decided to allow JPMC and its counsel to interview them, knowing that the notes of the interviews may be turned over to the government, but also knowing the JDA would continue, as modified. . . ." What are some of the reasons why counsel would allow the interviews to proceed with the knowledge that the information might be turned over to the government? Are you concerned at all by the fact that JPMC was paying the attorneys? If you were representing the defendants in *LeCroy*, would you have given different advice? What reasons might LeCroy and Snell have for continuing with the representation even if counsel had advised to the contrary?

5. *Joint defense agreement.* In *LeCroy*, the court defined a joint defense agreement as an extension of the attorney-client privilege that allows a privilege between defendants with a common interest. The *LeCroy* decision established the notion that the communication shared in the joint defense agreement must be made in confidence and be reasonably understood as confidential information. What would be the potential benefits and negative effects of such an undertaking? In your opinion, would the benefits sufficiently outweigh the risks? *See* Ed Magarian & Surya Saxena, Commentary, *Joint Defense Agreements: What Is a Responsible Company to Do?* 22 WHITE-COLLAR CRIME REP., No. 12, 1 (Sept. 2008).

Problem

15-6. Last year, the United States Securities and Exchange Commission (SEC) began an inquiry into whether certain accounting practices at an accounting firm, Delta Corp. (Delta) were in accordance with applicable law and regulations, and requested production of documents from Delta Corp.

As Delta reviewed the documents to be produced, it discovered documents suggesting that certain employees might have engaged in improper practices. Accordingly, Delta's Board of Directors resolved to conduct its own independent investigation of the disputed accounting practices and retained outside counsel, Felicia Franklin, to advise it.

Franklin reviewed thousands of documents and interviewed dozens of current and former employees. During Franklin's investigation, the SEC contacted her and informed Franklin that it, too, was investigating accounting practices at Delta. The SEC requested that Franklin share her findings, including determinations as to whether any wrongdoing had occurred and, if so, the identities of the persons responsible. After consulting with her client, Delta, Franklin agreed to share her documents and findings. The SEC, in turn, agreed to advise Franklin of its own findings. To govern Franklin's production of documents, the SEC entered into a written confidentiality agreement with Delta and Franklin.

After the above events, Paula Pailey, a customer of Delta, sued Delta alleging that it improperly handled her accounts. At Pailey's request, the court in the civil case issued a subpoena demanding that Delta produce all documents created or collected during the internal investigation.

Delta has moved to quash the subpoena. *How should the court rule? Why?*

C. Compliance Programs

In today's business climate, there is a high premium on corporate compliance programs. Good corporate citizenship through self-policing requires that corporations tailor compliance programs to meet their legal requirements, company- and industry-specific risks, and corporate culture. The development of compliance programs is one way that corporations have responded to highly publicized corporate scandals in order to demonstrate their integrity and social responsibility to investors and public onlookers. Moreover, a company receives powerful government incentives to establish an effective compliance policy. Some corporations, like banks, are required by law to have compliance programs. For the rest, compliance can influence how authorities exercise their discretion throughout the justice process.

1. Sarbanes-Oxley Act of 2002

The Sarbanes-Oxley Act was passed after the accounting scandals of 2001–2002. The Act requires corporations to improve accounting and auditing procedures in an effort to restore public trust and confidence and provides penalties for failure to do so. Most observers will agree that the Sarbanes-Oxley Act is the most significant piece of legislation affecting corporate governance, financial accounting, and public disclosure since the securities laws of the 1930s. The Act was an impetus for revision of the Sentencing Guidelines, which were amended for organizations effective November 1, 2004. The primary intent of the changes was to provide greater guidance to organizations and to encourage "effective programs to prevent and detect violations of law." The revised organizational sentencing guidelines encourage a corporate culture that is both ethical and committed to compliance with applicable laws and regulations. *See* Chapter 19, Sentencing, *infra*. In the "Effective Compliance and Ethics Program," U.S.S.G. § 8B2.1, the Sentencing Commission clearly stated that the purpose is to prevent and deter criminal conduct.

2. Department of Justice Policies

In 2008, the Department of Justice issued the most recent Principles of Federal Prosecution of Business Organizations. This is the current iteration of the policy that began as the "Thompson Memorandum," and then became the "McNulty Memorandum." The 2008 Principles were incorporated for the first time in the United States Attorneys' Manual (USAM), which later became the Justice Manual. The Justice Manual is a lengthy series of internal policies for and directions to DOJ personnel. The Justice Manual, however, states that the Manual provides only guidance and not rules enforceable by aggrieved outsiders. Justice Manual § 1-1.200 ("The Justice Manual provides internal DOJ guidance. It is not intended to, does not, and may not be relied upon to create any rights, substantive or procedural, enforceable at law by any party in any matter civil or criminal. Nor are any limitations hereby placed on otherwise lawful litigation prerogatives of DOJ.").

Justice Manual § 9-28.200 and the comment to it set out the overarching goal prosecutors considering charges against corporations should pursue.

> **A. General Principle:** Corporations should not be treated leniently because of their artificial nature nor should they be subject to harsher treatment. Vigorous enforcement of the criminal laws against corporate wrongdoers, where appropriate, results in great benefits for law enforcement and the public, particularly in the area of white collar crime. Indicting corporations for wrongdoing enables the government to be a force for positive change of corporate culture, and a force to prevent, discover, and punish serious crimes.

> **B. Comment:** In all cases involving corporate wrongdoing, prosecutors should consider the factors discussed in these guidelines.... Prosecutors have substantial latitude in determining when, whom, how, and even whether to prosecute for violations of federal criminal law. In exercising that discretion, prosecutors should consider the following statements of principles that summarize the considerations they should weigh and the practices they should follow in discharging their prosecutorial responsibilities. Prosecutors should ensure that the general purposes of the criminal law—appropriate punishment for the defendant, deterrence of further criminal conduct by the defendant, deterrence of criminal conduct by others, protection of the public from dangerous and fraudulent conduct, rehabilitation, and restitution for victims—are adequately met, taking into account the special nature of the corporate "person."

Justice Manual § 9-28.300 then sets out various factors prosecutors should consider when deciding whether and how to prosecute corporations:

A. *General Principle*: Generally, prosecutors apply the same factors in determining whether to charge a corporation as they do with respect to individuals. See JM 9-27.220, *et seq.* Thus, the prosecutor must weigh all of the factors normally considered in the sound exercise of prosecutorial judgment: the sufficiency of the evidence; the likelihood of success at trial; the probable deterrent, rehabilitative, and other consequences of conviction; and the adequacy of noncriminal approaches. *See id.* However, due to the nature of the corporate "person," some additional factors are present. In conducting an investigation, determining whether to bring charges, and negotiating plea or other agreements, prosecutors should consider the following factors in reaching a decision as to the proper treatment of a corporate target:

1. the nature and seriousness of the offense, including the risk of harm to the public, and applicable policies and priorities, if any, governing the prosecution of corporations for particular categories of crime (*see* JM 9-28.400);

2. the pervasiveness of wrongdoing within the corporation, including the complicity in, or the condoning of, the wrongdoing by corporate management (*see* JM 9-28.500);

3. the corporation's history of similar misconduct, including prior criminal, civil, and regulatory enforcement actions against it (*see* JM 9-28.600);

4. the corporation's willingness to cooperate, including as to potential wrongdoing by its agents (*see* JM 9-28.700);

5. the adequacy and effectiveness of the corporation's compliance program at the time of the offense, as well as at the time of a charging decision (*see* JM 9-28.800); 6. the corporation's timely and voluntary disclosure of wrongdoing (*see* JM 9-28.900);

7. the corporation's remedial actions, including, but not limited to, any efforts to implement an adequate and effective corporate compliance program or to improve an existing one, to replace responsible management, to discipline or terminate wrongdoers, to pay restitution (*see* JM 9-28.1000);

8. collateral consequences, including whether there is disproportionate harm to shareholders, pension holders, employees, and others not proven personally culpable, as well as impact on the public arising from the prosecution (*see* JM 9-28.1100);

9. the adequacy of remedies such as civil or regulatory enforcement actions, including remedies resulting from the corporation's cooperation with relevant government agencies (*see* JM 9-28.1200);

10. the adequacy of the prosecution of individuals responsible for the corporation's malfeasance (*see* JM 9-28.1300); and

11. the interests of any victims (*see* JM 9-28.1400).

Do these principles provide adequate guidance for prosecutors? How about to corporations facing potential indictment?

Notes and Questions

1. *Like natural persons?* Do you agree that "[c]orporations should not be treated leniently because of their artificial nature nor should they be subject to harsher treatment." Justice Manual § 9-28.200. Do you think prosecutors *actually do* treat corporations neither more leniently nor more harshly than natural persons?

2. *The Sentencing Guidelines.* Look through the factors judges are supposed to consider in Chapter 8 of the U.S. Sentencing Guidelines — Sentencing of Organizations (*see infra* Chapter 19). Do you see any overlap? Should the factors that bear on indictment and those that bear on sentencing be distinct or similar?

3. *The Yates Memo.* In 2015, then Deputy Attorney General Sally Yates issued a memo (the "Yates Memo") directing prosecutors to pay more attention to culpable individuals within corporations. "The guidance in this memo reflects six key steps to strengthen our pursuit of individual corporate wrongdoing, some of which reflect policy shifts and each of which is described in greater detail below: (1) in order to qualify for any cooperation credit, corporations must provide to the Department all relevant facts relating to the individuals responsible for the misconduct; (2) criminal and civil corporate investigations should focus on individuals from the inception of the investigation; (3) criminal and civil attorneys handling corporate investigations should be in routine communication with one another; (4) absent extraordinary circumstances or approved departmental policy, the Department will not release culpable individuals from civil or criminal liability when resolving a matter with a corporation; (5) Department attorneys should not resolve matters with a corporation without a clear plan to resolve related individual cases, and should memorialize any declinations as to individuals in such cases; and (6) civil attorneys should consistently focus on individuals as well as the company and evaluate whether to bring suit against an individual based on considerations beyond that individual's ability to pay." Memorandum from Deputy Att'y Gen. Sally Q. Yates, Sept. 9, 2015, *Individual Accountability for Corporate Wrongdoing*, 2–3. In 2019 the guidance of the Yates Memo was incorporated into Justice Manual § 9-28.000. Since its issuance, the Yates Memo has failed to bring about a significant increase in individual prosecutions. *See* FCPA PROFESSOR, *The Yates Memo — 5 Years Later* (June 19, 2020), https://fcpaprofessor.com/yates-memo-5-years-later/ ("[I]n the years prior to the Yates Memo approximately 75% of corporate FCPA enforcement actions lacked individual charges against company employees and five years since the Yates Memo 82% of corporate FCPA enforcement actions lack individual charges against company employees."). Why might that be?

4. *Self-reporting.* In recent years, the DOJ has firmed up its commitment to the importance of inducing corporations to self-report crime. Ordinarily, self-reporting is just one among many discretionary factors prosecutors consider at the charging stage. In 2017, the DOJ started a pilot program that created a presumption that the DOJ would decline foreign bribery charges if companies voluntarily self-disclosed misconduct, fully cooperated, and timely and appropriately remediated. *See* Just.

Manual §9-47.120 FCPA Corporate Enforcement Policy (replaced the Pilot Program). Why do you think the DOJ tested out this program with, among all possible types of violation, foreign bribery? Should the DOJ adopt this approach for other types of crime? The DOJ thought so. In 2019, it expanded the program to all matters handled by the Criminal Division. *See* Press Release, No. 19-452, U.S. Dep't of Just. Crim. Div., "Criminal Division Announces Publication of Guidance on Evaluating Corporate Compliance Programs" (Apr. 30, 2019), *available at* https://www .justice.gov/opa/pr/criminal-division-announces-publication-guidance-evaluating -corporate-compliance-programs. Note: The policy does not extend to misconduct that occurred in the parent company.

3. Critical Aspects of Effective Compliance Programs

Compliance programs also go hand-in-hand with internal investigations. Such programs frequently reveal the internal wrongdoing committed by employees, and internal investigations are one essential component of any effective compliance program. Compliance programs are especially important at sentencing, and the government also now regards the existence of a sound compliance program as relevant at the charging stage. Despite the rise of compliance programs, they are not an insurance policy. While such programs often give the company ammunition to address governmental investigations and provide strategies for reduced charges or defenses, an effective compliance program does not ensure that the government will refrain from instituting a criminal action.

An effective corporate compliance program can reduce corporate criminal charges or mitigate some ramifications of litigation. To be considered "effective," the program must ensure that the organization will exercise due diligence to detect unscrupulous conduct, remedy vulnerabilities, and promote an atmosphere that encourages ethical conduct. The organization has to establish basic standards and procedures to prevent and detect criminal conduct, and high-level personnel must be knowledgeable about the content and operations of the compliance program and promote the program throughout the organization. In addition, the organization is expected to take reasonable steps to communicate the proper procedures and training for the employees and ensure that the compliance programs are followed.

The hallmarks of an effective corporate compliance program vary according to the type of organization and the specific nature of the corporation. As one commentator notes, this variability among corporations should call for nuanced metrics for evaluating compliance.

> Corporations range in size from small mom-and-pop operations to familiar corporate giants such as Walmart and Amazon. Compliance and information management systems are quite different mechanisms for different sized organizations, involving wide-ranging real and proportional costs. Corporate risks and compliance needs also vary by industry. Some industries, such as the energy sector, involve notoriously high risk of criminal

misconduct; others, such as education, have fewer compliance needs. Doctrines that are invariant across industry and size will inevitably fail to produce satisfactory results in the majority of cases.

Mihailis E. Diamantis, *Functional Corporate Knowledge*, 61 Wm. & Mary L. Rev. 319, 364–65 (2019).

It may be surprising that, although the Justice Manual instructs prosecutors to evaluate a corporate suspect's compliance program before filing charges, for decades the Manual had less than one page's worth of guidance for prosecutors on the issue. The core of the guidance states:

> While the Department recognizes that no compliance program can ever prevent all criminal activity by a corporation's employees, the critical factors in evaluating any program are whether the program is adequately designed for maximum effectiveness in preventing and detecting wrongdoing by employees and whether corporate management is enforcing the program or is tacitly encouraging or pressuring employees to engage in misconduct to achieve business objectives. The Department has no formulaic requirements regarding corporate compliance programs. The fundamental questions any prosecutor should ask are: Is the corporation's compliance program well designed? Is the program being applied earnestly and in good faith? Does the corporation's compliance program work?

U.S. Dep't of Just., Just. Manual §9-28.800 Corporate Compliance Programs, B. Comment (revised July 2019).

In 2020, the DOJ issued updated Guidance for the Evaluation of Corporate Compliance Programs. *See* U.S. Dep't of Just. Crim. Division, Evaluation of Corporate Compliance Programs (Updated June 2020), *available at* https://www.justice.gov/criminal-fraud/page/file/937501/download. This new Guidance is built around three questions a prosecutor should ask:

1. "Is the corporation's compliance program well designed?"

2. "Is the program being applied earnestly and in good faith?" In other words, is the program adequately resourced and empowered to function effectively?

3. "Does the corporation's compliance program work" in practice?

Id. at 2. In answering those questions, the Guidance provides a checklist of more than 100 items for prosecutors to consider and balance against each other. The Guidance states that the DOJ "does not use any rigid formula to assess the effectiveness of corporate compliance programs." *Id.* at 1. Is having a 100-point balancing test and no rigid formula likely to make things better or worse?

Notes and Questions

1. *The Costs of Compliance.* Of course, compliance is not free. As one commentator has noted:

It is important to resist the urge to press corporations to spend whatever it takes to prevent as much misconduct as possible. No compliance program is failproof. No matter how much corporations spend on compliance, they cannot monitor their employees perfectly and some misconduct will pass under the radar. As such, there is always room for improvement and no limit to the amount corporations could invest in compliance for some marginal reduction in the risk of misconduct. It is too easy to discount the costs of compliance as private costs borne by faceless corporate fictions. Because of corporations' economic role and the porous line between corporations and the investing public, these costs can have detrimental social effects. . . . There is a socially optimal level for corporations to invest in compliance, and that level is less than everything.

Mihailis E. Diamantis, *Functional Corporate Knowledge*, 61 Wm. & Mary L. Rev. 319, 362 (2019). How should these observations figure into the DOJ's assessment of whether a corporation had effective compliance?

2. *Defense risks.* Can the presence of a corporate compliance policy work to the detriment of the company? "[C]ounsel and the employees of a corporation must consider that the questions asked, the answers received and the advice rendered may soon be in the hands of a prosecutor, competitors and civil litigants. This possibility has the effect of chilling the inquiry from the outset. . . ." David M. Zornow & Keith D. Krakaur, *Essay: On the Brink of a Brave New World: The Death of Privilege in Corporate Criminal Investigations*, 37 Am. Crim. L. Rev. 147, 156 (2000).

3. *Lessons from* Hilton Hotels. Should a corporation be held criminally liable for conduct that is contrary to its compliance policies and procedures? *See United States v. Hilton Hotels Corp.*, 467 F.2d 1000 (9th Cir. 1972). *See* Chapter 2, Corporate and Individual Liability, *supra*. When a corporation is the target of DOJ scrutiny, it is usually because its compliance program has failed to catch some employee misconduct. Does this necessarily mean that the program was ineffective? Is it harder to evaluate the effectiveness of a compliance program that has failed?

4. *Ethics.* Is it ethical for a corporation to refrain from investigating possible misconduct brought to its attention because it fears that the government might eventually ask for the results of the investigation? *See* Shirah Neiman, *Hallmark of an Effective Corporate Compliance Program and Waiver of the Privilege Under the Principles of Federal Prosecution of Business Organizations* (2004), *in* ABA-CLE Publication on White Collar Crime 2004, at D-1. In light of the fiduciary duties that executives have to corporate shareholders, is it ethical to conduct such an investigation?

Problems

15-7. Compliance programs do not provide a corporation with a barrier to litigation. Such programs do, however, mitigate potential charges against the corporation based on how effective those programs are.

Suppose that you are retained by ACME Corporation. ACME is concerned about potential investigations arising from faulty products that have caused serious injuries to customers.

What advice would you give your client relating to compliance programs to mitigate pending charges?

15-8. SpyD Corp. offers private investigation services to customers who want to find out details about someone's (the "target's") identification. They employ about 500 people, split into 50 divisions of 10 people, one division for each state. Jules is a manager in one of the divisions. He decides to use some target information (acquired by subverting SpyD's digital compliance protocols) to open credit cards in their names. He then uses these credit cards for some personal expenses and to throw morale-boosting pizza parties for his coworkers. SpyD quickly catches on, reports what happened to the government and fully cooperates in the investigation. However, to maintain public confidence in their services, SpyD insists on a public narrative that pins all the blame on Jules.

You're trying to persuade a DOJ prosecutor to resolve the investigation into SpyD. with a DPA. Can you persuade the prosecutor that SpyD has an effective compliance program? What additional information would you need?

D. Deferred and Non-Prosecution Agreements

Pretrial diversion had historically been used by the government as a way to steer individuals who committed minor offenses or who were juvenile offenders out of the criminal justice process. Such programs allowed individuals to avoid conviction if they satisfied the terms prosecutors stipulated in a pretrial diversion agreement. One goal was to assist in clearing the courts of minor cases so that judges could concentrate on more serious crimes. Additionally, upon successful completion of the probationary period, the offender was able to avert lifetime stigmatization by having the charges dropped and avoid a criminal record.

Beginning in 2003, these once-rare agreements became an important part of corporate criminal law. After the post-indictment collapse of Arthur Andersen and the disastrous collateral consequences of the Enron scandal, the DOJ signaled that pretrial diversion might be an option for corporations under investigation. As a result, a tool that was intended to clear the courts of minor cases and allow youthful or minor offenders to avoid conviction is now used to benefit large multinational corporations. In many industries, criminal conviction can lead to automatic and ruinous collateral effects, such as loss of license or debarment from conducting business with the federal government. Pretrial diversion is a means by which corporations can avoid conviction and prosecutors can still secure a fine and probation-like terms mandating reform.

Pretrial diversion agreements have become a fixture in the federal corporate law enforcement regime because they allow versatility in addressing complex and challenging corporate criminal matters. They come in two varieties: deferred prosecution agreements (DPAs) and non-prosecution agreements (NPAs). DPAs are more common, and are filed by prosecutors along with a charging document in federal court. They are therefore subject to some measure of judicial scrutiny. The charges are held in abeyance for the duration of the agreement and until the government seeks, and the court grants, dismissal of the charges following the successful conclusion of the DPA. In exchange, the corporation acknowledges that the government can prove its case and agrees to fully cooperate with the investigation. NPAs sidestep the courts altogether because prosecutors never even file charges. *See* Craig S. Morford, *Memorandum for Heads of Department Components and United States Attorneys*, 1 n.2 (Mar. 7, 2008), *available at* https://jenner.com/system/assets/assets /4954/original/Memo.pdf?1320337522. Both agreements allow the government to collect fines and impose other conditions during the probationary period, while at the same time monitoring and certifying compliance.

The DOJ *Principles of Federal Prosecution of Business Organizations* instruct prosecutors to consider when pretrial diversion, rather than filing or declining charges, may be appropriate:

> [W]here the collateral consequences of a corporate conviction for innocent third parties would be significant, it may be appropriate to consider a nonprosecution or deferred prosecution agreement with conditions designed, among other things, to promote compliance with applicable law and to prevent recidivism.... However, when considering whether to enter into a deferred prosecution or non-prosecution agreement with the defendant, prosecutors should consider the interests of any victims.... The appropriateness of a criminal charge against a corporation, or some lesser alternative, must be evaluated in a pragmatic and reasoned way that produces a fair outcome, taking into consideration, among other things, the Department's need to promote and ensure respect for the law.

U.S. Dep't of Just., Just. Manual § 9-28.1100 Collateral Consequences, B. Comment (revised July 2020).

The use of such agreements evidences a significant shift in prosecutorial discretion. Because these charges are dismissed, or never filed, the probationary period is supervised by the DOJ. Prosecutors are now in charge of both the prosecution as well as any probation under a DPA arrangement. Lacking judicial supervision, the government is the sole arbiter of determining whether the conditions have been met. As the next case discusses, this raises potential justice concerns that courts are powerless to address.

United States v. Fokker Services B.V.

818 F.3d 733 (D.C. Cir. 2016)

Srinivasan, Circuit Judge.

The Constitution allocates primacy in criminal charging decisions to the Executive Branch. The Executive's charging authority embraces decisions about whether to initiate charges, whom to prosecute, which charges to bring, and whether to dismiss charges once brought. It has long been settled that the Judiciary generally lacks authority to second-guess those Executive determinations, much less to impose its own charging preferences. The courts instead take the prosecution's charging decisions largely as a given, and assume a more active role in administering adjudication of a defendant's guilt and determining the appropriate sentence.

In certain situations, rather than choose between the opposing poles of pursuing a criminal conviction or forgoing any criminal charges altogether, the Executive may conclude that the public interest warrants the intermediate option of a deferred prosecution agreement (DPA). Under a DPA, the government formally initiates prosecution but agrees to dismiss all charges if the defendant abides by negotiated conditions over a prescribed period of time. Adherence to the conditions enables the defendant to demonstrate compliance with the law. If the defendant fails to satisfy the conditions, the government can then pursue the charges based on facts admitted in the agreement.

This case arises from the interplay between the operation of a DPA and the running of time limitations under the Speedy Trial Act.

. . .

The Speedy Trial Act establishes time limits for the completion of various stages of a criminal prosecution. *See* 18 U.S.C. §§ 3161–3174. For instance, the Act requires the commencement of trial within seventy days of the filing of an information or indictment by the government. *Id.* § 3161(c)(1). The Act also excludes various pretrial periods from the running of that seventy-day time clock. Of particular relevance, the Act excludes "[a]ny period of delay during which prosecution is deferred by the attorney for the Government pursuant to written agreement with the defendant, with the approval of the court, for the purpose of allowing the defendant to demonstrate his good conduct." *Id.* § 3161(h)(2).

That exemption exists to enable prosecutors to resolve cases through DPAs. . . . [A] DPA's viability depends on the specific exclusion of time for such agreements set forth in the Speedy Trial Act, 18 U.S.C. § 3161(h)(2). The filing of an information or indictment would ordinarily trigger the Act's seventy-day clock within which trial must commence. *See id.* § 3161(c)(1). But in the case of a DPA, if the defendant were to fulfill the agreement's conditions, the prosecution would move to dismiss all charges with prejudice at the end of the specified time period, ordinarily one to three years. Without the statutory exclusion of time for DPAs provided in § 3161(h)(2), the government would relinquish its ability to prosecute based on the conceded facts if the defendant were to violate the agreement after seventy days. That would largely eliminate the leverage that engenders the defendant's compliance with a DPA's conditions. The statutory exclusion of time for DPAs therefore is essential to the agreements' effective operation.

Fokker Services, a Dutch aerospace services company, provides technical and logistical support to owners of aircraft manufactured by its predecessor company. In 2010, Fokker voluntarily disclosed to the United States Departments of Treasury and Commerce that it had potentially violated federal sanctions and export control laws concerning Iran, Sudan, and Burma. At the time Fokker came forward, no government agency had initiated any investigation focused on the company.

Over the course of the next four years, Fokker cooperated in the wide-ranging investigation conducted by federal authorities. The company facilitated interviews of relevant witnesses, expedited the government's requests to Dutch authorities for documents under the Mutual Legal Assistance Treaty, and initiated its own internal investigation. Fokker's internal investigation revealed that, from 2005 to 2010, the company had participated in 1,147 illicit transactions through which it earned some $21 million in gross revenue. The company instituted remedial measures to improve its sanctions compliance program, adopting a set of procedures to track parts and bolstering its employee training requirements. It also fired its president and demoted or reassigned other employees who had been involved in the violations. The company's compliance efforts have been described by government officials as "a model to be followed by other corporations."

In light of Fokker's cooperation, remediation efforts, and other mitigating factors, federal agencies negotiated a global settlement with the company. The settlement included, as an integral component, an 18-month DPA. During the DPA's 18-month period, Fokker was to: continue full cooperation with the government, implement its new compliance policy, and pay fines and penalties totaling $21 million (a sum equaling the gross revenues gained by the company from the illicit transactions). Fokker also accepted responsibility for the acts described in the stipulated factual statement accompanying the DPA.

On June 5, 2014, pursuant to the agreement, the government filed with the district court a one-count information against Fokker, together with the DPA. The information charged Fokker with conspiracy to violate the International Emergency Economic Powers Act. See 18 U.S.C. § 371; 50 U.S.C. § 1705. The same day, the government and Fokker filed a joint motion for the exclusion of time under the Speedy Trial Act, in order to "allow [the company] to demonstrate its good conduct and implement certain remedial measures."

. . .

On February 5, 2015, the district court denied the joint motion for the exclusion of time. In explaining the reasons for its decision, the court criticized the government for failing to prosecute any "individuals . . . for their conduct." According to the court, approval of an agreement in which the defendant had been "prosecuted so anemically for engaging in such egregious conduct for such a sustained period of time and for the benefit of one of our country's worst enemies" would "promote disrespect for the law." The court further noted that certain employees had been permitted to remain with the company; that the DPA contained no requirement for an independent monitor; and that the amount of the fine failed to exceed the revenues Fokker gained from the illegal transactions. Based on those considerations, the court rejected the DPA as an "[in]appropriate exercise of prosecutorial discretion." ...

The Executive's primacy in criminal charging decisions is long settled. That authority stems from the Constitution's delegation of "take Care" duties, U.S. Const. art. II, § 3, and the pardon power, *id.* § 2, to the Executive Branch. Decisions to initiate charges, or to dismiss charges once brought, "lie[ ] at the core of the Executive's duty to see to the faithful execution of the laws." The Supreme Court thus has repeatedly emphasized that "[w]hether to prosecute and what charge to file or bring before a grand jury are decisions that generally rest in the prosecutor's discretion.

Correspondingly, "judicial authority is ... at its most limited" when reviewing the Executive's exercise of discretion over charging determinations. *Pierce,* 786 F.2d at 1201. The decision whether to prosecute turns on factors such as "the strength of the case, the prosecution's general deterrence value, the [g]overnment's enforcement priorities, and the case's relationship to the [g]overnment's overall enforcement plan." *Wayte v. United States,* 470 U.S. 598, 607 (1985). The Executive routinely undertakes those assessments and is well equipped to do so. By contrast, the Judiciary, as the Supreme Court has explained, generally is not "competent to undertake" that sort of inquiry. *Id.* Indeed, "[f]ew subjects are less adapted to judicial review than the exercise by the Executive of his discretion in deciding when and whether to institute criminal proceedings, or what precise charge shall be made, or whether to dismiss a proceeding once brought." *Newman v. United States,* 382 F.2d 479, 480 (D.C.Cir.1967). "Judicial supervision in this area" would also "entail[ ] systemic costs." Wayte, 470 U.S. at 608. It could "chill law enforcement," cause delay, and "impair the performance of a core executive constitutional function." *United States v. Armstrong,* 517 U.S. 456, 465. As a result, "the presumption of regularity" applies to "prosecutorial decisions and, in the absence of clear evidence to the contrary, courts presume that [prosecutors] have properly discharged their official duties." *Id.* at 464.

Those settled principles counsel against interpreting statutes and rules in a manner that would impinge on the Executive's constitutionally rooted primacy over criminal charging decisions. Of particular salience, Rule 48(a) of the Federal Rules of Criminal Procedure requires a prosecutor to obtain "leave of court" before dismissing charges against a criminal defendant. Fed. R. Crim. P. 48(a). That language could conceivably be read to allow for considerable judicial involvement in the determination to dismiss criminal charges. But decisions to dismiss pending criminal charges — no less than decisions to initiate charges and to identify which charges to bring — lie squarely within the ken of prosecutorial discretion. *See e.g.,*

Newman, 382 F.2d at 480. To that end, the Supreme Court has declined to construe Rule 48(a)'s "leave of court" requirement to confer any substantial role for courts in the determination whether to dismiss charges. Rather, the "principal object of the 'leave of court' requirement" has been understood to be a narrow one — "to protect a defendant against prosecutorial harassment . . . when the [g]overnment moves to dismiss an indictment over the defendant's objection." *Rinaldi v. United States,* 434 U.S. 22, 29 n.15 (1977). A court thus reviews the prosecution's motion under Rule 48(a) primarily to guard against the prospect that dismissal is part of a scheme of "prosecutorial harassment" of the defendant through repeated efforts to bring — and then dismiss — charges. *Id.*

So understood, the "leave of court" authority gives no power to a district court to deny a prosecutor's Rule 48(a) motion to dismiss charges based on a disagreement with the prosecution's exercise of charging authority. . . .

The same considerations govern our interpretation of the Speedy Trial Act provision at issue here. . . .

We see no reason to recognize a substantially broader authority for courts to scrutinize prosecutorial charging choices in the context of a DPA than in the context of Rule 48(a). Just as Rule 48(a)'s "leave of court" authority does not allow a court to withhold approval of a motion to dismiss charges based on a belief that more serious charges should be brought against the defendant (or against a third party), § 3161(h)(2)'s "approval of the court" authority does not permit a court to withhold approval of a motion to exclude time under a DPA based on that same belief. . . .

To be sure, the criminal charges filed as part of a DPA remain on the court's docket throughout the time of the agreement (i.e., pending assessment of whether the defendant has satisfied the agreement's conditions, upon which the prosecution seeks dismissal of the charges). But the existence of charges on the court's docket suggests no greater power on the part of the court to second-guess the underlying charging decisions than under Rule 48(a): there, too, criminal charges remain on the court's docket until dismissed. The key point is that, although charges remain pending on the court's docket under a DPA, the court plays no role in monitoring the defendant's compliance with the DPA's conditions. For instance, defendants who violate the conditions of their DPA face no court-ordered repercussions. Rather, the prosecution — and the prosecution alone — monitors a defendant's compliance with the agreement's conditions and determines whether the defendant's conduct warrants dismissal of the pending charges. Just as is the case under Rule 48(a), the prosecution, after taking stock of the circumstances, concludes that continued pursuit of a criminal conviction is unwarranted. . . .

. . .

Unlike a plea agreement — and more like a dismissal under Rule 48(a) — a DPA involves no formal judicial action imposing or adopting its terms. Whereas a district court enters a judgment of conviction and then imposes a sentence in the case of a plea agreement, the court takes no such actions in the case of a DPA. Rather, the entire object of a DPA is to enable the defendant to *avoid* criminal conviction and sentence by demonstrating good conduct and compliance with the law. And a DPA's provisions are agreed to by the parties, not the court, with no occasion for the court to adopt the agreement's terms as its own. The court never exercises its coercive power by entering a judgment of conviction or imposing a sentence. It instead merely approves the prosecution's judgment that further pursuit of criminal charges is unwarranted, as it does when it approves a prosecutor's motion to dismiss charges under Rule 48(a). And as is the case when confronted with a motion to dismiss charges under Rule 48(a), a district court lacks authority to disapprove a DPA under § 3161(h)(2) on the ground that the prosecution has been too lenient in its exercise of charging discretion. . . .

Notes and Questions

1. *Policy considerations.* Is there a fundamental concern in using programs designed for minor offenders to benefit huge, multinational corporations? Considering the factors that motivate the government to pursue white collar and corporate crime more aggressively today, is the use of DPAs consistent with the war on corporate crime?

2. *Inconsistencies.* The wide discretion that prosecutors have to design pretrial diversion agreements means that there can be a lot of variation, even between otherwise similarly situated corporate defendants. Some critics charge that this violates rule-of-law norms. *See* Jennifer Arlen, *Prosecuting Beyond the Rule of Law: Corporate Mandates Imposed through Deferred Prosecution Agreements*, 8 J. LEGAL ANALYSIS, 191, 197–205 (2016). One possible solution would be to make DOJ guidelines concerning DPAs and NPAs more detailed and less discretionary, perhaps with some sort of enforcement mechanism for corporations that believe the guidelines are being breached. Would that be an appealing approach?

3. *Charitable donations.* On occasion, the DOJ has set limits on what prosecutors can try to accomplish with pretrial diversion. Mandatory charitable donations were once an available term in DPAs and NPAs. In 2005, then-U.S. Attorney Chris Christie settled fraud charges with Bristol-Myers. One of the terms of the DPA required the corporation to endow an academic chair at Seton Hall, Christie's alma mater. *See* Paul Davies et al., *Bristol-Myers Ex-Officials Are Indicted*, WALL ST. J. (Jun. 16, 2005, 12:01 AM), https://www.wsj.com/articles/SB111885017740160374. When a congressional investigation ensued in 2008, the DOJ changed its policies to prohibit such terms in DPAs. *See* U.S. Dep't of Just. Manual § 9-16.325 ("Department attorneys may not enter into any agreement . . . that directs or provides for a payment or loan to any non-governmental person or entity that is not a party to the dispute.").

Today, pretrial diversion agreements are on the rise in white collar and corporate criminal cases, with more than 545 publicly disclosed agreements since only 2003. A running compilation is maintained by Brandon L. Garrett and Jon Ashley, through the Corporate Prosecution Registry of Duke University and University of Virginia School of Law, at http://lib.law.virginia.edu/Garrett/corporate-prosecution-registry /index. Between 2005 and 2019, prosecutors recovered an average of $4.8 billion per year through pretrial diversion agreements. *See* Gibson Dunn, 2020 Mid-Year Update on Corporate Non-Prosecution Agreements and Deferred Prosecution Agreements 2 (2020), https://www.gibsondunn.com/2020-mid-year-npa -dpa-update/. The terms of the probationary periods are as varied as a prosecutor can imagine. For example, traditional conditions require corporations to pay fines and penalties, cooperate with the government, and maintain or improve compliance programs. Prosecutors can demand that a company waive procedural rights, such as the right to a speedy trial and the statute of limitations. More innovative conditions direct corporations to restrict or modify merger decisions, oust directors or executives, create thousands of jobs, and adjust compensation packages.

Critics of such programs assert that career prosecutors have gained sweeping powers by inserting themselves into the routine management of major businesses without any judicial oversight or administrative background. Companies weigh the potentially huge penalties and other conditions of a DPA or NPA against the harsh consequence of a criminal conviction, debarment, or a corporate death sentence. The government can gain most of the benefits of conviction, while avoiding the risks associated with an investigation, indictment, and the uncertainty of an outcome at trial. Some critics find that prosecutors now impose DPAs and NPAs in cases where they previously would have declined charges altogether. Julie R. O'Sullivan, *How Prosecutors Apply the "Federal Prosecutions of Corporations" Charging Policy in the Era of Deferred Prosecutions, and What That Means for the Purposes of the Federal Criminal Sanction*, 51 Am. Crim. L. Rev. 29, 59 (2014).

It is unclear whether DPAs and NPAs have been effective in combatting corporate crime. Arguably, such programs allow the corporation to write a check and escape unscathed, furthering the public's impression of a dual system of justice. In addition, some believe that the rise in use of these programs has sent the wrong signal to corporations. By offering the corporation an option to avert conviction by cutting a deal with the government, corporations may be more willing to take risks with the knowledge that, if caught, they can seek a DPA or NPA. Moreover, a corporation can avoid criminal liability since it is deemed "too big to jail," and the individuals within the corporation escape prosecution:

> By seeking to prosecute the corporation rather than the individuals who were responsible for the criminal conduct, the government is sending the message that the individuals are too insulated to be prosecuted, and the companies are too big to jail. The corporation, under the auspices of a DPA, avoids prosecution, and the executives or other high ranking figures, avoid prosecution because the government has shifted its focus on corporate wrongdoing rather than individual wrongdoing within the corporation. [The prosecutor] and the company then agree that the company will enter into a deferred prosecution agreement that couples some immediate

fines with the imposition of expensive but internal prophylactic measures. For all practical purposes the case is now over. [The prosecutor is] happy because [they] believe that [they] helped prevent future crimes; the company is happy because it has avoided a devastating indictment; and perhaps the happiest of all are the executives, or former executives, who actually committed the underlying misconduct, for they are left untouched.

Why Have No High Level Executives Been Prosecuted in Connection with the Financial Crisis?, http://www.corporatecrimereporter.com/wp-content/uploads/2013/11 /rakoff.pdf (comments by U.S. District Court Judge Jed S. Rakoff, November 12, 2013); *see* Brandon Garrett, Too Big To Jail: How Prosecutors Compromise with Corporations (2016). In 2010, the Government Accountability Office studied the DOJ's use of pretrial diversion and concluded: "DOJ lacks performance measures to assess how DPAs and NPAs contribute to its efforts to combat corporate crime." U.S. Gov't Accountability Off., GAO-10-110, Corporate Crime: DOJ Has Taken Steps to Better Track Its Use of Deferred and Non-Prosecution Agreements, but Should Evaluate Effectiveness 2 (2009).

Notes and Questions

1. *Issues to consider.* Despite their history and critics, DPAs are gaining in popularity and usage. How does the DPA differ from negotiating a traditional civil resolution? Is a DPA noticeably distinct from ordinary probation and restitution?

2. *Corporate monitorships.* Most pretrial diversion agreements state that the corporation should improve its compliance. *See* Arlen *supra* at 199–203 (2016). Corporate monitorships are one tool the DOJ has for ensuring that happens. In some pretrial diversion agreements, the corporation will agree to hire (in consultation with the DOJ) an external specialist who, under the terms of the agreement, has various powers to implement reforms over a set period of years. The monitor then files reports with the DOJ, assessing the corporation's level of cooperation and progress. Some commentators believe that such monitorships are one of the best tools the DOJ has for effectuating reform. *See* Mihailis E. Diamantis, *An Academic Perspective, in* The Guide to Monitorships 79 (Anthony Barkow et al. eds., 2020). Does it surprise you that fewer than half of pretrial diversion agreements call for an external monitor? *See* Cindy R. Alexander & Mark A. Cohen, *The Evolution of Corporate Criminal Settlements: An Empirical Perspective on Non-Prosecution, Deferred Prosecution, and Plea Agreements,* 52 Am. Crim. L. Rev. 537, 588 (2015). When no monitor is appointed, the corporation is entrusted to reform itself and self-report on progress to the DOJ.

Problems

15-9. You are working for the Deputy Attorney General at the Department of Justice. Your assignment is to draft a memorandum that will be issued to all United States Attorneys concerning the use of deferred and non-prosecution agreements. Before you begin the draft of this memorandum for review, list the top five factors that weigh in favor of using these arrangements. Consider the benefits to the justice system, society, victims, and the accused.

15-10. You are connected with a national group of defense lawyers who practice in the area of corporate and white collar criminal defense. The group has asked you to advise them on the detriments of the deferred and non-prosecution agreements that the government is advocating. Prepare a short memorandum outlining the top five reasons why these arrangements are not in the best interests of the defense bar and their clients.

Chapter 16

The Grand Jury

"The war on white collar crime is frequently waged, and often won or lost, at the grand jury stage of the criminal process."[a]

A. Introductory Notes

Under the Fifth Amendment to the United States Constitution, "[n]o person shall be held to answer for a capital, or otherwise infamous crime, unless on a presentment or indictment of a Grand Jury." Rule 7(a) of the Federal Rules of Criminal Procedure further provides that, unless the defendant waives the right to a grand jury indictment, charges for any crime punishable by more than a year must be issued by a grand jury. When the grand jury finds probable cause that a crime has occurred, it issues the formal charge in the form of an indictment.

The federal right to a grand jury does not apply to the states. As discussed more fully below, however, many states do provide a right to a grand jury indictment in certain circumstances, and in other states prosecutors have the option of using grand juries to investigate criminal activities.

Grand juries are central to most white collar criminal investigations and often give rise to sophisticated strategic duels between prosecutors and defense attorneys. The grand jury's subpoena power allows the government to obtain crucial documents and compel testimony from potentially recalcitrant witnesses. This power is especially important when the government is investigating the conduct of corporations and other entities. Prosecutors typically employ the grand jury process to gather documents and obtain the testimony of current or former employees.

It is therefore vital for students and practitioners in the white collar field, and in corporate law in general, to have a thorough understanding of the grand jury system. Issues may arise, for example, with respect to possible criminal charges, related civil and/or investigative matters, and the representation of witnesses before grand juries.[b]

---

a. John R. Wing & Harris J. Yale, *Grand Jury Practice, in* WHITE COLLAR CRIME: BUSINESS AND REGULATORY OFFENSES § 8.02 (Otto Obermaier et al., eds., 2021).

b. Grand jury issues are also discussed *infra*, Chapter 17 (Self-Incrimination — Witness Testimony and Document Production) and Chapter 18 (Civil Actions, Civil Penalties, and Parallel Proceedings).

The Supreme Court described the grand jury's role as follows:

> The grand jury has always occupied a high place as an instrument of justice in our system of criminal law — so much so that it is enshrined in the Constitution. It serves the dual function of determining if there is probable cause to believe that a crime has been committed and of protecting citizens against unfounded criminal prosecutions. It has always been extended extraordinary powers of investigation and great responsibility for directing its own efforts. Traditionally, the grand jury has been accorded wide latitude to inquire into violations of criminal law. No judge presides to monitor its proceedings. It deliberates in secret and may determine alone the course of its inquiry.
>
> The grand jury may compel the production of evidence or the testimony of witnesses as it considers appropriate, and its operation generally is unrestrained by the technical procedural and evidentiary rules governing the conduct of criminal trials. It is a grand inquest, a body with powers of investigation and inquisition, the scope of whose inquiries is not to be limited narrowly by questions of propriety of forecasts of the probable result of the investigation or by doubts whether any particular individual will be found properly subject to an accusation of crime.
>
> These broad powers are necessary to permit the grand jury to carry out both parts of its dual function. Without thorough and effective investigation the grand jury would be unable either to ferret out crimes deserving of prosecution, or to screen out charges not warranting prosecution.

United States v. Sells Engineering, 463 U.S. at 418, 423–24 (1983).

In terms of investigative functions, the grand jury has broad subpoena powers. The Assistant United States Attorney or Attorneys assigned to a particular matter will lead the grand jury's investigation. Various government agencies, including the Federal Bureau of Investigation, do the legwork in gathering and presenting evidence to the grand jury. Because the grand jury has such broad powers and generally operates in secret, defense counsel face many challenges when representing a grand jury witness, subject, or target.[c]

Rule 6 of the Federal Rules of Criminal Procedure governs the operation of the federal grand jury. A grand jury consists of between 16 and 23 people drawn from

---

c. A grand jury "witness" is a person with information generally related to the matter under investigation. The "subject" of a grand jury investigation is one about whom the grand jury seeks more specific information and who may at some point become a focal point of the investigation. A grand jury "target" is "a person as to whom the prosecutor or the grand jury has substantial evidence linking him or her to the commission of a crime and who, in the judgment of the prosecutor, is a putative defendant." U.S. Dep't of Justice, U.S. Attorneys' Manual § 9-11.151. *See* Chapter 17, Self-Incrimination — Witness Testimony and Document Production, at § 17, A, *infra*.

across the judicial district and must represent a fair cross-section of the community. At least 12 grand jurors must vote to bring an indictment.[d]

The grand jury operates in secret. Generally, only the prosecutor, the witness, the grand jurors, and personnel such as court reporters and translators are present. Neither the witness nor the target may have counsel present. Prior to trial, only grand jury witnesses may disclose matters occurring before the grand jury, and public discussion of the criminal investigation must await the actual filing of an indictment. Even then, grand jury deliberations—which are not transcribed—remain confidential. Confidentiality protects the innocent by shielding the release of information that might fail to rise to the level of probable cause. Nonetheless, leaks do occur in grand jury investigations and may raise significant issues, including the defendant's right to a fair trial.

The prosecutors in charge of grand juries generally guide the proceedings. Because of this, it is commonly perceived that grand juries will ultimately follow the prosecutors' wishes in determining whether to indict and what charges to bring. This reality raises important questions. For example, given that a defendant in a federal case may waive the right to a grand jury indictment, why do most defendants decline to do so even though the grand jury will likely bring charges if the prosecutor believes they are warranted? In other words, what advantages does the grand jury process provide to a potential defendant? And in a state where prosecutors have the option of using a grand jury, when and why would they likely choose to do so?

This chapter discusses some of the most important issues relating to grand juries. These issues include the scope of the grand jury's investigative powers, the role of the grand jury in assessing evidence, grand jury secrecy, and practical considerations in grand jury practice.

B. Scope of the Grand Jury's Investigation

1. Relevancy, Admissibility, and Specificity

Many of the issues regarding the scope of the grand jury's investigation are addressed in the first case, a leading decision on the investigative powers of the federal grand jury.

---

d. Grand jurors, once empaneled, typically sit for 18 months or until discharged by the court, and hear evidence concerning a variety of criminal cases within the jurisdictional district. In many districts, a grand juror's obligations will be scheduled to recur every six weeks or so, when the jurors are called in for two to three days at a time to sit and receive evidence. In other, busier judicial districts, the grand jury members may appear weekly.

United States v. R. Enterprises

498 U.S. 292 (1991)

JUSTICE O'CONNOR delivered the opinion of the Court.

This case requires the Court to decide what standards apply when a party seeks to avoid compliance with a subpoena *duces tecum* issued in connection with a grand jury investigation.

Since 1986, a federal grand jury sitting in the Eastern District of Virginia has been investigating allegations of interstate transportation of obscene materials. In early 1988, the grand jury issued a series of subpoenas to three companies [Model, R. Enterprises and MFR, each distributing sexually oriented and adult materials]. . . . All three companies are wholly owned by Martin Rothstein. The grand jury subpoenas sought a variety of corporate books and records and, in Model's case, copies of 193 videotapes that Model had shipped to retailers in the Eastern District of Virginia. All three companies moved to quash the subpoenas, arguing that the subpoenas called for production of materials irrelevant to the grand jury's investigation and that the enforcement of the subpoenas would likely infringe their First Amendment rights.

The District Court, after extensive hearings, denied the motions to quash. . . . The court concluded that the subpoenas in this case were "fairly standard business subpoenas" and "ought to be complied with." Notwithstanding these findings, the companies refused to comply with the subpoenas. The District Court found each in contempt and fined them $500 per day, but stayed imposition of the fine pending appeal.

The Court of Appeals for the Fourth Circuit upheld the business records subpoenas issued to Model, but remanded the motion to quash the subpoena for Model's videotapes. Of particular relevance here, the Court of Appeals quashed the business records subpoenas issued to R. Enterprises and MFR. In doing so, it applied the standards set out by this Court in *United States v. Nixon*, 418 U.S. 683, 699–700 (1974). The court recognized that *Nixon* dealt with a trial subpoena, not a grand jury subpoena, but determined that the rule was "equally applicable" in the grand jury context. Accordingly, it required the Government to clear the three hurdles that *Nixon* established in the trial context — relevancy, admissibility, and specificity — in order to enforce the grand jury subpoenas. The court concluded that the challenged subpoenas did not satisfy the *Nixon* standards, finding no evidence in the record that either company had ever shipped materials into, or otherwise conducted business in, the Eastern District of Virginia. The Court of Appeals specifically criticized the District Court for drawing an inference that, because Rothstein owned all three businesses and one of them had undoubtedly shipped sexually explicit materials into the Eastern District of Virginia, there might be some link between the Eastern District of Virginia and R. Enterprises or MFR. It then noted that "any evidence concerning Mr. Rothstein's alleged business activities outside of Virginia, or his ownership of companies which distribute allegedly obscene materials outside of

Virginia, would most likely be inadmissible on relevancy grounds at any trial that might occur," and that the subpoenas therefore failed "to meet the requirements [*sic*] that any documents subpoenaed under [Federal] Rule [of Criminal Procedure] 17(c) must be admissible as evidence at trial." *Nixon, supra*, at 700. The Court of Appeals did not consider whether enforcement of the subpoenas *duces tecum* issued to respondents implicated the First Amendment.

We granted certiorari to determine whether the Court of Appeals applied the proper standard in evaluating the grand jury subpoenas issued to respondents. We now reverse.

The grand jury occupies a unique role in our criminal justice system. It is an investigatory body charged with the responsibility of determining whether or not a crime has been committed. Unlike this Court, whose jurisdiction is predicated on a specific case or controversy, the grand jury "can investigate merely on suspicion that the law is being violated, or even just because it wants assurance that it is not." *United States v. Morton Salt Co.*, 338 U.S. 632 (1950). The function of the grand jury is to inquire into all information that might possibly bear on its investigation until it has identified an offense or has satisfied itself that none has occurred. As a necessary consequence of its investigatory function, the grand jury paints with a broad brush. "A grand jury investigation 'is not fully carried out until every available clue has been run down and all witnesses examined in every proper way to find if a crime has been committed.'" *Branzburg v. Hayes*, 408 U.S. 665, 701 (1972).

A grand jury subpoena is thus much different from a subpoena issued in the context of a prospective criminal trial, where a specific offense has been identified and a particular defendant charged. "[T]he identity of the offender, and the precise nature of the offense, if there be one, normally are developed at the conclusion of the grand jury's labors, not at the beginning." *Blair v. United States*, 250 U.S. 273 (1919). In short, the Government cannot be required to justify the issuance of a grand jury subpoena by presenting evidence sufficient to establish probable cause because the very purpose of requesting the information is to ascertain whether probable cause exists.

This Court has emphasized on numerous occasions that many of the rules and restrictions that apply at a trial do not apply in grand jury proceedings. This is especially true of evidentiary restrictions. The same rules that, in an adversary hearing on the merits, may increase the likelihood of accurate determinations of guilt or innocence do not necessarily advance the mission of a grand jury, whose task is to conduct an *ex parte* investigation to determine whether or not there is probable cause to prosecute a particular defendant. In *Costello v. United States*, 350 U.S. 359 (1956), this Court declined to apply the rule against hearsay to grand jury proceedings. Strict observance of trial rules in the context of a grand jury's preliminary investigation "would result in interminable delay but add nothing to the assurance of a fair trial." *Id.* at 384. In *United States v. Calandra*, 414 U.S. 338 (1974), we held that the Fourth Amendment exclusionary rule does not apply to grand jury proceedings. Permitting witnesses to invoke the exclusionary rule would "delay and disrupt grand jury proceedings" by requiring adversary hearings on peripheral matters, *id.* at 349, and would effectively transform such proceedings into preliminary trials on the merits, 414 U.S. 338 at 349–50. The teaching of the Court's decisions is clear: A grand jury "may compel the production of evidence or the testimony of witnesses as it considers appropriate, and its operation generally is unrestrained by the technical procedural and evidentiary rules governing the conduct of criminal trials." *Id.* at 343.

This guiding principle renders suspect the Court of Appeals' holding that the standards announced in *Nixon* as to subpoenas issued in anticipation of trial apply equally in the grand jury context. The multifactor test announced in *Nixon* would invite procedural delays and detours while courts evaluate the relevancy and admissibility of documents sought by a particular subpoena. We have expressly stated that grand jury proceedings should be free of such delays. "Any holding that would saddle a grand jury with minitrials and preliminary showings would assuredly impede its investigation and frustrate the public's interest in the fair and expeditious administration of the criminal laws." *United States v. Dionisio*, 410 U.S. 1, 17 (1973). Additionally, application of the *Nixon* test in this context ignores that grand jury proceedings are subject to strict secrecy requirements. Requiring the Government to explain in too much detail the particular reasons underlying a subpoena threatens to compromise "the indispensable secrecy of grand jury proceedings." *United States v. Johnson*, 319 U.S. 503 (1943). Broad disclosure also affords the targets of investigation far more information about the grand jury's internal workings than the Federal Rules of Criminal Procedure appear to contemplate.

The investigatory powers of the grand jury are nevertheless not unlimited. *See Branzburg, supra*, 408 U.S. at 688. Grand juries are not licensed to engage in arbitrary fishing expeditions, nor may they select targets of investigation out of malice or an intent to harass. In this case, the focus of our inquiry is the limit imposed on a grand jury by Federal Rule of Criminal Procedure 17(c), which governs the issuance of subpoenas *duces tecum* in federal criminal proceedings. The Rule provides that "[t]he court on motion made promptly may quash or modify the subpoena if compliance would be unreasonable or oppressive."

This standard is not self-explanatory. As we have observed, "what is reasonable depends on the context." *New Jersey v. T.L.O.*, 469 U.S. 325, 337 (1985). In *Nixon*, this Court defined what is reasonable in the context of a jury trial. We determined that, in order to require production of information prior to trial, a party must make a reasonably specific request for information that would be both relevant and admissible at trial. But, for the reasons we have explained above, the *Nixon* standard does not apply in the context of grand jury proceedings. In the grand jury context, the decision as to what offense will be charged is routinely not made until after the grand jury has concluded its investigation. One simply cannot know in advance whether information sought during the investigation will be relevant and admissible in a prosecution for a particular offense.

To the extent that Rule 17(c) imposes some reasonableness limitation on grand jury subpoenas, however, our task is to define it. In doing so, we recognize that a party to whom a grand jury subpoena is issued faces a difficult situation. As a rule, grand juries do not announce publicly the subjects of their investigations. A party who desires to challenge a grand jury subpoena thus may have no conception of the Government's purpose in seeking production of the requested information. Indeed, the party will often not know whether he or she is a primary target of the investigation or merely a peripheral witness. Absent even minimal information, the subpoena recipient is likely to find it exceedingly difficult to persuade a court that "compliance would be unreasonable." As one pair of commentators has summarized it, the challenging party's "unenviable task is to seek to persuade the court that the subpoena that has been served on [him or her] could not possibly serve any investigative purpose that the grand jury could legitimately be pursuing." 1 S. Beale & W. Bryson, *Grand Jury Law and Practice* § 6:28 (1986).

Our task is to fashion an appropriate standard of reasonableness, one that gives due weight to the difficult position of subpoena recipients but does not impair the strong governmental interests in affording grand juries wide latitude, avoiding minitrials on peripheral matters, and preserving a necessary level of secrecy. We begin by reiterating that the law presumes, absent a strong showing to the contrary, that a grand jury acts within the legitimate scope of its authority. Consequently, a grand jury subpoena issued through normal channels is presumed to be reasonable, and the burden of showing unreasonableness must be on the recipient who seeks to avoid compliance. Indeed, this result is indicated by the language of Rule 17(c), which permits a subpoena to be quashed only "on motion" and "if *compliance* would be unreasonable" (emphasis added). To the extent that the Court of Appeals placed an initial burden on the Government, it committed error. Drawing on the principles articulated above, we conclude that where, as here, a subpoena is challenged on relevancy grounds, the motion to quash must be denied unless the district court determines that there is no reasonable possibility that the category of materials the Government seeks will produce information relevant to the general subject of the grand jury's investigation. Respondents did not challenge the subpoenas as being too indefinite nor did they claim that compliance would be overly burdensome. The Court of Appeals accordingly did not consider these aspects of the subpoenas, nor do we.

It seems unlikely, of course, that a challenging party who does not know the general subject matter of the grand jury's investigation, no matter how valid that party's claim, will be able to make the necessary showing that compliance would be unreasonable. After all, a subpoena recipient "cannot put his whole life before the court in order to show that there is no crime to be investigated." *Marston's Inc. v. Strand*, 114 Ariz. 260, 270 (1977). Consequently, a court may be justified in a case where unreasonableness is alleged in requiring the Government to reveal the general subject of the grand jury's investigation before requiring the challenging party to carry its burden of persuasion. We need not resolve this question in the present case, however, as there is no doubt that respondents knew the subject of the grand jury investigation pursuant to which the business records subpoenas were issued. In cases where the recipient of the subpoena does not know the nature of the investigation, we are confident that district courts will be able to craft appropriate procedures that balance the interests of the subpoena recipient against the strong governmental interests in maintaining secrecy, preserving investigatory flexibility, and avoiding procedural delays. For example, to ensure that subpoenas are not routinely challenged as a form of discovery, a district court may require that the Government reveal the subject of the investigation to the trial court *in camera*, so that the court may determine whether the motion to quash has a reasonable prospect for success before it discloses the subject matter to the challenging party.

Applying these principles in this case demonstrates that the District Court correctly denied respondents' motions to quash. It is undisputed that all three companies   Model, R. Enterprises, and MFR—are owned by the same person, that all do business in the same area, and that one of the three, Model, has shipped sexually explicit materials into the Eastern District of Virginia. The District Court could have concluded from these facts that there was a reasonable possibility that the business records of R. Enterprises and MFR would produce information relevant to the grand jury's investigation into the interstate transportation of obscene materials. Respondents' blanket denial of any connection to Virginia did not suffice to render the District Court's conclusion invalid. A grand jury need not accept on faith the self-serving assertions of those who may have committed criminal acts. Rather, it is entitled to determine for itself whether a crime has been committed.

Both in the District Court and in the Court of Appeals, respondents contended that these subpoenas sought records relating to First Amendment activities, and that this required the Government to demonstrate that the records were particularly relevant to its investigation. The Court of Appeals determined that the subpoenas did not satisfy Rule 17(c) and thus did not pass on the First Amendment issue. We express no view on this issue and leave it to be resolved by the Court of Appeals.

The judgment is reversed insofar as the Court of Appeals quashed the subpoenas issued to R. Enterprises and MFR, and the case is remanded for further proceedings consistent with this opinion.

JUSTICE STEVENS, with whom JUSTICE MARSHALL and JUSTICE BRENNAN join, concurring in part and concurring in the judgment. [Omitted.]

Notes and Questions

1. *Responding to a grand jury subpoena.* How should defense counsel advise a client who is served with a grand jury subpoena? Did the Supreme Court provide clear standards for determining the validity of a subpoena *duces tecum*? What evidence must be presented in order to challenge such a subpoena successfully? When and how must such a motion be presented to the court? *See United States v. Under Seal (In re Grand Jury Doe No. G.J. 2005-2)*, 478 F.3d 581 (4th Cir. 2007) (upholding district

court's granting of motion to quash subpoena and discussing parties' burdens and unreasonableness and oppressiveness). Given the Court's concern about the potential for an "arbitrary fishing expedition," how should defense counsel ensure that the government is *not* engaged in such prohibited information-gathering activities? Such circumstances may raise complex issues concerning challenges on the grounds that the subpoena is unduly burdensome or overly broad. In this regard, consider the case discussed in Note 2.c below.

2. *Subpoenas to third parties for production of documents.*

a. *A different standard for third party subpoenas?* Grand juries often seek materials from a third party, such as a bank or accounting firm, in possession of materials relating to the subject or target of the investigation. If those parties wish to object to the subpoena, they may seek to quash or modify the subpoena, as discussed in the note below. Is there a valid argument that some information held by third parties should not be subject to grand jury subpoena powers? Or that such subpoenas should require a higher than usual standard? *See* Christopher Slobogin, *Subpoenas and Privacy*, 54 DePaul L. Rev. 805 (2005). Professor Slobogin argues that a relevance standard "ought to be inadequate when personal information is sought from the subject (in which case a warrant should be required or immunity granted) or from a third-party record holder such as a bank, hospital, or Internet Service Provider." *Id.* at 836. Do you agree or disagree with this conclusion?

b. *May a grand jury subpoena third-party documents relating to a sitting President?* In 2019, the Manhattan District Attorney's Office served a grand jury subpoena *duces tecum* on Mazars USA, LLP, the personal accounting firm of President Donald J. Trump. The subpoena sought various financial records relating to Trump and his businesses. The press reported that prosecutors were examining potential crimes including tax fraud, insurance fraud, and falsification of business records. *See* Charlie Savage, *Trump Again Asks Supreme Court to Block Subpoena for His Tax Records*, N.Y. Times, Oct. 30, 2020, https://www.nytimes.com/2020/10/13/us/politics /trump-supreme-court-tax-records.html.

The President sued the district attorney and Mazars in federal district court, seeking to enjoin enforcement of the subpoena. He argued that a sitting President enjoys absolute immunity from state criminal process under Article II and the Supremacy Clause. The lower courts denied the motion and the President appealed to the Supreme Court. In its ruling, the Court found that the U.S. Constitution does not absolutely preclude, or require a heightened standard for, the issuance of a state grand jury subpoena to a sitting President. *See Trump v. Vance*, 140 S. Ct. 2412, 2421–31 (2020). The Court remanded to allow the President to challenge the subpoena on other grounds, including bad faith, overbreadth, and undue burden. *Id.* at 2428–31.

c. *Grounds for challenging subpoenas.*

On remand from the Supreme Court's decision in *Trump v. Vance*, the lower courts upheld the subpoena, rejecting the arguments that it was overly broad and intended to harm the President politically. *See Trump v. Vance*, 977 F.3d 198 (2d Cir.

2020). Trump again appealed to the Supreme Court. The Court subsequently denied Trump's motion for a stay. 209 L. Ed. 2d 115 (2021).

What are the competing policy concerns in this case? Although the decisions related to a state grand jury, consider whether the Supreme Court's initial decision was correct as a matter of the law relating to federal grand juries.

3. *Confidentiality and grand jury subpoenas.* How does the decision in *United States v. R. Enterprises*, 498 U.S. 292 (1991), apply to a subpoena for confidential information? In *In re United States v. Doe*, 434 F. Supp. 2d 377 (E.D. Va. 2006), the United States subpoenaed statements made by several police officers to the city's internal affairs office. The city moved to quash the subpoena on the grounds that the city had guaranteed that the statements would be confidential. The court quashed the subpoena, holding that the grand jury could avoid violating the confidentiality guarantee by subpoenaing witnesses directly. *Id.* at 382–383.

4. *Privileges, evidentiary rules, and grand jury subpoenas.* Generally, a grand jury may not obtain documents or testimony protected by the attorney-client privilege or the attorney work product doctrine. Assuming that the government can show that the evidence relates to an ongoing or future crime or fraud, however, then the grand jury may obtain the information. As one court explained,

> 'To circumvent [the attorney-client] privilege[] under the crime-fraud exception, the party seeking to overcome the privilege . . . must make a *prima facie* showing that (1) the client was committing or intending to commit a fraud or crime, and (2) the attorney-client communications were in furtherance of that alleged crime or fraud.' Because it is often difficult or impossible to prove that the exception applies without delving into the communications themselves, the Supreme Court has held that courts may use *in camera* review to establish the applicability of the exception.

In re Grand Jury Subpoena, 745 F.3d 681, 687 (3d Cir. 2014) (citations omitted).

5. *State grand jury practice.* State investigations into white collar criminal activities may also raise significant grand jury issues. Roughly half the states provide a right to a grand jury for felonious or other particularly serious offenses, and the other half provide state prosecutors with the option of using a grand jury. *See* R. Michael Cassidy, *Silencing Grand Jury Witnesses*, 91 IND. L.J. 823, 825n.9 (2016). In the latter circumstance, a prosecutor might choose to employ a grand jury, for example, in a controversial or otherwise highly publicized case. State grand juries have been used to investigate a number of high-profile cases. These include alleged police misconduct cases, particularly those involving police shootings of Black victims. Although these highly publicized grand jury proceedings do not generally involve white collar offenses, many of the complex issues they raise concerning grand jury practice also apply to grand jury investigations of white collar crimes, as discussed in the next note. For a detailed analysis of these issues, see Roger A. Fairfax, Jr., *The Grand Jury's Role in the Prosecution of Unjustified Police Killings — Challenges and Solutions*, 52 HARV. C.R.-C.L. L. REV. 397 (2017).

6. *The role of grand juries.* The materials in this chapter raise the question of how much control prosecutors can and should exercise over grand juries. As one commentator explained,

> The grand jury is an ancient, but often misunderstood, vehicle for community influence in the criminal justice system. It once enjoyed a reputation as a 'bulwark' of liberty, designed to shield individuals from meritless prosecutions by requiring the acquiescence of laypeople in the initiation of criminal charges. This reputation was cemented during the seventeenth and eighteenth centuries when grand juries in England and colonial America were seen as important safeguards against governmental overreaching. Indeed, the grand jury's prestige during these eras led to the right to grand jury indictment being enshrined in the Bill of Rights.

> In modern times, however, the grand jury has become known as the captive of the prosecutor. Instead of a protection for those accused of criminal offenses, today's grand jury is seen by many primarily as a potent investigative tool for the government. This perception is driven in large part by the fact that grand juries almost never vote to decline an indictment. Nearly every time a prosecutor asks a grand jury to return an indictment in a case, the grand jury complies.

Id. at 398–99 (citations omitted).

7. *Why have grand juries?* In light of the above commentary, what role do grand juries serve in the criminal justice system today? What role should they serve? *See* Roger A. Fairfax, Jr., *Grand Jury Discretion and Constitutional Design*, 93 CORNELL L. REV. 703 (2008) (arguing that a grand jury's discretion whether to bring criminal charges serves as an important check on government powers); Kevin K. Washburn, *Restoring the Grand Jury*, 76 FORDHAM L. REV. 2333 (2008) (arguing that the current grand jury system undermines respect for the grand jury and that reforms are needed so that the grand jury can serve an important role in promoting the criminal justice system's popular legitimacy).

More broadly, given that prosecutors generally control grand juries, why even use grand juries? Apart from the symbolic significance discussed in Note 6 above, grand juries present some real advantages to a potential defendant. Courts do exercise some, albeit limited, control over the process. In addition, the grand jury produces a written record that will be available to the defense at trial. Under *Brady v. Maryland*, 373 U.S. 83 (1963), the government must provide the defense with potentially exculpatory evidence, including grand jury materials.

The failure to produce exculpatory grand jury materials can have severe consequences for the government. For example, in *United States v. Aguilar*, 831 F. Supp. 2d 1180 (C.D. Ca. 2011), the court ordered that the government disclose the grand jury testimony of an FBI agent. The prosecutors did not provide the information, and the defendants were convicted. After the defendants filed a post-verdict motion to dismiss, the government provided the evidence. Although the government argued that the omission was unintentional and not prejudicial, the court vacated the convictions and dismissed the indictment with prejudice because of the government's misconduct. The court found that a "key FBI agent testified untruthfully before the grand jury" and that the government "recklessly failed to comply with [the court's] discovery obligations."

8. *Waiver.* Although the Fifth Amendment requires a grand jury indictment in felony cases, courts routinely allow defendants to waive this right under Rule 7(b) of the Federal Rules of Criminal Procedure ("An offense punishable by imprisonment for more than one year may be prosecuted by information if the defendant — in open court and after being advised of the nature of the charge and of the defendant's rights — waives prosecution by indictment."). In such cases, the charges can be filed with a charging instrument called an "information" signed by the prosecutor without presentment to a grand jury. Relatively few defendants waive their right to a grand jury indictment.

If you are defense counsel representing someone under investigation, what are the pros and cons of waiving the presentment of an indictment?

2. Exculpatory Evidence

One of the major criticisms of the grand jury system is its one-sidedness. The only individuals who are permitted to be present during the course of a grand jury investigation are the federal grand jurors, the court reporter, the witness, and the prosecutor who directs questioning. A witness may leave the grand jury room to consult with counsel as questions arise. Everyone except the grand jurors themselves must exit the room when the grand jury begins its deliberations to consider the issuance of an indictment. As you read the next case, consider what difference the presence of defense counsel would have made to the outcome.

United States v. Williams
504 U.S. 36 (1992)

JUSTICE SCALIA delivered the opinion of the Court.

The question presented in this case is whether a district court may dismiss an otherwise valid indictment because the Government failed to disclose to the grand jury "substantial exculpatory evidence" in its possession.

On May 4, 1988, respondent John H. Williams, Jr., a Tulsa, Oklahoma, investor, was indicted by a federal grand jury on seven counts of "knowingly mak[ing] [a] false statement or report . . . for the purpose of influencing . . . the action [of a federally insured financial institution]," in violation of 18 U.S.C. § 1014. According to the indictment, between September 1984 and November 1985 Williams supplied four Oklahoma banks with "materially false" statements that variously overstated the value of his current assets and interest income in order to influence the banks' actions on his loan requests.

Williams' misrepresentation was allegedly effected through two financial statements provided to the banks, a "Market Value Balance Sheet" and a "Statement of Projected Income and Expense." The former included as "current assets" approximately $6 million in notes receivable from three venture capital companies. Though it contained a disclaimer that these assets were carried at cost rather than at market value, the Government asserted that listing them as "current assets" — i.e., assets quickly reducible to cash — was misleading, since Williams knew that none of the venture capital companies could afford to satisfy the notes in the short term. The second document — the Statement of Projected Income and Expense — allegedly misrepresented Williams' interest income, since it failed to reflect that the interest payments received on the notes of the venture capital companies were funded entirely by Williams' own loans to those companies. The Statement thus falsely implied, according to the Government, that Williams was deriving interest income from "an independent outside source." Brief for United States 3.

Shortly after arraignment, the District Court granted Williams' motion for disclosure of all exculpatory portions of the grand jury transcripts. Upon reviewing this material, Williams demanded that the District Court dismiss the indictment, alleging that the Government had failed to fulfill its obligation under the Tenth Circuit's prior decision in *United States v. Page*, 808 F.2d 723, 728 (1987), to present "substantial exculpatory evidence" to the grand jury (emphasis omitted). His contention was that evidence which the Government had chosen not to present to the grand jury — in particular, Williams' general ledgers and tax returns, and Williams' testimony in his contemporaneous Chapter 11 bankruptcy proceeding — disclosed that, for tax purposes and otherwise, he had regularly accounted for the "notes receivable" (and the interest on them) in a manner consistent with the Balance Sheet and the Income Statement. This, he contended, belied an intent to mislead the banks, and thus directly negated an essential element of the charged offense.

The District Court initially denied Williams' motion, but upon reconsideration ordered the indictment dismissed without prejudice. It found, after a hearing, that the withheld evidence was "relevant to an essential element of the crime charged, created 'a reasonable doubt about [respondent's] guilt,'" App. to Pet. for Cert. 239–249, and thus "render[ed] the grand jury's decision to indict gravely suspect." App. Pet. for Cert. 269. Upon the Government's appeal, the Court of Appeals affirmed the District Court's order, following its earlier decision in *Page, supra.* It first sustained as not "clearly erroneous" the District Court's determination that the Government had withheld "substantial exculpatory evidence" from the grand jury. *See* 899 F.2d 898, 900–03 (10th Cir. 1990). It then found that the Government's behavior "'substantially influence[d]'" the grand jury's decision to indict, or at the very least raised a "'grave doubt that the decision to indict was free from such substantial influence.'" *Id.* at 903 (quoting *Bank of Nova Scotia v. United States*, 487 U.S. 250, 263 (1988)); *see* 899 F.2d at 903–04. Under these circumstances, the Tenth Circuit concluded, it was not an abuse of discretion for the District Court to require the Government to begin anew before the grand jury. We granted certiorari.

* * *

Respondent does not contend that the Fifth Amendment itself obliges the prosecutor to disclose substantial exculpatory evidence in his possession to the grand jury. Instead, building on our statement that the federal courts "may, within limits, formulate procedural rules not specifically required by the Constitution or the Congress," *United States v. Hasting*, 461 U.S. 499, 505 (1983), he argues that imposition of the Tenth Circuit's disclosure rule is supported by the courts' "supervisory power." We think not. *Hasting*, and the cases that rely upon the principle it expresses, deal strictly with the courts' power to control their *own* procedures. That power has been applied not only to improve the truth-finding process of the trial, but also to prevent parties from reaping benefit or incurring harm from violations of substantive or procedural rules (imposed by the Constitution or laws) governing matters apart from the trial itself. Thus, *Bank of Nova Scotia v. United States*, 487 U.S. 250 (1988), makes clear that the supervisory power can be used to dismiss an indictment because of misconduct before the grand jury, at least where that misconduct amounts to a violation of one of those "few, clear rules which were carefully drafted and approved by this Court and by Congress to ensure the integrity of the grand jury's functions," *United States v. Mechanik*, 475 U.S. 66, 74 (1986) (O'CONNOR, J., concurring in judgment).

We did not hold in *Bank of Nova Scotia*, however, that the courts' supervisory power could be used, not merely as a means of enforcing or vindicating legally compelled standards of prosecutorial conduct before the grand jury, but as a means of *prescribing* those standards of prosecutorial conduct in the first instance — just as it may be used as a means of establishing standards of prosecutorial conduct before the courts themselves. It is this latter exercise that respondent demands. Because the grand jury is an institution separate from the courts, over whose functioning the courts do not preside, we think it clear that, as a general matter at least, no such "supervisory" judicial authority exists, and that the disclosure rule applied here exceeded the Tenth Circuit's authority.

"[R]ooted in long centuries of Anglo-American history," the grand jury is mentioned in the Bill of Rights, but not in the body of the Constitution. It has not been textually assigned, therefore, to any of the branches described in the first three Articles. It "is a constitutional fixture in its own right." In fact the whole theory of its function is that it belongs to no branch of the institutional Government, serving as a kind of buffer or referee between the Government and the people. Although the grand jury normally operates, of course, in the courthouse and under judicial auspices, its institutional relationship with the Judicial Branch has traditionally been, so to speak, at arm's length. Judges' direct involvement in the functioning of the grand jury has generally been confined to the constitutive one of calling the grand jurors together and administering their oaths of office.

The grand jury's functional independence from the Judicial Branch is evident both in the scope of its power to investigate criminal wrongdoing and in the manner in which that power is exercised. "Unlike [a] [c]ourt, whose jurisdiction is predicated upon a specific case or controversy, the grand jury 'can investigate merely on suspicion that the law is being violated, or even because it wants assurance that it is not.'" *United States v. R. Enterprises, Inc.*, 498 U.S. 292, 297 (1991). It need not identify the offender it suspects, or even "the precise nature of the offense" it is investigating. The grand jury requires no authorization from its constituting court to initiate an investigation, nor does the prosecutor require leave of court to seek a grand jury indictment. And in its day-to-day functioning, the grand jury generally operates without the interference of a presiding judge. . . .

True, the grand jury cannot compel the appearance of witnesses and the production of evidence, and must appeal to the court when such compulsion is required. And the court will refuse to lend its assistance when the compulsion the grand jury seeks would override rights accorded by the Constitution, or even testimonial privileges recognized by the common law. Even in this setting, however, we have insisted that the grand jury remain "free to pursue its investigations unhindered by external influence or supervision so long as it does not trench upon the legitimate rights of any witness called before it." *United States v. Dionisio*, 410 U.S. 1, 17–18 (1973). Recognizing this tradition of independence, we have said that the Fifth Amendment's "constitutional guarantee *presupposes* an investigative body 'acting independently of either prosecuting attorney *or judge*'. . . ." *Id.* at 16.

No doubt in view of the grand jury proceeding's status as other than a constituent element of a "criminal prosecutio[n]," U.S. Const., Amdt. 6, we have said that certain constitutional protections afforded defendants in criminal proceedings have no application before that body. The Double Jeopardy Clause of the Fifth Amendment does not bar a grand jury from returning an indictment when a prior grand jury has refused to do so. We have twice suggested, though not held, that the Sixth Amendment right to counsel does not attach when an individual is summoned to appear before a grand jury, even if he is the subject of the investigation. And although "the grand jury may not force a witness to answer questions in violation of [the Fifth Amendment's] constitutional guarantee" against self-incrimination, *United States v. Calandra*, 414 U.S. 338, 346 (1974), our cases suggest that an indictment obtained through the use of evidence previously obtained in violation of the privilege against self-incrimination "is nevertheless valid." *Id.* at 346.

Given the grand jury's operational separateness from its constituting court, it should come as no surprise that we have been reluctant to invoke the judicial supervisory power as a basis for prescribing modes of grand jury procedure.

Respondent argues that the Court of Appeals' rule can be justified as a sort of Fifth Amendment "common law," a necessary means of assuring the constitutional right to the judgment "of an independent and informed grand jury," *Wood v. Georgia*, 370 U.S. 375, 390 (1962). Respondent makes a generalized appeal to functional notions: Judicial supervision of the quantity and quality of the evidence relied upon by the grand jury plainly facilitates, he says, the grand jury's performance of its twin historical responsibilities, *i.e.*, bringing to trial those who may be justly accused and shielding the innocent from unfounded accusation and prosecution. We do not agree. The rule would neither preserve nor enhance the traditional functioning of the institution that the Fifth Amendment demands. To the contrary, requiring the prosecutor to present exculpatory as well as inculpatory evidence would alter the grand jury's historical role, transforming it from an accusatory to an adjudicatory body.

It is axiomatic that the grand jury sits not to determine guilt or innocence, but to assess whether there is adequate basis for bringing a criminal charge. . . . As a consequence, neither in this country nor in England has the suspect under investigation by the grand jury ever been thought to have a right to testify or to have exculpatory evidence presented. Imposing upon the prosecutor a legal obligation to present exculpatory evidence in his possession would be incompatible with this system. If a "balanced" assessment of the entire matter is the objective, surely the first thing to be done — rather than requiring the prosecutor to say what he knows in defense of the target of the investigation — is to entitle the target to tender his own defense. To require the former while denying (as we do) the latter would be quite absurd. It would also be quite pointless, since it would merely invite the target to circumnavigate the system by delivering his exculpatory evidence to the prosecutor, whereupon it would *have* to be passed on to the grand jury — unless the prosecutor is willing to take the chance that a court will not deem the evidence important enough to qualify for mandatory disclosure. . . .

A complaint about the quality or adequacy of the evidence can always be recast as a complaint that the prosecutor's presentation was "incomplete" or "misleading." Our words in *Costello* bear repeating: Review of facially valid indictments on such grounds "would run counter to the whole history of the grand jury institution[,] [and] [n]either justice nor the concept of a fair trial requires [it]." 350 U.S. at 364.

Echoing the reasoning of the Tenth Circuit in *United States v. Page*, 808 F.2d at 728, respondent argues that a rule requiring the prosecutor to disclose exculpatory evidence to the grand jury would, by removing from the docket unjustified prosecutions, save valuable judicial time. That depends, we suppose, upon what the ratio would turn out to be between unjustified prosecutions eliminated and grand jury indictments challenged — for the latter as well as the former consume "valuable judicial time." We need not pursue the matter; if there is an advantage to the proposal, Congress is free to prescribe it. For the reasons set forth above, however, we conclude that courts have no authority to prescribe such a duty pursuant to their inherent supervisory authority over their own proceedings. The judgment of the Court of Appeals is accordingly reversed, and the cause is remanded for further proceedings consistent with this opinion.

JUSTICE STEVENS, with whom JUSTICE BLACKMUN and JUSTICE O'CONNOR join, and with whom JUSTICE THOMAS joins as to Parts II and III, dissenting.

* * *

Like the Hydra slain by Hercules, prosecutorial misconduct has many heads. Some are cataloged in Justice Sutherland's classic opinion for the Court in *Berger v. United States*, 295 U.S. 78 (1935):

> That the United States prosecuting attorney overstepped the bounds of that propriety and fairness which should characterize the conduct of such an officer in the prosecution of a criminal offense is clearly shown by the record. He was guilty of misstating the facts in his cross-examination of witnesses; of putting into the mouths of such witnesses things which they had not said; of suggesting by his questions that statements had been made to him personally out of court, in respect of which no proof was offered; of pretending to understand that a witness had said something which he had not said and persistently cross-examining the witness upon that basis; of assuming prejudicial facts not in evidence; of bullying and arguing with witnesses; and in general, of conducting himself in a thoroughly indecorous and improper manner. . . .

> The prosecuting attorney's argument to the jury was undignified and intemperate, containing improper insinuations and assertions calculated to mislead the jury. *Id.* at 84–85.

This, of course, is not an exhaustive list of the kinds of improper tactics that overzealous or misguided prosecutors have adopted in judicial proceedings.

Justice Sutherland's identification of the basic reason why that sort of misconduct is intolerable merits repetition:

> The United States Attorney is the representative not of an ordinary party to a controversy, but of a sovereignty whose obligation to govern impartially is as compelling as its obligation to govern at all; and whose interest, therefore, in a criminal prosecution is not that it shall win a case, but that justice shall be done. As such, he is in a peculiar and very definite sense the servant of the law, the twofold aim of which is that guilt shall not escape or innocence suffer. He may prosecute with earnestness and vigor — indeed, he should do so. But, while he may strike hard blows, he is not at liberty to strike foul ones. It is as much his duty to refrain from improper methods calculated to produce a wrongful conviction as it is to use every legitimate means to bring about a just one.

Berger v. United States, 295 U.S. at 88.

It is equally clear that the prosecutor has the same duty to refrain from improper methods calculated to produce a wrongful indictment. Indeed, the prosecutor's duty to protect the fundamental fairness of judicial proceedings assumes special importance when he is presenting evidence to a grand jury. As the Court of Appeals for the Third Circuit recognized, "the costs of continued unchecked prosecutorial misconduct" before the grand jury are particularly substantial because there the prosecutor operates without the check of a judge or a trained legal adversary, and virtually immune from public scrutiny. The prosecutor's abuse of his special relationship to the grand jury poses an enormous risk to defendants as well. For while in theory a trial provides the defendant with a full opportunity to contest and disprove the charges against him, in practice, the handing up of an indictment will often have a devastating personal and professional impact that a later dismissal or acquittal can never undo. Where the potential for abuse is so great, and the consequences of a mistaken indictment so serious, the ethical responsibilities of the prosecutor, and the obligation of the judiciary to protect against even the appearance of unfairness, are correspondingly heightened.

United States v. Serubo, 604 F.2d 807, 817 (3d Cir. 1979).

The standard for judging the consequences of prosecutorial misconduct during grand jury proceedings is essentially the same as the standard applicable to trials.

Unquestionably, the plain implication of that discussion is that if the misconduct, even though not expressly forbidden by any written rule, had played a critical role in persuading the jury to return the indictment, dismissal would have been required. In an opinion that I find difficult to comprehend, the Court today repudiates the assumptions underlying these cases and seems to suggest that the court has no authority to supervise the conduct of the prosecutor in grand jury proceedings so long as he follows the dictates of the Constitution, applicable statutes, and Rule 6 of the Federal Rules of Criminal Procedure. The Court purports to support this conclusion by invoking the doctrine of separation of powers and citing a string of cases in which we have declined to impose categorical restraints on the grand jury. Needless to say, the Court's reasoning is unpersuasive.

Explaining why the grand jury must be both "independent" and "informed," the Court wrote in *Wood v. Georgia*, 370 U.S. 375 (1962):

Historically, this body has been regarded as a primary security to the innocent against hasty, malicious and oppressive persecution; it serves the invaluable function in our society of standing between the accuser and the accused, whether the latter be an individual, minority group, or other, to determine whether a charge is founded upon reason or was dictated by an intimidating power or by malice and personal ill will.

Id. at 390.

It blinks reality to say that the grand jury can adequately perform this important historic role if it is intentionally misled by the prosecutor — on whose knowledge of the law and facts of the underlying criminal investigation the jurors will, of necessity, rely.

Unlike the Court, I am unwilling to hold that countless forms of prosecutorial misconduct must be tolerated — no matter how prejudicial they may be, or how seriously they may distort the legitimate function of the grand jury — simply because they are not proscribed by Rule 6 of the Federal Rules of Criminal Procedure or a statute that is applicable in grand jury proceedings. Such a sharp break with the traditional role of the federal judiciary is unprecedented, unwarranted, and unwise. Unrestrained prosecutorial misconduct in grand jury proceedings is inconsistent with the administration of justice in the federal courts and should be redressed in appropriate cases by the dismissal of indictments obtained by improper methods.

What, then, is the proper disposition of this case? I agree with the Government that the prosecutor is not required to place all exculpatory evidence before the grand jury. . . . But that does not mean that the prosecutor may mislead the grand jury into believing that there is probable cause to indict by withholding clear evidence to the contrary. I thus agree with the Department of Justice that "when a prosecutor conducting a grand jury inquiry is personally aware of substantial evidence which directly negates the guilt of a subject of the investigation, the prosecutor must present or otherwise disclose such evidence to the grand jury before seeking an indictment against such a person." U.S. Dept. of Justice, United States Attorneys' Manual ¶ 9-11.233, at 88 (1988).

Although I question whether the evidence withheld in this case directly negates respondent's guilt, I need not resolve my doubts because the Solicitor General did not ask the Court to review the nature of the evidence withheld. Instead, he asked us to decide the legal question whether an indictment may be dismissed because the prosecutor failed to present exculpatory evidence. Unlike the Court and the Solicitor General, I believe the answer to that question is yes, if the withheld evidence would plainly preclude a finding of probable cause. I therefore cannot endorse the Court's opinion. . . .

Notes and Questions

1. *Exculpatory evidence.*

a. *DOJ practice and policy.* The Department of Justice requires disclosure of exculpatory evidence as a matter of policy. This policy, however, creates no substantive rights for the defendant. *See* U.S. Dept. of Justice, Department of Justice Manual ¶ 9-11.233. Thus, failure to present such evidence forms no basis for dismissal of the indictment. Given the potential for prosecutorial abuses, should this policy be codified by Congress? Why or why not?

The DOJ has been criticized for failing to present exculpatory evidence to grand juries despite its policy requiring such disclosure. If such evidence need only be presented at the trial stage, does this create the potential for prosecutorial misconduct before the grand jury? Has the *Williams* case provided sufficient guidance as to how to avoid unfairness in this situation?

b. *State practice and policy.* Some states do require that prosecutors present exculpatory evidence to the grand jury. *See* R. Michael Cassidy, *Toward a More Independent Grand Jury: Recasting and Enforcing the Prosecutor's Duty to Disclose Exculpatory Evidence*, 13 GEO. J. LEGAL ETHICS, 361 (2000).

2. *Prosecutorial misconduct.* Misconduct by prosecutors has been the subject of major national concern. *See* Andrea Elliott & Benjamin Weiser, *When Prosecutors Err, Others Pay the Price,* N.Y. Times, June 24, 2007, http://www.nytimes.com/2004/03/21/nyregion/21prosecute.html. Other illustrations of prosecutorial misconduct were cited in Justice Stevens' dissent in the *Williams* case:

> Like the Hydra slain by Hercules, prosecutorial misconduct has many heads. . . . [It has not] been limited to judicial proceedings: the reported [lower court] cases indicate that it has sometimes infected grand jury proceedings as well. The cases contain examples of prosecutors presenting perjured testimony, questioning a witness outside the presence of the grand jury and then failing to inform the grand jury that the testimony was exculpatory, failing to inform the grand jury of its authority to subpoena witnesses, operating under a conflict of interest, misstating the law, and misstating the facts on cross-examination of a witness.

3. *Remedies for prosecutorial misconduct.* What other types of conduct might rise to the level of prosecutorial misconduct and infect the grand jury process? Should prosecutorial misconduct result in dismissal of the charges? Should dismissal apply if the defendant has not been prejudiced? The Court in *Williams* held that an indictment may not be dismissed merely because the prosecutor failed to present substantial exculpatory evidence. *See United States. v. Modica,* 663 F. 2d 1173 (2d Cir. 1981) ("Reversal is an ill-suited remedy for prosecutorial misconduct; it does not affect the prosecutor directly, but rather imposes upon society the cost of retrying an individual who was fairly convicted."). Prejudice will be presumed, however, in those circumstances where the "structural protections of the grand jury have been so compromised as to render the proceedings fundamentally unfair. . . ." *Bank of Nova Scotia v. United States,* 487 U.S. 250, 257–258 (1988) (the district court exercised its supervisory power over the grand jury where there were allegations of prosecutorial grand jury abuses; the court dismissed a 27-count indictment for tax fraud, obstruction of justice, and mail fraud).

Consider alternative ways to remedy grand jury errors that did not prejudicially affect a defendant: punishing the prosecutor via contempt of court for a knowing violation of Rule 6; referral of the misconduct to the bar to initiate appropriate attorney discipline; and chastising the prosecutor in a published opinion. Each of these remedies will avoid a windfall to the unprejudiced defendant, while at the same time address the culpable conduct of the prosecutor. Do these approaches have merit? Why or why not?

Problem

16-1. Doris Dern has been mayor of the town of Oakville for the last four years. Chris Chang, the President and sole shareholder of Construction Corp., is a political ally of Dern. Construction Corp. is regularly awarded contracts with the town of Oakville. Dern owns 10% of Construction Corp. A federal grand jury has been convened to explore indictment, with Dern and Chang as targets of the investigation.

The government believes that Dern failed to disclose her ownership interest in Construction Corp., in violation of state and local conflict of interest laws. The government also believes that this failure to disclose provides strong circumstantial evidence that Chang bribed Dern in connection with the award of the contracts.

The grand jury has seen documents and heard evidence from a number of witnesses, including Construction Corp. employees who testified that two years ago, Chang gave Dern an ownership interest in Construction Corp. in return for the award of city contracts. Chang mailed checks to Dern that represented Dern's interest in Construction Corp.'s profits. During the investigation, Anderson Andrews, the Assistant U.S. attorney in charge of the investigation received information showing that two years earlier, Dern filed documents that supplemented Dern's official conflict-of-interest disclosures and that fully revealed the arrangement between Construction Corp. and Dern. Andrews did not present this evidence to the grand jury.

You are counsel for Dern, and you have become aware of all the above facts. Assume that the grand jury has now indicted Dern on charges of honest services fraud. Apart from the substantive merits of the charges, what action, if any, should you take based on the government's conduct with respect to the grand jury in this case?

3. Irregularities and Abuse

The grand jury is the primary investigative tool in federal white collar and corporate criminal investigations. If there has been an irregularity in the grand jury process, what recourse does a putative defendant have prior to or after the indictment? The next case discusses the defense's options and addresses the limitations on the government's use of the grand jury after an indictment has been issued.

United States v. Arthur Andersen, L.L.P.

Crim. Action No. H-02-00121 (S.D. Tex. Apr. 9, 2002)

[Harmon, District Judge.]

Pending before the Court in the above referenced action is Defendant Arthur Andersen L.L.P.'s motion to quash subpoenas and limit grand jury proceedings.

Defendant contends that once an indictment has been returned, the government is prohibited from using the grand jury to conduct discovery or otherwise prepare its case for trial. Defendant charges that the government is abusing the grand jury process by seeking to use the grand jury to assist in its trial preparation and to conduct discovery and "freeze" testimony. Defendant complains that only now, after obtaining the indictment on March 7, 2002, charging it with obstruction of justice and after Defendant refused to plead guilty, is the government impermissibly subpoenaing Arthur Andersen personnel as fact witnesses to testify under oath about evidence relating to the obstruction of justice charge to strengthen its case, to "lock in — for trial purposes — those witnesses previously furnished through their voluntary interview." Defendant argues that not only the timing of these delayed subpoenas, but also the implausibility of the government's claim that it is now seeking to investigate whether to indict individuals in addition to the accounting institution, its subpoenas for Arthur Andersen witnesses whose testimony might constitute admissions attributable to their employer at trial support Defendant's charge of abuse by the government. Moreover, urges Defendant, the imminence of the trial setting eliminates any need to place witnesses before the grand jury now. Finally, Defendant asserts that "the government . . . made this bed; having rushed to indict on an extraordinarily expedited schedule, the Justice Department is in no position to complain if temporary restrictions on the grand jury are necessary to prevent the government from obtaining an unfair and improper advantage at trial."

In its memorandum in opposition, the government reiterates a point made in open court, i.e., that Andersen urged the Department of Justice to expedite a decision about whether to indict the firm for obstruction of justice based on document destruction; then after Defendant was indicted, Andersen reversed its position and asked the government to delay investigating individual employees, including those that Andersen has publicly blamed for the destruction of documents. The government further complains that in light of Andersen's campaign to enlist public sympathy by slanted statements and demonstrations, to influence the potential jury pool, and to signal its desired factual stance to current and former employees, including potential targets, subjects or witnesses in the grand jury investigation, expeditious investigation by the grand jury of current and former employees is necessary.

Emphasizing that the grand jury . . . is a separate entity from the courts, which have only a "very limited" supervisory power over grand jury proceedings, *United States v. Williams*, 504 U.S. 36 (1992), also underscores that grand jury proceedings are entitled to a presumption of regularity. The government points to the long settled principle that "where either primary purpose of the investigation is to determine whether others not indicted were involved in the same criminal activity, or whether the indicted party committed still other crimes, the government may go forward with the inquiry even though one result may be the production of evidence that could then be used at the trial of the pending indictment." Thus a grand jury subpoena may issue to assist the grand jury in its investigation even where the incidental effect might be that the prosecutor will use any information obtained for purposes other than that grand jury's investigation. Furthermore, the government's primary purpose for proceeding before the grand jury is not to collect evidence relating to the pending indictment against Arthur Andersen L.L.P. . . .

In support of its response, the government submits two declarations from attorneys working with the Enron Task Force, investigating all criminal matters associated with the collapse of Enron Corporation. The first, filed *ex parte* and under seal, was made by an Assistant United States Attorney and explains in detail that the challenged subpoenas were issued by a different grand jury than the one that indicted Defendant and were properly issued to investigate uncharged criminal conduct by individuals and entities. A second, unsealed declaration [was filed] by AUSU Leslie Caldwell delineating the procedural steps and negotiations between the government and Defendant up to the unsealing of the indictment for the instant case on March 14, 2002.

The Court has reviewed the applicable law and the record before it. A court should not intervene in the grand jury process absent a compelling reason. The existence of a pending indictment does not per se bar the government from using the grand jury to make a good faith, continuing inquiry into charges not included in that pending indictment. Abuse of the grand jury process occurs only when the government's sole or dominant purpose in convening a grand jury is to gather evidence for an already pending litigation. This sole or dominant purpose rule serves obvious purposes. It allows grand juries to continue investigations without having to wait to indict individuals or entities against which sufficient information to indict has already been uncovered, as well as to investigate additional individuals or entities who become suspects only after the indictment has been returned.

The government has explained with particularity and with documentary support that the government's expedited indictment was due to Arthur Andersen's urging. Thus the timing of the subpoena is not a factor bolstering Defendant' argument. Other than conclusory statements, Defendant has failed to show that the government's investigation in subpoenaing the Defendant's employees as witnesses is for the sole and dominant purpose of developing evidence for trial of its pending destruction-of-documents obstruction charge against Arthur Anderson L.L.P. The Court finds that the government's affidavits have shown it is acting in good faith to investigate unindicted charges against individuals and entities. As anyone following the news is fully aware, the collapse of Enron has spawned a complex and seemingly ever expanding investigation involving a wide range of parties and potential causes of action. The Court finds that there has been no abuse of grand jury process here. For these reasons the Court ORDERS that Defendant's motion to quash subpoenas and limit grand jury proceedings is DENIED.

Notes and Questions

1. *Motion to quash.* The motion to quash is a party's principal means for challenging grand jury irregularities. A motion to quash is directed to the federal district court supervising the grand jury. This court performs a limited supervisory role when considering motions to quash because grand jury proceedings are presumptively valid.

2. *Timing.* In the *Arthur Andersen* case, the pre-indictment negotiations worked to the disadvantage of the government. By presenting its case prior to the completion of the evidence-gathering process, it risked not securing all of the witnesses and evidence. On the other hand, a defendant will typically seek to delay an indictment.

Why did Andersen seek an expedited decision in this case? Why would a corporate defendant seek expedited resolution as a matter of defense strategy?

3. *Pre-indictment publicity.* One of the main reasons for grand jury secrecy is the potential adverse effect of pre-indictment publicity. By comparison, concerns over adverse *pretrial* publicity can sometimes be addressed by the trial court and eliminated through the petit jury selection process or by transferring the case to a different division in the federal district, if one is available. With pre-indictment publicity, on the other hand, the latter is not possible because the case must be presented in the district where the alleged offense occurred.

The investigation and prosecution of Arthur Andersen, along with potential civil liability, led to the firm's collapse and the loss of some 28,000 jobs. *See* Kurt Eichenwald, *Arthur Andersen is Said to be Near a Sale to a Rival*, N.Y. TIMES, March 11, 2002, https://www.nytimes.com/2002/03/11/business/arthur-andersen-is-said-to-be-ncar-a-sale-to-a-rival.html; David Stout, *Conviction of Arthur Andersen is Voided*, N.Y. TIMES, June 1, 2005, https://www.nytimes.com/2005/06/01/business/worldbusiness/conviction-of-arthur-andersen-is-voided.html.

After the case was reversed by the United States Supreme Court (*see* Chapter 11, Obstruction of Justice, *supra*), the Department of Justice abandoned its prosecution of Andersen. *See* Carrie Johnson, *U.S. Ends Prosecution of Arthur Andersen*, WASH. POST, Nov. 23, 2005, http://www.washingtonpost.com/wp-dyn/content/article/2005/11/22/AR2005112201852.html.

What do you think of the government's strategy in the case above? Was it unfair to the firm, as the firm argued? Why or why not?

4. *Impartiality and bias.* Although a defendant is entitled to an impartial petit jury, a defendant is not entitled to an impartial grand jury. As a result, lack of impartiality is not grounds for dismissal of the indictment. As one court commented,

> The basic theory of the functions of a grand jury, does not require that grand jurors should be impartial and unbiased. In this respect, their position is entirely different from that of petit jurors. The Sixth Amendment to the Constitution of the United States expressly provides that the trial jury in a criminal case must be 'impartial.' No such requirement in respect to grand juries is found in the Fifth Amendment. . . . A grand jury does not pass on the guilt or innocence of the defendant, but merely determines whether he should be brought to trial. It is purely an accusatory body.

United States. v. Knowles, 147 F. Supp. 19 (D.D.C. 1957).

5. *Multiple grand juries.* The *Arthur Andersen* case grew out of the Enron corporate fraud scheme, a complex scheme involving multi-district civil proceedings and criminal investigations. In such situations, more than one grand jury may be conducting an investigation. This case was coordinated by the Enron Task Force that was investigating matters arising from Enron's collapse. What particular dangers are presented for defendants in the case of multiple investigations?

Problem

16-2. Five former local police officers were being investigated by a federal grand jury for civil rights violations. The government called 16 witnesses before the grand jury, including the alleged victim, and thereafter issued an indictment against all the defendants. It was later revealed that the alleged victim in the case perjured himself before the grand jury. There is no evidence that the government knew, at the time of the victim's testimony, that it was perjurious, although there is evidence that the government suspected that some of the testimony might have been fabricated. The defendants sought to dismiss the indictment on the grounds that the alleged victim's "entire testimony before the grand jury is severely tainted by his perjury." The district court dismissed the indictment on the basis of the false testimony.

The government appeals. How should the court rule? Why?

C. Grand Jury Secrecy and Related Issues

The grand jury system is often criticized because of the secrecy in which grand juries operate when exercising their broad investigatory powers. While grand jury secrecy operates on the premise that it protects the innocent as well as the government, the reality is that secrecy is sometimes perceived as a potential shield for governmental abuse of the grand jury process. In addition, members of the public and the media often assert that disclosure of the nature and scope of high-profile grand jury investigations is in the public interest.

As you read through these materials, consider the five objectives of grand jury secrecy that the Supreme Court articulated in *United States v. Procter & Gamble*, 356 U.S. 677 (1958):

(1) to prevent the escape of those whose indictment may be contemplated;

(2) to insure the utmost freedom to the grand jury in its deliberations, and to prevent persons subject to indictment or their friends from importuning the grand jurors;

(3) to prevent subornation of perjury or tampering with the witnesses who may testify before grand jury and later appear at the trial of those indicted by it;

(4) to encourage free and untrammeled disclosures by persons who have information with respect to the commission of crimes; and

(5) to protect the innocent accused who is exonerated from disclosure of the fact that he has been under investigation and from the expense of standing trial where there was no probability of guilt.

Grand jurors do not hear both sides of a case. Defense counsel has no right to accompany the client into the grand jury room, to ask questions, or to submit evidence to the grand jury. During the course of a long-running criminal investigation, as can frequently occur in complex white collar cases, the defense has a limited ability to discern the details of the criminal investigation. Absent a court order or other authorization, only the witness may disclose the substance of the witness' testimony before the grand jury.

In high-profile investigations, a witness can take a proactive, aggressive approach by striking the first public blow and granting media interviews both pre- and post-grand jury appearance. By doing so, a witness can hope to "spin" the facts and generate public sympathy and support. Moreover, communication with the prosecutor early on in the investigation may persuade the prosecutor to label what would otherwise be a target or subject as a witness. Defendants have also claimed that the government agents and prosecutors have leaked grand jury information in order to prejudice the public and potential jurors.

Because secrecy rules are often unclear, issues involving grand jury secrecy can wreak havoc in investigations conducted by the Department of Justice. Leaks can potentially affect public opinion, taint a jury pool, and even affect the proceedings of the grand jury itself. When in doubt, prosecutors should err on the side of caution and maintain secrecy.

1. Leaks

The following case provides an example of the complex issues that can arise under Rule 6. Did the parties in this case have any motivation for attempting to "spin" the facts?

In re Sealed Case No. 99-3091
192 F.3d 995 (D.C. Cir. 1999)

PER CURIAM:

The Office of Independent Counsel (OIC) seeks summary reversal of the district court's order to show cause why OIC should not be held in contempt for violating the grand jury secrecy rule. . . .

On January 31, 1999, while the Senate was trying President William J. Clinton on articles of impeachment, the *New York Times* published a front page article captioned "Starr is Weighing Whether to Indict Sitting President." As is relevant here, the article reported:

> Inside the Independent Counsel's Office, a group of prosecutors believes that not long after the Senate trial concludes, Mr. Starr should ask the grand jury of 23 men and women hearing the case against Mr. Clinton to indict him on charges of perjury and obstruction of justice, the associates said. The group wants to charge Mr. Clinton with lying under oath in his Jones deposition in January 1998 and in his grand jury testimony in August, the associates added.

The next day, the Office of the President (the White House) and Mr. Clinton jointly filed in district court a motion for an order to show cause why OIC, or the individuals therein, should not be held in contempt for disclosing grand jury material in violation of Federal Rule of Criminal Procedure 6(e). The White House and Mr. Clinton pointed to several excerpts from the article as evidence of OIC's violations of the grand jury secrecy rule.

OIC responded that the matters disclosed in the article merely rehashed old news reports and, in any event, did not fall within Rule 6(e)'s definition of "matters occurring before the grand jury. . . ."

Notwithstanding the foregoing, Independent Counsel Kenneth W. Starr asked the Federal Bureau of Investigation to provide OIC assistance in conducting an internal leak investigation.

Troubled by these developments, the district court ordered OIC to show cause why they should not be held in civil contempt for a violation of Rule 6(e), concluding that the portion of the *New York Times* article quoted above revealed grand jury material and constituted a *prima facie* violation of Rule 6(e).

Because OIC has withdrawn its argument that none of its attorneys was the source of the disclosures in the *New York Times* article at issue here, the only remaining issue is whether those disclosures qualify as "matters occurring before the grand jury." Fed. R. Crim. P. 6(e)(2).

The district court concluded that only one excerpt from the *New York Times* article constituted a *prima facie* violation of Rule 6(e). That excerpt disclosed the desire of some OIC prosecutors to seek, not long after the conclusion of the Senate trial, an indictment of Mr. Clinton on perjury and obstruction of justice charges, including lying under oath in his deposition in the Paula Jones matter and in his grand jury testimony. These statements, according to the district court, reveal a specific time frame for seeking an indictment, the details of a likely indictment, and the direction a group of prosecutors within OIC believes the grand jury investigation should take. Not surprisingly, Mr. Clinton and the White House agree with the district court's expansive reading of Rule 6(e). OIC takes a narrow view of the Rule's coverage, arguing that matters occurring outside the physical presence of the grand jury are covered only if they reveal grand jury matters. DOJ generally supports OIC with respect to the Rule's coverage, but emphasizes the importance of the context and concreteness of disclosures.

The key to the district court's reasoning is its reliance on this court's definition of "matters occurring before the grand jury." In *In re Motions of Dow Jones & Co.*, 142 F.3d 496, 500 (D.C. Cir. 1998), we noted that this phrase encompasses "not only what has occurred and what is occurring, but also what is likely to occur," including "the identities of witnesses or jurors, the substance of testimony as well as actual transcripts, the strategy or direction of the investigation, the deliberations or questions of jurors, and the like." *Id.* Despite the seemingly broad nature of the statements in *Dow Jones*, we have never read Rule 6(e) to require that a "veil of secrecy be drawn over all matters occurring in the world that happen to be investigated by a grand jury." *Securities and Exchange Comm'n v. Dresser Indus.*, 628 F.2d 1368, 1382 (D.C. Cir. 1980). Indeed, we have said that "[t]he disclosure of information 'coincidentally before the grand jury [which can] be revealed in such a manner that its revelation would not elucidate the inner workings of the grand jury' is not prohibited." *Senate of Puerto Rico v. United States Dept. of Justice*, 823 F.2d 574, 582 (D.C. Cir. 1987). Thus, the phrases "likely to occur" and "strategy and direction" must be read in light of the text of Rule 6(e) — which limits the Rule's coverage to "matters occurring before the grand jury" — as well as the purposes of the Rule.

These purposes, as well as the text of the Rule itself, reflect the need to preserve the secrecy of the *grand jury* proceedings themselves. It is therefore necessary to differentiate between statements by a prosecutor's office with respect to its own investigation, and statements by a prosecutor's office with respect to a *grand jury's* investigation, a distinction of the utmost significance upon which several circuits have already remarked.

Information actually presented to the grand jury is core Rule 6(e) material that is afforded the broadest protection from disclosure. Prosecutors' statements about their investigations, however, implicate the Rule only when they directly reveal grand jury matters. To be sure, we have recognized that Rule 6(e) would be easily evaded if a prosecutor could with impunity discuss with the press testimony about to be presented to a grand jury, so long as it had not yet occurred. Accordingly, we have read Rule 6(e) to cover matters "likely to occur." And even a discussion of "strategy and direction of the investigation" could include references to not yet delivered but clearly anticipated testimony. But that does not mean that *any* discussion of an investigation is violative of Rule 6(e). Indeed, the district court's Local Rule 308(b)(2), which governs attorney conduct in grand jury matters, recognizes that prosecutors often have a legitimate interest in revealing aspects of their investigations "to inform the public that the investigation is underway, to describe the general scope of the investigation, to obtain assistance in the apprehension of a suspect, to warn the public of any dangers, or otherwise aid in the investigation."

It may often be the case, however, that disclosures by the prosecution referencing its own investigation should not be made for tactical reasons, or are in fact prohibited by other Rules or ethical guidelines. For instance, prosecutors may be prohibited by internal guidelines, *see, e.g.,* United States Attorney Manual §1-7.530, from discussing the strategy or direction of their investigation before an indictment is sought. This would serve one of the same purposes as Rule 6(e): protecting the reputation of innocent suspects. But a court may not use Rule 6(e) to generally regulate prosecutorial statements to the press. The purpose of the Rule is only to protect the secrecy of grand jury proceedings.

For these reasons, the disclosure that a group of OIC prosecutors "believe" that an indictment should be brought at the end of the impeachment proceedings does not on its face, or in the context of the article as a whole, violate Rule 6(e). We acknowledge, as did OIC, that such statements are troubling, for they have the potential to damage the reputation of innocent suspects. But bare statements that some assistant prosecutors in OIC wish to seek an indictment do not implicate the grand jury; the prosecutors may not even be basing their opinion on information presented to a grand jury.

The fact that the disclosure also reveals a time period for seeking the indictment of "not long after the Senate trial concludes" does not in any way indicate what is "likely to occur" before the grand jury within the meaning of Rule 6(e). That disclosure reflects nothing more than a desire on the part of some OIC prosecutors to seek an indictment at that time, not a decision to do so. The general uncertainty as to whether an indictment would in fact be sought (according to the article, only some prosecutors in OIC thought one should be) leads us to conclude that this portion of the article did not reveal anything that was "occurring before the grand jury."

Nor does it violate the Rule to state the general grounds for such an indictment — here, lying under oath in a deposition and before the grand jury — where no secret grand jury material is revealed. In ordinary circumstances, Rule 6(e) covers the disclosure of the names of grand jury witnesses. Therefore, the statement that members of OIC wished to seek an indictment based on Mr. Clinton's alleged perjury before a grand jury would ordinarily be Rule 6(e) material. In this case, however, we take judicial notice that the President's status as a witness before the grand jury was a matter of widespread public knowledge well before the *New York Times* article at issue in this case was written; the President himself went on national television the day of his testimony to reveal this fact. Where the general public is already aware of the information contained in the prosecutor's statement, there is no additional harm in the prosecutor referring to such information.

Similarly, it would ordinarily be a violation of Rule 6(e) to disclose that a grand jury is investigating a particular person. Thus, the statement that a grand jury is "hearing the case against Mr. Clinton" would be covered by Rule 6(e) if it were not for the fact that the *New York Times* article did not reveal any secret, for it was already common knowledge well before January 31, 1999, that a grand jury was investigating alleged perjury and obstruction of justice by the President. Once again, the President's appearance on national television confirmed as much.

[W]e reverse and remand with instructions to dismiss the Rule 6(e) contempt proceedings against OIC. . . .

Notes and Questions

1. *Scope of disclosure.* Rule 6(e)(2) governs disclosure of grand jury material. Although the government attorneys, personnel, and grand jurors are prohibited from disclosing matters occurring before the grand jury, the Supreme Court has held that the government may not prevent witnesses from discussing their own testimony before a grand jury. In addition, Rule 6(e)(2) allows for disclosure in certain circumstances including at trial and where there is a "particularized need."

2. *Witness testimony.* Does a witness have a right to review a transcript of the witness's own grand jury testimony? The circuits are split on this issue. *See In re: Grand Jury,* 490 F.3d 978, 986–88 (D.C. Cir. 2007) (reviewing circuit split and listing cases). In one decision, the D.C. Circuit reversed an order denying the witness such access, concluding that:

> In sum, grand jury witnesses have a strong interest in reviewing the transcripts of their own grand jury testimony. The government has little good reason to prevent witnesses from reviewing their transcripts. Weighing the interests of witnesses and the government, we therefore hold that the grand jury witnesses are entitled under Rule 6(e)(3)(E)(i) to review transcripts of their own grand jury testimony in private at the U.S. Attorney's Office or a place agreed to by the parties or designated by the district court.

Id. at 990. Was this the correct outcome? What are the competing interests in this situation? For an excellent overview of these and other issues relating to representation of a grand jury witness, see Jon May, *Advising the Grand Jury Witness: When Talk is Not Cheap,* 16 CRIM. JUST. 16, 17 (2008).

In *In re Grand Jury,* 566 F.3d 12 (1st Cir. 2009), the First Circuit took a different approach. The court declined to hold that witnesses are entitled to review their transcripts. The court went on to find, however, that "a less demanding requirement of particularized need applies when a grand jury witness demands access [in order to review] a transcript, rather than [to obtain] a copy of the transcript." *Id.* at 17. In that case, the court held that before reappearing before the grand jury the witness was entitled to review previous testimony where the subject matter was highly technical and the government had threatened a perjury charge. Does this approach make sense? Why or why not?

3. *Judicial notice.* The court in *In re Sealed Case* was quite willing to relax Rule 6 by taking judicial notice that the "President's status as a witness before the grand jury was a matter of widespread public knowledge. . . ." 192 F.3d 995, 1004 (D.C. Cir. 1999). Does this approach thwart the intention of Rule 6 to protect innocent citizens by prohibiting such disclosures? Any facts presented to a grand jury are probably already known by other persons. Should the grand jury secrecy rules cover this information because secrecy should protect *the fact that the grand jury had an interest in that information*? Would the answer be any more troubling if the witness were not a prominent public figure such as the President or a target who was not embroiled in a high-level, politically charged investigation?

4. *Leaks.* Leaks of grand jury materials to the press pose special dangers. Rule 6(e) is designed to prevent such dangers. Do you favor a rule that prohibits the disclosure that occurred in this case? Why or why not? Can a prosecutor leak grand jury material and later claim that the matter is no longer secret? The court discussed this scenario in footnote 13: "Of course, a prosecutor is not free to leak grand jury material and then make a self-serving claim that the matter is no longer secret. *Cf. In re North,* 16 F.3d 1234, 1245 (D.C. Cir. 1994) ('We do not intend to formulate a

rule that once a leak of Rule 6(e) material has occurred, government attorneys are free to ignore the pre-existing bond of secrecy,'" quoting *In re Sealed Case*, 192 F.3d at 1004 n.13).

5. *Parallel civil and criminal proceedings.* Complex issues relating to grand jury secrecy also arise in the context of parallel proceedings. For example, in a civil case brought by the government, may the civil government attorneys gain access to grand jury information? May a private civil litigant gain access to such information?

6. *Disclosure by grand jurors.* Grand jury secrecy rules apply to the grand jurors themselves. Should there be exceptions to this rule? What if a grand juror believes that the prosecutor has publicly misdescribed the grand jurors' deliberations or did not provide evidence that the grand jurors believed they needed? This issue has arisen in a number of cases, including those involving police shootings. For example, in *Doe v. Bell*, 969 F.3d 883 (8th Cir. 2020), a person who served on the grand jury that decided not to charge a police officer who fatally shot Michael Brown, a Black youth, in Ferguson, Missouri, brought a § 1983 civil rights action, arguing that the state's grand jury secrecy laws violated her First Amendment rights. The Eighth Circuit affirmed the dismissal of the case, holding that the secrecy laws did not violate the First Amendment even though prosecutor had already taken the "extraordinary" step of publicly releasing evidence and other grand jury materials. Is this outcome fair? Why or why not?

This issue of course will apply to all grand juries, including those involving white collar offenses. Should a grand juror have a First Amendment right to discuss matters occurring before a grand jury? As a matter of policy, should grand jury secrecy rules apply to grand jurors at all? Why or why not?

7. *Disclosure by grand jury witnesses.* Under federal law and the law of most states, grand jury secrecy rules do not apply to witnesses. Nonetheless, prosecutors sometimes attempt to muzzle grand jury witnesses. As one commentator explained:

> [A] small number of states . . . expressly prevent grand jury witnesses from disclosing their testimony to the press or to other witnesses. [In] the majority of . . . states and the federal system, obligations of grand jury secrecy do not extend to grand jury witnesses. In these jurisdictions, only persons performing an 'official function' before the grand jury are covered by the oath of secrecy. Absent a contract or court order, witnesses are free to talk with each other or with the press. Nevertheless, prosecutors often seek to handcuff grand jury witnesses in their exercise of First Amendment rights by drafting one-sided cooperation agreements or immunity orders that impose obligations of secrecy on grand jury witnesses, even though none exist under governing statutes or rules of criminal procedure.

R. Michael Cassidy, *Silencing Grand Jury Witnesses*, 91 IND. L.J. 823, 824 (2016) (citations omitted). Should the law, or prosecutorial practices, be allowed to prevent grand jury witnesses from disclosing their testimony? What are the competing concerns?

Problem

16-3. Defendants were indicted for fraud, bribery, and extortion. Three separate grand juries had investigated the allegations leading to the indictment, but the indictment came from the third grand jury. The defendants alleged that government attorneys leaked secret grand jury information relating to the second grand jury investigation, leading to news reports that discussed the identity, testimony, and demeanor of witnesses before the second grand jury. The defendants also alleged that the government eavesdropped on conversations by members of the second grand jury showing that they were not inclined to indict, which led the prosecution to engage in "grand jury shopping" when it chose to present the charges for indictment to a third grand jury. The government investigated all leaks of grand jury information that had allegedly been made, but found no misconduct, and said it did not engage in eavesdropping. The government also argued that its reasons for presenting the indictment to a third grand jury were not a proper subject for judicial inquiry. The district court stayed the trial indefinitely, pending completion of its own investigation into the alleged misconduct before the second grand jury.

The government appeals. How should the court rule? Why?

16-4. Assume that, in a small community of 20,000 residents, the public is speculating about the recent scandal involving the local (and only) bank president. Rumors suggest that she is being investigated for embezzling funds from the bank. There has been considerable media coverage on the allegations and suspicions. Assume the following people gave public statements:

   a. The prosecutor stated (as reported in the news media), "We are conducting an investigation into the criminal activities of the bank president."

   b. The prosecutor stated on the courthouse steps that the grand jury is investigating potential embezzlement of federally insured funds at the bank.

   c. The vice-president of the bank appeared before the grand jury and gave testimony. He also gave an interview to the news media revealing that he shared with the grand jury the dates and times of the embezzlement activities.

   d. A reporter for the local paper wrote that the grand jury is investigating the bank president, and attributed the story to an anonymous source.

Has anyone violated the secrecy restrictions of Rule 6(e)? If so, which person committed the violation, and what is the remedy for the violation(s)?

2. Disclosure to Government Attorneys

Frequently, in the performance of their duties, federal government attorneys seek to have access to grand jury material in order to further an investigation. Because of the long-standing rule that grand jury matters are secret and not generally subject to disclosure, codified in Rule 6, any such disclosures must be made within the confines of the rule or pursuant to court order. Two provisions of Rule 6 govern disclosures. Section 6(e)(3)(A)(i) states that "[d]isclosure of a grand-jury matter — other than the grand jury's deliberations or any grand juror's vote — may be made to an attorney for the government for use in performing that attorney's duty." By contrast, section 6(e)(3)(E)(i) [formerly 6(e)(C)(i)] states that a court may permit disclosure "at a time, in a manner, and subject to any other conditions that it directs of a grand-jury matter preliminarily to or in connection with a judicial proceeding."

Note on United States v. Sells Engineering

The Supreme Court in *United States v. Sells Engineering*, 463 U.S. 418 (1983), established the standard applicable to the disclosure of grand jury materials to government attorneys. In *Sells*, the investigation began as a combined civil and criminal matter handled by the Internal Revenue Service. The federal grand jury investigated charges of fraud and tax evasion by Sells Engineering in connection with certain governmental contracts. Sells Engineering reached an agreement with the government and entered a plea of guilty to one count in the indictment. All other charges were dismissed.

After the dismissal, the government sought disclosure of the grand jury material in connection with their civil fraud investigation under the False Claims Act. The district court granted the motion for disclosure, finding that the matter fell within [current section 6(e)(3)(A)(i)], and that the civil attorneys within the Department of Justice were entitled to the material "as a matter of right." The Court of Appeals reversed, finding that the disclosure was only authorized if the government could demonstrate a "particularized need" under 6(e)(C)(i) [currently 6(e)(3)(E)(i)].

The Supreme Court acknowledged the need for disclosure of grand jury materials in order to assist with further governmental investigations and business. The Court stated:

> [i]t does not follow, however, that any Justice Department attorney is free to rummage through the records of any grand jury in the country, simply by right of office. Disclosure under (A)(i) is permitted only 'in the performance of such attorney's duty.' The heart of the primary issue in this case is whether performance of duty, within the meaning of (A)(i), includes preparation and litigation of a civil suit by a Justice Department attorney who had no part in conducting the related criminal prosecution.

463 U.S. at 428.

The Court first recognized that governmental disclosures serve many investigative purposes. In reconciling the different disclosure sections of Rule 6, the Court ultimately concluded:

> [n]one of these considerations, however, provides any support for breaching grand jury secrecy in favor of government attorneys *other than prosecutors* — either by allowing them into the grand jury room, or by granting them uncontrolled access to grand jury materials. An attorney with only civil duties lacks both the prosecutor's special role in supporting the grand

jury, and the prosecutor's own crucial need to know what occurs before the grand jury.

Id. at 431. In deciding to limit the grand jury's extraordinary investigative powers, the Court held that "*no* disclosure of grand jury materials for civil use should be permitted without a court order." *Id.* at 440. Further, the Court held that the standard for this type of disclosure required the moving party to demonstrate a "particularized need," prior to any disclosure under Rule 6.

3. Disclosure in Connection with a Judicial Proceeding

Apart from disclosure to government attorneys, Rule 6(e) provides various other exceptions to grand jury secrecy rules. As noted above, under Rule 6(e)(3)(E)(1), for example, a "court may authorize disclosure — at a time, in a manner, and subject to any other conditions that it directs — of a grand-jury matter: (i) preliminarily to or in connection with a judicial proceeding."

This provision came into play when the United States House of Representatives' Judiciary Committee sought grand jury materials in connection with its investigation relating to the possible impeachment of President Donald Trump. The committee sought grand jury materials from Special Counsel Robert Mueller's investigation into alleged foreign interference with the 2016 presidential election. The Department of Justice had released a version of Mueller's report that was redacted in part due to asserted grand jury secrecy concerns. The Judiciary Committee subpoenaed the full report and other related grand jury materials on the grounds that the materials "bear on whether the President committed impeachable offenses by obstructing the FBI's and Special Counsel's investigation into Russian interference in the 2016 election and his possible motivations for doing so."

When the DOJ refused to comply with the subpoena, the committee requested that the federal district court in the District of Columbia order the disclosure of the materials. In its application, the committee relied upon Rule 6(e)(3)(E)(1), arguing that a potential Senate impeachment trial qualified as a "judicial proceeding." The committee also argued that it was irrelevant that the Senate had already voted to acquit the President because the committee's investigation of possible impeachable offenses was continuing. The district court agreed. The court also found that the committee had a specific need for the material that outweighed any grand jury secrecy concerns. The D.C. Circuit affirmed. The Supreme Court then stayed the order and granted certiorari for a full argument on the merits. *In re Application of Comm. on the Judiciary*, 414 F. Supp. 3d 129, 137, 147, 182 (D.D.C. 2019), *aff'd*, 951 F.3d 589 (D.C. Cir. 2020), *cert. granted*, No. 19-1328, 2020 WL 3578680 (U.S. July 2, 2020). The November 2020 election of Joe Biden as President caused the House Judiciary Committee to seek a postponement of the argument. Kyle Cheney, *House Asks Supreme Court to Postpone Mueller Grand Jury Case*, POLITICO, Nov. 17, 2020, 1:23 PM, https://www.politico.com/news/2020/11/17/house-asks-scotus-postpone-mueller-case-437014?cid=apn.

Assuming that the Court were to decide the issue, how would it likely rule? How should it rule? Why?

Problems

16-5. Please incorporate the facts from Problem 16-1 above.

During the grand jury's deliberations in this case, Andrews gave a press conference during which he made the following statement:

> A federal grand jury has been convened to explore wrongdoing at the highest levels of city government. We have information from witnesses that the mayor has taken kickbacks in return for awarding city business to a political ally, which is a crime under state and federal law, including the federal mail fraud and RICO statutes. We will vigorously pursue this investigation, and see to it that those responsible are brought to justice.

The day after the news conference, a local newspaper reported that Andrews had decided to ask the grand jury to return an indictment charging the mayor with mail fraud and RICO based upon the alleged kickback scheme.

Two weeks after the newspaper report, the grand jury returned an indictment against Dern under the RICO statute and mail fraud statutes.

a. Argue for the defense that the government's conduct in this case was inappropriate, and for the prosecution that it was not.

b. Assuming that the government's conduct was not appropriate, what recourse should the defense seek? How should the government respond to the defense's request for a remedy?

16-6. Baker & Tyler, Inc. ("B & T"), a wholesale bookseller, allegedly engaged in fraudulent pricing practices. Prior to the criminal grand jury proceedings at issue, former B & T employees initiated a civil suit alleging that B & T fraudulently overcharged institutional customers, including federally funded libraries, in violation of the civil provisions of the False Claims Act. The government also conducted a parallel civil investigation, "under seal," to determine whether or not to intervene in the action. The Department of Justice then commenced a criminal investigation.

During the parallel investigations, members of the government's civil and criminal teams met to exchange information and discuss how to proceed in the criminal case. In the meantime, discovery in the civil case had been stayed due to motions unrelated to the criminal case. Upon this occurrence, the government then decided to convene a grand jury. Several subpoenas were issued to B & T seeking "all business documents" for the five years in question. This request encompassed many of the same documents that were requested in discovery in the civil case prior to the stay.

B & T has filed a motion to quash the subpoenas. How should the court rule? Why?

Chapter 17

Self-Incrimination — Witness Testimony and Document Production

A. Introductory Notes

Under the Fifth Amendment to the United States Constitution, "[n]o person . . . shall be compelled in any criminal case to be a witness against himself. . . ." The protection against compelled self-incrimination allows a witness to remain silent in the face of government questioning and, in certain circumstances, to decline to produce documents or other materials to the government. If the government determines that the witness's testimony or documents are critical to the investigation, the government may seek a grant of immunity pursuant to a court order compelling the testimony or production of the documents. The statutory provisions governing this procedure are found in 18 U.S.C. §§ 6001–6005.

The unique nature of white collar investigations frequently centers on documentary evidence and testimony, raising particularly complex Fifth Amendment issues. The witness can assert the privilege against self-incrimination when compelled to appear and give testimony before a grand jury, in a trial court, in a civil deposition, or before Congress. In order for the government to compel the testimony, it must first serve a subpoena *ad testificandum* for testimony or a subpoena *duces tecum* for documentary evidence. If the witness has a valid Fifth Amendment privilege claim, then the government must resort to other measures in order to gain the information. It is most likely that a witness will first confront the Fifth Amendment dilemma in a white collar investigation during the grand jury stage of the proceedings.

Individuals suspected of engaging in white collar criminal activity are often respected members of their business and professional communities and occupy positions of prominence. Because they wish to maintain their reputations, such persons often strongly desire to speak with government investigators in an effort to convince the government that they are not culpable. As a result, when this type of "storytelling" is offered to the prosecutor in an effort to persuade the government that there was no wrongdoing, testimonial and documentary matters of self-incrimination arise.

B. Testimony

1. Witnesses, Subjects, and Targets

Defense counsel representing witnesses, subjects, or targets before the grand jury have different concerns because not all persons appearing before the grand jury are equal.

A. Witnesses. A witness is simply an innocent person with information generally related to the matter under investigation. For example, a records custodian, a victim of a crime, or a federal investigative agent can each be a witness subpoenaed to appear before the grand jury panel. Counsel representing a witness called before the grand jury will have to ascertain whether that witness falls within the category of either subject or target.

B. Subjects. A subject is one about whom the grand jury seeks general information of a more specific nature, although not approaching the threshold of a potential defendant. A subject is a witness "whose conduct is within the scope of the grand jury's investigation." Dep't of Justice, U.S. Attorneys' Manual § 9-11.151. Advice of Rights of Grand Jury Witnesses. Subjects can sometimes turn into targets, and it is often as a result of the grand jury appearance that this transformation occurs. Some defense attorneys will allow a subject to appear, especially where the appearance will be beneficial in establishing the non-involvement of the witness and the potential to eliminate that person from the roster of those of interest to the government.

C. Targets. By way of comparison, a target is "a person as to whom the prosecutor or the grand jury has substantial evidence linking him or her to the commission of a crime and who, in the judgment of the prosecutor, is a putative defendant." *Id.* A target is one who is the focus of the investigation for purposes of an indictment. As a matter of sound defense practice, counsel should generally not allow a target to appear before a federal grand jury. In situations where the target requests the opportunity to testify before the grand jury to tell his or her side of the story, the government has no obligation to grant the request. However, the USAM cautions that failure to allow the testimony might give the appearance of unfairness, and the USAM encourages the granting of such requests. USAM § 9-11.152. There are many risks in such a strategy mainly because a witness appears before a grand jury without counsel present. Because there is no opportunity for examination by the witness's attorney, the witness can be questioned by the prosecutor without any opportunity to clarify the testimony. Further, the testimony will give the government both an opportunity to learn information that it otherwise might not possess and a transcribed record that can be used to impeach the witness at a later proceeding.

Note

The decision whether to speak with an investigator. For corporate employees who are subjects or targets of criminal investigations, the decision whether or not to speak to a government investigator can be especially difficult. Often, such employees must decide whether or not to cooperate without knowing the extent of the investigation and/or their own potential exposure. *See* Chapter 2, Corporate and Individual Liability, *supra*. Further, employees generally are not privy as to what evidence already exists. They may also risk loss of employment if they decide to assert the privilege and not cooperate. Speaking has its own perils, given that any statement made could be used against them at a future legal proceeding.

These are difficult and often coercive dilemmas for employees. The coercive pressure to cooperate was integral to the decision in the KPMG case, *United States v. Stein*, 541 F.3d 130 (2d Cir. 2008) (discussed in Ch. 15, Internal Investigations, Compliance Programs, and Deferred and Non-Prosecution Agreements, *supra*), where the court suppressed the statements on the ground that the government's aggressive tactics were responsible for the pressure that KPMG exerted on its employees.

2. Immunity

Whenever a witness is subpoenaed to appear before a grand jury (or at trial) and provide sworn testimony, counsel for the witness must consider the witness's status prior to the appearance. In situations where the witness has useful and potentially self-incriminating information and declines to testify on Fifth Amendment grounds, the government must first offer immunity to obtain such testimony.

There are two types of immunity: transactional and use/derivative use. Transactional immunity shields an individual from prosecution for any matter concerning the transaction about which the testimony relates. This immunity includes protection from prosecution even where the evidence on which a prosecution would be based is from a source wholly unrelated to the witness. Although some states provide for transactional immunity, the Supreme Court has held that use/derivative use immunity is all that the Fifth Amendment requires. *Kastigar v. United States*, 406 U.S. 441 (1972).

Transactional immunity is much broader than use/derivative use immunity because it grants the witness full immunity from prosecution for any crimes about which the witness testifies. The federal government has eliminated transactional immunity in favor of use/derivative use immunity, which protects a witness against any adverse governmental use of the immunized testimony or documents in subsequent proceedings. This form of immunity is codified in 18 U.S.C. § 6002–6003:

> [N]o testimony or other information compelled under the order (or any information directly or indirectly derived from such testimony or other information) may be used against the witness in any criminal case, except in a prosecution for perjury, giving a false statement, or otherwise failing to comply with the order.

18 U.S.C. § 6002.

Use/derivative use immunity allows the government to prosecute the witness if the government has an independent source for the information on which the prosecution is based. In *Kastigar*, the Court held that the Fifth Amendment only requires that the government provide use/derivative use immunity; this guarantees that nothing learned from the witness's own testimony can be used against the witness, but allows other, independent evidence to be used. 406 U.S. at 453–454.

When the government initiates an investigation, it does not always know at the outset what wrongdoing occurred and who was involved in the wrongdoing. The government must seek testimony of individuals to provide evidence that will assist in the development of the theory of the case. Many, if not most, of these witnesses will not have any valid Fifth Amendment rights to assert. They neither have any potential criminal exposure nor any reason to resist testifying. On the other hand, individuals more closely associated with the investigation certainly could have reason to hesitate before responding to a subpoena or making an appearance at the grand jury.

It is imperative for defense counsel who is representing a witness in receipt of a grand jury subpoena to ascertain that witness' status by contacting the prosecutor handling the investigation. If it is determined that the client is a subject or target and faces criminal exposure, then the best defense strategy is to secure a favorable deal for the client. There are many "deals" that can favor a witness, but the most favorable for a subject or target is to obtain immunity from prosecution.

In addition, issues arise when a litigant in a civil proceeding seeks to gain access to immunized testimony. These issues are addressed in the Chapter 18, Civil Actions, Civil Penalties, and Parallel Proceedings, *infra*.

3. Prosecuting the Immunized Witness

Although the Department of Justice is the entity most likely to seek immunity during the course of a criminal investigation, the legislative branch of government also has this power and can grant immunity in order to obtain testimony for Congressional hearings. Such was the case during the "Iran-Contra" investigation, which arose from the following facts. During President Reagan's first term in office, Congress supported covert activity by the Central Intelligence Agency to aid the military and paramilitary activities of a counter-revolutionary group in Nicaragua known as the Nicaraguan Contras. The President viewed the Contras as necessary to counter the communist-leaning government of Nicaragua. Congress eventually terminated the CIA's authority to assist the Contras, but the President deployed his national security advisor, Robert McFarlane, to assist the Contras. McFarlane recruited Lt. Col. Oliver North to coordinate the secret mission.

Later, the President undertook an effort to obtain the release of seven U.S. hostages who were being held in Lebanon. Despite the official position of non-negotiation with terrorists, the President dealt indirectly with the kidnappers to gain the release of the hostages. The United States sold arms to Iran, which was at that time at war with Iraq, and Iran then negotiated with the kidnappers for the release of the hostages. North and his colleagues secretly funneled money to the Contras by selling weapons to Iran and secretly diverting the excess profits through private Swiss bank accounts.

When these events were discovered, they led to a six-year investigation, including the appointment of an Independent Counsel, Congressional hearings, and multiple criminal prosecutions, all known as the "Iran-Contra" affair. Congressional immunity was granted to Lt. Col. Oliver North and others during the course of a Congressional investigation into matters that were simultaneously being investigated by the Independent Counsel.

Witnesses testified under a grant of immunity before Congress in a widely viewed national broadcast that spanned several weeks during the summer of 1987. The independent counsel unsuccessfully sought to have Congress delay the public testimony until after the filing of the criminal charges. Members of the Office of Independent Counsel avoided exposure to this immunized public testimony through a variety of extreme measures in order to remain "untainted." Attorneys who were subsequently hired (including Professor Sandra D. Jordan, one of the co-authors of this text), were exposed to this immunized testimony.

Despite the grant of immunity, the Independent Counsel prosecuted North and others. North was convicted and appealed. The decision below is one of the leading cases on the prosecution of a previously immunized witness. As you read the case, consider the competing policy concerns addressed by the majority and dissenting opinions.

United States v. North

910 F.2d 843 (D.C. Cir. 1990), *modified*, 920 F.2d 940 (D.C. Cir. 1990)

[In the first *North* decision, the D.C. Circuit held, *inter alia*, that the district court erred by failing to hold a full hearing to determine whether North's immunized testimony had in any way been used during his criminal trial. The court remanded the case to the district court to conduct a hearing required by *Kastigar v. United States*, 406 U.S. 441 (1972), "to ensure that the IC (Independent Counsel) made no use of North's immunized congressional testimony." After issuing its original order, the D.C. Circuit court granted the petition for rehearing and issued the ruling that follows.]

PER CURIAM:

In its petition for rehearing, the Independent Counsel ("IC") has raised several new issues regarding our original disposition. As we explain below, we believe that all but one of the IC's claims lack merit. We therefore grant in part and deny in part the petition for rehearing and modify our original opinion, accordingly.

I. Immunized Testimony at Trial

The IC claims that we misapplied *United States v. Rinaldi*, 808 F.2d 1579 (D.C. Cir. 1987), in remanding "for a massive inquiry into 'the taint of the testimony and the derivation of the testimony.'" Petition for Rehearing at 7–8 ("Pet. for Reh'g").

The IC's argument rests on the *ipse dixit* that "the prosecution's freedom from taint establishes that its evidence was necessarily derived independently" and therefore that the inquiry mandated by *Rinaldi* would be "superfluous." Pet. For Reh'g at 8. This bold proposition, however, would convert *Kastigar*'s total prohibition on use, *Kastigar v. United States*, 406 U.S. 441 (1973), to a mere ban on significant prosecutorial exposure to the immunized testimony. It simply does not follow that insulating prosecutors from exposure automatically proves that immunized testimony was not used against the defendant. *Kastigar* is instead violated whenever the prosecution puts on a witness whose testimony is shaped, directly or indirectly, by compelled testimony, regardless of *how or by whom* he was exposed to that compelled testimony. Were the rule otherwise, a private lawyer for a witness sympathetic to the government could listen to the compelled testimony and use it to prepare the witness for trial. The government would presumably thereby gain the advantage of use of the immunized testimony so long as it did not actually cooperate in that effort. This interpretation of *Kastigar* ("Look ma, no hands") pressed by the IC, if accepted, would enormously increase the risk of providing immunized testimony. To reject it, it is unnecessary to decide whether, as North asserts, particular significance should be placed on the fact that other government personnel in the legislative and executive branches outside the Independent Counsel's office were, after exposure to immunized testimony, actively involved in preparing witnesses.

Indeed, *Rinaldi* explicitly recognizes that witnesses' exposure to immunized testimony can taint their trial testimony irrespective of the prosecution's role in the exposure and that an inquiry is therefore necessary into whether the content of witnesses' testimony was derived from or motivated by the immunized testimony. It specifically mandates an inquiry into what a witness knew prior to exposure to the immunized testimony and what information she gleaned from that exposure. . . . And even where the witness testifies from personal knowledge, use within the meaning of *Kastigar* may occur, if the immunized testimony influenced the witness' decision to testify. . . . Our opinion is thus entirely consistent with *Rinaldi* in calling for an inquiry on remand into the content and circumstances of witnesses' testimony.

Our dissenting colleague does not disagree with us on this central point so vigorously disputed by the IC—that the content and circumstances of testimony given by a witness exposed to the defendant's immunized testimony may constitute "use" of the immunized testimony in violation of a defendant's constitutional rights regardless of the prosecutor's "fault." But she does contend that we have extended *Rinaldi* by insisting that the testimony of any witness exposed to the immunized testimony be "pre-recorded" in much the same way as prosecutors memorialize their investigative material, including witnesses' statements, so as to be able to prove in a *Kastigar* hearing that the government has obtained no leads from the immunized testimony. . . .

To be sure, if such steps are not taken, it may well be extremely difficult for the prosecutor to sustain its burden of proof that a witness exposed to immunized testimony has not shaped his or her testimony in light of the exposure, or as the *Rinaldi* court observed, been motivated to come forward and testify in light of the immunized testimony. But we surely did not mean to preclude the use of any techniques of which we are not aware, nor did we mean to even suggest that the prosecutor was barred from trying to show in any fashion that a witness' testimony was not influenced by the immunized testimony.

What we did insist upon, however—and here we quite definitely part company with the Chief Judge—is that the prosecutor has to *prove* that witnesses who testified against the defendant did not draw upon the immunized testimony to use it against the defendant; the burden of disproving use cannot, under *Kastigar*, be shifted onto the defendant, nor can the defendant be required to assume the burden of going forward with evidence that puts in issue the question of use. Most important, the defendant is entitled to a *hearing* at which he would be able to challenge the prosecution's case for non-use.

If the prosecutor were to demonstrate through testimony that a particular witness exposed to the immunized testimony had not been affected by the exposure, for example, by showing that the witness had set down his story before exposure, then the burden of going forward would shift to the defendant to challenge that version. . . .

The IC (and the district court) obviously wished to avoid cross-examination of the exposed witnesses. Some might convincingly testify that their exposure had no effect on their trial or grand jury testimony. Others might well testify that they simply were unable to determine just how much exposure affected their testimony, in which case that uncertainty would surely be a grave problem for the party with the burden of proof—the prosecutor.

Government officials are subject to greater restraints on their behavior than private individuals. The Ethics in Government Act requires the Department of Justice to cooperate with an Independent Counsel. Other executive departments are expected to cooperate with the Department of Justice, the chief law enforcement arm of the executive. Moreover, the IC presumably has the power to bring charges of obstruction of justice against anyone who attempts to sabotage the investigation. We are not aware that the Independent Counsel made any efforts to prevent government officials who were to testify or who had already testified from exposing themselves to immunized testimony. . . .

Finally, and perhaps at the heart of the dissent's concerns, is the argument that a straightforward application of *Kastigar* in cases where a witness testifies before Congress, after Congress grants immunity under section 6005, unduly restricts Congress' role in exposing wrongdoing in the nation—including wrongdoing in the executive branch. . . . We do not think Congress would be so naive as lightly to grant use immunity to such prospective defendants. Surely Congress does so only when its perception of the national interest justifies this extraordinary step. When Congress grants immunity before the prosecution has completed preparing its "case," the prosecutor, whoever that may be, can warn that the grant of immunity has its institutional costs; in this case, the IC indeed warned Congress that "any grant of use and derivative use immunity would create serious — and perhaps insurmountable — barriers to the prosecution of the immunized witness." Memorandum of the Independent Counsel Concerning Use Immunity (Jan. 13, 1987) [Submitted to the Joint Congressional Iran Contra Committee J.A. at 2502]. . . . The political needs of the majority, or Congress, or the President never, never, never, should trump an individual's explicit constitutional protections.

II. Immunized Testimony Before the Grand Jury

The IC renews its argument that presentation of immunized testimony to the grand jury is permissible and that *no* inquiry into whether the grand jury considered evidence based upon North's congressional testimony is therefore appropriate. . . . The IC thus continues to miss the fundamental distinction between the presentation to the grand jury of evidence that has previously been unconstitutionally obtained and that of constitutionally-obtained evidence whose exposure to the grand jury amounts to a constitutional violation in and of itself. . . .

[T]he prosecution obtains the immunized testimony legally, but only by promising that neither the testimony or information itself nor any information directly or indirectly derived from it will "be used against [the defendant] in any criminal case." 18 U.S.C. § 6002. And it is only this promise that compels the defendant to testify in spite of his constitutional privilege: "immunity from use and derivative use is coextensive with the scope of the privilege against self-incrimination . . . [because i]t prohibits the prosecutorial authorities from using the compelled testimony in *any* respect." *Kastigar*, 406 U.S. at 453 (emphasis in original). When the prosecution reneges on this constitutionally-mandated bargain and presents the immunized testimony to the grand jury, the constitutional violation is part and parcel of the grand jury process. The presentation — "use" — of the testimony is precisely the proscribed act. The issue is thus not one of "derivative use . . . by the grand jury" and of the exclusionary rule (indeed, any use of the testimony is *per se* excluded under the statute and *Kastigar*). Rather, the situation is no different than if the grand jury had itself forced the defendant to give incriminating answers and any indictment based upon immunized evidence is no less tainted.

[The court then held that a *Kastigar* hearing was required into the content and circumstances of any testimony given by witnesses who were exposed to the defendant's immunized testimony.]

WALD, CHIEF JUDGE, dissenting as to Parts I, II, & III:

In his petition for rehearing, the Independent Counsel ("IC") argues that the prohibitions of the use-immunity statute, 18 U.S.C. § 6002, do not extend to the government's use of witnesses who have independently exposed themselves to immunized testimony. Although the claim that the statute does not cover any such witness exposure is problematical, I do agree, as my earlier dissent reflects, that the statute does not require that independent witness exposure and prosecutorial exposure be treated identically for prophylactic purposes. Since, as the IC's petition forcefully points out, my colleagues' original opinion effectively transformed a limited use immunity into a sweeping transaction immunity, I would grant the IC's petition for rehearing on the *Kastigar* issue. By exalting form over substance, the original *per curiam* eviscerates both the use-immunity and independent-counsel statutes; its consequences for future cases of public import are ominous.

III. *Kastigar* Requirements

A. *The Problem with the Original Opinion*

The Supreme Court has recognized that use immunity is coextensive with the Fifth Amendment privilege. Accordingly, restrictions on the use of immunized testimony are exacting.

> [T]he prosecution [bears] the affirmative duty to prove that the evidence it proposes to use is derived from a legitimate source wholly independent of the compelled testimony.

Kastigar at 460.

This "very substantial protection," *id.* at 461, while reflecting the importance of the constitutional values at stake, was not meant to make the prosecution's burden an impossible one. The use-immunity statute makes a precise accommodation between the privilege against self-incrimination and the public's legitimate interest in securing testimony; use immunity thus exists in a delicate tension with the Fifth Amendment.

By mandating additional — and practically unattainable — requirements not found in *Kastigar* itself, my colleagues have upset this tension. They have rendered impossible in virtually all cases the prosecution of persons whose immunized testimony is of such national significance as to be the subject of congressional hearings and media coverage. In their opinions, my colleagues have ruled that *Kastigar* requires at least *four* distinct showings, only the first two of which can be derived from *Kastigar* itself. First, the prosecutors must demonstrate that they avoided "significant exposure" to the immunized testimony. Majority Opinion ("Maj. op.") at 860. Second, the prosecution must demonstrate that its identification and questioning of witnesses was based solely on "independent leads" — without the use of immunized testimony. Maj. op. at 863. Third — a new requirement, appearing for the first time in the opinion denying rehearing — the prosecution must demonstrate that the immunized testimony did not "*motivate*" its witnesses to testify. And fourth, the prosecution must demonstrate that the testimony of witnesses "exposed" to immunized matter has been "canned" by the prosecution before such exposure. Maj. op. at 872.

The last and most stringent of these requirements — that witness testimony be pre-recorded — is certainly an unwarranted departure from current law.

My colleagues invoke *United States v. Rinaldi*, 808 F.2d 1579 (D.C. Cir. 1987), to support that radical extension of current law. Yet *Rinaldi* does not even suggest that the witness' original knowledge need be or was pre-recorded. Instead, the *Rinaldi* court indicated a far more lenient rule of inevitable discovery — the prosecution need only show that "the police *would* inevitably have learned the [facts] from [the witness]." 808 F.2d at 1583 (emphasis supplied).

A uniform requirement of pre-recording witness knowledge in exquisite detail is unworkable. As even the greenest trial lawyer knows, the accrual of evidence is interactive — the statements of one witness often suggest new questions for earlier witnesses. Pre-recording of every line of every witness' trial testimony in every prosecution in which a defendant might publicly offer immunized testimony would ultimately prove unfeasible.

The consequences of a pre-recording requirement are both predictable and troubling. Prospective targets of grand juries in national scandals would line up to testify before Congress, in exchange for what is effectively transaction immunity. A requirement of "nonuse" would be converted into a guarantee of nonprosecution.

The majority is correct in noting that, if *Kastigar* is read only to apply to exposure of *prosecutors*, then "a private lawyer for a witness sympathetic to the government could listen to the compelled testimony and use it to prepare the witness." Opinion on Petition for Rehearing at 942. But it is also true that if *Kastigar* is read to require pre-recording of all government-witness testimony, then a witness *hostile* to the government could "listen to the compelled testimony and use it" to insulate himself from testifying.

There must be a middle ground, and I believe the case should be reheard (by the panel or *en banc*) to find it. The significance of these issues for the prosecution of future governmental scandals and for the effective functioning of separation of powers is too great to let the overreach of the original opinion (or my colleagues' undefined backtracking) stand.

Notes and Questions

1. *Tainted prosecutors.* Courts enforce the *Kastigar* holding anytime that an individual previously protected under use and derivative use immunity is indicted in the same or a related matter. At the *Kastigar* hearing, the government bears the burden of showing that its case was not tainted in any way by the earlier immunized testimony. As the *North* case demonstrates, this is an extremely high burden.

Ultimately, individuals in the *North* case were deemed "tainted" in the following situations: those who had watched some or all of the immunized testimony; individuals exposed to news stories; and members of the public who did not take extraordinary steps to protect against exposure to immunized testimony. For example, Professor Jordan watched, along with the majority of the country, the congressional hearings some nine months before she joined the Independent Counsel's prosecution team. This broad category of "tainted" individuals ultimately includes potential witnesses for the prosecution who were under no obligation to avert their eyes and ears from the immunized testimony.

Given the court's ruling, what can a prosecutor's office do to maintain the separation of material gathered pursuant to an order of immunity? *See* Sandra D. Jordan, *Classified Information and Conflicts: Balancing the Scales of Justice After Iran-Contra*, 91 COLUM. L. REV. 1651 (1991).

2. *Immunity and other witness benefits.* Use/derivative use immunity is not the only benefit available to a witness. Other advantageous bargains include transactional immunity, cooperation agreements, informal immunity, dismissal of charges, sentencing recommendations, and outright declination of the prosecution.

One famous witness to whom the government granted full transactional immunity was Monica Lewinsky, whose affair with President Bill Clinton was a key component of the Office of Independent Counsel's investigation into alleged wrongdoing by Clinton and the subsequent impeachment proceedings. *See* Don Van Natta Jr. & John M. Broder, *Lewinsky, Given Immunity, Reportedly Agrees to Tell of Pact with Clinton to Lie*, N.Y. TIMES, July 29, 1998, https://archive.nytimes.com/www.nytimes .com/library/politics/072998clinton-starr.html (describing the "OIC's grant of full transactional immunity from prosecution"). Why did the OIC go to this extraordinary length to encourage Lewinsky's cooperation, do you think?

3. *DOJ procedures for prosecuting an immunized witness.* The United States Department of Justice has imposed strict procedures for situations where it is considering prosecution of an immunized witness. Although § 6002 immunity suggests the possibility of prosecuting an immunized witness, the United States Attorneys' Manual provides additional safeguards beyond the simple fact of the origin of the "independent evidence." U.S. Department of Justice, U.S.A.M. § 9-23.400. In addition to written authorization from the Attorney General, the prosecutor must "indicate the circumstances justifying prosecution and the method by which the government will be able to establish that the evidence it will use against the witness will meet the government's burden under *Kastigar v. United States.*" *Id.*

4. *Statements obtained by foreign authorities.* What if the compelled testimony occurred outside the United States? Do the *Kastigar* protections apply? In *United States v. Allen*, 864 F.3d 63 (2d Cir. 2017), the defendant had given testimony compelled by a foreign government authority in a financial fraud investigation conducted jointly with U.S. authorities. Before testifying at the defendant's trial, a witness reviewed the defendant's compelled testimony. The defendant was convicted.

The Second Circuit reversed the conviction and dismissed the case on Fifth Amendment grounds. The court found that *Kastigar*'s prohibition of use/derivative use evidence applies to testimony obtained by a foreign governmental authority. The court further found that the government had failed to meet its burden of proving that the witness's testimony was untainted by the defendant's compelled statement, and that the error was not harmless.

What is the significance of this holding? Commentators have suggested that it may be substantial:

The implications of the [*Allen*] decision are potentially far-reaching. In today's interconnected world, DOJ prosecutors often work hand-in-hand with foreign governments on joint investigations probing everything from financial frauds to suspected money laundering activities to violations of the Foreign Corrupt Practices Act. When foreign governments engage in questioning of potential suspects and compel those suspects to answer questions — as is permissible in many jurisdictions — DOJ prosecutors will have to establish procedures to ensure that the compelled testimony does not taint their case.

The *Allen* opinion demonstrates that avoiding such taint may be nearly impossible in many situations. Although the use of actual compelled statements can be avoided, witnesses, investigators, and prosecutors may be tainted by their exposure to information obtained in such a manner. . . .

This far-reaching decision turns cross-border investigative partnerships into a minefield for U.S. prosecutors.

Robert Anello, *Second Circuit Sends Shivers Down DOJ's Spine: Compelled Foreign Testimony Invalidates Prosecution*, FORBES, July 20, 2017, https://www.forbes.com /sites/insider/2017/07/20/second-circuit-sends-shivers-down-dojs-spine-compelled -foreign-testimony-invalidates-prosecution/?sh=12e1db9451f0.

Was this the correct outcome? Does the decision impose serious limitations on the ability of the U.S. government to conduct such joint investigations? If so, is there a remedy?

Problems

17-1. The defendant, an FBI agent, was charged with knowingly and willfully making a materially false statement on his federal disclosure report (DR) regarding gifts given to him by a cooperating witness. Because of his position in the FBI, the defendant was responsible for training other agents on the impropriety of accepting gifts in connection with their official duties. The defendant allegedly received several free trips to Las Vegas provided by a cooperating witness, and these trips were not reported on his annual DR.

In an internal government investigation, the lead investigator obtained a statement that the defendant had been compelled to give during a hearing "in an unrelated administrative investigation." In this unrelated statement, the defendant was under oath and was advised that none of the information obtained via the statement could be used against him in a later criminal or administrative proceeding. In the statement, the defendant described his role in "advising the other agents about the propriety of accepting free gifts."

The pertinent timeline shows the following:

- Defendant completed the DR in December 00.

- Defendant gave the statement in the administrative hearing in February 01.

- The investigation into the false statements in the DR was initiated in July 01.

- That July, the investigator requested a copy of the February statement.

- For a period of a year after the investigator requested the February statement, the investigator interviewed witnesses, reviewed the financial documentation supporting the Las Vegas trips, and began to construct a case theory.

- After this year-long investigation, the investigator received the copy of the February 01 statement in July 02. The investigator read the file of the administrative investigation and sent an email summarizing its contents to other investigators in the office. One of them replied, "Thanks. Have we looked for other instances where defendant gave advice on free gifts?"

- Two months later, in September 02, the investigator presented the case to the United States Attorney's Office for possible prosecution. The defendant was indicted the following month.

The defendant has filed a motion for a *Kastigar* hearing, which the court granted.

a. You represent the defendant. What specific questions do you ask your client in preparation for the Kastigar *hearing? What legal standard must you meet to be successful?*

b. You are the Assistant U. S. Attorney assigned to this case. After interviewing the chief investigative agent, what questions do you ask the agent in preparation for the Kastigar *hearing? Are there any other witnesses you should interview? What legal standard must you meet to be successful?*

c. Argue both the defense and government positions at the hearing.

d. How should the court rule? Why?

17-2. You represent a defendant who is serving five years of probation for possessing child pornography in violation of federal law. One of the conditions of his probation was that he submit to periodic and random polygraph examinations. Defendant raised a Fifth Amendment challenge, but the judge ruled that he had to submit to the polygraph on the ground that he was not entitled to immunity before he made incriminating statements. Defendant refused to submit to the polygraph without a grant of immunity, and the court revoked his probation.

Defendant appeals. What arguments should the defendant make? How should the government respond? How should the court rule? Why?

17-3. Robert is a real-estate agent who was involved in real-estate transactions with members of a real-estate fraud scheme. The United States Attorney wrote a letter to Robert's attorney granting Robert "informal immunity" for his testimony regarding the scheme. Robert was interviewed by the U.S. Attorney's office on two occasions, after which the government decided to seek formal use/derivative use immunity for

Robert and to call him to testify before the grand jury. Robert then testified before the grand jury.

One year later, the government is considering charging Robert with bank fraud, mail fraud, and money laundering in connection with the real-estate fraud scheme. The U.S. Attorney sought the authority to prosecute from the Department of Justice, providing a summary of the immunized grand jury testimony and stating that the government believed that Robert testified falsely. The government did not have sufficient evidence to prosecute Robert for perjury. The U.S. Attorney's office listed several independent sources from which it received evidence that Robert was involved in criminal activity in connection with the fraud scheme:

> a. Testimony from several of the fraud scheme leaders indicating that Robert had aided them in fraudulently purchasing real estate.

> b. Documents obtained from Robert after he testified under immunity as to their existence.

> c. Testimony from Robert's wife that ever since Robert appeared before the grand jury, she has suspected that Robert was involved in criminal activity because she heard him make incriminating statements on the phone.

> d. Testimony from Robert's assistant, whose identity was revealed by Robert's testimony before the grand jury.

Assume that you work for the Department of Justice and must approve the prosecution. Would you do so? Why or why not?

C. Documents

Because of the nature of white collar criminal investigations, the wrongdoing is frequently proven through documents. The paper trail often establishes both the mens rea and the actus reus. The money trail might be found in financial institution documents as well as business and personal records. Thus, an issue of critical importance in these types of paper investigations is the proper handling and production of documents, especially where the production of the documents can be incriminating.

Business records often provide critical evidence to prosecutors in a white collar case. Because the Fifth Amendment does not extend to artificial entities like corporations, there are no legitimate objections to the production of corporate documents pursuant to the grand jury subpoena. When a subpoena is served on the corporation for documents, the corporation must comply with the subpoena absent some other legal objection. Once a grand jury subpoena is properly issued to the holder of the records, the custodian must come forth and produce the records to the grand jury. A custodian of records can typically be an employee insulated from any allegations of criminal wrongdoing and, as a result, such subpoena *duces tecum* sparks no personal Fifth Amendment concerns. Examples of these types of witnesses are bank employees or corporate employees who work in the records divisions.

———————

As the next case shows, the question takes on a different character when the grand jury subpoena seeks the records of a sole proprietor who has a personal Fifth Amendment claim.

United States v. Doe

465 U.S. 605 (1984)

JUSTICE POWELL delivered the opinion of the Court.

This case presents the issue whether, and to what extent, the Fifth Amendment privilege against compelled self-incrimination applies to the business records of a sole proprietorship.

Respondent is the owner of several sole proprietorships. In late 1980, a grand jury, during the course of an investigation of corruption in the awarding of county and municipal contracts, served five subpoenas on respondent. The first two demanded the production of the telephone records of several of respondent's companies and all records pertaining to four bank accounts of respondent and his companies. The subpoenas were limited to the period between January 1, 1977 and the dates of the subpoenas. The third subpoena demanded the production of a list of virtually all the business records of one of respondent's companies for the period between January 1, 1976, and the date of the subpoena. The fourth subpoena sought production of a similar list of business records belonging to another company. The final subpoena demanded production of all bank statements and cancelled checks of two of respondent's companies that had accounts at a bank in the Grand Cayman Islands.

Respondent filed a motion in Federal District Court seeking to quash the subpoenas. The District Court for the District of New Jersey granted his motion except with respect to those documents and records required by law to be kept or disclosed to a public agency. In reaching its decision, the District Court noted that the Government had conceded that the materials sought in the subpoena were or might be incriminating. The court stated that, therefore, "the relevant inquiry is . . . whether the *act* of producing the documents has communicative aspects which warrant Fifth Amendment protection." *In re Grand Jury Empaneled March 19, 1980*, 541 F. Supp. 1, 3 (D.C.N.J. 1981). The court found that the act of production would compel respondent to "admit that the records exist, that they are in his possession, and that they are authentic." While not ruling out the possibility that the Government could devise a way to ensure that the act of turning over the documents would not incriminate respondent, the court held that the Government had not made such a showing.

The Court of Appeals for the Third Circuit affirmed. It first addressed the question whether the Fifth Amendment ever applies to the records of a sole proprietorship. After noting that an individual may not assert the Fifth Amendment privilege on behalf of a corporation, partnership, or other collective entity, the Court of Appeals reasoned that the owner of a sole proprietorship acts in a personal rather than a representative capacity. As a result, the court held that respondent's claim of the privilege was not foreclosed.

The Court of Appeals next considered whether the documents at issue in this case are privileged. The court noted that the contents of business records ordinarily are not privileged because they are created voluntarily and without compulsion. The Court of Appeals nevertheless found that respondent's business records were privileged under either of two analyses. First, the court reasoned that, the business records of a sole proprietorship are no different from the individual owner's personal records. Noting that Third Circuit cases had held that private papers, although created voluntarily, are protected by the Fifth Amendment, the court accorded the same protection to respondent's business papers. Second, it held that respondent's act of producing the subpoenaed records would have "communicative aspects of its own." *In re Grand Jury Empaneled March 19, 1980*, 680 F.2d 327, 335 (3d Cir. 1982). The turning over of the subpoenaed documents to the grand jury would admit their existence and authenticity. Accordingly, respondent was entitled to assert his Fifth Amendment privilege rather than produce the subpoenaed documents.

The Government contended that the court should enforce the subpoenas because of the Government's offer not to use respondent's act of production against respondent in any way. The Court of Appeals noted that no formal request for use immunity under 18 U.S.C. §§ 6002 and 6003 had been made. In light of this failure, the court held that the District Court did not err in rejecting the Government's attempt to compel delivery of the subpoenaed records.

We granted certiorari to resolve the apparent conflict between the Court of Appeals holding and the reasoning underlying this Court's holding in *Fisher v. United States*, 425 U.S. 391 (1976). We now affirm in part, reverse in part, and remand for further proceedings.

The Court in *Fisher* expressly declined to reach the question whether the Fifth Amendment privilege protects the contents of an individual's tax records in his possession. The rationale underlying our holding in that case is, however, persuasive here. As we noted in *Fisher*, the Fifth Amendment protects the person asserting the privilege only from *compelled* self-incrimination. 425 U.S. at 396. Where the preparation of business records is voluntary, no compulsion is present.[8] A subpoena that demands production of documents "does not compel oral testimony; nor would it

---

8. Respondent's principal argument is that the Fifth Amendment should be read as creating a "zone of privacy which protects an individual and his personal records from compelled production." Brief for Respondent 15. This argument derives from language in Boyd v. United States, 116 U.S. 616 (1886). This Court addressed substantially the same argument in *Fisher*:

> Within the limits imposed by the language of the Fifth Amendment, which we necessarily observe, the privilege truly serves privacy interests; but the Court has never on any ground, personal privacy included, applied the Fifth Amendment to prevent the

ordinarily compel the taxpayer to restate, repeat, or affirm the truth of the contents of the documents sought." *Id.* at 409. Applying this reasoning in *Fisher*, we stated:

> [T]he Fifth Amendment would not be violated by the fact alone that the papers on their face might incriminate the taxpayer, for the privilege protects a person only against being incriminated by his own compelled testimonial communications. *The accountant's workpapers are not the taxpayer's. They were not prepared by the taxpayer, and they contain no testimonial declarations by him. Furthermore, as far as this record demonstrates, the preparation of all of the papers sought in these cases was wholly voluntary, and they cannot be said to contain compelled testimonial evidence, either of the taxpayers or of anyone else. The taxpayer cannot avoid compliance with the subpoena merely by asserting that the item of evidence which he is required to produce contains incriminating writing, whether his own or that of someone else.*

Id. at 409–410.

This reasoning applies with equal force here. Respondent does not contend that he prepared the documents involuntarily or that the subpoena would force him to restate, repeat, or affirm the truth of their contents. The fact that the records are in respondent's possession is irrelevant to the determination of whether the creation of the records was compelled. We therefore hold that the contents of those records are not privileged.

Although the contents of a document may not be privileged, the act of producing the document may be. A government subpoena compels the holder of the document to perform an act that may have testimonial aspects and an incriminating effect.

In *Fisher*, the Court explored the effect that the act of production would have on the taxpayer and determined that the act of production would have only minimal testimonial value and would not operate to incriminate the taxpayer. Unlike the Court in *Fisher*, we have the explicit finding of the District Court that the act of producing the documents would involve testimonial self-incrimination. The Court of Appeals agreed. We therefore decline to overturn the finding of the District Court in this regard, where, as here, it has been affirmed by the Court of Appeals.

The Government, as it concedes, could have compelled respondent to produce the documents listed in the subpoena. Sections 6002 and 6003 of Title 18 provide for the granting of use immunity with respect to the potentially incriminating evidence. The Court upheld the constitutionality of the use immunity statute in *Kastigar v. United States*, 406 U.S. 441 (1972).

---

otherwise proper acquisition or use of evidence which, in the Court's view, did not involve compelled testimonial self-incrimination of some sort.
425 U.S. at 399.

The Government did state several times before the District Court that it would not use respondent's act of production against him in any way. But counsel for the Government never made a statutory request to the District Court to grant respondent use immunity. We are urged to adopt a doctrine of constructive use immunity. Under this doctrine, the courts would impose a requirement on the Government not to use the incriminatory aspects of the act of production against the person claiming the privilege even though the statutory procedures have not been followed.

We decline to extend the jurisdiction of courts to include prospective grants of use immunity in the absence of the formal request that the statute requires. . . . The decision to seek use immunity necessarily involves a balancing of the Government's interest in obtaining information against the risk that immunity will frustrate the Government's attempts to prosecute the subject of the investigation. Congress expressly left this decision exclusively to the Justice Department. If, on remand, the appropriate official concludes that it is desirable to compel respondent to produce his business records, the statutory procedure for requesting use immunity will be available.

We conclude that the Court of Appeals erred in holding that the contents of the subpoenaed documents were privileged under the Fifth Amendment. The act of producing the documents at issue in this case is privileged and cannot be compelled without a statutory grant of use immunity pursuant to 18 U.S.C. §§ 6002 and 6003. The judgment of the Court of Appeals is, therefore, affirmed in part, reversed in part, and the case is remanded to the District Court for further proceedings in accordance with this decision.

It is so ordered.

JUSTICE O'CONNOR, concurring. [Omitted.]

JUSTICE MARSHALL, with JUSTICE BRENNAN joins, concurring in part and dissenting in part. [Omitted.]

JUSTICE STEVENS, concurring in part and dissenting in part. [Omitted.]

Notes and Questions

1. *Delivery of records.* If John Doe had given the records to another individual to deliver to the grand jury, could the issue that concerned the Court have been avoided? Why or why not?

2. *Immunity guarantees.* During the oral argument, the Court questioned the government as to why it never requested the official use immunity pursuant to the statutory authority. The government "gave no plausible explanation," but simply promised that the documents would not be used against Doe after production. Why is this guarantee insufficient?

3. *Collective entity doctrine.* The United States Supreme Court has developed the "collective entity" rule, under which corporations and other collective entities are treated differently from individuals for Fifth Amendment purposes. *See Braswell*

v. United States 487 U.S. 99 (1988). In *Amato v. United States*, 450 F.3d 46 (1st Cir. 2006), the court established the rule in the First Circuit for the collective entity doctrine and its application to a corporation consisting of only one person. In *Amato*, the defendant was the "sole shareholder, director, officer and employee" of two corporations. *Id.* at 47. The U.S. Attorney's office served subpoenas on Amato for the corporation's records because he was the "records custodian." *Id.* at 47–48. The defendant moved to quash the subpoenas, arguing "that the act-of-production doctrine protects production of the records because the testimonial aspects of the production would incriminate him." *Id.* He asserted that the "collective-entity doctrine" did not apply to his case because "a footnote in *Braswell v. United States*, 487 U.S. 99 (1988) . . . left open the question of whether the collective-entity doctrine would apply if the custodian of corporate records is 'able to establish, by showing for example that he is the sole employee and officer of the corporation, that the jury would inevitably conclude that he produced the records.'" *Id.* at 48. *Braswell* held that "[a] corporation does not enjoy the privilege against self-incrimination guaranteed by the Fifth Amendment, as the privilege is a personal privilege enjoyed by natural individuals." *Id.* at 49. The magistrate judge refused to accept Amato's argument because "the First Circuit has rejected such an exception" and "*Braswell*'s footnote does not contradict the First Circuit's holdings." *Id.* at 48. The district court upheld the magistrate judge's decision. *Id.* at 49.

The First Circuit did not find the footnote in *Braswell* to be controlling and instead relied on its holding in *In re Grand Jury Proceedings (The John Doe Company, Inc.)*, 838 F.2d 624 (1st Cir. 1988). *Amato*, 450 F.3d at 51. In *John Doe Company*, the First Circuit held that "the act-of-production doctrine is not an exception to the collective-entity doctrine even when the corporate custodian is the corporation's sole shareholder, officer and employee." 838 F.2d at 627 n.3. *John Doe* held that "'production, including implied authentication, can be required of a corporation through a corporate officer regardless of the potential for self-incrimination.'" *Amato*, 450 F.3d at 52 (quoting *John Doe Company*, 838 F.2d at 626). Even though Amato was the sole employee and officer of the corporation, he still did not qualify for an "act of production" exception to the "collective-entity" doctrine. *Id.* at 51.

The Second Circuit reached a similar conclusion in *In re Grand Jury Subpoena Issued June 18, 2009*, 593 F.3d 155, 158 (2d Cir. 2010). The court held that there "simply is no situation in which a corporation can avail itself of the Fifth Amendment privilege." *Id.* at 158 (internal quotations and citations omitted). The court noted that "every other court to have considered this issue has reached the same conclusion for largely the same reasons." *Id.* at 159.

4. *The personal-corporate distinction.* Document gathering, processing, and review are inherent in any complex white collar criminal investigation. Because corporations act through their agents, it is critical to determine whether the documents in the possession of a person are corporate or personal documents when those documents are sought by a grand jury. This distinction is important because the corporation has no Fifth Amendment protection for its documents, while an individual

might be able to assert such privilege. Thus, a corporate employee in possession of subpoenaed documents faces a dilemma. The corporate custodian might be incriminated in the act of producing corporate documents.

Although the Supreme Court held that the content of voluntarily produced documents is not protected, because the documents themselves are not testimonial, *Fisher v. United States*, 425 U.S. 391 (1976), the "act of producing evidence in response to a subpoena nevertheless has communicative aspects of its own, wholly aside from the contents of the papers produced." *Id.* at 410. When addressing the question of whether the documents are personal or corporate, courts consider several factors: the purpose of the document; who produced the document; whether the document was necessary or incidental in the corporation's business; and who has possession of the document. *Bellis v. United States*, 417 U.S. 85, 92 (1974).

5. *Adverse inference against the corporation.* Statements made by an employee concerning matters within the scope of employment are vicarious admissions of a corporation under Federal Rule of Evidence 801(d)(2)(D). The vicarious relationship justifies informing the jury of the assertion of the privilege. When employees assert their individual Fifth Amendment privilege, in any subsequent civil action the jury can draw an adverse inference against the corporation based on the employee's assertion of privilege. This adverse inference, while not absolute, can be devastating and powerful when viewed by a jury. *See Brink's Inc. v. City of New York*, 717 F.2d 700, 707 (2d Cir. 1983) (involving company employees who asserted their Fifth Amendment privilege against self-incrimination at trial and did not testify; the judge instructed the jurors that they could assume that had the employees testified the testimony would have been adverse to the interests of the corporation).

Problems

17-4. You represent a real-estate firm, Howdy Real Estate, with one local office in your town, and the firm's owner, Howdy. The firm is a sole proprietorship and you discover that the government is investigating the illegal funneling of monies through certain bank accounts in a widespread money laundering scheme.

Federal authorities serve a grand jury subpoena on the office receptionist requesting that records for the previous three fiscal years be produced for the grand jury. Howdy's wife Happy is the receptionist for the firm. There are no more employees in the office because all of the other real-estate agents are independent contractors and maintain their offices in their homes.

You oppose the production of these business records. What motion do you file and what legal basis do you offer for your opposition?

17-5. Your motion has been denied. You now face the prospect of having Howdy or Happy appear before the grand jury with the records.

What other steps can you take to protect your client? Does your answer depend on whether Howdy or his wife appears with the records? Why or why not?

17-6. Regardless of how you analyzed question 17.5, your client is now ready to make the appearance before the grand jury. You know that you cannot accompany him into the grand jury room.

What precautions do you take to fully represent him at this critical stage of the investigation?

The next case involves the Whitewater investigation. Twenty years before President Bill Clinton was elected, he and Hillary Clinton joined a partnership with James and Susan McDougal called the Whitewater Development Corp. The partnership purchased 220 acres of land in Arkansas. James McDougal owned a savings and loan association that became insolvent in the 1980s as a result of a series of fraudulent loans. As a law firm partner of Webster Hubbell, Hillary Clinton performed legal services for the savings and loan.

During the 1980s, there were investigations of many savings and loan failures. The McDougals were both found guilty of fraud. An independent counsel, Kenneth Starr, was appointed, and the Whitewater investigation grew to include the Clintons' financial and legal activities associated with the savings and loan as well as the Clintons' response to questions about the transactions and improprieties in the White House travel office. The next case arose from the Whitewater investigation, and centers on document production and the Fifth Amendment privilege against self-incrimination.

United States v. Hubbell

530 U.S. 27 (2000)

JUSTICE STEVENS delivered the opinion of the Court.

The two questions presented concern the scope of a witness' protection against compelled self-incrimination: (1) whether the Fifth Amendment privilege protects a witness from being compelled to disclose the existence of incriminating documents that the Government is unable to describe with reasonable particularity; and (2) if the witness produces such documents pursuant to a grant of immunity, whether 18 U.S.C. §6002 prevents the Government from using them to prepare criminal charges against him.

This proceeding arises out of the second prosecution of respondent, Webster Hubbell, commenced by the Independent Counsel appointed in August 1994 to investigate possible violations of federal law relating to the Whitewater Development Corporation. The first prosecution was terminated pursuant to a plea bargain. In December 1994, respondent pleaded guilty to charges of mail fraud and tax evasion arising out of his billing practices as a member of an Arkansas law firm from 1989 to 1992, and was sentenced to 21 months in prison. In the plea agreement, respondent promised to provide the Independent Counsel with "full, complete, accurate, and truthful information" about matters relating to the Whitewater investigation.

The second prosecution resulted from the Independent Counsel's attempt to determine whether respondent had violated that promise. In October 1996, while respondent was incarcerated, the Independent Counsel served him with a subpoena *duces tecum* calling for the production of 11 categories of documents before a grand jury sitting in Little Rock, Arkansas. On November 19, he appeared before the grand jury and invoked his Fifth Amendment privilege against self-incrimination. In response to questioning by the prosecutor, respondent initially refused "to state whether there are documents within my possession, custody, or control responsive to the Subpoena." Thereafter, the prosecutor produced an order, which had previously been obtained from the District Court pursuant to 18 U.S.C. §6003(a) directing him to respond to the subpoena and granting him immunity "to the extent allowed by law." Respondent then produced 13,120 pages of documents and records and responded to a series of questions that established that those were all of the documents in his custody or control that were responsive to the commands in the subpoena, with the exception of a few documents he claimed were shielded by the attorney-client and attorney work-product privileges.

The contents of the documents produced by respondent provided the Independent Counsel with the information that led to this second prosecution. On April 30, 1998, a grand jury in the District of Columbia returned a 10-count indictment charging respondent with various tax-related crimes and mail and wire fraud. The District Court dismissed the indictment relying, in part, on the ground that the Independent Counsel's use of the subpoenaed documents violated §6002 because all of the evidence he would offer against respondent at trial derived either directly or indirectly from the testimonial aspects of respondent's immunized act of producing those documents. . . .

The Court of Appeals vacated the judgment and remanded for further proceedings. The majority concluded that the District Court had incorrectly relied on the fact that the Independent Counsel did not have prior knowledge of the contents of the subpoenaed documents. The question the District Court should have addressed was the extent of the Government's independent knowledge of the documents' existence and authenticity, and of respondent's possession or control of them. It explained:

> On remand, the district court should hold a hearing in which it seeks to establish the extent and detail of the [G]overnment's knowledge of Hubbell's financial affairs (or of the paperwork documenting it) on the day the subpoena issued. It is only then that the court will be in a position to assess the testimonial value of Hubbell's response to the subpoena. Should the Independent Counsel prove capable of demonstrating with reasonable particularity a prior awareness that the exhaustive litany of documents sought in the subpoena existed and were in Hubbell's possession, then the wide distance evidently traveled from the subpoena to the substantive allegations contained in the indictment would be based upon legitimate intermediate steps. To the extent that the information conveyed through Hubbell's

compelled act of production provides the necessary linkage, however, the indictment deriving therefrom is tainted.

United States v. Hubbell, 167 F.3d 552, 581 (D.C. Cir. 1999).

In the opinion of the dissenting judge, the majority failed to give full effect to the distinction between the contents of the documents and the limited testimonial significance of the act of producing them. In his view, as long as the prosecutor could make use of information contained in the documents or derived therefrom without any reference to the fact that respondent had produced them in response to a subpoena, there would be no improper use of the testimonial aspect of the immunized act of production. In other words, the constitutional privilege and the statute conferring use immunity would only shield the witness from the use of any information resulting from his subpoena response "beyond what the prosecutor would receive if the documents appeared in the grand jury room or in his office unsolicited and unmarked, like manna from heaven." *In re Minarik*, 166 F.3d 591, 602 (3d Cir. 1999).

On remand, the Independent Counsel acknowledged that he could not satisfy the "reasonable particularity" standard prescribed by the Court of Appeals and entered into a conditional plea agreement with respondent. In essence, the agreement provides for the dismissal of the charges unless this Court's disposition of the case makes it reasonably likely that respondent's "act [of] production immunity" would not pose a significant bar to his prosecution. The case is not moot, however, because the agreement also provides for the entry of a guilty plea and a sentence that will not include incarceration if we should reverse and issue an opinion that is sufficiently favorable to the Government to satisfy that condition. . . . We now affirm.

It is useful to preface our analysis of the constitutional issue with a restatement of certain propositions that are not in dispute. The term "privilege against self-incrimination" is not an entirely accurate description of a person's constitutional protection against being "compelled in any criminal case to be a witness against himself."

More relevant to this case is the settled proposition that a person may be required to produce specific documents even though they contain incriminating assertions of fact or belief because the creation of those documents was not "compelled" within the meaning of the privilege. Our decision in *Fisher v. United States*, 425 U.S. 371 (1976), dealt with summonses issued by the Internal Revenue Service (IRS) seeking working papers used in the preparation of tax returns. Because the papers had been voluntarily prepared prior to the issuance of the summonses, they could not be "said to contain compelled testimonial evidence, either of the taxpayers or of anyone else." Accordingly, the taxpayer could not "avoid compliance with the subpoena merely by asserting that the item of evidence which he is required to produce contains incriminating writing, whether his own or that of someone else." 425 U.S. at 409–10. It is clear, therefore, that respondent Hubbell could not avoid compliance with the subpoena served on him merely because the demanded documents contained incriminating evidence, whether written by others or voluntarily prepared by himself.

On the other hand, we have also made it clear that the act of producing documents in response to a subpoena may have a compelled testimonial aspect. We have held that "the act of production" itself may implicitly communicate "statements of fact." By "producing documents in compliance with a subpoena, the witness would admit that the papers existed, were in his possession or control, and were authentic." *United States v. Doe*, 465 U.S. 605, 613 (1984). Moreover, as was true in this case, when the custodian of documents responds to a subpoena, he may be compelled to take the witness stand and answer questions designed to determine whether he has produced everything demanded by the subpoena. . . .

Finally, the phrase "in any criminal case" in the text of the Fifth Amendment might have been read to limit its coverage to compelled testimony that is used against the defendant in the trial itself. It has, however, long been settled that its protection encompasses compelled statements that lead to the discovery of incriminating evidence even though the statements themselves are not incriminating and are not introduced into evidence. . . .

Compelled testimony that communicates information that may "lead to incriminating evidence" is privileged even if the information itself is not inculpatory. *Doe v. United States*, 487 U.S. 201, 208 n.6 (1988). It is the Fifth Amendment's protection against the prosecutor's use of incriminating information derived directly or indirectly from the compelled testimony of the respondent that is of primary relevance in this case.

Acting pursuant to 18 U.S.C. §6002, the District Court entered an order compelling respondent to produce "any and all documents" described in the grand jury subpoena and granting him "immunity to the extent allowed by law." In *Kastigar v. United States*, 406 U.S. 441 (1972), we upheld the constitutionality of §6002 because the scope of the "use and derivative-use" immunity that it provides is coextensive with the scope of the constitutional privilege against self-incrimination. . . .

We also rejected the petitioners' argument that derivative-use immunity under §6002 would not obviate the risk that the prosecutor or other law enforcement officials may use compelled testimony to obtain leads, names of witnesses, or other information not otherwise available to support a prosecution. That argument was predicated on the incorrect assumption that the derivative-use prohibition would prove impossible to enforce. But given that the statute contains a "comprehensive safeguard" in the form of a "sweeping proscription of any use, direct or indirect, of the compelled testimony and any information derived therefrom," we concluded that a person who is prosecuted for matters related to testimony he gave under a grant of immunity does not have the burden of proving that his testimony was improperly used. Instead, we held that the statute imposes an affirmative duty on the prosecution, not merely to show that its evidence is not tainted by the prior testimony, but "to prove that the evidence it proposes to use is derived from a legitimate source wholly independent of the compelled testimony." 406 U.S. at 460. Requiring the prosecution to shoulder this burden ensures that the grant of immunity has "le[ft] the witness and the Federal Government in substantially the same position as if the witness had claimed his privilege in the absence of a grant of immunity." 406 U.S. at 458–59.

The "compelled testimony" that is relevant in this case is not to be found in the contents of the documents produced in response to the subpoena. It is, rather, the testimony inherent in the act of producing those documents. The disagreement between the parties focuses entirely on the significance of that testimonial aspect.

The Government correctly emphasizes that the testimonial aspect of a response to a subpoena *duces tecum* does nothing more than establish the existence, authenticity, and custody of items that are produced. We assume that the Government is also entirely correct in its submission that it would not have to advert to respondent's act of production in order to prove the existence, authenticity, or custody of any documents that it might offer in evidence at a criminal trial; indeed, the Government disclaims any need to introduce any of the documents produced by respondent into evidence in order to prove the charges against him. It follows, according to the Government, that it has no intention of making improper "use" of respondent's compelled testimony.

The question, however, is not whether the response to the subpoena may be introduced into evidence at his criminal trial. That would surely be a prohibited "use" of the immunized act of production. But the fact that the Government intends no such use of the act of production leaves open the separate question whether it has already made "derivative use" of the testimonial aspect of that act in obtaining the indictment against respondent and in preparing its case for trial. It clearly has.

It is apparent from the text of the subpoena itself that the prosecutor needed respondent's assistance both to identify potential sources of information and to produce those sources. . . . The documents did not magically appear in the prosecutor's office like "manna from heaven." They arrived there only after respondent asserted his constitutional privilege, received a grant of immunity, and — under the compulsion of the District Court's order — took the mental and physical steps necessary to provide the prosecutor with an accurate inventory of the many sources of potentially incriminating evidence sought by the subpoena. It was only through respondent's truthful reply to the subpoena that the Government received the incriminating documents of which it made "substantial use . . . in the investigation that led to the indictment." Brief for United States 3.

For these reasons, we cannot accept the Government's submission that respondent's immunity did not preclude its derivative use of the produced documents because its "possession of the documents [was] the fruit *only* of a simple physical act — the act of producing the documents." *Id.* at 29. It was unquestionably neces-sary for respondent to make extensive use of "the contents of his own mind" in iden-tifying the hundreds of documents responsive to the requests in the subpoena. . . .

In sum, we have no doubt that the constitutional privilege against self-incrimination protects the target of a grand jury investigation from being compelled to answer questions designed to elicit information about the existence of sources of potentially incriminating evidence. . . . On appeal and again before this Court, how-ever, the Government has argued that the communicative aspect of respondent's act of producing ordinary business records is insufficiently "testimonial" to support a claim of privilege because the existence and possession of such records by any busi-nessman is a "foregone conclusion" under our decision in *Fisher v. United States*, 425 U.S. at 411. This argument both misreads *Fisher* and ignores our subsequent decision in *United States v. Doe*, 465 U.S. 605 (1984). . . .

Given our conclusion that respondent's act of production had a testimonial aspect, at least with respect to the existence and location of the documents sought by the Government's subpoena, respondent could not be compelled to produce those documents without first receiving a grant of immunity under § 6003. As we construed § 6002 in *Kastigar*, such immunity is coextensive with the constitutional privilege. *Kastigar* requires that respondent's motion to dismiss the indictment on immunity grounds be granted unless the Government proves that the evidence it used in obtaining the indictment and proposed to use at trial was derived from legitimate sources "wholly independent" of the testimonial aspect of respondent's immunized conduct in assembling and producing the documents described in the subpoena. The Government, however, does not claim that it could make such a showing. Rather, it contends that its prosecution of respondent must be consid-ered proper unless someone — presumably respondent — shows that "there is some substantial relation between the compelled testimonial communications implicit in the act of production (as opposed to the act of production standing alone) and some aspect of the information used in the investigation or the evidence presented at trial." Brief for United States at 9. We could not accept this submission without repudiating the basis for our conclusion in *Kastigar* that the statutory guarantee of use and derivative-use immunity is as broad as the constitutional privilege itself. This we are not prepared to do.

Accordingly, the indictment against respondent must be dismissed. The judg-ment of the Court of Appeals is affirmed.

JUSTICE THOMAS, with whom JUSTICE SCALIA joins, concurring. [Omitted.]

Notes and Questions

1. *"Communicative aspect" of production.* The Court rejected the government's argu-ment that "the communicative aspect of respondent's act of producing ordinary business records is insufficiently 'testimonial' to support a claim of privilege because the existence and possession of such records by any businessman is a 'foregone

conclusion' under our decision in *Fisher* [and *Doe*]." How did the government's conclusion misread *Fisher* and *Doe*?

2. *Scope of act of production immunity.* Despite the clarification the Court hoped to provide with *Fisher* and *Doe*, there remains a great deal of confusion as to the proper extent and scope of the act of production immunity. Does *Hubbell* offer any clear guidance? For an analysis of the issues arising from the assertion of the Fifth Amendment privilege in response to grand jury subpoenas, see Sara Sun Beale & James E. Felman, *The Fifth Amendment and the Grand Jury*, CRIM. JUSTICE 4 (Spring 2007).

Many uncertainties remain in this context. For example, what protection, if any, does a corporate employee have if the employee has terminated the employment, but still possesses corporate records? In *In Re three Grand Jury Subpoenas Duces tecum*, 191 F.3d 173 (2d Cir. 1999), for example, former corporate officers were in possession of corporate records and received a federal grand jury subpoena. Did the employees have a valid Fifth Amendment right to refuse production because the documents were in their personal possession? Or were the records corporate records that must be produced by the individuals as corporate representatives?

3. *Applying the* Hubbell *decision.* Courts are applying the *Hubbell* holding, with varying results. *See United States v. Ponds*, 454 F.3d 313 (D.C. Cir. 2006) (finding that *Hubbell* did not apply with respect to some subpoenaed documents because the government had prior knowledge of the existence and location of several types of documents subpoenaed, but that the government did not meet the particularity/prior knowledge requirements for many of the other document types listed in the subpoena); *United States v. Marra*, 2005 U.S. Dist. LEXIS 23411, at *14 (D.N.J. Oct. 5, 2005) (holding that accountant for client under investigation was required to produce and authenticate documents as custodian of record, but could not be compelled to give further testimony without implicating the Fifth Amendment). Also, in *Armstrong v. Guccione*, 470 F.3d 89 (2d Cir. 2006), the Second Circuit found that *Hubbell* did not undermine *Braswell v. United States*, 487 U.S. 99 (1988) (holding that a corporate custodian could not invoke the Fifth Amendment as a basis for refusing to produce corporate records, even though the act of producing those records has independent testimonial significance that might incriminate the custodian personally).

4. *Defense witness immunity.* What should defense counsel do when one of the witnesses asserts the Fifth Amendment privilege and refuses to testify (favorably) for the defense? Assume that the witness will not testify without immunity, that the government refuses to immunize the witness, and that the defendant, as a result, cannot call the witness. Should the government be required to grant immunity? If so, why and under what circumstances? If not, what policy reasons support your conclusions?

In the article by Reid H. Weingarten & Brian M. Heberlig, *The Defense Witness Immunity Doctrine: The Time Has Come to Give it Strength to Address Prosecutorial*

Overreaching, 43 AM. CRIM. L. REV. 1189 (2006), the authors argue that it is extremely difficult for a defendant to obtain immunity for defense witnesses because the prosecutors can manipulate the system in their favor through the guise of "prosecutorial discretion" and use of the co-conspirator exception to the hearsay rule. The authors argue that it should be easier for a defendant to show that the government has used immunity to gain a tactical advantage. *Id.* at 1192–1195. Also, they argue that "exculpatory evidence" should be defined broadly, especially in white collar cases, and that defendants should not have a hard time demonstrating that the testimony is unavailable from another source. *Id.* at 1196–1198. Do you agree?

In the Enron prosecution, *United States v. Skilling*, 2006 U.S. Dist. LEXIS 42664 (S.D. Tex. June 23, 2006), defendants Skilling and Lay filed a motion requesting court-ordered use immunity for proposed witnesses who had asserted their Fifth Amendment rights. The court denied the motion, finding a lack of authority under 18 U.S.C. § 6001 to grant immunity against the wishes of the government. The court held that the defendants had failed to show that the government had used its immunity privileges to unfairly skew the facts before the jury or that the government had no legitimate reason for refusing to immunize. The defendants also failed to show that the proposed witnesses would offer exculpatory testimony or that the government coerced the witnesses into asserting their Fifth Amendment rights. On appeal, the Fifth Circuit found the ruling of the district court to be harmless error. *United States v. Skilling*, 554 F.3d 529, 566–67 (5th Cir. 2009), *aff'd in part, vacated in part, and remanded*, *Skilling v. United States*, 561 U.S. 358 (2010) (*see* Chapter 4, Mail Fraud, Wire Fraud, and Related Crimes, *supra*, for a detailed discussion of the *Skilling* case).

In a Third Circuit case, the court recognized a Sixth Amendment right to immunization of witnesses who would provide exculpatory testimony for the defense. The defendant made the required showing that he was entitled to judicial use immunity by establishing that he was "prevented from presenting exculpatory evidence which is critical to his case." *United States v. Herman*, 589 F.2d 1191, 1204 (3d Cir. 1978). The court found that it had "inherent remedial power to require that the distortion be redressed by requiring a grant of use immunity to defense witnesses as an alternative to dismissal." *Id.*

5. *Electronically-stored information.* As discussed in Chapter 6, *supra*, searches of electronically-stored information may also raise complex act-of-production privilege issues. For example, the Eleventh Circuit has held that, absent a grant of full use and derivative use immunity, the government cannot compel a suspect to decrypt his computer hard drives when the decryption itself would be testimonial. *See In re Grand Jury Subpoena Duces Tecum*, 670 F.3d 1335 (11th Cir. 2012).

Problems

17-7. As an Assistant United States Attorney, you are handling the Howdy Real Estate investigation. You decide to offer immunity to one of the independent real-estate agents who works with the firm. During your investigation, you become aware of information leading you to believe that Howdy Real Estate is funneling monies through Caribbean bank accounts in an effort to hide revenue that should be taxable. Based on your investigation thus far, you believe that individuals may have committed the crimes of tax fraud, money laundering, and conspiracy.

One of the independent associates, Knowall, has been to several real estate closings where she assisted in the handling of the settlement of funds from the transactions. Knowall witnessed the division of the settlement accounts in such a way that she realized that the Howdys had created a separate account for the deposit of settlement proceeds. Although she is not sure where this account is located, she is willing to testify that the settlement records will show that monies were diverted into accounts other than the business account of the real estate firm. The main real estate account is the one from which she is paid her commissions, as is the case with the other agents working with Howdy Real Estate. The defense counsel says that Knowall will not testify without immunity. You do not know why she needs immunity.

Do you agree to seek immunity for her? What are the risks associated with this?

17-8. You have made the decision that Knowall is more valuable as a witness than as a subject or target, so you agree to proceed with the immunity request. Once you receive the approval to seek the court order granting immunity to Knowall, you take her into your office to prep her for the grand jury appearance. She tells you that she learned during conversations with the principals in the Howdy investigation that the money being used for mortgages "represents the proceeds of some form of unlawful activity." 18 U.S.C. § 1956(a)(1). Knowall denies having any direct connection with the diversion of the money to the Caribbean account or any other accounts. Once in the grand jury room, you begin to ask her questions related to separate bank accounts maintained by Mr. Howdy. During her testimony, it becomes evident to you that she was, in fact, the person who assisted in the funneling of the monies from the local agency bank to a bank account in the Caribbean. This directly contradicts her statement to you in your office as a proffer for the immunity request.

> *a. Because she told the grand jury a story that differs from what she told you in your office, could you prosecute her for perjury or false statements? What do you say as you discuss this situation with your superiors?*

> *b. If Ms. Knowall's involvement is more extensive that you had originally envisioned, should you use her as a witness in your case against Mr. and Mrs. Howdy? Why or why not?*

17-9. Consider the cases in this chapter on act of production immunity and the role of a records' custodian. As the AUSA in charge of an investigation, you issue a subpoena *duces tecum* to the custodian of records of the target company. Please consider the following questions:

a. Assume that the custodian invokes the privilege against self-incrimination.

Would you grant immunity for the act of producing the records? Why or why not? In answering this question, please assess the possible advantages and risks of such grant of privilege.

b. Now assume that, in light of the witness's assertion of the privilege against self-incrimination, you decide not to attempt to enforce the subpoena. You are concerned that seeking an immunity in order to obtain the evidence might mean that the evidence would be tainted in light of the *Hubbell* holding.

Would the invocation of the privilege affect how you conduct the investigation?

Chapter 18

Civil Actions, Civil Penalties, and Parallel Proceedings

A. Introductory Notes

1. Issues in Parallel Proceedings

This chapter builds upon the materials in Chapter 2, Corporate and Individual Liability, Chapter 16, The Grand Jury, and Chapter 17, Self-Incrimination — Witness Testimony and Document Production. The state and federal governments regulate white collar activities and impose civil penalties for a wide variety of business and other white collar conduct. Because federal and state agencies often impose civil penalties for regulatory wrongdoing, and then refer the matter for criminal investigation, astute counsel must closely monitor all civil and agency investigations. A corporation or individual may simultaneously confront parallel administrative, civil, and/or criminal actions based on the same or similar facts.

Moves made in one litigation context can affect strategic and legal options in the other. Admissions made in one proceeding may be available to opponents in others. Waiving privilege over some evidence for one purpose may waive privilege over it for all purposes. In addition, parallel proceedings present important issues concerning the right against self-incrimination, stays of parallel civil proceedings, and discovery. This chapter will explore the principal ethical and legal challenges resulting from the interplay between civil and criminal accountability.

2. Civil and Agency Investigations

Specific federal agencies have primary responsibility for enforcing the laws related to their respective zones of authority. Internal investigative power for each agency is located within its Office of Inspector General (OIG). The OIG and its staff monitor agency compliance, conduct audits of the agency and its providers, and supervise investigations regarding the laws specific to that agency. 5 U.S.C. app. 3 § 4(a). Some agencies, such as the Securities and Exchange Commission (SEC), also have a separate division of enforcement that conducts investigations into the public's possible violations of federal laws within the agency's authority, and that prosecutes civil enforcement actions through administrative proceedings and in the federal courts.

Agencies have the power to issue subpoenas. These subpoenas are very similar to grand jury subpoenas in that they compel the production of evidence in connection with the agencies' investigations. In addition, the Internal Revenue Service issues summonses, which are the equivalents of subpoenas. Courts have authority to review both the scope and propriety of subpoenas and summonses issued by federal agencies. A court exercises only limited review of an agency's actions in a subpoena enforcement proceeding, and does not normally consider the merits of a party's claim that it has not violated a statute or regulation administered by the agency.

Federal agencies depend on the courts for enforcement of both subpoenas and summonses. As a general rule, a court will enforce an administrative subpoena if: (1) it reasonably relates to an investigation within the agency's authority, (2) the specific inquiry is relevant to that purpose and is not too indefinite, (3) the proper administrative procedures have been followed, and (4) the subpoena does not demand information for an illegitimate purpose. *See, e.g., CFTC v. Tokheim*, 153 F.3d 474, 477 (7th Cir. 1998) (relying on *United States v. Powell*, 379 U.S. 48, 57–58 (1964)).

Standing alone, federal agencies cannot institute criminal actions. Instead, they must refer matters to the Department of Justice for a determination of whether criminal charges may be appropriate.

3. Deferred Prosecution

As discussed in Chapters 2 and 15, *supra*, the government has begun to use pretrial diversion as another tool to address corporate wrongdoing. Corporate diversion agreements — deferred and non-prosecution agreements — allow the government to impose terms of probation before or without conviction. This controversial procedure permits corporations to avoid criminal prosecution during a probationary period, and at the same time, gives the prosecutor extensive control over determining whether the corporation has complied with the terms and conditions of the probation. Such agreements have affected the attorney-client privilege, the work-product protections, restitution, parallel proceedings, fines, compliance, and individual rights within the corporation.

B. Civil Remedies

1. Fines

Conduct that gives rise to federal criminal liability will often also subject the corporation or individual to significant civil fines and regulations. Such matters may be resolved civilly through actions brought by a federal agency or private litigants with remedies that include injunctions, forfeitures, restitution, and/or fines. *See, e.g.,* Securities Fraud, Chapter 5 § E, *supra*, detailing some of the civil remedies available to the SEC and private litigants under the federal securities laws. When a corporation is obligated to pay a civil penalty, many of the constitutional protections that accompany criminal penalties do not apply. The question whether a civil penalty is sufficiently punitive to be equivalent to a criminal penalty has plagued the courts. In the next case, the Supreme Court addressed this issue under the Double Jeopardy Clause.

Hudson v. United States

522 U.S. 93 (1997)

CHIEF JUSTICE REHNQUIST delivered the opinion of the Court.

The Government administratively imposed monetary penalties and occupational debarment on petitioners for violation of federal banking statutes, and later criminally indicted them for essentially the same conduct. We hold that the Double Jeopardy Clause of the Fifth Amendment is not a bar to the later criminal prosecution because the administrative proceedings were civil, not criminal. Our reasons for so holding in large part disavow the method of analysis used in *United States v. Halper*, 490 U.S. 435, 448 (1989), and reaffirm the previously established rule exemplified in *United States v. Ward*, 448 U.S. 242, 248–49 (1980).

During the early and mid-1980's, petitioner John Hudson was the chairman and controlling shareholder of the First National Bank of Tipton (Tipton) and the First National Bank of Hammon (Hammon). During the same period, petitioner Jack Rackley was president of Tipton and a member of the board of directors of Hammon, and petitioner Larry Baresel was a member of the board of directors of both Tipton and Hammon.

An examination of Tipton and Hammon led the Office of the Comptroller of the Currency (OCC) to conclude that petitioners had used their bank positions to arrange a series of loans to third parties in violation of various federal banking statutes and regulations. According to the OCC, those loans, while nominally made to third parties, were in reality made to Hudson in order to enable him to redeem bank stock that he had pledged as collateral on defaulted loans.

On February 13, 1989, OCC issued a "Notice of Assessment of Civil Money Penalty." The notice alleged that petitioners had violated 12 U.S.C. §§ 84(a)(1) and 375b (1982 ed.) and 12 C.F.R. §§ 31.2(b) and 215.4(b) (1986) by causing the banks with which they were associated to make loans to nominee borrowers in a manner that unlawfully allowed Hudson to receive the benefit of the loans. The notice also alleged that the illegal loans resulted in losses to Tipton and Hammon of almost $900,000 and contributed to the failure of those banks. However, the notice contained no allegation of any harm to the Government as a result of petitioners' conduct. "After taking into account the size of the financial resources and the good faith of [petitioners], the gravity of the violations, the history of previous violations and other matters as justice may require, as required by 12 U.S.C. §§ 93(b)(2) and 504(b)," OCC assessed penalties of $100,000 against Hudson and $50,000 each against Rackley and Baresel.

Id. at 89a. [App. to Pet. for Cert.] On August 31, 1989, OCC also issued a "Notice of Intention to Prohibit Further Participation" against each petitioner. These notices, which were premised on the identical allegations that formed the basis for the previous notices, informed petitioners that OCC intended to bar them from further participation in the conduct of "any insured depository institution." *Id.* at 100a.

In October 1989, petitioners resolved the OCC proceedings against them by each entering into a "Stipulation and Consent Order." These consent orders provided that Hudson, Baresel, and Rackley would pay assessments of $16,500, $15,000, and $12,500 respectively. In addition, each petitioner agreed not to "participate in any manner" in the affairs of any banking institution without the written authorization of the OCC and all other relevant regulatory agencies.

In August 1992, petitioners were indicted in the Western District of Oklahoma in a 22-count indictment on charges of conspiracy, 18 U.S.C. § 371, misapplication of bank funds, §§ 656 and 2, and making false bank entries, § 1005. The violations charged in the indictment rested on the same lending transactions that formed the basis for the prior administrative actions brought by OCC. Petitioners moved to dismiss the indictment on double jeopardy grounds, but the District Court denied the motions. The Court of Appeals affirmed the District Court's holding on the nonparticipation sanction issue, but vacated and remanded to the District Court on the money sanction issue. The District Court on remand granted petitioners' motion to dismiss the indictments. This time the Government appealed, and the Court of Appeals reversed. That court held, following *Halper*, that the actual fines imposed by the Government were not as grossly disproportional to the proved damages to the Government as to render the sanctions "punishment" for double jeopardy purposes. We granted certiorari because of concerns about the wide variety of novel double jeopardy claims spawned in the wake of *Halper*. We now affirm, but for different reasons.

The Double Jeopardy Clause provides that no "person [shall] be subject for the same offence to be twice put in jeopardy of life or limb." We have long recognized that the Double Jeopardy Clause does not prohibit the imposition of all additional sanctions that could, "in common parlance," be described as punishment. *United States ex rel. Marcus v. Hess*, 317 U.S. 537, 549 (1943). The Clause protects only against the imposition of multiple criminal punishments for the same offense, *Helvering v. Mitchell*, 303 U.S. 391, 399 (1938).

Whether a particular punishment is criminal or civil is, at least initially, a matter of statutory construction. A court must first ask whether the legislature, "in establishing the penalizing mechanism, indicated either expressly or impliedly a preference for one label or the other." *Ward*, 448 U.S. at 248. Even in those cases where the legislature "has indicated an intention to establish a civil penalty, we have inquired further whether the statutory scheme was so punitive either in purpose or effect," as to "transfor[m] what was clearly intended as a civil remedy into a criminal penalty," *Rex Trailer Co. v. United States*, 350 U.S. 148, 154 (1956).

In making this latter determination, the factors listed in *Kennedy v. Mendoza-Martinez*, 372 U.S. 144, 168–169 (1963), provide useful guideposts, including:

> (1) [w]hether the sanction involves an affirmative disability or restraint; (2) whether it has historically been regarded as a punishment; (3) whether it comes into play only on a finding of *scienter*; (4) whether its operation will promote the traditional aims of punishment-retribution and deterrence; (5) whether the behavior to which it applies is already a crime; (6) whether an alternative purpose to which it may rationally be connected is assignable for it; and (7) whether it appears excessive in relation to the alternative purpose assigned.

It is important to note, however, that "these factors must be considered in relation to the statute on its face," *id*. at 169, and "only the clearest proof" will suffice to override legislative intent and transform what has been denominated a civil remedy into a criminal penalty, *Ward, supra*, at 249.

Our opinion in *United States v. Halper* marked the first time we applied the Double Jeopardy Clause to a sanction without first determining that it was criminal in nature. In that case, Irwin Halper was convicted of, *inter alia*, violating the criminal false claims statute, 18 U.S.C. §287, based on his submission of 65 inflated Medicare claims each of which overcharged the Government by $9. He was sentenced to two years' imprisonment and fined $5,000. The Government then brought an action against Halper under the civil False Claims Act, 31 U.S.C. §§3729–3731. The remedial provisions of the False Claims Act provided that a violation of the Act rendered one "liable to the United States Government for a civil penalty of $2,000, an amount equal to 2 times the amount of damages the Government sustains because of the act of that person, and costs of the civil action." *Id*. §3729. Given Halper's 65 separate violations of the Act, he appeared to be liable for a penalty of $130,000, despite the fact he actually defrauded the Government of less than $600. However, the District Court concluded that a penalty of this magnitude would violate the Double Jeopardy Clause in light of Halper's previous criminal conviction. While explicitly recognizing that the statutory damages provision of the Act "was not itself a criminal punishment," the District Court nonetheless concluded that application of the full penalty to Halper would constitute a second "punishment" in violation of the Double Jeopardy Clause. *Halper*, 490 U.S. at 438–439.

On direct appeal, this Court affirmed. As the *Halper* Court saw it, the imposition of "punishment" of any kind was subject to double jeopardy constraints, and whether a sanction constituted "punishment" depended primarily on whether it served the traditional "goals of punishment," namely, "retribution and deterrence." *Id*. at 448. Any sanction that was so "overwhelmingly disproportionate" to the injury caused that it could not "fairly be said solely to serve [the] remedial purpose" of compensating the Government for its loss, was thought to be explainable only as "serving either retributive or deterrent purposes." *See id*. at 448–449.

The analysis applied by the *Halper* Court deviated from our traditional double jeopardy doctrine in two key respects. First, the *Halper* Court bypassed the threshold question: whether the successive punishment at issue is a "criminal" punishment. Instead, it focused on whether the sanction, regardless of whether it was civil or criminal, was so grossly disproportionate to the harm caused as to constitute "punishment." In so doing, the Court elevated a single *Kennedy* factor — whether the sanction appeared excessive in relation to its nonpunitive purposes — to dispositive status. But as we emphasized in *Kennedy* itself, no one factor should be considered controlling as they "may often point in differing directions." 372 U.S. at 169. The second significant departure in *Halper* was the Court's decision to "asses[s] the character of the actual sanctions imposed," 490 U.S. at 447, rather than, as *Kennedy* demanded, evaluating the "statute on its face" to determine whether it provided for what amounted to a criminal sanction, 372 U.S. at 169.

We believe that *Halper*'s deviation from longstanding double jeopardy principles was ill considered. As subsequent cases have demonstrated, *Halper*'s test for determining whether a particular sanction is "punitive," and thus subject to the strictures of the Double Jeopardy Clause, has proved unworkable. We have since recognized that all civil penalties have some deterrent effect. If a sanction must be "solely" remedial (*i.e.*, entirely nondeterrent) to avoid implicating the Double Jeopardy Clause, then no civil penalties are beyond the scope of the Clause. Under *Halper*'s method of analysis, a court must also look at the "sanction actually imposed" to determine whether the Double Jeopardy Clause is implicated. Thus, it will not be possible to determine whether the Double Jeopardy Clause is violated until a defendant has proceeded through a trial to judgment. But in those cases where the civil proceeding follows the criminal proceeding, this approach flies in the face of the notion that the Double Jeopardy Clause forbids the government from even "*attempting* a second time to punish criminally." *Helvering*, 303 U.S. at 399 (emphasis added).

Finally, it should be noted that some of the ills at which *Halper* was directed are addressed by other constitutional provisions. The Due Process and Equal Protection Clauses already protect individuals from sanctions which are downright irrational. *Williamson v. Lee Optical of Okla., Inc.*, 348 U.S. 483 (1955). The Eighth Amendment protects against excessive civil fines, including forfeitures. *Alexander v. United States*, 509 U.S. 544 (1993); *Austin v. United States*, 509 U.S. 602 (1993). The additional protection afforded by extending double jeopardy protections to proceedings heretofore thought to be civil is more than offset by the confusion created by attempting to distinguish between "punitive" and "nonpunitive" penalties.

Applying traditional double jeopardy principles to the facts of this case, it is clear that the criminal prosecution of these petitioners would not violate the Double Jeopardy Clause. It is evident that Congress intended the OCC money penalties and debarment sanctions imposed for violations of 12 U.S.C. §§ 84 and 375b to be civil in nature. As for the money penalties, both §§ 93(b)(1) and 504(a), which authorize the imposition of monetary penalties for violations of §§ 84 and 375b respectively, expressly provide that such penalties are "civil." While the provision authorizing debarment contains no language explicitly denominating the sanction as civil, we think it significant that the authority to issue debarment orders is conferred upon the "appropriate Federal banking agenc[ies]." §§ 1818(e)(1)-(3). That such authority was conferred upon administrative agencies is prima facie evidence that Congress intended to provide for a civil sanction.

Turning to the second stage of the *Ward* test, we find that there is little evidence, much less the clearest proof that we require, suggesting that either OCC money penalties or debarment sanctions are "so punitive in form and effect as to render them criminal despite Congress' intent to the contrary." *United States v. Ursery*, 518 U.S. 267, 290 (1996). First, neither money penalties nor debarment has historically been viewed as punishment. We have long recognized that "revocation of a privilege voluntarily granted," such as a debarment, "is characteristically free of the punitive criminal element." *Helvering*, 303 U.S. at 399, and n.2. . . .

Second, the sanctions imposed do not involve an "affirmative disability or restraint," as that term is normally understood. While petitioners have been prohibited from further participating in the banking industry, this is "certainly nothing approaching the 'infamous punishment' of imprisonment." *Flemming v. Nestor*, 363 U.S. 603, 617 (1960). Third, neither sanction comes into play "only" on a finding of scienter. The provisions under which the money penalties were imposed, 12 U.S.C. §§ 93(b) and 504, allow for the assessment of a penalty against any person "who violates" any of the underlying banking statutes, without regard to the violator's state of mind. . . .

Fourth, the conduct for which OCC sanctions are imposed may also be criminal (and in this case formed the basis for petitioners' indictments). This fact is insufficient to render the money penalties and debarment sanctions criminally punitive, *Ursery, supra*, at 292 (slip op., at 24–25), particularly in the double jeopardy context, *see United States v. Dixon*, 509 U.S. 688, 704 (1993) (rejecting "same-conduct" test for double jeopardy purposes).

Finally, we recognize that the imposition of both money penalties and debarment sanctions will deter others from emulating petitioners' conduct, a traditional goal of criminal punishment. But the mere presence of this purpose is insufficient to render a sanction criminal, as deterrence "may serve civil as well as criminal goals." *Ursery*, 518 U.S. at 292. For example, the sanctions at issue here, while intended to deter future wrongdoing, also serve to promote the stability of the banking industry. To hold that the mere presence of a deterrent purpose renders such sanctions "criminal" for double jeopardy purposes would severely undermine the Government's ability to engage in effective regulation of institutions such as banks.

In sum, there simply is very little showing, to say nothing of the "clearest proof" required by *Ward*, that OCC money penalties and debarment sanctions are criminal. The Double Jeopardy Clause is therefore no obstacle to their trial on the pending indictments, and it may proceed.

The judgment of the Court of Appeals for the Tenth Circuit is accordingly affirmed.

[Concurring opinions omitted.]

Notes and Questions

1. *Successive punishments and successive prosecutions.* Is there a practical distinction between successive punishments and successive prosecutions? Is the Court's test for determining whether or not a sanction is punitive defensible? Why was the *Halper* test unworkable? Note that the Court in *Hudson* relied upon its earlier decision in *United States v. Ursery*, 518 U.S. 267 (1996), a forfeiture case discussed in Chapter 20, Forfeitures, *infra*.

2. *Post-*Halper *concerns.* The Court spoke of post-*Halper* "concerns about the wide variety of novel double jeopardy claims spawned in the wake of" the case. Justice Stevens pointed out in his concurrence, however, that there were only seven such cases, and that in each of those cases, the Court rejected the double jeopardy claim. *Hudson*, 522 U.S. at 106 (Stevens, J., concurring in the judgment.) Stevens questioned the Court's need to revisit *Halper* to reach the conclusion in *Hudson*. Why did the Court seemingly go out of its way to overturn *Halper*?

3. *Punitive civil fines.* Are some civil fines so punitive that they should preclude further prosecution? If so, in what circumstances?

Problems

18-1. Dana Doe was a stock broker. The Commodity Futures Trading Commission (the "Commission") entered an order revoking Doe's floor brokerage registration, barring Doe from trading in any market regulated by the Commission, and imposing a $10,000 fine. The order stemmed from an earlier investigation by the Commission into the possibility that Doe engaged in insider trading. Doe argues that this administrative sanction violates the Double Jeopardy Clause of the Fifth Amendment because it followed a criminal sentence for the same conduct.

Is Doe correct? Why or why not?

18-2. Daryl and his associates raised $5 million from investors by promising that they would earn spectacular returns from his plan to purchase Federal Communications Commission licenses and then resell them to major telecommunications companies. Daryl knew or should have known at the time he solicited these investments that these licenses could not be resold. Daryl's investors lost all of their money. The SEC brought a civil enforcement action against Daryl that resulted in a Consent Agreement, whereby Daryl consented to a judgment being entered against him "without admitting or denying the allegation of the SEC's complaint." The resulting judgment held Daryl liable for the penalty of disgorgement in the amount of $5 million. Six months later, a grand jury indicted Daryl for securities fraud. Daryl moves to dismiss the indictment, arguing that the penalty of disgorgement is effectively a criminal sanction and a subsequent criminal prosecution would therefore violate the Double Jeopardy Clause of the Fifth Amendment.

How should the court rule? Explain.

2. Qui Tam Actions

The False Claims Act, 31 U.S.C. §§ 3729–3733 (FCA), is based on the theory that "one of the least expensive and most effective means of preventing frauds on the Treasury is to make the perpetrators of them liable to actions by private persons acting, if you please, under the strong stimulus of personal ill will or the hope of gain." *United States v. Griswold*, 24 F. 361, 366 (D. Or. 1885) (quoted, *inter alia*, in *U.S. ex rel. Springfield Terminal Ry. Co. v. Quinn*, 14 F.3d 645, 649 (1994)). Through the FCA, the government has established incentives to promote enforcement of the laws. The FCA supplements governmental efforts by utilizing and rewarding the citizenry for investigative purposes. *Qui tam* is shorthand for the Latin phrase "*qui tam pro domino rege quam pro seipse*," meaning "he who sues for the king as for himself." There has been an explosion of qui tam actions in recent years, principally in the health care industry. Of the more than $3 billion recovered by the government in FCA actions in 2019, more than $2.1 billion arose from qui tam actions. *See Justice Department Recovers Over $3 Billion From False Claims Act Cases in Fiscal Year 2019*, Justice News Release (January 9, 2020), https://www.justice.gov/opa/pr /justice-department-recovers-over-3-billion-false-claims-act-cases-fiscal-year-2019.

The individual who brings a case under the FCA is called the relator. The next case discusses the standing of a private individual to bring an action under the FCA as a relator.

Vermont Agency of Nat. Res. v. United States ex rel. Stevens

529 U.S. 765 (2000)

Justice Scalia delivered the opinion of the Court:

This case presents the question whether a private individual may bring suit in federal court on behalf of the United States against a State (or state agency) under the False Claims Act, 31 U.S.C. §§ 3729–3733.

Originally enacted in 1863, the False Claims Act (FCA) is the most frequently used of a handful of extant laws creating a form of civil action known as *qui tam*. As amended, the FCA imposes civil liability upon "[a]ny person" who, *inter alia*, "knowingly presents, or causes to be presented, to an officer or employee of the United States Government . . . a false or fraudulent claim for payment or approval." 31 U.S.C. § 3729(a). The defendant is liable for up to treble damages and a civil penalty of up to $10,000 per claim. An FCA action may be commenced in one of two ways. First, the Government itself may bring a civil action against the alleged false claimant. § 3730(a). Second, as is relevant here, a private person (the relator) may bring a *qui tam* civil action "for the person and for the United States Government" against the alleged false claimant, "in the name of the Government." § 3730(b)(1).

If a relator initiates the FCA action, he must deliver a copy of the complaint, and any supporting evidence, to the Government, § 3730(b)(2), which then has 60 days to intervene in the action, §§ 3730(b)(2), (4). If it does so, it assumes primary responsibility for prosecuting the action, § 3730(c)(1), though the relator may continue to participate in the litigation and is entitled to a hearing before voluntary dismissal and to a court determination of reasonableness before settlement, § 3730(c)(2). If the Government declines to intervene within the 60-day period, the relator has the exclusive right to conduct the action, § 3730(b)(4), and the Government may subsequently intervene only on a showing of "good cause," § 3730(c)(3). The relator receives a share of any proceeds from the action — generally ranging from 15 to 25 percent if the Government intervenes (depending upon the relator's contribution to the prosecution), and from 25 to 30 percent if it does not (depending upon the court's assessment of what is reasonable) — plus attorney's fees and costs. § 3730(d)(1)-(2).

Respondent Jonathan Stevens brought this *qui tam* action in the United States District Court for the District of Vermont against petitioner Vermont Agency of Natural Resources, his former employer, alleging that it had submitted false claims to the Environmental Protection Agency (EPA) in connection with various federal grant programs administered by the EPA. Specifically, he claimed that petitioner had overstated the amount of time spent by its employees on the federally funded projects, thereby inducing the Government to disburse more grant money than petitioner was entitled to receive. The United States declined to intervene in the action. . . .

We first address the jurisdictional question whether respondent Stevens has standing under Article III of the Constitution to maintain this suit.

As we have frequently explained, a plaintiff must meet three requirements in order to establish Article III standing. First, he must demonstrate "injury in fact" — a harm that is both "concrete" and "actual or imminent, not conjectural or hypothetical." *Whitmore v. Arkansas*, 495 U.S. 149, 155 (1990). Second, he must establish causation — a "fairly . . . trace[able]" connection between the alleged injury in fact and the alleged conduct of the defendant. *Simon v. Eastern Kentucky Welfare Rights Organization*, 426 U.S. 26, 41 (1976). And third, he must demonstrate redressability — a "substantial likelihood" that the requested relief will remedy the alleged injury in fact. *Id.* at 45. These requirements together constitute the "irreducible constitutional minimum" of standing, which is an "essential and unchanging part" of Article III's case-or-controversy requirement, and a key factor in dividing the power of government between the courts and the two political branches. *See Lujan v. Defenders of Wildlife*, 504 U.S. 555, 559–60 (1992).

Respondent Stevens contends that he is suing to remedy an injury in fact suffered by the United States. It is beyond doubt that the complaint asserts an injury to the

United States—both the injury to its sovereignty arising from violation of its laws (which suffices to support a criminal lawsuit by the Government) and the proprietary injury resulting from the alleged fraud. But "[t]he Art. III judicial power exists only to redress or otherwise to protect against injury *to the complaining party.*" *Warth v. Seldin*, 422 U.S. 490, 499 (1975). It would perhaps suffice to say that the relator here is simply the statutorily designated agent of the United States, *in whose name* (as the statute provides, *see* 31 U.S.C. §3730(b)) the suit is brought—and that the relator's bounty is simply the fee he receives out of the United States' recovery for filing and/or prosecuting a successful action on behalf of the Government. This analysis is precluded, however, by the fact that the statute gives the relator himself an interest *in the lawsuit,* and not merely the right to retain a fee out of the recovery. Thus, it provides that "[a] person may bring a civil action for a violation of section 3729 *for the person and for the United States Government,*" §3730(b) (emphasis added); gives the relator "the right to continue as a party to the action" even when the Government itself has assumed "primary responsibility" for prosecuting it, §3730(c)(1); entitles the relator to a hearing before the Government's voluntary dismissal of the suit, §3730(c)(2)(A); and prohibits the Government from settling the suit over the relator's objection without a judicial determination of "fair[ness], adequa[cy] and reasonable[ness]," §3730(c)(2)(B). For the portion of the recovery retained by the relator, therefore, some explanation of standing other than agency for the Government must be identified.

There is no doubt, of course, that as to this portion of the recovery—the bounty he will receive if the suit is successful—a *qui tam* relator has a "concrete private interest in the outcome of [the] suit." *Lujan, supra,* at 573. But the same might be said of someone who has placed a wager upon the outcome. An interest unrelated to injury in fact is insufficient to give a plaintiff standing. The interest must consist of obtaining compensation for, or preventing, the violation of a legally protected right. A *qui tam* relator has suffered no such invasion—indeed, the "right" he seeks to vindicate does not even fully materialize until the litigation is completed and the relator prevails. This is not to suggest that Congress cannot define new legal rights, which in turn will confer standing to vindicate an injury caused to the claimant. *See Warth, supra,* at 500. As we have held in another context, however, an interest that is merely a "byproduct" of the suit itself cannot give rise to a cognizable injury in fact for Article III standing purposes. *See Steel Co. v. Citizens for Better Environment,* 523 U.S. 83, 93–102 (1998).

We believe, however, that adequate basis for the relator's suit for his bounty is to be found in the doctrine that the assignee of a claim has standing to assert the injury in fact suffered by the assignor. The FCA can reasonably be regarded as effecting a partial assignment of the Government's damages claim. Although we have never expressly recognized "representational standing" on the part of assignees, we have routinely entertained their suits. . . . We conclude, therefore, that the United States' injury in fact suffices to confer standing on respondent Stevens.

We are confirmed in this conclusion by the long tradition of *qui tam* actions in England and the American Colonies. That history is particularly relevant to the constitutional standing inquiry since, as we have said elsewhere, Article III's restriction of the judicial power to "Cases" and "Controversies" is properly understood to mean "cases and controversies of the sort traditionally amenable to, and resolved by, the judicial process." *Steel Co.*, 523 U.S. at 102; *see also Coleman v. Miller*, 307 U.S. 433, 460 (1939).

Qui tam actions appear to have originated around the end of the 13th century, when private individuals who had suffered injury began bringing actions in the royal courts on both their own and the Crown's behalf. Suit in this dual capacity was a device for getting their private claims into the respected royal courts, which generally entertained only matters involving the Crown's interests. Starting in the 14th century, as the royal courts began to extend jurisdiction to suits involving wholly private wrongs, the common-law *qui tam* action gradually fell into disuse, although it seems to have remained technically available for several centuries. . . .

Qui tam actions appear to have been as prevalent in America as in England, at least in the period immediately before and after the framing of the Constitution. . . . Moreover, immediately after the framing, the First Congress enacted a considerable number of informer statutes. Like their English counterparts, some of them provided both a bounty and an express cause of action; others provided a bounty only.

We think this history well nigh conclusive with respect to the question before us here: whether *qui tam* actions were "cases and controversies of the sort traditionally amenable to, and resolved by, the judicial process." *Steel Co.*, 523 U.S. at 102. When combined with the theoretical justification for relator standing discussed earlier, it leaves no room for doubt that a *qui tam* relator under the FCA has Article III standing.

* * *

Justice Breyer, concurring. [Omitted.]

Justice Ginsberg, with whom Justice Breyer joins, concurring in the judgment. [Omitted.]

Justice Stevens, with whom Justice Souter joins, dissenting. [Omitted.]

Notes and Questions

1. *Whistleblowers.* Qui tam actions enable the government to discover fraudulent conduct by using the eyes and ears of citizens and by encouraging insiders to "blow the whistle" on government corruption, fraud, and abuse. Both the private person acting "for the person and for the United States Government" against the alleged false claimant share in the proceeds of the lawsuit. 31 U.S.C. § 3730(b)(1). In some cases, the relator's share can be in the tens of millions of dollars. *See, e.g.*, James T. Ratner, *The 10 Largest Qui Tam Whistleblower Rewards*, https://www.qui-tam -attorney.com/10-largest-qui-tam-whistleblower-rewards.html. While, as the Court

noted in *Stevens*, the False Claims Act is the primary source of qui tam actions, whistleblower recoveries are permitted in other federal white collar contexts as well. For example, the Dodd-Frank Act (2010) required the SEC to adopt rules to pay whistleblowers 10%–30% of any sanctions over $1 million. *See* 15 U.S.C. §78u-6. Under SEC Rule 21F-3(a), the SEC will pay an award to a whistleblower who:

(1) Voluntarily provide[s] the Commission

(2) With original information

(3) That leads to the successful enforcement by the Commission of a Federal court or administrative action

(4) In which the Commission obtains monetary sanctions totaling more than $1,000,000.

According to a December 2020 press release, the SEC has awarded $728 million in whistleblower awards to 118 individuals since the program issued its first award in 2012. What are some of the principal social benefits and risks to the availability of qui tam and other whistleblower awards?

2. *History.* The qui tam law dates back to the Civil War, and it has brought billions of dollars in recovery to the government. In 1986, the law was strengthened to make it easier for individuals to sue and recover in matters of defense contractors. While qui tam actions can be brought in many types of cases, this area of law has exploded in recent years in the health care field. Why has this occurred?

3. *Monetary recovery.* The relator is entitled to a percentage of the potentially large monetary recovery as a reward for exposing the wrongdoing. According to the statute, recovery ranges from 15% to 25% if the government intervenes, and from 25% to 30% if the government does not — plus attorney's fees and costs. 31 U.S.C. §3730(d)(1)-(2). The government seeks to protect its interest in the integrity of the claim by joining the qui tam action and handling the negotiations in order to assure a successful outcome. However, the government does not always join a qui tam action. This decision can present ethical issues. For example, is it proper for the government to fail to promote litigation when the government is on notice that fraud is occurring? In addition, these cases can produce tension between the relators, the defendant, and the government. Why might the relationship between DOJ and the relator be strained? *See United States ex rel. Taxpayers Against Fraud v. General Electric Co.*, 41 F.3d 1032 (6th Cir. 1994).

Qui tam actions can extend for many years before they come to fruition. A recent trend is the involvement of private third-party litigation finance in qui tam claims. This practice is known as alternative litigation finance (ALF) and it provides funding to qui tam relators and their attorneys during the time that it takes for the lawsuit to run its course. *See* Matthew Andrews, *The Growth of Litigation Finance in DOJ Whistleblower Suits: Implications and Recommendations*, 123 YALE L.J. No. 7 (May 2014), http://www.yalelawjournal.org/note/the-growth-of-litigation-finance-in-doj-whistleblower-suits-implications-and-recommendations#_ftnref10. The author notes that qui tam actions provide lucrative investment opportunities for private hedge fund managers, providing enormous potential returns for investors. Financial assignments raise numerous policy and administrative questions, and this expanding trend may eventually become a staple in financing the costs of litigation and funding qui tam actions. *Id.* The Department of Justice has recently indicated that it may impose new disclosure rules where a qui tam action is funded by a third party. *See, e.g.,* Deputy Associate Attorney General Stephen Cox Provides Keynote Remarks at the 2020 Advanced Forum on False Claims and Qui Tam Enforcement, Justice News Release (January 27, 2020), https://www.justice.gov/opa/speech /deputy-associate-attorney-general-stephen-cox-provides-keynote-remarks-2020 -advanced. Why might disclosure of third-party funding for qui tam litigation be important to the government and defendants?

4. *The original source requirement.* Under the FCA, a relator must be an "original source" of the information that forms the basis for the suit, that is, the relator must have "direct and independent knowledge of the information on which the allegations are based." 31 U.S.C. § 3730(e)(4)(B). In *Rockwell Int'l Corp. v. United States,* 549 U.S. 457, 473–75 (2007), the Supreme Court found that the relator, a former employee of Rockwell, was not an original source as to events that occurred at Rockwell in 1987 and 1988. Because the relator had left Rockwell's employ in 1986, he had no personal knowledge of the events that occurred during 1987 and 1988, the timeframe upon which the qui tam action was based.

In addition, § 3730(e)(4)(A) provides that a court "shall dismiss" a qui tam action "if substantially the same allegations or transactions as alleged in the action ... were publicly disclosed" unless "the person bringing the action is an original source of the information." Under § 3730(e)(4)(B), an individual may still be deemed an "original source" after public disclosure if they have "knowledge that is independent of and materially adds to the publicly disclosed allegations or transactions, and ... has voluntarily *provided the information to the Government before filing an action* under this section."

The federal circuit courts have split over the meaning of the language "provided the information to the Government before filing an action." As outlined by the court in *United States ex rel. Duxbury v. Ortho Biotech Products, LP,* 579 F.3d 13 (1st Cir. 2009), the courts have followed three different approaches. Under the first approach, all that is required is that the relator voluntarily provide the information to the government before filing the qui tam action. Under the second approach, the relator must have been a source of the information provided to the entity that disclosed the allegations on which a suit is based. Under the third approach, an "original source" must provide the information to the government before any public disclosure, but the relator need not be the cause of the public disclosure.

5. *Claims made to private entities.* Does the FCA cover false claims made to a private entity that are subsequently paid with government funds? The Supreme Court addressed this issue in *Allison Engine Co., Inc. v. U.S. ex rel. Sanders,* 553 U.S. 662 (2008). In that case, the Navy had entered into contracts with shipyards to build destroyers. The shipyards subcontracted with a components subcontractor, which in

turn subcontracted with two other subcontractors. The subcontracts required that the components be accompanied by a certificate of conformance ("COC") certifying that the components were manufactured according to Navy specifications. The contracts and subcontracts were paid with funds from the federal government.

Former employees of the initial subcontractor brought a qui tam suit seeking damages from the subcontractors under the FCA. At trial, the plaintiffs showed that the defendants had issued COCs falsely stating that their work complied with Navy specifications, and presented invoices for payment to the shipyards. The proof did not, however, include the invoices the shipyards submitted to the Navy. The district court granted defendants' motion for summary judgment, concluding that, absent proof that false claims were presented with the purpose of obtaining payment by the government, the evidence was legally insufficient under the FCA. The Sixth Circuit reversed, holding that FCA claims do not require proof of an intent to cause a false claim to be paid by the government; proof of an intent to cause such a claim to be paid by a private entity using government funds was sufficient.

Agreeing with the district court that an FCA claim does not lie in such circumstances, the Supreme Court reversed. The Court held that:

> If a subcontractor or another defendant makes a false statement to a private entity and does not intend the government to rely on that false statement as a condition of payment, the statement is not made with the purpose of inducing payment of a false claim "by the government." In such a situation, the direct link between the false statement and the government's decision to pay or approve a false claim is too attenuated to establish liability.

Id. at 671–72. Reconsider the false statements statute, 18 U.S.C. §1001, discussed in Chapter 9, False Statements, *supra*. The Supreme Court's theory in *Allison Engine* appears to differ from the mens rea requirement for false statements under 18 U.S.C. §1001, where the defendant need not know the jurisdictional component that he is lying to a federal agent. Would the defendants be guilty of making false statements under §1001? Why or why not?

6. *Post-*Allison *legislation.* The FCA was amended in several important respects by the Fraud Enforcement and Recovery Act of 2009 ("FERA"), P.L. 111-21. Among those amendments was a provision designed to overturn the *Allison Engine* decision. New sections 3729(a)(1)(A), (B), (C), and (G) impose liability on one who:

(A) knowingly presents, or causes to be presented, a false or fraudulent claim for payment or approval;

(B) knowingly makes, uses, or causes to be made or used, a false record or statement material to a false or fraudulent claim;

(C) conspires to commit a violation of subparagraph (A), (B), (D), (E), (F), or (G); . . . or

(G) knowingly makes, uses, or causes to be made or used, a false record or statement material to an obligation to pay or transmit money or property to the government, or knowingly conceals or knowingly and improperly avoids or decreases an obligation to pay or transmit money or property to the government.

The definitional section of the statute, § 3729(b), overturns *Allison Engine* by, among other things, deleting the "by the government" language upon which the *Allison Engine* decision relied. FCA liability now requires a nexus to the government, covering requests for funds to a contractor, grantee, or other recipient, if the funds are "to be spent or used on the government's behalf or to advance a government program or interest." Also, FERA contains a materiality requirement for actions brought under the FCA, defining "material" as "having a natural tendency to influence, or be capable of influencing, the payment or receipt of money or property." Does the expanded liability create dangers for potential defendants? Why or why not?

Problem

18-3. Rhonda, a registered nurse, brought a qui tam action against the nursing home facilities at which she works for the submission of hundreds of fraudulent Medicare claims. The nursing home facilities moved to dismiss Rhonda's claim, arguing that she lacked standing because she entered into an alternative litigation finance agreement (ALF) with a hedge fund. Under the terms of Rhonda's ALF agreement, the hedge fund would finance her litigation expenses in exchange for 50% of any award she recovers. The facilities claim that by assigning her rights to the award to a third party, Rhonda forfeited her standing as a qui tam litigant under *Stevens*.

How should the court rule? Why?

C. Parallel Proceedings

Parallel proceedings exist when the government pursues simultaneous or successive civil and criminal investigations and/or cases relating to the same parties and activities. At the conclusion of a civil matter, the federal agency frequently turns the matter over to the Department of Justice for possible criminal proceedings. If the government has reasonable suspicion to believe that the federal criminal laws have been violated, then the matter may be referred to the appropriate U.S. Attorney's office for further investigation. Parallel proceedings complicate the legal and strategic landscape.

1. Fifth Amendment Risks

When civil matters threaten to become criminal matters, the risks for defendants are tremendous. A critical dilemma for the defendant involves the Fifth Amendment — should a defendant facing a possible criminal action refrain from testifying at a civil proceeding based on the right against self-incrimination?

United States v. Kordel

397 U.S. 1 (1970)

Mr. JUSTICE STEWART delivered the opinion of the Court.

The respondents are the president and vice president, respectively, of Detroit Vital Foods, Inc. They were convicted in the United States District Court for the Eastern District of Michigan, along with the corporation, for violations of the Federal Food, Drug, and Cosmetic Act. The Court of Appeals for the Sixth Circuit reversed the respondents' convictions on the ground that the Government's use of interrogatories to obtain evidence from the respondents in a nearly contemporaneous civil condemnation proceeding operated to violate their Fifth Amendment privilege against compulsory self-incrimination. We granted certiorari to consider the questions raised by the Government's invocation of simultaneous civil and criminal proceedings in the enforcement of federal law.

In March 1960 the Division of Regulatory Management of the Food and Drug Administration (hereafter FDA) instructed the agency's Detroit office to investigate the respondents' possible violations of the Food, Drug, and Cosmetic Act. Within a month the Detroit office recommended to the Division a civil seizure of two of the respondents' products, Korleen and Frutex; within another month the Division similarly recommended seizure to the FDA's General Counsel. On June 6, 1960, the General Counsel requested the United States Attorney for the Eastern District of Michigan to commence an in rem action against these products of the corporation, and the United States Attorney filed a libel three days later. The corporation, appearing as the claimant, answered the libel on September 12, 1960. An FDA official in the Division of Regulatory Management then prepared extensive interrogatories to be served on the corporation in this civil action. The United States Attorney filed the agency's interrogatories on January 6, 1961, pursuant to Rule 33 of the Federal Rules of Civil Procedure.

After the Division official had drafted the interrogatories, he recommended that pursuant to the Food, Drug, and Cosmetic Act the FDA serve upon the corporation and the respondents a notice that the agency contemplated a criminal proceeding against them with respect to the transactions that were the subject of the civil action. On January 9, 1961, three days after the filing of the interrogatories in the civil action, the Detroit office received an instruction from the Division to serve the statutory notice. The Detroit office complied 10 days later, and on March 8, 1961, the agency held a hearing on the notice.

On April 10, the corporation, having received the FDA's interrogatories but not yet having answered them, moved to stay further proceedings in the civil action or, in the alternative, to extend the time to answer the interrogatories until after disposition of the criminal proceeding.... Permitting the Government to obtain proof of violations of the Act by resort to civil discovery procedures, the movant urged, would be "improper" and would work a "grave injustice against the claimant;" it would also enable the Government to have pretrial discovery of the respondents' defenses to future criminal charges. Counsel expressly disavowed any "issue of a self-incrimination privilege in favor of the claimant corporation." And nowhere in the moving papers did counsel raise a claim of the Fifth Amendment privilege against compulsory self-incrimination with respect to the respondents.

On June 21, 1961, the District Court denied the motion upon finding that the corporation had failed to demonstrate that substantial prejudice and harm would result from being required to respond to the interrogatories. The court reasoned that the notice did not conclusively indicate the Government would institute a criminal proceeding, that six to 12 months could elapse from the service of the statutory notice to initiation of a criminal prosecution, and that the Government could obtain data for a prosecution from the testimony in the civil action or by subpoenaing the books and records of the corporation. Accordingly, the court concluded, the interests of justice did not require that the Government be denied the information it wanted simply because it had sought it by way of civil-discovery procedures. On September 5, 1961, in compliance with the court's directive, the corporation, through the respondent Feldten, answered the Government's interrogatories.

On July 28, 1961, five weeks after the District Court's order but more than a month before receipt of the answers to the interrogatories, the Director of the FDA's Detroit office recommended a criminal prosecution to the Division. The Division forwarded the recommendation to the General Counsel on August 31, 1961, still prior to receipt of Feldten's answers. While the matter was pending in the General Counsel's office, the Division officer who had originally drafted the proposed interrogatories recommended that additional violations of the statute be alleged in the indictment. On June 13, 1962, the Department of Health, Education, and Welfare requested the Department of Justice to institute a criminal proceeding, and about two months after that the latter department instructed the United States Attorney in Detroit to seek an indictment. The civil case, still pending in the District Court, proceeded to settlement by way of a consent decree in November 1962, and eight months later the Government obtained the indictment underlying the present judgments of conviction.

At the outset, we assume that the information Feldten supplied the Government in his answers to the interrogatories, if not necessary to the proof of the Government's case in the criminal prosecution, as the Court of Appeals thought, at least provided evidence or leads useful to the Government. . . .

The Court of Appeals thought the answers to the interrogatories were involuntarily given. The District Judge's order denying the corporation's motion to defer the answers to the interrogatories, reasoned the court, left the respondents with three choices: they could have refused to answer, thereby forfeiting the corporation's property that was the subject of the libel; they could have given false answers to the interrogatories, thereby subjecting themselves to the risk of a prosecution for perjury; or they could have done just what they did — disclose the requested information, thereby supplying the Government with evidence and leads helpful in securing their indictment and conviction.

In this analysis we think the Court of Appeals erred. For Feldten need not have answered the interrogatories. Without question he could have invoked his Fifth Amendment privilege against compulsory self-incrimination. Surely Feldten was not barred from asserting his privilege simply because the corporation had no privilege of its own, or because the proceeding in which the Government sought information was civil rather than criminal in character.

To be sure, service of the interrogatories obliged the corporation to appoint an agent who could, without fear of self-incrimination, furnish such requested information as was available to the corporation. The corporation could not satisfy its obligation under Rule 33 simply by pointing to an agent about to invoke his constitutional privilege. It would indeed be incongruous to permit a corporation to select an individual to verify the corporation's answers, who because he fears self-incrimination may thus secure for the corporation the benefits of a privilege it does not have. Such a result would effectively permit the corporation to assert on its own behalf the personal privilege of its individual agents.

The respondents press upon us the situation where no one can answer the interrogatories addressed to the corporation without subjecting himself to a real and appreciable risk of self-incrimination. For present purposes we may assume that in such a case the appropriate remedy would be a protective order under Rule 30(b), postponing civil discovery until termination of the criminal action. But we need not decide this troublesome question. For the record before us makes clear that even though the respondents had the burden of showing that the Government's interrogatories were improper, they never even asserted, let alone demonstrated, that there was no authorized person who could answer the interrogatories without the possibility of compulsory self-incrimination. To the contrary, the record shows that nobody associated with the corporation asserted his privilege at all. The respondents do not suggest that Feldten, who answered the interrogatories on behalf of the corporation, did so while unrepresented by counsel or without appreciation of the possible consequences. His failure at any time to assert the constitutional privilege leaves him in no position to complain now that he was compelled to give testimony against himself.

Kordel's claim of compulsory self-incrimination is even more tenuous than Feldten's. Not only did Kordel never assert the privilege; he never even answered any interrogatories.

The respondents urge that even if the Government's conduct did not violate their Fifth Amendment privilege against compulsory self-incrimination, it nonetheless reflected such unfairness and want of consideration for justice as independently to require the reversal of their convictions. On the record before us, we cannot agree that the respondents have made out either a violation of due process or a departure from proper standards in the administration of justice requiring the exercise of our supervisory power. The public interest in protecting consumers throughout the Nation from misbranded drugs requires prompt action by the agency charged with responsibility for administration of the federal food and drug laws. But a rational decision whether to proceed criminally against those responsible for the misbrand-ing may have to await consideration of a fuller record than that before the agency at the time of the civil seizure of the offending products. It would stultify enforce-ment of federal law to require a governmental agency such as the FDA invariably to choose either to forgo recommendation of a criminal prosecution once it seeks civil relief, or to defer civil proceedings pending the ultimate outcome of a criminal trial.

We do not deal here with a case where the Government has brought a civil action solely to obtain evidence for its criminal prosecution or has failed to advise the defendant in its civil proceeding that it contemplates his criminal prosecution; nor with a case where the defendant is without counsel or reasonably fears prejudice from adverse pretrial publicity or other unfair injury; nor with any other special circumstances that might suggest the unconstitutionality or even the impropriety of this criminal prosecution.

Overturning these convictions would be tantamount to the adoption of a rule that the Government's use of interrogatories directed against a corporate defendant in the ordinary course of a civil proceeding would always immunize the corpora-tion's officers from subsequent criminal prosecution. The Court of Appeals was cor-rect in stating that the Government may not use evidence against a defendant in a criminal case which has been coerced from him under penalty of either giving the evidence or suffering a forfeiture of his property. But on this record there was no such violation of the Constitution, and no such departure from the proper adminis-tration of criminal justice.

Accordingly, the judgment of the Court of Appeals is reversed, and the case is remanded to that court for further proceedings consistent with this opinion.

It is so ordered.

Notes and Questions

1. *Civil testimony.* Notice the timing of the legal proceedings in the *Kordel* case. *Kordel* raises the very real dilemma faced by litigants who are considering testifying in a civil proceeding while the potential for criminal prosecution looms. What are the precise dilemmas a defendant faces when considering whether or not to testify in the civil proceeding?

2. *Fifth Amendment risks.* Identify the risks a civil litigant faces if the litigant wants to assert the Fifth Amendment in a civil case and future criminal prosecution is likely. What are the implications in the civil case? In the upcoming criminal case?

3. *Adverse inferences*: Baxter v. Palmigiano. The law is well established that the Fifth Amendment protects a criminal defendant from having a judge or jury draw an adverse inference from the failure to testify. In civil proceedings, however, a wit-ness's assertion of the Fifth Amendment right to silence may have serious negative consequences. In *Baxter v. Palmigiano*, 425 U.S. 308 (1976), for example, a prison inmate was brought before a disciplinary board on charges of inciting a disturbance

in the prison. During the proceedings, he was told that the state might bring criminal charges against him. He was advised that if he chose to remain silent in the face of questioning by the board, his silence could be used against him in any subsequent criminal action. When he refused to answer questions based on his Fifth Amendment privilege, he was punished based on the assumption that his silence was equivalent to affirmative answers to the questions. The Supreme Court found that this use of the incriminating inference was proper and did not violate the Fifth Amendment. Lower courts have limited *Baxter* to those situations where there is independent evidence of the underlying facts.

4. *Corporate privilege against self-incrimination.* Why did Detroit Vital Foods not assert a Fifth Amendment privilege against self-incrimination?

2. Immunized Evidence

During the course of a civil matter, a litigant may seek to obtain evidence that has been produced in a prior proceeding. When a plaintiff seeks immunized evidence, several impediments exist. How can a civil attorney obtain information that is protected under a grant of immunity? Would it be admissible in a civil proceeding? Can judges or civil attorneys offer immunity to a witness in order to secure the testimony of a deponent in a civil case? The Supreme Court addressed this and related questions in the next case. (Refer to Chapter 17, Self-Incrimination — Witness Testimony and Document Production, *supra*, for a discussion of principles of immunity.)

Pillsbury Co. v. Conboy
459 U.S. 248 (1983)

JUSTICE POWELL delivered the opinion of the Court.

Pursuant to the federal use immunity provisions, 18 U.S.C. §§ 6001–6005, a United States Attorney may request an order from a federal court compelling a witness to testify even though he has asserted his privilege against self-incrimination. Section 6002 provides, however, that "no testimony or other information compelled under the order (or any information directly or indirectly derived from such testimony or other information) may be used against the witness in any criminal case. . . ." The issue presented in this case is whether a deponent's civil deposition testimony, repeating verbatim or closely tracking his prior immunized testimony, is immunized "testimony" that can be compelled over the valid assertion of his Fifth Amendment privilege.

Respondent John Conboy is a former executive of a defendant in the *In re Corrugated Container Antitrust Litigation*, M.D.L. 310 (S.D. Tex.). In January 1978, United States Department of Justice attorneys interviewed Conboy following a promise of use immunity. Conboy subsequently appeared before a grand jury investigating price-fixing activities and, pursuant to 18 U.S.C. § 6002, was granted formal use immunity for his testimony.

Following the criminal indictment of several companies, numerous civil anti-trust actions were filed in various United States district courts. . . . The District Court ordered that portions of the immunized government interview and grand-jury testimony of certain witnesses, including that of Conboy, be made available to lawyers for the class and opt-outs.

Pursuant to a subpoena issued by the District Court for the Northern District of Illinois, Conboy appeared in Chicago for a deposition at which he, his counsel, and petitioners' counsel had copies of his immunized testimony. The transcripts were marked as deposition exhibits so that all could follow the intended examination. The questioning fell into the following pattern: a question was read from the transcript; it then was rephrased to include the transcript answer (*i.e.*, "Is it not the fact that. . . ."); finally, Conboy was asked if he had "so testified" in his immunized interview and grand-jury examination. Conboy refused to answer each question, asserting his Fifth Amendment privilege against self-incrimination.

The District Court granted petitioners' motion to compel Conboy to answer the questions.

When Conboy continued to claim his privilege, the District Court held him in contempt, but stayed its order pending appeal. A panel of the Court of Appeals for the Seventh Circuit affirmed the contempt order, holding that, "[b]ecause the questions asked in this deposition were taken verbatim from or closely tracked the transcript of Conboy's grand jury testimony, we believe that his answers at the deposition would be 'derived from' the prior immunized [testimony] and therefore unavailable for use in any subsequent criminal prosecution." *In re Corrugated Container Antitrust Litigation*, 655 F.2d 748, 751 (1981).

On rehearing en banc, the Court of Appeals reversed the District Court. It first determined that Conboy's alleged fear of prosecution was more than "fanciful," and that Conboy therefore was entitled to assert his Fifth Amendment privilege unless his deposition testimony could not be used against him in a subsequent criminal action. The court then held that under §6002, absent a separate and independent grant of immunity, a deponent's civil deposition testimony that repeats verbatim or closely tracks his prior immunized testimony is not protected. While acknowledging that verbatim questions "of course [would be] derived" from the immunized testimony, the court reasoned that the answers to such questions "are derived from the deponent's current, independent memory of events" and thus "necessarily create a new source of evidence" that could be used in a subsequent criminal prosecution against Conboy. 661 F.2d 1145, 1155 (1981).

We granted certiorari to resolve the conflict in the Courts of Appeals, and now affirm.

It is not disputed that the *questions* asked of Conboy were directly or indirectly derived from his immunized testimony. The issue as presented to us is whether the causal connection between the questions and the *answers* is so direct that the answers also are derived from that testimony and therefore should be excluded under the grant of immunity.

Petitioners' argument is based on the language of § 6002 and on a common understanding of the words "derived from." The questions formulated on the basis of immunized testimony are clearly "derived from" the prior testimony. Thus, the answers that repeat verbatim or closely track a deponent's testimony are necessarily also "derived from" and "tainted by" such testimony. Petitioners therefore find no basis for the distinction made by the Court of Appeals between questions and answers responsive to those same questions. An answer by its very nature is evoked by and responds to information contained in a question.

Conboy's position is also straightforward: Questions do not incriminate; answers do. Unlike the questions, answers are not directly or indirectly derived from the immunized grand jury or interview transcripts, but from the deponent's current, independent memory of events. Even when a deponent's deposition answers are identical to those he gave to the grand jury, he is under oath to tell the truth, not necessarily as he told it before the grand jury, but as he knows it now. Each new statement of the deponent creates a new "source." In sum, the initial grant of [use] immunity does not prevent the prosecutor from prosecuting; it merely limits his sources of evidence.

Although the parties make their arguments in terms tracking those of the statute — whether the deposition testimony is "derived from" the prior testimony — it is clear that the crux of their dispute is whether the earlier grant of immunity itself compelled Conboy to talk. Petitioners contend that the prior grant of immunity *already* had supplanted Conboy's Fifth Amendment privilege at the time of the civil deposition. Petitioners would limit this immunity, of course, to testimony that "closely tracks" his prior immunized testimony. It is argued that this would not threaten the Government's need for admissible evidence or the individual's interest in avoiding self-incrimination. In the absence of such a threat, admissible evidence should be available to civil antitrust plaintiffs. But we cannot accept the assumptions upon which petitioners' conclusion rests. In our view, a District Court cannot compel Conboy to answer deposition questions, over a valid assertion of his Fifth Amendment right, absent a duly authorized assurance of immunity at the time.

We note at the outset that although there may be practical reasons for not testifying, as far as the deponent's Fifth Amendment right is concerned he should be indifferent between the protection afforded by silence and that afforded by immunity. A deponent's primary interest is that the protection be certain. The Government's interest, however, may be affected seriously by whether the deponent relies at the civil deposition on his Fifth Amendment privilege or on his prior grant of immunity. With due recognition of petitioners' need for admissible evidence, our inquiry then is whether this need can be met without jeopardizing the Government's interest in limiting the scope of an immunity grant or encroaching upon the deponent's certainty of protection.

Questions taken verbatim from a transcript of immunized testimony could evoke one of several responses from a deponent: (i) he could repeat or adopt his immunized answer; (ii) he could affirm that the transcript of his immunized answers accurately reflects his prior testimony; (iii) he could recall additional information responsive to the question but not disclosed in his immune testimony; or (iv) he could disclose information that is not responsive to the question. Petitioners do not contend, nor could they, that the prior grant of use immunity affords protection for all self-incriminating information disclosed by the immunized witness on any occasion after the giving of the immunized testimony. Rather, petitioners argue that only the first three responses would be "derived from" his immune testimony and therefore would be unavailable for use against the deponent in any subsequent criminal prosecution.

But even if the direct examination is limited to the questions and answers in the immunized transcript, there remains the right of cross examination, a right traditionally relied upon expansively to test credibility as well as to seek the truth. Petitioners recognize this problem, but maintain that the antitrust defendants "would be entitled to test the accuracy and truthfulness of Conboy's repeated immunized testimony without going beyond the confines of that testimony." Regardless of any limitations that may be imposed on its scope, however, cross examination is intended to and often will produce information not elicited on direct. We must assume that, to produce admissible evidence, the scope of cross examination at the deposition cannot easily be limited to the immunized testimony. This assumption implicates both the Government's and the individual's interests embodied in §6002.

Use immunity was intended to immunize and exclude from a subsequent criminal trial only that information to which the Government expressly has surrendered future use. If the Government is engaged in an ongoing investigation of the particular activity at issue, immunizing new information (*e.g.,* the answers to questions in a case like this one) may make it more difficult to show in a subsequent prosecution that similar information was obtained from wholly independent sources. If a District Court were to conclude in a subsequent civil proceeding that the prior immunity order extended to civil deposition testimony closely tracking the immunized testimony, it in effect could invest the deponent with transactional immunity on matters about which he testified at the immunized proceedings. This is precisely the kind of immunity Congress intended to prohibit. The purpose of §6002 was to limit the scope of immunity to the level that is constitutionally required, as well as to limit the use of immunity to those cases in which the Attorney General, or officials designated by him, determine that gaining the witness's testimony outweighs the loss of the opportunity for criminal prosecution of that witness.

Petitioners' interpretation of §6002 also places substantial risks on the deponent. Unless the grant of immunity assures a witness that his incriminating testimony will not be used against him in a subsequent criminal prosecution, the witness has not received the certain protection of his Fifth Amendment privilege that he has been forced to exchange. No court has authority to immunize a witness. That responsibility, as we have noted, is peculiarly an executive one, and only the Attorney General or a designated officer of the Department of Justice has authority to grant use immunity. Nor should a court, at the time of the civil testimony, predetermine the decision of the court in a subsequent criminal prosecution on the question whether the Government has met its burden of proving "that the evidence it proposes to use is derived from a legitimate source wholly independent of the compelled testimony." *Kastigar*, 406 U.S. 441, 460 (1972). Yet in holding Conboy in contempt for his Fifth Amendment silence, the District Court below essentially predicted that a court in any future criminal prosecution of Conboy will be obligated to protect against evidentiary use of the deposition testimony petitioners seek. We do not think such a predictive judgment is enough.

We hold that a deponent's civil deposition testimony, closely tracking his prior immunized testimony, is not, without duly authorized assurance of immunity at the time, immunized testimony within the meaning of § 6002, and therefore may not be compelled over a valid assertion of his Fifth Amendment privilege. The judgment of the Court of Appeals accordingly is *Affirmed*.

[Concurring opinions omitted.]

JUSTICE STEVENS, with whom JUSTICE O'CONNOR joins, dissenting. [Omitted.]

Notes and Questions

1. *The power of immunity.* Civil litigants do not have the authority to offer immunity to witnesses in order to secure their testimony. Immunity is solely a prerogative of the Executive. Why is this so?

2. *Alternatives to immunity.* If the government does not offer immunity, how can a civil litigant obtain the testimony of a witness who asserts a valid Fifth Amendment claim?

3. *Benefits and dangers from civil testimony.* Prosecutors do not have the opportunity to depose targets of grand jury investigations or defendants in criminal proceedings. Thus, if a criminal defendant has testified in a civil matter, this provides the prosecutor with desirable evidence that is otherwise not available. A prosecutor can determine whether the civil testimony is at odds with the trial testimony and use any testimonial discrepancies in cross-examination. Evidence is also useful to corroborate or discredit other witnesses in the case. What other benefits can the government derive from the civil matter testimony?

On the other hand, the government may face special challenges if one of its witnesses has testified under oath in a related civil matter prior to the criminal trial. Are there dangers for the government if its own witness has testified in a prior civil case?

4. *DOJ Transparency.* Not all investigating government agencies have been transparent with deponents about the possibility that their testimony will find its way into criminal proceedings. It was only in 2020 that the DOJ Antitrust Division updated its deposition procedures to include the following warning to deponents:

The information you provide may be used by the Department of Justice in other civil, criminal, administrative, or regulatory cases or proceedings. Individuals may refuse, in accordance with the rights guaranteed to them by the Fifth Amendment to the Constitution of the United States, to produce documents and/or answer any question that may tend to incriminate them.

Press Release 20-905, U.S. Dep't of Justice, *Antitrust Division Announces Updates to Civil Investigative Demand Forms and Deposition Process* (Sept. 10, 2020), https://www.justice.gov/opa/pr/antitrust-division-announces-updates-civil-investigative-demand-forms-and-deposition-process.

3. Grand Jury Risks

When a private civil litigant seeks disclosure of grand jury material, what standard must be met? In addition, logistical venue questions can be critical to the outcome, as the next cases demonstrate. (Refer to Chapter 16, The Grand Jury, *supra*, for principles relating to grand jury secrecy.)

Douglas Oil Co. v. Petrol Stops N.W.

441 U.S. 211 (1979)

JUSTICE POWELL delivered the opinion of the Court.

This case presents two intertwined questions concerning a civil litigant's right to obtain transcripts of federal criminal grand jury proceedings. First, what justification for disclosure must a private party show in order to overcome the presumption of grand jury secrecy applicable to such transcripts? Second, what court should assess the strength of this showing — the court where the civil action is pending, or the court that acts as custodian of the grand jury documents?

Respondent Petrol Stops Northwest is a gasoline retailer unaffiliated with any major oil company. In 1973, it operated 104 service stations located in Arizona, California, Oregon, Washington, and several other States. On December 13, 1973, respondent filed an antitrust action in the District of Arizona against 12 large oil companies, including petitioners Douglas Oil Co. of California and Phillips Petroleum Co. In its complaint, respondent alleged that on January 1, 1973, there had been a sharp reduction in the amount of gasoline offered for sale to it, and that this reduction had resulted from a conspiracy among the oil companies to restrain trade in gasoline, in violation of §§ 1 and 2 of the Sherman Act. As a part of this conspiracy, respondent charged, petitioners and their codefendants had fixed the prices of gasoline at the retail and wholesale distribution levels in California, Oregon and Washington.

Respondents Gas-A-Tron of Arizona and Coinoco also independently sell gasoline through service stations they own or lease. Unlike respondent Petrol Stops Northwest, however, their operations are limited to the vicinity of Tucson, Ariz.

On November 2, 1973, Gas-A-Tron and Coinoco filed an antitrust complaint in the District of Arizona naming as defendants nine large oil companies, including petitioner Phillips Petroleum Co. Like respondent Petrol Stops Northwest, Gas-A-Tron and Coinoco alleged that as of January 1, 1973, their supply of gasoline had been sharply reduced, and attributed this reduction to a conspiracy to restrain trade in violation of the Sherman Act. The specific charges of illegal behavior asserted by the two retailers substantially paralleled those made by Petrol Stops Northwest in its complaint, and included an allegation that the defendants had fixed the price of gasoline at the wholesale and retail levels.

Although the issues and defendants in the two actions were substantially the same, the cases were assigned to two different judges in the District of Arizona. In February 1974, respondents served upon petitioners a set of interrogatories which included a request that petitioners state whether either of their companies at any time between January 1, 1968, and December 14, 1974, had had any communication with any of their competitors concerning the wholesale price of gasoline to be sold to unaffiliated retailers. Petitioners also were asked to produce any documents they had concerning such communications. Petitioners responded that they were aware of no such communications, and therefore could produce no documents pertinent to the request.

In the meantime, the Antitrust Division of the Department of Justice had been investigating since 1972 the pricing behavior on the west coast of several major oil companies, including petitioners. As part of this investigation, employees of petitioners were called to testify before a grand jury empaneled in the Central District of California. The Government's investigation culminated on March 19, 1975, when the grand jury returned an indictment charging petitioners and four other oil companies with having conspired to fix the price of "rebrand gasoline" in California, Oregon, Washington, Nevada, and Arizona. The indictment alleged that the price-fixing conspiracy had begun in July 1970 and had continued at least until the end of 1971.

Although initially all six defendants charged in the criminal indictment pleaded not guilty, by December 1975, each had pleaded *nolo contendere* and was fined $50,000. Before changing their pleas, petitioners asked the District Court for the Central District of California to give them copies of the transcripts of testimony given by their employees before the grand jury. Their request was granted, and it appears that petitioners continue to possess copies of these transcripts.

In October 1976, respondents served upon petitioners requests for production of the grand jury transcripts in petitioners' possession. Petitioners objected to the requests for production, arguing that the transcripts were not relevant to the private antitrust actions and that they were not likely to lead to any admissible evidence. Respondents did not pursue their discovery requests by making a motion in the Arizona trial court to compel discovery. Rather, they filed a petition in the District Court for the Central District of California asking that court, as guardian of the grand jury transcripts to order them released to respondents. An attorney from the Antitrust Division of the Department of Justice appeared and indicated that the Government had no objection to respondents' receiving the transcripts already made available to petitioners. He suggested to the court, however, that the real parties in interest were petitioners, and therefore that they should be given an opportunity to be heard. The California District Court accepted this suggestion, and petitioners participated in the proceedings as parties adverse to respondents.

After briefing and oral argument, the court ordered the Chief of the Antitrust Division's Los Angeles Office "to produce for [respondents'] inspection and copying all grand jury transcripts previously disclosed to Phillips Petroleum Company or Douglas Oil Company of California or their attorneys relating to the indictment in *United States v. Phillips*." App. 48–49. The production order was subject, however, to several protective conditions. The transcripts were to "be disclosed only to counsel for [respondents] in connection with the two civil actions" pending in Arizona. Furthermore, under the court's order the transcripts of grand jury testimony "may be used . . . solely for the purpose of impeaching that witness or refreshing the recollection of a witness, either in deposition or at trial" in the Arizona actions. Finally, the court forbade any further reproduction of the matter turned over to respondents, and ordered that the material be returned to the Antitrust Division "upon completion of the purposes authorized by this Order."

On appeal, the Ninth Circuit affirmed the disclosure order. The Court of Appeals noted that under *United States v. Procter & Gamble Co.*, 356 U.S. 677 (1958), a party seeking access to grand jury transcripts must show a "particularized need." In evaluating the strength of the need shown in the present case, the Ninth Circuit considered two factors: the need for continued grand jury secrecy and respondents' need for the requested material. The court found the former need to be insubstantial, as the grand jury proceeding had concluded three years before and the transcripts already had been released to petitioners. As to respondents' claim, the court conceded that it knew little about the Arizona proceedings, but speculated that the transcripts would facilitate the prosecution of respondents' civil suits: Petitioners' answers to the 1974 interrogatories concerning price communications with competitors appeared to be at odds with their pleas of *nolo contendere* in the California criminal action.

Petitioners contend that the courts below erred in holding that, because the grand jury had dissolved and the requested material had been disclosed already to the defendants, respondents had to show only a "slight need" for disclosure. According to petitioners, this approach to disclosure is contrary to prior decisions of this Court indicating that "a civil litigant must demonstrate a compelling necessity for specified grand jury materials before disclosure is proper."

We consistently have recognized that the proper functioning of our grand jury system depends upon the secrecy of grand jury proceedings. . . .

At the same time, it has been recognized that in some situations justice may demand that discrete portions of transcripts be made available for use in subsequent proceedings. Indeed, recognition of the occasional need for litigants to have access to grand jury transcripts led to the provision in Fed. R. Crim. Proc. 6(e)(2)(C)(i) that disclosure of grand jury transcripts may be made "when so directed by a court preliminarily to or in connection with a judicial proceeding."

In *United States v. Procter & Gamble Co.*, the Court sought to accommodate the competing needs for secrecy and disclosure by ruling that a private party seeking to obtain grand jury transcripts must demonstrate that "without the transcript a defense would be greatly prejudiced or that without reference to it an injustice would be done." 356 U.S. at 682. Moreover, the Court required that the showing of need for the transcripts be made "with particularity" so that "the secrecy of the proceedings [may] be lifted discretely and limitedly." *Id.* at 683.

In *Dennis v. United States*, 384 U.S. 855 (1966), the Court considered a request for disclosure of grand jury records in quite different circumstances. It was there held to be an abuse of discretion for a District Court in a criminal trial to refuse to disclose to the defendants the grand jury testimony of four witnesses who some years earlier had appeared before a grand jury investigating activities of the defendants. The grand jury had completed its investigation, and the witnesses whose testimony was sought already had testified in public concerning the same matters.

From *Procter & Gamble* and *Dennis* emerges the standard for determining when the traditional secrecy of the grand jury may be broken: Parties seeking grand jury transcripts under Rule 6(e) must show that the material they seek is needed to avoid a possible injustice in another judicial proceeding, that the need for disclosure is greater than the need for continued secrecy, and that their request is structured to cover only material so needed. Such a showing must be made even when the grand jury whose transcripts are sought has concluded its operations, as it had in *Dennis*. For in considering the effects of disclosure on grand jury proceedings, the courts must consider not only the immediate effects upon a particular grand jury, but also the possible effect upon the functioning of future grand juries. Persons called upon to testify will consider the likelihood that their testimony may one day be disclosed to outside parties. Fear of future retribution or social stigma may act as powerful deterrents to those who would come forward and aid the grand jury in the performance of its duties. Concern as to the future consequences of frank and full testimony is heightened where the witness is an employee of a company under investigation. Thus, the interests in grand jury secrecy, although reduced, are not eliminated merely because the grand jury has ended its activities.

It is clear from *Procter & Gamble* and *Dennis* that disclosure is appropriate only in those cases where the need for it outweighs the public interest in secrecy, and that the burden of demonstrating this balance rests upon the private party seeking disclosure. It is equally clear that as the considerations justifying secrecy become less relevant, a party asserting a need for grand jury transcripts will have a lesser burden in showing justification. In sum, as so often is the situation in our jurisprudence, the court's duty in a case of this kind is to weigh carefully the competing interests in light of the relevant circumstances and the standards announced by this Court.

And if disclosure is ordered, the court may include protective limitations on the use of the disclosed material, as did the District Court in this case. Moreover, we emphasize that a court called upon to determine whether grand jury transcripts should be released necessarily is infused with substantial discretion.

Applying these principles to the present case, we conclude that neither the District Court nor the Court of Appeals erred in the standard by which it assessed the request for disclosure under Rule 6(e)....

Petitioners contend, irrespective of the legal standard applied, that the District Court for the Central District of California was not the proper court to rule on respondents' motion for disclosure. Petitioners note that the Court of Appeals and the District Court both purported to base their decisions in part upon the need for use of the requested material in the civil antitrust proceedings pending in Arizona. This determination necessarily involved consideration of the nature and status of the Arizona proceedings, matters peculiarly within the competence of the Arizona District Court.

Although the question is an important one, this Court heretofore has had no occasion to consider which court or courts may direct disclosure of grand jury minutes under Fed. Rule Crim. Proc. 6(e). The federal courts that have addressed the question generally have said that the request for disclosure of grand jury minutes under Rule 6(e) must be directed toward the court under whose auspices the grand jury was empaneled. Indeed, those who seek grand jury transcripts have little choice other than to file a request with the court that supervised the grand jury, as it is the only court with control over the transcripts.

Quite apart from practical necessity, the policies underlying Rule 6(e) dictate that the grand jury's supervisory court participate in reviewing such requests, as it is in the best position to determine the continuing need for grand jury secrecy.... Where, as in this case, the request is made for use in a case pending in another district, the judges of the court having custody of the grand jury transcripts will have no firsthand knowledge of the litigation in which the transcripts allegedly are needed, and no practical means by which such knowledge can be obtained. In such a case, a judge in the district of the grand jury cannot weigh in an informed manner the need for disclosure against the need for maintaining grand jury secrecy. Thus, it may well be impossible for that court to apply the standard required by the decisions of this Court, reiterated above, for determining whether the veil of secrecy should be lifted.

In the present case, the District Court for the Central District of California was called upon to make an evaluation entirely beyond its expertise. The District Judge readily conceded that he had no knowledge of the civil proceedings pending several hundred miles away in Arizona. Nonetheless, he was asked to rule whether there was a "particularized need" for disclosure of portions of the grand jury transcript and whether this need outweighed the need for continued grand jury secrecy.

Generally we leave it to the considered discretion of the district court to determine the proper response to requests for disclosure under Rule 6(e). We have a duty, however, to guide the exercise of discretion by district courts, and when necessary to overturn discretionary decisions under Rule 6(e).

We find that the District Court here abused its discretion in releasing directly to respondents the grand jury minutes they requested. Appreciating that it was largely ignorant of the Arizona civil suits, the court nonetheless made a judgment concerning the relative needs for secrecy and disclosure. The court based its decision largely upon the unsupported assertions of counsel during oral argument before it, supplemented only by the criminal indictment returned by the grand jury, the civil complaints, and petitioners' response to a single interrogatory that appeared to be inconsistent with petitioners' *nolo contendere* plea in the criminal case. Even the court's comparison of the criminal indictment and the civil complaints did not indicate unambiguously what, if any, portions of the grand jury transcripts would be pertinent to the subject of the Arizona actions, as only some of the same parties were named and only some of the same territory was covered.

The possibility of an unnecessary breach of grand jury secrecy in situations such as this is not insignificant. A court more familiar with the course of the antitrust litigation might have seen important differences between the allegations of the indictment and the contours of the conspiracy respondents sought to prove in their civil actions — differences indicating that disclosure would likely be of little value to respondents, save perhaps as a mechanism for general discovery. Alternatively, the courts where the civil proceedings were pending might have considered disclosure at that point in the litigation to be premature; if there were to be conflicts between petitioners' statements and their actions in the criminal proceedings, the court might have preferred to wait until they ripened at depositions or even during testimony at trial.

Under these circumstances, the better practice would have been for the District Court, after making a written evaluation of the need for continued grand jury secrecy and a determination that the limited evidence before it showed that disclosure might be appropriate, to send the requested materials to the courts where the civil cases were pending. The Arizona court, armed with their special knowledge of the status of the civil actions, then could have considered the requests for disclosure in light of the California court's evaluation of the need for continued grand jury secrecy. In this way, both the need for continued secrecy and the need for disclosure could have been evaluated by the courts in the best position to make the respective evaluations. . . .

Our decision today therefore is restricted to situations, such as that presented by this case, in which the district court having custody of the grand jury records is unlikely to have dependable knowledge of the status of, and the needs of the parties in, the civil suit in which the desired transcripts are to be used.

The judgment of the Court of Appeals is reversed, and the case is remanded for further proceedings consistent with this opinion.

It is so ordered.

JUSTICE REHNQUIST, concurring. [Omitted.]

JUSTICE STEVENS, with whom THE CHIEF JUSTICE and JUSTICE STEWART join, dissenting. [Omitted.]

Notes and Questions

1. *Secrecy interests.* What are the particular interests served by safeguarding the release of grand jury material? How are these interests adversely affected by simultaneous litigation in various courts? In what circumstances might the interests of litigants needing grand jury information outweigh the social interests in grand jury secrecy?

2. *Standard for release of grand jury material.* In *Douglas Oil*, the Supreme Court adopted a standard for allowing a civil litigant access to grand jury materials:

   a. The material is needed to avoid a possible injustice in a judicial proceeding;

   b. The need for disclosure is greater than the need for continued secrecy; and

   c. The disclosure required is structured to cover only necessary materials.

Does this set of standards adequately address a civil litigant's need for access to grand jury material?

3. *Availability to DOJ civil attorneys.* The Court in *United States v. Sells Eng'g, Inc.*, 463 U.S. 418 (1983), addressed the standard by which grand jury material could be released to attorneys in the civil division of DOJ. Although the government argued that the Rule 6 disclosure exemptions applied to all government attorneys, the Supreme Court held that it was limited to only those government attorneys who were engaged in the criminal investigation. The Court held that the *Douglas Oil* standard is a "highly flexible one, adaptable to different circumstances and sensitive to the fact that the requirements of secrecy are greater in some situations than in others." *Id.* at 445. However, DOJ civil attorneys may receive grand jury information only via court order based on a showing of particularized need.

On the same day the Court decided the *Sells* case, it also refined the limits on the disclosure of grand jury information in connection with an IRS investigation. The Court considered whether a tax audit is "preliminary to or in connection with a judicial proceeding" in order to come within the protection of FED. R. CRIM. P. 6(e). The Court in *United States v. Baggot*, 463 U.S. 476, 480 (1983), held that administrative agencies cannot inspect grand jury materials unless the "primary purpose" of disclosure is to "assist in preparation or conduct of a judicial proceeding." The Court concluded that the IRS proposed to use the materials to perform the "non-litigative function of assessing taxes rather than to prepare for or to conduct litigation," and thus that the rules of grand jury secrecy prohibited the disclosure of the materials in these circumstances. *Id.* at 483.

4. *Benefits for civil attorneys.* Why might a civil attorney want access to grand jury material? What are some of the ways in which a prior criminal litigation can assist a civil claimant? The *Douglas Oil* Court reasoned that civil attorneys were not in the same class as criminal attorneys who were conducting the investigation at hand. Why is this so?

4. Timing of Parallel Proceedings

The sequence of parallel proceedings has the potential to affect both the government and defense. A defendant, for example, may face a choice between asserting the Fifth Amendment privilege in the civil matter — and allowing an adverse inference to be drawn — or providing testimony in the civil case that could be used in a later criminal case. On the other hand, the government may have its own reasons for delaying a civil case, which might provide the defendant with depositions and other forms of discovery that would not be available in a criminal case. The government may also fear loss of evidence and witness tampering if the civil case is allowed to proceed. Parallel proceedings thus raise important tactical, ethical, strategic, and legal questions.

In the following case, the government conducted an extensive civil investigation with the cooperation of persons who were later charged in a related criminal case. The district court dismissed the criminal indictment, holding that the government's conduct had violated the defendants' constitutional rights. As you read the appeals court's decision, consider whether the government's conduct created the potential for unfairness or abuse.

United States v. Stringer

535 F.3d 929 (9th Cir. 2008)

SCHROEDER, CIRCUIT JUDGE:

The United States appeals from a final order of the district court dismissing criminal indictments against three individual defendants charging counts of criminal securities violations. The dismissal was premised on the district court's conclusion that the government had engaged in deceitful conduct, in violation of defendants' due process rights, by simultaneously pursuing civil and criminal investigations of defendants' alleged falsification of the financial records of their high-tech camera sales company. Foreseeing the possibility of an appeal, the district court held that the indictments must be dismissed, but ruled in the alternative that, should there be a criminal trial, all evidence provided by the individual defendants in response to Securities and Exchange Commission ("SEC") subpoenas should be suppressed....

. . .

We vacate the dismissal of the indictments because in a standard form it sent to the defendants, the government fully disclosed the possibility that information received in the course of the civil investigation could be used for criminal proceedings. There was no deceit; rather, at most, there was a government decision not to conduct the criminal investigation openly, a decision we hold the government was free to make. There is nothing improper about the government undertaking simultaneous criminal and civil investigations, and nothing in the government's actual conduct of those investigations amounted to deceit or an affirmative misrepresentation justifying the rare sanction of dismissal of criminal charges or suppression of evidence received in the course of the investigations.

Prior to the criminal action that forms the basis of this appeal, the SEC began investigating the defendants, J. Kenneth Stringer, III, J. Mark Samper, and William N. Martin, and their company for possible civil securities fraud violations. The company was FLIR Systems, Inc. ("FLIR"), an Oregon corporation headquartered in Portland that sells infrared and heat-sensing cameras for military and industrial use. The SEC began the investigation on June 8, 2000. About two weeks later, the SEC held the first of a series of meetings with the Oregon United States Attorney's Office ("USAO") to coordinate the ongoing SEC investigation with a possible criminal investigation. An SEC Assistant Director and an SEC Staff Attorney met with the supervisor of the white collar crime section of the USAO to discuss the possibility of opening a criminal investigation. The meeting apparently convinced the USAO supervisor to investigate. Within days, the USAO and the Federal Bureau of Investigation ("FBI") opened a criminal investigation.

Federal securities laws authorize the SEC to transmit evidence it has gathered to the USAO to facilitate a criminal investigation by the USAO. To gather evidence for its criminal investigation, the Oregon USAO in June of 2000 sent a letter to the SEC (the "Access Letter") requesting access to the SEC's non-public investigative files, and the SEC promptly granted access.

The civil and criminal investigations proceeded in tandem and the SEC continued to meet and communicate with the USAO and FBI. The SEC turned over documents the SEC collected through its civil investigation.

At the beginning of the criminal investigation, the USAO identified two of the three defendants, FLIR's former CEO, Stringer, and former CFO, Samper, as possible targets, and named them in the USAO's Access Letter to the SEC. A few months later, in October 2000, the Assistant United States Attorney ("AUSA") assigned to the case made a list of the subjects of the investigation and placed asterisks and the comment "knew what [was] going on" next to the entries for Samper and Stringer. A month later, the AUSA stated in his handwritten notes that Stringer had "lied [about] his role in" the company. In April 2001, an e-mail from the SEC Staff Attorney to the SEC Assistant Director stated the AUSA "define[d] [the] targets as Ken Stringer and Mark Samper."

The district court concluded that the third defendant, Martin, former VP of Sales, was also an early potential target of the criminal investigation. Martin appears on the AUSA's early list of the subjects of the investigation above the comment "knew pushing up sales." During a January 2001 meeting, the SEC advised the USAO and

FBI that FLIR was blaming Stringer and Martin for the fraudulent conduct at the heart of the investigation.

Early in the criminal investigation, the USAO decided the investigation should remain confidential. At an October 2000 meeting between the SEC, USAO, and FBI, the AUSA advised that the evidence collected by the SEC might support criminal wire fraud charges. Nonetheless, an internal FBI memo issued in late October stated that the AUSA had concluded, based on the defendants' cooperation with the SEC at that point, that the SEC should investigate "without the assistance or inclusion of the FBI." At the January 2001 meeting between the SEC, FBI, and USAO, the SEC revealed that FLIR was cooperative and was providing evidence that was damaging to Stringer and Martin.

By June 2001, the USAO was not yet ready to convene a grand jury and issue indictments. The SEC and USAO believed that FLIR and defendant Samper would settle with the SEC so long as the U.S. Attorney was not directly involved. During a December 2001 phone conversation between the AUSA assigned to the case and the SEC Assistant Director, the AUSA continued to believe it was "premature [sic] to surface" and that the presence of an AUSA would "impede" a meeting between the SEC and defendants. During a December 2002 phone call, the SEC and USAO decided that the USAO would not "surface," i.e., convene a grand jury and issue indictments, until the "end of Jan/early Feb" 2003.

The SEC facilitated the criminal investigation in a number of ways. The SEC offered to conduct the interviews of defendants so as to create "the best record possible" in support of "false statement cases" against them, and the AUSA instructed the SEC Staff Attorney on how best to do that. The AUSA asked the relevant SEC office, located in Los Angeles, to take the depositions in Oregon so that the Portland Office of the USAO would have venue over any false statements case that might arise from the depositions, and the SEC did so. Both the SEC and USAO wanted the existence of the criminal investigation kept confidential. The SEC Staff Attorney, at one of the Portland depositions, made a note that she wanted to "make sure [the] court reporters won't tell [FLIR's Attorney]" that there was an AUSA assigned to the case.

The SEC, however, did not hide from the defendants the possibility — even likelihood — of such an investigation. The SEC sent each of the defendants subpoenas in the summer of 2001, and attached to each was Form 1662, a form sent to all witnesses subpoenaed to testify before the SEC. Under the header "Routine Uses of Information," the four-page form states that "[t]he Commission often makes its files available to other governmental agencies, particularly the United States Attorneys and state prosecutors. There is a likelihood that information supplied by you will be made available to such agencies where appropriate."

Form 1662 also advises witnesses of their Fifth Amendment rights. After the heading "Fifth Amendment and Voluntary Testimony," the form states that:

> Information you give may be used against you in any federal . . . civil or criminal proceeding brought by the Commission or any other agency. You

may refuse, in accordance with the rights guaranteed to you by the Fifth Amendment of the Constitution of the United States, to give any information that may tend to incriminate you or subject you to fine, penalty, or forfeiture.

None of the defendants invoked his right against self-incrimination during his deposition, and all proceeded to testify in compliance with the subpoena. Each of the defendants was represented by counsel when he testified.

During the course of Stringer's deposition, taken in Portland in October 2001, Stringer's attorney actually questioned the SEC Staff Attorney about the involvement of the USAO. In response to those questions, the SEC Staff Attorney answered as follows:

MR. MARTSON: My first question is whether Mr. Stringer is a target of any aspect of the investigation being conducted by the SEC.

STAFF ATTORNEY: The SEC does not have targets in this investigation.

MR. MARTSON: The other questions I have relate to whether or not, in connection with your investigation, the SEC is working in conjunction with any other department of the United States, such as the U.S. Attorney's Office in any jurisdiction, or the Department of Justice.

STAFF ATTORNEY: As laid out in the 1662 form, in the "routine use of" section there are routine uses of our investigation, and it is the agency's policy not to respond to questions like that, but instead, to direct you to the other agencies you mentioned.

MR. MARTSON: And which U.S. Attorney's Office might I inquire into?

STAFF ATTORNEY: That would be a matter up to your discretion.

The record does not show the SEC did anything to impede an inquiry, nor does it disclose that any inquiry was made. The record reflects that the government never furnished defendants with any false information concerning the existence of a criminal investigation.

In September 2002, a year before the criminal indictments, defendants Samper and Martin entered into consent decrees in the civil action, agreeing to pay penalties, disgorgement, and pre-judgment interest.

The Supreme Court has held that the government may conduct parallel civil and criminal investigations without violating the due process clause, so long as it does not act in bad faith. *See United States v. Kordel,* 397 U.S. 1, 11 (1970). In *Kordel,* the Supreme Court held that the government did not violate the due process rights of corporate executives when it used evidence it obtained from an FDA civil investigation to convict them of criminal misbranding. The Court explained that the FDA did not act in bad faith when it made a request for information, which ultimately was used in the criminal investigation, for the agency made similar requests as a matter of course in 75% of its civil investigations. The Court suggested that the government may act in bad faith if it brings a civil action solely for the purpose of obtaining evidence in a criminal prosecution and does not advise the defendant of the planned use of evidence in a criminal proceeding. The Court thus distinguished the *Kordel* investigation from bad faith cases where

> the [g]overnment has brought a civil action solely to obtain evidence for its criminal prosecution or has failed to advise the defendant in its civil proceeding that it contemplates his criminal prosecution; . . . [or] any other special circumstances . . . might suggest the unconstitutionality or even the impropriety of this criminal prosecution.

Id. at 12–13. . . .

In this case, the district court concluded that the government should have told defendants of the criminal investigation and that it violated the standards laid down in *Kordel* when it failed to "advise defendants that it anticipated their criminal prosecution." It held that the government engaged in "trickery and deceit" when the SEC staff attorney instructed court reporters to refrain from mentioning the AUSA's involvement. When the SEC staff attorney responded to Stringer's attorney's question, during Stringer's deposition, by directing him to the U.S. Attorney, the district court concluded that the SEC attorney "evaded the question."

In its appeal, the government argues that it had no legal duty to make any further disclosure of the existence of the pending criminal investigation. It points to the warnings in Form 1662 in which the government disclosed the possibility of criminal prosecution, and it stresses that it did not make any affirmative misrepresentations. It maintains the SEC attorney's answer was appropriate and truthful.

The defendants argue that the district court properly held that the use of the evidence obtained by the SEC in a criminal prosecution would violate defendants' Fifth Amendment privilege against self-incrimination. The defendants were advised that the evidence could be used in a criminal investigation, but defendants did not invoke their Fifth Amendment privilege during the SEC investigation. The government on appeal correctly contends that defendants waived or forfeited their Fifth Amendment right against self-incrimination.

The privilege against self-incrimination protects an individual from being forced to provide information that might establish a direct link in a chain of evidence leading to his conviction. It may be waived if it is not affirmatively invoked. . . .

The district court therefore erred in holding that defendants' waivers of the privilege were ineffective because they were not told of the U.S. Attorney's active involvement. The SEC Form 1662 used in this case alerts SEC investigative witnesses that the information can be used in a criminal proceeding. Defendants were on sufficient notice, and so were their attorneys. . . .

The defendants next contend that the district court properly concluded that the government used the civil investigation solely to obtain evidence for a subsequent criminal prosecution, in violation of due process. The Supreme Court in *Kordel* made it clear that dual investigations must meet the requirements of the Fifth Amendment Due Process Clause. *See* 397 U.S. at 11–12. While holding that "[i]t would stultify the enforcement of federal law" to curtail the government's discretion to conduct dual investigations strategically, the Court suggested that a defendant may be entitled to a remedy where "the [g]overnment has brought a civil action solely to obtain evidence for its criminal prosecution." 397 U.S. at 11–12. In this case, the government argues that it did not violate defendants' due process rights because the civil investigation was not commenced solely to obtain evidence for a criminal prosecution.

It is significant to our analysis that the SEC began its civil investigation first and brought in the U.S. Attorney later. This tends to negate any likelihood that the government began the civil investigation in bad faith, as, for example, in order to obtain evidence for a criminal prosecution. . . .

United States v. Carriles, 486 F.Supp.2d 599, 619–21 (W.D. Tex.2007), on the other hand, is a clear example of government bad faith. The district court dismissed an indictment because the U.S. Citizenship and Immigration Services ("USCIS") interviewed the defendant solely to collect evidence in support of a criminal case against him. The defendant, a Cuban national, filed an application for naturalization. Although USCIS had already determined that the defendant was not eligible for citizenship, the agency nonetheless invited him to a pre-citizenship interview in order to collect evidence for a criminal false statements case. The interview protocol was altered in so many ways to serve the needs of the criminal investigation that it became an interrogation. The court described the "interview" as follows:

> (1) it lasted eight hours over the course of two days as opposed to the usual maximum of thirty minutes, (2) it involved two interviewers, (3) the [g]overnment provided an interpreter, (4) there were a total of four attorneys present — two defense attorneys and two Government attorneys, and (5) it was both audio and videotaped.

Because the "entire interview was . . . a pretext for a criminal investigation," the district court dismissed the indictment.

Our case is not remotely similar to *Carriles.* In this case the SEC's civil investigation was opened first, led to SEC sanctions and was conducted pursuant to the SEC's own civil enforcement jurisdiction. It was not a pretext for the USAO's criminal investigation of defendants. Congress has expressly authorized the SEC to share information with the Department of Justice to facilitate the investigation and prosecution of crimes. We must conclude the SEC interviewed the defendants in support of a bona fide civil investigation. There was no violation of due process.

The judgment of the district court dismissing the indictment is VACATED. The district court's suppression ruling is REVERSED. The case is REMANDED for further proceedings.

Notes and Questions

1. *Potential for abuse.* Was the district court correct that the government used "trickery and deceit" in this case? Was the manner in which the government conducted the parallel investigations unfair to the defendants? Even if so, did the unfairness amount to a due process violation? For a critical analysis of the *Stringer* decision, see W. Warren Hamel & Danette R. Edwards, *Parallel Investigations — 'Pay No Attention to the Man Behind the Curtain:'* United States v. Stringer *and the Government's Obligations to Disclose,* White Collar Crime Rep. (BNA) Vol. 3, No. 11, at 367 (May 23, 2008).

For a case raising similar issues, see *United States v. Scrushy,* 366 F. Supp. 2d 1134 (N.D. Ala. 2005). In that case, the court found that the government's criminal investigation was too closely connected with its civil action. The court therefore excluded the defendant's civil SEC testimony from use in the criminal case. The government did not appeal this decision. *See* Eli Ewing, Comment: *Too Close for Comfort:* United States v. Stringer *and* United States v. Scrushy *Impose a Stricter Standard on SEC/DOJ Parallel Proceedings,* 25 Yale L. & Pol'y Rev. 217 (2006).

2. *Priority of litigation.* When there are common facts between the parallel civil and criminal proceedings, courts give judicial deference to the criminal proceeding. A criminal prosecution will have priority in scheduling because of the constitutional right to a speedy trial. When a civil litigant seeks a stay of an administrative or civil proceeding, the district court will have discretion to grant the stay pending the outcome of the criminal action. What specific risks does a litigant face if the requested stay is not granted?

3. *The Fifth Amendment and stays of civil proceedings.* While courts have discretion to grant a stay, there is no constitutional requirement that a stay be granted pending the outcome of criminal proceedings. The challenges facing a defendant confronted with parallel proceedings were illustrated in *Keating v. Off. of Thrift Supervision,* 45 F.3d 322 (9th Cir. 1995), a case arising out of a major savings and loan scandal. In that case, the Office of Thrift Supervision (OTS) instituted a civil proceeding against Keating and refused to stay that proceeding while Keating faced parallel state and federal criminal proceedings. Because of the criminal proceedings, Keating asserted his Fifth Amendment privilege in the civil OTS matter. Keating argued on appeal that the failure to stay the OTS case violated his due process rights. The Ninth Circuit disagreed. The court found that Keating had sufficient time to prepare for the OTS proceeding, and had no absolute right to a stay. The court therefore concluded that there was no abuse of discretion in denying the stay.

4. *Benefits to litigants.* The government will often assert that its investigation would be impeded if civil discovery proceeds. Why is this? What are the possible costs and benefits for the government if the civil discovery proceeds? What are the possible costs and benefits for the criminal defendant if civil discovery proceeds?

5. *Martha Stewart.* Martha Stewart was indicted, found guilty, and served five months in prison for four counts of lying to federal agents and obstructing justice.

While her criminal case was pending, a consolidated class action was filed against her and some of the directors of her company, Martha Stewart Living Omnimedia, Inc. *See Semon v. Martha Stewart Living Omnimedia, Inc.*, 02 Civ. 6273, Hearing Tr. (S.D.N.Y. Sept. 30, 2003).

The parties sought a stay regarding some of the witnesses who were expected to testify in the criminal case. The government argued that, if the individuals were deposed, Stewart's lawyers would gain an unfair discovery advantage. The rules of criminal procedure do not provide for pretrial depositions of witnesses. The court denied the government's request, finding that the government made numerous public pronouncements about the case. In addition, the court discredited the government's assertion that it would be unfairly disadvantaged, saying that it did not want the civil case to "hang[] in the air" for years, while the criminal proceedings were ongoing. *Id.* at 22. Courts are willing to consider allegations of unfair discovery and prejudice when ruling on motions such as these.

6. *Settlements.* Settlement negotiations present another opportunity for the government to gain evidence for use in a criminal case. The subject of parallel proceedings has the opportunity to seek a global settlement in order to resolve criminal charges along with the civil claims simultaneously. Rule 408 of the Federal Rules of Evidence deals with settlement discussions and their use at trial. Rule 408 protects settlement discussions from disclosure at a subsequent trial or hearing. The rule's protection relates to civil matters but does not extend to criminal prosecutions. Most courts hold that settlement discussions can be used against a defendant in a criminal case. Why is this distinction made in the evidentiary rules?

7. *Overlapping fines.* When there are parallel civil and criminal actions by different government agencies against a corporation, the corporation may end up getting sanctioned twice for the same underlying conduct. In 2018, the DOJ updated its Justice Manual with the following language:

> In parallel and/or joint corporate investigations and proceedings involving multiple Department components and/or other federal, state, or local enforcement authorities, Department attorneys should remain mindful of their ethical obligation not to use criminal enforcement authority unfairly to extract, or to attempt to extract, additional civil or administrative monetary payments. In addition, in resolving a case with a company that multiple Department components are investigating for the same misconduct, Department attorneys should coordinate with one another to avoid the unnecessary imposition of duplicative fines, penalties, and/or forfeiture against the company.

U.S. Dep't of Just., Just. Manual § 1-12.100 (2018).

8. *Admissions.* Rule 801(d)(2)(A) of the Federal Rules of Evidence allows party admissions to be offered against a litigant. *See United States v. Cohen*, 946 F.2d 430 (6th Cir. 1991) (SEC consent decree is admissible as party admission, not under Rule 408). The government does not have the opportunity to depose a criminal defendant

or to obtain statements prior to the indictment or trial of a criminal case. Because the government does not know what the defendant's position will be on critical aspects of the criminal matter, the government benefits from any prior statements, especially those made under oath. If the government has available a deposition of the criminal defendant, the contents can be included in an indictment and assist the prosecutor in crafting cross-examination questions. Whenever a party is engaged in discussions with the government preliminary to the filing of charges, during the course of a civil investigation or during settlement negotiations, these statements or other documents can be admitted against the party as admissions.

Problem

18-4. You have a corporate client who is engaged in retail activities. The company has a network of stores across the country, and also conducts sales on the Internet. During the past few years, you have assisted the client in much of its business and legal dealings. The client comes to you and tells you the following:

a. A former group of employees is suing the client for discriminatory dismissal and seeks to depose the CEO.

b. The federal government has served a grand jury subpoena seeking the employment documents for the last five years.

c. The SEC is investigating improper activity with respect to the client's publicly traded stock. In connection with this action, the SEC is holding a significant amount of the client's money in escrow.

The client's executives tell you that they have done nothing wrong and are eager to get all of this behind them. The CEO wants to comply with the grand jury subpoena and is excited to be deposed in the civil matter to "straighten this matter out." *Counsel this client with respect to the three situations above.*

Chapter 19

Sentencing

A. Introductory Notes

1. Overview

Sentencing is supposed to be where the rubber meets the road in the criminal law. As discussed in the previous chapter, the largest corporations increasingly bypass the sentencing process entirely by entering into deferred prosecution agreements ("DPAs"). Even so, the terms of DPAs are often informed by sentencing norms. For individual white collar criminals, sentencing remains an important capstone to the criminal justice process. Whether by admission or jury verdict, the law views the defendant as guilty. The question now is about the nature and extent of punishment. Punishment is particularly important — and, at times, controversial — in white collar crime cases. As leading scholars have written, "white collar crimes are probably *more* significant than street crimes from a purely economic perspective, and such crimes often have the capacity to weaken trust and faith in the basic institutions of society." STANTON WHEELER ET AL., SITTING IN JUDGMENT: THE SENTENCING OF WHITE COLLAR CRIMINALS 2–3 (1988). Despite its outsized economic effects, many scholars believe white collar crime is less morally serious than street crime, which often involves the potential for physical violence.

Traditional goals of sentencing include: (1) retribution (or just deserts); (2) deterrence; (3) incapacitation; and (4) rehabilitation. These goals can be difficult to apply in practice and may even conflict in individual cases. Many scholars advocate for the hybrid theory of "limiting retributivism," which is closely associated with the great criminologist and law professor Norval Morris.

> Under this widely endorsed and adopted model, the offender's desert defines a range of morally justified punishments, setting upper and lower limits on the severity of penalties that may fairly be imposed on a given offender. Within the range of deserved penalties, case-specific incapacitation, rehabilitation, deterrence, and other sentencing goals may be pursued, but only to the extent that they are needed in a given case. Sentences within the desert range should be no more severe than necessary to achieve defined aims, a humane and utilitarian principle of necessity and efficiency which Morris referred to as "parsimony."

Richard S. Frase, *Punishment Purposes*, 58 STAN. L. REV. 67, 76–77 (2005). Views on retribution may be shifting as many advocates are pushing for less punishment across the board in criminal law. *See* Brian M. Murray, *Retributivist Reform of Collateral Consequences*, 52 Conn. L. Rev. 863 (2020). Whatever one's view of appropriate punishment, translating it for corporate defendants remains a conceptual and practical challenge. *See supra* Chapter 2, Corporate and Individual Criminal Liability.

Federal sentencing has undergone profound changes since the mid-1980s. First, the adoption of the United States Sentencing Guidelines ("Guidelines") in 1987 removed much of the sentencing discretion that trial judges previously had. Determination of criminal sentences had been largely committed to the discretion of trial judges, subject only to constitutional limits (e.g., the Eighth Amendment's proscription on cruel and unusual punishment) and statutory maximum and minimum sentences specified for certain crimes by statute. Second, beginning in 2005, the United States Supreme Court issued a series of decisions that restored much of that discretion.

The legal touchstone for federal sentencing is 18 U.S.C. § 3553. It directs courts to "consider the nature and circumstances of the offense and the history and characteristics of the defendant" and to "impose a sentence sufficient, but not greater than necessary . . .

(A) to reflect the seriousness of the offense, to promote respect for the law, and to provide just punishment for the offense;

(B) to afford adequate deterrence to criminal conduct;

(C) to protect the public from further crimes of the defendant; and

(D) to provide the defendant with needed educational or vocational training, medical care, or other correctional treatment in the most effective manner."

The portion of § 3553(a) that instructs sentencing courts to impose a sentence that is "sufficient but not greater than necessary" to satisfy the purposes of sentencing is often referred to as the "parsimony" clause. Section 3553 also lists several factors courts should consider, including "the need to avoid unwarranted sentence disparities among defendants with similar records who have been found guilty of similar conduct," "the need to provide restitution to any victims of the offense," and the Guidelines.

This chapter will briefly review the history of federal sentencing over the past several decades at both the policy and constitutional levels, and then explore how federal sentencing works today and why critics are calling for change.

2. The United States Sentencing Commission

The Guidelines are promulgated by the United States Sentencing Commission ("Commission"), which is an independent body within the judicial branch of the federal government. Unless Congress acts to block them within a specified timeframe, the Commission's Guidelines, and any subsequent amendments to them, become effective. The Commission consists of seven voting members, at least three of whom must be federal judges, and no more than four of whom can be from the same political party. The members are appointed by the President "after consultation with representatives of judges, prosecuting attorneys, defense attorneys, law enforcement officials [and others]" and "with the advice and consent of the Senate." 28 U.S.C. § 991(a). The Commission regularly reassesses and revises the Guidelines. *See* 28 U.S.C. § 994(o)–(p).

Among other responsibilities, the Commission is to consider a wide array of factors — including the sentencing purposes in § 3553(a)(2) — and craft the Guidelines to guide District Court sentencing discretion. The Supreme Court in *United States v. Rita* described the difference between the trial court and Commission functions this way:

> The upshot is that the sentencing statutes envision both the sentencing judge and the Commission as carrying out the same basic § 3553(a) objectives, the one, at retail, the other at wholesale.

551 U.S. 338, 348 (2007).

3. The Federal Sentencing Guidelines Framework

The Guidelines scheme requires that the sentencing judge calculate the sentencing range using a very specific set of rules and procedures. The following provides an overview of that process, and of current sentencing parameters under controlling United States Supreme Court precedent.

An Overview of the Federal Sentencing Guidelines[a]

United States Sentencing Commission

How the Sentencing Guidelines Work

The sentencing guidelines take into account both the seriousness of the offense and the offender's criminal history.

Offense Seriousness

The sentencing guidelines provide 43 levels of offense seriousness — the more serious the crime, the higher the offense level.

Base Offense Level

Each type of crime is assigned a base offense level, which is the starting point for determining the seriousness of a particular offense. More serious types of crime have higher base offense levels (for example, trespass has a base offense level of 4, while kidnapping has a base offense level of 32).

---

a. At the time of this text's publication, this document is freely *available at* https://www.ussc.gov /guidelines/2018-guidelines-manual-annotated.

Specific Offense Characteristics

In addition to base offense levels, each offense type typically carries with it a number of specific offense characteristics. These are factors that vary from offense to offense. They increase or decrease the offense level by adding or subtracting points from the base offense level. Some examples:

- One of the specific base offense characteristics for fraud (which has a base offense level of 7 if the statutory maximum is 20 years or more) increases the offense level based on the amount of loss involved in the offense. If a fraud involved more than a $6,500 loss, there is to be a 2-level increase to the base offense level, bringing the offense level up to 9. If a fraud involved more than a $40,000 loss, there is to be a 6-level increase, bringing the total to 13. A loss of more than $1,500,000 adds 16 levels.

- One of the specific offense characteristics for robbery (which has a base offense level of 20) involves the use of a firearm. If a firearm was brandished or possessed during the robbery, there is to be a 5-level increase, bringing the level to 25; if a firearm was discharged during the robbery, there is to be a 7-level increase, bringing the offense level to 27.

Adjustments

Adjustments are factors that can apply to any offense. Like specific offense characteristics, they increase or decrease the offense level. Categories of adjustments include: victim-related adjustments, the offender's role in the offense, and obstruction of justice. Examples of adjustments are as follows:

- If the offender was a minimal participant in the offense, the offense level is decreased by 4 levels.

- If the offender knew that the victim was unusually vulnerable due to age or physical or mental condition, the offense level is increased by 2 levels.

- If the offender obstructed justice, the offense level is increased by 2 levels.

Multiple Count Adjustments

When there are multiple counts of conviction, the sentencing guidelines provide instructions on how to achieve a "combined offense level." These rules provide incremental punishment for significant additional criminal conduct. The most serious offense is used as a starting point. The other counts determine whether and how much to increase the offense level.

Acceptance of Responsibility Adjustments

The final step in determining an offender's offense level involves the offender's acceptance of responsibility. The judge may decrease the offense level by two levels if, in the judge's opinion, the offender accepted responsibility for his offense.

In deciding whether to grant this reduction, judges can consider such factors as:

- Whether the offender truthfully admitted his or her role in the crime,

- Whether the offender made restitution before there was a guilty verdict, and

- Whether the offender pled guilty.

Offenders who qualify for the 2-level reduction and whose offense levels are 16 or greater, may, upon motion of the government, be granted an additional 1-level reduction if, in a timely manner, they declare their intention to plead guilty.

Criminal History

The guidelines assign each offender to one of six criminal history categories based upon the extent of an offender's past misconduct. Criminal History Category I is the least serious category and includes many first-time offenders. Criminal History Category VI is the most serious category and includes offenders with serious criminal records.

Determining the Guideline Range

Judges then use the offense level and the criminal history category to look up the applicable sentencing range on the Commission's sentencing table:

Offense Level	Criminal History Category (Criminal History Points)					
	I (0 or 1)	II (2 or 3)	III (4, 5, 6)	IV (7, 8, 9)	V (10, 11, 12)	VI (13 or more)
1	0–6	0–6	0–6	0–6	0–6	0–6
2	0–6	0–6	0–6	0–6	0–6	1–7
3	0–6	0–6	0–6	0–6	2–8	3–9
			• • •			
19	30–37	33–41	37–46	46–57	57–71	63–78
20	33–41	37–46	41–51	51–63	63–78	70–87
21	37–46	41–51	46–57	57–71	70–87	77–96
			• • •			
41	324–405	360–life	360–life	360–life	360–life	360–life
42	360–life	360–life	360–life	360–life	360–life	360–life
43	life	life	life	life	life	life

Sentences Within the Guideline Range

To select a sentence within the Guidelines range, "the court may consider, without limitation, any information concerning the background, character and conduct of the defendant, unless otherwise prohibited by law." U.S.S.G. §1B1.4.

Sentences Outside of the Guideline Range

After the guideline range is determined, if an atypical aggravating or mitigating circumstance exists, the court may "depart" from the guideline range. That is, the judge may sentence the offender above or below the range. When departing, the judge must state in writing the reason for the departure. The Guidelines state that a "sentencing court may depart from the applicable guideline range if . . . there exists an aggravating or mitigating circumstance . . . of a kind, or to a degree, not adequately taken into consideration by the Sentencing Commission in formulating the guidelines that, in order to advance the objectives set forth in 18 U.S.C. § 3553(a)(2), should result in a sentence different from that described." U.S.S.G. § 5K2.0(a)(1). The Guidelines then list more than 20 different factors that could qualify for departure, including refusal to assist authorities, causing the death of a victim, or disrupting a government function (which tell in favor of an upward departure), and provocative conduct from the victim, voluntary disclosure of the offense, or diminished capacity (which tell in favor of a downward departure). U.S.S.G. § 2K2.0.

Of course, unless the defendant pleads guilty, the jury must find the facts required for conviction beyond a reasonable doubt. *See, e.g., In re: Winship*, 397 U.S. 358, 364 (1970). But through a series of cases starting in the late 1990s and continuing until the late 2000s, the Supreme Court reinterpreted the Sixth Amendment and required jury fact-finding in such a way as to completely upend the United States Sentencing Guidelines.

In 1998, the Supreme Court concluded that a defendant's prior conviction was *not* an element of the offense and thus not one of those facts a jury must find. *Almendarez-Torres v. United States*, 523 U.S. 224, 227 (1998).

In *Apprendi v. New Jersey*, 530 U.S. 466, 490 (2000), however, the Supreme Court held that "other than the fact of a prior conviction, any fact that increases the penalty for a crime beyond the prescribed statutory maximum must be submitted to a jury, and proved beyond a reasonable doubt." As long as the "statutory maximum" in *Apprendi* meant the traditional, legislatively set maximum punishment, the Federal Guidelines (and most other sentencing guideline systems) were safe because most punishments called for by the Guidelines were well below the frequently sky-high legislative statutory maximums. Four years later, in *Blakely v. Washington*, 542 U.S. 296 (2004), the court expanded *Apprendi* by holding that "the relevant 'statutory maximum' is not the maximum sentence a judge may impose after finding additional facts, but the maximum he may impose without any additional findings." In other words, any facts that would increase the maximum applicable sentence must be found by a jury, and not just by a sentencing judge after conviction.

Then, in January 2005, the U.S. Supreme Court decided the landmark case *United States v. Booker*, 543 U.S. 220 (2005). The *Booker* decision addressed whether the Sixth Amendment right to jury trial applies to the Federal Sentencing Guidelines. Because the Guidelines were mandatory, they required judges to make findings of fact that could increase the maximum applicable sentence. That, the Court held, violated *Apprendi*'s understanding of the Sixth Amendment. Rather than invalidate the Guidelines in their entirety, the Court imposed the narrower remedy of excising only the statutory provisions that made the Guidelines mandatory, 18 U.S.C. § 3553(b)(1) and 18 U.S.C. § 3742(e). As a consequence, the Guidelines became advisory for sentencing judges.

Under the approach set forth by the Court, "district courts, while not bound to apply the Guidelines, must consult those Guidelines and take them into account when sentencing," subject to review by the courts of appeal for "unreasonableness." *Booker*, 543 U.S. at 264. The subsequent Supreme Court decision in *Rita v. United States*, 551 U.S. 338 (2007), held that courts of appeal may apply a presumption of reasonableness when reviewing a sentence imposed within the Guidelines sentencing range. The Supreme Court continued to stress the importance of the federal sentencing guidelines in subsequent sentencing-related cases. *See Gall v. United States*, 128 S. Ct. 586, 596 (2007) ("As a matter of administration and to secure nationwide consistency, the Guidelines should be the starting point and initial benchmark" at sentencing); *Kimbrough v. United States*, 128 S. Ct. 558, 564 (2007) (After *Booker*, "[a] district judge must include the Guidelines range in the array of factors warranting consideration"). As a matter of fact, sentencing decisions largely tend to fit within Guidelines ranges, deviating from them in only 48.8% of cases. *See* U.S. Sentencing Comm'n, 2019 Sourcebook of Federal Sentencing Statistics 84 (2020), https://www.ussc.gov/research/sourcebook-2019 (Of all federal sentences imposed in 2019, 75% of cases received sentences under the Guidelines Manual and of those 56,995 cases, 51.4% were within the Guidelines range.).

Notes and Questions

1. *Procedure.* To arrive at the Guideline range, the United States Probation Office completes a Sentencing Worksheet. The worksheets identify the base offense level, specific offense characteristics, adjustments, and criminal history to determine the Guidelines range. The Probation Office also prepares a Pre-Sentence Report ("PSR"), which helps the lawyers and the judge in advance of and during sentencing. The PSR may go through multiple revisions as the parties object to the information it contains. The sentencing judge resolves all disputes about the proper Guideline calculation.

2. *National guidelines.* Are sentencing guidelines a good idea? What are the pros and cons of having a single sentencing standard that applies across the nation?

3. *Grouping.* If the defendant was convicted of multiple counts, the court may combine or "group" those counts for sentencing if the counts involved substantially the same harm. Thus, multiple counts of mail fraud—each mailing can be a separate count—will be grouped together if they are part of the same fraudulent scheme. *See* U.S.S.G. § 3D1.2, comment. (n.4). What effect do these grouping rules have on prosecutorial charging discretion?

4. *Relevant conduct.* The Guidelines instruct the judge to consider relevant conduct, which includes "all acts and omissions . . . that occurred during the commission of the offense, in preparation for that offense, or in the course of attempting to avoid detection or responsibility for that offense. . . ." U.S.S.G. § 1B1.3(a)(1). Further, relevant conduct includes "all acts and omissions . . . that were part of the same course of conduct or common scheme or plan as the offense of conviction." U.S.S.G. § 1B1.3(2). This includes conduct found by the judge by a preponderance of the evidence even

if the jury — following the beyond a reasonable doubt standard — acquitted or never even had the facts presented to it. *See, e.g., United States v. Watts*, 519 U.S. 148 (1997). Is it fair to increase a defendant's sentence based on acquitted or uncharged conduct?

5. *Substantial assistance.* Under § 5K1.1 of the Guidelines, the government has the discretion to file a motion for a downward departure based upon a defendant's substantial assistance to the government in an ongoing criminal investigation or prosecution. Only the government may make such a motion. Judges often grant such motions. They then decide what departure size is warranted. About 26% of cases receive a below-Guidelines sentence at the request of the government; however, only 9.6% of downward departures were for substantial assistance. *See* 2019 Source-book, *supra*. As a policy matter, which actor — the prosecutor or the judge — is in a better position to decide whether a defendant has provided enough assistance to the government to warrant a lower sentence (and by how much)?

6. *What is unreasonable? Booker* provided for appellate review guarding against "unreasonable" sentences. What could that mean in practice? Is it helpful to know that the Court in *Rita* described the issue on appeal of a sentence as "whether the trial court abused its discretion"?

7. *What about Congress?* In his *Booker* remedial majority opinion, Justice Breyer stated: "Ours, of course, is not the last word: The ball now lies in Congress' court. The National Legislature is equipped to devise and install, long term, the sentencing system, compatible with the Constitution, that Congress judges best for the federal system of justice." 543 U.S. at 265. Indeed, Congress can take some or all of the trial court's post-*Booker* sentencing discretion away as long as it complies with the Supreme Court's interpretation of the Sixth Amendment and has the jury find all the relevant facts. To date, it has not done so. Why do you think Congress has not acted and thus allowed the remedial majority's vision of the Guidelines to remain in effect?

B. Modern Federal Appellate Review in Action

Courts continue to struggle with the discretionary nature of federal sentencing in the post-*Booker* world. The next case provides an interesting example of the types of sentencing issues that may arise on appeal. As you read the case, pay particular attention to the procedural and policy issues that the court discusses and consider whether you agree with the sentence and the underlying rationale.

United States v. Cavera

550 F.3d 180 (2d Cir. 2008) (en banc)

CALABRESI, CIRCUIT JUDGE.

Defendant-Appellant Gerard Cavera appeals from a judgment entered on August 23, 2005 in the United States District Court for the Eastern District of New York. Cavera pled guilty to a firearms trafficking offense. The district court imposed an above-Guidelines sentence after finding that the Sentencing Guidelines failed to take into account the need to punish more severely those who illegally transport guns into areas like New York City. On appeal, Cavera contends, among other things, that the district court erred when it relied on local conditions to justify a higher sentence.

A panel of this Court held that the district court rested its decision on impermissible considerations, and determined that the sentence should be vacated and the case remanded for resentencing. We ordered rehearing en banc, and directed the parties to submit briefs on the effect of the Supreme Court's intervening decisions in *Gall v. United States*, 128 S. Ct. 586 (2007), and *Kimbrough v. United States*, 128 S. Ct. 558 (2007). With the benefit of the guidance afforded by those rulings, we now affirm the judgment of the district court.

Cavera, a septuagenarian army veteran with residences in New York and Florida, was arrested by the FBI with the aid of a confidential informant. Beginning in July 2003, the informant purchased guns illegally in New York City on several occasions from a man named Peter Abbadessa. Abbadessa told the confidential informant that his uncle, Anthony Lucania, had a friend named Gerry (Cavera), who acted as Abbadessa's Florida gun supplier. In April 2004, the confidential informant flew to Florida, along with Abbadessa and Lucania, for the express purpose of procuring firearms. At the FBI's direction, the informant paid Lucania $11,500 for sixteen guns. Abbadessa and Lucania then went to Cavera's residence in Deerfield Beach, Florida, where they gave Cavera money in exchange for two boxes containing sixteen firearms. The boxes were later given to the informant, who turned them over to the FBI. Abbadessa, Lucania, and the confidential informant returned to New York on separate flights.

On June 23, 2004, a grand jury returned an indictment charging Cavera, Abbadessa, and Lucania with various violations of the federal gun trafficking laws. Cavera pled guilty to one count of conspiracy to deal in and to transport firearms, in violation of 18 U.S.C. § 371.

Cavera first appeared for sentencing on June 9, 2005. At this point, Judge Sifton gave notice that he was considering an above-Guidelines sentence, "simply because I think the sentencing guidelines may understate the seriousness of this offense because of the consequences for the community of bringing or transporting . . . firearms into New York City." The district court adjourned the proceedings to give the parties an opportunity to address the issue.

The parties appeared again for sentencing on July 28, 2005. The court determined that the Guidelines recommended a sentence of twelve to eighteen months' imprisonment and a fine of $3,000 to $30,000. But Judge Sifton concluded that a higher sentence was appropriate, stating in open court that the Guidelines range did not adequately meet the "crying need to do what can be done to deter gun trafficking into the large metropolitan area[s] of this country." At the same time, the district court filed a detailed written opinion further explaining its reasoning.

In this opinion, Judge Sifton began by noting that the Guidelines, "[i]n the pursuit of national uniformity in sentencing practices," do not take local circumstances into account, and instead reflect a national average. For this reason, the Guidelines were "less persuasive" in Cavera's case than they would otherwise be.

The district court explained its decision to impose an above-Guidelines sentence in terms of two of the § 3553(a) factors. Focusing first on the need for the sentence to reflect the seriousness of the offense, as directed by 18 U.S.C. § 3553(a)(2)(A), Judge Sifton found that Cavera's offense was more harmful than the national average offense contemplated by the Guidelines. "Firearms smuggled into New York City commonly end up in the hands of those who could not otherwise legally acquire them, are frequently used for illegitimate purposes, and have the potential to create a substantially greater degree of harm when in an urban environment . . . than in the United States generally." In this respect, the district court referred to statistical studies indicating that homicide rates were substantially higher in large urban areas than in suburban and rural locales. Judge Sifton also noted that population density in the state of New York, in New York City, and especially in particular parts of the Eastern District of New York, exceeded the national average.

The district court also relied on a greater-than-average need, in this case, to achieve strong deterrence. *See* 18 U.S.C. § 3553(a)(2)(B). The purpose of gun trafficking laws "is to prevent lax firearm laws in one state from undermining the more restrictive laws of other states." In states with strict gun laws, like New York, a higher percentage of guns used in crimes arrive from out of state than is the case in jurisdictions with less restrictive firearms laws. New York's strict gun control laws create a "larger black market" for guns than in places with less strict laws. The district court cited an article describing New York City as "one of the 'unusual areas' to which running guns is a profitable enterprise." Accordingly, Judge Sifton concluded that a more severe penalty for trafficking guns into New York City was necessary to bring about adequate deterrence.

The district court noted next that a sentencing judge is also directed to consider "the need to avoid unwarranted sentencing disparities among defendants with similar records who have been found guilty of similar conduct." 18 U.S.C. § 3553(a)(6). Judge Sifton recognized that his approach would lead to different sentences for otherwise-similar firearms traffickers in different federal districts. Such disparities, however, were not "unwarranted." Rather, they were based on "objectively demonstrated, material differences between the impact of the offenses in those districts."

In one respect, Cavera benefited from Judge Sifton's willingness to disagree with the Guidelines. Judge Sifton noted that the Guidelines also failed to take into account "the inverse relationship between age and recidivism." Judge Sifton stated that he would consider the lesser need for specific deterrence when sentencing Cavera, who was over seventy.

On these bases, the court imposed a sentence of twenty-four months' imprisonment — six months longer than the top end of the applicable Guidelines range. Cavera was also sentenced to three years' supervised release, a $60,000 fine, and a $100 special assessment.

Cavera appealed the sentence. Initially, the government agreed with Cavera that the sentence could not stand. Writing before *Gall* and *Kimbrough*, a panel of this Court held that Judge Sifton erred in his analysis of the §3553(a) factors "by sentencing Cavera on the basis of a policy judgment concerning the gravity of firearms smuggling into a heavily populated area, like New York City, rather than on circumstances particular to the individual defendant and his crime." For this reason, the panel determined that the sentence was procedurally and substantively unreasonable. A majority of the Court's active judges voted to rehear the case en banc.

In *United States v. Booker*, the Supreme Court held that the mandatory application of the Sentencing Guidelines was incompatible with the Sixth Amendment. 543 U.S. 220, 226–27 (2005). Accordingly, the Court excised the portion of the Sentencing Reform Act of 1984 that ordinarily required district courts to impose Guidelines-range sentences. In Justice Breyer's "Remedial Opinion," the Court retained an important role for the Sentencing Commission, leaving untouched the statutory direction to district courts that they should consult the Guidelines range when imposing sentence. *Booker* rendered the Guidelines "effectively advisory," and permitted sentencing courts to tailor the appropriate punishment to each offense in light of other concerns. After *Booker*, appellate courts were to review sentences for "unreasonableness." Review for "unreasonableness" amounts to review for abuse of discretion.

The resulting regime is, at first glance, beguilingly simple. The district courts have discretion to select an appropriate sentence, and in doing so are statutorily bound to consider the factors listed in §3553(a), including the advisory Guidelines range. The courts of appeals then review for abuse of discretion. . . .

The Supreme Court recently offered further guidance. See *Gall v. United States*, 128 S. Ct. 586 (2007); *Kimbrough v. United States*, 128 S. Ct. 558 (2007); *Rita v. United States*, 551 U.S. 338 (2007). In these cases, the Court expressed its view of the respective competencies of the Sentencing Commission, the district judges, and the courts of appeals. From those opinions, and from our own experience with the advisory Guidelines system, we derive the following principles.

A sentencing judge has very wide latitude to decide the proper degree of punishment for an individual offender and a particular crime. . . .

Even after *Gall* and *Kimbrough*, sentencing judges, certainly, are not free to ignore the Guidelines, or to treat them merely as a "body of casual advice." *See United States v. Crosby*, 397 F.3d 103, 113 (2d Cir. 2005). A district court should normally begin all sentencing proceedings by calculating, with the assistance of the Presentence Report, the applicable Guidelines range. The Guidelines provide the "starting point and the initial benchmark" for sentencing, *Gall*, 128 S. Ct. at 596, and district courts must "remain cognizant of them throughout the sentencing process," *id.* at 596 n. 6. It is now, however, emphatically clear that the Guidelines are guidelines — that is, they are truly advisory. A district court may not presume that a Guidelines sentence is reasonable; it must instead conduct its own independent review of the sentencing factors, aided by the arguments of the prosecution and defense. District judges are, as a result, generally free to impose sentences outside the recommended range. When they do so, however, they "must consider the extent of the deviation and ensure that the justification is sufficiently compelling to support the degree of the variance." *Id.* at 597. In this way, the district court reaches an informed and individualized judgment in each case as to what is "sufficient, but not greater than necessary" to fulfill the purposes of sentencing. 18 U.S.C. § 3553(a).

After *Gall* and *Kimbrough*, appellate courts play an important but clearly secondary role in the process of determining an appropriate sentence. We review the work of district courts under a "deferential abuse-of-discretion standard." *Gall*, 128 S. Ct. at 591. This form of appellate scrutiny encompasses two components: procedural review and substantive review.

As to substance, we will not substitute our own judgment for the district court's on the question of what is sufficient to meet the § 3553(a) considerations in any particular case. We will instead set aside a district court's substantive determination only in exceptional cases where the trial court's decision "cannot be located within the range of permissible decisions." *United States v. Rigas*, 490 F.3d 208, 238 (2d Cir. 2007) (internal quotation marks omitted). To the extent that our prior cases may be read to imply a more searching form of substantive review, we today depart from that understanding.

This degree of deference is only warranted, however, once we are satisfied that the district court complied with the Sentencing Reform Act's procedural requirements, and this requires that we be confident that the sentence resulted from the district court's considered judgment as to what was necessary to address the various, often conflicting, purposes of sentencing.

A district court commits procedural error where it fails to calculate the Guidelines range (unless omission of the calculation is justified), makes a mistake in its Guidelines calculation, or treats the Guidelines as mandatory. It also errs procedurally if it does not consider the § 3553(a) factors, or rests its sentence on a clearly erroneous finding of fact. Moreover, a district court errs if it fails adequately to explain its chosen sentence, and must include "an explanation for any deviation from the Guidelines range." Where we find significant procedural error, one proper course would be to remand to the district court so that it can either explain what it was trying to do, or correct its mistake and exercise its discretion anew, rather than for the appellate court to proceed to review the sentence for substantive reasonableness.

These broad statements, however, require more specificity, both as to substantive and procedural reasonableness review if they are to guide us in particular cases, including the one before us. Thus, when conducting substantive review, we take into account the totality of the circumstances, giving due deference to the sentencing judge's exercise of discretion, and bearing in mind the institutional advantages of district courts. Unlike some of our sister circuit courts, we do not presume that a Guidelines-range sentence is reasonable. Nor can we presume that a non-Guidelines sentence is unreasonable, or require "extraordinary" circumstances to justify a deviation from the Guidelines range. *Gall*, 128 S. Ct. at 595. Where, as in the case before us, we review a non-Guidelines sentence, we may "take the degree of variance into account and consider the extent of a deviation from the Guidelines." *Id.* But we must not employ a "rigid mathematical formula that uses the percentage of a departure as the standard for determining the strength of the justifications required for a specific sentence." *Id.* . . .

Accordingly, we will continue to patrol the boundaries of reasonableness, while heeding the Supreme Court's renewed message that responsibility for sentencing is placed largely in the precincts of the district courts. As the Supreme Court strongly suggested in *Kimbrough*, a district court may vary from the Guidelines range based solely on a policy disagreement with the Guidelines, even where that disagreement applies to a wide class of offenders or offenses.

When, moreover, we examine a district court's justification for differing from the Guidelines recommendation, our review must be informed by the "discrete institutional strengths" of the Sentencing Commission and the district courts. *Kimbrough*, 128 S. Ct. at 574. As a result, a district court's decision to vary from the Guidelines "may attract greatest respect when the sentencing judge finds a particular case outside the 'heartland' to which the Commission intends individual Guidelines to apply." *Id.* at 574–75 (internal quotation marks omitted). Where, instead, the sentencing judge varies from the Guidelines "based solely on the judge's view that the Guidelines range fails properly to reflect § 3553(a) considerations even in a mine-run case," the Supreme Court has suggested that "closer review may be in order." *Id.* at 575 (internal quotation marks omitted). Nevertheless, in *Kimbrough* itself, the Supreme Court found that no "closer review" was warranted where a district court based its sentence on a policy disagreement with the 100-to-1 crack cocaine vs. powder cocaine weight ratio, because the crack cocaine Guidelines are not based on empirical data and national experience, and hence "do not exemplify the Commission's exercise of its characteristic institutional role." *Id.*

We do not, however, take the Supreme Court's comments concerning the scope and nature of "closer review" to be the last word on these questions. More will have to be fleshed out as issues present themselves. For instance, we note that some Guidelines enhancements and reductions apply without modulation to a wide range of conduct. [M]any Guidelines such as those covering "offenses involving taxation," U.S.S.G. § 2T4.1, "antitrust offenses," see *id.* § 2R1.1, and larceny, embezzlement, fraud, and similar crimes, see *id.* § 2B1.1, drastically vary as to the recommended sentence based simply on the amount of money involved. Here again a district court may find that even after giving weight to the large or small financial impact, there is a wide variety of culpability amongst defendants and, as a result, impose different sentences based on the factors identified in § 3553(a). *Cf. United States v. Ebbers,* 458 F.3d 110, 129 (2d Cir. 2006) (concluding that the sentencing disparity between co-defendants in a securities fraud case was reasonable in light of the "varying degrees of culpability and cooperation between the various defendants"). Such district court decisions, if adequately explained, should be reviewed especially deferentially.

But what does the procedural requirement, that the district court must explain its reasons for its chosen sentence, entail? The statutory scheme has long required sentencing judges, "at the time of sentencing," to state their reasons for imposing the particular sentence "in open court." 18 U.S.C. § 3553(c). And where a non-Guidelines sentence is selected, the district court must also explain its reasons for doing so "with specificity in the written order of judgment and commitment." *Id.*§ 3553(c) (2). . . .

When all is said and done, once we are sure that the sentence resulted from the reasoned exercise of discretion, we must defer heavily to the expertise of district judges. This circumspect form of review, it is true, may result in substantial variation among district courts. But "some departures from uniformity [are] a necessary cost" of the *Booker* remedy. *Id.* at 574. And in its recent cases, the Supreme Court has made clear its view that disparities in sentences imposed by different district judges are more likely to reflect justified differences than are those arising from differences of opinion among appellate panels. This last point may not be easy for appellate panels to accept, but we believe that it is what the Supreme Court has instructed.

In this respect, we emphasize that sentencing discretion is like an elevator in that it must run in both directions. Under *Gall, Kimbrough,* and *Irizarry v. United States,* 128 S. Ct. 2198 (2008), district courts have the power to impose sentences both above and below the Guidelines range. . . .

We begin by asking whether the court below committed any "significant procedural error." *Gall,* 128 S. Ct. at 597. We find no error in the district court's calculation of the Guidelines range. Judge Sifton, moreover, clearly considered the Guidelines, and certainly did not treat that range as mandatory nor presume that it was reasonable. . . .

Whether or not the district court's decision in this case reflected a categorical policy disagreement with the Guidelines, the Supreme Court's recent teachings strongly suggest that such a disagreement does not suffice to render that decision either procedurally or substantively unreasonable. It is now clear that, in appropriate circumstances, district courts may rely on categorical factors to increase or decrease sentences. There is, in addition, no special reason to think that reliance on a locality-based categorical factor is — without more — suspect. The environment in which a crime was perpetrated may, in principle, inform a district court's judgment as to the appropriate punishment in any number of ways. We agree with Judge Sifton that, while a district court should not rely on "subjective considerations such as 'local mores' or feelings about a particular type of crime," a finding "that the crime will have a greater or lesser impact given the locality of its commission is appropriately considered in crafting a reasonable sentence post-*Booker*." As always, the more specifically in the purposes of sentencing a district court's rationale is grounded, the more likely it is to survive appellate inspection.

Judge Sifton stated expressly that he did not base his decision on "local feelings" in New York that gun trafficking is more serious. The district court can properly be read to have rested its decision that a sentence above the Guidelines range was necessary to satisfy the § 3553(a)(2) factors on two independent grounds. The first ground was the nonspecific geographical and demographic fact that New York City is a large metropolitan area. In this respect, Judge Sifton observed that urban areas have higher homicide rates than suburban and rural areas; that in those parts of New York City included in the Eastern District of New York, population density sometimes exceeded 35,000 persons per square mile when the national average was only 78 persons per square mile; and that guns smuggled into New York City frequently end up in the hands of persons not legally authorized to possess them and are used for illegitimate purposes. *Id.* at 295. From these circumstances, he concluded that firearm trafficking into New York City, and specifically into those boroughs in the Eastern District of New York, presented a greater risk of harm. The district court's second ground focused instead on New York's stricter gun regulatory scheme. More stringent local regulation in New York, the district court found, "renders gun running a more serious problem and creates a larger [and more profitable] black market" than in other places. *Id.* Accordingly, on the district court's view, "a more severe penalty is necessary to produce adequate deterrence." *Id.*

As to the district court's first ground, our Court is divided. Were it necessary to reach the issue, some of us would hold that the district court, in its wide discretion, permissibly relied on a determination that trafficking guns into an urban area is likely to create more harm than the national average offense envisaged by the Guidelines. Others would hold that the district court erred to the extent that it based the sentence on the notion that guns are more dangerous in metropolitan areas. Still others are unsure whether reference to such broad, nonspecific geographical and demographic factors is appropriate in the context of this case.

We need not resolve that disagreement today, because the district court's second ground, that of deterrence, provides an independently sufficient justification for its variation from the Guidelines. The court clearly concluded that the existence and enforcement of strict local gun laws in a particular jurisdiction is likely to make the cost of getting a gun in that jurisdiction higher than in a jurisdiction with lax anti-gun laws. This, the court indicated, will increase the profits to be had from trafficking guns into the strong-enforcement jurisdiction. There is considerable support for this opinion. Where the profits to be made from violating a law are higher, the penalty needs to be correspondingly higher to achieve the same amount of deterrence.

Like any economic theory, these points are not uncontroversial, but it is not an abuse of discretion for courts to rely on this form of reasoning in deciding on an appropriate sentence. Indeed, the statutory requirement that sentencing courts consider, on a case by case basis, what is necessary for "deterrence to criminal conduct," 18 U.S.C. § 3553(a)(2)(B), almost inevitably makes judges focus on notions and theories that may be controversial to some. . . .

In the course of an unusually detailed explanation of his reasoning, Judge Sifton discussed the relevant § 3553(a) considerations, and explained with particularity his basis for disagreeing with the Guidelines recommendation in the specific context of Cavera's case. Judge Sifton, moreover, reached an individualized judgment as to what the purposes of sentencing required in this case. In view of Cavera's advanced age, the district court chose to reduce the sentence it would otherwise have imposed based on its perception that Cavera was less likely than the average offender to reoffend. In addition, Judge Sifton explicitly considered the need to avoid unwarranted sentence disparities, and concluded that sentencing disparities among different federal districts were warranted by, among other things, the greater need for deterrence in New York, with its more profitable black market in firearms. Given the deference we owe to district judges, especially after *Gall* and *Kimbrough*, this deterrence-based rationale easily suffices to justify the sentence. It follows that it would not be an abuse of discretion to impose a prison sentence of twenty-four months that exceeded the top end of the Guideline range by just six months, and a fine that surpassed the Guidelines maximum by $30,000. In relation to both the recommended Guidelines sentence and the § 3553(a) factors, the sentence is substantively reasonable.

What then of the broad demographic and geographic factors the district court considered? It seems clear to us from the record that the district court would have imposed the same sentence had it relied solely on the New York-specific rationale that the local gun regulatory scheme created a heightened need for deterrence in this case. In these circumstances, we need not decide whether the district court erred when it also relied, in the alternative, on the wider notions of geographic and demographic variation because, even if we were to identify error, it would be harmless in the light of the alternative independent ground for the challenged sentence. Since any such error would be harmless, the sentence imposed in this case withstands appellate review.

The panel decision is VACATED, and the judgment of the district court is AFFIRMED.

Notes and Questions

1. *The significance of the* Booker *line of cases.* How much discretion does the decision give to trial judges? To what degree should appeals courts defer to trial judges?

2. *The* Kimbrough *decision.* Is a policy disagreement a "reasonable" basis for a departure? For example, if a judge disagrees with the policy underlying the Guidelines' former 100-to-1 crack-to-powder cocaine sentencing ratio — treating each gram of crack cocaine as the equivalent to 100 grams of powder cocaine — may the judge use that disagreement to justify a below-Guidelines sentence? The disparity was based upon an initial assessment that crack cocaine was more dangerous and addictive than powder cocaine. This policy came under widespread attack, however, largely because of racial disparities between powder and crack cocaine sentencing; the vast majority of defendants in crack cocaine cases are African American. *See Kimbrough v. United States*, 128 S. Ct. 558, 566–68 (2008). The ratio has since been narrowed by Congress.

3. *Shifting patterns.* Although many sentencing judges continued to sentence close to the Guidelines at first, that pattern has started to shift. The United States Sentencing Commission reported that the rate of within-Guidelines' recommended range sentences (for theft, property destruction, and fraud offenses) has leveled in recent years — 46.1% in fiscal year 2014 to 43.9% in fiscal year 2019. This is a distinct shift from 2008, when 64.5% of § 2B1.1 crimes were within-range. *See* U.S. Sentencing Comm'n, *Quick Facts: Theft, Property Destruction, and Fraud*, https://www.ussc .gov/research/quick-facts (referencing current and archived reports for fiscal years 2012–2019).

C. Economic Offenses

1. Overview

In the post-*Booker* environment, the discretion of the sentencing judge is crucial. This is particularly true in white collar crime cases because the relevant Guidelines are both complex and controversial.

In 2001, the Commission merged the theft and fraud Guidelines into U.S.S.G. § 2B1.1. Section 2B1.1 starts with a base offense level of 7 in many cases, which by itself would result in a Guidelines range of 0 to 6 months in custody for a defendant with no criminal history. There are 19 specific offense characteristics and 20 Application Notes, which themselves span more than 15 pages of dense text.

Arguably at the core of § 2B1.1 is the first specific offense characteristic, which deals with "loss." There are 16 different loss levels ranging from more than $6,500 (which produces no increase in the offense level) to more than $550,000,000 (which adds 30 to the offense level). Offense level 37 (base offense level 7 plus 30) results in a Guidelines range of 210–262 months in custody for a defendant with no criminal history. While each of the other specific offense characteristics is potentially significant, none of them alone can have that much influence over the offense level. Is the centrality of loss in § 2B1.1 a good or bad policy? How can and should judges react in individual cases post-*Booker*?

Selected portions of § 2B1.1:

(a) Base Offense Level:

    (1) **7**, if (A) the defendant was convicted of an offense referenced to this guideline; and (B) that offense of conviction has a statutory maximum term of imprisonment of 20 years or more; or

    (2) **6**, otherwise.

(b) Specific Offense Characteristics

    (1) If the loss exceeded $6,500, increase the offense level as follows:

    (2) (Apply the greatest) If the offense —

        (A) (i) involved 10 or more victims; (ii) was committed through mass-marketing; or (iii) resulted in substantial financial hardship to one or more victims, increase by **2** levels;

        (B) resulted in substantial financial hardship to five or more victims, increase by **4** levels; or

        (C) resulted in substantial financial hardship to 25 or more victims, increase by **6** levels.

    (3) If the offense involved a theft from the person of another, increase by **2** levels.

    (4) If the offense involved receiving stolen property, and the defendant was a person in the business of receiving and selling stolen property, increase by **2** levels.

    . . .

    (7) If (A) the defendant was convicted of a Federal health care offense involving a Government health care program; and (B) the loss under subsection (b)(1) to the Government health care program was (i) more than $1,000,000, increase by **2** levels; (ii) more than $7,000,000, increase by **3** levels; or (iii) more than $20,000,000, increase by **4** levels.

    . . .

    (16) If the offense involved (A) the conscious or reckless risk of death or serious bodily injury; or (B) possession of a dangerous weapon (including a firearm) in connection with the offense, increase by **2** levels. If the resulting offense level is less than level **14**, increase to level **14**.

    (17) (Apply the greater) If—

(A) the defendant derived more than $1,000,000 in gross receipts from one or more financial institutions as a result of the offense, increase by **2** levels; or

(B) the offense (i) substantially jeopardized the safety and soundness of a financial institution; or (ii) substantially endangered the solvency or financial security of an organization that, at any time during the offense, (I) was a publicly traded company; or (II) had 1,000 or more employees, increase by **4** levels.

(C) The cumulative adjustments from application of both subsections (b)(2) and (b)(17)(B) shall not exceed **8** levels, except as provided in subdivision (D).

(D) If the resulting offense level determined under subdivision (A) or (B) is less than level **24**, increase to level **24**.

(18) If (A) the defendant was convicted of an offense under 18 U.S.C. § 1030 [computer fraud], and the offense involved an intent to obtain personal information, or (B) the offense involved the unauthorized public dissemination of personal information, increase by **2** levels.

. . .

(20) If the offense involved —

(A) a violation of securities law and, at the time of the offense, the defendant was (i) an officer or a director of a publicly traded company; (ii) a registered broker or dealer, or a person associated with a broker or dealer; or (iii) an investment adviser, or a person associated with an investment adviser; or

(B) a violation of commodities law and, at the time of the offense, the defendant was (i) an officer or a director of a futures commission merchant or an introducing broker; (ii) a commodities trading advisor; or (iii) a commodity pool operator,

increase by **4** levels.

Notes and Questions

1. *Congressional concern.* Since before the dawn of the Guidelines era, Congress was concerned about lenient sentences for white collar offenses. As one court noted:

As the legislative history of the adoption of § 3553 demonstrates, Congress viewed deterrence as 'particularly important in the area of white collar crime.' S. Rep. No. 98-225, at 76 (1983), *reprinted in* 1984 U.S.C.C.A.N. 3182, 3259. Congress was especially concerned that prior to the Sentencing Guidelines, '[m]ajor white collar criminals often [were] sentenced to small fines and little or no imprisonment. Unfortunately, this creates the impression that certain offenses are punishable only by a small fine that can be written off as a cost of doing business.' *Id.*

United States v. Martin, 455 F.3d 1227, 1240 (11th Cir. 2006). Does combining the theft and fraud guidelines fix that? Consider one the following comments on the Guidelines' effect of leveling the playing field between white collar fraud and robbery:

> In 1985 [as the Guidelines were being promulgated], the Bureau of Justice Statistics released *The National Survey of Crime Severity*, which polled Americans on the "seriousness" of various sorts of crimes. . . . These numbers indicate that, at least in the eyes of the average American, fraud and robbery are roughly on a moral par. That data is forty years old, but more recent studies suggest it is still good. . . .

> There is no straightforward way to tell whether the Sentencing Guidelines reflect a moral equivalence between fraud and robbery. Each crime has different factors that can raise the offense level (e.g., causing substantial financial hardship versus using a gun) and the offense level for fraud scales up faster with the magnitude of the economic loss than does robbery. One sensible test could be to compare the Sentencing Guidelines offense levels for the average fraud and the average robbery. The average fraud causes a loss of roughly $5.5M. Assuming no other aggravating offense characteristics, the average fraud has an offense level of 24 (6 for the base offense level plus 18 for the loss). The average robbery is for $1,167 and involves some kind of dangerous weapon (gun, knife, or "other"). Again assuming no other additional aggravating offense characteristics, the average robbery has an offense level of . . . *exactly the same*, 24 (20 for the base offense level plus 4 for using a dangerous weapon).

Mihailis E. Diamantis, *White-Collar Showdown*, 102 Iowa L. Rev. 320, 332–33 (2017). Do you agree that robbery and fraud are morally equivalent? What do you think of the author's approach to testing whether the Guidelines reflect moral equivalence between the two?

2. *Intentional increase.* The first Commission noticed that "data revealed inconsistencies in treatment, such as punishing economic crime less severely than other apparently equivalent behavior." U.S.S.G. Ch.1, Pt. A, Subpt. 1 (original 1987 introduction to the Guidelines Manual). This initial Commission went on to describe its very much pre-*Booker* solution as follows:

> Under present [pre-Guidelines] sentencing practice, courts sentence to probation an inappropriately high percentage of offenders guilty of certain economic crimes, such as theft, tax evasion, antitrust offenses, insider trading, fraud, and embezzlement, that in the Commission's view are 'serious.' If the guidelines were to permit courts to impose probation instead of prison in many or all such cases, the present sentences would continue to be ineffective.

The Commission's solution to this problem has been to write guidelines that classify as 'serious' (and therefore subject to mandatory prison sentences) many offenses for which probation is now frequently given. At the same time, the guidelines will permit the sentencing court to impose short prison terms in many such cases. The Commission's view is that the definite prospect of prison, though the term is short, will act as a significant deterrent to many of these crimes, particularly when compared to the status quo where probation, not prison is the norm.

Id.

Over the subsequent decades, the Commission has continued to respond to concerns about inappropriate leniency in white collar cases and has continued to increase the recommended sentences. Should the Commission have kept its focus on the prison versus probation divide? Has the Commission not gone far enough? Or, as some commentators think, has the commission gone too far? One study posing a hypothetical to "240 sitting federal and state judges, representing all federal circuits and eight states . . . found that three in four federal district court judges sentenced [are inclined to sentence a hypothetical] defendant to the exact minimum sentence possible (151 months) of a seven-year range." Mark W. Bennett et al., *Judging Federal White-Collar Fraud Sentencing: An Empirical Study Revealing the Need for Further Reform*, 102 Iowa L. Rev. 939, 944 (2017). Other empirical analysis confirms this pattern for actual sentencing decisions in white collar cases. *See* Jillian Hewitt, *Fifty Shades of Gray: Sentencing Trends in Major White-Collar Cases*, 125 Yale L. Rev. 1018 (2016). What might the relevance of that study be for sentencing policy?

3. *Insider trading.* Insider trading cases are governed by U.S.S.G. § 2B1.4. The Commission amended the Guidelines in 2010, in response to the Dodd-Frank Wall Street Reform and Consumer Protection Act. It "increase[d] the base offense level for organized schemes to engage in insider trading; and [] it broaden[ed] the existing 'abuse of trust' enhancement to include virtually all financial professionals." Christopher P. Conniff et al., *Sentencing Guidelines for Insider Trading: Recent Amendments Create Greater Disparity*, 26 Fed. Sent'g Rep. 43, 43 (2013). Whether as a result of those changes or other factors, a 2011 *Wall Street Journal* analysis concluded that "[i]nside traders are facing considerably harsher sentences than they did in the past." Chad Bray & Rob Barry, *Long Jail Terms on Rise*, Wall St. J (Oct. 13, 2011), *available at* http://online.wsj.com/news/articles/SB100014240529702047746045766269919551 96026. According to the Sentencing Commission, "Securities and investment fraud offenders received the longest average sentences at 52 months, more than twice as long as the average sentence for all economic crime offenders of 23 months." Courtney Semisch, U.S. Sentencing Comm'n, What Does Federal Economic Crime Really Look Like? 2 (2019). Even so, there are salient exceptions to this trend. In a major 2020 case, a banker at Goldman Sachs convicted of insider trading received a sentence of 12 months of home detention; the Guidelines range was 30–37 months imprisonment. *See* Kadhim Shubber & Claire Bushey, *'Flash Crash' Trader Avoids*

Further Jail Time, Fɪɴ. Tɪᴍᴇs (Jan. 28, 2020), https://www.ft.com/content/ea94b64c-41e1-11ea-a047-eae9bd51ceba/.

4. *Race and economic crime.* There seems to be a racial dimension to economic crime. According to a 2019 study by the Sentencing Commission: "White offenders accounted for a substantial majority of securities and investment fraud (79.9%), computer related fraud (70.5%), and government procurement fraud (62.3%), while Black offenders accounted for the largest proportion of tax fraud (55.0%), identity theft (49.4%), and credit card fraud (45.0%)." Sᴇᴍɪsᴄʜ, *supra.* What is the social and economic significance of these statistics? How, if at all, should these racial disparities affect sentencing policy for economic crime?

2. Sentencing Discretion in Fraud Cases

Several federal trial judges find the fraud Guidelines to be unhelpful, particularly in high-loss cases. One of the most prominent critics of the fraud guidelines is Judge Jed Rakoff of the United States District Court for the Southern District of New York. He expresses those concerns in this case.

United States v. Adelson

441 F. Supp. 2d 506 (S.D.N.Y. 2006)

Rᴀᴋᴏꜰꜰ, Dɪsᴛʀɪᴄᴛ Jᴜᴅɢᴇ.

This is one of those cases in which calculations under the Sentencing Guidelines lead to a result so patently unreasonable as to require the Court to place greater emphasis on other sentencing factors to derive a sentence that comports with federal law.

[The indictment] charged defendant Richard P. Adelson with one count of securities fraud, eight counts of causing false reports to be filed with the U.S. Securities and Exchange Commission ("S.E.C."), two counts of soliciting proxies through false statements, and one count of conspiring with others to commit such acts. The gist of the indictment was that Adelson, as Chief Operating Officer and, (eventually) President of Impath, Inc. — a public company specializing in cancer diagnosis testing — joined a conspiracy, initially concocted by others, to materially overstate Impath's financial results, thereby artificially inflating the price of its stock.

It was the government's theory that the conspiracy began in late 1999, that Adelson joined it in 2001, and that it continued until mid-2003. However, on February 16, 2006, following a two-week trial, a jury, while convicting Adelson of conspiracy, securities fraud, and the three of the false filing counts that related to filings made in the latter half of 2002, acquitted him of all seven counts that related to earlier filings.

The most likely reading of the jury's verdict — and one that the Court accepted at sentencing — was that Adelson only joined the conspiracy toward its end. Specifically, the evidence credited by the jury shows that the conspiracy — essentially an accounting fraud—was hatched by various Impath accounting executives and employees who were under strong pressure from the Chief Executive Officer, Anuradha Saad, to maintain the company's healthy financial results and thereby buttress its "high-flying" status in the securities markets. The fraud was sufficiently sophisticated to fool the company's outside auditors, and it also fooled Dr. Saad, from whom the government, after originally charging her with complicity in the fraud, eventually accepted a plea to misappropriating company funds for personal expenses (a misconduct unearthed, ironically, by Adelson). However, as the jury's split verdict attests, Adelson, who had more financial acumen than Saad, ultimately became aware of the fraud toward its latter stages, but, rather than expose it, chose to conceal it and to participate in its continuation, thus leading to his conviction.

After the fraud was uncovered, the accounting employees who actually designed the fraud entered into cooperation agreements with the government, in return for which they became eligible for the substantially reduced sentences that they ultimately received. For her misappropriation of funds for personal expenses, Dr. Saad was given a "non-guideline" sentence of 3 months' imprisonment, which the government did not appeal.

However, at Adelson's sentencing, on May 30, 2006, the government argued that the Sentencing Guidelines, if properly calculated in Adelson's case, called for a sentence of life imprisonment, cabined only by the maximum of 85 years permitted under the counts of which Adelson was convicted. Short of that, the government argued, the Court should at least impose a sentence somewhere in the range of 15 to 30 years' imprisonment. Adelson's counsel, by contrast, argued that the proper guideline calculation resulted in a guideline range of 21 to 27 months' imprisonment, and urged that the actual sentence be well below that range. In the end, however, the Court imposed a non-guideline sentence of 42 months imprisonment (i.e., three-and-a-half years), plus restitution in the amount of $50 million, immediate forfeiture of $1.2 million, three years of supervised release to follow imprisonment, and a life-time ban from being an officer or director of a public company. (Adelson also faces additional monetary sanctions in a parallel proceeding brought against him by the S.E.C.).

The Court's first job was to calculate what the sentence would be under the Sentencing Guidelines (using the version of the Guidelines that was in effect when the conspiracy ended in 2003). Since Adelson had had no prior brushes with the law—indeed, as undisputed evidence submitted by his counsel showed, his life prior to the events here in question was, as the Court concluded, exemplary his Criminal History Category was "I" (the lowest score possible).

The government argued, however, that his total Offense Level score was no less than 55. This was rather remarkable in itself, for the official Sentencing Guidelines Table—the grid from which guideline sentences are ultimately derived—only lists Offense Levels from 1 to 43. This is because everything above level 42 is "life imprisonment," so there is no need to go higher. Put differently, an Offense Level of 55 is a level normally only seen in cases involving major international narcotics traffickers, Mafia dons, and the like. How could it possibly apply here?

What drove the government's calculation in this case, more than any other single factor, was the inordinate emphasis that the Sentencing Guidelines place in fraud cases on the amount of actual or intended financial loss. As many have noted, the Sentencing Guidelines, because of their arithmetic approach and also in an effort to appear "objective," tend to place great weight on putatively measurable quantities, such as the weight of drugs in narcotics cases or the amount of financial loss in fraud cases, without, however, explaining why it is appropriate to accord such huge weight to such factors. *See generally* Kate Stith & José A. Cabranes, *Fear of Judging: Sentencing Guidelines in the Federal Courts* 69 (1998). Specifically, under §2B1.1 of the guidelines, a defendant who violates the federal anti-fraud laws starts with a base offense level of either 6 or 7 (depending on the date of the offense), to which is added, e.g., 16 points if the loss is more than $1 million, or 24 points if the loss is more than $50 million, or 28 points if the loss is more than $200 million. United States Sentencing Guidelines ("U.S.S.G.") §2B1.1(b)(1). Since successful public companies typically issue millions of publicly traded shares—in Impath's case, there were 16.6 million shares of common stock outstanding as of 2003—the precipitous decline in stock price that typically accompanies a revelation of fraud generates a multiplier effect that may lead to guideline offense levels that are, quite literally, off the chart.

The problem is further exacerbated by the fact that the ordinary measure of loss in a criminal securities fraud case is the decline in the price of stock when the fraud is revealed. Since this occurs at the end of the conspiracy, even someone like Adelson who had no role in originating the conspiracy but only joined it in its latter stages will still be legally responsible under the guidelines for the full loss amount that he could reasonably foresee.

In the instant case, the government calculated that the revelation of accounting irregularities at Impath in press releases issued on July 30, 2003 and August 22, 2003 caused the stock price to decline by 88%, thereby causing Impath's thousands of shareholders to suffer a combined loss of no less than $260 million. In response, defendant's counsel submitted a report from Dr. Bala Dharan, a distinguished professor of accounting at Rice University, who, after noting that several material accounting irregularities referenced in the July 30 and August 22 press releases were not attributable to the fraud of which Adelson was convicted, concluded that numerous other contemporary marketplace factors also contributed to the decline in Impath's stock (which, indeed, had been steadily declining since 2001). Because of these "confounding factors," Dr. Dharan opined, it was literally impossible to determine what portion of the actual loss was attributable to the fraudulent conspiracy.

Confronted with these two extreme positions, the Court chose to focus, not on actual loss, but on the alternative measure of intended loss, see Application Note 3(A) to U.S.S.G. §2B1.1, which the Court concluded was more than $50 million but less than $100 million. [The] Court found that, notwithstanding the substantial decline in Impath stock that occurred before Adelson joined the conspiracy, Adelson would have reasonably foreseen when he joined the conspiracy that the eventual revelation of the overstatement of financial results would still likely cause at least a 20% further decline in the price of the stock. This 20% figure — the Court's rough approximation based on the modest extent of the actual overstatements in the context of the public loss of confidence in Impath's future that had already led to a large decline in share price even before Adelson joined the conspiracy — translates to a loss of around $50 million or so at the time of the July 30 and August 22 press releases that first revealed the accounting irregularities to the marketplace. (The precise calculation is 20%/88% multiplied by $260 million = $59 million). Although Adelson was a Johnny-come-lately to the conspiracy, he was still liable for this full $50 million-plus loss that he foreseeably understood would likely occur after he joined and furthered the conspiracy, and thus 24 points had to be added to his base offense level of 6.

At the sentencing hearing, the government also argued that another 6 points had to be added to the offense level because the offense involved more than 250 victims, U.S.S.G. §2B1.1(b)(2), that another 4 points had to be added because Adelson was an officer of a publicly-traded company, id. §2B1.1(b)(15)(A)(i), that another 4 points had to be added because Adelson, although not an originator of the fraud, ultimately played a leadership role, id. §3B1.1(a), that another 2 points had to be added because the offense endangered the financial security of a publicly traded company, id. §2B1.1(b)(13)(B)(ii), that another 2 points had to be added because the fraud involved sophisticated means, id. §2B1.1(b)(9)(C), and that another two points had to be added because Adelson had allegedly induced one of the co-conspirators, Peter Torres, to lie to investigators, thereby obstructing justice, id. §3C1.1.

While one might theorize as to why the Sentencing Commission promulgated each of these additions, "the [Sentencing] Commission has never explained the rationale underlying any of its identified specific offense characteristics, why it has elected to identify certain characteristics and not others, or the weights it has chosen to assign to each identified characteristic." Stith & Cabranes, *supra*, at 69. Here, their combined effect — an added 20 points under the government's approach — ill-fits the situation of someone like Adelson. It represents, instead, the kind of "piling-on" of points for which the guidelines have frequently been criticized. Nonetheless, a district court is obligated to add such points where, on a preponderance standard, they are supported by the evidence; and, in the end, the Court found that each of the aforementioned additions except the 2-point adjustment for endangering the financial security of a publicly-traded company and the 2-point adjustment for obstruction of justice were sufficiently supported by the evidence to require their addition.

Despite these additions, the total offense level of 46 determined by the Court (i.e., a base level of 6, plus a 24 points for loss, plus 16 points for adjustments and enhancements) was 9 points less than the level of 55 recommended by the government (i.e., a base level of 7, plus 28 points for loss, plus 20 points for adjustments and enhancements). But, under the guidelines, this 20% reduction in the offense level made absolutely no difference in the recommended guideline sentence — for as noted, the guidelines recommend life imprisonment for every offense level over 42. Moreover, as a practical matter, a sentence of life imprisonment was effectively available here, for the statutory maximum sentence for the combined five counts of which Adelson had been convicted was 85 years, which, given his current age of 40, would have led to his imprisonment until the age of 125.

Even the government blinked at this barbarity. Pressed repeatedly by the Court as to whether he was asking for a guideline sentence (which, under the Justice Department's prevailing policy he was obligated to do), government counsel refused to answer the question directly. For example, the following colloquy occurred:

THE COURT: Anything above 43 is lifetime in prison.

THE GOVERNMENT: Yes, your Honor.

THE COURT: And then presumably, then, it's your position, since you take the position that the sentencing guidelines are presumptively reasonable, that I should sentence the defendant to as close to lifetime imprisonment as I can, which would be 85 years.

THE GOVERNMENT: Well, your Honor, our position is a sentence that's consistent with the sentencing guidelines —

THE COURT: Well, the guidelines say life.

THE GOVERNMENT: Right.

THE COURT: So what else could be consistent with that, other than life? Presumably 85 years would do that trick, so whereas two or three or four or five years would not, right?

THE GOVERNMENT: Yes, your Honor, but —

THE COURT: So you want Mr. Adelson to spend the rest of his life in prison. That's your position, yes?

THE GOVERNMENT: Your Honor, I think our position is slightly more nuanced than that.

THE COURT: That would be a welcome change.

THE GOVERNMENT: That we respectfully submit that a sentence that is consistent with the terms of the applicable guidelines —

THE COURT: The applicable guidelines in your view is life imprisonment. What could be consistent with that other than life imprisonment?

THE GOVERNMENT: And consistent with other sentences in other similar cases. We think that by coupling those two together, that would be an appropriate reasonable —

THE COURT: So you think I should impose a non-guideline sentence?

THE GOVERNMENT: Your Honor, as the Court is well aware, our policy is that the guidelines sentence is —

THE COURT: I don't think you can have it both ways. I think you either have to take this position that you seem to be taking in your papers, that this defendant should be sentenced to life imprisonment, or not. I don't think you can wiggle out of that with this what you call "nuanced" equivocation.

THE GOVERNMENT: Well, your Honor, I think that the guidelines set forth a series of different aggravating factors that are applicable here and that lead to an end result which is something that Congress has determined should be appropriate or as a severe sentence for these type of corporate fraud offenses, and I think that in light of other similarly situated cases and the sentences imposed there, taking into account all of the factors that your Honor should look at all of the factors under 3553(a).

On any fair reading of this and similar colloquies throughout the sentencing hearing, it is patent that the government was asking the Court not to impose a guideline sentence or, indeed, a sentence of anything like 85 years. What this exposed, more broadly, was the utter travesty of justice that sometimes results from the guidelines' fetish with abstract arithmetic, as well as the harm that guideline calculations can visit on human beings if not cabined by common sense.

The government was therefore right to ultimately suggest, as indicated above, that the Court fashion a sentence that, while taking some account of the guidelines, focuses more on the statutory factors set forth in 18 U.S.C. § 3553(a). Although the government also argued that the Court should fashion a sentence "consistent with other sentences in other similar cases," specifically citing in its papers to the 25 years given Bernard Ebbers, the 15 and 20 years given John and Timothy Rigas, the 30 years given Patrick Bennet, and the 20 years given Steven Hoffenberg, neither in its written submissions nor in its oral argument did the government attempt to show any detailed similarities between the particular facts pertaining to those defendants and to Adelson. Nor is any such comparison justified. Indeed, this Court, which presided over the S.E.C.'s case against WorldCom, S.E.C. v. WorldCom, is specifically aware of how hugely different that case, involving the largest fraud in history (with losses of anywhere from $2 billion to $11 billion) is from this case, let alone how totally removed the situation of Adelson (a belated entrant to the Impath conspiracy) is from that of Ebbers (an active leader of the WorldCom conspiracy through many of its most critical phases).

Thus, Adelson's counsel was far more on point in reminding the Court that the only other defendant involved in Impath misconduct who had been sentenced at the time of Adelson's sentence, Dr. Saad, had received a three-month sentence, from which the government had sought no appeal. But here again, the analogy was far from perfect, for even though the government had originally charged Saad with participation in the fraud, and never backed off its belief that she had participated in it, the government conceded that it could not prove this beyond a reasonable doubt and permitted her to plead to a much lesser charge.

In the end, the Court, confronted with an absurd guideline result that not even the government seriously defended, and with inapt analogies to other cases and defendants, chose to focus its primary attention on the non-guidelines factors set forth in § 3553(a), including both those of general applicability and those that had special relevance to Adelson's particular circumstances.

As the Court noted at the time of sentence, section 3553(a), entitled "Factors to be considered in imposing a sentence," gives first position to "(1) the nature and circumstances of the offense and the history and characteristics of the defendant." The offense here was egregious: an accounting fraud extending over several years that had an intended loss of more than $50 million. But, as the government conceded, Adelson was not the originator of the fraud, and, as the jury found in effect, Adelson did not participate in the fraudulent conspiracy until its final months. During the time of his participation, the price of Impath's stock was not further inflated. On the contrary, after having declined from a high of $81 per share in early November 2000 to $18 per share in June 2002 (the earliest date that, based on the jury's verdict, it is likely Adelson joined the conspiracy), the price remained at $18 per share or lower until the issuance of the press releases in July and August 2004.

Put another way, the evidence showed that Adelson was sucked into the fraud not because he sought to inflate the company's earnings, but because, as President of the company, he feared the effects of exposing what he had belatedly learned was the substantial fraud perpetrated by others. While his efforts in this regard, which included signing certain false filings with the S.E.C., qualified him as a "leader" in guidelines argot, the reality of his situation was that of an executive who, upon learning of his subordinates' misconduct at a time when, for other reasons, the company is already losing shareholder confidence, makes the improper decision to conceal what has occurred. In this sense, Adelson was closer (though not identical) to an accessory after the fact, a position that has historically been viewed as deserving lesser punishment than that accorded the instigators of the wrongdoing.

As for "the history and characteristics of the defendant," it was undisputed at the time of sentencing that Adelson's past history was exemplary. Over 100 persons from all walks of life submitted detailed letters attesting, from personal knowledge, to Adelson's good works and deep humanity. Several letter writers described Adelson's "generosity of spirit," his ever-present willingness to go above and beyond the call of duty to help others. As one friend recounted, Adelson would "speak to [another friend who was suffering from mental illness] on the phone at all hours and drive 3 to 4 hours at a moment's notice to care for him." These letters from friends and family also detail numerous acts of compassion and generosity that date back to the defendant's childhood and have continued to the present. Not only friends, but also prominent business colleagues (such as the chairman of a large public company), educators (such as a Harvard dean), lawyers, doctors, accountants, health care specialists, clergymen, policemen, and other people whose lives were touched by Adelson's acts of kindness, wrote to the Court to express their admiration for the defendant's integrity and generosity. Numerous colleagues at Impath who personally suffered from the fraud here perpetrated nevertheless also wrote the Court on Adelson's behalf, describing the defendant's commitment to Impath and to its mission to improve the lives of cancer patients.

As these examples attest, Adelson's good deeds were not performed to gain status or enhance his image. Most of them were unknown to all but a few people until the time of his sentencing. But, surely, if ever a man is to receive credit for the good he has done, and his immediate misconduct assessed in the context of his overall life hitherto, it should be at the moment of his sentencing, when his very future hangs in the balance. This elementary principle of weighing the good with the bad, which is basic to all the great religions, moral philosophies, and systems of justice, was plainly part of what Congress had in mind when it directed courts to consider, as a necessary sentencing factor, "the history and characteristics of the defendant."

Subsection 2 of section 3553(a) then calls upon the Court to take account of some of the broad general purposes of sentencing, specifically, "the need for the sentence imposed-(A) to reflect the seriousness of the offense, to promote respect for the law, and to provide just punishment for the offense; (B) to afford adequate deterrence to criminal conduct; (C) to protect the public from further crimes of the defendant; and (D) to provide the defendant with needed educational or vocational training, medical care or other correctional treatment in the most effective manner." At the time of sentence, neither party remotely suggested that either "C" (more commonly called "specific deterrence") or "D" (more commonly called "rehabilitation") had any relevance to Adelson. With his reputation ruined by his conviction, it was extremely unlikely that he would ever involve himself in future misconduct. Just to be sure, however, the Court, as part of the sentence here imposed, barred Adelson from ever again serving as an officer or director of a public company.

As for "A" and "B", more commonly referred to as "retribution" and "general deterrence," the Court had no doubt that Adelson's misconduct called for serious punitive measures. In the case of financial fraud, however, an important kind of retribution may be achieved through the imposition of financial burdens. Accordingly, the Court imposed on Adelson a restitution requirement of no less than $50 million, the first $1.2 million of which was obtained by the Court's ordering the immediate forfeiture of most of Adelson's current assets. The rest, the Court ordered, must be paid at the rate of 15% of Adelson's monthly gross income following his release from prison, a requirement that virtually guarantees that Adelson will be making substantial restitution payments for the rest of his life. So far as monetary sanctions are concerned, therefore, the Court did indeed impose a life sentence.

As for prison time, the Court concluded that, notwithstanding all the mitigating factors outlined above, meaningful prison time was necessary to achieve retribution and general deterrence. But as to the latter, there is considerable evidence that even relatively short sentences can have a strong deterrent effect on prospective "white collar" offenders. *See, e.g.,* Richard Frase, *Punishment Purposes*, 58 STANFORD L. REV. 67, 80 (2005); Elizabeth Szockyj, *Imprisoning White Collar Criminals?*, 23 S. ILL. U. L.J. 485, 492 (1998). *Cf.* UNITED STATES SENTENCING COMMISSION, FIFTEEN

YEARS OF GUIDELINES SENTENCING 56 (2004) (noting that the Sentencing Guidelines were written, in part, to "ensure a *short but definite* period of confinement for a larger proportion of these 'white collar' cases, both to ensure proportionate punishment and to achieve deterrence") (emphasis supplied).

Not that the three-and-a-half years imposed by the Court is a short sentence in any practical sense. It is, for example, many times the sentence imposed on Dr. Saad, on the other co-conspirators, and on such high visibility "white collar" offenders as Martha Stewart. Moreover, the government at no time here presented any evidence or cited to any studies indicating that a sentence of more than three-and-a-half years was necessary to achieve the retributive and general deterrence objectives applicable to a case like this one. And "necessary" is the operative word, for section 3553(a) expressly dictates that "[t]he court shall impose a sentence sufficient, but not greater than necessary, to comply with the purposes set forth in paragraph (2) of this subsection" (emphasis supplied). Accordingly, the Court was convinced that three-and-a-half years of prison time was all that was necessary to achieve the purposes set forth in § 3553(a)(2).

The remainder of section 3553(a) is largely concerned with making certain that the sentencing court take account of the guidelines, see § 3553(a)(4), and of "the need to avoid unwarranted sentence disparities among defendants with similar records who have been found guilty of similar conduct," § 3553(a)(5). As already indicated, the Court here considered the guidelines at length, but, like the government itself, found them wildly off-base in this case. As for the need to avoid unwarranted disparities, the Court rejected both the government's claim that Adelson's conduct was comparable to that of Ebbers' and the like, as well as defendant's claim that Adelson's conduct was only slightly more egregious than that of Dr. Saad. But, between these extremes, the sentence the Court did impose was, the Court believes, not unlike sentences that other district courts have imposed in cases involving persons like Mr. Adelson who are belated entrants to substantial financial conspiracies.

Lastly, section 3553(a)(7) reminds the district court of "the need to provide restitution to any victims of the offense." Here, as noted, the Court imposed a restitution requirement of the full $50 million in estimated loss. The Court recognized, of course, that it was unlikely that Adelson, once released from prison, with his reputation destroyed and his employment limited to non-public companies, would ever be positioned to make full restitution. But, by requiring him to make monthly payments of 15% of his gross monthly income, the Court believes that the maximum restitution realistically obtainable from this defendant will in fact be obtained.

To put this matter in broad perspective, it is obvious that sentencing is the most sensitive, and difficult, task that any judge is called upon to undertake. Where the Sentencing Guidelines provide reasonable guidance, they are of considerable help to any judge in fashioning a sentence that is fair, just, and reasonable. But where, as here, the calculations under the guidelines have so run amok that they are patently absurd on their face, a Court is forced to place greater reliance on the more general considerations set forth in section 3553(a), as carefully applied to the particular circumstances of the case and of the human being who will bear the consequences. This the Court has endeavored to do, as reflected in the statements of its reasons set forth at the time of the sentencing and now in this Sentence Memorandum. . . . Whether those reasons are reasonable will be for others to judge.

Notes and Questions

1. *Reasonableness.* What sentence would you have imposed if you were the trial judge? Why? Do you agree that Adelson's sentence was reasonable?

2. *Community support.* In upholding the sentence, Judge Rakoff noted that Adelson had many people write letters of support on his behalf. "Not only friends, but also prominent business colleagues (such as the chairman of a large public company), educators (such as a Harvard dean), lawyers, doctors, accountants, health care specialists, clergymen, policemen, and other people whose lives were touched by Adelson's acts of kindness, wrote to the Court to express their admiration for the defendant's integrity and generosity." A defendant has to have significant social status to receive letters like these. What role should such letters have for sentencing? How does support from the defendant's community interact with the Guidelines' goal of equalizing sentences for street crime and white collar crime?

3. *Charitable donations.* A similar concern may arise from taking charitable works into account at sentencing. While section 5H1.11 of the Sentencing Guidelines states that charitable service is "not ordinarily relevant," some judges see large charitable donations as evidence of extraordinary service that warrants a lower sentence. As one commentator noted, "[J]udges may not render inequitable results based on the defendant's socioeconomic status, race, or gender. And yet, when judges make sentencing decisions based on charitable donations, they do just that." Jessica Baldwin Bowes, *Freedom Futures: Charitable Donations in White-Collar Sentencing*, 106 Iowa L. Rev. 897 (2021).

4. *Quantitative focus.* The Guidelines' focus on quantitative harm—whether the weight of illegal drugs offered or sold, or the amount of money fraudulently sought or obtained—allows for a level of apparent precision in the Guidelines that many criticize as misleading or false. Is the amount of loss always a good proxy for the amount of harm inflicted and the defendant's moral culpability? Some commentators criticize focusing exclusively on "loss" as the economic measure. They advocate looking at a defendant's pecuniary gain as well. One "reform proposal is for the Commission to adopt a downward departure to adequately respond to situations where an offender's gain is substantially lower than the loss the offender caused, with the largest decrease for offenders who derive little or no gain." Mark W. Bennett et al., *Judging Federal White-Collar Fraud Sentencing: An Empirical Study Revealing the Need for Further Reform*, 102 Iowa L. Rev. 939, 988 (2017). Does that sound like a step in the right direction?

5. *Disparities.* As mentioned earlier, federal trial judges tend to sentence white collar criminals at or below the Guidelines' minimum. Thirty-two percent of white collar

offenders receive no prison sentence, compared to nine percent of narcotics offenders. Katherine McBroom, *Avoid Lip Service in Criminal Justice Reform: Start with Sentencing*, 33 No. 08 WESTLAW J. WHITE-COLLAR CRIME 02 (Apr. 26, 2019). The median narcotics prison sentence is more than eight times greater than the median white collar sentence — 58 versus 7.5 months. *Id.* As you read the next note about cognitive bias, bear in mind the familiar racial disparities between defendants convicted of white collar and narcotics violations.

6. *Cognitive bias.* What might explain why the disparities described in the previous note persist, even as the Guidelines strive to stiffen white collar sentences? One commentator has a suggestion:

> [G]ood old cognitive bias. "Bias" sounds like an evil word, but the kind of cognitive bias at issue here is the sort of bias that we all exhibit; it is unconscious and out of our control. Still, we should counteract it to the extent possible. That is what the Sentencing Commission was trying to do by raising the ranges for white-collar fraud to their present level. Before the reforms, sentences for white-collar criminals were too light, especially when compared to street-crime sentences. One leading explanation was that judges are much more likely to overlap demographically with the sorts of upper-echelon folks who end up committing white-collar crimes. Beneath their robes and powdered wigs, judges are just humans subject to human foibles; like us all, they are more likely to empathize (even if unconsciously) with one of their own. The Sentencing Commission could not cure this suspected cognitive bias, but they could counteract it by raising the sentencing ranges for white-collar crimes. Which is what they did.

Mihailis E. Diamantis, *White-Collar Showdown*, 102 IOWA L. REV. 320, 322–23 (2017). Is it a coincidence that Judge Rakoff went to Harvard Law School and specifically mentioned Adelson's letter from a Harvard Dean as justification for the low sentence? What else might explain a trial judge's inclination to sentence white collar offenders at or below the Guidelines range minimum?

7. *Restitution.* The Mandatory Victim Restitution Act (18 U.S.C. § 3663A) requires federal courts to order payment of restitution to victims. The Sentencing Guidelines also prioritize restitution, saying any money paid by defendant is first applied to the order of restitution and then to any punitive fines. U.S.S.G. § 5E1.1(c). Is Judge Rakoff right that "an important kind of retribution may be achieved through the imposition of [restitution]"? Or is restitution more of a civil-style remedy that has no bearing on what punishment a defendant deserves?

8. *Criminal history.* While Adelson's prior history may have been "exemplary," half of all fraud offenders have at least one prior conviction (usually not another economic crime). Tracey Kyckelhahn & Emily Herbst, U.S. SENTENCING COMM'N, THE CRIMINAL HISTORY OF FEDERAL OFFENDERS 6 (2018). How should sentencing for economic crime address recidivism?

———————

Although federal trial judges have significant latitude in imposing sentences, their discretion is not unlimited.

United States v. Peppel

707 F.3d 627 (6th Cir. 2013)

Karen Nelson Moore, Circuit Judge.

Defendant-Appellee Michael Peppel, former President, CEO, and Chairman of the Board of Directors of MCSi, Inc. ("MCSi"), conspired with CFO Ira Stanley to falsify MCSi accounting records and financial statements in order to conceal the actual earnings from shareholders, while at the same time laundering proceeds from the sale of his own shares in a public stock offering. For this conduct, the sentencing guidelines provided a sentencing range of 97–121 months' imprisonment. The district court, based almost solely on its estimation of Peppel as "a remarkably good man," varied downward drastically from this advisory range, imposing a custodial sentence of only seven days — a 99.9975% reduction. Plaintiff-Appellant the government appeals the substantive reasonableness of the seven-day sentence, arguing that a seven-day sentence does not adequately reflect the seriousness of the offense, serve the goal of general deterrence, or avoid national sentencing disparities, and that the district court placed disproportionate weight on disfavored factors. Peppel contests the government's arguments and proffers a conditional cross-appeal, contending that the district court erred in its amount-of-loss and number-of-victims calculations that formed the basis of two sentencing enhancements.

We conclude that the district court abused its discretion by imposing an unreasonably low seven-day sentence, but did not err in calculating the amount of loss or number of victims. We therefore VACATE Peppel's sentence and REMAND for resentencing consistent with this opinion.

From 1996 to March 2003, Peppel was employed at MCSi, a publicly traded company specializing in computer technology and visual-communication products. In 1998, Peppel was elected President and CEO of MCSi and was subsequently elected as Chairman of the Board of Directors in 2000. After success in the late 1990s, MCSi began experiencing financial difficulties. In 2000, Peppel and MCSi CFO Ira Stanley conspired to falsify MCSi accounting records and financial statements in order to conceal the actual earnings from shareholders. This conspiracy, to which Peppel pleaded guilty, ended on or about April 30, 2003. These falsified records "were based upon fraudulent MCSi transactions involving a firm known as Mercatum, Ltd." Although the specifics of these transactions are debated, it appears that in December 2001 Peppel set up a sale of $37.1 million of MCSi product to Mercatum under terms that allowed Mercatum to pay for the MCSi product upon resale. Peppel then arranged, through false documents, to record this sale as a "bill and hold," which indicated that Mercatum was billed prior to receipt of the goods. MCSi therefore was able falsely to report $37.1 million in revenue in connection with this purported sale in the fourth quarter of 2001. These false revenues were included in a February 26,

2002 public announcement. This scheme also included additional sham transactions involving FedEx, Skytron, and ClearOne Communications.

During the same time period that he was orchestrating the Mercatum transaction, Peppel sold 300,000 shares of his personal MCSi stock in a public stock offering. In this December 21, 2001 transaction, "Peppel generated gross proceeds before commission and expenses in the amount of $6,862,500." Peppel then deposited these proceeds into personal bank accounts, and these transactions formed the factual basis of the money-laundering count to which Peppel pleaded guilty.

In January 2003, several class actions were filed against Peppel and MCSi, alleging various forms of fraudulent conduct. On February 14, 2003, MCSi announced in a press release that the SEC had commenced an investigation, and on February 18, 2003, the first day of trading following the announcement, MCSi stock fell $0.87 per share. Peppel was terminated from MCSi on March 11, 2003, and MCSi was delisted from NASDAQ on April 17, 2003. An SEC civil-enforcement action followed, and certain restrictions were instituted against Peppel, including a lifetime bar from serving as an officer or director of a public company.

On December 13, 2006, the government filed a twenty-six count indictment against Peppel. On August 11, 2010, Peppel pleaded guilty to conspiracy to commit securities, mail, and wire fraud in violation of 18 U.S.C. §§ 371 and 1349; willful false certification of a financial report by a corporate officer in violation of 18 U.S.C. § 1350; and money laundering in violation of 18 U.S.C. § 1957.

Because of the numerous objections to the [pre-sentence report], the district court held an evidentiary hearing; in particular, the district court focused on calculating the amount of loss caused by Peppel's conduct. At the evidentiary hearing, the district court heard testimony and received reports on five competing amount-of-loss theories. The first was proffered by the probation officer, who recommended attributing a loss of $18 million to Peppel as a result of his conduct. To reach this number, the probation officer calculated the loss per share from February 14 to February 18, 2003, and multiplied this number ($0.87) by the number of publicly held shares (approximately 21 million). The government put forth three amount-of-loss calculations. The first, which was calculated by John Hlavacek, the SEC expert, estimated the total loss to be $298 million. "This was based on the average weekly market price of MCSi stock from May 14, 2001 to November 14, 2002 ($13.59), less the closing price on February 18, 2003 ($1.25), times the total shares held by non-insiders (24,158,776)." The government then called Dr. Marlena Akhbari, who "generally opined that public disclosure of four separate pieces of adverse information about MCSi from January 15 to February 14, 2003, caused a decline in value of $2.91 per share." Additionally, Joseph Geraghty testified for the government and "opined that Peppel's fraud with respect to the Mercatum transaction caused an actual loss to MCSi's secured lenders of approximately $88 million."

Peppel, however, continued to argue that "shareholder loss simply cannot be reasonably calculated, and that at best, the Court should utilize his gain from the sale of MCSi stock in December 2001 during the public offering," valued at $6,862,500. Ultimately, the district court applied the probation officer's calculation, which resulted in a 20-level enhancement under U.S.S.G. § 2B1.1(b)(1)(K) and a 4-level enhancement under U.S.S.G. § 2B1.1(b)(2)(B). These enhancements, in conjunction with other factors not at issue in this appeal, resulted in an adjusted offense level of 30 and an advisory sentencing range of 97–121 months' imprisonment.

The district court held an extensive sentencing hearing, at which Peppel called numerous witnesses to testify as to his character, accomplishments, and charitable works. Peppel argued for a sentence of probation and supervised release, whereas the government maintained that a within-guidelines sentence would be appropriate. The district court imposed a seven-day custodial sentence, three years of supervised release, and a $5 million fine.

The government argues that Peppel's sentence is substantively unreasonable in light of the 18 U.S.C. § 3553(a) factors and the advisory 97-month minimum sentence under the guidelines. The government offers the following five bases for this contention:

> [The sentence] (1) fails to adequately reflect the seriousness of Peppel's offense conduct, promote respect for the law, and provide just punishment for the offense; (2) fails to afford adequate general deterrence to similar offense conduct; (3) fails to adequately avoid unwarranted sentencing disparities among defendants with similar records who have been found guilty of similar conduct; (4) is based, in part, on an unreasonable amount of weight given to Peppel's history and characteristics; and (5) is based, in part, on the consideration of impermissible factors.

Peppel counters each reason separately and also argues that the district court correctly considered the totality of the factors and selected a sentence that is sufficient on the whole.

"A sentence may be considered substantively unreasonable when the district court selects a sentence arbitrarily, bases the sentence on impermissible factors, fails to consider relevant sentencing factors, or gives an unreasonable amount of weight to any pertinent factor." United States v. Robinson, 669 F.3d 767, 774 (6th Cir.2012) (internal quotation marks omitted). "The applicable Guidelines range represents the starting point for substantive-reasonableness review because it is one of the § 3553(a) factors and because the Guidelines purport to take into consideration most, if not all, of the other § 3553(a) factors." *United States v. Haj-Hamed*, 549 F.3d 1020, 1025 (6th Cir. 2008). "While the standard of review does not change based on whether a sentence is inside, just outside, or significantly outside the Guidelines range, the greater the district court's variance, the more compelling the evidence must be." *United States v. Christman*, 607 F.3d 1110, 1118 (6th Cir. 2010).

A. Seriousness of the Conduct, Respect for the Law, and Just Punishment

The government argues that the district court committed error "by failing to explain how Peppel's sentence of only seven days in jail, a 97-month downward variance, satisfies the § 3553(a) goals of adequately reflecting the seriousness of Peppel's offense conduct, of promoting respect for the law, and of providing just punishment for Peppel's conduct." Peppel rejoins that the district court considered the seriousness of the offense and that the government's argument ignores the non-custodial components of Peppel's sentence, the totality of which reflects the seriousness of the offense.

We have previously asserted that a district court must explain how a sentence comports with the level of seriousness of the crime committed: "While the district court recognized that the offenses of conviction were 'serious,' it did not explain how the one-day sentence it gave Davis meshed with Congress's own view of the crimes' seriousness. . . ." *United States v. Davis*, 537 F.3d 611, 617 (6th Cir. 2008) (internal citations omitted). It is plain that the district court acknowledged the seriousness of the offense in broad terms at Peppel's sentencing hearing. Notably, however, the district court never explained why the seven-day sentence was sufficient to reflect the seriousness of Peppel's crimes. The most applicable statement made by the district court to this analysis was its reasoning that a double-digit sentence would be greater than necessary given the facts of this case. However, reasoning that a twenty-five-year sentence is inappropriate in light of the facts of the case does not satisfy the requirement to state affirmatively why the chosen sentence reflects the seriousness of the offense.

Peppel responds that the totality of his sentence adequately reflects the seriousness of the offense. Peppel notes that in addition to the seven-day custodial sentence, he "has forfeited substantial personal assets, . . . the SEC has barred [him] from ever again serving as a director or officer of a public company," and the district court imposed a $5 million fine. The government rejoins that custodial sentences are qualitatively different and reiterates its argument that the district court failed to explain how the totality of these components is sufficient to reflect the seriousness of the conduct.

The existence of additional components of Peppel's sentence does not cure the district court's failure to explain how a seven-day custodial sentence adequately reflects the seriousness of the offense. Moreover, as argued by the government, many of the statements made by the district court in this portion of its analysis are improper under our established law. For example, the district court considered collateral consequences of the prosecution and conviction: "The Court accepts Mr. Peppel and his family's representation that the last five years have been punishing, literally and figuratively, for Mr. Peppel, and the Court takes that into consideration as well." Such assertions are in direct contradiction of [*United States v.*] *Bistline*, where we explained that "[t]he district court's recitation of these collateral consequences therefore does nothing to show that Bistline's sentence reflects the seriousness of his offense. Were it otherwise, these sorts of consequences — particularly ones related to a defendant's humiliation before his community, neighbors, and friends — would tend to support shorter sentences in cases with defendants from privileged backgrounds, who might have more to lose along these lines." 665 F.3d [758, 765–66 (6th Cir. 2012)].

Peppel further argues that there is consensus among judges, academics, the American Bar Association, and the Department of Justice that the guidelines for white collar crimes are flawed and require amendment. In support of his argument, Peppel relies on a letter from the Director of the Office of Policy and Legislation. Letter from Jonathan J. Wroblewski, Director, Office of Policy and Legislation, to the Honorable William K. Sessions III (June 28, 2010), *available at* http://sentencing .typepad.com/files/annual_letter_2010_final_062810.pdf. The substance of this letter, however, undermines Peppel's argument not only with respect to the seriousness of the offense, but also regarding nearly every other sentencing factor at issue. The letter focuses on the sentencing disparity between certain classes of crimes, noting that a different regime exists for certain frauds "that has largely lost its moorings to the sentencing guidelines." *Id.* at 2. Regarding economic crimes specifically, Mr. Wroblewski writes that "[u]nfortunately, we have seen with increasing frequency district courts sentencing fraud offenders — especially high-loss fraud offenders — inconsistently and without regard to the federal sentencing guidelines." *Id.* at 4. He further opines that "[t]he current sentencing outcomes in these cases are unacceptable, and the Commission should determine whether some reforms are needed." *Id.* at 5.

For these reasons, we find Peppel's arguments unpersuasive and conclude that the district court abused its discretion by failing to explain why a seven-day sentence of imprisonment adequately reflects the seriousness of Peppel's offense and that the court erred by considering impermissible factors.

B. General Deterrence

The government also argues that the seven-day sentence does not effectuate § 3553(a)'s goal of general deterrence. Peppel counters that the negative publicity garnered from the proceedings would deter an executive from following in his footsteps and that a custodial sentence would not add to general deterrence. The district court stated the following concerning general deterrence:

> And with regard to general deterrence, several jurists and commentators have concluded that relatively short sentences of incarceration for white collar economic crimes are generally more than sufficient to serve this goal. And I would refer counsel to the case of United States versus Adelson. . . .

As an initial matter, the district court based its ruling on an out-of-circuit case that relies upon a theory that we have expressly rejected. In *Davis*, we reversed a district court that imposed a one-day sentence for bank fraud, explaining that "[w]hile the district court indicated that this sentence would serve the goals of societal deterrence, . . . it is hard to see how a one-day sentence for a lucrative business crime satisfies that goal." 537 F.3d at 617 (internal citation omitted). In reaching this conclusion, we cited with approval an Eleventh Circuit case which reasons that "[t]he

7-day sentence imposed by the district court also utterly fails to afford adequate deterrence to criminal conduct. Because economic and fraud-based crimes are more rational, cool, and calculated than sudden crimes of passion or opportunity, these crimes are prime candidates for general deterrence." *United States v. Martin*, 455 F.3d 1227, 1240 (11th Cir. 2006) (internal quotation marks, alteration, and citation omitted). The Eleventh Circuit further concludes: "Yet the message of Martin's 7-day sentence is that would-be white collar criminals stand to lose little more than a portion of their ill-gotten gains and practically none of their liberty. . . . The district court's 7-day sentence not only fails to serve the purposes of § 3553, but even worse, undermines those purposes." *Id.*

Moreover, the sentence imposed by the district court in this case bears little resemblance to that imposed by the district court in *United States v. Adelson*, 441 F. Supp. 2d 506 (S.D.N.Y. 2006), as is made clear when the principle cited by the district court is placed in context. To begin, the potential sentence for Adelson under the guidelines was eighty-five years, which is significantly greater than the eight-to-ten-year sentence advised for Peppel. In *Adelson*, the government recommended a sentence in the range of fifteen to thirty years, the defendant proposed a sentence of two years, and the district court ultimately imposed a three-and-a-half year sentence. The district court noted that the factor that drove the government's recommendation was the "inordinate emphasis that the Sentencing Guidelines place in fraud cases on the amount of actual or intended financial loss." *Id.* at 509. Even after taking that factor into account, though, the district court noted the importance of considering general deterrence in financial-fraud cases and imposed a three-and-a-half-year sentence: "notwithstanding all the mitigating factors outlined above, meaningful prison time was necessary to achieve retribution and general deterrence." *Id.* at 514. *Adelson* thus advocates implementing a meaningful custodial sentence in fraud cases, even when "it was undisputed at the time of sentencing that [a defendant's] past history was exemplary." *Id.* at 513.

A seven-day custodial sentence does not adequately serve the goal of general deterrence, particularly in light of our binding precedent. The district court's imposition of a seven-day sentence and its assertion that such a sentence would effectuate general deterrence was thus an abuse of discretion.

C. National Sentencing Disparities

Further, the government contends that Peppel's sentence does not avoid "unwarranted disparity with other defendants whose fraudulent conduct results in similar dollar losses to multiple victims and similar personal enrichment for the defendant." Peppel argues that such a low sentence is not unusual in the white collar-crime context and that it was appropriate to consider the sentence of Stanley, Peppel's codefendant, in imposing Peppel's sentence.

Section 3553(a)(6) provides that a sentencing court shall consider "the need to avoid unwarranted sentence disparities among defendants with similar records who have been found guilty of similar conduct." 18 U.S.C. § 3553(a)(6). We have previously held that this provision refers to national sentencing disparities rather than sentencing disparities among codefendants. "One of the central reasons for creating the sentencing guidelines was to ensure stiffer penalties for white collar crimes and to eliminate disparities between white collar sentences and sentences for other crimes." *Davis*, 537 F.3d at 617.

> The district court addresses the national-sentencing-disparities factor as follows:

> The Court must also consider avoiding unwarranted sentencing disparities among similarly situated defendants. And this is a broad consideration that goes beyond any co-defendant in this case or in this set of circumstances.

> Mr. Peppel has argued that a within Guideline sentence would be unduly harsh when compared with sentences imposed on other corporate criminals. Clearly, the aim of this statutory directive is to avoid sentencing disparities on a national basis, and the advisory Guidelines serve as a basis for avoiding such disparities. In cases where the ultimate sentence lies outside of the Guidelines range, it is difficult to assess disparity without some consideration of other similarly situated defendants.

> . . . [T]he Court nevertheless feels that and believes that specific knowledge of the myriad of facts that resulted in the particular sentences to which we are attempting to compare Mr. Peppel's situation is probably not very productive. The amount of loss, however calculated, is not the critical point, not always the critical point, and so I think other cases, specific cases, are not helpful.

> . . .

> While the Court [in *United States v. Parris*, 573 F. Supp.2d 744 (E.D.N.Y. 2008),] noted that there is undoubtedly a host of factors that entered into these sentences, it was plain to the Court that the defendants were not in the same league with offenders who directly caused enormous losses and received lengthy double-digit sentences [(in terms of years)]. In the latter category, the primary defendants in Enron, WorldCom, and Global Crossing cases were particularly mentioned.

> In this case the Court agrees that a double-digit sentence would be greater than necessary and likely would contribute to perceived sentencing disparity in the broad sense. The Court's estimate of actual loss in this case of approximately $18 million is not and cannot be exact for the reasons discussed in the Court's prior order.

> Mr. Peppel's admitted conduct of improperly reporting the Mercatum income and certifying MCSi's Form 10-Q is not comparable to the conduct that led to lengthy sentences for, among others, Enron and WorldCom officers. Cases involving outright theft of company or investor funds or looting

company resources to enrich oneself obviously calls for much harsher sentences than this case merits.

As with its discussion of *Adelson*, we disagree with the district court's portrayal of *Parris*. In *Parris*, the defendants faced an advisory sentence of 360 months to life imprisonment under the guidelines. Finding this to be extreme under the circumstances, the district court asked the government and the defendants to provide the court with a compendium of factually analogous cases nationally. The result of this collaborative effort was a finding that on the whole, "[t]hose who were not cooperators and were responsible for enormous losses were sentenced to double-digit terms of imprisonment (in years); those whose losses were less than $100 million were generally sentenced to single-digit terms." *Id.* at 753. After considering this factor, along with the other § 3553(a) factors, the district court sentenced the defendants to sixty months of incarceration. Although this is a significant variance from the guideline range, it is a substantially greater term than a sentence of seven days. Moreover, a review of the compendium attached to the *Parris* case establishes that the sentences imposed nationally were all in terms of months or years, with the exception of one case where the defendant was imprisoned for thirty days. *Parris*, if anything, establishes the opposite of what was attributed to it by the district court. The compendium makes clear that a seven-day sentence does nothing to avoid national sentencing disparities.

In addition to relying on inapposite cases, the district court failed to offer an explanation as to how a seven-day sentence avoids national sentencing disparities, an omission of even greater import when imposing a sentence so decidedly below the guideline range. As discussed with respect to the seriousness of the offense, the rejection of a twenty-five-year sentence does not demonstrate how the chosen sentence avoids national sentencing disparities. We therefore conclude that the district court abused its discretion in imposing a sentence that does not avoid national sentencing disparities.

D. History and Characteristics

Additionally, the government asserts that the district court gave undue weight to Peppel's personal history and characteristics, particularly with respect to factors discouraged by the guidelines such as education and vocational skills, family ties and responsibilities, and civic, charitable, or prior good works. Peppel responds that the district court was within its discretion to consider these factors and that it engaged in a thorough analysis of each of the cited characteristics.

The district court relied extensively on Peppel's history and characteristics in fashioning the seven-day sentence, focusing on two characteristics in particular: (1) the monetary, emotional, and charitable support Peppel provides to his family, friends, and community, and (2) his business expertise. Examples of the court's statements concerning the first characteristic are as follows:

> Mr. Peppel's sentencing memorandum and the many letters, in excess of
> 100, that the Court has received from friends and business acquaintances

note Mr. Peppel's humble beginnings and his many community and charitable activities both before and after the charges in this case. Mr. Peppel has five dependent children and provides financial and emotional support to his brother, who is stricken with multiple sclerosis and has suffered from that disease for many years. To his credit, Mr. Peppel is now involved in a business venture that is apparently a growing success and provides a very much needed service to a large number of people, not to mention jobs.

. . .

Mr. Peppel is key to the welfare of his mother and brother, his wife and children, a company that depends on him in a difficult economic situation, and the Court is satisfied, as I previously stated, that Mr. Peppel will not engage in this type of behavior again.

With respect to the second characteristic, the court reasoned:

Mr. Peppel is a talented businessman, entrepreneur, and the Court considers imposing a substantial fine upon Mr. Peppel, and a significant, actually maximum under the law, period of supervised release, but the Court sees very little benefit to be gained by incarcerating Mr. Peppel for an extended period of time as the Guidelines suggest.

. . .

'I see it to be wasteful for the government to spend taxpayers' money to incarcerate someone that has the ability to create so much more for this country and economy.' [This was a quotation from a letter in support of the defendant. — Eds.]

Although we have recognized that in certain instances a district court may weigh heavily factors such as financial and emotional support when considering the appropriate sentence, we cannot agree that the circumstances identified by the district court justify varying downward in such a significant manner. Based on the record in this case, there is nothing to indicate that the support provided by Peppel to his family, friends, business associates, and community is in any way unique or more substantial than any other defendant who faces a custodial sentence. Further, Peppel's status in the community and chosen profession cannot alone be the basis for such a conclusion.

The second characteristic — Peppel's business expertise — is troubling for related reasons. We reject the inference drawn from the district court's statements, and infused in Peppel's defense, that individuals with certain professional qualifications, such as Peppel, should be sentenced lightly on the asserted ground that they offer more to society than those who do not possess such knowledge and skill. To that end, the district court seems to reason, society receives a greater value from allowing individuals such as Peppel to continue to work in their chosen field than from imposing a custodial sentence on them.

The district court's heavy reliance on unremarkable aspects of Peppel's characteristics constituted an abuse of discretion. Nothing in the record establishes unique circumstances other than his chosen profession and status in the community, both of which are decidedly inappropriate to form the basis of such a large downward variance. Because the district court not only placed far too great of an emphasis on Peppel's history and characteristics, but also considered improper factors that we have previously repudiated, we conclude that the district court abused its discretion.

For the reasons stated, the district court abused its discretion by imposing a sentence that does not reflect the seriousness of the offense, avoid national sentencing disparities, or effectuate general deterrence, and by affording too much weight to Peppel's history and characteristics. We therefore vacate Peppel's sentence and remand for resentencing.

Notes and Questions

1. *Unreasonable?* Do you agree that Peppel's sentence was unreasonable? If so, why do you think the sentencing judge imposed such a low sentence? If you now had to resentence Peppel, after having read the Sixth Circuit's decision, what sentence would you impose? Remember that the advisory Guidelines recommend a sentence of 97–121 months of imprisonment.

2. *Rationale.* The Sixth Circuit found the seven-day sentence to be unreasonable. Do you believe that an explanation focused more on the trial court's disagreement with the Guidelines, rather than on its view of Peppel as a "remarkably good man," would have led to a different result on appeal?

3. *Resentencing.* Judge Sandra Beckwith, the same judge who originally sentenced Peppel, resentenced him in June 2013 to two years in prison along with the original fine and other requirements. According to the DAYTON DAILY NEWS, Judge Beckwith rejected the government's request for a 121-month sentence and said that she "struggled" with the deterrence aspect of the sentence. She concluded that, "[t]he modest sentence in this case should be more than enough to serve that goal." Thomas Gnau, *Peppel Sentenced to Two Years*, DAYTON DAILY NEWS (June 4, 2013), *available at* https://www.daytondailynews.com/business/peppel-sentenced-two -years/LsvJ7s5zUNmFMpJfxuzd1K/.

4. *Loss amount.* The *Peppel* case demonstrates some of the different ways in which loss amounts can be conceived. Is it appropriate to consider changes in stock price? Would Peppel's proposal to focus on his gain have underestimated the harm inflicted by his crimes?

Problems

19-1. Defendant worked as a property manager for Mallow Properties. As part of his duties, he was authorized to approve invoices for work performed on the properties under his supervision. For two years, defendant used his position to steal from Mallow. His scheme worked in two ways. First, he took payment checks for legitimate invoices and deposited them into several bank accounts at his disposal. He then took the same invoices, broke them down into several smaller invoices, and resubmitted them for payment, using the smaller checks to pay the vendors. Second, he created fraudulent invoices for work never performed. In some cases, the listed contractor on these invoices did not even exist. He then deposited the payment checks into various bank accounts to which he had access. Defendant stole a total of $180,000. As a result, Mallow had to institute new policies and procedures to verify invoice payments. Based on these facts, defendant has pleaded guilty to bank fraud.

Defendant has stated that, at the time of the offense, he was going through a difficult divorce and was concerned about providing for his children. He also admitted to living beyond his means. Defendant was 47 years old and had no prior criminal record. He had two sons, ages 15 and 13, and was by all accounts an excellent parent. Despite strained relations with his ex-wife, she had agreed to allow the youngest son to live with defendant. Other family members also made positive statements about defendant's character.

Defendant's mental and physical health appeared to be sound, and he had no substance abuse issues. A high-school graduate with some college education, defendant compiled a solid work history. Following his termination by Mallow, he obtained a well-paying job as a property manager for another company, but that employer terminated defendant when it learned about this offense via an anonymous phone call. The loss of this job clearly affected defendant's ability to make restitution. Defendant intended to re-pay Mallow and, shortly after the offense was discovered, signed over a motorcycle worth about $18,000 as a sign of good faith. He also took up residence in his office at his new workplace in an effort to save money. Once he lost the property manager job, he became a self-employed contractor performing remodeling and drywall work, earning much less. Further, because his child support payments were based on his old salary, he quickly amassed arrears and was unable to make restitution. He also sat down with his two sons and admitted to them what he had done, and expressed genuine remorse for his crime, indicating that he was humiliated by his downfall.

This case is now before the trial judge for sentencing.

> *a. Calculate the Guidelines sentence range, assuming a base level of 7, U.S.S.G. § 2B1.1(a)(1), and a criminal history category of I.*

> *b. For the prosecution and the defense, (1) determine the sentence that you believe should be imposed and (2) make the arguments in support of your recommended sentence.*

> *c. Now assume that you are the trial judge. What sentence would you impose? Why?*

19-2. Casey Madden was a bank teller at Central Federal Credit Union, a federally insured credit union. He was approached by Danielle Roberts, who worked for an identity theft ring in the area. Roberts offered Madden $100 for each set of 10 names, Social Security numbers, and account numbers that Madden provided to her.

Madden retrieved the information for 80 customers from the credit union's computer and gave the information to Roberts. Roberts then gave the information to Darrel Park, who was the mastermind behind the identity theft ring. Park used the personal information obtained from the customers to defraud them of over $500,000.

After receiving complaints from numerous Central Federal Credit Union customers, federal agents launched an investigation. They soon determined that Madden was involved in the scheme. The agents approached Madden and offered him a plea bargain in exchange for his cooperation. Thereafter, Madden cooperated fully with the government's investigation of Roberts and Park. Park was the principal target of the investigation. However, because Roberts had also agreed to plead guilty and cooperate, and because Madden had never met Park and could not provide any information as to Park, the government determined that Madden was unable to provide substantial assistance in the investigation.

Madden has pleaded guilty to one count of computer fraud in violation of 18 U.S.C. § 1030(a)(2)(A). The government has declined to bring a substantial assistance motion.

a. Calculate Madden's advisory Guidelines range.

b. Impose the sentence you deem appropriate as the District Judge. What do you need to say by way of explanation to protect the sentence if it is appealed?

c. Assume the District Judge imposed a sentence at the lower two-thirds end of the Guidelines range. Would you find that sentence reasonable if you were an appellate judge? Why or why not?

19-3. Wesley Snipes is a popular movie actor and the owner of a film production company. At some point, he became involved with a group called the American Rights Litigators ("ARL"). ARL would help its customers in their struggle with the Internal Revenue Service ("IRS") by questioning the IRS's lawful ability to collect taxes. ARL claims, in part, that domestic earnings are not "income" that can be taxed.

During the years in question, Snipes earned more than $37 million in gross income, but he did not file individual tax returns for those years. Rather, Snipes sent the IRS various documents arguing that the IRS could not collect taxes from him. Among other things, Snipes claimed that, "as a 'fiduciary of God,' who is a 'nontaxpayer,' he was a 'foreign diplomat' who was not obliged to pay taxes." *United States v. Snipes*, 611 F.3d 855, 860 (11th Cir. 2010). Tax attorneys who had worked for Snipes told him that he had to pay taxes and stopped representing him when he insisted on failing to file his tax returns.

Snipes was indicted on various charges, including conspiracy, felony filing a false claim, and six counts of willful failure to file taxes, a misdemeanor. The jury convicted Snipes only of three counts of willful failure to file taxes. The maximum sentence the Court could impose was thus three years in prison.

The Probation Office determined that Snipes's intended tax loss was just over $41 million and recommended the statutory maximum sentence of three years. Snipes objected on several grounds, including that a three-year sentence is not appropriate for misdemeanor convictions. Snipes also presented character witnesses on his behalf.

The case is now before the trial judge for sentencing.

> *a. Calculate Snipes's advisory Guidelines range.*
>
> *b. Impose the sentence you deem appropriate as the District Judge and explain why. What is your dominant purpose of punishment in imposing that sentence?*
>
> *c. Assume the District Judge imposed a three-year sentence. Would you find that sentence reasonable if you were an appellate Judge? Why or why not?*

3. Fraud Guidelines: Controversy and Potential Reform

The fraud Guidelines are controversial and have prompted criticism from lawyers, judges, and academics. The following concurrence frames the issue.

United States v. Corsey

723 F.3d 366 (2d Cir. 2013)

[In a *Per Curiam* decision, the Second Circuit affirmed the defendants' mail and wire fraud convictions, but reversed their 20-year, statutory maximum sentences as procedurally unreasonable. The Court described the case as follows: "This appeal arises out of a conspiracy to defraud a non-existent investor of three billion dollars." The defendants tried to "lure a broker [who was actually an informer working with the FBI] into procuring financing for an imaginary Siberian oil pipeline. The two sides exchanged information about possible partners, and the best structure for a loan. But in reality each side duped the other — [the defendants] had no plans to build a pipeline across the Russian tundra, and [the informer] never represented a hedge fund interested in lending billions to the defendants to do so."]

UNDERHILL, DISTRICT JUDGE, concurring:

Although I agree that appellants' sentences should be vacated and remanded for procedural error, the real problem is that those sentences are shockingly high. For that reason, I would reach the question of substantive reasonableness and would reverse on the merits.

In my view, the loss guideline is fundamentally flawed, and those flaws are magnified where, as here, the entire loss amount consists of intended loss. Even if it were perfect, the loss guideline would prove valueless in this case, because the conduct underlying these convictions is more farcical than dangerous. If substantive review of sentences actually exists other than in theory, it must be undertaken at least occasionally. This would have been an appropriate case in which to do so, because it raises so starkly the problems with the loss guideline. Until this Court weighs in on the merits of the loss guideline, sentences in high-loss cases will remain wildly divergent as some district judges apply the loss guideline unquestioningly while others essentially ignore it. The widespread perception that the loss guideline is broken leaves district judges without meaningful guidance in high-loss cases; that void can only be filled through the common law, which requires that we reach the substantive reasonableness of these sentences.

Substantive review of sentences provides "a backstop for those few cases that, [even if] procedurally correct, would nonetheless damage the administration of justice because the sentence imposed was shockingly high, shockingly low, or otherwise unsupportable as a matter of law." [*United States v.*] *Rigas*, 583 F.3d [108,] 123 [(2nd Cir. 2009)](citation and footnote omitted). Not surprisingly, we have only rarely held that a sentence is substantively unreasonable. In sum, we will set aside a district court's substantive determination of the appropriate sentence only "in exceptional cases where the trial court's decision cannot be located within the range of permissible decisions." *United States v. Cavera*, 550 F.3d 180, 189 (2d Cir.2008) (citation and internal quotation marks omitted). This is such a case.

The twenty-year sentences imposed on appellants are not merely harsh, they are dramatically more severe than can be justified by the crime the appellants committed. This was a clumsy, almost comical, conspiracy to defraud a non-existent investor of three billion dollars. That scheme never came close to fruition. Even the terms of the proposed deal itself were laughable: the lender of three billion dollars would, according to the appellants, receive fourteen billion dollars in profit over five years. This scheme amounted to a series of absurd lies piled on top of even more absurd lies. Appellants' conduct was not dangerous because they had absolutely no hope of success.

A single factor—loss, specifically intended loss—drove the Guidelines calculation, and a single section 3553(a) factor—deterrence—provided the basis for accepting the Guidelines recommended sentence. A district court may not presume that a sentence within the Guidelines range is reasonable. Although the District Court used the intended loss amount correctly for purposes of calculating the Sentencing Guidelines range, the Court erred by failing to dramatically discount that calculation when weighing the section 3553(a) factors against the totality of the circumstances of this case. This conspiracy to defraud involved no actual loss, no probable loss, and no victim. The scheme was treated as sophisticated, but could be more accurately described as a comedic plot outline for a "Three Stooges" episode. Because the plan was farcical, the use of intended loss as a proxy for seriousness of the crime was wholly arbitrary: the seriousness of this conduct did not turn on the amount of intended loss any more than would the seriousness of a scheme to sell the Brooklyn Bridge turn on whether the sale price was set at three thousand dollars, three million dollars, or three billion dollars. By relying unquestioningly on the amount of the intended loss, the District Court treated this pathetic crime as a multi-billion dollar fraud — that is, one of the most serious frauds in the history of the federal courts.

The error of accepting intended loss as a proxy for the seriousness of this crime was "compounded by the fact that the district court was working with a Guideline that is fundamentally different from most and that, unless applied with great care, can lead to unreasonable sentences that are inconsistent with what § 3553 requires." [*United States v.*] *Dorvee*, 616 F.3d [174,] 184 [(2nd Cir. 2010)]. The loss guideline, like the child pornography guideline at issue in *Dorvee*, was not developed by the Sentencing Commission using an empirical approach based on data about past sentencing practices. As such, district judges can and should exercise their discretion when deciding whether or not to follow the sentencing advice that guideline provides.

The fraud guideline was initially set forth in Guideline section 2F1.1. The Sentencing Commission set the original 1987 Guidelines for economic offenses higher than historical sentences in order to further the deterrence and just punishment goals of sentencing. In 1989, in response to the savings and loan crisis, Congress passed legislation increasing the maximum penalties for financial fraud offenses and directing the Sentencing Commission to include specific offense characteristic enhancements in the fraud guideline. In 2001, the Sentencing Commission amended the Guidelines to combine the fraud, theft and embezzlement, and property destruction guidelines into a single guideline, section 2B1.1. That change was accompanied by the publication of a new loss table that had the effect of increasing offense level calculations, especially for high-dollar-value crimes. Most recently, the fraud guideline was amended in 2003 in response to Congressional directives in the Sarbanes-Oxley Act. Those amendments included further changes to the loss table that added offense level points in the highest loss cases. The three sets of amendments to the loss table of the fraud guideline alone have effectively multiplied several times the recommended sentence applicable in 1987 for large-loss frauds, which itself was set higher than historic sentences. Each of the three increases in the recommended Guideline ranges for fraud crimes was directed by Congress, without the benefit of empirical study of actual fraud sentences by the Sentencing Commission.

The history of bracket inflation directed by Congress renders the loss guideline fundamentally flawed, especially as loss amounts climb. The higher the loss amount, the more distorted is the guideline's advice to sentencing judges. As a well-known sentencing commentator has put it, "For the small class of defendants . . . convicted of fraud offenses associated with very large guidelines loss calculations, the guidelines now are divorced both from the objectives of Section 3553(a) and, frankly, from common sense. Accordingly, the guidelines calculations in such cases are of diminished value to sentencing judges." Frank O. Bowman III, *Sentencing High-Loss Corporate Insider Frauds After* Booker, 20 FED. SENT'G REP. 167, 168 (2008).

When the Guidelines range zooms off the sentencing table, sentencing judges are discouraged from undertaking close examination of the circumstances of the offense and the background and characteristics of the offender. That certainly happened here. But the low marginal utility of the guideline in this very high intended loss case should have prompted greater, not lesser, reliance on the section 3553(a) factors other than the Guidelines.

In this case, it is impossible to describe the sentences imposed on appellants as substantively reasonable. In my view, none of the section 3553(a) factors, singly or in combination, can justify these shockingly high punishments, which are far greater than necessary to punish or deter appellants' conduct. The District Court provided "no reason why the maximum sentence of incarceration was required to deter [the appellants] and offenders with similar history and characteristics." *Dorvee*, 616 F.3d at 184. The bare assertion of the need to deter, unconnected to the background and characteristics of a defendant or the nature and circumstances of a crime, provides only superficial support for a sentence of imprisonment. Here, the factor of deterrence simply cannot "bear the weight assigned it under the totality of circumstances in the case." *Cavera*, 550 F.3d at 191. None of the appellants had ever served a significant term of imprisonment and two of the three had spent no time in prison whatsoever. This raised the question whether a statutory maximum sentence is necessary to deter future wrongdoing. That is especially true here because appellants are older than most defendants and, accordingly, can be expected to have a lower risk of recidivism than most. Indeed, one of the appellants will surely die in prison, if required to serve a sentence anywhere close to twenty years; although an effective life sentence, by definition, provides complete deterrence, imposing such a sentence for the conduct underlying this conviction would be senseless.

The absence of any actual loss whatsoever and especially the absence of a victim significantly undercut any argument that this crime was particularly serious. Outside the context of Sentencing Guidelines calculations, intended loss is always less serious than actual loss, so its value as a proxy for seriousness of a crime must be carefully examined. And not all actual loss is equally serious. A fraud that results in the loss of even a few thousand dollars by an elderly or sick person who, as a result of the loss, becomes unable to afford the necessities of life or medical care is much more serious than a fraud that results in ten or a hundred times that loss by a large corporation able to absorb the financial consequences without a need to close plants, fire employees, or even declare the loss as material in public financial reports. Simply put, contrary to the assumption underlying the loss guideline, not all dollars of loss are fungible.

Moreover, the convictions in this case were for conspiracy, which proscribes an agreement to commit fraud and punishes that agreement the same whether or not a fraud was actually committed. "[W]e punish unconsummated efforts to cause harm as 'attempts' or 'conspiracies' (albeit usually less severely than completed crimes) so long as the would-be-perpetrator has come close enough to success that we can be confident his malignant designs were real and not mere fantasy, and thus that his conduct was morally blameworthy." Frank O. Bowman, III, *Coping with 'Loss': A Re-examination of Sentencing Federal Economic Crimes Under the Guidelines*, 51 VAND. L. REV. 461, 559 (1998). The circumstances of these convictions put them very close to the boundary of mere fantasy (or perhaps the boundary of mental competence) and the sentences should have reflected that fact. As with most attempt crimes and unconsummated conspiracies, the actual loss here was zero. The wrongfulness of the appellants' conduct does not turn in any meaningful sense on the amount that the conspirators sought to obtain; all other things equal, an effort to secure $3 billion for construction of an imaginary pipeline is not 100 times as serious as an effort to secure $30 million for construction of an imaginary factory. Accordingly, factors other than intended loss become critical in distinguishing the seriousness of unconsummated criminal conduct.

District judges are not permitted to treat the Sentencing Guidelines as reasonable. The corollary of that proposition is that district judges have an obligation to consider whether a sentence other than a Guidelines sentence would be sufficient, but not greater than necessary, to serve the purposes of sentencing. 18 U.S.C. § 3553(a). Accordingly, district judges have an obligation to consider whether to depart from the Guidelines sentencing range or to impose a non-Guidelines sentence in every case. That duty will frequently require judges applying the loss guideline to evaluate whether the calculated Guidelines range substantially overstates the seriousness of a crime. *See* U.S.S.G. § 2B1.1 application note 19(C) ("There may be cases in which the offense level determined under this guideline substantially overstates the seriousness of the offense. In such cases, a downward departure may be warranted."). That duty went unfulfilled in this case, and the result was the imposition of shockingly high sentences on the appellants.

The Court of Appeals missed an opportunity in this case to provide much needed guidance to district judges who must apply the misguided loss guideline. Thankfully, the District Court will have the opportunity at resentencing to undertake the difficult task of weighing all of the section 3553(a) factors under the circumstances of these cases to reach sentences that are sufficient, but not greater than necessary, to serve the purposes of sentencing.

Notes and Questions

1. *Section 2B1.1.* Do you think that § 2B1.1 appropriately captures the harm inflicted by the defendants in this case?

2. *Substantive reasonableness review.* Do you think it is easier for the Court of Appeals to engage in substantive reasonableness review when the sentence is very lenient as in *Peppel* or very severe as in *Corsey*?

3. *Resentencing.* What do you think is the likely result on resentencing in this case?

4. *More disparity?* Judges are imposing fewer federal fraud sentences in compliance with the Guidelines. There are many reasons for this, including requests by the government, but the judges are also exercising their post-*Booker* authority to vary from

the Guidelines on their own. In congressional testimony in 2011, Chief Judge Patti Saris, the Chair of the Commission, said: "There are troubling trends in sentencing, including growing disparities among circuits and districts and demographic disparities, which the Commission has been evaluating." *Hearing Before the Subcomm. on Crime, Terrorism, and Homeland Security of the H. Comm. on the Judiciary*, 112th Cong. (Oct. 12, 2011) (prepared testimony of Judge Patti B. Saris, Chair of the U.S.S.G. Commission). Are you concerned about these trends?

5. *Scrap the Guidelines.* In 2013, Judge Rakoff suggested that "the Federal Sentencing Guidelines should be scrapped in their entirety and replaced with a nonbinding, nonarithmetic multifactor test." Jed S. Rakoff, *Why the Federal Sentencing Guidelines Should Be Scrapped*, 26 FED. SENT'G REP. 6, 6 (2013). Judge Rakoff expounded on his vision for a post-Guidelines world:

> Now in the Guidelines context, what I would suggest is that for every category of crime the Sentencing Commission devise a list of factors, unweighted but fairly detailed, each of which a sentencing judge would be required to address in writing, stating how it applied (or did not apply) to the case at hand, what other factors might also be relevant, and how the combination should be viewed in the context of that particular case in arriving at the sentence imposed. This analysis would then be subject to fairly robust review on appeal. . . .
>
> Would this approach lead to more disparity? Yes, if by 'disparity' one means any deviation from an artificial numbering system dictating a sham consistence. But no, if one is concerned with true disparities, that is, like cases not being treated alike: for the combination of having to consider every factor and state in writing how they interplay in a given case, when coupled with a searching appellate review, would soon develop a common law of sentencing that would eliminate outliers without sacrificing individual circumstances. . . . [I]f you believe that sentencing is more properly the role of judges than of adversarial prosecutors or distant, number-crunching commissions, and that judges are serious when they tell you that sentencing is among the most important things they do, you might be willing to give this new approach a try.

Id. at 9. Do you think that Congress would or should adopt this kind of a system? Judge Rakoff calls for "robust review on appeal." What would robust review of an amorphous, multifactor balancing test look like?

Problems

19-4. A jury found Rajat Gupta, a 63-year-old chief of consulting for a major international firm, guilty of three counts of securities fraud and one count of conspiracy. Gupta was also a member of the Board of Directors of Goldman Sachs Group and was convicted of breaching his fiduciary duty to Goldman by giving its inside information to a trader friend of his, although Gupta himself did not directly profit by passing along the tips.

Based on the trader's gain from Gupta's offense, the sentencing judge concluded that the loss attributable to Gupta was in excess of $5 million. The court found that the total offense level was 28. Combined with a Criminal History Category of I, the advisory Guidelines range was 78 to 97 months of imprisonment.

The government sought a Guidelines sentence. It argued that Gupta and the trader, who had already been convicted and sentenced to 11 years in prison, were "very close friend[s]" and that Gupta was to benefit indirectly from his friend's illicit gains.

Before his conviction, Gupta was a widely admired business person with a long record of philanthropic achievements. Gupta's attorneys emphasized the duration and magnitude of his good works, including his efforts fighting diseases like AIDS, tuberculosis, and malaria around the world. The sentencing court observed that it could "say without exaggeration that it has never encountered a defendant whose prior history suggest such an extraordinary devotion, not only to humanity writ large, but also to individual human beings in their times of [n]eed." *United States v. Gupta*, 904 F. Supp. 2d 349, 354 (S.D.N.Y. 2012). Gupta's lawyers sought a term of probation with a community service requirement and suggested that Gupta might work with youth in New York or poor people in Rwanda.

This case is now before the trial judge for sentencing.

a. Assuming that the judge followed the government's recommendation, should the Court of Appeals find that to be a substantively reasonable sentence?

b. Assume that the judge followed Gupta's recommendation, should the Court of Appeals find that to be a substantively reasonable sentence?

c. What sentence would you impose and why? Why do you think that the Court of Appeals would find it substantively reasonable?

D. Organizational Sentencing Guidelines

1. Overview

The government enforces the criminal laws against organizations as well as against individuals. Chapter 2, *supra*, explores the ways in which organizations such as corporations, partnerships, and labor unions may be found guilty of violating the criminal law. Since 1991, the Commission has provided a set of Organizational Guidelines for these cases. Broadly speaking, the Commission wants the convicted organization to: (1) remedy the harm it caused; (2) be stripped of all its assets if the offense was primarily criminal in nature; (3) pay a fine based on the severity of the offense and the responsibility of the organization (which can be increased for such things as "tolerance of criminal activity," and decreased because of "the existence of an effective compliance and ethics program") (*see infra*); and (4) serve probation if needed to effectuate other sanctions or "reduce the likelihood of future criminal conduct." U.S.S.G. Ch. 8, intro. comment.

Two commentators offer this overview of the Organizational Guidelines structure:

> Rather than adhering to any single goal, the Guidelines state numerous objectives: "to provide just punishment, adequate deterrence, and incentives for organizations to maintain internal mechanisms for preventing, detecting, and reporting criminal conduct" (Chapter 8). Some provisions of the Guidelines also ensure that criminal corporations pay restitution to their victims. Others disgorge corporations of criminal profits.
>
> The centerpiece of the Guidelines is the rubric for calculating fines. The Guidelines authorize judges to impose a financial death sentence (a fine exceeding corporate assets) on any corporation "operated primarily for a criminal purpose." (§ 8C1.1). For other corporations, the calculation is more complex, balancing the seriousness of the crime with case-specific considerations.
>
> 1. Judges begin by calculating the "base fine," which is the greatest of three numbers: the loss caused by the corporate crime, the gain realized by the corporation, or the fine listed on a table [ranging from $8,500 to $150,000,000].
>
> 2. They then determine the "culpability score," which incorporates several factors, including: size of the corporation, pervasiveness of the misconduct, involvement of senior personnel, prior history of misconduct, the presence or absence of an effective compliance program, and whether the corporation cooperated with authorities.
>
> 3. The base fine and the culpability score give judges a "fine range," which can go as low as five percent of the base fine and as high as four-hundred percent.
>
> 4. After calculating the fine range, judges select a fine within the range. In doing so, they balance factors such as the need to fulfill the purposes of criminal law, the collateral consequences of conviction, and whether the offense targeted vulnerable victims.
>
> 5. Alternatively, judges consider whether to depart above or below the fine range. Relevant considerations include whether the corporation provided substantial assistance to authorities (depart down) or whether the criminal conduct involved substantial risk of death or bodily injury (depart up).
>
> The Organizational Sentencing Guidelines close with provisions for placing corporate convicts on probation. The Guidelines direct courts to impose

a one- to five-year term of probation when needed to ensure payment of penalties, to implement compliance enhancements, or "to accomplish one or more of the purposes of sentencing" (§ 8D1.1). The Guidelines give judges wide latitude to impose any condition "reasonably related to the nature and circumstances of the offense or the history and characteristics of the organization" (§ 8D1.4). In some circumstances, courts may appoint a monitor to implement the probation conditions.

In addition to the Sentencing Guidelines, a series of other statutes and regulations impose "collateral consequences" on convicted corporations. These consequences can disqualify corporations from receiving licenses or other business privileges, like contracting with the government. In many sectors — like accounting and healthcare — such collateral consequences can be fatal.

Mihailis E. Diamantis & William S. Laufer, *Prosecution and Punishment of Corporate Criminality*, 15 ANNU. REV. L. SOC. SCI. 453, 464–65 (2019).

2. Culpability Score

Much like the individual Guidelines, the Organizational Guidelines describe various factors that add or subtract points in an effort to calculate a measure of the seriousness of the crime. For organizational defendants, this measure is called the "culpability score." Relevant culpability scores range from 0 to 10, and can have a dramatic effect on the Guidelines fine range.

Sentencing of Organizations § 8C2.5: Culpability Score

(a) Start with 5 points and apply subsections (b) through (g) below.

(b) <u>Involvement in or Tolerance of Criminal Activity</u>

If more than one applies, use the greatest:

(1) If—

    (A) the organization had 5,000 or more employees and

        (i) an individual within high-level personnel of the organization participated in, condoned, or was willfully ignorant of the offense; or

        (ii) tolerance of the offense by substantial authority personnel was pervasive throughout the organization; or

    (B) the unit of the organization within which the offense was committed had 5,000 or more employees and

        (i) an individual within high-level personnel of the unit participated in, condoned, or was willfully ignorant of the offense; or

        (ii) tolerance of the offense by substantial authority personnel was pervasive throughout such unit, add **5** points; or

(2) If—

    (A) the organization had 1,000 or more employees and

        (i) an individual within high-level personnel of the organization participated in, condoned, or was willfully ignorant of the offense; or

        (ii) tolerance of the offense by substantial authority personnel was pervasive throughout the organization; or

    (B) the unit of the organization within which the offense was committed had 1,000 or more employees and

        (i) an individual within high-level personnel of the unit participated in, condoned, or was willfully ignorant of the offense; or

        (ii) tolerance of the offense by substantial authority personnel was pervasive throughout such unit,

add **4** points; or

(3) If—

    (A) the organization had 200 or more employees and

        (i) an individual within high-level personnel of the organization participated in, condoned, or was willfully ignorant of the offense; or

        (ii) tolerance of the offense by substantial authority personnel was pervasive throughout the organization; or

    (B) the unit of the organization within which the offense was committed had 200 or more employees and

        (i) an individual within high-level personnel of the unit participated in, condoned, or was willfully ignorant of the offense; or

        (ii) tolerance of the offense by substantial authority personnel was pervasive throughout such unit,

add **3** points; or

(4) If the organization had 50 or more employees and an individual within substantial authority personnel participated in, condoned, or was willfully ignorant of the offense, add **2** points; or

(5) If the organization had 10 or more employees and an individual within substantial authority personnel participated in, condoned, or was willfully ignorant of the offense, add **1** point.

(c) <u>Prior History</u>

If more than one applies, use the greater:

(1) If the organization (or separately managed line of business) committed any part of the instant offense less than 10 years after (A) a criminal adjudication based on similar misconduct; or (B) civil or administrative adjudication(s) based on two or more separate instances of similar misconduct, add **1** point; or

(2) If the organization (or separately managed line of business) committed any part of the instant offense less than 5 years after (A) a criminal adjudication based on similar misconduct; or (B) civil or administrative adjudication(s) based on two or more separate instances of similar misconduct, add **2** points.

(d) <u>Violation of an Order</u>

If more than one applies, use the greater:

(1) (A) If the commission of the instant offense violated a judicial order or injunction, other than a violation of a condition of probation; or (B) if the organization (or separately managed line of business) violated a condition of probation by engaging in similar misconduct, <u>i.e.</u>, misconduct similar to that for which it was placed on probation, add **2** points; or

(2) If the commission of the instant offense violated a condition of probation, add **1** point.

(e) <u>Obstruction of Justice</u>

If the organization willfully obstructed or impeded, attempted to obstruct or impede, or aided, abetted, or encouraged obstruction of justice during the investigation, prosecution, or sentencing of the instant offense, or, with knowledge thereof, failed to take reasonable steps to prevent such obstruction or impedance or attempted obstruction or impedance, add **3** points.

(f) <u>Effective Compliance and Ethics Program</u>

(1) If the offense occurred even though the organization had in place at the time of the offense an effective compliance and ethics program, as provided in § 8B2.1 (Effective Compliance and Ethics Program), subtract **3** points.

. . .

(g) <u>Self-Reporting, Cooperation, and Acceptance of Responsibility</u>

If more than one applies, use the greatest:

(1) If the organization (A) prior to an imminent threat of disclosure or government investigation; and (B) within a reasonably prompt time after becoming aware of the offense, reported the offense to appropriate governmental authorities, fully cooperated in the investigation, and clearly demonstrated recognition and affirmative acceptance of responsibility for its criminal conduct, subtract **5** points; or

(2) If the organization fully cooperated in the investigation and clearly demonstrated recognition and affirmative acceptance of responsibility for its criminal conduct, subtract **2** points; or

(3) If the organization clearly demonstrated recognition and affirmative acceptance of responsibility for its criminal conduct, subtract **1** point.

Notes and Questions

1. *Prosecution guidelines.* What are some points of overlapping concern between the Organizational Guidelines and the Department of Justice's charging manual (*see supra* Chapter 15)? Why the overlap? Is it a good thing?

2. *Incentives.* What incentives are each section of the Organizational Guidelines trying to give corporations? Are the incentives great enough? Some scholars think the Organizational Guidelines do not give corporations adequate reason to self-report. *See* Jennifer Arlen, *The Failure of the Organizational Sentencing Guidelines*, 66 U. MIAMI L. REV. 321, 325–26 (2012) ("[P]erversely, the Guidelines offer the least percentage mitigation for policing to large firms convicted of crimes involving managers and to firms with a past history of wrongdoing . . . the Guidelines [thus] discourage firms from monitoring, self-reporting, and cooperating. . . .") It can be very hard for the Department of Justice to detect corporate crime, so self-reporting can be a powerful enforcement tool.

3. *Recent stats.* Eighteen percent of corporate convicts pay no fine or restitution, 13.5% pay both, 62.7% pay a fine but no restitution, and 14.4% pay restitution but no fine. U.S. SENTENCING COMM'N, FISCAL YEAR 2019 OVERVIEW OF FEDERAL CRIMINAL CASES 21 (Apr. 2020), https://www.ussc.gov/research/data-reports/overview-federal-criminal-cases-fiscal-year-2019. The average fine is almost $10,500,000 and, in total, organizations were ordered $1,105,956,355 in restitution and fines in 2019. *Id.* Do any of these numbers surprise you?

Problem

19-5. *What is the culpability score for each the following firms that have engaged in criminal activity?* Explain how you arrive at the number. If you think you need more information, indicate what information and what bearing it has on the sentence.

1. The firm has more than 6,000 employees. It has no history of prior bad conduct. A manager in an overseas division (which has 3,000 employees) was involved. Once the government detected the crime, the firm instantly cooperated.

2. The firm has 150 employees. It has civil judgments against it for similar misconduct in the past, but this is its first criminal conviction. The firm has an effective compliance program that detected the crime, but the firm did not report it to the government. Once the government detected the crime, the firm instantly cooperated.

3. Compliance Programs

In addition to retribution and deterrence, the Organizational Guidelines are also concerned with corporate rehabilitation. The Guidelines largely accomplish this by giving corporations an incentive to be proactive about compliance. The Commission has written:

> These guidelines offer incentives to organizations to reduce and ultimately eliminate criminal conduct by providing a structural foundation from which an organization may self-police its own conduct through an effective compliance and ethics program. The prevention and detection of criminal conduct, as facilitated by an effective compliance and ethics program, will assist an organization in encouraging ethical conduct and in complying fully with all applicable laws.

U.S.S.G. Ch. 8, intro. comment. Corporations that have an effective compliance program can receive a three-point reduction to their culpability score.

The Organizational Guidelines define what counts as effective compliance:

Sentencing of Organizations § 8B2.1: Effective Compliance and Ethics Program

(a) To have an effective compliance and ethics program . . . an organization shall —

   (1) exercise due diligence to prevent and detect criminal conduct; and

   (2) otherwise promote an organizational culture that encourages ethical conduct and a commitment to compliance with the law. Such compliance and ethics program shall be reasonably designed, implemented, and enforced so that the program is generally effective in preventing and detecting criminal conduct. The failure to prevent or detect the instant offense does not necessarily mean that the program is not generally effective in preventing and detecting criminal conduct.

(b) Due diligence and the promotion of an organizational culture that encourages ethical conduct and a commitment to compliance with the law within the meaning of subsection (a) minimally require the following:

   (1) The organization shall establish standards and procedures to prevent and detect criminal conduct.

   (2) (A) The organization's governing authority shall be knowledgeable about the content and operation of the compliance and ethics program and shall exercise reasonable oversight with respect to the implementation and effectiveness of the compliance and ethics program.

      (B) High-level personnel of the organization shall ensure that the organization has an effective compliance and ethics program, as described in this guideline. Specific individual(s) within high-level personnel shall be assigned overall responsibility for the compliance and ethics program.

(C) Specific individual(s) within the organization shall be delegated day-to-day operational responsibility for the compliance and ethics program. Individual(s) with operational responsibility shall report periodically to high-level personnel and, as appropriate, to the governing authority, or an appropriate subgroup of the governing authority, on the effectiveness of the compliance and ethics program. To carry out such operational responsibility, such individual(s) shall be given adequate resources, appropriate authority, and direct access to the governing authority or an appropriate subgroup of the governing authority.

(3) The organization shall use reasonable efforts not to include within the substantial authority personnel of the organization any individual whom the organization knew, or should have known through the exercise of due diligence, has engaged in illegal activities or other conduct inconsistent with an effective compliance and ethics program.

(4) (A) The organization shall take reasonable steps to communicate periodically and in a practical manner its standards and procedures, and other aspects of the compliance and ethics program, to the individuals referred to in subparagraph (B) by conducting effective training programs and otherwise disseminating information appropriate to such individuals' respective roles and responsibilities.

(B) The individuals referred to in subparagraph (A) are the members of the governing authority, high-level personnel, substantial authority personnel, the organization's employees, and, as appropriate, the organization's agents.

(5) The organization shall take reasonable steps —

(A) to ensure that the organization's compliance and ethics program is followed, including monitoring and auditing to detect criminal conduct;

(B) to evaluate periodically the effectiveness of the organization's compliance and ethics program; and

(C) to have and publicize a system, which may include mechanisms that allow for anonymity or confidentiality, whereby the organization's employees and agents may report or seek guidance regarding potential or actual criminal conduct without fear of retaliation.

(6) The organization's compliance and ethics program shall be promoted and enforced consistently throughout the organization through (A) appropriate incentives to perform in accordance with the compliance and ethics program; and (B) appropriate disciplinary measures for engaging in

criminal conduct and for failing to take reasonable steps to prevent or detect criminal conduct.

(7) After criminal conduct has been detected, the organization shall take reasonable steps to respond appropriately to the criminal conduct and to prevent further similar criminal conduct, including making any necessary modifications to the organization's compliance and ethics program.

(c) In implementing subsection (b), the organization shall periodically assess the risk of criminal conduct and shall take appropriate steps to design, implement, or modify each requirement set forth in subsection (b) to reduce the risk of criminal conduct identified through this process.

By encouraging the creation of innumerable compliance plans, the Organizational Guidelines have had a dramatic impact on the way corporations operate. The Organizational Guidelines' emphasis on compliance led to explosive growth in the compliance industry as firms sought to implement programs that would qualify as "effective." The Ethics Resource Center expressed this concern in a 2012 report, which was drafted on the occasion of the Organizational Guidelines' 20th anniversary:

> By offering reduced sentences for corporate offenders that cooperated with investigators and/or established effective compliance and ethics programs to promote respect for the law, the Guidelines extended a metaphorical 'carrot' to induce good corporate behavior. Bad actors, on the other hand, would receive stiffer sentences. Because of subsequent trends in law enforcement, including the preference for negotiated plea agreements instead of trial, the [Organizational Guidelines] have turned out to have minimal impact on sentencing. But evidence shows that the Guidelines have achieved significant success in reducing workplace misconduct by nurturing a vast compliance and ethics movement and enlisting business organizations in a self-policing effort to deter law-breaking at every level of their business.

ETHICS RESOURCE CENTER, THE FEDERAL SENTENCING GUIDELINES FOR ORGANIZATIONS AT TWENTY YEARS: A CALL TO ACTION FOR MORE EFFECTIVE PROMOTION AND RECOGNITION OF EFFECTIVE COMPLIANCE AND ETHICS PROGRAMS i (2012). *See also* Frank O. Bowman III, *Drifting Down the Dnieper with Prince Potemkin: Some Reflections About the Place of Compliance Programs in Federal Criminal Sentencing*, 39 WAKE FOREST L. REV. 671 (2004).

Some commentators are more hesitant to call the Organizational Guidelines an unmitigated success. From one perspective, the Guidelines have not done enough. The criteria defining "effective compliance" are abstract. This can incentivize firms to implement "paper" programs that check all of the formal boxes but have little efficacy. *See* David Hess, *Ethical Infrastructures and Evidence-Based Corporate Compliance and Ethics Programs: Policy Implications from the Empirical Evidence*, 12

N.Y.U.J.L. & Bus. 317, 318–20 (2016). The effective compliance criteria are also rather unsophisticated since they take a one-size-fits-all approach to all firms, sidestepping the inconvenient fact that compliance needs vary widely from industry to industry. From another perspective, the Organizational Guidelines have done too much. Compliance costs have increased exponentially, draining resources that businesses could put to productive use. *See* William S. Laufer, *The Missing Account of Progressive Corporate Criminal Law*, 14 N.Y.U.J.L. & Bus. 71, 112–14 (2017). These might be necessary costs of doing business; however, in light of the fact that the Organizational Guidelines are not based on any actual data about what effective compliance looks like, there is legitimate concern about waste.

Notes and Questions

Ordered to improve compliance. Only about 19% of convicted corporations are ordered to improve their compliance programs. U.S. Sentencing Comm'n, Fiscal Year 2019 Overview of Federal Criminal Cases 21 (Apr. 2020), https://www.ussc.gov/research/data-reports/overview-federal-criminal-cases-fiscal-year-2019. Does this seem consistent with the importance that the Organizational Guidelines place on compliance?

Problem

19-6. SpyD Corp. offers private investigation services to customers who want to find out details about someone's (the "target's") identification. They employ about 500 people, split into 50 divisions of 10 people, one division for each state. Jules is a manager in one of the divisions. He decides to use some target information (acquired by subverting SpyD's digital compliance protocols) to open credit cards in their names. He then uses these credit cards for some personal expenses and to throw morale-boosting pizza parties for his coworkers. SpyD quickly catches on, reports what happened to the government, and fully cooperates in the investigation. However, to maintain public confidence in their services, SpyD insists on a public narrative that pins all the blame on Jules.

You're negotiating a DPA with a prosecutor. The prosecutor has asked for your calculation of SpyD's culpability score. How do you respond? Did you subtract three points for effective compliance? If you are uncertain, what further facts do you want to investigate? Note that this is the same scenario posed in Problem 15-8, discussing the DOJ's guidelines for charging business organizations. Does your reasoning about what counts as effective compliance differ under the Sentencing Guidelines?

Chapter 20

Forfeitures

A. Introductory Notes

1. Purpose, Scope, and Controversy

Congress enacted the forfeiture laws with the express purposes of deterring illegal activity and depriving wrongdoers of the fruits of their acts. Federal forfeiture statutes provide the government with the power to both seize and obtain ownership of private property that is related to criminal activity, including such white collar crimes as money laundering and RICO violations.[a] The United States Department of Justice has also sought to make aggressive use of forfeitures in electronic fraud cases, including those involving virtual assets such as cryptocurrency. *See* U.S. DEPT. OF JUSTICE, CRYPTOCURRENCY: AN ENFORCEMENT FRAMEWORK (Oct. 2020).

The forfeiture statutes apply to virtually all types of property, whether the property was actually used in the illegal activity or represents proceeds of such activity. For the purposes of this text, the most important avenues of federal forfeitures are the financial crimes statutes and the RICO statute. Although many of the forfeitures discussed in the cases below did not arise in the context of white collar crime, the legal principles in those cases apply equally in the white collar context.

Depending upon the statute used in the particular case, the forfeiture may occur as part of a criminal case or a civil proceeding. Criminal forfeitures did not come into widespread use at the federal level until the enactment of the RICO statute in 1970. Such forfeitures occur as part of the penalty phase in a criminal case. The principal criminal forfeiture provisions are set forth in the financial crimes statutes, the RICO statute, and the narcotics statutes. *See* 18 U.S.C. §§ 982, 1963; 21 U.S.C. § 853.

Unlike criminal forfeitures, civil forfeitures have a long history in Anglo-American law. A civil forfeiture case is an *in rem* proceeding in which the property itself is named as the defendant. Such a case is based upon the legal fiction that the property itself is the wrongdoer. Thus, a civil forfeiture proceeding may be brought

---

a. Although most states also have their own forfeiture laws, this chapter focuses primarily on federal forfeiture proceedings. The controversies over forfeiture laws described in this chapter have led some state governments to limit forfeitures or ban the practice entirely. *See, e.g., Policing for Profit: New Mexico*, INST. FOR JUSTICE (2d ed. Jan 1, 2020), https://ij.org/pfp-state-pages/pfp-new-mexico/#:~:text=In%202015%2C%20New%20Mexico%20enacted,its%20owner%20of%20a%20crime.

even where the alleged wrongdoer has not been convicted of or even charged with a crime.

The forfeiture statutes have generated substantial revenues for the government, but have also produced significant controversy.[b] Much of the controversy arises from the government's financial stake in these proceedings. In *United States v. James Daniel Good Real Property*, 510 U.S. 43, 56 n.2 (1993), the Supreme Court tacitly acknowledged the potential for a conflict between the government's budgetary needs and property owners' rights:

> The extent of the government's financial stake in drug forfeiture is apparent from a 1990 memo, in which the Attorney General urged United States Attorneys to increase the volume of forfeitures in order to meet the Department of Justice's annual budget target: 'We must significantly increase production to reach our budget target. Failure to achieve the $470 million projection would expose the Department's forfeiture program to criticism and undermine confidence in our budget projections. Every effort must be made to increase forfeiture income during the remaining three months of [fiscal year] 1990."

Critics thus have argued that "the forfeiture laws . . . are producing self-financing, unaccountable law enforcement agencies divorced from any meaningful oversight." *See* Eric D. Blumenson & Eva Nilsen, *Policing for Profit: The Drug War's Hidden Economic Agenda*, 65 U. Chi. L. Rev. 35, 41 (1998). These criticisms have led to broad challenges to statutes' constitutionality. *See* Note, *How Crime Pays: The Unconstitutionality of Modern Civil Asset Forfeiture as a Tool of Criminal Law Enforcement*, Harv. L. Rev. 131, 2387–2388 (2018) (noting that "[c]ivil forfeiture has come under bipartisan fire with stories of abuse and claims that it provides law enforcement with excessive power . . . current practices have become entwined with criminal law enforcement and thus are unconstitutionally punitive.").

In addition, forfeiture laws, particularly civil forfeiture statutes, disproportionately affect people of color and lower income groups. As one commentator noted, "[c]ivil forfeitures fall disproportionately on minorities and the poor. Anecdotal accounts and some in-depth studies show troubling racial disparities, with more innocent minority owners losing their property and being impacted by excessive forfeitures." Nora V. Demleitner, *Will the Supreme Court Rein in "Excessive Fines"*

---

b. The U.S. Department of Justice issues annual reports listing the total value of the property subject to seizure and forfeiture. The most recent reports put the amount in the federal Assets Forfeiture Fund and the Seized Asset Deposit Fund at well over $6 billion. *See* https://oig.justice.gov /reports/2019/a20014.pdf.

For a disturbing account of asset forfeiture abuse, see Sarah Stillman, *Taken: Under Civil Forfeiture, Americans Who Haven't Been Charged with Wrongdoing Can Be Stripped of Their Cash, Cars, and Even Homes. Is That All We're Losing?*, The New Yorker (Aug. 12, 2013), http://www .newyorker.com/magazine/2013/08/12/taken.

and Forfeitures? Don't Rely on Timbs v. Indiana, FED. SENT. REP. Vol. 32, No. 1 (Oct. 2019), at 11.

In reaction to these criticisms, both state governments and the federal government have undertaken forfeiture reform efforts. Congress enacted the Civil Asset Forfeiture and Reform Act (CAFRA), Pub. L. No. 106-185, 114 Stat. 202 (codified as amended in 42 U.S.C. §§ 8, 18, 19, 21, 31). As discussed more fully below, CAFRA does provide some protections to property owners, including a uniform "innocent owner" defense and certain procedural safeguards.

Despite reform efforts, forfeiture laws remain extremely controversial. Property owners have raised various constitutional challenges to forfeitures, and the United States Supreme Court has addressed a number of these challenges. For this reason, more than in any chapter in this text, the law of forfeitures raises a broad array of important constitutional law issues, including issues arising under the Fifth Amendment's Due Process Clause and Double Jeopardy Clause, the Sixth Amendment's right to counsel, and the Eighth Amendment's Excessive Fines Clause.

2. The Statutory Provisions

a. Civil Forfeitures

The most important federal civil forfeiture statutes relate to financial crimes, 18 U.S.C. § 981, and narcotics offenses, 21 U.S.C. § 881. The provisions of 18 U.S.C. § 981(a)(1)(A) make forfeitable all real and personal property related to money laundering, currency transaction reporting crimes, and dozens of other crimes involving financial transactions, financial institutions, or fraud against the United States. Under 21 U.S.C. § 881, the government may obtain forfeiture of a wide range of property, including materials used to manufacture narcotics, conveyances, and all proceeds of a controlled substances transaction, whether direct or indirect, as well as "all moneys, negotiable instruments, securities, or other things of value furnished or intended to be furnished by any person in exchange for a controlled substance or listed chemical in violation of this subchapter, all proceeds traceable to such an exchange, and all moneys, negotiable instruments, and securities used or intended to be used to facilitate any violation of this subchapter." Under subsection 881(a)(7), all real property used or intended for use in committing, or facilitating the commission of, a federal drug law violation is also subject to forfeiture.

These statutes contain provisions allowing the government, in certain circumstances, to seize or otherwise assume control over property prior to obtaining forfeiture. Such a seizure must be supported by probable cause that the property is subject to forfeiture.

The government files a civil complaint to initiate the forfeiture proceeding, at which the government must prove by a preponderance of the evidence that the property is forfeitable. As seen in § C below, a bona fide purchaser or seller of the property may have standing to contest the forfeiture, as may those who use the property as a primary residence.

b. Criminal Forfeitures

A criminal forfeiture occurs as an *in personam* proceeding against the defendant, and the property is forfeited as part of the penalty phase of the case. As seen in § C below, however, criminal forfeitures may affect the property interests of innocent persons.

Since 1970, Congress has adopted an increasingly broad range of criminal forfeiture provisions. Three forfeiture statutes provide the basis for most of the federal criminal forfeitures. First, § 982 of the federal criminal code focuses on property involved in financial crimes. That statute covers property related to violations of the currency transaction reporting statutes, the money laundering statutes, and other specified crimes. *See* 18 U.S.C. § 982. Second, the RICO statute contains a broad forfeiture provision. *See* 18 U.S.C. § 1963. Finally, violations of the federal drug laws can also give rise to forfeitures under 21 U.S.C. § 853. The criminal forfeiture statutes, like their civil counterparts, allow the government to assume control over the potentially forfeitable property prior to determination of forfeitability at trial. The statutes allow this in order to preserve the property for forfeiture.

Under § 982, the government may obtain forfeiture of property involved in, or traceable to, an offense that violates one of the currency transaction reporting or money laundering statutes, as well as property constituting or derived from the proceeds of additional specified crimes. Under § 853, the government likewise may obtain forfeiture of a broad range of property, including real property and tangible and intangible personal property interests. Section 1963 similarly covers a broad range of property, and makes such property forfeitable when the defendant has been convicted for violating one of the RICO provisions.

All three criminal forfeiture statutes allow forfeiture of "substitute" assets. *See* 21 U.S.C. § 853(p); 18 U.S.C. § 982(b)(2); 18 U.S.C. § 1963(I)(1). This occurs when, for example, the specific assets subject to forfeiture cannot be located. This may occur when assets have been transferred or sold to an innocent third party, or when such assets have been commingled with nonforfeitable property and cannot be easily separated.

Under 28 U.S.C. § 2461(c), a provision enacted as part of CAFRA and amended in 2006, whenever civil forfeiture is authorized, the government may seek criminal forfeiture based upon the civil forfeiture provision. The statute provides:

> If a person is charged in a criminal case with a violation of an Act of Congress for which the civil or criminal forfeiture of property is authorized, the Government may include notice of the forfeiture in the indictment or information pursuant to the Federal Rules of Criminal Procedure. If the defendant is convicted of the offense giving rise to the forfeiture, the court shall order the forfeiture of the property as part of the sentence in the

criminal case pursuant to [1] the Federal Rules of Criminal Procedure and section 3554 of title 18, United States Code. . . .

Courts have rejected restrictive interpretations of this statute and have held that the full range of civil forfeiture provisions now may be employed in criminal cases. *See, e.g., United States v. Schlesinger*, 514 F.3d 277, 278 (2d Cir. 2008) (finding that mail fraud cases, which are subject to civil forfeiture under 18 U.S.C. § 981, are also subject to criminal forfeiture under § 2461(c)); *United States v. Vampire Nation*, 451 F.3d 189 (3d Cir. 2006) (same).

B. The Scope of Forfeitable Property

1. Statutory Scope

a. Civil Forfeitures

Prior to the enactment of CAFRA, the courts had adopted a number of approaches for determining the extent of forfeitable property. Congress resolved this conflict by codifying the approach that had been adopted by a number of courts. Thus, CAFRA requires the government to establish a "substantial connection" between the illegal activity and the property. As you read the next cases, (a) identify the theories of forfeiture that the government employed, and (b) consider whether the courts correctly analyzed each theory.

United States v. One 1998 Tractor

288 F. Supp. 2d 710 (W.D. Va. 2003)

JONES, DISTRICT JUDGE.

The claimant in this in rem civil forfeiture proceeding is Karapet Shimshiryan, a truck driver who transports goods in his tractor-trailer for a living. Shimshiryan's tractor and the trailer are the defendant property. Shimshiryan has previously pleaded guilty to violating the federal criminal laws that prohibit transporting, concealing, or possessing contraband cigarettes.[1] In the present action, the government seeks the forfeiture of Shimshiryan's tractor and trailer pursuant to the statute permitting the forfeiture of "an aircraft, vehicle, or vessel involved in" transporting,

---

1. *See* 18 U.S.C.A. § 2342 ("It shall be unlawful for any person knowingly to ship, transport, receive, possess, sell, distribute, or purchase contraband cigarettes."); 49 U.S.C.A. § 80302(b) ("A person may not — (1) transport contraband in an aircraft, vehicle, or vessel; (2) conceal or possess contraband on an aircraft, vehicle, or vessel; or (3) use an aircraft, vehicle or vessel to facilitate the transportation, concealment, receipt, possession, purchase, sale, exchange, or giving away of contraband."). "Contraband cigarettes" are a quantity in excess of 60,000 cigarettes, which bear no evidence of the payment of applicable State cigarette taxes in the State where such cigarettes are found, if such State requires a stamp, impression, or other indication to be placed on packages or other containers of cigarettes to evidence payment of cigarette taxes. 18 U.S.C.A. § 2341(2).

concealing, or possessing contraband cigarettes. 49 U.S.C. §80303. I agree with Shimshiryan that the trailer is not subject to forfeiture because it was his tractor and not his trailer that carried the contraband and because the government has failed to establish that the trailer was substantially connected to the offense, as required under the Civil Asset Forfeiture Reform Act of 2000 ("CAFRA"), 18 U.S.C.A. §983. I reject Shimshiryan's argument that the forfeiture is barred on constitutional grounds.

A bench trial has been held on the government's complaint for forfeiture. . . .

The basic facts are not in dispute. On September 6, 2002, while returning to California after having delivered his trailer's cargo of produce to its destination in New York, driver-owner Shimshiryan and a companion stopped at a tobacco sales outlet in Virginia in this judicial district. The two men purchased and loaded approximately twenty-three half cases of cigarettes (approximately 282,400 cigarettes) into the cab of the tractor and went on their way. Shimshiryan intended to take the cigarettes back to California and from there send them to his brother in Armenia who in turn would sell them for a profit. The sales outlet had been under surveillance by law enforcement officers and Shimshiryan was followed a few miles into the neighboring state of Tennessee. Agents from the Bureau of Alcohol, Tobacco, and Firearms, along with state and local law enforcement officers, stopped the tractor-trailer in Tennessee and recovered the cigarettes from the tractor. These cigarettes did not bear Tennessee state tax stamps as required by law. Shimshiryan's criminal prosecution and this in rem forfeiture action followed.

The government has two arguments as to why the trailer should be subject to forfeiture, even though the contraband cigarettes were never transported there. First, the government argues that the tractor-trailer constitutes a single "vehicle" under 49 U.S.C.A. §80303. Second, the government claims that even if the tractor-trailer does not constitute a single vehicle for the purposes of §80303, the trailer should still be subject to forfeiture because it provided the illegal activity with an air of legitimacy and thus shielded it from the government's suspicion.

Section 80303 permits the forfeiture of "an aircraft, vehicle, or vessel involved in" transporting contraband. The government argues that the trailer should be forfeited even though it did not carry the contraband because it should not be viewed as separate from the tractor—the tractor-trailer should be considered one vehicle. Section 80303 does not define "vehicle." There are two cases applicable to this issue, *The Dolphin*, 3 F.2d 1 (1st Cir. 1925), and *United States v. Santoro*, 866 F.2d 1538 (4th Cir. 1989).

The Dolphin addressed the issue of what constitutes a "vessel" for the purposes of what was then a forfeiture statute directed at vessels delivering foreign cargo to the United States without a government permit. In that case, a tugboat towed a barge that delivered foreign liquor to a Brooklyn pier without the requisite permit. The applicable forfeiture statute permitted the forfeiture of "the vessel, tackle, apparel, and furniture" that illegally unloaded the cargo. The district court had construed the term "vessel" to include the tug as well as the barge, even though the contraband had not been unloaded from the tug. In holding that the tugboat was not subject to forfeiture, the court of appeals found that (1) there was no applicable law to support the assertion that "the tug and its tow constitute one vessel" and (2) the tugboat was not part of the "tackle" attached to the barge.

A Fourth Circuit case that also provides guidance in interpreting § 80303 answered the question of whether a twenty-six acre lot that was separated by a road into two parts should be wholly forfeited when the criminal activity only occurred on one part of the land. In *United States v. Santoro*, five acres of the land at issue lay across the road from the other nineteen acres, and it was on the five-acre parcel that the claimant had sold drugs. The claimant challenged the forfeiture on the basis that the two parcels were separate, and only the smaller parcel should be forfeited because her illegal activity was confined to that area.

First, the court looked to the language of the statute, which permitted the forfeiture of "[a]ll real property, including any right, title, and interest *in the whole of any lot or tract of land* and any appurtenances or improvements." *Id.* at 1543 (alteration in original). The court of appeals then adopted the reasoning of the trial court and held that the "'whole of any lot or tract of land' must be determined from the duly recorded instruments and documents filed in the county offices where the defendant property is located." *Id.* at 1543. Because the property's deed described it as a single, undivided tract, the court held that the twenty-six acre lot was subject to forfeiture in its entirety, even though it was taxed as two separate parcels.

Shimshiryan's tractor and trailer were purchased separately, had separate titles, and separate vehicle identification numbers. Based on the First Circuit's holding in *The Dolphin* and the Fourth Circuit's reasoning in *Santoro*, I hold that the tractor and the trailer do not constitute one vehicle.

The government's second argument for forfeiture of the trailer is that § 80303 permits the forfeiture of a vehicle "involved in" a violation of the federal laws that prohibit transportation, concealment, or possession of contraband cigarettes. CAFRA provides that if the government's theory of forfeiture is that the property was "involved in the commission of a criminal offense," then the government must show, "by a preponderance of the evidence," that there was a "substantial connection between that property and the offense." 18 U.S.C.A. § 983(c). Therefore, in order for the government to gain forfeiture of the trailer on the basis that it was "involved in" Shimshiryan's violation, CAFRA requires that it establish, by a preponderance of the evidence, that there was a substantial connection between the trailer and the offense.

Although the Fourth Circuit has yet to apply CAFRA's "substantial connection" test, *see United States v. Mondragon*, 313 F.3d 862, 865 (4th Cir. 2002) (discussing CAFRA in the context of the sufficiency of pleading), its pre-CAFRA decisions in civil forfeiture cases are still instructive in applying that test because the only change in this circuit in that area of civil forfeiture law is in the government's burden of proof. Before the passage of CAFRA in 2000, "the government's trial burden was to show probable cause for forfeiture; the burden of proof then shifted to the claimant. Now, after CAFRA's enactment, the government must prove by a preponderance of the evidence that the property is subject to forfeiture." *Mondragon*, 313 F.3d at 865. Thus, the only difference between the Fourth Circuit's pre-CAFRA case law determining whether property involved with transporting contraband should be forfeited and the current test under CAFRA is in the government's heightened burden of proof — the government must now establish a substantial connection by a preponderance of the evidence, and not just probable cause.

In *United States v. Two Tracts of Real Property*, 998 F.2d 204 (4th Cir. 1993), the defendant in the underlying criminal case permitted marijuana to be transported by boat to his father's marina. After it was delivered, it was driven from the marina across another lot of land, also owned by the defendant's father, in order to access a public road. Crossing that lot of land was the only means by which the smugglers could reach the public road. The government sought the forfeiture of the land with access to the public road because it was allegedly substantially connected to the criminal activity on the basis that (1) it provided access to a public road following the unloading of the marijuana and (2) it tended to shield the illegal activity from public view. As for the first claim, the court found that it was "physically impossible" for the smugglers to reach the road from the marina without crossing the land in question, but it held that this "geographic fact" did not establish a substantial connection. *Id.* at 212.

As for the second argument that the property's shielding effect created a substantial connection to the activity, the court held that the "mere fact that a physical obstruction tends to conceal crime does not, without more, make the obstruction forfeitable." *Id.* In further explaining its decision, the court of appeals distinguished the facts of a case it decided three years earlier, *United States v. Schifferli*, 895 F.2d 987 (4th Cir. 1990), in which it upheld the forfeiture of a dental office used by the dentist to write illegal prescriptions.[4] It stated that the "use of an office building to commit crimes that closely resemble the owner's or tenant's lawful work is a far cry from a natural object's inherent, irrepressible ability to conceal whatever lies behind it" because in the former case "the guilty owner's intent establishes a sufficient connection with crime to render the property forfeitable." *Id.* at 212.

The decision in *Two Tracts of Real Property* establishes that when the government seeks the forfeiture of property on the basis that it was substantially connected to the

---

4. In *Schifferli*, the claimant was a dentist who had used his office over forty times during a four-month period to write illegal prescriptions for eight individuals. 895 F.2d at 989. *Schifferli* is like many other cases in that forfeiture of the office was upheld on the basis that it was the situs of the illegal prescription writing. It is well settled that the use of property as a situs for conducting illegal activities establishes a substantial connection between the property and the underlying criminal activity.

crime by shielding the illegal activity from public view, it must show "more" than that the property "tends to conceal" the crime. Furthermore, proof of the owner's intent to use the property for the purpose of shielding his or her criminal activity qualifies as the something "more" required to establish a substantial connection. In this case, the government merely alleges that the trailer shielded the criminal activity from detection by creating the appearance that the claimant was engaged in a legitimate trucking business. Because the government has not provided any evidence indicating that Shimshiryan's trucking business was a sham, or that he operated it with the intent of concealing his criminal activity, it has not met its burden of proof. The government has failed to establish a substantial connection between the trailer and the offense, as required by CAFRA, and the trailer is not subject to forfeiture. . . .

Notes and Questions

1. *The government's theories.*

a. *The conveyance theory.* Why did the court conclude in *One 1998 Tractor* that the trailer did not qualify as a "vehicle"? Did the court correctly apply the reasoning from *The Dolphin* and *Santoro*?

b. *The substantial connection theory.* Based on the cases above and the precedent they discuss, what is required for a "substantial connection"? Can you divine factors to use in making this determination? Do the cases that the court in *One 1998 Tractor* cites (*Two Tracts of Real Property* and *Schifferli*) support its conclusion? According to the court, what more did the government need to show? If the contraband had been in the trailer, would the tractor have been forfeitable under either theory? Why or why not?

2. *The burden of proof.* Who had the burden pre-CAFRA? Post-CAFRA? What were the standards pre- and post-CAFRA? Would CAFRA's changes to the law affect the analysis in the two cases above? Why or why not? Why did Congress change the standard? What is the practical effect of the changes in the two cases above?

3. *The USA PATRIOT Act.* The USA PATRIOT Act added a new forfeiture statute that provides for forfeiture of:

(G) All assets, foreign or domestic—

(i) of any individual, entity, or organization engaged in planning or perpetrating any act of domestic or international terrorism . . . against the United States, citizens or residents of the United States, or their property, and all assets, foreign or domestic, affording any person a source of influence over any such entity or organization;

(ii) acquired or maintained by any person with the intent and for the purpose of supporting, planning, conducting, or concealing an act of domestic or international terrorism . . . against the United States, citizens or residents of the United States, or their property; or

(iii) derived from, involved in, or used or intended to be used to commit any act of domestic or international terrorism . . . against the United States, citizens or residents of the United States, or their property.

18 U.S.C. § 981(a)(1)(G). What is the scope of forfeitable property under this section? What connection is required between a specific act of terrorism and the property at issue? Are there dangers inherent in this approach? Why or why not?

b. Criminal Forfeitures

Federal Rule of Criminal Procedure 32.2(b) governs the determination of the scope of forfeitable property. Under that rule, upon a determination of the defendant's guilt, the court or jury identifies the property subject to forfeiture and determines whether the "requisite nexus between the property and the offense" has been established by the government. One issue that had split the federal courts of appeal is whether coconspirators are jointly and severally liable for criminal forfeitable property under the federal narcotics laws. Under this rule, a minor participant in a criminal scheme, such as Terry Honeycutt in the case below, could be subject to a money judgment for the entire amount of illegally generated assets. Most courts of appeal allowed for joint and several liability, but the Supreme Court rejected that rule in the case that follows. What are the competing concerns ?

Honeycutt v. United States
137 S. Ct. 1626 (2017)

Justice SOTOMAYOR delivered the opinion of the Court.

Terry Michael Honeycutt managed sales and inventory for a Tennessee hardware store owned by his brother, Tony Honeycutt. After observing several "'edgy looking folks'" purchasing an iodine-based water-purification product known as Polar Pure, Terry Honeycutt contacted the Chattanooga Police Department to inquire whether the iodine crystals in the product could be used to manufacture methamphetamine. An officer confirmed that individuals were using Polar Pure for this purpose and advised Honeycutt to cease selling it if the sales made Honeycutt "'uncomfortable.'" Notwithstanding the officer's advice, the store continued to sell large quantities of Polar Pure. Although each bottle of Polar Pure contained enough iodine to purify 500 gallons of water, and despite the fact that most people have no legitimate use for the product in large quantities, the brothers sold as many as 12 bottles in a single transaction to a single customer. Over a 3-year period, the store grossed roughly $400,000 from the sale of more than 20,000 bottles of Polar Pure. . . .

A federal grand jury indicted the Honeycutt brothers for various federal crimes relating to their sale of iodine while knowing or having reason to believe it would be used to manufacture methamphetamine. Pursuant to the Comprehensive Forfeiture Act of 1984, 21 U.S.C. § 853(a)(1), which mandates forfeiture of "any proceeds the person obtained, directly or indirectly, as the result of" drug distribution, the government sought forfeiture money judgments against each brother in the amount of $269,751.98, which represented the hardware store's profits from the sale of Polar Pure. Tony Honeycutt pleaded guilty and agreed to forfeit $200,000. Terry went to trial. A jury acquitted Terry Honeycutt of 3 charges but found him guilty of the remaining 11, including conspiring to and knowingly distributing iodine in violation of §§ 841(c)(2), 843(a)(6), and 846.

The District Court sentenced Terry Honeycutt to 60 months in prison. Despite conceding that Terry had no "controlling interest in the store" and "did not stand to benefit personally," the government insisted that the District Court "hold [him] jointly liable for the profit from the illegal sales." The government thus sought a money judgment of $69,751.98, the amount of the conspiracy profits outstanding after Tony Honeycutt's forfeiture payment. The District Court declined to enter a forfeiture judgment, reasoning that Honeycutt was a salaried employee who had not personally received any profits from the iodine sales.

The Court of Appeals for the Sixth Circuit reversed. . . . The Court granted certiorari to resolve disagreement among the Courts of Appeals regarding whether joint and several liability applies under § 853.[1]

Criminal forfeiture statutes empower the government to confiscate property derived from or used to facilitate criminal activity. Such statutes serve important governmental interests such as "separating a criminal from his ill-gotten gains," "returning property, in full, to those wrongfully deprived or defrauded of it," and "lessen[ing] the economic power" of criminal enterprises. *Caplin & Drysdale, Chartered v. United States*, 491 U.S. 617, 629–630 (1989). The statute at issue here — § 853 — mandates forfeiture with respect to persons convicted of certain serious drug crimes. The question presented is whether § 853 embraces joint and several liability for forfeiture judgments.

A creature of tort law, joint and several liability "applies when there has been a judgment against multiple defendants." *McDermott, Inc. v. AmClyde*, 511 U.S. 202, 220–221 (1994). If two or more defendants jointly cause harm, each defendant is held liable for the entire amount of the harm; provided, however, that the plaintiff recover only once for the full amount. *See* Restatement (Second) of Torts § 875 (1977). Application of that principle in the forfeiture context when two or more defendants conspire to violate the law would require that each defendant be held liable for a forfeiture judgment based not only on property that he used in or acquired because of the crime, but also on property obtained by his co-conspirator.

An example is instructive. Suppose a farmer masterminds a scheme to grow, harvest, and distribute marijuana on local college campuses. The mastermind recruits

---

1. *Compare United States v. Van Nguyen*, 602 F.3d 886, 904 (8th Cir. 2010) (applying joint and several liability to forfeiture under § 853); *United States v. Pitt*, 193 F.3d 751, 765 (3d Cir. 1999) (same); *United States v. McHan*, 101 F.3d 1027 (4th Cir.1996) (same); and *United States v. Benevento*, 836 F.2d 129, 130 (2d Cir. 1988) (*per curiam*) (same), with *United States v. Cano-Flores*, 796 F.3d 83, 91 (D.C. Cir. 2015) (declining to apply joint and several liability under § 853).

a college student to deliver packages and pays the student $300 each month from the distribution proceeds for his services. In one year, the mastermind earns $3 million. The student, meanwhile, earns $3,600. If joint and several liability applied, the student would face a forfeiture judgment for the entire amount of the conspiracy's proceeds: $3 million. The student would be bound by that judgment even though he never personally acquired any proceeds beyond the $3,600. This case requires determination whether this form of liability is permitted under § 853(a)(1). The Court holds that it is not.

Forfeiture under § 853 applies to "any person" convicted of certain serious drug crimes. Section 853(a) limits the statute's reach by defining the property subject to forfeiture in three separate provisions. An understanding of how these three provisions work to limit the operation of the statute is helpful to resolving the question in this case. First, the provision at issue here, § 853(a)(1), limits forfeiture to "property constituting, or derived from, any proceeds the person obtained, directly or indirectly, as the result of" the crime. Second, § 853(a)(2) restricts forfeiture to "property used, or intended to be used, in any manner or part, to commit, or to facilitate the commission of," the crime. Finally, § 853(a)(3) applies to persons "convicted of engaging in a continuing criminal enterprise" — a form of conspiracy — and requires forfeiture of "property described in paragraph (1) or (2)" as well as "any of [the defendant's] interest in, claims against, and property or contractual rights affording a source of control over, the continuing criminal enterprise." These provisions, by their terms, limit forfeiture under § 853 to tainted property; that is, property flowing from (§ 853(a)(1)), or used in (§ 853(a)(2)), the crime itself. The limitations of § 853(a) thus provide the first clue that the statute does not countenance joint and several liability, which, by its nature, would require forfeiture of untainted property.

Recall, for example, the college student from the earlier hypothetical. The $3,600 he received for his part in the marijuana distribution scheme clearly falls within § 853(a)(1): It is property he "obtained . . . as the result of" the crime. But if he were held jointly and severally liable for the proceeds of the entire conspiracy, he would owe the government $3 million. Of the $3 million, $2,996,400 would have no connection whatsoever to the student's participation in the crime and would have to be paid from the student's untainted assets. Joint and several liability would thus represent a departure from § 853(a)'s restriction of forfeiture to tainted property.

In addition to limiting forfeiture to tainted property, § 853(a) defines forfeitable property solely in terms of personal possession or use. . . . Neither the dictionary definition nor the common usage of the word "obtain" supports the conclusion that an individual "obtains" property that was acquired by someone else. Yet joint and several liability would mean just that: The college student would be presumed to have "obtained" the $3 million that the mastermind acquired.

Section 853(a)(1) further provides that the forfeitable property may be "obtained, directly or indirectly." The adverbs "directly" and "indirectly" modify — but do not erase — the verb "obtain." In other words, these adverbs refer to how a defendant obtains the property; they do not negate the requirement that he obtain it at all. For instance, the marijuana mastermind might receive payments directly from drug purchasers, or he might arrange to have drug purchasers pay an intermediary such as the college student. In all instances, he ultimately "obtains" the property — whether "directly or indirectly." . . .

Section 853(a)'s limitation of forfeiture to tainted property acquired or used by the defendant, together with the plain text of § 853(a)(1), foreclose joint and several liability for co-conspirators. . . .

It would also render futile one other provision of the statute. Section 853(p) — the sole provision of § 853 that permits the government to confiscate property untainted by the crime — lays to rest any doubt that the statute permits joint and several liability. That provision governs forfeiture of "substitute property" and applies "if any property described in subsection (a), as a result of any act or omission of the defendant" either:

(A) cannot be located upon the exercise of due diligence;

(B) has been transferred or sold to, or deposited with, a third party;

(C) has been placed beyond the jurisdiction of the court;

(D) has been substantially diminished in value; or

(E) has been commingled with other property which cannot be divided without difficulty.

§ 853(p)(1).

Only if the government can prove that one of these five conditions was caused by the defendant may it seize "any other property of the defendant, up to the value of" the tainted property — rather than the tainted property itself. § 853(p)(2). This provision begins from the premise that the defendant once possessed tainted property as "described in subsection (a)," and provides a means for the government to recoup the value of the property if it has been dissipated or otherwise disposed of by "any act or omission of the defendant." § 853(p)(1).

Section 853(p)(1) demonstrates that Congress contemplated situations where the tainted property itself would fall outside the government's reach. To remedy that situation, Congress did not authorize the government to confiscate substitute property from other defendants or co-conspirators; it authorized the government to confiscate assets only from the defendant who initially acquired the property and who bears responsibility for its dissipation. Permitting the government to force other co-conspirators to turn over untainted substitute property would allow the government to circumvent Congress' carefully constructed statutory scheme, which permits forfeiture of substitute property only when the requirements of §§ 853(p) and (a) are satisfied. There is no basis to read such an end run into the statute.

Against all of this, the government asserts the "bedrock principle of conspiracy liability" under which "conspirators are legally responsible for each other's foreseeable actions in furtherance of their common plan." Brief for United States 9; see also *Pinkerton v. United States*, 328 U.S. 640 (1946). Congress, according to the government, must be presumed to have legislated against the background principles of conspiracy liability, and thus, "when the traceable proceeds of a conspiracy are unavailable, [§] 853 renders conspirators jointly and severally liable for the amount of the proceeds foreseeably obtained by the conspiracy."

The plain text and structure of § 853 leave no doubt that Congress did not incorporate those background principles. Congress provided just one way for the government to recoup substitute property when the tainted property itself is unavailable — the procedures outlined in § 853(p). And, for all the government makes of the background principles of conspiracy liability, it fails to fully engage with the most important background principles underlying § 853: those of forfeiture.

Traditionally, forfeiture was an action against the tainted property itself and thus proceeded in rem; that is, proceedings in which "[t]he thing [was] primarily considered as the offender, or rather the offence [was] attached primarily to the thing." *The Palmyra*, 12 Wheat. 1, 14, 6 L.Ed. 531 (1827). The forfeiture "proceeding in rem st[ood] independent of, and wholly unaffected by any criminal proceeding in *personam*" against the defendant. *Id.* at 15. Congress altered this distinction in enacting § 853 by effectively merging the *in rem* forfeiture proceeding with the in *personam* criminal proceeding and by expanding forfeiture to include not just the "thing" but "property . . . derived from . . . any proceeds" of the crime. § 853(a)(1). But as is clear from its text and structure, § 853 maintains traditional *in rem* forfeiture's focus on tainted property unless one of the preconditions of § 853(p) exists. . . .

Forfeiture pursuant to § 853(a)(1) is limited to property the defendant himself actually acquired as the result of the crime. In this case, the government has conceded that Terry Honeycutt had no ownership interest in his brother's store and did not personally benefit from the Polar Pure sales. The District Court agreed. Because Honeycutt never obtained tainted property as a result of the crime, § 853 does not require any forfeiture.

The judgment of the Court of Appeals for the Sixth Circuit is reversed.

Notes and Questions

1. *Joint and several liability.* The government in *Honeycutt* argued that the tort principle of joint and several liability should apply to the criminal forfeiture in the case. As noted in footnote 1 of the decision, four courts of appeal had agreed with the government, while one disagreed. In rejecting the government's position, the Court relied both upon principles of statutory construction and legislative intent. Are you persuaded by the Court's analysis? Why or why not?

2. *Money judgments.* Given that forfeitures are directed to specific property, including the instrumentalities of or proceeds from the illegal activity, does it make sense to allow for money judgments in criminal forfeiture cases? The federal courts of

appeal that have considered the issue have held in the affirmative. For example, in *United States v. Hall*, 434 F.3d 42, 59 (1st Cir. 2006), the court found two justifications for money judgments in criminal forfeiture proceedings: criminal forfeitures, unlike civil forfeitures, are against a person rather than property and, in any event, "permitting a money judgment, as part of a forfeiture order, prevents a drug dealer from ridding himself of his ill-gotten gains to avoid the forfeiture sanction." *Accord United States v. Awad,* 598 F.3d 76 (2d Cir. 2010). Is this the correct result? Why or why not? Should money judgments likewise be permitted in *civil* forfeitures?

3. *Substitute assets.* As the Court discussed in *Honeycutt,* some forfeiture statutes allow the government to obtain forfeiture of "substitute assets" when the forfeitable assets cannot be located, have been transferred or sold to a third party, are beyond the court's jurisdiction, have been reduced in value, or were commingled with non-forfeitable property and cannot be easily separated. *See* 21 U.S.C. § 853(p); 18 U.S.C. § 982(b); 18 U.S.C. § 1963(m). In such a case, and subject to certain statutory limitations, the court will order the forfeiture of substitute assets up to the value of the otherwise forfeitable assets. Why did Congress allow for the forfeiture of substitute assets? Are there dangers in this approach?

4. *Right to a jury trial?* In *Libretti v. United States,* 516 U.S. 29, 49 (1995), the United States Supreme Court held that the Constitution does not provide the right to a "jury verdict on forfeitability" in a criminal case because this is a statutory factor of the sort that sentencing judges may decide. Later, in *Apprendi v. New Jersey,* 530 U.S. 466 (2000), the Court held that any fact that increases the penalty for a crime beyond the prescribed statutory maximum must be submitted to a jury and proven beyond a reasonable doubt. Does the *Apprendi* decision effectively overrule *Libretti* and grant a jury trial right to determinations of the scope of criminal forfeitures? Does the outcome in *United States v. Booker,* 125 S. Ct. 738 (2005), discussed in Chapter 19, Sentencing, *supra,* affect this result? Why or why not? *See* Comment, Matthew R. Ford, *Criminal Forfeiture and the Sixth Amendment's Right to Jury Trial Post*-Booker, 101 Nw. U. L. Rev. 1371 (2007) (arguing that *Booker* should apply to forfeiture proceedings in some circumstances).

So far, the federal courts of appeal have held that the amount of forfeiture need not be submitted to the jury because a judge's fact-finding on this issue during sentencing does not increase a statutory maximum sentence. In *United States v. Phillips,* 704 F.3d 754, 769–770 (9th Cir. 2012), for example, the court reasoned:

> Although criminal forfeiture undoubtedly constitutes an element of punishment, there is no statutory (or guideline) maximum limit on forfeitures. Rather, criminal forfeitures are indeterminate and open-ended, and may include all property 'constituting, or derived from, any proceeds the person obtained, directly or indirectly,' from his unlawful conduct. The Second, Fourth, and Seventh Circuits have all explicitly distinguished *Booker* and denied the right to a jury determination in the forfeiture context

because forfeiture is not a 'determinate sentencing scheme' with a 'statutory maximum.'

Id. at 770 (citing cases). *Accord United States v. Christensen*, 828 F.3d 763, 821–22 (9th Cir. 2015); *United States v. Simpson*, 741 F.3d 539 (5th Cir. 2014). Do these cases seem consistent with *Apprendi*? *See* Brynn Applebaum, Note, *Criminal Asset Forfeiture and the Sixth Amendment after* Southern Union *and* Alleyne: *State-Level Ramifications*, 68 VAND. L. REV. 549, 552 (2015) (arguing that "the Court should, and eventually will, overrule *Libretti*: the same constitutional standard that applies to *Apprendi* facts should apply to the facts necessary to authorize and determine the amount of forfeiture").

Problems

20-1. Defendant Clarissa Clement was addicted to the prescription pain killer hydrocodone. To support her addiction, she called in phony prescriptions to pharmacies, using numerous aliases. Last January, a pharmacist informed the police that he suspected defendant of fraud. The pharmacist gave the police a physical description of defendant and of the defendant's vehicle, which Ms. Clement used to pick up the prescription. In April, another pharmacist from a different pharmacy contacted police about suspected fraud. On that occasion, defendant picked up the prescription using the pharmacy's drive-thru window, and the pharmacist identified the customer as Ms. Clement using a police photograph. The pharmacist also described the defendant's vehicle and gave its license plate number. The police were able to document five other such occasions when defendant used the vehicle to pick up hydrocodone with phony prescriptions.

In May, police arrested defendant for obtaining drugs with fraudulent prescriptions. The government now seeks civil forfeiture of the vehicle under 21 U.S.C. § 881(a)(4). The vehicle is a minivan that served as the sole family vehicle for Ms. Clement and her three children. The evidence shows that driving related to the prescription drug scheme constituted only about two percent of the vehicle's use over the relevant time period.

Is the vehicle subject to forfeiture? Why or why not?

20-2. Defendant was convicted of mail fraud, wire fraud, securities fraud, and money laundering in connection with a fraudulent investment scheme. The government now seeks a criminal forfeiture order of a house owned by defendant. The government's theory is that the property was the address of record for the companies that the defendant used as the vehicles for his fraudulent scheme.

Should the court grant the government's request? Why or why not?

20-3. Defendant purchased 19 acres of land, built a house and large barn on the property, and lived there with defendant's spouse. Defendant purchased the acreage in one land sale contract, and county land records described the property as a single unit. The defendant and his spouse used eight acres of the property to grow vegetables and hay. The barn was used to store a tractor and other equipment used in farming. The property was worth $180,000.

Over several months, defendant engaged in online conversations with a law enforcement agent who was posing as a mother of two minor children. On several occasions, defendant transmitted images of child pornography to the agent. Defendant expressed an interest in performing sexual activities with the children and encouraged them to view his child pornography. He discussed the possibility of the group meeting at some point. Defendant conversed with the agent, and transmitted child pornography to the agent from his desktop computer, which was located in the computer room of his house.

When executing a search warrant for defendant's home, officers found 272 images of child pornography on defendant's computer. Evidence showed that defendant received and distributed the images through a hardwired Internet connection set up in the house. Defendant pleaded guilty to two counts of distributing child pornography. The court then considered the government's request for criminal forfeiture of the entire property, including the acreage and buildings, under the "substantial connection" test of the applicable forfeiture statute. The court ordered forfeiture of the entire property, and defendant appeals.

How should the court of appeals rule? Why?

C. Constitutional Limitations

1. Forfeitures as "Punishment"

a. Civil Forfeitures

After long declining to place constitutional constraints on civil forfeitures, see *Calero-Toledo v. Pearson Yacht Leasing Co.*, 416 U.S. 663, 680–90 (1974), the Supreme Court in *Austin v. United States*, 509 U.S. 602 (1993), squarely addressed the issue whether the Eighth Amendment's Excessive Fines Clause potentially limits the scope of such forfeitures. Three years later, in *United States v. Ursery*, 518 U.S. 267 (1996), the Court addressed the question whether civil forfeiture constitutes punishment under the Double Jeopardy Clause. Are these cases consistent?

Note on Austin v. United States

In *Austin*, the defendant pleaded guilty to the state crime of possessing cocaine with the intent to distribute and was sentenced to seven years in prison. The defendant used his auto body shop and mobile home when committing the crime. The federal government obtained civil forfeiture of the home and business. The Supreme Court granted certiorari to address the threshold question whether the Eighth Amendment's Excessive Fines Clause, which provides that "excessive fines [shall not be] imposed," applies to in rem forfeitures. The government took the position that the clause only applies to *criminal* punishments.

The Court disagreed. The Court reasoned that, while some constitutional amendments expressly only apply to criminal actions, that limitation does not apply to the Eighth Amendment. 509 U.S. at 607–09. The Court thus held that the Excessive Fines Clause limits the "Government's power to extract payments, whether in cash or in kind, '*as punishment* for some offense.'" *Id.* at 609–10, *citing Browning-Ferris Industries v. Kelco Disposal, Inc.*, 492 U.S. 257, 265 (1989). Thus, the issue is whether the forfeiture itself constitutes punishment.

To this point, the government argued that the civil forfeiture statutes at issue are not punitive, but remedial. According to the government, these forfeitures both remove the "instruments" of the drug trade and serve to compensate the government for expenses incurred in enforcing narcotics laws.

The Court unanimously rejected these arguments, finding that the value of the forfeited property demonstrated that the forfeiture was more than merely remedial. Further, the Court held, a civil sanction can have both remedial and punitive purposes. If a nominally civil sanction is punitive at least in part, then the Excessive Fines Clause applies. In its holding, the Court did not adopt a test for determining when a civil forfeiture is excessive under the Eighth Amendment.

Note on United States v. Ursery

The Court in *Austin* unanimously held that civil forfeitures constitute "punishment" and are therefore subject to Excessive Fines Clause analysis. Are civil forfeitures also "punishment" under the Fifth Amendment's Double Jeopardy Clause? That clause provides that "[n]o person shall . . . be subject for the same offense to be twice put in jeopardy of life or limb." Would it violate the Clause to subject a defendant both to: (a) punishment in a criminal case and (b) civil forfeiture arising out of the same act(s)?

In *United States v. Ursery*, 518 U.S. 267 (1996), the Supreme Court held not. That case involved a consolidated appeal from two circuit court decisions holding that the above scenario violated the Double Jeopardy Clause. In one case, the government obtained civil forfeiture of the defendant's home, which was used for narcotics transactions. Subsequently, the defendant was criminally convicted of those same transactions. In the other case, two defendants were convicted of violating drug and money laundering statutes. In a later civil forfeiture proceeding, the district court ordered forfeiture of assets relating to those offenses. In both cases, the circuit courts found that the defendants' Double Jeopardy rights were violated, and the government appealed.

In considering whether the Double Jeopardy Clause applies in these situations, the Court concluded that the definition of "punishment" under the Double Jeopardy Clause is narrower than the definition of "punishment" under the Excessive Fines Clause. Therefore, the Double Jeopardy Clause is not triggered by civil forfeitures.

Only Justice Stevens dissented, stating that "the Court today stands *Austin* on its head—a decision rendered only three years ago, with unanimity on the pertinent points." Are these two decisions in fact inconsistent? Can you explain the considerations that might have produced the outcome in *Ursery*? Is it fair to subject a person both to criminal punishment for an offense and to civil forfeiture for the same offense? Why or why not?

Of course, the government need not obtain a criminal conviction in order to seek civil forfeiture. But in *Ursery*, the government, in two different instances, initiated both a civil in rem forfeiture proceeding and a criminal proceeding against the property owner. Why would the government choose to initiate a civil forfeiture proceeding, rather than simply obtain criminal forfeiture as part of the penalty phase of its criminal case?

Notes and Questions

1. *Defining "punishment."* What is the test for determining whether a "civil" sanction constitutes punishment under the Double Jeopardy Clause? The *Austin* majority relied upon *United States v. Halper*, 490 U.S. 435, 448 (1989), which held that "a civil sanction that cannot fairly be said *solely* to serve a remedial purpose, but rather can only be explained as also serving either retributive or deterrent purposes, is punishment, as we have come to understand the term."

In *Hudson v. United States*, 522 U.S. 93, 99–104 (1997), however, the Court changed course and rejected the *Halper* test, relying in part on *Ursery*. As discussed more fully in Chapter 18, Civil Actions, Civil Penalties, and Parallel Proceedings, *supra*, the Court in *Hudson* stated that "the Double Jeopardy Clause does not prohibit the imposition of any additional sanction that could . . . be described as punishment" but "only protects against the imposition of multiple criminal punishments for the same offense."

In order for a civil penalty to trigger the Double Jeopardy Clause under *Hudson*, then, a court must first determine whether the civil penalty is either: (a) explicitly criminal or (b) "so punitive in form and effect as to render [it] criminal despite Congress' intent to the contrary. . . ."

In light of *Hudson*, "challenges based on violations of the double jeopardy clause have virtually disappeared in the federal and state jurisdictions. . . ." Dee R. Edgeworth, Asset Forfeiture: Practice and Procedure in State and Federal Courts 289 (ABA Publishing 3d ed. 2014).

2. *The constitutionality of civil forfeitures.* Civil forfeitures continue to be subject to substantial criticism. As one commentator noted:

> Increasingly civil forfeitures, excessive fines, and rampant fees seem far removed from the goals of the criminal justice system. They are ineffective as crime fighting tools; they distort law-enforcement priorities; they raise revenue on the backs of those with the least resources; they are an ongoing reminder of the unequal enforcement of the laws.

Nora V. Demleitner, *Will the Supreme Court Rein In "Excessive Fines" and Forfeitures? Don't Rely on* Timbs V. Indiana, FED. SENT'G REP., Vol. 32, No. 1 (Oct. 2019).

Given the controversy over and criticism of civil forfeiture laws, are these laws likely to withstand constitutional challenges to their validity? *Compare* Caleb Nelson, *The Constitutionality of Civil Forfeiture*, 125 YALE L.J. 2446 (2016) (arguing that the Supreme Court is unlikely to hold civil forfeiture laws unconstitutional), *with* Kevin Arlyck, *The Founders' Forfeiture*, 119 COLUM. L. REV. 1449 (2019) (arguing that civil forfeitures may be vulnerable to constitutional challenge).

As discussed throughout this chapter, the Supreme Court has subjected forfeiture laws to various constitutional limitations, including the Eighth Amendment's Excessive Fines Clause and the Fifth Amendment's Due Process Clause. Might the Court one day hold civil forfeiture laws unconstitutional in their entirety? Consider this question as you read the materials in this chapter.

b. Criminal Forfeitures

The same year it decided *Austin*, the Court held in *Alexander v. United States*, 509 U.S. 544, 558–59 (1993), that criminal forfeitures under the RICO statute, 18 U.S.C. §1963, are also subject to the Eighth Amendment's Excessive Fines Clause. The Court did not provide guidance, in either *Austin* or *Alexander*, as to the sorts of factors that lower courts might use when applying the Excessive Fines Clause to forfeiture cases. The Court finally turned to that task in the case that follows.

United States v. Bajakajian

524 U.S. 321 (1998)

JUSTICE THOMAS delivered the opinion of the Court.

Respondent Hosep Bajakajian attempted to leave the United States without reporting, as required by federal law, that he was transporting more than $10,000 in currency. Federal law also provides that a person convicted of willfully violating this reporting requirement shall forfeit to the government "any property . . . involved in such offense." 18 U.S.C. §982(a)(1). The question in this case is whether forfeiture of the entire $357,144 that respondent failed to declare would violate the Excessive Fines Clause of the Eighth Amendment. We hold that it would, because full forfeiture of respondent's currency would be grossly disproportional to the gravity of his offense.

On June 9, 1994, respondent, his wife, and his two daughters were waiting at Los Angeles International Airport to board a flight to Italy; their final destination was Cyprus. Using dogs trained to detect currency by its smell, customs inspectors discovered some $230,000 in cash in the Bajakajians' checked baggage. A customs inspector approached respondent and his wife and told them that they were required to report all money in excess of $10,000 in their possession or in their baggage.

Respondent said that he had $8,000 and that his wife had another $7,000, but that the family had no additional currency to declare. A search of their carry-on bags, purse, and wallet revealed more cash; in all, customs inspectors found $357,144. The currency was seized and respondent was taken into custody.

A federal grand jury indicted respondent on three counts. . . .

Respondent pleaded guilty to the failure to report in Count One; the government agreed to dismiss the false statement charge in Count Two; and respondent elected to have a bench trial on the forfeiture in Count Three. After the bench trial, the District Court found that the entire $357,144 was subject to forfeiture because it was "involved in" the offense. The court also found that the funds were not connected to any other crime and that respondent was transporting the money to repay a lawful debt. The District Court further found that respondent had failed to report that he was taking the currency out of the United States because of fear stemming from "cultural differences": Respondent, who had grown up as a member of the Armenian minority in Syria, had a "distrust for the government."

Although § 982(a)(1) directs sentencing courts to impose full forfeiture, the District Court concluded that such forfeiture would be "extraordinarily harsh" and "grossly disproportionate to the offense in question," and that it would therefore violate the Excessive Fines Clause. The court instead ordered forfeiture of $15,000, in addition to a sentence of three years of probation and a fine of $5,000 — the maximum fine under the Sentencing Guidelines — because the court believed that the maximum Guidelines fine was "too little" and that a $15,000 forfeiture would "make up for what I think a reasonable fine should be."

The United States appealed, seeking full forfeiture of respondent's currency as provided in § 982(a)(1). The Court of Appeals for the Ninth Circuit affirmed. . . .

The Eighth Amendment provides: "Excessive bail shall not be required, nor excessive fines imposed, nor cruel and unusual punishments inflicted." U.S. Const., Amdt. 8. This Court has had little occasion to interpret, and has never actually applied, the Excessive Fines Clause. We have, however, explained that at the time the Constitution was adopted, "the word 'fine' was understood to mean a payment to a sovereign as punishment for some offense." *Browning-Ferris Industries of Vt. v. Kelco Disposal, Inc.*, 492 U.S. 257, 265 (1989). The Excessive Fines Clause thus "limits the government's power to extract payments, whether in cash or in kind, as punishment for some offense." *Austin v. United States*, 509 U.S. 602, 609–610 (1993) (emphasis deleted). Forfeitures — payments in kind — are thus "fines" if they constitute punishment for an offense.

We have little trouble concluding that the forfeiture of currency ordered by § 982(a)(1) constitutes punishment. The statute directs a court to order forfeiture as an additional sanction when "imposing sentence on a person convicted of" a willful violation of § 5316's reporting requirement. The forfeiture is thus imposed at the culmination of a criminal proceeding and requires conviction of an underlying felony, and it cannot be imposed upon an innocent owner of unreported currency, but only upon a person who has himself been convicted of a §5316 reporting violation.[3]

The United States argues, however, that the forfeiture of currency under §982(a)(1) "also serves important remedial purposes." The government asserts that it has "an overriding sovereign interest in controlling what property leaves and enters the country." It claims that full forfeiture of unreported currency supports that interest by serving to "dete[r] illicit movements of cash" and aiding in providing the government with "valuable information to investigate and detect criminal activities associated with that cash." Deterrence, however, has traditionally been viewed as a goal of punishment, and forfeiture of the currency here does not serve the remedial purpose of compensating the government for a loss. Although the government has asserted a loss of information regarding the amount of currency leaving the country, that loss would not be remedied by the government's confiscation of respondent's $357,144.

The United States also argues that the forfeiture mandated by §982(a)(1) is constitutional because it falls within a class of historic forfeitures of property tainted by crime. In so doing, the Government relies upon a series of cases involving traditional civil *in rem* forfeitures that are inapposite because such forfeitures were historically considered nonpunitive. . . .

The theory behind such forfeitures was the fiction that the action was directed against "guilty property," rather than against the offender himself. Historically, the conduct of the property owner was irrelevant; indeed, the owner of forfeited property could be entirely innocent of any crime. . . .[6]

The forfeiture in this case does not bear any of the hallmarks of traditional civil *in rem* forfeitures. The Government has not proceeded against the currency itself, but has instead sought and obtained a criminal conviction of respondent personally. The forfeiture serves no remedial purpose, is designed to punish the offender, and cannot be imposed upon innocent owners.

---

3. [T]the dissent's speculation about the effect of today's holding on "kingpins" and "cash couriers" is misplaced. Section 982(a)(1)'s criminal *in personam* forfeiture reaches only currency owned by someone who himself commits a reporting crime. It is unlikely that the government, in the course of criminally indicting and prosecuting a cash courier, would not bother to investigate the source and true ownership of unreported funds.

6. It does not follow, of course, that all modern civil *in rem* forfeitures are nonpunitive and thus beyond the coverage of the Excessive Fines Clause. Because some recent federal forfeiture laws have blurred the traditional distinction between civil *in rem* and criminal *in personam* forfeiture, we have held that a modern statutory forfeiture is a "fine" for Eighth Amendment purposes if it constitutes punishment even in part, regardless of whether the proceeding is styled *in rem* or *in personam*. *See Austin v. United States, supra*, at 621–622 (although labeled *in rem*, civil forfeiture of real property used "to facilitate" the commission of drug crimes was punitive in part and thus subject to review under the Excessive Fines Clause).

The government specifically contends that the forfeiture of respondent's currency is constitutional because it involves an "instrumentality" of respondent's crime.[8] According to the government, the unreported cash is an instrumentality because it "does not merely facilitate a violation of law," but is "the very *sine qua non* of the crime." The government reasons that "there would be no violation at all without the exportation (or attempted exportation) of the cash.

Acceptance of the government's argument would require us to expand the traditional understanding of instrumentality forfeitures. This we decline to do. Instrumentalities historically have been treated as a form of "guilty property" that can be forfeited in civil *in rem* proceedings. In this case, however, the government has sought to punish respondent by proceeding against him criminally, *in personam*, rather than proceeding *in rem* against the currency. It is therefore irrelevant whether respondent's currency is an instrumentality; the forfeiture is punitive, and the test for the excessiveness of a punitive forfeiture involves solely a proportionality determination.[9]

Because the forfeiture of respondent's currency constitutes punishment and is thus a "fine" within the meaning of the Excessive Fines Clause, we now turn to the question whether it is "excessive."

The touchstone of the constitutional inquiry under the Excessive Fines Clause is the principle of proportionality: The amount of the forfeiture must bear some relationship to the gravity of the offense that it is designed to punish. Until today, however, we have not articulated a standard for determining whether a punitive forfeiture is constitutionally excessive. We now hold that a punitive forfeiture violates the Excessive Fines Clause if it is grossly disproportional to the gravity of a defendant's offense.

The text and history of the Excessive Fines Clause demonstrate the centrality of proportionality to the excessiveness inquiry; nonetheless, they provide little guidance as to how disproportional a punitive forfeiture must be to the gravity of an offense in order to be "excessive." Excessive means surpassing the usual, the proper,

---

8. Although the term "instrumentality" is of recent vintage, it fairly characterizes property that historically was subject to forfeiture because it was the actual means by which an offense was committed. "Instrumentality" forfeitures have historically been limited to the property actually used to commit an offense and no more. A forfeiture that reaches beyond this strict historical limitation is *ipso facto* punitive and therefore subject to review under the Excessive Fines Clause.

9. The currency in question is not an instrumentality in any event. The Court of Appeals reasoned that the existence of the currency as a "precondition" to the reporting requirement did not make it an "instrumentality" of the offense. We agree; the currency is merely the subject of the crime of failure to report. Cash in a suitcase does not facilitate the commission of that crime as, for example, an automobile facilitates the transportation of goods concealed to avoid taxes. In the latter instance, the property is the actual means by which the criminal act is committed. *See* Black's Law Dictionary 801 (6th ed. 1990) ("Instrumentality" is "[s]omething by which an end is achieved; a means, medium, agency").

or a normal measure of proportion. The constitutional question that we address, however, is just how proportional to a criminal offense a fine must be, and the text of the Excessive Fines Clause does not answer it.

Nor does its history. The Clause was little discussed in the First Congress and the debates over the ratification of the Bill of Rights. . . .

We must therefore rely on other considerations in deriving a constitutional excessiveness standard, and there are two that we find particularly relevant. The first, which we have emphasized in our cases interpreting the Cruel and Unusual Punishments Clause, is that judgments about the appropriate punishment for an offense belong in the first instance to the legislature. The second is that any judicial determination regarding the gravity of a particular criminal offense will be inherently imprecise. Both of these principles counsel against requiring strict proportionality between the amount of a punitive forfeiture and the gravity of a criminal offense, and we therefore adopt the standard of gross disproportionality articulated in our Cruel and Unusual Punishments Clause precedents.

In applying this standard, the district courts in the first instance, and the courts of appeals, reviewing the proportionality determination *de novo*, must compare the amount of the forfeiture to the gravity of the defendant's offense. If the amount of the forfeiture is grossly disproportional to the gravity of the defendant's offense, it is unconstitutional.

Under this standard, the forfeiture of respondent's entire $357,144 would violate the Excessive Fines Clause.[11] Respondent's crime was solely a reporting offense. It was permissible to transport the currency out of the country so long as he reported it. Section 982(a)(1) orders currency to be forfeited for a "willful" violation of the reporting requirement. Thus, the essence of respondent's crime is a willful failure to report the removal of currency from the United States.[12] Furthermore, as the District

---

11. The only question before this Court is whether the full forfeiture of respondent's $357,144 as directed by § 982(a)(1) is constitutional under the Excessive Fines Clause. We hold that it is not. The government petitioned for certiorari seeking full forfeiture, and we reject that request. Our holding that full forfeiture would be excessive reflects no judgment that "a forfeiture of even $15,001 would have suffered from a gross disproportion," nor does it "affir[m] the reduced $15,000 forfeiture on *de novo* review." Those issues are simply not before us. Nor, indeed, do we address in *any* respect the validity of the forfeiture ordered by the District Court, including whether a court may disregard the terms of a statute that commands full forfeiture: respondent did not cross-appeal the $15,000 forfeiture ordered by the District Court. The Court of Appeals thus declined to address the $15,000 forfeiture, and that question is not properly presented here either.

12. Contrary to the dissent's contention, the nature of the nonreporting offense in this case was not altered by respondent's "lies" or by the "suspicious circumstances" surrounding his transportation of his currency. A single willful failure to declare the currency constitutes the crime, the gravity of which is not exacerbated or mitigated by "fable[s]" that respondent told one month, or six months, later. The government indicted respondent under 18 U.S.C. § 1001 for "lying," but that separate count did not form the basis of the nonreporting offense for which § 982(a)(1) orders forfeiture. Further, the District Court's finding that respondent's lies stemmed from a fear of the government because of "cultural differences," does not mitigate the gravity of his offense. The dissent's charge of

Court found, respondent's violation was unrelated to any other illegal activities. The money was the proceeds of legal activity and was to be used to repay a lawful debt. Whatever his other vices, respondent does not fit into the class of persons for whom the statute was principally designed: He is not a money launderer, a drug trafficker, or a tax evader.[13] And under the Sentencing Guidelines, the maximum sentence that could have been imposed on respondent was six months, while the maximum fine was $5,000. Such penalties confirm a minimal level of culpability.[14]

The harm that respondent caused was also minimal. Failure to report his currency affected only one party, the government, and in a relatively minor way. There was no fraud on the United States, and respondent caused no loss to the public fisc. Had his crime gone undetected, the government would have been deprived only of the information that $357,144 had left the country. The government and the dissent contend that there is a correlation between the amount forfeited and the harm that the government would have suffered had the crime gone undetected. We disagree. There is no inherent proportionality in such a forfeiture. It is impossible to conclude, for example, that the harm respondent caused is anywhere near 30 times greater than that caused by a hypothetical drug dealer who willfully fails to report taking $12,000 out of the country in order to purchase drugs.

Comparing the gravity of respondent's crime with the $357,144 forfeiture the government seeks, we conclude that such a forfeiture would be grossly disproportional to the gravity of his offense. It is larger than the $5,000 fine imposed by the District Court by many orders of magnitude, and it bears no articulable correlation to any injury suffered by the government.

For the foregoing reasons, the full forfeiture of respondent's currency would violate the Excessive Fines Clause. The judgment of the Court of Appeals is affirmed.

---

ethnic paternalism on the part of the District Court finds no support in the record, nor is there any indication that the District Court's factual finding that respondent "distrust[ed] . . . the government," was clearly erroneous.

13. Nor, contrary to the dissent's repeated assertion, is respondent a "smuggl[er]." Respondent owed no customs duties to the government, and it was perfectly legal for him to possess the $357,144 in cash and to remove it from the United States. His crime was simply failing to report the wholly legal act of transporting his currency.

14. In considering an offense's gravity, the other penalties that the Legislature has authorized are certainly relevant evidence. Here, as the government and the dissent stress, Congress authorized a maximum fine of $250,000 plus five years' imprisonment for willfully violating the statutory reporting requirement, and this suggests that it did not view the reporting offense as a trivial one. That the maximum fine and Guideline sentence to which respondent was subject were but a fraction of the penalties authorized, however, undercuts any argument based solely on the statute, because they show that respondent's culpability relative to other potential violators of the reporting provision—tax evaders, drug kingpins, or money launderers, for example—is small indeed. This disproportion is telling notwithstanding the fact that a separate Guideline provision permits forfeiture if mandated by statute. That Guideline, moreover, cannot override the constitutional requirement of proportionality review.

**JUSTICE KENNEDY, with whom THE CHIEF JUSTICE, JUSTICE O'CONNOR, and JUS-
TICE SCALIA join, dissenting.**

For the first time in its history, the Court strikes down a fine as excessive under
the Eighth Amendment. The decision is disturbing both for its specific holding
and for the broader upheaval it foreshadows. At issue is a fine Congress fixed in
the amount of the currency respondent sought to smuggle or to transport without
reporting. If a fine calibrated with this accuracy fails the Court's test, its decision
portends serious disruption of a vast range of statutory fines. The Court all but says
the offense is not serious anyway. This disdain for the statute is wrong as an empirical matter and disrespectful of the separation of powers, . . .

Turning to the question of excessiveness, the majority states the test: A defendant
must prove a gross disproportion before a court will strike down a fine as excessive.
This test would be a proper way to apply the Clause, if only the majority were faithful in applying it. The Court does not, however, explain why in this case forfeiture
of all of the cash would have suffered from a gross disproportion. The offense is a
serious one, and respondent's smuggling and failing to report were willful. The cash
was lawful to own, but this fact shows only that the forfeiture was a fine; it cannot
also prove that the fine was excessive.

The majority illuminates its test with a principle of deference. Congress deems the
crime serious, but the Court does not. Under the congressional statute, the crime is
punishable by a prison sentence, a heavy fine, and the forfeiture here at issue. As the
statute makes clear, the government needs the information to investigate other serious crimes, and it needs the penalties to ensure compliance. . . .

Congress considered currency smuggling and non-reporting a serious crime and
imposed commensurate penalties. It authorized punishments of five years' imprisonment, a $250,000 fine, plus forfeiture of all the undeclared cash. Congress found
the offense standing alone is a serious crime, for the same statute doubles the fines
and imprisonment for failures to report cash "while violating another law of the
United States." Congress experimented with lower penalties on the order of one year
in prison plus a $1,000 fine, but it found the punishments inadequate to deter lucra-
tive money laundering. The Court today rejects this judgment.

The Court rejects the congressional judgment because, it says, the Sentencing
Guidelines cap the appropriate fine at $5,000. The purpose of the Guidelines, how-
ever, is to select punishments with precise proportion, not to opine on what is a
gross disproportion. In addition, there is no authority for elevating the Commission's judgment of what is prudent over the congressional judgment of what is constitutional. The majority, then, departs from its promise of deference in the very case
announcing the standard.

The Court's argument is flawed, moreover, by a serious misinterpretation of the
Guidelines on their face. The Guidelines do not stop at the $5,000 fine the major-
ity cites. They augment it with this vital point: "Forfeiture is to be imposed upon a
convicted defendant as provided by statute." United States Sentencing Commission,

Guidelines Manual § 5E1.4 (Nov.1995). The fine thus supplements the forfeiture; it does not replace it. Far from contradicting congressional judgment on the offense, the Guidelines implement and mandate it.

The crime of smuggling or failing to report cash is more serious than the Court is willing to acknowledge. The drug trade, money laundering, and tax evasion all depend in part on smuggled and unreported cash. Congress enacted the reporting requirement because secret exports of money were being used in organized crime, drug trafficking, money laundering, and other crimes. Likewise, tax evaders were using cash exports to dodge hundreds of millions of dollars in taxes owed to the government.

The Court does not deny the importance of these interests but claims they are not implicated here because respondent managed to disprove any link to other crimes. Here, to be sure, the government had no affirmative proof that the money was from an illegal source or for an illegal purpose. This will often be the case, however. By its very nature, money laundering is difficult to prove; for if the money launderers have done their job, the money appears to be clean. The point of the statute, which provides for even heavier penalties if a second crime can be proved, is to mandate forfeiture regardless. . . .

In my view, forfeiture of all the unreported currency is sustainable whenever a willful violation is proved. The facts of this case exemplify how hard it can be to prove ownership and other crimes, and they also show respondent is far from an innocent victim. For one thing, he was guilty of repeated lies to government agents and suborning lies by others. . . .

Respondent told these lies, moreover, in most suspicious circumstances. His luggage was stuffed with more than a third of a million dollars. All of it was in cash, and much of it was hidden in a case with a false bottom.

The majority ratifies the District Court's see-no-evil approach. It dismissed the lies as stemming from "distrust for the Government" arising out of "cultural differences." While the majority is sincere in not endorsing this excuse, it nonetheless affirms the fine tainted by it. This patronizing excuse demeans millions of law-abiding American immigrants by suggesting they cannot be expected to be as truthful as every other citizen. Each American, regardless of culture or ethnicity, is equal before the law. Each has the same obligation to refrain from perjury and false statements to the government.

In short, respondent was unable to give a single truthful explanation of the source of the cash. The multitude of lies and suspicious circumstances points to some form of crime. Yet, though the government rebutted each and every fable respondent proffered, it was unable to adduce affirmative proof of another crime in this particular case. . . .

Given the severity of respondent's crime, the Constitution does not forbid forfeiture of all of the smuggled or unreported cash. Congress made a considered judgment in setting the penalty, and the Court is in serious error to set it aside. . . .

In these circumstances, the Constitution does not forbid forfeiture of all of the $357,144 transported by respondent. I dissent.

Notes and Questions

1. *A split court.* As is so often true in white collar cases, the Court in *Bajakajian* was sharply split; the dissent is written in particularly vehement terms. The dissent does not quarrel with the test for determining whether a fine is excessive, but does dispute the outcome in the case. Can you explain why the issue divided the Court so narrowly? The majority and dissent have very different views both of the seriousness of the crime at issue and of Bajakajian's individual culpability. Which side has the better of the debate? Why?

2. *Application to civil forfeitures.* In CAFRA, Congress codified the *Bajakajian* rule for civil forfeitures. That provision, codified at 18 U.S.C § 983(g) (General Rules for Civil Forfeiture Proceedings), provides:

> (g) Proportionality.
>
> (1) The claimant . . . may petition the court to determine whether the forfeiture was constitutionally excessive.
>
> (2) In making this determination, the court shall compare the forfeiture to the gravity of the offense giving rise to the forfeiture.
>
> (3) The claimant shall have the burden of establishing that the forfeiture is grossly disproportional by a preponderance of the evidence at a hearing conducted by the court without a jury.
>
> (4) If the court finds that the forfeiture is grossly disproportional to the offense it shall reduce or eliminate the forfeiture as necessary to avoid a violation of the Excessive Fines Clause of the Eighth Amendment of the Constitution.

3. *The "cultural" defense.* What role did the defendant's background play in the decision? What was the dissent's point in this regard? Is the dissent right? Why or why not?

4. *The congressional response to* Bajakajian.

a. *The "cash smuggling" statute.* As part of the "USA PATRIOT Act" of 2001, Congress enacted a law, titled "Bulk Cash Smuggling into or out of the United States." 31 U.S.C. § 5332. That statute makes it a criminal offense to knowingly conceal more than $10,000 in cash and to transport or attempt to transport that cash in or out of the country with the intent to evade the currency reporting requirements.

b. *Forfeitures.* In addition to imprisonment of not more than five years, the statute provides for both criminal and civil forfeiture of all property "involved in" or "traceable to" the crime. The statute further provides that "any currency or other monetary instrument that is concealed or intended to be concealed in violation of . . . *shall be considered property involved in the offense.*" 31 U.S.C. § 5332 (emphasis added). The preamble to the statute states that prior statutes forced criminals to eschew traditional financial institutions in favor of carrying bulk cash and "only the confiscation of [this cash] can effectively break the cycle of criminal activity" of which it is a part, requiring a new crime so that the cash can be "confiscated as the *corpus delicti*" of the offense.

This language appears to respond to language in *Bajakajian* concluding that: (1) cash is not an "instrumentality" of the crime of failing to report currency, and (2) merely failing to report, as part of the "gross proportionality" analysis, does not cause substantial harm to the government. In particular, the *Bajakajian* majority had rejected the dissent's conclusion that the defendant was a "smuggler." In response, the preamble to § 5332 states that carrying and failing to report the currency "is the equivalent of, and creates the same harm as, the smuggling of goods."

In light of this language, are civil and criminal forfeitures based upon violations of § 5332 subject to Excessive Fines Clause analysis? Despite apparent congressional intent to the contrary, lower federal courts have subjected § 5332 forfeitures to Excessive Fines Clause review. *See, e.g., United States v. $132,245.00 in U.S. Currency*, 764 F.3d 1055, 1061 (9th Cir. 2014) ("Comparing the gravity of [the] offense with the amount to be forfeited, we find that forfeiture of all $132,245 does not violate the Excessive Fines clause of the United States Constitution."); *United States v. Jose*, 499 F.3d 105, 111–114 (1st Cir. 2007) (holding that the forfeiture on the facts of the case was not excessive, and declining to decide the threshold question whether the Excessive Fines Clause even applies to § 5332 forfeitures); *United States v. $120,856*, 394 F. Supp. 2d 687, 695–696 (D.V.I. 2005) (holding that forfeiture under § 5332 of $120,856 that legal immigrant attempted to bring into United States "would be extraordinarily harsh and grossly disproportionate to the offense," and reducing the forfeiture to $7,500); *United States v. $293,316 in United States Currency*, 349 F. Supp. 2d 638, 650–651 (S.D.N.Y. 2004) (Weinstein, J.) (reducing forfeiture under § 5332 on facts similar to those presented in *Bajakajian*, and rejecting the government's argument that § 5332 compels forfeiture of the entire amount).

5. *The applicability of* Bajakajian *to forfeitures of illegal drug sale proceeds.* Does the Court's ruling apply to forfeitures of illegal drug sale proceeds under 21 U.S.C. § 881(a)(6)? In *United States v. $185,336.07*, 731 F.3d 189 (2d Cir. 2013), the Second Circuit held as follows:

> [Appellant argues that] the District Court's decision, which permitted the seizure of the $185,336.07 in illegal drug sale proceeds under 21 U.S.C. § 881(a)(6), violated the Eighth Amendment's ban on disproportionate punishment. We have not spoken directly on the question of whether the Eighth Amendment's prohibition on disproportionate punishment applies to § 881(a)(6); we do so now, and hold that it does not. In *Austin v. United States*, 509 U.S. 602 (1993), the Supreme Court held that, notwithstanding statutory language that 'no property right . . . exist[s]' in the property described under 21 U.S.C. § 881(a)(1)–(11), the Excessive Fines Clause of the Eighth Amendment applies to forfeitures of conveyances and real estate under 21 U.S.C. § 881(a)(4) and 21 U.S.C. § 881(a)(7). In reaching this conclusion, the Court stated

that 'Congress understood those provisions as serving to deter and to punish' rather than 'serv[ing] solely a remedial purpose.'

The current case, however, deals with subsection (a)(6) — which concerns proceeds from illicit drug sales. All of our sister courts of appeal that have considered this provision have concluded that the forfeiture of 'guilty property,' such as illicit drug proceeds, 'has been traditionally regarded as nonpunitive' as to which the Eighth Amendment's restrictions on punishment do not apply. In so doing, these courts have viewed the forfeiture of drug proceeds as categorically distinct from the forfeiture of conveyances and real estate. *See United States v. Tilley,* 18 F.3d 295, 300 (5th Cir. 1994) ('[T]he forfeitures of conveyances and real estate have no correlation to, or proportionality with, the costs incurred by the government and society because of the large and unpredictable variances in the values of real estate and conveyances in comparison to the harm inflicted upon government and society by the criminal act,' whereas 'the forfeiture of drug proceeds will always be directly proportional to the amount of drugs sold. The more drugs sold, the more proceeds that will be forfeited.'). We agree with this view and hold that the Eighth Amendment does not apply to forfeitures under 21 U.S.C. § 881(a)(6). We hold, therefore, that Pellegrino's Eighth Amendment argument is meritless.

Do you agree with the court's holding and reasoning? Why or why not?

6. *Extending* Bajakajian *to the states.* In *Timbs v. Indiana,* 139 S. Ct. 682 (2019), the Supreme Court held that the Excessive Fines Clause applies to state civil forfeitures through the Fourteenth Amendment's incorporation doctrine. Will this lead to substantial constraints on state forfeitures? Consider the following commentary:

Despite the ostensible limitation the Excessive Fines Clause provides on forfeitures, so far it has proved an insufficient backstop on most federal civil forfeitures.

It is unlikely to play a more robust role in the states going forward. Most of the states permit civil forfeitures. In a number of states, investigative reports have called into question the legitimacy of forfeiture as a valid law-enforcement tool. Some police forces appear to use it to procure resources rather than fight crime. They proceed against property owners without sufficient proof of criminal conduct. Yet the property owners often lack the resources to dispute a forfeiture. The procedural setup creates a substantial burden to dispute a forfeiture. In the forfeiture of cell phones or items of similar or lower price, the cost of disputing the forfeiture can be substantially higher than the replacement cost, which provides a disincentive to challenging the police action.

Most problematically, law enforcement agencies in most states have a direct stake in forfeitures. They are permitted to retain a substantial percentage of the proceeds from forfeitures, and in some cases all the proceeds.

Those incentives may even change the emphasis of police work. For example, police may become more interested in seizing cash proceeds of drug exchanges than in seizing the drugs themselves.

Nora V. Demleitner, *Will the Supreme Court Rein in "Excessive Fines" and Forfeitures? Don't Rely on* Timbs v. Indiana, FED. SENT'G. REP. Vol. 32, No. 1 (Oct. 2019), at 10–11. Are these concerns valid? Why or why not? If so, should civil forfeitures be abolished? What are the competing policy concerns?

Problems

20-4. Robert appeals from a December Year 10 judgment of civil forfeiture against his 29.6 acres of property, including his own barn-art studio of 1,000 square feet, another residence of 2,000 square feet occupied by Robert and his husband, Harry, and three small storage buildings. The residence sits on a half-acre of property that was originally part of the entire 29.6-acre tract, but was subdivided and separately titled at the time the residence was completed in January Year 06. The residence, including the half-acre lot, is worth $250,000 and is jointly owned by Robert and Harry, each of whom contributed half of the construction costs for the home. The half-acre that was formerly part of the entire 29.6-acre tract was transferred to joint ownership at the time they occupied the home in January Year 06.

The police arrested Robert in January Year 10 after they discovered 20 marijuana plants being grown in a large shed (one of the three storage buildings) on Robert's property. Robert had been growing the marijuana in the shed for three years. Each plant had a market value of approximately $4,000. Robert is an artist and part-time nurse who had an art studio in the loft area of the barn.

Robert was charged under state law with cultivation of marijuana without a license in violation of applicable state law. Marijuana possession and cultivation were legalized in the state by voter initiative enacted in November Year 05, but commercial cultivation must be licensed by the state. Failure to obtain a license is a criminal offense. To avoid a longer sentence, Robert immediately pleaded guilty to cultivation of marijuana without a license. Although subject to a possible maximum five-year prison term and $100,000 fine, he was sentenced to two years' probation and no fine because he had no prior criminal record.

Almost seven months after Robert's guilty plea, the United States entered the case and filed a complaint in the United States district court for in rem forfeiture of the entire 29.6-acre tract and all structures thereon under 21 U.S.C. § 881(a)(7). Both the government and Robert moved for summary judgment. The district court granted the government's motion for summary judgment, denied Robert's motion, and entered a judgment of forfeiture against the 29.6 acres of property, including all structures and the residence.

In ordering the forfeiture, the court made the following factual findings: Robert acquired the 29.6-acre tract in Year 00; the shed where the marijuana was grown and the shed's curtilage are worth $100,000; the remaining part of the 29.1 acre tract is worth $500,000; the barn is the defendant's art studio; the defendant owns all the 29.1 acres and structures thereon in full (i.e., there is no mortgage); Robert has been employed as an artist and nurse for the last 10 years and has earned an average of approximately $75,000 a year during that time; Robert is 45 years old, and his only other asset is $250,000 in a retirement account; Robert bought the 29.6-acre tract with money he inherited from his parents; Robert grew the marijuana for personal use, sold marijuana to friends, neighbors, and acquaintances, and also gave marijuana to friends and acquaintances who suffer from illnesses, including cancer, for whom marijuana provided medical benefits. Robert's annual sales totaled an average of $20,000 over the three years in question.

> *a. Does the forfeiture violate the Eighth Amendment? Why or why not? If there is an Eighth Amendment violation, what level of forfeiture would pass constitutional muster?*
>
> *b. Is the "substantial connection" test met on the facts of this case? Why or why not?*

20-5. A government agent posing as a drug dealer paid cash to buy $25,000 worth of jewelry from a jewelry store. The store clerk did not file the required currency transaction report, and deposited the cash in several transactions of under $10,000 in a bank account created in a fictitious name. Based upon the store clerk's actions, the store was convicted of money laundering and currency transaction reporting violations. The government sought forfeiture of the store's entire $2 million in inventory. The court ordered forfeiture in the entire amount, and imposed a fine of $100,000. The statutory maximum fine was $600,000.

Does the forfeiture violate the Eighth Amendment? Why or why not? If there is an Eighth Amendment violation, what level of forfeiture would pass constitutional muster?

2. Third-Party Interests

Issues relating to ownership interests of potentially innocent third parties — that is, those who are not the suspected wrongdoers — frequently arise in civil forfeitures, where there is no requirement that the property owner be convicted of or even charged with a crime. Criminal forfeitures, on the other hand, *do* depend upon the determination of the defendant's guilt before the defendant's property can be seized or forfeited. People other than the defendant may also have an interest in the potentially forfeitable property, however. The cases discussed below deal with these "third-party" interests.

a. Civil Forfeitures

Notes on United States v. 92 Buena Vista Avenue *and* Bennis v. Michigan

Civil forfeiture statutes provide that title to forfeitable property "vests" with the federal government at the time that the underlying crime occurs. *See* 21 U.S.C.

§ 881(h). Federal forfeiture statutes provide, however, that property belonging to innocent third parties is not forfeitable. Are these provisions reconcilable? In other words, how could an innocent property owner retain title to property that already belongs to the government?

The United States Supreme Court confronted this issue in *United States v. 92 Buena Vista Avenue*, 507 U.S. 111 (1993). In *Buena Vista*, the third party claimant purchased her home with cash generated from drug sales. Even though the claimant asserted that she did not know the origin of the cash, the government sought forfeiture of the home. The government argued that the claimant was not the owner of the house because title vested with the government at the moment the house was purchased with drug money. *Id.* at 124. The Court rejected the government's argument, holding that title does not pass to the government until a court enters a forfeiture order and that a third party may assert an innocent owner defense to forfeiture.

After the *92 Buena Vista Avenue* decision, those who possessed proceeds from criminal activity began to transfer property to family members to avoid potential forfeiture. In an attempt to deal with this practice, CAFRA limits third-party "innocent owner" claims in situations where the third party acquired the property interest *after* the conduct giving rise to forfeiture took place. In such a circumstance, the third party must show (1) that the claimant was "a bona fide purchaser or seller for value (including a purchaser or seller of goods or services for value)," and (2) that the claimant "did not know and was reasonably without cause to believe that the property was subject to forfeiture."

In CAFRA, Congress provided a defense that a qualifying innocent owner can assert in all federal civil forfeiture cases. Does the Constitution mandate an innocent owner defense in all civil forfeiture cases, including in states where such a defense in unavailable? The Supreme Court addressed this issue in *Bennis v. Michigan*, 516 U.S. 442 (1996). In that case, police arrested the petitioner's husband for having sex with a prostitute in the husband and wife's car in violation of Michigan law. Thereafter, the state sought civil forfeiture of the car. The defendant's wife argued that the forfeiture violated the Due Process Clause because she was not allowed to contest the forfeiture by showing that she was unaware of her husband's crime. *Id.* at 446.

The Court rejected the claim by a five-to-four vote. The Court held that "a long and unbroken line of cases holds that an owner's interest in property may be forfeited by reason of the use to which the property is put *even though* the owner did not know that it was to be put to such use." *Id.* Although federal law and many state statutes now require that the innocent owner defense be available, there is no constitutional right to such a defense in all forfeiture cases.

Notes and Questions

1. *A uniform innocent owner defense.* Prior to the passage of CAFRA, federal civil forfeiture statutes varied widely in the degree to which they provided an innocent

ownership defense. CAFRA provides an innocent owner defense applicable to all federal civil forfeitures. 18 U.S.C. § 983(d).

2. *Property owned at the time of the illegal activity.* With respect to property owned at the time of the illegal activity, under CAFRA, the third party claimant has the burden of proving by a preponderance of the evidence that the claimant:

> (i) did not know of the conduct giving rise to forfeiture; or

> (ii) upon learning of the conduct giving rise to the forfeiture, did all that reasonably could be expected under the circumstances to terminate such use of the property.

The statute provides examples of the latter, including giving timely notice to law enforcement of the illegal activity, or revoking or attempting to revoke permission for the wrongdoer to use the property. Is the defense too narrow? Too broad? Why?

3. *The exclusion for primary residences.* In an attempt to avoid overly harsh results from CAFRA's limitations on the innocent owner defense discussed above, CAFRA also provides that:

> An otherwise valid claim . . . shall not be denied on the ground that the claimant gave nothing of value in exchange for the property if—

> (i) the property is the *primary residence* of the claimant;

> (ii) depriving the claimant of the property would deprive the claimant of the *means to maintain reasonable shelter* in the community for the claimant and all dependents residing with the claimant;

> (iii) the property *is not, and is not traceable to, the proceeds of any criminal offense*; and

> (iv) the claimant acquired his or her interest in the property through *marriage, divorce, or legal separation*, or the claimant was *the spouse or legal dependent of a person whose death resulted in the transfer of the property to the claimant* through inheritance or probate, except that the court shall limit the value of any real property interest for which innocent ownership is recognized under this subparagraph to the value necessary to maintain reasonable shelter in the community for such claimant and all dependents residing with the claimant. . . .

18 U.S.C. § 983(d)(3)(B)(i) (emphasis added). This exclusion only applies to property used to facilitate a criminal offense, and does not apply to property purchased with proceeds from illegal activity. Also note that this exclusion does not apply to criminal forfeitures under the narcotics laws, which requires any third-party claimant to be a bona fide purchaser for value. *See* 21 U.S.C. § 853(n)(6)(B).

What would have been the result in *92 Buena Vista Avenue* under CAFRA? Is this provision unnecessarily limited? What competing policy concerns are at issue? For a history and analysis of this section of CAFRA, see Stefan D. Cassella, *The Uniform Innocent Owner Defense to Civil Asset Forfeiture: The Civil Asset Forfeiture*

Reform Act of 2000 Creates a Uniform Innocent Owner Defense to Most Civil Forfeiture Cases Filed by the Federal Government, 89 KY. L.J. 653 (2001).

Problem

20-6. Acting on an anonymous tip, a United States customs official stopped and questioned Linda as she was about to board her flight at Los Angeles International Airport en route to visit her sister in London, England. The official advised Linda of the relevant currency reporting requirements and told her that she must declare any currency, travelers' checks, and other negotiable monetary instruments totaling more than $10,000.00. Linda stated that she was carrying $9,000.00 in cash. The customs official offered Linda the opportunity to amend her declaration and specifically advised her of the need to report the transportation of monetary instruments on behalf of others. Linda, however, declined this invitation, and again stated that she was carrying only $9,000.00 in cash. Upon searching Linda's purse, Clark discovered $8,900 in cash, along with six negotiable checks totaling nearly $200,000.

Linda stated that the negotiable checks were the proceeds of a sale of certain land in Florida. These checks were made out to, and appeared to be endorsed by, Linda's husband, Armando. According to the customs official, Linda claimed that she had forged the signatures on these checks, and that Armando was not aware that she had these checks in her possession or that she planned to take them out of the country.

Customs agents then telephoned Armando. Armando contradicted his wife on a number of points, stating that he had, in fact, signed the checks bearing his name, and that he was aware that his wife had these checks in her possession as she left the United States. According to Armando, his wife kept the checks so that he would not, in her absence and without her final approval, invest these funds in the purchase of another parcel of property in Florida.

Linda was charged with violating the reporting requirements of 31 U.S.C. § 5316 and making false statements to the customs official. The government also seeks civil forfeiture of the cash and negotiable checks under 18 U.S.C. § 981(a)(1)(A). The cash and checks are the joint property of Linda and Armando.

Armando and Linda both assert an innocent owner defense. Will either likely succeed? Why or why not?

b. Criminal Forfeitures

As noted above, under Federal Rule of Criminal Procedure 32.2, the court is required to promptly enter a preliminary forfeiture order once the "requisite nexus between the property and the offense" has been established, regardless of the property interests of those other than the defendant. Once that nexus has been established, the order may be entered *regardless* of any such existing third-party interests. After such order has been entered, however, Rule 32.2(b)(3) authorizes the Attorney General "to commence proceedings that comply with any statutes governing third-party rights." Thus, the statutes allow for protection of third-party interests, but only after the criminal forfeiture proceeding has been concluded. As discussed below, some courts allow third parties to intervene prior to the conclusion of the case.

3. The Sixth Amendment

Recall that, in a criminal case, the government may obtain an order freezing a defendant's assets prior to trial in order to preserve the assets for possible forfeiture. Do the criminal forfeiture statutes allow the government to obtain such an order even where the defendant needs the frozen property to pay attorneys' fees? Even if so, would such a result violate the Sixth Amendment's right to counsel?

Note on Monsanto *and* Caplin & Drysdale

In *United States v. Monsanto*, 491 U.S. 600 (1989), the Court confronted the question whether the criminal forfeiture statute at issue provided for the forfeiture of assets necessary for the defendant to pay attorney's fees. In that case, the government alleged that the assets were the products of illegal narcotics transactions and were forfeitable under 21 U.S.C. § 853. The district court issued an order freezing the assets. On appeal, the defendant argued that assets needed for attorney's fees are not not forfeitable under the statute.

The Court rejected the defendant's argument, noting that the statute's plain language requires that "all assets falling within its scope . . . be forfeited upon conviction, with no exception existing for the assets used to pay attorney's fees — or anything else, for that matter." *Id.* at 606. The Court thus refused to recognize an exception for property that was to be used to pay attorney's fees. *Id.* at 613 ("Permitting a defendant to use assets for his private purposes that, under this provision, will become the property of the United States if a conviction occurs cannot be sanctioned.").

In *Caplin & Drysdale v. United States*, 491 U.S. 617 (1989), a case decided the same day as *Monsanto*, the Court addressed the question whether the freezing of assets needed for attorney's fees violates the Sixth Amendment right to counsel. The Court held that the Sixth Amendment guarantees adequate representation for defendants in criminal cases. That right, however, does not provide a defendant with the right to hire counsel of choice; appointment of a public defender ensures the right to counsel. *Id* at 624. Thus, forfeitable assets may be restrained without violating a defendant's right to counsel; the Sixth Amendment only requires that the defendant be given adequate representation. The Court relied on the relation-back doctrine, under which the forfeitable property belongs to the government as of the time of the criminal activity. The Court stated that a wrongdoer (such as a robber) has no right to use the ill-gotten property. Writing for a four-member dissent, Justice Blackmun stated that "it is unseemly and unjust for the government to beggar those it prosecutes in order to disable their defense at trial." 491 U.S. at 635. (Blackmun, J., dissenting).

Which side has the better of the argument? Why did the dissent employ such unusually harsh language? And why, as in so many forfeiture cases, was the Court so narrowly split? Is there something about the nature of forfeitures that produces such sharp divisions?

4. Procedural Due Process

Recall that both civil and criminal forfeiture statutes allow for the government to assume control of the property prior to the civil forfeiture trial or the criminal trial of the defendant. When evaluating the constitutionality of such pretrial restraints, federal courts have struggled to balance the government's need to maintain the property for forfeiture and the defendant's due process rights.

a. Pretrial Seizures and Attorneys' Fees

In its decisions in *Monsanto* and *Caplin & Drysdale*, the Supreme Court held that the forfeiture of funds needed to pay attorneys' fees does not violate the Sixth Amendment right to counsel. A separate but related issue arises when the government seeks pretrial restraint of such funds. What constitutional rights are at play in that circumstance?

The latter issue raises concerns under both the Fifth Amendment's Due Process Clause and the Sixth Amendment right to counsel. In *United States v. Monsanto*, 924 F.2d 1186, 1203 (2d Cir. 1991) (en banc), the Second Circuit held that "the [F]ifth and [S]ixth Amendments, considered in combination, require an adversary, post-restraint, pretrial hearing as to probable cause that (a) the defendant committed the crimes that provide a basis for forfeiture, and (b) the properties specified as forfeitable in the indictment are properly forfeitable." In *Kaley v. United States*, 134 S. Ct. 1090 (2014), the government agreed as to the second point, but argued that a defendant has no constitutional right to a hearing on the first issue.

Note on Kaley *and* Luis

In *Kaley*, the defendants were charged with interstate transportation of stolen medical devices and money laundering. The district court issued a pretrial order restraining the defendants from transferring potentially forfeitable assets, including those needed to pay their attorney's fees. The court also denied the defendants' request for a hearing to determine the adequacy of the criminal charges underlying the forfeiture. The appeals court affirmed.

The Supreme Court agreed with the lower courts that the defendants had no constitutional right to such a hearing. The Court noted that lower courts have generally held that defendants do have a right to a pretrial hearing to determine whether there is probable cause that the frozen assets themselves would be forfeitable, a point that the government conceded in *Kaley*. That right, though, does not extend to a pretrial determination of the sufficiency of underlying criminal charges.

The Court reasoned that under the applicable forfeiture statute, 21 U.S.C. § 853(e), a trial court may order pretrial seizure of forfeitable assets. The Court cited *Monsanto* and *Caplin & Drysdale* to hold that a hearing is not required on the substance of the underlying charges. Otherwise, the trial court would simply be second-guessing probable cause determinations that the grand jury had already made.

The *Kaley* defendants also asserted a due process challenge under *Mathews v. Eldridge*, 424 U.S. 319 (1976). Under that holding, a court weighs the burdens that the proceeding would impose on the government against the private interest. The court also analyzes "the risk of an erroneous deprivation" of that interest without the proceeding and "the probable value, if any, of [the] additional . . . procedural safeguard[ ]."

The Court in *Kaley* found that those factors weighed in favor of the government. The Court found that the government has a substantial interest in obtaining pretrial seizure of the assets in order to preserve their forfeitability. Concerning the private interests, the Court found that "in this context — when the legal standard is merely probable cause and the grand jury has already made that finding — both our precedents and other courts' experience indicate that a full-dress hearing will provide little benefit." Chief Justice Roberts dissented in an opinion joined by Justices Breyer and Sotomayor. The dissent viewed the majority's decision as "fundamentally at odds with our constitutional tradition and basic notions of fair play."

After *Kaley*, one open issue was whether the government may obtain pretrial restraint of a defendant's "untainted" assets necessary for the defendant to hire counsel. The government took the position that such assets, even though not the proceeds or instrumentalities of the alleged illegal activity, were subject to pre-forfeiture seizure to ensure that a defendant would be able to pay restitution and other penalties after conviction.

In *Luis v. United States*, 136 S. Ct. 1083 (2016), the Court addressed the question whether the government could obtain pretrial seizure of such untainted assets. In a split decision, five justices found in two separate opinions that a defendant is entitled to use such assets to pay for attorney's fees. The government argued allowing defendants to use untainted assets to pay attorneys' fees would deprive the government of funds necessary for restitution and other post-conviction penalties. The Court rejected this argument, finding that the Sixth Amendment right to counsel requires that defendants have access to untainted funds to pay attorneys' fees. Three justices dissented; Justice Kennedy wrote the principal dissent, which Justice Alito joined. In her separate dissent, Justice Kagan opined that *Monsanto* is "a troubling decision." Justice Kagan found, however, that absent an overturning of *Monsanto*, the government's position was supported by controlling case law. *Id.* at 1112 (Kagan, J., dissenting).

Notes and Questions

1. *The role of the grand jury.* In *Kaley*, the government argued strongly that a pretrial hearing would require an inappropriate inquiry into the grand jury proceedings. The Court agreed. Do you agree with its conclusion? Why or why not?

2. *The Fifth and Sixth Amendments.* Is the majority in *Kaley* correct that its decision was compelled by *Monsanto* and *Caplin & Drysdale*? If so, were those cases correctly decided? If so, then how can you justify the Court's holding in *Luis*?

3. *The Due Process Clause.* On this issue as well, the *Kaley* majority and dissent strongly disagreed. Do you agree with the majority's analysis? Why?

4. *Presumption of innocence.* Quoting *Caplin & Drysdale*, the Court in *Kaley* stated, "'A defendant has no Sixth Amendment right to spend another person's money' for legal fees — even if that is the only way to hire a preferred lawyer. Consider the example of a 'robbery suspect' who wishes to 'use funds he has stolen from a bank to retain an attorney to defend him if he is apprehended.'" What implications, if any, does this statement have for the presumption of innocence?

5. *Fairness.* In dissent, Chief Justice Roberts argued in *Kaley* that the majority's decision is "fundamentally at odds with our constitutional tradition and basic notions of fair play." Is he correct? Why or why not?

6. *Criticism of* Kaley. Many commentators criticized the Court's decision in *Kaley*. Typical comments included: "I worry that the *Kaley* decision may contribute to . . . a growing imbalance in the adversarial process." The Court "was not concerned about how anomalous this [result] is for both presumed and actually innocent defendants." Commentators also suggested that the remedy for the issue may now lie with Congress. *See* Alisa Johnson, *Supreme Court Restricts Judge's Inquiry in Hearings Challenging Freezing of Assets*, WHITE COLLAR CRIME REP. (BNA) (March 7, 2014). Should Congress address the *Kaley* holding? If so, how?

In the wake of *Kaley*, members of Congress placed renewed emphasis on overhauling the federal asset forfeiture scheme. One proposal would directly overturn *Kaley* and require a pretrial adversarial hearing on the issue whether the underlying criminal charges are supported by probable cause. *See* Jeffrey D. Koelemay, *Asset Forfeiture Reform Long Overdue, Senators, Witnesses Indicate at Hearing*, 10 WHITE COLLAR CRIME REP. (BNA), No. 9 at 335 (April 21, 2015).

7. *The votes.* In both *Kaley* and *Luis*, the Court was sharply split along lines that were highly unusual in criminal cases. What is it about those cases that produced such strong divisions among the Justices? Are there unique policy concerns at play in right to counsel issues?

b. Restraints on Real Property

Note on James Daniel Good Real Property

In what circumstances may the government seize property prior to a trial without notice or a hearing? In *Calero-Toledo v. Pearson Yacht Leasing Co.*, 416 U.S. 663, 680 (1974), a civil forfeiture case, the Court approved such seizures in "extraordinary" circumstances. Such circumstances may exist, for example, when there is a risk that the property could be hidden or destroyed. *Id.*

In 1993, the Supreme Court addressed the issue of *ex parte* seizures of *real* property in *United States v. James Daniel Good Real Property*, 510 U.S. 43 (1993). In that case, the government sought forfeiture of the defendant's home and land because the property had been used to violate the federal drug laws. Without notice or a hearing, a federal magistrate found probable cause that the property was subject to forfeiture under § 881(a)(7). The magistrate issued a warrant of arrest in rem that authorized the seizure of the property. By a five-to-four majority, the Court found that the owner's due process rights had been violated. The Court stated that notice and a hearing are generally required by due process, acknowledging that such notice and hearing may not be required in exceptional circumstances. Such circumstances are not present, the Court held, with respect to real property, which cannot be moved or hidden.

Congress codified this decision in CAFRA, 18 U.S.C. § 985, which provides in part that "real property that is the subject of a civil forfeiture action shall not be seized before entry of an order of forfeiture" pursuant to hearing and that the government must notify the property owner before seeking such an order. The statute provides an exception to the notice and hearing requirement where the court "makes an *ex parte* determination that there is probable cause for the forfeiture and that there are exigent circumstances that permit the government to seize the property without prior notice and an opportunity for the property owner to be heard." CAFRA states that "[a]n exigency could be shown if, for example, the defendant threatened to damage or destroy a building or other property, or if the property were used in ongoing criminal activity." CAFRA further provides that "to establish exigent circumstances, the government shall show that less restrictive measures such as a *lis pendens*, restraining order, or bond would not suffice to protect the government's interests in preventing the sale, destruction, or continued unlawful use of the real property."

Why did Congress provide special protections for seizures of real property? Are such protections justified? What sort of "exigent circumstances" might warrant seizure of real property without notice and a hearing?

Problems

20-7. A man, Jim Jarman, and his two small children live in a rent-controlled, one-bedroom apartment in Chicago. Mr. Jarman has a part-time job as a waiter and barely makes ends meet. Without a rent-controlled apartment, he and his children would not be able to afford housing. Mr. Jarman's younger brother, Sam, is a truck-driver who spends an average of a couple of nights a week sleeping on a fold-out couch in the living room. Sam does not contribute to the rent but does buy food for members of the household. Jim is much older than Sam and raised Sam from the time Sam was 12 years old when their parents were killed in a car accident.

The apartment building and its grounds are known to the police and the residents as the location of narcotics sales. The sales are often accompanied by violence; within the past year, 15 residents who were innocent bystanders, including four small children, have been wounded in shootings associated with drug sales. Six residents, including two small children, died from the gunshot wounds. The police have strong hearsay evidence that Sam was responsible for at least several of the shootings and are continuing their investigation in the hopes of obtaining sufficient evidence to arrest him on that charge.

While residing at Jim's apartment, Sam, on occasion, brings in small packages from his truck and keeps them in the closet in the living room. When Jim asked Sam about the contents of the packages, Sam told Jim to mind his own business. Jim has also seen Sam take the packages down to the street below, where Sam sometimes meets with and takes cash from people Jim does not know. Jim has advised Sam in no uncertain terms that he never wants any drugs brought into his household.

Jim told his neighbor, Martha Mills, that he wonders what Sam is doing when he leaves the apartment with the packages. Martha told Jim that she did not know what Sam is up to, but that she had a friend, Alice, whose apartment had been used by Alice's son to store drugs that he sold. Martha also told Jim that, if Jim thinks Sam is selling drugs, he should kick Sam out of the apartment because Jim could lose his lease just like Alice did. Jim told Martha that he had helped raise Sam and could never bring himself to kick Sam out. Martha advised Jim to retain an attorney.

Assume that you are a criminal defense attorney with a great deal of experience in civil and criminal forfeitures. Jim has come to you for advice about the foregoing. He is adamant that his brother remain in the apartment, but wants to know how to protect himself. How do you advise him?

20-8. Please incorporate the facts from the preceding problem. Early in the morning of the Monday after Jim met with his attorney, there were several drug-related shootings at Jim's building, resulting in one death. Federal agents arrived at Jim's apartment at 2:00 a.m. and broke down the door. They entered the bedroom, where Jim and the children were sleeping. The agents had their guns drawn. Terrified, Jim demanded that they leave. The agents refused to do so, and informed Jim that they had a warrant issued by a United States magistrate one hour earlier authorizing them to seize the apartment under 21 U.S.C. § 881. The agents gave Jim 15 minutes to pack his belongings and leave with his children; Sam was not present. Jim and his children spent the following week in a shelter.

The government then entered into an occupancy agreement that allowed the family to return to the apartment but required them to obtain prior governmental approval for any guests that visited the apartment. Jim and his children have returned and are abiding by the occupancy agreement; they have not seen or heard from Sam since the evening the agents appeared. The government has initiated a civil forfeiture proceeding under 21 U.S.C. § 881(a)(7).

Assume that the government has established by a preponderance of the evidence that the lease is a forfeitable property interest. Jim argues both that (1) the lease cannot be forfeited because the seizure was invalid under the Due Process Clause, and (2) in any event he is an innocent holder of the lease. Should Jim prevail on either of his arguments? Why or why not?

Table of Cases

Table of Statutes

Code of Federal Regulations
Title:Sec., Page

Federal Rules of Civil Procedure
Rule, Page

Federal Rules of Criminal Procedure
Rule, Page

Index